CLASS 1 EARNINGS BRACKETS (continued)

1998–99

Earnings bracket		Earnings period/Earnings		
No	Secondary	Weekly	Monthly	Yearly
No primary earnings brackets	—	£0 to £63.99	£0 to £277.99	£0 to £3,327.99
	1	£64.00 (LEL) to £109.99	£278.00 (LEL) to £476.99	£3,328.00 (LEL) to £5,719.99
	2	£110.00 to £154.99	£477.00 to £671.99	£5,720.00 to £8,059.99
	3	£155.00 to £209.99	£672.00 to £909.99	£8,060.00 to £10,919.99
	4	£210.00 to £485.00 (UEL)	£910.00 to £2,102.00 (UEL)	£10,920.00 to £25,220.00 (UEL)
	4	£485.01 or more	£2,102.01 or more	£25,220.01 or more

Note
There are no earnings brackets after 5 April 1999: see Chapter 51.

CLASS 1 CONTRIBUTION RATES 1988–89 to 1989–90 (to 4 ... 1989)

| | Primary | | | | | Secondary | | | |
EB	SR%[1]	RR%[1]	COSR%[2,3]	COSR%[2,4]	EB	SR%[1]	RR%[1]	COSR%[2,3]	COSR%[2,4]
1	5.00	3.85	2.85	3.00	1	5.00	5.00	0.90	1.20
2	7.00	3.85	4.85	5.00	2	7.00	7.00	2.90	3.20
3	9.00	3.85	6.85	7.00	3	9.00	9.00	4.90	5.20
					4	10.45	10.45	6.35/10.45[5]	6.65/10.45[5]

CLASS 1 CONTRIBUTION RATES 1989–90 (from 5 October 1989) and 1990–91

| | Primary | | | | Secondary | | | |
	SR%[6]	RR%[1]	COSR%[6]	EB	SR%[1]	RR%[1]	COSR%[2]
LEL to UEL	9.00	3.85	7.00	1	5.00	5.00	1.20
				2	7.00	7.00	3.20
				3	9.00	9.00	5.20
				4	10.45	10.45	6.65/10.45[5]

CLASS 1 CONTRIBUTION RATES 1991–92 and 1992–93

| | Primary | | | | Secondary | | | |
	SR%[6]	RR%[1]	COSR%[6]	EB	SR%[1]	RR%[1]	COSR%[2]
LEL to UEL	9.00	3.85	7.00	1	4.60	4.60	0.80
				2	6.60	6.60	2.80
				3	8.60	8.60	4.80
				4	10.40	10.40	6.60/10.40[5]

[1] Rate applies to all earnings by which the earnings bracket has been identified.
[2] Rate applies only to that part of earnings which exceeds the LEL; the relevant standard rate applies to that part of earnings equal to the LEL.
[3] Rates in force 6 October 1985 to 5 April 1988.
[4] Rates in force from 6 April 1988.
[5] Lower rates apply only to earnings which exceed the LEL but do not exceed the UEL; higher rate applies to any earnings above the UEL.
[6] Rate applies only to that part of earnings which exceeds LEL; rate of 2.00% is applied on earnings up to and including the LEL.

CLASS 1 CONTRIBUTION RATES 1993–94

	Primary			Secondary			
	SR%[3]	RR%[1]	COSR%[3]	EB	SR%[1]	RR%[1]	COSR%[2]
LEL to UEL	9.00	3.85	7.20	1	4.60	4.60	1.60
				2	6.60	6.60	3.60
				3	8.60	8.60	5.60
				4	10.40	10.40	7.40/10.40[4]

CLASS 1 CONTRIBUTION RATES 1994–95

	Primary			Secondary			
	SR%[3]	RR%[1]	COSR%[3]	EB	SR%[1]	RR%[1]	COSR%[2]
LEL to UEL	10.00	3.85	8.2	1	3.60	3.60	0.60
				2	5.60	5.60	2.60
				3	7.60	7.60	4.60
				4	10.20	10.20	7.20/10.20[4]

CLASS 1 CONTRIBUTION RATES 1995–96 to 1996–97

	Primary			Secondary			
	SR%[3]	RR%[1]	COSR%[3]	EB	SR%[1]	RR%[1]	COSR%[2]
LEL to UEL	10.00	3.85	8.2	1	3.00	3.00	—
				2	5.00	5.00	2.00
				3	7.00	7.00	4.00
				4	10.20	10.20	7.20/10.20[4]

[1]Rate applies to all earnings by which the earnings bracket has been identified.
[2]Rate applies only to that part of earnings which exceeds the LEL; the relevant standard rate applies to that part of earnings equal to the LEL.
[3]Rate applies only to that part of earnings which exceeds the LEL; the rate of 2% is applied on earnings up to and including the LEL.
[4]Lower rate applies only to earnings which exceed the LEL but do not exceed the UEL; the higher rate applies to any earnings above the UEL.

CLASS 1 CONTRIBUTION RATES 1997–98 and 1998–99

	Primary				Secondary				
	SR%[3]	RR%[1]	COSR%[3]	COMP%	EB	SR%[1]	RR%[1]	COSR%[2]	COMP%[2]
LEL to UEL	10	3.85	8.40	8.40	1	3.00	3.00	0.00	1.50
					2	5.00	5.00	2.00	3.50
					3	7.00	7.00	4.00	5.50
					4	10.00	10.00	7.00/10.00[3]	8.50/10.00[4]

[1]Rates apply to all earnings by which the earnings bracket has been identified.
[2]Rates apply only to that part of earnings which exceeds the LEL; the relevant standard rate applies to that part of earnings equal to the LEL.
[3]Rate applies only to that part of earnings which exceeds the LEL; the rate of 2% is applied on earnings up to and including the LEL.
[4]Lower rate applies only to earnings which exceed the LEL but do not exceed the UEL; the higher rate applies to any earnings above the UEL.

CLASS 1 CONTRIBUTION RATES 1999–2000

	Primary				Secondary			
	SR%	RR%	COSR%	COMP%	SR%	RR%	COSR%[3, 4]	COMP%[3, 4]
	10	3.85	8.40	8.40	12.20	12.20	9.20	11.60

[1]All primary rates apply only to earnings between the LEL and the UEL.
[2]All secondary rates apply only to earnings in excess of the employers earnings threshold (without limit).
[3]The contracted-out rate shown applies only on earnings up to the UEL; any balance will be subject to the SR (ie not contracted-out rate).
[4]In addition, an employer's contracted-out rebate is due on earnings falling between the LEL and the employer's earnings threshold, amounting to 3% of such earnings (COSR) or 0.6% of such earnings (COMP).

CLASS 1 CONTRIBUTION RATES 2000–01

	Primary				Secondary			
	SR%	RR%	COSR%[5]	COMP%[5]	SR%	RR%	COSR%[3, 4]	COMP%[3, 4]
	10	3.85	8.40	8.40	12.20	12.20	9.20	11.60

[1]All primary rates apply only to earnings between the employee's earnings threshold and the UEL.
[2]All secondary rates apply only to earnings in excess of the employer's earnings threshold (without limit).
[3]The contracted-out rate shown applies only on earnings up to the UEL; any balance will be subject to the SR (ie not contracted-out rate).
[4]In addition, an employers contracted-out rebate is due on earnings falling between the LEL and the employer's earnings threshold, amounting to 3% of such earnings (COSR) or 0.6% of such earnings (COMP).
[5]In addition, an employee's contracted out rebate is due on earnings falling between the LEL and the employee's earnings threshold, amounting to 1.6% of such earnings.

Tables of rates of Class 2, 3 and 4 Contributions, annual maxima and SSP/SMP rebates can be found on the inside back cover.

Tolley's
National Insurance
Contributions
2000–01

Edited by Jon Golding ATT TEP,
with consulting editor Peter Arrowsmith FCA

Tolley Publishing

Whilst every care has been taken to ensure the accuracy of the contents of this work, no responsibility for loss occasioned to any person acting or refraining from action as a result of any statement in it can be accepted by the author or publishers.

Inland Revenue texts are Crown copyright and are reproduced by kind permission of the Agency and the Controller of Her Majesty's Stationery Office.

Tax Bulletins and Contributions Agency National Insurance News contain certain qualifications that appear on the back page of each issue. These should be referred to before reliance is placed on an interpretation.

Published by
Tolley
2 Addiscombe Road
Croydon
Surrey CR9 5AF England
020–8686 9141

Typeset by Kerrypress Ltd
Luton, Beds., England

Printed and bound in Great Britain by
The Bath Press, Bath

© Reed Elsevier (UK) Limited 2000
ISBN 0 75450 659–2

Preface

The text of this 2000–01 edition states the law as it stood up to and including 30 April 2000. In addition, a supplement will be issued in December 2000 giving details of the changes in law and practice relating to National Insurance Contributions from the publication of Tolley's National Insurance Contributions 2000–01 to the 2000 'Green' Budget.

This 2000-01 edition is being published at an earlier date than usual. This is to ensure that the many changes in the area of National Insurance contributions are readily accessible to practitioners. Also, this year, as well as the changes mentioned below, a new chapter is included at chapter 58 called 'Working Case Study.' This case study is cross-referenced to chapters in the earlier part of the book with typical examples. It also includes useful Internet website addresses and other source information references.

This work is published shortly after the introduction of a new threshold for the payment of employee's contributions and a shift in emphasis for the self-employed between Class 2 and Class 4 following the 1998 Taylor Report. The extended Class 1A charge on all taxable benefits in kind will operate from 6 April 2000, imposing further financial burden on employers– but is not yet enshrined in legislation. The employee's threshold, whilst welcome, does nothing at all to alleviate employers' record keeping requirements and creates a great deal of complication for contracted-out workers and/or where earnings from different employments have to be aggregated. As ever, this book aims to provide an up to date and comprehensive guide to all aspects of the contribution system.

Butterworths Tolley is pleased again this year to have the expertise of Peter Arrowsmith FCA as consulting editor. Peter is an independent specialist in National Insurance matters, offering consultancy services as well as writing and speaking widely on the subject.

Whilst the book seeks to give comprehensive coverage in the text and examples, Butterworths Tolley always welcomes comments on the book's coverage and suggestions for improvement.

Tolley Publishing
2 Addiscombe Road
Croydon
Surrey
CR9 5AF

Contents

Contents

Abbreviations and References

For the full names and numbers of statutory instruments which appear in the text, see the Table of Statutory Instruments at the back of the book.

AC	=	Law Reports, Appeal Cases
A-G	=	Attorney-General
AER	=	All England Law Reports
afr	=	armed forces rate
ALU	=	Appeals Liaison Unit
AOG	=	Adjudication Officers' Guide
APP	=	Appropriate personal pension
Art	=	Article
BTC	=	British Tax Cases
CA	=	Contributions Agency
cf	=	compare
Ch	=	Law Reports, Chancery Division
CIR	=	Commissioners of Inland Revenue
cl	=	clause
Cm	=	Command (1986 to date)
Cmnd	=	Command (1956–1986)
CMLR	=	Common Market Law Reports
CP	=	Decision of the Social Security Commissioners (Pension)
c-o	=	contracted-out
Comm	=	Community
COMP	=	Contracted-out money-purchase schemes
COR/cor	=	contracted-out rate
COSR	=	Contracted-out salary related
Col	=	Column
DC	=	Divisional Court
DSS	=	Department of Social Security
DLR	=	Dominion Law Reports (Canada)
DoE	=	Department of Employment
EAT	=	Employment Appeal Tribunal
E & B	=	Ellis and Blackburn's Reports
EB	=	Earnings bracket
E & E	=	Ellis and Ellis's Reports
EC	=	European Community
ECJ	=	European Court of Justice
ECR	=	European Court Reports
EEA	=	European Economic Area
EEC	=	European Economic Community
EEET	=	Employee's (i.e. primary) earnings threshold
EO	=	Executive Officer
ERET	=	Employer's (i.e. secondary) earnings threshold
ESC	=	Extra-statutory concession
EU	=	European Union
FA	=	Finance Act
FICA	=	Federal Insurance Contributions Act
HCP	=	House of Commons Paper
HL	=	House of Lords
ICAEW	=	The Institute of Chartered Accountants in England and Wales
ICR	=	Law Reports, Industrial Cases Reports
ICTA	=	Income and Corporation Taxes Act

Abbreviations and References

IR	=	Inland Revenue
IRLR	=	Industrial Relations Law Reports
ITR	=	Industrial Tax Reports
J	=	Mr Justice
JP	=	Justice of the Peace Reports
JSA	=	Jobseeker's Act
Kay	=	Kay's Reports, Chancery
KB	=	Law Reports, King's Bench Division
KIR	=	Knight's Industrial Reports
LEL	=	Lower Earnings Limit
LJ	=	Lord Justice
LTR	=	Law Times Reports
MSC	=	Manpower Services Commission
NAO	=	National Audit Office
n-c-o	=	not contracted-out
NI	=	National Insurance
NICO	=	National Insurance Contributions Office
No	=	Number
O	=	Order
ODCQ	=	Office for the Determination of Contribution Questions
P	=	page
Para	=	paragraph
PAYE	=	Pay As You Earn
PC	=	Personal Contact Manual (Inland Revenue)
PD	=	Law Reports, Probate, Divorce and Admiralty Division
PEB	=	Primary earnings bracket
PSA	=	Pensions Schemes Act
Pt	=	Part
QB	=	Law Reports, Queen's Bench Division
Reg	=	Regulation
r	=	rule
RR/rr	=	reduced rate
RSC	=	Rules of the Supreme Court
R(P)	=	Reports of the Social Security Commissioners (Retirement Pension)
R(S)	=	Reports of the Social Security Commissioners (Sickness Benefits)
R(U)	=	Reports of the Social Security Commissioners (Unemployment Benefit)
s/Sec	=	Section
SC	=	Court of Session Cases (Scotland)
Sc & Div	=	Law Reports, Scots and Divorce Appeals
Sch	=	Schedule
SEB	=	Secondary earnings bracket
SEO	=	Senior Executive Officer
SI	=	Statutory Instrument
SLT	=	Scots Law Times Reports
SMP	=	Statutory maternity pay
SR/sr	=	standard rate
SSA	=	Social Security Act
SSAA	=	Social Security Administration Act
SSAC	=	Social Security Advisory Committee
SSALE	=	Social Security Advice Line for Employers
SSCBA	=	Social Security Contributions and Benefits Act

SSC(TF)A	=	Social Security Contributions (Transfer of Functions, etc.) Act
SSP	=	Statutory sick pay
SSPA	=	Social Security Pensions Act
STC	=	Simon's Tax Cases
STI	=	Simon's Tax Intelligence
TC	=	Tax Cases
TLR	=	Times Law Reports
TMA	=	Taxes Management Act 1970
UEL	=	Upper Earnings Limit
UK	=	United Kingdom
US	=	United States Supreme Court Reports
Vol	=	Volume
WLR	=	Weekly Law Reports
WR	=	Weekly Reporter
WWR	=	Western Weekly Reports (Canada)
YT	=	Youth Training

1 Introduction

1.1 THE BACKGROUND TO THIS WORK

A little under 90 years ago, David Lloyd George stood before Parliament and introduced to the honourable members the novel concept of national insurance. Anticipating a hostile response to the new levy, however, he described his contribution scheme as nothing more than a 'temporary expedient' and he hastened to assure the House that it was something which would 'at no distant date' become 'unnecessary'. Ironically, Lloyd George's 'temporary expedient' has now achieved a permanence even greater than that of income tax (another 'temporary' measure, but one which, unlike national insurance, requires an annual Finance Act to revive it), and has established itself as, with some regularity, the State's second or third largest source of income. In 2000–01 alone, for example, the yield is expected to exceed *fifty-nine thousand million pounds*! (See NATIONAL INSURANCE FUND (45)).

1.2 A neglected area of law

It is a curious fact, however, that, despite the size and permanence of this levy, few people know very much about it. Even those who have the task of advising others of their financial responsibilities to the State—accountants, solicitors, business consultants and the like—have (until more recent times) treated it with a disregard that they would not dream of according to any other of Parliament's taxation measures; and they have done so, it seems, in the belief that it cannot 'bite' in the way that other taxes can and that the way in which it 'gnaws' is beyond anyone's control or influence. (As to whether it is correct to refer to national insurance contributions as a tax, see 8.1 ANTI-AVOIDANCE).

1.3 Increasing activity

Whether or not the hitherto widespread disregard for contribution law has been attributable to the reasons suggested at 1.2 above, developments in this field of law have been such as to bring that disregard suddenly and forcibly to an end. With effect from 6 October 1985, a graduated structure for national insurance contributions was introduced and, so far as an employer's liability for secondary CLASS 1 CONTRIBUTIONS (15) is concerned, the upper earnings limit (which until then, had provided a contribution ceiling for an employer irrespective of the amount of earnings paid to any particular employee) was removed. (see 30.1 EARNINGS LIMITS AND THRESHOLDS). Those two changes, along with the abolition of the entry fee in April 1999 and increase in employer's contribution rate to 12.2% (although reducing slightly to 11.9% in April 2001) while easing the contribution burden for low-paid employees and their employers, *increases* that burden for many employers. And, since 1991–92, employers have been faced with a further burden—CLASS 1A CONTRIBUTIONS (16)—which, it is estimated, will, even after tax relief, cost them, collectively, nearly £900 million in 1999–2000. Added, in April 1999, to this is yet another category of contributions—Class 1B and, from April 2000, the extension of the existing Class 1A charge to virtually all benefits in kind. Faced with all this, and with the increasing vigilance of the authorities in all areas of compliance, the majority of employers and their advisers have now become aware that they have been ignoring a tiger which is by no means as toothless as it once appeared.

1.4 THE AIM OF THIS WORK

Placed in the situation outlined at 1.3 above, many employers and their advisers are now finding themselves in positions of some difficulty. They are asking—or being asked—questions to which they have no ready answers. Is a profit-sharing trust still an effective means of avoiding contribution liabilities? Can we split Sally's remuneration between our six subsidiaries so as to take both her and ourselves out of contribution liability? Will contribution liabilities be avoided if we pay for Alan's children's school fees instead of giving him a bonus? Are benefits in kind still an effective way of providing Roger's remuneration package?

When things go wrong and one is faced with a demand for contribution arrears or when one is given notice of an adverse decision on a contribution matter, even the apparently simple question 'Can one appeal?' formerly had no simple answer. There is now a *formal* appeal procedure which is fully considered in Chapter 9.

Then there are all the problems of a more routine nature. Now that Mrs Jones has received her decree nisi may she still pay reduced rate contributions? Should Alan pay contributions on his earnings from his school-holiday job? What do we do about Tony's contributions if we send him to the Paris office for twelve months? The new fellow says he wants to be treated as self-employed—what could be the consequences? How do we calculate Alex's contributions if we appoint him director before the end of the tax year? See case studies at WORKING CASE STUDY (58).

The aim of this work is simply to provide a comprehensive reference guide for employers, company secretaries and managers, as well as for accountants, solicitors and other professional advisers, who, in the course of their work, are obliged to answer these and the host of other such questions which arise in the area of contribution law.

1.5   Key principles

Three particular principles have been adhered to throughout. First, because the statutory source material is extensive (see 1.6 below) and not readily accessible to many potential users of this work, the wording of provisions and regulations has been adhered to as closely as possible wherever this has been consistent with the overall principle of clarity. Second, worked examples with, in some cases, forms and standard letters have been provided to illustrate every major point of practical difficulty. Third, because of the increasing mobility of labour throughout the European Union and the rest of the western world, the international aspect of each topic is considered wherever relevant, full reference being made to Community law and, more generally, to bilateral treaties where these bear on the topic in question.

1.6   SOURCES OF CONTRIBUTION LAW

Apart from the relationship created by statute, there is no antecedent relationship between an individual (or company) and the State which could require the payment of contributions. National insurance contributions are, like taxes, creatures of statute, and the main statutes in question are *Social Security Contributions and Benefits Act 1992, Social Security Administration Act 1992* and *Social Security Act 1998*. The first two of these Acts are consolidations of earlier legislation and are largely skeletal. They require the flesh of secondary legislation to make them an effective body of law. The secondary legislation takes the form of regulations and orders made by statutory instrument and there are now scores of these which, either in whole or in part, are of current application in the field of contributions.

1.7   Case law

There is very little case law concerning the contribution legislation itself, but such as there is has been drawn upon fully in this work, as has case law of more general application where it is seen as relevant to the subject in hand. The concept of 'residence', for example, is a concept common to both tax law and contribution law but defined in neither. As the courts have pronounced very fully on its meaning in its tax law context, however, their pronouncements are a useful guide to its meaning in the present context. So, too, with the meaning of 'contract of service' which lies at the very root of all categorisation questions. Here, case law arising out of employment protection legislation provides an additional useful insight into the judicial mind as it approaches the question whether a person is truly an employee or not.

1.8 Ministers' decisions

The old appeal procedure (such as it was) that applied until 1 April 1999 under contribution law resulted in decisions which, for a time, were published. These are no longer in print but, where relevant, reference has been made to them in this work. They are of no binding force but will, of course, tend to be followed by the authorities where the circumstances surrounding a current problem are on all fours with the circumstances in a decided case.

1.9 Adjudication Officers' Guide

Adjudication Officers are civil servants within the DSS and the DoE who, independent of Ministers and other departmental officials, decide (at first instance) claims to social security benefits. In furtherance of his duties under *SSAA 1992, s 39(2)*, The Chief Adjudication Officer provides for adjudication officers a multi-volume Adjudication Officers' Guide (published by The Stationery Office Ltd) which, although 'it should not. . . be quoted as authority before any tribunal or court' gives much detailed interpretation on many matters of general concern (residence and presence conditions etc.) as well as on the law relating to particular benefits. Where relevant, reference is made to the AOG in this work.

1.10 Leaflets

The Inland Revenue and Benefits Agency publish a large number of LEAFLETS (40) dealing with contribution matters and the editions of these noted at 40.2 are referred to throughout the text. Although providing a useful insight into departmental views on the meaning of the legislation, they do not, however, profess to give an authoritative statement of the law and they have no binding force. The new Contributor's Charter is reproduced at 40.3 LEAFLETS.

1.11 TERRITORIAL SCOPE OF THIS WORK

This work attempts to give a comprehensive statement of contribution law as it applies in England and Wales. The legislation is equally applicable in Scotland, apart from the modifications necessitated by the fact that Scotland possesses separate court and legal systems (e.g. for 'High Court' read 'Court of Session'). The work does not apply to Northern Ireland, though contribution law there is virtually identical with that in Great Britain (see 49.18 OVERSEAS MATTERS).

1.12 APPROACH

The remaining chapters in this work are arranged in strict alphabetical order. This is an ideal arrangement for the person using the work for reference purposes in that each major topic of contribution law has been allotted its own chapter and may thus be accessed without recourse to the index. It may, however, pose difficulties for the person wishing merely to 'read a book about national insurance' and it is suggested that any such person should begin with CATEGORISATION (14) and let the cross-referencing system lead him on from there. In addition to Tables of Contents, Statutes, Statutory Instruments, Cases and Published Decisions, the work contains a

1.13   Introduction

WORKING CASE STUDY (58) which has been designed to enable readers to apply the procedures in the earlier chapters to a situation that reflects real-life problems. In the case study there are cross-references to relevant chapters in the book and Internet web site addresses for further external reference.

1.13   THE FUTURE OF NATIONAL INSURANCE CONTRIBUTIONS

In May 1993, the Secretary of State for Social Security, the Rt Hon Peter Lilley, set up a working group under the government's deregulation initiative. Its terms of reference were

'To review how employees' earnings and expenses are defined for national insurance and tax purposes and, having regard to

- the contributory principle for national insurance

- the importance of a broad tax and NICs base in order to make further progress towards lower tax rates

to identify changes which would reduce burdens on employers.'

The working party's report was published in September of the same year and was intended as a discussion document. It did, however, recommend that, as an essential first step, there should be a single definition of earnings/emoluments for both tax and NIC. This should be closer to the current tax definition to ensure a wider base on which tax and contributions could be calculated. Following such alignment, the group envisaged further steps being taken to reduce the burden on employers which arises from their having to operate two different systems of deductions from remuneration. Initiatives were announced by the Secretary of State for Social Security on 30 November 1994 for harmonisation of income tax and NIC. The transfer of the Contributions Agency to the Inland Revenue occurred on 1 April 1999 and confirmed the closer working ties. The *Social Security Contributions (Transfer of Functions, etc.) Act 1999* became law in February 1999 and transferred certain functions relating to national insurance contributions to the Commissioners of Inland Revenue from the Secretary of State. Further, a letter in The Times on 15 February 2000 prompted some emotive responses:

'Crisis in NI system

Sir, Writing from an association representing employer's payroll interests, [we] fully endorse . . . comments (letters, 9 February) but wish to add that the system is in crisis. National Insurance no longer has any insurance element. The only purpose it now serves is as a means for government to increase the overall tax take at the same time claiming an income tax reduction.

National Insurance rules and operation are so complex as to defy comprehension except among a few specialists. It imposes a huge compliance burden on employers, and this will increase further in April when NI is extended to cover perks and some expenses incurred by employees.

The Inland Revenue's computerised NI recording system appears to be at meltdown. Pension payments are being estimated or delayed rather than based on accurate contribution records, and every year £18 million pounds of taxpayers' money is spent correcting errors. Worse still, hundreds of pounds of workers' contributions are never properly recorded or allocated to contributor records—they just sit in a sort of "suspense" account.

There can be no better time than this year's Budget for the Chancellor to announce a merger of income tax and national insurance.

Yours sincerely,

MIKE NICHOLAS

(Chairman) Payroll Alliance.'

The Chancellor of the Exchequer did not merge income tax and national insurance in his Budget on 21 March 2000!

Also, copies of the memorandum of understanding between the Inland Revenue and DSS are available on the Internet under Inland Revenue http://www.inlandrevenue.gov.uk and DSS http://www.dss.gov.uk and also in Tolley's Practical NIC 1999, p 48.

2 Administration

Cross-references. See 9.3 to 9.6, 9.15 and 9.19 APPEALS AND REVIEWS for jurisdiction of the Secretary of State and remedies for dissatisfaction with his exercise of it; 32.1 to 32.4 ENFORCEMENT for powers of inspectors; INLAND REVENUE (37); NATIONAL INSURANCE FUND (45); NATIONAL INSURANCE NUMBER (46) for contribution-recording procedures and inaccuracy of records; 49.13 and 49.17 OVERSEAS MATTERS for derogation of authority to international bodies; 51.1 RATES AND LIMITS for the Secretary of State's power to alter contribution rates; WORKING CASE STUDY (58).

Other Sources. Simon's NIC, Part I, Section 9.

2.1 DEPARTMENT OF SOCIAL SECURITY AND INLAND REVENUE

Until 1 April 1999, the DSS was the Government Department responsible for giving effect to parliamentary legislation on matters of social security. Between 1 November 1968 and 25 July 1988 the functions of the DSS and those of the Department of Health were combined as functions of a single Department of Health and Social Security, but on 25 July 1988 the pre-1 November 1968 division of responsibility was restored. The DSS also still administers the various contributory and non-contributory State benefit schemes throughout Great Britain, including the statutory sick pay and statutory maternity pay schemes. It has a total staff of nearly 90,000. (Social Security Press Release 96/035, 28 February 1996).

Since April 1991, all social security operations have been undertaken by Agencies—though still within the framework of ministerial responsibility (see 2.2 below).

The two main agencies (each of which is a Next Steps agency and has its own business plan approved by Ministers and which together cover the DSS's major executive functions) are:

(*a*) *The Information Technology Services Agency* (ITSA). This agency came into being on 2 April 1990 and services the computing and telecommunications needs of the DSS. Its chief executive is George McCorkell. (DSS Press Releases 90/52, 7 February 1990; 90/170, 2 April 1990; 93/12, 21 January 1993; ITSA Annual Report and Accounts 1993–94; 95/042, 29 March 1995; 96/286, 12 December 1996; 99/039, 22 February 1999).

(*b*) *The Benefits Agency* (BA). This agency came into being in April 1991 and its head office is located in Leeds. It is responsible for the administration of all social security benefit claims and entitlements, and for the payment annually of approximately £47 billion in contributory benefits as well as non-contributory benefits such as Income Support and non-contributory jobseeker's allowance. It has 65,000 staff in around 470 local offices and about 600 staff in its Leeds headquarters. (DSS Press Releases 89/490, 14 November 1989; 90/52, 7 February 1990; 90/78, 16 February 1990; 90/240, 15 May 1990; 91/1(BA), 10 April 1991; 95/042, 29 March 1995; 96/056, 20 March 1996).

The former Contributions Agency was set up in 1991 and replaced the National Insurance Contributions Unit which was formed as a transitional measure on 5 April 1990. From 1 April 1999 all 8,000 Contribution Agency staff at Newcastle and 115 local office locations joined the Inland Revenue and a new executive office called the National Insurance Contributions Office (NICO) replaced the CA. The NICO is run from a head office in Newcastle upon Tyne and is responsible for

(i) collecting national insurance contributions, 'with particular emphasis on ensuring full compliance by employers with payment and notification requirements';

(ii)   for maintaining about 77 million individual records of which 47 million are active (see CA Specialist Conference notes, October 1997 page 19 and 46.4 NATIONAL INSURANCE NUMBER); and

(iii)   providing NI-related information to enable benefits to be paid promptly and accurately.

NICO's first Director is George Bertram, previously the chief executive of the Contributions Agency. On 4 January 2000 Ann Chant was appointed Director General, Strategic Services Delivery which will include management responsibilities of NICO. See IR Press Release 1 December 1999.

In March 1997, the former CA published two charters—an employers' charter and a contributors' charter—which stated the Inland Revenue/CA's service standards. The employer's charter replaced the one written in January 1994. The Contributors' Charter was updated by the Inland Revenue in April 1999. See 40.3. (CA Press Release, 24 April 1995; DSS Press Releases 91/117, 1 August 1991 and 94/3, 17 January 1994 and CA Business Plan 1998–1999).

Specialised groups within Inland Revenue NICO may be contacted as follows

Longbenton, Newcastle upon Tyne, NE98 1ZZ

Class 1A Group	Class 1A remittances and collection	Tel 0645 155176
Deferment Group	Deferment of Class 1, 2 and 4 contributions	Tel 0645 157141
Self Employment Directorate	Class 2 and Class 3 (including direct debit)	Tel 0645 154655
		Fax 0645 153 417
Magnetic Media	End of year returns in computer format	Tel 0191 2257936
Overseas Conts Helpline		Tel 0645 154811
Overseas Conts (EC)	NI for persons moving in EC/EEA	Tel 0191 2253886
Overseas Conts (RA)	NI for persons moving outside EC/EEA	Tel 0191 2253299
Refunds Group	Refunds on NI paid in error or excess	Tel 0645 155628
COEG	All aspects of contracted-out employment	Tel 0645 150150
Posting Check Group	Computer check problems re reduced rate elections, age exception etc.	Tel 0645 154553

There are other Agencies within the DSS, e.g. the Child Support Agency and the War Pensions Agency.

2.2   The Secretary of State for Social Security and the Treasury

At the head of the DSS is the Secretary of State for Social Security (at present The Rt Hon Alistair Darling MP) who is also a member of the Cabinet and is politically responsible to Parliament for the proper administration of the law on matters of social security. For this reason, social security legislation imposed duties on and granted powers to the Secretary of State *per se* and not (as might be expected) to the Department over which he presides, though, in practice, the discharge of such duties and the exercise of such powers was almost invariably delegated to DSS inspectors and other officers who are authorised to act in his name. This is fully in accordance with the common law constitutional principle that powers given to a Secretary of State in a statute may be exercised under his authority by responsible officials of his department unless the common law right to delegate has been negatived or confined by express statutory provisions. (*Carltona Ltd v Comr of Works [1943] 2 All ER 560 per Lord Greene MR at 563; R v Secretary of State for the Home Dept ex p Oladehinde [1990] 2 All ER 367 per Lord Donaldson MR at 381*).

The Social Security Acts granted wide legislative powers to the Secretary of State and these are exercised by statutory instrument in the making of numerous orders and regulations. Once the drafts of such orders and regulations have been laid before Parliament and approved by a resolution of each House in accordance with the procedures prescribed in *Statutory Instruments Act 1946*, they become law and acquire the force of the enabling statute. [*SSAA 1992, ss 189, 190; SSCBA 1992, ss 175, 176*].

2.3   Administration

These legislative powers are now transferred to the Inland Revenue and/or the Treasury by *SSC(T)A 1999*, but the concurrence of the Secretary of State is still required in certain instances. These are mainly circumstances where the proposed instrument would have an effect on potential contributory benefit entitlement (including statutory sick pay and statutory maternity pay) for which the Secretary of State still retains policy responsibility, notwithstanding the transfer of functions on 1 April 1999.

The Secretary of State is assisted in his task by a Minister of State for Social Security and Welfare Reform, Stephen Timms MP. He has responsibility for, *inter alia* operational matters and National Insurance Contributions.

The DSS spokesperson in the House of Lords is Baroness Hollis of Heigham. Her responsibilities include the War Pensions Agency and the Child Support Agency.

The three under-secretaries are Baroness Hollis of Heigham, Angela Eagle MP and Hugh Bayley MP. National Insurance contributions, the Contributions Agency, its transfer to the Inland Revenue and deregulation are within the list of responsibilities of Mr Bayley.

The Inland Revenue is accountable to HM Treasury where the Chancellor of the Exchequer, Gordon Brown MP, is assisted by the Chief Secretary to the Treasury, Andrew Smith MP, and the Paymaster General, Dawn Primarolo MP.

2.3   Headquarters

The address of the Inland Revenue is Somerset House, Strand, London WC2R 1LB though it operates through numerous divisions and many local offices. The principal of these, so far as the contribution side of the social security scheme is concerned, is the National Insurance Contributions Office, Longbenton, Newcastle upon Tyne NE98 1ZZ, tel. 0191 213 5000 at which all contribution records are held on computer (Records Division) and attention is given to specialist matters such as liability for contributions when working abroad (International Services Section); deferment of contribution liability in multiple employment situations (Deferment Group); refund of overpaid contributions (Refunds Group); questions relating to contracting-out of the State pension scheme (Contracted-Out Employments Group); administration of appeals (Appeals Liaison Unit) and liability of mariners (Maritime Section).

The efficient administration of benefits, the implementation of information technology within the DSS, and the smooth-running of the reforms introduced by *SSA 1986* is the responsibility of the Social Security Management Board which is chaired by the DSS Permanent Secretary. Its members are senior DSS and DoE officials, plus two non-executive members. (DSS Press Release 88/405, 17 November 1988).

There was also an Occupational Pensions Board (dissolved on 5 April 1997) which was set up under *Social Security Act 1973* now consolidated into the *Pensions Schemes Act 1993*. It advised the Secretary of State on occupational and personal pensions matters and administering the contracting-out, equal access and preservation requirements of occupational pensions legislation. Its address was PO Box 1NN, Newcastle upon Tyne, NE99 1NN. The Chairman of the Board was Peter Carr CBE. The OPB ceased in April 1997 by way of provision in the *Pensions Act 1995* and at first the CA and now IR NICO is responsible for the contracting out requirements and certification thereof. (CA Specialist Conference, 20 February 1996). The Occupational Pensions Regulatory Authority (OPRA), Invicta House, Trafalgar Place, Brighton BN1 4DW headed by John Hayes CBE took over the remaining functions of the OPB. Tel. 01273 627600. Fax. 01273 627688. (DSS Press Release 96/084, 1 May 1996).

2.4   Field Operations

All contributions and compliance work which requires a local presence is dealt with by Inland Revenue staff, many of whom will have been CA employees before 1 April 1999.

2.5   Local offices

Local DSS offices come under regional control and number approximately 450. Each is staffed by a manager (a senior executive officer or principal), an assistant manager (a higher executive officer) and up to six executive officers and other staff. Some 115 local offices had, on 31 March 1999, a contribution section manned by CA staff. On 1 April 1999 those sections became Inland Revenue offices and most that have not already done so are likely to merge into one physical location within the next year. In some instances the DSS, CA and Inland Revenue already shared the same building as at March 1999 so physical merger will not need to be addressed separately.

2.6   Employer compliance officers (NIC)

Former CA inspectors have now become employer compliance officers and currently number around 2,000 and are almost exclusively deployed in monitoring and enforcing compliance with contribution law, although since 1992–93 their activities have been extended to include educational visits under the title Customer Service Manager. For that reason, their powers are necessarily wide and include those of entry, inquiry and examination (see 32.1 to 32.4 ENFORCEMENT).

2.7   Information

The Inland Revenue publication 'Tax Bulletin' may be obtained by subscription at an annual cost of £22 (cheques payable to 'Inland Revenue'). Application should be made to Inland Revenue, Finance Division, Barrington Road, Worthing, West Sussex BN12 4XH. Alternatively, 'Tax Bulletin' and IR Press Releases may be found on the Internet at the following address: http://www.inlandrevenue.gov.uk. The CA's 'NI News' is no longer published.

Explanatory leaflets may be obtained from local Inland Revenue offices, including those that were not part of the DSS organisation prior to April 1999. Those employers who have computer systems can obtain a copy of the Information Package for computer bureaux and computer users which is usually available in January.

On 22 February 1988 the DSS established a free, social security advice line for employers and the self-employed (SSALE) which was accessed by dialling a freephone number. SSALE, based in Glasgow, provided general advice on procedural matters relating to national insurance contributions, statutory sick pay and statutory maternity pay, and offered clarification on matters dealt with in the various guides for employers published by the DSS. (DSS Press Release, 16 February 1988). The service was extended and reviewed in 1992–93, with more up-to-date telecommunications equipment being added in 1993–94 and 1994–95. It dealt with 327,703 calls in 1995–96 and attained Charter Mark status. Following the close workings between the CA, Inland Revenue and Customs and Excise a tripartite telephone helpline was field-tested in Scotland. This number is in use nationally from 7 October 1996; the number is 0845 7143143 with calls charged at the local rate. This number now replaces the former freephone facility and continues in operation after the transfer to the IR.

In April each year the Benefits Agency information service issues CAT 1 'A catalogue of leaflets, posters and information' which details all the publicity material for the DSS agencies and all national insurance contributions leaflets. The latter are now also included in the Inland Revenue 'Catalogue of Leaflets'. See 40.2 LEAFLETS.

2.8 Administration

2.8 Inland Revenue Schedule E Compliance section

A special compliance unit of the former Contributions Agency was set up in 1994-95 operating out of Bromley in Kent. The main purpose of the unit was to administer the national insurance system by way of visits to the major employers who have employees totalling 2,000–2,500 or more. The employer was given 6–8 weeks' notice of an impending visit unless there was or it was suspected that an NIC mitigation scheme was in operation in which case the visit would be unannounced. See [**Case Study 9**] in WORKING CASE STUDY (58). It is understood that significant amounts of NICs were being recouped by these visits which involved teams of Inspectors spending up to six weeks at the employer's establishment and consequently there was invariably a large amount of arrears payable at the end of the visit. The Inspectors were usually satisfied with going back six years but under the *Limitation Act 1980, s 32* in the case of fraud, concealment and mistake this limit could be breached. However, although *s 37(1)* states that the Act applies to proceedings by or against the Crown it does not apply in the case of recovery of any tax, duty or interest. [*LA1980, s 37(2)*]. These activities went on to form part of the Large Employers Group, controlled from Newcastle and upon transfer to the IR merged with the IR's Schedule E Compliance section in the Midlands.

3   Age Exception

Cross-references. See 7.2 ANNUAL MAXIMUM; 15.2 CLASS 1 CONTRIBUTIONS; 18.2 CLASS 2 CONTRIBUTIONS; 19.2 CLASS 3 CONTRIBUTIONS; 20.3 CLASS 4 CONTRIBUTIONS; WORKING CASE STUDY (58).

Other Sources. Simon's NIC, Part I, Section 2, Chapter 8.267; Tolley's Social Security and State Benefits Handbook 2000–01.

3.1   PERSONS UNDER 16

No liability for either primary or secondary CLASS 1 CONTRIBUTIONS (15) can arise where earnings are paid to an employed earner who has not attained the age of 16. [*SSCBA 1992, s 6(1)*]. Earnings of school children on work experience schemes, school children working as newspaper delivery boys/girls, etc. are entirely exempt from contribution liability. This exception ceases with the commencement of the sixteenth anniversary of the employed earner's date of birth and any earnings paid to him or for his benefit on or after that anniversary attract a contribution liability in the normal way, even if earned before the relevant date and even if the employed earner is still undergoing full-time education (see also APPRENTICES, TRAINEES AND STUDENTS (10)). [*Family Law Reform Act 1969, s 9(1); SSCBA 1992, ss 6(1), 173*].

An employed earner who attains the age of 16 is under no legal obligation to inform his employer of the fact but the employer is legally obliged to discharge any contribution liability which arises on or after that date. Accordingly, any employer who takes into his employment a person who is not yet 16 would be well advised to record the date of the employee's sixteenth birthday on that person's pay record and to request the individual to obtain an appropriate age exception certificate, making application on Form CA 2835U.

3.2   Class 2 contributions

The 'under 16' exception provision in relation to CLASS 2 CONTRIBUTIONS (18) corresponds to that set out at 3.1 above but, because Class 2 contributions are flat-rated and relate to contribution weeks, a self-employed earner whose sixteenth birthday falls within a contribution week is liable to pay a Class 2 contribution for that week even though he is, for part of it, below the specified age. [*SSCBA 1992, ss 2(5), 11(1); Contributions Regs, Reg 54(2)*].

A 'contribution week' is a period of seven days beginning with midnight between Saturday and Sunday. [*Contributions Regs, Reg 1(2)*].

3.3   Class 3 contributions

No liability to pay CLASS 3 CONTRIBUTIONS (19) can ever arise as such contributions are of an entirely voluntary nature. [*SSCBA 1992, s 1(2)*]. The entitlement to pay such contributions is, however, subject to age exception in that payment is prohibited in respect of

(a)   any week before that in which the sixteenth anniversary of the date of birth occurs [*SSCBA 1992, ss 13(1), 173; Family Law Reform Act 1969, s 9(1)*]; and

(b)   the year in which the seventeenth or eighteenth anniversary of the date of birth occurs if, in an earlier tax year, Class 1, Class 2 or Class 3 contributions sufficient to yield a qualifying EARNINGS FACTOR (29) for that year have been paid [*Contributions Regs, Reg 28(1)(f)*].

3.4 Age Exception

3.4 Class 4 contributions

In the case of CLASS 4 CONTRIBUTIONS (20), exception from liability, though available to anyone who at the beginning of the year of assessment is under the age of 16, will not be obtained unless application is made. The Secretary of State and now the Inland Revenue, by issuing a certificate of exception, signifies acceptance that the age condition has been fulfilled. [*SSCBA 1992, s 17(1)(2); Contributions Regs, Reg 60(2)–(4), (6)*]. As no possible benefit can accrue to a contributor from the payment of Class 4 contributions [*SSCBA 1992, s 21(1)(2)*], exception should be claimed whenever it is available.

3.5 Application for Class 4 exception

Application is by form CA 2835U which is obtainable from Deferment Group (see 2.3 ADMINISTRATION) and should be made before the beginning of the year of assessment for which exception is sought or, if later, before contributions become due and payable. The certificate of exception is issued directly to the Inland Revenue local office dealing with the Self-assessment tax return and, in accordance therewith, the Inland Revenue will not be expecting to receive any Class 4 contributions for which the applicant would otherwise be liable. [*Contributions Regs, Reg 60(3)–(5)*].

3.6 Rectification of erroneous Class 4 assessment

If Class 4 contributions are paid for a year of assessment and a certificate of exception is issued for that year or would have been so issued if application had been made in good time, those contributions must be repaid to the earner, unless (and except to the extent that) they are treated (at the Inland Revenue's option) as paid on account of other contributions properly payable under contribution legislation. [*Contributions Regs, Regs 68, 69(1)*]. Repayment is subject to time limits and application rules (see 53.2 REPAYMENT AND RE-ALLOCATION).

3.7 PERSONS OVER PENSIONABLE AGE

An employed earner who attains pensionable age is to be excepted from liability for Class 1 primary contributions on any earnings paid to him or for his benefit *after* that date, unless those earnings would normally have fallen to be paid to him or for his benefit *before* that date, in which case the exception is not to apply. [*SSCBA 1992, s 6(2); Contributions Regs, Reg 20A, as amended by Contributions Amendment No 2 Regs 1985, Reg 3*]. Where a payment of earnings is made to or for the benefit of an employed earner in the tax year in which he attains pensionable age but *before* the date in that tax year on which he reaches that age, and the relevant payment of earnings would normally fall to be made *after* that date, the general rule concerning mis-timed payments applies (see 31.4 EARNINGS PERIODS) so that the earner is to be excepted from liability for Class 1 primary contributions on those earnings also. [*Contributions Regs, Reg 6(1)(a)*]. That general rule is of no application, however, where the normal payment date and the actual payment date of a mis-timed payment of earnings fall within different tax years. [*Reg 6(3)*]. A special rule has been introduced, therefore, to except a person from liability for primary Class 1 contributions on earnings which, though paid to him before he attains pensionable age, would normally fall to be paid to him in a subsequent tax year. [*Contributions Regs, Reg 20, as amended by Contributions Amendment No 4 Regs 1985, Reg 3*].

Example
Andrew and Bill each became 65 on 18 March 2000. Each normally received an annual bonus from his employer: Andrew on 31 March and Bill on 30 April. In 2000, however, each received his bonus on 28 February. Although each received his bonus before he reached pensionable age, neither has a primary Class 1

liability as regards that bonus as, in each case, the bonus would normally have fallen to be paid after pensionable age had been attained: in Andrew's case, within the same tax year, and in Bill's case, within a subsequent tax year.

Since 6 April 1978, it has been of no relevance for age exception purposes whether retirement from regular employment actually takes place on the attainment of pensionable age or not.

Pensionable age is, in the case of a man, 65, and in the case of a woman born before 6 April 1950, 60. For women born after 5 April 1955 it is 65, and for those born between these dates a sliding scale operates to determine the day on which pensionable age is attained. See table below for graph regarding approximate new state pension ages and in the *Pensions Act 1995, 4 Sch, Part 1*. See also, leaflet EQP1a and Social Security Departmental Report, Cmnd 3213 page 45.

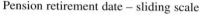

Pension retirement date – sliding scale

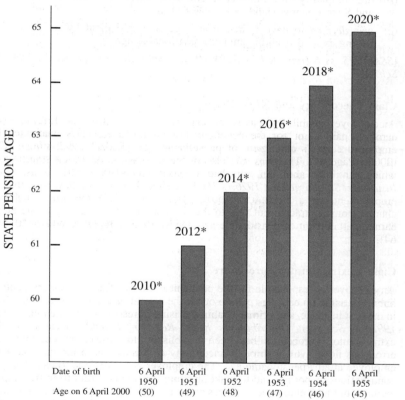

Date of birth	6 April 1950	6 April 1951	6 April 1952	6 April 1953	6 April 1954	6 April 1955
Age on 6 April 2000	(50)	(49)	(48)	(47)	(46)	(45)

*Year of retirement

If the number of tax months or part tax months between 5 April 1950 and the woman's date of birth is an odd number, that number of months is added to the date of the woman's 60th birthday. The day on which she attains pensionable age is deemed to fall on the immediately following 6th of the month. If the number of whole or part tax months falling between 5 April 1950 and her date of birth is an even number, that number of months is added to the date of her 60th birthday, but the day on which she attains pensionable age is deemed to fall on the immediately preceding

6th of the month. A tax month runs from the 6th of one calendar month to the 5th of the next calendar month. [*SSCBA 1992, s 122(1)* and *Pensions Act 1995, 4 Sch*].

Example
Imogen was born on 29 March 1954. This falls within the 48th tax month after 5 April 1950. 48 months are therefore added to the date of her 60th birthday, bringing the date to 29 March 2018. As the addition was an even number of months, she attains pensionable age on 6 March 2018.

3.8 Class 1 exception pre-6 April 1978

Prior to 6 April 1978, exception from contribution liability on the grounds of being over pensionable age was only permitted if the person concerned

(*a*) had actually retired from regular employment; or

(*b*) did not qualify for a category A retirement pension (see Tolley's Social Security and State Benefits Handbook 2000–01); or

(*c*) was *deemed* to have retired from regular employment by reason of 5 years having expired from his attaining pensionable age.

[*SSA 1975, ss 6 (repealed by SSPA 1975, 5 Sch), 27(5) (repealed by SSA 1989, 1 Sch 1)*].

3.9 Class 1 secondary and NI surcharge exclusion

An employer's liability to pay secondary CLASS 1 CONTRIBUTIONS (15.2) in respect of earnings paid to or for the benefit of an employed earner is unaffected by the employed earner's attainment of pensionable age. [*SSCBA 1992, s 6(2)*] (CWG 2 (2000), Page 64). This was true also of the NATIONAL INSURANCE SURCHARGE (47) which, until its abolition, attached to such secondary contributions. [*National Insurance Surcharge Act 1976, s 1(1)*]. It should be noted, however, that, if the employment was a CONTRACTED-OUT EMPLOYMENT (23.2), the *rate* of liability will change from contracted-out rate to the not contracted-out rate upon the employed earner's attainment of pensionable age. [*SSPA 1975, s 30(1)*] (CWG 2 (2000), Page 64).

3.10 Class 1 extra-statutory procedure

An employer is responsible for the payment not only of any secondary contribution liability arising on earnings paid to or for the benefit of an employed earner but also, in the first instance, any primary liability arising in respect of those earnings. [*SSCBA 1992, 1 Sch 3(1); Contributions Regs, Reg 46, 1 Sch*]. Because of this an extra-statutory procedure has been established to protect an employer against erroneous non-payment through uncertainty or mistake as to the date on which an employee attains pensionable age. The employer is to continue to calculate primary contributions as normal and to make the appropriate deduction from the employee's earnings until the employee produces either a certificate of age exception on form CA 4140 or CF 384 or a certificate of earner's non-liability on form CA 2700 or CF381. (CWG 2 (2000), Page 64 and CA 38, Page 43). An employed earner now reaching pensionable age and applying to the Class 1 Caseworker for a certificate authorising his employer not to make primary contribution deductions will receive a CA 4140. It must be stressed that this procedure has no foundation in law and an employer is free to disregard it if he so wishes. Indeed, if he has definite evidence (e.g. sight of a birth certificate) that an employee is, in fact, over pensionable age, he has no legal right—even in the absence of an exception certificate—to continue to make deductions in respect of primary Class 1 contributions and should cease to do so. (CWG 2 (2000), Page 64).

Certificates CF 384, CA 4140, CA 2700 and CF381are DSS/IR property and should be returned to the DSS/IR if they have not been given back to an employee when he leaves his employment. (CWG 2 (2000), Page 64). A certificate is sent to anyone who has stated on a retirement pension claim form (BR 1) to DSS Pensions Section that he or she intends to continue in employment. Anyone who does not automatically receive a certificate and who applies for one will be asked to complete a form CF 13. If it can be verified that the applicant is over retirement age, a certificate will be issued in respect of each employment.

3.11 Rectification of erroneous Class 1 primary deduction

Where, in the absence of a certificate of exemption and because of adherence to the extra-statutory procedure described at 3.10 above, an employer has deducted primary Class 1 contributions for which his employee was not liable, rectification may be effected by the employer within the tax year in which the over-deduction occurred (see 21.4 COLLECTION), but not otherwise. [*Contributions Regs, 1 Sch 13 (2A)*]. The overpayment should be refunded to the employee, the deductions working sheet (P11) and all pay records should be amended and the next payment to the Collector of Taxes should reflect the adjustment. (CWG 2 (2000), Page 64, para 91). Over-deductions in tax years before that in which discovery of the error occurs may be rectified only by the IR. (CWG 2 (2000), Page 64, para 91). This is because, once deduction documentation has been passed to the Collector of Taxes at the end of a tax year, contribution records are updated and must, therefore, be directly amended to reflect any subsequent adjustment (see 46.1 NATIONAL INSURANCE NUMBER).

3.12 Class 2 contributions

An exception from liability to pay CLASS 2 CONTRIBUTIONS (18) corresponding to that described at 3.7 above in relation to Class 1 contributions is given in respect of any period after pensionable age is attained. [*SSCBA 1992, s 11(2)*]. If the sixty-fifth or, as the case may be, sixtieth anniversary of the date of birth occurs during a contribution week (see definition at 3.2 above) and the wording of this provision is strictly construed, no liability can arise for that week as the contribution otherwise payable would, in part, relate to a period after the attainment of pensionable age.

3.13 Class 3 contributions

Because payment of CLASS 3 CONTRIBUTIONS (19) is voluntary, no question of exception from liability to pay such contributions can ever arise. There is, however, a form of 'over pensionable age' exception as regards Class 3 contributions in that payment of such contributions in respect of the tax year in which pensionable age is attained (not merely of any part of it falling after the date on which that age is attained) and of any subsequent tax year is prohibited. [*Contributions Regs, Reg 28(1)(e)*].

As the year in which pensionable age is attained must be disregarded when considering whether or not the contribution conditions for retirement pension have been satisfied, and as payment of Class 3 contributions is to be allowed only with a view to enabling a contributor to satisfy contribution conditions of entitlement to benefit, this age exception from entitlement is entirely necessary. [*SSCBA 1992, ss 13(2), 44(1), 3 Sch 5 as amended by the Pensions Act 1995, 4 Sch 4*].

The above points are somewhat forcefully put in the former CA's Field Operations Manual at paragraphs 3805 and 3806 as follows:

3805   Having made a belated enquiry about pension entitlement or paying voluntary NICs, often years later, they have expected entitlement to RP from the age of 60 by paying voluntary NICs.

3.13   Age Exception

3806   BA and CA use the following check list of points to investigate these cases:

Question	Answer
Is the contributor aged 59 years eight months or over?	If not, consider whether a pension forecast would be more appropriate.
Has the contributor made an earlier enquiry?	If so, what was it about ? Where did they make the enquiry? What were they told?
	If the contributor has not made an earlier enquiry, do not backdate the date of payment of NICs and inform the contributor.
Consider married woman's election position	Do they have a current non-paying election? Have they had one in the past? If so, obtain details. Can they revoke their election to pay voluntary NICs? Have they made earlier enquiries about revoking an election? If so, obtain details.
	If they have enquired before, could they have revoked their election at the time of the original enquiry?
	Has their election lapsed under the two year rule? If the contributor had a valid non-paying election at age 60 and did not make an earlier enquiry about pension entitlement, payment of NICs or revoking their election, they cannot pay voluntary NICs. Inform the contributor.
Voluntary NICs	Are they entitled to pay? Have they asked about paying voluntary NICs before? If so, obtain details. If they have enquired before, could they have revoked their election at the time of the original enquiry to pay voluntary NICs? Consider the time limits for payment. If necessary, can they be extended locally, see *paras 5150–5152.* If not, consider whether they can be extended. Consider the possible effect of payment on other benefits, both their own and their husband's. There may also be an effect on non-DSS benefits, eg private pension. Consider the husband's age. When will he be 65 and when will the contributor be entitled to a pension on his record? Will paying voluntary NICs be worthwhile?

Question	Answer
Pre-48 insurance	Was there pre-48 insurance? If so, consider *Circular PIP/13*. Obtain details of employment history if necessary. If the enquiry concerns pre-48 NICs, take action as per *Circular PIP/13*.
Is there a claim to RP?	When and where was the claim made? What was the outcome? If the previous claim was disallowed, are there now grounds for the Adjudication Officer to consider a review? If the contributor has not made a claim, ask Pensions to issue a claim and advise the contributor to claim but emphasise that the Agency cannot predict the outcome.
Contributor insists they have been inadequately advised.	Obtain details of their reasons for this. If the contributor does not accept any explanation you give refer all papers to CATS3.

3.14 Class 4 contributions

Automatic exception from liability for CLASS 4 CONTRIBUTIONS (20) is given to any earner who, at the beginning of the year of assessment, is over pensionable age. [*SSCBA 1992, s 17(1)(2); Contributions Regs, Reg 58(a)*]. Under *Family Law Reform Act 1969, s 9(1)* and *SSCBA 1992, s 173*, a person is deemed to attain a given age at the commencement of the relevant anniversary of the date of his birth. In law, therefore, a person born on 6 April 1935 will attain the age of 65 at midnight on 5 April 2000 and, although his sixty-fifth birthday falls on the first day of the year of assessment 2000–01, he is nevertheless regarded as being over pensionable age at the beginning of that year of assessment for Class 4 contribution exception purposes. A person who attains pensionable age during the course of a year of assessment remains liable for Class 4 contributions for the whole of that year. (Leaflet CWL2).

It may be observed that, because of the 'preceding year' basis of assessment which formerly applied for the purposes of income tax under Sch D, Cases I and II, profits earned and drawn before the attainment of pensionable age may nevertheless escape assessment to Class 4 contributions.

Example
Donald was 65 on 5 April 1995. His adjusted profits for the years ended 30 April 1994, 30 April 1995 and 30 April 1996 were £10,000, £12,000 and £13,000 respectively. As his business is continuing, those profits are assessable to income tax under Sch D, Case I for the tax years 1995–96 (£10,000 preceding year basis *ICTA 1988, s 60(3)*), 1996–97 (£12,500 adjusted i.e. 12/24ths × £12,000 + £13,000, see *FA 1994, s 200; 20 Sch 2, 5*) and 1997–98 (£13,000 current year basis *ICTA 1988, s 60(3)(b); FA 1994, s 200*) but, because Donald was over pensionable age at the beginning of the first of those years, he is automatically excepted from Class 4 contribution liability on *all* the profits in question—despite the fact that nearly two years worth of those profits were earned *before* his sixty-fifth birthday.

3.15 Age Exception

It will be appreciated that under the new current year basis of tax assessment the effect of this basis of calculation of Class 4 liability will lessen the effect illustrated above. Indeed, for those with a 5 April year-end the apparent anomaly exists no longer.

3.15 Rectification of erroneous Class 4 assessment

If Class 4 contributions are erroneously assessed for any year of assessment at the start of which the earner was over pensionable age, a refund may be obtained by applying to Inland Revenue National Insurance Contributions Office, Deferment Group, General Administration Section, Longbenton, Newcastle upon Tyne NE98 1ZZ (Leaflet CWL2). Any repayment falling due in respect of contributions wrongly paid by reason of such erroneous assessment will, however, (as the tax assessment is not affected) be made by the NICO and not by the Inland Revenue local office responsible for the Tax Return (see 53.2 REPAYMENT AND RE-ALLOCATION). [*Contributions Regs, Regs 68, 69*].

A further anomaly arises in that for women the pensionable age is 60 and therefore a Class 4 exception will arise five years prior to that of a man of equal age. However, the alignment of pensionable ages for men and women will rectify this anomaly. [*Pensions Act 1995, 4 Sch 4*].

Example
George and Alice, who are twins, were born on 30 March 1940 and are equal partners in Twin Peaks Enterprises. The profit under the self-assessment provisions for 2000–01 amount to £23,000 each. George will pay Class 4 contributions amounting to £1,303.05 but Alice will be excepted from payment of Class 4 notwithstanding *Pensions Act 1995, 4 Sch 4* as she was born before 1950.

4 Agency Workers

Cross-references. See 5.2 and 5.6 AGGREGATION OF EARNINGS for the aggregation rules relating to agency workers; 14.14 CATEGORISATION for categorisation by regulation; CLASS 1 CONTRIBUTIONS (15); ENTERTAINERS (33); EXAMINERS (34); HOMEWORKERS AND OUTWORKERS (35); LABOUR-ONLY CONTRACTORS (38).

Other Sources. Simon's NIC, Part I, Section 2, Chapter 4.65–4.120; Leaflet CA 25.

4.1 CATEGORISATION

A person who, on general principles, would fall to be categorised as a self-employed earner (see 14.10 CATEGORISATION) is nonetheless to be treated as an employed earner if, not being a member of one of the excluded groups described at 4.5 below, he

(*a*) obtains employment by or through some third party; *and*

(*b*) renders, or is under an obligation to render, personal service; *and*

(*c*) is subject to (or to the right of) supervision, direction and control as to the manner of rendering of such service; *and*

(*d*) there is a continuing financial relationship between him and the third party (see 4.2 below).

[*Categorisation Regs, Reg 2(1)(2), 1 Sch Pt I para 2*] (CWG 2 (2000), Page 66).

The effect of these rules is to bring within the category of employed earner all persons such as secretaries, clerks, teachers, nurses, draughtsmen and computer programmers who, obtaining through agencies temporary employment which is not under a contract of service in offices, schools, hospitals and nursing homes, etc. would otherwise fall to be treated as self-employed earners for social security purposes. It has been held, for instance, that secretarial 'temps', registered at an employment agency on terms which place no obligation on the agency to find the temps work and which place no obligation on the temps to accept work offered, are *in an employment law context*, employed under contracts for services, not under contracts of service (*Wickens v Champion Employment [1984] ICR 365*); yet such persons will (if the conditions stated above apply) nonetheless fall to be treated as *employed earners* in the context of *national insurance law*. Parallel provisions in *ICTA 1988, s 134* as amended by *FA 1998, ss 55, 56* ensure that such persons are treated as employees for income tax purposes.

4.2 The four criteria

If the IR is to succeed in categorising a person as an employed earner for national insurance contribution purposes merely by virtue of the agency rules, it must be able to show that the person concerned meets all four of the requirements set out at 4.1 above; but, because of the way in which those requirements are set, the IR may find that task easier than one might imagine.

The terms of (*a*), for instance, do *not* require that employment be obtained through a formal employment agency of some kind. If, because of C's involvement, A obtains employment with B, the terms of (*a*) are met, whoever or whatever C might be, and whatever C's normal activities happen to be. The width of the expression 'by or through' ensures that the terms of (*a*) also remain satisfied if a second agency, D, is interposed between C and B.

Likewise, the terms of (*b*) do *not* rule out the possibility of A sending a substitute to work for B in his stead. The DSS used to say that, if substitution takes place, it will need to establish 'how often, what the actual arrangements are and most importantly who pays the replacement worker before deciding what effect this might have on the application of the regulations'. (DSS letter 8 December 1987). Occasional substitution, where the substitute worker is paid instead of the worker whose place he takes, will, it seems, be regarded as leaving unaffected the worker's ongoing obligation to render personal service.

It is worth observing, however, that (b) does require that the supply by the agency is the supply of personal *service*. If, instead, the agency is supplying a package of some kind, e.g. a promotional campaign which merely includes the provision of personnel as part of the package, the agency rules do *not* apply. The personnel involved in such a situation may, however, be employees of the agency itself, i.e. a contract of service may be in existence between the persons concerned and the agency (see 14.3 CATEGORISATION).

As regards (c), the DSS said:

'The rule that the worker must be subject to supervision, direction or control, or right of control, "as to the manner" of the rendering of services generally generates the most arguments. To satisfy this control test, which is more specific than the one in the contract of service rules (see 14.5 CATEGORISATION), we need to look not just at what jobs are to be done and when, but at the right to control *how* the duties are carried out. It matters not whether anyone actually does tell the worker how to go about his work but requires simply to show that someone could. The regulation purposely does not specify who must have that right.' (DSS letter 8 December 1987).

The right may, in other words, lie *either* with the third party who has placed the worker *or* with the person with whom the worker has been placed. In either circumstance, the terms of (c) will be met. If it is once established that, at the outset, the person supplied has been told that he or she must perform duties in a particular manner or in accordance with established practices, the IR can be expected to regard the right of control as subsisting throughout the engagement.

The DSS views expressed here reflect the judgment in the unreported case of *Staples v Secretary of State for Social Services* (15 March 1985) which concerned a chef who could be told what food to prepare but not how to prepare it.

So far as (d) is concerned, there is a 'continuing financial relationship' between a person and a third party through whom he obtains employment when either

(i) earnings for services such as are described at 4.1 above are paid by, or through, or on the basis of accounts submitted by, that third party, or in accordance with arrangements made with that third party; or

(ii) payments, other than to the person employed, are made by way of fees, commission or other similar payments which relate to the continued employment of that person in the employment concerned.

[*Categorisation Regs, 1 Sch Pt I para 2(a)(b)*].

There is *no* continuing financial relationship, however, where the only payment to the agency is an introductory fee (Leaflet CA 25 and CWG 2 (2000), Page 66) and the only continuing financial arrangement is one which arises between the person employed and the person to whom the agency has introduced him on the basis of a contract of service entered into as a result of the introduction e.g. an audit clerk supplied to an accountant through an agency who works on the premises of the accountant's clients. [*Categorisation Regs, 1 Sch Pt I para 2(c)*].

4.3 Secondary contributor

The third person by whom, or through whose agency, the person employed is supplied will fall to be treated as the secondary contributor as regards Class 1 contribution liability on the earnings of the person supplied (see 14.15 CATEGORISA-TION). If, however, the 'third person' is a partnership subject to English law and the person supplied is himself one of its members, the other members of the partnership will be treated as the secondary contributor. [*SSCBA 1992, s 7; Categorisation Regs, Reg 5 and 3 Sch para 2(a)*].

Where the person who should, according to these rules, be the secondary contributor cannot be treated as such because he has no place of business in Great Britain and is neither resident nor present here (see 49.9 OVERSEAS MATTERS), the person to whom the person employed is supplied will be treated as the secondary contributor instead. [*Reg 5 and 3 Sch para 2(c)*].

For some years there was uncertainty as to whether this rule could be applied in situations where a person is sent by a foreign employer to work for someone in GB while remaining under a contract of service with that foreign employer. Having sought information from a number of companies in the UK who are host to such seconded employees, the DSS issued an undated and unreferenced note early in 1993, the text of which is reproduced below:

'WORKERS SECONDED FROM ABROAD —LIABILITY FOR NATIONAL INSURANCE CONTRIBUTIONS (NICs)

1. This Note announces the conclusions of a DSS review of the liability for employers' secondary NICs for certain overseas workers (in the main, those from countries outside the EEC or with which there is no bi-lateral agreement) seconded to the UK by a foreign employer to work temporarily for a subsidiary or independent company.

2. Generally, under the provisions of the Social Security (Contributions) Regulations 1979 SI No 591, NICs do not become payable until such workers have been resident in GB for a period of 52 weeks. Thereafter, liability for primary (employee) Class 1 NICs arises but, where the worker remains under a contract of service only with the foreign employer, and that employer has no place of business in GB, the Contributions Regulations do not impose secondary (employer) liability on the UK company or organisation to which the worker is seconded.

3. Against a background of increasing numbers of such workers and doubts raised in individual cases, the DSS has been reviewing the position in regard to provisions within the Social Security (Categorisation of Earners) Regulations 1978 SI 1689, which, inter alia, provide for certain persons to be treated as secondary Class 1 contributors. Following full and detailed consideration, however, it has now been accepted that those provisions are not appropriate in these cases. Secondary liability, therefore, will continue currently to be based solely on the considerations described in paragraph 2 above.

4. It should be noted, however, that it is the policy of the DSS that, in the interests of equity, a primary Class 1 liability should normally be matched by a secondary NIC liability. Accordingly, the DSS will be considering bringing forward amending Social Security legislation, at some future date, to put the matter beyond doubt.

5. It is expected that, in the majority of past and current cases, primary Class 1 NICs only are being paid or will have been paid. In other cases, however, it may be that secondary NICs are being or have been paid where, in the light of this Note, no liability existed. In such cases, refunds may be appropriate, subject to satisfactory confirmation that the conditions are met.

6. Guidance on the outcome of the review has been issued to staff of the Contributions Agency. Anyone wishing to apply for a refund should write for an application form to:

Contributions Agency, Refunds Group, Room 101E, Longbenton, Newcastle upon Tyne, NE98 1YX (now NICO, Refunds Group, Longbenton, Newcastle upon Tyne, NE98 1ZZ), or telephone 0645 154450 (local-rate call charges), quoting reference "SW". Any other enquiries about this Note should be addressed in the first instance and preferably in writing quoting the same reference to their local Social Security office. Addresses and telephone numbers are listed under "Social Security—Department of" in the telephone directory.'

The amending legislation referred to in paragraph 4 of that note is contained in *Categorisation Amendment Regs 1994, Regs 2 and 4*, and is described at 49.9 OVERSEAS MATTERS. In addition, the *Social Security (Contributions) Amendment (No 4) Regulations 1994, SI 1994 No 2299* which came into force on 30 September 1994 brought into effect for NIC purposes similar provisions to those for PAYE that were introduced by the *Finance Act 1994* in respect of seconded workers. Where an employee works for another person who is not his employer then that person ('the principal employer') is deemed to be the employer for the collection purposes of *Contributions Regs 1979, Sch 1*. This means that the principal employer is responsible for the payment of Class 1 contributions of the seconded employee and can deduct an amount equal to the employee's contributions from the payments to the immediate employer. This amendment will only apply where the Inland Revenue has issued a direction under *ICTA 1988, s 203E* that payments should be deducted from any payments made. [*Contributions Regs 1979, 1 Sch 3, as amended*].

Where a member of a partnership obtains temporary employment through an agency (other than the partnership itself) in such a way as to bring about his categorisation as an employed earner under the rules described at 4.1 above, the basic rules stated above as regards the identification of the secondary contributor apply in their entirety; in other words, the agency will be treated as the secondary contributor. Where, however, a director or employee of a limited company obtains temporary employment through an agency in the manner described, the company and not the agency will be treated as the secondary contributor, *unless* the employee or director obtains his temporary employment *independently* of the company, in which case the normal rules will apply. (Leaflet CA 25).

4.4   AGGREGATION OF EARNINGS

A special aggregation rule operates so as to ensure that where earnings in respect of different employments are paid by different persons and some other person is, in accordance with the rule stated at 4.3 above, treated as the secondary contributor, all earnings paid in a given earnings period are treated as a single payment of earnings in respect of a single employment (see EARNINGS PERIODS (31) and 5.2 and 5.6 AGGREGATION OF EARNINGS).

4.5   EXCEPTIONS TO THE AGENCY RULE

The modified rule of categorisation described at 4.1 above does not apply to

(*a*)   anyone who, although falling to be categorised under the modified rule, does so under some other regulation (see 36.1 HUSBAND AND WIFE; 38.13 LABOUR-ONLY CONTRACTORS and 43.1 MINISTERS OF RELIGION);

(*b*)   anyone who, although satisfying the conditions set out at 4.1 above, renders his services in his own home or on other premises not under the control or management of the person to whom he is supplied e.g. an audit clerk supplied to an accountant through an agency who works on the premises of the accountant's clients (see 35.1 and 35.2 HOMEWORKERS AND OUTWORKERS); or (*c*)   anyone who is employed as an actor, singer, musician or other entertainer or as a fashion, photographic or artist's model (see 33.1 ENTERTAINERS and CWG 2 (2000), Page 66).

[*Categorisation Regs, 1 Sch Pt I para 2*].

4.6   SPECIFIC TYPES OF AGENCY

Many employment agencies specialise in particular kinds of placement and some such types of agency warrant special comment.

4.7   Nursing and home-care agencies

Nurses etc. supplied to hospitals, institutions, old people's homes etc. by a nursing agency will, if the agency has a continuing financial relationship with the nurses etc., usually fall to be treated as employees of the agency according to the rules described in this chapter, because a matron or some other senior person will have the right to direct how the nurses etc. will perform their duties. Special considerations apply, however, where nurses or other forms of helpers or carers are supplied to disabled, elderly, or incapacitated people in their own homes. In such cases, the IR will look closely at the position regarding the right of control over how duties are performed. Normally, such a right will be possessed by the person who is being cared for, or by another member of that person's household; but if the person lives alone and is so incapacitated as to be wholly reliant upon the carer or virtually so, the right of control may, effectively, be non-existent or may have been totally abrogated, and in such a case, if the agency itself exercises no control, the agency rules will not apply. It is worth noting that the DSS never considered that medical guidance given by the GP, consultant or hospital responsible for the patient's health, amounts to supervision, direction or control of the nurse or carer. (Leaflet CA 25). See also IR Schedule E Manual, Vol III, para SE 7751. Nursing 'banks' are known to cause particular difficulties because of the AGGREGATION OF EARNINGS (5.2) rules.

4.8   Agricultural agencies

Some agencies specialise in the supply of agricultural workers to farms, including herd managers and farm managers. The DSS accepted that, so far as many such placements are concerned, the right of supervision, direction or control may be entirely lacking (e.g. where the farm owner is absent) and that, where it is lacking, the agency rules do not apply.

4.9   Promotional agencies

Demonstrators and merchandisers are often agency-supplied workers who are placed in stores and supermarkets or at shows, exhibitions, sports grounds, race tracks etc. and given the task of promoting and/or shelf-stocking the products of the agency's client, i.e. the product manufacturer. The question whether the agency rules apply in such situations often, again, resolves itself into the question whether the demonstrators and merchandisers concerned are subject to the right of control over how they carry out their duties. The fact that such persons are unsupervised at the time they carry out their task does not mean that the right to control is lacking; and, indeed, if it can be established that preliminary instructions are issued to the persons concerned or that initial training is supplied, the IR will maintain that a right of control is proved to exist.

4.10 Agency Workers

4.10 Professional services agencies

Many agencies supply professionally qualified personnel to their clients, e.g. draughtsmen, architects, management consultants, engineers, computer programmers, chefs. Often, such people have businesses of their own and use agency work to supplement their income. Again, the test of whether the agency rules apply will come down to the question of the right of control. If the person's expertise in his or her particular field is such that all the agency's client can do is to recognise the professional's independence and to give him or her a free hand to produce in his or her own way the result which the client requires, the agency rules are unlikely to apply. But if, while carrying out his or her assignment for the agency, the professional has to work under the same constraints as employees of the client, the agency rules will serve to attribute him or her with employed earner status.

4.11 Construction industry workers

In a development following the review of construction industry workers (see 38.4 LABOUR-ONLY CONTRACTORS) there has been concern expressed about the position of agencies who engage workers in the construction industry. Where agency provisions apply there will be a liability for Class 1 NICs but the tax position was different until 6 April 1998 in that there will be a liability for Schedule D tax and, in the first instance, Class 4 contributions. (CA Specialist Conference, 15 October 1996). It would then be necessary to claim relief against the Class 4 liability in respect of the earnings in which Class 1 has been paid, following the same procedure as for SUBPOSTMASTERS (55). The following statement was made at the CA Specialist Conference in February 1997:

> 'Under the Categorisation of Earners Regulations 1978 (SI 1689) a liability for Class 1 NIC's arises where a worker is supplied by, or through a third party, has to provide personal service, is paid through that third party and is subject to control (or the right of control). Inland Revenue have similar legislation but workers supplied to the construction industry are specifically excluded from them. The position is that, provided the criteria is satisfied, workers and agencies will be liable to pay Class 1 NICs but the workers will continue to be treated as self-employed for tax purposes'.

CA Specialist Conference February 1997 notes, pages 56 and 57. See also IR Tax Bulletin, April 1997, page 413.

Since the status reviews of subcontractors had to be performed by 6 April 1997 the incidence of agency-supplied subcontractors has increased indicating that many who had failed the status review have now been taken on by agencies. This trend towards the employment of agency-supplied subcontractors had been evident in some large construction projects and had enabled construction companies to relieve themselves of the administrative tax burden of deducting tax at basic rate and accounting for it to the Collector of Taxes (Class 1 NICs still being due though). The Financial Secretary to the Treasury announced on 31 July 1997 that the exemption for construction workers from the agency tax rules would be removed with effect from 6 April 1998. Those agencies who now supply workers to the construction industry will, subject to the conditions set out in those rules, be required to operate PAYE on payments to construction workers in the same way as other agency workers. This change now aligns tax with the NICs treatment of agency workers. Further evidence of the removal of the exemption was seen in the Inland Revenue Press Release dated 9 February 1998 in which the draft clauses enabling the agencies to deduct and account for PAYE as well as Class 1 NICs were published. The legislation proposed was given effect in advance of the Royal Assent to the Finance Bill 1998 by way of a resolution under the authority of the *Provisional Collection of Taxes Act 1968*. See Inland Revenue Press Release 9 February 1998 and also CA National Insurance

News, Summer 1997 page 3, where the CA stated that agency workers who find themselves being charged Class 4 contributions on earnings that are subject to Class 1 contributions can apply for a certificate of exemption. Special application forms for agency-supplied workers were available from Contributions Agency, Deferment Group for years up to and including 1997–98.

5 Aggregation of Earnings

Cross-references. See AGENCY WORKERS (4); CLASS 1 CONTRIBUTIONS (15); 18.3 CLASS 2 CONTRIBUTIONS for small earnings exception; CLASS 4 CONTRIBUTIONS (20); 50.4 PARTNERS.

Other Sources. Simon's NIC, Part I, Section 2, Chapter 6; Tolley's National Insurance Brief, March 1996, page 19, April 1997, pages 25–28 and June 1999, pages 42 and 43.

5.1 UNDERLYING PRINCIPLES

A fundamental tenet of the contribution scheme is that, where earnings are paid to or for the benefit of an earner in respect of any one of his employments as an employed earner, primary and secondary Class 1 contributions are to be paid without regard to any other earnings in respect of any other employment. [*SSCBA 1992, s 6(1)(4)*]. However, because there are certain situations in which this rule would (or could be made to) work to a contributor's advantage, aggregation rules which become operative in such situations have been introduced into the legislation.

5.2 THE AGGREGATION RULES

Subject to certain modifications in the case of an earner who has been, but is no longer, a director of a company (see 5.8 below) and subject also, in some instances, to a test of practicability (see 5.7 below), the legislation provides that *all* earnings paid to an earner in a given earnings period (see EARNINGS PERIODS (31)) in respect of one or more employed earner's employments must be aggregated and treated as a single payment of earnings in respect of one such employment if the earnings are in respect of

(a) employments under the same employer (see 5.3 below) [*SSCBA 1992, 1 Sch 1(1)(a); Contributions Regs, Reg 10*]; or

(b) different employments and are paid by different secondary contributors (see 14.15 CATEGORISATION) who, in respect of those employments, carry on business in association with each other (see 5.4 below) [*SSCBA 1992, 1 Sch 1 (1)(b); Contributions Regs, Reg 12(1)(a), as amended by Contributions Amendment Regs 1984, Reg 6(a) and Contributions Transitional Regs 1985, Reg 5(5)*]; or

(c) different employments and are paid by different employers of whom one is, by regulation, treated as the secondary contributor (see 14.15 CATEGORISATION) in respect of each employment (see 5.5 below) [*SSCBA 1992, 1 Sch 1(b); Contributions Regs, Reg 12(1)(b), as amended by Contributions Amendment Regs 1984, Reg 6(a)*]; or

(d) different employments and are paid by different persons in respect of work performed for those persons by the earner in those employments, and, in respect of those earnings, some other person is, by regulation, treated as the secondary contributor (see 4.3 AGENCY WORKERS and 5.6 below) [*SSCBA 1992, 1 Sch 1(b); Contributions Regs, Reg 12(1)(c), as amended by Contributions Amendment Regs 1984, Reg 6(a)*].

A payment of earnings made at an irregular interval (see 31.4 EARNINGS PERIODS) is, however, not to be aggregated with any other earnings except where it and the other earnings would, if paid at the normal time, have been paid within the same earnings period. [*Contributions Regs, Reg 6(4)(5), as amended by Contributions Amendment Regs 1984, Reg 5*]. Nor is a payment of earnings made to an earner in the tax year in which he attains pensionable age but before he attains that age to be aggregated with other earnings if that payment of earnings would, under normal circumstances, fall to be paid in a following tax year (see 3.7 AGE EXCEPTION). [*Contributions Regs, Reg 12A, as amended by Contributions Amendment No 4 Regs 1985, Reg 2*].

5.3   Rule 1—employments under the same employer

The first aggregation rule (see 5(2)(a) above) is of dual effect. *Firstly*, it ensures that, where earnings in respect of an employed earner's employment are of different parts, those parts will, whether paid at the same or at different pay intervals, be aggregated and treated as a single amount of earnings, insofar as they are paid within the same EARNINGS PERIOD (31).

Example

Arnold is employed by Bauble Bros as a sales representative. He receives a weekly salary, quarterly commission and an annual bonus. Under the earnings period rules, his earnings period is a week (unless the Secretary of State has directed otherwise). In the week ended 1 July 2000, A receives

	£
Salary for the week ended 1 July 2000	100
Commission for the quarter ended 30 June 2000	387
Bonus for the year ended 31 December 1999	3,300
	£3,787

By virtue of *SSCBA 1992, 1 Sch 1(1)(a)*, the contribution liabilities of A and of B for that week will be assessed by reference to a single amount of earnings of £3,787.

Secondly, it precludes the avoidance or reduction of Class 1 contribution liabilities which might otherwise be attained through the fragmentation of an earner's earnings over two or more separate employments within the same company, firm or organisation. Although the operation of this rule is not dependent on the amount of earnings in at least one of the employments being below the current lower earnings limit or, from 6 April 1999, below the earnings threshold, the rule is of no anti-avoidance effect unless that is so.

Example

Throughout 2000–01, Cyril is employed by the Dainty Dish Restaurant under two separate contracts of service. As barman, he is paid earnings of £50 per week and, as wine waiter, he is paid earnings of £150 per week. If each amount of earnings were to be viewed in isolation from the other amount of earnings and contribution liabilities were to be assessed on that basis in accordance with *SSCBA 1992, s 6(4)*, no liability for either primary or secondary contributions would arise as regards C's earnings as barman (those earnings being below the 2000–01 employees' earnings threshold of £76 per week) and a Class 1 liability of only £7.80 primary (i.e. £76 @ Nil + £78 @ 10%) and £8.05 (i.e. £150-£84 × 12.2%) secondary would arise as regards C's earnings as wine waiter. Because C's two employments are under the same employer, however, the provisions of *SSCBA 1992, 1 Sch 1(1)(a)* take effect and override *s 6(4)* by requiring that all his earnings in respect of those employments be aggregated and treated as a single weekly payment of £200 in respect of a single employment. Instead of a total liability of only £15.85, therefore, a liability of £26.55 per week arises, viz.

Class 1

		£
Primary	£76 @ Nil	Nil
	£124 @ 10%	12.40
	£200	12.40
Secondary	£84 @ Nil	Nil
	£116 @ 12.2%	14.15
	£200	£26.55

5.4   Aggregation of Earnings

The expression 'under the same employer' is not defined in the legislation, nor has it been subjected to judicial interpretation nor is it explained in the article on this subject in CA National Insurance News, Issue 2, page 3. In May 1985, however, the ICAEW asked the DSS to give its interpretation of the term and to say, in particular, whether it considered that (*a*) different divisions of the same company and (*b*) wholly owned subsidiaries and their parent company constituted 'the same employer'. The DSS replied on 7 August 1985 in the following terms:

'Firstly, as regards divisions of the same company we assume that they are in fact sections of that company and not separate legal entities like subsidiary companies. If this is so, then even though a person has more than one job within the company concerned, his contracts will lie with the *company*. Earnings from each job will normally be aggregated and national insurance contributions levied on the total. If however, aggregation is not reasonably practicable because the earnings in the respective jobs are separately calculated, contribution liability may be assessed on each separate payment.

Turning to your point about subsidiaries and the parent company, the fact that they are wholly owned subsidiaries does not cause them to be regarded as "the same employer". What determines whether one company is liable (as the secondary contributor) to pay contributions on all the earnings or whether various companies are *each* liable to do so in respect of the earnings they pay depends on the answer to the question—in respect of which contract of service or directorship (as an office holder) is/are the payment(s) made?'

The impracticability exception referred to in the first paragraph of this reply is discussed at 5.7 below. Further, although a parent company and a subsidiary will not be considered to be the same employer, if they are carrying on business in association Rule 2 (see 5.4 below) will operate and have the same arithmetical effect.

5.4   Rule 2—different employments, but secondary contributors in association

The second aggregation rule (see 5.2(*b*) above) is more complex than the first and contains four terms which frequently give rise to difficulty and which, therefore, require elaboration.

(*a*)   The rule relates to earnings in respect of different employments paid by different secondary contributors. A secondary contributor is the person who, in respect of earnings from an employed earner's employment is—or but for the operation of the earnings threshold would be (see 30.1 to 30.3 EARNINGS LIMITS AND THRESHOLDS)—liable to pay a secondary contribution under *SSCBA 1992, s 6* and *Contributions Regs, Reg 1(2)* and will not necessarily, therefore, be the employed earner's employer (see 14.15 CATEGORISATION).

(*b*)   The secondary contributors who pay the earnings must carry on business in association. Although the term 'association' has acquired a precise legal meaning in tax law (see *ICTA 1988, s 416*) and employment law (see *Employment Protection (Consolidation) Act 1978, s 153(4)*), it remains undefined in social security legislation. The question whether or not particular secondary contributors 'carry on business in association' is, therefore, purely a question of fact and cannot be decided merely by reference to any 'associated' status which those secondary contributors possess under other branches of law. The IR takes the view, for social security purposes, that the expression means that the businesses 'serve a common purpose and to a significant degree they share such things as accommodation, personnel, equipment or customers'. (CWG 2 (2000), Page 36, item 65). Some light was shed on the meaning of these words in a letter from the DSS dated 30 November 1983 in which it was stated that:

'for the purpose of the Contribution Regulations, what is considered is the actual relationship between the companies. What we therefore look for is some degree of common purpose, substantiated by, for example, the sharing of facilities, personnel, accommodation, customers etc. Basically, the greater the interdependence the greater the likelihood of our treating the companies as being in association. Companies in association would normally share profits or losses and, to a significant degree, resources. When I say 'sharing profits or losses' I mean that one would expect the companies' relationship to be such that the fortunes of one would be reflected in those of the other(s). So, for example, where two companies share expenses—say for staff or premises—this would tend to affect the profits or losses of both.'

The stress is on the nature of the *trading* relationship between two businesses, not on their *constitutional* links. This was made plain in an earlier letter dated 25 October 1982, in which the DSS said:

'The Department's intention is that the phrase should be used in a restricted sense as the principle [set out at 5.1 above] of contributions liability arising in each separate employment is one of the central features of the Act. . . We are obliged to ensure that in any circumstances where the provision may be invoked we are satisfied that the secondary contributors. . . are acting in concert to a common goal. . . For instance, the fact that two companies associate together for mutual aid or that one company has one or more directors common to each does not of itself cause these two companies to be carrying on business in association. If however, two companies agree together to undertake together a definite business project, say, one to manufacture goods and the other to sell them, both companies sharing in agreed proportions the overall costs and profits, the two companies should be regarded as carrying on business in association. Alternatively the companies could also be regarded as carrying on business in association if they constitute a group. Conversely if one company manufactures goods and sells them to another company which in turn markets them, each charging and making its own profits, one can hardly say that the "businesses are carried on in association". This would also apply where two or more companies were set up to carry on different facets of the same enterprise and were linked through a holding company.'

It should probably be noted, however, that recent activity by the former Contributions Agency suggests that greater importance is now being attached to constitutional links alone although it is arguable that this is not justified by the wording of the regulation. Conversely, the guidance now stresses that the sharing of facilities must be 'to a significant degree'; a small amount of sharing is not sufficient to cause two employers to be carrying on business in association. This was covered at the October 1997 Contributions Conference where it was stated that it is not sufficient that two employers occupy the same premises and have the same directors. 'There are many aspects that we would need to look at to arrive at a decision on trading in association, such as: whether or not they are sharing resources; whether or not they are sharing staff; if they are involved in contracts where they would both share etc;'.

(c)   The carrying on of a business in association is to be in respect of those employments to which the earnings relate. Where, therefore, two or more companies etc. carry on business in association but also engage in other unassociated activities, the earnings of a person employed by two or more of those companies etc. in the unassociated aspects of their businesses will not be aggregable under the rule.

Example
Throughout 2000–01, Edward is paid earnings of £110 per week in respect of his employment with Fabrications Ltd; £120 per week in respect of his employment

with Gudroofs; £76 per week in respect of his employment with Homemakers Ltd and £80 per week with Interiors Ltd. H is in voluntary liquidation under John, a liquidator, but is continuing to play its part in a joint project with F, G and I involving the development of a residential building site. E is employed by G, H and I in connection with that joint project but his employment with F is in connection with unassociated activities in which that company is involved. There are four secondary contributors who pay earnings to E: F, G, J (as liquidator of H—see 14.15 CATEGORISATION) and I, but of these only F, G and I are carrying on business in association (J, as liquidator, is not), and of these only G and I are doing so in respect of E's employments. Accordingly, only the earnings E receives from G and I fall to be aggregated under *Reg 12(1)(a)*, with contribution liabilities arising as follows.

	£	Primary* %	£	Secondary† %	£
		Class 1			
F	110.00	Nil/10	3.40	Nil/12.2	3.17
G	120.00				
I	80.00				
	200.00	Nil/10	12.40	Nil/12.2	14.15
J	76.00	Nil	Nil	Nil	Nil

(* Nil% × £76, 10% × remainder.)   (†Nil% × £84, 12.2% × remainder.)

5.5 Rule 3—different employments, different employers one of whom is secondary contributor

The third aggregation rule (see 5.2(c) above) is of limited application as there are presently only six circumstances in which a person who is an employed earner's employer will also fall to be treated as a secondary contributor under the *Categorisation Regs, 3 Sch* as regards earnings paid to that earner in respect of other employed earner's employments (see 14.15 CATEGORISATION). Such circumstances will arise where an earner is employed

(a) by a head of chambers and also as a barrister's clerk by one or more barristers in those chambers; or

(b) by a liquidator and also as an employee of one or more companies in voluntary liquidation but carrying on business under that liquidator; or

(c) by the Church Commissioners for England and also as a minister of the Church of England; or

(d) by the person responsible for the administration of a fund from which a minister of religion is remunerated and also as a minister of religion remunerated from that fund; or

(e) by an agency and also as an office cleaner or other type of agency worker remunerated through that agency; or

(f) by a UK employer and also as a secondee from a foreign employer providing personal service to the UK 'host' employer.

Example
From 6 April 2000, Keith is employed by the Lively Lazarites Central Fund as an accountant at a salary of £110 per week. He is also remunerated by that fund at the rate of £100 per week as minister of the LL Free Church in Lincoln. Under the provisions of *SSCBA 1992, s 6(4)* (which require the earnings from each employment to be viewed in isolation from the other) Class 1 contribution liabilities of £3.40 primary and £3.17 secondary would arise on the earnings of

£110 per week as those earnings exceed the earnings thresholds (see EARNINGS LIMITS AND THRESHOLDS (30)) and attract a main primary contribution rate of 10%, and also attract a secondary contribution rate of 12.2%. On the earnings of £100 per week, Class 1 contribution liabilities of £2.40 primary and £1.95 secondary would arise as those earnings also exceed the earnings threshold and attract both the main primary contribution rate of 10% and a secondary contribution rate of 12.2%, in respect of earnings exceeding the respective thresholds. As the fund is not only K's employer, however, but also the secondary contributor as regards the earnings paid to him as a minister of religion (see 43.2 MINISTERS OF RELIGION), his earnings must, by virtue of *Reg 12(1)(b)*, be aggregated and, in consequence, Class 1 contributions of £13.40 primary and £15.37 secondary will be payable on the combined earnings of £210 as these attract a main primary contribution rate of 10% on the combined earnings over £76 and for secondary contribution purposes they attract a contribution rate of 12.2% on combined earnings over £84.

5.6 Rule 4—different employments, secondary contributor other than one of the employers

The fourth aggregation rule (see 5.2(*d*) above) currently relates only to persons who have a continuing financial relationship with agencies through which they are employed by other persons (see AGENCY WORKERS (4)).

Example
In 2000–01, Marveltipe Agencies obtain temporary employment for Norma, a secretary, with Oliver Ltd, Petersco and Quill Ltd. Through M, N is paid weekly earnings of £49 from O, £50 from P and £51 from Q. Although the earnings are in respect of different employments and are paid by different persons, M (though not itself one of N's employers) is the secondary contributor as regards those earnings (see 4.3 AGENCY WORKERS) and, accordingly, by virtue of *Reg 12(1)(c)*, the earnings must be aggregated. Contributions will, in consequence, be payable on earnings of £150 per week. Were it not for *Reg 12(1)(c)*, all N's earnings would, under *SSCBA 1992, s 6(4)*, have escaped liability as each amount falls below the 2000–01 weekly earnings thresholds of £76 (employee) and £84 (employer) respectively.

5.7 Impracticability exception

Aggregation under the first or second of the aggregation rules (see 5.3 and 5.4 above) is *not* to take place if such aggregation is not reasonably practicable. [*Contributions Regs, Regs 11, 12(1)*]. The term 'reasonably practicable' has created difficulties for employers and the DSS once looked at an option whereby the employer agrees non-aggregation before the event (see CA Consultation Panel and CA Specialist Conference written response, 20 February 1996). As regards the first aggregation rule, however, the exception is, in law, confined to situations in which the earnings in the respective employments are separately calculated. [*Reg 12(1)*]. The DSS used to illustrate this kind of impracticability by the example of a business which had several branches and which paid its employees locally rather than centrally (obsolete DSS Leaflet NI 269/CA 28, 1989 edition, Para 91) but now it describes the matter in its published guidance as follows.

'If the earnings from each job are separately calculated, you do not have to add the earnings from the separate jobs together if it is not reasonably practicable to do so. For example, it might not be practicable to do so if you operate a computerised payroll system which is unable to perform the calculation and you would then have to do it manually. In such cases, you may be required to show why it has not been reasonably practicable to add the earnings together.' (CWG 2 (2000), Page 36, para 67).

It is understood that the inclusion of a person in different PAYE schemes has, on occasions, been regarded by the DSS as rendering the aggregation of that person's earnings impracticable, but that is not an exclusive test. The DSS said:

'In the Department's view, the question practicable/impracticable can only be determined by examination of the specific circumstances of each individual case taking into consideration such factors as the physical/geographical position of the business concerned, the location of pay points and associated payroll documentation, the variety and range of pay practices operated, and the percentage of the workforce affected. We do not accept that, simply because separate PAYE schemes exist, it will necessarily be impracticable to aggregate earnings'. (Letter 11 July 1988).

The term 'reasonably practicable' is not defined in the legislation, but it is one which has received judicial interpretation in other contexts. It is 'a narrower term than "physically possible"' and implies that the potential loss which might result from failure to do the thing called for (here, presumably, the contribution loss to the NI Fund as a result of non-aggregation) must be balanced against the costs of doing the thing called for (here, aggregation of earnings)—not only in terms of money but in terms of time and trouble also. Where there is a 'gross disproportion' between the two, the doing of the thing called for will not be 'reasonably practicable'. (*Edwards v National Coal Board [1949] 1 AER 743 at 747 per Asquith LJ*). The 'disproportionately costly in terms of time, trouble and expense' test was approved by Lord Oaksey in *Marshall v Gotham Co Ltd [1954] 1 AER 937 at 939* and, more recently, by Lord Goff in *Mailer v Austin Rover Group plc [1989] 2 AER 1087*.

5.8   Exclusion of earnings relating to periods of former directorship

Where an earner who was, but is no longer, a director of a company (see COMPANY DIRECTORS (21)) receives earnings in any tax year after that in which he ceased to be a director, those earnings, insofar as they are paid in respect of any period during which he was a director, are *not* to be aggregated with any other earnings with which they would otherwise fall to be aggregated. [*Contributions Regs, Reg 6A(5)(a), as amended by Contributions Amendment Regs 1983, Reg 4*].

The qualification contained in this regulation is of time only and it is, therefore, irrelevant whether the earnings actually relate to the former directorship or relate to other non-directorial activities performed during the earlier period in question.

Example
Throughout 2000–01, Richard is employed by Stiffs Ltd as an embalmer at a salary of £2,000 per month. Until 31 December 1999 he had been a director of the company but had, on that date, resigned because of worsening health. In September 2000, the board votes him a bonus of £3,000 in respect of his services as director during the year ended 31 December 1999 and a further £2,000 in respect of his services as embalmer during the same period. Were it not for *Reg 6A(5)(a)*, R's earnings of £2,000 (salary) and £5,000 (bonuses) in September 2000 would fall to be aggregated as the amounts are derived from different employments under the same employer, and, in consequence of that and the earnings period rules (see EARNINGS PERIODS (31)), contribution liabilities would arise as follows.

	Class 1			
	*Primary**		*Secondary†*	
	%	£	%	£
£7,000 (limited for primary contribution purposes to *monthly* UEL £2,319)	Nil/10	<u>199.00</u>	Nil/12.2	<u>809.47</u>

(*Nil% × £329, 10% × remainder.)   († Nil × £365, 12.2% × remainder.)

That primary contribution liability is only slightly more than the primary contribution liability on R's regular monthly earnings of £2,000 (i.e. £167.10) and this would mean that, were the earnings of £5,000 to be added to that £2,000, virtually the whole of the £5,000 bonuses would escape the contribution net. Because both elements of the £5,000 are in respect of a period during which R was a director of the company, however, *Reg 6A(5)(a)* prohibits aggregation of the £5,000 with R's other earnings and, because *Reg 6A(5)(b)* imposes an annual earnings period on the earnings relating to the period when R was a director, contribution liabilities will, in fact, be as follows.

		Class 1			
		*Primary**		*Secondary†*	
Salary		%	£	%	£
£2,000	(less than *monthly* UEL for primary contribution purposes £2,319)	Nil/10	167.10	Nil/12.2	199.47
Bonuses £5,000	(less than *annual* UEL for primary contribution purposes £27,820)	Nil/10	<u>104.80</u>	Nil/12.2	<u>75.03</u>
<u>£7,000</u>			<u>271.90</u>		<u>274.50</u>

(* Nil% × £329, monthly/£3,952   († Nil% × £365 monthly/£4,385
yearly, 10% × remainder.)   yearly, 12.2% remainder.)

If R's total primary contributions paid in 2000–01 exceed (as they almost certainly will) the annual maximum of £2,432.70, one might assume that R will be able to obtain repayment of the excess, but the DSS denies this (see 7.1 ANNUAL MAXIMUM).

5.9   Exclusion of SMP paid by the Secretary of State

Where statutory maternity pay is paid by the Secretary of State rather than by an employer under the *Statutory Maternity Pay General Regs 1986, Reg 7* (e.g. where an employer has become insolvent and a maternity pay period has not expired), that payment is not to be aggregated with any other earnings for contribution purposes. [*Contributions Regs, Reg 6B, as amended by Contributions Amendment No 2 Regs 1987, Reg 3*].

5.10   Aggregation of earnings where related earnings periods are of different lengths

The treatment of earnings paid at different intervals in respect of a single employment has been discussed at 5.3 above. Where, however, earnings in respect of two or more employed earner's employments fall to be aggregated under any of the rules described above, the earnings period (see EARNINGS PERIODS (31)) relative to the earnings derived from each employment is first to be determined under the normal earnings period rules or, as the case may be, under the director's earnings period rules. [*Contributions Regs, Reg 2, as amended by Contributions Amendment Regs 1983, Reg 3*]. Should the earnings periods so determined for the employments in question then be found to be of different lengths, a common earnings period is to be determined by application of the following rules.

(*a*) Where at least one of the earnings periods in question has been determined under the director's earnings period rules (see 31.11 EARNINGS PERIODS), the common earnings period is to be the earnings period (or, if there is more than one, the *longer or longest* earnings period) so determined. [*Contributions Regs, Reg 6A(4)*].

(*b*) Where none of the earnings periods has been determined under the directors' earnings period rules but the earnings are derived from different types of employment, e.g. contracted-out, not contracted-out with an approved personal pension scheme (APP), not contracted-out without an APP scheme, the common earnings period is to be the earnings period (or, if there is more than one, the shorter or shortest earnings period) derived from

  (i)   the not contracted-out employment(s), if the employee has an APP scheme, or

  (ii) the contracted-out employment(s), if there is no not contracted-out employment with an APP scheme,

  (iii) the employment contracted out by virtue of a COMP scheme, if shorter than (ii) above and if there is no not contracted-out employment with an APP scheme.

The authority for giving precedence to the earnings period derived from contracted-out employments was *Contributions Regs, Reg 5A(2)(a) as amended by Contributions Amendment Regs 1980, Reg 2*, but there appeared to be no authority for giving precedence to the earnings period derived from not contracted-out employments where the employee has an APP scheme. DSS instructions were, however, that such precedence must be given and this has now been confirmed for those employees who

● have more than one job with the same employer (or different employers carrying on business in association) and their earnings are aggregated, and

● have different earnings periods in each job, and

● are members of their employer's contracted-out occupational pension scheme in at least one of their employments.

  (See CA Press Release 96/1, 15 March 1996) and [*Pensions Act 1995, s 148 and Social Security (Contributions) Amendment (No 3) Regs 1996, Reg 2*].

(*c*) Where none of the earnings periods has been determined under the directors' earnings period rules and the earnings are all derived from the same types of employment, the common earnings period is to be the shorter or shortest earnings period derived from such employments. [*Contributions Regs, Reg 5A(2)(b) as amended by Social Security (Contributions) Amendment (No 5) Regulations 1996, SI 1996 No 2407, Reg 3*].

Example
Throughout 2000–01, Terry is employed by Upholstery Ltd and by Veneer Ltd. The two companies are jointly engaged in producing and marketing a new range

of office furniture and T's employments both relate to the associated operations. His employment by U is not contracted-out and he is paid £200 per month. He has no appropriate personal pension scheme. His employment by V is contracted-out and he receives earnings of £350 per week. On 1 February 2001 he is appointed a director of that company. In accordance with *Reg 12(1)(a)*, T's earnings from his two employments fall to be aggregated (unless it is impracticable to do so—see 5.7 above) but, because the earnings in each employment are paid at different intervals and thus give rise to different earnings periods, a common earnings period must be determined. As T does not become a director of V until 1 February 2001, the common earnings period as regards earnings paid before that date falls to be determined in accordance with *Contributions Regs, Reg 5A(2)* and, as there is a 'mix' of employments, is to be the earnings period relating to the contracted-out employment, i.e. a week. The common earnings period as regards earnings paid after that date falls to be determined under *Reg 6A(4)* in consequence of T's appointment as director of V and, as that directorship will attract an earnings period of nine weeks, is to be nine weeks.

It follows, therefore, that, in the month of July 2000, for example, contribution liabilities will fall to be determined by reference to earnings of £350 for each of the weeks ended 1, 8, 15 and 22 July but by reference to earnings of £550 (i.e. £350 + £200) for the week ended 29 July. This basis will continue to 31 January 2001. The period from 1 February 2001 to 5 April 2001 then forms a single earnings period, however, contribution liabilities will fall to be determined by reference to earnings of £3,550 (i.e. [9 × £350] + [2 × £200]).

5.11 Calculation of contributions on aggregated earnings

Where earnings from different employments fall to be aggregated and all the employments are of the same type (i.e., contracted-out by reason of a salary related scheme, contracted-out by reason of a COMP scheme, not contracted-out with an appropriate personal pension (APP) scheme, or not contracted-out without an APP scheme), calculation of the Class 1 contribution liabilities gives rise to no particular difficulty. Where the employments are mixed, however, a question of precedence arises and, unless this is resolved in accordance with certain rules, Class 1 contribution liabilities will be incorrectly calculated. The current procedure is as follows (see the 1998–99 edition of this work for the effect on aggregation of the previous rate structure):

(a) Add together for the earnings period arrived at under 5.10 above all the aggregable earnings paid in that earnings period. If the total earnings thus ascertained are below the lower earnings limit (LEL) appropriate to the earnings period concerned (see 30.3 EARNINGS LIMITS AND THRESHOLDS), go no further: no contributions are due and no entries are required on forms P11 and P14.

(b) If the total earnings arrived at in (a) equal or exceed the relevant lower earnings limit, divide the total earnings into

   (i) earnings from not contracted-out employments ('*category 1 earnings*'), and

   (ii) earnings from contracted-out employments ('*category 2 earnings*').

(c) If the employee has an APP scheme, proceed to (g) below; otherwise proceed as follows.

Note: EEET = Employee's earnings threshold.

       ERET = Employer's earnings threshold.

No APP scheme

(d) If category 2 earnings alone reach the appropriate upper earnings limit (UEL) for the relevant earnings period, the total primary Class 1 contribution liability on total earnings for the earnings period is:

5.11 Aggregation of Earnings

[UEL – EEET] × contracted-out rate (8.4%, 2000–01);

and the total secondary Class 1 contribution liability on total earnings for the earnings period is:

(1) [UEL – ERET] × contracted-out rate (9.2%, 2000–01), plus

(2) [total earnings – UEL] × not contracted-out rate (12.2%, 2000–01),

and the employer's contracted-out rebate is due in respect of earnings between the LEL and the ERET. The employee's contracted-out rebate is also available in respect of the earnings between the LEL and the EEET, but it will be treated in accordance with the rules in 22.3 CONTRACTED-OUT EMPLOYMENT.

(e) If category 2 earnings alone do not reach the appropriate UEL but total earnings do, then:

(A) If category 2 earnings reach the appropriate employer's earnings threshold, the total primary Class 1 contribution liability on total earnings for the earnings period is:

(1) [category 2 earnings – EEET] × contracted-out rate (8.4%, 2000–01), plus

(2) [UEL – category 2 earnings] × not contracted-out rate (10%, 2000–01);

and the total secondary Class 1 contribution liability on total earnings for the earnings period is:

(1) [category 2 earnings – ERET] × contracted-out rate (9.2%, 2000–01), plus

(2) category 1 earnings × not contracted-out rate (12.2%, 2000–01),

and the employer's contracted-out rebate is due in respect of earnings between the LEL and the ERET. The employee's contracted-out rebate is also available in respect of the earnings between the LEL and the EEET, but it will be treated in accordance with the rules in 22.3 CONTRACTED-OUT EMPLOYMENT.

(B) If category 2 earnings reach the appropriate employee's earnings threshold but not the appropriate employer's earnings threshold, the total primary Class 1 contribution liability on total earnings for the earnings period is:

(1) [category 2 earnings – EEET] × not contracted-out rate (8.4%, 2000–01); plus

(2) [UEL – category 2 earnings] x not contracted-out rate (10%, 2000–01);

and the total secondary Class 1 contribution liability on total earnings for the earnings period is:

[total earnings – ERET] × not contracted-out rate (12.2%, 2000–01),

and the employer's contracted-out rebate is due in respect of the excess earnings over the LEL. The employee's contracted-out rebate is also available in respect of the earnings over the LEL, but it will be treated in accordance with the rules in 22.3 CONTRACTED-OUT EMPLOYMENT.

(C) If category 2 earnings reach the appropriate LEL but not the appropriate employee's earnings threshold, the total primary Class 1 contributions liability on total earnings for the earnings period is:

[UEL – EEET] × not contracted-out rate (10%, 2000–01);

and the total secondary Class 1 contribution liability on total earnings for the earnings period is:

[total earnings – ERET] × not contracted-out rate (12.2%, 2000–01),

and the employer's contracted–out rebate is due in respect of the excess of category 2 earnings over the LEL. The employee's contracted–out rebate is also available in respect of the excess of category 2 earnings over the LEL, but it will be treated in accordance with the rules in 22.3 CONTRACTED–OUT EMPLOYMENT.

(D) If category 2 earnings do not reach the appropriate LEL, the total primary Class 1 contributions liability on total earnings for the earnings period is:

[UEL – EEET] × not contracted-out rate (10%, 2000–01);

and the total secondary Class 1 contribution liability on total earnings for the earnings period is:

[total earnings – ERET] × not contracted-out rate (12.2%, 2000–01).

(f) If neither category 2 earnings alone nor total earnings reach the appropriate UEL, then:

(A) If category 2 earnings reach the appropriate employer's earnings threshold, the total primary Class 1 contribution liability on total earnings for the earnings period is:

(1) [category 2 earnings – EEET] × contracted-out rate (8.4%, 2000–01), plus

(2) category 1 earnings × not contracted-out rate (10%, 2000–01);

and the total secondary Class 1 contribution liability on total earnings for the earnings period is:

(1) [category 2 earnings – ERET] × contracted-out rate (9.2%, 2000–01), plus

(2) category 1 earnings × not contracted-out rate (12.2%, 2000–01),

and the employer's contracted-out rebate is due in respect of earnings between the LEL and the ERET. The employee's contracted-out rebate is also available in respect of the earnings between the LEL and the EEET, but it will be treated in accordance with the rules in 22.3 CONTRACTED-OUT EMPLOYMENT.

(B) If category 2 earnings reach the appropriate employee's earnings threshold but not the appropriate employer's earnings threshold, the total primary Class 1 contribution liability on total earnings for the earnings period is:

(1) [category 2 earnings – EEET] × contracted-out rate (8.4%, 2000–01), plus

(2) category 1 earnings × not contracted-out rate (10%, 2000–01);

and the total secondary Class 1 contribution liability on total earnings for the earnings period is:

[total earnings – ERET] × not contracted-out rate (12.2%, 2000–01),

and the employer's contracted-out rebate is due in respect of the excess of category 2 earnings over the LEL. The employee's contracted-out rebate is also available in respect of the earnings between the LEL and the EEET, but it will be treated in accordance with the rules in 22.3 CONTRACTED-OUT EMPLOYMENT.

(C) If category 2 earnings reach the appropriate LEL but not the appropriate employee's threshold, the total primary Class 1 contribution liability on total earnings for the earnings period is:

[total earnings – EEET] × not contracted-out rate (10%, 2000–01),

and the total secondary Class 1 contribution liability on total earnings for the earnings period is:

[total earnings – ERET] × not contracted-out rate (12.2%, 2000–01),

and the employer's contracted-out rebate is due in respect of earnings between the LEL and the ERET. The employee's contracted-out rebate is also available in respect of the earnings between the LEL and the EEET, but it will be treated in accordance with the rules in 22.3 CONTRACTED-OUT EMPLOYMENT.

(D) If category 2 earnings do not reach the appropriate LEL, the total primary Class 1 contribution liability on total earnings for the earnings period is:

[total earnings – EEET] × main not contracted-out rate (10%, 2000–01);

and the total secondary Class 1 contribution liability on total earnings for the earnings period is:

[total earnings – ERET] × not contracted-out rate (12.2%, 2000–01).

Paragraphs (d), (e) and (f) all assume that the category 2 earnings derive solely from employments contracted-out by reason of salary related schemes. If the contracted-out employment has, instead, a COMP scheme then the employer's contracted-out rates will be the higher rate of 11.6% rather than 9.2%. If there are at least two contracted-out employments and at least one relates to a salary related scheme and at least one relates to a COMP scheme refer to the end of this section.

APP scheme

(g) If category 1 earnings alone reach the appropriate upper earnings limit (UEL) for the relevant earnings period, the total primary Class 1 contribution liability on total earnings for the earnings period is:

[UEL – EEET] × not contracted-out rate (10%, 2000–01);

and the total secondary Class 1 contribution liability on total earnings for the earnings period is:

[total earnings – ERET] × not contracted-out rate (12.2%, 2000–01).

(h) If category 1 earnings alone do not reach the appropriate UEL but total earnings do, then:

(A) If category 1 earnings reach the appropriate employer's earnings threshold, the total primary Class 1 contribution liability on total earnings for the earnings period is:

(1) [category 1 earnings – EEET] × not contracted-out rate (10%, 2000–01), plus

(2) [UEL – category 1 earnings] × contracted-out rate (8.4%, 2000–01);

and the total secondary Class 1 contribution liability on total earnings for the earnings period is:

(1) [category 1 earnings – ERET] x not contracted-out rate (12.2%, 2000–01), plus

(2) [UEL – category 1 earnings – ET] × not contracted-out rate (9.2%, 2000–01), plus

(3) [total earnings – UEL] × not contracted-out rate (12.2%, 2000–01).

(B) If category 1 earnings reach the appropriate employee's earnings threshold but not the appropriate employer's earnings threshold, the total primary Class 1 contribution liability on total earnings for the earnings period is:

(1) [category 1 earnings – EEET] × not contracted-out rate (10%, 2000–01), plus

(2) [UEL – category 1 earnings] × contracted-out rate (8.4%, 2000–01);

and the total secondary Class 1 contribution liability on total earnings for the earnings period is:

(1) [UEL – ERET] × contracted-out rate (9.2%, 2000–01), plus

(2) [total earnings – UEL] × not contracted-out rate (12.2%, 2000–01),

and the employer's contracted-out rebate is due on the amount by which category 1 earnings fall short of the employer's earnings threshold.

(C) If category 1 earnings reach the appropriate LEL, but not the appropriate employee's earnings threshold, the total primary Class 1 contribution liability on total earnings for the earnings period is:

[UEL – EEET] × contracted-out rate (8.4%, 2000–01);

and the total secondary Class 1 contribution liability on total earnings for the period is:

(1) [UEL – ERET] × contracted-out rate (9.2%, 2000–01), plus

(2) [total earnings – UEL] × not contracted-out rate (12.2%, 2000–01),

and the employer's contracted-out rebate is due on the amount by which category 1 earnings fall short of the employer's earnings threshold. The employee's contracted-out rebate is due on the amount by which category 1 earnings fall short of the employee's earnings threshold but will be dealt with according to the rules in 22.3 CONTRACTED-OUT EMPLOYMENT.

(D) If category 1 earnings do not reach the appropriate LEL, the total primary Class 1 contribution liability on total earnings for the earnings period is:

[UEL – EEET] × contracted-out rate (8.4%, 2000–01);

and the total secondary Class 1 contribution liability on total earnings for the period is:

(1) [UEL – ERET] × contracted-out rate (9.2%, 2000–01), plus

(2) [total earnings – UEL] × not contracted-out rate (12.2%, 2000–01),

and the employer's contracted-out rebate is due in respect of earnings between the LEL and ERET. The employee's contracted-out rebate is due on the amount of earnings between the LEL and the EEET but will be dealt with according to the rules in 22.3 CONTRACTED-OUT EMPLOYMENT.

(*i*) If neither category 1 earnings alone nor total earnings reach the appropriate UEL, then:

(A) If category 1 earnings reach the appropriate employer's earnings threshold, the total primary Class 1 contribution liability on total earnings for the earnings period is:

(1) [category 1 earnings – EEET] × not contracted-out rate (10%, 2000–01), plus

(2) category 2 earnings × contracted-out rate (8.4%, 2000–01);

and the total secondary Class 1 contribution liability on total earnings for the earnings period is:

(1) [category 1 earnings – ERET] × not contracted-out rate (12.2%, 2000–01), plus

(2) category 2 earnings × contracted-out rate (9.2%, 2000–01).

(B) If category 1 earnings reach the appropriate employee's earnings threshold but not the appropriate employer's earnings threshold, the total primary Class 1 contribution liability on total earnings for the earnings period is:

(1) [category 1 earnings – EEET] × not contracted-out rate (10%, 2000–01), plus

(2) category 2 earnings × contracted-out rate (8.4%, 2000–01),

and the total secondary Class 1 contribution liability on total earnings for the earnings period is:

[total earnings – ERET] × contracted-out rate (9.2%, 2000–01),

and the employer's contracted-out rebate is due on the amount by which category 1 earnings fall short of the employer's earnings threshold.

(C) If category 1 earnings reach the appropriate LEL but not the appropriate employee's earnings threshold, the total primary Class 1 contribution liability on total earnings for the earnings period is:

[UEL – EEET] × contracted-out rate (8.4%, 2000–01);

and the total secondary Class 1 contribution liability on total earnings for the earnings period is:

[total earnings – ERET] × contracted-out rate (9.2%, 2000–01).

and the employer's contracted-out rebate is due on the amount by which the category 1 earnings fall short of the employer's earnings threshold. The employee's contracted-out rebate is due on the amount by which category 1 earnings fall short of the employee's earnings threshold but will be dealt with according to the rules in 22.3 CONTRACTED-OUT EMPLOYMENT.

(D) If category 1 earnings do not reach the appropriate LEL, the total primary Class 1 contribution liability on total earnings for the earnings period is:

[total earnings – EEET] × contracted-out rate (8.4%, 2000–01);

and the total secondary Class 1 contribution liability on total earnings for the earnings period is:

[total earnings – ERET] × contracted-out rate (9.2%, 2000–01).

and the employer's contracted-out rebate is due in respect of earnings between the LEL and ERET. The employee's contracted-out rebate is due on the amount of earnings between the LEL and ERET but will be dealt with according to the rules in 22.3 CONTRACTED-OUT EMPLOYMENT.

Paragraphs (g), (h) and (i) above all assume that the category 2 earnings derive solely from employments contracted-out by reason of salary related schemes. If the contracted-out employment has, instead, a COMP scheme the employer contracted-out rates will be the higher rate of 11.6% rather than 9.2%. If there are at least two contracted-out employments and at least one relates to a salary related scheme and at least one relates to a COMP scheme, refer to the end of this section.

The authority for giving priority to contracted-out contributions (as described above where there is no APP scheme) is found in *SSCBA 1992, 1 Sch 1(2)–(6)*, but authority for reversing the priority where there *is* an APP scheme appears to be lacking in the legislation—though such a reversal is entirely logical.

Example (1)
Throughout 2000–01, Wendy is employed by X–Press Printers Ltd both as cashier and as safety officer. Her employment as cashier is a contracted-out (COSR) employment and carries a salary of £400 per month. Her employment as safety officer is not contracted-out and carries a wage of £35 per week. There is no APP. Because W's salary and wage are earnings in respect of employments under the same employer, they must be aggregated in accordance with the provisions of *SSCBA 1992, 1 Sch 1(1)(a)* (see 5.3 above). The common earnings period must be a month (see 5.10 above) and the aggregated earnings will, accordingly, be £540 in most months (i.e. £400 + (4 × £35)) which, since it exceeds the current monthly employee's earnings threshold of £291 and since the employments are a mix of contracted-out and not contracted-out, brings the provisions of *SSCBA 1992, 1 Sch 1(2)–(6)* into effect. These dictate that, as the total amount of earnings from the contracted-out employments (£400 per month) does not exceed the current upper earnings limit of £2,319, contributions must first be calculated on those earnings at rates attributable to contracted-out employments, then on the balance of earnings from the not contracted-out employment using the not contracted-out rates.

			Class 1		
		Primary		Secondary	
		%	£	%	£
291.00	(monthly LEL)	Nil	0.00	Nil	0.00
38.00		Nil	0.00	Nil	0.00
329.00	(monthly EEET)				
36.00		8.4	3.02	Nil	0.00
365.00	(monthly ERET)				
35.00	(balance of c–o earnings)	8.4	2.94	9.2	3.22
400.00					
140.00	(n–c–o earnings)	10	14.00	12.2	17.08
540.00	(aggregated earnings)		19.96		20.30

The employer's contracted-out rebate is £2.79 i.e. (£38 + £55) × 3% and the employee's contracted-out rebate is £0.61 i.e. £38 x 1.6%. As 61p is less than £3.02, it may be deducted from the employee's liability leaving a reduced employee's national insurance deduction of £19.35. See 22.3 CONTRACTED-OUT EMPLOYMENT.

Example (2)
Yvonne is similarly employed by Zap Computer Games Ltd, but her contracted-out (COMP) employment carries a salary of £1,287 per month and her not contracted-out employment carries a wage of £259 per week. Again, there is no APP. In most months, therefore, her aggregated earnings are £2,323 (i.e. £1,287 + (4 × £259)).

			Class 1		
		Primary		Secondary	
		%	£	%	£
291.00	(monthly LEL)	Nil	0.00	Nil	0.00
38.00	(monthly EEET)	Nil	0.00	Nil	0.00
329.00					
36.00		8.4	3.02	Nil	0.00

5.11   Aggregation of Earnings

		Class 1			
		Primary		Secondary	
		%	£	%	£
365.00	(monthly ERET)				
922.00	(balance of c–o earnings)	8.4	77.45	11.6	106.95
1,287.00					
1,032.00	(n–c–o earnings to UEL)	10	103.20	12.2	125.90
2,319.00	(monthly UEL)		183.67		
4.00	(balance of n–c–o earnings)			12.2	0.49
2,323.00	(aggregated earnings)				233.34

The employer's contracted-out rebate is £0.56 i.e. (£38 + £55) x 0.6% and the employee's contracted-out rebate is £0.61 i.e. £38 x 1.6%. As 61p is less than £3.02, it may be deducted from the employee's liability leaving a reduced employee's national insurance deduction of £183.06. See 22.3 CONTRACTED-OUT EMPLOYMENT.

Where, from 6 April 1997, there are different types of contracted-out scheme the earnings relating to the COMPS employment are considered first. The procedure is as follows.

(a) Add together for the earnings period arrived at under 5.10 above all the aggregable earnings paid in that earnings period. If the total earnings thus ascertained are below the lower earnings limit (LEL) appropriate to the earnings period concerned (see 30.3 EARNINGS LIMITS AND THRESHOLDS), go no further: no contributions are due.

(b) If the total earnings arrived at in (a) equal or exceed the relevant lower earnings limit, divide the total earnings into

  (i) earnings from COMP contracted-out employments ('category 2A earnings') and

  (ii) earnings from COSR contracted-out employments ('category 2B earnings')

(c) If category 2A earnings alone reach the appropriate upper earnings limit (UEL) for the relevant earnings period, the total primary Class 1 contribution liability on total earnings for the earnings period is:

  (1) [UEL – EEET] × COMP contracted-out rate (8.4%, 2000–01);

  and the total secondary Class 1 contribution liability on total earnings for the earnings period is:

  (1) [UEL – ERET] × COMP contracted-out rate (11.6%, 2000–01), plus
  (2) [total earnings – UEL] × not contracted-out rate (12.2%, 2000–01),

  and the employer's COMP contracted-out rebate is due on earnings between the LEL and the employer's threshold. The employee's contracted-out rebate is due on earnings between the LEL and the employee's earnings threshold.

(d) If category 2A earnings alone do not reach the appropriate UEL but total earnings do, then:

  (A) If category 2A earnings reach the appropriate employer's earnings threshold, the total primary Class 1 contribution liability on total earnings for the earnings period is:

    (1) [category 2A earnings – EEET] × COMP contracted-out rate (8.4%, 2000–01), plus

(2) [UEL – category 2A earnings] × COSR contracted-out rate (8.4%, 2000–01);

and the total secondary Class 1 contribution liability on total earnings for the earnings period is:

(1) [category 2A earnings – ERET] × COMP contracted-out rate (11.6%, 2000–01), plus

(2) [UEL – category 2A earnings] × COSR contracted-out rate (9.2%, 2000–01), plus

(3) [total earnings – UEL] × not contracted-out rate (12.2%, 2000–01),

and the employer's COMP contracted-out rebate is due on earnings between the LEL and the employer's earnings threshold. The employee's contracted-out rebate is due on earnings between the LEL and the employee's earnings threshold.

(B) If category 2A earnings reach the appropriate employee's earnings threshold but not the appropriate employer's earnings threshold, the total primary Class 1 contribution liability on total earnings for the earnings period is:

(1) [category 2A earnings – EEET] × COMP contracted-out rate (8.4%, 2000–01), plus

(2) [UEL – category 2A earnings] × COSR contracted-out rate (8.4%, 2000–01);

and the total secondary Class 1 contribution liability on total earnings for the earnings period is:

(1) [UEL – ERET] × COSR contracted-out rate (9.2%, 2000–01), plus

(2) [total earnings – UEL] × not contracted–out rate (12.2%, 2000–01),

and the employer's COMP contracted-out rebate is due on the amount of COMP earnings which exceed the LEL and the employer's COSR contracted-out rebate is due on the amount by which COMP earnings fall short of the employer's earnings threshold. the employee's contracted–out rebate is due on earnings between the LEL and the employee's earnings threshold.

(C) If category 2A earnings reach the appropriate LEL but not the appropriate employee's earnings threshold, the total primary Class 1 contributions liability on total earnings for the earnings period is:

[UEL – category 2A earnings] × COSR contracted-out rate (8.4%, 2000–01);

and the total secondary Class 1 contribution liability on total earnings for the earnings period is:

(1) [UEL – ERET] × COSR contracted-out rate (9.2%, 2000–01), plus

(2) [total earnings – UEL] × not contracted-out rate (12.2%, 2000–01),

and the employer's COMP contracted-out rebate is due on the amount of the COMP earnings which exceed the LEL and the employer's COSR contracted-out is due on the amount by which the COMP earnings fall short of the employer's earnings threshold. The employee's contracted-out rebate is due on earnings between the LEL and the employee's earnings threshold.

(D) If category 2A earnings do not reach the appropriate LEL, the total primary Class 1 contributions liability on total earnings for the earnings period is:

(1) [UEL – EEET] × COSR contracted-out rate (8.4%, 2000–01);

and the total secondary Class 1 contribution liability on total earnings for the earnings period is:

(1) [UEL − ERET] × COSR contracted-out rate (9.2%, 2000–01), plus

(2) [total earnings − UEL] × not contracted-out rate (12.2%, 2000–01),

and the employer's COMP contracted-out rebate is due on earnings between the LEL and the employer's earnings threshold. The employee's contracted-out rebate is due on earnings between the LEL and the employee's earnings threshold.

(e) If neither category 2A earnings alone nor total earnings reach the appropriate UEL, then:

(A) If category 2A earnings reach the appropriate employer's earnings threshold, the total primary Class 1 contribution liability on total earnings for the earnings period is:

(1) [category 2A earnings − EEET] × COMP contracted-out rate (8.4%, 2000–01), plus

(2) category 2B earnings × COSR contracted-out rate (8.4%, 2000–01);

and the total secondary Class 1 contribution liability on total earnings for the earnings period is:

(1) [category 2A earnings − ERET] × COMP contracted-out rate (11.6%, 2000–01), plus

(2) category 2B earnings × COSR contracted-out rate (9.2%, 2000–01),

and the employer's COMP contracted-out rebate is due on the amount between the LEL and the employer's earnings threshold. The employee's contracted-out rebate is due on earnings between the LEL and the employee's earnings threshold.

(B) If category 2A earnings reach the appropriate LEL but not the earnings threshold but not the appropriate employer's earnings threshold, the total primary Class 1 contribution liability on total earnings for the earnings period is:

(1) [category 2A earnings − EEET] × COMP contracted-out rate (8.4%, 2000–01), plus

(2) category 2B earnings × COSR contracted-out rate (8.4%, 2000–01);

and the total secondary Class 1 contribution liability on total earnings for the earnings period is:

[total earnings − ERET] × COSR contracted-out rate (9.2%, 2000–01),

and the employer's COMP contracted-out rebate is due on the amount of COMP earnings which exceed the LEL and the employer's COSR contracted-out rebate is due on the amount by which COMP earnings fall short of the employer's earnings threshold. The employee's contracted-out rebate is due on earnings between the LEL and the employee's earnings threshold, but will be dealt with according to the rules in 22.3 CONTRACTED-OUT EMPLOYMENT.

(C) If category 2A earnings reach the appropriate LEL but not the employee's earnings threshold, the total primary Class 1 contribution liability on total earnings for the earnings period is:

category 2B earnings × COSR contracted-out rate (8.4%, 2000–01);

and the total secondary Class 1 contribution liability on total earnings for the earnings period is:

[total earnings – ERET] × COSR contracted-out rate (9.2%, 2000–01),

and the employer's COMP contracted-out rebate is due on the amount of COMP earnings which exceed the LEL and the employer's COSR contracted-out rebate is due on the amount by which COMP earnings fall short of the employer's earnings threshold. The employee's contracted-out rebate is due on earnings between the LEL and the employee's earnings threshold, but will be dealt with according to the rules in 22.3 CONTRACTED-OUT EMPLOYMENT.

(D) If category 2A earnings do not reach the appropriate LEL, the total primary Class 1 contribution liability on total earnings for the earnings period is:

(1) [total earnings – EEET] x COSR contracted-out rate (8.4%, 2000–01);

and the total secondary Class 1 contribution liability on total earnings for the earnings period is:

(1) [total earnings – ERET] × COSR contracted-out rate (9.2%, 2000–01),

and the employer's COSR contracted-out rebate is due earnings between the LEL and the employer's earnings threshold. The employee's contracted-out rebate is due on earnings between the LEL and the employee's earnings threshold, but will be dealt with according to the rules in 22.3 CONTRACTED-OUT EMPLOYMENT.

Example
A is a car salesman for B Ltd and earns £1,500 per month (COSR). He also assists at the forecourt till and is paid £100 per week (COMP). The relevant earnings period is one week as the COMP employment takes precedence.

In most weeks the liabilities are:

		Class 1			
		Primary		*Secondary*	
		%	£	%	£
67.00	(weekly LEL)	Nil	0.00	Nil	0.00
9.00	(balance)	Nil	0.00	Nil	0.00
76.00	(weekly EEET)				
8.00		8.4	0.67	Nil	0.00
84.00	(weekly ERET)				
16.00	(balance of COMP earnings)	8.4	1.34	11.6	1.86
100.00	(COMP earnings)		2.01		1.86

The employer's contracted-out rebate is £0.10 i.e. (£9 + £8) = £17 × 0.6% and the employee's contracted-out rebate is £0.14 i.e. £9 x 1.6%. As 14p is less than £2.01 it may be deducted giving a reduced employee's national insurance liability of £1.87—see 22.3 CONTRACTED-OUT EMPLOYMENT. Once a month the position will be:

		Class 1			
		Primary		*Secondary*	
		%	£	%	£
67.00	(weekly LEL)	Nil	0.00	Nil	0.00
9.00		Nil	0.00	Nil	0.00
76.00	(weekly EEET)				
8.00		8.4	0.67	Nil	0.00

5.12 Aggregation of Earnings

		Class 1			
		Primary		Secondary	
		%	£	%	£
84.00	(weekly ERET)				
16.00	(balance of COMP earnings)	8.4	1.34	11.6	1.86
100.00					
435.00	(COSR earnings to UEL)	8.4	36.54	9.2	40.02
535.00	(weekly UEL)		38.55		
1,065.00	(balance of COSR earnings)			12.2	129.93
1,600.00	(aggregated earnings)				171.81

The employer's contracted-out rebate is £0.10 i.e. (£9 + £8) = £17 × 0.6% and the employee's contracted-out rebate is £0.14 i.e. £9 × 1.6%. As 14p is less than the COMP liability of £2.01, it may be deducted giving an overall, reduced employee's national insurance liability of £38.41—see 22.3 CONTRACTED-OUT EMPLOYMENT.

5.12 Aggregation of earnings with gratuities etc. paid separately

In certain circumstances, tips, gratuities and service charges are earnings for contribution purposes (see 28.33 EARNINGS). Where that is so, but where the allocation of gratuities is not carried out by the person who is the secondary contributor as regards the ordinary earnings of the employed earner to whom such gratuities etc. are allocated, the secondary contributor must aggregate with ordinary earnings the amount of the gratuities etc. allocated and account for Class 1 contributions on the aggregated amount. (CWG 2 (2000), Pages 30 and 31, flowchart).

Example
Anthony runs a small hotel in which he employs Bonnie and Clyde as waiters. For the week ending 7 August 2000, B's earnings are £50 and C's earnings are £90. On the face of it, no contribution liabilities arise as regards B's earnings as they fall below the limit of £76, and liability for primary and secondary Class 1 contributions as regards C's earnings are at only Nil% initial and 10% main primary, and 12.2% secondary on the earnings over £84. In the week concerned, however, guests have asked for tips of £55 to be added to their bills and A has passed those tips to David, the hall porter, instructing him that B is to receive £30 and C is to receive £25. In those circumstances, contribution liabilities for which A is accountable are as follows:

		£		£
B	Class 1 primary:	76 @ Nil%		0.00
		4 @ 10%		0.40
		80		0.40
	Class 1 secondary:	80 @ Nil%		0.00
C	Class 1 primary:	76 @ Nil%		0.00
		39 @ 10%		3.90
		115		3.90
	Class 1 secondary:	84 @ Nil%		0.00
		31 @ 12.2%		3.78
		115		3.78

5.13   **APPORTIONMENT OF SECONDARY CONTRIBUTIONS ON AGGREGATED EARNINGS**

Where earnings fall to be aggregated under Rule 2 of the aggregation rules described at 5.4 above, liability for Class 1 secondary contributions payable in respect of those earnings is to be apportioned between the secondary contributors in such proportions as they agree between themselves or, in the absence of any such agreement, in the proportions which the earnings paid by each bear to the aggregated earnings. [*SSCBA 1992, 1 Sch 1(3); Contributions Regs, Reg 12(2), as amended by Contributions Amendment Regs 1984, Reg 6*].

Primary contributions payable by an employed earner in respect of aggregated earnings may be deducted either wholly from one of the two or more aggregated payments or partly from the other or any one or more of the others (see 21.4 COLLECTION). [*Contributions Regs, 1 Sch 13(1A)*].

5.14   **RECORDS**

Where earnings fall to be aggregated under any of the aggregation rules described above, the relevant employments will be either

(*a*)   all not contracted-out; or

(*b*)   all contracted-out under the same occupational pension scheme; or

(*c*)   all contracted-out but under different occupational pension schemes; or

(*d*)   not contracted-out and contracted-out under the same occupational pension scheme; or

(*e*)   not contracted-out and contracted-out but under different occupational pension schemes and/or one or more COMP schemes.

In cases falling within (*a*) or (*b*) above, separate records need not be kept for each employment and contributions should be entered on a single deduction working sheet.

In cases falling within (*c*) above, separate records must be kept for each employment and must show the earnings on which Class 1 primary contributions are payable at contracted-out rate and the amount of contributions payable at that rate in respect of each employment. Contributions should, however, be entered on a single deduction working sheet.

In cases falling within (*d*) above, separate records (as in (*c*) above) *and* separate deduction working sheets must be maintained: one for the contracted-out employments and one for the not contracted-out employments.

In cases falling within (*e*) above, separate records must be kept for each COSR contracted-out employment (as in (*c*) above), for each COMP employment and for the not contracted-out employments. Only *three* deduction working sheets should be maintained, however: one for the COSR contracted-out employments, one for the COMP employments and one for the not contracted-out employments.

In *all* cases, a *single* amount of contributions should be entered on each deduction working sheet. [*Contributions Regs, 1 Sch 13(6B)*].

On the first occasion when, in cases falling within (*d*) or (*e*) above, *two or more* deduction working sheets are opened in respect of one employee, the Inspector of Taxes must be notified. If, for PAYE purposes, all earnings are recorded on only one of the deduction working sheets, the one on which COMP contracted-out rate contributions are to be recorded should be used or, if there is no COMP scheme, the deduction working sheet on which COSR contracted-out rate contributions are to be recorded should be used. The other deduction working sheet(s) should have 'NI' entered in the tax code box.

5.15 Aggregation of Earnings

In cases falling within (*b*), (*c*), (*d*) or (*e*) above, records should be retained throughout the period of the employment concerned and for three years after it ends.

Where a computer payroll system is in use and is programmed to prevent two deduction documents being maintained for the same employee, both contributions may, exceptionally, in cases falling within (*d*) or (*e*) above, be recorded on one document but each must be identified by its appropriate contribution table letter (see 15.5 CLASS 1 CONTRIBUTIONS) and separate details must be shown in the pay records.

5.15 BENEFICIAL USE OF AGGREGATION RULES

Although the aggregation rules are an anti-avoidance device, it was possible, until 6 October 1985, in certain circumstances, for a secondary contributor to turn the rules to his advantage. If, for instance, an earner was being paid earnings in respect of two or more employments and those earnings *together* exceeded the upper earnings limit (which, before 6 October 1985, applied for secondary as well as for primary contribution purposes) but *separately* did not, the application of the aggregation rules (if that could be brought about) would ensure that less secondary Class 1 contributions would be paid than would otherwise be the case.

A detailed description of the principle involved and of its application will be found in earlier editions of this work. Here, it is necessary to say only that the removal of the upper earnings limit for secondary Class 1 contribution purposes has now neutralised the beneficial effect of arrangements built on the aggregation rules.

If aggregation does not take place where it seems that it may be appropriate, employers should have clear evidence for their reasons for not aggregating. The former CA found that local authorities often give reasons why aggregation *does* not take place but not why it *cannot* take place (CA Annual Conference 11 October 1994).

5.16 AGGREGATION FOR CLASS 2 SMALL EARNINGS EXCEPTION PURPOSES

A self-employed earner may be excepted from liability to pay CLASS 2 CONTRIBUTIONS (18.3) in respect of any period in which his earnings from such employment are, or are treated as being, less than a specified amount. [*SSCBA 1992, s 11(4)*]. For this purpose, 'earnings' are defined by *Contributions Regs, Reg 25(2)* as 'net earnings from employment as a self-employed earner' and, though the term 'net earnings' is not further defined in the legislation, it is taken to mean earnings such as would be shown in a profit and loss account prepared in accordance with proper accounting principles (see 28.49 EARNINGS and Leaflet CA 02). As a person has but a single 'self' by whom to be employed, the term must be taken to embrace all self-employed activities in which a person is engaged, and, accordingly, the net earnings from each activity must be aggregated and any net loss must be set against those aggregated profits. However, a surplus of loss(es) in any year cannot be carried forward for Class 2 purposes.

The earnings in question relate to tax years and, accordingly, in strict law, time apportionment will be a prerequisite to aggregation unless the accounting periods already run from 6 April in one year to 5 April in the next. [*Contributions Regs, Regs 1(2), 25(1)*].

Example
Esmerelda has been self-employed as a dressmaker and also as a hairdresser for many years. Her accounts reveal the following trading results

Year ended	Trade		£
31 December 1999	Dressmaker	Loss	(2,000)
31 December 2000	Dressmaker	Profit	5,000
30 September 1999	Hairdresser	Profit	4,000
30 September 2000	Hairdresser	Profit	6,000

Her 1999–2000 earnings for Class 2 exception purposes are

	£
9/12 × £(2,000)	(1,500)
3/12 × £5,000	1,250
6/12 × £4,000	2,000
6/12 × £6,000	3,000
	£4,750

It used to be DSS practice to accept an account ending in a tax year as being co-terminous with the tax year. Thus, in the case of Esmerelda above, it would have been expected that the DSS would have regarded her earnings as being £4,000 – £2,000 (loss), i.e. £2,000, for 1999–2000 but the practice was discontinued during 1990–91.

5.17 AGGREGATION FOR CLASS 4 PURPOSES

CLASS 4 CONTRIBUTIONS (20) are payable in respect of all annual profits or gains which are immediately derived from the carrying on or exercise of one or more trades, professions or vocations, and are profits or gains chargeable to income tax under Case I or II of Schedule D. [*SSCBA 1992, s 15(1)*]. The Class 4 contribution for any tax year is to be an amount equal to a prescribed percentage of so much of those profits or gains as exceeds a prescribed lower annual limit and does not exceed a prescribed upper annual limit. [*Sec 15(3)*]. Clearly, therefore, profits or gains must be aggregated for Class 4 purposes but, because social security legislation has, in this instance, adopted the basis of assessment applied by the Inland Revenue for the purposes of income tax, no question of time apportionment arises and aggregation is simply a matter of totalling the adjusted profits assessable to tax in a particular tax year. In the case of a partner, it will be his share of the adjusted profits. [*SSCBA 1992, 2 Sch 4(1)*]. (See further 50.4 PARTNERS.)

Example
Francis is in business as an interior decorator and as a furniture renovator. He is also a partner in a firm which supplies fitted kitchens. His interior decorating business was established several years ago with a 31 October accounting date but the furniture renovating business commenced only on 1 May 1996 with a 30 April accounting date. The fitted kitchen partnership is long-established (with a 31 December accounting date) and F's share of profits one-half. Trading results adjusted in accordance with the tax and Class 4 rules are

Year ended	Trade	
31 October 1997	Interior decorator	£6,000
31 October 1998	Interior decorator	£7,500
31 October 1999	Interior decorator	£8,500
31 October 2000	Interior decorator	£9500
30 April 1997	Furniture renovator	£520
30 April 1998	Furniture renovator	£1,250
30 April 1999	Furniture renovator	£1,300
30 April 2000	Furniture renovator	£1,200

5.17 Aggregation of Earnings

31 December 1997	Fitted kitchens	£14,000
31 December 1998	Fitted kitchens	£16,000
31 December 1999	Fitted kitchens	£18,000
31 December 2000	Fitted kitchens	£26,000

Schedule D, Case I assessments for 1997–98 will be as follows

	£
Interior decorator (current year basis)	6,000
Furniture renovator (current year basis)	520
Fitted kitchens (current year basis split according to profit share in 1997–98:1/2 × £14,000)	7,000
	£13,520

Schedule D, Case I assessments for 1998–99 will be as follows

	£
Interior decorator (current year basis)	7,500
Furniture renovator (current year basis)	1,250
Fitted kitchens (current year basis split according to profit share in 1998–99:1/2 × £16,000)	8,000
	£16,750

Schedule D, Case I assessments for 1999–2000 will be as follows

	£
Interior decorator (current year basis)	8,500
Furniture renovator (current year basis)	1,300
Fitted kitchens (current year basis split according to profit share in 1999–2000:1/2 × £18,000)	9,000
	£18,800

Schedule D, Case I assessments for 2000–01 will be as follows

	£
Interior decorator (current year basis)	9,500
Furniture renovator (current year basis)	1,200
Fitted kitchens (current year basis split according to profit share in 2000–01:1/2 × £26,000)	13,000
	£23,700

Note: Tax and NICs are payable in two instalments for 2000–01 on 31 January 2001 and 31 July 2001 based on previous year's *liability* (even though the lower limit has changed). The balance of tax and NICs is payable on 31 January 2002. Francis's Class 4 liability will increase substantially on the previous year's amount i.e. £23,700 – £4,385 × 7% = £1,352.05 as compared with 1999–2000 Class 4 of £676.20. Francis will have to pay the balance of Class 4 NIC (and tax) on 31 January 2001 in respect of 1999–2000 amounting to £675.85 and also the first instalment of Class 4 for 2000–01 of £676.02 — a grand total of £1,351.87!

Losses (arising from activities the profits or gains of which would be brought into computation for Class 4 contribution purposes) are available for relief against the aggregated profits or gains arrived at on the principles outlined above (see 28.80 EARNINGS). [*SSCBA 1992, 2 Sch 3(1)*].

6   Airmen

Cross-references. See ARMED FORCES (11) for members of the regular air forces of the Crown; CLASS 1 CONTRIBUTIONS (15); OVERSEAS MATTERS (49) for domicile, residence and EC/EEA and reciprocal agreements.

Other Sources. Simon's NIC, Part I, Section 8, Chapter 49.31; IR Booklet 490 (1998).

6.1   GENERAL CONSIDERATIONS

The social security system is, like the tax system, subject to territorial limitations (see 49.2 OVERSEAS MATTERS). Where an insured person works outside the UK, he ceases to be 'gainfully employed in Great Britain', with the result that he can be neither an 'employed earner' nor a 'self-employed earner' for contributions purposes (see 14.2 and 14.10 CATEGORISATION). This implies that there is no liability to pay Class 1, Class 2 or Class 4 contributions. In the absence of special rules to change the position, those UK residents employed in international transport would often cease to be compulsorily insured when they left the UK and might have to rely on voluntary contributions under Class 3 to maintain their entitlement to the basic state pension.

The system copes with any temporary overseas absences for those normally within Class 1 liability by deeming the individuals concerned to continue to be 'employed earners' for 52 weeks after departure. There is a corresponding 52-week period of non-liability for those sent to work only temporarily in the UK by non-UK employers (see 49.8 OVERSEAS MATTERS). [*Contributions Regs, Regs 119(2), 120(2)(a)*].

Workers in international transport, however, do not fit neatly into that framework. Because of the brevity of their stays in many different jurisdictions and the length of time they spend outside national jurisdictions, they may not qualify for the protection of any state's social security system. To provide such protection for essentially UK-based workers in international air transport, the *Contributions Regs, Regs 81–84* include provisions governing the UK national insurance liabilities of 'airmen', broadly limiting liability to those domiciled in the UK or having a place of residence in the UK, subject to the provisions of reciprocal agreements and EC/EEA regulations.

6.2   DEFINITION

An *airman* is any person, other than a serving member of the ARMED FORCES (11), who is, or has been, employed under a contract of service (see 14.3 CATEGORISATION) and falls into one of two categories:

(*a*)   a pilot, commander, navigator or other member of crew (e.g. stewards and stewardesses) of any aircraft, wherever the contract of service is entered into; or

(*b*)   in any other capacity on board any aircraft for the purposes of the aircraft, its crew, or any passengers or cargo or mails carried thereby, where the contract of service is entered into in the UK with a view to its performance, wholly or partly, while the aircraft is in flight.

[*Contributions Regs, Reg 81*].

It should be noted that the definition does not extend to self-employed earners working under a contract for services (see 14.3 CATEGORISATION), whose liability to CLASS 2 CONTRIBUTIONS (18) therefore depends on the normal rules and, in particular, the ordinary residence test prescribed by *Contributions Regs, Reg 119(1)(d)*.

6.3 THE AMENABILITY RULE IN CONTRIBUTION LEGISLATION

The primary factor linking an employed airman to the UK social security system is a UK base. Contributions are payable by or in respect of an airman only if he is either domiciled (see 49.5 OVERSEAS MATTERS) or has a place of residence in the UK. [*Contributions Regs, Reg 82(2)*]. This is subject to contrary provisions in reciprocal agreements. [*Contributions Regs, Reg 82(3)*].

However, a UK-domiciled airman and non-domiciled airman with a UK place of residence can spend significant periods overseas and, as mentioned above, under the general rules of categorisation a person must be gainfully employed in Great Britain (see 49.2 OVERSEAS MATTERS for definition of Great Britain) if he is to fall within the category of employed earner. [*SSCBA 1992, s 2(1)(a)*]. He must then fulfil certain conditions of residence or presence (see 49.8 OVERSEAS MATTERS) if he is to be liable to pay CLASS 1 CONTRIBUTIONS (15).

Although an airman may fail to meet these requirements by the very nature of his employment, he is, nevertheless, to be *treated* as being employed in employed earner's employment and as present in Great Britain if he fulfils two conditions:

(i) he is employed as an airman on board an aircraft; and

(ii) • his employer, or
  • the person paying his earnings in respect of that employment (whether as agent for the employer or not), or
  • the person under whose directions the terms of his employment and the amount of his earnings are determined,

where the aircraft is British (see below), has a place of business in Great Britain.

Where the aircraft is not British, the deeming provision applies only if the person referred to in (ii) has his principal place of business in Great Britain. [*Contributions Regs, Reg 82(1)*].

This amenability rule is, however, subject to any different rule arising under reciprocal agreements given effect in Great Britain by Order in Council (see 6.4 below) or under EC Regulations (see 6.5 below). [*Contributions Regs, Reg 82(3); European Communities Act 1972, ss 2, 3*].

A *place of residence* is a factual matter and is to be distinguished from the status of residence. The latter is a qualitative attribute which a person may or may not possess whether he has a place of residence or not (see 49.4 OVERSEAS MATTERS). Many non-UK airmen who fly regularly into the UK rent a flat near the airport, but a caravan may also be a place of residence, as may a yacht anchored in territorial waters. (*Makins v Elson [1977] STC 46; Bayard Brown v Burt (1911) 5 TC 667*). For the meaning of *place of business* see 49.7 OVERSEAS MATTERS.

A *British aircraft* is an aircraft which 'belongs to Her Majesty' (i.e. is owned by the Crown) or is registered in the UK with an owner, or managing owner if there is more than one owner, who resides or has his principal place of business (see 49.4, 49.7 OVERSEAS MATTERS) in Great Britain. For this purpose, a charterer or sub-charterer entitled as hirer for the time being to possession and control of the aircraft is to be taken to be the owner. [*Contributions Regs, Reg 81*].

6.4 RECIPROCAL AGREEMENT RULES

Where an airman falls within the scope of a reciprocal agreement which has effect in Great Britain, the general amenability rule (see 6.3 above) will usually be superseded by rules contained in the agreement. The provisions of reciprocal agreements as regards travelling personnel of an undertaking engaged in the transport of passengers or goods by air tend to imitate the terms of *EC Reg 1408/71, Art 14(2)(a)* which deals with 'travelling or flying personnel' in EC member states (see 6.5 below). Such provisions are generally that

(*a*) subject to (*b*) and (*c*) below, where a person is employed by an undertaking which has its principal place of business in the territory of one of the parties to the reciprocal agreement, the legislation of that party is to apply to him, even if he is employed in the territory of the other party;

(*b*) subject to (*c*) below, where the undertaking has a branch or agency in the territory of one of the parties to the reciprocal agreement and a person is employed by that branch or agency, the legislation of that party is to apply to him;

(*c*) where a person is ordinarily resident (see 49.4 OVERSEAS MATTERS) in the territory of one of the parties to a reciprocal agreement and is employed wholly or mainly in that territory, the legislation of that party is to apply to him, even if the undertaking which employs him does not have its principal place of business or a branch or an agency in that territory.

The provision made for determining the relevant contribution legislation as regards airmen in agreements originating prior to 1973 may differ considerably from the provision set out above and reference to the appropriate agreement will be necessary in every case. (See 49.21 OVERSEAS MATTERS for a complete list of reciprocal agreements currently in force.) The agreements between the UK and Austria, Barbados, Belgium, Bermuda, Cyprus, Denmark, Finland, France, Germany, Guernsey, Italy, Jamaica, Jersey, Luxembourg, Mauritius, the Netherlands, Norway, the Philippines, Portugal, Spain, Sweden, Switzerland, Turkey and former Yugoslavia all contain special provisions regarding airmen.

6.5 OTHER MATTERS

EC regulations

For the provisions of EC regulations concerning travelling or flying personnel engaged in international transport of goods or passengers by air, see 49.15 OVERSEAS MATTERS. Unless individual EC/EEA member states elect otherwise, EC Regulations supersede any reciprocal agreements between such states, and no elections are currently in force relating to airmen. See also *Civil Aviation Act 1982* and *Air Navigation Orders*.

6.6 Time limits

Where an airman is outside Great Britain by reason of his employment as an airman and is, in consequence, unable to comply at or within the allotted time with a requirement of the contributions legislation, he is to be deemed to have complied if he meets the requirement as soon thereafter as is reasonably practicable. [*Contributions Regs, Reg 83*].

6.7 Travel expenses

Expenses of travelling between home and airport may sometimes qualify for deduction for the purposes of Schedule E income tax under *ICTA 1988, ss 193, 194* (see *Nolder v Walters, KB 1930, 15 TC 380* and 28.62 EARNINGS). Where an airman is within Class 1 liability but is not taxable on payments of, or contributions towards, expenses which are deductible from Schedule E emoluments by virtue of *s 193(3), (4)* or *(6)* or *s 194(1)* because they relate to duties performed wholly or partly outside the UK, such payments are excluded from earnings for contribution purposes. [*Contributions Regs, Reg 19(1)(q)*]. The cost of travel to an airport other than the

6.8 Airmen

normal base should also be excluded from earnings by virtue of the normal business expenses rule (see 28.62 EARNINGS and IR Booklet 490, Chapter 7).

Furthermore, if the employer books and pays for the transport, the normal rule for payments in kind (see 28.24 EARNINGS) should apply to exclude the cost from the airman's earnings.

6.8 Airmen born abroad

An airman born outside Great Britain who is not covered by EC Regulations or a reciprocal agreement is not liable for payment of Class 1 contributions unless he is resident or domiciled in Great Britain. If there is no primary (employee's) liability, there can be no secondary liability either [*Contributions Regs, Reg 82(2)*]. Such an airman should write to International Services, NICO, Longbenton, Newcastle upon Tyne, NE98 1ZZ seeking a ruling to confirm non-liability.

7   Annual Maximum

Cross-references. See CLASS 1 CONTRIBUTIONS (15); CLASS 2 CONTRIBUTIONS (18); CLASS 3 CONTRIBUTIONS (19); CLASS 4 CONTRIBUTIONS (20); 44.1 MULTIPLE EMPLOYMENTS for circumstances in which excessive contributions may be paid; DEFERMENT OF PAYMENT (27) for circumstances in which excess payment of contributions may be prevented; 53.5 REPAYMENT AND RE-ALLOCATION for repayment of excess contributions; 58 WORKING CASE STUDY.

Other Sources. Simon's NIC, Part I, Section 2, Chapter 8.161, Section 3, Chapters 12.91 and 13.111.

7.1   GENERAL CONSIDERATIONS

This chapter is mainly concerned with the specific statutory rules which apply so as to limit the amount of contributions payable where a person has multiple employments; but a preliminary question which must be addressed is: Is there, in law, an annual maximum so far as a person with a single employment was concerned? The DSS answer to that question was, no; but the position is far from clear.

Liability for Class 1 contributions is imposed where 'in any tax week' earnings are paid to or for the benefit of an earner. [*SSCBA 1992, s 6(1)*]. A 'tax week' is 'one of the successive periods in a tax year beginning with the first day of that year and every 7th day thereafter; the last day of the tax year (or, in the case of a tax year ending in a leap year, the last 2 days) to be treated accordingly as a separate tax week', while a 'tax year' is 'the 12 months beginning with 6th April in any year'. [*SSCBA 1992, s 122(1)*]. It follows, therefore, that there can *never* be more than 53 tax weeks in a tax year and that, in the case of the weekly-paid earner around whom the provisions of *Sec 6* (the charging section) are framed, there can never be a liability for more than 53 primary Class 1 contributions at the rates set by *Sec 8(2)* on the earnings defined by *Sec 8(1)*. Thus, it is surely arguable that the terms of *Sec 6* themselves create an annual maximum for any earner in a single employment, i.e. 53 primary Class 1 contributions at the maximum standard rate on weekly earnings equivalent to the weekly upper earnings limit. The section makes no special provision for earners paid at other than weekly intervals (except to say that references to earnings limits are to be taken as references to prescribed equivalents—*Sec 8(3)*) and it must surely follow, therefore, that that same annual maximum applies to such earners without the need for any other provision to limit their liability.

This is of importance because there are circumstances in which an employed earner in a single employment will, in a tax year, pay more than the maximum referred to.

Example

Avocet works for Bittern and is paid £2,204 every four weeks. The employment is not contracted-out. Each pay day, B calculates the contributions due by dividing £2,204 by 4 and looking up the resultant £551 in Table A of the National Insurance Tables 1 (CA 38 (April 2000), Page 15). The tables in Table A extend only to gross pay of £535 (the weekly UEL) for which the employer's contribution is £55.02 and the employee's contribution is £45.90; but the tables instruct Bittern to go to the end of the book (Page 62) to see how to deal with the remaining £16 of gross pay. There he is told that there is an additional employer's contribution of £1.95. Armed with the combined amounts of £56.97 employer and £45.90 employee, Bittern now multiplies those amounts by four and pays over to the collector of taxes £227.88 employer's contributions and £183.60 employee's contributions after deducting £183.60 from A's salary. The first of these four-weekly pay days in 2000–01 fell on 6 April 2000 and the last will fall on 5 April 2001; 14 of them in all. So that, once the 5 April contributions have been collected from his pay, A will have paid $14 \times £183.60$ in the tax year, i.e. £2,570.40. But the annual maximum implicit in *SSCBA 1992, s 6* is only £2,432.70, i.e. $[53 \times £76 \times Nil\%] + [53 \times £459 \times 10\%]$. In other words, the annual maximum implicit in *Sec 6* has been exceeded by £137.70.

Only where an earner has more than one employment, does the annual maximum implicit in *Sec 6* not serve to limit liability. Because *Sec 6(4)* imposes liability 'without regard to any other payment of earnings ... in respect of any other employment' the annual maximum created by *Sec 6* only serves to limit contribution liability in each employment and does not limit the earner's *combined* liabilities. Thus there is every reason why, in the case of an earner with two or more employments, the special liability-limiting provision supplied by *SSCBA 1992, s 19* and *Contributions Regs, Reg 17* (see 7.2 below), should have been introduced. But it seems inconceivable that Parliament would have made that provision (which limits the contributions paid by an employee with two or more employments to 53 weeks of contribution at the maximum standard rate on weekly earnings equivalent to the weekly upper earnings limit) while leaving an employee in a single employment with the open-ended liability for which the DSS contended. On the contrary, it seems clear that Parliament *must* have considered that the very terms of *Sec 6* themselves imposed that same limitation on any earner in a single employment.

The DSS claimed, however, that, in the circumstances illustrated by the above example,

'. . . there has not been an overpayment of contributions by the relevant employees of the Company. Contributions become payable by an employee in accordance with *SSA 1975, s 4(1)(2)* [now *SSCBA 1992, s 6(1)(4)*] where in any tax week . . . earnings are paid which exceed the lower earnings limit and up to the upper earnings limit as specified in *s 4(1)* [now *SSCBA 1992, s 5(1)*]. The prescribed equivalent shall apply where employees are paid other than on a weekly basis; this equivalent is provided by *Contributions Regs, Reg 8A*. The employees have paid the correct amount of contributions calculated in accordance with *Reg 8A*. Since liability can arise only on payment, it would appear that no overpayment can be made as if an extra contribution is made in year 1, this will of necessity result in one less contribution being made in year 2. If other provisions in the legislation were intended to alter the liability to contributions under the above provisions, they would do so expressly and unambiguously. The relevant legislation contains no such provisions. Regulation 17 of the Regulations was introduced to ensure that excess contributions could be refunded to employees with more than one employment as it was perceived by the Department that an overpayment could arise in certain circumstances. No such possible inequity may arise regarding contributions payable by employees in a single employment.'. (DSS Letter, 30 July 1991).

In other words, the DSS not only rejected the contention that any annual maximum is implicitly imposed by the terms of *Sec 6* itself but also claimed that the absence of such a maximum cannot lead to inequity! It is, however, clearly in error when it claims that the 'extra' contributions paid in one year are necessarily compensated for by 'less' contributions paid in the next year. As may easily be demonstrated, they are not. A 14-period year (as in the above example) will be preceded and succeeded by a number of 13-period years, *never* by a 12-period year. And it must surely be inequitable if two employees with identical earnings pay different amounts of contributions merely because one is paid at weekly or monthly intervals while the other is paid at four-weekly intervals. It is, furthermore, in fundamental breach of the contributory principle that, where earnings are paid at or above the upper earnings limit, that should be so. Contributions in excess of 53 primary Class 1 contributions at maximum standard rate on weekly earnings equivalent to the weekly upper earnings limit can *never* increase an entitlement to SERPS or any other state benefit (see 13.2 BENEFITS).

This argument then leads to the question: If there *is* an implicit annual maximum imposed by the terms of *Sec 6* itself so far as the earnings of an employed earner in a single employment are concerned, is there any provision which will enable a return of contributions to be made where contributions have been paid in excess of that maximum. Again, the DSS said, no; but that appears to contradict the plain terms of *Contributions Regs, Reg 32* which states that 'where . . . there has been any payment of contributions in excess of the amount prescribed in regulation 17 of these regulations . . . such contributions shall be returned . . .'. The amount prescribed in regulation 17 is 'an amount equal to 53 primary Class 1 contributions at the maximum standard rate', so, carrying that definition back into *Reg 32*, we arrive at a regulation which reads: 'where . . . there has been any payment of contributions in excess of 53 primary Class 1 contributions at the maximum standard rate . . . such contributions shall be returned . . .'.

Regulations may, of course, only operate within the limitations imposed on them by the Act under which they are made. So it is necessary to ask from which provisions of *SSCBA 1992, Reg 32* derives its authority. At first glance the enabling provision for *Reg 32* is *Sec 19(2)* which relates exclusively to the 'multiple employment' annual maximum; but then there is *1 Sch 8(1)(m)*. That paragraph enables regulations which provide 'for the return of . . . contributions paid . . . in such circumstances that, under any provision . . . of regulations, they fall to be repaid'. It may be argued, therefore, that there is indeed authority for contributions paid in excess of the annual maximum implicit in the terms of *Sec 6* to be repaid; but the DSS rejected this view also. It said:

'. . . *Reg 17* is empowered by *SSA 1975, s 11(1)* [now *SSCBA 1992, s 19(1)*] and *Reg 32* empowered by *SSA 1975, s 11(2)* [now *SSCBA 1992, s 19(2)*], for the purpose of *s 11(1)* [now *SSCBA 1992, s 19(1)*]. Therefore as *Reg 32* is subordinate to *Reg 17* (and therefore imports all of its conditions) you seek to rely on the provisions of *SSA 1975, 1 Sch 6(1)(h)* [now *SSCBA 1992, 1 Sch 8(1)(m)*]. This paragraph provides an enabling power to make regulations for "the return of . . . contributions . . . in such circumstances that under any provision of Part I of the Act or of Regulations, they fall to be repaid". In the Department's view paragraph *6(1)(h)* [now *8(1)(m)*] grants the power to make a regulation to repay in certain circumstances where there is *already* a provision in the Act or another regulation which specifically provides for a repayment to be made. It does not simply provide for the return of contributions in such circumstances as may be prescribed—but in such circumstances that, under any provision of Part I of the Act or of Regulations, they fall to be repaid. It looks to the existence of other provisions. Therefore *1 Sch 6(1)(h)* [now *1 Sch 8(1)(m)*] does not empower *Reg 32* in the manner outlined in your letter. As *Reg 32* is subordinate to *Reg 17*, all the conditions of *Reg 17* apply in any instance where a refund is claimed under *Reg 32* (except in cases of error).' (DSS Letter, 30 July 1991).

In other words, the DSS claimed that *Reg 32* is applicable *only* in the multiple employment situations to which *Reg 17* refers. A careful reading of *Reg 32* makes it difficult to see, however, how that can be so. *Reg 32* contains no reference whatsoever to multiple employment situations. The draftsmen *could* easily have built in such a limitation (had they so wished) by simply following the reference to 'regulation 17 of these regulations' with the words 'and the circumstances prescribed in that regulation apply'; but they did not do so.

The position remains, however, that in the view of the National Insurance Contributions Office of the Inland Revenue, there is no annual maximum which may be applied to limit the contributions liability of an employed earner in a single employed earner's employment.

As indicated above, the position is quite different where an earner has more than one employment and/or self-employment. Then, specific statutory provisions and regulations serve to limit as described below. However, the insertion of *Reg 32(1A)*

7.2 Annual Maximum

prevents the refund of Class 1 primary contributions to an individual in cases where the *Social Security (Additional Pension) (Contributions Paid in Error) Regulations 1996, SI 1996 No 1245, Reg 3* applies. See 23.6 CONTRACTED-OUT EMPLOYMENT.

7.2 THE LIMITATIONS ON CONTRIBUTIONS

Class 1 and Class 2 limitation

Where an earner is employed in more than one employment (irrespective of whether the employments are employed earner's employments or self-employments), liability in any tax year for

(*a*) primary Class 1 contributions; or

(*b*) where both Class 1 and Class 2 contributions are payable, both primary Class 1 and Class 2 contributions,

is not to exceed an amount equal to 53 primary Class 1 contributions at the primary percentage payable on earnings at the upper earnings limit. [*Contributions Regs, Reg 17, as amended by Social Security (Contributions and Credits)(Miscellaneous Amendments) Regs 2000, Reg 7*]. For 2000–01 this amount is £2,432.70, i.e. 53 × [£76 × Nil%] + 53 × [£459 × 10%].

This annual maximum is, in the case of VOLUNTEER DEVELOPMENT WORKERS (57) (but not in the case of SHARE FISHERMEN (54)) to be reduced by the amount of any special Class 2 contributions which have been paid in respect of the year in question. [*Contribution Regs, Reg 123D(1)(c) as amended by Contribution Amendment Regs 1986, Reg 2*]. The effect of this is to ensure that, where a volunteer development worker pays contributions in excess of the maximum in a year, any repayment obtained by him will consist entirely of contributions other than any special Class 2 contributions which he may have paid in respect of that year (see 53.5 REPAYMENT AND RE-ALLOCATION).

There are no provisions enabling the annual maximum to be reduced if the contributor attains pensionable age during the year, thereby ceasing to be liable to primary Class 1 and Class 2 contributions (see 3.7 and 3.12 AGE EXCEPTION).

Example

For the whole of 2000–01, Finch is employed by Grebe in a contracted-out employment at a salary of £2,200 per month. From 6 October 2000 to 5 April 2001, she is also employed by Heron in a not contracted-out employment at a salary of £1,000 per month; and from 1 January 2001, she is also self-employed. The Class 1 primary contributions paid on her earnings from her employed earner's employments are as follows

	£			£		£
Grebe	329.00	(monthly EEET) @ Nil%		0.00 × 12 =		0.00
	1,871.00		@ 8.4%	157.16 × 12 =		1,885.92
	2,200.00					1,885.92
Heron	329.00	(monthly EEET) @ Nil%		0.00 × 6 =		0.00
	671.00		@ 10%	67.10 × 6 =		402.60
	1,000.00					402.60
						2,288.52

Finch also pays:

Class 2 contributions		2.00 × 14 =	28.00
			2,316.52

On the face of it, F will not have paid excessive contributions since the annual maximum for 2000–01 is £2,432.70. Such a judgement is premature however. Before the question of any excess can be decided, the primary Class 1 contributions paid at less than standard rate (i.e. £1,885.92) must be converted to contributions at the appropriate standard rate (i.e. £1,885.92 × 10/8.4 = £2,245.14) and a fresh total must be arrived at (i.e. £2,675.74). As this fresh total *exceeds* £2,432.70, excess contributions have, in fact, been paid and, provided the necessary conditions are met, the excess, suitably adjusted, will be repayable (see 53.5 REPAYMENT AND RE-ALLOCATION).

7.3   Class 4 limitation

Although *Contributions Regs, Reg 17* effectively ensures that an earner's liability for primary Class 1 contributions and Class 2 contributions is limited to the annual maximum amount which he would pay were he employed in a single employed earner's employment with earnings at the upper earnings limit (see 7.2 above), that regulation does nothing to limit liability for Class 4 contributions which the earner may also have paid or be due to pay. Class 4 limitation is, however, provided by *Reg 67(1), as amended by Contributions Amendment No 3 Regs 1985, Reg 3 and Contributions Transitional Regs 1985, Reg 6*, as follows. Where for any year such contributions are payable *in addition to*

(*a*)   primary Class 1 contributions; or

(*b*)   Class 2 contributions; or

(*c*)   both primary Class 1 contributions and Class 2 contributions,

the liability of the earner for Class 4 contributions for that year is not to exceed such amount as, *when added to the amount of primary Class 1 contributions and Class 2 contributions ultimately payable* by him for the year (i.e. after applying the Class 1 and Class 2 annual maximum rule described at 7.2 above) *equals* in value *the sum of*

(i)   the amount of Class 4 contributions which would be payable by that earner on profits or gains equal to the upper annual limit (see 30.8 EARNINGS LIMITS AND THRESHOLDS); and

(ii)   for 1985–86 only, £218; but for any other year, 53 times the amount of a Class 2 contribution payable for the year.

For 2000–01, the sum of items (i) and (ii) will normally be £1,746.45, *viz*

		£	
£27,820 – £4,385 @ 7%	=	1,640.45	(Class 4)
£2.00 × 53	=	106.00	(Class 2)
		£1,746.45	

It should be noted, however, that where Class 2 contributions are, by reason of their late payment, payable at a rate other than the rate set for the tax year, that other rate is the rate which must be used for the purposes of the calculation shown above. [*Reg 67(1)*]. Were it not for this provision, the penal effect of the late-paid contribution rules (see 39.7 LATE-PAID CONTRIBUTIONS) might, in some circumstances, be frustrated. Similarly, in the case of SHARE FISHERMEN (54) who pay a special higher rate of Class 2 contributions, the higher rate must be used for the purposes of the calculation. [*Contribution Regs, Reg 98(d)*].

For 2000–01, the share fisherman's annual maximum will be £1,780.90, *viz*

$$
\begin{array}{lll}
 & \pounds & \\
\pounds 27,820 - \pounds 4,385 \text{ @ } 7\% = & 1,640.45 & \text{(Class 4)} \\
\pounds 2.65 \times 53 \qquad\qquad = & \underline{140.45} & \text{(Class 2)} \\
 & \underline{\underline{\pounds 1,780.90}} &
\end{array}
$$

Because the Class 4 limiting amount, calculated as explained above, is invariably less than the Class 1 and Class 2 annual maximum described at 7.2 above (£2,432.70 for 2000–01), it is clear that no liability for Class 4 contributions can possibly arise where liabilities have already been limited by reference to the Class 1 and Class 2 annual maximum.

The regulation also affords relief from Class 4 liability, however, in situations where earnings are too low for the Class 1 and Class 2 annual maximum to be of any effect.

Example
Iris is a self-employed dressmaker with profits assessable to income tax under self-assessment basis for 2000–01 (and requiring no further adjustment) of £17,000. Throughout the year she pays Class 2 contributions but, intermittently, when business is poor, she supplements her income by taking employment with Jeans Ltd. Her earnings from J during the year were 32 weeks at £476. Contributions are paid as follows

		£
Class 1 primary	£76 × Nil% × 32	0.00
	£400 × 10% × 32	1,280.00
Class 2	£2.00 × 52	104.00
		1,384.00

In the absence of a relieving provision, Class 4 contributions of £883.05 (i.e. [£17,000 – £4,385 (LAL)] @ 7%) would also be payable. Under the terms of *Reg 67(1)*, however, the Class 4 liability is not to exceed the amount by which £1,746.45 (the Class 4 limiting amount) exceeds £1,384.00, i.e. £362.45 and, in consequence, I's liability is limited to that of someone deriving equivalent total earnings exclusively from self-employment.

For the purpose of determining the extent of an earner's liability for Class 4 contributions under *Reg 67(1)*, the amount of any primary Class 1 contributions paid at a rate less than the standard rate is to be converted into its standard rate equivalent. *[Reg 67(2)]*. This applies, for example, to contracted-out contributions and married women's reduced rate contributions.

7.4   SECONDARY CONTRIBUTORS

Because secondary Class 1 contributions have no insurative content whatsoever, the considerations which give rise to a limitation of contribution liability to an annual maximum in the case of a primary Class 1 contributor are of no relevance in the case of a secondary contributor. Accordingly, no provision is made to limit the amount of secondary contributions payable by an employer or other secondary contributor in respect of any particular employed earner.

8 Anti-Avoidance

Cross-references. See AGGREGATION OF EARNINGS (5) for circumstances in which aggregation of fragmented earnings may be enforced; CATEGORISATION (14) for criteria to be applied in determining an earner's status; 31.3 and 31.11 EARNINGS PERIODS for *Reg 3(2)* direction and for anti-avoidance rules for company directors.

Other Sources. Simon's NIC, Part I, Section 12, Chapter 61; Tolley's Tax Planning 2000–01.

8.1 AVOIDANCE DEVICES

Attempts at avoidance of contribution liability generally involve either

(a) the concealment or removal of factors which would evidence the existence of a 'master/servant' relationship, and the exposure or creation of factors which would suggest that the 'servant' is, in fact, an independent contractor who may properly be categorised as a self-employed earner; or

(b) the fragmentation of a single employment into multiple concurrent employments, one or more of which give rise to earnings at a level below the lower earnings limit or at a level on which Class 1 contributions are payable at a rate lower than the rate at which Class 1 contributions would be payable were the employment not fragmented (see 30.1 to 30.7 EARNINGS LIMITS AND THRESHOLDS); or

(c) the creation of a pay structure which features two or more regular pay intervals of different lengths (see 31.3 EARNINGS PERIODS) and such a division of earnings between those pay intervals as ensures that earnings paid at the longer intervals are subject to, and exceed for primary contribution purposes, the upper earnings limit (see 30.7 EARNINGS LIMITS AND THRESHOLDS) applicable to the shortest interval; or

(d) the substitution of payments which may be disregarded in arriving at EARNINGS (28) for contribution purposes for payments which may not so be disregarded, although such action is likely in most cases to result, from 6 April 2000, in a Class 1A charge on the employer instead.

Where avoidance activity of the kind described at (a) above is encountered, it may be remedied by re-categorisation grounded on the various judicial tests whereby the existence of a contract of service may be revealed (see 14.3 to 14.7 CATEGORISATION).

Where avoidance of contribution liability takes the form described at (b) above, the application of the aggregation rules (see 5.2 to 5.7 AGGREGATION OF EARNINGS) will, wherever possible, be enforced.

Where avoidance of liability has been achieved through a pay structure of the kind described at (c) above and the greater part of earnings has been paid at intervals of greater length than the shortest, future avoidance by those means will be prevented by notifying the persons concerned that the normal earnings period rule is thereafter to be reversed (*Reg 3(2)* direction, see 31.3 EARNINGS PERIODS).

For the counteraction of the activity described at (d) above and other avoidance activities, the DSS relied on powers granted to the Secretary of State under *SSCBA 1992, 1 Sch 4(c)* and contained in *Contributions Regs, Regs 21, 22*, considered below. These powers now rest in the Inland Revenue by virtue of the transfer of the CA on 1 April 1999 [*SSC(T)A 1999, 3 Sch 34*].

Until 1999 the DSS showed little enthusiasm for seeking the application to contribution avoidance schemes of the anti-avoidance principles enunciated by the courts in the tax cases of *W T Ramsay Ltd v CIR [1981] 1 AER 865* and *Furniss v*

Dawson [1984] *STC 153*, though it seems clear that the judiciary could extend into an area such as that of national insurance contributions the 'abuse of rights' doctrine which lies at the heart of those principles, should it see fit to do so. Hitherto, however, the courts have confined themselves to applying the doctrine only where clearly identifiable *taxes* have been avoided. It is worth observing, however, that the courts are moving towards the view that national insurance contributions are, in reality, a tax. In *Westwood v Secretary of State for Employment [1984] 1 AER 874* Lord Bridge stated that 'the payments which sustain the [national insurance] fund, by whatever name called, are made by way of compulsory levies on citizens in different circumstances, and to some extent on the general body of taxpayers, so that *they may properly be regarded as much more closely analogous to a tax than to a contractual premium under an insurance policy*' and, in the recent case of *Minister of Housing and National Insurance and Another v Smith [1990] PC*, the Privy Council decided that '*the contributions of employed persons, employers and self-employed persons* [payable under the Bahamian National Insurance Act 1972] *are properly to be regarded as taxes ... they are a tax on employment*'. Given that the Bahamian contribution scheme is closely modelled on the UK contribution scheme, that decision must potentially have great persuasive authority should the issue of whether or not UK contributions are a tax ever be taken before the English or Scottish courts. Early in 1999, a number of Secretary of State's decisions (see 9 APPEALS AND REVIEWS) cited the *Ramsay* case in concluding that national insurance contributions were payable in a number of avoidance schemes. It is believed that such decisions were made in the cases of gold jewellery, insurance policies and platinum sponge. It is expected that challenges to these decisions will be made in the High Court (see 9 APPEALS AND REVIEWS).

In the case of *DTE Financial Services v Wilson [1999] STC 1061* an avoidance scheme involving reversionary interests in offshore trusts and which therefore also had tradeable assets implications for NICs (see point 14 at 28.26 EARNINGS) expounded on the *Ramsay* principle. The Special Commissioner in that case perhaps gives the latest view:

'I am happy to accept the analysis of *Ramsay* provided by my learned colleagues in the *Dunstall* case (see [1999] STC (SCD) 26 at 39–41, paras 65 to 70). In particular, to repeat para 68 of that case (at 40):

"The principles were further developed by Lord Oliver of Aylmerton in *Craven (Inspector of Taxes) v White* [1988] STC 476 at 507, [1989] AC 398 at 514 in the following way: "as the law currently stands, the essentials emerging from *Furniss (Inspector of Taxes) v Dawson* [1984] STC 153, [1984] AC 474 appear to me to be four in number: (1) that the series of transactions was, at the time when the intermediate transaction was entered into, pre-ordained in order to produce a given result; (2) that the transaction had no other purpose than tax mitigation; (3) that there was at that time no practical likelihood that the pre-planned events would not take place in the order ordained, so that the intermediate transaction was not even contemplated practically as having an independent life; and (4) that the pre-ordained events did in fact take place. In these circumstances the court can be justified in linking the beginning with the end so as to make a single composite whole to which the fiscal results of the single composite whole are applied."

I have no hesitation in finding that all these four essentials are to be found in the present case. The series of transactions was pre-ordained in order to produce the result that Mr MacDonald received £40,000; the intermediate transactions had no other purpose than tax mitigation; there was no practical likelihood (despite what I say in para 15 above) that the pre-planned events would not take place in the order ordained; those events did in fact so take place.

Mr Thornhill QC for the company contends that *WT Ramsay Ltd v IRC* [1981] STC 174, [1982] AC 300 cannot apply in this case unless one postulates an independent life for one of the transactions which, on *Ramsay* principles, cannot be regarded as having been contemplated as having that independent life. It would be odd if *Ramsay* could be circumvented by planning the intermediate transactions in this particular way. The company decided that Mr MacDonald should have a £40,000 bonus; Mr MacDonald got a bonus; that is—in both senses—the beginning and end of the matter. £40,000 started off in the company's bank account; it ended up in Mr MacDonald's bank account. The £40,000 appears in the company's accounts as a bonus paid and in Mr MacDonald's return as an emolument received; those entries reflect the reality of the situation which is that, in effect, the company paid Mr MacDonald a bonus of £40,000. How the company should have deducted tax from the sum is a question which, as in *Paul Dunstall Organisation Ltd v Hedges (Inspector of Taxes)* [1999] STC (SCD) 26, I find it unnecessary to address; the essential point is that the company should have accounted for that tax.

It might perhaps be argued that, while it is permissible to use *Ramsay* to bring something within a charging section, it is less clearly permissible to use it to bring something within a pure machinery section, which is what s 203 is. I should not be convinced by such an argument. Section 203 is an exceedingly important section in its own right; the machinery which it provides applies to a majority of the taxpayers in this country and is essential for the regular flow of money to the Exchequer. Even if the main object of the present scheme was the avoidance of national insurance contributions, a further and by no means negligible object was the avoidance, by deferral, of PAYE—by keeping the Exchequer out of its money for a year or more. I see no reason why *Ramsay* should not be used to counter such a scheme; in the present case I find that, in accordance with *Ramsay* principles, the company is to be treated as having made a payment within s 203. The appeal is accordingly dismissed.'

The dicta in the judgment suggests that the *Ramsay* principle, even if upheld in this case on appeal, may be less applicable in some other similar cases where the outcome for the employee is less certain.

8.2   NEGATION OF ABNORMAL PAY PRACTICES

The Secretary of State was given powers with a view to securing that liability for the payment of CLASS 1 CONTRIBUTIONS (15) is not avoided or reduced by a secondary contributor (see 14.15 CATEGORISATION) following any practice in the payment of earnings which is abnormal for the employment in respect of which the earnings are paid. The Secretary of State may, if he thought fit, determine any question relating to a person's Class 1 contributions where any such practice has been or is being followed, as if the secondary contributor concerned had not followed any abnormal pay practice, but had followed a practice or practices normal for the employment in question. [*Contributions Regs, Reg 21(2)*].

These powers, following the transfer of the CA on 1 April 1999, are now exercisable by the Board of Inland Revenue. [*SSC(T)A 1999, s 1(2), and 2 Sch*].

8.3   Retrospective effect

Reg 21(2) may be of limited retrospective effect, it being stated that its provisions are *not* to apply in so far as the decision relates to contributions based on payments made more than one year before the beginning of the year in which that decision is given. [*Reg 21(1)*]. 'Year' does, as usual, mean 'tax year'. [*Reg 1(2)*]. Although this retrospective limitation was no doubt introduced to *favour* the contributor (in that it will usually be at least two years before a decision is reached on any dispute concerning contribution liability), its introduction may well have rendered the regulation *ultra vires*. That is because the primary legislation under which *Reg 21* is made (*SSCBA 1992 1 Sch 4(c)*) does not itself authorise the retrospective creation of contribution liabilities and the application of *Reg 21* in a retrospective manner would, therefore, be an attempt on the part of the Board or, previously, the Secretary of State to levy money for the use of the Crown without the authority of Parliament. Such action contravenes the *Bill of Rights 1688* and has in the past been declared unlawful by the courts (see *Congreve v Home Office [1976] 1 AER 697*).

8.4 The meaning of 'abnormal'

The legislation provides no definition of 'abnormal for the employment'. On 7 August 1985, however, in response to a request by the ICAEW for a note of the DSS's view on the meaning of the expression, the DSS stated that 'any "abnormality" must be tested against normal procedures in the employment in question' and that 'the abnormality has to be in the act of making payments and not in the payments themselves'.

It is understood that, in practice, a compliance officer will look at past pay practices within the organisation itself, within the particular sector of industry or commerce in which the organisation operates, and within other similar organisations in the locality but, given that the employment to which *Reg 21* relates is the 'employment in respect of which the earnings are paid', that approach is surely incorrect. How other employees in the same organisation, industrial sector or locality are paid would seem to be irrelevant. The only legitimate comparison would seem to be a comparison between the contractually correct payment procedure (as established by any written contract of service or by past practice) as regards the individual concerned and the payment procedure which is in fact being followed.

The DSS took the view that, as dividends and payments in kind are not EARNINGS (28) for contribution purposes, the substitution of dividends or payments in kind for remuneration which would be earnings for contribution purposes cannot be regarded as an abnormal pay practice for the purposes of *Reg 21*.

8.5 Appeal and review

It would seem that, if an appeal against a decision on the question of whether or not a particular pay practice was abnormal for the employment in respect of which earnings had been paid were to be taken before the court, the court would ask itself whether, in the light of such evidence as had been offered of normal procedures in the employment in question, any reasonable person could have come to the conclusion arrived at by the Board or, previously, the Secretary of State. An affirmative answer would then conclude the matter. Accordingly, there would seem to be little scope for challenge of a decision of this kind.

8.6 Liability for additional contributions

Contributions Regs, Reg 21 is silent on the question of who is to bear any additional contribution burden which arises as a result of a determination under those powers. Where, however, the contributions relate to the current year and the under-deduction can be shown to have occurred by reason of an error made in good faith, there would appear to be no grounds on which to prohibit recovery of primary contributions from the employed earner to whom they relate, provided the recovery rules are properly observed (see 21.4 COLLECTION). [*1 Sch 13(2A)(b)*]. The April 1981 version of DSS Leaflet NI 35 (now superseded) bore this out by stating that, in the application of *Reg 21* to abnormal pay practices concerning company directors, 'in many cases' (i.e. not all) 'the company will not be entitled to deduct from the director's earnings his share of arrears to be paid' (page 5).

8.7 **NEGATION OF PRACTICES INVOLVING IRREGULAR OR UNEQUAL PAYMENTS**

In addition to any anti-avoidance action which may be taken under *Reg 21*, the Board may, where it is satisfied as to the existence of any practice in respect of the payment of earnings whereby the incidence of Class 1 contributions is *avoided or reduced by means of irregular or unequal payments*, give directions for securing that such contributions are payable as if that practice were not followed. [*Contributions Regs, Reg 22*].

Regulation 22 directions are often made in situations where employees are remunerated largely by means of irregular or unequal commission payments and basic remuneration (if any) is at only a low level.

These powers now exercisable by the Board of Inland Revenue were previously the remit of the Secretary of State. [*SSC(T)A 1999, s 1(2) and 2 Sch*].

8.8 **Lack of intent to avoid of no relevance**

Reg 22 is of extremely wide application in that, in order to justify the giving of a direction, the Board needs merely to demonstrate that earnings amenable to payment at regular intervals or in equal amounts would, had they been so paid, have attracted a greater contribution liability than they did, in fact, attract. The motive for the irregularity or inequality of the payments is of no consequence and, even where it is unrelated to the consequential reduction or avoidance of contributions, will be disregarded.

8.9 **Non-retrospective effect**

The tenses of the verbs used in *Reg 22* suggest that a direction made under its provisions is of only current and future effect and this was specifically confirmed by the April 1981 version of DSS Leaflet NI 35 (now superseded) which stated that a direction under *Reg 22* 'cannot be applied retrospectively' (page 5).

8.10 **Application**

Despite the fact that *Reg 22* (negation of practices avoiding liability) may not be applied with retrospective effect, it is nevertheless of far greater use for anti-avoidance purposes than is *Reg 21* (negation of abnormal pay practices). This is not due merely to the fact that the area of avoidance activity which will justify its use is far wider than that of *Reg 21* but to the fact that the power it grants is that of a 'direction' rather than a 'determination of a question'. Administratively, the former merely requires the writing of a letter, whereas the latter will normally require a formal inquiry at which the parties involved may make representations, call witnesses etc., and a formal decision.

It will be noted that *Reg 22* contains no *de minimis* amount which avoided contribution liability must exceed before a direction may be made. In practice, however, the DSS previously set a criterion for deciding whether or not a direction should be made and it was observable (though the DSS did not publish its criterion) that directions were not made unless contribution liability would be increased by at least 1/3rd or £100, whichever was the less.

A direction under *Reg 22* almost inevitably takes the form of an earnings period rule designed to frustrate the particular avoidance arrangement which gave rise to the direction (see EARNINGS PERIODS (31)).

8.11   Anti-Avoidance

8.11   Appeals

Reg 22 itself contains no provision for appeal against a direction made within its terms but, as such a direction must necessarily 'relate to a person's contributions', any question arising in connection with it must inevitably be capable of being the subject of an appealable decision (see 9 APPEALS AND REVIEWS).

9 Appeals and Reviews

Cross-references. See 2.2 ADMINISTRATION in earlier editions for administrative (rather than judicial) status also enjoyed by the Secretary of State; WORKING CASE STUDY (58).

Other Sources. Simon's NIC, Part I, Setion 11, Chapter 58; Tolley's National Insurance Brief, January 1997, page 7; Tolley's Practical NIC, May 1999, page 33; Leaflets IR 37 and CA14F.

9.1 GENERAL CONSIDERATIONS

In earlier editions of this work it has been necessary to explain that there was, in the Social Security Acts, no provision for appeals in connection with contribution matters and that the appellate bodies which operate in connection with State benefits have no jurisdiction so far as the contribution side of the State scheme is concerned. Although there was *effectively* an appeal procedure in connection with contributions it was not widely known or understood and, if described under its correct title, would not immediately have been recognised as such. (Indeed, only 1,500 or so persons a year employed the procedure, including the courts and insurance officers).

However, with the transfer of the former Contributions Agency to the Inland Revenue with effect from 1 April 1999 and the transfer of contributions policy functions from DSS to the Treasury from the same date, the opportunity was taken to modernise the appeals system, such as it was. It is now brought almost entirely into line with those procedures encountered in dealing with other imposts for which the Inland Revenue is responsible.

The fact that there remain some small differences, and the previous absence of a formal appeal system in relation to contributions, is explained by the fact that the Social Security Acts (unlike the Taxes Acts) make no provision for formal assessments of their levies—other than CLASS 4 CONTRIBUTIONS (20), for appeals against which see 9.16 below. The liability is either self-assessed at a fixed rate or employer-assessed by reference to earnings paid (see CLASS 1 CONTRIBUTIONS (15), CLASS 2 CONTRIBUTIONS (18)) or to cars and fuel made available to employees (see CLASS 1A CONTRIBUTIONS (16)).

The Social Security Act 1998 proposed a new scheme for challenging National Insurance contributions decisions with effect from 6 April 1999. This was superseded by the transfer but would have created a system uniform with that for all State benefits, having three stages:

– appeal tribunal;

– Social Security Commissioners;

– Court of Appeal.

This process that had been proposed for contributions appeals generally is, however, retained in respect of contracting-out matters (see 9.13).

The new system has operated from 1 April 1999 and is largely regulated by *Social Security Contributions (Transfer of Functions, etc.) Act 1999* and *Social Security Contributions (Decisions and Appeals) Regulations 1999 (SI 1999 No 1027)*.

The remainder of this chapter deals with:

● Current procedure for appeals to the Inland Revenue Commissioners (9.2 to 9.12)

● Decisions under the *Pension Schemes Act 1993* (9.13)

● An outline of the previous system (9.14), but a more detailed description of it can be found in the 1998–99 and earlier editions of this work

- Transitional arrangements where the former procedures had been instigated, but the Secretary of State for Social Security had not made a decision by 1 April 1999 (9.15)

- Disputes concerning Class 4 contributions (9.16)

9.2 DECISIONS OF OFFICERS OF THE BOARD OF INLAND REVENUE

Where a contributor or his employer is faced with a demand for payment which is considered to be wrong or excessive the matter will first be considered informally. If the dispute cannot be resolved in this way, it will then be for an officer of the Board of Inland Revenue to issue a formal 'decision' under, *SSC(T)A 1999, s 8*. Such decisions are currently co-ordinated by the Appeals Liaison Unit in Newcastle upon Tyne and, at first, such decisions will only be issued by one or, at the most, two senior ex-Contributions Agency staff in each region or from Newcastle.

The formal decision is then appealable (see 9.5 below) in much the same way as an old style tax assessment or an amendment to a self-assessment.

9.3 The subject matter of a decision

An officer of the Board may decide —

(a) whether a person is or was an earner and, if he is or was, in which category of earners he should be included (see CATEGORISATION (14));

(b) whether a person is or was employed in employed earner's employment for industrial injuries purposes (*SSCBA 1992, Part V*);

(c) whether a person is or was liable to pay any contributions of any class and the amount of the liability:

(d) whether a person is or was entitled to pay contributions, notwithstanding that there is no liability to pay, e.g., payment of voluntary contributions (see CLASS 3 CONTRIBUTIONS (19));

(e) whether contributions of a particular class have been paid for any period;

(f) on any issue in connection with Statutory Sick Pay or Statutory Maternity Pay;

(g) on matters concerning the issue or content of any notice under *SSCBA 1999, s 121C* (notices of company officer's personal liability for unpaid contributions);

(h) any issue arising under *Jobseekers Act 1995, s 27* (Back To Work schemes for long-term unemployed):

(i) whether a person is liable to pay interest;

(j) whether a person is liable to a penalty;

(k) the amount of interest and/or penalty;

(l) other issues as may be prescribed by regulations made by the Board of Inland Revenue.

[*SSC(T)A 1999, s 8(1)*].

Items (c) and (e) above do not include decisions relating to Class 4 contributions which have, because they are invariably collected along with income tax, always been dealt with under tax appeal procedures. [*SSC(T)A 1999, s 8(2)*.

Item (f) does not extend to any decision as to the making of sub-ordinate legislation since policy for Statutory Sick Pay and Statutory Maternity Pay remains with the Secretary of State for Social Security, even though it is now administered by the Inland Revenue. Nor does it extend to any decision as to whether the liability to pay

Statutory Sick Pay or Statutory Maternity Pay is that of the Board or the employer. [*SSC(T)A 1999, s 8(3)*].

The Board may make regulations with regard to the making of decisions and officers may direct that he shall have the assistance of an 'expert' where it appears that a question of fact requires special expertise. [*SSC(T)A 1999, s 9 (1)(2)*].

'Expert' means a person appearing to the officer of the Board to have knowledge or experience which would be relevant in determining the question of fact. [*SSC(T)A 1999, s 9(3)*].

The Board may make regulations enabling decisions under *section 8* to be varied or superseded. [*SSC(T)A 1999, s 10*].

A decision must be made to the best of the officers information and belief and must state the name of every person in respect of whom it is made, and

— the date from which it has effect, or

— the period for which it has effect.

[*Social Security Contributions (Decisions and Appeals) Regulations 1999, Reg 3(1)*].

An officer may entrust responsibility for completing procedures to some other officer, whether by means involving the use of a computer or not, including the responsibility for serving the notice on any person named in it. [*Social Security Contributions (Decisions and Appeals) Regulations 1999, Reg 3(2)*].

9.4 Giving notice of the decision

Notice of a decision must be given to every person named in it or, in the case of a decision relating to entitlement to Statutory Sick Pay or Statutory Maternity Pay, to the employee and employer concerned. [*Social Security Contributions (Decisions and Appeals) Regulations 1999, Reg 4(1)*].

In the case of Class 1 contributions the notice will name the employer and each affected employee. Where the number of employees exceeds six the Inland Revenue will seek to agree a representative sample of employees with the employer or the agent and will name only those selected employees (as well as the employer) in the Notice. This is an extra-statutory arrangement, there being no legal basis for the selection of six employees as the number beyond which not to look at each case individually.

Where the dispute relates to Class 1A contributions only the employer is affected as no employee contribution arises. However, whilst there is therefore no obligation on the part of the Inland Revenue to name employees in the notice, it will usually do so where the decision concerns the provision of particular cars. Presumably, similar procedures will apply in due course in the case of disputed Class 1B liability.

In the case of Class 2, Class 3 or Class 4 decisions (the latter relating only to cases where Class 4 is not collected through the self-assessment Tax Return), there will invariably be only one person named in the notice.

The notice must state the date on which it is issued and may be served by post addressed to any person at his usual or last known place of residence or his place of business or employment. Notice to a company may be addressed to its registered office or its principal place of business. [*Social Security Contributions (Decisions and Appeals) Regulations 1999, Reg 4(2)(3)*].

A decision may be varied by an officer of the Board if he has reason to believe that it was incorrect at the time it was made. Notice of such variation must be given to the same persons and in the same manner as the original decision. [*Social Security Contributions (Decisions and Appeals) Regulations 1999, Reg 5(1)(2)*].

9.4 Appeals and Reviews

If a decision is under appeal, it may be varied at any time before the tax appeal Commissioners determine the appeal. [*Social Security Contributions (Decisions and Appeals) Regulations 1999, Reg 5(4)*].

A decision may be made superseding an earlier decision, including a varied decision, which has become inappropriate *for any reason*. A superseding decision will have effect from the date of the change in circumstances which rendered the previous decision (or varied decision) inappropriate. The previous decision ceases to have effect immediately the superseding decision comes into effect. [*Social Security Contributions (Decisions and Appeals) Regulations 1999, Reg 6(1)(2)*].

Decisions are issued on Form DAA1(A) and it tells the recipient to let their professional adviser or agent, if they have one, see it. Copies will be issued direct to agents, if acting. Where copies have to be sent to more than one person, the notes on the face of the notice will be varied on each copy to reflect the differing effects of the decision on different categories of people affected, e.g. where copies are sent to employers and one or more employees. The Notice of Decision also includes a payslip for making payment of the National Insurance contributions in question and will be sent with a letter of explanation which will, in practice, usually be a summary of what has been established in previous correspondence. A guide, DAA2 'A Guide to Your Notice of Decision', will also be sent to every recipient.

INLAND REVENUE	*NOTICE OF DECISION*
L Ltd	Inland Revenue (NI) Contributions Office
10 Any Road	Class 1 Caseworker
Any Town	Instructions and Planning Team
Any County	Room H2002
AN10 2YZ	Longbenton
	Newcastle Upon Tyne NE98 1YZ
Date of Issue 1 April 2000	Tel 0191 225 8159 Fax 0191 225 8344
	Reference
	AB123456C
	Please use this reference if you write or call it will help avoid delay

National Insurance contributions, Statutory Sick Pay or Statutory Maternity Pay
My decision is as follows:
1. That L Ltd is liable to pay primary and secondary Class 1 contributions for the period 6 April 1996 to 5 April 1999 in respect of the earnings of Mrs F Smith.
2. The amount that L Ltd is liable to pay in respect of those earnings is £5,490.
3. The amount that L Ltd has paid in respect of those earnings is £4,270.
4. The difference is due to Class 1 contributions on school fees.

A N Other
Officer of the Board

Notes

General

This Notice of Decision is addressed to you personally as required by law. If you have a professional adviser or agent Please let them see this notice at once.

This notice contains my formal decision. You will find details of how the decision has been reached and additional information in the accompanying letter and/or *DAA2 Guide*, 'A 'Guide to your Notice of Decision'.

Appeals

If you do not accept this decision please appeal telling us why you think the decision is wrong. The appeal must be made in writing to me within 30 days of the date of issue shown above.

If agreement cannot be reached we will arrange for your appeal and any other appeal to be heard by the Appeal Commissioners who are anindependent tribunal. See page 4 of the *DAA2 Guide*.

Payment If you accept this decision please pay any outstanding amount of National Insurance contributions due from you using the enclosed payslip. Pay any Statutory Sick Pay or Statutory Maternity Pay to the employee.

Variation of Decision
A decision is varied when agreement has been reached or the decision is incorrect. See page 6 of the *DAA2 Guide.*

Interest Charges on late payment
Interest may be charged on National Insurance Contributions paid late. See page 6 of the *DAA2 Guide.*

DAA1(A)

In a letter to all Clerks to the General Commissioners of Income Tax from the Lord Chancellor's Department on 3 August 1999 the following guidelines were given on the new system of appeals procedure:

THE NEW SYSTEM

The new Decisions and Appeals (DAA) process for NICs, SSP and SMP provides, for the first time, a right of appeal on a point of fact or law to an independent appeals tribunal (Tax Commissioners). Responsibility for making formal decisions rests with NICs staff in the Inland Revenue. The aim is to produce a more consistent and efficient system, as well as granting the contributor a statutory right of appeal.

Broadly speaking, the new DAA process can be broken down into three separate stages —

Stage 1—the informal opinion

This reflects part of the pre-DAA system of dealing with NICs, SSP and SMP disputes. A member of the Inland Revenue staff might offer an initial opinion on the contributor's liability to pay NICs, for example. On the SSP/SMP front, an officer of the Board might discover that an employer is doing something wrong, or an employer might ask for an opinion.

At this stage, disputes can be settled by discussion and agreement. Usually a formal decision is needed only when the normal process of discussion is exhausted and agreement cannot be reached.

Stage 2—the formal decision

Where agreement cannot be reached or a request for a decision is received, a formal decision will be made. That decision has to be made to the best of the officer's information and belief.

Each person in respect of whom the decision is made will be sent a Notice of Decision (form DAA1) and will have a right of appeal. The Notice of Decision will be accompanied by "A Guide to your Notice of Decision" (DAA2), which explains the action to be taken if the recipient does not agree with the decision. A copy of the leaflet DAA2 was sent to Clerks with the circular dated 23 April. Further copies can be obtained from your local office. (The Notice of Decision will also be accompanied by an explanatory letter in cases where it would be helpful.) The DAA2 Guide contains an appeal form (DAA3) which can be used to make an appeal. Once the formal decision has been made and the Notice of Decision issued, the contributor or employer has 30 days from the date of issue in which to lodge a written appeal.

cont'd

9.5 Appeals and Reviews

> For SSP and SMP, there will often be an established dispute when the case is referred to Inland Revenue. In those cases, a formal decision will be made and a Notice of Decision issued when requested by the employee or the Secretary of State for Social Security (DHHS in NI).
>
> There is no statutory time limit for making a NICs decision. It may be necessary to make a decision on whether NICs were paid for a period many years ago because it affects basic retirement pension entitlement. **Unlike NICs, requests for a SSP or SMP decision must be made within 6 months of a dispute first arising.**
>
> **Stage 3—the appeal**
> Appeals against formal decisions can be settled in one of three ways—
>
> By the Inland Revenue and appellant(s) coming to an agreement,
>
> By the appellant(s) withdrawing the appeal(s),
>
> By the General or Special Commissioners.

9.5 APPEALS AGAINST OFFICER'S DECISIONS

Any person named in a notice of decision, which in the case of decisions relating to entitlement to Statutory Sick Pay or Statutory Maternity Pay will be both the employee and the employer, has the right of appeal to the tax appeal Commissioners. The same right also extends to personal liability notices issued to company officers in respect of company contribution debts. [*SSC(T)A 1999, s 11(1)(2)(4); SSAA 1992, s 121D as inserted by SSA 1998 s 64*].

In the letter to all Clerks to the General Commissioners of Income Tax from the Lord Chancellor's Department mentioned in 9.4 above it is stated:

> **Joining non-appellants to the proceedings**
> Where someone named in a decision has not appealed, they should have the opportunity to attend the hearing and present their case if they so wish—thus avoiding any accusation of unfairness. To illustrate, an employee who has claimed SSP and SMP, and who has received a decision in their favour, is unlikely to appeal against that decision. But the employer might appeal. The employee will clearly have an interest and may wish to have an input at the hearing of the appeal.
>
> Under Regulation 7(1) of the General Commissioners (Jurisdiction and Procedures) Regulations 1994, the General Commissioners have the power to join parties to the proceedings. Inland Revenue can readily identify these cases. Inspectors in Tax Offices have been advised to approach the Clerk to the General Commissioners and ask if non-appellants, who have been named in the decision, can be invited to the hearing. It has been suggested that they do this when the first case arises. Agreement could be given on an individual case basis or on a general basis but the joining of a non-appellants to the proceedings in these particular circumstances should be a formality. Tax Offices have been provided with a suitably worded invitation to the non-appellant to attend the hearing. These can be prepared, along with the usual notification of hearing to appellants, for issue by the Clerk.

9.6 Manner of making an appeal

An appeal must be made in writing within 30 days after the date on which the notice of decision was issued and must be made to the officer who gave notice of the decision. The Guide DAA2 contains a tear-off appeal form (DAA3) which may be used but an appeal made in any format in writing and within the specified 30 days is legally valid. [*SSC(T)A 1999, s 12(1)(2)*].

The notice of appeal must specify the grounds of appeal but on hearing by the Commissioners they may allow additional grounds, not stated in the notice of appeal, to be put forward if satisfied that the omission was neither wilful nor unreasonable. [*SSC(T)A 1999, s 12(3)*].

Appeals will be heard by the General Commissioners unless the appellant elects under *TMA 1970 s.46(1)*, at the time of making the appeal, that the hearing shall be before the Special Commissioners. *TMA 1970, s.31 (5A) to (5E)* have effect in relation to such an election. [*SSC(T)A 1999, s 12(4)(5)*].

Appeals against notices issued under *SSAA 1992, s 121C* (see 9.2 above) will always be heard by the Special Commissioners.

In practice, as a matter of policy, the Inland Revenue will always exercise it's own right to have the case heard by the Special Commissioners if the dispute relates to a NIC-avoidance case.

The Board have the power to make regulations, with the concurrence of the Lord Chancellor and the Lord Advocate, in respect of contributions, Statutory Sick Pay and Statutory Maternity Pay appeals and may also make regulations regarding matters arising pending a decision of an officer under s.8, pending the determination by the tax appeal Commissioners, out of the variation of a decision or out of the superseding of a decision. [*SSC(T)A 1999, ss 13, 14*].

9.7 Place of hearing of appeal

An appeal to the General Commissioners shall be heard in the division in which one of the following places, specified by election made by the appellant, is situated

— the appellant's usual place of residence in the United Kingdom at the time the election is made

— if any, the appellant's place of business in the United Kingdom at the time the election is made

— if any, the appellant's place of employment in the United Kingdom at the time the election is made.

'Place of business' means the place where the trade, profession or vocation is carried on and, if it is carried on at more than one place, the head office or the place where it is mainly carried on.

The division covering the place of employment may be the subject of an election whether or not the subject matter of the appeal relates to matters connected with the employment. [*Social Security Contributions (Decisions and Appeals) Regulations 1999, Reg 7(1)(2)(3)(8)(9)*].

The election must be made at the time that the appeal against the decision of the officer of the Board is made or else before such later date as the Board may allow and it is irrevocable. [*Social Security Contributions (Decisions and Appeals) Regulations 1999, Reg 7(5)*].

Where no election is made, or is not made in time, an officer of the Board may make an election specifying one of the above three locations. If there is no such location, an officer of the Board may give directions to determine a place for the appeal to be heard but such direction does not have effect unless the officer notifies the appellant of his direction. [*Social Security Contributions (Decisions and Appeals) Regulations 1999, Reg 7(4)(6)(7)*].

9.8 Appeals and Reviews

9.8 Multiple appeals

Where more than one appeal is made to the General Commissioners in respect of the same decision (e.g., both employer and employee, or more than one affected employee), all such appeals must be heard at the same time and, where none of the appellants has made an election concerning the division of the General Commissioners which is to hear the appeal, an officer of the Board may give directions for determining the location. [*Social Security Contributions (Decisions and Appeals) Regulations 1999, Reg 8(1)(2)*].

Where more than one appeal has been made and, collectively, more than one location for hearing has been specified for the hearing, then any such election made by the employer shall be ignored—whether the appeal relates directly to contributions or to entitlement to Statutory Sick Pay or Statutory Maternity Pay. [*Social Security Contributions (Decisions and Appeals) Regulations 1999, Reg 8(3)(4)*].

If there then remains only one division which is the subject of an election, an officer of the Board may direct that the General Commissioners for that division shall determine the division of General Commissioners that shall hear the appeal. In determining the matter, the Commissioners shall consider any representations made orally or in writing by any of the appellants (i.e., including the employer). [*Social Security Contributions (Decisions and Appeals) Regulations 1999, Reg 8(3)(5)*].

If there is, however, more than one division which is the subject of an election, an officer of the Board may give directions as to the division of General Commissioners which shall determine the division of General Commissioners that shall hear the appeal. In determining the matter, the Commissioners shall consider any representations made orally or in writing by any of the appellants (i.e., including the employer). [*Social Security Contributions (Decisions and Appeals) Regulations 1999, Reg 8(3)(6)*].

If there is no election made by any appellant, an officer of the Board may give directions for determining the division of General Commissioners that shall hear the appeal, taking into account factors which appear to him to be relevant. [*Social Security Contributions (Decisions and Appeals) Regulations 1999, Reg 8(3)(7)*].

No such directions as are mentioned above shall have effect in relation to any appeal unless the officer of the Board serves on each appellant a notice stating the effect of the directions made. [*Social Security Contributions (Decisions and Appeals) Regulations 1999, Reg 8(8)*].

In a letter to all Clerks to the General Commissioners of Income Tax from the Lord Chancellor's Department on 3 August 1999 the following guidelines were given on the place of appeal hearing:

Place of appeal hearing

The appellant can choose, within the time limit for making an appeal or such later period as the Board of Inland Revenue allows, to have the appeal heard by the Commissioners for the Division where he/she lives, works or has business premises.

Where the decision names more than one person, all appeals against that decision must be heard at the same time and place.

Where there is more than one appeal against a decision and the appellants choose different places for the appeals to be heard, Regulation 8 of the Social Security Contributions (Decisions and Appeals) regulations 1999 contains the rules for

---

cont'd

deciding which Division of the General Commissioners should hear the appeals. These rules introduce a stage before the appeal hearing takes place, and are intended to be as fair as possible to the appellants.

Where multiple appeals involve elections for places within the boundary of one Division of General Commissioners, there is no issue and the appeals will be determined in the Division chosen.

In other cases, the Inland Revenue will try to obtain agreement amongst the appellants to the place of the hearing. Where agreement is reached amongst a number of appellants, the Revenue will issue directions nominating a Division, and that Division will decide which Division will hear the appeals (it is anticipated that the appeals will normally be heard in the Division agreed by the appellants). The Inland Revenue will liaise with Clerks over the arrangements for appeal hearings.

Where agreement on the place of the hearing is not readily achievable, Inland Revenue will issue directions in writing to the appellants, nominating a Division which will decide the Division to hear the appeals. The letter will also notify the appellants of their right to make representations to the Commissioners through the Clerk about the Division they consider should hear the appeals. If an appellant wishes to make his/her representations in person, the Clerk will arrange for this to happen — we suggest that such representations be made at the end of a general appeal meeting, and that there will be no need to arrange a special meeting for this. When the Commissioners have decided which Division will hear the appeals, arrangements can be made for a hearing in the normal way. As our circular of 23 April explained, these appeals can be dealt with as part of the Division's general programme of appeal meetings, and will be reflected in the triennial review formula for remuneration purposes.

Where there is more than one appeal against a decision and one or more appellants elect for the Special Commissioners, the appeal will normally be heard by the Special Commissioners (subject to inappropriate elections being disregarded).

9.9   Late appeals

Late appeals may be admitted if the officer of the Board is satisfied that there was a reasonable excuse for not bringing the appeal within the normal time limit, provided that application is made without undue delay thereafter. [*Social Security Contributions (Decisions and Appeals) Regulations 1999, Reg 9, applying the provisions of TMA1970, s 49*].

9.10   Determination by Commissioners

A notice giving the time, date and place of hearing will be sent to the appellant(s) and any agent or professional adviser, normally at least 28 days before the hearing (Inland Revenue Tax Bulletin, June 1999, p 664).

The Commissioners may decide by a majority of those present at the hearing that the decision shall be varied in any manner or that it shall stand good. The Commissioners may examine the appellant on oath or affirmation or take other evidence. [*Social Security Contributions (Decisions and Appeals) Regulations 1999, Reg 10*].

9.11   Settling appeals by agreement

Appellants may, before an appeal is heard by the Tax Commissioners, come to an agreement with an officer of the Board that the decision under appeal should be treated as

— upheld without variation, or

— varied in a particular manner, or

— superseded by a further decision,

and the same consequences will then ensue as would have ensued if the officer had made a decision in the same terms as that under appeal, had varied the decision or made a superseding decision, as the case may be.

In any of these circumstances, all appeals against the original decision shall lapse and notice of the agreement must be given by the officer of the Board to all persons named in the decision who did not appeal against it. [*Social Security Contributions (Decisions and Appeals) Regulations 1999, Reg 11(1)(2)(3)*].

If such an agreement is not made in writing it is necessary for the officer of the Board to confirm by written notice to every appellant the fact that an agreement was come to and details of it's terms. [*Social Security Contributions (Decisions and Appeals) Regulations 1999, Reg 11(4)*].

An appellant may, before an appeal is heard by the Tax Commissioners, notify the officer of the Board and every other person named in the decision, either orally or in writing, that he does not wish to proceed with the appeal. Unless, within 30 days, any person to whom that notice is given indicates that he is unwilling that the appeal should be treated as withdrawn then the appellant, the officer of the Board and every person named in the decision are treated as having reached an agreement that the decision should be upheld without variation. [*Social Security Contributions (Decisions and Appeals) Regulations 1999, Reg 11(5)*].

Where an appeal is to be settled by agreement in any manner mentioned above, the agreement may be made with any person acting on behalf of an appellant or any other person named in the decision and notices may be validly given to such persons. [*Social Security Contributions (Decisions and Appeals) Regulations 1999, Reg 11(6)*].

9.12 Dissatisfaction with Commissioners determination

If the Inland Revenue, the appellant or another party to the proceedings think that the Commissioners decision is wrong on a point of law, then the appeal can be taken further through the Courts. At this stage, the contributions in dispute must, if that is not already the case, be paid. If the appellant is successful, the amount will be repaid. If the hearing is with regard to Statutory Sick Pay or Statutory Maternity Pay, employers do not have to pay Statutory Sick Pay or Statutory Maternity Pay until the Courts have finally settled the appeal.

In the case of a decision by the General Commissioners, within 30 days the Clerk to the Commissioners must be requested in writing to provide a Case to be stated for the opinion of the High Court (the Court of Session in Scotland, or the Court of Appeal (Northern Ireland) in Northern Ireland).The statutory fee of £25 must be enclosed. The Clerk must prepare a draft within 56 days, and there is then 56 days from receipt to make representations, which must be copied to the Inland Revenue. The Inland Revenue may also make representations within the same period. These must be copied to the appellant, who then has a further 28 days to make further representations in response to those of the Revenue. Any such further representations must also be copied to the Revenue. The Commissioners then sign the case in it's final form and send it to the appellant. If the case is to be taken further, it must be sent to the High Court, etc., within 30 days of receipt (and a copy sent to the Revenue). This time limit cannot be extended.

Appeal from the High Court may be made to the Court of Appeal and then the House of Lords. [*Social Security Contributions (Decisions and Appeals) Regulations 1999, Reg 12 applying the provisions of TMA 1970, s 56*].

If the appeal was heard by the Special Commissioners, they will issue a written decision. If the decision is to be contested, notice must be sent direct to the High Court within 56 days stating the grounds of appeal. Copies of the notice must be sent to the Inland Revenue and the Special Commissioners.

Appeal from the High Court may be made to the Court of Appeal and then the House of Lords. Alternatively, the case may be heard initially by the Court of Appeal, with the leave of the Court of Appeal. [*Social Security Contributions (Decisions and Appeals) Regulations 1999, Reg 12, applying the provisions of TMA 1970, s 56A*].

9.13 DECISIONS UNDER THE PENSION SCHEMES ACT 1993

The new appeals process for contracted-out decisions took effect from 5 July 1999. It differs in a number of ways from the tax appeal process and, in some instances, very speedy action indeed is required.

In the same way as contributions, Statutory Sick Pay and Statutory Maternity Pay; decisions about contracting-out matters are, from 1 April 1999, made by an officer of the Board of Inland Revenue. [*SSCTA 1999, s 16(1)*]. However, appeals against contracted-out decisions are not heard by the Tax Appeal Commissioners under the system set out above but by the new unified independent Appeal Tribunal that also deals with all state benefit claims. [*Social Security Act 1999, s 12 as amended by SSCTA 1999, s 16(6)*]. Decisions are likely to be in regard to such matters as the issue, cancellation and variation of a contracting-out certificate and will have been made under *ss 8, 9* and *10* of the *Social Security Act 1998*. Informal notifications, such as Guaranteed Minimum Pension statements, are not classed as decisions but as opinions see *Technical Guidance on Contracted-Out Decision Making and Appeals* (Leaflet CA 14F), page 4. This means that there is no right of appeal in such matters but contributors and employers are encouraged to query discrepancies. Only if a query of this kind cannot be resolved and it is still disputed will a formal decision then be issued, and at that point the decision may then be appealed.

This appeals mechanism has three layers

— appeals tribunal;

— Social Security Commissioners;

— Court of Appeal.

[*Social Security Act 1998, ss 12-18*]

Disagreement with a decision

Where a contributor or employer disagrees with a decision, the person who made the decision should be contacted within one calendar month. They should be advised why the decision is disputed and be provided with any new evidence or information that may be available. The officer at Contracted-Out Employments Group will then advise whether or nor not the decision can be revised. If it cannot, then the person affected has one calendar month from the date of this notification within which any appeal must be received. Alternatively, the appeal can simply be made straight away so as to be received within one calendar month of the making of the decision.

Before the case is referred to the Appeals Tribunal, the officer who made the decision will review the contents of the appeal application in order to determine whether the decision may be revised. If any revised decision is to the advantage of the appellant, the appeal will lapse—although a fresh appeal may be made against the revised decision. If the decision is revised, but not to the appellant's advantage, the appeal will proceed in just the same way as if the decision had not been revised.

9.13 Appeals and Reviews

Late appeals

If an appeal is made outside the time limit, the person who made the decision will, if the late appeal is to be accepted, have to be satisfied that there were good reasons why the appeal could not have been made in time. If the officer is not so satisfied, then it is for The Appeals Service to consider the application. Their decision on the matter is final and cannot be the subject of a further appeal. The Appeals Service is the body which handles the administration of contracted-out and benefits appeals, and arranges for appeals to be heard.

Who may appeal?

An appeal against a decision may be made by

- a member of a pension scheme,
- a trustee or manager of a pension scheme, or
- an employer of earners in an employment to which a scheme applies.

How to appeal

The appeal must be made in writing and be signed by the person making it. There is no special form and form DAA3, used for contributions, Statutory Sick Pay and Statutory Maternity Pay appeals, will not be appropriate. The letter should specify

- the reference number shown on the Notice of Decision,
- the date of issue of the Notice of Decision,
- details of the decision being appealed, and
- why it is thought that the decision is wrong.

Any appropriate supporting evidence should also be enclosed.

Processing the appeal

When the appeal is received, The Appeals Service is notified. Contracted-Out Employments Group will send to the appellant a 'pre-hearing' enquiry form. The form asks whether the appellant and/or a representative will be attending the hearing or whether the appellant is content for the appeal to proceed without an oral hearing. This form must be completed and returned to The Appeals Service so as it be *received* by them within *fourteen* days of it's *date of issue*. It is not known whether the 'pre-hearing' enquiry will be sent by first class post. Hopefully it will, but even if so it still leaves only a few days, in practice, to respond. It should be recalled that this is the same system that applies to benefit claimants. But in a large company, the appropriate personnel may not, even if they are not ill or on holiday, be immediately available due to other work commitments, to respond in such a time scale.

Withdrawing an appeal

An appeal can be withdrawn at any time until the Appeals Tribunal considers the appeal. In that eventuality, The Appeals Service must be notified. This can be done by letter or on the 'pre-hearing' enquiry form, which even has a specific 'tick-box' for this purpose. It can also be done verbally at any oral hearing. No reason needs to be given for the withdrawal of an appeal.

'Misconceived appeals'

If the person who made the original decision is of the opinion that the appeal has no reasonable chance of success the appellant will be told of this, the reason why this view is held, and will be provided with the usual 'pre-hearing' enquiry form. The appellant must then give reasons on the 'pre-hearing' form why the appeal can succeed. Alternatively, an oral hearing can be requested to explain those reasons. Either way, this is getting into complex areas but the enquiry form must still nonetheless be *received within* the usual *fourteen* days of its *date of issue*. Furthermore, if The Appeals Service does not receive the form on time then, of course, the appeal may not be heard.

Upon receipt, a legally qualified tribunal member will consider the case and decide whether there are sufficient grounds for the appeal to be heard. If it is decided that there are insufficient grounds for the appeal to be heard, the appellant may inform the clerk to the Appeals Tribunal that he requires a tribunal to determine, as a preliminary issue at an oral hearing, whether or not the appeal is misconceived.

Appeal hearing

The Appeals Service will give at least fourteen days notice of the date of the hearing. If anyone stated on the 'pre-hearing' enquiry form as to be attending is, in fact, unable to attend on the date specified then the appellant should contact The Appeals Service as soon as possible.

The Appeal Tribunal will consist of one, two or three members chosen by the President of Appeals Tribunals from a panel of people appointed by the Lord Chancellor. Since it is a requirement that at least one member of a tribunal shall be legally qualified, then where a hearing is before only one person, that person must be legally qualified. Where there is more than one member to a tribunal, the President will have nominated one of those persons as chairman and this will usually be the legally qualified member. Decisions are made by a majority of votes. Where the appeal is complex, the tribunal will be attended by an expert witness, invited by The Appeals Service, to provide appropriate advice and guidance.

Disagreement with the Appeal Tribunal's decision

A further appeal may be made to the Office of Social Security and Child Support Commissioners (The Commissioner). However, this requires the approval of the chairman of the Appeal Tribunal and may, in any event, only be on a point of law. Application for leave to appeal to The Commissioner can be made in writing to the chairman of the tribunal via the relevant Appeals Service office. If the tribunal announces its decision orally at the end of a hearing the application for leave may, optionally, also be made orally at the hearing. The application should refer to the grounds on which it is made and The Appeals Service must receive it within one calendar month of the date on which the copy of the record of the full decision was issued.

Disagreement with the Commissioner

An appeal on a question of law only can be made from The Commissioner's decision to

● the Court of Appeal (in England and Wales),

● the Court of Session (in Scotland), or

● the Court of Appeal in Northern Ireland

Such an appeal requires the leave of The Commissioner who made the decision, the leave of The Chief Commissioner in certain cases or, if The Commissioners refuse leave, with the leave of the appropriate court. Applications must be received within one calendar month from the date of issue of The Commissioner's decision.

In rare cases it may be possible to apply to the High Court for a Judicial Review with a view to it quashing The Commissioner's decision, but only if there are compelling reasons in the interest of justice for it to do so.

9.14   SECRETARY OF STATE'S DETERMINATIONS (PRE-1 APRIL 1999)

Under *SSAA 1992, s 17* (now repealed), the determination of all questions arising in connection with contribution matters was placed within the jurisdiction of the Secretary of State for Social Security, who is, of course, the head of the Department of Social Security. However, the Secretary of State for Social Security (who is, perforce, distanced from the day-to-day running of the DSS by the Minister of State who assists him) did not personally take part in the determination procedure but delegated his judicial powers to senior members of the Office for the Determination of Contributions Questions. The ODCQ was located at Newcastle upon Tyne and had status independent of the former Contributions Agency although it was part of, and responsible to, the DSS. It took no part in the determination of departmental policy, practice or procedure. Support for the propriety of this process of delegation may be found in decisions of the courts. (*Carltona Ltd v Commr of Works [1943] 2 AER 543*).

The Secretary of State was given jurisdiction in respect of specific contribution questions referred to within the DSS as 'principal questions'. The Secretary of State was also given jurisdiction as regards any question *otherwise relating to a person's contributions* or his earnings factor. [former *Sec 17(1)(b)*]. The only limitation placed on this 'otherwise' clause is that questions relating to Class 4 contributions were excluded from the Secretary of State's jurisdiction (other than questions as to whether a person is excepted from liability to such contributions, whether his liability for such contributions is deferred or whether he is liable for such directly-collectable contributions (see CLASS 4 CONTRIBUTIONS (19)). [*Sec 17(2)*]. These always used to, and still do, lie within the jurisdiction of the General or Special Commissioners on an appeal under *Taxes Management Act 1970, s 31*.

Apart from adjudicating authorities (such as the courts, adjudication officers, local tribunals and the Social Security Commissioners) who had to refer *SSAA 1992, s 17(1)* questions to the Secretary of State, application for a determination of a question relating to contributions liability could be made only by a 'person interested'. [*Adjudication Regs, Reg 13(3)*]. A 'person interested' is defined as a person whose interest in the application or decision relates to *that person's own liability* or *actual or potential rights* under the Social Security Acts. [*Reg 12*]. The contributions to which a question relates may be secondary contributions and a secondary contributor may, therefore, be a 'person interested' in, for example, a question concerning the categorisation of a person who works for him. (*Secretary of State for Social Services v Maclean [1972] SLT (Sh Ct) 34*).

One effect of the provisions described is that the DSS itself was precluded from applying to the Secretary of State for the determination of a question (but see 8.3 ANTI-AVOIDANCE) although an Inspector of the Contributions Agency could apply in SSP or SMP cases only [*Reg 13(3)*]. If, therefore, a person with whom the DSS could not reach agreement on a contribution matter was himself unwilling to apply for a determination, the DSS had no alternative but to institute proceedings in order that, when the matter was brought before the court, the court could refer the question (Letter from the ODCQ dated 6 January 1993).

Anyone who wished to obtain a determination by the Secretary of State on a *SSAA 1992, s 17(1)* question had to make written application to him in an approved form. [*Adjudication Regs, Reg 13(1)*]. This involved the completion of a form CF 90 or a form CF 93 which was issued by the DSS and sent or delivered to the prospective applicant or his agent only in liaison with that prospective applicant's local Contributions Agency office. This intra-department procedure was intended to give scope for reappraisal of the applicant's case in order that the formal determination procedure might be dispensed with if possible.

No time limit on the filing of an application was imposed by either *SSAA 1992* or the relevant regulations.

An application for a determination by the Secretary of State of a *Sec 17(1)* question could, with the Secretary of State's leave, be withdrawn at any time before the decision was given. [*Adjudication Regs, Reg 6(4)*].

Where the DSS issued a form CF 90 or CF 93 for completion, the issuing officer would, in accordance with ODCQ practice, insert for the applicant the question to be asked of the Secretary of State. This practice was followed because an applicant's knowledge of contribution law and the issues involved is generally insufficient for him to draft his question in a comprehensive and meaningful way. For example, to ask, 'Are contributions payable on the bonus of £5,000 paid by XYZ Co to J Bloggs?' is to beg the question 'Whether by virtue of his association with XYZ Co, Joe Bloggs was, during the period . . . to . . ., included in the category of employed earners for the purposes of the Social Security Contributions and Benefits Act 1992 and, if so: (*a*) Whether the said XYZ Co was the secondary contributor within the meaning of Sections 6 and 7 of that Act in relation to any earnings paid to or for the benefit of the said Joe Bloggs in respect of any employment under the said company, and if so, (*b*) What is the amount of Class 1 contributions (if any) payable in respect of the said Joe Bloggs by the said XYZ Co?'

It remained the case that, whatever the merits of a question drafted by the DSS might be, an applicant was not obliged to endorse it but could (though the forms did not tell him this) amend it or reject it entirely in favour of a relevant alternative question which he himself supplied

Forms CF 90 (which were used where categorisation is an issue) and CF 93 (which were used where categorisation is *not* an issue) contained merely a list of standard questions and spaces for the applicant's replies. If the applicant wished to add a statement for the Secretary of State's consideration, he could do so. (Letter from ODCQ dated 6 January 1993).

Where a question was to be referred to the Secretary of State by himself (see 8.3 ANTI-AVOIDANCE), by the court or by an insurance officer, a local tribunal or the Social Security Commissioners, it was for the Secretary of State, the court or the insurance officer respectively to decide on the question which was to be asked.

When the Secretary of State received an application for determination of a *SSAA 1992, s 17(1)* question, he had to take steps to bring the application to the notice of anyone who appeared to him to be interested in it. Form CF 91 was used for this purpose.

Before determining a question coming within *SSAA 1992, s 17(1)*, the Secretary of State could, if he thought fit, appoint a person to hold an inquiry into, and report to him upon, the question itself or any matters arising in connection with it. [*SSAA 1992, s 17(4)*].

Despite the discretionary nature of the provision, the holding of an oral inquiry was normal practice 'in cases where the issues are factually complex or where important points of law arise' (Superseded DSS Leaflet NI 260, p 76) and such inquiries are designated for the purposes of *Tribunal and Inquiries Act 1971, s 19* so that the safeguards for which that Act and *Tribunals and Inquiries (Discretionary Inquiries) Order 1975* provide are to apply. The Secretary of State (though he could in fact appoint whomsoever he pleased to hold an inquiry) usually appointed a lawyer either from the Solicitor's Office of his own Department or from a panel of non-DSS lawyers.

A DSS inquiry was never intended to be an adversarial forum and for that reason the law gave the DSS only a limited right of presence and no right whatsoever to be heard. DSS inquiry holders were, however, latterly circumventing those strictures by the simple expedient of calling DSS officers as witnesses and inquiry holders often recorded but overruled any objection which was made to them concerning such a practice.

A person required to attend an inquiry could be paid travelling expenses and, if the necessary period of absence from a person's home or place of work was two and a half or more hours, a subsistence allowance at a scale rate. Compensation for loss of remunerative time could also be paid. [*SSAA 1992, 2 Sch 7*]. Details of rates were given in leaflet CF 100.

Legal costs in connection with an inquiry could not be awarded irrespective of whether or not the inquiry was related to court proceedings. (Case 5/560/K HCP 246 1977–78). Nor was legal aid available. It seems, however, that costs of obtaining the referral of a question to the Secretary of State could be obtained. (*DHSS v Envoy Farmers Ltd [1976] 2 AER 173*).

After an inquiry had been held, the person who held it prepared a report and sent it to ODCQ advising the senior officer acting for the Secretary of State as to the answer to be given to the question which was asked. The senior officer did not need to accept the inquiry-holder's advice but would have placed the Secretary of State in an exposed position as regards any external review which might follow if he did not do so. Indeed, there was evidence that the advice would be followed even where it directly contradicted the long-standing opinion and long-followed practice of the DSS, though, where that was the case, the Secretary of State could, in his administrative, as opposed to his judicial, capacity seek to reverse the effect of the decision by the introduction of suitable regulations. Inquiry-holders' reports were not published, nor were they available to the applicant or other persons interested in the application.

The Secretary of State had to give written notice of his decision (which was done on Form CF 261) and of the right to request a statement of grounds to the applicant and to any other persons appearing to him to be interested in that decision. [*Adjudication Regs, Reg 15(1)*]. No obligation was imposed on him (as it is on the chairman of an appeal tribunal, for example—see *Reg 23(2)*) to volunteer a *reasoned* answer, however; and no such answer was given in practice, unless a statement of grounds was requested by the applicant or any other person appearing to the Secretary of State to be interested. A statement of the grounds of the Secretary of State's decision must be such as would have enabled the person requesting it to determine whether any question of law had arisen upon which he could appeal to the High Court (see below). [*Reg 16(2)*].

The Secretary of State was authorised to publish his decision in such manner as he thought fit but, on the grounds that confidentiality should be preserved, did not do so after 1958. [*Reg 15(1)*]. Between 1950 and 1958 'Selected Decisions of the Minister on Questions of Classification and Insurability' were published but are now out of print. Such decisions are, when cited, referred to as 'M Decisions'.

Unless an applicant availed himself of one of the remedies for dissatisfaction with a decision of the Secretary of State set out below, that decision was final, though this was not to be taken as meaning that any finding of fact or other determination on which the decision is based or which it embodies was conclusive for the purpose of any further decision. [*SSAA 1992, s 60*]. The significance of this qualification is that if, for example, the Secretary of State decided that Joe Bloggs was included in the category of employed earners by virtue of his association with XYZ Co, that decision was not conclusive if, later, another question came before the Secretary of State which concerns either Joe Bloggs or the XYZ Co.

The Secretary of State could, at any time, correct any accidental errors in a decision of his or in the record of such a decision and, as any such correction is to be deemed to be part of the decision itself or of that record, written notice of the correction must be given as soon as practicable to every party to the proceedings. In calculating any time for appealing against a decision (see below) days falling before the day on which notice of a correction is given were to be disregarded. [*Regs 9, 11(1)(2)*].

There could be no appeal against a correction made by the Secretary of State nor against a refusal by the Secretary of State to make a correction. [*Reg 11(3)*].

An applicant who was dissatisfied with a determination by the Secretary of State could seek to have the matter remedied by

(a) applying to the Secretary of State for the decision to be *set aside on procedural grounds*;

(b) applying to the Secretary of State for the decision to be *reviewed on factual or legal grounds*;

(c) appealing to the High Court on a point of law; or

(d) applying to the court for the decision to be *judicially reviewed*.

Alternatively, the dissatisfied applicant could, if the circumstances were such that it was not reasonable to expect him to resort to any of the stated remedies and there had been maladministration, complain to the Parliamentary Commissioner through a Member of Parliament and ask the Commissioner to investigate the matter. [*Parliamentary Commissioner Act 1967, s 5(1)(2)*].

Where new facts were brought to the notice of the Secretary of State or where he was satisfied that his decision of a '*s 17(1)* question' was made in ignorance of, or was based on a mistake as to, some material fact, or was erroneous in point of law, he could review that decision provided no appeal to the High Court from that decision was pending and that the time for so appealing had expired (see below). [*SSAA 1992, s 19*].

Only a person interested could seek a review of a decision by the Secretary of State and could do so by written application by applying in writing to the DSS office from which notice of the Secretary of State's decision was issued. The application had to be received within three months beginning with the date on which the Secretary of State gave written notice of his decision or, upon application for extension of time, within such further period as the Secretary of State for special reasons allowed. [*Adjudication Regs, Regs 1(3)(a), 3(1)–(3) and 2 Sch 10*].

Where, on a review, the Secretary of State revises his determination of a question, the revised determination was normally be retrospective in its effect to the date on which the original determination took effect.

Any person aggrieved by the determination of the Secretary of State on any question of law arising in connection with that determination (and not referred to the High Court by the Secretary of State) could appeal from that determination to the High Court or Court of Session in Scotland. [*SSAA 1992, s 18(3)*]. This procedure will apply currently to Secretary of State decisions made before 1 April 1999.

In order to be able to determine whether a question of law had arisen in connection with the Secretary of State's determination, the applicant for the determination or anyone else who appeared to the Secretary of State to be interested could request a formal statement of the grounds on which the Secretary of State based his decision.

Most questions which fell to be determined by the Secretary of State were questions of mixed fact and law in the sense that, once the primary facts were established, it is a question of law as to what is the true inference from those facts. It is, for example, a question of fact as to whether A takes orders from B, but it is a question of law as to whether that justifies the conclusion that A is under a contract of service and thus belongs in the category of employed earners. Where a determination by the Secretary of State involved an inference from fact, there was, therefore, a question of law on which an appeal to the High Court could be made. Such an appeal will always fail, however, if the Secretary of State's inference from the primary facts before him was reasonable. It will only succeed if the court finds that the Secretary of State's application of facts to law was one that *no* reasonable person in his place *could* have made. (*Argent v Minister of Social Security* [*1968*] *3 AER 208, per Roskill J*). The duty of the court is to see whether the Secretary of State could properly come to the conclusion which he did on the available evidence and, if so, whether any conclusion so reached could be falsified by a strict approach, by way of construction, to the facts so found, including any written arrangements assented to by the parties. (*Warner Holidays Ltd v Secretary of State for Social Services, [1983] ICR 440, per McNeill J*). The court will never disturb findings of fact and if such findings are thought to be erroneous the remedy lies in an application for review.

A person who is entitled to appeal to the High Court and who wishes to do so must, within 28 days of receipt of the Secretary of State's notice of determination (or of the statement of grounds if such a statement has been requested), give notice in writing to the Secretary of State requiring a case to be stated setting forth the facts on which his decision was based and the decision he arrived at on those facts, [*SSAA 1992, s 18(5); RSC, Order 111, r 2*]. In order to facilitate the drafting of the case, the appellant should, when giving notice, indicate the question of law on which he wishes to appeal. (DSS guidance note CF 263, 'Action to dispute a decision of the Secretary of State', para 3). These time limits may be extended if there is good reason for the delay. On receipt of the appellant's notice requiring a case to be stated, the case will be prepared and a draft will be submitted to the appellant for his comments before the case is finalised, engrossed, signed and sent to him. [*SSAA 1992, s 18(5); RSC, Order 56, r 9*]. If the appellant then wishes to proceed, he must prepare a notice of originating motion in the form laid down in *RSC, Appendix A* (i.e. Form No 13) and, within 28 days of receipt of the finalised stated case, enter the notice for hearing and serve a copy of it on the Secretary of State and a copy of it and the stated case on any other party to the proceedings. [*SSAA 1992, s 18(5); RSC, Order 111, rr 3 and 56, r 10*]. To enter the notice for hearing, the appellant must lodge two copies of it and the stated case (one for the court and one for the judge) at the Crown Office, Royal Courts of Justice, Strand, London WC2 2LL, paying the appropriate fee. The appeal will then be placed in the court list and will, eventually, come on for hearing before a single judge of the Queen's Bench Division. [*SSAA 1992, s 18(5); RSC, Order 111, r 1*]. At the hearing, the appellant (or his counsel) must address his arguments to the judge, but these must be confined to the correctness or otherwise *at law* of the Secretary of State's decision. No evidence or disputations of fact will be admitted.

The Secretary of State is entitled to appear and be heard on a reference or appeal to the High Court in connection with a determination of a *s 17(1)* question but, whether he appears or not, may be ordered by the court to pay the costs of any other person. [*SSAA 1992, s 18(4)(7); RSC, Order 56, r 12*].

The judge's decision is final and is retrospective to the date when the question for determination first arose. Where the issue is one of CATEGORISATION (14), however, the Secretary of State may, in the interests of a contributor or claimant, prevent the decision being applied retrospectively. [*Categorisation Regs, Reg 4(1)*].

Where it is considered that the Secretary of State (or the department which he heads) failed to perform some administrative duty laid upon him by law, or to have exceeded his powers, or to have acted contrary to natural justice (e.g. with bias) or in excess of his jurisdiction, and no other avenue of redress is or was open, a party with a 'sufficient interest' in the matter may seek a judicial review.

Judicial review is a remedy that lies exclusively in public law and, on application, the court has jurisdiction to grant a declaration or injunction or to make a prerogative order of *mandamus* (commanding the performance of a duty), *prohibition* (prohibiting the exceeding of jurisdiction), or *certiorari* (removing a decision into the Queen's Bench Division for inquiry into its legality and, if necessary, for correction). Prior to 11 January 1978, a person seeking redress had himself to decide which of these procedures was most appropriate, but, since that date, the court has exercised discretion as to which interlocutory directions should be made. [*RSC Order, 53, r 1(1)(2)*].

There are two stages to the procedure for judicial review.

(*a*)   Application (within 3 months of the decision, on form 86A) to a divisional court of the Queen's Bench Division for leave to apply for judicial review. [*RSC Order 53, rr 3(1), 4(1)*]. This is, initially, made *ex parte* but the application may be adjourned for persons or bodies against whom relief is sought to be represented [*RSC Order 53, r 3(2)*]. The court cannot grant leave unless it considers the applicant has a sufficient interest in the matter to which the application relates. [*RSC Order 53, r 3(5)*].

(*b*)   If leave is granted, the second stage is the hearing of the application itself and, if the court so decides, the granting of a declaration or injunction or the making of a prerogative order.

For judicial review generally, see *R v CIR (ex p National Federation of Self-Employed and Small Businesses Ltd) HL [1981] STC 260.*

See 53.7 REPAYMENT AND RE-ALLOCATION for remission of interest on late-paid Class 1 and Class 1A contributions when a question is submitted to the Secretary of State (but not when a decision of an officer of the Board (see 9.3 above) is the subject of an appeal).

9.15   TRANSITIONAL PROCEDURES

Where a person had made an application before 1 April 1999 for a question to be determined by the Secretary of State for Social Security but, as at that date, the question had not been determined, the matter is thereafter treated as being one for a decision of an officer of the Board of Inland Revenue. [*Social Security Contributions (Decisions and Appeals) Regulations 1999, Reg 4*].

It will now therefore be necessary in such cases for a formal decision to be issued under *SSC(T)A 1999, s 8* so that an appeal may then be made, within 30 days, to the tax Commissioners. Affected parties may feel aggrieved that delay by the DSS/CA/Secretary of State in dealing with the 'appeal' (such as it was) under the old system results in them now having to follow what is, arguably, a less favourable route. Whilst the old system was little-known and had fallen into disrepute, it had the advantage that the DSS/CA could not counter-appeal if the determination was in the contributor's favour. For cases dealt with by correspondence, rather than an oral hearing, it was also relatively inexpensive.

The Inland Revenue issued, in May 1999, a temporary extra-statutory concession as regards interest on amounts of National Insurance contributions disputed by employers and others before 1 April 1999. Under these arrangements, the disputed NIC and the interest on it need not currently be paid while an appeal to the General or Special Commissioners is pending (although the *Transfer Act* does enable regulations to be introduced to require payment before an appeal may be heard). Normally, if the liability is confirmed, interest runs under the usual rules, e.g., for Class 1, from fourteen days after the end of the tax year to which the contributions relate.

The previous mechanism (see 9.14 above and 53.7 REPAYMENT AND RE-ALLOCATION) provided that interest did not accrue from, broadly, the time the dispute arose and the time the question 'was disposed of'.

Where an application had been submitted before 1 April 1999 for a determination by the Secretary of State but no determination had been made by that time, then interest will continue to be remitted until 1 August 1999 or the date the *section 8* decision is made—whichever is the later.

If, before 1 April 1999, a contributor had advised the Contributions Agency that they disputed liability, but it had been agreed that no formal application would be made pending the outcome of a lead case, then interest will also be remitted until the later of 1 August 1999 and a *section 8* decision on the individual case (not the lead case).

Where a determination was made before 1 April 1999, but a Statement of Grounds (see 9.14) was requested but not received until after that date, then interest will be remitted until the later of 1 August 1999 or 14 days after the issue of the Statement of Grounds.

This ESC will apply to about 100 formal cases and about another 2,300 cases where the same points arise and it had been agreed with Contributions Agency before 1 April 1999 that the outcome would await the result of a lead case. It also affects about 40 cases where the Secretary of State had confirmed liability but the matter is likely to go to the High Court. This requires the issue of a "Statement of Grounds" for the Secretary of State's determination, a process that has recently taken an inordinate amount of time. Many of these cases are where payments of substantial bonuses have been made by way of rhodium, platinum sponge or in other non-cash forms. According to the Inland Revenue, about £250–£300 million of National Insurance contributions may be due if the authorities' challenges are successful. (See Inland Revenue Press Release 100/99, 18 May 1999)

Regulation 28D, which provided for the 'freezing' of interest under the pre-1 April regime has now been largely repealed but the amended provision continues to provide for the remission of interest in cases of official error. (See Inland Revenue Press Release 100/133, 9 July 1999).

9.16 CLASS 4 QUESTIONS

Because CLASS 4 CONTRIBUTIONS (20) are payable in accordance with assessments made under the Income Tax Acts, the provisions of *Taxes Management Act 1970, Pt V* have always applied with necessary modifications in relation to such contributions as they apply in relation to income tax and this continues to be the case after 31 March 1999. [*SSCBA 1992, s 15(1)(2)(5), 2 Sch 8*]. The effect of this is that an appeal against a Class 4 assessment must be made in writing within 30 days of the issue of the notice of assessment, must state the grounds on which it is based and must be to the General Commissioners, unless the appellant elects for it to be taken before the Special Commissioners. An appeal may be brought out of time if there is a reasonable excuse for the delay. An appeal against the decision of the Commissioners may be made to the High Court by way of Stated Case *on a point of law* and thence to the Court of Appeal and the House of Lords. (See, for example, *Martin v O'Sullivan [1982] STC 416*.) [*TMA 1970, ss 31(1)(4)(5), 49(1), 56*].

Under 'self-assessment' from 6 April 1996, there will be few assessments issued now. However, in the case of a dispute, whether for income tax, Class 4 contributions or both, it will be necessary for the Inland Revenue, exceptionally, to issue an assessment in order to enable an appeal to be made by the taxpayer/contributor.

The only questions concerning Class 4 contributions which are excluded from this jurisdiction are

(*a*) whether by regulations made under *SSCBA 1992, s 17(1)* a person is excepted from Class 4 liability or his liability is deferred; and/or

(*b*) whether he is liable for Class 4 contributions that may be collected directly by the NICO under *SSCBA 1992, ss 17(3)–(6), 18*.

[*SSAA 1992, s 17(2), 2 Sch 8*].

These two matters previously fell within the Secretary of State's remit (see 9.14 above). However, from 1 April 1999, they become matters for a decision of an officer of the Board under *SSC(T)A, 1999 s 8* (see 9.2 to 9.12 above) and then, only by those means, will the matter now fall to be put before the tax Commissioners.

10   Apprentices, Trainees and Students

Cross-references. See 3.1 to 3.4 AGE EXCEPTION for those under 16; 14.3 to 14.7 CATEGORISATION for contract of service; CLASS 1 CONTRIBUTIONS (15); 24.4 to 24.9 CREDITS for contributions awarded in early years and during and after training etc.; NATIONAL INSURANCE NUMBER (46) for entry into the social security scheme; 49.3 and 49.4 OVERSEAS MATTERS for meaning of present, resident and ordinarily resident; WORKING CASE STUDY (58).

Other Sources. Simon's NIC, Part I, Section 2, Chapter 4; Section 4, Chapter 14 and Section 8, Chapter 46; Tolley's National Insurance Brief, February 1997, page 15; Tolley's Social Security and State Benefits Handbook 2000.

10.1   AGE LIMITATIONS

No liability for either primary or secondary CLASS 1 CONTRIBUTIONS (15) or for CLASS 2 CONTRIBUTIONS (18) can arise in respect of a person who has not yet attained the age of 16, and exception from CLASS 4 CONTRIBUTIONS (20) may be claimed by anyone who is not over that age at the beginning of a year of assessment (see 3.1 to 3.6 AGE EXCEPTION).

10.2   APPRENTICES

A person who is gainfully employed in Great Britain under a contract of service (see 14.3 CATEGORISATION) is an employed earner for contribution purposes, and a contract of service includes a contract of apprenticeship. [*SSCBA 1992, ss 2(1)(a), 122(1)*].

A 'contract of apprenticeship' is a contract by which a person is bound to and *serves* another for the purpose of learning something which the other is to teach him. (*St Pancras Parish v Clapham Parish (1860) 2 E & E 742, per Lord Cockburn CJ at p 750*). Where, however, the primary purpose of a contract is not service but is teaching or learning, the contract is neither a contract of apprenticeship nor a contract of service. (*Wiltshire Police Authority v Wynn [1980] ICR 649*). A person engaged under a training contract which is neither a contract of service nor a contract of apprenticeship is not an employed earner for contribution purposes, and any allowances paid to him will, therefore, attract no contribution liability.

The DSS regarded apprentice jockeys and stable boys who receive board and lodgings as employed earners (see 14.2 CATEGORISATION).

10.3   PARTICIPANTS IN GOVERNMENT TRAINING SCHEMES

Where a participant in Youth Training receives only the YT allowance (£40.00 a week at age 16 or 17), no contribution liability will arise as the amount of such allowances falls below the lower earnings limit (see EARNINGS LIMITS AND THRESHOLDS (30)). Where, however, the allowance is topped-up by the 'managing agent' (i.e. the employer who has charge of the participant) to a level which equals or exceeds the lower earnings limit, the contribution position will depend on whether, in the particular circumstances of his case, the participant is, in law, under a contract of service, a contract of apprenticeship or a training contract. A managing agent has considerable freedom in the arrangements he enters into with the participant, and he may, with the participant's consent, write into the training agreement a declaration that the agreement is not intended to establish a contractual relationship between himself and a participant. Such a declaration will result in a contract which is binding only in honour (*Rose & Frank Crompton Co v J R Crompton & Bros Ltd [1923] 2 KB 261*) and which, therefore, it seems, precludes the participant from falling into the category of employed earners for contribution purposes. If, on the other hand, the training agreement expressly states that the participant is to be regarded as an employee, the training agreement will, it seems, bring the participant within the category of employed earners for contribution purposes and contribution liabilities will ensue. In the absence of such an express statement, a participant will not be an employee (*Daley v Allied Suppliers Ltd [1983] IRLR 14*), but he may be a trainee or an apprentice and, in order to decide which, the tests outlined at 10.2 above must be applied. If the primary purpose of the training agreement is merely to formalise an arrangement under which the participant may be taught certain skills, the contract is a training contract, not a contract of service or apprenticeship, and, because it does not bring the participant into the category of employed earners, no contribution liabilities can arise. If, however, the primary purpose of the training agreement is to formalise an arrangement under which the participant is to serve the managing agent in order to learn a trade, the contract may be construed as a contract of apprenticeship and contribution liabilities will arise if the earnings paid are sufficiently great. It is thought that a clause within the agreement which guarantees the participant employment at the end of the training period will be strongly indicative of apprenticeship.

The *Health and Safety (Training for Employment) Regs 1990 (SI 1990 No 1380)* provide that, for the purposes of health and safety legislation, trainees are to be *treated as* employees. By implication, their status as trainees means that they would not otherwise qualify as employees and the deeming regulation is required to bring them under the cover of health and safety law.

The Training Agreement held by the participant will indicate whether the participating young person has employee status or not. A further indication will be the position on paid overtime which may not be worked by a person with trainee-only status.

Where a participant has employed earner status, Class 1 contributions must be calculated by reference to the total pay the participant receives, *including* the YT allowance.

Training premiums paid to participants in Employment Training (which commenced on 5 September 1988 and replaced the Community Programme, the old and new Job Training Schemes, the Wider Opportunities Training Programme and various other employment and training programmes for those aged 18 or over) attract neither primary or secondary Class 1 contribution liability nor Class 2 contribution liability if the participant is in receipt of a training premium under *Employment and Training Act 1973, s 2* (effective 5 September 1988) or *Enterprise and New Towns (Scotland) Act 1990, s 2* (effective 1 April 1991). [*Employment Training Payments Order 1988, Art 2 as amended*].

Under the Jobstart Scheme (which aimed to encourage the long-term unemployed to take up full-time employment at under £90 a week gross but which was discontinued on 28 February 1991) a top-up payment of £20 a week was made for the first six months of the employment. The DSS did not regard the top-up payment as EARNINGS (28) for contribution purposes, though the wage itself was.

With effect from 1 October 1991, any payment made to a person using the facilities provided under the Employment Action Programme is not to be treated as a payment of earnings for contribution purposes. [*Employment Action (Miscellaneous Provisions) Order 1991, Reg 3*].

As from 6 April 1996 the payments of £50.00 per week and £300 worth of training vouchers under the pilot Jobmatch Scheme by way of work incentive allowance were to be excluded from tax by extra statutory concession. The amount was payable for a maximum of 26 weeks to people who come off the unemployment register after two years of being unemployed and commence part-time work. Similarly, the payments under the permanent Jobmatch Scheme which came into effect on 6 April 1997 were also exempt from NICs as well as vouchers received for training. [*Social Security (Contributions) Regs 1979, Reg 19(1)(w)(x)*] (see also CA Press Release 96/1, 15 March 1996 and IR Press Release 14 March 1997). When the pilot scheme was introduced in 1995 the Treasury decided not to tax the payments or the vouchers and to put this on a formal footing the Inland Revenue removed the tax charge by means of *ESC A90*. New regulations widened the exclusion from charge to NICs to cover the permanent scheme. [*Social Security (Contributions) Amendment (No 3) Regs 1997 (SI 1997, No 820)*] and the tax exclusion was extended by *ESC A97*. There was unlikely to be any involvement in the scheme by employers because they are not directly involved in the payment of the allowance or vouchers (CA National Insurance News extracts Number 8, Summer 1997). The scheme did, however, cease on 31 March 1998.

Under the 'New Deal' for 18–24 year olds from April 1998 there are three main options:

- full time education and training;

- subsidised employment;

- Environmental Task Force and voluntary sector work.

In the case of subsidised employment, the subsidy paid to the employer is a maximum of £60 per week in the case of 30 hours or more per week and a maximum of £40 per week otherwise. In addition, £750 is provided towards training costs. The actual wage paid by the employer will be liable to NIC in the usual way, regardless of subsidy received but the training allowance is not subject to NIC (CA National Consultation Panel, 14 January 1998 and CWG2 (2000), page 29). Of course, usually the training allowance will not find itself reaching the hands of the employee so NIC liability or otherwise would not be in point. See also *Social Security (New Deal Pilot) Regulations 1999, SI 1999 No 3156*.

This contrasts with payments under the 'New Deal 50 Plus' training programme to those aged 50 or more going back into work. They will not pay tax or NICs on the payments they receive through the scheme, even though these mirror the amounts above of £60 per week and an in-work training grant of £750. The employment credit payment of £60 and the training grant should not be chargeable to NICs as earnings from employment (Class 1) or assessable for self-employment (Class 2).

[*Social Security (Contributions) (Amendment No 5) Regulations 1999, SI 1999 No 2736*].

10.4   TRAINING OR OCCUPATIONAL CENTRE ATTENDERS

Some local authorities and other organisations provide work, training or occupational centres directed to the welfare and rehabilitation of persons who are physically or mentally handicapped. The question whether a person attending such a centre is or is not gainfully employed is determined by the arrangements and conditions applying at the centre. (R(U)2/67). The DSS normally accepted that an attender is not in gainful employment, however, if

(a)   the main object of any work performed is therapeutic, not commercial;

(b)   arrangements for attendance are elastic and informal; and

(c)   payments do not depend on output but are in the nature of pocket money given as an incident of rehabilitation.

(AOG Vol 6 para 50120).

10.5 STUDENTS

In accordance with the principle stated at 10.2 above, students who are required to undertake practical work as part of their education do not thereby become party to a contract of service, even though they receive a maintenance allowance or fees for the work they perform. (*M7 (1950); M16 (1951); M19 (1951)*). A person who, *while under a contract of service* with an employer, enters upon a course of study (either full-time or as part of a sandwich course) does not, however, cease thereby to be under a contract of service and is, accordingly, liable as an employed earner for contributions on pay or financial assistance which constitutes earnings received from his employer, even if received during the periods of education.

10.6 Post-graduate students and researchers

The position of post-graduate students and researchers will be determined by application of the tests relating to the existence or otherwise of a contract of service (see 14.3 to 14.7 CATEGORISATION). A person who is remunerated for teaching, demonstrating or assisting in research will, however, normally be regarded as either an employed earner (*Vandyk v Minister of Pensions and National Insurance [1954] 2 AER 723*), or a self-employed earner (*M39 (1954)*). However, training in research has been held to be education not employment, as has research supervised by teaching staff and beyond the control of the person paying a grant towards that research. (*M56 (1956); M6 (1950)*).

10.7 Vacation studentships

The UK Atomic Energy Authority, the Post Office and various government departments award vacation studentships to university students whom they wish to recruit into their service at the end of the university course. Such students usually receive travelling expenses and an allowance but, as their activity does not constitute gainful employment, the allowances attract no contribution liability.

10.8 Registered seafarers and cadets

Training allowances paid to a registered seafarer or cadet who is undergoing Merchant Navy Establishment Administration approved training do not attract contribution liabilities unless the seafarer's agreement or the cadet's indentures continue throughout the period of training.

10.9 ARTICLED CLERKS

A *solicitor's* articled clerk will normally occupy the dual position of being concurrently under both a training contract (which is not a contract of service) with his principal *and* a contract of employment (which is a contract of service) with the firm of which his principal is a member. (*Oliver v J P Malnick & Co [1983] 3 AER 795*).

The position of an *accountant's* articled clerk is somewhat different, however. Under the Education and Training Regulations of the Institute of Chartered Accountants in England and Wales, training contracts are, from 1 January 1983, between a firm and a student and not, as formerly, between an authorised principal and a student. Thus, an accountant's articled clerk will be under two contracts (one of training and one of service) but both will be with the firm concerned.

The Secretary of State has, in the past, formally determined that the articled clerks of both accountants and auctioneers are, quite apart from their training contracts, under contracts of service with the firms to which their principals belong. (*M29 (1953); M53 (1956)*).

10.10 BARRISTERS' PUPILS

Before a barrister can practice unsupervised in England and Wales he or she is required first to complete at least twelve months pupillage. During this time he or she is known as a pupil. The DSS regarded the whole of the first twelve months of any period of pupillage as a period of training and not of gainful occupation, even though work may be done for a fee under the guidance of the pupil master after the first six months pupillage has been completed.

If a period of pupillage extends beyond twelve months, the DSS had regard to the frequency of paid briefs in deciding whether the extended pupillage constitutes training or gainful occupation. If training is minimal and paid briefs are accepted regularly the DSS regarded the barrister as a SELF-EMPLOYED EARNER (see 14.10).

A barrister who has completed his or her pupillage but cannot find a full tenancy in chambers may become a 'squatter' in chambers. The DSS regarded a squatter as a SELF-EMPLOYED EARNER (see 14.10).

In Scotland, an advocate's pupillage lasts for between nine and twelve months (depending on admission dates) during which time no paid legal work may be undertaken. The DSS regarded the whole period of pupillage as one of training.

10.11 STUDENTS AND APPRENTICES NOT ORDINARILY RESIDENT IN GREAT BRITAIN

Where, provided he is not ordinarily resident in Great Britain (see 49.4 OVERSEAS MATTERS),

(a) a full-time student, other than a national of another EEA member state, who is following a course of studies outside the United Kingdom undertakes, during his vacation, temporary employment of a nature similar or related to his course of studies as an employed earner in Great Britain; or

(b) a person who has a relationship with someone outside the UK comparable with the relationship which exists between an apprentice and his master in Great Britain commences, before he attains the age of 25, a period of employment in Great Britain which is of a nature similar or related to his employment under the relationship outside the UK,

liability for contributions is not to arise until the student or apprentice has been resident in Great Britain for a *continuous* period of 52 contribution weeks beginning with the contribution week following the date of his *last* entry into Great Britain. [*Contributions Regs, Reg 119(2), (3)(a)(b)*]. A contribution week is a period of seven days beginning with midnight between Saturday and Sunday. [*Reg 1(2)*].

The reciprocal agreement between the UK and France provides that students and apprentices who, having been insured under the French contribution scheme, are temporarily employed in the UK are to be insured under the UK contribution scheme from the outset and that the provisions of *Reg 119* described above are *not* to apply. [*National Insurance (France) Order 1958, Art 6(1)*]. That agreement is superseded by the EC regulations so far as EEA nationals are concerned, but it remains in force so far as non-EEA nationals are concerned.

10.12 BENEFIT ENTITLEMENTS

Credits may be awarded to

(a) new entrants to the contribution scheme;

(b) persons undergoing a course of full-time approved training (special rules apply to disabled people who can only attend a course part-time);

(*c*)   persons who have reached the end of a course of full-time education, a course of approved training, or an apprenticeship,

so as to enable them to fulfil the *second* contribution condition for certain benefits (see 13.2 BENEFITS and 24.4 to 24.9 CREDITS).

If the last tax year before the benefit year in which a person's claim for state benefit arises is the tax year in which or before which his liability to pay contributions first arises, that person may, for the purpose of enabling the contribution condition for widow's payment to be met (see 13.2 BENEFITS),

(i)   aggregate all EARNINGS FACTORS (29) derived from the aggregate of earnings on which he has paid or has been treated as having paid primary Class 1 contributions and from Class 2 contributions he has actually paid before the date of claim, and

(ii)   treat that aggregate sum as his earnings factor for the last complete year before the beginning of the benefit year in which a claim arises.

[*SSCBA 1992, 3 Sch 7*].

11 Armed Forces

Cross-references. See CLASS 1 CONTRIBUTIONS (15); CROWN SERVANTS AND STATUTORY EMPLOYEES (25); 49.3 and 49.4 OVERSEAS MATTERS for meaning of resident, ordinarily resident and present.

Other Sources. Simon's NIC, Part I, Section 1, Chapters 4.211–4.213; Section 6, Chapter 7.213, 17.64; Section 7, Chapter 32.54 and Section 9, Chapter 55.351; DSS leaflet GL 26.

11.1 DEFINITION

A serving member of the forces is any person who, being over the age of 16 and not absent on desertion, is a member (giving full pay service) of any establishment or organisation listed below, subject to the exceptions stated below. [*Contributions Regs, Reg 1(2)*].

Prescribed establishments and organisations are

1 any of the regular naval, military or air forces of the Crown

2 Retired and Emergency Lists of Officers of the Royal Navy

3 Royal Naval Reserves (including Women's Royal Naval Reserve and Queen Alexandra's Royal Naval Nursing Service Reserve)

4 Royal Marines Reserve

5 Army Reserves (including Regular Army Reserve of Officers, Regular Reserves, Long Term Reserves and Army Pensioners)

6 Territorial and Army Volunteer Reserve

7 Royal Air Force Reserves (including Royal Air Force Reserve of Officers, Women's Royal Air Force Reserve of Officers, Royal Air Force Volunteer Reserve, Women's Royal Air Force Volunteer Reserve, Class E Reserve of Airmen, Princess Mary's Royal Airforce Nursing Service Reserve, Officers on the Retired List of the Royal Air Force and Royal Air Force Pensioners)

8 Royal Auxiliary Air Force (including Women's Royal Auxiliary Air Force)

9 The Royal Irish Regiment to the extent that its members are not members of any force within para 1 above.

[*Contributions Regs, 3 Sch Pt I, as amended by Contributions Amendment Regs 1980, Reg 6 and Contributions Amendment No 2 Regs 1994, Reg 4*].

None of the following is within the term 'serving member of the forces':

(i) a serving member of any naval force of HM forces who locally entered that force at an overseas base and who had not previously been insured under the UK scheme;

(ii) a serving member of any military force of HM forces who entered that force, or was recruited for that force, outside the UK and the depot of whose unit is situated outside the UK; and

(iii) a serving member of any air force of HM forces who entered that force, or was recruited for that force, outside the UK and is liable under the terms of his engagement to serve only in a specified part of the world outside the UK.

[*Contributions Regs, 3 Sch Pt II*].

11.2 CATEGORISATION

A serving member of the forces is to be treated as an employed earner in respect of his membership of those forces and as present in Great Britain even if he is, in fact, serving overseas. [*SSCBA 1992, s 116; Contributions Regs, Reg 114*]. This accords with EC rules which provide that, irrespective of his presence in another State, a person called up or recalled for service in the armed forces is to be subject to the social security legislation of that State. [*EC Reg 1408/71, Art 13(2)(e)*].

Members of the forces are excepted from the provisions of *Arts 6 and 9* of the agreement between the United Kingdom and Cyprus which state that the Cypriot scheme is to apply to all persons employed in the British Sovereign Base areas of Akrotiri and Dhekelia. [*Social Security (Cyprus) Order 1983, Art 8 as amended by Social Security (Cyprus) Order 1994*].

11.3 EARNINGS

The EARNINGS (28) of serving members of the forces are, for contribution purposes, to exclude

(*a*) Emergency Service grants [*Contributions Regs, Reg 117(1)(a)*];

(*b*) bounties in recognition of liability for immediate call-up in times of emergency [*Reg 117(1)(c)*];

(*c*) gratuities at the end of a voluntarily-undertaken further period of service [*Reg 117(1)(b); ICTA 1988, s 316(1)(2)*];

(*d*) payments in lieu of food and drink normally supplied in kind to members of the armed forces [*Reg 117(1)(b); ICTA 1988, s 316(3)(a)*];

(*e*) contributions to mess expenses [*Reg 117(1)(b); ICTA 1988, s 316(3)(b)*].

11.4 EARNINGS PERIOD

The earnings period (see EARNINGS PERIODS (31)) of a serving member of the forces is

(*a*) in the case of a member of the regular forces, the accounting period under the Naval Pay Regulations, Army Pay Warrant or Queen's Regulations, as appropriate; or

(*b*) in the case of a person undergoing training in any of the prescribed establishments numbered 2 to 9 at 11.1 above, a month.

[*Contributions Regs, Reg 117(2)*].

11.5 CONTRIBUTION RATES

Although a serving member of the forces is eligible for only a restricted range of State benefits [*Members of the Forces Benefits Regs 1975*], recognition is no longer made for this factor in determining the rates of Class 1 contributions by, and in respect of, such a person. Until 5 April 1996, however, the percentage rate of Class 1 contributions payable in respect of a person's earnings as such a member was *reduced* by

(*a*) 0.4 in the case of the main primary percentage where the percentage would be at the standard rate, i.e. for 1995–96, 9.6% instead of 10% (with the initial primary percentage remaining at 2%);

(*b*) 0.4 in the case of both the initial and the main primary percentage where the percentage would be at the reduced rate, i.e. for 1995–96, 3.45% initial and 3.45% main instead of 3.85%; and

(c) 0.4 in the case of secondary contributions, i.e. for 1995–96:

secondary earnings bracket 1 2.60%
secondary earnings bracket 2 4.60%
secondary earnings bracket 3 6.60%
secondary earnings bracket 4 9.80%;

(see EARNINGS LIMITS AND THRESHOLDS (30)).

[*Contributions Regs, Reg 115(1)(2) as amended by Contributions Transitional Regs 1989, Reg 3(9), Contributions Amendment Regs 1990, Reg 2(3), Contributions Amendment No 2 Regs 1992, Reg 2(3), Contributions Amendment No 2 Regs 1993, Reg 2(3), Contributions Amendment No 2 Regs 1995, Reg 2(3) and Contributions Amendment No 2 Regs 1996, Reg 2(3)*].

Contributions were to be calculated in accordance with the normal rules (see CLASS 1 CONTRIBUTIONS (15)) and paid into the NATIONAL INSURANCE FUND (45).

11.6 LATE-PAID CONTRIBUTIONS

For the purpose of any entitlement to BENEFITS (13), any Class 1 contributions paid after the due date in respect of earnings paid to or for the benefit of a person in respect of his employment as a member of the forces are to be treated as paid on the due date (see 21.3 COLLECTION). [*Contributions Regs, Reg 116*].

11.7 NON-COMPLIANCE WITH TIME LIMITS

Where a serving member of the forces is unable to comply with a time limit laid down in the legislation by reason of being at sea or outside Great Britain because of his employment, he will be deemed to have complied if he does whatever is required of him as soon as is reasonably practicable. [*Reg 118*].

11.8 EMPLOYMENT IN OR BY VISITING FORCES

Employment as a member of the naval, military or air forces of a country to which *Visiting Forces Act 1952* applies is to be entirely disregarded for contribution purposes, and this applies equally to any civilian employed by such a force unless he is ordinarily resident in the United Kingdom (see 49.4 OVERSEAS MATTERS). [*Categorisation Regs, Reg 2(4), 1 Sch Pt III para 11, as amended by Categorisation Amendment Regs 1980, Reg 2*].

11.9 EMPLOYMENT AS A MEMBER OF INTERNATIONAL HEADQUARTERS OR DEFENCE ORGANISATIONS

Employment as a member of any international headquarters or defence organisation designated under *International Headquarters and Defence Organisations Act 1964, s 1* is to be entirely disregarded for contribution purposes unless the person so employed is

(a) a serving member of Her Majesty's regular forces raised in the UK and any officer in the Brigade of Gurkhas holding Her Majesty's Commission who is not a Queen's Gurkha officer; or

(b) a civilian ordinarily resident in the United Kingdom (see 49.4 OVERSEAS MATTERS) who is not a member of any scheme which the headquarters or organisation has established for the provision of pensions, lump sums, gratuities or like benefits to persons who cease to be in its employment.

[*Categorisation Regs, Reg 2(4), 1 Sch Pt III para 12, as amended by Categorisation Amendment Regs 1980, Reg 2 and Categorisation Amendment Regs 1984, Reg 3*].

11.10 BRITISH FORCES IN GERMANY

In the case of members of the UK forces (and the civilian component of such forces) stationed in Germany, *Reg 114* and *EC Reg 1408/71, Art 13(2)(e)* are overridden in appropriate cases by *Reciprocal Agreement (SI 1961 No 1202)—Germany, Arts 3(6) and 7(5)* and *Reciprocal Agreement (SI 1961 No 1513)—Germany, Arts 2(5) and 5(5)*. [*EC Reg 1408/71, Annex III, Point A, Para 30*].

Serving members of HM Forces remain within UK Class 1 liability when stationed in Germany although this will be of less consequence now fewer HM Forces are regularly stationed in Germany. However, the following provisions of the reciprocal agreement remain applicable notwithstanding *Art 6 of EC Reg 1408/71*:

(i) UK nationals are to enjoy the rights and be subject to the obligations of German social security legislation under the same conditions as German nationals;

(ii) British forces, members of the civilian component and their dependants mentioned in a 1959 agreement supplementary to the Status of Forces Agreement are to be covered by the reciprocal agreement in the same way as other persons;

(iii) where a person is employed in Germany in UK Government service or in the service of a UK public corporation, UK legislation is to apply as if the person were employed in the UK;

(iv) where a person is employed as in (iii) in Germany and his contract of service has been concluded by a person employed in Germany in UK Government service or in the service of a UK public corporation, German legislation is to apply unless and until the person gives notice, within three months of the commencement of the employment, that UK legislation is to apply;

(v) personal servants of anyone within (iii) or (iv) above may also choose which social scheme to join in relation to that employment;

(vi) a person not ordinarily resident in Germany employed in a civilian capacity by the UK forces there or by a designated organisation serving those forces is to be subject to UK social security law as if the person were employed in the UK.

A list of the designated organisations referred to in (vi) above is set out in the now superseded DSS Leaflet FB5. In addition to the Ministry of Defence and the NAAFI, a number of religious and welfare-related organisations were specified in the April 1998 edition of FB5 as follows:

Malcolm Clubs;

Services Sound and Vision Corporation;

SSAFA/Forces Help;

Order of St John of Jerusalem and the British Red Cross Society Joint Committee Service Hospitals Welfare Department (SHWD);

St Andrew's Ambulance Association;

CVWW (Council for Voluntary Welfare Work) and the following organisations which are attached to it:

Catholic Women's League;

Church Army;

Church of England Soldiers', Sailors' and Airmen's Clubs;

Methodist Church Forces' Board;

Mission to Military Garrisons;

Royal Sailors' Rest;

Salvation Army Red Shield Services;

Sandes Soldiers' and Airmen's Centres;

Soldiers' and Airmen's Scripture Readers Association;

Toc H;

WRVS (Women's Royal Voluntary Service);

YMCA (Young Men's Christian Association);

YWCA (Young Women's Christian Association).

Under the terms of the reciprocal agreement, civilian dependants of British forces personnel working for non-designated organisations or for German employers are usually subject to the German social security system. This is particularly true of German nationals married to UK forces personnel.

11.11 **BRIGADE OF GURKHAS**

Employment (other than as a member of any designated international headquarters or defence organisation (see 11.9 above)) as a Queen's Gurkha officer or as any other member of the Brigade of Gurkhas of a person who was recruited for that Brigade in Nepal is to be disregarded. [*Categorisation Regs, Reg 2(4), 1 Sch Pt III Para 13*]. This provision was introduced with effect from 6 April 1994 (by *Categorisation of Earners (Amendment) Regs 1994, Reg 3*) at the same time as provisions which imposed a secondary Class 1 liability on 'host employers' using the services in the UK of employees supplied by a 'foreign employer' (see 49.9 OVERSEAS MATTERS).

12 Arrears of Contributions

Cross-references. See CLASS 1 CONTRIBUTIONS (15) for liability; CLASS 1A CONTRIBUTIONS (16) for liability; CLASS 2 CONTRIBUTIONS (18) for liability; CLASS 4 CONTRIBUTIONS (20) for liability and assessment; 21.3, 21.8 and 21.13 COLLECTION for dates when contributions fall due; 32.9 ENFORCEMENT for prosecution procedure; 49.13 OVERSEAS MATTERS for recovery of foreign contribution arrears; WORKING CASE STUDY (58).

12.1 GENERAL CONSIDERATIONS

Contribution arrears (which may include unpaid contributions under legislation prior to 1975 [*Contributions Regs, Reg 129*]) will frequently be associated with arrears of income tax. Where they are, they will invariably, following the transfer of the CA on 1 April 1999, be recovered under the extensive powers enjoyed by the Inland Revenue (see 12.2 and 12.3 below and 37.4 INLAND REVENUE: CO-ORDINATION WITH THE DSS). Where they are not so associated, or the association is disregarded, they may be recovered either as a debt due to the Crown or by means of prosecution under powers contained in *SSAA 1992* (see 12.4 below). Additionally, until 12 November 1984, where the person prosecuted was a limited company, arrears could, in certain circumstances, be recovered from the company's directors as a civil debt (see earlier editions of this work). One of the reasons cited for the original abolition of this provision was that it discouraged the appointment of non-executive directors and was a disincentive to new entrepreneurs to take over an ailing business with a view to attempting to secure its recovery. Such arguments do not apply, however, in the case of 'phoenix' companies where directors incur large debts through non-payment of creditors then liquidate the company relying on its limited liability status to protect themselves. Such businesses then re-appear in a new company, free of debt, but typically with the same directors and staff. The former CA successfully prosecuted such a director under *section 115(1), Social Security Administration Act 1992* (see 12.4 below and 22.10 COMPANY DIRECTORS). In the case in question the director was fined £2,400, ordered to pay costs of £500 and National Insurance arrears of over £50,000. The CA indicated that it would make similar prosecutions in the future (CA Press Release 95/14, 27 September 1995. See also Department of Trade and Industry press notice P/96/848 on 12 November 1996 and notice P/99/79 on 28 January 1999). The change of 1984 is partially reversed with the introduction of *section 64, Social Security Act 1998 (introducing new section 121C, SSAA 1992)*, brought into effect from 6 April 1999. [*Social Security Act 1998 (Commencement No. 4) Order 1999, Reg 2*]. This enables any failed company's unpaid national insurance contributions to be recharged to, *inter alia*, one or more directors or the company secretary by way of a 'personal liability notice' where the failure of the company to pay appears to the Secretary of State to be attributable to fraud or neglect on the part of such persons.

Methods of recovery vary as to the time within which, and the amount for which, an action may be brought. Clearly, the Inland Revenue will be influenced by such factors in arriving at its decision as to how to proceed in any particular case.

12.2 CONTRIBUTION ARREARS RECOVERABLE AS INCOME TAX

Any primary or secondary Class 1 contributions which an employer is liable to pay to the collector of taxes for any income tax month (see 21.3 COLLECTION) may be recovered by application of the recovery provisions contained in income tax legislation and PAYE regulations *as if those contributions were tax* due under *ICTA 1988, s 203* and the related PAYE regulations. [*Contributions Regs, 1 Sch 28(1)*].

The recovery provisions referred to include the following

(*a*) distraint in relation to goods and chattels of the person by whom the unpaid amount is due (see 'Assessing effects', PC Manual para 3.17 issue 12/94 and Enforcement Manual, paras E2412 issue 10/98 and E2514, issue 10/97);

(*b*) summary proceedings commenced in the name of a collector for recovery of the unpaid amount as a civil debt;

(*c*) county court proceedings commenced in the name of a collector for recovery of the unpaid amount as a debt due to the Crown;

(*d*) High Court proceedings subject to the Rules of the Supreme Court and commenced in the name of the DSS for recovery of the unpaid amount as a debt due to the Crown.

[*TMA 1970, ss 61–68; Crown Proceedings Act 1947, ss 13, 15 and 17(2); The Distraint by Collectors (Fees, Costs and Charges) (Amendment) Regulations 1995*].

Proceedings may only be brought (see also 'Warning of enforcement proceedings', PC Manual para 3.17 issue 12/94) under (*b*) above where the amount due (or any instalment) is less than £2,000 (from 6 April 1996) and under (*c*) above where the amount due is less than £5,000. [*TMA 1970, ss 65(1), 66(1); FA 1984, s 57; County Courts Act 1984, s 16; Recovery of Tax in Summary Proceedings (Financial Limits) Order 1991 (SI 1991 No 1625); Finance Act 1994, 19 Sch 19(1)*]. However, in applying this provision, the tax element and the contribution element in a debt which includes both elements are each to be viewed *without regard to the other*, i.e. an action for recovery of a debt of £3,999.98, being £1,999.99 tax and £1,999.99 contributions, is within the limit for proceedings in a magistrates' court, and an action for recovery of a debt of £9,999.98, being £4,999.99 tax and £4,999.99 contributions is within the limit for proceedings in a county court. Furthermore, earnings-related contributions and Class 1A contributions may be treated as separate debts for these purposes. [*Contributions Regs, 1 Sch 28(1)(2)*].

12.3   Class 4 contribution arrears

Class 4 contributions which become payable in accordance with assessments made under income tax legislation *are* (not merely may be) recoverable as if they were income tax chargeable under Case I or Case II of Schedule D. [*SSCBA 1992, s 16(1)*]. Only special CLASS 4 CONTRIBUTIONS (20.5) and such ordinary Class 4 contributions as, following upon the issue of a certificate of deferment, are separately calculated at the National Insurance Contributions Office, cannot be recovered in this way (see 27.8 to 27.10 DEFERMENT OF PAYMENT). [*SSCBA 1992, ss 16(2), 18(2); Contributions Regs, Reg 66(1)(b)*].

It follows that the recovery provisions summarised at 12.2 above must be applied in relation to any Class 4 contribution arrears.

Furthermore, the penalty provisions of *TMA 1970, Pt X* apply in relation to Class 4 contributions assessable by the Inland Revenue as do the interest provisions of *TMA 1970, s 88(1)(4)(5)(a)(b)* in relation to tax recovered to make good loss due to a taxpayer's fault. The interest provisions of *TMA 1970, s 86* in relation to amounts overdue did not, however, apply to arrears of Class 4 contributions until 19 April 1993. [*SSCBA 1992, s 16(1)(2), 2 Sch 6; SSCPA 1992 Appointed Day Order 1993 (SI 1993 No 1025)*] (see Inspector's Manual, para 6035, issue 12/94).

The *Social Security Act 1998* amends *SSCBA 1992, 2 Sch 6(1)* so that references to *TMA 1970, s 88* in that section are repealed, since such provision is no longer required following the replacement of the *section 88* interest regime with new interest and penalty provisions under 'self-assessment'. [*SSCBA 1992, 2 Sch 6 as repealed by Social Security Act 1998, s 59*].

12.4   PROSECUTION FOR NON-PAYMENT OF CONTRIBUTIONS

Where contribution arrears are not associated with arrears of tax (or where any such association is disregarded), the DSS could, by High Court writ, proceed for the recovery of the arrears as a debt due to the Crown. Such a course of action has the advantage of being without monetary limits (see 12.6 below and 12.2 above), but is costly, subject to delay and, above all, where the debtor is a limited company, confined to the company itself. Summary proceedings have none of these detriments and, as the power to commence such proceedings is given to the Secretary of State by *SSAA 1992*, he may, unless a time or monetary limit presents an insurmountable obstacle, be expected to take the magistrates' court recovery route instead. From 6 April 1999, recovery may be made more easily by distraint under new *SSAA 1992, s 121A* in England and Wales or under new *s 121B* containing similar recovery provisions under Scottish law, both sections inserted by *Social Security Act 1999, s 63* with effect from 6 April 1999. [*The Social Security Act 1998 (Commencement No 4) Order 1999, Reg 2*].

If a person fails to pay, at or within the time prescribed for the purpose, any contribution which he is liable to pay, he was liable on summary conviction to a fine of not more than £1,000. [*SSAA 1992, s 114(1), Criminal Justice Act 1982, s 37(2), Criminal Justice Act 1991, s 17*]. If the contribution remains unpaid at the date of the conviction, he was liable to pay a sum equal to the amount which he failed to pay. [*Sec 119(1)*]. It is no defence against an action for non-payment of contributions to show that there had been no intent to avoid payment, nor is it a defence to have paid the amount outstanding by the time of the court appearance. (*R v Highbury Corner Stipendiary Magistrate, ex p DHSS, The Times, 4 February 1987*). These offences are decriminalised from 6 April 1999 (*Social Security Act 1999 (Commencement No 4) Order 1999, Reg 2*) but some of the replacement civil offences have yet to carry any penalties as the introduction of various measures has been deferred. New interest and penalty (both fixed and tax-related) provisions in relation to the direct payment of Class 1A contributions (i.e. by the 'Alternative Payment Method') are, however, effective from 20 April 1999 (*Regs 47F and 47K introduced by The Social Security (Contributions) Amendment (No 3) Regulations 1999*).

The *Social Security Act 1998* introduced with effect from 6 April 1999 a new *criminal* offence of fraudulent evasion and being knowingly involved in fraudulent evasion of contributions. [*The Social Security Act 1998 (Commencement No 4) Order 1999, Reg 2*]. The offence is brought to trial summarily or on indictment. When tried summarily the maximum fine is to be level 5 (£5,000) on the standard scale. When tried on indictment the maximum penalty will be seven years imprisonment and/or an unlimited fine. [*SSAA 1992, s 114 (1) (2) as amended by Social Security Act 1998, s 61*]. Also, a *civil* penalty is to be introduced for those who fail to pay contributions within the prescribed time limit and removes the need to prove failure to make payment of the particular contribution. Regulations, so far not made because Ministers have decided to delay introduction, will prescribe the amount of the penalty or how it is to be ascertained and the time limits for imposing it. [*SSAA 1992, s 114A as inserted by Social Security Act 1998, section 61*].

Where the offence of non-payment has been committed by a body corporate and is proved to have been committed with the consent or connivance of, or to be attributable to any neglect on the part of, a director, manager, secretary or other similar officer of the body corporate, he, as well as the body corporate, is guilty of the offence and is liable to be proceeded against accordingly. If, furthermore, the affairs of a body corporate are managed by its members, this provision applies to any member who acts or defaults in the manner described in connection with his managerial functions as if he were a director of the body corporate. [*SSAA 1992, s 115*]. In practice, these provisions will, from April 1999, be short-circuited by involving the new offence under *s 114(1)* and *(2)*, mentioned above and/or *s 122K* (see 12.1).

See 39.3 LATE-PAID CONTRIBUTIONS for the meaning of 'connivance'.

In *Dean v Hiesler* [*1942*] *2 AER 430* it was held that the word 'director', if unqualified, means only a person who has been validly appointed a director in accordance with the provisions of the *Companies Acts* and does not extend to a person whose appointment is defective (e.g. by his failure to take up qualification shares as required by the company's articles of association or by the failure of the board of directors properly to convene the meeting at which he is appointed), even though that person may act as a director, describe himself as such, and even give proper notice of his appointment to the registrar of companies.

Because the DSS usually commenced proceedings against a company for a small specimen offence only (see 12.7 below), the Department has, in the past, seldom then moved against the company's directors under *SSAA 1992, s 115* (or its pre-consolidation equivalent) as, by so doing, it would have limited its right of recovery to the amount of that specimen debt. Instead, it was DSS practice, until 12 November 1984, to pursue the directors under *SSA 1975, s 152(4)* and thus, in many cases, recover total arrears (see earlier editions of this work). Following the suspension of the use of *SSA 1975, s 152(4)* on the date mentioned and its repeal by *Insolvency Act 1985, s 235(3), 10 Sch, SSA 1986, s 57(1)* (now consolidated as *SSAA 1992, s 115*) has usually been relied on instead. Similar provisions, intended to be used only against 'phoenix companies' are now to be found at *SSAA 1992 s 121C* (see 12.1 above).

For a detailed description of *prosecution procedure* see 32.9 to 32.15 ENFORCEMENT.

12.5   Evidence of non-payment

Where the contributions in question (however recoverable) are contributions which fall to be paid in the same way as income tax under the PAYE scheme (see 21.2 COLLECTION), a certificate of a collector of taxes that any amount of contributions which a person is liable to pay to that collector for any period has not been paid either to him or, to the best of his knowledge or belief, to any other person to whom it might lawfully be paid, is, until the contrary is proved, to be sufficient evidence in any proceedings before a court that the sum stated in the certificate is unpaid and due. [*SSAA 1992, s 118(1)(2)*]. A document purporting to be such a certificate is to be treated as being such a certificate until the contrary is proved. [*Sec 118(3); Contributions Regs, 1 Sch 27(3)*].

Where non-payment of any contribution, interest or penalty is contested, a certificate of an authorised officer that the searches specified in the declaration for a record of a particular contribution have been made, and that the record in question has not been found, is admissible in any proceedings for an offence as evidence of the facts stated in the declaration *unless*

(*a*)   oral evidence to like effect would not have been admissible; or

(*b*)   a copy of the declaration has not been served on the person charged with the offence seven days or more before the hearing or trial; or

(*c*)   the person charged with the offence gives notice to the prosecutor, not later than three days before the hearing or trial or within such further time as the court may in special circumstances allow, requiring the person who made the declaration to attend the trial. [*SSAA 1992, s 118(4)(6)*].

(*d*) the contrary is proved. [*SSAA 1992, s 118(1), amended by Social Security Act 1998, s 62*, with effect from 6 April 1999 (*The Social Security Act 1998 (Commencement No 4) Order 1999, Reg 2*)].

12.6 Time limits on the recovery of arrears

Where proceedings for the recovery of unpaid contributions are commenced under the recovery provisions relating to income tax (see 12.2 and 12.3 above), the time limits are as follows.

(*a*) Distraint. The date on which the collector of taxes closes his accounts for the year in which the unpaid contributions became due. (*Elliott v Yates [1900] CA 2 QB 370*).

(*b*) Summary proceedings. In the case of Class 4 contributions, six months from the date when the contributions became due irrespective of when the demand was made. (*Mann v Cleaver (1930) 15 TC 367*). In the case of Class 1 contributions, one year from the time the matter complained of first arose. [*Magistrates' Courts Act 1980, s 127(1); TMA 1970, s 65(3)*].

(*c*) County Court and High Court Proceedings. The *Limitation Act 1980*, which applies a general six year bar on action to recover statutorily imposed debts, is of no application to proceedings by the Crown for the recovery of any tax or duty [*Limitation Act 1980, s 9(1), s 37(2)(a)*]. In early editions of this work it was therefore stated that, in view of the taxative nature of social security contributions (see *Metal Industries (Salvage) Ltd v Owners of the S T Harle [1962] SLT 114*), there was no time limit on the commencement of High Court proceedings for their recovery. However, in a letter to the editor of the Payroll Journal, the Chief Executive of the Contributions Agency at the time, Ann Chant, stated that 'the Limitation Act 1980 restricts the time allowed for us to enforce payment of those arrears by civil proceedings to six years from when the debt arose,' and this is clearly the reverse position. In the same letter, justifying the Agency's practice of requesting payment of contributions for periods of more than six years, she wrote, 'As you will no doubt appreciate, we have a duty to protect the public purse and collect all arrears of national insurance contributions whenever they are discovered. If unmet liability exists the amount must be assessed and requested. Failure to do this would be unfair to those contributors and employers who pay correctly and on time.'

The Inland Revenue Enforcement Manual states; 'For NIC, the time limit is six years from the date that it became due and payable *but* the six year period starts afresh from the date the person liable (or their agent) acknowledges the debt in writing or makes part payment.' Paras E1305–1306, issue 4/96.

Because all the provisions of the Income Tax Acts, including those relating to collection and recovery are to apply in relation to Class 4 contributions, the Crown exception to the Limitation Act in respect of tax or duty will apply to unpaid Class 4 contributions which may therefore be recovered in respect of periods more than six years before. [*Limitation Act 1980, s 37(2)(a), SSCBA 1992, s 16(2)*]. Again, the Inland Revenue Enforcement Manual comments as follows; 'The time limit within which proceedings can be started in the County Court is governed generally by *section 9(1) Limitation Act 1980*. This provides that an action must be brought within six years from the date of the cause of action but, *section 37(2)* of the same Act, *excludes* proceedings for recovery of tax (but not NIC) from this restriction.' Paras E1305–1306, issue 4/96.

In December 1999 the Revenue served a statutory demand relating to a judgment debt, comprising unpaid income tax, which was more than six years' old. The debtor applied to have the demand set aside, on the grounds that the judgment debt was statute-barred under *Limitation Act 1980, s 24*. The registrar dismissed the application and authorised the Revenue to present a bankruptcy petition, but the Ch D allowed the debtor's appeal. Hart J held that presenting a bankruptcy petition based on a judgment debt was within *Limitation Act 1980, s 24*, and that in the case in question, it was not permissible to present a bankruptcy petition in respect of the debt. *Re A Debtor (No 647of 1999), Ch D 22 February 2000 unreported. (Note.* At the time of writing, no transcript of this judgment is available).

As the payment of Class 3 contributions is voluntary, no question of enforcing their payment can arise.

Although the *Limitation Act 1980, s 9(1)* prevents an action to recover any sum recoverable by virtue of any enactment from being brought after the expiration of six years from the date on which the cause of action accrued, *s 29(5)* of that Act treats the cause of action as having accrued on the date that any person liable for a debt, or his authorised agent, acknowledges it in a signed document or makes any payment in respect of it. Acknowledgment of a smaller sum than that demanded is an acknowledgment only of that smaller sum (*Surrendra Overseas Ltd v Government of Sri Lanka [1977] 2 AER 481*), whereas a general admission of debt will be regarded as an acknowledgment of the whole of the debt if the precise amount can be ascertained by extrinsic evidence (*Dungate v Dungate [1965] 3 AER 818*).

Since the *Limitation Act 1980, s 9(1)* does not extinguish the right to a debt over six years' old, but merely deprives the authorities of a remedy of action for its enforcement, the authorities are entitled to apply any payment that is less than the amount demanded and which does not identify the debts that it is to settle, to the statute-barred debts first. More recently the CA acknowledged that it was bound by the *Limitation Act* to the six year time limit but it would still send a 'request for payment' for the whole amount in the first instance (CA Consultation Panel, 11 December 1995).

The expression 'cause of action' means the factual situation stated by a plaintiff which (if substantiated) entitles the plaintiff to a remedy at law against the defendant (*Letang v Cooper [1964] 2 AER 929*). In the case of a national insurance contribution, it is simply the date on which the payment of the contribution first becomes overdue. (See 21.6 and 21.9 COLLECTION for due dates). An action is 'brought' in the High Court when a writ or originating summons is issued and in a county court when a summons or originating application is issued, and time continues to run until that date. It follows, therefore, that a mere request or even a demand for payment of outstanding contributions not yet six years overdue will be of no consequence if they are more than six years overdue by the time a writ or summons is issued.

Limitation Act 1980, s 32 merits careful attention, however. It provides that where any fact relevant to the plaintiff's right of action has been deliberately concealed from him by the defendant, the period of limitation does not begin to run until the plaintiff has discovered the concealment or could with reasonable diligence have discovered it. That section then goes on to provide that, for this purpose, deliberate commission of a breach of duty in circumstances in which it is unlikely to be discovered for some time amounts to deliberate concealment of the facts involved in that breach of duty. In the majority of cases where the IR seeks to recover arrears of contributions, those arrears will have arisen through ignorance and there will have been no deliberate concealment of liability or deliberate commission of a breach of duty by the contributor. If, however, the IR can show that in any particular case there *was* deliberate concealment of liability or deliberate commission of a breach of duty by the contributor *and* that the IR could not with reasonable diligence have discovered it, time will run not from the due date of the contributions in question but from the date of discovery by the IR.

From correspondence, it appears that the DSS equated any ignorance or misunderstanding of the law, giving rise to a potential contributor's failure to make contributions (or to claim exception therefrom), with a *deliberate* breach of duty by that individual. This interpretation of *Limitation Act 1980, s 32*, which effectively denies that the commission of an offence can be an honest blunder (see *King v Victor Parsons & Co [1973] 1 WLR 29*) is unsupportable and, were it correct, would prevent that section applying to any situation in which there has been a failure to make proper contributions.

Where summary proceedings under the old *SSAA 1992, s 114(1)* were the chosen means of recovery (see 12.4 above), they must be commenced within the period of *three months* from the date on which evidence, sufficient in the opinion of the Secretary of State to justify a prosecution for the offence, comes to his knowledge. [*SSAA 1992, s 116(2)*]. A certificate signed by or on behalf of the Secretary of State as to that date is conclusive evidence of the date. [*SSAA 1992, s 116(3)*]. Alternatively, proceedings may be commenced within the period of *twelve months* after the commission of the offence, if that period expires later than the three month period. [*SSAA 1992, s 116(2)*]. In practice, the three month provision is rarely needed for reasons which the following example will make clear.

Example
On 7 October 1998, Arnold deducts a primary Class 1 contribution from the wage he pays to Brian, his employee, but fails to pay this or his related secondary Class 1 contribution to the Collector of Taxes. The remittance is due within 14 days after the end of the tax month in which the deduction took place and A, therefore, commits an offence on 19 November 1998. Even if the offence comes to the knowledge of the DSS before 18 November 1999, no proceedings need be commenced until then since that is when the twelve month period expires. If, however, the DSS does not become aware of the offence until *after* 18 November 1999 (a most unlikely eventuality as failure to submit end-of-year returns to the collector of taxes by then will have resulted in an inspection, and the returns or the inspection will have revealed the non-payment) it will have three months from the date of discovery in which to commence proceedings.

12.7 **Practice regarding prosecution**

For the sake of clarity, it must be stated that a separate offence is committed each time an employer fails to pay a contribution in respect of one of his employees and each time a self-employed earner fails to pay a Class 2 contribution which he is liable to pay. In periods before April 1993, when Class 2 contributions were due weekly and a contributor was expected to buy a Class 2 stamp, each failure to buy a stamp was a separate offence.

Example
Cliff had 100 monthly-paid employees. In paying their wages for the month ended 31 August 1999 he deducted primary Class 1 contributions but by 20 September had failed to make a remittance to the collector of taxes. He also failed to purchase a Class 2 stamp for himself for each week in August. C had committed 105 separate offences!

If, in a situation such as that given above, the DSS commenced proceedings in the magistrates' court under the old provisions of *SSAA 1992, s 114(1)*, doing so for only one of the latest offences of which it had concrete proof and, having obtained a conviction for that offence, would then offer a single certificate supplied by a Collector of Taxes (see 12.5 above) as evidence of the other offences and would ask for an order to be made for the total amount. Because the size of debt has an equal bearing on the choice of forum in which proceedings may be brought, whether brought under the old *Sec 114(1)* or under the tax recovery provisions (see 12.6 above), the specimen offence which is chosen would, where possible, relate to an unpaid contribution of under £2,000 (from 6 April 1996) in order that the proceedings may be brought in a magistrates' court (see 12.2 above).

The introduction of quarterly billing for Class 2 contributions and the abolition of the requirement to pay weekly with effect from 6 April 1993 reduces the opportunity for an offence to be committed.

Further, from 6 April 1999 distraint procedures will, in preference, be followed (*SSAA 1992, s 121A* — England and Wales — or *SSAA 1992, s 121B* — Scotland).

12.8 Arrears recoverable as a penalty

Any sum which a person is liable to pay on conviction for non-payment of contributions is recoverable from him as a penalty. [*SSAA 1992, s 121(4)*]. This does not mean that the sum is a penalty: it is not; and the sum cannot, therefore, be mitigated, for example, under *Magistrates Court Act 1980, s 34(1)*, in the way that a penalty can be mitigated. (*Leach v Litchfield [1960] 3 AER 739*). Nor do the words 'liable to pay' import any discretion. They are equivalent in meaning to 'shall be ordered to pay' and magistrates cannot, therefore, decline to make an order for payment of arrears where such arrears have been proved. (*Shilvock v Booth [1956] 1 AER 382 per Lord Goddard CJ at p 384; R v Melksham Justices, ex p Williams, The Times, 15 March 1983*). Once an order has been made, it is not appropriate for the prosecution to be requested to commence civil proceedings for recovery (see 12.2 above). (*Morgan v Quality Tools and Engineering (Stourbridge) Ltd [1972] 1 AER 744*).

A sum ordered to be paid under *SSAA 1992, s 120* (i.e. after summary proceedings), is not enforceable against the defendant as a civil debt. (*R v Marlow (Bucks) JJ, ex p Schiller [1957] 2 AER 783*). A defendant who fails to comply with an order is, therefore, liable to be committed to prison under *Magistrates' Courts Act 1980, 4 Sch* for up to 90 days.

The *Social Security Act 1998* provides for distraint action to be taken in England and Wales where a person served with a certificate confirming their debt, fails to make payment within 30 days. A magistrate's warrant is required for forced entry to premises and, where necessary, the assistance of a constable may also be secured. Any goods distrained will be held for a five-day period and then sold by auction. After recovery of the debt the balance of the proceeds, if any, are to be paid to the debtor. Premises does not include a private dwelling house unless an authorised officer has reasonable grounds to believe that a trade or business is being carried on from those premises. [*SSAA 1992, s 121A inserted by Social Security Act 1998, s 63*].

DISTRESS WARRANT   SO No. *2/99*

Derby & South Derbyshire Magistrates' Court (Code)

Date	*2 May 1999*
Debtor	*A Smith T/A Racing Services*
Address	*1–5 Epsom Road, Derby*
Amount ordered	
To be paid	*£867.00*
Costs	*£16.50* (including the fee paid by the complainant for the minute of the order)

The debtor was on   20. . .   at   Magistrates' Court ordered to pay the sums specified above [by...] [immediately]. The debtor has been served with a copy of a minute of the order and default has been made in the payment.

Total amount still outstanding	*£883.50*
Costs of issuing this warrant	*£6.50*
Amount now payable	*£890.00*

Direction:

You [the Constables of   Police Force] are required immediately to make distress of the money and goods of the debtor (except the clothing and bedding of the debtor and the debtor's family and the tools and implements of the debtor's trade; and if the amount shown as now payable, together with the costs and charges of taking and keeping the distress, is not paid, then not earlier than the sixth day after the making of the distress, unless the debtor consents in writing to an earlier sale, to sell the goods and pay the proceeds of the distress to the Clerk of the   Magistrates' Court and if [no] [insufficient] distress can be found, to certify the same to that Magistrates' Court.

Magistrate/Justice of the Peace
[By order of the Court/Clerk of the Court]

In Scotland, pointing proceedings under *Debtors (Scotland) Act 1987, Sch 5* can be instituted where a person has been served with a certificate confirming the debt (*s 118(1)* above) but fails to make payment within 30 days. A sheriff's summary warrant is required for recovery and sale by way of pointing. Applications must be accompanied by the certificate of debt and a certificate stating that it (the certificate of debt) was served on the person in question and the debt remains unpaid. [*SSAA 1992, s 121B inserted by Social Security Act 1998, s 63*].

12.9   BANKRUPTCY, LIQUIDATION AND RECEIVERSHIP

In the winding-up of a company and in the distribution of a bankrupt's estate, certain unpaid national insurance contributions are preferential debts and rank equally with, and fall to be paid along with, other preferential debts in priority to all other debts. The Collector of Taxes at Worthing (Central Office) will initially advance the bankruptcy process against the debtor with a statutory demand. This provides a period of 21 days during which the debt must be paid or 18 days in which to make an application to the court to set aside the demand. In this latter case there must be a very strong argument for success in setting aside the demand. A figure of £750 or greater must be shown by the Revenue for their application to proceed. [*Insolvency Act 1986, ss 175, 328(1), 6 Sch, paras 6 and 7*].

The contributions in question are

(a) all sums which, on the relevant date (see below) are due from the company which is being wound up or, as the case may be, the bankrupt, on account of

Class 1 or Class 2 contributions which became due from the company or the bankrupt concerned in the twelve months preceding the relevant date; and

(*b*) all sums (not exceeding, in the whole, any one year's assessment) which have been assessed on the bankrupt up to 5 April next before the relevant date and are due to the Inland Revenue (rather than to the DSS) from the bankrupt on account of Class 4 contributions.

[*Insolvency Act 1986, 6 Sch, paras 6 and 7*].

In relation to a company, the *relevant date* is,

(i) in the case of a company being wound up by the court where the winding-up order was made immediately upon the discharge of the administration order, the date of the making of the administration order;

(ii) in a case not falling within (i) above where a company being wound up by the court had not commenced to be wound up voluntarily before the date of the making of the winding-up order, the date of the appointment (or first appointment) of a provisional liquidator, or, if no such appointment has been made, the date of the winding-up order, and

(iii) in any other case, the date of the passing of the resolution for the winding-up of the company.

[*Insolvency Act 1986, s 387(3)*].

In relation to a bankrupt, the *relevant date* is,

(A) where at the time the bankruptcy order was made, there was an interim receiver of the debtor's estate appointed under *Insolvency Act 1986, s 286*, the date on which the interim receiver was first appointed after the presentation of the bankruptcy petition; and

(B) in any other case, the date of the making of the bankruptcy order.

[*Insolvency Act 1986, s 387(6)*].

Example
The dissolution of a company may come to the notice of NICO where there are outstanding NICs due and the following letter is likely to be sent to Companies House in accordance with instructions in the CA Field Operations Manual, standard letter. [*Companies Act 1985, ss 652, 652A*]:

'I understand that action under Section 652 of the Companies Act 1985 has started for the above-named company. This company has failed to pay contributions under the Social Security Contributions and Benefits Act 1992 and it may be necessary to start proceedings against the company to recover the unpaid contributions. Please do not take any further steps to strike-off the name of the company from the Register.'

12.10 Set-off of Crown debts

Under *Insolvency Act 1986, s 323* (in the case of the distribution of a bankrupt's estate) and *Insolvency Rules 1986, Rule 4.90* (in the case of the distribution of the property of a company which is being wound up), sums due from and to parties involved in mutual dealings are to be set off against each other, and this applies to Crown debts such as VAT, income tax and social security contributions. (*Re Cushla Ltd [1979] STC 615*). The set-off rules were formerly contained in *Bankruptcy Act 1914, s 31* (now repealed) which, by virtue of *Companies Act 1985, s 612* (also repealed) applied also in the case of the winding-up of an insolvent company. Thus, in *R A Cullen Ltd v Nottingham Health Authority, The Times, 1 August 1986* it was held that a health authority obtaining services and materials from an outside supplier did so as an agent of the Crown and that the supplier of such services and materials could, therefore under *Bankruptcy Act 1914, s 31* as applied by *Companies Act 1985, s 612*, set money due to it from the health authority in that respect against its arrears of national insurance contributions.

In the case of *CIR v Lawrence & Another, Ch D 10 February 2000 All ER (D) 157* administration orders were made in respect of a number of associated companies. One of the companies continued to trade and to pay its employees. The administrators failed to pay PAYE and NIC deductions to the Revenue. The Revenue applied to the Ch D, which held that the administrators were required to pay these sums. The effect of *Insolvency Act 1986, s 19 (5)* was that PAYE and primary Class 1 National Insurance contributions enjoyed special priority over the general expenses of the administrators, since 'administrators should not be encouraged to fund an administration with PAYE or NIC deductions they have made or will make from the salary roll'. However, the Ch D held that this special priority did *not* extend to secondary Class 1 NICs.

12.11 WAIVER OF ARREARS

Standing instructions (unpublished) provide for officials to waive proceedings for arrears where, for example, a person would have been entitled to exception from contribution liability had he claimed it, or where it would not be practicable to recover the arrears because of a person's financial circumstances. (Hansard 24 February 1978 Vol 944 No 67 Col 836). There is no limit to the amount which may be so waived and authority for granting waivers has, since April 1983, been delegated to local office management. Previously, authority rested with regional financial officers. DSS guidance to its local offices suggested that, in deciding whether a waiver should be granted, they should take account of such factors as whether there was a genuine and reasonable doubt about the class of contribution payable, whether the DSS or another Government Department may have misdirected the employer on national insurance contribution liability, and the size of the arrears. In combination with one or more of those factors, local offices may take into account the assets of the employer (Hansard 20 July 1988 Vol 137 Col 683). It is understood, for example, that individuals will not normally be pursued for arrears of contributions if they are in receipt of income support (or jobseeker's allowance) and unlikely to be able to pay any sums demanded. There are grounds for believing also that, where liability is contested and recovery of alleged arrears would involve costly litigation, the DSS *might* have been prepared to settle for significantly less than the amount due.

12.12 PAYMENT OF ARREARS BY INSTALMENTS

Rather than take proceedings against a defaulting contributor, NICO will, wherever possible, make an arrangement which will enable him to discharge his liabilities over a period of time. The arrangement will normally involve the contributor's agreement to pay by instalments an agreed amount of contribution arrears (possibly a lesser amount than the actual contribution debt—see 12.11 above) over a period of 12 months or longer. The arrangements will be set down in writing on a form CA 5719 (for a company or other business) or form CA 5721 (self-employed contributor) which must be signed by the contributor and will contain, in addition to the instalment terms, both an admission of liability and a declaration of inability to pay in full. Failure to adhere to the arrangement will, of course, result in the proceedings being taken against the contributor and, in that event, the admission of liability on the form CA 5719 or CA 5721 will be evidence of the unpaid debt.

12.13 TAX RELIEF FOR CLASS 1 CONTRIBUTION ARREARS

No tax relief may be obtained in respect of any primary element of Class 1 contribution arrears which are paid by an employer. [*ICTA 1988, s 617(3)(a)*]. This is so despite the fact that the employer may be debarred from recovering the primary contributions from the employee to whose earnings they relate. (See 15.8 CLASS 1 CONTRIBUTIONS, 14.13 CATEGORISATION and 21.4 COLLECTION). Relief may be obtained in respect of the secondary element of the arrears, however, but difficulties may be encountered with the Inland Revenue in this respect. Inspectors of taxes have been known to cite *James Spencer and Co v IRC (1950) 32 TC 111* as authority for the proposition that secondary Class 1 contribution arrears paid must be allowed as a deduction from trading profits in the year in which they are paid rather than in the years to which they relate. The case cited establishes no such principle. The liabilities there in question were contingent liabilities, not matured liabilities. By contrast, Class 1 arrears comprise liabilities which have fully matured in earlier years and it is, therefore, in those earlier years that relief should be given (*Simpson v Jones (1968) 44 TC 599*). The machinery for obtaining relief in years for which tax assessments have become final is the 'error or mistake' claim provided for by *TMA 1970, s 33*.

The *FA 1997, s 65* change to *ICTA 1988, s 617* gives effect to the fact that the section needed amendment due to the requirement to legislate ESC B48 so that Class 1A national insurance contributions be allowed as a deduction in arriving at profits or gains. *FA 1997, s 65(3)* inserts *subsection 4* to *ICTA 1988, s 617* that allows the deduction of Class 1A contributions from profits and gains where the Class 1A contributions are paid on or after 26 November 1996. In practice relief will be given on an extra statutory basis for earlier payments.

13 Benefits: Contribution Requirements

Cross-references. See CONTRACTED-OUT EMPLOYMENTS (23); CREDITS (24) for circumstances in which contributions will be awarded rather than paid; 26.4 DEATH OF CONTRIBUTOR for widow's right to make good her deceased husband's contribution record; EARNINGS FACTORS (29) for calculation of factors; NATIONAL INSURANCE NUMBER (46) for contribution records; WORKING CASE STUDY (58).

Other Sources. Tolley's Social Security and State Benefits Handbook 2000–01.

13.1 GENERAL CONSIDERATIONS

Contributions payable under the provisions and regulations described in this work are levied with the primary objective of providing funds for the payment of contributory benefits (see NATIONAL INSURANCE FUND (45)). [*SSCBA 1992, s 1(1)*]. Non-contributory benefits (with the exception of guardian's allowance) are paid by the Exchequer and include the following

— social fund payments (maternity, funeral, cold weather);
— attendance allowance;
— severe disablement allowance;
— invalid care allowance;
— category C and D retirement pensions;
— age addition;
— child benefit;
— guardian's allowance;
— one-parent benefit;
— family credit;
— housing benefit;
— income support (see jobseeker's allowance below);
— disability living allowance;
— council tax benefit.

[*SSCBA 1992, ss 63–79 as amended by the Social Security (Severe Disablement Allowance and Invalid Care Allowance) Amendment Regulations 1994; Social Security Pensions Act 1975, s 22*].

Non-contributory benefits are of no further concern in this work. Contributory benefits (marked with an asterisk in the table of rates below) and the particular class of contribution are of concern, however, and include

		Class
(*a*)	contribution-based jobseeker's allowance;	1
(*b*)	statutory sick pay†;	1
(*c*)	statutory maternity pay†;	1
(*d*)	incapacity benefit;	1 and 2
(*e*)	maternity allowance;	1 and 2
(*f*)	widow's payment;	1, 2 and 3
(*g*)	widowed mother's allowance;	1, 2 and 3
(*h*)	widow's pension;	1, 2 and 3
(*i*)	category A and B retirement pensions.	1, 2 and 3

† Strictly no contribution is necessary but the receipt of SSP and SMP is compromised for an employee with *average* earnings below the NIC lower earnings limit. This remains the applicable earnings limit notwithstanding that, from 6 April 2000, employees do not pay contributions until earnings reach the primary earnings threshold.

SOCIAL SECURITY
Benefit Rates for 2000/2001

	Old rate	New rate
Attendance Allowance		
Higher rate	£52.95	£53.55
Lower rate	£35.40	£35.80
Child Benefit		
First or only child	£14.40	£15.00
Lone parent – first or elder child	£17.10	£17.55
Each subsequent child	£9.60	£10.00
Disability Living Allowance		
Care component		
– highest	£52.95	£53.55
– middle	£35.40	£35.80
– lowest	£14.05	£14.20
Mobility component		
– higher	£37.00	£37.40
– lower	£14.05	£14.20
Earnings rule		
Invalid Care Allowance	£50.00	£50.00
Incapacity Benefit*		
Long term benefit	£66.75	£67.50
– increase for age (higher)	£14.05	£14.20
– increase for age (lower)	£7.05	£7.10
Short-term benefit (under pension age)		
– lower rate	£50.35	£50.90
– higher rate	£59.55	£60.20
Short-term benefit (over pension age)		
– lower rate	£64.05	£64.75
higher rate	£66.75	£67.50
Invalidity allowance (transitional)		
– lower rate	£4.45	£4.50
– middle rate	£8.90	£9.00
– higher rate	£14.05	£14.20
Exemption limit	£58.00	£58.50
Income Support		
Single/lone parent		
– under 18 (usual)	£30.95	£31.45
– 18 to 24	£40.70	£41.35
– 25 or over	£51.40	£52.20
Couple		
– both under 18	£61.35	£62.35
– one/both over 18	£80.65	£81.95

	Old rate	New rate
Industrial Death Benefit		
Widow's pension		
– higher rate	£66.75	£67.50
– lower rate	£20.03	£20.25
Industrial Disablement Pension		
18 or over (max)	£108.10	£109.30
Under 18 (max)	£66.20	£67.50
Invalid Care Allowance	£39.95	£40.40
Jobseeker's Allowance		
Single 25 or over	£51.40	£52.20
Couple both 18 or over	£80.65	£81.95
Maternity Allowance		
Higher rate	£59.95	£60.20
Lower rate	£51.70	£52.25
Retirement Pension*		
Category A or B	£66.75	£67.50
Category B (lower)		
– husband's contribution	£39.95	£40.40
Category C or D		
– non-contributory	£39.95	£40.40
Category C (lower)		
– non-contributory	£23.90	£24.14
Additional pension		
Addition at age 80	£0.25	£0.25
Severe Disablement Allowance		
Basic rate	£40.35	£40.80
Age related addition		
– higher rate	£14.05	£14.20
– middle rate	£8.90	£9.00
– lower rate	£4.45	£4.50
Statutory Maternity Pay*		
Earnings threshold	£66.00	£67.00
Lower rate	£59.55	£60.20
Statutory Sick Pay*		
Earnings threshold	£66.00	£67.00
Standard rate	£59.55	£60.20
Widow's Benefit*		
Widow's payment (lump sum)	£1000.00	£1000.00
Widowed mother's allowance	£66.75	£67.50
Widow's pension (standard)	£66.75	£67.50

13.2   Benefits: Contribution Requirements

[*SSCBA 1992, s 20(1)*].

The new weekly rates of the major benefits shown above apply from the first full week in April, i.e. week commencing 10 April 2000 which represents for most of the benefits an increase in line with the retail prices index up to September 1999 of 1.1%.

A category A pension is a retirement pension claimed on a person's own contribution record whereas a category B pension (see above) is the same retirement pension claimed on the record of a spouse, former spouse or deceased spouse. Category C and D pensions are, however, non-contributory retirement pensions payable respectively to people who reached pensionable age before 5 July 1948 (and thus have no contribution record) and people aged 80 or over whose contribution record is so inadequate that they receive no category A pension or one which is very small.

For a person to become entitled to any of these benefits, he must satisfy not only any circumstantial conditions attaching to the benefit concerned (for which see Tolley's Social Security and State Benefits Handbook 2000–01) but also various contribution conditions.

13.2   CONTRIBUTION CONDITIONS

All references below to the payment of Class 1 contributions includes, from 6 April 2000, receipt of earnings subject to Class 1 equal to or exceeding the lower earnings limit but on which no contributions have actually been paid due to the earnings not exceeding the earnings threshold. [*SSCBA 1992, s 6A(2) inserted by Welfare Reform and Pensions Act 1999, Sch 9, para 3 , and The Social Security Contributions (Notional Payment of Primary Class 1 Contributions) Regulations 2000, SI 2000/747*].

Most contributory benefits have two contribution conditions attached. The first contribution condition for

(*a*) contribution-based jobseeker's allowance (and, previously, unemployment benefit) is that, before the day in respect of which benefit is claimed, the claimant has actually paid primary Class 1 contributions in respect of one of the last two complete tax years before the benefit year in which the beginning of the period of interruption of employment falls, and that the EARNINGS FACTORS (29) derived from earnings on which primary Class 1 contributions have been paid or treated as paid is not less than 25 *times* that year's weekly lower earnings limit (see *SSCBA 1992, s 21, 3 Sch 1; JSA 1995, s 2* and 30 EARNINGS LIMITS);

(*b*) short-term incapacity benefit (and, previously, sickness benefit) is that, before the day in respect of which benefit is claimed, the claimant has actually paid primary Class 1 contributions or Class 2 contributions in respect of any one tax year and that the EARNINGS FACTOR (29) derived from earnings on which primary Class 1 contributions have been paid or treated as paid or from Class 2 contributions is not less than 25 *times* that year's weekly lower earnings limit (see *SSCBA 1992, s 21, 3 Sch 2* and 30 EARNINGS LIMITS);

(*c*) maternity allowance is that the claimant has actually paid primary Class 1 contributions (other than at the reduced rate) or Class 2 contributions in respect of at least each of 26 weeks in the 66 weeks immediately preceding the fourteenth week before the expected week of confinement [*SSCBA 1992, s 35(1), 3 Sch 3*];

(*d*) widow's payment is that the contributor concerned (i.e. the claimant, the claimant's spouse, or the claimant's former spouse, etc.) has actually paid primary Class 1 contributions or Class 2 contributions or Class 3 contributions in respect of any tax year ending before the date on which the contributor concerned attained pensionable age or died under that age, and that the EARNINGS FACTOR (29) derived from earnings on which primary Class 1 contributions have been paid or treated as paid and from any Class 2 contributions or Class 3 contributions is not less than *25 times* that year's weekly lower earnings limit (see *SSCBA 1992, 3 Sch 4, 7* and 30 EARNINGS LIMITS);

(*e*)   widowed mother's allowance, widow's pension, category A and B retirement pensions is that the contributor concerned (i.e. the claimant, the claimant's spouse, or the claimant's former spouse, etc.) has actually paid primary Class 1 contributions or Class 2 contributions or Class 3 contributions in respect of any one tax year ending before the date on which the contributor concerned attained pensionable age or died under that age, and that the EARNINGS FACTOR (29) derived from earnings on which primary Class 1 contributions have been paid or treated as paid and from any Class 2 contributions or Class 3 contributions is not less than *52 times* that year's weekly lower earnings limit (see *SSCBA 1992, 3 Sch 5* and 30 EARNINGS LIMITS).

[*SSCBA 1992, s 21(1)(2) and 3 Sch 1, 2, 3, 4, 5*].

There is no first contribution condition in respect of long-term incapacity benefit because that benefit rests on eligibility for, and is in continuation of, short-term incapacity benefit, statutory sick pay or, previously, sickness benefit.

The second contribution condition for

(i)   contribution-based jobseeker's allowance (and, previously, unemployment benefit) is that, in respect of the last two complete tax years before the beginning of the benefit year in which the beginning of the period of interruption of employment falls, the claimant has paid (or is treated as having paid) primary Class 1 contributions on earnings, or has been credited with earnings, from which he has derived an EARNINGS FACTOR (29) of not less, in each of those years, than *50 times* the year's weekly lower earnings limit (see 30 EARNINGS LIMITS);

(ii)   short-term incapacity benefit (and, previously, sickness benefit) is that, in respect of the last two complete tax years before the beginning of the benefit year in which the beginning of the period of interruption of employment falls, the claimant has either paid or been credited with Class 2 contributions, or has paid (or is treated as having paid) primary Class 1 contributions on earnings, or been credited with earnings, from which he has derived an EARNINGS FACTOR (29) of not less, in each of those years, than *50 times* the year's weekly lower earnings limit (see 30 EARNINGS LIMITS);

(iii)   widowed mother's allowance, widow's pension, category A and B retirement pensions is that, in respect of each of the requisite number of tax years of his working life, the contributor concerned has either paid or been credited with Class 2 or Class 3 contributions, or has paid (or is treated as having paid) primary Class 1 contributions on earnings, or been credited with earnings, from which he has derived an EARNINGS FACTOR (29) of not less, in each of those years, than *52 times* the year's weekly lower earnings limit (see 30 EARNINGS LIMITS).

[*SSCBA 1992, s 21(1)(2) and 3 Sch 1, 2, 3, 4, 5*].

The requisite number of tax years in respect of each of which the *second* contribution condition must have been satisfied in connection with a claim for widowed mother's allowance, widow's pension, or category A or B retirement pension depends on the duration of the working life of the contributor concerned. A person's 'working life' is the period between (inclusive) the tax year in which he attained the age of 16 and (exclusive) the tax year in which he attained pensionable age or died under that age. [*SSCBA 1992, 3 Sch 5(8)*].

13.3 Benefits: Contribution Requirements

Duration of 'working life'	'Requisite number of years' = the number of years of the working life minus
10 years or less	1
20 years or less (but more than 10)	2
30 years or less (but more than 20)	3
40 years or less (but more than 30)	4
more than 40 years	5

[*SSCBA 1992, 3 Sch 5(5)*].

There is no second contribution condition for maternity allowance or widow's payment.

13.3 ADDITIONAL PENSIONS

Insofar as the contribution conditions described at 13.2 above relate to long-term incapacity benefit, widow's pension, widowed mother's allowance and category A or B retirement pension, they relate only to the *basic* pension and allowance. An *additional* pension or allowance is payable also if the contributor concerned is not in CONTRACTED-OUT EMPLOYMENT (23). [*SSCBA 1992, ss 33(3), 39(1)(2), 41(4)(5), 44(3)(4), 48B(3)(4), 51(2) amended by Pensions Act 1995, 4 Sch*].

The additional Category A pension is the weekly equivalent of a specified percentage applied to the amount of the surpluses (if any) in the pensioner's EARNINGS FACTORS (29) in tax years beginning with the year 1978–79. The percentage rate and the surpluses to which it is to be applied are determined by reference to the tax year in which the pensioner attains pensionable age, viz:

(a) 1998–99 or earlier—$1\frac{1}{4}\%$ of the surplus in 1978–79 and each subsequent year.

(b) 2008–09 or earlier but after 1998–99—25/N% of the surplus in 1978–79 and each subsequent year up to and including 1987–88, plus (20 + X)/N% of the surplus in 1988–89 and each subsequent year, where N is the number of tax years in the pensioner's working life and X is 0.5 for each tax year by which the tax year in which the pensioner attains pensionable age precedes the tax year 2008–09.

(c) 2009–10 or later—25/N% of the surplus in 1978–79 and each subsequent year up to and including 1987–88, plus 20/N% of the surplus in 1988–89 and each subsequent year, where N is the number of tax years in the pensioner's working life.

[*SSCBA 1992, s 45(1)*].

With the phased movement of the pensionable age for women from 60 to 65 over the period 2010–2020, the calculation in (c) will vary between women over the ten year period from 2010 (see 3.7 AGE EXCEPTION).

The additional Category B pension for a widower is to be calculated as above except that references to the pensioner are to be taken as references to his wife. [*SSCBA 1992, s 51(2)*].

The additional Category B pension for a widow, widowed mother's allowance, widow's pension or invalidity pension for widowers in a case where the deceased spouse dies under pensionable age is to be calculated as above except that N is the lesser of 49 (where the deceased spouse was male) or 44 (where the deceased spouse was female) and the number of tax years beginning with 1978–79 and ending with the tax year preceding the tax year in which entitlement to the additional pension begins. [*SSCBA 1992, s 46(2) as amended by Pensions Act 1995, 4 Sch 5*].

Similarly, until 5 April 1995, the additional invalidity pension for persons under pensionable age was to be calculated as above except that N was the lesser of 49 (where the person entitled to the pension was male) or 44 (where the person entitled to the pension was female) and the number of tax years beginning with 1978–79 and ending with the tax year preceding the first day of entitlement to the additional pension in the period of interruption of employment in which that day falls. [*SSCBA 1992, s 46(1)*].

There is a surplus in an earnings factor of a contributor concerned for a relevant year if that factor, revalued under the *Revaluation of Earnings Factors Orders 1979 to date* exceeds the qualifying earnings factor (see 29.6 EARNINGS FACTORS) for the tax year immediately preceding the tax year in which pensionable age is attained. A contributor's earnings factor for these purposes is the aggregate of his earnings factors from earnings upon which primary Class 1 contributions were paid or treated as paid in respect of that year and earnings factors derived from Class 2 and Class 3 contributions actually paid by him in respect of a year. [*SSCBA 1992, s 44(5)–(7)*].

13.4 European law

EC Reg 1408/71 co-ordinates benefit entitlement for migrant workers within the EEA. The detailed rules are beyond the scope of this work, but one example of co-ordination may be found in *Art 18*. Where UK legislation makes the acquisition, retention or recovery of the right to sickness and maternity benefits conditional upon the completion of periods of insurance, employment or residence, the DSS must (to the extent necessary) take account of periods of insurance, employment or residence completed under the legislation of any other member state as if they were periods completed under UK legislation. In this connection also see *Lurlalo v Instituto Nazionale della Previdenza Sociale [1998] All ER (ECJ) 366* for treatment of unemployment periods in one member state extending the reference period in another member state in respect of invalidity benefit.

However, European Regulations will not always hold sway. This may be amply demonstrated by *Art 48* and the case of *Graf v Filzmoser Maschinenbau Gmb H [2000] All E R (ECJ) 170* where a German national terminated his contract of employment in Austria to commence new employment in Germany and claimed compensation (two months' salary). The Advocate General concluded that

'... Art 48 of the Treaty does not preclude national provisions which deny a worker entitlement to compensation on termination of the employment if he terminates his contract of employment in another member state, when those provisions grant him entitlement to such compensation if the contract ends without termination being at his own initiative or attributable to him.'

A further example was the Northern Irish Court of Appeal case regarding full pay for maternity leave known as the 'Gillespie' case referred to by the ECJ. In the judgment on 13 February 1996 the Court stated that account must be taken of any backdated pay rises where a woman's maternity pay is calculated without taking account of pay increases during maternity leave. Regulations effective from June 1996 redress the balance.

14 Categorisation

Cross-references. See AGENCY WORKERS (4); AIRMEN (6); APPEALS AND REVIEWS (9) for means of contesting categorisation decisions; APPRENTICES, TRAINEES AND STUDENTS (10); ARMED FORCES (11); COMPANY DIRECTORS (22); CROWN SERVANTS AND STATUTORY EMPLOYEES (25); ENTERTAINERS (33); EXAMINERS (34); HOMEWORKERS AND OUTWORKERS (35); HUSBAND AND WIFE (36); LABOUR-ONLY CONTRACTORS (38); LECTURERS, TEACHERS AND INSTRUCTORS (41); MARINERS (42); MINISTERS OF RELIGION (43); OIL-RIG WORKERS, DIVERS, ETC. (48); PARTNERS (50); SHARE FISHERMEN (54); SUBPOSTMASTERS (55); VOLUNTEER DEVELOPMENT WORKERS (57); WORKING CASE STUDY (58).

Other Sources. Simon's NIC, Part I, Section 2, Chapter 4; Tolley's National Insurance Contributions Brief, July 1996, pages 53–55 and August 1996, pages 57–60; Inland Revenue leaflets IR 56/NI 39 and IR 148/CA 69.

14.1 GENERAL CONSIDERATIONS

An 'earner' is anyone who derives remuneration or profit from an employment and an 'employment' includes any trade, business, profession, office or vocation and the exercise of the powers and duties of a public or local authority. [*SSCBA 1992, ss 3(1), 122(1)*]. 'Business', according to Lord Diplock, is 'a wider concept than a trade' (*American Leaf Blending Co Sdn Bhd v Director-General of Inland Revenue [1978] STC 561*) and has been held by Rowlatt J to mean 'an active occupation . . . continuously carried on' (*CIR v Marine Steam Turbine Co (1920) 12 TC 174*) and by Widgery J to mean 'a serious undertaking earnestly pursued'. (*Rael-Brook Ltd v Minister of Housing and Local Government [1967] 1 AER 262*). (See 14.10 below for the significance of these judicial comments.) In order to establish whether a person is liable to pay contributions, however, and, if so, of which class (or classes), it is necessary to ascertain whether or not he falls within either or both of the two categories of earner around which the contribution legislation has been framed. Those categories are

(*a*) employed earners; and

(*b*) self-employed earners.

[*SSCBA 1992, s 2(1)*].

If a person falls within the first of these categories, contributions will, in normal circumstances, be payable not only by that person himself but also by some other person (usually his employer) who is known as the *secondary contributor*. Though not specifically referred to as such by the legislation it is useful to regard secondary contributors as forming a separate category of person for contribution purposes and they are so regarded in this chapter.

A fourth type of person to which the contribution legislation applies is the person who, whether already belonging to one of the categories mentioned or not, wishes to pay contributions on a voluntary basis in order to provide or make up his entitlement to benefit. Although forming a group of sorts, such persons attract no categorisation problems of any kind and are, accordingly, afforded no separate treatment in this chapter (but see CLASS 3 CONTRIBUTIONS (19)).

It should also be noted that the Secretary of State for Social Security has the power to determine by Statutory Instrument that certain particular groups of workers should be treated as Class 1 (employed) or Class 2 (self–employed) contributors. The DSS made use of these powers for certain groups and the NICO will apply the regulations whenever it is appropriate:

- Electoral workers (generally exempt from NIC)

- Examiners, moderators, etc. of certain examining bodies (generally treated as self employed, see 34 EXAMINERS).

- Domestic employment by close relatives (generally exempt from NIC) see 38.12.

- Ministers of Religion (generally treated as employees) see 43 MINISTERS OF RELIGION.

- Office cleaners (generally treated as employees).

- Part-time or visiting lecturers, teachers or instructors (generally treated as employees) see 41 LECTURERS, TEACHERS AND INSTRUCTORS.

- Employment of a person by his or her spouse (generally treated as an employee) see 36 HUSBAND AND WIFE.

- certain actors, musicians and other performers (generally treated as employees) see 33 ENTERTAINERS.

Where these regulations do apply it can mean that national insurance treatment differs from the income tax and/or PAYE treatment. See Inland Revenue Schedule E Manual, para SE 827 (8/96). [*SSCBA 1992, s 2(2)*].

14.2   EMPLOYED EARNERS

An 'employed earner' is any person who is gainfully employed in Great Britain either

(*a*)   under a *contract of service*, or

(*b*)   in an *office* (including elective office) with emoluments chargeable to income tax under Schedule E.

[*SSCBA 1992, s 2(1)(a)*].

Any contribution liability which arises as a result of a person's categorisation as an employed earner is a liability under Class 1 (see CLASS 1 CONTRIBUTIONS (15)) and is, therefore, wholly earnings-related. [*SSCBA 1992, s 1(2)*]. It follows that no liability can possibly arise unless an employed earner is 'gainfully' employed and that, in the context of this definition (though not in the definition of a self-employed earner—see 14.10 below), the qualification is otiose. Under the earlier legislation from which the phrase was borrowed, however, Class 1 contributions were flat-rated and 'gainfully' was held by the courts to mean 'for the purposes of gain'. (*Vandyk v Minister of Pensions and National Insurance [1954] 2 AER 723*). The phrase thus once served, in certain circumstances, to permit contributions to be collected where no true earnings actually arose from an employment. (*Benjamin v Minister of Pensions and National Insurance [1960] 3 WLR 430; Re J B Griffiths, Quinn & Co (1963) 5 KIR 128*).

An employment must be regarded as 'gainful' if a person is engaged in it with a desire, hope and intention of obtaining remuneration or profit in return for services or efforts. (*CP 7/49*). Thus, a person will be regarded as gainfully employed throughout any period for which he is under a contract of service whether or not he actually works during that period. (*R(U) 4/60, R(U) 5/83*). However, where work *is* done, the absence of any hope or intention to profit from it will not prevent the employment being gainful if the person doing the work is in fact paid for doing it. (*CP 7/49, R(P) 1/65*). (See AOG Vol 6 paras 50055–50059).

An important DSS observation on the wording of *SSCBA 1992, s 2(1)(a)* was that:

'The words "in Great Britain" (see 49.2 OVERSEAS MATTERS) qualify the words "gainfully employed", not the following words "under a contract of service". When read together with the definitions of "employed" and "employment" to be found in [*Sec 122(1)(2)*] of the Act, the words "gainfully employed in Great Britain" clearly require no more than that the person concerned should undertake in Great Britain, with a view to gain, activities in the course of, *inter alia*, some trade, business, office, profession or vocation.' (Letter, 10 October 1986).

14.2   Categorisation

Example

The wages clerk at Benevolent Ltd has written to the NICO asking for their determination on the employment status of the Managing Director's wife who is to provide consultancy services to the company for the period 27 October 2000 to 13 April 2001. The NICO replies to the wages officer as follows:

Dear Sir,

Under the provisions of Section 2(1)(a) of the Social Security Contributions and Benefits Act 1992 ('the 1992 Act') the distinction between employed earner's employment and self-employment depends mainly on the existence of a contract of service.

Where there is a contract of service, then in general, the person is regarded as an employee.

A contract of service need not be in writing. Section 122 of the 1992 Act provides that it can also be an oral agreement and can be an expressed one or one implied from the working arrangements.

There is however no precise legal definition of what constitutes a contract of service, i.e. what makes the relationship in law between the two parties that of employer and employee.

The National Insurance Contributions Office relies on principles established from the case law of the Courts over many years and applies these to the facts of the individual case concerned.

Some of the facts which the Courts consider important are:

1.   is the person in business on their own account;

2.   must the person give personal service for which they are paid;

3.   can the 'employer' control what the person does, when they do it and how they do it, even if the control is not exercised;

4.   is the person part and parcel of the 'employers' business or organisation;

5.   does the person supply tools, equipment and materials and, if so, to what extent;

6.   who makes a profit or loss from work;

7.   is the person paid for the job or for the hours or days they work;

8.   can the 'employer' select, suspend or dismiss the person; and

9.   is the self-employment the intention of both parties.

The National Insurance Contributions Office weighs all the factors in a working relationship, including those mentioned above, before deciding if a contract of service exists.

A person may say that they are self-employed or work on a casual basis but this does not alter the fact that if the work is carried out under conditions which amount to a contract of service the person is an employed earner under the 1992 Act.

Our ruling

In this case Jennifer Bransdon-Smith

I consider the weight of evidence of these factors in the working relationship between

27 October 2000 and 13 April 2001 shows that there is a contract of service.

---

cont'd

> National Insurance contributions and income tax may be payable on different basis.
>
> Keep this letter safe in a case you have to show it to the Inland Revenue.
>
> **Further information**
>
> If you think this decision or ruling is incorrect, please let us know, in writing within 28 days. Please include:
>
> - reasons why you think it is wrong and
> - any further information and/or documentation which you think is relevant.
>
> *Letter continues*

Note to the example: CA National Insurance News, summer 1997 page 4 states that if new information is put forward CA, as it then was, will consider whether the ruling can be changed. If not, there is now a right to have the matter formally considered by the Tax Commissioners on appeal (see 9 APPEALS AND REVIEWS).

14.3   The meaning of 'contract of service'

A 'contract of service' is any contract of service or apprenticeship, whether written or oral and whether expressed or implied and is, therefore, synonymous with a contract of employment. [*SSCBA 1992, s 122(1); Employment Protection (Consolidation) Act 1978, s 153(1)*].

Whether or not such a contract exists is a question to be determined only after looking at the totality of the evidence. (*Argent v Minister of Social Security [1968] 3 AER 208, per Roskill J*). That determination will be a conclusion of law and will depend both on the rights conferred and the duties imposed by the contract. If the rights conferred and the duties imposed are such that the relationship created is one of master and servant, it is irrelevant that the parties may have declared it to be something else. (*Ready Mixed Concrete (South East) Ltd v Minister of Pensions and National Insurance [1968] 1 AER 433, per MacKenna J*). The parties cannot alter the truth of their relationship by putting a different label on it. (*Massey v Crown Life Insurance Co [1978] 2 AER 576, per Lord Denning*). It is equally irrelevant that a statutory authority such as the Inland Revenue may have accepted the relationship as being other than what it, in fact, is: a convenient arrangement for tax or national insurance purposes is not determinative. (*Tyne & Clyde Warehouses Ltd v Hamerton [1978] ICR 661; Young & Woods Ltd v West [1980] IRLR 201; Warner Holidays Ltd v Secretary of State for Social Services [1983] ICR 440*). However, unless there are obvious indicators that a person's employment status is other than that claimed by him, the Inland Revenue usually accepts without query the status claimed. This would also include persuasive authority in connection with, say, *Employment Rights Act, Part X* and *Sex Discrimination Act 1975, Part II*. (See *Carver v Saudi Arabian Airlines, Times Law Reports, 24 March 1999*).

It is not necessary that bad faith should be proved before a written contract may be disregarded. (*Reade v Brearley (1933) 17 TC 687*). It is merely necessary that the contract is inconsistent with the realities of a relationship. (*Global Plant Ltd v Secretary of State for Health and Social Security [1971] 3 AER 385*). If, however, the parties' relationship is ambiguous, any agreement between them then becomes the best material from which to gather the true legal relationship between them. (*Massey v Crown Life Insurance Co [1978] 2 AER 576, per Lord Denning; BSM (1257) Ltd v Secretary of State for Social Services [1978] 2 AER 576*). In construing a written agreement one must look at all the circumstances at the time the agreement was entered into and the intention of the parties must be determined from the words of the agreement in the light of those circumstances. (*Plumb Brothers v Dolmar (Agriculture) Ltd, The Times, 7 April 1984, per Lord Justice May*). The parties' *subjective* intentions are of no relevance. (*Ibid, per Lord Justice Purchas*). If the agreed terms accurately reflect the parties' intentions and are given practical effect, the status of the parties is that to which the agreed terms point. (*McMenamin v Diggles [1991] STC 419*).

If the true relationship between parties to an agreement of the kind envisaged is not that of master and servant, it will usually be that of employer and independent contractor and, because such a contract (which is known as a 'contract for services') is indicative of self-employment rather than employment, the distinction between the one and the other has assumed great importance and has led to the evolution of various tests by which the true nature of a contract may be decided. It is a question of law as to what are the right tests to be applied in determining whether a contract falls into the one or the other class. (*Construction Industry Training Board v Labour Force Ltd [1970] 3 AER 220, per Fisher J*).

It is sometimes the case that a person who is about to perform work for another will arrange to provide his service through the medium of a limited company which he owns and of which he is the sole director. Underlying such arrangements is the mistaken belief that what might otherwise be a contract *of* service between *the worker* and the person for whom he is to work is thereby turned into a contract *for* services between the *limited company* and that person. This is not necessarily so. If the truth of the arrangement is that the worker is obliged to render personal service, is subject to personal control as to the manner of doing his work (see 14.5) and is not, as a matter of economic reality, in business on his own account (see 14.7), it has always been open to the IR and others to draw aside the corporate veil and to have regard to the unwritten contract of service which the veil is intended to conceal. See also the Chancellor's Budget Statement on 9 March 1999 countering the avoidance of tax and NICs by those who set up personal service companies and similar intermediaries. This counter avoidance legislation has effect from 6 April 2000 and is arguably directed at those in the computer industry but it will nonetheless apply to many others as well. IR Budget Press Release IR 35, 9 March 1999. See 14.17 below.

14.4   The mutual obligations test

It is intrinsic to any contract that its parties incur obligations towards each other; and a contract of service is no exception. Where, therefore, a situation arises in which no obligations exist, there can be neither a contract of service nor a contract for services—even though one party might be found to be performing a service for the other and the other might be found to be remunerating the first party in some way. Accordingly, a fundamental task of any tribunal which is addressing itself to the question whether a person is an employed earner or a self-employed earner is to ascertain whether or not a certain irreducible minimum of obligation lies on the person receiving service and on the person giving service. For there to exist a contract of service, the minimum obligation required of the alleged employee is that he accepts and performs some reasonable amount of work for the alleged employer (*Nethermere (St Neots) Ltd v Gardiner [1984] ICR 615, per Kerr LJ*), that he makes himself available to the alleged employer and that he refrains from seeking or accepting employment from another employer during the continuance of his relationship with the alleged employer. (*Hellyer Brothers Ltd v McLeod, [1986] ICR 122, per Slade LJ*). So far as the alleged employer is concerned, that minimum obligation is that he offers continuing employment to the alleged employee. (The *Hellyer* case). (It is worth noting that, in the German language, the words for employer and employee actually encapsulate a brief description of these minimum mutual obligations: *Arbeitgeber* and *Arbeitnehmer* — work-giver and work-acceptor). Thus, where a person *may*, but *need not*, be asked to perform a service and, if asked, is free to decline to provide the service asked for, there exists no mutuality of obligation and thus no contract of service, even though the person's services may frequently be requested and those services may frequently be supplied. (*Mailway (Southern) Ltd v Willsher [1978] IRLR 322; O'Kelly v Trusthouse Forte plc [1983] 3 AER 456*).

It may be, however, that, despite the initial absence of mutual obligations, the regular giving and taking of work over periods of a year or more may give rise to expectations which harden into such obligations and such obligations may, in turn, give rise to an enforceable contract of service. (*Nethermere (St Neots) Ltd v Gardiner [1984] ICR 615, per Stephenson LJ*). In other words, the conduct of the parties to a relationship may, over a substantial period of time, turn that relationship into a contract of service by creating mutual obligations between the parties. (*Airfix Footwear Ltd v Cope [1978] ICR 1210*). Mutuality of obligation may also, in some instances, be inferred from the economic dependence of each party on the other, e.g. if a situation exists where, should work offered to an alleged employee be refused, further work would be withheld and where, should further work not be offered, the alleged employee would look elsewhere (*Four Seasons (Inn on the Park) Ltd v Hamarat, 17 April 1985, EAT 369/84*). Furthermore, where evidence discloses what, on the face of it, is a series of contracts for services entered into between the same parties and covering a substantial period of time, it might be open to a tribunal properly to infer from the parties' conduct, notwithstanding the absence of any evidence as to any express agreement of that nature, the existence of a continuing overriding arrangement which governs the whole of their relationship and itself amounts to a contract of service, i.e. a 'global' or 'umbrella' contract. (The *Hellyer* case). In such cases, it will be the gaps between each period of service that become significant. Does the alleged employee have an obligation to make himself available to the alleged employer during those intervening periods and must he, during those periods, refrain from seeking or accepting other employment? Does the alleged employer have an ongoing obligation to offer the alleged employee any employment which is available throughout those intervening periods? If the answer is affirmative, a global contract of employment will probably exist. (*Boyd Line Ltd v Pitts [1986] ICR 244*). The NICO attitude where there is a series of short-term assignments carried out by a person, with no obligation to offer or accept further such assignments at any point, appears to be that there is no continuous contract of employment, but when each assignment is carried out there may very well exist a short-term contract. The terms of each short-term assignment will determine whether the contract is one 'of service' or 'for services'.

14.5   The control test

Having established that there exists a contract which gives rise to mutual obligations, for however short a period, the next step is to determine whether or not that contract is a contract of service. The principal test to be applied is whether a person who has agreed, in consideration of a wage or other remuneration, to provide his *own* work and skill in the performance of some service for some other person, has also agreed, expressly or impliedly, to be 'subject to that other person's control in a sufficient degree to make that other person master'. If he has, and if other provisions of the contract between them are not sufficiently inconsistent with it being a contract of service to outweigh the control factor, the contract is a contract of service. (*Ready Mixed Concrete (South East) Ltd v Minister of Pensions and National Insurance [1968] 1 AER 433, per MacKenna J at pp 439 to 440*). The reference to the provision of *personal* service and the reference to the method of remuneration are both important. A person's obligation to do work himself rather than hiring someone else to do it for him is a strong indication that the contract is a contract *of service* rather than a contract *for services* (*Pauley v Kenaldo Ltd [1953] 1 WLR 187*). (*Leaflet IR 56/NI 39*). Conversely, an arrangement under which payment is to be of a specified amount for the whole of the work to which the contract relates, rather than by weekly or monthly wage or salary, is a strong indicator that the contract is a contract for services. (*Writers Guild of Great Britain v BBC [1974] ICR 234*). The working of set hours, or of a given number of hours a week or month, and payment by the hour, the week, or the month will be indicative of employed earner status, as will the ability to earn overtime pay. (*Short v J and W Henderson Ltd (1946) 62 TLR 427*). (Leaflet IR 56/NI 39).

The control question will always have to be considered. (*Market Investigations Ltd v Minister of Social Security [1969] 3 AER 732, per Cooke J*). However, the emphasis has shifted over the years so that it can be said that control need no longer be the decisive factor, but it remains of very great importance. (*Argent v Minister of Social Security [1968] 3 AER 208, per Roskill J*). In 1984, the Privy Council held that, in most cases, the decisive criterion for determining the relationship between the parties to a contract is the extent to which the person, whose status as an employee or independent contractor is in issue, is under the direction and control of the other party to the contract with regard to the manner in which he does his work under it. (*Narich Pty Ltd v Commissioner of Pay-roll Tax [1984] ICR 286*).

In a 1995 case, Mr Justice Lightman said 'The lack of "control". . . does not have the significance today that it once may have had as the litmus test for a contract of employment. It is certainly not a universal litmus test, and its importance (and indeed relevance) must depend in particular on the role to be played by the "employee" in the "employer's" business'. (*Horner v Hasted [1995] 67 TC 439*).

In practice, of course, many employees have considerable independence. Accordingly, when applying the control test, the IR has regard to any *right* of control which exists—even if it is seldom or never exercised—and to whether that control extends beyond the duties imposed to the method and performance of those duties. This is as it should be for 'a servant is a person subject to the command of his master as to the manner in which he shall do his work' and 'the ultimate question is not what specific orders, or whether any specific orders, were given but who is entitled to give the orders as to how the work should be done and reference should be made to *Express and Echo Publications Ltd v Tanton [1999] All ER (D) 256*. See also (*Yewens v Noakes (1880) 6 QBD 530; Simmons v Heath Laundry Co [1910] 1 KB 543; Mersey Docks and Harbour Board v Coggins and Griffith (Liverpool) Ltd [1946] 2 AER 345*). The IR considers that, in general, if a person can be told 'at any time what to do or when and how to do it' he is under a contract of service (*Ferguson v John Dawson & Partners (Contractors) Ltd [1976] 3 AER 817*). (Leaflet IR 56/NI 39). Where a right to suspend or dismiss exists, this too will be indicative that the contract is a contract of service. (*Willard v Whiteley Ltd [1938] 3 AER 779; Morren v Swinton and Pendlebury Borough Council [1965] 1 WLR 576*) (Leaflet IR 56/NI 39).

14.6   The integration test

Another test (which increasingly is seen as but part of the economic reality test—see 14.7) involves a consideration of the relationship between the services a person performs and the business of the person for whom he performs them. If the services are performed as an integral part of the business rather than being merely accessory to it, the contract under which those services are performed will be a contract of service. (*Stevenson, Jordan and Harrison Ltd v MacDonald and Evans [1952] RPC 10, per Lord Denning*). This is because the person will be 'part and parcel' of the business, whether the services he renders are subject to control or not. (*Bank voor Handel en Scheepvaart NV v Slatford [1952] 2 AER 956*). Thus, though a hospital board may be in no position to tell its surgeons what to do or how to do it, those surgeons may well be under contracts of service with the board as the operations they perform are an integral part of the hospital's activity. (*Cassidy v Minister of Health [1951] 1 AER 574; see also Amalgamated Engineering Union v Minister of Pensions [1963] 1 AER 864*).

14.7 The economic reality test

The economic reality test approaches matters from yet another direction. (It originated in the United States and Canada—see *US v Silk (1946) 331 US 704* and *Montreal Locomotive Works Ltd v Montreal and Attorney-General for Canada (1947) 1 DLR 161*.) The test asks whether a person who has engaged himself to perform services is performing them as a person 'in business on his own account'. (*Market Investigations Ltd v Minister of Social Security [1969] 3 AER 732, per Cooke J*) or, to put the question into the vernacular, is the person 'his own boss'. (*Withers v Flackwell Heath Football Supporters' Club [1981] IRLR 307*). If the answer is negative, the person is a party to a contract of service.

Among the relevant factors which will need to be considered in applying the economic reality test are whether (and to what degree) a person performing services

(*a*) provides his own equipment,

(*b*) hires his own helpers,

(*c*) takes financial risk,

(*d*) takes responsibility for investment and management, and

(*e*) has an opportunity of profiting from sound management in the performance of his task

(*Market Investigations Ltd v Minister of Social Security [1969] 3 AER 732*). See also 38.5 and IR Tax Bulletin, February 2000, page 716.

As far as (*a*) is concerned, the IR points out that it is the provision of *major* items of equipment that is of relevance—many employees provide the small tools which are needed for them to perform their tasks. (Leaflet IR 56/NI 39). IR Tax Bulletin, February 2000, page 716 states:

> '. . . a self-employed contractor generally provides whatever equipment is needed to do the job (though in many trades, such as carpentry, it is common for employees, as well as self-employed workers, to provide their own hand tools). The provision of significant equipment (and/or materials) which are fundamental to the engagement is of particular importance.'

As far as (*b*) is concerned, the IR suggests a distinction between being free to hire people on terms of one's own choice to do the work which one has taken on, paying them out of one's own pocket, and merely being authorised to delegate work or to engage others on behalf of one's employer (Leaflet IR 56/NI 39).

As far as (*c*) is concerned, the IR asks: 'Do you risk your own money in the business? Are you responsible for meeting the losses as well as taking the profits? Do you have to correct unsatisfactory work in your own time and at your own expense?' (Leaflet IR 56/NI 39). IR Tax Bulletin, February 2000, page 716 states:

> '. . . A person who has the freedom to choose whether to do the job himself or hire somebody else to provide substantial help is probably self-employed.'

Method of remuneration (see 14.5 above) is also an important consideration in relation to this test. If a person is paid by way of a fixed wage or salary, financial risk will be virtually non-existent, whereas remuneration by commission only may indicate that a person is risking his own money in carrying out a contract. The issue of leaflet IR 148/CA 69 for the construction industry 'Are your workers employed or self-employed?' in 1995 goes some way to clarifying the position; the leaflet reiterates the standard tests of control, mutual obligation and integration from the point of view of sub-contractors. Whilst this view clarifies a number of matters by setting out indicators each case will be viewed according to its own particular circumstances (see 38.4 LABOUR-ONLY CONTRACTORS).

14.8   Categorisation

In *Hall v Lorimer 1993 BTC 473*, the Court of Appeal rejected a checklist approach to categorisation, but added to the tests summarised by Cooke J in *Market Investigations*. In particular, it will be important to determine whether a person has set up a business-like organisation of his own and whether there is a degree of continuity in the relationship between the person performing the services and the person for whom they are performed. In *Lorimer*, the taxpayer regularly worked for over twenty different clients and took on over 500 separate engagements over four years, the longest lasting two weeks and most only a day or less. Although the taxpayer provided none of his own equipment, the engagements he undertook were merely incidents in his professional career. He ran the risk of bad debts, which an employee would not face, and he incurred significant expenditure on obtaining more engagements. His expenses were different in nature and scale from those incurred by employees. The Inland Revenue argued that the taxpayer could not be treated as self-employed as he had no capital tied up in the productions on which he was working, but the Special Commissioner, quoted approvingly by Nolan LJ in the Court of Appeal, noted that the production company was not Lorimer's business. *His* business was to exploit his undoubted skills as a vision mixer, controlling his own costs and profiting from being successful, thereby attracting more work as his reputation grew.

14.8   Contracts of apprenticeship

See 10.2 APPRENTICES, TRAINEES AND STUDENTS.

14.9   The meaning of 'office'

An 'office' is a post which can be recognised as existing, whether it be occupied for the time being or vacant, and which, if occupied, does not owe its existence in any way to the identity of the incumbent or his appointment to the post. (*Edwards v Clinch [1980] 3 AER 278, per Buckley LJ*). A company director occupies an office though he may also be under a contract of service (see 22.3 COMPANY DIRECTORS and *McMillan v Guest [1942] 1 AER 606, per Lord Atkin*). So does a member of Parliament, a minister of the Crown and a judge. (Hansard 16 December 1975 Vol 902 No 20 Col 578). A bishop of the Church of England is an office-holder (DSS Leaflet NP 21, now out of print) as is a member of the Church of England clergy, a NHS consultant, a stipendiary reader in the Church of England, a police officer, a justice of the peace, a trustee or executor, a company auditor, a local land charges registrar, a student union president, a club secretary, a trade union officer, a company registrar and a superintendent registrar of births, deaths and marriages. (*Re Employment of Church of England Curates [1912] 2 Ch 563; Mitchell and Edon v Ross [1961] 3 AER 49; Barthorpe v Exeter Diocesan Board [1979] ICR 900; Ridge v Baldwin [1964] AC 40; Knight v A-G [1979] ICR 194; Dale v CIR [1951] 2 AER 517; Ellis v Lucas [1966] 2 AER 935; Ministry of Housing and Local Government v Sharp [1969] 3 AER 225; Oleskar v Sunderland Polytechnic Students' Union EAT 482/79; 102 Social Club & Institute v Bickerton [1977] ICR 911; Stevenson v United Road Transport Union [1977] ICR 893; CIR v Brander and Cruickshank [1971] 1 AER 36; Miles v Wakefield Metropolitan District Council [1985] IRLR 108*). This list is not exhaustive and it is clear that elected members of local authorities, CROWN SERVANTS (25), SUBPOSTMASTERS (55) and the like are all officers within the terms of the definition.

The occupation of an office is not in itself sufficient to place a person in the category of employed earners. The office has to be with emoluments chargeable to income tax under Schedule E. [*SSCBA 1992, s 2(1)(a)*]. Emoluments include all salaries, fees, wages, perquisites and profits whatsoever. [*ICTA 1988, s 131(1)*]. For emoluments to be chargeable to income tax under Schedule E in respect of an office, they must be emoluments *therefrom*. [*ICTA 1988, s 19(1)*]. This means that a payment is not chargeable to tax under Schedule E unless it has been made to a person 'in return for acting as or being an employee'. (*Hochstrasser v Mayes [1959] 3 AER 817, per Lord Radcliffe*). 'Chargeable' is not, of course, the same thing as 'charged'. The Inland Revenue may fail to charge to tax under Schedule E payments made to an office holder which should be so charged, or may charge to tax under Schedule E payments made to an office holder which should not be so charged. In the first event the office is nonetheless an office with emoluments chargeable to tax under Schedule E for the purpose of *SSCBA 1992, s 2(1)(a)* while in the latter event it is not.

If, as is usually the case, a partnership holds the office of auditor of a limited company, each of the partners is (if the partnership is subject to English, rather than Scottish, law) jointly and severally responsible for the discharge of the duties attaching to that office. (*Saddler v Whiteman [1910] 1 KB 868, per Farwell LJ at p 889*). As the auditor's remuneration or fee is clearly an emolument chargeable to income tax under Schedule E, each partner of the firm falls within the category of employed earner by reason of the office and is, in law, liable for Class 1 contributions on the earnings received. Revenue practice is, however, to allow such earnings to be included in the profits of the partnership chargeable to income tax under Schedule D, and the DSS always followed suit, effectively collecting CLASS 4 CONTRIBUTIONS (20) on the earnings.

14.10 SELF-EMPLOYED EARNERS

A 'self-employed earner' is any person who is gainfully employed in Great Britain otherwise than in employed earner's employment (whether or not he is also employed in such employment). [*SSCBA 1992, s 2(1)(b)*].

Because this definition is largely negative and because categorisation as a self-employed earner will result in liability for contributions being determined under the Class 2 (i.e. earnings-*un*related) contribution rules (see CLASS 2 CONTRIBUTIONS (18)), much depends on the meaning of the words 'gainfully employed'. This phrase differs slightly from the pre-1975 phrase 'gainfully occupied in employment' but not, it is thought, sufficiently to alter the test to which those original words gave rise, i.e. 'whether or not a person holds himself out as being anxious to become employed for the purposes of gain', not whether or not he has in fact received some net profit from his activities as a self-employed person. (*Vandyk v Minister of Pensions and National Insurance [1954] 2 AER 723*).

A person's business or occupation must, of course, have actually *begun* before that person can be regarded as 'gainfully employed' as a self-employed earner. Pre-commencement preparatory activity, e.g. finding premises, obtaining finance, researching the likely market etc., will not constitute gainful employment as a self-employed earner. But, once the business or occupation has begun, its profitability or otherwise becomes irrelevant to the determination of status for national insurance purposes. The motive of gain is there, whatever the trading results might be, and self-employed earner status will continue until the business or occupation is actually discontinued. In deciding whether or not a person is gainfully employed as a self-employed earner for any week, the test to be applied is, therefore: Has he begun to run a business or practice a profession or engage in an occupation on his own account and is that business, profession or occupation continuing—even if dormant and inactive—or has it been discontinued, temporarily or permanently? A person does not cease to be gainfully employed as a self-employed earner merely because, for a time, no work is actually done. (AOG Vol 6 para 50064).

Thus, the Secretary of State has, for instance, formally determined that a theatrical producer who specialises in summer shows and Christmas pantomimes but who holds himself out as available to put on productions at other times of the year is consequently self-employed during his periods of inactivity. (*M37 (1953)*). The

Secretary of State has similarly determined that the proprietor of a boarding house is a self-employed earner throughout a year even though the greater part of the year is spent in cleaning and decorating in preparation for the holiday season during which actual gain arises. (*M36 (1953)*). It should be noted that this may also be true of a person deriving profits or gains from the commercial letting of furnished holiday accommodation. Although such an activity is not a trade but is merely treated as such for taxation purposes (see *ICTA 1988, s 503(1)*), it may well constitute a 'business' (see 14.1 above and Vinelott J's comments in *Griffiths v Jackson [1983] STC 184*) and, if it does, the presence of a profit-motive will render the person letting the accommodation liable to categorisation as a self-employed earner. The DSS stated its policy as being that a person who has furnished holiday lettings must be self-employed because the activity of taking bookings, dealing with payments, keeping accounts, cleaning etc constitutes business activity. (Letter, 29 January 1993). However, in subsequent correspondence it has been acknowledged that where very little time is spent working (i.e. collecting rents, taking bookings, etc.) then the question whether a business is being carried on for these purposes may be disregarded. The words 'very little time', were originally supposed to have been representative of a limit of 8 hours per week. However, the CA wrote to point out that it is not possible to define a set number of hours that may be considered inconsiderable. Its view was that it is necessary to look at the facts present in each case. It goes on to state that if Inspectors are in doubt about the level of activity they should *not* treat it as inconsiderable and in those circumstances it relies on the level of earnings to decide whether or not liability exists. (Letter from CA, 16 October 1995). If, though, the person carries on other business and is therefore self-employed in another capacity then if, taking the two businesses together, the individual would be classed as self-employed with regard to the two combined incomes under self-employment activities, then it would not be possible to disregard the furnished holiday lettings element. In order to resolve the matter a question was put to the Secretary of State for his determination and the results of an enquiry held on 8 June 1994 decided that in the particular circumstances mentioned above there was no gainful employment as a self-employed earner for the purposes of *SSA 1975* and *SSCBA 1992*. In contrast, in a determination by the Secretary of State in a more recent case, the fact that an individual with lettings had responsibilities which required him to be on call 24 hours a day with no pattern to his working hours did not preclude self-employed status. In fact, it was stated that although the business was not as active as he would have wished he continued to be engaged in it and the position was analogous to that of a shopkeeper who remains open for business but has few customers.

The mere receipt of rents from property is, however, to raise no *presumption* in law that a business is being carried on. (*American Leaf Blending Co Sdn Bhd v Director-General of Inland Revenue [1978] STC 561, per Lord Diplock*).

However, in a written reply the CA more recently stated that it is not possible to define what constitutes 'trivial' but in the circumstances noted above i.e. collecting rents, furnishing and maintaining the property, repairing/contracting for repairs, then the person letting the property will be considered gainfully employed as a self-employed earner and thereby liable to Class 2 contributions (CA Specialist Conference written response, 20 February 1996).

Although, under this test, the motive of gain is, alone, sufficient to place a person within the category of self-employed earners, the absence of the motive of gain is not sufficient to remove him from that category where actual gain has in fact occurred. (*Benjamin v Minister of Pensions and National Insurance [1960] 3 WLR 430*). Thus, for instance, the DSS took the view that fee-earning foster parents who receive a separate or distinct 'reward element' are self-employed earners for contribution purposes (AOG Vol 6 para 50408). (*Foster Care Allowances and Income Tax*, National Foster Care Association Booklet). If, however, both motive and actual gain become absent, a person will cease to be within the category of self-employed earners, as, for instance, a cricket umpire and an ice-cream salesman, each of whom were, according to the formal determinations of the Secretary of State, non-employed during the winter months. (*M38 (1954); M45 (1954)*).

The National Insurance Commission have held that a sleeping partner in a business is not a self-employed earner so long as he renders no services to the business. (*R(S)10/79, CP 5/75*). He may have a motive of gain but, as there is no employment of any kind, he cannot be said to be 'gainfully employed'.

Unfortunately, interpretative problems do not end with the 'gainfully' test for even if, by application of that test, a person is seen to be within the category of self-employed earners, he will be removed from that category and his earnings from that self-employed earner's employment disregarded for contribution purposes if he is not *ordinarily* employed in such employment. [*Categorisation Regs, Reg 2(4), 1 Sch Pt III para 9*].

Though the meaning of 'ordinarily' has never been considered by the courts in the context of employment, it has been so considered in the context of residence and has been held to mean habitually, regularly, normally, with a settled purpose, not extraordinarily (see 49.4 OVERSEAS MATTERS). (*Lysaght v CIR HL (1928) 13 TC 511*). It is submitted that, in order to be able to judge whether or not these qualities are attached to an employment, it is necessary to consider a person's activities over a period of time, and that the period of time should be a whole year or, if the nature of the activity is seasonal, that season within a year. If, then, within the selected period, a person is gainfully employed in a self-employed earner's employment on a regular basis for more than 50% of the time (disregarding holidays and days of incapacity), he should be regarded as being ordinarily self-employed.

The only published statement by the DSS of its views on the meaning of the word 'ordinarily' in this context was contained in an early version of the long obsolete leaflet NI 192 which informed non-NHS nurses and midwives that, if their only self-employment is occasional home nursing at long and irregular intervals, e.g. less than once a fortnight, they might be regarded as not ordinarily self-employed.

A test of what constitutes ordinary, gainful self-employed earner's employment is applied where (but only where) the earner in question is also employed in an employed earner's employment from which he derives substantial earnings. The test asks whether the earnings from the spare-time self-employment exceed an amount set annually, i.e. £250 for 1977–78 and 1978–79, £400 for 1979–80 and 1980–81, and £800 for 1981–82 and each subsequent tax year to date. If the answer is negative, the employment is disregarded. (Leaflet CA 02). This test has no actual basis in law, however.

Under regulations revoked in 1978, self-employment was to be disregarded if it occupied the person concerned for less than eight hours a week. Until relatively recently, some DSS inspectors continued to apply that test (extra-statutorily) to determine whether a person should be regarded as 'ordinarily' self-employed, but the DSS subsequently disclaimed the validity of such an approach. The DSS did admit, however, that 'if a person's self-employment only involves a couple of hours per week then we deem it to be "inconsiderable" and do not enforce payment of a self-employed contribution'. (Letter, 29 January 1993). But see Secretary of State's determination regarding an individual who was 'on-call' 24 hours a day but was not as active as desired due to the property industry depression (see above).

However, the CA has confirmed in writing (16 October 1995) that 'The Agency's view is that we need to look at the facts present in each case. Inspectors may still disregard self-employment as *inconsiderable* but that is a matter for individual judgement depending on the nature of employment. They are specifically told it is not possible to define a set number of hours that may be considered to be inconsiderable.

14.11   Categorisation

Inspectors are also instructed that if they are in doubt about the level of activity they should not treat it as inconsiderable. In those circumstances the Agency relies on the level of earnings to decide whether or not liability exists.' Part of the reason for this is that it may be possible for some businesses to generate enough income to attract NICs without investing a great deal of effort. If an arbitrary limit was imposed on the time invested then a clear route to being excused NIC has been created. Another contributor may do similar work, earn the same amount, but do longer hours and therefore have a NIC liability. This is perceived by NICO as being unfair so it prefers to rely on the level of earnings to decide liability in the majority of cases.

Categorisation as a self-employed earner will be of significance only where earnings from the self-employed earner's employment exceed the small earnings exception level (see 28.76 EARNINGS, 18.3 CLASS 2 CONTRIBUTIONS AND 51.8 RATES AND LIMITS).

14.11 **THE RELEVANCE OF TAX TREATMENT**

The intention of Parliament in redefining the categories of employed earner and self-employed earner was to align CLASS 1 CONTRIBUTIONS (15) with Schedule E and CLASS 2 CONTRIBUTIONS (18) with Schedule D. (See 847 House of Commons Debates 5th Series Col 124). It must be expected, therefore, that, where the Inland Revenue brings a person's earnings within the charge to Schedule E, it will also, through its NICO, seek to categorise that person as an employed earner for NICs. Prior to 1 April 1999, there was never any obligation on either the IR or DSS to follow the rulings of the other and the cautious attitude which the DSS generally maintained is well illustrated by the Secretary of State's confirmation that possession of a sub-contractor's tax exemption certificate is *normally* accepted as evidence of self-employment *unless* investigation reveals that a contract of service is in existence. (Hansard 13 November 1981 Vol 12 No 8 Pt II Col 188). DSS practice was, apparently, to proceed on the basis that, unless suitable evidence to the contrary was produced, the Inland Revenue had issued a subcontractor's certificate without full enquiry into the applicant's circumstances. The DSS would therefore make its own decision on employment status and inform the Inland Revenue of that decision. In an effort to clarify the uncertainty in this area leaflet IR 148/CA 69 was issued jointly by the Inland Revenue and Contributions Agency and addresses whether workers taken on in the subcontracting industry are employees or self-employed notwithstanding the fact that a subcontractor's certificate may have been issued to the individual.

The problems which have arisen where the DSS and the Inland Revenue have insisted on their right to make independent decisions on employment status were, in July 1985, the subject of Governmental comment. The White Paper 'Lifting the Burden' (*Cmnd 9571*) said:

'In deciding about a person's employment status, the two Departments principally involved—the DSS and the Inland Revenue—rely on the same body of general law. But sometimes decisions by the two Departments have differed, particularly when one decision is more recent and based on new information. They will be taking a number of steps before the end of the year to ensure that in future decisions taken are consistent. In particular, they will be reviewing the guidelines to staff derived from case law and will be improving staff training. They will be arranging for better liaison where views over a person's employment status differ between the two Departments. This liaison will seek to ensure a consistent, swift and clear decision, once differences of view have been identified, with the minimum of inconvenience to the person concerned.' (*Chp 4, Para 14*).

These steps were implemented in 1987. An Inland Revenue Press Release dated 19 March 1987 stated that:

'From 6 April 1987—

(a) each Inland Revenue and DSS local office will have one nominated officer who will be responsible for all enquiries and decisions about employment status;

(b) Revenue and DSS offices will confirm these decisions in writing, if requested; and

(c) a written decision made after investigation by one Department will be accepted by the other, provided all the relevant facts were accurately and clearly given at the time and circumstances remain the same.'

This policy was affirmed in a review of what is known as the 'Common Approach', the report of which was published in 1994.

Although these arrangements might have been administratively convenient, their validity is questionable. Where one government department reaches a decision in the exercise of its statutory powers, another government department cannot be estopped by that decision from reaching a different decision in the exercise of its own statutory powers. Furthermore, it is *ultra vires* for one government department to delegate its decision-making powers to another government department. (*Western Fish Products Ltd v Penwith DC [1981] 2 All ER 204; Lavender & Son Ltd v MHLG [1970] 3 All ER 871*).

The courts have indicated that, where they make a decision as to the employment status of an individual, they expect the Inland Revenue (and, presumably, the DSS) to give full effect to it, even though the decision may have been made in some connection other than income tax or social security contributions. (*Young and Woods Ltd v West [1980] IRLR 201*). The courts consider such consistency necessary if an individual is to be discouraged from asserting (as he otherwise might) that he had one employment status for, say, tax and national insurance purposes, but a different status for, say, redundancy and unfair dismissal purposes.

The *Social Security Contributions (Transfer of Functions, etc.) Act 1999, ss 8–19; 7 Sch* provides the Inland Revenue with the right for their staff to take decisions on matters that have in the past been administered by the CA. Similar or identical issues such as whether a person is employed or self-employed will now be determined by Inland Revenue staff and appeals against such decisions will be to the Tax Commissioners. See APPEALS AND REVIEWS (9).

14.12 DETERMINATION OF DOUBTFUL CASES

The DSS advised that, where there is any doubt as to the category or categories in which a person belongs, the local office should be consulted. (Leaflet IR 56/NI 39). There is often a reluctance to heed this advice as it is thought that the local office will always err in favour of employed earner status. It should be borne in mind, however, that no decision given by Inland Revenue officers is final and that a question whether a person is an earner and, if he is, as to the category of earners in which he is to be included, is subject to appeal to the Tax Commissioners (and beyond). [*SSC(T)A 1999, s 11*]. (see APPEALS AND REVIEWS (9)).

For cross-references to the various categorisation determinations made by the Secretary of State and noted in this work, see PUBLISHED DECISIONS (62).

14.13 RETROSPECTIVE EFFECT OF A CATEGORISATION DECISION

The IR will invariably take steps to remedy any case of mis-categorisation which comes to its knowledge, but the extent to which corrective action will be retrospective will depend on the nature of the mis-categorisation.

If it is found that a person who has been treated as an employed earner properly belongs in the category of self-employed earners, its decision to that effect will normally relate only to the present, thus ensuring that re-categorisation will be effective only from the date of the decision and that no question of repayment of excess contributions arises. (But see 38.10 for an exception in the case of film and TV industry workers.) If, therefore, a person wishes to obtain a repayment of contributions in such circumstances, it will be necessary to obtain the Department's agreement that during the past period for which the repayment is sought, he properly belonged in the category of self-employed earners (see REPAYMENT AND RE-ALLOCATION (53)). This may not easily be obtained but, should the Department decline to give a ruling on the matter, a formal decision of the Board may be requested and, if necessary, insisted upon (see APPEALS AND REVIEWS (9)) [*SSC(T)A 1999, s 8*].

If, on the other hand, it is found that a person who has been treated as a self-employed earner properly belongs in the category of employed earners, the date from which it will re-categorise the earner concerned will depend on the circumstances of the case. Guidance is as follows.

'Each case has to be considered on its merits. If after investigation it is decided that a person should be reclassified as an employed earner for national insurance purposes the Department's main responsibility is to ensure that the correct contributions are being paid *currently*. The date of change of classification could however be effective from an earlier date. In those circumstances any Class 2 contributions which the contributor has paid erroneously as a result of the change of status from self-employed to employed earner are reallocated as primary Class 1 contributions. Any balance of primary contributions due and any arrears of secondary contributions are generally requested from the employer. If the erroneous Class 2 contributions amount to more than the primary Class 1 contributions due the excess is refundable. The Inland Revenue deals with Class 4 contributions overpaid as a result of a change of status.' (Hansard 27 February 1984 Vol 55 No 108 Cols 62–63).

Four points must be made concerning that Parliamentary answer.

(*a*) There are grounds for supposing that the date of re-categorisation *will* (not 'may') be effective from a date earlier than the date the mis-categorisation is discovered—particularly if the DSS or, now, IR was not asked to give a ruling when the contractual relationship in question was entered into (see 14.12) and if there are grounds for supposing that the mis-categorisation was deliberate rather than accidental. The DSS partially confirmed that this is the case by stating that 'the normal practice is to assess earlier liability under Class 1 when a person previously paying Class 2 contributions is re-categorised as an employee. However, full account is taken of all the circumstances before a decision is made to require payment by the employer of any amounts due'. (Hansard 6 March 1986 Vol 93 Col 243). Where 'normal practice' is followed and where the DSS (rather than the Inland Revenue) is the department initiating the re-categorisation, the effective date may be as early as 6 April 1975 or, if the contractual relationship concerned was entered into after that date, the date the relationship began. Where the Inland Revenue initiates re-categorisation, the period of re-categorisation will be limited to six years. Whilst the DSS had historically taken the view that it can recover arrears without time limit, latterly the CA accepted that the provisions of the *Limitation Act 1980* apply and it must be expected that the Inland Revenue will follow the same approach (see 12.6 ARREARS OF CONTRIBUTIONS).

(*b*) Erroneously-paid Class 2 contributions *may* be re-allocated as primary Class 1 contributions, but no legal obligation to re-allocate is imposed on the Department. The matter is within the discretion of the Secretary of State. [*Contribution Regs, Reg 31*].

(*c*) Any balance of primary and secondary Class 1 contributions which remain outstanding after any erroneously-paid Class 2 contributions have been re-allocated are *invariably demanded* (not 'generally requested') from the secondary contributor concerned.

(*d*) The secondary contributor may recover from his employee only such part (if any) of the contributions demanded from him as are *primary* contributions which should have been deducted from his employee's earnings in the *current* tax year but which he did not deduct *by reason of an error* which he made in good faith. [*Contribution Regs, 1 Sch 13(2A)(a), (b)(i)*]. In addition, the amount of arrears which can be deducted in any earnings period is limited to the amount that equals the correct deduction for that earnings period itself. [*Contributions Regs, 1 Sch 13(3A)*]. Any other recovery from the employee will be unlawful.

An example will help to underline the significance of these various comments.

Example
In the early 1990s, Algernon began to undertake television maintenance work for Bloggs TV Rentals Ltd. It was agreed between A and B that A would be treated as self-employed and would discharge his own tax and national insurance liabilities. A's earnings from B, and the contributions he paid, were as follows

Year ended 5 April	Earnings £	Class 2 £	Class 4 £
1991	20,500	236.60	774.90
1992	22,000	267.80	850.50
1993	23,500	278.20	941.22
1994	25,000	288.60	976.50
1995	26,500	293.80	1,158.51
1996	27,000	299.00	1,185.52
1997	28,000	314.60	1,008.00
1998	30,000	325.95	1,030.20
1999	32,000	330.20	1,074.60
2000	34,000	340.60	1,108.20
		£2,975.35	£10,108.15

In August 2000, an employer compliance officer calls on B to make a routine inspection of the wages records and, in the course of that examination, sees a note in the wages book reading 'Algernon—£660 per week from 6 April 2000'. The officer inquires further into the matter and decides that A has properly belonged in the category of employed earners since the engagement began. He computes the Class 1 liabilities to be

Year ended 5 April	Primary £	Secondary £	Total £
1991	1,470.56	2,090.00	3,560.56
1992	1,635.92	2,288.00	3,923.92
1993	1,698.84	2,444.00	4,142.84
1994	1,761.76	2,600.00	4,361.76
1995	1,998.88	2,703.00	4,701.88
1996	2,046.72	2,754.00	4,800.72
1997	2,112.24	2,856.00	4,968.24
1998	2,160.08	3,000.00	5,160.08
1999	2,253.76	3,200.00	5,453.76
2000	2,256.80	4,148.00	6,404.80
	£19,395.56	£28,083.00	£47,478.56

Even assuming the Inland Revenue permits the set-off of Class 2 contributions already paid by A, the amount due from B (but see 12.6 ARREARS OF CONTRIBUTIONS

131

as regards its enforceability) will be £44,503.21 (i.e. £47,478.56 – £2,975.35) and *no part of this amount will be recoverable from A*. If, however, A had misled B the position might alter. See 21.7 COLLECTION.

One point to take into account in the above example is the effect of the *Limitations Act 1980* on 'demands' for payment of contributions; in an interview with Payroll Manager's Review in April 1996 the former Chief Executive of the then CA, Mrs Faith Boardman stated 'If there is no response to the request then we will issue a demand warning that legal action will be taken in the event of non-payment. But when we issue that demand the arrears are restricted to six years, in accordance with the *Limitations Act*. I'm certainly not aware of demands, as such, being issued for periods up to twenty years ago, in part because, frankly, it would be quite unusual for us to query the payments made by an employer as far back as that!'

The effect of this is that Bloggs TV Rentals Ltd should pay only £29,585.33 (£44,503.21 *less* the total Class 1 liabilities (as reduced by Class 2 paid) for the years ended 5 April 1991, 5 April 1992, 5 April 1993 and 5 April 1994). The company should, when making the payment, make clear that the payment being made relates to 1994–95 to 1999–2000 inclusive. Otherwise, the NICO is entitled to, and will, allocate the payment as part-payment against the total amount it has computed i.e. including the out of date years. It can then pursue the outstanding amount due for 'in-date' years.

Where a person is re-categorised in consequence of a formal determination by the Secretary of State or on appeal to the Tax Commissioners and then, later, the decision is reversed on review or overturned by the High Court on appeal, there are certain discretionary powers. These are to prevent the new decision becoming retrospective in its effect by directing that the person in question is, up to the date of the decision on review or appeal, to be treated as though he properly belonged in the category of earners corresponding to the contributions which are now seen to have been incorrectly paid. The right to exercise this power is conditional upon it appearing that it would be in the interest of the person by or in respect of whom such contributions have been paid, or of any claimant or beneficiary by virtue of that person's contributions. [*Categorisation Regs, Reg 4*]. In practice, this power is only exercised where a self-employed earner has been re-categorised as an employed earner, has paid Class 1 contributions, and has then had his re-categorisation reversed (i.e. back to self-employed earner) on review or appeal.

The *Social Security Act 1998* contains new provisions (*section 54*) where an individual has been treated as an employed earner but is subsequently recategorised as self-employed. In respect of contributions for tax years 1998–99 onwards contributions will be refunded only for the current tax year and the most recently closed tax year.

Example
In June 1996 Derek engages Rodney to clean his car every day and to occasionally drive him in the car. Derek deals with PAYE and NICs as though Rodney is an employee. However, because Rodney can carry out the work at any time and can refuse to carry out those requirements if engaged on similar work for his other customers. Rodney is, on 6 May 2001, recategorised as a self-employed earner.

Contributions	Refund position	
1996-97	Refund due ⎱	
1997-98	Refund due ⎰	'Old' rules apply (i.e. current)
1998-99	No refund due ⎱	*Social Security Act 1998, s 54* rules
1999-2000	No refund due ⎰	apply
2000-01	Refund due	
2001-02	Refund due	Adjusted by employer 'in year'.

This draconian measure is partially eased with effect from 6 April 2000 by *The Social Security (Contributions) (Amendment No 3) Regulations 2000, SI 2000 No 736*. The rule as illustrated in the above example will not apply where either an appeal has been lodged by the end of 'year 2' or, within the same time scale, a written request has been made that an officer of the Board of Inland Revenue decides the categorisation question. [*Reg 37A as inserted by The Social Security (Contributions) (Amendment No 3) Regs 2000, Reg 2*].

14.14 CATEGORISATION BY REGULATION

In order to enable difficult or inconvenient categorisation questions to be resolved in an administratively convenient manner, regulations may be made to provide

(*a*) for employment of any prescribed description to be disregarded in relation to the liability for contributions which would otherwise arise from employment of that description; and

(*b*) for a person in employment of any prescribed description to be treated as falling within a category of earner *other than that in which he would otherwise fall*.

[*SSCBA 1992, s 2(2)*].

In accordance with regulations which have been made under these provisions, the following employments are to be *disregarded* entirely.

(i) Certain employments by close relatives (see 38.12 LABOUR-ONLY CONTRACTORS).

(ii) Certain employments of a person by his or her spouse (see 36.1 HUSBAND AND WIFE).

(iii) Extra-ordinary employment as a self-employed earner (see 14.10 above).

(iv) Employments on or after 6 April 1978 as a returning (or acting returning) officer or as counting officer for the purpose of any parliamentary or local government election or referendum authorised by Act of Parliament; or employments by any such officers for such purposes. [*Categorisation Regs, 1 Sch Pt III Para 10(c)*].

(v) Certain employments in a visiting force or as a member of an international headquarters or defence organisation (see 11.8, 11.9, and 11.11 ARMED FORCES).

Also, as stated in 14.1, in accordance with such regulations, earners in respect of employments of the following kinds are to be treated as falling within the category of *employed earner*.

(A) Employment as an office cleaner (see 38.13 LABOUR-ONLY CONTRACTORS).

(B) Employment as a cleaner of telephone apparatus and associated fixtures (see 38.15 LABOUR-ONLY CONTRACTORS).

(C) Certain employments through agencies (see 4.1 AGENCY WORKERS).

(D) Certain employments of a person by his or her spouse (see 36.1 HUSBAND AND WIFE).

(E) Certain employments as LECTURERS, TEACHERS AND INSTRUCTORS (41.2).

(F) Certain employments as MINISTERS OF RELIGION (43.1).

(G) Certain actors, musicians and other performers (see 33 ENTERTAINERS).

Certain earners gainfully employed as EXAMINERS (34.1) are, on the other hand, to be treated by regulation as falling within the category of self-employed earner.

VOLUNTEER DEVELOPMENT WORKERS (57) working outside Great Britain are to be categorised as self-employed earners, provided they do not derive from their employment earnings in respect of which Class 1 contributions are payable. [*Contributions Regs, Reg 123B as amended by Contributions Amendment Regs 1986, Reg 2*].

Rent officers and deputy rent officers appointed under a rent registration scheme are to be regarded as employed under a contract of service and are thus to be treated as employed earners for contribution purposes. [*Rent Act 1977, s 63(3)*]. Likewise, magistrates' clerks are to be regarded as employed under a contract of service with the local authority in the area in which they are based. [*Justices of the Peace Act 1979, ss 5, 57, 58*].

14.15 SECONDARY CONTRIBUTORS

A secondary contributor can only exist in relation to any payment of earnings to, or for the benefit of, an employed earner. [*SSCBA 1992, s 7(1)*]. Subject to certain exceptions listed below, the secondary contributor will be

(*a*) in the case of an earner employed under a contract of service (see 14.3 to 14.7 above), his employer;

(*b*) in the case of an earner employed in an office with emoluments chargeable to income tax under Schedule E (see 14.9 above),

    (i) any person who is prescribed in relation to that office under, for example, the charter, statute, declaration of trust or other instrument creating the office or, if no such person is prescribed,

    (ii) the government department, public authority or body of persons responsible for paying the emoluments of the office.

[*SSCBA 1992, s 7(1)*].

The *exceptions* are as follows.

(A) Where a person works under the general control and management of a person other than his immediate employer, that person rather than the immediate employer is to be treated as the secondary contributor [*SSCBA 1992, s 7(2)(b); Categorisation Regs, Reg 5, 3 Sch 2; Contributions Regs, 1 Sch 3(1)*]; or

(B) Where a person falls to be treated as an employed earner by application of the regulations described at 14.14 above, the person prescribed by those regulations is to be treated as the secondary contributor (see 4.3 AGENCY WORKERS, 36.1 HUSBAND AND WIFE, 38.13 and 38.15 LABOUR-ONLY CONTRACTORS, 41.2 LECTURERS, TEACHERS AND INSTRUCTORS and 43.2 MINISTERS OF RELIGION) [*SSCBA 1992, s 7(2); Categorisation Regs, Reg 5, 3 Sch 1, 2, 3, 6, 7, 8 as amended by Categorisation Amendment Regs 1990, Reg 3(1)*]; or

(C) Where a person is employed by a company in voluntary liquidation which is carrying on business under a liquidator, the liquidator is to be treated as the secondary contributor [*Categorisation Regs, Reg 5, 3 Sch 4*]; or

(D) Where a person is employed as a barrister's clerk, the head of chambers is to be treated as the secondary contributor [*Categorisation Regs, Reg 5, 3 Sch 5*]; or

(E) Where a person is employed by a foreign employer and, in pursuance of that employment, his personal service is first made available to a host employer on or after 6 April 1994 and is rendered for the purposes of the host employer's business, the host employer to whom the personal service is made available is to be treated as the secondary Class 1 contributor. (See 4.3 AGENCY WORKERS and 49.9 OVERSEAS MATTERS) [*Categorisation Regs, Reg 5, 3 Sch 9 as inserted by Categorisation Amendment Regs 1994, Reg 4*]. For this purpose, a 'foreign employer' is a person who does not fulfil the conditions as to residence or presence in Great Britain and who, if he did fulfil those conditions, would be the secondary contributor in relation to any payment of earnings to or for the benefit of the person employed; and a 'host employer' is a person who has a place of business in Great Britain. [*Categorisation Regs, Reg 1(2) as amended by Categorisation Amendment Regs 1994, Reg 2*]. It should be noted that the word 'employer' in this context does not impart any of the common law considerations such as mutual obligations, control and economic reality into the identification of the employer. It is important to note that the change to the regulations only apply to secondments taking place on or after 6 April 1994. In view of the operation of the '52-week rule' (see 49.8 OVERSEAS CONTRIBUTIONS) the first actual liability for secondary contributions cannot have arisen in respect of such employees until at least 5 April 1995.

(F)   Where a person is employed as a mariner (see 42.8 MARINERS) and his employer does not satisfy conditions of residence and presence (see 49.9 OVERSEAS MATTERS), the person who pays his earnings is to be treated as the secondary contributor [*Contributions Regs, Reg 93*].

(G)   Where a person is employed as an entertainer the person who has engaged the entertainer under that contract of services is to be treated as the secondary contributor. [*Categorisation Regs, Reg 5, 3 Sch as amended by Categorisation Amendment Regs 1998, Reg 4*].

The rule in (C) above was necessitated by a determination by the Secretary of State (see 14.12 above) that, in law, the appointment of a liquidator or receiver does not terminate a contract of service under which a person working for a company supplies his services and that, in consequence, the company and not the liquidator is liable as secondary contributor for contributions on earnings paid after the date of the appointment. (*M30 (1953)*). Likewise, the rule in (D) above was necessitated by a determination by the Secretary of State that, in law, a barrister's clerk (if employed rather than self-employed—see *McMenamin v Diggles* [1991] *STC 419*) is employed under a separate contract of service between himself and each of the barristers occupying the chambers in which he works. (*M49 (1956)*).

A local authority is to be regarded as the secondary contributor in relation to earnings paid to rent officers and clerks to the justices (and their staff) based in its area. [*Rent Act 1977, s 63(3); Justices of the Peace Act 1979, ss 5, 57, 58*].

A person who would otherwise fall to be treated as a secondary contributor according to the rules stated will not be so treated if he fails to satisfy conditions of residence or presence in Great Britain (see 49.9 OVERSEAS MATTERS).

14.16   ILLEGAL CONTRACTS OF SERVICE

It has been explained at 14.2 and 14.10 that for a person other than an office holder to be an *employed earner* for contribution purposes he must be gainfully employed in Great Britain *under a contract of service*; and that anyone gainfully employed in Great Britain otherwise than in employed earner's employment will be a *self-employed earner*. It follows, therefore, that anyone who enters a contract of service which, in law, is or becomes void will, for contribution purposes, fall to be categorised as a self-employed earner rather than an employed earner and that his employer under the contract will cease to be a secondary contributor (See 14.5 above).

Certain contracts of service are void by operation of statute. Examples are as follows.

(*a*)   A contract under which a person works for a bookmaker, commission agent or turf accountant and whose duties involve taking bets

(i)   as a tout or street betting runner;

(ii) at a racecourse — unless he is 21 or over and has written and registered authority and the bookmaker has a current permit issued by the Betting Licensing Authority; or

(iii) at a betting shop — unless he is 18 or over.

[*Betting, Gaming and Lotteries Act 1963, ss 3, 8, 21*].

(*b*) A contract under which a non-patrial within the terms of *Immigration Act 1971, s 2* is employed contrary to restrictions placed on his freedom to work under *Sec 3* of that Act as amended by the *Asylum and Immigration Act 1996, 2 Sch.* (See *Rastegarnia v Richmond Designs Ltd 19 May 1978 IT Case Number 11141/78/A*).

Other contracts of service may be void at common law. These are contracts of service which require the commission of crimes or torts or the perpetration of fraud; contracts of service which are for sexually immoral purposes or are prejudicial to public safety or to the administration of justice; and contracts of service tending to corruption in public life.

Example (1)
Arthur is engaged by Knight Hotels Ltd as a concierge. At his interview he was told that he would have to procure prostitutes for hotel guests should he be asked to do so. That makes his contract of service void as the contract has a sexually immoral purpose, and Arthur is, for contribution purposes, a self-employed earner. Neither Knight Hotels nor Arthur will have any Class 1 liabilities as regards the earnings paid to Arthur.

Example (2)
Guinevere is engaged by Lancelot Enterprises Ltd as a sales representative. At her interview she is told that she will receive two-thirds of her agreed salary as declared gross pay but that the other third will be paid to her as expenses so as to evade tax and national insurance. That makes her contract void as one of its objects is to defraud the Inland Revenue, and she is, therefore, a self-employed earner for contribution purposes. (See *Napier v National Business Agency Ltd [1951] 2 AER 264*).

14.17 **PERSONAL SERVICE COMPANIES**

Under proposals announced by the Chancellor in the March 1999 Budget, people who would otherwise be employees of their clients will no longer be able to avoid paying their share of tax and National Insurance contributions by working through personal service companies and other intermediaries. The new rules apply from 6 April 2000. See **www.inlandrevenue.gov.uk/IR35**.

This is a revised approach which corresponds to concerns expressed during consultation that the new rules were too wide in scope, and that they would make it impossible for people to work through intermediaries even if they were prepared to pay the right amount of tax and NICs. The main points are.

- The rules will rely on the *existing* tests (see 14.3–14.6) which are currently used to determine the boundary between employment and self-employment for tax and National Insurance contributions purposes, instead of the alternative test put forward originally. Using these more familiar tests will help understanding of the new rules and ensure they are targeted on the right people.

- The responsibility for ensuring that the new rules are followed will belong to the *intermediaries* themselves, not the clients, as originally proposed. As a result of this approach, there will be no need for a certification scheme to allow clients to identify intermediaries who could continue to receive gross payments.

- The *intermediaries* will be responsible for applying PAYE and National Insurance contributions to all earnings from relevant engagements, after a limited allowance for expenses and pension contributions. See Example below.

'Intermediary' is widely defined, including a company in which the worker, together with associates, controls more than *only* five per cent of a company. 'Associate' is similarly very widely defined including, for the first time ever in tax and contribution law, unmarried partners (of the opposite sex, but not the same sex!). [*The Social Security Contributions (Intermediaries) Regulations 2000, SI 2000 No 727, Regs 2(5) and 3*].

14.18 Identifying engagements where the new rules will apply

The new rules will apply to engagements ('relevant engagements') where:

(a) a worker provides services under a contract between a client and an intermediary; and

(b) but for the presence of the intermediary, the income arising would have been treated as coming from an office or employment held by the worker under the existing rules used to determine the boundary between employment and self-employment income for tax/NICs purposes, if the individual had contracted directly with the client.

Guidance on the existing rules is included in Inland Revenue leaflet IR56 (available on the Internet). The rules will be applied in respect of each engagement, in the same way as they apply to individuals who operate without intermediaries. See 14.23 Contracts below.

The rules do not apply to such engagements where:

(a) the client is an individual and not in business (so services for a householder should not be affected); or

(b) the worker only receives income from the intermediary in a form which falls within Schedule E/Class 1 (e.g. straightforward employees of consultancy firms) and has no other rights to income or capital from the intermediary. Exceptions have been made for income from certain investments (e.g. holdings of small numbers of shares in the employing company). Similar rules exempt some partners in larger partnerships.

14.19 Tax and NICs treatment where the new rules apply

Under the modified approach intermediaries, and not the clients, are responsible for operating the legislation. It is not necessary for the clients to check whether the legislation applies when they enter into a contract with an intermediary. There is no certification scheme.

The intention is that all the money received by the intermediary in respect of a relevant engagement, minus certain deductions listed below, should be treated as paid to the worker in a form subject to Schedule E tax and Class 1 NICs.

14.20 The intermediary

(a) Intermediaries who are companies

Where a company intermediary receives income in respect of a relevant engagement, then:

I. the intermediary will operate PAYE and pay NICs on payments of salary to the worker during the year, in the normal way;

II.   if, at the end of the tax year, the total of the worker's employment income from the intermediary, including benefits in kind, amounts to less than the intermediary's income from all that worker's relevant engagements, then the difference (net of allowable expenses described below) will be deemed to have been paid to the worker as salary on 5 April, and Schedule E tax/NICs will be due.

III.   Where salary is deemed in this way:

- appropriate deductions will be allowed in arriving at corporation tax profits; and

- no further tax/NICs will be due if the worker subsequently withdraws the money from the company.

(b) Where the intermediary is a partnership

Where a partnership receives gross payment under a relevant contract:

I.   Income of the partnership from all relevant engagements in the year (net of allowable expenses described below) will be deemed to have been paid to the worker on 5 April as salary from a deemed employment held by the worker, and Schedule E tax/NICs will be due accordingly.

II.   Any amount deemed to be income within Schedule E/Class 1 under (I) above will not be included when computing the worker's share of Schedule D partnership profits.

However, the Inland Revenue's current practice of including small amounts of Schedule E income in the calculation of Schedule D profits for the self-employed, including partners, will apply also in these cases.

The deemed payment will be aggregated with other payments already made in the tax year concerned and the total amount will be assessed as if the recipient were a director (i.e. annual or pro rata annual earnings period) whether or not the person is in fact a director. [*The Social Security Contributions (Intermediaries) Regulations 2000, SI 2000 No 727, Reg 8(2)*].

14.21 **Expenses**

It is proposed that an intermediary should be allowed to deduct the following expenses from payments in respect of a relevant engagement in calculating whether any 'deemed payment' is required:

I.   all expenses otherwise eligible for deduction under the normal schedule E expenses rule (*ICTA 1988, s 198*): i.e. qualifying travelling expenses and those expended wholly and exclusively and necessarily in the performance of the duties of the employment (guidance on the expenses rules is included in Inland Revenue booklets 480 and 490 (available on the Internet at **www.inlandrevenue.gov.uk**)); plus

II.   any employer pension contributions made to an approved scheme which are allowable under normal rules; plus

III.   a further flat rate 5% of the gross payment for the relevant contract to cover other miscellaneous expenses, such as running costs of the intermediary;

IV.   the amount of the employer's NICs paid during the year, plus any due on the deemed payment.

14.22 Failure cases

Where an intermediary fails to deduct and account for PAYE/NICs on payments to the worker under the new rules, the normal penalty provisions for employer failures will apply. If the intermediary does not meet its obligations to account for PAYE/NICs then the amount may be collected from the worker — as happens in certain circumstances under existing PAYE and NIC legislation.

14.23 Contracts

As mentioned above the terms of contracts used by service company workers are all important. Agency contracts in the IT industry normally require the worker to perform his/her duties at the client's premises, using the client's equipment, work standard hours and be paid at an hourly rate, etc. Where a worker is engaged on a contract for a period of a month or more and cannot demonstrate a recent history of work including engagements which have the characteristics of self-employment then the Inland Revenue will likely as not say that the work constitutes employment and is therefore covered by the new rules. Where the period is less than a month the position will be considered on a case by case basis.

Example

Graham is an IT consultant working through his own service company and has secured a job with Benevolent Ltd through an agency to work on the computerised accounts system for six months. In accounts a team leader (another IT contractor) tells Graham what work he is to carry out but he is left to his own experience to determine 'how' the work is carried out. Graham is expected to be in attendance at Benevolent Ltd a regular 40 hours per week. Graham's company is paid an hourly rate for his services at 1.5 times the normal hourly rate. Billed monthly, Benevolent Ltd pays the agency who in turn are invoiced by Graham's company. The total invoices for the six months will amount to £25,000. Graham draws a salary of £10,000 from his company over the period. Allowable expenses amount to £750 and there are pension contributions of £2,000. The main indications that self-employment arises here is the minimal financial risk from invoicing, the ability to work for others and the existence of Graham's company. In contrast, the engagement is relatively long and he must carry out the services personally. Also Benevolent Ltd provides the equipment and working accommodation and he works the usual working hours of the client. The engagement with Benevolent Ltd would appear to have been an employment had it been directed between Graham and the client direct rather than through the service company. The new rules therefore apply as follows:

	£	
Relevant income received		£25,000
Deduct	£	
Pension contributions	2,000.00	
Expenses (allowable)	750.00	
Flat rate all'ce (5% of £25,000)	1,250.00	
Salary paid	10,000.00	
Class 1 NICs (on £10,000)	685.00	(14,685)
Net deemed payments before NICs		10,315
Employer's NICs		(1,122)
Deemed payment (£10,315 × 100/112.2)		£9,193

The post-expense figure before NICs (i.e. £10,315) is multiplied by 100/112.2 to reach the deemed payment figure since the employers earnings threshold has already been taken into account on the £10,000 salary. The PAYE and NICs on the deemed payment will be payable on or before 19 April 2001. Late payment will

14.23 Categorisation

incur an interest charge and possible penalty and therefore an estimate of PAYE/NICs should be paid by 19 April in the year following the end of the tax year. The service company is responsible for the compliance aspect of PAYE/NICs regarding the new rules.

15 Class 1 Contributions: Employed Earners

Cross-references. See AGE EXCEPTION (3) for age limitations on liability; AGGREGATION OF EARNINGS (5); ANTI-AVOIDANCE (8); APPEALS AND REVIEWS (9) for remedies for dissatisfaction with amounts assessed; ARREARS OF CONTRIBUTIONS (12) for recovery provisions; CATEGORISATION (14); COLLECTION (21); COMPANY DIRECTORS (22); CONTRACTED-OUT EMPLOYMENT (23); CREDITS (24) for circumstances in which Class 1 contributions are awarded; DEATH OF CONTRIBUTOR (26) for non-liability on earnings paid thereafter; DEFERMENT OF PAYMENT (27); EARNINGS (28); EARNINGS LIMITS AND THRESHOLDS (30); EARNINGS PERIODS (31); ENFORCEMENT (32); INLAND REVENUE (37) for links with PAYE and disclosure of information; MARINERS (42); MULTIPLE EMPLOYMENTS (44); NATIONAL INSURANCE NUMBER (46); NATIONAL INSURANCE SURCHARGE (47); OVERSEAS MATTERS (49); RATES AND LIMITS (51); REDUCED LIABILITY ELECTION (52); REPAYMENT AND RE-ALLOCATION (53); WORKING CASE STUDY (58).

Other Sources. Simon's NIC, Part I, Section 2, Chapter 8; Tolley's Tax Planning 2000–01; Leaflets CA 01, CA29, CA30, CA 35/36, CWG2 (2000).

15.1 GENERAL CONSIDERATIONS

Class 1 contributions account for over 96% of the National Insurance Fund's contribution income. In monetary terms, this will amount to some £50,805,000,000 in the year 2000–01 and, of this, some £29,654,000,000 will represent secondary contributions from employers and others paying earnings. The balance of £21,151,000,000 represents primary contributions payable by employees (see 45.4 NATIONAL INSURANCE FUND). In addition, a further £6,271,000,000 of Class 1 contributions collected is diverted directly to the National Health Service (£3,532,000,000 secondary and £2,739,000,000 primary).

In 1995–96, the most recent year for which detailed figures are currently available, 22.153 million persons paid Class 1 contributions either alone or along with CLASS 2 CONTRIBUTIONS (18) and or CLASS 3 CONTRIBUTIONS (19) (Contributions and Qualifying Years for Retirement Pension 1995–96, Government Statistical Service, May 1998).

15.2 LIABILITY

Subject to the qualification stated below, both a primary (i.e. employed earner's) and a secondary (i.e. employer's) Class 1 contribution is payable where, in any tax week, EARNINGS (28) are *paid* (see 15.3 below) to or for the benefit of an earner in respect of any one employment of his and

(a) he is categorised as an employed earner in relation to that employment (see 14.2 to 14.9 CATEGORISATION); and

(b) he is over the age of 16 (see 3.1 AGE EXCEPTION); and

(c) as regards primary contributions, the amount paid exceeds the current employee's earnings threshold — or, up to 5 April 2000, lower earnings limit — (scaled-up as appropriate in either case if his EARNINGS PERIODS (31) are longer than a week; see 30.1 to 30.3 EARNINGS LIMITS AND THRESHOLDS) and as regards secondary contributions, the amount paid exceeds the current employer's earnings threshold — or, up to 5 April 1999, lower earnings limit (scaled-up as appropriate in either case if his EARNINGS PERIODS (31) are longer than a week; see 30.1 to 30.3 EARNINGS LIMITS AND THRESHOLDS).

[*SSCBA 1992, s 6(1) as amended by Social Security Act 1998, s 51(2)*].

If, however, the earnings relate to a period after the earner has attained pensionable age, a secondary contribution *only* is payable in respect of those earnings (see 3.7 AGE EXCEPTION). [*SSCBA 1992, s 6(2)*].

15.3 Class 1 Contributions: Employed Earners

For the meaning of 'secondary contributor' see 14.15 CATEGORISATION.

In thus determining liability, no regard need be given to any other payment of earnings to, or for the benefit of, the earner in respect of any other employment unless one or other of the AGGREGATION OF EARNINGS (5) rules applies. [*SSCBA 1992, s 6(1)*].

15.3 The meaning of 'paid'

Class 1 contribution liability arises in relation to earnings *paid*, not earnings earned. Unlike income tax,—which is an annual charge—Class 1 contributions are due on earnings paid in an EARNINGS PERIOD (31). It is of considerable importance, therefore, to determine precisely when, in law, payment of earnings takes place. The general rule is that payment of earnings takes place when a sum equivalent to those earnings is placed unreservedly at the disposal of the earner. (*Garforth v Newsmith Stainless Ltd [1979] 2 AER 73*). It is sufficient, therefore, that they are placed to the credit of an account (whether with the employer or with a bank or some other third party) on which the earner is free to draw, whether he does, in fact, draw on the account or not. It is suggested, however, that a mere book entry is not sufficient to constitute a payment of earnings and that, for example, a credit to a director's current account with his company is *not* a payment of earnings unless the company places an equivalent monetary resource at the director's disposal. Insofar as the *Garforth* case purports to state otherwise it is thought to be bad law. An absence of funds to support a credit entry in a director's current account with his company will necessarily impose a restriction on his right to draw on the sum placed to his credit, and any restriction on the right to draw a sum placed to an earner's credit will prevent payment from taking place until the restriction is removed. It was important that an employer kept these principles in mind if he decided to pay to an employee a bonus in kind rather than in cash so as to avoid Class 1 contribution liabilities (see 28.24 EARNINGS). If the bonus was voted to the employee unconditionally, payment (in the form of a credit against which the employee was thereupon free to draw) was deemed to be made at the time of voting and Class 1 liabilities then arose. The form in which drawings were later made was, accordingly, quite irrelevant. Contribution liabilities were avoided only if the bonus etc. was voted subject to the condition that it was paid and received in the specified non-cash form selected by the employer and not otherwise. Since there is a Class 1A charge on all taxable benefits in kind from 6 April 2000, such arrangements are now unlikely to be entered into in practice.

It is interesting to note in connection with the above comments on restrictions on the right to draw remuneration the provisions of *FA 1989, s 45(2)* which provide that, for PAYE purposes, any 'fetter' on the right to draw sums credited to a director's account with a company is to be disregarded in determining when those sums are paid. The Revenue has confirmed in relation to income tax (Press Release, 28 July 1989) that earnings voted subject to a condition having been fulfilled are not 'fettered'— entitlement to those earnings does not arise until the condition is fulfilled, at which point it is possible that PAYE and Class 1 liability arise.

Where a loan or advance is made in anticipation of earnings, payment of earnings will normally take place only when the obligation to repay is released. (*Clayton v Gothorp [1971] 2 AER 1311*). (But it should be noted that the mere writing-off by an employer of a loan made to an employee does not release the employee from the obligation to repay and consequently does *not* constitute a payment of earnings—contrary to what the Inland Revenue say. (See EARNINGS (28)). In the case of COMPANY DIRECTORS (22.3) only, this general rule is reversed so that a loan or advance in anticipation of earnings is earnings at the time of the advance itself. Until 5 April 1994, the DSS also took the view that, where an employee used a company credit card or company charge card to purchase goods or services for private purposes, a payment of earnings took place if and when the employer waived the right to recover such amounts from the employee. (April 1993 Green Book NI 269, Page 56, Item (13)). However, since 1995 the guidance has changed to exclude from earnings any goods or services that an employee purchases on his employer's behalf, so long as the employee had prior authority to make the purchase and the employee explained to the supplier in advance of the contract being made, and the supplier accepted, that the purchase was being made on the employer's behalf. See CWG2 (2000), Page 76.

Where an employed earner's regular remuneration is, as a term of his employment, in advance, the amounts paid are, because of the earner's unfettered right to them, earnings paid at the time of payment.

Certain irregular payments of earnings made in respect of regular periods have, by regulation, a deemed date of payment (see 31.4 EARNINGS PERIODS).

Payment need not be to the earner himself for it to be liable to Class 1 contributions: it is sufficient that it is for his benefit. [*SSCBA 1992, s 6(1)*]. (Though it is arguable that no primary Class 1 contribution is collectible—see 21.1 COLLECTION.) Thus, the discharge of an earner's pecuniary obligation by his employer will (if the payment is made in return for the earner acting as or being an employee and for no other reason—see 28.45 EARNINGS) be a payment of earnings. (*Hartland v Diggines (1926) 10 TC 247*). Thus, for example, the amount paid by an employer in settlement of *private* telephone charges made to one of his employees is, if the employee himself is the telephone subscriber, earnings for contribution purposes (see 28.60 EARNINGS).

The question then arises whether, if an employer declines to recover primary Class 1 contributions from an employee, the same principle applies. Has the employer effectively discharged his employee's indebtedness and do the primary contributions themselves become earnings on which further contributions are due? Although the DSS never took the point (see 21.3 COLLECTION), the answer may be yes. The liability for primary Class 1 contributions is clearly the liability of the earner [*SSCBA 1992, s 6(3)(a)*] and, even though the employer is obliged by law to discharge that liability [*1 Sch 3*], the employee normally has no choice but to 'pay' by suffering a deduction from his earnings equivalent to the amount which the employer has discharged. If the employer declines to make the deduction, the employee is relieved of the liability to suffer the deduction and that is arguably equivalent to an additional payment of earnings.

15.4 RATES

The amount of a primary Class 1 contribution for which liability arises as described at 15.2 above, is, from 6 April 2000, to be the percentage of so much of the earnings paid in the tax week as exceeds the current primary earnings threshold but does not exceed the current upper earnings limit. This is currently 10%.

In 1999–2000, it was the percentage of so much of the earnings paid in the tax week as exceeded the lower earnings limit but did not exceed the upper earnings limit.

Prior to 6 April 1999, it was the initial primary percentage of so much of the earnings paid in the week, in respect of the employment in question, as did not exceed the lower earnings limit and the main primary percentage of so much of those earnings as exceeded the lower earnings limit but did not exceed the upper earnings limit (the lower and upper earnings limits being scaled up as appropriate if the EARNINGS PERIODS (31) are longer than a week; see 30.1 to 30.3 EARNINGS LIMITS AND THRESHOLDS). [*SSCBA 1992, s 8(1)*]. Earnings in excess of the upper earnings limit are ignored for primary Class 1 contribution purposes.

Example
Kevin employed Glenn at a rate of £200 per week from 27 March to 7 April 2000, making payment on Friday each week. Primary contributions due are

15.4 Class 1 Contributions: Employed Earners

Week ended 31 March 2000	66 × Nil%	Nil
	134 × 10%	13.40
	£200	£13.40
Week ended 7 April 2000	76 × Nil%	Nil
	124 × 10%	12.40
	£200	£12.40

The amount of a secondary Class 1 contribution for which liability arises as described at 15.2 above, is, from 6 April 2000, to be the secondary percentage of so much of the earnings paid in the tax week as exceeds the current secondary (i.e. employer's) earnings threshold. This is currently 12.2%.

Prior to 6 April 1999 it was to be the appropriate secondary percentage of the earnings paid in the week in respect of the employment in question. [*SSCBA 1992, s 9(1)*]. There has, from 6 October 1985, been no upper earnings limit which might restrict the amount to which the appropriate secondary percentage is to be applied.

From 5 October 1989 to 5 April 1999 the initial standard rate primary percentage had been 2% and thereafter the rate was reduced to nil. From 6 April 1994 to 5 April 1999 the main standard rate primary percentage has been 10% and the 10% remained for 1999–2000. [*SSCBA 1992, s 8(2)*]. The appropriate secondary percentages were previously determined by reference to the secondary earnings brackets in which the earnings fall (see 30.4 to 30.6 EARNINGS LIMITS AND THRESHOLDS) i.e. for 1998–99 (standard rate):

EB	%	EB	%	EB	%	EB	%
1	3	2	5	3	7	4	10

Following the previous example, Kevin's secondary contributions in respect of Glenn's employment are:

Week ended 31 March 2000	83 × Nil%	Nil
	117 × 12.2%	14.27
	£200	£14.27
Week ended 7 April 2000	84 × Nil%	Nil
	116 × 12.2%	14.15
	£200	£14.15

The above rates will not always be appropriate, however (see 51.3 RATES AND LIMITS). Certain married women and widows (but not their secondary contributors) are entitled to contribute at a *reduced* rate (see REDUCED LIABILITY ELECTIONS (52)) and, where an employed earner's earnings are derived from a CONTRACTED-OUT EMPLOYMENT (23), both the employed earner and his secondary contributor are to pay contributions at a special *contracted-out* rate on earnings falling between the lower and upper earnings limits being either a contracted-out salary related (COSR) or contracted-out money purchase (COMP) scheme (see 30.1 EARNINGS LIMITS AND THRESHOLDS and 51.2 to 51.5 RATES AND LIMITS). For 2000–01 the reduced rate is 3.85% on earnings between the lower and upper earnings limits and the primary contracted-out rate is 8.4% on earnings between the lower and upper earnings limits. The secondary contracted-out rates, after taking account of all contracted-out rebates, are:

On weekly earnings		COSR scheme	COMP scheme
From	*To*		
£0.00	£67.00	Nil	Nil
£67.01	£84.00	3% rebate	0.6% rebate
£84.01	£535.00	9.2%	11.6%
Over £535.00		12.2%	12.2%

See also 22.3 CONTRACTED–OUT EMPLOYMENT. [*Contributions Regs, Reg 104, as amended by Contributions Amendment No 2 Regs 1982, Reg 2 and SI 1989 No 1677, Reg 3(8); SSCBA 1992, s 8(1)–(2); SSCBA 1992, s 9(1)–(3) as amended by Social Security Act 1998, s 51; Pension Schemes Act 1993, s 41*].

Certain of these rates are reduced (or further reduced) where the employed earner in question is

(*a*)   a serving member of the ARMED FORCES (11.5) (primary and secondary, standard and reduced rates) but only up to 5 April 1996; or

(*b*)   a mariner (primary and secondary, standard and contracted-out rates, with a further secondary reduction where the earnings relate to employment on a foreign-going ship—see 42.9 to 42.11 MARINERS).

If it is considered necessary, the Treasury (subject to Parliamentary approval) may, at any time, make an order altering

(*a*)   the primary percentage; and/or

(*b*)   the secondary percentage

provided that neither the primary percentage nor the secondary percentage is increased to a rate more than 0.25% higher than the relevant rate applicable for the preceding tax year.

These powers were vested in the Secretary of State for Social Security prior to 1 April 1999.

[*SSAA 1992, ss 143, 145(1)–(3) as amended by SSC(T)A 1999, 3 Sch 46–49*].

Changes which overstep these restrictions must be brought about by statute.

15.5   **CALCULATION**

Class 1 contributions may be calculated by one of two methods. The first is the 'exact percentage method' and is mainly used in connection with computerised payrolls or the calculation of contributions payable on the earnings of COMPANY DIRECTORS (22.4). Under this method primary and secondary contributions are each to be calculated separately at each of whichever rates apply and each such calculation is to be to the nearest penny with any amount of a halfpenny or less being disregarded. [*Contributions Regs, Reg 9(1)(a)(b)*].

The alternative (and usual) method of calculation is in accordance with scales and a contributions calculator prepared by the Board of Inland Revenue. [*Contributions Regs, Reg 9(2) as amended by Contributions Transitional Regs 1985, Reg 5(4)(a) and SSC(T)A 1999, s 1(2) and 2 Sch*]. These take the form of tables lettered A to W. Volumes containing selections of these tables appropriate to the needs of different types of employer are available from the Inland Revenue. These volumes are as follows.

CA 38—not contracted-out contributions for employers.
CA 39—contracted-out contributions for employers with COSRS.
CA 40—employees with no secondary contributor.
CA 41—members of armed forces (to 1995–96 only).
CA 42—mariners with foreign-going rebate.
CA 43—contracted-out contributions and minimum payments for employers with COMPS.

15.5   Class 1 Contributions: Employed Earners

There are also 'Simplified Deduction Scheme' tables (CA 37) for employers of low paid persons, without pension schemes. Although described as 'simplified' they are simply shorter than the CA 38 tables and can only be used for earnings up to (in 2000–01) £284 per week or £1,175 per month (note that these amounts do not match).

The tables most commonly in use (and included in several of the volumes described) are the following.

Table A — not contracted-out standard rate contributions.
Table B — not contracted-out reduced rate contributions.
Table C — not contracted-out employer-only contributions.
Table D — contracted-out COSR standard rate contributions.
Table E — contracted-out COSR reduced rate contributions.
Table F — contracted-out COMPS standard rate contributions.
Table G — contracted-out COMPS reduced rate contributions.
Table S — contracted-out COMPS employer only contributions.

When the NICO speaks of a person's table letter, it is the letter indicated above to which it refers.

The tables cater for EARNINGS PERIODS (31) of one week or one month only, so that, where the earnings period is a multiple of a week or a month, the earnings in question must be divided as necessary and the contributions shown by the tables as appropriate to the result must then be multiplied by the divisor. In the case of weekly earnings periods, the tables are banded in earnings steps of £1 and, in the case of monthly earnings periods, in earnings steps of £4 except where earnings reach the earnings threshold. Where the amount of earnings on which contributions are to be calculated does not appear in the tables, the next lower figure on the scale is to be used. [*Contributions Regs, Reg 9(3)(4)*]. The contribution liability revealed by use of the tables has been calculated on the mid-point of each table band except at the lower and upper earnings limit where it has been calculated on the limit itself.

Example
Alistair is in a contracted-out (COSR) employment. His earnings for the quarter ended 30 June 2000 are £9,000 and, in accordance with the normal procedures of the company by which he is employed are paid to him on 5 July 2000. Class 1 contributions could be calculated by either the exact percentage method or the tables method (see Cards CWG1 (2000), Card 12), as follows.

Exact percentage method

Employee's earnings threshold = 13 × £76.00 = £988.00

Employer's earnings threshold = 13 × £84 = £1,092.00†

Employee's upper earnings limit = 13 × £535.00 = £6,955.00

	£				£
Primary:	898.00	×	Nil%	=	0.00
	6,057.00	×	8.4%	=	501.23
	£6,955.00				£501.23
Secondary:	1,092.00	×	Nil%	=	0.00
	5,863.00	×	9.2%	=	539.40
	£6,955.00				539.40
	2,045.00	×	12.2%	=	249.49
	£9,000.00				£788.89

146

Tables method
Tables CA 39, either:
Weekly Table D
£9,000.00/13 = £692.31
Table entry £535.00

Primary: £38.56 × 13 =	£501.28
Secondary: £41.49 × 13 =	£539.37
† (per calculator at end of Table) £19.15 × 13	248.95
	£788.32

or:
Monthly Table D
£9,000.00/3 = £3,000
Table entry £2,319.00

Primary: £167.16 × 3 =	£501.48
Secondary: £179.77 × 3 =	£539.31
+ (per calculator at end of Tables) £83.08 × 3 =	249.24
	£788.55

Two notes need to be made about the above example. First, from the total contributions would also be deducted the employee's and employer's contracted-out rebate on earnings falling between the respective lower earnings limit and the earnings thresholds. This rebate is considered further in 23 CONTRACTED-OUT EMPLOYMENT. Secondly, the calculations are not strictly correct so far as the employer's contributions is concerned since the employer's earnings threshold, as well as being expressed in terms of a weekly amount, is also expressed in terms of monthly or annual amounts. [*Reg 7, as amended by The Social Security (Contributions and Credits)(Miscellaneous Amendments) Regulations 2000, Reg 3*]. The earnings threshold is not to be multiplied in the conventional way where the earnings period is a multiple of either a week or a month and, in this example, should strictly be £4,385 ÷ 12 × 3 = £1,096.25, rounded up to £1,097.00. However, it is impossible for standard tables to accommodate this and the instructions for use of the tables have not been amended since the introduction of the earnings thresholds. [*Reg 8(3), as amended by The Social Security (Contributions and Credits)(Miscellaneous Amendments) Regulations 2000, Reg 4*].

Although either method may be used, all the contributions payable in a particular tax year as regards the earnings paid to or for the benefit of an employed earner in respect of his employed earner's employment (or employments, if he has more than one and they fall to be aggregated) are, unless the Inland Revenue agrees to the contrary, to be calculated wholly in accordance with one method or the other. [*Contributions Regs, Reg 9(5)*]. Permission to change from one method to the other is not required, however, where the change is attributable to a change in payroll procedure (e.g. payroll computerisation) or to an employed earner being transferred from an 'exact percentage' payroll to a 'tables' payroll, or vice versa. (CWG2 (2000), Page 36).

Special calculation rules are to be applied where an earner's earnings in respect of different employed earner's employments are to be aggregated and those employments include both contracted-out and not contracted-out employments (see 5.11 AGGREGATION OF EARNINGS).

Special calculation rules applied also for 1985–86 in the case of company directors and other employed earners with *annual* EARNINGS PERIODS (31) (see the 1986–87 edition of this work) and 1989–90 in the case of company directors who held office and received payments of earnings during periods which straddled 5 October 1989 (see 22 COMPANY DIRECTORS).

15.6 **COLLECTION**

Where earnings are paid to an employed earner and a liability for a primary and a secondary Class 1 contribution arises in respect of the payment, the secondary contributor is liable not only for his own secondary contribution but, in the first instance, to pay the earner's primary contribution also. [*SSCBA 1992, 1 Sch 3(1)*]. This is so *unless*

(a) he is a person against whom the contribution legislation cannot be enforced (because he is, for example, an employer who is neither resident nor present in Great Britain and who has no place of business here—see 49.9 OVERSEAS MATTERS); or

(b) the earner has agreed (under, for example, a DEFERMENT OF CONTRIBUTIONS (27) arrangement) that he himself will pay any primary contributions payable in respect of his earnings.

The machinery for the discharge of these liabilities and for the recovery of primary contributions from the earnings to which they relate was created by the DSS and lies in the PAYE system which, with the concurrence of the Inland Revenue, has been adapted and extended so as to be suitable for use in such a way.

For a detailed explanation of collection procedures see 21.1 to 21.7 COLLECTION and, for a description of the powers of recovery available where normal collection procedures are ineffective, see ARREARS OF CONTRIBUTIONS (12).

15.7 **COMPENSATION FOR SECONDARY CONTRIBUTIONS PAID ON SSP AND SMP**

With the introduction of statutory sick pay (SSP) and statutory maternity pay (SMP), employers became responsible for paying what was, effectively, a state benefit to employees. However, both SSP and SMP have always been treated as pay (see 28.20 EARNINGS), so employers must account for Class 1 contributions on any SSP or SMP payments. Employers were therefore paying secondary contributions in respect of a state benefit. Until 5 April 1991, employers were entitled under *Statutory Sick Pay Compensation Regs 1983, Reg 2* to recover by deduction from payments due to the collector of taxes in respect of contributions, or under *Reg 3* to have refunded by the Secretary of State, all SSP paid, together with an amount by way of compensation for secondary Class 1 contributions which they were deemed to have accounted for on such SSP.

From 6 April 1991, for most employers the recovery of SSP was restricted to 80% of SSP paid and the additional compensation was abolished [*Statutory Sick Pay Act 1991, s 3*]. However, a measure of relief was provided for 'small' employers, defined as those employers whose gross contributions bill in the 'qualifying year' had not exceeded £16,000. The 'qualifying year' was the last complete tax year. The limit was pro-rated for those businesses which had not been employers throughout the last complete tax year or who became employers for the first time in the current year.

Where an employer qualified as 'small', recovery of all SSP was still possible as a result of Small Employers' Relief ('SER'), but only in respect of those employees who were absent through sickness for at least six weeks. The limits for 1994–95 were eased, so that employers with a gross contributions liability of up to £20,000 in the qualifying year would be eligible, and the six week waiting period was reduced to four weeks.

However, when these changes were announced, the Secretary of State also announced proposals for a different form of SSP relief, to apply from 6 April 1995.

This scheme, known as the Percentage Threshold Scheme ('PTS'), differs from the SER scheme in that there is no £20,000 limit and no four week waiting period. It is intended to help employers deal with exceptionally high levels of sickness absence and is not strictly related to the size of the payroll, although there was originally believed to be around 87% overlap between the employers covered by SER and PTS.

Under the PTS, employers must calculate each month the ratio of SSP paid (N.B. paid, not due) to Class 1 contributions liability in the month. If SSP exceeds 13% of the contributions liability, the employer may recover the excess from the monthly remittance to the collector of taxes. The effect is to help employers with a large proportion of the workforce sick at any time. [*Statutory Sick Pay Percentage Threshold Order 1995* and *Statutory Sick Pay Percentage Threshold Order 1995 (Consequential) Regulations 1995*].

Example
Sickly Limited has ten employees and a total monthly liability for primary and secondary contributions of £698.40. The PTS threshold is therefore £90.79. If one employee becomes entitled to SSP of £60.20 (i.e. one week's absence following the waiting days), no recovery is possible, as the SSP paid is below the limit. However, if three employees become entitled to SSP of £60.20 each in the month, Sickly may recover (£180.60-£90.79) = £89.81 from the normal remittance of £698.40.

The compensation arrangements for SMP remained in place for all employers until 4 September 1994 and continue in place for 'small' employers. In order to pay for improvements to maternity benefits required under the EC's Pregnant Workers Directive from 16 October 1994, the government reduced the SMP recovery rate to 92% for most employers in respect of SMP paid on or after 4 September 1994. For 'small' employers (using the £20,000 rule originally set for SSP), recovery continued in 1994–95 at the rate of 104%, including compensation, and 105% for 1995–96. [*Statutory Maternity Pay Compensation Amendment Regs 1994*]. The rate for 1996–97 was 105.5%. [*Statutory Maternity Pay Compensation Amendment Regs 1996*]. The rate increased to 106.5% from 6 April 1997 [*Statutory Maternity Pay Compensation Amendment Regs 1997*], to 107% from 6 April 1998 [*Statutory Maternity Pay (Compensation of Employers) Amendment Regs 1998*] and then down to 105% from 6 April 1999 and continuing at this rate for 2000–01. [*Statutory Maternity Pay (Compensation of Employers) Amendment Regs 1999*].

In the case of SMP 'small' employers need to check their gross Class 1 contributions liability for the 'qualifying year'. The 'qualifying year' is the last complete tax year before each employee's qualifying week. For qualifying weeks beginning Sunday

● 9 April 1995 to 31 March 1996 inclusive, the qualifying tax year is 1994–95.

● 7 April 1996 to 30 March 1997 inclusive, the qualifying tax year is 1995–96.

● 6 April 1997 to 5 April 1998 inclusive, the qualifying tax year is 1996–97.

● 12 April 1998 to 4 April 1999 inclusive, the qualifying tax year is 1997–98.

● 11 April 1999 to 2 April 2000 inclusive, the qualifying tax year is 1998–99.

● 9 April 2000 to 1 April 2001 inclusive, the qualifying tax year is 1999–2000.

Before the introduction of the PTS, where compensation has been available, the employer's entitlement has been, as regards any payment of SSP and SMP made in a particular tax year, a fixed percentage of the total SSP or SMP paid. The rates applied have been as follows:

Year	*Compensation rates*			
	SSP%	SER%	SMP%	SER%
1985–86	9	n/a	n/a	n/a
1986–87	8	n/a	n/a	n/a
1987–88	7	n/a	7	n/a
1988–89	7	n/a	7	n/a

15.7 Class 1 Contributions: Employed Earners

Year	SSP%	SER%	SMP%	SER%	
		Compensation rates			
1989–90	7.5	n/a	7.5	n/a	
1990–91	7	n/a	7	n/a	
1991–92	–	–†	4.5	n/a	
1992–93	–	–†	4.5	n/a	
1993–94	–	–†	4.5	n/a	
1994–95	–	–†	4	n/a	6 April to 3 Sept.
			–	4	4 Sept. to 5 April
1995–96	n/a	n/a	–	5	
1996–97	n/a	n/a	–	5.5	
1997–98	n/a	n/a	–	6.5	
1998–99	n/a	n/a	–	7.0	
1999–00	n/a	n/a	–	5.0	
2000–01	n/a	n/a	–	5.0	

†Employers recovered 100% instead of only 80% of SSP.

[*Statutory Sick Pay Additional Compensation Regs 1985, Reg 3 as amended by Statutory Sick Pay Additional Compensation Amendment Regs 1987, Reg 3; Statutory Maternity Pay Compensation Regs 1987, Reg 3; Statutory Sick Pay Additional Compensation Amendment Regs 1988, Reg 2; Statutory Maternity Pay Compensation Amendment Regs 1988, Reg 2; Statutory Sick Pay Additional Compensation Amendment Regs 1989, Reg 2; Statutory Maternity Pay Compensation Amendment Regs 1989, Reg 2; Statutory Maternity Pay Compensation Amendment Regs 1990, Reg 2; Statutory Sick Pay Additional Compensation Amendment Regs 1990, Reg 2; Statutory Maternity Pay Compensation Amendment Regs 1991, Reg 2; Statutory Maternity Pay Compensation Amendment Regs 1994, Regs 1–9; Statutory Maternity Pay (Compensation of Employers) Amendment Regs 1995, Reg 2; Statutory Maternity Pay (Compensation of Employers) Amendment Regs 1996, Reg 2; Statutory Maternity Pay (Compensation of Employers) Amendment Regs 1997, Reg 2; Statutory Maternity Pay (Compensation of Employers) Amendment Regs 1998, Reg 2, Statutory Maternity Pay (Compensation of Employers) Amendment Regs 1999, Reg 2*].

The rates for 1991–92, 1992–93, 1993–94 and to 3 September 1994 have been arrived at by expressing as a percentage of the total amount of SMP payable by all employers in the preceding year the total amount of secondary Class 1 contributions payable by all employers in that year on that SMP. [*Statutory Sick Pay Additional Compensation Regs 1985, Reg 3; Statutory Maternity Pay Compensation Amendment Regs 1991, Reg 2*].

An employer may compensate himself to the extent of his entitlement by deducting the amount due to him from his contribution payments to the Collector of Taxes except where and insofar as

(i) the contribution payments relate to earnings paid before the beginning of the income tax month in which the payment of statutory maternity pay was made;

(ii) the contribution payments are made by him later than 6 years after the end of the tax year in which the payment of statutory maternity pay was made;

(iii) the amount has been paid to him by the Secretary of State or by the Inland Revenue in the circumstances described below; or

(iv) he has made a written request for direct payment of the compensation and has not, or not yet, received notification that the request is refused.

Where the contribution payments due to the Collector are insufficient to enable full compensation and recovery to be made, an employer is permitted, in practice, to compensate himself by making a deduction from any tax which is also due to be paid to the Collector for that month. (CA 29 page 38, para 78 and CA 30, page 54 para 76).

Example

In the month ended 5 June 2000, Brandon paid £120.40 SSP and £60.20 SMP to employees.

His payments due to the Collector for that month, before recoveries, were £102.85 contributions and £82.60 PAYE. He is entitled to SMP recovery as a 'small employer'.

He may recover:

	£
SSP £120.40 – (13% × £102.85)	107.03
SMP £60.20 × 105%	63.21
	£170.24

This amount is first set off against Class 1 contributions leaving a difference of £67.39. This may be deducted from the PAYE of £82.60 leaving only £15.21 payable to the Collector.

[*Statutory Sick Pay Percentage Threshold Order 1995, Reg 3 and Statutory Maternity Pay Compensation Amendment Regs 1994, Reg 5*].

As indicated above, an employer can make written request to the Inland Revenue (previously the Secretary of State) for direct payment to him of all or part of the compensation due to him. Such payment would be made *provided* the Inland Revenue was satisfied that

(A) after the employer had recovered by deduction from contributions payable by him to the collector of taxes all or part of statutory sick pay or statutory maternity pay paid by him, the balance of contributions payable was insufficient to enable him to deduct all or part of the compensation due; or

(B) the employer was not liable to pay any primary or secondary Class 1 contributions.

[*Statutory Sick Pay Percentage Threshold Order 1995; Reg 4 and Statutory Maternity Pay Compensation Amendment Regs 1994, Reg 6 as amended by SSC(T)A 1999, 2 Sch*].

In practice, as explained above, an employer was expected to recover any statutory sick pay, statutory maternity pay and the related compensation not only from any contributions due to be paid to the Collector but also from any tax so payable. Only if the combined amount of tax and contributions due were insufficient to enable full recovery and compensation to be made should he have requested direct payment of the balance, and not even then if he was able to recover the balance in the following month. Requests for direct payment should be made to the Inland Revenue Accounts Office. (CA 30, Page 54, para 76 and CA 29, Page 38, para 78).

From 6 April 1997 where the employer provides contractual remuneration (wages or occupational sick pay) that equals or exceeds the rate of SSP there will no longer be the requirement to maintain records of the calculation of SSP. The change in legislation arises from the *Statutory Sick Pay (General) Regs 1996, SI 1996, Reg 2* and it entitles the employer to voluntarily apply the easement arrangements. The regulations provide that payment of contractual remuneration equal to or exceeding the amount of SSP payable in respect of a day of incapacity will not be regarded as a payment of SSP for the purposes of record keeping requirements of *Statutory Sick Pay (General) Regs 1982, Reg 13*. Once the easement arrangements have been undertaken, and it is not necessary to give any notification of this, the following procedures may be effected by the employer:

• the easement may apply to some or all of the employees

• the contractual sick pay arrangements may vary according to the length of incapacity

- informal or discretionary arrangements for sick pay also allow easement entitlement where contractual pay is at least as good as SSP

- recovery of SSP costs under the percentage threshold scheme (PTS) still applies as long as the amount the employer would have paid in SSP for pay-days falling between the sixth of the month and the following fifth exceeds the current threshold of thirteen per cent of NICs for the month.

In these cases where the employer opts out of the SSP rules the payment will effectively become occupational sick pay when paid to the employee. Any employer who wishes to take advantage of the easement is obliged to formally advise his/her employees by reason of *Employment Rights Act 1996, s 1(4)(d)(ii)* in writing, in the case of new employees, of the terms and conditions relating to incapacity for work due to sickness or injury. Existing employees do not have to be advised in writing as they will still retain an underlying right to SSP anyway but it is probably appropriate to advise them or their representatives of the new arrangements.

Example
Death's Door Ltd has decided that it will take advantage of the SSP easement arrangement for all its employees (from 6 April 1999). However, although there is not a requirement to advise the existing employees of the change, new employees must be advised within two months of the date when the employee's employment begins. Death's Door Ltd's personnel department takes the opportunity to advise existing employees by way of a revised notice to their Staff Handbook rather than a personalised letter. New and recently joined employees will receive a similar notice incorporated within their Staff Handbook along the same lines as what follows:

To: Ivor Sickness

From: Personnel Department, Death's Door Ltd.

Date:

I attach a revised page . . ., Appendix . . . and index which should be inserted into your Staff Handbook. We believe that our obligations under the Employment Rights Act 1996, sections 1(4)(d)(ii) and 2(2) have been fulfilled. Your co-operation with this change would be appreciated.

Sickness Absence

In accordance with statutory regulations, if you are absent from work due to sickness, the company will pay Company Sick Pay (full basic pay including Statutory Sick Pay) for up to 28 weeks after which period the payments will be made by the DSS.

Company Sick Pay, which is the full basic pay being not less than the SSP equivalent, is payable, dependent on length of continuous company service as follows:

Period of service at the date of commencement of illness	*Period during which payment will be made*	
	Full basic salary	*Followed by ½ basic salary*
Up to 6 months	4 weeks	4 weeks
6 months–2 years	8 weeks	8 weeks
2–5 years	13 weeks	13 weeks
5–10 years	26 weeks	26 weeks
Over 10 years	52 weeks	

Cont'd

For the purposes of calculating Company Sick Pay, periods of sickness separated from each other by 12 months or less will be added together.

Please note the following in relation to **Sickness Absence.**

1. The payment of Company Sick Pay will be withheld unless a signed Statement of Reasons for Absence (SRA form) is received.

2. A medical certificate must be produced on request.

3. The Company reserves the right to require you to be examined by a Doctor of its own choosing.

4. The Board will take into consideration special circumstances which might warrant extending the period of Company Sick Pay.

5. Unexplained absences could lead to pay being withheld.

6. Holiday entitlement will not accrue during absence of over 4 weeks.

7. The Company reserves the right to request the return of a Company car if this is required for operational reasons.

Your attention is also drawn to the notification procedure in Section . . ., the Grievance procedure in section . . . and Appendix . . .

As a result of the Sally Brown (Child Poverty Action Group-sponsored) case any individual who is employed on a series of contracts with the same employer, linked by a period of not more than 8 weeks, and the period in employment exceeds 13 weeks, then this will be regarded as being continuous employment. Their contract should be regarded as being for an indefinite period and therefore cannot be terminated without 7 days' notice. See CA National Insurance News, Summer 1997 page 6 and CA30, page 3, para 8.

15.8   TAX RELIEF AND NIC HOLIDAY

Under no circumstances may tax relief be given or a tax deduction allowed in respect of primary Class 1 contributions. [*ICTA 1988, s 617(3)(a)*]. Accordingly, no relief will be available even to an employer who has accounted for primary Class 1 contributions in circumstances which preclude his recovery of such contributions from the employed earner concerned (see 14.13 CATEGORISATION and 21.4 COLLECTION). Class 1 *secondary* contributions and Class 1A contributions paid by a secondary contributor will be allowable as a deduction in computing his profits and gains, however, provided those secondary contributions have been wholly and exclusively laid out or expended for the purposes of his trade, profession or vocation or, in the case of an investment company, insurance company or the owner of mineral rights, have been disbursed as expenses of management. [*ICTA 1988, s 617(4)* and Inland Revenue ESC (see Inland Revenue Press Release 30 May 1996)]. This proviso will operate so as to preclude a deduction from profits for tax purposes in respect of secondary Class 1 contributions on earnings which are themselves disallowed, e.g. where the earnings are considered excessive as in *Copeman v William Flood & Sons Ltd (1940) 24 TC 53*. Up until 25 November 1996 relief under *ICTA 1988, s 617* applied only to secondary Class 1 contributions paid by employers. Previously, relief for Class 1A contributions had been allowed by reason of extra–statutory concession but this is now enshrined in *ICTA 1988, s 617(4) as substituted by FA 1997, s 65(3)*. Class 1A (or for that matter secondary Class 1) contributions are now allowable as a deduction in computing profits or gains where these are claimed as a deduction under *ICTA 1988, s 198* (relief for necessary expenses) or *ICTA 1988, s 332(3)(a)* (performance of duties as a clergyman or minister) in order to cover the situation where office holders, and ministers of religion engage assistance in connection with their work.

Section 617 is further amended by *FA 1999, s 61* so as to give tax relief for the payment of Class 1B contributions (see Chapter 17).

In the November 1994 Budget an initiative was put forward called 'Back to Work Incentives' which was to encourage employers to take on the unemployed, lone parents, carers and some Government trainees (not YTS) who have been out of the job market for at least two years. The scheme, which ceased for new employments commencing on or after 1 April 1999, offered the participating employer a secondary NIC holiday of 52 weeks and could be claimed after the qualifying employee was employed for at least one quarter of the period. [*Jobseekers Act 1995*; *Employer's Contributions Reimbursement Regs 1996 as amended by Employer's Contributions Reimbursement Regs 2000*]. The scheme continued to run for existing employees up to 31 March 2000 when it finally ceased. In the past an employer wishing to participate in the holiday provided the Benefits Agency with the evidence from the employee of the prospective entitlement to the NIC holiday on Form A503. This was then sent to the Contributions Agency after it had been checked and the Agency then issued the certificate of authorisation CA 4138 to the employer. The certificate was then retained by the employer and if the employee left after the first thirteen weeks but before the expiry of fifty two weeks then the tear-off section CA 4138A was completed and returned to the CA NIC Holiday Section. Once the employer had the certificate he could then operate the scheme claiming the equivalent of all secondary contributions paid in respect of that employee but had to wait until the 13 week qualifying period expires before doing so. This NIC holiday was not only for standard rate NIC payers but included women with reduced rate certificates CA 4139, CF 383 or CF 380A. The employer could then claim the appropriate NICs when they made their monthly or quarterly remittance to the Inland Revenue or at a time that was convenient to them (see Inland Revenue Collection PAYE manual Vol 1, para PA 1614 (5/97)). The employer could keep details of the NIC holiday calculations on the reverse of certificate CA 4138 thereby reducing the burden of compliance that besets so many incentives. If an employee has two or more jobs with the same employer or associated employers then the employer holding the CA 4138 was able to claim the amount equivalent to the aggregated secondary contributions. (See CA National Insurance News, Issues 4 and 5).

Example

Florence owns the Roundabout Rest Home for the aged and requires three new auxiliary nurses due to an extension of the premises. She interviews a number of applicants in March 1999 but on the advice of her accountant husband takes on three auxiliaries who have been out of the job market for at least two years one of whom is also going to work for another Roundabout carework subsidiary. One of the new auxiliaries cannot commence work until 6 April 1999 due to illness. She sends the completed forms A503, Parts A and B to the Benefit Office and the Contributions Agency subsequently send her Certificates CA 4138 for two of the new employees. Roundabout will not be able to claim NIC holiday in respect of the auxiliary who was not able to commence employment before 1 April 1999.

Although Florence pays secondary contributions in respect of the contracted-out scheme that she operates for the rest home employees she can in fact claim the not contracted-out rate of contributions for the two employees, which are higher. So although the employees are 'Category D' the employer can reclaim 'Category A' secondary contributions. Florence may, as the main employer, also claim the secondary contribution in respect of the additional job that one of her new staff is proposing to undertake with the subsidiary company. The option for Florence to claim the higher not contracted-out rate and the aggregated secondary contribution for all the new employees gives a further benefit.

16   Class 1A Contributions: Benefits in kind

Cross-references. See APPEALS AND REVIEWS (9) for remedies for dissatisfaction; ARREARS OF CONTRIBUTIONS (12) for recovery provisions; CATEGORISATION (14) for meaning of secondary contributor; CLASS 1 CONTRIBUTIONS (15) for rates etc; COLLECTION (21); EARNINGS (28) for payments in kind; ENFORCEMENT (32); INLAND REVENUE (37) for links with PAYE etc; WORKING CASE STUDY (58).

Other Sources. Simon's NIC, Part I, Section 2, Chapter 9; Tolley's Pay and Benefits Handbook; Tolley's Income Tax 2000–01; Leaflet CA 33, CA 34 and Cards CWG1 (2000), Nos 13 and 14; CWG5 (2000), Issue 1. See also IR Leaflet 480 (2000), sections 11–16. See Inland Revenue Collection PAYE manual Vol 1, paras PA 1654–1658 (15/98) and Tolley's Practical NIC Service, 1999, page 56.

16.1   GENERAL CONSIDERATIONS

Class 1A contributions were introduced by *Social Security (Contributions) Act 1991* with effect from 6 April 1991 'to fill . . . an important gap in the national insurance contributions system, as a result of which employers do not pay contributions to the national insurance fund if they pay their employees in cars rather than in cash' (Hansard 9 May 1991 col 849). The first such contributions were payable in respect of the year 1991–92 and it is estimated that they will increase the income of the NATIONAL INSURANCE FUND (45) by £896 million in 2000–01. Although there was, until *Finance Act 1997*, a general prohibition against Class 1A contributions being allowed under *ICTA 1988, s 617* a concession published 30 May 1996 allows the deduction of Class 1A contributions in computing business profits.

Up until 5 April 2000, Class 1A contributions have been charged only on the provision by employers of cars and fuel for private use but Class 1As are extended to most benefits in kind after that date.

In this connection, it was announced in the March 1999 Budget that from 6 April 2000 employer national insurance contributions will be charged on all taxable benefits in kind. This will be achieved by way of an extension to the existing Class 1A structure, rather than the creation of any new charge. These new procedures which are detailed in CWG5 (2000) Issue 1 are explained in more detail below and at 16.18. It should be borne in mind that CWG5 is a preliminary guide and subject to change.

In a press release issued on 19 November 1999 it was stated that the new return and payment arrangements would be designed to minimise employer's end of year work. The Class 1A return will be merged with existing P11D reports and payment will be made to the employer's existing PAYE/NICs reference at the Accounts Office. The first returns and payment under the new arrangements will be due on 19 July 2001. Currently further consultation is preceding the issue of guidance to employers and software providers. Class 1A will not apply in the following cases where benefits in kind are:

(a)   covered by Class 1 NICs; or

(b)   covered by a dispensation; or

(c)   included in a PAYE Settlement Agreement; or

(d)   provided for employees earning less than £8,500 per year; or

(e)   otherwise not required to be reported via the P11D return arrangements.

Also, from 6 April 2000 to reflect the developments in modern working practices and reduce reporting requirements, certain benefits will be exempted from tax and NICs. These are small amounts of private use by an employee of items e.g. tools provided by the employer for the employee's work, qualifying beneficial loans and general welfare counselling provided by an employer. See IR Press Release 19 November 1999.

Paragraphs 16.4 to 16.7 below relate largely to the provision of cars and fuel for private use.

16.2   LIABILITY

A Class 1A contribution is payable, by the employer only, for any tax year in respect of an earner, certain directors and employees, to whom benefits are made available if,

(a)   for that tax year, the earner is, by virtue of *ICTA 1988, s 157*, chargeable to income tax under Sch E on an amount in respect of that benefit; and

(b)   the employment by reason of which the benefit is made available is employed earner's employment (see 14.2 CATEGORISATION).

[*SSCBA 1992, s 10(1)*].

This effectively confines the Class 1A charge to 'returnable benefits' as well as the past Class 1A situations where a 'car' (see below) is made available (without transfer of title) to an employed earner (or to members of his family or household) who is a 'company director' (see below) or who has 'emoluments' (see below) of £8,500 a year or more and is so available by reason of his employment and is available for his (or their) travel other than 'business travel' (see below). [*ICTA 1988, ss 157(1), 167*].

A *returnable benefit* (see 16.18 *et seq* below), is a benefit that is not excluded by reason of (a) to (e) above in 16.1 and is reportable on form P11D (2001). Class 1A will therefore be extended to cover most benefits in kind and the Table at 16.18 details the NICs treatment. See CWG5 (2000) Issue 1, pages 11–16.

A '*car*' (see 16.3–16.17 below) is any mechanically propelled road vehicle other than

(i)   a vehicle of a construction primarily suited for the conveyance of goods or burden of any description, e.g. a lorry or pickup truck;

(ii)   a vehicle of a type not commonly used, and not suitable to be used, as a private vehicle, e.g. a Grand Prix racing car;

(iii) a motor cycle or an invalid carriage.

[*ICTA 1988, s 168(5); FA 1993, 3 Sch*].

A '*company director*', in this context (see also CA33, Page 40, paras 130–133), is,

(i)   in relation to a company whose affairs are managed by a board of directors, a member of that board;

(ii)   in relation to a company whose affairs are managed by a single director, that director;

(iii) in relation to a company whose affairs are managed by the members themselves, a member of the company; or

(iv)   anyone (other than a mere professional adviser) in accordance with whose instructions the directors are accustomed to act;

unless, either on his own or in conjunction with his associates and relatives, he does not own or control more than 5% of the company's ordinary share capital and

(1)   he is required to devote substantially the whole of his time to the service of the company in a managerial or technical capacity; or

(2) the company

    (*a*) does not carry on a trade and its functions do not consist wholly or mainly in the holding of investments or other property, or

    (*b*) is established for charitable purposes only.

[*ICTA 1988, ss 167(1)(5), 168(8)–(11)*].

'*Emoluments*', in this context, includes all salaries, fees, pay, wages, overtime pay, leave pay, bonuses, commissions, perquisites, tips, gratuities, benefits in kind (whether provided to the employee himself or to members of his household or family), expense payments and allowances, before the deduction of any expenses allowable for tax purposes other than

    (i) contributions to an approved superannuation fund in respect of which the individual is entitled to tax relief as an expense;

    (ii) exempt profit-related pay; and

    (iii) contributions under an approved payroll giving scheme;

and, for the purpose of deciding whether the emoluments amount to £8,500 or more, emoluments derived from two or more offices or employments with the same employer or from a number of offices or employments with inter-connected companies are to be treated as if they were emoluments derived from a single office or employment.

[*ICTA 1988, ss 167(1)–(4), 168(2), 171, 202*].

It is important to note that although certain full-time working directors etc. may fall to be treated as being outside the scope of *ICTA 1988, s 157 etc.* under the definition of 'company director' given above, those same directors may fall to be treated as within the scope of *s 157 etc.* by reason of the quantum of their 'emoluments'.

'*Business travel*', in this context, is travelling which a person is necessarily obliged to do in the performance of the duties of his employment. [*ICTA 1988, s 168(5)(c)*]. It does *not* include home-to-business travel.

The tying of Class 1A liability on cars and fuel to the coat-tails of *ICTA 1988, ss 157 and 158* is a deliberate attempt by Parliament to obviate all the problems which would have arisen had Parliament decided to create an entirely free-standing set of charging rules and definitions, similar, but not identical, to those used in revenue law and thus to ease the compliance burden for those on whom the new charge falls. As Mr Nicholas Scott, the then Minister for Social Security, said during the second reading debate on the *Social Security (Contributions) Bill* which introduced Class 1A contributions:

'In devising these arrangements we have paid careful attention to the need to produce a scheme which employers can operate with the minimum of extra work. We have therefore decided to stick very closely to existing Inland Revenue rules with which employers are already familiar. Accordingly, the Bill will impose a contribution liability in respect of those employees provided with cars only where a scale charge would apply for tax purposes. Broadly speaking, these are company directors and employees earning more than £8,500 a year, including benefits in kind. The substantial advantage of this approach is that employers are already required to report annually to the Inland Revenue the details of such cars and we see no reason why they should face any particular difficulty in combining the reporting process with assessment of contribution liability under the terms of this Bill.' (Hansard 9 May 1991 col 852).

An area where the tax and NIC rules diverge is where an employee remains under contract to his home country employer outside the UK and continues to pay contributions to his home country scheme; if, in such cases, no UK NIC is paid by the secondee, then there will be no liability to Class 1A. Also, where no contributions treaty exists (e.g. Japan, Korea, Australia, New Zealand, etc.) there will be no Class 1 liability until the employee has been resident in the UK for 52 weeks and only then will there be a Class 1A liability. (Tolley's Practical NIC, Vol 3, number 12, p 90).

16.3   The person liable

The charge to income tax under Sch E which arises by virtue of *ICTA 1988, s 154 et seq* where a benefit is made available to an employee or director for his private use is on the employee or director himself; but the Class 1A contribution is payable by

(a)   the person who is liable to pay the secondary Class 1 contribution relating to the last (or only) 'relevant payment of earnings' in the tax year in relation to which there is a liability to pay such a contribution (see 14.15 CATEGORISATION and CA33, Page 40, para 132); or

(b)   if no such contribution is payable in relation to a relevant payment of earnings in the tax year, the person who, if the benefit in respect of which the Class 1A contribution is payable were earnings in respect of which Class 1 contributions would be payable, would be liable to pay the secondary Class 1 contribution; or

(c)   the third party provider of non-cash incentives and benefits can be liable for Class 1A contributions as a secondary contributor from 6 April 2000 rather than the employer.

[*SSCBA 1992, s 10(2) as amended by Social Security Act 1998, s 52;* Child Support, Pensions and Social Security Bill 1999].

The above section (*b*) was replaced by virtue of *Social Security Act 1998 (Commencement No 1) Order 1998, SI 1998 No 2209* with effect from 8 September 1998.

This would, for instance, apply in circumstances where a director who is over the age of 65 receives the use of a company car but has no other source of emoluments from the company. Prior to the change, no Class 1A charge could have arisen because there were no earnings (even below the lower earnings limit) subject to Class 1. The DSS said that because the change was made on September 1998 and Class 1A is an annual charge a liability will exist in such circumstances for the whole of 1998–99 (CA33, Page 36, Para 116) but the accuracy of this statement is surely questionable, especially if a car ceased to be provided before 8 September 1998. The point is similar to that arising in respect of an earlier charge in respect of car fuel benefits, see 16.6 below.

For these purposes, a '*relevant payment of earnings*' is defined as 'a payment of earnings . . . made to or for the benefit of an earner in respect of the employment by reason of which the car is made available'. [*SSCBA 1992, s 10(3)*].

There is a possibility that both Class 1A and Class 1 NICs could arise at the same time. However, the Contributions Agency never intended such a dual liability and will not pursue the Class 1 NICs which arise on such motoring expenses. (See CA National Insurance News, Issue 4, page 8. Also, CA Press Release 96/1, 15 March 1996). This practice has the force of law from the 6 April 1996 with the insertion of new *Contributions Regs 1979, Reg 19(1)(y)*). [*Social Security (Contributions) Amendment (No 3) Regs 1996*].

In some instances where the benefit of the car is freely convertible into cash, the benefit of providing a car is taxable under the general income tax rules rather than the special provisions for company cars. These cash alternative schemes have meant that some employers have avoided their Class 1A NIC liability. In order to rectify this loophole where a cash alternative is offered, the employer will pay Class 1A NICs if the employee has the benefit of the car or Class 1 NICs if the employee takes the cash alternative. Employers are so liable from 6 April 1995. (CA National Insurance News, Issue 2, page 1 and *ICTA 1988, s 157A, inserted by FA 1995, s 43.*)

Where, in relation to his employment, an earner is paid by one person but has a car made available to him by another, the effect of these provisions will be to impose a Class 1A charge on the person paying the earner, not on the person who makes the car available.

Example
Avant is a sales representative. Throughout 2000–01, his contract of service is with Ballade and they pay Avant his salary and commission; but the car he uses is owned and made available to him by Cavalier, Ballade's parent company. Because Avant has private use of the car, he is chargeable to income tax under Sch E on an amount arrived at under *ICTA 1988, s 157*, and, in consequence, a Class 1A contribution is payable for 2000–01 in respect of Avant and the car made available to him. But, because the secondary Class 1 contribution on the last payment of earnings made to Avant in 2000–01 is paid by Ballade, Ballade must pay the Class 1A contribution even though Cavalier, not Ballade, is the person who owns the car and has made it available to Avant.

It should be noted that, even if the last payment of earnings to Avant by Ballade in 2000–01 happens to be below the lower earnings limit for 2000–01 so that no secondary Class 1 contribution is in fact payable by Ballade in respect of that payment of earnings, the terms of *SSCBA 1992, s 10(2)(b)* as amended by *Social Security Act 1999, s 52* ensure that a liability to Class 1A still exists, but it would, in those circumstances, become payable by Cavalier.

Where a person works successively for two or more employers in a tax year and is provided with a car in respect of each employment for both private and business use, *SSCBA 1992, s 10(1)(2)* will ensure that a Class 1A contribution will be payable in respect of each.

Example
Herald works for Integra until 5 January 2001 when he changes jobs and takes up employment with Jetta. He is provided with a car (which is available for his private use) in each job. A tax charge will arise in respect of each car for 2000–01 so a Class 1A contribution will be payable in respect of each car for that year. Integra will pay secondary Class 1 contributions in relation to Herald's last earnings in his employment with Integra so Integra will be liable to pay a Class 1A contribution in respect of the car provided in that job, while Jetta will pay secondary Class 1 contributions in relation to Herald's last earnings in the tax year so Jetta will be liable to pay a Class 1A contribution in respect of the car provided in the second job.

In such circumstances, each Class 1A charge will reflect the length of time for which the car has been made available and the business mileage in each employment (see 16.9 below).

Where a person succeeds to a business and pays emoluments to a person who was an employee in the business before the succession took place, the successor employer will be liable for the whole of any Class 1A contribution which is payable in respect of the employee for the tax year of change as the successor employer will be the person making the last 'relevant payment of earnings' to the earner in the tax year.

Example
Orion works for Panda by whom he is provided with a car which is available for his private use. In October 2000, Panda sells his business to Quinta and Quinta continues to employ Orion and to allow him the private use of the car. As Quinta will pay a secondary Class 1 contribution in relation to Orion's last payment of

earnings in 2000–01 in respect of the employment by reason of which the car is made available, he (to the exclusion of Panda) will be liable to pay the Class 1A contribution in respect of the car provided throughout the year.

If, of course, Orion had left Panda's employment before the change took place, the Class 1A liability in respect of the car provided to Orion from 6 April 2000 to the date of his leaving would, for the same reason, rest with Panda.

16.4 COMPUTATION

Where a liability to pay a Class 1A contribution arises for 1999–2000, the amount of that contribution is the 'Class 1A percentage' of

(a) the 'car benefit' in respect of the car(s) provided to the earner in the tax year; and

(b) if, by virtue of *ICTA 1988, s 158*, a Sch E charge is also imposed on the earner in respect of fuel provided for the car, the cash equivalent of the benefit of the fuel to the earner in the tax year.

[*SSCBA 1992, s 10(4)*].

It should be noted in connection with (b) above that fuel is provided for a car if

(i) any liability in respect of the provision of fuel for the car is discharged;

(ii) a non-cash voucher or a credit-token is used to obtain fuel for the car or money which is spent on such fuel;

(iii) any sum is paid in respect of expenses incurred in providing fuel for the car;

but that no Sch E charge is imposed in respect of such fuel if the fuel is made available *only* for business travel. [*ICTA 1988, s 158(3) and (6)(b)* and CWG1 (2000), Card 14].

The '*Class 1A percentage*' is a rate equivalent to the secondary Class 1 percentage rate appropriate for the highest secondary earnings bracket for the tax year in question, i.e. 12.2% for 2000–01. [*SSCBA 1992, s 10(5)*].

For 1994–95 onwards, the car benefit for any car is 35% of its list price. This is defined as the inclusive price, including any accessories, published by the car's manufacturer, importer or distributor, in respect of a single UK retail sale in the open market, on the day before the car's first registration. It includes delivery costs and car tax. No account can be taken of bulk purchase terms or other favourable discounts. [*ICTA 1988, s 168A as amended by FA 1993, 3 Sch*]. The NICO consider 'price' to be the manufacturer's, importer's or distributor's list price on the day before it was first registered and delivery charges, taxes (but not road tax) are included. Also included are accessories and the cost of fitting them. As well as the invoice, specialist lists such as Glass's Guide or GAP Nationwide Motor Research Limited can also be used (CA National Insurance News, Issue 4, page 4). Some questions have been raised as to the meaning of 'distributor' for the purposes of gauging the list price. The Inland Revenue remains of the opinion that the list price that matters is the manufacturer's, importer's or distributor's published list price (see also IR leaflet 480 (2000) para 12.4) and they comment on the suggestion that the dealer can be the distributor as follows:

'Such an interpretation could result in multiple price lists for each car, published by everyone involved right from its original manufacture to its final sale. In the Inland Revenue's view there is nothing within the structure or language of Section 168A to warrant that interpretation. It includes no provision for choosing between different prices for the same car. It also draws a distinction between "manufacturer, importer or distributor" and the "seller".'

From 6 April 1998, any premium on the price of the car which is manufactured to run on road fuel gases will be disregarded when calculating the price of a car. Road fuel gas means any substance which is gaseous at a temperature of 15°C and under pressure of 1013.25 millibars, and which is for use as fuel in road vehicles. Currently, the two types of fuel in use which fall within this definition are compressed natural gas and liquid petroleum gas. [*ICTA 1988, s 168AB*].

As a result of *FA 1995, s 44* certain accessories needed by disabled persons who qualify for an 'orange badge' to enable them to drive the car may be disregarded, with effect from 6 April 1995, in calculating the list price. This not only includes accessories specifically designed for disabled drivers such as special steering wheels but also features which are of particular assistance to disabled drivers such as electric windows and automatic transmission, provided they are not standard accessories. (See also IR leaflet 480 (2000) para 12.8).

For cars costing more than £80,000, the list price is limited to that figure. [*ICTA 1988, s 168G*].

The list price of second-hand cars is more difficult to determine but the Contributions Agency stated that they would accept the reported price agreed for tax purposes.

For cars which are more than 15 years old, which have a market value of at least £15,000, and which have appreciated in value since they were first purchased (referred to as classic cars in the legislation), the cash equivalent is the market value on the last day in the tax year that the car was available to the employee. [*ICTA 1988, s 168F*]. Values of classic cars may be determined by recent valuations for insurance purposes, prices in the 'market' or published prices. The value is restricted to £80,000. (See also IR leaflet 480 (2000) paras 12.24–25 and 12.28).

The list price is increased by the cost of optional accessories, excluding mobile telephones. If an accessory costing more than £100 is added after the car is first made available, then the cost of that accessory is added to the list price of the car for each year during any part of which it is available provided that the accessory was first made available after 31 July 1993. [*ICTA 1988, ss 168B, 168C*]. Certain accessories for disabled drivers may be disregarded from 6 April 1995 as well as, from 6 April 1998, equipment to run on road fuel gas. [*ICTA 1988, s 168A(11); s 168AA inserted by FA 1995, s 44; s 168AB inserted by FA 1998, s 60*].

If an employee makes a capital contribution towards the provision of the car or accessories, that contribution, limited to a maximum of £5,000, is deducted from the list price in the year that the contribution is made, and in all subsequent years. [*ICTA 1988, s 168D*].

For 1991–92 to 1993–94, the 'cash equivalent' of the benefit of a car was to be ascertained in accordance with *ICTA 1988, s 157* and *Sch 6* using a table of values based on the car's engine capacity, age and original market value.

From 6 April 2002, the tax and Class 1A National Insurance charge in respect of cars will be a percentage of the car's price graduated according to the level of the car's carbon dioxide (CO_2) emissions. See **[Case Study 5]**. The charge will range from 15% to 35% (maximum) of the list price. Discounts for business mileage over 2,499 and 17,999 miles per annum will also cease at that time (Inland Revenue Press Release REV 6, 21 March 2000).

For 2000–01, the cash equivalent of the benefit of fuel supplied for private use is ascertained in accordance with *ICTA 1988, s 158* as amended by *The Income Tax (Cash Equivalents of Car Fuel Benefits) Order 2000, Reg 2*, from the following table:

16.5 Class 1A Contributions: Benefits in kind

Cash equivalent of fuel benefit for 2000–01

	£
Table A	
Petrol	
Cars with cylinder capacity of	
Up to 1,400 cc	1,700
1,401 cc to 2,000 cc	2,170
2,001 cc or more	3,200
Table B	
Cars without a cylinder capacity	3,200
Table AB	
Diesel	
Cars with cylinder capacity of	
Up to 2,000 cc	2,170
2,001 cc or more	3,200

Similar tables applied to earlier years. See Tolley's Income Tax 2000–01. The rates for 2000–01 constitute a 40.9% increase over 1999–2000.

The adjustments to these cash equivalents of car and fuel benefits which are permitted or required by *ICTA 1988, Sch 6 as amended by FA 1999, s 47* are described at 16.5 to 16.11 below.

16.5 Car used for business purposes

For *tax* purposes, the cash equivalent of the car, but not car fuel, described at 16.4 above is to be *reduced* if it is shown to the Inspector of Taxes' satisfaction that the employee was required by the nature of his employment to make (and did in fact make) use of the car for business travel amounting to at least 2,500 miles (proportionally reduced for periods of unavailability) in the relevant tax year. Where business travel is shown to be at least 2,500, but less than 18,000 miles (proportionately reduced, if appropriate), benefit is 25% of the car's price. Business mileage in excess of 17,999 a year attracts a charge of 15% of the car's price. [*ICTA 1988, Sch 6, para 2 as amended by FA 1999, s 47*].

For 1994–95 to 1998–99 inclusive, the car benefit was two-thirds of 35% of the car's list price or one-third thereof respectively.

The same rule applies for Class 1A purposes, but the person liable to pay the Class 1A contribution must treat the employee's business mileage as giving rise to no reduction unless he, the Class 1A contributor, has information to the contrary. [*SSCBA 1992, s 10(6)(b)(i)* and also CWG1 (2000), Card 14]. The nature of the information required is discussed at 16.11 below.

The income tax rules were different for 1991–92, 1992–93 and 1993–94. In those years the cash equivalents, ascertained as described at 16.4 above, were to be *reduced* by half if it was shown to the Inspector's satisfaction that the employee was required by the nature of his employment to make (and did in fact make) use of the car for business travel amounting to at least 18,000 miles (proportionally reduced for periods when the car was unavailable) in the relevant tax year. The same rule applied for Class 1A purposes except that use of the car for the earner's business travel was to be taken to have amounted to *less* than 18,000 miles (proportionally reduced, if appropriate) unless the person liable to pay the Class 1A contribution had information to show the contrary. [*SSCBA 1992, s 10(6)(b)(i)*]. The nature of the information which was required by this provision is discussed at 16.11 below. The 50% reduction also applied to the fuel scale charges for 1991–92 and 1992–93, but see 16.6 below as regards 1993–94 and later years.

In 1991–92, 1992–93 and 1993–94, the cash equivalent ascertained as described at 16.4 above, was to be *increased* by half for income tax purposes if, in the relevant tax year, the car was not used for the employee's business travel or its use for such travel did not amount to more than 2,500 miles (proportionally reduced if appropriate). [*ICTA 1988, Sch 6, Pt II, para 5(1)(2)*]. The same rule applied for Class 1A purposes except that the use of the car for the earner's business travel was to be taken to have amounted to less than 2,500 miles (proportionally reduced, if appropriate) unless the person liable to pay the Class 1A contribution had information to show the contrary. [*SSCBA 1992, s 10(6)(b)(ii)*]. The nature of the information which was required by this provision is discussed at 16.11 below. (See also IR leaflet 480 (2000) para 12.30–31).

16.6 Business use and fuel

For 1991–92 and 1992–93, the fuel scale charge was to be reduced by one half for income tax purposes where business use was at least 18,000 miles. This reduction applied for both income tax and Class 1A purposes.

From 6 April 1993, for income tax purposes the fuel scale charge was not to be adjusted to reflect business travel of more than 18,000 miles. The same change was applied to Class 1A contributions, but because of the way the legislative amendments were made, opinion was divided as to whether the abolition of the reduction for Class 1A purposes took effect from 6 April 1993 or only from 30 November 1993 when the amending regulations were laid. The DSS took the former view, so that the fuel scale charge for 1993–94 *et seq* is not adjusted for Class 1A purposes in respect of business travel of 18,000 miles or more.

The only exception to this is when Class 1A contributions have been correctly paid before 30 November 1993, for example a 1993–94 contribution in respect of an employee who left employment before that date (see 16.8 below). (DSS Press Release, 14 December 1993).

16.7 Additional cars

If, for *tax* purposes, a charge arises in respect of two or more cars which are made available concurrently, the car benefit described at 16.4 above in respect of each of the cars, other than the one used to the greatest extent for the employee's business travel, is not to be reduced when business travel is at least 2,500 but less than 18,000 miles, and is only to be reduced by one quarter (one third for periods prior to 6 April 1999) when business travel is 18,000 miles or more. [*ICTA 1988, Sch 6, para 4 as amended by FA 1999, s 47*]. The same rule applies for Class 1A purposes, except that *no* car is to be treated as the one used to the greatest extent for the employee's business travel unless the person liable to pay the Class 1A contribution has information to show the contrary. [*SSCBA 1992, s 10(6)(c)*]. (The nature of the information required by this provision is discussed at 16.11 below.) As it stands, this rule gives rise to one or more increased Class 1A liabilities even where two or more cars are concurrently made available for private use by reason of different employed earner's employments under different employers who are *not* 'associated'. Clearly, in such circumstances, the two or more unassociated employers involved may not even be aware that more than one car is being made available to their employee and may, therefore, be ignorant of their obligation to alter the reductions which would otherwise apply to the scale amount. This difficulty has been overcome by providing that, in such circumstances, liabilities arrived at under *SSCBA 1992, s 10(6)(c)* are to be reduced to the liabilities which would have arisen had *6 Sch 4* been omitted from *ICTA 1988*. [*Contributions Regs, Reg 22C*]. That reduction does not apply, however, where two or more cars are made available for private use by reason of

(*a*) any one employed earner's employment; or

(*b*) two or more employed earner's employments under the same employer; or

(*c*) two or more employed earner's employments under different employers who are associated.

[*Reg 22C(3)*].

For the purpose of *Reg 22C(3)*, two or more employers are to be treated as associated if they are carrying on business in association (see 5.4 AGGREGATION OF EARNINGS), or if one has control (whether alone or in conjunction with someone who controls him) of the other or others or any person has control of both or all of them. 'Control' in relation to a partnership employer means having the right to a share of more than one-half of the assets or income of the partnership, and, in relation to other employers, having the power to secure that the affairs of the employer are conducted in accordance with the wishes of the person concerned. In the case of a body corporate, such power means power derived from articles of association or other regulatory document or exercisable by means of holding shares or possessing voting rights. [*Reg 22C(4)*].

Example
Esprit concurrently works for both Favorit and Galant, driving more than 2,500 business miles for each. (Favorit is a wholly-owned subsidiary of Hatchback and Hatchback and Favorit each owns 30% of the shares in Galant.) Each employer provides Esprit with a car costing £10,000 and makes it available to Esprit for his private use. Neither employer has any information about the extent of Esprit's business motoring in his other employment so, under the rule in *SSCBA 1992, s 10(6)(c)*, each is liable to pay a Class 1A contribution for 2000–01 on £3,500 without any reduction. *Reg 22C* does nothing to alleviate the position because Favorit and Galant are associated within the terms of *Reg 22C(4)*. If the two companies were *not* associated, the Class 1A liabilities would each be reduced to 25% of the list price i.e. £2,500 by virtue of *Reg 22C*.

16.8 Cars more than four years old

For cars which are more than four years old at the end of the tax year, the car benefit found as described at 16.4 above is reduced by one quarter after any reduction for business travel (see 16.6 above) but before any reductions for unavailability (see 16.9 below) and payments made by the employee for his private use of the car (see 16.10 below). [*ICTA 1988, 6 Sch 5 as amended by FA 1999, s 47*].

Prior to 6 April 1999, the reduction was one third.

16.9 Reduction for periods when car not available for use

If, for any part of the relevant tax year, the car in question was 'unavailable', the car benefits as described at 16.4 above are, for *tax* purposes, to be *reduced* by multiplying them by the fraction

$$\frac{365 - number\ of\ days\ of\ unavailability}{365}$$

The figure of 365 in the equation is always used, even if the year is a leap year.

A car is to be treated as 'unavailable' for a particular day if

(i) it was not made available to the employee until after that day; or

(ii) it had ceased to be available to him before that day; or

(iii) it was incapable of being used at all throughout a period of not less than 30 consecutive days of which that day was one.

[*ICTA 1988, s 158(5) and 6 Sch 9* and see also CWG1 (2000), Card 14; CA33 (2000), Pages 13, 43 and 44].

The former Contributions Agency confirmed that the car would not be regarded as unavailable for use when the employee/director is disqualified from driving, nor when he is on an overseas business trip lasting more than 30 days, unless the car is in fact no longer available to the employee/director or his family. (*Letter from CA to local General Practitioners Group*).

Example

Kadette takes up employment by Legend on 1 June 2000 and a new, 1,800 cc car, costing £10,000 is made available for his business and private use. Petrol is also provided. On 15 June, Kadette is involved in an accident and the car is off the road until 8 July. On 21 September, Kadette is involved in another accident and this time the car is off the road until 29 October. On 1 November, Kadette is moved into a clerical post within the company where he no longer has the use of a company car. The cash equivalent of the car and fuel benefits for 2000–01 are £3,500 and £2,170 respectively, but the car is unavailable for 56 days at the start of the tax year, for 37 days in September/October, and for 156 days at the end of the tax year. The period of repair in June/July does not count as unavailability because it lasted for only 22 consecutive days. The cash equivalents of £3,500 and £2,170 are, therefore, reduced by 249/365 to £1,112 and £689.

The same rules apply for Class 1A purposes except that a car is *not* to be regarded as unavailable for a day under (iii) above unless the person liable to pay the Class 1A contribution has information to show that the condition specified at (iii) is satisfied as regards the day in question. [*SSCBA 1992, s 10(6)(a)*]. The nature of the information required by this provision is discussed at 16.11 below.

A specimen letter is shown below:

Legend Ltd

Kadette

....

....

Dear K,

Provision of company car and fuel

The company has decided that, with immediate effect, it shall no longer provide you with a company vehicle for either business and/or private use.

You are required to return the vehicle .... [make, model] .... [Reg no.] .... to .... [Name] .... at .... [Location] .... by .... [Time] .... on .... [Date] .... along with all sets of ignition and related keys. You will wish to remove all personal possessions before doing so.

On return from .... [Country] /the end of your disqualification/the company will consider whether to make available the same, or another, company vehicle, which may or may not extend to permission to use such vehicle for non-business travel.

16.10 Reduction for employee paying for use of car and/or fuel

If, in the relevant tax year, an employee is required, as a condition of the car being available for his private use, to pay any amount of money (whether by deduction

16.11 Class 1A Contributions: Benefits in kind

from his emoluments or otherwise) for that use, the car benefit for the car described at 16.4 above is to be reduced (or if already reduced under the rules described at 16.5, 16.8 and 16.9 above, further reduced) by the amount so paid in, or in respect of, that year. [*ICTA 1988, 6 Sch 7*].

If, in the relevant tax year, an employee is required to make good to the person providing the fuel the *whole* of the expense incurred by the fuel-provider in, or in connection with, the provision of fuel for the employee's private use and the employee does so, the cash equivalent shown by the Table at 16.4 above is reduced to nil. [*ICTA 1988, s 158(6)*].

16.11 The 'information' required

The effect of the modifications made by *SSCBA 1992, s 10* to *ICTA 1988, 6 Sch*, as described at 16.5 to 16.8 above, is, *in the absence of appropriate information*, to impose a charge to Class 1A contributions on the car benefit, as if the car was used for less than 2,500 business miles (see 16.6 above) in respect of any car or cars made available for the private use of an employee, subject to any reductions described at 16(9)(i) and (ii) above.

Example
Metro, one of the company's typical salesmen, is employed by Benevolent Ltd throughout 2000–01. Benevolent Ltd concurrently makes available for Metro's business and private use two new cars: one (car 1) of 1,800 cc (petrol) costing £10,000 and another (car 2) of 2,200 cc (diesel) costing £16,000, and Benevolent Ltd also provides petrol/diesel for business and private motoring in both cars. But Benevolent Ltd keeps no records and has no information available as to business mileage or the degree of use of either car. For Class 1A purposes, the benefits described at 16.4 above (i.e. £3,500 and £5,600 for cars, £2,170 and £3,200 for fuel i.e. a total of £14,470) cannot be reduced under the rules described at 16.9 and 16.5 above. The rule described at 16.8 above has no additional effect.

If, however, Benevolent Ltd obtains information to show that Car 1 had been off the road for 48 days (thus bringing entitlement to a reduction under 16.9 above) and that business mileage in cars 1 and 2 had been 8,000 and 20,000 respectively (thus bringing potential entitlement to a reduction under 16.5 above to 25% in respect of car 1 and to 15% in respect of car 2, but identifying car 2 as the only car whose cash equivalent is to be adjusted under the rule described at 16.7 above), the cash equivalent for Class 1A purposes will be as follows:

			£
Car 1	£10,000 × 35% (i.e. £3,500) × $^{317}/_{365}$	=	3,039
Car 2	£16,000 × 15%	=	2,400
Fuel 1	£2,170 × $^{317}/_{365}$	=	1,884
Fuel 2	£3,200	=	3,200
			£10,523

That example demonstrates the importance to a Class 1A contributor of having suitable 'information' to hand; but it gives no indication of what form the information must take. The Act is not specific on this point and merely states that regulations may be made for requiring persons to maintain, in such form and manner as may be prescribed, records of such matters as may be prescribed for the purpose of enabling the incidence of liability for Class 1A contributions to be determined, and to retain the records for so long as may be prescribed. [*SSCBA 1992, Sch 1, para 8(1)(aa)*]. The only regulations made under that power deal with the form-filling aspects of the Class 1A contributions charge rather than laying down rules about mileage records etc.

A clear statement on what is required in the way of evidence of high mileage etc. was given by Mr Nicholas Scott in the Second Reading debate on the Social Security (Contributions) Bill. Referring to the concern about additional record-keeping expressed by employers both to the DSS and to the press, he had this to say:

'I do not believe that such concern is well founded. As I have explained, details of company cars already have to be provided to the Inland Revenue each year. Only a small amount of additional information will be needed to calculate the appropriate contribution charge. If, for example, the employer intends to claim one of the discounts for high mileage, he will have to satisfy himself that the car was used for more than 2,500 or more than 18,000 business miles during the course of the year. I do not believe that that will represent an insuperable problem. We believe that in the majority of cases the information will already be available from the employer's records. First, it will be generally clear from the nature of the employee's job whether a discount for business use over 2,500 or 18,000 miles a year is appropriate. Secondly, the employer will be able to check details of business mileage with his employees. Finally, since the employer will be meeting the cost of petrol used for business mileage and may be keeping records for VAT purposes, further information will be available. So I do not believe that this will put any substantial extra burden on employers. There will be no requirement to maintain comprehensive business mileage records in every case and, generally speaking, we shall be adopting precisely the same approach to this as the Inland Revenue does at the moment in assessing individual liability; and after consulting employers, we shall be providing them with detailed guidance about what information will be required to comply with the requirements . . .'.

(Hansard 9 May 1991 col 853).

That statement was supported by the DSS's view expressed during the course of the Social Security (Contributions) Bill's passage through Parliament and made public in advance of the detailed guidance notes in leaflet CA 33.

Such concerns will, however, cease to be of any relevance when, from 6 April 2002, the measure of business miles undertaken in a tax year ceases to be of any relevance (see 16.4).

16.12 Car made available by reason of more than one employment

Where a car is made available to an employee by reason of two or more employments of his, whether under the same or different employers, the amount of any Class 1A contribution which would be payable for the year in accordance with the rules described in the foregoing paragraphs is to be reduced in accordance with the following rules.

(a) If the aggregate use of the car for business travel in the two or more employments is not less than 18,000 miles (as reduced, where relevant, by reference to periods of unavailability—see 16.9 above), each employer's Class 1A liability is to be reduced to the amount which would have been payable if the car had been used for business travel for at least 18,000 miles (again, as reduced where relevant) in each of the employments. [*Contributions Regs, Reg 22D(1), (2)(a), (3)(a)*].

(b) If the aggregate use of the car for business travel in the two or more employments is more than 2,500 miles but less than 18,000 miles (each mileage limit as reduced, where relevant, by reference to periods of unavailability—see 16.9 above), each employer's Class 1A liability is to be reduced to the amount which would have been payable if the car had been used for business travel for more than 2,500 miles but less than 18,000 miles (again, each mileage limit as reduced where relevant) in each of the employments. [*Contributions Regs, Reg 22D(1), (2)(b), 3(b)*].

(c) The amount (= 'Y') arrived at under (*a*) or (*b*) (or, if the aggregate use of the car for business travel in the two or more employments does not exceed 2,500 miles, the amount which remains unadjusted under (*a*) or (*b*)) is then to be further reduced (or reduced) by deducting from it an amount equal to

$$Y \times \frac{Z-1}{Z}$$

where 'Z' is the number of employments in question. [*Contributions Regs, Reg 22E*].

Example
Robin works for Senator, Trevi and Uno and, by reason of those three employments, is provided with a 1,800 cc car costing £10,000 which is available for his private use. In 2000–01 he travels 7,000 miles on business for Senator, 4,000 miles on business for Trevi and 8,000 on business for Uno. Apart from the provisions of *Reg 22D*, Senator, Trevi and Uno (who each remunerate him separately under his contracts of employment with them) would each be liable for a Class 1A contribution on a cash equivalent of 25% of the list price, i.e., £2,500 but, because of *Reg 22D*, each is to be liable on a cash equivalent of 15% of the list price, i.e., £1,500 (see 16.5 above). That amount is then, in each case, further reduced under *Reg 22E* by deducting from it

$$£1,500 \times \frac{3-1}{3} = £1,000$$

In other words, each will be liable for a Class 1A contribution on £500 and the aggregate of those reduced scale amounts (3 × £500) is £1,500, i.e., the reduced scale amount on which a single employer of Robin would have been liable for a Class 1A contribution.

16.13 Cars and fuel for severely disabled employees

In addition to the *FA 1995* rules excluding certain accessories from the list price of the car, no Schedule E charge is made by the Inland Revenue where a specially adapted car is made available to a severely and permanently disabled employee only for home to work travel and business travel or where fuel is provided only for such travel. (ESC A59). For Class 1A purposes, the following rules apply in respect of a car made available by reason of his employment and on account of his disability to a disabled employed earner who is disabled for purposes of (or for purposes which include) assisting, on account of his disability, his travelling between his home and place of employment. [*Contributions Regs, Regs 22F(1), 22G(1)(a)*].

(a) Where the terms on which the car is made available to the employed earner prohibit private use other than use by that employed earner in travelling between his home and place of employment, and no prohibited private use of the car has been made in the tax year, the person who would otherwise be liable to pay a Class 1A contribution for the year in respect of that employed earner and that car is to be excepted from that liability. [*Reg 22G*].

(b) Where the terms on which the car is made available to the employed earner do *not* prohibit private use other than use by that employed earner in travelling between his home and place of employment, or where, though prohibited, such private use has been made in the tax year, and

  (i) treating the private use of the car by the employed earner in travelling between his home and place of employment as business travel would increase the use of the car for business travel to an amount of not less than

18,000 miles (as reduced, where relevant, by reference to periods of unavailability—see 16.9 above), or

(ii) treating the private use of the car by the employed earner in travelling between his home and place of employment as business travel would increase the use of the car for business travel to an amount of more than 2,500 miles but less than 18,000 miles (each mileage limit being reduced, where relevant, by reference to periods of unavailability—see 16.9 above),

the employed earner's travelling between his home and place of employment is to be regarded as business travel. [*Reg 22F*].

Example
Viva is so disabled as not to be able to use public transport but is able to drive an adapted 1,800 cc car costing £10,000 and made available to him by Windsor, his employer. Windsor permits him unlimited private use of the car. In 2000–01, Viva travels 2,000 miles on business and 5,000 miles between his home and his place of employment. In the absence of *Reg 22F*, Windsor would be liable for a Class 1A contribution on the full cash equivalent of £3,500, but, because of *Reg 22F*, the reduced 25% charge for business mileage between 2,500 and 17,999 is to apply.

16.14 Pooled cars

For *tax* purposes, a car is treated as *not* having been available for the private use of any of the employees to whom it was made available if, in the relevant tax year, it was included in a car pool and

(*a*) it was made available to and used by more than one employee and was not ordinarily used by any one employee to the exclusion of the others;

(*b*) any private use of it by any employee was merely incidental to (see IR leaflet 480 (2000) para 15.1) its business use; and

(*c*) it was not normally kept overnight at or near the residence of any of the employees unless it was kept on premises occupied by the provider of the car.

[*ICTA 1988, s 159*].

If a car is recognised as a pooled car by the Inland Revenue, no Sch E charge will arise in respect of that car under *ICTA 1988, s 157* and it follows, therefore, that no Class 1A liability will arise either (see 16.2 above). [*SSCBA 1992, s 10(1)*].

16.15 Shared cars

By concession, for Schedule E purposes, the Inland Revenue apportions between the users of a shared car the cash equivalent of the benefit of that car. (ESC A71). So far as Class 1A contribution liability is concerned, where a car is made available for private use to two or more employed earners concurrently by reason of their respective employments under the same employer, the amount of any Class 1A contribution which would be payable for the year in accordance with the rules described in the foregoing paragraphs is to be reduced in accordance with the following rules.

(*a*) If the aggregate use of the car for business travel in the two or more employments is not less than 18,000 miles (as reduced, where relevant, by reference to periods of unavailability—see 16.9 above), the employer's Class 1A liability is to be reduced to the amount which would have been payable if the car had been used for business travel for at least 18,000 miles (again, as reduced where relevant) in each of the employments. [*Contributions Regs, Reg 22D(1), (2)(a), (3)(a)*].

(b) If the aggregate use of the car for business travel in the two or more employments is more than 2,500 miles but less than 18,000 miles (each mileage limit as reduced, where relevant, by reference to periods of unavailability—see 16.9 above), the employer's Class 1A liability is to be reduced to the amount which would have been payable if the car had been used for business travel for more than 2,500 miles but less than 18,000 miles (again, each mileage limit is reduced where relevant) in each of the employments. [*Contributions Regs, Reg 22D(1), (2)(b), 3(b)*].

(c) The amount (= 'Y') arrived at under (a) or (b) (or, if the aggregate use of the car for business travel in the two or more employments does not exceed 2,500 miles, the amount which remains unadjusted under (a) or (b)) is then to be further reduced (or reduced) by deducting from it an amount equal to

$$Y \times \frac{Z - 1}{Z}$$

where 'Z' is the number of employments in question. [*Contributions Regs, Reg 22E*].

Example
Accord, Bacara and Clio work for Dedra and, by reason of their employments, are concurrently provided with one 1,800 cc car costing £10,000 which is available for their private use. In 2000–01, Accord travels 7,000 miles on business, Bacara travels 4,000 miles on business and Clio travels 8,000 miles on business. Apart from the provisions of *Reg 22D*, Dedra would be liable for three Class 1A contributions, each on a scale amount of £2,500 but, because of *Reg 22D*, he is to be liable, instead, on three scale amounts of only £1,500 each. These three amounts are then each further reduced under *Reg 22E* by deducting

$$£1,500 \times \frac{3 - 1}{3} = £1,000$$

In other words, Dedra will be liable for three Class 1A contributions on £500 and the aggregate of those reduced scale amounts (3 × £500) is £1,500, i.e., the reduced scale amount on which he would have been liable for a Class 1A contribution if he had made the car available to just one employee who travelled the three employees' combined business miles.

16.16 Cars made available to relatives of an employee

Where a person and a relative of his both work for the same employer and a car is made available for the private use of the relative, that car is, for *tax* purposes, deemed to be made available to the relative by reason not only of the relative's employment but also of the employment of the employee to whom the relative is related. [*ICTA 1988, s 168(6)(b)*]. That being so, a dual liability may arise in law for Sch E purposes: once on the relative and once on the employee to whom the relative is related; or, even if no dual liability arises because the relative is not a director and does not earn £8,500 or more a year, a liability may still arise in law on the employee to whom the relative is related. [*ICTA 1988, s 157*].

By concession, however, for Sch E purposes, a director or employee will not be taxed on the benefit of a car made available for the private use of a member of his family or household if

(a) the relative etc. is himself charged to tax on the benefit; or

(b) the relative etc. is *not* himself charged to tax on the benefit but he receives the car in his own right as an employee, and

(i) it can be shown that equivalent cars are made available on the same terms to employees in similar employment with the same employer who are unrelated to directors or higher-paid employees, or

(ii) the provision of an equivalent car is in accordance with normal commercial practice for the employment concerned.

(ESC A71).

The terms of this concession are paralleled for Class 1A purposes by *Contributions Regs, Reg 22B* which provides that the person who, in the circumstances described above, would be liable to pay a Class 1A contribution in respect of the employee to whom the relative is related is to be excepted from liability if:

(*a*) a Class 1A contribution is payable in respect of the relative and the car; or

(*b*) no Class 1A contribution is payable in respect of the relative and the car because the relative is not chargeable to tax (by reason of not being a director and not having earnings of £8,500 or more a year) and

(i) cars equivalent to that made available to the relative are made available on the same terms to other employed earners who are in similar employment with the same employer and who are not related to other employed earners under that employer; or

(ii) the making available for private use of a car equivalent to that made available to the relative is in accordance with normal commercial practice for employment of the type concerned.

[*Reg 22C(1)–(3)*].

For these purposes, a 'relative' is a spouse, a parent or remoter forbear, a child or remoter issue, a brother or sister, or a spouse of any of these. [*Reg 22C(4)*].

16.17 **Cars in the motor industry**

If, as part of his normal duties, a car salesman or demonstrator has to take a demonstration, test or experimental car home for the purpose of calling on a prospective customer, it is Inland Revenue practice not to regard the car, on that account alone, as being available for private use; but if such cars are otherwise available for the employee's private use, they attract a tax charge, and will therefore attract a Class 1A charge, in the normal way. In practice, the Inland Revenue is prepared to agree an estimated benefit with a motor industry employer and the DSS would generally accept the figures agreed. See IR 480 (2000), para 11.10–11.

16.18 **RETURNABLE BENEFITS**

The Child Support, Pensions and Social Security Bill 1999, due to be enacted Summer 2000, contained the original provisions for extending Class 1A NICs to all benefits that are not already assessable under Class 1A or excluded by reason of separate classification or exemption. For instance, in the latter category benefits provided to those employees earning less than £8,500 inclusive of benefits and expenses will not attract Class 1A NICs irrespective of whether a P9D is required for tax purposes. The extended Class 1A charge applying to all returnable benefits applies from 6 April 2000. If Class 1 NICs are currently payable on items such as readily convertible assets (such as a bonus paid in fine wines or non-cash vouchers) then no Class 1A charge will apply. See 16.1(*a*)–(*e*) for other exclusions. In the case of most benefits where there is a mix of both business and private the full amount of the benefit will be assessable to Class 1A NICs. However, where the private element is small then it is intended that there is a relaxation in the reporting rules. 'Small' is not defined but the IR Press Release of 19 November 1999 suggests a case such as

16.18   Class 1A Contributions: Benefits in kind

tools used in the business and privately begging the question that if the individual took the tools home for weekend use would this be 'small'? CWG 5 (2000) Issue 1 states that '... if there is some small amount of non-work use or where the benefit is provided solely for work outside the workplace but there is some small amount of private use.' This therefore would seem to preclude the use of tools by the individual over the weekend but would be allowable if the individual returned home directly from a job and used the tool that evening only. The distinction is obviously very fine and one can imagine the regular use of an employer's laptop computer used at home over the weekend by the individual to surf the Internet would not be considered 'small'. The CWG 5 (2000) Issue 1 contains a helpful table of expenses and their treatment from the Class 1 and Class 1A NICs point of view. However, the table is not comprehensive and even the CWG 5 states that it has no legal force. Issue 2 of CWG5 is to be issued late Summer/early Autumn 2000. The table is reproduced for reference purposes only below:

Type of expense or benefit provided	Circumstances	Class 1 NICs due (include in gross pay)	Class 1A NICs due
Assets placed at the employee's disposal	Provided mainly for business use and private use is small	No	No
	Provided for mixed business and private use	No	Yes
Assets transferred to the employee but not Readily Convertible Assets	Can be turned into cash only by sale, such as furniture, kitchen appliances, property and clothes	No	Yes
Car fuel for private motoring in a company owned car	Any means or supply and purchase—see para 62 of leaflet CA33 for exceptions	No	Yes
Car fuel for private motoring in a privately owned car	Supplied using a company credit card or garage account or agency card or from your own fuel pump and the conditions described on page 76 of CWG2 apply	No (see 2)	Yes
	Any other circumstances	Yes	No
Car parking facilities including motorcycles and bicycles	At or near place of work	No	No
	Elsewhere—unless the parking is part of a journey which is qualifying business travel	No	Yes
Car parking fees at normal place of employment paid for or reimbursed to employee	Employer contract (see 3)	No	No
	All other circumstances	Yes	No
Car parking fees for business related journeys paid for or reimbursed to employee	In all circumstances	No	No
Cars made available for private use		No	Yes
Childcare help provided by you in qualifying nurseries or playschemes	See booklet 480 for special conditions	No	No
Childcare help—any other means	Employer contract (see 3)(* See footnote)	No	Yes
	Employee contract (see 4)	Yes	No
Childcare vouchers	Provided for the cost of childcare for children up to the age of 16	No	No
Christmas boxes	In cash	Yes	No
	In goods	No	Yes
Protective clothing or uniforms (may have a logo) which are necessary for work	All circumstances	No	No

		Class 1	Class 1A
Protective clothing or uniforms which can be worn at any time	Provided by you	No	Yes
	See page 75 of booklet CWG2	Yes	No
	Employee contracts (see 4)		
Computers supplied by you for private use	Annual value and running expenses of £500 or less	No	No
	Amount in excess of £500	No	Yes
Council tax	See page 75 of CWG2	No	No
	All other circumstances	Yes	No
Credit cards, Charge cards, employee uses your card to purchase:	Goods or services bought on your behalf and the conditions described on page 76 of booklet CWG2 apply	No	No (see 2)
	Items for the personal use of the employee	Yes	No
	Items relating to specific and distinct business expenses actually incurred by the employee	No	No
Employee's liability insurance	See page 76 of booklet CWG2 for conditions	No	No
Entertaining clients expenses/ allowances	Employer contracts (see 3)	No	No
	Employee contracts (see 4)	No	No
Entertaining staff expenses/ allowances	Employer contracts (see 3)	No	Yes
	Employee contracts (see 4)	Yes	No
Expenses not covered by dispensation	Specific and distinct business expenses included in the payment	No	No
	Any profit element in the payment	Yes	No
Expenses and benefits covered by a dispensation		No	No
Food, groceries and farm produce	Employer contracts (see 3)	No	Yes
Goods, such as TV, Furniture, etc transferred to the employee	Employer contracts (see 3)	No	Yes
	Employee contracts (see 4)	Yes	No
Holidays	Employer contracts (see 3) (unless vouchers)	No	Yes
		Yes	No
	Employee contracts	Yes	No
Income Tax paid	But not deducted from directors	Yes	No
Income Tax paid	On notional payments not borne by employee with 30 days of receipt of each notional payment	Yes	No
Insurance premiums for pensions, annuities, etc on the employee's death or retirement. See pages 60 and 90 of CWG2 for exceptions	Employee contracts (see 4)	Yes	No
Living accommodation provided by you	See page 83 of CWG2	No	No
	In all other circumstances	No	Yes
Loans, beneficial arrangements	Qualifying loans	No	No
	Non-qualifying loans	No	Yes
Loans written off	At the time you decide not to seek repayment	Yes	No
Meal vouchers	Which cannot be transferred to another person, used only for meals and not worth more than 15p per day	No	No
Meals provided by you	At canteen open to your staff generally or on your business premises on a reasonable scale and all employees may obtain free or subsidised meals	No	No
	Any other circumstances	No	Yes

16.18 Class 1A Contributions: Benefits in kind

		Class 1	1AClass
Medical, dental etc treatment or insurance to cover such treatment	Employer contracts (see 3)	No	Yes
	Employee contracts (see 4)	Yes	No
	Outside the UK where the need for treatment arises while the employee is outside the UK working for you	No	No
Mobile phones provided by you		No	No
Mobile phones costs of private calls	Employer contracts (see 3)	No	No
	Employee contracts (see 4)	Yes	No
Office accommodation, supplies/services on employer's premises used by employee doing his/her work		No	No
Personal bills of the employee paid by you	Employee contracts (see 4)	Yes	No
Personal incidental expenses	See booklet 480 for special conditions	No	No
Readily convertible assets, remuneration provided in non-cash form such as stocks and shares, bullion, commodities etc	See page 97 of CWG2 for detailed information	Yes	No
Relocation expenses/benefits	Non-qualifying expenses	Yes	No
	Non-qualifying benefits	No	Yes
	Qualifying expenses/benefits of £8,000 or less	No	No
	Qualifying expenses/benefits in excess of £8,000	No	Yes
Retirement benefit schemes	You contribute towards an unapproved scheme	Yes	No
Round sum allowances	Specific and distinct business expenses identified	No	No
	Profit element	Yes	No
Scholarships awarded to students because of their parent's employment	Employer contracts (see 3)	No	Yes
	Employee contracts (see 4)	Yes	No
School fees	Employer contracts (see 3)	No	Yes
	Employee contracts (see 4)	Yes	No
Social functions	See page 84 of CWG2 for special conditions	No	Yes
	Any other type of function	No	No
Sporting or recreational facilities provided by you such as fishing, horse racing, etc	See booklet 480 for special conditions	No	No
	All other circumstances	No	Yes
Stocks and shares and share options	See Readily Convertible Assets		
Non-RCA shares or options		No	No
Subscriptions and professional fees membership is voluntary	Employer contracts (see 3)	No	Yes
	Employee contracts (see 4)	Yes	No
Suggestion schemes awards to employees	Not part of the employee's normal duties to make suggestions and award is wholly discretionary with no contractual entitlement or expectation	No	No
	Above conditions not fully satisfied	Yes	No
Third party benefits/ payments	Made available to employee by reason of the employee's employment	See 16.3 above	

		Class 1	Class 1A
Training payments for course fees, books etc	Training is work-related or encouraged or required by you in connection with the employment	No	No
	All other circumstances and employer contracts (see 3)	No	Yes
	All other circumstances and employee contracts (see 4)	Yes	No
Vans—available for private use		No	Yes
Vouchers	See page 79 of booklet CWG2 for exceptions	Yes	No

1. From April 2000, where assets (apart from vehicles, boats and aircraft) and services made available to employees to use for work on your premises or elsewhere and there is only a small amount of incidental private use no Class 1A contributions will be due.

2. Where an employee purchases goods or services on your behalf and you later transfer ownership of these to the employee Class 1A NICs will be due.

3. Contract is between you, the employer, and the provider of the benefit.

4. Contract is between the employee and provider and you, the employer, pay the provider or reimburse the employee.

5. Specific and distinct business expenses may feature in a number of payments you make to employees and should be recorded in the appropriate P11D section.

6. Round Sum Allowances may feature in a number of payments you make to employees and should be recorded in the appropriate P11D section.

Footnote: The position regarding childcare provided under an employer's contract is to change following the Budget on 21 March 2000. There will not, in fact be a Class 1A liability on this item even if a tax charge arises because the provision is 'outside' the workplace.

The above Inland Revenue list and notes should be read in conjunction with the P11D (2001) and P11D(b) (2001) expenses, benefits and Class 1A NICs returns 2000–01. In a majority of benefit cases Class 1As will be due on the full amount of the benefit where there is a mix of private use but see above for where private use is small. Under a change announced for inclusion in the Finance Bill 2000 and to take effect from 6 April 2000, loans where the interest would qualify for full tax relief, will be exempted from the beneficial loans charge and Class 1As and will no longer need to be reported on the P11D. Other loans, including those, which partly qualify for tax relief, will continue to be reported as at present.

The use of company credit cards varies. It depends on whether the individual is acting on his/her own right or they are acting as a representative of the company when they use the card. It is a difficult distinction and the use of the credit card to obtain money, goods or services for personal gain is treated as payment of earnings and subject to Class 1 NICs. Business expenses are disregarded. Two exceptions arise in respect of the credit card so that no Class 1 NICs is due on:

- Private fuel purchased by means of a company credit card where a Class 1A contribution liability already exists on the provision of free private fuel. See 16.4.

- Any purchase made using a company credit card which can be regarded as motoring expense associated with a car liable to Class 1A contributions.

16.19 COLLECTION

Existing regulations which provide for the collection of Class 1 contributions along with income tax are extended to cover the collection of Class 1A contributions also. [*SSCBA 1992, Sch 1, para 6*]. The statutory collection arrangements are as follows in respect of the 1999–2000 liability and that for earlier years.

(*a*)   Subject to (*b*) below, an employer who is liable to pay a Class 1A contribution must,

   (i)   if he is paying Class 1 contributions quarterly (see 21.3 COLLECTION), pay that contribution to the Collector of Taxes not later than 19 July in the tax year immediately following the end of the tax year in respect of which that contribution is payable;

   (ii)   if he is not paying Class 1 contributions quarterly (see 21.3 COLLECTION), pay that contribution to the Collector of Taxes not later than 19 July in the tax year immediately following the end of the tax year in respect of which that contribution is payable or, if the liability is in respect of 1995–96 or earlier, 19 June in the tax year immediately following the end of the tax year in respect of which that contribution is payable.

See also CA Press Release 96/8, 23 September 1996. The change of payment date mentioned in (ii) above is a logical consequence of the later filing date for forms P11D, as part of the various changes that were made in connection with self-assessment. [*Contributions Regs, 1 Sch 26C(1)(2) as amended by Social Security Contributions Amendment (No 5) Regs 1996, SI 1996 No 2407 Reg 7(3)*].

(*b*)   Where there is a change in the employer who is liable to pay emoluments to or for the benefit of all the persons who are employed in a business in respect of their employment in the business (i.e. a succession) and one or more employees have ceased to be employed in the business before the change of employer occurs, the employer before the change must,

   (i)   not later than 12 days after the end of the final income tax month in which he pays emoluments, record on the deductions working sheet for the tax year for each employee who has left and in respect of whom a Class 1A contribution is payable the amount of the Class 1A contribution and the category letter, and

   (ii)   not later than 14 days after the end of the final income tax month mentioned in (i), pay the Class 1A contribution mentioned in (i) to the Collector of Taxes and, if the final income tax month is that beginning on 6 April, 6 May, or in 1997–98 onwards 6 June, pay also any Class 1A contribution in respect of the tax year immediately preceding the tax year in which the final income tax month occurs.

The employer before the change must also include the amount of the Class 1A contribution mentioned in (i) on the annual return relating to the tax year in which the final tax month falls. See Inland Revenue Collection PAYE Manual Vol 1, Para PA 1654 (5/98).

[*1 Sch 26D*].

Example
On 28 April 2000, Egg sells his business to Chicken. Yolk, one of Egg's employees to whom Egg had made a car available for Yolk's private use throughout his employment, left Egg's employment on 25 April 2000. Egg made his final payment of emoluments to the remaining employees on 30 May. By 17 May 2000, Egg must record on the 2000–01 deductions working sheet for Yolk the Class 1A

contribution due for the 20 days from 6 April 2000 to the date of Yolk's departure and, by 19 May 2000, he must pay to the Collector that Class 1A contribution and the Class 1A contribution due in respect of Yolk for 1999–2000. Normally, the Class 1A contributions due for 1998–99 would be payable on 19 July 2000. Egg must also now pay the 1998–99 Class 1A contribution in respect of Yolk on 19 May 2000. The equivalent liability for any other employees to whom cars have been provided will be met, in respect of both 1998–99 and 1999–2000, by the purchaser.

(*c*) Where an employer ceases to carry on business and upon that cessation no other person becomes liable to pay emoluments to or for the benefit of any employee in respect of his employment in that business (i.e. no succession), the employer must,

 (i) not later than 12 days after the end of the final income tax month in which he pays emoluments, record on the deductions working sheet for the tax year for each employee in respect of whom a Class 1A contribution is payable the amount of the Class 1A contribution and the category letter, and

 (ii) not later than 14 days after the end of the final income tax month mentioned in (i), pay the Class 1A contribution mentioned in (i) to the collector of taxes and, if the final income tax month is that beginning on 6 April, 6 May or, in 1997–98 onwards, 6 June, pay also any Class 1A contribution in respect of the tax year immediately preceding the tax year in which the final income tax month occurs.

The employer must also include the amount of the Class 1A contribution mentioned in (i) on the annual return relating to the tax year in which the final tax month falls.

[*1 Sch 26D*].

(*d*) An employer who pays to the Collector an amount in respect of Class 1A contributions which he was not liable to pay may deduct the overpayment from any payment of secondary Class 1 contributions which he is liable to pay subsequently for any income tax period in the same tax year. [*1 Sch 26C(3)*].

(*e*) If an employer has paid no Class 1A contribution by the date mentioned at (*a*), (*b*)(ii) or (*c*)(ii) above, or has paid an amount which the Collector is not satisfied is the full amount due, and the Collector is unaware of the full extent (if any) of the employer's liability, the Collector may give notice to the employer requiring him to make a return within 14 days showing the extent of his liability. [*1 Sch 27(2A)(3)*].

(*f*) If, after 14 days following the date mentioned at (*a*), (*b*)(ii) or (*c*)(ii) above the employer has paid no amount of Class 1A contributions to the Collector of Taxes in respect of the year in question and there is reason to believe that the employer has a liability to pay, the Collector may specify the amount due to the best of his judgment and give the employer seven days notice to pay after which he may, in the absence of payment, certify the amount for recovery purposes as described at 21.6 COLLECTION.

(*g*) With effect from 6 April 1999, in calculating Class 1A contributions, employers are to round fractional amounts to the nearest whole penny, with £0.005 or less being disregarded. [*Social Security (Contributions) Amendment (No 3) Regs 1998, Reg 7*].

Class 1A contributions in respect of an employee who leaves may, by concession, be recorded and paid as soon as possible after the time of departure, and in any event before the end of the tax year. The concession avoids the creation of a payroll record for an ex-employee in the year following cessation of the employment, which would be necessary if the statutory payment method is used. (CA 33, Paragraph 106).

For Class 1A contributions due in respect of 1991–92 the DSS introduced an extra-statutory direct payment procedure known as the 'alternative payment method', which was extended for 1992–93 and subsequent years. Under the arrangement, employers who make cars available for the private use of employees are permitted (following registration with the Contributions Agency or, now, Inland Revenue NICO) to pay the Class 1A contributions due on 19 July (or, historically, as the case may be—19 June) following the year, directly to Newcastle using a special declaration and remittance form. The arrangement was restricted for 1991–92, 1992–93, 1993–94 to employers who made ten or more cars available but for 1994–95 and subsequent years no restriction in the arrangement applied. Applications (Form CA 34) by the employer to pay contributions by the alternative payment method in respect of cars provided during 1999–2000 must have been received no later than 20 May 2000 by the Class 1A Group, stating the company name, address, telephone number, tax district, PAYE reference, collection reference, number of vehicles and a contact point at the company. Adoption of the alternative payment method will mean that Class 1A details are not entered on forms P11 (deductions working sheets), P14 (OCR), P35, see CA 33 and CWG1 (2000), Card 15. See Inland Revenue Collection PAYE Manual Vol 1, paras PA 1657–1658 (5/98).

The 'alternative payment method' operated informally until 1999, when it was regularised by *Social Security (Contributions) Amendments (No 3) Regulations 1999* which replaces part of the *1979 Regs* and inserts new provisions. New *Reg 47* provides for payment other than to the Collector of Taxes. *Reg 47A* specifies the payment date in normal circumstances, being 19 July after the end of the tax year to which the contributions relate. *Reg 47B* replicates the existing provisions, advancing the payment date where there is a succession to a business but some employees left on or before the succession and *Reg 47C* does likewise in the case of the cessation of a business. *Reg 47J* specifies that returns are to be made in each of the three foregoing circumstances. *Reg 47D* enables the Inland Revenue to require a return to be made where no payment has been made by the due date. Additionally or alternatively, they are empowered to estimate the contribution due by virtue of *Reg 47E* and, if still unpaid, certify the amount due for enforcement.

The alternative payment method will form the basis of the only method of payment of Class 1A in respect of the liability for 2000–01 and subsequent years. The recording of information on PAYE documentation will no longer apply. Those employers who did not use the alternative method will make their final entries on 2000–01 forms P11 and P14/P60 in respect of the 1999–2000 liability due on 19 July 2000.

16.20 REPAYMENT

The provision for repayment of wrongly paid Class 1A contributions is very restrictive and applies only where a person has paid a Class 1A contribution in respect of a particular employee and the car made available to him, and, in calculating the cash equivalent of the benefit of the car or fuel for the purposes of ascertaining the amount of the Class 1A contribution,

(*a*)   he made that calculation by reference to information which had been made available to him by the employee and that information was inaccurate or incomplete; or

(*b*)   he had been unable to obtain information from the employee because of the employee's absence from Great Britain or absence from work through sickness, injury, pregnancy or confinement, or because the employee had left the employment; or (*c*) he had become liable to pay the contribution as a successor to the business and the information available to him was inaccurate or incomplete.

[*Contributions Regs, Reg 33A(2)*].

In such circumstances, the person who has paid the Class 1A contribution may apply for repayment of the overpaid element of the contribution and, if the IR is satisfied in the light of the information provided (see 16.11 above) that the overpayment has occurred, repayment will be made. [*Reg 33A(1)*]. The application must be in writing and must be made within six years of the end of the tax year in which the contribution was paid, or, where there has been a good cause for delay, within such longer period as may be allowed. [*Reg 33A(3)*]. (CA 33, Page 35, para 119).

It seems that there is no provision under which a repayment of Class 1A contributions may be made in other circumstances, e.g. where a person who has complete and accurate information simply miscalculates the contribution—though, if the person discovers his error before the end of the tax year in which payment took place, he may deduct the overpayment from any subsequent payment of secondary Class 1 contributions in that year (see 16.19(*d*) above).

16.21 PENALTIES AND INTEREST

The penalty provisions for late, fraudulent or negligent returns made to the Collector of Taxes are extended to returns required in connection with Class 1A contributions; though not—until 20 April 1999 (see below)—to the extra-statutory return mentioned at 16.19 above. [*SSCBA 1992, 1 Sch 7(11)(a)*]. (See 21.8 COLLECTION).

From 19 April 1993 interest has been chargeable on Class 1A contributions which are paid late. (See 39.9 LATE-PAID CONTRIBUTIONS.)

Where the 'alternative payment method' has been used then no interest or penalties for non-payment or non-compliance apply until 1999. New provisions in the *1979 Regs* inserted by *Social Security (Contributions) Amendment No 3 Regulations 1999*, will, in practice, apply to payments for 1998–99 (normally due 19 July 1999) onwards.

The Social Security (Contributions) Amendment (No 3) Regs 1999, SI 1999 No 975 formalises the APM for the first time since it's introduction in April 1991. New *Reg 47A* inserted into the *1979 Regs* specifies 19 July as the payment date. New *Regs 47B* and *47C* replicate the payroll system provisions for earlier payment than usual where on a succession to a business there are some employees who had left before the succession took place or where a business ceases completely.

The Inland Revenue are given the power to require a return to be rendered (*Regs 47D* and *47J*) and, in the event of non-payment, to specify an amount which it estimates is properly due (*Reg 47E*). Such an estimated amount can then be recovered as though it was actual Class 1A National Insurance contributions.

Reg 47F provides that interest shall be charged on an overdue payment at the rate applicable under *SSCBA 1992, 1 Sch 6(3)* from the due date until payment. This is, it should be noted, more onerous than if the 'alternative payment method' had not been used since then interest would not run until 19 April 2000 on a payment of Class 1A contributions in respect of 1998–99. Under the 'alternative payment method' interest will, under the new provisions, run from 20 July 1999—nine months earlier than would have been the case if returns had been made to the Collector of Taxes.

Provisions have been made to permit the payment of interest on a refund of overpaid Class 1A contributions (*Reg 47G*); the repayment of overpaid interest (*Reg 47H*) and the remission of interest in the case of official error (*Reg 47I*). Where a return under the 'alternative payment method'—

(*a*) is made incorrectly due to fraud or neglect a penalty may be charged, the amount not exceeding the amount of contributions underpaid (*Reg 47K(1)*);

(*b*) is not made, then the following penalties may be imposed:

(i) for each of the first twelve months, £100 per ten cars or part thereof (e.g. £200 per month if there are eleven cars in respect of which Class 1A contributions are due) and

(ii) if the failure extends beyond twelve months, a further penalty not exceeding the amount of contributions unpaid. [*Regs 47K(2) and (3)*].

These penalties may be recovered as if they were Class 1A contributions due. [*Reg 47K(4)*].

The due date for payment of a penalty under these provisions is 30 days from the date of issue (including that day) of the penalty notice. [*Reg 47K(5)*].

The Inland Revenue may mitigate or remit any penalty at it's discretion. [*Reg 47K(6)*].

As with the charge to interest under the 'alternative payment method', these penalty provisions are more onerous than those applying in the case of payment via returns made to the Collector of Taxes.

16.22 APPEALS

The procedure for an appeal (see 9 APPEALS AND REVIEWS) is extended to cover a question whether a Class 1A contribution is payable or otherwise relating to a Class 1A contribution.

17   Class 1B Contributions: PAYE settlement agreements

Cross-reference. See APPEALS AND REVIEWS (9) for remedies for dissatisfaction.

Other Sources. Simon's NIC, Part 1, Section 2, Chapter 9A; Leaflet IR155; CWG2 (2000), Page 86; CA30, Page 34; CA29, Page 24.

17.1   PAYE settlement agreements

The introduction of legislation concerning Annual Voluntary Settlements, now called PAYE settlement agreements (PSAs), which enabled the Inland Revenue to exact the tax liability from the employer without recourse to the employee, had an impact on NICs treatment. [*ICTA 1988, s 206A as inserted by FA 1996, s 110*]. PSAs came into being from 6 April 1996 to formally replace the more informal (and relatively secretive) Annual Voluntary Settlements. It is a voluntary arrangement between an employer and the local tax office whereby the employer agrees to pay the tax that is due on certain expenses and possibly benefits in kind. Having entered into a PSA in respect of particular items, those items do not then appear on the Forms P11D/P9D or on the employee's self-assessment tax return. See also Inland Revenue leaflet IR155. There was originally no appropriate legislation for the then CA to introduce a PSA for NICs unlike the Inland Revenue who already held powers of care and management which provide a practical solution in this respect. As far as the CA was concerned there was no such practical solution and where the payment attracted NIC then it should have been assessed correctly to Class 1 as it should always have been in the past. This created difficulties but as many PSAs were in respect of benefits in kind on which the tax was paid by the employer and as those payments were normally covered by *Contributions Regs 1979, Reg 19(1)(d)* this did not give rise to a NI charge. [*Income Tax (Employments) (Amendment No 6) Regs 1996*, Statement of Practice SP 5/96].

It was confirmed by the *Social Security Act 1998 (Commencement No 1) Order 1998, Reg 2* that PSAs and NICs alignment would apply from 6 April 1999 onwards. However, *sections 53* and *65* of the Act were brought into force on 8 September 1998 for the purpose of making the further detailed regulations in respect of the operation of Class 1B NICs. [*Social Security Act 1998 (Commencement No 1) Order 1998, Reg 2*].

Class 1B arises at the rate of 12.2% only from 6 April 1999 when the employer has entered into a PAYE Settlement Agreement (PSA) with the Inland Revenue. No employee's contribution is due under the Class 1B system.

17.2   The *Social Security Act 1998* introduced the power to make regulations in respect of Class 1B contributions. Class 1B is payable, instead of Class 1 or Class 1A, for example on cash vouchers, but not on the benefit of a corporate golf club subscription, since that is an employer's contract and would not have attracted Class 1 NICs. It is also due on all the tax payable under the PSA, whether that tax relates to items otherwise liable to NICs or not. In other words, the tax due on the corporate golf club subscription mentioned above will attract Class 1B, even though the subscription itself does not. [*SSCBA 1992, s 10A as inserted by Social Security Act 1998, s 53*]. Under the rule in *Hartland v Diggines* [*1926*] *10 TC 247* the discharge of employees' tax liabilities is equivalent to cash payments to those employees. The CA always alleged that the payment of tax under an old annual voluntary settlement constituted such a personal discharge even though no individual personal liability was ever calculated. The income tax legislation creating the replacement PSAs specifically

17.3 Class 1B Contributions: PAYE settlement agreements

provided that the tax due under a PSA is, for the avoidance of doubt, deemed to be the employer's liability. Hence there cannot be a Class 1 charge on the tax, even if the particular item itself falls to be treated as earnings so that Class 1 is due. However, from 6 April 1999, the tax is now liable to Class 1B contributions instead. It remains the case that no class of National Insurance contributions liability arises on the *tax* element of a PSA for the years 1996–97, 1997–98 and 1998–99.

17.3 Rates and collection

Class 1B is payable by 19 October following the end of the year to which it relates (i.e. at the same time as the tax due under the PSA) so that the first such payment will be due by 19 October 2000. There will be a liability for tax under a 1998–99 PSA on 19 October 1999 but there is no Class 1B to add to it for that year. The rate is initially set at 12.2%, which is the same as the not contracted-out employer's rate. This is an employer-only charge similar to Class 1A and, like Class 1A, not generating any benefit entitlement in return for the payment. The Class 1B rate can be increased by statutory instrument by two percentage points per annum above the Class 1 rate if required. [*SSAA 1992, s143A (2) as inserted by Social Security Act 1998, s 65*]. The *Welfare Reform and Pensions Act 1999, ss 77, 78,* however, provides that, as with Class 1A previously, the rate will now be tied to the Class 1 secondary rate. Fortunately, the collection mechanism is much clearer than that for Class 1A, being kept totally separate from the Form P35 process for everyone.

For the years 1996/97, 1997/98 and 1998/99 items such as the cash vouchers mentioned above remained subject to Class 1 (but no NICs were payable on the related tax) and should strictly have been accounted for on the Form P11 or equivalent in just the same way as if they were normal salary/wage payments.

17.4 Exclusions

Employers are allowed under the regulations to exclude from their calculations amounts in respect of employees normally excluded by reason of a social security agreement and where the EC rules, reciprocal agreement or standard residence and presence conditions result in there being no Class 1 liability at all. One of the purposes of a PSA is to dispense with the need to keep detailed records and calculations of small amounts for every individual employee. Employers will therefore be allowed to pay Class 1B in these cases if they want to. This approach will be favourable in many cases. [*Reg 21J inserted by The Social Security Contributions Statutory Maternity Pay and Statutory Sick Pay (Miscellaneous Amendments) Regs 1999, Reg 4*].

Example
Benevolent Ltd has 500 employees who are all provided with benefits in kind (hairdressing on site) of £50 each which are not liable for NICs during the year ended 5 April 2001. Of these employees, 400 are basic rate taxpayers and the other 100 are higher rate taxpayers. Also, 100 employees receive expenses amounting to £2,000 relating to home to work travel for the higher rate taxpayers. Benevolent Ltd wishes to avoid having to submit P11Ds and P9Ds for the employees as well as the administrative burden of advising employees of the necessity to notify the Inland Revenue of the benefit under the self-assessment legislation. The PSA negotiation might be as follows:

	£	£
Tax due under PSA.		
Value of benefits provided to basic rate taxpayers		
(400 × £50)	20,000.00	
Tax thereon @ 22%	4,400.00	
Gross up tax £4,400 × $\frac{100}{100-22}$		5,641.03
Value of benefits provided to higher rate taxpayers		
(100 × £50)	5,000.00	
Value of expenses provided to higher rate taxpayers	2,000.00	
	7,000.00	
Tax thereon @ 40%	2,800.00	
Gross up tax £2,800 × $\frac{100}{100-40}$		£4,666.67
Total tax		£10,307.70
NICs due under PSA.		
Value of expenses liable for NICs	2,000.00	
Class 1B NICs due @ 12.2% on £2,000		244.00
Tax paid by employer liable to Class 1B charge	10,307.70	
Class 1B NICs due re tax paid by employer @ 12.2%		1,257.54
Total NICs and tax payable by Benevolent Ltd		£11,809.24

The tax and Class 1B is payable to the Inland Revenue on or before 19 October 2001.

17.5 Incorrect payments

Provision is included for rounding of contributions and recovery of unpaid contributions. [*Reg 22I inserted by The Social Security Contributions Statutory Maternity Pay and Statutory Sick Pay (Miscellaneous Amendments) Regs 1999, Reg 4*]. Interest will be charged on unpaid amounts from 20 October following the year to which the payment relates at the same rate as applies to underpayments of Class 1 and Class 1A. [*Reg 28A as amended by The Social Security Contributions Statutory Maternity Pay and Statutory Sick Pay (Miscellaneous Amendments) Regs 1999, Reg 4*]. Interest that is not properly due will be repayable. Interest will be added to repayments of overpaid Class 1B at the same rate as applicable to Class 1/Class 1A and will run from the same 20 October date as mentioned above or, if later, the actual date of payment. Class 1B overpaid will also be able to be treated as contribution paid on account of secondary Class 1, and also 1A and 2 will be able to be offset against Class 1B. [*Reg 31(2) as inserted by The Social Security Contributions Statutory Maternity Pay and Statutory Sick Pay (Miscellaneous Amendments) Regs 1999, Reg 4*].

17.6 Recording requirements

No new records are required to be kept over and above those needed for tax purposes and to distinguish between items, which would or would not otherwise have been liable to NICs. However, where an employee fails to qualify for SSP or SMP only because the average weekly earnings fall below the specified limit, it will be a requirement that if any amounts included in the PSA relate to that employee and would otherwise have been liable to Class 1, the relevant value must be treated as earnings and included in average earnings calculations, if falling in the relevant weeks. [*Statutory Maternity Pay (General) Regs 1986, Reg 20(2) and Statutory Sick Pay (General) Regs 1982, Reg 17(2) as amended by The Social Security Contributions Statutory Maternity Pay and Statutory Sick Pay (Miscellaneous Amendments) Regs 1999, Regs 12 and 13*]. Any details required for inspection must be kept for three years following the year to which they relate.

17.7 Class 1B Contributions: PAYE settlement agreements

17.7 Timing of PSA

Class 1B only applies once a PSA is entered into. So if this is done during the tax year, or even after it, then the Class 1 applies to relevant payments and not Class 1B. Class 1B will be due on all tax paid under PSAs relating to 1999–2000 and subsequent years regardless of the time at which the PSA is entered into and even if there are no payments at all included in it which would otherwise have been liable to Class 1/Class 1A. [*SSCBA 1992, s10(5) as inserted by Social Security Act 1998, s 53*].

18   Class 2 Contributions: Self-employed Earners

Cross-references. See AGE EXCEPTION (3) for age limitations on liability; 5.16 AGGREGATION OF EARNINGS for small earnings exception; APPEALS AND REVIEWS (9); ARREARS OF CONTRIBUTIONS (12) for recovery powers and procedures; CATEGORISATION (14); COLLECTION (21); CREDITS (24) for circumstances in which Class 2 contributions may be awarded; DEFERMENT OF PAYMENT (27); EARNINGS (28); ENFORCEMENT (32); LATE-PAID CONTRIBUTIONS (39); MULTIPLE EMPLOYMENTS (44); NATIONAL INSURANCE NUMBER (46); OVERSEAS MATTERS (49); PARTNERS (50); RATES AND LIMITS (51); REDUCED LIABILITY ELECTIONS (52); REPAYMENT AND RE-ALLOCATION (53); SHARE FISHERMEN (54); SUBPOSTMASTERS (55); VOLUNTEER DEVELOPMENT WORKERS (57); WORKING CASE STUDY (58).

Other Sources. Simon's NIC, Part I, Section 3, Chapter 12; Tolley's Social Security and State Benefits Handbook 2000–01; Leaflets CA 02, CA 04, CA 06, CWL 1 and CWL 2.

18.1   GENERAL CONSIDERATIONS

Class 2 contributions are paid by about 2.4 million self-employed earners and, in the year 2000–01, are expected to produce £280,000,000 of National Insurance Fund income (see 45.4 NATIONAL INSURANCE FUND). In addition, a further £51,000,000 collected is diverted directly to the National Health Service. When compared with total contributions from employed earners (£23,889,000,000) and their secondary contributors (£33,186,000,000), however, the amount is small and represents just over ½% of total fund income from contributions. The amount has reduced for 2000–01 due to the substantial reduction in the weekly rate. A discussion document 'The Self Employed and National Insurance' was published in 1980 and representations to this were made by the Consultative Committee of Accountancy Bodies and other interested institutions. On 3 November 1983, however, it was announced that, because of a lack of any clear preference for specific reforms, no fundamental changes were to be made to the existing system. (Hansard Vol 47 Col 456).

The 'Taylor Report' published on 17 March 1998 (Budget day) recommended that Class 2 contributions be abolished and subsumed into a higher, but revenue-neutral, Class 4 charge. The Chancellor agreed to consider these proposals and in the 1999 Budget announced that there would be a re-distribution as between the Class 2 and Class 4 elements of contribution, both of which most self-employed persons have to pay, but that the Class 2 contribution would nonetheless be retained, albeit falling to £2.00 per week from April 2000.

An awareness in the DSS that there are many self-employed persons who should be, but are not, registered for Class 2 contribution purposes led the former CA to set as one of its targets the identification of a further 40,000 such persons in each of the years 1995–96 and 1996–97. In fact, 39,791 such persons were identified in 1995–96 and 40,916 in 1996–97 (see CA Annual Report July 1997, page 15). The CA also developed a Class 2 database which will improve Class 2 compliance by keeping track of non-payers and identifying them at earlier stages. Nonetheless the Report on the National Insurance Fund account for the year ended 31 March 1999, released in March 2000, reflects the problems created by the failings of NIRS 2 computer system and contains the following comment:

> 'The Inland Revenue estimate broadly that some £416 million of recorded debt was outstanding at 31 March 1999. However, because of problems with information technology systems some elements of this amount are unreliable.'

18.2 Class 2 Contributions: Self-employed Earners

The debt figure of £416 million is equivalent to nearly 60% of the total Class 2 contributions due to be collected in 1999–2000!

In 1995–96, the most recent year for which detailed figures are currently available, 2.346 million persons paid Class 2 contributions either alone or along with other classes of contribution (Contributions and Qualifying Years for Retirement Pension 1995–96, Government Statistical Service, May 1998).

18.2 LIABILITY

Every self-employed earner is, if he is over the age of 16 and under pensionable age, liable to pay Class 2 contributions at a prescribed weekly rate (see 14.10 CATEGORISATION, 3.2, 3.12 AGE EXCEPTION AND 51.7 RATES AND LIMITS). [*SSCBA 1992, s 11(1)(2)*].

Liability will always be measured in complete weeks as a person is to be treated as a self-employed earner in respect of any week during any part of which he is such an earner. [*SSCBA 1992, s 2(5)*]. Liability will, furthermore, continue unless and until a person is no longer ordinarily gainfully employed in his self-employed earner's employment. [*Categorisation Regs, Reg 3, 2 Sch*]. The effect of this latter regulation is to impose a liability even for weeks of holiday, weeks of inactivity and weeks where there are no earnings from the self-employment, provided the self-employment has not ceased or become so irregular and exceptional and non-gainful as to be disregarded under *Categorisation Regs, Reg 2(4) and 1 Sch Pt III Para 9* (see 14.10 CATEGORISATION).

Once a person ceases to be ordinarily self-employed, however, his liability will cease, on 'doctrine of source' principles. (*National Provident Institution v Brown (1921) 8 TC 57*). This is so even if his self-employed activities were such that they will continue to produce earnings for him into the future (e.g. book royalties from ceased self-employed authorship).

18.3 Exception from liability on grounds of small income

An earner who would otherwise be liable for Class 2 contributions in respect of his employment as a self-employed earner may be excepted from such liability in respect of any period in which his EARNINGS (28.77) from such employment are, or are treated as being, less than a specified amount (see 51.8 RATES AND LIMITS). [*SSCBA 1992, s 11(4)*]. For 2000–01 the prescribed amount is £3,825. [*SSCBA 1992, s 11(4) as amended by Contributions Re-rating and National Insurance Funds Order 2000, SI 2000/755, Reg 2(b)*].

Exception under these provisions is not granted automatically, but must be on the earner's own application. [*SSCBA 1992, s 11(5)*]. If granted, the exception may, at the Inland Revenue's discretion and as is considered appropriate to the circumstances of the case, commence on a date earlier than the date of application, but not more than 13 weeks earlier. [*Sec 11(5); Contributions Regs, Reg 24(5)(b)*].

Where Class 2 contributions have not been paid but small earnings exception would have been available had an application been made within the time limit prescribed, waiver of the Class 2 liabilities may be granted by concession (see 12.11 ARREARS OF CONTRIBUTIONS).

Where Class 2 contributions have been paid but small earnings exception would have been available had an application been made within the time limit prescribed, a repayment of those contributions may, under certain conditions, be obtained (see 53.6 REPAYMENT AND RE-ALLOCATION).

The earnings for any particular tax year are to be treated as less than the specified amount for that year (see 51.8 RATES AND LIMITS) if it is shown to the satisfaction of the Inland Revenue that

(a) in the tax year preceding the particular tax year concerned, the applicant's EARNINGS (28.77) were less than the amount specified for the preceding tax year and that there has since been no material change of circumstances; or

(b) in the particular tax year concerned, the applicant's EARNINGS (28.77) are expected to be less than the specified amount

[*Contributions Regs, Reg 25(1)*].

Example
Ambrose is a florist. His accounts (prepared in October 2000) show that his net profits for the year ended 5 April 2000 are only £2,800. As trade is continually worsening and as he is already behind with his Class 2 payments, he decides to apply for 2000–01 Class 2 exception and does so on 8 November 2000. As his earnings in 1999–2000 were less than £3,770 (the specified amount for 1999–2000) and as things are changing only for the worse, exception will be granted—but only from (and including) the week beginning 13 August 2000. Ambrose should, of course, have applied for 2000–01 Class 2 exception *before* 6 April 2000 on the grounds that he expected his net profits for the year ended 5 April 2001 to be less than £3,825 (the specified amount for 2000–01).

Application for Class 2 exception on the grounds of small income is to be made to the Inland Revenue in a form approved by it. In practical terms, this involves completing and signing a form CF10 (contained in Leaflet CA 02) and lodging it with the Inland Revenue NICO, Self Employment Directorate, Customer Accounts Section, Longbenton, Newcastle upon Tyne NE98 1ZZ. The application is to be supported by such information and evidence may be required and until 27 May 1996 this usually took the form of accounts, tax assessments or records of receipts and payments. For years up to 5 April 1993, the contribution card also had to accompany the application. (Leaflet CA 02). [*Contributions Regs, Reg 24(1)–(3) as amended by SSC(T)A 1999, s 1(2) and 2 Sch*].

One of the problems connected with the small earnings exception has been that a person starting up in business finds it difficult to produce evidence of his likely earnings from that business and frequently discovers these have been below the exception limit only after the time-limit for application for exception has passed. In July 1985, the Government addressed itself to this problem and announced that, from Autumn 1985, there would be a change of approach in such circumstances:

'It is perhaps not widely known that if earnings from self-employment are below a certain level . . . national insurance contributions need not be paid if exemption from payment has been agreed by the DHSS. This exemption . . . is to be given greater publicity in future. People whose earnings are likely to be low will be encouraged to apply for it and the DHSS proposes to apply the exemption from Autumn 1985 to all new traders who apply for it.' ('Lifting the Burden', *Cmnd 9571, Chp 4, Para 15*).

In a letter to the ICAEW on 15 November 1985, Lady Trumpington (then a Parliamentary Under Secretary of State at the DHSS) expanded on this and said that 'newly self-employed people . . . will no longer be required to produce specific evidence of their likely earnings. Instead, all they need do is sign a statement saying they expect their earnings to be below the specified amount and they will be given the SEE until the end of the contribution year.' These rules were explained in Leaflet CA 02.

From 27 May 1996 evidence of earnings no longer has to be produced in support of the declaration of earnings on Form CF10 (CA notice CA6813, June 1996) whether the applicant is newly self-employed or not.

If the application is approved, the Inland Revenue will issue to the applicant a 'certificate of exception' (CA5445) which will state the period for which the exception is to apply. This period will be three years unless a shorter period is thought to be appropriate (e.g. in the case of a new business) and will end on a Saturday immediately following a 5 April. If the conditions attaching to a certificate of exception cease to be fulfilled, the certificate automatically ceases to be in force and the Inland Revenue must be notified. [*Contributions Regs, Reg 24(4), (5)(a) as amended by SSC(T)A 1999, s1(2) and 2 Sch*]. It should be noted that the increase of earnings to a level in excess of the small earnings exception limit is *not* a breach of the conditions attaching to a certificate and does *not* automatically terminate any exception which has been granted. Indeed, the DSS was usually content to let a certificate of exception run to its expiry in such circumstances, even when made aware that earnings are excessive. If, however, the holder of a certificate wishes to cancel it for that or any reason (other than termination of self-employment) he may do so by completing and signing declaration 11(2) on the certificate itself and by returning the certificate to the Inland Revenue. If self-employment ceases, the same procedure should be followed using declarations 11(2) and 11(3). Cancellation of a certificate takes place from such date as the Inland Revenue determines. [*Reg 24(6)(b) as amended by SSC(T)A 1999, s 1(2) and 2 Sch*].

Anyone holding a certificate of exception must produce it for inspection if required to do so. [*Reg 24(6)(a)*].

Although a certificate of exception excepts the holder from liability to pay a Class 2 contribution for any contribution week during the whole of which it is in force, the holder is nonetheless entitled to pay a contribution if he so wishes. Section 11(1) of the certificate is used for this purpose. He may wish to do so to protect his benefit entitlement (see BENEFITS (13)) as no CREDITS (24) are awarded during periods of exception on grounds of small income. [*Contributions Regs, Reg 26*]. See 28.77 EARNINGS regarding the exclusion of enterprise allowance payments in arriving at profits for Class 2 small earnings exception purposes.

See 55.3 SUBPOSTMASTERS for the application of these rules to a subpostmaster who carries on an ancillary business as a self-employed earner.

18.4   Exception from liability on other grounds

A self-employed earner is to be excepted from liability to pay a Class 2 contribution for any contribution week if, as regards that week, he satisfies any of the following conditions.

(a) He is, in respect of the whole of the week, in receipt of incapacity benefit. [*Contributions Regs, Reg 23(1)(a) as amended by Contributions Amendment No 4 Regs 1987, Reg 5* and *Incapacity Benefit (Consequential and Transitional Amendments and Savings) Regs 1995, Reg 13(2)*]. From 13 April 1995, incapacity benefit replaced the previous invalidity and sickness benefits which were not taxable but most elements of the new incapacity benefit are taxable. It comprises three rates which increase with the duration of the incapacity; that is the lower short-term rate of £50.90 per week will be payable for the first 28 weeks (and is not taxable), the higher short-term rate of £60.20 per week will be payable after 28 weeks and the long-term incapacity benefit is payable after 52 weeks (both of the latter elements being taxable). Anyone already receiving invalidity benefit on 13 April 1995 will not pay tax on their incapacity benefit so long as they remain incapable of work. Long term incapacity benefit is £67.50 per week for 2000–01. [*Social Security (Incapacity for Work) Act 1994, s 13* and *Income Tax (Employments) Regulations 1993*]. See also Inland Revenue Press Release 22 March 1995 and DSS Press Release 9 November 1999.

(*b*)   He is, throughout the whole of the week, incapable of work. Incapacity for work is the primary test of eligibility for sickness/incapacity benefit and for statutory sick pay and, that being so, the words will, it is submitted, be accorded no wider meaning here than they are accorded in their benefit context (see Tolley's Social Security and State Benefits Handbook 2000–01). [*Contributions Regs, Reg 23(1)(b); SSCBA 1992, ss 25(1), 151(1)*]. In a sickness benefit context, however, the National Insurance Commissioners were known to hold that a person who becomes incapable of doing work himself may continue to be capable of work for the purpose of the legislation if he remains capable of *supervising* the work done by others in his stead. (*R(S) 2/61*).

(*c*)   She is, in respect of the week, in receipt of maternity allowance. [*Contributions Regs, Reg 23(1)(c)*].

(*d*)   He is, throughout the whole of the week, undergoing imprisonment or detention in legal custody. [*Contributions Regs, Reg 23(1)(d)*]. Legal custody covers detention by reason of a legal proceeding or as the result of a court proceeding whether the detention has a punitive or corrective purpose or not. (*R v National Insurance Commissioner, Ex p Timmis [1954] 3 AER 292*). It thus includes detention in a mental hospital or a similar institution following a court order (*R(S) 20/53*, and numerous other reported decisions of the National Insurance Commissioners in the sickness benefit series) but, as in that decision, the Commissioners have made it clear that the related proceedings must be criminal proceedings or be grounded on a criminal act. A detainee allowed out of a mental hospital to work under daily licence is nonetheless under detention. (*R(S) 23/54*). Whether, or when, a person will cease to be 'ordinarily self-employed' by reason of a period of imprisonment or detention in legal custody will presumably depend largely on the length of the period for which actual self-employment is suspended (see 14.10 CATEGORISATION).

(*e*)   He is, in respect of any part of the week, in receipt of unemployability supplement or invalid care allowance. [*Contributions Regs, Reg 23(1)(e)*].

(*f*)   He is a VOLUNTEER DEVELOPMENT WORKER (57). [*Contributions Regs, Reg 123C(a) as amended by Contributions Amendment Regs 1986, Reg 2*].

A whole week for these purposes is a period of seven days beginning with midnight between Saturday and Sunday but excluding Sunday or some religiously-acceptable alternative day. [*Contributions Regs, Regs 1(2), 23(2)(a)(b)*].

A self-employed earner who is excepted from Class 2 liability in accordance with these regulations remains entitled to pay a contribution for any week of exception, should he wish to do so. [*Regs 23(3) and 123C(b)*].

Certain married women and widows are effectively excepted from liability by reason of a reduced rate election (see 18.5 below).

18.5   RATES

Class 2 liability arises at a *specified flat rate* for each contribution week in the tax year. [*SSCBA 1992, s 11(1)*]. Provision is made for the imposition of liability at a higher flat rate than normal in the case of earners who, by virtue of the *Categorisation Regulations* are moved from the category of employed earner to that of self-employed earner. [*Sec 11(3)*]. However, to date, this power has not been exercised. The only group of earners who could currently be affected were that to be so are certain EXAMINERS (34). For 2000–01 the weekly rate has been set at £2.00. [*SSCBA 1992, s 11(1) as amended by Contributions Re-rating and National Insurance Funds Payments Order 2000, Reg 2(a)*]. (See 51.8 RATES AND LIMITS for earlier years).

18.6   Class 2 Contributions: Self-employed Earners

A *special higher rate* of Class 2 contributions is imposed under *Sec 117(1)* in respect of SHARE FISHERMEN (54.3) because, though self-employed earners, such persons are eligible for jobseeker's allowance. For 2000–01 the special higher rate is £2.65. [*Contribution Regs, Reg 98(c) as amended by Contributions Re-rating Consequential Amendment Regs 2000, Reg 2*]. The rate at which VOLUNTEER DEVELOPMENT WORKERS (57) are entitled to pay a Class 2 contribution, should they wish to do so is £3.35 for 2000–01. [*Contribution Regs, Reg 123D(b)*].

Certain married women and widows who would, were they employed earners, be entitled to pay primary Class 1 contributions at a reduced rate are, if they are self-employed earners, under *no liability* to pay Class 2 contributions. [*Contributions Regs, Reg 100(1)(b)*]. The enabling provision under which this regulation was made, *SSCBA 1992, s 19(4)(b)*, permits, as an alternative to nil liability, the imposition of a reduced liability, but no such reduced Class 2 liability has ever yet been imposed (see REDUCED LIABILITY ELECTIONS (52)).

If it is considered necessary, the Treasury (previously the Secretary of State) but subject to Parliamentary approval may, at any time, make an order altering the weekly rate of Class 2 contribution. [*SSAA 1992, ss 143(1), 144(1), 189(9 as amended by SSC(T)A 1999, 3 Sch 46, 49*].

Where a Class 2 contribution is paid late it will, in certain circumstances, be payable at a rate other than the rate at which it would have been payable had it been paid on or by its due date (see 39.7 LATE-PAID CONTRIBUTIONS).

18.6   COLLECTION

A Class 2 contribution liability may be discharged either by paying a quarterly bill or by direct debit of a bank account, or for years before 1993–94, affixing a stamp of appropriate value to a contribution card (see 21.9 to 21.12 COLLECTION). Where these collection methods are ineffective, recovery proceedings may be taken (see ARREARS OF CONTRIBUTIONS (12)). (CA Press Release 25 March 1993).

18.7   TAX RELIEF

No tax relief may be given or a tax deduction allowed in respect of any Class 2 contribution paid. [*ICTA 1988, s 617(3)(a)*].

18.8   VOLUNTARY CLASS 2 CONTRIBUTIONS

In certain limited circumstances, Class 2 contributions may be paid voluntarily in order to protect entitlement to short-term benefits (other than jobseeker's allowance) and basic retirement pension and widows' benefits during absence from the UK (see OVERSEAS MATTERS (49.8)). See Leaflet CA 04.

19   Class 3 Contributions: Voluntary

Cross-references. See AGE EXCEPTION (3) for age limitations on entitlement to pay; APPEALS AND REVIEWS (9) for procedure for questioning a decision on entitlement to pay; BENEFITS (13) for relevance of Class 3 contributions to benefit entitlement; 21.13 COLLECTION for payment procedure; DEATH OF CONTRIBUTOR (26); EARNINGS FACTORS (29) for relationship of factors with entitlement to pay Class 3 contributions; LATE-PAID CONTRIBUTIONS (39); NATIONAL INSURANCE NUMBER (46) for contribution records; RATES AND LIMITS (51).

Other Sources. Simon's NIC, Part I, Section 4, Chapter 14; Leaflet CA 08.

19.1   GENERAL CONSIDERATIONS

As may be expected, Class 3 contributions, being entirely voluntary in nature, account for only a minute proportion of the National Insurance Fund's contribution income (see 45.4 NATIONAL INSURANCE FUND). The figure is, in fact 0.11% which, in 2000–01, will represent income of some £54,000,000 to the National Insurance Fund. These amounts compare to total expected contribution receipts of £59,428,000,000.

In 1995–96, the most recent year for which detailed figures are currently available, 93,000 persons paid Class 3 contributions either alone along with other classes of contributions (Contributions and Qualifying Years for Retirement Pension 1995–96, Government Statistical Service, May 1998).

Class 3 contributions can serve no purpose but that of enabling a person to satisfy the contribution conditions for entitlement to basic category A or B retirement pension, widow's payment, basic widowed mother's allowance and basic widow's pension (see BENEFITS (13)). [*SSCBA 1992, s 13(2); Contributions Regs, Regs 27(1) and 13(1)*]. This being so, however, the entitlement to pay Class 3 contributions may be of particular importance to persons who are excluded by regulation from both the category of employed earners and the category of self-employed earners and who cannot, therefore, create such an entitlement by normal means (see 14.14 CATEGORISATION). It is also of use both to those who, though paying Class 1 or Class 2 contributions, fail to do so in a particular year or years at a sufficiently high level and, in some instances, those working abroad, see OVERSEAS MATTERS (49).

19.2   ENTITLEMENT TO CONTRIBUTE

Payment of Class 3 contributions is allowed only with a view to enabling a person to satisfy conditions of entitlement to BENEFITS (13). [*SSCBA 1992, s 13(2); Contributions Regs, Reg 27(1)*]. Entitlement to pay a Class 3 contribution does not, therefore (as it does in the case of Class 1 or Class 2 contributions) rest on a person's CATEGORISATION (14) but merely on the level of Class 1, Class 2 or Class 3 contribution which has already been attained with regard to a particular tax year. This level is quantified in terms of EARNINGS FACTORS (29), and only where a person's earnings factor (or the aggregate of his earnings factors) for a tax year has neither equalled nor exceeded the qualifying earnings factor for that year may a Class 3 contribution be paid (subject to the prohibitions described below). [*SSCBA 1992, s 14(1)*].

A *qualifying earnings factor* in relation to a tax year means an earnings factor equal to the lower earnings limit for that year multiplied by 52 (see EARNINGS LIMITS (30)). [*SSCBA 1992, s 14(2); Contributions Regs, Reg 28(3)*].

Even if the condition described above has been met, a person is *not* entitled to pay a Class 3 contribution in respect of a year if

19.3 Class 3 Contributions: Voluntary

(*a*) he would, but for the payment of a Class 3 contribution, be entitled to be credited with a contribution (see CREDITS (24)); *or*

(*b*) the aggregate of his earnings factors derived from earnings upon which primary Class 1 contributions have been paid, credited earnings, or Class 2 or Class 3 contributions paid or credited (see EARNINGS FACTORS (29)) is less than the qualifying earnings factor and

    (i) the period has passed within which any Class 3 contributions may be treated as paid for that year (see 39.5 LATE-PAID CONTRIBUTIONS); or

    (ii) he has previously applied for the return of any Class 3 contributions paid in respect of that year (see 53.4 REPAYMENT AND RE-ALLOCATION); *or*

(*c*) it would cause the aggregate of his earnings factors derived from earnings upon which primary Class 1 contributions have been paid, credited earnings, or Class 2 or Class 3 contributions paid or credited to exceed the qualifying earnings factor by an amount which is half or more than half that year's weekly lower earnings limit; *or*

(*d*) he is subject to the age limitation rules (see 3.3 and 3.13 AGE EXCEPTION); *or*

(*e*) she has made a reduced rate election and that election is in force (see REDUCED LIABILITY ELECTIONS (52)).

[*Contributions Regs, Regs 28(1), 105 as amended by Contributions Amendment No 2 Regs 1987, Reg 7*].

Prohibitions (*a*) and (*b*) above (but *not* prohibitions (*c*) (*d*) and (*e*)) may, however, be disregarded if the payment of a Class 3 contribution in respect of a year would enable a person to satisfy

(A) the first contribution condition for retirement pension or widow's pension or widowed mother's allowance if that condition has not been satisfied at the beginning of that year (see 13.2 BENEFITS); or

(B) the contribution condition for widow's allowance if that condition has not been satisfied at the beginning of that year (see 13.2 BENEFITS); or

(C) until 12 April 1995 the second contribution condition for unemployment or sickness benefit in transitional cases involving the termination of training or education begun before 5 April 1975 (see 13.2 BENEFITS).

[*Contributions Regs, Reg 28(2)(a)(b)(d), as amended by Contributions Amendment Regs 1984, Reg 10(a)(b) and Incapacity Benefit (Consequential and Transitional Amendments and Savings) Regs 1995, Reg 13(3)*].

In the foregoing description of prohibited Class 3 contributions, 'credited' means credited for the purpose of retirement pension, widowed mother's allowance and widow's pension, and, therefore, *excludes* primary Class 1 starting credits or credits in relation to the termination of training or education (see CREDITS (24)). [*Reg 28(3)*].

19.3 Appropriation of Class 3 contributions

Class 3 contributions paid in one year may be appropriated to the earnings factor of another year if such contributions may be paid for that other year according to the entitlement conditions described at 19.2 above. Such appropriation may be made either at the contributor's request or by the Inland Revenue with the contributor's consent. [*Contributions Regs, Reg 30 as amended by SSC(T)A 1999, s 1(2) and 2 Sch*].

19.4   RATE

A Class 3 contribution is of a specified fixed amount (set out in 51.9 RATES AND LIMITS). For 2000–01 this has been set at £6.55. [*SSCBA 1992, s 13(1), as amended by Contributions Re-rating and National Insurance Funds Payments Order 2000, Reg 3*].

If it is considered necessary, the Treasury (previously the Secretary of State) but subject to Parliamentary approval may, at any time, make an order altering the amount of a Class 3 contribution. [*SSAA 1992, ss 143(1), 144(1), 189(9) as amended by SSC(T)A 1999, 3 Sch 46, 49*].

Where a Class 3 contribution is paid after the end of the contribution year to which it relates, it may be payable at a rate other than that applicable for the contribution year to which it relates (see 39.7 LATE-PAID CONTRIBUTIONS).

19.5   COLLECTION

A Class 3 contribution may be made by either paying a quarterly bill or by direct debit of a bank account, or for years before 1993–94, affixing a stamp of appropriate value to a contribution card (see 21.12 COLLECTION). In practice, it is also possible to pay by cheque in a lump sum during or after the tax year in question, subject only to the proviso as to the rate of contribution that may then be payable (see 19.4 above and 39.7 LATE-PAID CONTRIBUTIONS).

In any event, application will need to be made on form CA5603 'Application to pay Class 3 NI contributions'.

19.6   TAX RELIEF

No tax relief may be given or a tax deduction allowed in respect of any Class 3 contribution paid. [*ICTA 1988, s 617(3)(a)*].

20   Class 4 Contributions: On Profits of a Trade Etc.

Cross-references. See AGE EXCEPTION (3) for age limitations on liability; 5.17 AGGREGATION OF EARNINGS; 7.3 ANNUAL MAXIMUM for Class 4 limiting maximum; APPEALS AND REVIEWS (9); 12.3 ARREARS OF CONTRIBUTIONS for recovery provisions; 21.13 to 21.18 COLLECTION; DEFERMENT OF PAYMENT (27); 28.77 to 28.85 EARNINGS; 30.6 EARNINGS LIMITS; INLAND REVENUE (37); 48.2 OIL-RIG WORKERS, DIVERS, ETC.; 49.12 OVERSEAS MATTERS; PARTNERS (50); 51.7 RATES AND LIMITS; REPAYMENT AND RE-ALLOCATION (53); SUBPOSTMASTERS (55); WORKING CASE STUDY (58).

Other Sources. Simon's NIC, Part I, Section 3, Chapter 13; Inspector's Manual, Vol II, Inland Revenue Collection Manual, Vol 1, Leaflets IR 24, CWL1 and CWL2.

20.1   GENERAL CONSIDERATIONS

Class 4 contributions account for 1.76% of the National Insurance Fund's contribution income (see 45.4 NATIONAL INSURANCE FUND). In monetary terms, this will amount to some £847,000,000 in 2000–01 and a further £201,000,000 of that collected will be diverted directly to the National Health Service.

This class of contribution was created in 1975 and, because liability for contributions within it cannot (except in special circumstances—see 20.5 below) arise without an income tax assessment under Schedule D Case I or II and can neither create nor augment a benefit entitlement for the contributor, has been seen by self-employed earners as a thinly-disguised additional tax on a specific range of their profits. Strong feelings have, therefore, brought even the validity of the imposing provisions under attack, but without success. (*Martin v O'Sullivan [1984] STC 258*). See 18.1 CLASS 2 CONTRIBUTIONS in relation to government discussion documents and Reports on the national insurance position of the self-employed.

20.2   LIABILITY

Although Class 4 contributions are effectively payable by self-employed earners, liability is not dependent on such CATEGORISATION (14) as it is in the case of Class 2 contributions. Instead, Class 4 contributions are payable in respect of profits or gains 'immediately derived' from the carrying on or exercise of one or more trades, professions or vocations, being profits or gains *chargeable to income tax under Case I or II of Schedule D* for any year of assessment beginning on or after 6 April 1975. [*SSCBA 1992, s 15(1)*]. (See also Inspector's Manual, paras 6010–6017, issue 12/94).

For these purposes, profits or gains chargeable to income tax under Case I or II of Schedule D are deemed to include profits or gains consisting of a payment of an enterprise allowance made on or after 18 March 1986 (or made before that date as part of a distinct series of payments one or more of which is made on or after 16 March 1986) by the appropriate body (originally the Manpower Services Commission, later the Training Commission, now the local TEC or LEC) under *Employment and Training Act 1973, s 2(2)(d)* or *Enterprise and New Towns (Scotland) Act 1990, s 2(4)(c)* and chargeable to income tax under Case VI of Schedule D. [*ICTA 1988, s 127, 29 Sch*]. (See 28.78 EARNINGS for the position as regards enterprise allowance payments made before 18 March 1986 and see 28.76 for the exclusion of enterprise allowance payments in arriving at profits for Class 2 small earnings exception purposes.)

There is no similar provision with regard to profits or gains derived from the commercial letting of furnished holiday accommodation (also chargeable to income tax under Case VI of Schedule D) and, accordingly, no Class 4 liability can arise in respect of such profits. (See *Gittos v Barclay [1982] STC 390; Griffiths v Jackson [1983] STC 184, and ICTA 1988, s 503(1)*). (See 14.10 CATEGORISATION for the Class 2 implications of commercially letting such accommodation.)

The wording of *SSCBA 1992, s 15(1)* is borrowed largely from *ICTA 1988, s 833(4)(c)* which would indicate that, though not bound to do so, the DSS would follow established case law in deciding what are, and what are not, profits or gains 'immediately derived' from the carrying on of a trade etc. If that is so, a person will not be liable for Class 4 contributions on profits or gains in the creation of which he has had no direct involvement. Thus, a pension to a retired partner under a partnership deed will not be an immediately derived profit or gain. (*Pegler v Abell (1972) 48 TC 564; Lawrence v Hayman [1976] STC 227*). Neither will a consultancy share of profits paid to a retired partner where the services are minimal, nor a sleeping partner's share in partnership profits. (*Hale v Shea (1964) 42 TC 260*). (Leaflets CWL2, IR 24; Inspector's Manual, para 6025, issue 12/94).

Profits or gains immediately derived from the carrying on of a trade etc. and chargeable to tax under Schedule D, Case I or II are subject to various adjustments before they become earnings for Class 4 contribution purposes, and Class 4 contributions are then payable only on so much of earnings as falls between a lower and an upper annual limit (see 28.78 to 28.86 EARNINGS and 30.8 EARNINGS LIMITS AND THRESHOLDS).

For the effect of Schedule D, Case I or II losses set against other income see 28.81.

20.3 Exception from liability

Exception from liability for Class 4 contributions will be granted to

(*a*) anyone who, at the beginning of a year of assessment, is over pensionable age (see 3.14 AGE EXCEPTION and Inspector's Manual, para 6063, issue 12/94);

(*b*) anyone who, at the beginning of a year of assessment is under the age of 16 and applies for exception (see 3.4 to 3.6 AGE EXCEPTION and Inspector's Manual, para 6065, issue 12/94);

(*c*) anyone who is non-resident for tax purposes (see 49.12 OVERSEAS MATTERS and Inspector's Manual, para 6061, issue 12/94);

(*d*) anyone who, though deriving profits or gains from a trade, profession or vocation, does not *immediately* so derive them (see 20.2 above);

(*e*) any trustee, guardian, tutor, curator, or committee of an incapacitated person who would otherwise be assessable and chargeable to Class 4 contributions under *TMA 1970, s 72 [SSCBA 1992, 2 Sch 5(a)]* (see also Inspector's Manual, para 6062, issue 12/94);

(*f*) any trustee who would otherwise be liable for Class 4 contributions under *ICTA 1988, s 59* which imposes a charge to tax under Schedule D on persons entitled to or receiving profits or gains [*SSCBA 1992, 2 Sch 5(b)*];

(*g*) certain divers and diving supervisors who, though working as employees in the North Sea are charged to tax under Schedule D on their earnings (see 48.2 OIL-RIG WORKERS, DIVERS, ETC. and Inspector's Manual, para 6064, issue 12/94) [*Contributions Regs, Reg 59*]; and

(*h*) certain Class 1 contributors whose earnings are chargeable to income tax under Schedule D (see 20.4 below).

See also Inland Revenue Collection manual Vol 1, para CM 1703, issue 11/97.

20.4 Exception of Class 1 contributors in respect of earnings chargeable to tax under Schedule D

It is often the case that persons employed as self-employed earners in certain trades, professions or vocations receive certain earnings, for example, fees from offices held and salaries under contracts of service, which, though assessable to income tax under

20.4 Class 4 Contributions: On Profits of a Trade Etc.

Case I or II of Schedule D as part of their trading profits, attract (or are, for precautionary reasons (see 14.13 CATEGORISATION), treated by persons for whom they provide services as attracting) a liability for Class 1 contributions. Examples of such people are solicitors, accountants, ENTERTAINERS (33), film technicians and (possibly) SUBPOSTMASTERS (55). Any such person (and any person treated as an employed earner for contribution purposes but assessed to tax under Schedule D Case I or II as a self-employed earner—see 14.14 CATEGORISATION) may apply for exception from any Class 4 liability which would otherwise arise. This exception applies to so much of a person's profits or gains for a year of assessment as

(a) exceed the Class 4 lower annual limit for that year but do not exceed the Class 4 upper annual limit for that year; *and*

(b) equal an amount of earnings paid in that year, calculated by reference to primary Class 1 contributions which he has paid in respect of those earnings or, but for exception following DEFERMENT OF PAYMENT (27), would have paid in respect of those earnings.

[*Contributions Regs, Reg 61*].

The formula for the calculation of earnings under (b) above is,

(i) if the contributions ('C') were paid (or, but for deferment, would have been payable) at a *standard rate* ('SR') $100 \times C/SR$;

(ii) if the contributions ('C') were paid (or, but for deferment, would have been payable) at a *contracted-out rate* for salary related schemes ('COSR') $100 \times C/COSR$;

(iii) if the contributions ('C') were paid (or, but for deferment, would have been payable) at a COMP *contracted-out rate* ('COMP') $100 \times C/COMP$;

(iv) if the contributions ('C') were paid (or, but for deferment, would have been payable) at the *reduced rate* ('RR') $100 \times C/RR$.

[*Contributions Regs, Reg 61(1)(a)(b)(c), as amended by Contributions Transitional Regs 1985, Reg 6(a) and Contributions Transitional Regs 1989, Reg 3(6)*].

Example

Ariadne is a practising solicitor and also the company secretary of Web Ltd. Her accounting year ends on 30 June and her 2000–01 assessable profits for Class 4 purposes (based on her accounts to 30 June 2000 under *ICTA 1988, s 60(3)(b); FA 1994, s 200*) are £29,000. During 2000–01 she is paid secretarial fees (under deduction of standard rate primary Class 1 contributions, as appropriate) on a quarterly basis as follows

	Gross fees £	Class 1 £	
June 2000	500.00	—	(below EEET)
September 2000	500.00	—	(below EEET)
December 2000	1,080.00	Nil	(Nil% on EEET [13 × £76 = £988])
		9.20	(10% on remainder [£1,080 – £988 = £92])
March 2001	7,000.00	Nil	(Nil% on EEET [13 × £76 = £988])
		596.70	(10% on remainder up to the UEL [13 × £535 = £6,955])
	£9,080.00	£605.90	

The gross fees of £500 received in June 2000 will be included in Ariadne's accounts for the year ended 30 June 2000. The remaining £8,580 falling into the accounts for the year ended 30 June 2001 will be within the basis period for 2001–02. The fact that some of this income is taxed and subject to Class 4 contributions in 2001–02 does not affect the Class 4 exception for 2000–01 on an amount of profits arrived at as follows:

	£
Earnings below the employee's earnings threshold charged at Nil%	988.00
9.20 × 100/10 =	92.00
Earnings below the employee's earnings threshold charged at Nil%	988.00
596.70 × 100/10 =	5,967.00
	£8,035.00

Profits on which Class 4 contributions would be payable for 2000–01 would, therefore, be

	£
Profits as stated	29,000
Less: lower annual limit	4,385
	24,615
Less: excess of profits over the upper annual limit £29,000 – £27,820	1,180
	23,435
Less: Class 4 exception (as computed above)	8,035
	£15,400

If, however, Ariadne's assessable profits for 2000–01 had been only £4,465, a Class 4 exception of only £80 would have been available, thus

	£
Profits as stated	4,465
Less: lower annual limit	4,385
	80
Less: excess of profits over the upper annual limit	—
	80
Class 4 exception limited to	£80

Exception from Class 4 liability in these circumstances is conditional upon an application being made by the earner to the Inland Revenue before the beginning of the year to which the exception relates or before such later date as the Inland Revenue allows. [*Contributions Regs, Reg 61(2) as amended by SSC(T)A 1999, s 1(2) and 2 Sch*]. The application is to be made in such manner as the Inland Revenue directs and must be supported by such information and evidence as is required for the purpose of confirming the earner's entitlement to exception. [*Reg 61(3) as amended by SSC(T)A 1999, s 1(2) and 2 Sch*]. A successful application will result in the issue of a certificate of exception, but, if relevant information has been withheld or the information supplied was erroneous, the certificate may be revoked by the Inland Revenue and thereupon the earner will become liable to pay all Class 4 contributions which, but for the certificate, would have been due. Prior to 1 April 1999, contributions would, in that event, have been calculated by, and become payable to, the Secretary of State, not the Inland Revenue. [*Regs 64(5)(a)(b), 65(a)(b)(ii)*].

The practical difficulty intrinsic to these exception provisions is that the total amount of Class 1 contributions paid during a year of assessment cannot be ascertained until after the year has ended, by which time the first self-assessment payment on account of Class 4 contributions for that year of assessment will have fallen due (see 21.13 COLLECTION). Accordingly, an application for exception which is made (as it should be) *before* the beginning of a year of assessment is treated as an application for Class 4 DEFERMENT OF PAYMENT (27.8) [*Contributions Regs, Reg 61(4)*], while an application made *after* the end of the year of assessment is treated as an application for repayment of contributions (see 53.5 REPAYMENT AND RE-ALLOCATION).

The ICAEW suggested to the DSS that these complex and impracticable provisions could be dispensed with entirely if the DSS had issued to any self-employed earner whose status had been established to the satisfaction of the DSS and who undertook to include all earnings from whatever source in his assessable profits, a certificate of self-employment authorising anyone paying earnings to pay those earnings without deduction of Class 1 contributions. The DSS, however, rejected the suggestion on the grounds that such a scheme would be too onerous to administer.

20.5   Special Class 4 contributions

Special Class 4 contributions are payable by any earner who is, by regulation, treated as being self-employed (see 14.14 CATEGORISATION) and who has, in any tax year, earnings from that self-employment which

(*a*)   would otherwise be Class 1 earnings; and

(*b*)   are chargeable to tax under Schedule E; and

(*c*)   exceed the special Class 4 lower annual limit.

[*SSCBA 1992, s 18(1); Contributions Regs, Reg 71*].

Such earnings are to be calculated as if they were employed earner's earnings and the total is to be rounded *down* to the nearest pound (see EARNINGS (28)). [*Reg 73*].

Where both ordinary and special Class 4 contributions are payable for any year, the amount of special Class 4 contributions is not to exceed the difference (if any) between the ordinary Class 4 contributions payable and the amount of Class 4 contributions which would be payable on profits or gains equal to the upper annual limit for the year. [*Reg 76*].

The only group of earners to whom these provisions currently relate are certain EXAMINERS (34) and SHARE FISHERMEN (54).

20.6   **RATE**

Class 4 ordinary and special contributions are payable at a prescribed percentage rate on so much of Class 4 earnings as exceeds the lower annual limit but does not exceed the upper annual limit (see 28.77–28.86 EARNINGS and 51.10–51.11 RATES AND LIMITS). [*SSCBA 1992, ss 15(3), 18(1)*]. For 2000–01 the lower annual limit is £4,385, the upper annual limit is £27,820 and the rate is 7%. [*SSCBA 1992, ss 15(3), 18(1), as amended by Contributions Re-rating and National Insurance Funds Payments Order 2000, Reg 4*]. The rate may at any time be changed by order of the Treasury (previously the Secretary of State) provided the new rate does not exceed 8.25%. [*SSAA 1992, s 143(1)–(4) as amended by SSC(T)A 1999, 3 Sch 46, 49*]. Any greater increase must be effected by statute.

20.7   **ASSESSMENT AND COLLECTION**

While, in certain circumstances, ordinary Class 4 contributions were, like special Class 4 contributions, collected by the Secretary of State and may now be collected directly by Inland Revenue NICO, ordinary Class 4 contributions are normally collected by the Inland Revenue along with income tax due under Case I or II Schedule D assessments (see 21.14, 21.16 COLLECTION). However, an assessment for

Class 4 purposes is to be raised in accordance with the Income Tax Acts. [*SSCBA 1992, s 16(1)*]. This formerly resulted in a *partnership* being jointly assessed to, and becoming liable to pay, Class 4 contributions relating to the partners *individually* in respect of the profits or gains of that partnership where the pre–'self-assessment' tax rules applied. As an administrative move where an individual was both in earned employment and has self-employment income and was dealt with by two separate tax districts then for administrative ease only the General Claims District dealt with the issue of the assessments. See IR Letter P137 sent to taxpayers and their advisers. Under self-assessment there is no joint and several liability for tax and Class 4 contributions (see 50.4 PARTNERS).

Where an assessment has become final and conclusive for income tax purposes, it is final and conclusive for Class 4 contribution purposes also and no subsequent adjustment is permissible except in relation to relief for interest, annuities or other annual payments made in the year of assessment (see 28.83 EARNINGS). [*SSCBA 1992, 2 Sch 3(5), 7*].

Now that self-assessment of personal tax has come into effect for 1996–97 and subsequent years, the basis of calculating Class 4 contributions and the way in which they are collected has changed (e.g. interim payments will be required on 31 January and 31 July with the Schedule D tax). [*FA 1996, s 147*].

20.8   **TAX RELIEF**

From 1985–86 to 1995–96 inclusive, a deduction from total income for income tax purposes could be claimed of an amount equal to one-half of Class 4 contributions payable in respect of the year of assessment. [*ICTA 1988, s 617(5), repealed by FA 1996, s 147, 41 Sch 15 and FA 1997, s 65(2)*].

Where Class 4 contribution liability was deferred (see 27.8 DEFERMENT OF PAYMENT), the amount of Class 4 contributions on which tax relief was available was not determined until after the tax assessment for the relevant year had been finalised. Accordingly, once the Class 4 amount was known, the tax assessment needed to be amended, but, in practice, the initiative for such amendment had to be taken by the taxpayer or his agent.

21 Collection

Cross-references. See ARREARS OF CONTRIBUTIONS (12) for overdue contributions recovery provisions; CLASS 1 CONTRIBUTIONS (15); CLASS 1A CONTRIBUTIONS (16); CLASS 1B CONTRIBUTIONS (17); CLASS 2 CONTRIBUTIONS (18); CLASS 3 CONTRIBUTIONS (19); CLASS 4 CONTRIBUTIONS (20); DEFERMENT OF PAYMENT (27); ENFORCEMENT (32) for offences and penalties and powers of inspectors; INLAND REVENUE (37); NATIONAL INSURANCE NUMBER (46) for recording of contributions.

Other Sources. Simon's NIC, Part I, Sections 10 and 11, Chapters 56–60.

21.1 **CLASS 1 CONTRIBUTIONS**

Social security legislation contains no provision for formal assessment or determination of Class 1 liability, other than where such liability, or its amount, is in dispute. Instead, rules are laid down in relation to the kind of employment in which Class 1 liabilities will arise, the kind of EARNINGS (28) to which such liability will relate, the basis period by reference to which the liability must be computed, the extent to which earnings in such a period may be disregarded, and the rate at which calculation must take place. The task of assessment and discharge of liability is then left to any person who, finding he is liable to contribute under these rules, is directed by the legislation to perform that task (see CATEGORISATION (14), EARNINGS LIMITS AND THRESHOLDS (30), EARNINGS PERIODS (31) AND RATES AND LIMITS (51)).

Normally, that person will be the *secondary contributor* (see 14.15 CATEGORISATION). This is because where earnings are paid to an employed earner and a liability for primary and secondary CLASS 1 CONTRIBUTIONS (15) arises in respect of that payment, the secondary contributor, as well as being liable for his own secondary contribution, is liable in the first instance to pay the earner's primary contribution also, on behalf of and to the exclusion of the earner. [*SSCBA 1992, 1 Sch 3(1)*]. He is, however, entitled to recover such primary contributions from the earner's earnings as the primary contribution is the liability of the earner. [*SSCBA 1992, s 6(3)*].

It is arguable that, where earnings are paid not *to* the earner but to someone else *for the benefit of* the earner (e.g. when an employer discharges an employee's personal debt to a third party), any primary Class 1 liability imposed by *SSCBA 1992, s 6* becomes uncollectible in law. This is because *s 6(3)* requires the primary liability imposed on the earner to be discharged in the manner provided for in *1 Sch 3*, but *1 Sch 3* addresses itself only to the situation where earnings are paid *to* an earner and makes no mention of the situation where earnings are paid *for the benefit of* an earner. It follows that, where a payment is made to someone other than the earner (even though for his benefit) no primary Class 1 contribution becomes due from the employer and, in consequence, the collection machinery of *Contributions Regs, 1 Sch* can be applied only to the secondary Class 1 contribution which is due. It might be thought that the authorities could have resort to direct collection procedures in order to obtain payment of the primary Class 1 contribution which is due, but such procedures are available only in deferment situations and situations where the employer is outside the jurisdiction of Parliament. [*Contributions Regs, Regs 47, 48, 1 Sch 50*].

21.2 **Collection as income tax**

The principle on which the imposition of Class 1 contribution liability is based is the same as that which underlies the collection of tax on earnings chargeable to tax under Schedule E (see 21.1 above). It follows, therefore, that, as the objective of the CATEGORISATION (14) rules is to align Class 1 with Schedule E, and as an elaborate and developed PAYE system already enables tax on earnings within Schedule E to be collected in accordance with the principle enunciated, the PAYE system is itself the ideal means of collecting Class 1 contributions. Accordingly, it is provided that, subject to any alternative arrangements which might be made (see 21.5 below), Class 1 contributions are to be *paid, accounted for and recovered in like manner as income tax* deducted from the emoluments of an office or employment by virtue of PAYE arrangements under *ICTA 1988 s 203*, and that extended and modified PAYE regulations are to apply to, and for the purpose of, such contributions. [*Income Tax (Employments) Regulations 1993; SSCBA 1992, s 6(1); Contributions Regs, Reg 46*].

The modified PAYE regulations appear in social security legislation as *Contributions Regs, 1 Sch*. Amendments to the *Income Tax (Employments) Regulations 1993* made in February 1995 by *Income Tax (Employments) (Amendment No 2) Regs 1995*, in May 1996 by *Income Tax (Employments) (Amendment No 3) Regs 1996 SI 1996 No 1312* and in October 1998 by *Income Tax (Employments) Amendment Regs 1998, SI 1998 No 2484* have not, at the time of writing, been reflected in *Contributions Regs, 1 Sch*.

FA 1989, s 45 inserted *ICTA 1988, s 203A* to define 'payment' for PAYE purposes. *Reg 46* does not, however, import into contribution law principles of income tax law, rather it borrows the collection and recovery machinery of the PAYE system. The new definition of 'payment' for income tax purposes is therefore not applicable for contribution purposes. [*Income Tax (Employments) Regulations 1993 as amended by Income Tax (Employments)(Amendment) Regulations 1998, SI 1998 No 2484*].

21.3   Liability of a secondary contributor

Where earnings are paid to an employed earner and, in respect of that payment, liability arises for primary and secondary Class 1 contributions, the secondary contributor is, except where a special alternative arrangement has been made, to discharge the *whole* liability (see 21.1 above and 21.5 below). This is done by paying to the Collector of Taxes, within 14 days of the end of the income tax month (or, where quarterly remittances are permitted, the income tax quarter—see below) during which the earnings were paid, the amount of those contributions less any amount which he has deducted from such contributions by way of recovery of payments of statutory maternity pay and statutory sick pay or by way of compensation for secondary Class 1 contributions paid on payments of statutory maternity pay and, until April 1991, statutory sick pay (see 15.7 CLASS 1 CONTRIBUTIONS). [*Contributions Regs, 1 Sch 26, as amended by Contributions Amendment No 4 Regs 1991, Reg 2(3)*].

The amount to be paid to the Collector in accordance with the foregoing paragraph is not to include any amount which could have been, but was not, deducted from a payment of earnings which fell to be aggregated with another payment of earnings (see 5.13 AGGREGATION). A secondary contributor will, however, be deemed to have deducted from the last of any payments of earnings which fell to be aggregated any Class 1 contributions deductible but not deducted from those payments, and will, accordingly, be obliged to include in his payment to the Collector the amount of the deemed deduction. [*Contributions Regs, 1 Sch 26(2)*].

Where an Inspector of Taxes has authorised a secondary contributor to deduct tax from each payment of earnings which he makes to an earner who is in receipt of a fixed salary or wage by reference only to the amount of that payment, payment of Class 1 contributions related to those earnings is to be made to the Collector of Taxes only quarterly, i.e. payment of such contributions for the three months ended 5 July 2000 will not, in such circumstances, be due for payment until 19 July 2000. [*1 Sch 26A(1)(b)*].

Likewise, with effect from 14 August 1991, where an employer has reasonable grounds for believing that, for income tax months falling within the current tax year, the average monthly total amount to be paid to the Collector will be less than a specified amount (£400 to 9 July 1992, £450 from 10 July 1992 to 5 April 1995, £600 from 6 April 1995 to 5 April 1999, £1,000 from 6 April 1999 to 5 April 2000 and £1,500 from 6 April 2000) in respect of PAYE, Class 1 contributions and deductions made from payments made to subcontractors in the construction industry and student loan repayments *less* reimbursement for payments made to employees in respect of working families tax credit (WFTC) and disabled persons tax credit (DPTC), Class 1 contributions need only be paid over to the Collector quarterly. [*1 Sch 26A as inserted by Contributions Amendment No 4 Regs 1991, Reg 2 and as amended by Contributions Amendment No 6 Regs 1992, Reg 7; Contributions Amendment No 3 Regs 1995, Reg 3(2); Social Security (Contributions) Amendment (No 2) Regs 1999, Reg 2; Social Security (Contributions) Amendment (No 5) Regs 2000, Reg 2*].

The Inland Revenue formerly considered the *effective date of payment* to be as follows. In the case of

(*a*) an in-dated cheque sent through the post, the date of posting (which, because of the impossibility of referring to all postmarks, is taken as the third working day before the day on which the Collector receives the cheque);

(*b*) cash or an in-dated cheque tendered personally, the date of tender;

(*c*) a post-dated cheque, the date of the cheque;

(*d*) a bank giro credit, the date stamped on the payslip by the bank's cashier;

(*e*) a Girobank in-payment, the date stamped on the payslip by the Post Office counter clerk;

(*f*) a Girobank transfer, the date of the Inland Revenue's National Giro bank statement on which the item appears;

(*g*) electronic funds transfer, one working day immediately before the date value is received by the Inland Revenue.

(Tolley's Practical Tax 1981, p 42).

(Inland Revenue Press Release, 1 April 1993).

However, with effect from 6 April 1996, a payment made by cheque to an officer of the Board of Inland Revenue, or to the Board, will be treated for all purposes of *TMA 1970* as made on the day on which the cheque was received by the officer or the Board, provided the cheque is paid on its first presentation to the bank on which it is drawn. [*TMA 1970, s 70A inserted by virtue of FA 1994, 19 Sch 22; Income Tax (Employments) (Amendment No 2) Regs 1996, Regs 3–5 and Contributions Amendment No 4 Regs 1996, Reg 2*]. See also IR Press Release 1 April 1996 regarding cheques received on or after 19 April 1996 whereby interest is charged from different dates for Class 1 and 1A depending on the payment method. See also Inland Revenue Collection Manual, Vol 1 paras CM 5101 *et seq.*

Where a secondary contributor has made a deduction from a contributions payment by way of recovery of payments of statutory sick pay and/or statutory maternity pay made by him or by way of compensation for secondary Class 1 contributions paid on such statutory maternity pay (or, before 6 April 1991, on such statutory sick pay), the deemed date of payment of the contributions included in the extinguished contributions payment is:

(i) if the deduction by way of recovery or compensation does not wholly extinguish the contributions payment, the first date on which any part of the remainder is paid, or

(ii) if the deduction by way of recovery and/or compensation wholly extinguishes the contributions payment, the fourteenth day after the end of the income tax month during which there were paid the earnings in respect of which the contributions payment was payable.

[*Statutory Sick Pay Compensation Regs 1983, Reg 4; Statutory Maternity Pay Compensation Regs 1987, Reg 6*].

Where an employer pays the annual Class 1A contribution (see 16.18 CLASS 1A CONTRIBUTIONS: BENEFITS IN KIND) through the PAYE system by entering the amounts on forms P11 and P14/P60 for the years up to and including 2000–01 documents in respect of liabilities for years up to and including 1999–2000, the due date of payment is now 19 July. See 16.18 for payment dates for Class 1 contributions relating to 1995–96 and earlier years. The above rules apply to determine the effective date of payment. However, where an employer uses the Class 1A 'Alternative Payment Method', the Inland Revenue NICO is unable to accept electronic funds transfers. See Inland Revenue Collection PAYE manual, Vol 1 paras PA 1655–1656 (5/97). [*Contributions Regs, 1 Sch 13A as amended by Contributions Amendment No 5 Regs 1996, Reg 7(2)*].

Where an amount of tax as well as of contributions becomes due for payment, a single remittance may cover both amounts but the payslip (P 30BC(Z)) must distinguish between them. In this context from 6 April 2000 'tax' means PAYE income tax, *plus* student loan repayments *less* WFTC/DPTC. This is because, although all amounts paid to the Collector of Taxes are paid into the Inland Revenue account, the Inland Revenue accounts for and pays to the National Insurance Fund (when directed to do so by the Treasury) sums which it estimates have been paid to it as contributions. [*SSCBA 1992, 1 Sch 6(8)*]. It is suggested that, where an insufficient amount is paid to satisfy both tax and contributions which are due, the secondary contributor may, because both debts are due to a single creditor (i.e. the Crown), appropriate the payment he makes to either the tax debt or the contribution debt or partly to each. The Inland Revenue has, in the case of contributions but not tax, the power of proceeding against the directors of a limited company for certain of the company's unpaid debts (see 12.4 ARREARS OF CONTRIBUTIONS). Thus, prudence dictates that the directors of a company which is encountering difficulties should ensure that sums paid to the Inland Revenue are expressly appropriated to contribution debts rather than to debts for tax under the PAYE scheme. It is an established maxim of law that, when money is paid, it is to be applied according to the will of the payer not of the receiver, and, if the party to whom the money is offered does not agree to apply it according to the expressed will of the party offering it, he must refuse it. (*Croft v Lumley (1858) 5 E & B, per Lord Campbell*). Non-return of a cheque sent to the Inland Revenue, therefore, signifies acceptance of any expressed application by the payer. Where a Collector of Taxes agrees to accept a payment which is less than an employer's full tax and Class 1 contribution liability, he is instructed to agree with the employer how the payment is to be apportioned. (Hansard 22 February 1984 Vol 54 No 104 Cols 543–544).

Receipts for remittances will be issued only if requested. [*Contributions Regs, 1 Sch 26B(1)*].

Where, by reason of an error made by the secondary contributor in good faith or as a result of a change from not contracted-out to CONTRACTED-OUT EMPLOYMENT (23) or because a refund has been made under *Social Security (Refunds) (Repayment of Contractual Maternity Pay) Regs 1990, Reg 2*, an overpayment of contributions is made to the Collector of Taxes, the amount overpaid may be deducted in arriving at any amount subsequently remitted to the Collector *within the same tax year*. This is so provided that, if there was a corresponding over-deduction from any payment of earnings to an employed earner, the employed earner has been reimbursed. [*Contributions Regs, 1 Sch 26B(2)(3), as amended by Contributions Amendment No 4 Regs 1991, Reg 2(3)*]. Regulations may also provide for repayment of contributions

21.3 Collection

paid by reference to earnings which have become repayable. [*SSCBA 1992, 1 Sch 8(1)(h)*].

If a secondary contributor dies, anything which he would have been liable to do under the *Contribution Regs* is to be done by his personal representative or, if he paid earnings only as an agent, the person succeeding him or, if there is no successor, his principal. [*1 Sch 33*].

Similarly, but to a more restricted degree, a person who becomes a secondary contributor by succeeding to a trade or business is to do under the *Contributions Regs* anything which the former secondary contributor would have been liable to do, except that he is not to be liable for contributions which were deductible from earnings paid to an employed earner before the succession took place but are no longer so deductible (see 21.4 below). [*Contributions Regs, 1 Sch 34*].

A secondary contributor against whom, by reason of some international treaty or convention, liability to pay and account for contributions cannot be enforced may pay and account for contributions on a voluntary basis. [*Contributions Regs, Reg 50(2)*]. In cases where a secondary contributor neither chooses, nor can be made, to pay and account for contributions, a direct collection arrangement for primary contributions only will be made with the primary contributor concerned (see 21.5 below).

As the Crown are entitled to preferential status with regard to PAYE and NICs prior to the date of a bankruptcy order a robust argument will be needed for an application to set aside a Statutory Demand. The debtor must be able to prove that there is a distinct possibility that the Revenue is owed less than £750. The Statutory Demand provides for a period of 21 days in which the debtor must pay the debt or 18 days in which an application to court to set aside the demand must be made. [*Insolvency Act 1986, Sch 6*]. See Tolley's Practical Tax, 9 February 2000 page 25 and also *CIR v Lawrence and Another* [*2000*] *All ER(D) 157* at 12.10 ARREARS OF CONTRIBUTIONS.

No *quantum meruit* for work which compliance with the regulations necessitates may be deducted from the amount which a secondary contributor is liable to pay, and the failure of the regulations to provide for such remuneration does not render them *ultra vires*. (*Meredith v Hazell (1964) 42 TC 435*).

Where funds which have been set aside by a secondary contributor to meet his liabilities are stolen, the liabilities cannot on those grounds be treated as discharged. (*A-G v Jeanne Antoine* [*1949*] *2 AER 1000*).

If a secondary contributor agrees to pay earnings without any deductions or taxes, the agreement must be treated as being to pay such earnings as, after deductions, would leave the specified amount. (*Jaworski v Institution of Polish Engineers in Great Britain Ltd* [*1950*] *2 AER 1191*). It seems that, in practice, the authorities do not strictly apply this rule but are content to recover from the employer Class 1 contributions calculated on an amount which, after the deduction of tax calculated in accordance with the PAYE code issued in respect of the employee in question, is reduced to the agreed free-of-tax pay.

Example
Zebedee has agreed to pay Dougal £500 per month throughout 2000–01, free of all tax and national insurance. D has been issued with a BR tax code, i.e. he has no surplus allowances and is liable to tax at 22%. Free-of-tax pay of £500 is equivalent to £641.03 gross of tax at 22% and the Inland Revenue will, therefore, require Z to account to it for a deemed tax deduction of £141.03. But the Inland Revenue requirement will not end there. The primary Class 1 liability on earnings of £641.03 is £31.20 (i.e. Nil% × £329.00 + 10% × £312.03) and as Z has agreed to discharge that primary Class 1 liability also, the Inland Revenue will require Z to account for tax of £8.80, being tax on the gross equivalent of £31.20, i.e. £40.00.

The position will then be as follows:

		£
Gross pay = £641.03 + £40.00 =		681.03
Deemed tax deduction therefrom @ 22%		149.83
		531.20
Deemed primary Class 1 deduction		31.20
Net pay		£500.00
PAYE payable by Z to Inland Revenue		149.83
NIC payable by Z to Inland Revenue:		
Class 1 primary	31.20	
Class 1 secondary (12.2% × £641.03 – £365)	33.68	
		64.88
		£214.71

It is understood that this position is currently accepted as being correct by the Inland Revenue as it was, previously, by the DSS even though, as will have been noted, the DSS was losing Class 1 contributions under the arrangement. It was collecting only £31.20 primary and £33.68 secondary Class 1 contributions on £681.03 whereas it should be collecting £35.20 primary (i.e. £329 × Nil% + £352.03 × 10%) and £38.56 secondary (i.e. 12.2% × £681.03 – £365.00). For the authorities to insist on more would, however, be to create an endless spiral. Revision of the contribution liability would necessitate a revision of the true gross pay which, in turn, would necessitate a revision of the contribution liability which, in turn . . .!

It is, however, understood that this matter is currently the subject of an internal legal review. It is submitted that the legal position is quite clear — contributions should be due on the higher amount of £681.03 in the above example — but the practicalities of the required calculations should a change in policy result from the current review is quite a separate matter.

Inland Revenue guidance is to be found in Inland Revenue Leaflet FOT 1, P11 (FOT) and FOT Tax Tables (Tables G).

21.4 Recovery by a secondary contributor of primary contributions paid

Under no circumstances may a secondary contributor make, from earnings paid by him, any deduction in respect of his own or any other person's secondary contributions or otherwise recover such contributions from any earner to whom he pays earnings, even if he has contracted with the earner that he will do so.

A secondary contributor is, however, entitled to recover from an earner the amount of any primary contribution paid, or to be paid, by him on behalf of the earner, but recovery must be made by deduction from the earner's earnings in accordance with the rules set out below *and not in any other way*. [*SSCBA 1992, 1 Sch 3(3); Contributions Regs, 1 Sch 6(1)(b), (2)*]. The amount of primary contributions which a secondary contributor is entitled to deduct from an earner's earnings is the amount of the primary contributions based on those earnings, except that, where two or more payments of earnings fall to be aggregated (see AGGREGATION OF EARNINGS (5)), the secondary contributor may deduct the primary contributions based on those earnings either wholly from one such payment or partly from one and partly from the other or any one or more others. [*Contributions Regs, 1 Sch 13(1)(1A)*].

Where a secondary contributor has not deducted from an earner's earnings the full amount of primary contributions which he was entitled to deduct, he may (subject to the limitations set out below) recover the under-deduction by deduction from any subsequent payment of earnings to that earner *during the same tax year* if, but only if, the under-deduction occurred

21.4 Collection

(*a*) by reason of an error made by the secondary contributor in good faith; or

(*b*) in respect of payments made under employment protection legislation and treated as earnings by virtue of *SSCBA 1992, s 112* (see 28.11 EARNINGS); or

(*c*) as a result of the cancellation, variation or surrender of a contracting-out certificate issued in respect of the employment in respect of which the payment of earnings was made except where the cancellation is of a *further* contracting-out certificate under *PSA 1993, s 36(3) (formerly SSPA 1975, s 51A(5))* and recovery is prohibited by *Contracting-Out (Recovery of Class 1 Contributions) Regs 1982, Reg 2* (see CONTRACTED-OUT EMPLOYMENT (23)); or

(*d*) in respect of a sickness payment treated as earnings under *SSCBA 1992, s 4(1)* and paid by a person other than the secondary contributor.

[*Contributions Regs, 1 Sch 13(2A)(a)(b)(i)–(v), as amended by Contracting-Out (Recovery of Class 1 Contributions) Regs 1982, Reg 2, Contributions Amendment No 4 Regs 1983, Reg 8(a) and Contributions Amendment Regs 1984, Reg 16(a)*].

The amount which may be deducted from a payment (or from payments which fall to be aggregated) in respect of an under-deduction is an amount in addition to but not in excess of the amount otherwise deductible. [*Contributions Regs, 1 Sch 13(3A)(a), as amended by Contributions Amendment Regs 1984, Reg 16(b)*].

Example
Anne works for Boleyn Ltd and is paid £119 per week. When preparing the wages for 25 March 2001, B realises that an incorrect amount of primary contributions has been deducted from A's wage for each of the previous three weeks, thus

Pay day	Gross pay	Primary contribution due	Primary contribution deducted
	£	£	£
4 March	119	4.30	0.70
11 March	119	4.30	0.70
18 March	119	4.30	0.70

The correct normal deduction on 25 March is £4.30 and an additional £4.30 may, therefore, be deducted on that date as a partial recovery of the £10.80 under-deduction. Similarly, a further £4.30 may be recovered by way of an additional deduction on 1 April. The balance of £2.20 will, however, be *irrecoverable* as the next pay day is not in the same year as that in which the under-deduction occurred.

As stated in 21.3 where there is a succession to a trade or business the purchaser is liable for anything the former secondary contributor would have been liable to do. [*Contributions Regs, 1 Sch 34* and see also *Transfer of Undertakings (Protection of Employment) Regulations 1981*].

Example
Clips Hair Salon employs a number of assistants to assist the stylists with washing and preparation prior to cut. The owner has not deducted tax or NICs in respect of the assistants' wages all of whom earned over £67 per week including tips during 1999–2000. The owner sells the business to one of the existing stylists and contracts are exchanged on 21 April 2000. The total tax and NICs unpaid by the previous owner for 1999–2000 amounts to £1,207.80 and £1,057.68 (primary), £257.40 (secondary). The new owner will take on the total liability of £2,522.88 even though this was originally due to be paid by the previous owner. Also, an appropriate return should have been made by 19 May 2000 in respect of tax and

NICs. If the new owners miss the deadline of 19 April 2000 for payment of outstanding tax and NICs i.e. the amount of £2,522.88, then interest will run from 20 April 2000. Clearly, unless there is a case of fraud the previous owners have no liability.

21.5   Records

If, during any year, a secondary contributor makes to an employed earner any payment of earnings in respect of which Class 1 contributions are payable, he must prepare and maintain a deductions working sheet P11 (2000) for that earner. [*SSCBA 1992, 1 Sch 6(1); Contributions Regs, 1 Sch 6(1)(a), as amended by Contributions Amendment Regs 1981, Reg 4 and Contributions Amendment No 4 Regs 1983, Reg 7 and Contributions Amendment No 2 Regs 1987, Reg 11(2)*]. On the deductions working sheet he must record (see CWG1 (2000), Cards 8–11):

(*a*)   the tax year to which the deductions working sheet relates;

(*b*)   the name and NATIONAL INSURANCE NUMBER (46) of the employed earner;

(*c*)   the employed earner's category letter (see 15.5 CLASS 1 CONTRIBUTIONS); and

(*d*)   in relation to each payment of earnings which he makes to the employed earner

(i)   the date of payment;

(ii)   the amount of any statutory sick pay (optional from 6 April 1996 unless recovery is made under the Percentage Threshold Scheme—see 15.7 CLASS 1 CONTRIBUTIONS);

(iii)   the amount of all the Class 1 contributions payable on the earnings;

(iv)   the amount of primary contributions included in (iii);

(v)   the amount of any employer's contracted-out rebate due on earnings between the lower earnings limit and the earnings threshold;

(vi)   the amount of any statutory maternity pay;

(vii)   the amount of earnings up to the lower earnings limit, if that limit is equalled or exceeded;

(viii)   the amount of earnings falling between the lower earnings limit and the employee's earnings threshold;

(ix)   the amount of earnings falling between the employee's earnings threshold and the employer's earnings threshold;

(x)   the amount of earnings falling between the employer's earnings threshold and the upper earnings limit.

[*Contributions Regs, 1 Sch 13(6)(a)–(b), as amended by Contributions Amendment Regs 1981, Reg 5(a), Contributions Amendment No 4 Regs 1983, Reg 8(b)(c), Contributions Amendment Regs 1984, Reg 16(d), Contributions Amendment No 2 Regs 1987, Reg 11(3), Contributions Amendment No 3 Regs 1991, Reg 3(2), Contributions Amendment No 6 Regs 1992, Reg 4; Social Security (Contributions and Credits)(Miscellaneous Amendment) Regulations 1999, Reg 19(3) and Social Security Contributions (Notional Payment of Primary Class 1 Contributions) Regulations 2000, Reg 9(2), SI 2000/747*].

He must also retain for the three succeeding tax years a record of the date and amount of earnings paid in a tax year, excluding from earnings and recording separately the amount of any allowable superannuation contributions. [*Contributions Regs, 1 Sch 13(6C), as substituted by Contributions Amendment Regs 1984, Reg 16(d)*]. The requirement to record earnings as well as contributions for 1987–88 onwards was imposed because of the new method of calculating EARNINGS FACTORS (29) for 1987–88 and later years. The requirement to record the earnings at the lower earnings limit from 6 April 1999 is a result of the government's policy to treat employees not paying contributions as having paid contributions nonetheless provided that they would have done so under the Class 1 structure prior to the changes in April 1999 and April 2000. The reason put forward for the recording of other bands of earnings includes the same factor but it is submitted that these are, in fact, superfluous.

See 5.14 AGGREGATION OF EARNINGS for recording of aggregated earnings and contributions thereon.

A secondary contributor must render to the Inspector or Collector of Taxes an end-of-year return not later than 44 days after the end of a tax year i.e. 19 May (see CWG1 (2000) Card 18). This is form P 14 (OCR) (see CWG1 (2000) Card 21) (or such other form as the Inland Revenue approves or prescribes) and must be submitted in respect of each employed earner in respect of whom the secondary contributor was required, at *any* time during the year, to prepare or maintain a deductions working sheet, summarising that employed earner's deductions working sheet and showing

(*a*) particulars identifying the employed earner;

(*b*) the year to which the return relates;

(*c*) under each category letter:

  (i) the total amount of all Class 1 contributions payable on earnings;

  (ii) the total amount of primary contributions included in (i); and

  (iii) in the case of contracted-out employment, the amount of employer's rebate or earnings between the lower earnings limit and the earnings threshold;

(*d*) the total amount of statutory maternity pay paid during the year;

(*e*) the amount of earnings up to and including the lower earnings limit, but only if that limit is reached or exceeded;

(*f*) the amount of earnings between the lower earnings limit and the employee's earnings threshold;

(*g*) the amount of earnings between the employee's earnings threshold and the employer's earnings threshold;

(*h*) the amount of earnings between the earnings threshold and the upper earnings limit;

(*i*) the total amount of statutory sick pay paid during the year (optional from 6 April 1996 unless recovery is made under the Percentage Threshold Scheme—see 15.7 CLASS CONTRIBUTIONS: EMPLOYED EARNERS and also below);

(*j*) the amount of any Class 1A contribution payable in respect of the year preceding the year to which the return relates;

(*k*) where Class 1A contributions are payable other than on 19 July due to a cessation of, or succession to, a business, the amount of any such Class 1A contribution payable in respect of the year to which the return relates;

(*l*) where contracted-out contributions are payable by virtue of a money purchase scheme, a scheme contracted-out number ('SCON').

[*Contributions Regs, 1 Sch 30(1), as substituted by Contributions Amendments Regs 1981, Reg 7 and as amended by Contributions Amendment No 4 Regs 1983, Reg 11, Contributions Amendment Regs 1985, Reg 5, Contributions Amendment No 2 Regs 1987, Reg 11(7)(b), Contributions Amendment No 2 Regs 1990, Reg 2(3), Contributions Amendment No 6 Regs 1992, Reg 13, Contributions (Miscellaneous Amendments) Regs 1994, Reg 3; Social Security (Contributions and Credits)(Mis-*

cellaneous Amendments) Regs 1999, Reg 19(5) and Social Security Contributions (Notional Payment of Primary Class 1 Contributions) Regulations 2000, Reg 9(4) SI 2000/747].

As regards (i) above, it is only necessary to record, from 6 April 1996, statutory sick pay where a recovery is made under the Percentage Threshold Scheme. Employers still have the option to record all statutory sick pay paid, whether recovered or not, if they wish, or some other meaningful figure between the amount actually recovered and the total amount paid, again if they wish. The intention of the change is to reduce the burden of record-keeping and prescribe the *minimum* requirement rather than the precise manner in which all employers *must* keep records (CA Specialist Conference, 20 February 1996).

Not later than 44 days after the end of a tax year i.e. 19 May, a secondary contributor must render to the Inspector of Taxes an annual statement and declaration (P 35 or such other form as the Inland Revenue approves or prescribes) summarising those end-of-year returns and showing

(*a*) the total amount of all Class 1 contributions payable by him in respect of each employee during the year;

(*b*) the total amount of all Class 1 contributions payable by him in respect of all employees during the year;

(*c*) in relation to any employment contracted-out by virtue of a salary-related scheme, the employer's number recorded on his contracting-out certificate issued by the Occupational Pensions Board (in practice, this is known as the 'ECON' or employer's contracting-out number);

(*d*) the total amount of all statutory sick pay paid by him to each employee during the year but, from 6 April 1996, only to the extent that such amounts have been recovered under the Percentage Threshold Scheme (see 15.7 CLASS 1 CONTRIBUTIONS: EMPLOYED EARNERS);

(*e*) the total amount of all statutory sick pay paid by him to all employees during the year but, from 6 April 1996, only to the extent that such amounts have been recovered under the Percentage Threshold Scheme (see 15.7 CLASS 1 CONTRIBUTIONS: EMPLOYED EARNERS);

(*f*) the total amount deducted, in respect of statutory sick pay paid by him during the year, as compensation for secondary Class 1 contributions paid on such statutory sick pay (see 15.7 CLASS 1 CONTRIBUTIONS: EMPLOYED EARNERS);

(*g*) the total amount of all statutory maternity pay paid by him to each employee during the year;

(*h*) the total amount of all statutory maternity pay paid by him to all employees during the year;

(*i*) the total amount deducted, in respect of statutory maternity pay paid by him during the year, as compensation for secondary Class 1 contributions paid on such statutory maternity pay (see 15.7 CLASS 1 CONTRIBUTIONS: EMPLOYED EARNERS);

(*j*) the total amount of Class 1A contributions paid by him in respect of each employee during that year; and

(*k*) the total amount of Class 1A contributions paid by him in respect of all his employees during that year.

See CA Press Release CA14/97 for details of the most common errors arising from the preparation of Form P14.

[Contributions Regs, 1 Sch 30(1)(2), as amended by Contributions Amendment Regs 1981, Reg 7, Contributions Amendment No 4 Regs 1983, Reg 11, Contributions

21.6 Collection

Amendment No 2 Regs 1987, Reg 11(7)(d), Contributions Amendment (No 2) Regs 1990, Reg 2(3); Contributions Amendment Regs 1992, Reg 19 and Social Security Contributions (Notional Payment of Primary Class 1 Contributions) Regulations 2000, Reg 9(4), SI 2000/747].

Item (*f*) ceased to be required in respect of the annual statement for 1991–92 as no compensation was payable on SSP paid after 5 April 1991 (see 15.7 CLASS 1 CONTRIBUTIONS: EMPLOYED EARNERS). Even 'small' employers who qualified for recovery of 100% of SSP payments under the Small Employers' Relief scheme ceased to be eligible for compensation. With the advent on 6 April 1995 of the Percentage Threshold Scheme, even the 100% recovery by small employers was abolished.

In the case of a corporate body, the declaration must be signed by a director or the company secretary. The Inland Revenue may require the end-of-year returns to be in some form other than that prescribed for tax purposes and, if so required, the return is to be made in accordance with the conditions prescribed. [*Contributions Regs, 1 Sch 30(3)(6A)*].

Where a computerised payroll system is in use, the system must be capable of producing the detailed records described above, and computer print-outs must be retained for three years (or, in the case of CONTRACTED-OUT EMPLOYMENT (23) where separate records are required, see 5.12 AGGREGATION OF EARNINGS, for the period of the employment concerned and for three years after that employment ends) as in the case of manual records. (CWG2 (2000), Pages 1 and 2). Year-end returns which provide the required details may be made on magnetic tape or flexible disk cartridge (e.g. floppy disk) instead of on forms P14 and P35. Details of requirements in this respect may be obtained from The Inland Revenue (Magnetic Media) at the NICO at Lindisfarne House, Room BP2102, Longbenton, Newcastle upon Tyne, NE98 1ZZ (tel 0191–225 7932/3605, fax 0191–225 9403). The Inland Revenue does not help employers to decide which commercially available software products meet their legal obligations but until the 1999 CWG2 directed businesses to the Institute for the Management of Information Systems (IMIS) at The Business Centre, 6 Church Street, Twyford, Berks, RG10 9DR (tel 0118 934 5262, fax 0118 934 4043) or the British Computer Society, Specialist Groups Liaison, 1 Sanford Street, Swindon SN1 1HJ (tel 01793 417417, fax 01793 480270, e-mail *sg@bcs.org.uk*) for further advice. The authorities actively promote the use of magnetic media returns and produces an information pack for employers and payroll software producers together with an explanatory leaflet CA49, available from the above address. Employers can design and operate their own computer program and should obtain the notes by writing to Inland Revenue Notes for Payroll Software Developers, PO Box 1460, Bristol, BS99 3NW.

21.6 Enforcement

The following provisions apply in case of default.

If, within 14 days of the end of any income tax month, a secondary contributor has

(*a*) paid no Class 1 contributions to the Collector of Taxes for that month, and the Collector is unaware of the amount if any which the secondary contributor is liable to pay; or

(*b*) has paid an amount, but the Collector is not satisfied that it is the *full* amount which the secondary contributor is liable to pay,

the Collector may give notice to the secondary contributor requiring him to render a return within 14 days informing the Collector of the amount of Class 1 contributions which he, the secondary contributor, is liable to pay the Collector for that month or for that and earlier months. [*Contribution Regs, 1 Sch 27 as substituted by Contributions Amendment (No 2) Regs 1990, Reg 2(1)*].

Similarly, if the employer has

(i) paid no amount of Class 1A contributions to the Collector by the date which applies to him (i.e. normally 19 July and for cessations/successions 14 days from the end of the relevant tax month), or

(ii) paid an amount, but the Collector is not satisfied that it is the full amount which the employer is liable to pay,

the Collector may take the same steps to issue a notice requiring a return. [*Contributions Regs, 1 Sch 27(2A)(3)(b), amended by Contributions Amendment Regs 1992, Reg 16 and Contributions Amendment No 6 Regs 1992, Reg 10*].

If no return is made by the secondary contributor, the Collector has two alternatives.

(A) He may require the secondary contributor to produce for his inspection at the 'prescribed place' all (or such as he specifies) of the wages sheets, deductions working sheets, and other documents and records relating to the calculation of earnings or of Class 1 contributions or of Class 1A contributions payable for such tax years or income tax months as he specifies; and, by reference to information obtained from his inspection, may prepare a certificate showing the amount of Class 1 and/or Class 1A contributions which the secondary contributor appears to be liable to pay.

Until 10 July 1992, the regulation required the production of documents etc. only 'at the employer's premises'. This has now been extended to 'at such time as the officer may reasonably require, at the prescribed place'. That place is

(*a*) such place in Great Britain as the employer and the authorised officer may agree upon; or

(*b*) in default of such agreement, the place in Great Britain at which the documents and records referred to are normally kept; or

(*c*) in default of such agreement, and if there is no such place in Great Britain, the employer's principal place of business in Great Britain.

The extension of the provision also specifically allows the officer to take copies of, or make extracts from, any documents produced to him for inspection and, if it appears to him to be necessary to do so, at a reasonable time and for a reasonable period, to take any such document with him when he leaves, giving the employer a receipt for the same. If such documents are reasonably required for the proper conduct of the business, the officer is obliged to provide a copy, at no charge, to the person by whom it was produced to him.

(B) He may, upon consideration of the secondary contributor's record of past payments, specify, to the best of his judgment, the amount of Class 1 contributions which he considers the secondary contributor is liable to pay and give notice to him of that amount. This provision also extends to Class 1A contributions paid through the PAYE system, but only from 20 April 1999 where the employer pays the Class 1A contributions by the Alternative Payment Method.

If the amount or any part of the amount specified in the notice remains unpaid 7 days after the date specified in the notice, the Collector may certify the amount due, which will be treated as unpaid earnings-related contributions or Class 1A contributions as appropriate. The certificate is sufficient evidence of the debt for the Collector to initiate proceedings against the employer.

[*Contributions Regs, 1 Sch 32(1)(1A)(1B)(2), as amended by Contributions Amendment Regs 1981, Reg 8, Contributions Amendment No 4 Regs 1983, Reg 12, Contributions Amendment No 2 Regs 1987, Reg 11(9), Contributions Amendment Regs 1992, Reg 20 and Contributions Amendment No 6 Regs 1992, Reg 15;*

21.7 Collection

Contributions Regs, 1 Sch 27A as amended by Contributions Amendment Regs 1985, Reg 3 and Contributions Amendment No 3 Regs 1995, Reg 3(3); Contributions Regs, 1 Sch 27B(1), as inserted by Contributions Amendment Regs 1992, Reg 17 and amended by Contributions Amendment No 3 Regs 1995, Reg 3(4)].

If the Collector takes course (B) above and the secondary contributor fails, within the 7 days allowed by the notice, either

(1) to pay the full amount specified by the notice; or

(2) to pay the amount of Class 1 or Class 1A contributions *actually* due for the income tax period or periods concerned; or

(3) to satisfy the collector that no amount of Class 1 or Class 1A contributions is due for the income tax period or periods concerned,

the Collector may then certify the amount as if it were an amount he had arrived at by taking course (A) above. [*Contributions Regs, 1 Sch 27A(2)(3), as amended by Contributions Amendment Regs 1985, Reg 3 and Contributions Amendments No 3 Regs 1995, Reg 3(3); Contributions Regs, 1 Sch 27B(2)(3), as inserted by Contributions Amendment Regs 1992, Reg 17 and amended by Contributions Amendment No 3 Regs 1995, Reg 3(4)].*

The procedure under course (B) above is not confined to situations where there has been *no* payment of Class 1 or Class 1A contributions by a secondary contributor within the relevant time limit, but may be followed by the Collector where, after seeking the secondary contributor's explanation as to an amount of Class 1 or Class 1A contributions which has been paid, he is not satisfied that the amount is the full amount which the secondary contributor is liable to pay for that period. [*Contributions Regs, 1 Sch 27A(6), as amended by Contributions Amendment Regs 1985, Reg 3; Contributions Regs, 1 Sch 27B(5), as inserted by Contributions Amendment Regs 1992, Reg 17].* If, however, during that 7 days allowed by the notice, the secondary contributor claims, but does not satisfy the Collector, that the payment of Class 1 or Class 1A contributions which he has made is the full amount of Class 1 or Class 1A contributions for which he is liable, the secondary contributor may require the Collector to follow the procedure laid down as course (A) above as if the Collector had required the production of documents etc. [*Contributions Regs, 1 Sch 27A(7), as amended by Contributions Amendment Regs 1985, Reg 3; Contributions Regs, 1 Sch 27B(6) as inserted by Contributions Amendment Regs 1992, Reg 17].*

Any excess of Class 1 or Class 1A contributions paid as the result of a secondary contributor's compliance with a Collector's notice under course (B) may be set off against any amount which the secondary contributor is liable to pay to the Collector for any subsequent income tax period, and if any such excess (verified by reference to the end-of-year returns etc.) remains unrecovered by the end of the tax year, it will be repaid. [*Contributions Regs, 1 Sch 27A(8)(9), as amended by Contributions Amendment Regs 1985, Reg 3; Contributions Regs, 1 Sch 27B(7) as inserted by Contributions Amendment Regs 1992, Reg 17].*

21.7 Direct collection of primary contributions

An employed earner will himself be liable to pay and account for primary Class 1 contributions in respect of his earnings from an employed earner's employment in the following circumstances.

(a) Where under a DEFERMENT OF PAYMENT (27.2) arrangement authorised by the Inland Revenue, the earner has agreed that he himself will pay any such contributions on such earnings.

(*b*)   Where such contributions should have, but have not, been paid by a secondary contributor and the failure to pay is due to an *act or default of the earner* and not to any negligence on the part of the secondary contributor.

(*c*)   Where the secondary contributor is a person against whom, by reason of an international treaty or convention (see 25.9 CROWN SERVANTS AND STATUTORY EMPLOYEES), the collection provisions are *not enforceable* and who is not willing to comply with those provisions on a voluntary basis.

(*d*)   Where the earner's employer who would otherwise fall to be treated as the secondary contributor cannot be so treated by reason of his *failure to fulfil prescribed conditions as to residence and presence* in Great Britain and no 'host employer' can be specified to be the secondary contributor in accordance with *Categorisation Regs, Reg 1(2) as amended by Categorisation Regs 1994, Reg 2* (see 49.9 OVERSEAS MATTERS).

[*Contributions Regs, Regs 47, 48(1), 50(1) and 1 Sch 50(1)*].

In a case falling within (*b*) to (*d*) above, the employed earner himself will be subject to all the regulations (suitably modified) as to payment, recording and enforcement of primary Class 1 contributions, as described at 21.3, 21.5 and 21.6 above. In a case falling within (*a*) above, where an amount has been deferred in excess of the contribution liability which is ultimately excepted, the Inland Revenue NICO will inform the earner of the amount of primary Class 1 contributions yet to be paid. (Leaflet CA 01).

It is arguable that *1 Sch 50(1)* (which covers the circumstance described at (*d*) above) is *ultra vires* for the following reasons. Whenever a payment of earnings is made to an earner, the secondary contributor in relation to that payment of earnings is the employer of the employee concerned irrespective of who makes the payment. [*SSCBA 1992, s 7(1)(a)*]. That employer is liable for the secondary contribution on the payment and the employee is liable for the primary contribution but the *manner* in which those liabilities fall to be discharged is governed entirely by *SSCBA 1992, 1 Sch 3*. [*SSCBA 1992, s 6(3)*]. The terms of *1 Sch 3* are mandatory, not merely permissive, and provide that where earnings are paid to an employed earner and in respect of that payment liability arises for primary and secondary Class 1 contributions, the secondary contributor *shall* (except in prescribed circumstances), as well as being liable for his own secondary contribution, be liable in the first instance to pay also the earner's primary contribution, on behalf of and to the exclusion of the earner. 'Prescribed' means 'prescribed by regulations' [*s 122(1)*] and the *only* regulation which does in fact prescribe circumstances in which the secondary contributor shall *not* be liable to pay an earner's primary contributions is *Contributions Regs, Reg 47*. This provides that the Inland Revenue may, if thought fit, *authorise* a direct collection arrangement, but, as *Reg 48* makes clear, the provisions of *SSCBA 1992, 1 Sch 3* are only set aside by such an arrangement if the earner himself has *agreed* to pay the primary contribution. If there is no such agreement by the employee, liability for both primary and secondary contributions lies with the secondary contributor and it would seem that that incidence of liability cannot be altered or varied by anything in *Contributions Regs, 1 Sch*. That Schedule (which applies the PAYE regulations to Class 1 contributions) is brought into operation only by, and for the purposes of, *Reg 46* (as *Reg 46* itself and the sidenote to the Schedule make plain) and, insofar as *1 Sch 50(1)* purports to impose a direct collection procedure on the employee where the person paying emoluments is beyond the jurisdiction of Parliament, it would seem to go beyond the enabling power. *1 Sch 50(1)* is not made under *SSCBA 1992, 1 Sch 3* which it would need to be in order to alter the incidence of liability for which *1 Sch 3* provides.

Even if *1 Sch 50(1)* is *intra vires*, however, it may not be of any effect in situations where payments to a UK employee are made by someone who is not his contractual employer and who does not fulfil prescribed conditions as to residence and presence in GB. 'Employer' means, for the purpose of *Contributions Regs, 1 Sch*, 'any person paying emoluments' [*1 Sch 2(1)*], and *1 Sch 3(1)* provides that where an employee works under the general control and management of a person who is not his 'immediate employer', that person is to be deemed to be the employer for the purpose of *1 Sch*. In other words, although an overseas third party pays the employee and would thus, in the absence of *1 Sch 3(1)* be the 'employer' who, under *1 Sch*, would have to pay and account for contributions, the UK employer is, instead, deemed to be 'the employer' for the purpose of *1 Sch* generally *and* for the purpose of *1 Sch 50(1)* in particular. But *1 Sch 50(1)* is of effect only where 'the employer' (ie, the UK employer, not the overseas payer of earnings) is non-resident etc, which is not the case in the situation referred to here. The consequences are as follows:

(i) The employee has no obligation to pay and account for his own primary contributions because only *1 Sch 50(1)* imposes such an obligation.

(ii) The UK employer has an obligation to pay and account for primary and secondary contributions under *1 Sch 26(1)*, but that obligation extends only to the total amount of earnings-related contributions *due* in respect of the emoluments paid by the overseas payer but which the UK employer is (under *1 Sch 3(1)*) deemed to have paid.

The use of the term 'contributions due' presupposes that the liability for contributions can be quantified, but, in the circumstances being considered here, where the emoluments are paid by someone other than the person who, under the deeming provisions of *1 Sch 3(1)*, is liable to pay the contributions, the person liable can know what the liability is only if the person actually paying the emoluments informs the deemed employer (the UK employer) of the necessary particulars. *1 Sch 3(1)* recognises this by purporting to require the person paying the emoluments to provide just such information, but it seems that, in law, such a requirement is *ultra vires* where the person paying the emoluments is outside the jurisdiction. (*Colquhoun v Heddon (1890) 2 TC 621*). It is now, of course, possible to request the relevant information from elsewhere in the Inland Revenue under *SSAA 1992, s 122(1)* (on the assumption that the employee concerned will make a return of his income from the overseas source). But, even were the information to be obtained by such means, the information would be of no use because the Inland Revenue is prohibited by *s 122(3)* from passing it on to anyone, including the UK employer. It would seem, therefore, that, in the situation where an employee receives a payment of earnings from someone who is not his contractual employer and who is outside the jurisdiction of Parliament, the employee cannot be required to pay or account for his primary contributions and the UK employer cannot be required to pay or account for either primary or secondary contributions unless the overseas payer of the earnings informs the UK employer directly, on a voluntary basis, of the payment made to the employee concerned. Arguably, this remains the case even though, since 6 April 1994, *Categorisation Regs 1978, 3 Sch 9* has deemed a 'host employer' to be the secondary contributor in respect of an employee sent to work for the host employer by a 'foreign employer'. Accounting for any contributions requires knowledge of the amount and date of any payment of earnings, but these facts may not be known to the UK host employer. A similar problem affects the operation of PAYE under *ICTA 1988, s 203C* (inserted by *FA 1994, s 126* with effect from 3 May 1994).

21.8   Penalties

In response to poor levels of compliance with PAYE regulations, *FA 1989, ss 164, 165* introduced substantial changes to the penalty regime for PAYE returns, including a new *TMA 1970, s 98A* which applies to the late submission of employers' year-end returns (e.g. P14 and P35) and to the fraudulent or negligent completion of incorrect year-end returns by virtue of *Income Tax (Employments) Regs 1993, Reg 43(12)*.

The new regime, from 20 May 1995, involves automatic penalties for late returns, but an interim system operated from 1989 to 1995. The change to automatic penalties was brought about by *FA 1989, s 165(2) (Appointed Day) Order 1994 (SI 1994 No 2508)*, made on 23 September 1994 to take effect from 20 May 1995.

Until the change took place, the Inland Revenue had to ask the General Commissioners to impose a penalty. It was announced in 1989 that the change to automatic penalties would occur in 1995 and that the year-end time limits applied in practice before penalty proceedings were brought would be gradually moved into line with the statutory limits (IR Press Release, 14 March 1989). Over the period from 1989 to 1994, by concession, the statutory filing deadline of 19 May was ignored and an alternative, later date was used for determining whether penalties should be sought, each year's date advancing closer to 19 May. When the *Appointed Day Order* was made, the Inland Revenue also announced a new extra statutory concession B45 to assist those persons required to make company returns or employers' and contractors' end-of-year returns to adjust to the new automatic penalty systems. The concession has been amended by reducing to seven days after the strict filing date the extra period during which, if a return is lodged late, no penalty will be imposed. The concession will be kept under review (Inland Revenue Press Release, 14 September 1995 and amended concession B45).

Under the concession the Board allowed, for the first year in which the new penalties were due, a short 'period of grace' following the statutory time limits during which automatic penalties would not be charged. It was explicitly stated that this concession should not be taken as an extension of the statutory filing dates and every effort should be made to ensure that the returns were received by the Inland Revenue by the statutory filing dates. For the P14 and P35 returns due by 19 May 1999, therefore, automatic penalties would not be applied if the returns were received by 26 May 1999 (IR Press Release, 8 September 1994, see also IR Press Release 14 September 1995).

The penalty for the submission of an *incorrect* PAYE return made fraudulently or negligently is an amount *up to* the difference between the amount paid for the year of assessment to which the return relates and the amount which would have been payable had the return been correct. [*TMA 1970, s 98A(4)*].

The initial regime for *late* returns was geared to the number of employees covered by the P35. This was achieved by relating the penalty to a 'relevant monthly amount', which was set at £100 per 50 employees or part thereof. A late return for 51 employees would therefore attract a relevant monthly amount of £200, as the number of employees is rounded up to the nearest 50. [*s 98A(3)*].

The penalty created by *FA 1989, s 165(2)* could apply in three stages:

— for the initial failure to make a return, an employer was liable to a penalty of *up to* twelve times the relevant monthly amount [*s 98A(2)(a)(i)*];

— if the failure continued after a penalty was imposed under *s 98A(2)(a)(i)*, the employer faced a further penalty or penalties of the relevant monthly amount (apparently non-mitigable) for each month, or part month, during which the failure continued, but excluding any month after the twelfth or for which a further penalty had already been imposed [*s 98A(2)(a)(ii)*];

— if the failure continued beyond twelve months, in addition to any penalties under *s 98A(2)(a)*, the employer faced a penalty of *up to* the amount unpaid as at 19 April after the end of the year of assessment to which the return related (i.e. the last date by which month 12 remittances should have been paid). [*s 98A(2)(b)*].

From 20 May 1995, the initial penalty of £1,200 per 50 employees under *s 98A(2)(a)(i)* no longer applies. Instead, *s 98A(2)(a)* simply provides for a penalty of the relevant monthly amount for each month, or part month, during which the failure continues, for up to twelve months. [*FA 1989, s 165(1)*].

With effect from 22 October 1990, the above penalties for late, fraudulent and negligent returns for tax purposes also apply in relation to the 'contributions returns' described at 20.5 above and the provisions of *TMA 1970, ss 100–100D and 102–104* apply in relation to such penalties. [*SSCBA 1992, 1 Sch 6(7), 7; Contributions Regs, 1 Sch 30(7), 51(10) as inserted by Contributions Amendment No 4 Regs 1990, Reg 2(3)*]. The PAYE returns mainly involve only Class 1 contributions, but some employers account for Class 1A contributions through the PAYE system. Where this is so, this penalty regime applies to both Class 1 and Class 1A contributions. [*SSCBA 1992, 1 Sch 6(2)(c), 7(11); Contributions Regs, Reg 30(7)*].

For contributions purposes, the penalty provisions are modified as follows:

(*a*)   Where a person has failed to render a *tax* return for a particular tax year within the time prescribed and is thus liable for a penalty for a default in the first twelve months, he is *not* liable for a similar penalty in respect of the associated *contributions* return (which is effectively constituted by the same piece of paper or electronic return). [*SSCBA 1992, 1 Sch 7(3)*]. The *Social Security Act 1998* changes the wording 'is liable to' and 'be liable to' in *SSCBA 1992, 1 Sch 7(3)* to 'has been required to pay' and 'be required to pay' with effect from 6 April 1999. [*Social Security Act 1999 (Commencement No. 4) October 1999*].

(*b*)   Where a person has failed to render a tax return and associated contributions return for a particular tax year and the failure has continued beyond twelve months, a single penalty may apply of *up to* the sum of any tax and contributions remaining unpaid at the end of 19 April following the end of the tax year to which the return relates. An authorised officer of the Inland Revenue must determine that a penalty is to be imposed in respect of both returns. [*SSCBA 1992, 1 Sch 7(4)(5)*].

(*c*)   Where a person has fraudulently or negligently made an incorrect tax return and an associated contributions return for a particular tax year, a single penalty may apply of *up to* the sum of any tax and contributions remaining unpaid at the end of 19 April following the end of the tax year to which the return relates. Again, an authorised officer of the Inland Revenue must determine that a penalty is to be imposed in respect of both returns. [*SSCBA 1992, 1 Sch 7(4)(5)*].

Any contributions-related penalties collected by the Inland Revenue under the foregoing rules are, net of collection costs, paid to the National Insurance Fund. [*SSCBA 1992, 1 Sch 7(6) and (8) as amended by SSC(T)A 1999, 3 Sch 36*].

The above penalties in relation to contribution returns could only be imposed by the Inland Revenue. Whilst the *Social Security Act 1998* introduced new powers to enable the equivalent penalties to be charged by the CA, the transfer of the CA to the Inland Revenue on 1 April 1999 made further action in this regard unnecessary.

Enabling regulations may also prescribe circumstances in which contributions are to be paid and collected direct at Newcastle rather than through the Collector of Taxes. It also provides for regulations to set out the requirements for making the payments of contributions and the imposition of interest and penalties where the requirements are not met. Regulations shall also prescribe the circumstances where the payment is not required, the rate of penalty and how it is to be ascertained, time limits and other administrative matters. Regulations will also provide for interest and penalties to be charged for a period prior to the passing of the *Social Security Act 1998* where the Inland Revenue could have done so. [*SSCBA 1992, 1 Sch 7B as inserted by Social Security Act 1998, s 57*].

Such regulations have been made in respect of Class 1A contributions (see 16.20 CLASS 1A CONTRIBUTIONS: BENEFITS IN KIND).

Penalties under *s 98A* may be levied notwithstanding that a contributions question had been put to the Secretary of State for determination by him under *SSAA 1992, s 17* or had been referred to the Court under *s 18* or is the subject of an appeal to the Tax Commissioners under the new procedure from 1 April 1999 (see 9 APPEALS AND REVIEWS), but if the outcome will affect the person's liability for a penalty, the penalty may not be imposed until the question has been determined. *SSCBA 1992, 1 Sch 7(12)* as amended by *SSC(T)A 1999, 7 Sch 10*]. See also IR press release dated 18 May 1999.

Despite the existence of the legislation since 1990, none of these penalty provisions is reflected in the Employers Further Guide to PAYE and NICs, CWG2 (2000) (see 32.5 ENFORCEMENT). The Contributions Agency had no legal authority to apply the civil penalty regime as set out in *TMA 1970, s 98A* and it could not summon an employer to appear before the General Commissioners for a penalty hearing. Any cases potentially open to such proceedings therefore had to be referred to the Inland Revenue.

In practice, Contributions Agency investigations rarely resulted in prosecution and were usually settled simply by the payment of any arrears and, since 1992–93, interest. When errors are discovered by a PAYE auditor and the employer settles the underpaid tax and contributions, the settlement will often include a negotiated amount by way of interest and penalties.

Since the advent of *TMA 1970, s 98A* in 1989, the starting point has been 100% of the error.

This figure is then discounted for three factors:

Factor	Maximum discount
Disclosure	20%–30%
Cooperation	40%
Size and gravity	40%

For further information on Inland Revenue practice in this area, see Tolley's Tax Compliance and Investigations.

Interest on late-paid Class 1 and Class 1A contributions (currently 8.5%) and on refunds (currently 3.5%) of such contributions was introduced from 19 April 1993 by *Contributions Amendment No 5 Regs 1993* which inserted *Regs 28A–D* into the *Contributions Regulations 1979* (see 39.9 LATE-PAID CONTRIBUTIONS, 53.7 REPAYMENT and RE-ALLOCATION and NI News, Issue 7, page 12).

21.9 **CLASS 2 CONTRIBUTIONS**

Irrespective of contributions of other classes which may be payable, a single Class 2 contribution is to be paid in respect of every contribution week during any part of which an earner is ordinarily employed in one or more self-employed earner's employments unless the earner has been excepted from liability for that week (e.g. by reason of receipt of incapacity benefit, incapability for work, receipt of maternity allowance or detention in legal custody) or his liability has been deferred (see 18.3 and 18.4 CLASS 2 CONTRIBUTIONS and 27.8 DEFERMENT OF PAYMENT).

Such a contribution is, unless an alternative arrangement has been approved, (see 21.10 below), due for payment 28 days after the issue of a notice at the end of a contribution quarter. [*Contribution Regs, Reg 54, as substituted by Contributions Amendment Regs 1993, Reg 4*].

For Class 2 purposes, a contribution week which falls partly in one tax year and partly in another is to be treated as falling wholly in the tax year in which it begins. [*Reg 131*].

21.10 Collection

A penalty can be imposed for late payment, although if payment is made sufficiently late, payment may be due at a higher rate (see 39.7 LATE-PAID CONTRIBUTIONS). The *Social Security Act 1998* enables regulations to be made to impose a penalty in such circumstances. It is understood that it was originally proposed that the penalty would be a fixed amount of £30 where a quarterly bill is paid more than 28 days after the date of issue. It is also expected that, where a penalty has been imposed, the higher rate of charge referred to in 39.7 will *not* apply. These penalties were due to be introduced on 6 April 1999 but introduction has been deferred by Ministers (CA Press Release 05/99, 30 March 1999). It remains to be seen whether the power to introduce such a penalty will now ever be exercised given that the bill amounts to £26 per quarter in 2000–01 — which is rather less than the level of penalty reputedly borne in mind. The *SSC(T)A 1999, 4 Sch 1–3* enables the recovery of contributions, interest and penalties summarily as a civil debt in proceeding commenced in the name of an authorised officer on application to a Magistrate's Court. 'Authorised officer' means an officer of the Board of Inland Revenue authorised by them for that purpose.

21.10 Contribution cards

In respect of contribution weeks ending before 11 April 1993, anyone who was liable to pay a Class 2 contribution or who, being entitled though not liable to pay such a contribution, wished to do so, was required, unless liability had been deferred (see 27.8 DEFERMENT OF PAYMENT), to apply to the Secretary of State for a contribution card. [*Contribution Regs, Reg 51(1)(a), (3)*]. Failure to make such an application was an offence punishable on summary conviction by a penalty, which increased for each day after conviction during which the offence continued.

For further details of the regulations concerning contribution cards, readers should refer to earlier editions of this work.

21.11 Methods of payment

A Class 2 contribution liability may be discharged by

(a) making a payment to the Inland Revenue of the amount of contributions specified in a written notice issued within fourteen days of the end of the quarter in question; or

(b) making payment by *direct debit* of a bank or Girobank account under an arrangement authorised by the Inland Revenue; or

(c) consenting to a *deduction* of the appropriate amount by the Secretary of State from a war disablement pension or a pension or allowance specified in *Supplementary Benefits Act 1976, 1 Sch 23(5)(6)*, where such a pension or allowance is being received. Although *SBA 1976, 1 Sch* was repealed by *SSA 1986, 11 Sch* with effect from 11 April 1988, it is specifically provided that this rule applies to any pension or allowance analogous to those paid under *SBA 1976, 1 Sch.*

[*SSCBA 1992, 1 Sch 8(2), 10(1); Contributions Regs, Regs 54(1), (2), (3), 54A as substituted and inserted by Contributions Amendment Regs 1993, Reg 5 and amended by SSC(T)A 1999, 2 Sch*].

In respect of contribution weeks ending before 11 April 1993, a Class 2 contribution liability could be discharged by affixing a stamp of appropriate value to a contribution card (see 21.10 above) in the space indicated on the card for the purpose and immediately cancelling that stamp by writing or over-stamping in ink across the face of it the date on which it was affixed.

Since 11 April 1993, anyone who is liable to pay a Class 2 contribution or who, being entitled though not liable to pay such a contribution, wishes to do so, has been liable to notify the Inland Revenue (previously the Secretary of State) in writing of the date upon which he commenced or ceased to be a self-employed earner, or of the date upon which he wishes to commence or cease paying Class 2 contributions as appropriate. [*Contributions Regs, Reg 53A as inserted by Contributions Amendment Regs 1993, Reg 4 and amended by SSC(T)A 1999, 2 Sch*].

A Class 2 contributor, whether paying compulsorily or voluntarily, must notify the Inland Revenue (previously the Secretary of State) in writing of any change of his address. [*Contributions Regs, Reg 53B as inserted by Contributions Amendment Regs 1993, Reg 4 and amended by SSC(T)A 1999, 2 Sch*].

Failing to notify is an offence punishable on summary conviction by a penalty which increases for each day after conviction during which the offence continues. The maximum level of the penalty is as follows.

Offence committed
- before 22 September 1991 .... £200
- after 21 September 1991, but before 1 October 1992 .... £400
- after 30 September 1992 (level 3 on the standard scale) £1,000

Continuing contravention for each day
- before 22 September 1991 .... £20
- after 21 September 1991 .... £40

[*Contribution Regs, Reg 132, as amended by Contributions Amendment No 2 Regs 1983, Reg 2, Contributions Amendment No 5 Regs 1991, Regs 4, 5 and Criminal Justice Act 1991, s 17*].

The payment date specified in (*a*) above may be delayed until 28 days after the date specified as the date of notification in the payment notice in the following circumstances:

(*a*) when a notice has been issued, but the recipient has informed the Inland Revenue immediately that the notice he received has since been lost, destroyed or defaced and the notice is re-issued; or

(*b*) when a notice has been issued, but the recipient informs the Inland Revenue immediately that he disputes the amount of contributions shown in the notice and the notice is re-issued; or

(*c*) when the contributor has notified the Inland Revenue within 28 days after the end of the quarter that he has not received a notice and one is subsequently issued; or

(*d*) when the contributor has, after more than fourteen days from the end of the quarter have elapsed, not received a written notice in respect of any week or weeks in that contribution quarter and he notifies the Inland Revenue accordingly. [*Contributions Regs, Reg 54(4), (5), (6) as substituted by Contributions Amendment Regs 1993, Reg 5 and amended by SSC(T)A 1999, 2 Sch*].

A contribution quarter is one of the four periods of not less than 13 weeks beginning on the first, fourteenth, twenty-seventh or fortieth Sundays of any tax year. [*Contribution Regs, Reg 54(7) as substituted by Contributions Amendment Regs 1993, Reg 5*].

Although it had been the practice of clerks at local DSS offices to accept payment of arrears of Class 2 contributions, the practice lacks authority and is not, therefore, a permitted method of payment. In particular, a person who, after the end of a contribution year, pays to a local office the Class 2 contributions for which he was liable during that year, has committed the offence of failing to pay, at or within the time prescribed for the purpose, a number of Class 2 contributions which he was liable to pay and is, therefore, liable on summary conviction to a fine. (*R v Highbury*

Corner Stipendiary Magistrate, ex p DHSS, The Times, 4 February 1987). See 21.12 below and 12.5 ARREARS OF CONTRIBUTIONS.

A question as to whether payment of contributions has been properly made within the terms of (*d*) above will be a matter for a decision of an officer of the Board of Inland Revenue and not one which the justices may decide (see APPEALS AND REVIEWS (9)). (*DHSS v Walker Dean Walker Ltd [1970] 1 AER 757*).

The provisions of *Stamp Duties Management Act 1891* and *Post Office Act 1953, s 63* applied, with adaptations, to contribution stamps. [*SSCBA 1992, 1 Sch 8(3); Contributions Regs, Reg 57*]. Thus, to forge stamps or to handle forged stamps was a criminal offence punishable by up to 14 years imprisonment while mere possession, without lawful excuse, of a fictitious stamp (whether it was known to be fictitious or not) was an offence punishable by a fine of up to £500. [*SDMA 1891, s 13; POA 1953, s 63; as adopted by Contributions Regs, 2 Sch Pts I, II; Criminal Justice Act 1982, ss 37(2) and 46(1), and Criminal Justice Act 1991, s 17*]. There could be no lawful excuse where stamps were bought from an unauthorised person. (*Winkle v Wiltshire [1951] 1 AER 479.*) These provisions are now effectively spent.

It was also an offence to buy, sell, offer for sale, take or give in exchange, pawn, or take in pawn, a used (i.e. cancelled) contribution stamp, or to affix a used contribution stamp to a contribution card. To remove or erase a contribution stamp from a contribution card amounted to defacement of the contribution card itself. [*SSAA 1992, s 114(4); Contributions Regs, Reg 56(3)*].

Contribution stamps were withdrawn from sale at Post Offices on 21 April 1993.

If a contributor wishes to discharge his liability by direct debit, he should complete and send to Inland Revenue National Insurance Contributions Office, Self Employment Directorate (APC), Longbenton, Newcastle upon Tyne, NE98 1ZZ a form CF 351 N (which forms part of Leaflet CA 04) or Form CA5601 (which forms part of Leaflet CWL 1). The form will be transmitted to the bankers concerned who will then make contribution payments from the contributor's account monthly, normally on the second Friday in each month. Each debit will cover four or five contributions depending on the number of Sundays in the preceding tax month, but will not include contributions for weeks of proven incapacity. If the authority necessary for a bank or the Post Office to make such payments is withdrawn or ceases, any payment made thereafter by the bank or the Post Office will not be accepted as a payment of contributions. [*Contributions Regs, Reg 54A(3)*].

21.12 **Enforcement**

A contribution card to which there had not been affixed a stamp for a contribution week for which a contribution was due would have been evidence sufficient to justify proceedings for non-payment in respect of weeks before 6 April 1993. Where the card itself was missing or could not be produced, however, a statutory declaration to that effect by an officer of the Secretary of State was, subject to certain conditions, sufficient in such proceedings (see 12.5 ARREARS OF CONTRIBUTIONS). [*SSAA 1992, s 118(4)*].

See 21.11 above for the validity of proceedings where Class 2 contributions, though paid, have been paid late in accordance with an established but unauthorised practice.

See ARREARS OF CONTRIBUTIONS (12) for means of recovery where ordinary collection procedures fail.

For the purpose of summary proceedings under *SSAA 1992, s 114 as substituted by Social Security Act 1998, s 61* (see 12.4 ARREARS OF CONTRIBUTIONS) or of proceedings in the High Court or a county court (see 12.1 ARREARS OF CONTRIBUTIONS), the amount of each Class 2 contribution which a contributor is to be treated as having failed to pay is the amount he would have paid under the rules for late-paid Class 2 contributions (see 18.5 CLASS 2 CONTRIBUTIONS) if he had paid the outstanding contributions on the date the proceedings commenced. [*SSCBA 1992, s 12(5)*]. Summary proceedings commence on the date an information is laid (see 32.10 ENFORCEMENT) and proceedings in the High Court or a county court commence when an action commences. [*SSCBA 1992, s 12(7)*].

21.13 CLASS 3 CONTRIBUTIONS

Where a person wishes, and may be permitted, to pay CLASS 3 CONTRIBUTIONS (19), he may do so, since 6 April 1993, by either method (*a*) or (*b*) described at 21.11 above or by making a remittance at, or after the end of, the tax year to which they are to relate. If, for periods before 6 April 1993, contributions stamps were used, the rules described at 21.10 and 21.11 above in relation to contribution cards and contribution stamps then applied in their entirety. Until 6 April 1984, payment of Class 3 contributions was regarded as taking place only when a contribution card to which stamps had been affixed was surrendered to a DSS local office or to a DSS inspector or a remittance was received. From 6 April 1984 until 5 April 1993, payment took place when the stamp was affixed. The 'due date' for payment of a Class 3 contribution is not later than 42 days after the end of the tax year in respect of which it is paid but, since payment of Class 3 contributions cannot be enforced and since late paid contributions may, in certain circumstances, be admitted and will, if paid within the two tax years next following the tax year to which they relate, be payable at the rate at which they would have been payable had they been paid within the tax year to which they relate, the requirement is of little significance (see 39.5 and 39.7 LATE-PAID CONTRIBUTIONS). Furthermore, where a contributor shows to the satisfaction of the Inland Revenue that the late payment has been made through ignorance or error rather than through failure to exercise due care and diligence, the two-year time limit may be extended so that the contributor may pay the contributions at the original rate rather than a higher rate (see 39.7 LATE-PAID CONTRIBUTIONS). [*Contributions Regs, Regs 27(3)(a), 54(1), as amended by Contributions Amendment Regs 1984, Reg 14; Reg 43D and SSC(T)A 1999, 2 Sch*].

The established procedure whereby employers may make *annual* payments to the NICO in respect of the Class 3 contributions of their employees overseas is unaffected by the change to quarterly billing.

21.14 CLASS 4 CONTRIBUTIONS

Class 4 contributions are payable in the same manner as any income tax which is, or would be, chargeable in respect of the profits or gains which form the basis of assessment or self-assessment (whether or not income tax in fact falls to be paid) and are payable by the person on whom the income tax is (or would be) charged in accordance with assessment or self-assessment made under the Income Tax Acts (see 20.7 CLASS 4 CONTRIBUTIONS). [*SSCBA 1992, s 15(1)(2)(5)*]. Except where liability for such contributions has been deferred or the contributions are special Class 4 contributions, the provisions of those Acts as to collection and recovery apply, with necessary modifications, in relation to Class 4 contributions. Contributions are to be subject to the collection and recovery provisions of the Income Tax Acts *as if they were income tax* chargeable under Schedule D, Case I or II. It should be noted particularly that the penalty provisions of *TMA 1970, Pt X* apply to Class 4 contributions separately from the associated income tax liability. Therefore, a penalty for, e.g. failure to render a return, may be levied twice by some Inspectors of Taxes, who treat the failure as two separate contraventions in respect of income tax and contributions, despite the fact that only one return would, in fact, be made. (See 27.8 DEFERMENT OF PAYMENT and 21.16, 21.17 below). [*Sec 16(1)(2)(6)*].

Until the introduction of self-assessment in 1996–97, Class 4 contributions for a particular tax year are payable in two equal instalments, the first on or before

21.14 Collection

1 January falling within that tax year or, if later, at the expiration of a period of 30 days following the date of the issue of the notice of assessment and the second on or before the following 1 July or, if later, at the expiration of the 30 day period mentioned. [*ICTA 1988, s 5(2)*].

For 2000–01, under self-assessment, the Class 4 (and tax) demands will, in principle, be based on the following dates

31 January 2001	50% of the total income tax and Class 4 liability for 1999–2000 as finally computed
31 July 2001	50% of the total income tax and Class 4 liability for 1999–2000 as finally computed
31 January 2002	Balancing payment on tax and Class 4

Note that 31 January 2002 is also the first instalment date for NICs (and tax) for 2001–02 [*TMA 1970, s 59A* as amended by *FA 1995, 21 Sch 2(5)*].

Example
Brian commenced in business on 1 January 1996. In April 1997 his first year's accounts are agreed with the Inland Revenue and he receives notices of assessment dated 25 April 1997 which include Class 4 contributions as follows

	£
1995–96	18.00
1996–97	248.86

In August 1998, Brian completes his first self-assessment tax return. He computes his 1997–98 Class 4 liability to be £450.00. In July 1999, he completes his 1998-99 tax return and computes his Class 4 liability for that year to be £250.

The normal due dates for 1995–96 were 1 January 1996 and 1 July 1996, but these have both passed. The £18.00 Class 4 liability falls due, therefore, on 25 May 1997 being 30 days after the date of the notice of assessment. Of the normal due dates for 1996–97, 1 January 1997 has also passed and the first instalment of the £248.86 Class 4 liability (£124.43) also falls due, therefore, on 25 May 1997. The second instalment, however, does not fall due until 1 July 1997, i.e. its normal due date. The two interim payments of tax and NICs for 1997–98 will initially be based on the agreed assessment for 1996–97 and paid in equal instalments on 31 January 1998 and 31 July 1998. On 31 January 1999 Brian's tax payment included the balance of the 1997–98 Class 4 liability being £201.14 and the first instalment of the 1998–99 year, due on the same date, will include £225.00 in respect of Class 4 (i.e. 50% of the finally computed 1997–98 liability). On 31 July 1999 the second interim payment for 1998-99 of £225.00 is due. Having determined, however, that the 1998–99 actual liability of £250.00 is less than the scheduled interim payments, Brian may consider making a claim to reduce the payment due on 31 July 1999 so that he then pays only a further £25.00 on that date. In practice, Brian will consider both his income tax liability on those profits as well as income tax due on all other taxable income since, under self-assessment, the amount payable is considered globally and is not allocated to different sources of income or between income tax and Class 4 contributions. The final liability of £250.00 also fixes the interim payments for 31 January 2000 and 31 July 2000 i.e. £125.00 to be included in each instalment regarding Class 4 contributions.

Prior to self-assessment, a single payslip for each instalment covered, but distinguished between, the amounts due in respect of both income tax (if any) and Class 4 contributions, and a remittance was to be made in a single amount to the Collector of Taxes. This was to be so even where no income tax was payable.

For effective dates of payment see 21.3 above.

All sums received by the Collector of Taxes are initially paid into the Inland Revenue account but then, when directed to do so by the Treasury, the Inland Revenue accounted for, and paid over to, the Secretary of State, sums estimated to have been collected in respect of Class 4 contributions. [*SSCBA 1992, s 16(4) as repealed by SSC(T)A 1999, 3 Sch 16*].

Where, under the provisions of *ICTA 1988, s 559(4)* as amended by *FA 1996, s 72(3)* and *FA 1998, ss 55, 56, 8 Sch 2*, a contractor deducts from a payment made to a subcontractor under a contract relating to construction operations a sum equal to 18% (but see 38.4 LABOUR-ONLY CONTRACTORS) of so much of the payment as does not represent the direct cost of materials to be used in the construction operations and pays that sum over to the Inland Revenue, the excess (if any) of that sum over the subcontractor's liability to income tax in respect of his profits or gains is to be treated (to the extent of the subcontractor's liability, if any, for Class 4 contributions) as Class 4 contributions paid in respect of his profits or gains. (See also 38.4 LABOUR-ONLY CONTRACTORS). Where a return of deductions on form P35 (and, previously, SC35) is delayed and there is a claim that the failure to comply was 'minor and technical' any reason to expect that the obligations would not be timeously complied with will preclude relief. (*T & C Hill (Haulage) (a firm) v Glieg [2000] STI 162 Sp C 227*). [*ICTA 1988, ss 559(5)(8), 562(10) and Income Tax (Sub-contractors in the Construction Industry)(Amendment) Regs 1998, SI 1998 No 2622*].

Example
Chris has for some years been a labour-only subcontractor, but he does not possess an exemption certificate but does posses a registration card. His accounts for the year ended 30 June 2000 under the self-assessment rules show assessable profits of £13,000 for 2000–01. In the tax year 2000–01 he receives sub-contract payments from which £1,600 has been deducted at source. The position for 2000–01 is

	£	£
Schedule D, Case I profit	13,000	
Less: personal and other tax allowances	6,000	
Taxable income	7,000	
Tax liability: £1,520 @ 10%		
£5,480 @ 22%		1,357.60
Class 4 profit	13,000	
Less: lower annual limit	4,385	
	8,615	
Class 4 liability: £8,615 at 7%		603.05
		1,960.65
2000–01 deductions at source		1,600.00
Class 4 payable		£360.65

Note: the timing of the payment of £360.65 will be influenced by the size of the previous year's total liability and the interim payments resulting.

21.15 Assessments

Class 4 contributions are to be paid by the person from whom the corresponding income tax is (or, if there were any, would be) due. [*SSCBA 1992, s 15(1)(2)(5)*].

21.16 Special Class 4 contributions

Where a person is liable to pay special Class 4 contributions, the responsibility for collection of those contributions lies with the Inland Revenue NICO (see 20.5 CLASS 4 CONTRIBUTIONS). [*SSCBA 1992, s 18(2) as amended by SSC(T)A 1999, 3 Sch 18*].

21.17 Collection

The Inland Revenue NICO must notify the earner of the special Class 4 contribution due from him for the tax year concerned unless some other arrangement is made with the earner concerned. The earner must, unless he appeals against a decision of an officer of the Board of Inland Revenue, pay that contribution to the Inland Revenue within 28 days from the receipt of the notice (see APPEALS AND REVIEWS (9) and 21.18 below). [*Contributions Regs, Reg 74 as amended by SSC(T)A 1999, 2 Sch*].

21.17 Collection of deferred contributions

The assessment of an earner's profits or gains (and the earner's right of appeal against such an assessment) is unaffected by the issue of a certificate of deferment (see 27.10 DEFERMENT OF PAYMENT). However, the notice of assessment or, as applicable, the self-assessment is to show no figure representing Class 4 contributions payable and the collection provisions of the *Income Tax Acts* are *not* to apply. Instead, responsibility for the calculation, administration and recovery of Class 4 contributions ultimately payable in respect of the profits or gains assessed for the year of assessment to which the certificate of deferment relates is to pass to the Inland Revenue NICO. [*Contributions Regs, Reg 66(1) as amended by SSC(T)A 1999, 2 Sch*].

For the purpose of enabling the NICO to make the necessary calculations, the NICO may obtain from elsewhere in the Inland Revenue the amount of the earner's profits or gains (as adjusted for Class 4 purposes) or those adjusted profits or gains exceed the Class 4 upper annual limit, the fact that they do exceed that limit (see 30.8 EARNINGS LIMITS). [*Reg 66(3)(4) as amended by SSC(T)A 1999, 2 Sch*].

Any exception from Class 4 contribution liability available by reason of Class 1 contributions being paid on earnings chargeable to income tax under Case I or II of Schedule D is to be recognised in calculating an earner's Class 4 liability (see 20.4 CLASS 4 CONTRIBUTIONS). [*Reg 66(2)*].

When the NICO has made its calculation of the earner's liability for Class 4 contributions deferred but payable it must give the earner notice of the amount. [*Reg 66(5)*]. The earner must then, within 28 days of receipt of the notice, pay the stated amount before the expiry of that period, unless

(A) he disputes a decision of an officer of the Board of Inland Revenue by lodging an appeal (see APPEALS AND REVIEWS (9) and 21.18 below); or

(B) he has made some claim or late appeal which affects the certified profits or gains, and has notified the NICO that he has done so.

[*Contributions Regs, Reg 66(6) as amended by SSC(T)A 1999, 2 Sch*].

If the Inland Revenue makes any amendment to an assessment and that amendment affects the amount of profits or gains computed for Class 4 contribution purposes, the altered amount must be supplied forthwith to the earner and to the NICO. [*Reg 66(7) as amended by SSC(T)A 1999, 2 Sch*].

21.18 Collection of deferred or special Class 4 contributions after appeal

Following claims, appeals and (formerly) questions for determination, the earner will receive notice to pay the Class 4 contributions owing. The collection procedure is set out below.

Following

(*a*) a claim or appeal in connection with an assessment of deferred Class 4 contributions made by NICO (see 21.17 above); or

(*b*) an appeal in connection with special Class 4 contributions (see 21.16 above) the Inland Revenue NICO must, after the time stated below, give the earner notice (or revised notice) of such Class 4 contributions as are due from the earner, having regard to the outcome of the appeal, claim or determination. The earner must, within 28 days of receipt of that notice pay the amount specified. [*Contributions Regs, Reg 75(1)*].

The time after which notice or revised notice may be given is

(i) in the case of an altered amount of profits or gains being certified by the Inland Revenue, the date on which they are certified;

(ii) in the case of a late appeal (other than one resulting in (*a*)), the date of the determination of the appeal;

(iii) in the case of a claim or appeal against a decision on a claim made under the Income Tax Acts (other than one resulting in (*a*)), the date on which the time for appealing against the decision on the claim expires, or, if later, the date of the determination of the appeal;

(iv) in the case of a decision under *SSC(T)A 1999, s 8* by an officer of the Board of Inland Revenue, the date on which the time for appealing expires, or, if later, the date of the determination of the appeal.

[*Contributions Regs, Reg 75(2)*].

21.19 Enforcement

For the means of recovery available to the Inland Revenue where normal methods of collection fail, see ARREARS OF CONTRIBUTIONS (12) and ENFORCEMENT (32).

21.20 Interest and penalties

Interest can be charged under *TMA 1970, s 86* on overdue Class 4 contributions in just the same way as it is charged on overdue tax when the contribution is included in an assessment issued on or after 19 April 1993. From 6 April 1995, overpaid Class 4 contributions attract a repayment supplement under *ICTA 1988, s 824* upon repayment, although *Contributions Regs 1979, Reg 70* prevented the application of repayment supplement before that date. [*Contributions Amendment No 3 Regs 1995, Reg 2*]. The Inland Revenue have the same powers in relation to the remission of interest on Class 4 contributions under *TMA 1970, s 86* as they have in relation to the remission of interest on tax. [*SSCBA 1992, 2 Sch 6(1) and (2), Social Security (Consequential Provisions) Act 1992 Appointed Day Order 1993*].

Interest may also be charged on unpaid Class 4 contributions where the liability for those contributions arises as a result of a *tax* assessment being made to recover for the Crown a loss of tax wholly or partly attributable to the taxpayer's fault. (See Inspector's Manual, para 6035, issue 12/97). Then, the related Class 4 contributions will attract an interest charge just as the tax does, and the tax provisions relating to the discretionary mitigation of interest, the staying or compounding of proceedings for its recovery, and the determination of the date from which it is to run, are to apply as regards the interest on Class 4 contributions also. [*SSCBA 1992, 2 Sch 6 and Taxes (Interest Rate) (Amendment) Regulations 1999, SI 1999 No 419*].

Until 19 April 1993, the provisions of *TMA 1970, s 86* did not apply and the only way for the Inspector of Taxes to charge interest on Class 4 contributors paid late was under *s 88*. *Section 88* ceased to have effect upon the introduction of self-assessment for income tax (see below).

The provisions of *TMA 1970, Pt X* in relation to penalties for failure to make a return or for making a return fraudulently or negligently specifically apply as regards Class 4 contributions. [*SSCBA 1992, s 16(1)(2)(6)*]. It may also be that *TMA 1970, s 7* (failure to notify liability) applies because of the generality of the wording of *SSCBA 1992, s 16(1)(2)(6)*. (See 39.9 LATE-PAID CONTRIBUTIONS).

The *Social Security Act 1998* amends *SSCBA 1992, 2 Sch 6(1)* so that references to *TMA 1970, s 88* are repealed and the appointed day was 8 September 1998. [*SSCBA 1992, 2 Sch 6 as repealed by Social Security Act 1998, s 59*]. The repealed provisions are superfluous following the changes to the interest regime applicable to self-assessment. However, for the tax year 1996–97 *section 88* shall continue to apply where an assessment has been made for the purpose of making good to the Crown a loss of tax attributable to:

- a failure to give a notice;
- make a return, produce or furnish a document; or
- provide other information

under the Taxes Acts, or, an error in any information, return, accounts or other documents delivered to the Inland Revenue. The above provisions apply to a partnership whose trade, profession or business commenced before 6 April 1994.

21.21 CLASS 1A CONTRIBUTIONS

The collection provisions relating to Class 1A contributions are fully described at 16.18 CLASS 1A CONTRIBUTIONS. Due to the link between Class 1 and Class 1A in recording and enforcement procedures, the relevant Class 1A provisions may be found at 21.5 and 21.6 above.

21.22 CLASS 1B CONTRIBUTIONS

The collection provisions relating to Class 1B contributions are fully described at 17 CLASS 1B CONTRIBUTIONS. Due to the fact that Class 1B liability arises on the value of all items included in a PSA which would otherwise be liable for Class 1 or Class 1A contributions, interest is also due on unpaid tax on PSAs. Where interest has been paid by a secondary contributor the interest will be repaid where it is found not to have been due although the contribution in respect of which it was paid was due. Also, the interest will be repaid where the Class 1B contribution paid is returned or repaid in accordance with the provisions of *Regs 32* or *33A*. [*Social Security Contributions Statutory Maternity Pay and Statutory Sick Pay (Miscellaneous Amendments) Regs 1999, Reg 11*].

22   Company Directors

Cross-references. See AGE EXCEPTION (3); 4.3 AGENCY WORKERS for position where director obtains temporary employment through an agency; AGGREGATION OF EARNINGS (5); 12.4 ARREARS OF CONTRIBUTIONS for personal liability of directors for company contribution arrears; CATEGORISATION (14); CLASS 1 CONTRIBUTIONS (15); EARNINGS (28); 31.11 EARNINGS PERIODS; 44.2 MULTIPLE EMPLOYMENTS; 49.3 OVERSEAS MATTERS for position of non-resident director of a UK company; WORKING CASE STUDY (58).

Other Sources. Simon's NIC, Part I, Section 2, Chapters 7.191–7.230 and 11.1–11.70; Tolley's Tax Planning for Family Companies, para 5.9; Tolley's Tax Planning 2000–01; Tolley's National Insurance Brief, September 1996, pages 65–66 Tolley's Practical NIC Service, January 2000; Leaflet CA 44.

22.1   GENERAL CONSIDERATIONS

Because pre-1975 national insurance legislation did not bring office-holders within its definition of an employed earner, company directors who were *not* under contracts of service were, until 6 April 1975, regarded as self-employed earners (see CATEGORISATION (14) and *M4 (1950)* and *M10 (1950)*). The operation of *SSA 1975, s 2(1)(a)* (which re-defined an employed earner) brought this to an end, however, and, from 6 April 1975, *all* company directors who derive at least part of their remuneration from their office were (and continue to be) categorised as *employed earners*.

Such categorisation meant that all company directors became liable for Class 1 contributions on their earnings in accordance with the normal rules but that they alone among employed earners were in a position to exploit those rules by carefully contrived arrangements of salaries, bonuses and pay intervals. Attempts in 1980 by the DSS to render many such arrangements ineffective by a strict application of a court ruling on the meaning of 'payment' in relation to the voting of remuneration were largely unsuccessful (see 15.3 CLASS 1 CONTRIBUTIONS). Pressured by the Public Accounts Committee of the House of Commons in 1981 to bring to an end the avoidance by company directors of an estimated £8,000,000 per annum (see HC Paper 369 (1981–82)), the Secretary of State introduced regulations which came into effect on 6 April 1983 changing the basis on which the Class 1 liability of a director would, thereafter, arise (see 22.3 and 22.4 below).

On 31 January 1996 proposals were announced which would have, if implemented, eased from 6 April 1997 the administration procedures necessary to operate the special basis for directors. A Consultative Document was issued inviting comments by 29 March 1996. The result of the consultation was that the proposals were shelved in the light of the feedback received but similar provisions in the *Social Security Act 1998* enable, from 6 April 1999, contributions to be paid on account in the case of a company director. These provisions will place on a legal footing at least some of the practices adopted by employers in recent years.

[*Social Security Act 1998, s 49 and Social Security (Contributions) Amendment (No 3) Regs 1998, Reg 3 introducing new Reg 6A(6)*].

22.2   THE MEANING OF 'COMPANY DIRECTOR'

With effect from 6 April 1997 a director is defined for social security purposes as:

(*a*)   where a company is managed by a board or similar body, a member of that board or body;

(*b*)   where a company is managed by a single director or person, that person;

(c) any person in accordance with whose instructions the directors are accustomed to act.

In the case of (c), this will not apply if the other person's instructions are limited to professional advice e.g. a solicitor. [*Contributions Regs, Reg 1(2), as amended by Contributions Amendment (No 5) Regs 1996, Reg 2*].

This definition bears a close resemblance to that in *ICTA 1988, s 202B(5) and (6)*, although, interestingly, it differs in that for tax purposes where a company's affairs are managed by the members themselves such members are 'directors'. This does not apply for NIC purposes.

A director is *not* a company director for social security contribution purposes if the company in relation to which he is a director is *neither*

(a) a company within the meaning of *Companies Act 1985, s 735(1)*; *nor*

(b) a body corporate to which, by virtue of *CA 1985, s 718*, any provision of *CA 1985* applies.

[*Contributions Regs, Reg 1(2), as amended by Contributions Amendment Regs 1983, Reg 2*]. A director of a non-British based foreign company or of an unincorporated association is, therefore, outside the definition of company director. So, too, is the director of a building society within the meaning of *Building Societies Act 1986* unless of course, the society has de-mutualised. (Leaflet CA 44, Para 4). But see 22.5 below for an exception to this rule.

There was, until 6 April 1997 (see below), no substantive definition of the term 'company director' either in social security legislation or in company legislation but the DSS took it to mean 'a person who occupies the position, or exercises the function, of a director of a company within the meaning of *Section 735 of the Companies Act 1985*, whether or not the appointment as a director is in accordance with the provisions of the Act' (CA 44 April 1995 edition – now superseded, Para 3) i.e., the definition of a director in *section 741 of the Companies Act 1985* was not considered to apply. In a letter to the author of 14 August 1990, the DSS said that its lawyers had confirmed that 'the restrictive interpretation of a "director" in the [then] current edition of NI 35' (i.e. a person appointed under *CA 1985, ss 291–294*) 'will not prevent the Department from taking enforcement action in appropriate cases'.

Whether the DSS's position as clarified above is correct or not is a matter of conjecture. In *Re Lo-Line Electric Motors Ltd* [1988] 2 AER 692 it was confirmed that the word 'director' when used without qualification or definition is capable of including *de facto* directors, but whether it does so or not in any specific instance depends on the context. If the context is penal, a strict construction might be necessary (and that would exclude *de facto* directors); but where the context is non-penal, the word 'director' probably includes a person validly appointed a director, a person invalidly appointed a director, and a person merely *de facto* acting as director. Thus, in relation to the matters with which this chapter is concerned and in relation to periods prior to 6 April 1997, the word should be widely construed, but in relation to the penal provisions described at 12.4 ARREARS OF CONTRIBUTIONS a narrow construction is, arguably, to be preferred.

22.3 EARNINGS

Every company director is, *ipso facto*, an office-holder. (*McMillan v Guest* [1942] 1 AER 606, per Lord Atkin). But that leaves open the question whether he derives his remuneration from his office or from a contract of service or even a contract for services with the company concerned. In *Allen v Minister of National Insurance (1956) QBD reported as M59 (1958)*, for instance, it was held that although Mr Allen was chairman and director of a company called Woodcrafts (Leigh-on-Sea) Ltd in which he held all but one of the shares, he derived his remuneration not from his office but from a contract with the company for his services as a self-employed woodworker. More frequently, an executive director of a company will be found to derive his remuneration from a contract of service with the company in which he also holds office. (*Lee v Lee's Air Farming Ltd [1960] 3 AER 420; Ferguson v Telford Greir Mackay & Co Ltd (1967) 2 ITR 387; Eaton v Robert Eaton Ltd [1988] ICR 302*).

The distinction may be more important than is generally recognised. If a company director derives all his remuneration from a contract *for services*, he is a *self-employed earner* for contribution purposes because he is not 'gainfully employed . . . under a contract of service or in an office . . . with emoluments' (see 14.2 CATEGORISATION). And, if that is so, the special rules which, from 6 April 1983, govern the calculation of earnings for contribution purposes, are, it seems, of no application. (See below.)

The treatment of the earnings of company directors who derive all their earnings from their office, or derive it partly from their office and partly from a contract of service, has varied over the years.

Between 6 April 1975 and 1 September 1980, a fee-paid director was treated, for both PAYE and contribution purposes, as receiving earnings on each occasion of payment during a tax year, even though the payment would usually be an advance drawing of the amount to be voted to the director for the year at some future date. Only the amount of any undrawn balance of the voted fees would then be earnings at the date of voting. The latter payment was regarded as annual and the earlier advances were, if made monthly, regarded as monthly payments, and, thus the way was open for the avoidance or reduction of contribution liability by advantageous use of the earnings period rules (see 31.3 EARNINGS PERIODS).

In a press release dated 1 September 1980, the DSS announced that this treatment of advance drawings was incorrect in law and that fees would, in future, not be regarded as earnings for contribution purposes until voted and placed unreservedly at the disposal of the directors concerned. Advance drawings of such fees (though still subject to PAYE) would accordingly be *disregarded* for contribution purposes. Although this brought the treatment of directors' fees into conformity with general law on the payment of earnings, it was difficult both to apply and to enforce and widespread contribution avoidance continued (see 22.1 above and 15.3 CLASS 1 CONTRIBUTIONS: EMPLOYED EARNERS). New rules were introduced, therefore, legitimately to place the treatment of directors' fees on their old (incorrect) basis and to impose an *annual* earnings period (see 31.11 EARNINGS PERIODS) on all directors.

Thus, *from 6 April 1983*, any payment made by a company to or for the benefit of any of its directors is to be treated as remuneration derived from employed earner's employment if that payment would not otherwise be earnings for contribution purposes but is made on account of, or by way of an advance on, a sum which would be earnings for contribution purposes. [*SSCBA 1992, s 4(5); Contributions Regs, Reg 17A, as amended by Contributions Amendment Regs 1983, Reg 5*]. This rule has led to a number of difficulties over the last 17 years which are discussed below in relation to directors' current accounts and loan accounts.

It should be noted that the tax treatment of a director's earnings, which used to differ significantly from the national insurance contributions treatment of those same earnings, has now been broadly aligned with the established NIC treatment, although minor differences remain. With effect from 6 April 1989, the basis of taxation of directors' emoluments was changed to that set out in *ICTA 1988, ss 202A, 202B* (created by *FA 1989, s 37*). Broadly, Schedule E emoluments, except for pensions and social security benefits, are now assessed for the tax year in which they are received, rather than for the tax year to which they relate. The change in the overall basis of assessment is also reflected in the introduction by *FA 1989, s 45* of a definition of the time when emoluments are treated as paid for the purposes of the PAYE collection system.

22.3　Company Directors

While *s 202A* taxes emoluments of an office or employment on the basis of their receipt, it relies on the definition in *s 202B* of the time of receipt. This can be summarised in the case of directors as the earlier or earliest of the following times:

(*a*)　when payment is made of or on account of the emoluments;

(*b*)　when a person becomes entitled to payment of or on account of the emoluments;

(*c*)　when sums on account of emoluments are credited to the director's current or loan account by the company;

(*d*)　where the amount of the emoluments for a period is determined before the period ends, the time when the period ends; and/or

(*e*)　where the amount of the emoluments for a period is not known until the amount is determined after the period has ended, the time when the amount is determined.

The PAYE rules introduced by *FA 1989, s 45* simply restate rules (*a*) and (*b*) above to 'the time when payment is actually made' and 'the time when a person becomes entitled to the payment' respectively, and broadly copy rules (*c*) to (*e*).

It will be noted that the effect of the above rules is to charge emoluments to income tax when payment is made, whether already earned or on account of a sum which will be earnings in due course. This results in a situation broadly similar to that for national insurance contribution purposes, which arises from the combination of the rule established in *Garforth v Newsmith Stainless Ltd [1979] 2 AER 73* (see 15.3) and *Reg 17A* outlined above.

However, it should not be overlooked that rule (*d*) above is likely to be the rule which conflicts most readily with the national insurance contribution law as follows.

Example
Gary Newsmith is a director of Lesstain Ltd. L has an accounting date of 5 July. G has no balance standing to his credit with L at 6 July 2000 and fees already voted and paid have exactly equalled his drawings up to that date. G has substantial earnings from other sources and takes only one payment annually from L in respect of his services. A meeting is held on 4 April 2001 at which G's fees for the year ending 5 July 2001 are determined at £10,000, but this amount is neither credited to his current account nor made available to him. Due to cash flow problems and the desire to tie G to the company, it is agreed that G will only become entitled to his emoluments on 1 October 2001.

Under the *FA 1989* rules, G is taxable under Schedule E in 2001–02, since that is the year in which the end of the accounting period falls, and L has to apply PAYE to the emoluments on 5 July 2001, despite the fact that G may not draw the emoluments before 1 October 2001. When that date arrives, L must deduct and account for National Insurance contributions, since it is only then that the money is put unreservedly at G's disposal.

The above example is, of course, somewhat contrived and in reality there is likely to be little doubt about when PAYE and NICs are to be applied to a director's earnings and about the year into which earnings then fall. See earlier editions of this work for the contrast between the pre-6 April 1989 tax rules and the national insurance rules.

If fees are voted to a director in advance, the fees will become earnings for contribution purposes on the date when he has an unreserved right to draw them.

Example
Dawn is a director of East Ltd. On 31 March 2000 E votes fees to D of £800 payable on the last Friday in each month for the next twelve months. D will have earnings for contribution purposes thus:

	£
28 April 2000	800
26 May 2000	800
23 June 2000	800
etc.	

Difficulties with National Insurance contribution liabilities arising from the operation of directors' current accounts were referred to above. For a full discussion of earlier DSS policies, please refer to past editions of this work.

The difficulty is caused by the fact that the typical close company director does not have a service contract and is remunerated in accordance with the Articles of Association. The standard 'Table A' articles under *Companies (Tables A to F) Regs 1985* provide: '82 The directors shall be entitled to such remuneration as the company may by ordinary resolution determine and, unless the resolution provides otherwise, the remuneration shall be deemed to accrue from day to day.' This leads to a situation in many companies where the owner-directors simply take money as needed during the year, debiting the drawings to a drawings or current account and bringing that account back into credit by voting remuneration at the AGM, when the accounts for the year are approved.

Clearly, a drawing by a director in *repayment of a loan* which he had earlier made to the company is *not* earnings since it is not a payment of earnings or a payment on account of a sum which would be earnings. Where a director's account goes into credit following the AGM, subsequent drawings against the *credit* balance are irrelevant for contributions purposes. However, if the account becomes overdrawn, or further overdrawn, as a result of the debiting of a particular transaction by the director, *Reg 17A* becomes relevant.

Whether the director draws cash, equivalent to salary, or uses a company cheque to settle a personal bill, the company must consider whether the debiting of the transaction to the director's account constitutes a payment of earnings or deemed earnings. In other words, does the payment represent remuneration or profit derived from the employment, or an advance on such remuneration which would be treated as earnings by *Reg 17A*?

Because *Reg 17A* deems certain payments to be liable when they otherwise would not be so liable, care is needed to avoid double counting when fees are voted into such an account. Earnings are only liable once to Class 1 contributions, so any amounts charged under *Reg 17A* must be excluded from earnings when fees are later voted into the account to clear or reduce the overdrawn balance.

In the past, the DSS misinterpreted the series of transactions which has taken place, insisting for a time that any payment of a director's personal bill was a payment of earnings, even if the bill was paid using money which already stood to the director's credit in a current account and which had already suffered a Class 1 liability at the time of credit to the account. The policy was revised in a 1994 supplement to the Manual for Employers on NIC for company directors, NI 35, and the new policy is set out in some detail in paras 30–31 of CA 44.

The DSS subsequently accepted that, if a director's personal bill is paid by the company, liability will arise only if and to the extent that:

- the payment is treated by the company as remuneration and charged to the profit and loss account as such; or

- the payment is charged to the director's account with the company *and* the transaction makes the account overdrawn or further overdrawn *and* it is anticipated that the drawing is on account of an amount which will be voted into the account as earnings in due course.

Debiting amounts for cash drawings or personal bills to the account which leave it in credit will not constitute paying earnings. Similarly, debiting cash drawings or personal bills to the account which create or increase an overdrawn balance will not constitute earnings *provided* the overdrawing is not in anticipation of the future crediting of remuneration. If a director intends to clear the overdrawn balance by the introduction of cash from another source (e.g. dividends, matured life assurance policies, legacies, or other personal income), *Reg 17A* is of no application and there can be no Class 1 liability. Remuneration taken in a form which does not constitute earnings for contribution purposes might also be used to clear the balance.

The DSS went further in the April 1995 edition of Leaflet CA 44 and the Inland Revenue has put its name to the same viewpoint in subsequent editions of CA 44. If a director draws money out of a current account making it overdrawn or further overdrawn and the director does not normally receive advance or anticipatory payments of remuneration, the amount overdrawn will not be regarded as earnings unless the company authorises payment of the amounts overdrawn. Authorisation may be in writing or by the other directors agreeing verbally that they know about the situation. According to the CA 44, Para 31 guidance, Class 1 liability arises at the point where the amounts overdrawn are authorised.

This guidance is based correctly on the premise that, if a director takes money from the company, the payment to him cannot represent a payment of earnings if it is unauthorised. As was explained above, payment may take place only when an amount is placed unreservedly at the disposal of the director, so any unauthorised payment cannot constitute payment. An authorised drawing on account of future remuneration will be liable. However, the guidance is nevertheless flawed in that it ignores the requirements of *Reg 17A* when dealing with an authorised payment. If an 'authorised' drawing is made in the knowledge that it will be debited to the director's account and the balance will be cleared in due course by something other than a vote of remuneration (e.g. dividends), *Reg 17A* cannot apply to treat the payment as an advance on future earnings. There can accordingly be no Class 1 liability on the authorised drawing.

In typical situations, the position may be summarised by the following examples.

(a) *Account overdrawn, fees etc. credited.* To the extent that the items creating the overdraft have already been treated as earnings for contribution purposes (see (c) and (d) below), the fees etc. credited will *not* be earnings for contribution purposes, but any other part of the fees etc. credited will be earnings. (CA 44, Para 30).

Example
Sherlock is a director of Holmes Ltd. On 24 July 2000, his current account with H is overdrawn by £2,800 of which £2,000 has been treated as earnings for contribution purposes. On 25 July 2000, fees of £30,000 are voted to him and credited to the account. £28,000 of those fees are earnings for contribution purposes.

(b) *Account in credit, fees etc. credited.* The whole of the fees credited will be earnings for contribution purposes. (CA 44, Para 30).

(c) *Account overdrawn, items debited.* All the items debited will be earnings for contribution purposes as long as the drawing is made in anticipation of an earnings payment (e.g. fees or bonuses). (CA 44, Para 30).

Example
Watson is a director of Elementary Ltd. On 22 June 2000, his current account with E is overdrawn by £5,000. On 23 June 2000, E pays W cash of £4,000. The £4,000 is debited to his account. The whole £4,000 is earnings for contribution purposes.

(*d*) *Account in credit, items debited.* To the extent that the total of the items debited do not exhaust the credit balance, they will *not* be earnings for contribution purposes, but to the extent that they throw the account out of credit and into overdraft they will be earnings as long as the drawing is made in anticipation of an earnings payment (e.g. fees or bonuses). (CA 44, Para 30).

Example
Moriarty is a director of Reichenbach Ltd. On 22 August 2000, his current account with R is in credit to the tune of £3,700. On 23 August 2000, R pays M cash of £5,000. The £5,000 is debited to his account. Only £1,300 is earnings for contribution purposes.

In (*c*) and (*d*) above, it is assumed that the director concerned was *authorised* to receive the amounts paid to him or *authorised* to have amounts paid to others on his behalf.

It must be stressed that the absence of, or lateness of, accounting entries relating to a director's current or drawings account will have no bearing on the date on which payments fall to be regarded as earnings. If a company pays cash to a director on 19 September 2000, that is the date on which (depending on the true state of the director's current account with the company on that date) earnings equal to the payment are paid to the director. Likewise, if fees are voted to the director unconditionally on 17 October 2000, that is the date on which (again subject to the true state of his current account up to that date) those fees are earnings paid to him.

For the treatment of fees paid to nominee directors see 28.74 EARNINGS.

It should be noted that, until 31 March 1989, where a disallowance of director's remuneration for corporation tax purposes was negotiated with the Inspector of Taxes and the amount disallowed was formally waived and refunded to the company by the director so as to obtain a reduction in the Schedule E liability equivalent to the amount disallowed (see Inland Revenue Press Release 6 November 1967, later incorporated in Statement of Practice C4 Para 4), the DSS was not permitted to allow any similar reduction in Class 1 contribution liabilities (see 37.5 INLAND REVENUE). Thus, a director who, by reason of such a waiver, reduced his fees below the upper earnings limit for a tax year would pay primary Class 1 contributions on some part, if not all, of the earnings which he had refunded to the company, and the company would suffer secondary Class 1 contributions on the whole of the amount refunded. (CA 44, Para 30). Although close company apportionment was abolished in 1989 and SP/C4 was withdrawn, it became clear from ICAEW Tax Faculty Technical Release Tax 11/93, para 38, that the practice outlined in SP/C4, para 4, still applies and that waivers are still used in exceptional circumstances, despite the fact that Class 1 liabilities have arisen. Such liabilities will be avoided only if it can successfully be argued that the fees waived were never freely available to the director concerned but had been voted only on condition that the director would not be free to draw upon them until a deduction from profits for corporation tax purposes in respect of those fees had been agreed by the Inland Revenue (see 15.3 CLASS 1 CONTRIBUTIONS).

Although what is now *SSCBA 1992, 1 Sch 8(1)(h)* contains provision for refunds to be made of contributions paid by reference to earnings which have become repayable, the DSS made it known that it would use this power only in connection with repayments of contractual maternity pay (i.e. where an earner on maternity leave receives pay from her employer and, on deciding not to return to work, is obliged to refund the wages paid to her). [*Refunds (Repayment of Contractual Maternity Pay) Regs 1990*].

22.4   CALCULATION OF CONTRIBUTIONS

Calculation of primary and secondary Class 1 contribution liabilities in respect of the earnings of a company director proceeds largely in the same manner as does the calculation of contribution liabilities in respect of the earnings of any other employed earner. However, the following special rules apply:

(*a*) payments made to a company director may be regarded as earnings for contribution purposes before they would be so regarded in general law (see 22.3 above); *and*

(*b*) a company director's *earnings period* will be a *year* (or, if he is appointed a director during the course of a year, so much of the tax year as remains), whether or not he remains a director throughout the year or throughout so much of it as remains after his appointment (see 31.11 EARNINGS PERIODS); *and*

(*c*) where a company director has one or more other employed earner's employments the earnings of which fall to be aggregated with his earnings as a company director, special rules are to apply as to the length of the common earnings period (see 5.10 AGGREGATION OF EARNINGS); *and*

(*d*) a company director's earnings period will be a *year* in respect of any earnings paid to him in any tax year *after he ceases to be a director* if those earnings relate to a period during which he was a director (see 31.11 EARNINGS PERIODS), and such earnings are under no circumstances to be aggregated with other earnings (see 5.8 AGGREGATION OF EARNINGS).

[*Contributions Regs, Regs 6A, 17A, as amended by Contributions Amendment Regs 1983, Regs 4, 5*].

The combined effect of (*a*) and (*b*) above is to require Class 1 contributions in respect of each payment of earnings made to a company director during a tax year to be paid to the Collector of Taxes within 14 days of the end of the tax month (or, if quarterly payments are permitted, the quarter) in which each such payment of earnings is made, but to require the amount of contribution liability in respect of each such payment to be calculated by reference to the *annual* upper and lower earnings limit and earnings threshold applicable for the tax year as a whole in which the payments fall (see 21.3 COLLECTION and EARNINGS LIMITS AND THRESHOLDS (30)). This being so, neither the normal exact percentage method nor the normal tables method of calculation may be used (see 15.5 CLASS 1 CONTRIBUTIONS: EMPLOYED EARNERS). Instead, a modified version of one or the other method must be applied.

The *modified exact percentage method* requires the carrying-out of the following procedure on each occasion of payment of earnings to a director during 2000–01.

(i) Add the amount of the payment of earnings in question to the total of all other payments of earnings to the director since 6 April 2000 or, if he was not appointed director until after 6 April 2000, since the date of his appointment.

(ii) Compare the total arrived at in (i) with the annual (or, where the director was appointed after the start of the tax year, pro-rata annual) lower and upper earnings limits and employee's and employer's earnings thresholds for the tax year in which the payment falls (see 30.3 EARNINGS LIMITS AND THRESHOLDS).

(iii) If the total arrived at in (i)

(A) does not exceed the lower earnings limit arrived at in (ii), proceed no further for there is *no* liability on any of the payments to date in the tax year, including the payment in question nor do any entries fall to be made on the P11 deductions working sheet;

(B) equals or exceeds the lower earnings limit but does not exceed the employee's earnings threshold, there is *no* liability on any of the payments to date in the tax year, including the payment in question, *but* entries will fall to be made in columns 1a and 1b on the P11 deductions working sheet;

(C) exceeds the employee's earnings threshold but does not exceed the upper earnings limit arrived at in (ii), calculate contribution liabilities on the *total* arrived at in (i) (albeit that the secondary contribution will amount to nil if the annual—or pro-rata annual, as the case may be—employer's earnings threshold has not been exceeded) and *deduct* therefrom the contribution liabilities already accounted for on *all* previous payments of earnings contained in the total. The remainders are the contribution liabilities on the payment in question;

(D) exceeds the upper earnings limit arrived at in (ii), calculate the primary Class 1 contribution liability on an amount equal to the upper earnings limit as arrived at in (ii) and the secondary Class 1 contribution liability on the total amount arrived at in (i), then *deduct* from the contribution liabilities so calculated the contribution liabilities already accounted for on *all* previous payments of earnings contained in the total. The remainders are the contribution liabilities on the payment in question.

The *modified tables method* also requires step (i) above to be taken, but then, if the director concerned was a director at the beginning of the tax year, the total thus arrived at has to be *divided by 12*. If the director concerned was not appointed a director until after the start of the tax year, the total arrived at in (i) has to be divided by the number of remaining contribution weeks in the tax year including that in which his appointment took place. An average monthly (or, as the case may be, weekly) amount is thus obtained based on earnings to date. The monthly (or, as the case may be, weekly) contribution tables (and, if necessary, the contribution calculator located at the end of the contribution tables) is then used to ascertain the primary and secondary Class 1 contribution liabilities appropriate to such average earnings, *and those liabilities must then be multiplied by the divisor* which was used to obtain those average earnings. The total contribution liabilities already accounted for on the total earnings arrived at in (i) has then to be deducted from the total contribution liabilities thus calculated and the remainders are the contribution liabilities due on the payment of earnings in question. Where the average earnings exceed the highest band figure in the contribution tables, that highest band figure has to be used to ascertain the primary Class 1 contribution liability in the manner described and, thereafter, no further such liability will arise whether further earnings are paid to the director during the remainder of the tax year or not. Secondary Class 1 liabilities continue to arise whenever earnings are paid but if the average earnings exceed the highest band figure in the contribution tables, the contribution calculator located at the end of the contribution tables has to be used to determine the extent of that secondary Class 1 liability. (Leaflet CA 44, Paras 39 to 44).

Example
Frederick is appointed a director of Great Ltd on 1 November 2000. There are 23 whole or part contribution weeks left in 2000–01, not counting for this purpose the one day which constitutes week 53 (Leaflet CA 44, Para 23) and his earnings period as a director is, therefore, 23 weeks. As the employee's weekly earnings threshold and the employee's upper earnings limit for 2000–01 are £76.00 and £535.00 respectively, F's earnings threshold and upper earnings limit are £1,748.00 (i.e. £76.00 × 23) and £12,305.00 (i.e. £535.00 × 23). The employer's earnings threshold is £1,932 (i.e. £84 × 23) after which the earnings are subject to the 12.2% rate. (The calculation of these limits and thresholds is necessary only if contributions in respect of earnings are to be calculated by use of the modified exact percentage method.) Not contracted–out earnings are paid to F as follows:

22.4 Company Directors

Date	Payment £	Cumulative £
30 November	700	700
31 December	800	1,500
31 January	5,000	6,500
29 February	900	7,400
31 March	2,700	10,100

Contributions could be calculated by use of either the *modified exact percentage method* or the *modified tables method*.

The *modified exact percentage procedure* would operate thus:

Cum. pay £		Cum. primary £	Primary payable £	Cum. secondary £	Secondary payable £
700		—	—	—	—
1,500	Nil% × £1,500	—	—	—	—
6,500	Nil% × £1,748				
	10% × £4,752	475.20	475.20		
	Nil% × £1,932				
	12.2% × £4,568			557.30	557.30
7,400	Nil% × £1,748				
	10% × £5,652	565.20	90.00		
	Nil% × £1,932				
	12.2% × £5,468			667.10	109.80
10,100	Nil% × £1,748				
	10% × £8,352	835.20	270.00		
	Nil% × £1,932				
	12.2% × £8,168			996.50	329.40
			£835.20		£996.50

Alternatively, the *modified tables procedure* could have operated, thus:

Cum.Pay ÷ 23 £	Weekly table band £	Primary per table × 23 £	Primary payable £	Secondary per table × 23 £	Secondary payable £
30.43	—	—	—	—	—
65.22	—	—	—	—	—
282.61	282.00	474.95	474.95	557.06	557.06
321.74	321.00	564.65	89.70	666.31	109.25
439.13	439.00	836.05	271.40	997.51	331.20
			£836.05		£997.51

It will be noted that there are only minor discrepancies between the two results.

Because it will very often be some time before a director's earnings in a tax year reach the employee's earnings threshold for that year, the authorities are agreeable to amounts of contributions being paid on account during that period of nil liability. Furthermore, if the level of earnings which a director will attain by the end of the tax year can be estimated with some degree of certainty, the authorities are agreeable to the primary and secondary Class 1 contribution rates appropriate to earnings at that anticipated level being applied throughout the year. The effect of both practices will be to spread contribution liabilities as evenly as possible over the period to the date on which the director's earnings reach the UEL for the director himself. (CA 44, Paras 45 to 49). If contribution-spreading of the type permitted is put into effect but, for some reason, the anticipated level of earnings is not attained, any overpayment of contributions which arises will be repayable. (Leaflet CA 44, Paras 49 and 65).

The DSS did not consent to contribution liability being spread evenly over the whole earnings period if this would result in less contributions being accounted for than were actually due. However, from 6 April 1999 payments may be made on account provided that there is a regular pattern of payments to the director, they exceed the relevant lower earnings limit and the director agrees to this method being adopted (CA 44, Paras 6 to 9). [*Reg 6A, as inserted by Social Security (Contributions) Amendment (No 3) Regs 1998, Reg 3*].

The above procedures are as set out in CA 44, Paras 38 to 44 and CWG1 (2000), Card 12 but the modified tables procedure will, in fact, give rise to small excess payments of secondary contributions since the annual and monthly earnings thresholds have been set specially for 2000–01 at £4,385 and £365 respectively, rather than the usual 52 or 4 1/3 times the weekly limit (see 30 EARNINGS LIMITS AND THRESHOLDS).

22.5 **NON-EXECUTIVE AND NOMINEE DIRECTORS**

Contribution liabilities in respect of earnings paid to a non-executive director are to be calculated and discharged in just the same way as they would be calculated and discharged in the case of any other director, except, from 6 January 1988, where

(*a*) the director is a partner in a firm carrying on a profession, and

(*b*) being a director of a company is a normal incident of membership of that profession and of membership of the director's firm, and

(*c*) the director is required by the terms of his partnership to account to his firm for the payment, and

(*d*) the payment forms an insubstantial part of the gross returns of the firm.

In such circumstances, the payments made to the director are to be excluded from his earnings for contribution purposes. [*Contributions Regs, Reg 19B(1)(2) as inserted by Contributions Amendment No 4 Regs 1987, Reg 4*]. (CA 44, Para 55). Instead, the payments will be included in the Schedule D profits subject to Class 4 liability as part of the profits of the partnership. *Reg 19B(1)(2)* gives legal force to an extra-statutory concession (almost matching IR ESC A37 (1980), Para 1) which has been available since 6 April 1984. (See 37.4 INLAND REVENUE.) Further, from 6 April 1996, for the purpose of *Reg 19B* only, 'company' is defined so as to match the definition in *ICTA 1988, s 832(1)(2)*. [*Social Security (Contributions) Amendment (No 3) Regulations 1996, Reg 3*].

From 6 April 1991, this rule applies not only to company directors but also to building society directors. [*Contributions Regs, Reg 19B(5) as amended by Contributions Amendment No 3 Regs 1991, Reg 2*].

It should be noted that neither the law nor the concession applies where a non-executive director, although holding his directorship as an incident of his profession, is a *sole practitioner*. In such a case, fees paid to him in his capacity as a non-executive director are liable to Class 1 contributions in the normal way. If such a practitioner chooses to include as a receipt of his practice fees which he has received in his capacity as a non-executive director, he will render those fees—which will already have suffered a primary Class 1 deduction—liable, as part of his profits or gains, to CLASS 4 CONTRIBUTIONS (20). In such circumstances he may be excepted from part of his Class 4 liability (see 20.4 CLASS 4 CONTRIBUTIONS). However, certain payments to nominee directors and also professional advisers (fees) come within ESC A37 and will be excluded from Class 1 liability but may be included as self-employed earnings for Class 2/4 NIC purposes (see CA Press Release 96/1, 15 March 1996).

22.6   Company Directors

Nominee directors who do not benefit personally from the fees paid for their services are also covered by *Reg 19B*. The exclusion of their fees from earnings is discussed at 28.74 EARNINGS. See also CA 44, Para 58.

22.6 MULTIPLE DIRECTORSHIPS

Where a person is both a director and an employee of but a single company, his earnings in both capacities must be aggregated for contribution purposes (see AGGREGATION OF EARNINGS (5)). (Leaflet CA 44, Para 51). If, however, his directorships (other than nominee directorships—see 28.74 EARNINGS) and/or employments extend to more than one company, contribution liabilities will arise in each company in respect of his earnings from that company without regard to his earnings from the other company or companies (see 15.2 CLASS 1 CONTRIBUTIONS) *unless* the circumstances are such that AGGREGATION OF EARNINGS (5) may, or must, take place. (Leaflet CA 44, Paras 52–54).

22.7 DIRECTORS WHO ARE ALSO SELF-EMPLOYED

A company director who is also a self-employed earner will generally be liable for Class 1, Class 2 and Class 4 contributions if, in the case of Class 1 and Class 4, his earnings reach a sufficiently high level for such liabilities to arise (see EARNINGS LIMITS AND THRESHOLDS (30)). He will not be so liable if he is not normally self-employed (see 14.10 CATEGORISATION) or has been *excepted* from, or has *deferred*, his Class 2 and/or Class 4 liabilities (see 18.3 CLASS 2 CONTRIBUTIONS; 20.3 CLASS 4 CONTRIBUTIONS; 27.8 DEFERMENT OF PAYMENT). If, however, the total contributions paid exceed the ANNUAL MAXIMUM (7) he will be able to obtain repayment of the excess (see 53.5 REPAYMENT AND RE-ALLOCATION).

In the Budget statement on 9 March 1999 it was announced that the hiring of individuals through their own service companies will, from 6 April 2000, no longer benefit from the fiscal advantages offered by a corporate structure. The use of such personal service companies has resulted in less tax and NICs being paid. It is intended that the changes will ensure that people working in such 'disguised employment' will be paying the same tax and NICs as someone employed directly. see Personal Service Companies in 14.7 CATEGORISATION, CWG2 (2000), Page 86 and Employer's Bulletin Issue 4, February 2000, Page 11.

22.8 CHANGES DURING THE EARNINGS PERIOD

Where, after 6 April 1983, a director attains pensionable age during the course of a tax year, his earnings period is, according to normal rules, the tax year during which the change occurs, but the only earnings to be taken into account for *primary* Class 1 contribution purposes are those both paid and due for payment before pensionable age is attained and those paid after pensionable age is attained but due for payment before that date (see 3.7 AGE EXCEPTION). (CA 44, Para 61).

Where, during the course of a tax year, the *reduced liability election* of a director who is a married woman or widow ceases to be valid (see 52.5 REDUCED LIABILITY ELECTION), standard rate primary Class 1 contributions are payable on all earnings paid after the date on which the reduced rate certificate is cancelled. (CA 44, Para 62).

Where, during the course of a tax year, a director's employment changes from CONTRACTED-OUT EMPLOYMENT (23) to not contracted-out employment, or *vice versa* and total earnings reach or exceed the annual (or pro-rata annual) employee's earnings threshold but contracted-out earnings do not reach or exceed that amount, the primary Class 1 liability for the year will be arrived at by applying the not contracted-out primary percentage to the chargeable earnings up to and including the annual (or pro-rata annual) upper earnings limit (i.e. those exceeding the lower earnings limit).The secondary liability will be arrived at by applying the secondary not contracted-out percentage to the earnings which exceed the earnings threshold.

If there is such a change but contracted-out earnings reach or exceed the annual (or pro-rata annual) employee's earnings threshold then (unless the director has an approved personal pension scheme—see below) the primary Class 1 liability for the year will be arrived at by

(a) treating the employee's earnings threshold as comprising wholly contracted-out earnings,

(b) then applying the primary contracted-out percentage to the balance of contracted-out earnings up to and including the annual (or pro-rata annual) upper earnings limit, and

(c) then applying the primary not contracted-out percentage to any balance of not contracted-out earnings up to and including the annual (or pro-rata annual) upper earnings limit.

The secondary liability will be arrived at by applying the secondary contracted-out percentage to the contracted-out earnings which exceed the employer's earnings threshold and the secondary not contracted-out percentage to the not contracted-out earnings.

If there is such a change where contracted-out earnings reach or exceed the annual (or pro-rata annual) employee's earnings threshold and the director has an appropriate personal pension, the primary Class 1 liability for the year will be arrived at by applying

(a) the not contracted-out percentage to the chargeable not contracted-out earnings up to and including the annual (or pro-rata annual) upper earnings limit (i.e. those exceeding the employee's earnings threshold), and

(b) the contracted-out percentage to any balance of contracted-out earnings up to and including the annual (or pro-rata annual) upper earnings limit.

The secondary liability will be arrived at by applying the not contracted-out percentage to the not contracted-out earnings exceeding the employer's earnings threshold and the contracted-out percentage to the contracted-out earnings.

It should be noted that a director who chooses to contract out with an appropriate personal pension continues to pay contributions at the not contracted-out rates (Table A). This would *not* therefore be a 'change in employment status' for the purpose of the rules described above. Those rules would, however, become relevant if the director ceased to contribute to the personal pension and joined the company's contracted-out occupational scheme. (CA 44, Para 63).

Example (1)
Greenfinch, a director of Starling Ltd, leaves S's occupational pension scheme on 20 April 2000. His earnings were £1,000 before the change and £13,000 after the change. As G's earnings from his contracted-out employment do not exceed the annual EEET (£3,952), Class 1 liabilities arise as follows:

Primary:

£3,952 × Nil% =	£0.00
£10,048 × 10% =	£1,004.80
£14,000	£1,004.80

Secondary:

£4,385 × Nil% =	£0.00
£9,615 × 12.2% =	£1,173.03
£14,000	£1,173.03

22.9   Company Directors

Example (2)
Redwing is appointed a director of Starling Ltd on 5 May 2000 so his pro-rata
employee's earnings threshold and upper annual earnings limit are £3,648 (i.e. £76
× 48) and £25,680 (i.e. £535 × 48) respectively. The pro-rata employer's earnings
threshold is £4,048 (£4,385 ÷ 52 × 48, rounded up). He was not an employee of
S at all prior to that date. He joins S's salary–related occupational pension scheme
on 2 August 2000. His earnings were £5,000 before the change and £29,000 after
the change. As R's earnings from his contracted-out employment exceed the
pro-rata UEL, Class 1 liabilities arise as follows:

Primary:

£3,648 × Nil% =	£0.00
£22,032 × 8.4% =	£1,850.69
£25,680	£1,850.69

Secondary:

£4,048 × Nil% =	£0.00
£21,632 × 9.2% =	£1,990.14
£25,680	£1,990.14
£8,320 × 12.2% =	£1,015.04
£34,000	£3,005.18

Example (3)
The facts are as in Example (2) but Redwing has an APP before joining the
occupational scheme. Class 1 liabilities arise as follows:

Primary:

£3,648 × Nil% =	£0.00
£1,352 × 10% =	£135.20
£5,000	£135.20
£20,680 × 8.4% =	£1,737.12
£25,680	£1,872.32

Secondary:

£4,048 × Nil% =	£0.00
£952 × 12.2% =	£116.14
£5,000	£116.14
£20,680 × 9.2% =	£1,902.56
£25,680	£2,018.70
£8,320 × 12.2% =	£1,015.04
£34,000	£3,033.74

Note: The above three examples disregard the employer's contracted-out rebate in
respect of earnings falling between the lower earnings limit and the earnings
thresholds (see 23 CONTRACTED-OUT EMPLOYMENT).

22.9   MITIGATION OF CLASS 1 CONTRIBUTION LIABILITIES

Class 1 contribution liabilities in respect of earnings paid to company directors may be
mitigated or avoided by various means. Payments may, for instance, be made in kind
rather than in cash but that contribution-free method of paying remuneration is not
confined to company directors. From 6 April 2000, most payments in kind will be
subject to Class 1A contributions (see 16.18 CLASS 1A CONTRIBUTIONS: BENEFITS IN
KIND). The one method which is generally so confined is the payment of remuneration
by way of a dividend on shares. A dividend, being derived from shares rather than from

an employment, is not brought within the definition of earnings for Class 1 contribution purposes [*SSCBA 1992, s 3(1)*] nor will be liable to the extended Class 1A charge. Where a dividend is paid, therefore, it will attract no contribution liability and, because the main corporation tax rate for small companies is presently 20% and no additional rate of income tax is charged on an individual's investment income, no adverse tax consequences will follow, provided the company profits out of which it is paid do not exceed £300,000 (for the year to 31 March 2001) i.e. the level of profits beyond which the fully-reduced small companies rate of corporation tax ceases to apply. [*ICTA 1988, s 13*]. For 2000–01 the tax credit for individuals is 10% and since dividend income is taxed at either this rate of 10% or the rate of 32½% for higher rate taxpayers (but not at basic rate), only higher rate taxpayers will suffer an additional tax charge.

Example

Alan Bransdon-Smith and Geoff Legit are directors of Benevolent Ltd and each holds 500 £1 shares in that company. On 17 July 2000 it is clear that the corporation tax profits of Benevolent for the accounting period to 31 July 2000 will be approximately £170,000 and it is decided to pay Bransdon–Smith and Legit £50,000 each immediately. This might be achieved by the payment of either £100,000 in bonuses or £80,000 in dividends that will carry £8,888 (10% of the gross equivalent) in related tax credits. (Since the 10% tax credit for dividends attracts no further liability to a basic rate taxpayer this is as good as the 20% tax credit on most other forms of savings income).

From 6 April 1999, there is no longer any ACT payable by the company when it pays a dividend. The dividend figure of £80,000 rather than £90,000 (i.e. equivalent to £100,000 gross) is appropriate because of the reduced tax credit and tax liability on dividends for 40% taxpayers which leaves the same total liability in the hands of such a taxpayer now as was the case when the tax credit was actually 20%. This gives an additional income tax advantage to those still wholly or partially below the 40% income tax bracket.

A comparison of the two routes is as follows:

	Bonus route		Dividend route	
	£	£	£	£
B				
Pre-bonus profit		170,000		170,000
Gross bonuses	(100,000)			
Class 1 secondary @ Nil/12.2%	(11,130)			
		(111,130)		—
Post-bonus profit		58,870		170,000
Corporation tax @ 20%		(11,774)		(34,000)*
Post-tax profit		47,098		136,000
Dividend		—		(80,000)
Retained Profit		£47,098		£56,000
Bransdon-Smith and Legit				
Gross bonuses		100,000		—
Class 1 primary @ Nil%/10% on UEL £27,820 × 2		(4,774)		—
Post-NIC bonuses		95,226		—
Dividends				80,000
Post-NIC dividends				80,000
and bonuses		95,226		
Income tax*		(25,904)	(13,258)	
Tax credits		—	8,888	
				(4,370)

Post-tax and NI income		£69,322	£75,630

Assuming reliefs of £4,385 each, income tax would be charged for each individual as follows:

	Bonus route		*Dividend route*	
		£		£
Taxable income		50,000		44,444
Personal allowances		(4,385)		(4,385)
		45,615		40,059
	1,520 @ 10% = £152		28,400 @ 10% = £2,840	
	26,880 @ 22% = £5,914		— @ 22%	
	17,215 @ 40% = £6,886		11,659 @ 32½% = £3,789	
Liability before credits		12,952		6,629
Tax credits		—	£40,000 @ ⅑%	4,444
Tax not collected at source		—		2,185

The individual's tax liability in the above example is affected (in both cases) by the availability of personal allowances and (under the dividend route) by the lack of income other than dividend income. If other income covered the allowances and the lower and basic rate bands, the tax liability under both routes would be identical. The only difference in net income would then be the primary contribution liability (if any) on the bonuses.

For the company, the benefit of the dividend route is the post-tax saving of secondary NIC liability, reduced by the excess of the corporation tax relief lost by not paying the bonus.

Where a company's profits are such that it pays corporation tax at the full rate of 30% or marginal rate of 32½% (2000–01), the payment of a bonus rather than a dividend will result in an absolute saving of corporation tax, as the bonus is deductible from profits for Schedule D purposes. In contrast, dividends are paid out of post-tax earnings.

It should be noted that, where directors require income at regular intervals throughout the year, e.g. monthly, interim dividends may be paid at the required intervals. In the above example, for instance, Bransdon-Smith and Legit could have received an interim monthly dividend of £3,704 (including related tax credit of 10%) each.

Where it is undesirable that all shareholders should participate *pro rata* in any profits which are to be distributed, waivers (or part waivers) may be obtained from non- (or only part-) participating shareholders as necessary. For a waiver to be effective, however, it must be made and delivered to the company before the shareholder obtains the right to receive the dividend, which, in the case of an interim dividend, arises at the time of payment and, in the case of a final dividend, arises at the time the directors' recommendation is approved by the shareholders in general meeting. (*Lagunas Nitrate Co Ltd v Schroeder & Co (1901) 85 LTR 22; Re Severn and Wye and Severn Bridge Rail Co (1896) 74 LTR 219*). If a waiver is made voluntarily it must be made under seal.

Possible drawbacks to arrangements of the kind described should not be overlooked. These include

(a) the possibility that a dividend declared *before* the end of the accounting period to which it relates will (because the profits are not finally ascertainable at the time of payment) exceed the profits ultimately found to have been available for distribution and will thus be wholly or partly illegal. [*Companies Act 1985, ss 263–268*];

(*b*)   the possibility that the value of any minority shareholdings will be enhanced if a high dividend record is established by the company;

(*c*)   the fact that dividends are neither remuneration for occupational pension scheme purposes nor relevant earnings for retirement annuity or personal pension purposes. This must be a major point for consideration in the case of any director who is approaching retirement age or a younger director who wishes to take maximum advantage of a good trading year to direct earnings into a tax-free savings scheme;

(*d*)   the fact that entitlement to State benefits will be impaired unless remuneration by way of salary is maintained at a level equal to or above the lower earnings limit (see 13.2 BENEFITS and 30.1 EARNINGS LIMITS AND THRESHOLDS).

In February 1994, the Contributions Agency issued a note to the ICAEW and other professional bodies in which they admitted that, until August 1992, their view had been that *disproportionate* dividends were not genuine dividends but earnings. The note confirms, however, that, from that date, their view has been that a lawful dividend (i.e. one paid in accordance with the rights laid down in a company's Memorandum and Articles of Association and out of profits available for distribution) should not (even if disproportionate by reason of waivers) be regarded as earnings for contribution purposes. The note also goes on to state that an unlawful dividend *will* be regarded as earnings, but there seems to be no justification for such a stance. A dividend, whether lawful or unlawful, is derived from shares, not from an employment, and is not therefore within the terms of *SSCBA 1992, s 3(1)*.

22.10 DIRECTOR'S LIABILITY FOR COMPANY'S CONTRIBUTION ARREARS

Where a company cannot or will not meet its contribution liabilities and proceedings were taken against it under *SSAA 1992, s 114(1)* prior to its amendment with effect from 6 April 1999 for the offence of failing to pay, within the time prescribed for the purpose, a contribution which it is liable to pay, its guilt may extend to its directors and they may be proceeded against for the same criminal offence (see 12.4 ARREARS OF CONTRIBUTIONS). [*SSAA 1992, s 115*]. The CA undertook its first criminal case against a director of a 'phoenix' company in 1995 for non-payment of NICs amounting to over £50,000. A fine and costs of £2,400 and £500 respectively were imposed on the director in this case. A 'phoenix' company is one which goes into liquidation only to set up again very often with a similar name and close proximity to the original company with the same assets transferred at an undervalue. One of the areas that concerns the CA is the failure by the company to send tax and NICs deducted to the CA/IR prior to the liquidation. In this connection, statutory powers were announced on 1 August 1996 by the Secretary of State for Social Security that would allow the Courts to freeze personal assets of offenders who failed to pay NICs. This course of action would have been restricted to cases where an offence had been committed by a body corporate under *SSAA 1992, s 114(1)* and it was proved to have been committed with the consent of or connivance of, or was attributed to any neglect on the part of a director, manager, secretary or other similar officer of the body corporate (see DSS Press Release, 1 August 1996). This was a wider power, which may not have been restricted to cases of 'phoenix' companies. See also the Department of Trade and Industry Press Release P/96/848 on 12 November 1996. [*SSAA 1992, ss 114, 115(1); Criminal Justice Act 1988, s 71* and *Criminal Justice Act 1988 (Confiscation Orders) Order 1996, SI 1996 No 1716*]. See also Tolley's National Insurance Brief, September 1996 'Phoenix in the Frame'.

The pressure on 'phoenix directors' has been maintained subsequently and in this connection a new section to the *Social Security Act 1998–SSA 1998, s 64* effective from 6 April 1999 by virtue of *Social Security Act 1998 (Commencement No 4) Order 1999, Reg 2* establishes the new offence of 'fraudulent evasion of national insurance' allowing culpable directors to be personally liable. As well as being liable for their proportion of debt applicable to their culpability they are liable for accrued and future interest and penalties thereon as well. The previous sanctions were limited to a fine of up to £1,000 and the deduction of the director's personal contributions from his NI account and are now replaced with the potential seizure of the culpable director's home and personal assets where relevant. See also DSS Press Release 98/020, 5 February 1998.

Directors, as well as others, might also fall foul of the new offence where *any* person 'is knowingly concerned in the fraudulent evasion of any contributions which he or any other person is liable to pay'. [*SSCBA 1992, s 114 as amended by s 61, Social Security Act 1998,* effective from 6 April 1999. *Social Security Act 1998 (Commencement No. 4) Order 1999, Reg 2*].

A person guilty of this new offence shall be liable to imprisonment for a term not exceeding seven years, or a fine, or both.

In a further attack on individuals accepting nominee directorships the Department of Trade and Industry obtained a 12 year disqualification order on 28 January 1999 against a Sark-based nominee director. The use of Sark-based directors has in the past enabled those who are already disqualified to continue to trade anonymously. The Sark individual, Mr Croshaw, had acted as director of over 1,300 UK companies. The nominee directorships involved Mr Croshaw in no duties and the Court took a dim view of his abrogation of responsibility.

In a separate but interesting case of *Pawlowski v Dunnington (1999) STC 550* the Revenue discovered that a company was failing to deduct tax from a director's emoluments. The Revenue therefore issued determinations under *Income Tax (Employments) Regulations 1993, Reg 49*. The company failed to pay the tax determined, and subsequently went into liquidation. The Revenue then made a direction under *Reg 49(5)* that the tax should be recovered from the director. (The Revenue also made a direction under *Reg 42(3)* covering previous years.) The director failed to pay the tax demanded, and Collector of Taxes took proceedings in the Wigan County Court. The County Court judge ruled that the Collector had failed to prove that the director knew that the company had not been deducting PAYE. The Revenue appealed to the Court of Appeal, which allowed the appeal and remitted the case of the County Court for rehearing. Simon Brown LJ observed that the County Court judge had approached the case in 'the wrong way' and had 'dismissed the claim on an impermissible basis'. The Collector did not have to prove that the director knew that the company had not been deducting PAYE, but simply had to show that there was material on which the Board could properly have formed such an opinion. The Court of Appeal also held that a defendant was entitled to raise a public law defence in collection proceedings of this kind, rejecting the Revenue's contention that the directions could only be challenged by judicial review. Simon Brown LJ observed that there were 'practical disadvantages which flow from raising a public law challenge like this by way of defence instead of judicial review' but held that 'the Revenue's solution to the problem raised by the present case is a simple one: they should confer on taxpayers a right of appeal against directions comparable to that which arises on assessment'.

23   Contracted-Out Employment

Cross-references. See 13.8 BENEFITS for additional pension component; CLASS 1 CONTRIBUTIONS (15); 51.3 RATES AND LIMITS for contracted-out rates.

Other Sources. Simon's NIC, Part I, Section 2, Chapter 10; Leaflets CA 14, CA 14A, CA 15, CA 17, PEC 5, 6 and 8.

23.1   THE STATE PENSION SCHEME

On 6 April 1978, the *Social Security Pensions Act 1975* came into force and brought into existence a state earnings-related pension scheme (SERPS). Under that scheme basic retirement pension, widow's pension, widowed mother's allowance and invalidity pension are each augmented by an *additional component* which is related to such of a contributor's earnings as fall between the lower and upper earnings limits (see 30.1 EARNINGS LIMITS AND THRESHOLDS and 13.3 BENEFITS). Invalidity pension has since been replaced by long-term incapacity benefit with which there is no longer an earnings related component. The scheme is not funded, however, and it has now been acknowledged that the likely future costs of providing the additional component could be met only by 'handing down an irresponsibly large financial bill to the next generation' of contributors. ('Reform of Social Security: Programme for Action', *Cmnd 9691, Para 1.15*). Accordingly, provisions were enacted in *Social Security Act 1986* which reformed the scheme and aimed to cut the future cost by one-half — although due to the misleading content of DSS leaflets over the intervening period some benefit reductions due to have taken place from April 2000 have been deferred. The provisions of *SSPA 1975* have now mainly been incorporated into the *Pensions Schemes Act 1993*.

23.2   Contracting-out

Although the government is committed to the continued provision of earnings-related pensions, SERPS is only one part of the government's pension strategy. The 'central aim remains to see an extension of individual pension provision—while at the same time widening choice for the individual and increasing competition among the providers of pensions'. (*Cmnd 9691, Para 1.18*). Where an employer makes such independent arrangements for the provision of earnings-related pensions to his employees through a private occupational pension scheme, his employees are *contracted-out* of SERPS *provided* the private scheme meets certain stringent statutory requirements. [*PSA 1993, ss 40–49*]. The original arrangement was that the private scheme then shoulders, in place of the State, the responsibility for providing a *guaranteed minimum pension* related to earnings, but because this open-ended responsibility has deterred many small employers from making private arrangements for pensions, the reformed scheme has, from 6 April 1997, offered an employer, as an alternative commitment, responsibility for a *guaranteed minimum level of contributions* to a private occupational pension scheme. Such schemes are known as contracted-out money-purchase schemes (COMPS). This guaranteed minimum contribution level is equivalent to the contracted-out rebate (see 23.3). (*PSA 1993, ss 7, 8*).

In order to encourage the establishment of occupational pension schemes of either kind, the Secretary of State was committed, where an occupational pension scheme first became a contracted-out scheme on or after 1 January 1986 and before 6 April 1993, to making directly to the trustees of the scheme an incentive payment equal to 2% of the upper band earnings of each employee within the scheme or £1, whichever was the greater, for each tax week between 6 April 1988 and 5 April 1993 inclusive spent in such contracted-out employment [*SSA 1986, s 7*]. After 5 April 1993 the rate is 1% and the incentive is limited to personal pension policyholders aged over thirty at the start of the tax year (*SSA 1986, s 3 as amended by SSA 1993, s 1, PSA 1993, s 45 now amended by PSA 1995, s 138*).

In 1995-96, the most recent year for which detailed figures are available, 8.651 million persons paid Class 1 contributions at the contracted-out rate (Contributions and Qualifying Years for Retirement Pension 1995-96, Government Statistical Service, May 1998).

The employment of an earner in employed earner's employment is *contracted-out employment* in relation to him during any period in which

(*a*) he is under pensionable age; and

(*b*) his service is, for the time being, service which qualifies him for a guaranteed minimum pension provided by an occupational pension scheme or his employer makes minimum payments in respect of the earner's employment to a money purchase contracted-out scheme; and

(*c*) the scheme is a contracted-out scheme in relation to that employment; and

(*d*) a contracting-out certificate, issued by the Occupational Pension Board, is in force.

[*PSA 1993, ss 7(1), 8(1)*].

Every employer is required to inform each of his employees, as part of the written particulars of his employment, whether or not his employment is a contracted-out employment. [*Employment Protection (Consolidation) Act 1978, s 1(4)(d)*]. Employees that become retrospectively members of the employer's occupational scheme will, along with the employer, be entitled to a refund of the difference between the not contracted-out contributions and the contracted-out contributions since the retrospective joining date. See CWG2 (2000) Page 58.

The Occupational Pensions Board was the body formerly responsible for overseeing contracting-out arrangements. It was the OPB which issued to the employer the contracting-out certificate, showing the Employer Contracted-Out Number ('ECON') which must appear on year-end returns which include contributions at the contracted-out rate. From April 1997 the Occupational Pensions Board ceased to exist and many of its functions, including the approval of schemes contracting-out, were taken over by the Contracted-out Employments Group ('COEG') at the Contributions Agency. Following the transfer on 1 April 1999, this is also now part of the Inland Revenue and may be contacted at Inland Revenue NICO, Contracted-out Employment Group, Longbenton, Newcastle upon Tyne, NE1 1ZZ (Tel. 08459 150150).

From 1 July 1988, an employee has been able, if he wishes, in preference to remaining within SERPS or joining or remaining within any occupational pension scheme for membership of which he is eligible, to join a personal pension scheme of his own choosing and, provided that scheme complies with the requirements of the *Appropriate Schemes Regs 1988* so that it is approved by the Secretary of State for Social Security, the Secretary of State will pass on to the scheme an amount equivalent to the contracted-out rebate (see 23.3 below) which would have been obtained on the standard rate primary and secondary Class 1 contributions paid on that employee's earnings had that employee's employment been a contracted-out employment (i.e. the employee and employer pay contributions as if the employment were not contracted-out and the Inland Revenue (previously the DSS), on processing the year-end return, remits the contracted-out rebate (see 23.3 below) to the pension provider). Additionally, until 6 April 1993, the Secretary of State would pay into the personal pension scheme an amount equivalent to 2% of the earnings on which the contracted-out-rebate-equivalent was calculated or £1 per week of relevant employment, whichever was the greater. [*SSA 1986, ss 1–3*].

It was announced in February 1992, following the Government Actuary's quinquennial review of the State pension scheme, that the incentive payment would continue for a further five years in respect of some appropriate personal pensions, but not occupational schemes, when the current arrangements ended. However, the incentive has been set at 1% rather than 2% with effect from 6 April 1993 and is limited to policy-holders aged over thirty at the start of the tax year (*SSA 1986, s 3 as amended by SSA 1993, s 1*). The intention of this revision to the incentive scheme is to ensure that the majority of personal pension holders will find it advantageous to maintain their policy rather than opt back into SERPS. (DSS Press Release 92/40, 27 February 1992). During 1993–94 5.7 million people were members of an appropriate personal pension scheme of whom 3.6 million were men and 2.1 million were women (DSS Press Release 95/136, 25 October 1995). The intention of the change is to make private pension provision more attractive than state provision across the age range of the working population by increasing the rebate for older contributors who remain outside SERPS. From April 1997, firms have found it easier to contract-out. From that date contracted-out money purchase schemes (COMPS) attract different contracted-out rebates to COSR schemes, although initially the employee's rate is the same and only the secondary contributor's rates differ.

From 6 April 1998 contracted-out money purchase schemes (COMPS) are allowed to open up a contracted-out salary related scheme (COSRS) part and operate as a contracted-out mixed benefit scheme (COMB) either offering protected rights or salary related benefits depending on which part of the COMB an individual is in.

From April 2001, 'stakeholder pensions' are being introduced, along with enhanced earnings-related state pension accrual for lower earners. These proposals are likely to have yet further impact on contracting-out matters in due course.

Where effect is given to protected rights the NICO need, in certain circumstances, to collect the date this occurred. As a result of membership of a COMP scheme the state additional pension entitlement of the member, or, in the case of death, any widow(er) is reduced by an amount known as the contracted-out deduction (COD). Currently, in the case of a widow(er) the amount of COD is related to whether the member died before state pension age (SPA). From 6 April 1996, in recognition of the fact that men and women can use their protected rights for pension/annuity purposes from age 60, the amount of the COD applied in widow(er) cases is related to whether or not effect was given to the protected rights by the member before he or she died.

To enable the NICO to apply the correct amount of COD they need to know and record the date effect was given to the protected rights by the member. This additional information will be collected via new style forms CA 1577 (RD2025A) and CA 1594 (RD2025). Date of effect means:

- in the case of a pension/annuity, the date of entitlement to payment first arises

- in the case of commutation, the date the lump sum is paid to the member

When a COMP scheme winds up without effect being given to protected rights they can be assured or taken out through an appropriate insurance policy. This applies to current members and past early leavers (including any potential pensioners), who have not given effect to their protected rights. The new option is available to COMP schemes which are in the process of winding-up.

From 6 April 1997 onwards a new range of national insurance contributions were introduced for members of contracted-out money purchase schemes. The new categories are:

23.3 Contracted-Out Employment

TYPE OF CONTRIBUTION	CATEGORY TABLE LETTER
COMPS CONTRACTED-OUT STANDARD RATE	F
COMPS CONTRACTED-OUT REDUCED RATE	G
COMPS CONTRACTED-OUT STANDARD RATE MARINER (Foreign Going)	H
COMPS CONTRACTED-OUT REDUCED RATE MARINER (Foreign Going)	K
COMPS CONTRACTED-OUT STANDARD RATE EMPLOYERS ONLY*	S
COMPS CONTRACTED-OUT MARINER RATE EMPLOYERS ONLY*	V

* e.g. deferment granted.

Where the date of birth field on the P14 has been completed a comparison will be made with the date of birth held by the NICO which could result in enquiries being made with the individual or ultimately the scheme. Any age related payment will, in these circumstances, be suspended until NICO enquiries are complete. Where the date of birth field on the P14 has not been completed the date of birth held by the NICO will be used to calculate any age related rebate.

The date of birth used in the calculation will be included in the payment details provided to the scheme (either magnetic tape or paper schedule depending on the method chosen by the scheme). The new National Insurance category letters set out in the table above reflect the fact that the employer rebate levels are different for COMP and COSRS and to enable COMP earnings to be separately identified on the end of year return.

Form P14 (OCR) includes a space for the Scheme Contracted-Out Number (SCON) to be entered against the relevant COMP earnings. [*Pensions Act 1995, ss 137, 138*].

23.3 CONTRIBUTION REDUCTION

Because an employed earner who is contracted-out of the State scheme will nevertheless receive the basic component of his pension from the State, and because that basic component is linked with contributions on earnings at the lower earnings limit, the rate of contribution required on earnings up to that level is the same as that required from an employed earner who is not contracted-out (see BENEFITS (13)). [*PSA 1993, s 41(1)*]. With effect from 6 April 1999, that rate is nil. Prior to this the rate had been 2% on this slice of the earnings for a number of years. Similarly, but because it is not linked with benefit entitlement at all, the rate of secondary Class 1 contribution required on earnings in excess of the upper earnings limit is the normal rate of secondary Class 1 contribution. [*PSA 1993, s 41(1)*]. Because, however, contributions on earnings between the lower and upper earnings limits are linked with the additional component which a contracted-out earner forgoes, those primary and secondary Class 1 contributions are reduced to a contracted-out rate (see 51.4 RATES AND LIMITS). [*PSA 1993, s 41(1)*]. From 6 April 1989 to 5 April 1993, the contracted-out rate was

(*a*) in the case of a primary Class 1 contribution, a percentage which was 2% lower than the normal percentage; and

(*b*) in the case of a secondary Class 1 contribution, a percentage which was 3.8% lower than the normal percentage.

[*SSPA 1975, s 27(1)(b)(2), as amended by Contracted-out Percentages Order 1987, Art 2*].

From 6 April 1993 these percentages were respectively 1.8% and 3% but from 6 April 1997 onwards the percentages were 1.6% and 3% respectively for contracted-out salary related schemes (COSRS) and 1.6% and 1.5% respectively for contracted-out money purchase schemes (COMPS). In the case of APPs (where the COSR rebate is relevant) and COMPS, additional age-related rebates are paid by DSS over and above the basic flat rate percentage rebates. (DSS Press Release 92/40, 27 February 1992 and 96/47, 13 March 1996; 96/81, 29 April 1996; CWG2 (2000) page 59, items 74–79 [*Class 1 Contributions—Contracted-out Percentages Order 1992, Arts 1, 2 and PSA 1993, s 41(1) as amended by Social Security (Reduced Rates of Class 1 Contributions) (Salary Related Contracted-out Schemes) Order 1996, Art 2]*).

The employer's rebate in respect of COMPS schemes was further reduced to 0.6% with effect from 6 April 1999. [*Social Security (Reduced Rates of Class 1 Contributions, and Rebates) (Money Purchase Contracted-out Schemes) Order 1998, Reg 2(a)*].

Example 1
Aphid, Bollweevil, Chafer and Dungbeetle are all employed in *contracted-out salary related scheme* employment with Earwig Ltd. During June 2000, their weekly earnings are £70, £77, £90 and £600 respectively. Their contribution rates and those of E are, therefore, determined as follows.

A   £70 falls above the lower earnings limit but below the employee's (i.e. primary) earnings threshold of £76, so no contributions are due (see 30.4 EARNINGS LIMITS AND THRESHOLDS).

However, the employer's contracted-out rebate is due on the earnings from £67 to £70 i.e. £3 at 3%, notwithstanding that there are no employer's contributions due and there is an employee's contracted-out rebate due of £3 × 1.6%. As no employees contributions are due at this level of earnings the employee's rebate is given to the employer.

B   £77 falls above the employee's (i.e. primary) earnings threshold but below the employer's (i.e. secondary) earnings threshold, so only primary contributions are due (see 30.4 EARNINGS LIMITS AND THRESHOLDS). Therefore,

on £67 (LEL)	Nil
on £9 (LEL to EEET)	Nil
on £1 (balance)	the primary contracted-out rate is $(10 - 1.6)\%$ = 8.4%.

However, the employer's contracted-out rebate is due on the earnings from £67 to £77 i.e. £10 at 3%, notwithstanding that there are no employer's contributions due and there is an employee's contracted-out rebate due of £9 × 1.6%. This amounts to 14p. As the employee's contribution is only 8p (£1 × 8.4%), 8p of the rebate goes to the employee so that nothing is deducted from the employee's gross pay in respect of NIC. The balance of the employee's rebate (6p) benefits the employer.

C   £90 falls above the lower earnings limit and both the primary and secondary earnings thresholds so both primary and secondary contributions are due (see 30.4 EARNINGS LIMITS AND THRESHOLDS). Therefore,

on £67 (LEL)	Nil
on £9 (LEL to EEET)	Nil
on £8 (EEET to ERET)	the primary contracted-out rate is $(10 - 1.6)\%$ = 8.4%

| on £6 (balance) | the primary contracted-out rate is $(10 - 1.6)\%$ = 8.4% and the secondary contracted-out rate is $(12.2 - 3.0)\% = 9.2\%$. |

In addition, the employer's contracted-out rebate is due on the earnings from £67 to £84 i.e. £17 at 3% and there is an employee's contracted-out rebate due of £9 × 1.6%, i.e. 14p. As this is exceeded by the employee's contributions due at 8.4% on £(90 – 76) = 14, i.e. £1.18, all of it may be used to reduce to £1.04 the deduction made from gross pay in respect of NIC. The employer benefits only to the extent of the employer's contracted-out rebate.

D   £600 falls above the UEL of £535 so primary contributions are due up to the UEL and secondary contributions on all earnings above the earnings threshold as follows (see 30.4 EARNINGS LIMITS AND THRESHOLDS).

on £67 (LEL)	Nil
on £9 (LEL to EEET)	Nil
on £8 (EEET to ERET)	the primary contracted-out rate is $(10 - 1.6)\%$ = 8.4% and there are no secondary contributions.
on £451 (balance from ERET to UEL)	the primary contracted-out rate is $(10 - 1.6)\%$ = 8.4% and the secondary contracted-out rate is $(12.2 - 3.0)\% = 9.2\%$.
on £65 (remainder)	the primary contracted-out contribution rate is nil and the secondary contracted-out contribution rate is 12.2%.

In addition, the employer's contracted-out rebate is due on the earnings from £67 to £84 i.e. £17 at 3% and there is an employee's contracted-out rebate due of £9 × 1.6%, i.e. 14p. As this is exceeded by the employee's contributions due, all of it benefits the employee by reducing by 14p the NIC calculated for deduction from gross pay. The employer benefits only to the extent of the employer's contracted-out rebate.

Example 2
Aphid, Bollweevil, Chafer and Dungbeetle are all employed in *contracted-out money purchase scheme* employment with Earwig Ltd. During June 2000, their weekly earnings are £70, £77, £90 and £600 respectively. Their contribution rates and those of E are therefore determined as follows:

A   £70 falls above the lower earnings limit but below the employee's (i.e. primary) earnings threshold, so no contributions are due. However, the employer's contracted-out rebate is due on the earnings from £67 to £70 i.e. £3 at 0 6%, notwithstanding that there are no employer's contributions due and there is an employee's contracted-out rebate due of £3 x 1.6%, i.e. 14p. As no employee's contributions are due at this level of earnings the employee's rebate is given wholly to the employer.

B   £77 falls above the employee's (i.e. primary) earnings threshold but below the employer's (i.e. secondary) earnings threshold, so only primary contributions are due (see 30.4 EARNINGS LIMITS AND THRESHOLDS). Therefore,

on £67 (LEL)	Nil
on £9 (LEL to EEET)	Nil
on £1 (balance)	the primary contracted-out rate is $(10 - 1.6)\%$ = 8.4%.

However, the employer's contracted-out rebate is due on earnings from £67 to £77, i.e. £10 × 0.6%, notwithstanding that there are no employer's contributions due and there is an employee's contracted-out rebate due of £9 × 1.6%. This amounts to 14p. As the employee's contribution is only 8p (£1 × 8.4%), 8p of the rebate goes to the employee so that nothing is deducted from the employee's gross pay in respect of NIC. The balance of the employee's rebate (6p) benefits the employer.

C   £90 falls above the lower earnings limit and both the primary and secondary earnings thresholds so both primary and secondary contributions are due. Therefore,

on £67 (LEL)	Nil
on £9 (LEL to EEET)	Nil
on £8 (EEET to ERET)	the primary contracted-out rate is (10 − 1.6)% = 8.4% and there are no secondary contributions.
on £6 (balance)	the primary contracted-out rate is (10 − 1.6)% = 8.4% and the secondary contracted-out rate is (12.2 − 0.6)% = 11.6%.

In addition, the employer's contracted-out rebate is due on the earnings from £67 to £84 i.e. £17 at 0.6% and there is an employee's contracted-out rebate due of £9 × 1.6%, i.e. 14p. As this is exceeded by the employee's contributions due at 8.4% on £(90 − 76) = 14 i.e. £1.18, all of it may be used to reduce to £1.04 the deduction to be made from gross pay in respect of NIC. The employer benefits only to the extent of the employer's contracted-out rebate.

D   £600 falls above the UEL of £535 so primary contributions are due up to the UEL and secondary contributions on all earnings above the earnings threshold as follows. Therefore,

on £67 (LEL)	Nil
on £9 (LEL to EEET)	Nil
on £8 (EEET to ERET)	the primary contracted-out rate is (10 − 1.6)% = 8.4% and there are no secondary contributions.
on £451 (balance from ERET to UEL)	the primary contracted-out rate is (10 − 1.6)% = 8.4% and the secondary contracted-out rate is (12.2 − 0.6)% = 11.6%.
on £65 (remainder)	the primary contracted-out rate is nil and the secondary contracted-out rate is 12.2%.

In addition, the employer's contracted-out rebate is due on the earnings from £67 to £84 i.e. £17 at 0.6% and there is an employee's contracted-out rebate due of £9 × 1.6%, i.e. 14p. As this is exceeded by the employee's contributions due, all of it benefits the employee by reducing by 14p the NIC calculated for deduction from gross pay. The employer benefits only to the extent of the employer's contracted-out rebate.

23.4   Termination of contracted-out employment

Any payments of earnings (including statutory maternity pay) made to a former employee within the six weeks following the date of termination of his employment are to continue to attract contribution liabilities at the relevant contracted-out rates if

23.5 Contracted-Out Employment

his former employment was a contracted-out employment. Any payment made thereafter, however, attracts contributions at the appropriate not contracted-out rates. [*PSA 1993, s 41(2)*].

23.5 Reduced rate elections

Married women and widows who have the right to pay contributions at a reduced rate (see REDUCED LIABILITY ELECTIONS (52)) may also be in contracted-out employment. No further reduction of the reduced rate of primary contribution (3.85% in 2000–01) is available in respect of the contracted-out rebate, although the secondary contributor is entitled to the appropriate percentage reduction (i.e. 3.0% for COSR schemes in 2000–01 and 0.6% for COMPS in 2000–01) in the secondary liability. [*PSA 1993, s 41(3)*].

23.6 Retained pensions

A problem that arose from the broadcasting and film industry with regard to the payment of Class 1 NICs as employees meant that on reclassification as self-employed workers their contributions were refunded. This meant that their entitlement to SERPS or additional incapacity benefit built up by the payments would be given up. However, those fee paid staff can choose to leave their past Class 1 contribution record alone, forego the repayment that they are otherwise entitled to and instead retain entitlement to the extra pension under the SERPS rules. This change effectively bypasses the normal categorisation rules and is made effective by the *Pensions Act 1995*. The CA stated that this only applies where there has been a genuine miscategorisation of employment status of workers in that industry. See DSS Press Release 14 May 1996.

24   Credits

Cross-references. See BENEFITS (13) for circumstances in which credits may be used to satisfy contribution conditions for benefit entitlement; EARNINGS FACTORS (29) for inclusion or otherwise of credited contributions.

Other Sources. Leaflets CA 09, CA 10, CA 12, CA 13 and DSS Leaflet CF411.

24.1   GENERAL CONSIDERATIONS

In relation to periods before 6 April 1987, a credit was a contribution which a person was entitled to have added to his contribution record without any payment being made, for the purpose of bringing his EARNINGS FACTORS (29) for any tax year to a figure which would enable him to satisfy contribution conditions of his own or some other person's entitlement to benefit. [*SSA 1975, s 13(4)*]. Because of a change in the basis on which EARNINGS FACTORS (29) are calculated for 1987–88 and later years, however, that definition was, from 6 April 1987, extended to include an amount of notional earnings which a person is entitled to have added to his record of earnings for the purpose of increasing his earnings factors. [*SSCBA 1992, s 22(5)*]. The credit consists of an amount of earnings sufficient to raise the individual's earnings factor for the year in question to the annual lower earnings level. The earnings will be credited in multiples of the weekly lower earnings level (2000-01: £67).

Where two contribution conditions are specified in relation to a particular benefit, a credit may only be awarded for the purpose of enabling the *second* of those conditions to be satisfied (see 13.2 BENEFITS). Where a person would be entitled to more credits than are required to bring his earnings factor to the required level, the award is to be limited to the minimum amount necessary for that purpose. [*Credits Regs, Reg 3(1)*].

In 1994–95 some 10.5 million people in the UK were awarded an average of 39.4 national insurance credits (1% sample of national insurance records) (see Hansard, 22 January 1996, Col 109). In 1995–96, the most recent year for which figures are available, 10 million people were awarded credits (Contributions and Qualifying Years For Retirement Pension 1995–96).

24.2   Types and rates of credit

A credit may be of either a Class 3 contribution or (before 6 April 1987), a Class 1 contribution or (after 6 April 1987) earnings, depending on the circumstances in which it falls to be awarded. The amount of the credit awarded is:

(*a*) in the case of a Class 3 contribution, the amount of a Class 3 contribution at the rate set for a Class 3 contribution in the year concerned; and

(*b*) in the case of a Class 1 credit for a week, the amount of a primary Class 1 contribution calculated earnings equal to the lower earnings limit for that week (see EARNINGS LIMITS AND THRESHOLDS (30) and 51.4 RATES AND LIMITS); and

(*c*) in the case of Class 1 credits for a year, such amount as is needed to bring the person's earnings factor (see EARNINGS FACTORS (29)) to the level at which the second contribution condition for entitlement to benefit will be satisfied for that year (see 13.2 BENEFITS); and

(*d*) in the case of a credit of earnings for a year, such amount as is needed to bring the person's earnings factor (see EARNINGS FACTORS (29)) to the level at which the second contribution condition for entitlement to benefit will be satisfied for that year (see 13.2 BENEFITS).

24.3   Credits

[Credits Regs, Reg 3(2), as amended by Credits Amendment Regs 1978, Reg 2(2) and Contributions Transitional Regs 1985, Reg 7, and as amended by Credits Amendment Regs 1987, Reg 11 for 1986–87 and earlier years and Reg 3(c) for 1987–88 and subsequent years].

Where a person is entitled to a credit in respect of a week which is partly in one tax year and partly in another, he is to be entitled to be credited with earnings or a contribution for the tax year in which the week began and not for the tax year in which it ends. *[Reg 3(3), as amended by Credits Amendment Regs 1987, Reg 3(d)].*

24.3   Age limitations

A person cannot be brought within the contribution scheme until he attains the age of 16 and cannot continue in it after he has attained pensionable age, therefore credits will not be awarded to persons for any years before that in which the 16th birthday was reached or for any years in which state pensionable age was reached or subsequently (see AGE EXCEPTION (3)).

24.4   STARTING CREDITS

On the principle that a person who had entered, but had not yet had the opportunity to do more than make minimal contributions to, the contribution scheme should not be penalised as regards his ability to benefit under the scheme, credits were, if necessary, awarded to all new scheme-entrants for both short- and long-term benefit purposes. Since 2 October 1988 starting credits have only been awarded for long-term benefit purposes.

24.5   Class 1 credits or credited earnings

For the purpose of enabling a person to fulfil the second contribution condition (see 24.1 above) for entitlement to unemployment benefit, sickness benefit or maternity allowance, that person (provided she is not a married woman with a reduced rate election in force immediately before the end of any tax year concerned—see REDUCED LIABILITY ELECTIONS (52)) was, until 1 October 1988, entitled to

(*a*)   Class 1 credits for the year in which he or she attained the age of 17 or for any previous year if the year concerned is 1986–87 or an earlier year; or

(*b*)   be credited with earnings equal to the lower earnings limit then in force (see EARNINGS LIMITS AND THRESHOLDS (30) and 51.4 RATES AND LIMITS) for any week in the year in which he or she attained the age of 17 or in any previous year.

[Credits Regs, Reg 5(1)(a)(2) as amended by Credits Amendment Regs 1987, Reg 11 for 1986–87 and earlier years and Reg 4 for 1987–88 and, until 1 October 1988, 1988–89].

Such credits were, until 1 October 1988, also awarded for years after the year in which a person attained the age of 17 up to and including that in which a person (not being a married woman as described above and not having been insured under a pre-1975 scheme) paid, or was treated as paying, for the first time, a Class 1 or Class 2 contribution. *[Credits Regs, Reg 5(1)(b)(2)].*

With effect from 2 October 1988, *Reg 5* was revoked so that, after that date, no starting credit of earnings can be made. *[Credits Amendment No 2 Regs 1988, Reg 3(1)].*

24.6   **Class 3 credits**

For the purpose of enabling a person to fulfil the second contribution condition (see 24.1 above) for entitlement to retirement pension, widowed mother's allowance or widow's pension, that person is to be credited with sufficient Class 3 contributions to bring his earnings factor in respect of the tax year in which he attained the age of 16 and each of the two following tax years to the required level. [*Credits Regs, Reg 4(1)*]. No such credits are, however, to be given in respect of tax years prior to 1975–76 unless the person was in Great Britain on 6 April 1975 and, though over the age of 16, was not then insured under the pre-1975 legislation. In such a case Class 3 credits for 1974–75 are to be awarded. [*Reg 4(2)*].

24.7   **EDUCATION AND TRAINING CREDITS**

Credits are available both during, and at the end of, a period of training, and at the end of a period of full-time education or apprenticeship. Although they appear to belong together, approved training credits and termination credits are connected only superficially and must be considered in isolation from each other.

24.8   **Approved training credits**

For the purpose of enabling the second contribution condition (see 24.1 above) for any benefit to be fulfilled, a person who has undergone a course of training is, until 3 September 1988, entitled to a Class 1 credit in respect of each week of the course which fell in 1986–87 or an earlier year and to be credited with earnings equal to the lower earnings limit then in force (see EARNINGS LIMITS AND THRESHOLDS (30) and 51.4 RATES AND LIMITS) in respect of each week of the course falling in 1987–88 or a later year, provided that the following conditions were fulfilled.

(*a*) The course

    (i) was full-time; and

    (ii) was not undertaken in pursuance of the employment of the person concerned as an employed earner; and

    (iii) was approved by the Secretary of State for Social Security; and

    (iv) was, when begun, not intended to last for more than twelve months or, in a case where the person concerned is a disabled person (within the meaning of *Disabled Persons (Employment) Act 1944*) who was undergoing training under *Employment and Training Act 1973* or *Enterprise and New Towns (Scotland) Act 1990* such longer period as was reasonable in the circumstances of the case; *and*

(*b*) The person concerned

    (i) had attained the age of 18 before the beginning of the tax year in which the week in question began; and

    (ii) had, for at least one of the last three tax years ending before the course began, derived from

        (A) Class 2 contributions paid or credited, and either

        (B) Class 1 contributions paid or credited, if the year was 1986–87 or an earlier year, or

        (C) earnings upon which primary Class 1 contributions have been paid or treated as paid or from earnings credited, if the year is 1987–88 or a later year, an earnings factor amounting in the aggregate to at least 50 times the lower earnings limit for that year, unless in the circumstances of his case there is reasonable ground for waiving this requirement; and

(iii)   was not a married woman with a reduced rate election in effect in any part of the week in question (see REDUCED LIABILITY ELECTIONS (52)).

[*Credits Regs, Reg 7(1)–(3), as amended by Credits Amendment Regs 1978, Reg 2(2); Credits Amendment Regs 1987, Reg 11 for 1986–87 and earlier years and Reg 5 for 1987–88 and, until 3 September 1988, 1988–89*].

The term 'full-time' has been considered by the National Insurance Commissioners in the context of full-time education for child benefit purposes and held to carry its natural and ordinary meaning so that a course involving morning-only attendance was, though a full course, not a full-time course. (*R(F) 4/62*). If a course is to be approved by the Secretary of State for Social Security, it must (in addition to being a full-time course) be 'vocational, technical or rehabilitative'. (now obsolete DSS Leaflet NI 125). Approval was automatically granted to any such course run by the Training Commission (formerly the Manpower Services Commission), but, in other cases, a Certificate of Attendance at a Course of Training had to be sought by application on form CF 55C.

From 4 September 1988, the conditions under which approved training credits were awarded were changed and, in some respects, relaxed. From that date onwards it has been a requirement that the trainee had attained the age of 18 before the beginning of the tax year in which the relevant week of training began, that the course, when it began, was not intended to continue for more than 12 months (or, in the case of a disabled person within the meaning of the *Disabled Persons (Employment) Act 1944* who is receiving the training under the *Employment and Training Act 1973* or, with effect from 1 April 1991, the *Enterprise and New Towns (Scotland) Act 1990*, such longer period as is reasonable in the circumstances) and that the course is either

(i)   a course of full-time training, or

(ii) if the trainee is a disabled person within the meaning of the *Disabled Persons (Employment) Act 1944*, a course of training which is attended for not less than 15 hours in the week in question, or

(iii) a course of training introductory to either (i) or (ii).

[*Credits Regs, Reg 7 as amended by Credits Amendment No 3 Regs 1988, Reg 2 from 4 September 1988 and Enterprise (Scotland) Consequential Amendments Order 1991, Art 3(a)*].

Courses sponsored by the Department of Education and Employment are acceptable for credits which will be awarded automatically. Such courses are arranged by Training and Enterprise Councils (TECs) in England and Wales, Local Enterprise Companies (LECs) in Scotland and the Training and Employment Agency in Northern Ireland. Students on other courses which satisfy the rules for credits should apply on Form CA5483 (Leaflet CA12).

24.9   Termination credits

For the purpose of enabling a person to fulfil the second contribution condition for unemployment benefit or sickness benefit (see 24.1 above), that person (provided she was not a married woman with a reduced rate election in force immediately before the end of any tax year concerned—see REDUCED LIABILITY ELECTIONS (52)) was, until 1 October 1988, to be entitled either to Class 1 credits for 1986–87 or an earlier tax year or to be credited with earnings equal to the lower earnings limit then in force (see EARNINGS LIMITS AND THRESHOLDS (30) and 51.4 RATES AND LIMITS) for 1987–88 or 1988–89 if, during any part of the year, he or she was (*a*)   undergoing a course of full-time education; or

(*b*)   undergoing a course of training approved in this connection by the Secretary of State; or

(*c*)   an apprentice.

The credits were, however, conditional upon, in the case of (*a*) and (*b*), the course or, in the case of (*c*), the apprenticeship having commenced before the person attained the age of 21 and having terminated.

[*Credits Regs, Reg 8(1)(2), as amended by Credits Amendment Regs 1978, Reg 2(2); Credits Amendment Regs 1987, Reg 11 for 1986–87 and earlier years and Reg 7 for 1987–88 and, until 1 October 1988, 1988–89*].

Though the regulation does not specify that a course of full-time education must be undergone at an educational establishment, it is probable that the term 'undergoing' precludes private or home study from the term 'education', even where the studies are directed (see the National Insurance Commissioners reported decision *R(F) 4/61*). For the meaning of 'full-time' see 24.8 above.

It is not stated that a course of training need, in this context, be full-time (cf. 24.8 above and see the revised requirements below) though earlier editions of Leaflet CA 12 have implied that, in deciding whether or not to approve a course of training for the purpose of either this or *Reg 7* (see 24.8 above), identical tests will be applied.

For the definition of a 'contract of apprenticeship' see 10.2 APPRENTICES, TRAINEES AND STUDENTS. In the present context, the term 'apprentice' may be more loosely used and may extend to any person undergoing a full-time training for any trade, business, profession, office, employment or vocation and not in receipt of earnings which provide him wholly or substantially, with a livelihood. [*Family Allowances Act 1965, s 23, now repealed*].

From 2 October 1988 to 30 September 1989 the requirements were more stringent in that termination credits could be awarded only if, of the two tax years on which the claim for unemployment or sickness benefit depended (see 13.2 BENEFITS), the year other than the year for which termination credits were to be awarded was a year for which the EARNINGS FACTOR (29) was not less than 50 times that year's lower earnings limit (see EARNINGS LIMITS AND THRESHOLDS (30)) and the tax year for which the credits were to be awarded was a year after the year in which the trainee attained the age of 17.

[*Credits Regs, Reg 8, as amended by Credits Amendment No 2 Regs 1988, Reg 2 from 2 October 1988*].

The conditions under which, from 1 October 1989, termination credits of earnings equal to the lower earnings limit will be awarded to a person for either of the last two years before the beginning of a relevant benefit year for the purpose of entitlement to contributions-based jobseeker's allowance (previously unemployment benefit) and short-term incapacity benefit (previously sickness benefit) are as follows.

(*a*)   during at least part of the year concerned the person must have been either an apprentice or someone undergoing

(i)   a course of full-time education (see above); or

(ii)   a course of full-time training arranged under *Employment and Training Act 1973, s 2(1)* or, with effect from 1 April 1991, *Enterprise and New Towns (Scotland) Act 1990, s 2(3)*; or

(iii)   any other full-time course the sole or main purpose of which was the acquisition of occupational or vocational skills; or

      (iv) in the case of a disabled person within *Disabled Persons (Employment) Act 1944*, a part-time course attended for at least 15 hours a week which, if full-time, would fall within (ii) or (iii) above;

  (*b*) the course or apprenticeship must have begun before the person attained the age of 21;

  (*c*) the course or apprenticeship must have terminated;

  (*d*) the year other than that for which credits are sought must be a year for which the EARNINGS FACTOR (29) is not less than 50 times that year's lower earnings limit (see 30 EARNINGS LIMITS AND THRESHOLDS); and

  (*e*) the year for which credits are sought must not be a year before the person attains the age of 18.

[*Credits Regs, Reg 8 as amended by Credits Amendment Regs 1978, Reg 2(2), Credits Amendment No 2 Regs 1988, Reg 2, Credits Amendment Regs 1989, Reg 3, Enterprise (Scotland) Consequential Amendments Order 1991, Art 3(b) and Incapacity Benefit Consequential Transitional Amendments and Savings Regs 1995, Reg 6*].

24.10 **UNEMPLOYMENT AND INCAPACITY CREDITS**

For the purpose of enabling the second contribution condition for any benefit to be fulfilled (see 24.1 above), a person (provided not a married woman with a reduced rate election in force during any part of a week concerned—see REDUCED LIABILITY ELECTIONS (51)) is entitled to a *Class 1 credit* in respect of each week of unemployment or incapacity falling in 1986–87 or an earlier tax year or to be credited with earnings equal to the lower earnings limit then in force (see EARNINGS LIMITS AND THRESHOLDS (30) and 51.4 RATES AND LIMITS) in respect of each week of unemployment or incapacity falling in 1987–88 or a later tax year (see 24.11, 24.12 below). This is subject to the proviso that, where the benefit concerned is *contributions-based jobseeker's allowance* or *short-term incapacity benefit*, the person must, in respect of one of the last two complete tax years before the beginning of the benefit year in which the period of interruption of employment falls have

  (*a*) derived an EARNINGS FACTOR (29) of *not less than 25 times the weekly lower earnings limit* for that year (see EARNINGS LIMITS AND THRESHOLDS (30)). Where the benefit concerned is contributions-based jobseeker's allowance, the earnings factor must have been derived from earnings upon which Class 1 contributions have *actually been paid* or treated as paid. When the benefit concerned is sickness or short-term incapacity benefit, the earnings factor must have been derived from such earnings or from Class 2 contributions; or

  (*b*) been entitled to (or, but for *Overlapping Benefits Regulations 1979*, would have been entitled to) either invalidity pension (from 13 April 1995, short-term incapacity benefit at the higher rate or long-term incapacity benefit) invalid care allowance, or unemployability supplement in respect of any day in, or any week falling in or partly in, that year; or

  (*c*) claimed contributions-based jobseeker's allowance, sickness benefit or short-term incapacity benefit or maternity allowance for some period of that year and has satisfied or may be treated as having satisfied the contribution conditions for such benefit; or

  (*d*) been entitled to an approved training credit for any week in that year (see 24.8 above); or

  (*e*) been entitled to a Class 1 credit or to be credited with earnings under these provisions for a week during that year and had exhausted his right to contributions-based jobseeker's allowance or unemployment benefit or sickness benefit or incapacity benefit for that week; or

(f) been entitled to be credited with earnings from a week which included a day which would have been a day of incapacity but for the fact that the person concerned was a local authority councillor and was, for the week in which the day fell, entitled to an attendance allowance payable under *Local Government Act 1972, s 173(1)* or *Local Government (Scotland) Act 1973, s 45(1)* which exceeded the permitted maximum amount of earnings under *Unemployment, etc. Regs 1983, Reg 3(3)*.

[*Credits Regs, Reg 9(1)(6)(9), as amended by Credits Amendment Regs 1977, Reg 2; Credits Amendment Regs 1978, Reg 2(2); Credits Amendment Regs 1983, Reg 2; Credits Amendment Regs 1987, Reg 11 for 1986–87 and earlier years, Credits Amendment No 2 Regs 1987, Reg 2, and Credits Amendment No 4 Regs 1988, Reg 2(3)(b), for 1987–88 and later years, and Credits Amendment Regs 1988, Regs 2 and 3 for 1988–1989 and later years and Incapacity Benefit Consequential and Transitional Amendments and Savings Regs 1995, Reg 6*].

Credits under this regulation are to be awarded for weeks of proven incapacity or unemployment between a claim for benefit and its determination even if the claim is disallowed for other reasons. If an appeal against disallowance of benefit is upheld, such credits are to be awarded for the period covered by the claim, if they have not already been awarded. (18 House of Commons Debates 6th Series Col 414, 24 February 1982).

24.11 Week of unemployment

A 'week of unemployment' is a week in which each of the days (excluding Sunday or some religiously acceptable alternative day) are *days of unemployment* for jobseeker's allowance purposes, or would have been such days had benefit been claimed within the prescribed time. In this latter event, a day will be a day of unemployment only if the person concerned attended an Employment Service Jobcentre, etc. and made a written declaration of unemployment and availability for employment on that day or provided alternative evidence of unemployment and availability for employment. [*Credits Regs, Reg 9(2)(3)(7)(a)(b)*].

Employment during a day will not preclude that day from being a day of unemployment provided that the person concerned was available on that day to be employed full-time in some employed earner's employment (including employment as a share fisherman—see SHARE FISHERMEN (54)) *and* the employment in which he was engaged

(a) did not engage him for a total of more than eight hours in the week; and

(b) was (if employed earner's employment) not his usual main occupation or was done for or organised through a charity etc.

[*Reg 9(4)(a), as amended by Unemployment etc. Amendment Regs 1982, Reg 5(3) and Credits Amendment Regs 1994, Reg 2*].

Employment may also be disregarded if, even though failing to meet these conditions, the employment was engaged in on only one day of the week and the EARNINGS (28) in that day did not exceed the weekly lower earnings limit then in force (see EARNINGS LIMITS AND THRESHOLDS (30)) and he was engaged in no other employment in that week [*Reg 9(4)(b), as amended by Miscellaneous Amendment Regs 1976, Reg 4(1)(3) and Credits Amendment Regs 1994, Reg 2*].

A day is not to be regarded as a day of unemployment if the person concerned is a sea-going share fisherman (see SHARE FISHERMEN (54)) and does not satisfy the requirements of *Mariners' Benefits Regs 1975, Reg 8(5)(6)*.

24.12 Credits

For the purpose of the rules relating to unemployment and incapacity credits, the day on which there begins a period of employment which extends beyond midnight into the following day is not to be treated as a day of interruption of employment if the employment before midnight is of longer duration than the period after midnight, and, conversely, if the employment after midnight is of longer duration than the unemployment before midnight, or if the employment before and after midnight is of equal duration, the second day is not to be treated as a day of interruption of employment. [*Credits Regs, Reg 9(8A), as inserted by Credits Amendment No 4 Regs 1988, Reg 2(3)*].

From 6 April 1992, a day which is not a 'day of unemployment' for benefit purposes because it is a day covered by a compensation payment made in connection with the termination of employment may, on written notice of the grounds of claim, be treated as a 'day of unemployment' for the purpose of unemployment credits. *Credit Regs, Reg 9(3A) as inserted by Credits Amendment Regs 1992*].

24.12 Week of incapacity

A week of incapacity is a week in which each day (other than Sunday or some religiously acceptable alternative day)

(*a*) was a day of incapacity for work under *SSCBA 1992, s 30C* (incapacity benefit: days and periods of incapacity for work); or

(*b*) would have been such a day had short-term incapacity benefit (or, previously, sickness benefit) or maternity allowance been claimed within the prescribed time; or

(*c*) formed part of a period for which injury benefit (now abolished) was payable or would have been payable had a claim been made within the prescribed time; or

(*d*) was a day of incapacity for work for statutory sick pay purposes under *SSCBA 1992, s 151* and fell within a period of entitlement under *SSCBA 1992, s 153*; or

(*e*) would have been a day of incapacity but for the fact that the person concerned was a local authority councillor and was, for the week in which the day fell, entitled to an attendance allowance payable under *Local Government Act 1972, s 173(1)* or *Local Government (Scotland) Act 1973, s 45(1)* which exceeded the permitted maximum amount of earnings under *Unemployment etc. Regs 1983, Reg 3(3)*.

[*Credits Regs, Reg 9(2)(5), as amended by Credits Amendment Regs 1983, Reg 2, Credits Amendment No 2 Regs 1987, Reg 2 and Incapacity Benefit Consequential and Transitional Amendments and Savings Regs 1995, Reg 6(4)*].

24.13 OVER-60 CREDITS

For the purpose of enabling the second contribution condition for any benefit to be fulfilled (see 24.1 above), a person is (subject to the limitation described below) entitled, for 1986–87 and earlier years, to be credited with so many Class 1 contributions or, for 1987–88 and later years, such earnings as are necessary to bring his EARNINGS FACTOR (29) to the required level in respect of the tax year in which he attained the age of 60 and each of the four succeeding years (but not a tax year before 1983–84 and not any tax year in which he is absent from Great Britain for more than 182 days). [*Credits Regs, Reg 9A(1)(2)(5), as amended by Supplementary Benefit Miscellaneous Provisions Amendment Regs 1983, Reg 2; Credits Amendment No 2 Regs 1983, Reg 2(4); Credits Amendment Regs 1987, Reg 11 for 1986–87 and earlier years and Reg 9 for 1987–88 and later years; Credits Amendment Regs 1994, Reg 3*].

Where, in any of the tax years concerned, a person is liable to pay a Class 2 contribution in respect of any week, he is to be credited with a Class 1 contribution or with earnings, as the case may be, only for weeks in respect of which no contribution of any class is payable and for which he is not entitled to a credit of any description under any other of the Credit Regulations. From 8 August 1994, a self-employed earner is eligible for such a credit of earnings equal to the lower earnings limit only if he or she is liable to pay Class 2 contributions in respect of any week or is excepted from liability on the grounds that his or her earnings are expected to be less than the self-employed earners exception (SEE) limit set by *SSCBA 1992, s 11(4). [Credits Regs, Reg 9A(3) (4), as amended by Supplementary Benefit etc. Regs, Reg 2; Credits Amendment Regs 1987, Reg 11 for 1986–87 and earlier years and Reg 9 for 1987–88 and later years; Credits Amendment Regs 1994, Reg 3].*

24.14 MARRIAGE TERMINATION CREDITS

For the purpose of enabling the second contribution condition for *unemployment benefit, sickness benefit and maternity allowance* to be fulfilled (see 24.1 above), a woman whose marriage had been terminated for any reason was entitled, until 5 April 1987, to be credited with so many Class 1 contributions as were necessary to bring to the required level her EARNINGS FACTOR (29) for any tax year during the whole or part of which the marriage subsisted, provided that, during the tax year (if the marriage had by then taken place) before that in which the marriage ended, or during any subsequent tax year, she had derived an earnings factor of at least 25 times the weekly lower earnings limit for the year in question from Class 1 or Class 2 contributions actually paid (see EARNINGS LIMITS AND THRESHOLDS (30)). *[Married Women etc. Regs, Reg 2, repealed with effect from 6 April 1987 by Credits Amendment Regs 1987, Reg 10].*

A marriage ended by divorce terminates on the date of the decree absolute. A voidable marriage which has been annulled is treated as if it was a valid marriage terminated by divorce at the date of the annulment. A woman who has obtained a decree absolute of presumption of death and dissolution of marriage is to be treated as a person whose marriage is terminated otherwise than on death, unless the date of her husband's death has been satisfactorily established. *[Married Women etc. Regs, Reg 10].*

24.15 Widows

Where a woman ceases to be entitled either to a widow's allowance or to a widowed mother's allowance (other than by reason of remarriage or cohabitation with a man as his wife), she is to be treated as having satisfied the first contribution condition for contributions-based jobseeker's allowance, incapacity benefit or maternity allowance *and*, for the purpose of enabling the second contribution condition for any of those benefits to be fulfilled, she is to be credited with such Class 1 contributions as are necessary for every year up to and including that in which she ceased to be so entitled. *[Married Women etc. Regs, Reg 3(1)(a)(b), as amended by Home Responsibilities Regs 1978, Reg 3(1)].*

A woman will be *treated* as having ceased to be entitled to a widow's allowance or widowed mother's allowance if, although she did not receive widow's allowance or widowed mother's allowance, she would have been entitled to receive it but for her failure to claim, or delay in claiming, the benefit, or for her disqualification for receipt of the benefit for reasons other than cohabitation with a man as his wife, and the entitlement would have ceased. *[Married Women etc. Regs, Reg 3(7)].*

A woman who would otherwise be entitled to the credits referred to above but who is receiving a widow's industrial death benefit or a war or service widow's pension at a rate equal to or greater than the rate of contributions-based jobseeker's allowance, incapacity benefit or maternity allowance, will *not* be entitled to the credits for short term benefit purposes until she has, in respect of any one year beginning after her husband's death, derived an earnings factor of at least 25 times that year's weekly lower earnings limit from Class 1 or Class 2 contributions actually paid. *[Reg 3(5)(a)].*

24.16   Credits

Class 3 credits sufficient to enable certain widows and former widows to fulfil the contribution conditions necessary for entitlement to long-term benefits were, as a transitional measure, granted for the tax years 1975–76 to 1977–78. [*Married Women etc. Regs, Reg 6, as amended by Married Women and Widows Transitional Regs 1975, Reg 6(3) and Married Women and Widows Special Provisions Amendment Regs 1977, Reg 2*].

24.16 **INVALID CARE CREDITS**

For the purpose of enabling the second contribution condition for entitlement to any benefit to be fulfilled, a person (other than a married woman with a reduced rate election in force for the week concerned—see REDUCED LIABILITY ELECTIONS (52)—or a person entitled to an unemployment or incapacity credit for that week—see 24.10 above) was, on or after 12 April 1976 but before 6 April 1987, entitled to a Class 1 credit in respect of each week for any part of which an invalid care allowance was paid to him or, in the case of a widow, would have been so payable but for her receipt of other benefits. For qualifying weeks after 5 April 1987, the person is entitled to be credited with earnings equal to the lower earnings limit then in force (see EARNINGS LIMITS AND THRESHOLDS (30) and 51.4 RATES AND LIMITS) [*Credits Regs, Reg 7A(1)(2), as amended by Invalid Care Allowance Regs 1976, Reg 19; Credits Amendment Regs 1978, Reg 2(2); Credits Amendment Regs 1987, Reg 11 for 1986–87 and earlier years and Reg 6 for 1987–88 and later years*].

24.17 **JURY SERVICE CREDITS**

For the purposes of enabling the contribution conditions for entitlement to any benefit to be fulfilled, a person (other than a married woman with a reduced rate election in force for the week concerned—see REDUCED LIABILITY ELECTIONS (52)) is, from 6 April 1988, entitled to be credited with earnings equal to the lower earnings limit then in force (see EARNINGS LIMITS AND THRESHOLDS (30) and 51.4 RATES AND LIMITS) in respect of each week falling wholly within 1988–89 or within a later tax year for any part of which he attended at Court for jury service, provided that:

(*a*) his EARNINGS (28) as an employed earner for the week concerned are below the lower earnings limit then in force, and

(*b*) he claims the credit in writing before the end of the benefit year which immediately follows the tax year in which the week falls or within such further time as may be reasonable in the circumstances of the case.

A person who in any part of the week is a self-employed earner is, from 8 August 1994, precluded from receiving jury service credits for that week.

[*Credits Regs, Reg 9B, as inserted by Credits Amendment Regs 1988, Reg 2(3) and amended by Credits Amendment Regs 1994, Reg 4*].

The CA Field Operations Manuals at paragraphs 9763 and 9765 state:

9763   Any contributor whose contribution record is deficient because of jury service can get JSCs unless they are:

1   a married women with a reduced rate election;

2   getting SDA or Incapacity credits only; or

3   self-employed and not entitled to SEE.

9765 Contributors normally enquire about JSCs after the deficiency notice exercise.

In these circumstances the following letter is normally sent out by the CA:

> **Letter to contributor who enquires about Jury Service credits**
>
> Dear [ ]
>
> Thank you for your enquiry about credits when you were on Jury Service.
>
> I can confirm that someone who is called for Jury Service is entitled to a credit for each week they attend. Part of a week also counts. A married woman who has chosen to pay a reduced rate of contribution is not entitled to credits on the grounds of unemployment or Jury Service.
>
> You only need credits to make up a deficiency in your contribution record for a particular year, so you may not need them. If you do, the Department of Social Security will notify you. You will also get a form RD171A, on which you can claim the credits. When you return that form, we will ask you to provide a statement confirming the period you spent on Jury Service.
>
> However, if you claim Sickness or Unemployment Benefit before you claim the credits, tell your local Social Security or Unemployment Benefit office about your Jury service. This will ensure that we take account of any credits due if they affect your benefit claim.
>
> If you change your address, tell your local Social Security office.
>
> Further information
>
> Please get in touch with the person or manager of the section shown above if you:
>
> - need further information
>
> - are dissatisfied with the service you have received.
>
> Full details of our complaints system are given in leaflet CA62—'Unhappy with our service?', available from this or any other Social Security office.
>
> Yours sincerely,

24.18 MATERNITY PAY PERIOD CREDITS

For the purposes of enabling the contribution conditions for entitlement to any benefit to be fulfilled, a woman (other than a married woman with a reduced rate election in force for the week concerned—see REDUCED LIABILITY ELECTIONS (52)) is, from 6 April 1987, entitled to be credited with earnings equal to the lower earnings limit then in force (see EARNINGS LIMITS AND THRESHOLDS (30) and 51.4 RATES AND LIMITS) in respect of each week during a maternity pay period for which statutory maternity pay was paid to her, provided that she claims the credit in writing before the end of the benefit year which immediately follows the tax year in which the week falls or within such further time as may be reasonable in the circumstances of her case.

[*Credits Regs, Reg 9C, as inserted by Credits Amendment Regs 1988, Reg 2(3)*].

24.19 MISCELLANEOUS CREDITS

Contribution schemes prior to the 1975 scheme provided for the awarding of credits and such credits are preserved for the purpose of satisfying the contribution conditions attaching to current benefits. [*Social Security (Consequential Provisions) Act 1975, s 2*]. They are in certain cases augmented by non-employed (i.e. Class 3 equivalent) contributions. [*Widow's Benefit, Retirement Pension and Other Benefits Transitional Regs 1979, Reg 7*].

Where for any year a contributor's earnings factor derived from Class 1, Class 2 or Class 3 contributions paid by, or credited to, him falls short of a figure which is 52 times that year's weekly lower earnings limit for Class 1 contributions by an amount which is equal to, or less than, half that year's weekly lower earnings limit, that contributor is to be credited with a Class 3 contribution for that year (see EARNINGS FACTORS (29)). [*Contributions Regs, Reg 36*].

24.20 OVERSEAS EMPLOYMENT CREDITS

Although not described as such within the legislation, a kind of credit will nonetheless be awarded to any person who

(*a*)   has been absent from Great Britain and, by virtue of *Contribution Regs, Reg 120,* a reciprocal agreement or EC Reg 1408/71 (see 49.8, 49.14 and 49.17 OVERSEAS MATTERS) has paid Class 1 contributions at standard rate for the first 52 weeks of a continuing employment overseas or would have paid such contributions for the first 52 weeks of his employment overseas (or for such shorter period as his overseas employment continued) under *Reg 120* but for the operation of a reciprocal agreement or *EC Regs 1408/71*;

(*b*)   has returned to Great Britain; and

(*c*)   remained ordinarily resident in Great Britain throughout his absence (see 49.4 OVERSEAS MATTERS).

Any such person is to be treated as having paid Class 1 contributions on earnings at the lower earnings limit for any tax week of absence for which Class 1 contributions have not in fact been paid if that tax week is relevant to a claim for contributions-based jobseeker's allowance or short-term incapacity benefit and the person concerned is not entitled to corresponding benefits under the social security scheme of the foreign country in which he was employed. [*Unemployment, Sickness and Invalidity Benefit Regs 1983, Reg 20 as amended by Incapacity Benefit Consequential and Transitional Amendments and Savings Regs 1995, Reg 17(12)*].

24.21 DISABILITY WORKING ALLOWANCE CREDITS

With effect from 6 April 1992, a person may be credited with earnings equal to the lower earnings limit then in force in respect of each week for any part of which a disability working allowance is paid to him. To qualify, the person in receipt of the DWA must either be an employed earner or a self-employed earner who is excepted from Class 2 contributions on account of small earnings. No DWA credit may be awarded if the person is also entitled to an unemployment or incapacity credit, or is a married woman with a valid reduced rate election. *Credits Regs, Reg 7B, as inserted by Credits Amendments Regs 1991, Reg 3*].

The CA Field Operations Manual states at paragraphs 9804–9807 the following:

DWA credit entitlement

9804   DWA credits are available for any week, or part week, a contributor receives DWA. Self-employed and employed earners can get credits, but different rules apply.

Self-employed contributors

9805   Credits are available for self-employed contributors for any week or part week they receive DWA, providing for the relevant period, they:

1   hold a SEE certificate; or

2   have received a refund of Class 2 NICs because of low earnings.

9806   Self-employed contributors can only get DWA credits for the period of the refund. The refund must be for a period after 6 April 1992.

9807   If the contributor's earnings are above the SEE limit, there is no credit entitlement. Class 2 NICs are payable.

DWA was replaced in October 1999 by the Disabled Person's Tax Credit.

24.22 HOME RESPONSIBILITY PROTECTION CREDITS

A person who has to stay at home to look after a child or children and does not therefore undertake full time work will in many cases be covered by the home responsibility protection in relation to his or her pension rights. The effect of this is that the years of home responsibility protection are used to reduce the total number of years for which the contribution conditions for retirement pension must be met (see 13.2 BENEFITS: CONTRIBUTION REQUIREMENTS). In addition, rules also provide for certain individuals with home responsibilities to be credited with contributions such as when receiving invalid care allowance in respect of severely disabled children. See DSS Leaflet CF 411 'Home Responsibilities Protection'. [*Home Responsibilities Regs, Reg 2*].

The CA Field Operations Manual advises at paragraph 3012 the following:

Contributor entitlement to Home Responsibilities Protection (HRP)

3012   Do not accept Class 3 NICs if the contributor wants to pay for them for a year when they were entitled to HRP, unless you can confirm it would be more beneficial for them to pay Class 3 NICs. See the example below:

Example

A contributor has 10 years HRP and has paid NICs for 20 years, resulting in a 69% pension entitlement. If they pay for a year which HRP already covers, although they will lose that HRP year, the extra year paid results in a 70% pension entitlement, i.e.

HRP 10   HRP 9

   +   = 20/29 = 69%   +   = 21/30 = 70%

PAY 20   PAY 21

(See also CLASS 3 CONTRIBUTIONS: VOLUNTARY (19)).

25   Crown Servants and Statutory Employees

Cross-references. See ARMED FORCES (11); OVERSEAS MATTERS (49); SUBPOSTMASTERS (55).

Other Sources. Simon's NIC, Part I, Section 2, Chapter 8.46, Leaflet CA 65.

25.1   GENERAL CONSIDERATIONS

A significant percentage of the working population are employed in the public sector either as Crown servants or as employees of statutory corporations. A Crown servant is 'appointed to an office and is a public officer remunerated by moneys provided by Parliament so that his appointment depends not on a contract but on appointment by the Crown'. (*CIR v Hambrook [1956] 2 QB 641*). An employee of a statutory corporation will be a Crown servant if the Act creating the corporation expressly provides that the corporation is to act on behalf of the Crown, otherwise (even if the corporation is controlled by a government department) he will be an ordinary employee. (*Tamlin v Hannaford [1950] 1 KB 18*). Thus employees of the National Health Service are Crown servants, but employees of the British Broadcasting Corporation and employees of the Post Office are ordinary employees. (*Wood v Leeds Area Health Authority [1974] 2 IRLR 204; British Broadcasting Corporation v Johns [1956] Ch 32; Malins v Post Office [1975] ICR 60*).

Employment protection legislation narrows the definition of Crown servants set out above so as to bring certain Crown servants within its ambit [*Employment Protection (Consolidation) Act 1978, s 138*] but such narrowing of definition is irrelevant in the context of contribution law.

25.2   CATEGORISATION

Apart from members of the ARMED FORCES (11) who are Crown servants but are subject to special contribution provisions, a Crown servant is to be treated for contribution purposes as if he is a private person. [*SSCBA 1992, s 115(1)*]. This means that a liability for contributions on his earnings will arise only if he is an employed earner or self-employed earner according to the normal rules of CATEGORISATION (14). A Crown servant cannot *per se* be in business on his own account and cannot, therefore, be a self-employed earner. To be an employed earner he must, however, be gainfully employed in Great Britain under a contract of service or in an office with emoluments chargeable to tax under Schedule E. [*SSCBA 1992, s 2(1)(a)*]. The traditional view has been that no contract of service can exist between the Crown and its servants (*Dunn v R [1896] 1 QB 116*) but a modern view is that it can. (*Kodeeswaran v A-G for Ceylon [1970] 2 WLR 45*). Be that as it may, 'all servants ... of the Crown hold office' (*Ridge v Baldwin [1963] 2 AER 66*) and, assuming they are remunerated and that their emoluments are chargeable to tax under Schedule E, that will be sufficient to bring them within the category of employed earner for contribution purposes.

25.3   Police and prison officers

A police officer is a ministerial officer exercising statutory rights independent of contract. (*A-G for New South Wales v Perpetual Trustee Co Ltd [1955] AC 457*). He falls in a class of his own being neither a Crown servant nor an ordinary employee. (*Ridge v Baldwin [1963] 3 AER 66*). He does, however, hold an office with emoluments and is, therefore, an employed earner for contribution purposes.

Police cadets are neither office holders nor persons under a contract of service, and cannot, therefore, be categorised as employed earners or self-employed earners for contribution purposes. (*Wiltshire Police Authority v Wynn* [*1981*] *ICR 649*). (See APPRENTICES, TRAINEES AND STUDENTS (10).)

A prison officer, while acting as such, has all the powers, authority, protection and privileges of a constable. [*Prison Act 1952, s 8*]. He, like a police officer, holds an office with emoluments and is an employed earner for contribution purposes.

25.4   CROWN SERVANTS ETC. EMPLOYED OVERSEAS

It will generally be the case that, if a Crown servant, an employee of a statutory corporation, or a person in the private service of such a person, is employed overseas but does not fall within the contribution exemption provisions of the *Diplomatic Privileges Act 1964* or the *Consular Relations Act 1968* (see 25.5 etc. below), he will, if he is not permanently settled in the foreign state in which he is working and if there is a reciprocal agreement between the UK and that foreign state or the foreign state is another EEA member state, remain subject to the contribution legislation of Great Britain. [*National Insurance (Finland) Order 1984, Art 8(2), etc.; EC Regs 1408/71, Art 13(2)(d)*]. (See 49.14 and 49.21 OVERSEAS MATTERS.) Where a Crown Servant is posted to an overseas location within the EEA (see 49.1 OVERSEAS MATTERS) there is no requirement for certificates of coverage from the home state and no provision for such certificates in the *EC Reg 1408/71*.

The DSS had, historically, considered that certain allowances paid to crown employees serving overseas were not subject to national insurance contributions. However, it received legal advice suggesting that, on the basis of the legislation, contributions were in fact due from 6 April 1975. In response, the Government laid new regulations to put the previous, long-standing practice on a legislative footing from 6 April 1997 [*Social Security Amendment No 3 Regs 1997, Reg 2*]. The Contributions Agency have decided not to pursue arrears of contributions from 6 April 1975 to 5 April 1997, '*since to do so would entail considerable administrative costs ... and would not result in an overall increase in Government revenue*'. (National Insurance Fund Account 1996–97).

25.5   Contribution exemption

The Vienna Convention on Diplomatic Relations (*Cmnd 1368*) and the Vienna Convention on Consular Relations (*Cmnd 2113*) have the force of law in the United Kingdom by virtue of the *Diplomatic Privileges Act 1964* and the *Consular Relations Act 1968*. Those conventions confer exemption from contribution liability on certain groups of persons employed in the state receiving a diplomatic mission or accepting the establishment of a consular post (see 25.6, 25.7 below). Similar exemption is conferred on certain persons employed here by international organisations (see 25.8). Where the sending and receiving states are members of the EC, however, special rules apply (see 25.9 below).

25.6   Diplomatic agents etc.

A diplomatic agent is, as regards services rendered for the sending state but not as regards any other services, exempt from any social security provisions in force in the receiving state. [*Diplomatic Privileges Act 1964, 1 Sch 33(1)*].

A *diplomatic agent* is either the person charged by the sending state with the duty of acting as the head of a diplomatic mission or a member of the staff of such a mission having diplomatic rank (e.g. secretaries, counsellors and attachés). [*DPA 1964, 1 Sch 1*].

Similarly exempt from the social security provisions of the receiving state are

(a) private servants who are in the sole employ of a diplomatic agent, provided they are neither nationals of nor permanently resident in the receiving state *and* they are covered by social security provisions in force in the sending state or some other state;

(b) the members of the family of a diplomatic agent forming part of his household, provided they are not nationals of the receiving state;

(c) any members of the administrative and technical staff of the mission, together with members of their families forming part of their respective households, provided they are neither nationals of nor permanently resident in the receiving state; and

(d) members of the service staff of the mission, provided they are neither nationals of nor permanently resident in the receiving state.

[*DPA 1964, 1 Sch 33(2), 37*].

A *private servant* is a person who is in the domestic service of a member of the mission and who is not an employee of the sending state. *Members of the administrative and technical staff* are the members of the staff of a mission employed in the administrative and technical service of the mission (e.g. clerks, typists, archivists and radio and telephone operators). *Members of the service staff* are the members of the staff of a mission in the domestic service of the mission (e.g. butlers, cooks, maids and chauffeurs). [*DPA 1964, 1 Sch 1*].

Anyone who is not covered by these exemptions is subject to the social security provisions in force in the receiving state in the normal way, and any diplomatic agent employing such a person must observe the obligations which the social security provisions of the receiving state impose on employers. [*DPA 1964, 1 Sch 33(3)*].

The head of a diplomatic mission will normally supply the Foreign and Commonwealth Office with a list of the staff of the mission etc. and, once such persons have been accepted as *persona grata*, exemption from liability will apply where appropriate. Any question which arises as to whether a person is entitled to privilege or immunity is to be settled conclusively by a certificate issued by or under the authority of the Secretary of State. [*DPA 1964, s 4*].

All these provisions are subject to provisions to the contrary (if any) contained in bilateral or multilateral agreements affecting the sending and receiving states (see 49.17 to 49.23 OVERSEAS MATTERS). [*DPA 1964, 1 Sch 33(5)*]. In particular, they are subject to the EC regulations governing diplomatic staff described at 25.9 below.

25.7 **Members of consular posts**

Identical provisions to those described at 25.6 above apply in the case of members of a consular post, members of their families forming part of their households, and members of the private staff who are in the sole employ of members of the consular post. [*Consular Relations Act 1968, 1 Sch 48*].

A *member of a consular post* means a consular officer, a consular employee or a member of the service staff. A *consular officer* means the person charged with the duty of acting as head of a consular post and any other person entrusted with the exercise of consular functions. A *consular employee* means any person employed in the administrative or technical service of a consular post; and a *member of the service staff* means any person employed in the domestic service of the consular post. [*CRA 1968, 1 Sch 1*].

All those provisions are again subject to provisions to the contrary (if any) contained in bilateral or multilateral agreements affecting the sending and receiving states (see 49.17 to 49.23 OVERSEAS MATTERS). [*CRA 1968, s 1(7)*]. In particular, they are subject to the EC regulations governing consular staff described at 25.9 below.

25.8   International organisations

Exemption as described at 25.6 and 25.7 above will, if conferred by Order in Council, be granted to senior officers and staff members of committees and missions of international organisations provided the persons concerned are neither nationals of nor permanently resident in the receiving state. [*International Organisations Act 1968, s 1, 1 Sch Pt III, as amended by Diplomatic and other Privileges Act 1971 and European Communities Act 1972, s 4(1), 3 Sch Pt IV*]. Such organisations include the United Nations, the Commission of the European Communities, the Council of Europe, the International Labour Organisation, the World Health Organisation and the International Court of Justice.

25.9   Diplomatic and consular staff of EEA member states

A person employed by a diplomatic mission or a consular post within the European Community or other European Economic Area member state, or a member of the private domestic staff of an agent of such a mission or post, is, contrary to the rules described at 25.6 and 25.7 above, subject to the social security legislation of the state in whose territory he is employed *unless*

(*a*)   he is a national of the EEA member state which is the accrediting or sending State; and

(*b*)   he opts to be subject to the social security legislation of that state.

[*EC Reg 1408/71, Art 16(1)(2)*].

The option referred to at (*b*) above must be exercised within three months of the date on which the person concerned was engaged by the diplomatic mission or consular post concerned or on which he entered into the personal service of an agent of such a mission or post, and, once exercised, takes effect on the date of entry into the employment. [*EC Reg 574/72, Art 13*]. The right of option may be renewed at the end of each calendar year and, if renewed, will take effect on the first day of the following calendar year. [*EC Regs 1408/71, Art 16(2) and 574/72, Art 13(1)*].

Auxiliary staff of the European Communities may opt to be subject to the social security legislation of either

(i)   the member state in whose territory they are employed; or

(ii)   the member state to whose social security legislation they were last subject; or

(iii)   the member state whose nationals they are.

That right of option may be exercised once only, at the time when the contract of employment is concluded, and takes effect from the date of entry into employment. [*EC Regs 1408/71, Art 16(3) and 574/72, Art 14(1)*].

25.10   Non-exempt employees of exempt employer

Where a non-exempt employed earner is employed by an exempt employer, the employer will not fall to be treated as a secondary contributor (see 14.15 CATEGORISATION). He will, therefore, have no liability to pay or account for primary or secondary Class 1 contributions payable on earnings paid to that non-exempt earner. In such cases, the exempt employer may voluntarily undertake a secondary contributor's responsibilities (see Leaflet CA 65, pages 10 and 11) but, should he decline to do so, direct collection procedures will be imposed on the employed earner in relation to any liability for primary Class 1 contributions which arises (see Leaflet CA 65, pages 12–14 and 21.7 COLLECTION).

This situation may arise where a UK national is employed overseas by an overseas government agency or body. Despite the fact that the individual is employed outside the UK, a diplomatic presence of some kind in the UK may be argued to create a UK place of business (see 49.7 OVERSEAS MATTERS) of that overseas government. An individual who is ordinarily resident in the UK and resident here immediately before the commencement of the employment with the overseas government may therefore be required to pay primary contributions for the first 52 weeks of absence from the UK under *Contributions Regs, Reg 120.*

Where, however, a UK civil servant or a servant of a UK public corporation, or a UK national in the private service of such a person, is

(*a*) employed in Germany, *and*

(*b*) his contract of service has been concluded with a person employed in Germany in the Government service of the UK or in the service of a public corporation of the UK,

Art 13(2)(d) is superseded by *Reciprocal Agreement (No 1202) – Germany, Art 7(3)* and *Reciprocal Agreement (No 1513) – Germany, Art 5(3)* and the person concerned is to be subject to German social security legislation unless, within three months of the beginning of his employment, he chooses to be subject to UK social security legislation and gives notice of his choice to his employer and the Federal Minister of Labour and Social Affairs. [*EC Reg 1408/71, Annex III, Point A, Para 39*].

Similarly, and by operation of the same provisions, where a German national in the service of Germany or of some other public authority in Germany, or a German national in the private service of such a person,

(i) is employed in the UK, *and*

(ii) in accordance with his contract of service, is employed for service with a specified office in the UK,

he is to be subject to UK social security legislation unless, within three months of the beginning of his employment, he chooses to be subject to German social security legislation and gives notice of his choice to his employer and the Inland Revenue.

In both cases, the choice takes effect from the date of notification and, from that date, the person concerned is treated as if he were employed in the territory of the state to the social security legislation of which he has chosen to be subject.

25.11 Staff of the European School

Staff members of the European School at Culham (i.e. headmaster, deputy heads, secondary school teachers, primary school teachers, kindergarten teachers and educational advisers) are excepted from any class of employment for social security contribution purposes provided that they are seconded to the School by an EEA member state other than the UK and are subject to that state's social security legislation. [*EC (Privileges of the European School) Order 1990, Art 7(a)*].

26   Death of Contributor

Cross-references. See BENEFITS (13); CLASS 3 CONTRIBUTIONS (19).

Other Sources. Simon's NIC, Part I, Section 2, Chapter 8.291, Tolley's Social Security and State Benefits Handbook 2000–01.

26.1 CESSATION OF LIABILITY ON DEATH

Liability for national insurance contributions is *personal* to an earner and cannot, therefore, arise once an earner has died. [*SSCBA 1992, ss 6(1), 11(1)*]. However, contributions which have become due for payment before a person's death remain a debt due to the Inland Revenue by the estate of the deceased earner (in the case of Class 2 contributions) or by the secondary contributor concerned (in the case of Class 1 contributions).

There is, accordingly, no liability for either primary or secondary Class 1 contributions in respect of payments of *inter vivos* earnings made to the earner's estate after his death. (Leaflet CWG2 (2000), Page 16). Nor can there be a liability for a Class 2 contribution in respect of the week in which a self-employed earner dies, as a Class 2 contribution is not due until the last day of the contribution week. [*Contributions Regs, Reg 54(2)*].

There are grounds for believing that it is NICO policy to waive a claim for Class 2 contributions due from a deceased self-employed earner at the date of his death if, after distribution of his estate, his widow is in financial difficulty.

26.2 Class 4 contributions

Class 4 contributions are payable in the same manner as income tax, and liability arises in accordance with assessments raised by the Inland Revenue, or self-assessments made in respect of 1996–97 and later years. [*SSCBA 1992, s 15(1)(2)(5)*]. Tax under Case I or II of Schedule D which would, but for a person's death have been chargeable on him, is, however, to be assessed and charged on his executors or administrators. [*ICTA 1988, s 60(8)*]. It follows, therefore, that liability for Class 4 contributions on profits or gains to the date of death arises and also becomes a debt due from the estate of the deceased.

26.3 Death of secondary contributor

If a secondary contributor dies, anything which he would have been liable to do under the Contribution Regulations is to be done by his personal representatives or, if the secondary contributor was acting merely as an agent, by the person who succeeds him as agent or, if no one succeeds him, by the person on whose behalf he paid earnings. [*Contributions Regs, 1 Sch 33*].

26.4 Voluntary contributions

If a person dies, any contributions which, immediately before his death he was entitled but not liable to pay, may be paid notwithstanding his death, subject to compliance with any time limits to which the deceased person would have been subject. [*Contributions Regs, Reg 43*]. Thus, Class 2 contributions which the deceased was entitled but not liable to pay at the date of his death, and Class 3 contributions which he was entitled to pay, may be paid by *anyone* (not only his spouse but, for example, a former spouse) after his death. Such payments may be important, in relation to long-term benefits available to persons other than the contributor, on the contributor's record (e.g. retirement pension, widowed mother's

26.5 Death of Contributor

allowance). See Tolley's Social Security and State Benefits Handbook 2000–01, Chapter 12 for details of benefits and contributor/beneficiary relationships.

26.5 Return of contribution cards

On the death of a person to whom a contribution card was issued any person having, or thereafter obtaining, possession of that person's contribution card was to deliver it to a DSS local office. [*Contributions Regs, Reg 53(4)*]. This requirement has become obsolete with the abolition of contribution cards and stamps. It now only applies to cards issued before 11 April 1993. [*Contributions Amendment Regs 1993, Reg 7*].

27   Deferment of Payment

Cross-references. See ANNUAL MAXIMUM (7); CLASS 1 CONTRIBUTIONS (15); CLASS 2 CONTRIBUTIONS (18); CLASS 4 CONTRIBUTIONS (20); COLLECTION (21); MULTIPLE EMPLOYMENTS (44); RATES AND LIMITS (51); REPAYMENT AND RE-ALLOCATION (53).

Other Sources. Simon's NIC, Part I, Section 1, Chapter 56.211; Leaflets CA 01, CWL2 and CA 72.

27.1   GENERAL CONSIDERATIONS

Whenever a person who is employed in one employed earner's employment also becomes employed in one or more other such employments or self-employments, there arises the possibility that the total amount of contributions paid by him in the year will exceed his ANNUAL MAXIMUM (7) liability. Should this, in fact, occur, the excess amount of contributions paid is not lost and may be repaid, but it is obviously preferable that the payment of excessive contributions is avoided wherever possible (see 53.5 REPAYMENT AND RE-ALLOCATION). To this end, the Inland Revenue will, on a contributor's application and if satisfied that the likelihood of over-payment is great, arrange for deferment of the contributions which would otherwise be due in respect of one or more of the contributor's employments or self-employments.

For those applying for deferment (or their accountants on their behalf) the Inland Revenue NICO Deferment Group has requested that telephone callers to the Group (General enquiries tel. 06451 57141) should be aware of the last two digits of the NI number so that the correct telephone or fax number may be dialled. If the deferer's NI number is, say, AB 12 34 **66** C the telephone number called should be 08459 155653, 157227 or 159703, i.e.

Last two NI numbers	Telephone	Fax
00–33	08459 155425 or 155006 or 155651	08459 159595
34–**66**	08459 155653 or 157227 or 159703	08459 159595
67–99	08459 159383 or 155654 or 159463	08459 159224

27.2   CLASS 1 DEFERMENT

Where, in any tax year, an earner has earnings from two or more employed earner's employments, an arrangement may be authorised by the Inland Revenue under which the normal collection procedures are *not* to apply to earnings paid in respect of one or more of those employments but *are* to apply in respect of earnings paid in one or more of the others (see 21.1 to 21.4 COLLECTION). [*SSCBA 1992, s 19(1)(2); Contributions Regs, Regs 47, 49(1)*]. Payment of contributions on the earnings to which the normal collection procedures are *not* to apply will then be deferred. (Leaflets CA 01 and CA 72).

Such an arrangement will only be authorised where the earner has reason to believe that, during the year, he will pay contributions in respect of earnings to which the normal collection procedures *are* to apply of a sum equal to at least 52 primary Class 1 contributions at the rate applicable to him on earnings at the weekly upper earnings limit, or twelve such contributions at the monthly upper earnings limit (see EARNINGS LIMITS AND THRESHOLDS (30) and 51.2–51.4 RATES AND LIMITS). [*Contributions Regs, Reg 49(2)(3)*].

27.3   Application procedure

Application for deferment is to be made by sending a completed form CA 72A contained in Leaflet CA 72, supported (if requested by the Inland Revenue) by

27.4 Deferment of Payment

payslips or other documentary evidence of earnings from each employment, to the Deferment Group at Longbenton, Newcastle-upon-Tyne NE98 1ZZ (see 2.3 ADMINISTRATION). The application should reach the Group as soon as possible *before 6 April* of the year for which deferment is sought in order that any arrangement made might be operative from the first pay day in the new tax year. Arrangements will not normally be made for a year if the deferment application has not been made on or before *14 February* in the year (i.e. before the end of PAYE week 45), or for a year in which the applicant will reach pensionable age. (Leaflets CA 01 and CA 72).

27.4 Contracted-out and not contracted-out employments

An earner has no choice as to which of his employments are to be included in a deferment arrangement. That decision lies with the Deferment Group. Where, however, an earner is employed both in contracted-out employment and in not contracted-out employment, Deferment Group will always defer *not contracted-out contribution liability rather than contracted-out liability*, whenever this is possible (unless the earner has taken out an appropriate personal pension). In the latter instance Deferment Group will try to defer the contracted-out liability.

Similarly, deferment will usually be given in respect of COSR contracted-out employment, leaving payments in a COMPS employment payable to the maximum extent that those earnings will allow.

Example
Afghan is employed by Beagle Ltd (contracted-out, salary £290 per week); Collie Ltd (contracted-out, salary £400 per week); and Doberman Ltd (not contracted-out, salary £300 per week). He seeks Class 1 deferment for 2000–01. There are two possibilities: either liability on earnings from B may be deferred (leaving contributions payable on earnings from C and D which, together, will exceed the 2000–01 weekly upper earnings limit of £535), or liability on earnings from D (leaving contributions payable on earnings from B and C which, together, will also exceed £535). As A's employment with D is a not contracted-out employment, however, whereas his employment with B is not, deferment will be granted in relation to A's employment with D. Note, however, that if A's employment with B carried a salary of only £90 per week so that the only deferment arrangement possible would relate to the employment with B, that arrangement would be approved irrespective of the fact that the employment with B is a contracted-out employment. Where A has taken out an appropriate personal pension, deferment will not be granted in relation to A's employment with D.

Alternatively, if the employment with B was COSR, C was COMP and A had an APP in respect of earnings from D, then deferment would be granted in respect of earnings from B leaving those from C and D to take priority. At the end of the tax year a balancing repayment would be due which would be made out of the COMP earnings from C first.

27.5 Notification and operating procedure

An earner is notified of the Contributions Agency Deferment Group's decision on form CA 2717 and deferment certificates (CA 2700) are sent to the secondary contributors in the employments to which the deferment is to relate. (See CWG2 (2000), Page 58). The certificate informs the secondary contributor of the period to which it relates and instructs the secondary contributor that, during that period, he is no longer to deduct primary Class 1 contributions from the earnings paid to the earner in question, unless he is given written notification that the arrangement has been cancelled (CA 2702), though it offers him no explanation as to why that should be so and gives him no indication that the earner has one or more other employments. [*Contributions Regs, Reg 48*]. Nonetheless, although the Form CA2700 itself may remain silent on the matter, the astute employer who is conversant with the instructions on Page 58 of CWG2 will be only too well aware that his employee probably has at least one other job.

The secondary contributor himself is unaffected by the arrangement and must continue to pay and account for *secondary* Class 1 contributions on the earner's earnings as normal, using Table C, S, or V for the purpose of his calculations (see 15.5 CLASS 1 CONTRIBUTIONS and CWG2 (2000), Page 58).

A secondary contributor to whom a deferment certificate has been issued in respect of one of his employees is asked to maintain a record of both the primary Class 1 contribution liabilities which would have arisen had the deferment certificate not been issued and the relevant earnings. Such a record should be retained for three years after the end of the tax year concerned and may be required by the Deferment Group at Newcastle upon Tyne on form CA 2701 (CWG2 (2000), Page 58).

Where an application is approved *after 6 April*, one or more pay days may have passed before a deferment certificate can be sent to the secondary contributor (or contributors) concerned. In that event, the secondary contributor will be instructed to repay to the earner concerned all primary contributions thus far deducted from earnings paid to that earner since the previous 6 April. The secondary contributor will then be permitted to recoup from subsequent remittances to the Collector of Taxes amounts already paid to the Collector in respect of those refunded primary Class 1 contributions. Any unrecouped amount outstanding at the end of the tax year will be repaid by the Collector.

27.6 Post-deferment assessment

If the earner's expectations are proved to have been correct after the tax year has ended, it is found that maximum contributions have, in fact, been paid, exception from liability to pay contributions in respect of the earnings on which contribution liability was deferred will be granted automatically. [*SSCBA 1992, s 19(3); Contributions Regs, Reg 49(2)*]. If, however, it is found that contributions actually paid have fallen short of the total contribution liability arising on all the earner's earnings (subject to the annual maximum), *direct collection* procedures (see 21.7 COLLECTION) will be instituted so as to recover the shortfall. [*Reg 47*]. In making application for deferment, a contributor has to agree to pay any such shortfall within 28 days of demand (see form CA 72A in Leaflet CA 72 and 26.10 below).

Example
Eel is employed by Flounder Ltd, Grunion Ltd and Hake Ltd. In March 1999, when his earnings from the three companies were £330, £50 and £290 per week respectively, he applied for Class 1 deferment for 2000–01. As his anticipated earnings from F and H together exceeded the upper earnings limit for 2000–01 (£535), deferment was granted in respect of the primary Class 1 contribution liability which would otherwise have arisen on his earnings from G. If, when the year ends, it is found that earnings from F and H have, contrary to expectations, not reached the upper earnings limit throughout the year, the Inland Revenue will issue a demand for the balance of contributions due (relating those contributions to E's earnings from G but calculating the amount by reference to his actual total earnings in the year). If (as is more likely), however, the earnings from F and H have together exceeded the upper earnings limit throughout the year, any excess contributions paid on those earnings will be refunded (see 53.5 REPAYMENT AND RE-ALLOCATION) and the earnings from G will be automatically excepted from the liability which, until its exception, had been merely deferred.

27.7 Change in circumstances

Once a deferment arrangement has been brought into operation, there is an obligation on the earner to inform the Inland Revenue of

27.8 Deferment of Payment

(a) the termination of any employment in which contributions should, as part of the arrangement, have continued to be payable;

(b) the change to contracted-out employment of any not contracted-out employment; and

(c) the taking out of a personal pension.

Where a new employment is begun during a year for which deferment arrangements are already in effect, a further completed form CA 72A should be sent to the Deferment Group in order that an additional deferment certificate may, if appropriate, be issued. (Leaflet CA 72).

27.8 CLASS 2 AND/OR CLASS 4

Where a person is both an employed earner and a self-employed earner during a tax year, the Inland Revenue may make special arrangements to avoid excess payments of contributions. He must first be satisfied that the total amount of Class 1 contributions which are likely to be paid by or in respect of that person will exceed the Class 1 and Class 2 limiting amount for that year (see 7.2 ANNUAL MAXIMUM). The Inland Revenue may then make special arrangement with the person as to the manner and date for any (or any further) payment by him of Class 2 contributions in respect of that year (i.e. a 'deferment arrangement'). [*SSCBA 1992, s 19(1)(2); Contributions Regs, Reg 54(3)(a)*].

Similarly, the Inland Revenue may issue a 'certificate of deferment' for any year of assessment if

(a) there is doubt as to the extent, if any, of an earner's liability to pay Class 4 contributions for that year; or

(b) it is not possible to determine whether or not the earner is, or will be, liable to pay Class 4 contributions for that year.

The certificate of deferment will defer the earner's liability for Class 4 contributions until such later date as the Inland Revenue directs. [*SSCBA 1992, s 17(1)(b), (2)(c); Contributions Regs, Reg 62*].

There will be doubt as to the extent of an earner's liability to pay Class 4 contributions whenever that earner has, in addition to earnings from self-employment, earnings from an employed earner's employment at or above the employee's earnings threshold (see EARNINGS LIMITS AND THRESHOLDS (30)). This is because, where the total of primary Class 1 and Class 2 contributions paid in a tax year falls short of that year's Class 4 limiting amount any Class 4 liability is to be restricted to the amount of the shortfall, and if the combined Class 1 and Class 2 liabilities are *above* the Class 4 limiting amount, any potential Class 4 liability will be extinguished entirely (see 7.3 ANNUAL MAXIMUM).

Example

Inigo is a self-employed architect whose 2000–01 assessable Class 4 profits were £26,000. He is, however, also retained by Jones Ltd at an amount of £134 per week and expects the retainer to continue throughout 2000–01, but at an increased rate. His anticipated contribution liability for 2000–01 is, therefore,

	£
Class 1: £200 : Nil% on £76 × 52 weeks	0.00
+ 10% on £58 (balance) × 52 weeks	301.60
Class 2: 52 × £2.00	104.00
	405.60
Class 4: £26,000 – £4,385 (lower limit) × 7%	1,513.05
	£1,918.65

As the estimated Class 1 and Class 2 total (£405.60) falls short of the 2000–01 Class 4 limiting amount (£1,746.45) (see 7.3 ANNUAL MAXIMUM), Class 4 contributions will be reduced from £1,513.05 to whatever the shortfall (estimated at £1,746.45 – £405.60 = £1,340.85) is ultimately found to be. Because the amount may not be determined with accuracy until 6 April 2001 or later, however, he may apply for deferment of all Class 4 liability. In practice, the Inland Revenue does not make refunds of 50p or less and therefore works on a limiting amount of £1,746.95.

Were Inigo's anticipated earnings from his employed earner's employment to be in excess of £535 per week, Class 2 liabilities could be deferred also as, in that case, his Class 1 contributions alone would approximate to the overall annual maximum.

27.9 Application

If a person wishes to defer his liability to pay Class 4 contributions for any year of assessment, he must make formal application to the Inland Revenue in such manner as it approves. [*Contributions Regs, Reg 64(1)*]. In practical terms, this means that an applicant must complete and send to the Inland Revenue NICO Deferment Group at Longbenton, Newcastle-upon-Tyne NE98 1ZZ (see 2.3 ADMINISTRATION) a form CA 72B which may be found in the back of Leaflet CA 72. Where appropriate, this form (and renewal form RD 1301, issued automatically to previous year's successful applicants) serve as an application for Class 2 deferment also.

The applicant must be prepared to furnish the Inland Revenue with all such information and evidence as he requires and inadequate or erroneous information may result in the revocation of any certificate of deferment which is issued. In such a case contribution liability will revive in respect of the whole year. [*Contributions Regs, Reg 64(5)*].

An application for deferment is to be made before the beginning of the tax year to which it relates or before such later date as the Inland Revenue may allow. [*Contributions Regs, Reg 63(2)(a)*].

In practice, claims (except some renewal claims) are usually made well into the tax year to which the claim relates as the application forms are contained in leaflets dated April and invariably not physically available some time into the tax year.

27.10 Notification and procedure

Notification of a deferment decision is made to an applicant on form RD904A. Where the decision is favourable, a certificate of deferment is issued to the relevant Inland Revenue income tax office. Responsibility for the calculation and collection of any Class 4 contributions ultimately payable then becomes the responsibility of the NICO (see 21.16 COLLECTION) even if the certificate is revoked. [*Contributions Regs, Regs 65(a), 66(1)(b)*]. The tax office continues to note the self-assessed profits or gains for Class 4 purposes, however, and certifies these (or, if they exceed the Class 4 upper annual limit—see 30.8 EARNINGS LIMITS AND THRESHOLDS—the fact that they do so), to the NICO for each deferment year. [*Reg 66(3)*].

Any deferred contributions which are ultimately found to be due are payable within 28 days of demand. [*Reg 66(6)*].

Prior to 1996–97 where there was a deferment of Class 4 contributions, but an amount was ultimately paid, the 50% income tax relief was not granted until the Inspector of Taxes had been informed by the DSS that a payment of Class 4 contributions had been made. The DSS has said that such notification was automatic, using internal form RD905 (ICAEW Technical Release 21/92, paras 111, 112) but this was clearly, in practice, very often not so.

28 Earnings

Cross-references. See CLASS 1 CONTRIBUTIONS (15); CLASS 1A CONTRIBUTIONS (16) for treatment of cars and fuel supplied by an employer to an employee; CLASS 2 CONTRIBUTIONS (18) for small income exception; CLASS 4 CONTRIBUTIONS (20).

Other Sources. Simon's NIC, Part I, Section 2, Chapters 6 and 7; Tolley's Tax Planning 2000–01; Tolley's Income Tax 2000–01; Tolley's National Insurance Brief, February 1997; Leaflets CWG2 (2000) and CA 02. See also Leaflets 480 (2000) and 490 (January 1998).

28.1 GENERAL CONSIDERATIONS

The term 'earnings', when used in the context of social security legislation, includes any remuneration or profit derived from any trade, business, profession, office or vocation. It applies equally, therefore, to the income of an employed earner and that of a self-employed earner, though the amount of a person's earnings for any period, or the amount of his earnings to be treated as comprised in any payment made to him or for his benefit, are to be calculated or estimated in the manner and on the basis prescribed in the legislation and such prescriptions do, in fact, differ in the case of employed earners and self-employed earners. [*SSCBA 1992, ss 3(1)(2), 122(1)*].

When liability to pay contractual remuneration was limited by law in 1975 in an attempt to counter inflation, 'remuneration' was statutorily defined as including, in relation to any person, 'any benefit, facility or advantage, whether in money or otherwise, provided by the employer or by some other person under arrangements with the employer, whether for the first-mentioned person or otherwise, by reason of the fact that the employer employs him'. [*Remuneration, Charges and Grants Act 1975, s 7*]. It seems, however, that, in common law, remuneration is not so wide a concept as that. In *S & U Stores Ltd v Lee [1969] 2 AER 417* it was said that the term remuneration carries a narrower meaning than emoluments but is 'not mere payment for work done, but is what the doer expects to get as the result of the work he does insofar as what he expects to get is quantified in terms of money'. This definition was clarified in *S & U Stores Ltd v Wilkes [1974] 3 AER 401* where it was held that in order to ascertain a person's remuneration in the context of employment protection law, one must

(*a*) include any sum which is paid as a wage or salary without qualification;

(*b*) disregard the value of any benefit in kind (e.g. free accommodation) and any sum paid in cash by someone other than the employer (e.g. the Easter offering received by a minister of religion);

(*c*) examine any sum which is agreed to be paid by way of reimbursement or on account of expenditure incurred by the employee and see whether *in broad terms* the whole or any part of it represents a profit or surplus in the hands of the employee, and, to the extent that it does represent such a profit or surplus, include that sum.

It was stressed that (*c*) calls not for an involved accountancy exercise but for a broad common sense view of the realities of the situation.

S & U Stores v Wilkes was not a national insurance case but was concerned with redundancy pay. Its authority is at best persuasive in the present context, therefore. Furthermore, the addition of the word 'profit' to the definition of earnings for contribution purposes will, it seems, catch the items which are to be disregarded under (*b*) above, but *not* anything disregarded under (*c*) as being a legitimate reimbursement of expenses. The view that the word 'profit' brings payments in kind within the meaning of the word 'earnings' in *SSCBA 1992, s 3(1)* is rejected by at least two leading Counsel but the DSS clearly believed that it does as *Contributions Regs, Reg 19(1)(d)* was specifically introduced to *remove* such payments from the amount of earnings on which Class 1 contributions are exigible. (See 28.24 below).

The calculation or estimation of earnings is not merely a matter of deciding what should be *included* but of deciding also what should be *excluded*. The various regulations concerned govern both aspects of the computation and provide for certain receipts to be disregarded entirely and for certain items of expenditure to be deducted from receipts. [*SSCBA 1992, s 3(3)*].

Earnings paid in a foreign currency are to be converted to their sterling equivalent at the date of payment.

It should be noted in the context of employees, where an item is *not* earnings for Class 1 purposes it may, from 6 April 2000, fall within the extended charge to Class 1A National Insurance contributions.

28.2 EARNINGS FOR CLASS 1 PURPOSES

For the purpose of Class 1 contributions the amount of a person's earnings is, subject to the exclusion of various types of payment (see 28.7 to 28.75 below), to be calculated on the basis of that person's gross earnings (see 28.4 below) from the employment or employments concerned. [*Contributions Regs, Reg 18*].

The fact that, in this Chapter, various types of payment will be stated or argued to be outside the scope of Class 1 contributions will not, of itself, prevent a Class 1A charge arising in respect of the provision of cars and fuel for private use or, from 6 April 2000, on benefits in kind generally. Where a Class 1A charge arises on the provision of a benefit in kind and the recipient already has earnings in excess of the upper earnings limit there will be no difference in the National Insurance cost to the employer since the Class 1 (employer) and Class 1A (employer-only) rates are identical.

In the absence of any directions to the contrary, therefore, payments received by an employed earner will fall to be attributed or not attributed to his employments on the same causative principle as was enunciated in the leading tax case of *Hochstrasser v Mayes* [*1959*] *3 AER 817*. In that case it was stated that not every payment made to an employed earner by his employer is necessarily derived from his employment but that, for a payment to be so derived, the payment must be made 'in return for acting as or being an employee' and for no other reason. It is not sufficient to render a payment assessable that an employee would not have received it unless he had been an employee.

Despite the words of Lord Radcliffe in the *Hochstrasser* case quoted above, there has always been a tendency, when considering whether or not an item constitutes earnings, to seek only a link to services rendered or to be rendered (i.e. to see whether the item in question has been received in return for *acting* as an employee) and to disregard the alternative causative link of status (i.e. to see whether the item has been received in return for *being* an employee). The case of *Hamblett v Godfrey* [*1987*] *STC 60* serves as a strong reminder that that alternative causative link cannot be ignored. June Hamblett, a civil servant employed by GCHQ at Cheltenham by the Crown, had her right to belong to a trade union and certain other employment protection rights withdrawn, and in recognition of her loss of those previously-enjoyed rights she was paid £1,000. The court found that the £1,000 was not received by her in return for *acting* as an employee but that, as all the rights in question were directly connected with her employment, it *was* received by her in return for *being* an employee and was, therefore, emoluments for tax purposes. The DSS is understood to have found this judgment of particular interest and, in the light of the court's decision, reconsidered its views on what should not be included in earnings for contribution purposes. Pages 75–79 of Leaflet CWG2 (2000) reflect the latest views of the Inland Revenue and its NICO.

The more recent case of *Wilcock v Eve* [*1995*] *STC 18* concerned whether an ex gratia payment to a former employee could be charged to tax under Schedule E. The judgment contains a useful review of the case law in this area, although part of the Inland Revenue case turned on the benefits in kind legislation in *ICTA 1988, Pt V,*

Chapter II, which is irrelevant to Class 1 contributions, as the test for P11D purposes merely requires a benefit to be provided 'by reason of' employment, which is much wider than 'from' the employment.

Mr Eve was employed by a company which was sold out of a group to its management. Had he remained an employee of a group company for five months longer, he would have been entitled to exercise share options under an approved SAYE share option scheme and would have made a tax-free gain of around £10,000, depending on the share price on the actual day of exercise. The vendor company decided, a year after the notional exercise date, to pay him £10,000 as compensation for the loss of his rights under the SAYE scheme, which had been caused by its decision to sell the subsidiary. It was under no contractual obligation to do so, nor had any promise been made to the taxpayer: indeed, Mr Eve knew nothing of the payment until it was received. The company's reason for making the payment was given as a wish to maintain its reputation of dealing fairly with its employees and ex-employees.

The Inland Revenue claimed that the payment was either an emolument from the employment, taxable under what is now *ICTA 1988, s 19* or, alternatively, a benefit by reason of employment, taxable under what is now *ICTA 1988, s 154*. Only the former argument would be relevant to Class 1 liability. In support of the *s 19* argument, the Inland Revenue relied on the decisions in *Laidler v Perry [1966] AC 16*; *Brumby v Milner [1976] 1 WLR 1096* and *Hamblett v Godfrey*. The first concerned £10 vouchers given to employees at Christmas, held to be taxable emoluments. The second concerned a company merger which led to a payment being made to employees following the winding up of a profit-sharing trust, again held to be taxable emoluments.

Carnwath J felt able to distinguish Mr Eve's case from the three main authorities cited by the Inland Revenue. While accepting that an emolument 'from' employment is not necessarily confined to something in the nature of a reward for continuing employment (following *Hamblett*), he noted a distinction between rights intimately linked with the employment (e.g. trades union rights) and rights enjoyed in some other capacity (e.g. as a house-owner required to move). In his view, the share option scheme rights would have fallen on the borderline, were it not for the decision in *Abbott v Philbin HL 1960, 39 TC 82*. There it had been held that the *grant* of an option might be a taxable emolument, but the value realised on *exercise* was not — only the introduction of what is now *ICTA 1988, s 135* deemed a share option gain to be taxable under Schedule E, and then not by deeming it to be an emolument from the employment, but by simply including it within the Schedule E charge. In the absence of *s 135*, the exercise of Mr Eve's option after five years would not have constituted a taxable emolument on basic principles. Carnwath, J held that the payment made by the vendor to compensate him for the loss of the right to exercise the option should have the same character, i.e. it was not 'from the employment' but from his rights as the owner of an option.

28.3   Relevance of tax and 'earnings rule' decision

Although the underlying principle is the same whether the nature of a payment is being determined for contribution purposes, tax purposes, statutory sick pay purposes, statutory maternity pay purposes or State benefit purposes (see 28.2 above), the Secretary of State was *not bound* by decisions in these other areas. Indeed, the legislation in each area has its own incompatible rules of inclusion and exclusion. Earnings for the purposes of deciding the availability of benefits are governed by *Benefit (Computation of Earnings) Regs 1978*, and earnings for the purposes of deciding the earnings level in connection with statutory sick pay and statutory maternity pay are governed by *Statutory Sick Pay General Regs 1982* as amended by *Social Security Contributions, Statutory Maternity Pay and Statutory Sick Pay (Miscellaneous) Amendments Regs 1996* and *Statutory Maternity Pay General Regs 1986* respectively, which, despite their obvious similarities, are confined in their application to the area of law to which they belong.

Where the nature of a payment falls to be determined solely on general principles, however, a person may be *estopped* from arguing that a payment which he has conceded to be earnings for one purpose is not earnings for another. 'Blowing hot and cold in this way is something which the law does not tolerate'. *(R(P) 4/67)*. (See also *R(P) 1/69* and AOG Vol 6 Para 50552).

28.4 Gross earnings

The definition of earnings discussed at 28.2 above means that all wages, salaries, commissions and overtime payments fall to be included. (CWG2 (2000) Page 79).

There are many other kinds of payment which are made to employees and which, in certain circumstances, will fall, or not fall, to be included in earnings. These are discussed at 28.7 to 28.75 below in the following order.

28.5 Earnings

It should be noted that, where an item falls to be included in earnings, the requirement that Class 1 contribution liability is to be assessed on the basis of *gross* earnings precludes all deductions. [*Contributions Regs, Reg 18*]. That preclusion extends to deductions permitted for tax purposes such as relief for

(*a*) superannuation and personal pension contributions [*ICTA 1988, ss 594, 639*];

(*b*) necessary expenses of the employment [*ICTA 1988, s 198*];

(*c*) foreign earnings [*ICTA 1988, s 193*];

(*d*) personal allowances [*ICTA 1988, ss 256–278*];

(*e*) interest on qualifying loans [*ICTA 1988, ss 353–368*];

(*f*) charitable donations under the payroll deduction scheme [*ICTA 1988, s 202*];

(*g*) profit-related pay under a registered scheme [*ICTA 1988, s 171*].

It should also be noted, in the context of employees, where an item is *not* earnings for Class 1 purposes it may, from 6 April 2000, nonetheless fall within the extended charge to Class 1A National Insurance contributions.

28.5 Timing problems

The timing of a payment will often create confusion as to whether or not the payment forms part of earnings for contribution purposes.

The mere fact that a payment of an amount which is clearly earnings is made *in advance* of the period to which it relates does not prevent that amount being earnings at the date of payment if such payments are regularly made in advance. The question is one of unconditional entitlement. If, for example, an employee's contract provides that he is to receive a salary monthly in advance, his unconditional entitlement to the salary arises at its due date each month irrespective of the fact that he has yet to perform a month's work in connection with the payment. If, on the other hand, an employee who is not entitled to be paid until the end of the month requests and obtains a 'sub' or advance payment in the second week of the month, the amount paid to him is not earnings until the due date arrives. (CA28, April 1995 (now superseded), Page 72, Item 2). In that case, the 'sub' or advance is, in reality, a loan, see 28.44.

These principles apply equally to advance payments (if any) made to agricultural workers engaged on six-monthly or yearly hirings. Unless advance payments are made at regular intervals, they are to be treated as loans not earnings and the whole amount payable for the hiring will be earnings at (and not until) the end of the hiring period.

All payments made to COMPANY DIRECTORS (22) in advance or on account of fees yet to be voted are earnings at the point of payment (see 22.3 COMPANY DIRECTORS). (CWG2 (2000), Page 76).

Where pay is held back from an employee or set aside until some later date or event (e.g. Christmas or the annual holiday), the question whether the reserved amount is earnings or not again depends on whether or not the employee is unconditionally entitled to it at the date of reservation. If he is, the amount is earnings at that point; if he is not, the amount does not become earnings until entitlement does arise or payment is actually made (whichever is the earlier). (CWG2 (2000), Pages 25–28). For holiday pay, see 28.21 below.

Care must be taken in the kind of situation described above to ensure that amounts of pay are not treated as earnings *twice* for contribution purposes. Any payment made to an employee which would otherwise be earnings for contribution purposes is to be *excluded* from the computation of his earnings if, and to the extent that, it represents sums which have previously been included in earnings for Class 1 contribution purposes. [*Contributions Regs, Reg 19(1)(a)*].

Arrears of pay (e.g. from a back-dated pay award) become earnings only when entitlement to them arises—normally on the date of payment.

Where a payment of earnings is made either before an employment begins or after an employment has ended, it seems that no Class 1 liabilities can arise as regards that payment—despite the fact that *Contributions Regs, Reg 3(4)* is framed on a contrary assumption. Under the primary legislation, the Class 1 charge is confined to situations where, in any tax week, earnings are paid to or for the benefit of an earner in respect of any one employment of his which *is* employed earner's employment. [*SSCBA 1992, s 6(1)*]. It is not extended to a payment of earnings in respect of an employment which *was* or which *will be* employed earner's employment. The term 'which is' in the present principal Act replaced the more ambiguous term 'being' in the former principal Act with effect from 1 July 1992 and thus narrowed the range of interpretation which the charging section is able to sustain. [*SSA 1975, s 4(2)*]. See 28.7 and 28.8 below.

The DSS rejected this view and is understood to have the support of leading counsel, although the alternative view expressed above is also known to be supported by leading counsel. It is clear from literature issued after 1 April 1999 that the Inland Revenue reject it also. It is argued for the DSS view that a payment after termination remains earnings if it represents remuneration or profit derived from the employment and that the word 'is' must be read as meaning 'is, was or will be'. The Contributions Agency argued that regulations setting earnings periods for payments after termination indicate that the intention of the law is to include such payments within the Class 1 charge. In a letter quoted in *Booth's NIC Brief*, May 1994, the then Contributions Agency wrote:

'Our Agency does not accept that subordinate legislation is any less legal or effective than primary legislation, provided it is made within the confines of the powers granted by the latter.'

The counter-argument centres on three points.

- The change from 'being' to 'is' arose from a consolidation. It is accepted that a consolidating act cannot change the law. The new wording is less ambiguous than the old, so there is a presumption that the new wording represents the intention of the legislature more clearly and that the intention has not changed.

- Secondary legislation may not alter or vary the construction of an Act of Parliament, per Slade J in *Vandyk v Minister of Pensions and National Insurance [1954] 2 AER 723*. That being so, the existence of regulations covering post-termination payments is of no relevance in construing the primary legislation, the plain wording of which suggests that such payments are not subject to the Class 1 charge.

- Payments after termination were considered for Schedule E purposes in *Bray v Best [1989] 1 AER 969*. Oliver LJ held that, for an emolument to be chargeable under Schedule E, it had not only to be an emolument 'from the employment' but also an emolument for the year of assessment in respect of which the charge was sought to be raised. It was an established principle that a receipt or entitlement arising in a year of assessment was not chargeable to tax unless there existed in that year a source from which it arose. On the facts, the payments made could not be attributed to a chargeable period. Accordingly, the payments were not taxable. Legislation was subsequently introduced to attribute post-termination payments to the final year in which the source existed (see *ICTA 1988, s 19(4A) inserted by FA 1989, s 36(3)*).

28.6 Earnings

Although this is an income tax case, it is possible to compare the Class 1 charge with the Schedule E charge. If in a tax week (or month, or other earnings period) no source exists for a payment, it is arguable that no Class 1 charge may arise, particularly in view of the 1992 version of the wording of the charging section, *SSCBA 1992, s 6(1)*. The tax legislation reversing the *Bray v Best* decision was not replicated in contributions law.

The matter was considered further in National Insurance News, No 10, Spring 1998, where the CA reiterated its view that payments made before or after employment commences or ceases can be 'earnings', and will be 'earnings' unless one of the various exceptions, e.g. *Regulation 19(1)(d)*, applies.

28.6 Assignment or waiver of entitlement to pay

Once an unconditional entitlement to remuneration arises from an employed earner's employment, the amount of the entitlement is earnings for contribution purposes irrespective of the use to which it is put. Thus, for example, a member of a religious order may covenant to his or her order the whole of the remuneration to which he or she is entitled under, say, a contract to teach in a local school, but the remuneration remains nonetheless earnings for contribution purposes.

Likewise, charitable gifts under the payroll giving scheme (GAYE) deducted from pay for tax purposes remain part of earnings for contribution purposes. (CWG2 (2000), Page 22).

If, however, an employed earner waives his entitlement to remuneration *before* that entitlement arises, that remuneration will not, it seems, be earnings for contribution purposes. Thus, an employed earner who wishes, for example, to give £20 a month to the NSPCC could, instead of using the GAYE scheme (under which he would gain only tax relief, not NI relief), give a waiver to his employer in respect of £20 of his remuneration each month in consideration for his employer paying £20 a month to the NSPCC. By so doing, the employed earner would obtain both tax and NI relief as the £20 would be neither emoluments for tax purposes nor earnings for contribution purposes. Information on the GAYE scheme is obtainable from the Inland Revenue, FICO Repayments Section, St John's House, Merton Road, Bootle, Merseyside, L69 9BB (tel. 0151 472 6029/6053).

Waivers and repayment of remuneration already paid must (with the exception of contractual maternity pay — see 28.19 below), however, be disregarded for contribution purposes, even if they are recognised for tax purposes. (See 22.3 COMPANY DIRECTORS).

28.7 STARTING PAYMENTS

The DSS asserted and the Inland Revenue continues to assert that all 'golden hellos' and 'golden handcuffs' are earnings for contribution purposes. (CWG2 (2000), Page 76). This is quite simply wrong. Certainly, if the payment is made as a reward for services to be rendered to the payer in the future, it will be earnings. (*Hochstrasser v Mayes [1959] 3 AER 817; Riley v Coglan [1969] 1 AER 314*). And this will be so even if the payment is made by a party who has no direct or indirect interest in the performance of the contract of service which the recipient is being induced to enter and takes the form of a 'golden goodbye' from his former employer. (*Shilton v Wilmshurst [1991] STC 88*). But, if the 'golden hello' is an inducement for a person to surrender a personal advantage and a compensation for the loss caused to him by such surrender (other than the loss of earnings in his previous employment!), the amount should, on the grounds that it is not derived from the *employment*, not be regarded as earnings for contribution purposes. (*Jarrold v Boustead [1964] 3 AER 76; Pritchard v Arundale [1971] 3 AER 1011; Glantre Engineering Ltd v Goodhand [1983] STC 1; Vaughan-Neil v IRC [1979] STC 644*). In accordance with this principle (and despite the statements in CWG2 (2000), Page 76), the DSS is understood to have agreed that (in line with Revenue treatment from 6 April 1987) a sum of up to £6,000 paid unconditionally by a Rugby Football League club to an individual as part of a signing-on fee and representing compensation for the individual player's loss of amateur status will not be earnings for contribution purposes. (Taxation, 19 July 1990, Page 448). The inclusion in the original DSS leaflet CA 28, Page 76, Item 25, of a sentence advising employers to contact their local Social Security office in cases of doubt, suggests that discretion may be exercised although this is not clear from CWG2 (2000). It was reported in Taxation (26 January 1995, Page 383) that the agreement between the RFL and the Revenue had been updated, increasing the allowable tax-free payment to £8,500 with effect from 1 December 1993. It must be assumed that this new agreement will also be respected, especially now that contribution matters are the responsibility of the Inland Revenue.

It is important to note that, even where a starting payment *is* a payment of earnings, it is arguable that it is not within the charge to Class 1 contributions if it is made *before* the employment begins. (See 28.5 above).

28.8 LEAVING PAYMENTS

Generally

Subject to the comments at 28.5 above, any regular payments of earnings made to an employed earner after he has left his employment will (unless he is over pensionable age—see 3.7 AGE EXCEPTION) fall to be included in earnings for contribution purposes, whether, at the time of payment, he has commenced employment with a different employer or not. (CWG2 (2000), Page 15).

Also to be included in earnings is any additional payment made to the employed earner such as a deferred bonus, pay arrears from a back-dated pay award or (provided it does not represent amounts which have already been included in earnings—see 28.5 above) an accrued holiday pay entitlement (but see 28.9 below for an alternative view).

Other payments made on or after the termination of an employment may, or may not, be earnings for contribution purposes, depending on the circumstances. The same general principle enunciated earlier holds good. If the payment is made to the employed earner in return for him acting as or being an employee, it will be earnings; if it is made for some other reason or on other grounds, it will not. For this reason, it will be almost impossible to argue that any payment made to an employed earner on or after termination in satisfaction of an entitlement arising under the earner's contract of service is not earnings; and the same problem will arise wherever it can be shown that there was a firm expectation and understanding that the payment would be made for then there may be an *implied* term in the contract or service that such a payment will be made.

It is important to note, however, that even where a leaving payment *is* a payment of earnings, it may not be within the charge to Class 1 contributions if it is made *after* the employment has ended. (See 28.5 above).

28.9 Compensation for loss of office

In accordance with the general principle laid down at 28.8 above, any payment which is made voluntarily by an employer to compensate an employed earner for the loss of his office or employment (rather than as a disguised additional reward for past services—see *Bray v Best [1989] 1 AER 969*) will *not* be earnings for contribution purposes. (*Henley v Murray [1950] 1 AER 908; Clayton v Lavender (1965) 42 TC 607*). But an involuntary payment, i.e. one made under the express or implied terms of the employed earner's contract of service (see 28.8 above), will be caught. (*Henry v Foster (1931) 16 TC 605; Dale v de Soissons [1950] 2 AER 460; Williams v Simmonds [1981] STC 715*).

It is arguable that even accrued holiday pay included in a termination payment may, in appropriate circumstances, be treated as a compensation payment. If the contract of employment is silent on the treatment of accrued holiday entitlement at the time of termination, it is possible that any payment in respect of holiday entitlement accrued but not taken could quite correctly be characterised as compensation rather than earnings. However, in many businesses, it is the invariable practice to pay accrued holiday pay on termination and it may therefore have become an implied contractual term for all the employees concerned. In such circumstances, the payment is very likely to be earnings.

If the circumstances under which termination has taken place are such that the employed earner has a claim against the employer for breach of contract, i.e. wrongful dismissal, but the employed earner agrees (preferably *following* termination) to accept a compensation payment in satisfaction of his claim for damages, the payment by the employer will hardly be voluntary but it will nonetheless *not* be regarded as earnings for contribution purposes. It will, in fact, be treated as damages (see 28.10 below). (CWG2 (2000), Page 92). If a settlement of compensation is negotiated *before* the contract has been terminated, care must be taken to ensure that the negotiations do not merely result in a variation of the contract so as to provide for an agreed sum on termination; for such a sum will constitute earnings for contribution purposes.

The DSS sought to recover contributions in respect of employers' payments intended as compensation for breach of contract. The Department argued that they are in fact restrictive covenant payments, taxable by virtue of *SSCBA 1992, s 4(4)*. Whilst that section would at first sight appear to be inapplicable because such payments are made to compensate the former employee for his loss of rights and not in return for any restriction on his future actions, the section uses the very wide definition of restrictive covenant contained in *ICTA 1988, s 313(1)*. That refers to 'an undertaking [given by an individual in connection with his holding an office or employment] (whether absolute or qualified, and whether legally valid or not) the tenor or effect of which is to restrict him as to his conduct or activities'. This definition, the DSS maintained, includes situations where the individual agrees not to pursue his legal remedy for breach of contract in consideration of his former employer paying him a certain sum, which is often quantified, under normal breach of contract principles, by reference to the salary that he has lost.

This interpretation is at odds with the DSS's own original guidance in the 1995 leaflet CA 28, Page 90, Item (95), namely, 'If an employee seeks redress through the courts and payment is made to prevent, or as a result of, legal action, no NICs are due.' This has now been superseded by CWG2 (2000), Page 93, Item 7 which states 'the termination was a breach of contract. For example . . . you agree, or the Courts or an Industrial Tribunal rule, that the employee was unfairly or wrongly dismissed'. However, that guidance also states that if the payment of compensation on termination of employment is contractual or contains a contractual element, the contractual element should be included in gross pay. As contributions can only be levied in respect of earnings (see 28.1 above), the contract referred to in the guidance must therefore be the contract of employment and not the agreement that the employee reaches with his employer. This is borne out by the example given of a contractual element, namely arrears of pay.

28.10 Damages

Damages are not earnings for contribution purposes, and that extends to payments made to compromise an action for damages. (*Du Cros v Ryall (1935) 19 TC 444*).

Thus, the DSS regarded as damages which are not earnings for contribution purposes any payment made by an employer to his former employee in connection with a breach of contract if

(a)   court proceedings have started, or

(b)   there is a threat of court proceedings, or

(c)   the payment is made to prevent legal action being taken.

28.11 **Employment protection payments**

Certain payments made under the *Employment Rights Act 1996* and the *Trade Union and Labour Relations (Consolidation) Act 1992* to an employed earner are to be treated as earnings for contribution purposes. These are

(a)   guarantee payments;

(b)   medical suspension payments;

(c)   maternity pay payments;

(d)   payments of arrears of pay under an order for reinstatement;

(e)   payments of arrears of pay under an order for re-engagement;

(f)   payments of pay due as a result of an order for the continuation of a contract of employment;

(g)   payments of pay due as a result of a protective award.

[*SSCBA 1992, s 112; Contributions (Employment Protection) Regs 1977, Reg 2(a)(b); Employment Rights Act 1996, s 240, 1 Sch 51(1)(4)*].

An award by an industrial tribunal of compensation for unfair dismissal is *not* regarded as earnings for contribution purposes.

The amount to be *included* in earnings is, in a case falling within

(i)   (a) or (b), the amount actually paid;

(ii)   (c), the amount actually paid or, if normal wages are paid, the gross wage net of any maternity pay handed over to the employer;

(iii)   (d) or (e), the gross amount of the award including wages in lieu of notice, *ex gratia* payments and other benefits;

(iv)   (f), the gross amount of the award including payments under the contract of employment, damages for breach of the contract in respect of any part of the pay period covered by the order and any lump sum payment in lieu of notice;

(v)   (g), the gross amount of the award including payments under the contract of employment and damages for breach of the contract in respect of a period falling within the protected period.

(1995 DSS Leaflet CA 28, Paras 124–133; Page 92, Item (105). See also CWG2 (2000), pages 95 and 96 regarding the time at which contributions are due).

The above rules are to apply even if the actual amount payable to the earner is, after PAYE and national insurance deductions and deductions made by the awarding tribunal, very small or non-existent (Leaflet CWG2 (2000), Page 95).

If an award includes an element which would normally have been excluded from earnings for contribution purposes (e.g. loss of tips direct from customers), that element of the award should be excluded for contribution purposes.

Where there is difficulty in ascertaining the gross amount which is to be included in earnings for contribution purposes, the clerk to the awarding tribunal may be consulted.

28.12 Earnings

28.12 Ex gratia payments

An *ex gratia* payment is simply a payment not compelled by any legal right. (See *Edwards v Skyways Ltd [1964] 1 WLR 349*). It thus strictly covers voluntary compensation for loss of office (see 28.9 above). The term is more commonly confined, however, to payments which an employer makes to an employed earner following termination of the earner's contract of service but which he has no obligation to make and which are not primarily compensatory in nature. It is axiomatic that a contract of service cannot provide for an *ex gratia* payment on termination. Such payments are not earnings for contribution purposes provided they are made in recognition of loyalty, length of service etc., rather than to the past services provided.

The DSS advised that, if it is an employer's practice to make '*ex gratia*' payments when employees leave, such payments constitute earnings for contribution purposes. (CWG2 (2000), Page 92). This is correct only if the employer's past practice has given rise to an implied term in the contract of service of the person to whom the *ex gratia* payment is now being made; and for that to be so the practice must have been well known to the employees. A past practice, however consistent, will not bring an *ex gratia* payment into earnings for contribution purposes if the practice has been kept confidential.

See also 28.2 above for details of *Wilcock v Eve* concerning an *ex gratia* payment to a former employee.

28.13 Golden handshakes

'Golden handshake' is not a term of precise meaning and is generally used to cover the whole of any lump-sum which an employee receives on leaving his employment, however that lump-sum is constituted. In order to determine the contribution consequences of making the payment, therefore, each of its separate elements will need to be identified and examined in the light of 28.8 to 28.12 above and 28.14 to 28.17 below. The DSS was quite wrong in the past in stating that all golden handshakes should be treated as earnings.

28.14 Payments in lieu

Previously CA 28 made it clear that what the DSS meant by pay in lieu of remuneration is payments of compensation for the loss of earnings resulting from premature termination of a fixed term contract of service (See 1995 DSS leaflet CA 28, Page 90, Item (94)).

The legal principles underlying the guidance are these. The phrase 'payment in lieu of notice' may be used both where a contract of service ends on an agreed date with an agreed payment and where the contract is terminated immediately with the employee having the right to damages for breach of contract or compensation for unfair dismissal. In the former case, the employee surrenders no rights. He merely receives what he is entitled to receive by virtue of his contract of service. (*Dale v de Soissons [1950] 2 AER 460*). In the latter case, the employer might decide to make a payment to meet any anticipated claim for damages which the employee might have in respect of the failure to work out his notice and to earn his wages. The true nature of the latter payment is to meet any anticipated claim for loss by the employee; it is not referable to the provision of services and it should thus be regarded as damages (see 28.10 above). (*Dixon v Stenor Ltd [1973] ICR 157; Gothard v Mirror Group Newspapers Ltd [1988] ICR 729; Delaney v Staples [1990] ICR 364; Foster Wheeler (London) Ltd v Jackson, 24 August 1990, Times*).

The DSS confirmed its position to be as follows: 'Legal advice available to the Department confirms that any payments made under the provisions of a contract of service will, unless excluded by regulations, attract NIC liability. Payments in lieu of notice are made because the provisions of a contract cannot be fulfilled. As such they are regarded as damages for breach of contract and not earnings. Clearly a payment which is provided for in a contract cannot represent damages for breach of contract.' (Letter to author, 4 April 1990).

There has, in the past, been some difficulty over a typical clause in a service contract reserving a right to the employer to make a payment in lieu of notice. Generally, this clause, which may also provide for liquidated damages, is intended to protect the employer after termination. If the employer is in fundamental breach of the contract, the former employee may be able to refuse to abide by restrictive covenants in the contract, citing the employer's breach as a defence if enforcement of those covenants is sought. Reservation of the right to pay damages under the contract allows the employer to avoid such actions by the ex-employee.

The view was supposedly clarified by the Contributions Agency when they stated

'Because a PILON is a payment to compensate an employee's legal claim for damages for loss due to a breach of contract and to forestall a legal action for such breach its compensatory character prevents it being regarded as earnings. It does not, therefore, attract liability for NICs.

In addition to specifying the period of notice, a contract of employment may provide *expressly* for a sum to be paid *instead* of that notice. In other words, the contract provides that in the event of the employment being terminated prematurely, a payment in lieu of notice *will* be made.

This payment too is intended to replace the employee's entitlement to damages in the event of notice *not* being given. It too has the character of a payment made to forestall a legal action, and to compensate for a breach of contract.

But, the payment *is* earnings for NIC purposes. This is because it is something to which the employee becomes entitled as part of the terms on which they agreed to provide their services. It is therefore treated as, and constitutes part of, the employee's rewards for their labour.'

(CA Specialist Conference written responses, 20 February 1996.)

If payment is made, it is often difficult to determine whether the payment is contractual 'earnings' (and therefore subject to Class 1 liability) or non-contractual compensation (and therefore not earnings). In *Dale v de Soissons*, the contract of employment provided for a payment of £10,000 as 'compensation for loss of office' if termination occurred after twelve months of a contract which purported to be for three years. The court held that, in fact, termination after twelve months did not constitute a breach, as specific provision had been made for just such an eventuality. A breach would only have occurred if the £10,000 had not been paid on termination after one year. The £10,000 paid was therefore held to be an emolument from the employment rather than compensation derived from the termination. The Contributions Agency has used this line of argument to charge Class 1 contributions on payments in lieu.

This matter was further addressed by the CA as follows

'If the contract provides that in the event of the fixed term being curtailed in any way the employer will make a payment in lieu of remuneration for the remaining period, then the right to that payment arises from the terms of the contract. The employer and employee have agreed that as part of the terms on which the employee will provide his services, that the employee shall in certain circumstances be entitled to certain payments. The right to the payment specified in the contract forms part of the rewards for the employee's services. It is earnings, and attracts liability for NICs.

If the contract does not provide for the making of a payment in lieu of remuneration in the event of the employer terminating the contract before the expiry date, then any payment on account of lost remuneration is compensatory only. It is not earnings, and therefore there is no liability for NICs.

If an employee has contracted to work for a fixed term and the employer has contracted to provide work for that period, any termination by the employer in advance of the expiry date constitutes a breach of contract by them, and entitles the employee to claim damages. The employer's payment is compensation for a legal claim to damages, and is made to forestall such a claim. For the reasons given in paragraph 7 it does not constitute earnings and does not attract liability for NICs.'

(CA Specialist Conference written responses, 20 February 1996.)

However, in the recent case in the Court of Appeal of *EMI Group Electronics Ltd v Coldicott [1999] STC 803* the question of whether pay in lieu of notice is taxable has fallen on the side of the Inland Revenue. In this case the Inland Revenue had asserted that termination payments made to two senior executives in lieu of their notice, written into their contracts, were assessable to PAYE (and NICs). The specific part of the termination provisions were as follows:

'NOTICE OF TERMINATION

The senior manager is required to give the Company three months' notice in writing of the intention to terminate employment. The Company will give its senior managers six months' notice in writing of its intention to terminate employment, except during the first six months' of service, when this will be reduced to three months' notice.

The Company reserves the right to make payment of the equivalent of salary in lieu of notice and to terminate employment without notice or payment in lieu for gross misconduct.'

In the Court of Appeal Chadwick LJ supported the decisions reached by the Commissioners and the High Court and came to the conclusion that ' . . . there is nothing in the authorities which requires this court to reach the conclusion that a payment in lieu of notice, made in pursuance of a contractual provision, agreed at the outset of the employment, which enables the taxpayer company to terminate the employment on making that payment, is not properly to be regarded as an emolument *from* that employment. In my view, for the reasons which I have set out, such a payment is an emolument from the employment.' Leave to appeal to the House of Lords was refused. Now that the matter has been resolved it might be in the interests of employers to review the discretionary pay in lieu contracts and in the above circumstances deduct PAYE and NICs (where relevant).

See also Tolley's Practical NIC, June 1999, page 41.

Delaney v Staples, although a *Wages Act* case, may provide a persuasive counter-argument. Browne-Wilkinson, LJ stated there that 'a payment in lieu is not a payment of wages in the ordinary sense since it is not a payment for work to be done under the contract of employment.' Something that is not wages for work done or a reward for services cannot be remuneration or profit derived from the employment on the principles outlined above in relation to *Hochstrasser v Mayes*.

Furthermore, the principles applied in *Hamblett v Godfrey* need not present a difficulty. Following Carnwath, J's reasoning in *Wilcock v Eve* (see 27.2 above), Miss Hamblett was taxed on the £1,000 compensation she received not simply because she was an employee under a contract of service but because the payment derived from a right intimately linked with that employment. It is submitted that, where payment in lieu is *permitted, but not required*, by the contract of employment, but only at the discretion of the employer, no contractual *right* to the payment exists and any payment made cannot be earnings. Thus, no contribution liability can arise in this circumstance and this was confirmed, for the first time, in CWG2 (1998), Page 81 (although the Inland Revenue still asserted that such payments are both taxable and subject to PAYE). The CA view was in line with what is expressed in its Specialist Conference written responses, 20 February 1996. Before its demise, the Contributions Agency, however, rebutted that advice (CA National Insurance News No 12, Winter 1998/99) and the 1999 and 2000 editions of CWG2 again revert back to the statement that such payments *are* liable to contributions. This is supported by the outcome of the *EMI* case referred to above. See CWG2 (2000), Page 93, Item 1.

If it can be demonstrated that the payment is derived directly from the termination rather than from the services (i.e. it would not have been made if the employment had not been terminated and no right to receive it was written into the contract), it should not represent earnings. Even if the payment might have been made in another form in due course, it is likely that it would still not be liable. In *Henley v Murray*, a director with a fixed term contract was asked by the board to resign early. He was paid on termination the amount he would have received if the appointment had continued to the contractual termination date. The sum was held by the Court of Appeal not to be assessable. The payment was clearly *related to and based on* the contract, but was derived from its termination, not from its being carried out. Also, if the employer and the employee both agree that the employment should terminate forthwith on payment of *a sum in lieu of notice* this subsequent agreement between the parties does not constitute a term on which the employee agreed to provide their labour. It is in fact the price the employer is prepared to pay the employee to forego notice to which they would otherwise be entitled and no NICs would be due in respect of it, but for the outcome of the *EMI* case referred to above. For a review of the Inland Revenue position see IR Tax Bulletin, August 1996, pages 325–327.

28.15 Redundancy pay

Any payment by way of redundancy pay, whether provided for within the terms of a contract or not, is to be excluded from earnings. [*Contributions Regs, Reg 19(4)(a)*]. (CWG2 (2000), Page 93). The exclusion stated applies to all redundancy payments, not merely to statutory redundancy payments. A redundancy payment is merely compensation for the loss of the accrued right in a person's job (*Lloyd v Brassey [1969] 1 AER 382*) which, were it not excluded from earnings for contribution purposes by regulation, would fall to be excluded or included by reference to the principles set out at 28.9 above. A redundancy payment is made in return for an employee ceasing to be an employee rather than for acting as or being one. (See *Mairs v Haughey [1992] STC 495*, and 28.2 above).

In practice, for these purposes, the definition of 'redundancy' is drawn from *Employment Rights Act 1996, Part XI* and *s 199(2)* or *209*. Redundancy, for employment protection purposes, is defined as dismissal wholly or mainly due to the fact that the employer has ceased, or intends to cease, to carry on the business for the purposes of which the employee was employed or has ceased or intends to cease to carry on that business in the place where the employee was employed. Alternatively, redundancy can occur where the requirements of that business for employees to carry out work of a particular kind, or for employees to carry out work of a particular kind in the place where they were so employed, have ceased or diminished or are expected to cease or diminish.

The CA added further clarification

'A company may embark on a series of comprehensive redundancies where payments in lieu of notice are common, and become an expectation by those who are affected. However, it is unlikely to be the intention of any employer that whatever may be offered by way of a payment in lieu of notice as part of a redundancy package shall become incorporated into an employee's existing terms of and conditions of service, and, as a consequence, form part of the rewards that employee receives in exchange for providing services. The usual intention is that the payment should be received as compensation for losing the right to provide services. The payment therefore remains one to compensate the employee for the breach of contract in giving no notice or less than the requisite amount of notice, and does not attract liability for NICs.'

(CA Specialist Conference written responses, 20 February 1996.)

28.16 Restrictive covenant payments

Guidance on this topic is that payments made by an employer to an employed earner in consideration of the earner agreeing not to compete against the employer are earnings for contribution purposes. (CWG2 (2000), Page 93). That has been correct advice since 21 July 1989 for, since that date, any sum paid to or for the benefit of an employed earner which is chargeable to tax by virtue of *ICTA 1988, s 313* (other than by *s 313(4)* — until 10 July 1997), i.e. a cash payment made to an employee in return for some undertaking, such as an undertaking not to compete, is to be treated as earnings for contribution purposes. [*SSCBA 1992, s 4(4)*].

It is worth observing that *ICTA 1988, s 313(4)* relates to circumstances where valuable consideration other than money is given. As *SSCBA 1992, s 4(4)* was not to apply in such a case, it has previously been possible for an employer to transfer, say, gilts to a former employee in consideration for a restrictive covenant without the gilts being earnings for contribution purposes. However, this 'loophole' has now been blocked, with effect from 10 July 1997. [*Social Security Act 1998, s 50 (1) and (3)*].

It is worth emphasising that payments in respect of restrictive covenants are *not* within *SSCBA 1992, s 3(1)(a)* unless *Sec 4(4)* puts them there; and a careful reading of *Sec 4(4)* will show that it cannot put them there unless, *at the point of payment*, the person to whom or for whose benefit they are paid is not just an 'earner' but an '*employed earner*', i.e. someone 'gainfully employed in Great Britain either under a contract of service, or in an office (including an elective office) with emoluments chargeable to income tax under Schedule E'. [*Sec 2(1)(a)*]. If, therefore, at the time of payment of a restrictive covenant payment, the person concerned is *not* such an 'employed earner' (because, for example, he is between jobs), *Sec 4(4)* does not appear to apply to him and the payment cannot, therefore, ever reach *Sec 6(1)*, the Class 1 charging section.

The DSS also once took the view that an employment relationship between payer and recipient is a prerequisite for liability. Where a company buys a competing business and pays the vendors a sum in consideration of an agreement not to compete with the new combined business, there will be a tax liability under *s 313* but it is arguable that there can be no Class 1 liability if the individuals concerned do not become employees of the purchaser.

See also 28.9 above for commentary on the policy of applying *s 4(4)* to termination payments.

28.17 Pensions

Any payment by way of a pension is to be excluded from earnings for contribution purposes. [*Contributions Regs, Reg 19(1)(g)*]. (CWG2 (2000), Page 93).

The term 'pension' is not defined in the legislation and there is no judicial definition of the term. It has been held, however, that, for payments to be pension payments,

(*a*)   the employment in respect of which the payments are made must have ceased;

(*b*)   the employment need not have ceased because of retirement but may have ceased through, for example, incapacity;

(c) the payments need not be for past services in the sense of being deferred pay but may be on account of, for example, disability; and

(d) the payments need not continue for life but may end, for example, on the cesser of disability.

(*Johnson v Holleran* [*1989*] *STC 1*).

This accords with the usual meaning of the term 'pension' which is a periodic allowance made to a person who has either retired, become disabled or permanently incapacitated, reached old age, or become widowed or orphaned.

Until 5 April 1993, DSS Leaflet NI 269 stated that 'for a payment to be regarded as a pension the employment must have ceased,' but this has now been deleted.

As regards (c) above, it is important to note that, though a payment need not relate to *past* services in order to be a pension, if it relates to *present or future* services it will *not* be a pension in accordance with any accepted understanding of the term.

DSS guidance was that neither periodic payments by way of pension for long service, retirement, ill health or widowhood nor lump sum commutation payments in respect of such pensions are earnings for contribution purposes. The DSS appeared to draw no distinction between pensions under schemes approved under *ICTA 1988, s 590* and unapproved pension schemes such as are referred to in *ICTA 1988, s 595*. It does, however, stress that if payments are made under a trust arrangement during the course of employment, such payments will constitute earnings for contribution purposes (1995 DSS Leaflet CA28, Page 83, item (72)). This comment presumably related to attempted contributions avoidance by means of payments through funded unapproved retirement benefits schemes or 'FURBS' trusts where money is paid out of the trust before retirement. Payments from pension trust funds after the employment has ended are, however, to be excluded from earnings.

FURBS were heavily marketed as a supposed NIC avoidance scheme and the rules are sometimes written in such a way that a relatively young person can take a supposed pension but then commute that payment into a lump sum. This way FURBS have been used regularly as a conversion medium for annual bonuses which are then in turn converted into cash in the hands of that employee with no Class 1 NICs liability. It was announced on 22 July 1997 that clauses would be included in the Social Security Bill to bring FURBS payments into charge to contributions from 6 April 1999. However, the CA then declared:

'Having examined the issue, we consider that we may have been somewhat cautious in our view of the current legislation in relation to FURBS. We also know that there has been comments regarding the guidance we have issued. We have never issued specific guidance on FURBS. However we are aware that there is a need to provide clear guidance on the issue of FURBS.'

CA Specialist Conference, 29 October 1997.

Subsequently, the Agency confirmed in a Press Release on 17 November 1997 that in their view FURBS have always, technically, been liable to contributions and that they will expect employers to comply by 6 April 1998. They also stated that they may look again at earlier alleged FURBS transactions where payments have been made out of the FURBS very quickly. This view by the Agency, as it applies to a genuine FURBS, is widely thought to be incorrect and may well be challenged (see APPEALS AND REVIEWS (9); DSS Press Release 97/127, 22 July 1997; CA 47/97, 17 November 1997; CWG2 (2000), Page 61; CA National Insurance News extracts, Summer 1997 and CA National Insurance News extracts, Spring 1998).

Further provision is made by *The Social Security (Contributions and Credits) (Miscellaneous Amendments) Regulations 1999, SI 1999 No 568*. These regulations make various provisions from 6 April 1999 with regard to FURBS and other pension schemes. These are all arguably superfluous, since a payment 'by way of a pension' is to be excluded from earnings and a pension contribution — whilst clearly a payment to or for the *benefit* of the earner — is arguably excluded by *Reg 19(1)(d)*, but these regulations stem from the authorities' questionable belief that payments by employers to pension schemes are, nonetheless, earnings.

- Provision is made for the apportionment of payments into a FURBS which relate to two or more earners [*Reg 18(zl) as inserted by SI 1999 No 568, Reg 8*],

- No National Insurance contributions are to arise on employer's contributions to an Inland Revenue approved scheme, including funds under *ICTA 1988, s 607* and *s 608*, nor (for the avoidance of doubt) on benefits deriving from such schemes [*Reg 19(1)(zn) as inserted by SI 1999 No 568, Reg 9(2)*]

- No National Insurance contributions are to arise on certain benefits from a FURBS which are attributable to payments made to schemes prior to 6 April 1998. Broadly, benefits which would be 'relevant benefits' under *ICTA 1988, s 612* were the fund 'approved', will escape NIC liability. [*Reg 19(1)(zo) as inserted by SI 1999 No 568, Reg 9(2)*]

- No National Insurance contributions are to arise on benefits from a FURBS which are attributable to payments made to schemes on or after 6 April 1998 and which have themselves been subjected to National Insurance contributions [*Reg 19(1)(zp) as inserted by SI 1999 No 568, Reg 9(2)*]

- No National Insurance contributions are to arise on payments into a new scheme for which Inland Revenue approval under *ICTA 1988, s 604* has been made (subject to various conditions and, also, certain small self-administered schemes are excluded) [*Reg 19(1)(zq) as inserted by SI 1999 No 568, Reg 9(2)*]

- No National Insurance contributions are to arise on payments into certain French, Irish and Danish schemes [*Reg 19(1)(zr) as inserted by SI 1999 No 568, Reg 9(2)*]

- Refunds of National Insurance contributions may be obtained in respect of payments to a scheme before application was made for Inland Revenue approval or, notwithstanding the esception mentioned above, if contributions were nonetheless paid, and the scheme is subsequently granted approval [*Reg 32A as inserted by SI 1999 No 568, Reg 12*].

The Press Release accompanying the new *Regulations* again states that where payments have been made to a discretionary FURBS before 6 April 1999 the Contributions Agency (now National Insurance Contributions Office) 'will closely scrutinise such arrangements and will seek National Insurance if it can establish a payment of earnings to or for the benefit of an employee'.

28.18 PAY DURING ABSENCE

General

An employed earner may be absent from his employment for a variety of reasons: sickness, maternity, holiday, jury service, trades union activities, etc.; but may still receive payments from his employer or from third parties during such absences. The question whether or not such payments are earnings for contributions purposes is to be answered by looking at the contract of service (written or oral, express or implied) and seeing whether the payments arise under the contract or not. If they do, they are earnings.

It is sometimes the case that an employer who pays his employee during the employee's absence because of sickness or maternity will require the employee to pass to him any social security benefits received. In those circumstances, only the payments by the employer *net* of the benefits handed over are earnings for contribution purposes because that is all that the employer is actually paying to the employee. (See 1995 DSS Leaflet CA 28, Page 77, Item (36)).

28.19 **Maternity pay and SMP**

From 6 April 1987, those provisions of the *Employment Protection (Consolidation) Act 1978* which conferred a right to maternity pay were repealed and replaced by provisions in *SSA 1986* which conferred a right to statutory maternity pay (SMP). Any sum paid to or for the benefit of an employed earner in whole or part satisfaction of any entitlement of that person to statutory maternity pay is to be treated as earnings for contribution purposes. [*SSCBA 1992, s 4(1)*].

Following the *European Directive 92/85/EEC* on the protection of pregnant women at work the SMP scheme has been altered. The changes apply to any woman whose baby is born on or after 16 October 1994. The three length of service tests have been reduced to one of 26 weeks continuous service at the qualifying week (see also CWG1 (2000), Card 17). Also, the ECJ decision in *Gillespie and others v Northern Ireland Health and Social Services Board and others C-342/93* ensures that retrospective pay rises must also apply to those on maternity leave but see *Alabaster v Woolwich plc and Another [2000] TLR 19 April 2000*. This was effective from 12 June 1996. Women eligible for SMP will receive:

(*a*)   the higher rate of 90% of their average earnings for the first 6 weeks and

(*b*)   up to 12 weeks at the lower rate of £60.20.

Note: Exceptionally, where (*b*) is greater than (*a*) the employer should pay the amount in (*b*) throughout the maternity pay period but this is not mathematically possible in 2000–01 as 90% x the lower earnings limit (£67) equals £60.30.

See leaflet CA 29 and CA National Insurance News, Issue 2 Page 5. Note that none of the changes referred to above affect the treatment of SMP as earnings.

If an employer chooses to pay an employed earner the whole or part of her normal pay during a period of maternity leave in consideration for her promise to return to work at the end of her leave, that pay, too, is, on general principles, earnings for contribution purposes. (See 1995 DSS leaflet CA 28, Page 76, Item (30)). Contractual maternity pay refunded by an employee who fails to return to her employment after her maternity leave ends can be excluded retrospectively from earnings and a refund claimed. [*Refunds (Repayment of Contractual Maternity Pay) Regs 1990, Reg 2*].

See 28.20 below for the treatment of any maternity pay which is provided under an insurance scheme or through either a trust fund or a stamp fund.

Example
The wages department of Maternity Pay Ltd are told by one of their long-standing workers, Barbara Bloggs, that she is pregnant and is expecting to give birth on 10 November 2000. After checking her medical evidence (MATB1) and reviewing the action required on form SMP3, the wages department look to see what the expected week of confinement is in column 1 of the Statutory Maternity Pay tables (CA 35/36, Page 13) and this is 5–11 November 2000. Also, the qualifying week must be ascertained and this is found in column 2 of the table which indicates the week commencing of 23 July 2000. Barbara has been continuously employed since before 5 February 2000 (column 3) (i.e. more than 26 weeks up to and including the qualifying week) so she will meet the condition of continuous employment. Barbara's average earnings for the eight weeks ending on the last pay-day on or before the Saturday of the qualifying week must be looked at and this figure is £196.18 which is more than the lower earnings limit for NICs. A bonus payment for exceeding her sales quota is paid on 18 August amounting to £750.

Barbara wants to start her maternity absence on 14 October 2000 so the start of the Maternity Pay Period is 15 October 2000. The higher rate of SMP is payable for six weeks:

Average earnings £196.18 × 9/10 = £176.56 per week.

Maternity Pay Ltd must continue to pay SMP at the lower rate of £60.20 for the next 12 weeks. The company cannot pay her any SMP after 20 January 2001. Note that because the bonus payment was made after the qualifying week this amount would not fall to be included in the calculation of average weekly earnings.

A change in the method of calculation of average weekly earnings was advised at the CA's Specialist Conference on 29 October 1997 when it was stated:

'For example someone receives holiday pay in advance and it falls within the relevant period, then the average calculation would be boosted or someone may have received holiday pay — or other payments — before the period starts, which took the payments out and depressed the payments within the relevant period, so you could have 7 payments, you could have 11 payments and that should allow us to get the the thing better, get it right.'

Following this, the CA 35/36 issued in April 1998 had a new paragraph inserted on page 2 to give effect to the statement above and this instruction is now contained in the SMP Manual, CA29 at page 20, item 42. Employers should also have regard to the *Maternity and Parental Leave etc. Regulations 1999*, which confer new rights on maternity and parental leave in respect of their employees from 15 December 1999.

28.20 Sick pay and SSP

Any sum paid to or for the benefit of an employed earner in whole or part satisfaction of any entitlement of that person to statutory sick pay (SSP) is to be treated as earnings for contribution purposes. [*SSCBA 1992, s 4(1)*]. (CWG2 (2000), Page 20, Item (22), see also CWG1 (2000) card 16). The weekly rate of Statutory Sick Pay from 6 April 2000 is £60.20 per week and is payable for days of incapacity for work for employees with average weekly earnings of £67 or more.

Following the abolition from 6 April 1994 of the employer's right to recover 80% of SSP paid, SSP ceased to be a state benefit and became 'pay' for the purposes of the Equal Treatment Directive. Women over 60 but below 65 therefore became entitled to SSP. For such women, although SSP constitutes earnings, no primary contributions are due because they are over state pension age.

Any occupational sickness payment is to be treated as remuneration derived from an employed earner's employment if such a payment is made to or for the benefit of an employed earner in accordance with arrangements (e.g. with trustees or with an insurance company) under which the secondary contributor in relation to the employment concerned has made, or remains liable to make, payments towards the provision of that sickness payment. [*SSCBA 1992, s 4(1)*].

Where, however, the funds for making such a sickness payment are in part attributable to contributions made by the employed earner, the part of any sickness payment attributable to such contributions is to be disregarded. [*SSCBA 1992, s 4(2); Contributions Regs, Reg 19(1A) as amended by Contributions Amendment No 4 Regs 1983, Reg 3(b)*].

A 'sickness payment' is any payment made in respect of absence from work due to incapacity for work by reason of some specific disease or bodily or mental disablement. [*SSCBA 1992, s 4(3)*]. The DSS understood this definition to include pregnancy. However, there are now specific provisions to preclude the claiming of SSP where a pregnant woman is absent in 'the disqualifying period'. (CA 30, Page 29, Para 40 and CWG1 (2000) Card 16).

Where a sickness payment falls to be treated as earnings under these provisions, it is to be made through the person who is the secondary contributor in relation to the employment concerned unless it is payable by some other person who has agreed to make the payment and has arranged to provide the secondary contributor with all the information he needs in order to be able to pay and account for any Class 1 contribution liability arising. [*SSCBA 1992, 1 Sch 11; Contributions Regs, Reg 17B as amended by Contributions Amendment No 4 Regs 1983, Reg 2*]. Authorisation may be needed for such an alternative arrangement. Occupational sick pay paid for a period after an earner's contract of service has ended, for example as an ill-health pension, is not to be so regarded, even if it would otherwise fall to be regarded as earnings under the above provisions.

It is often the case where, for example, an employee is covered by permanent health insurance that the insurer's liability when a claim is made specifically includes the employer's Class 1 contribution liability on the 'earnings' paid to the invalid employee. Contributions are paid until State pension age and a full contribution record is thereby maintained.

For the purposes of entitlement to statutory sick pay, agency workers and short-term contract workers will be treated as being in continuous employment and their contract should be regarded as being for an indefinite period without the employer giving seven days notice when the:

- employee is engaged on a series of contracts with the same employer, and
- individual contracts are linked by periods of not more than eight weeks; and
- overall time in the employment with that employer exceeds 13 weeks.

(CA Specialist Conference, 29 October 1997 and CA30, Para 8). See also 28.19 for the CA's view on average weekly earnings which applies also to statutory sick pay.

28.21 Holiday pay

Holiday pay (whether or not a holiday is actually taken) is earnings for contribution purposes and falls to be included in gross pay when paid *unless*

(a) it is directly or indirectly derived or reimbursable from a central fund to which a number of secondary contributors contribute but which they neither manage nor control [*Contributions Regs, Reg 19(1)(b) as amended by Contributions Amendment Regs 1984, Reg 8(a)*]; or

(b) it represents sums to which the earner concerned had an earlier unconditional right but which, with his consent, were set aside (e.g. under a holiday credits scheme operated by the secondary contributor concerned) until such time as a holiday was taken (CWG2 (2000), Page 25, Item (33)).

See 31.8 EARNINGS PERIODS for special rules concerning the assessment of contribution liability on holiday pay.

Payments made under schemes falling within (a) above (which are widespread in the building and civil engineering, electrical contracting and heating, ventilating and domestic engineering industries) are to be entirely excluded from gross earnings. The amounts expended by the secondary contributor in the purchase of the special stamps which are used to build up entitlement under such schemes are also to be excluded. (CWG2 (2000), Page 25, Item (33)). Under the *Income Tax (Holiday Pay) Regs 1981*, holiday payments under such schemes have, from 1 January 1982, been subject to a basic rate tax deduction.

Payments made under the kind of arrangement described at (b) above should be excluded from gross earnings only if the set-aside sums which they represent have (as they should have) been included in gross earnings at the time the earner acquired his unconditional right to them (see 15.3 CLASS 1 CONTRIBUTIONS). In cases where the earner's right to a set-aside amount is restricted to such time as he takes his holiday, the amount should be excluded from gross earnings until the restriction is removed. (Leaflet CWG2 (2000), Page 25, Item (33)).

See 28.8 for the treatment of holiday pay paid after the earner concerned has left his employment.

28.22 Lost-time payments

Payments made to an employed earner to compensate him for the loss of earnings he has sustained in undertaking jury service or engaging in trade union activities etc. is *not* earnings for contribution purposes *providing* the payment is made by someone other than the employer or, if made by the employer, is made on behalf of some other person or organisation.

28.23 Damages advances

It is sometimes the case that, if an employed earner has an accident at work, his employer will, instead of paying him sick pay, make a loan to him pending settlement of his claim for damages. Once the claim is settled and the amount of damages (if any) is ascertained, the whole or part of the loan becomes repayable. If, at that point, the employed earner is released from the obligation to repay any part of the loan which does not represent damages, that part becomes earnings for contribution purposes (see 28.44 below).

DSS guidance here has been that the loans should be included in gross pay unless the employee will be obliged to make repayment whether or not his damages claim is successful.

28.24 PAYMENTS IN KIND

It should be noted that most payments in kind that are not subject to Class 1 contributions will, from 6 April 2000, attract a Class 1A liability.

Any payment in kind or by way of the provision of board or lodging or of services or other facilities is (with some specific exceptions — see 28.26 below) to be excluded from earnings for Class 1 contribution purposes. [*Contributions Regs, Reg 19(1)(d)*].

The terms of that regulation clearly presuppose that payments in kind *are* earnings and that, but for the excluding effect of the regulation's terms, would remain so. That presupposition has been increasingly brought into question outside the DSS and the Inland Revenue. In particular, it is being said that the terms 'remuneration' and 'profit' which are used by *SSCBA 1992* to define earnings are (unlike 'emoluments' in *ICTA 1988, s 131(1)* which are defined so as to include 'perquisites') not sufficiently wide to bring benefits in kind within their ambit. The point becomes of increasing importance as the scope of *Reg 19(1)(d)* is restricted further (see 28.26 below).

The DSS view was that if a payment in kind is to be brought within the excluding provisions of *Reg 19(1)(d)* it must be 'payment by a means which cannot be directly negotiated for a known cash value' and must, therefore, be something which cannot 'be exchanged for cash by surrender' but which 'can only be turned into cash if a willing purchaser can be found' ('Review of DSS/Inland Revenue Definitions of Gross Earnings: Consultation Paper', July 1991). For items which fail this test see 28.25 below.

A further condition which, though axiomatic, is often overlooked is that the goods or services concerned must belong to the employer before they can constitute a payment in kind to the employee. If, for example, an employee contracts for a package holiday abroad and his employer pays the bill, the employer has not made a payment in kind (i.e. a holiday package) to the employee: he has paid off the employee's debt for a package holiday which has 'belonged' to the employee from the outset (see 28.45 below). In the case of a holiday, even if the contract is properly made with the employer rather than the employee, tickets will be passed to the employee. From 6 April 1999, this latter act will attract a contributions liability, since the tickets are likely to constitute a non-cash voucher which has been provided to the employee.

Even if a particular item can, however, withstand both the tests described, it may still be taken out of the excluding provisions of *Reg 19(1)(d)* by operation of *Reg 19(5)* (see 28.26 below) and if it is not, then the item may very well, from 6 April 2000, attract a Class 1A charge.

As the wording of *Reg 19(1)(d)* makes plain, free board and lodging provided for an employed earner is not earnings for contribution purposes; but the expression 'services or other facilities' is somewhat vague. The word 'facilities' has three common meanings: the means of rendering something readily possible; things specially arranged or constructed to provide recreation; and monies available for use or borrowing. But the DSS had expressed no view on which of those meanings it considers the word to carry. Some have sought to argue that the term is wide enough to cover not only the provision to an employee of a company credit card but even any personal expenditure for which the card is used (see 28.47 below). That argument was rejected, however, in *R v DSS, ex p Overdrive Credit Card Ltd [1991] STC 129.*

28.25 Premium bonds etc.

A payment to an employed earner in the form of premium bonds or national savings certificates cannot be regarded as a payment in kind within *Reg 19(1)(d)* as the nature of such bonds and certificates is such that they are capable of encashment by mere surrender and thus fail one of the fundamental tests which the DSS believed that the law imposes (see 28.24 above). They are, therefore, earnings for Class 1 purposes. (See CWG2 (2000), page 77).

28.26 Financial instruments, shares and share options

In contrast to premium bonds etc. (see 28.25 above), most financial instruments are incapable of encashment by mere surrender and require a willing buyer and a mutually agreed price before they may be converted into cash by either sale or redemption. In principle, therefore, such instruments offer themselves as potential vehicles for the payment of remuneration in kind, i.e. in a form which does not attract Class 1 liabilities.

Gilt-edged securities are the prime example of such financial instruments: they are readily available, readily valued (with only a small bid-offer spread), easily transferred and readily sold for cash settlement. However, in the face of widespread contribution avoidance using gilts, the Government acted to render their use ineffective with effect from 12 May 1988. Employers' attention then switched to other financial instruments, such as equities, units in unit trusts and life assurance policies. This perceived abuse of the payment in kind rule was blocked with effect from midnight on 6 November 1991 by *Contributions Amendment No 6 Regs 1991*. For detailed descriptions of the use of gilts, units etc., reference should be made to earlier editions of this work.

The 1991 regulations amended the *Contributions Regs 1979, Regs 18, 19* in order to bring a wide range of financial instruments, including certain life assurance policies, into charge for Class 1 purposes when used to remunerate employees or directors. Technically, the new *Regulation 19(5)* prevents the 'conferment of any beneficial interest in' the specified assets being treated as a payment in kind under *Reg 19(1)(d)*. A list of financial instruments, based on (but with much wider scope than) the list of 'investments' in *Financial Services Act 1986, 1 Sch Pt I*, was added to the *Contributions Regs 1979* as *Schedule 1A*, headed 'Assets not to be disregarded as payments under regulation 19(1)(d)'. As the assets in question are not cash, valuation provisions were added as an amendment to *Reg 18*.

The list was further extended with effect from 1 December 1993 by *Contributions Amendment No 7 Regs 1993* which added two further items to *Schedule 1A*. The amendment was intended to block the use of gold bullion, but it is of wider application, as discussed below. When employers' attention switched to assets outside that wider application, e.g. diamonds and fine wines, the list was extended yet again with effect from 23 August 1994 to include gemstones and alcoholic liquors (see below) and, with effect from 6 April 1995 to include any assets for which 'trading arrangements' exist. Due to perceived defects in the 'trading arrangements' definition, this is extended to include, for PAYE purposes from 6 April 1998, 'readily convertible assets'. This definition also extends to National Insurance contributions with effect from 1 October 1998 by the amendment of *Reg 18* and the inclusion of *Sch 1B. [Social Security (Contributions) (Amendment No 3) Regs 1998]*. (CWG2 (2000), Page 97).

As a result, any payment in kind will now only be free of Class 1 liability if it satisfies the two tests already outlined (i.e. whatever is given or provided must be non-encashable and must be supplied by the employer to the employee) *and* falls outside the group of assets specified by *Reg 19(5)* and *Schedules 1A* and *1B*. (If it does — a Class 1A charge is nonetheless likely to arise in respect of transactions on and after 6 April 2000).

The investments which may not now be treated under *Reg 19(1)(d)* as payments in kind when given by employer to employee are now divided into sixteen broad categories. The first fourteen, set out in *Schedule 1A*, the fifteenth in *Schedule 1B* and the sixteenth in *Reg 19(5)(b)*, are as follows.

1.   *Shares and stock in the capital of a company. [1A Sch 1]*.

     It should be noted that, while there was a general trend after 1987 to reward employees in quoted securities, which are usually readily saleable, this category covers both listed and unlisted shares.

     'Company', for these purposes, includes any body corporate constituted under the law of any country or territory and any unincorporated body constituted under the law of a country or territory outside the UK. Unlike the *FSA 1986* definition, it also includes bodies incorporated under the law of any part of the UK relating to building societies within the meaning of *Building Societies Act 1986, s 119(1)*, and industrial and provident societies registered or deemed to be registered under the *Industrial and Provident Societies Act 1965* or the *Industrial and Provident Societies Act (Northern Ireland) 1969. [1A Sch 10]*.

     This simple change would itself, in the absence of some other relieving provision, have brought share option gains under approved or unapproved employee share schemes into the scope of Class 1 contributions. However, this point was, for a time, dealt with by three specific exclusions from the definition of earnings:

     (*a*)   *Shares or stock*. Regulations excluded from earnings payment by way of shares or stock (including a payment by way of or derived from shares appropriated under an *ICTA 1988, s 186* profit sharing scheme) where such shares or stock form part of the 'ordinary share capital' of the secondary contributor, a 'company' which has 'control' of that secondary contributor, or a 'company' which either is or has 'control' of a 'body corporate' which is a member of a consortium owning either that secondary contributor or a body corporate having control of that secondary contributor. From 5 December 1996, the exclusion from earnings will not apply if the shares are outside an approved scheme and the shares are tradeable assets. From 1 October 1998 the exclusion will not apply if the shares are readily convertible assets. [*Reg 19(1)(l) as amended by Contributions Amendment No 6 Regs 1996, Reg 4; Social Security (Contributions) Amendment (No 3) Regs 1998, Reg 6; Sch 1B as inserted by Social Security (Contributions) Amendment (No 3) Regs 1998, Reg 10*].

'Body corporate', for these purposes, includes a body corporate constituted under the law of a country or territory outside the UK and an unincorporated association, wherever constituted. However, it does not include partnerships, local authorities within the definition of *ICTA 1988, s 842A* or local authority associations within the definition of *ICTA 1988, s 519*. [*Reg 19(7)(a)*].

The definition of 'consortium' follows broadly that applied for the purposes of corporation tax loss surrenders, albeit without the geographical restrictions imposed by *ICTA 1988, s 413(5)*. For the purposes of this relief, a body corporate ('A') is treated as a member of a consortium owning another body corporate ('B') if A is one of a number of bodies corporate which own in total at least 75% of B's ordinary share capital and each owns at least 5% of that capital. There is no requirement that the member of the consortium be UK resident. [*Reg 19(7)(b)*].

'Company', for these purposes, simply means any body corporate having a share capital. [*Reg 19(7)(c)*].

'Control' means the power of a person to secure that the affairs of the controlled company are conducted in accordance with the wishes of that person. This power may derive from the holding of shares or the possession of voting power in or in relation to a body corporate (i.e. indirect control is taken into account) or from the articles of association or other document regulating the controlled company or another body which controls it. [*Reg 19(7)(d)*].

'Ordinary share capital' means all the issued share capital (by whatever name called) of the company other than capital the holders of which have a right to a dividend at a fixed rate but no other right to share in the profits of the company. [*Reg 19(7)(e)*]. Participating preference shares are therefore 'ordinary shares' for the purposes of *Sch 1A*.

(b) *Options*. Also excluded from earnings are certain payments by way of an option to acquire any shares specified in (a) above (broadly, options granted under an Inland Revenue approved share scheme). [*Reg 19(1)(m) as amended by Contributions Amendment No 6 Regs 1996, Reg 4; Social Security (Contributions) Amendment (No 3) Regs 1998, Reg 6; Sch 1B as inserted by Social Security (Contributions) Amendment (No 3) Regs 1998, Reg 10*].

Where options did not fall within the exclusions mentioned above e.g. 'unapproved' options, then a national insurance charge arose only on the grant of the option (and even then only if the grant was at 'undervalue'), rather than the date of exercise as applies for tax purposes. See **[Case study 1]** in WORKING CASE STUDY (58). This changed on 6 April 1999 so that the NICs treatment is brought into line with the tax treatment which charges the gain at the time of the exercise of the option. As with income tax, there will continue to be an NIC charge on the occasion of the grant of a 'long option' (see below as regards the 1998 Budget changes and WORKING CASE STUDY (58). There will also be an NICs liability if shares can still be subject to forfeiture or conversion more than 5 years after they were first awarded.

This prevents NICs being postponed indefinitely as was the case before the new rules were tabled. This latter change only takes effect from the date the new clause in the Social Security Bill was tabled i.e. 9 April 1998. It was also announced in the Budget on 17 March 1998 that the 'seven year' rule for income tax in connection with the grant of options will be altered to ten years i.e. where the option is exercisable more than ten years after the grant. This change is to be mirrored for NIC purposes so that a charge to NICs also only arises on grant if the option is capable of being exercised after more than ten years. [*ICTA 1988, s 135 as amended by FA 1998, s 49*]. See also Press Release 97/127, 22 July 1997, CA Press Release CA12/98, 1 April 1998 and also CA National Insurance News extract, Summer 1997.

This evolvement of NIC rules in connection with 'unapproved' share options has been tortuous and difficult to follow. The position was that there was a charge on the grant of such options, unless the shares are not subject to 'trading arrangements' or, from 1 October 1998, are not 'readily convertible assets' or the grant is made under an Inland Revenue approved scheme. For options *granted* on or after 6 April 1999, where a charge would otherwise have arisen on grant only, the charge now arises on exercise only unless the options are exercisable after more than ten years, in which case there will be a charge on grant (if at undervalue) as well as on exercise. Concern has been expressed, particularly on behalf of e-commerce and high-tech companies, at the current charging of the employer's national insurance contribution at 12.2% on gains arising on the exercise of unapproved schemes. Following the 2000 Budget, the Government is considering suggestions that would involve all or part of the employer's NIC liability being met by the employee by mutual agreement. Further details on this proposal are awaited. See also CWG2 (2000), Page 98 and Society of Share Scheme Practitioners November 1996, Budget Press Release.

As well as the exclusions for shares and options which are not readily convertible assets (*Reg 19(1)(zh)*) and the grant of share options which are not exercisable more than ten years after grant (*Reg 19(1)(zi)*), there are also the following exceptions:

- certain conditional shares where there exists a charge under *ICTA 1988, s 135* and that interest is treated as earnings under *Reg 17AB* [*Reg 19(1)(zj)*];

- certain rights granted before 9 April 1998 [*Reg 19(1)(zk)*];

- certain option swaps (e.g. in company takeover situations) except where the first option was granted before 6 April 1999 and substantial discount is obtained on the replacement options [*Reg 19(1)(zl)*];

- most payments for the assignment or release of options granted before 6 April 1999 [*Reg 19(1)(zm)*];

[*Reg 19(1)(zh)–19(1)(zm) as inserted by Social Security Contributions, Statutory Maternity Pay and Statutory Sick Pay (Miscellaneous Amendments) Regs 1999, Reg 3(2)*].

(c) *Employee priority share allocations.* Similarly excluded from earnings is any payment by way of any benefit which is free of Schedule E income tax liability by virtue of *FA 1988, s 68(1)*. [*Reg 19(1)(n)*]. This exclusion is arguably of no value, as the benefit excluded from income tax liability by *Sec 68(1)* is the value of the opportunity offered to employees to apply for shares in priority to members of the public. As the employees will inevitably acquire shares (which are excluded from Class 1 earnings by *Reg 19(1)(l)*) rather than cash, it is difficult to see how this exclusion would apply.

2. *Commercial debt instruments. [1A Sch 2].*

This includes debentures, debenture stock, loan stock, bonds, certificates of deposit and other instruments creating or acknowledging indebtedness, other than instruments falling within paragraph 3 below. This provision merely replaces that part of former *Reg 19C* (repealed with effect from 7 November 1991) which brought into Class 1 earnings payment in the form of commercial debt instruments. It should be noted that simple debts, as opposed to debt instruments, are not within the scope of this paragraph but are included in the definition of readily convertible assets with effect from 1 October 1998.

3. *Public debt instruments. [1A Sch 3].*

Loan stock, bonds and other instruments creating or acknowledging indebtedness issued by or on behalf of any of the following three categories of public body are included under this heading.

(*a*) Any government, of the UK, Northern Ireland or any other country or territory outside the UK. *[1A Sch 11(a)].*

(*b*) Any local authority, in the UK (within the definition of the term given by *ICTA 1988, s 842A*) or elsewhere. *[1A Sch 11(b)].*

(*c*) Any public authority, meaning 'any international organisation, the members of which include the UK or another member State'. *[1A Sch 11(c)].* This wording is arguably somewhat confusing. Although the term 'member State' is most commonly used in the context of the EC, there is nothing to indicate that the meaning here is so limited. It seems to mean that the international organisation must be a grouping of states rather than other lesser bodies before it may be regarded as a 'public authority' for this purpose.

The origins of these definitions in *FSA 1986, 1 Sch Pt I* specifically exclude bank notes, but this is unnecessary in contribution law as foreign currency is cash, which cannot be treated as a payment in kind.

4. *Warrants. [1A Sch 4].*

This category covers warrants or other instruments entitling the holder to subscribe for assets falling within paragraphs 1, 2 or 3 above. It is specifically provided that it is immaterial whether the assets to which the warrants etc. relate are for the time being in existence or identifiable. *[1A Sch 12].*

5. *Certificates representing securities. [1A Sch 5].*

Also excluded from relief under *Reg 19(1)(d)* are certificates or other instruments which confer

(*a*) property rights in respect of any asset falling within paragraphs 1 to 4 above;

(*b*) any right to acquire, dispose of, underwrite or convert an asset, being a right to which the holder would be entitled if he held any such asset to which the certificate or instrument relates; or

(*c*) a contractual right (other than an option—see paragraph 7 below) to acquire any such asset otherwise than by subscription.

6. *Units in collective investment scheme.* [*1A Sch 6*].

    This includes shares in or securities of an open-ended investment company as defined in *FSA 1986, s 75(8)* (typically, an offshore unit trust).

    The pre-7 November 1991 schemes for paying NIC-free bonuses in units in an authorised unit trust become ineffective because of this paragraph. The definition of collective investment scheme for this purpose is drawn from *FSA 1986, s 75(1)* and covers any arrangements with respect to property of any description, including money, the purpose or effect of which is to enable persons taking part in the arrangements (whether by becoming owners of the property or any part of it or otherwise) to participate in or receive profits or income arising from the acquisition, holding, management or disposal of the property or sums paid out of such profits or income. The participants must not have day-to-day control over the management of the property in question. The arrangements must also involve either the pooling of the contributions of the participants and of the profits or income, or the management of the property as a whole by or on behalf of the operator of the scheme. Important exclusions from the definition are occupational pension schemes, contracts of insurance (but see below), franchise arrangements, employee share schemes and arrangements the predominant purpose of which is to enable participators to share in the use or enjoyment of a particular property (e.g. time share properties).

7. *Options.* [*1A Sch 7*].

    Options to acquire or dispose of the following may not be treated as a payment in kind when the beneficial ownership of the option is transferred to an employee or director.

    (*a*) Any asset within any other paragraph of *Schedule 1A*.

    (*b*) Currency of the UK or of any other country or territory.

    (*c*) Gold, silver, palladium or platinum.

    (*d*) Options to acquire or dispose of any of the options listed in (*a*) to (*c*) above.

    This paragraph covers only *options* over the securities and commodities in question, not the underlying assets themselves. From 1 December 1993, those are included in *1A Sch 9A* (see below). Until that date, commodities within (*c*) might be used in appropriate circumstances to pay remuneration free of Class 1 liability.

8. *Futures.* [*1A Sch 8*].

    Also excluded from *Reg 19(1)(d)* is any contract for the sale of a commodity or property of any other description under which delivery is to be made at a future date and at a price agreed upon when the contract is made. A price is taken to have been agreed upon when a contract is made even if it is left to be determined by reference to the price at which a contract is to be entered into on a market or exchange or could be entered into at a time and place specified in the contract. Equally, a price is taken to have been agreed in a case where the contract is expressed to be by reference to a standard lot and quality even if provision is made for a variation in the price to take account of any variation in quantity or quality on delivery. [*1A Sch 14*]. For *FSA 1986* purposes, futures contracts made for commercial rather than investment purposes are not to be treated as 'investments', but no such distinction is drawn in *Schedule 1A*.

9. *Contracts for differences.* [*1A Sch 9*].

    Reg 19(1)(d) no longer applies to a contract for differences or any other contract, the purpose or pretended purpose of which is to secure a profit or avoid a loss by reference to fluctuations in the value or price of property of any description or in an index or other factor designated for that purpose in the contract. Again, for *FSA 1986* purposes, such a contract is not an 'investment' if the parties to the contract intend that the profit is to be obtained or the loss avoided by taking delivery of any property to which the contract relates, but no such exception applies for contributions purposes.

10. *Assets dealt on investment exchanges. [1A Sch 9A].*

From 1 December 1993, commodities or any others assets capable of being sold on an investment exchange which has been recognised under the *FSA 198, s 37* are excluded from *Reg 19(1)(d)*. The regulation therefore plugs the gap that payments in gold bullion and other traded commodities used to exploit.

The UK investment exchanges recognised under the *FSA 1986, s 37* as at November 1997 are

London Stock Exchange Ltd
The London Metal Exchange Ltd
The International Petroleum Exchange of London Ltd
The London Commodity Exchange 1986 Ltd (London Fox)
LIFFE Administration and Management (London International Financial Futures Exchange)
OMLX, The London Securities and Derivatives Exchange
Tradepoint Financial Networks Plc

The overseas investment exchanges recognised under the *FSA 1986, s 37* by the Treasury as at January 2000 are

NASDAQ (National Association of Securities Dealers Automated Quotations)
Sydney Futures Exchange Ltd (SFE)
Chicago Mercantile Exchange (CME)
Chicago Board of Trade (CBOT)
New York Mercantile Exchange (NYMEX)
Swiss Exchange
Cantor Financial Futures Exchange
Eurex Zurich
Warenterminborse Hannover

Recognition of the Delta Government Options Corporation (DELTA) was revoked on 5 July 1999.

11. *Vouchers. [1A Sch 9B].*

Any voucher, stamp or similar document that can be exchanged for an asset in one of the ten categories above is, from 1 December 1993, also excluded from *Reg 19(1)(d)*. Until 6 April 1999, non-encashable vouchers for use in High Street stores remained outside the scope of earnings provided that, as will usually be the case, they cannot be exchanged for items described in *Schedule 1A*. However, all non-cash vouchers are liable to NICs from 6 April 1999 with the exception of childcare vouchers by virtue of *Social Security (Contributions) Amendment Regs 1999, Reg 4* and *Social Security (Contributions)(Amendment No 4) Regs 2000, SI 2000/760*. Where a third party provides workers with awards in non-cash vouchers as part of an incentive scheme, that third party may, from 6 April 2000, pay the NICs rather than employers having to report and pay NICs on incentives over which they have no control. In such circumstances the liability for non-cash vouchers is altered from Class 1 to Class 1A from 6 April 2000. [See IR Leaflet 480 (2000), para 26.1 and CWG2 (2000), Page 79].

12. *Alcoholic liquor. [1A Sch 9ZA].*

With the inclusion of gold bullion in *1A Sch*, some employers began to pay bonuses in the form of cases of fine wines stored in bond (i.e. where no VAT or duty had been paid). From 24 August 1994, *1A Sch* includes any alcoholic liquor within the meaning of *Alcoholic Liquor Duties Act 1979, s 1* in respect of which no duty has been paid under that Act. [*1A Sch 17, inserted by Contributions Amendment No 3 Regs 1994*]. ALDA 1979, s 1 does not cover angostura bitters or methylated spirits (but see 14 *Tradeable assets* below).

13. *Gemstones.* [*1A Sch 9ZB*].

From 24 August 1994, *1A Sch* was also extended to include any gemstone, defined as including stones such as diamond, emerald, ruby, sapphire, amethyst, jade, opal or topaz and organic gemstones such as amber or pearl, whether cut or uncut and whether or not having an industrial use. [*1A Sch 18 inserted by Contributions Amendment No 3 Regs 1994*]. Because of *1A Sch 9B* (above), payments of bonuses in the form of vouchers exchangeable for diamonds ceased at the same time to be effective in avoiding Class 1 liability.

14. *Tradeable assets.* [*1A Sch 9C*].

With effect from 6 April 1995, *Contributions Amendment No 4 Regs 1995* added to *1A Sch* payment in the form of 'any other asset, including any voucher, for which trading arrangements exist and any voucher capable of being exchanged for such an asset.' For this purpose, 'trading arrangements' has the meaning given in *ICTA 1988, s 203K(2)(a) (Reg 1(2) as amended by Contributions Amendment No 6 Regs 1996, Reg 2)* and so for these purposes gross pay now includes

- any payments made by way of an asset for which 'trading arrangements' exist

- vouchers capable of being exchanged for such assets, or

- vouchers which are themselves subject to 'trading arrangements'.

[*1A Sch 19*] (See also CWG2 (1997), Page 93).

The definition in *s 203K* was introduced by *FA 1994, s 131* with effect from 3 May 1994 as part of the Inland Revenue's revision of the PAYE rules to ensure that payment in kind for contributions avoidance purposes did not automatically entail a deferral of the tax liability on the same transactions. From that date, payment in the form of tradeable assets became subject to PAYE (see *ICTA 1988, s 203F as amended by FA 1998, s 65*). 'Tradeable assets' are defined for the purposes of *1A Sch* more narrowly than for PAYE (presumably because the earlier parts of *1A Sch* are felt to cover the other situations covered by the PAYE rules):

'Trading arrangements for an asset are arrangements for the purpose of enabling the person to whom the asset is provided to obtain an amount similar to the expense incurred in the provision of the asset.' [*ICTA 1988, s 203K(2)(a)*].

References in *s 203K(2)* to enabling a person to obtain an amount are to include both a reference to enabling a class or description of persons which includes that person to obtain the amount and a reference to enabling an amount to be obtained by any means, including in particular by using an asset or goods as security for a loan or an advance. [*s 203K(3)(a)*].

An amount is 'similar to' an expense incurred if it is greater than, equal to or not substantially less than that expense. [*s 203K(3)(b)*].

This amendment to *1A Sch* effectively ended the use of a number of avoidance schemes where dealers were prepared to make arrangements, formal or informal, for assets to be sold to employers and bought back from employees at a price close to the original selling price. Bonuses paid in the form of platinum sponge (i.e. powder rather than the sheet metal which is traded on the London Metal

Exchange), demonetarised gold coins (not being bullion deals which are regulated by the London Bullion Market Association), long-case clocks and rare metals (e.g. lithium, rhodium, cobalt, antimony, molybdenum etc.), which had received some press attention, seem to have been the target of the amendment.

15. *Readily convertible assets. [1B Sch 1]*.

Following the introduction of *1A Sch 9C*, a number of companies and their advisors have continued to advocate the use of these and similar items. The authorities say that they do not accept the 'narrow interpretation' of this law but to prevent further doubt a new term 'readily convertible asset' applies for PAYE purposes from 6 April 1998 (*FA 1998, s 65*) and also applies for NIC purposes from 1 October 1998.

Schedule 1B imposes a liability in respect of a readily convertible asset which *ICTA 1998, s 203F* defines as

- an asset capable of being sold or otherwise realised on a recognised investment exchange (within the meaning of the *FSA 1986, s 37*) or on the London Bullion Market;

- an asset capable of being sold or otherwise realised on a market for the time being specified in PAYE regulations;

- an asset consisting in the rights of an assignee, or any other rights, in respect of a money debt that is or may become due to the employer or any other person;

- an asset consisting in, or in any right in respect of, any property that is subject to a fiscal warehousing regime;

- an asset consisting in anything that is likely (without anything being done by the employee) to give use to, or become, a right enabling a person to obtain an amount or total amount of money which is likely to be similar to the expense incurred in the provision of the asset;

- an asset for which trading arrangements are in existence; or

- an asset for which trading arrangements are likely to come into existence in accordance with any arrangements of another description existing when the asset is provided or with any understanding existing at that time.

Paragraph 2 of *Schedule 1B* extends the provisions to an asset treated by *ICTA 1988, s 203FA* as falling within *s 203F* (i.e. expenditure to enhance an existing readily convertible asset). In the case of *DTE Financial Services Ltd v Wilson, Ch D [1999] STI 1741* a widely marketed scheme designed to avoid NICs failed. The anti-avoidance principles laid down by *Ramsay* were deemed to have applied, subject to an appeal, but had they not then the provisions relating to tradeable assets in *s 203F* would have applied to impose a liability. *Paragraph 3* of *Schedule 1B* includes vouchers exchangeable for any asset referred to in *Paragraphs 1, 2* of *Schedule 1B*. [*Social Security (Contributions) Amendment (No 3) Regs 1998 (SI 1998 No 2211), Regs 5(3)(4), 10; new Schedule 1B to the Contributions Regulations and Social Security (Contributions) Amendment (No 3) Regulations 1998*].

16. *Long term insurance contracts*.

Before 6 November 1991, it seems that some employers were remunerating their employees by taking out investment-type life assurance policies and assigning the benefit to those employees.

The sixteenth category of asset within the scope of the anti-avoidance regulations is any contract, the effecting and carrying out of which constitutes long term business falling within Class I (life and annuity business), Class III (linked long term business) or Class VI (capital redemption business) specified in *Insurance Companies Act 1982, 1 Sch. [Reg 19(5)(b)]*. The other classes of business in *ICA 1982, 1 Sch* are birth and marriage contracts, permanent health contracts and tontines, none of which would be of importance in the context of employee remuneration.

Where the provisions of a contract of insurance are such that the effecting and carrying out of the contract constitutes both long term business and general business (within the meaning of *ICA 1982*) or long term business despite the inclusion of subsidiary general business provisions, the contract is deemed to be long term business for the purposes of *Reg 19(5)(b)*. *[Reg 19(6)]*.

As *Reg 19(5)(b)* is confined to circumstances in which a beneficial interest is conferred, some employers have tried to circumvent the regulations by making payments into single premium life policies already owned by their employees, arguing that this merely inflates the value of the policy but does not represent the conferment of a beneficial interest. Alternatively, the employer may make the single premium life contract himself with a nominal premium, assign the benefit of the almost worthless policy to the employee and follow this with a large payment into the policy. While the initial transfer confers a beneficial interest, the value of the earnings is minimal, and the second premium does not confer an interest in the policy. It is, however, doubtful whether this route successfully avoids Class 1 liability. The second premium is in cash, not kind, it clearly represents remuneration or profit derived from the employment, and is made for the benefit of the earner. It is therefore arguably chargeable to Class 1 contributions under *SSCBA 1992, s 6(1)*. The counter-argument is that the payment must also be received in kind, as 'earnings' are defined in *SSCBA 1992, s 3(1)(a)* as remuneration or profit derived from an employment, i.e. by reference to their receipt rather than their payment. The Contributions Agency challenged a number of such schemes and the absence until recently of new anti-avoidance legislation suggests that the DSS lawyers may have felt that none was needed to defeat the schemes. *Finance Act 1998, s 66 inserting ICTA 1988, s 203FA as amended by Income Tax (Employments) (Notional Payments) (Amendment) Regs 1998*, seeks to make the authorities intentions clear as regards the operation of PAYE from 6 April 1998 (enhancement expenditure to existing assets). The same change took place for NIC purposes with effect from 1 October 1998. *[Social Security (Contributions) Amendment (No 3) Regs 1998, Regs 5(3)(4), 9, 10 and new Schedule 1B]*.

No specific timing provisions were added to the regulations bringing transfers of assets within *1A Sch* into earnings for Class 1 purposes. Because of this, the transfer to the employee must be treated as if it were a cash payment of earnings when it is made. No separate year-end reporting procedures were introduced, as none was required. (This may be contrasted with the tax provisions, which involve annual reporting on form P9D or P11D rather than inclusion in gross pay for PAYE purposes where transfers of assets are outside the scope of *ICTA 1988, s 203F*.) However, if the transfer is to be treated as a cash payment, the employer must know the value to be included in gross pay for Class 1 purposes. No valuation provisions are included in the revised regulations in respect of life policies assigned by way of remuneration. However, detailed provisions exist to deal with the first fourteen categories set out above (i.e. those included in *Schedule 1A*). These are as follows.

(a) *The basic rule*

Where a payment of earnings comprises the conferment of a beneficial interest in any asset specified in *1A Sch* (i.e. not life policies, which are covered by *Reg 19(5)(b)*), the amount of those earnings for Class 1 purposes is to be calculated or estimated at a price which that beneficial interest might reasonably be expected to fetch if sold in the open market on the day on which it is conferred. [*Reg 18(2)*].

Where any such asset is not quoted on a recognised stock exchange (as defined by *ICTA 1988, s 841*), it is to be assumed that there is available to any prospective purchaser of the beneficial interest all the information which a prudent prospective purchaser might reasonably require before buying by private treaty at arm's length. [*Reg 18(3)*].

(*b*) *Stock Exchange securities*

Where the payment consists of the conferment of the beneficial interest in shares or securities listed in the Stock Exchange Daily Official List, the valuation rules for Class 1 purposes are similar to those for capital gains tax where gifts are made, i.e. the lower of

(i) the 'quarter-up' value (the amount which is the lower of the two prices shown in the quotations for the shares or securities in the SEDOL on the date of payment plus one-quarter of the difference between the two figures); or

(ii) the mid-bargain point (the amount which is halfway between the highest and lowest prices at which bargains, other than those done at special prices, were recorded in the shares or securities for the date of that payment).

If the transfer occurs on a non-business day, the above test is applied to the last preceding and the next following business days and the lower result is taken as the appropriate value.

[*Reg 18(4)*].

If the Stock Exchange provides a more active market elsewhere than the London trading floor, the basic rule in (a) above applies. [*Reg 18(5)*].

Similarly, securities quoted only overseas are covered by the basic valuation rule, as *Reg 18(4)* refers to 'The Stock Exchange' rather than to any recognised stock exchange.

(*c*) *Unit trusts and marketable commodities*

Units in a unit trust (as defined in *FSA 1986, s 75(8)*) and marketable commodities (as defined in *1A Sch 9A*) must be valued when an employer confers a beneficial interest in them on an employee. The basic rule in (*a*) applies unless the items have a published selling price, in which case the earnings are to be calculated or estimated by reference to the lowest selling price on the date of payment. If no selling price was published on the date of payment, the price applies which was the lowest published on the last previous date before the date of payment. [*Reg 18(6), (7)*].

(*d*) *Alcoholic liquor, gemstones and vouchers*

The amount of earnings comprised in a payment in the form of assets within *1A Sch 9ZA, 9ZB and 9B* is to be calculated or estimated on the basis of the *cost* of the asset in question. [*Reg 18(8) inserted by Contributions Amendment No 3 Regs 1994*]. This differs from the valuation for PAYE purposes under *ICTA 1988, s 203F*, which refers to the 'amount which is obtained' under the trading arrangements. [*s 203F(3)(b)*].

(*e*) *Trading arrangements*

Where earnings are paid on or before 30 September 1998 in the form of assets for which trading arrangements exist, the value of those earnings for the purposes of *1A Sch* is to be calculated or estimated by reference to the amount 'obtainable' under the trading arrangements in question as if that amount were obtained on the day on which the beneficial interest was conferred. [*Reg 18(9) inserted by Contributions Amendment No 4 Regs 1995, Reg 2 and Contributions Amendment No 6 Regs 1996, Reg 3*]. This also differs subtly from the equivalent PAYE provision (see *(d)* above), which requires that an amount actually be obtained before PAYE is due.

This point has been identified as a possible flaw in the PAYE anti-avoidance provisions, as the *Income Tax (Employments) (Notional Payments) Regs 1994* permit the operation of PAYE on notional payments only in the income tax period of payment. It has been argued that, if the employee does not sell the tradeable asset and no amount 'is obtained', no PAYE deduction is required. The amendment to *Reg 18* appears to avoid this difficulty by using the notional value on the day on which the beneficial interest in the asset is conferred on the employee.

(f)   Readily convertible assets

The amount of earnings chargeable to national insurance contributions is to be the best estimate that can reasonably be made of the amount of income likely to be chargeable to tax under Schedule E in respect of, as the case may be, the provision or enhancement of the asset. In the case of a voucher exchangeable for such assets, similar rules apply. [*Reg 18(10) as inserted by Social Security (Contributions) Amendment (No 3) Regs 1998, Reg 5(4)*].

On closing the loopholes involving diamonds and fine wines, Peter Lilley, the then Secretary of State for Social Security asserted the Government's dislike of such 'abuses', stating, 'These regulations are clear evidence of the Government's intention to act speedily to close National Insurance loopholes if they come to light.' (DSS Press Release 94/123, 23 August 1994). The announcement on 5 April 1995 of the tradeable assets rules was accompanied by a similar statement (DSS Press Release 95/050, 5 April 1995).

John Denham MP, when Parliamentary Secretary at the Department of Social Security stated:

'We will be tough on avoidance and abuse, but we will also be fair on employers. Employers can expect us to challenge rigorously any attempts to abuse the system, but they can also look to us for a modern, efficient and fair system of decision-making and settling disputes.'

The Tax Journal, Issue 430, 1 December 1997; CA National Insurance News, Issue 9, Winter 1997–98 and CWG2 (2000), Page 97.

All the anti-avoidance rules against schemes exploiting the payment in kind rule have been aimed at cash conversion schemes, where assets can be easily traded for a fairly certain value. Where employers choose to give employees, e.g. works of art or expensive cars without making arrangements for their resale, *1A Sch* does not apply. However, without such trading arrangements, most employees will presumably be reluctant to accept such assets by way of remuneration, particularly when 40% of the cost to the employer must be paid in income tax in due course. It therefore seems unlikely that *1A Sch* will be further extended to such items, especially since such transactions will, from 6 April 2000, attract a Class 1A charge and most recipients of such assets are likely to have earnings subject to Class 1 already in excess of the upper earnings limit.

28.27 **Commodities**

As mentioned in relation to *Contributions Regs, 1A Sch 7* above, until 1 December 1993 transfers of commodities to employees were not within the scope of the revised regulations and so any commodity for which there was a ready market could potentially be used to pay remuneration. The most popular seemed to be gold bullion. For a discussion of remuneration planning using gold bullion, readers should consult earlier editions of this work.

28.28 **Vouchers and warrants**

From 6 April 1993 the DSS temporarily (i.e. until 6 April 1999) reintroduced its earlier advice that vouchers and warrants which carry no cash option are payments in kind for contribution purposes. Certain vouchers e.g. Marks & Spencers which can only be exchanged for goods come within this category. The advice was withdrawn whilst the DSS Policy Division reviewed its policy in the light of the decision in *R v DSS, ex parte Overdrive Credit Card Ltd [1991] STC 129*. For a discussion of the arguments in favour of this treatment, the 1992–93 edition of this work should be consulted. For the position regarding fuel vouchers after the *Overdrive* case, see 28.67 below. From 1 December 1993, vouchers which can be exchanged for any commodity traded on an investment exchange recognised under the *Financial Services Act 1986* or on the London Bullion Market or for shares, unit trusts, loan stock, gilts, debentures and other securities, constitute earnings. [*Contributions Regulations 1A Sch 9B*]. From 24 August 1994 vouchers exchangeable for alcoholic liquor or gemstones were added to this list, while vouchers exchangeable for tradeable assets were added on 6 April 1995 and vouchers exchangeable for readily convertible assets on 1 October 1998. [*Contributions Amendment No 3 Regs 1994; Contributions Amendment No 4 Regs 1995 1B Sch 3 as inserted by Social Security (Contributions) Amendment (No 3) Regs 1998, Reg 10*]. (CWG2 (2000), Page 79).

New provisions effective from 6 April 1999 make it easier to collect NICs from non-cash vouchers. Whilst cash vouchers were already chargeable to NICs, vouchers such as Marks & Spencer, Asda and frequent flyer programmes e.g. Air Miles are now liable too for NICs in the same way as cash earnings. The only non-cash vouchers that are specifically exempt from the new arrangements are those for childcare. See DSS Press Release 97/127, 22 July 1997 and CA National Insurance News, Summer 1997. [*Social Security (Contributions)(Amendment No 4) Regs 2000, SI 2000/760*].

From 6 April 1999 onwards all non-cash vouchers, excepting those in respect of childcare, will be liable to NICs. The CA originally envisaged that that there would be no exceptions to this rule even to the extent that no *de-minimis* limit for seasonal rewards/gifts will be allowed. However, in *Regulations* coming into force 6 April 2000 the following categories of non-cash voucher will be disregarded for NICs:

- vouchers provided to, or for the benefit of, an employee by a person who is not the secondary contributor but who provides that voucher; and

- vouchers to obtain goods and services in connection with a company car which are exempt for tax reasons. [*ICTA 1988, s 157 (3)(b)*].

See CA Specialist Conference response, 29 October 1997. [*Social Security (Contributions)(Amendment No 4) Regs 2000, SI 2000/760, Regs 3,4*].

Example
Generous Ltd gives a B&Q retail voucher costing £600 for the benefit of three employees in the proportions of 50% to X, 30% to Y and 20% to Z. The following amounts must be included in the employees' gross pay for tax and NICs:

X	Y	Z
£	£	£
300	180	120

Z is an employee earning under £8,500 per annum and therefore form P9D (2000) should be completed and the value of £120 placed in 1.13 of that form. X and Y earn in excess of £8,500 per annum and the values for them will have to be reported on Forms P11D.

[*Reg 19(5)(c) and 1C Sch as inserted by Social Security (Contributions) Amendment Regs 1999, Regs 4,5*].

28.29 GIFTS AND AWARDS

According to the DSS, any payment made to an employed earner, however described, will be earnings for contribution purposes if it is made under contract or in accordance with a scheme or an established practice or in fulfilment of a firm expectation that it would be made. The first three conditions are clearly correct because, in any of those circumstances, the payment will be one of the rewards in return for which the employed earner is, in fact, providing his service (see 28.2 above). But the last condition is questionable *if the payment is purely personal* (see 28.30 below).

28.30 Birthday presents etc.

In accordance with the principle described at 28.29 above, guidance is that gifts from an employer to an employed earner are earnings for Class 1 purposes if they are paid under the employee's contract of service or the employee could expect such a payment because, for example, it is an acknowledged practice within the company to make such payments. (See 1995 leaflet CA 28, Page 73, Item (6)). Only personal and totally unexpected gifts may be excluded. But that cannot be right. A birthday gift made each year to an employee because of a close *personal* relationship between the employer and the employee will not be earnings for contribution purposes whether it is expected or not. It will not be made to the person 'in return for acting as or being an employee' (*Hochstrasser v Mayes [1959] 3 AER 817*). The second condition imposed by CA 28 is, therefore, invalid. The kind of gifts most likely to pass this test are birthday, anniversary and wedding presents; though the DSS recognised that a gift in recognition of long service or the passing of an examination (see 28.32 below) may also qualify.

28.31 Bonus payments

Bonus payments made in the normal course of an employment, e.g. for productivity, performance, job completion, Christmas, will always be earnings for contribution purposes in accordance with the principle described at 28.2 and 28.29 above.

There appear to be only two circumstances in which that may not be so. The first is where the bonus is paid by some unconnected third party who bears the ultimate cost. The DSS was, for example, understood not to regard as earnings a bonus paid by a car manufacturer to a car salesman working for one of the manufacturer's distributors in recognition of his performance. But it may well be that the DSS regarded such a bonus as a gratuity or offering falling within the special rules described at 28.33 below. Certainly, there would seem to be no other justification for the practice as such a bonus is quite clearly 'derived from' the salesman's employment. The case of *Booth v Mirror Group Newspapers plc [1992] BTC 455* should have caused the DSS to review its policy but there was never any evidence of such a review. Although the case concerned the deductibility of PAYE from payments to a non-employee, the PAYE provision on which the case turned is imported into contributions law as *Contributions Regs, 1 Sch 2(1)*. This defines 'employer' and 'employee' respectively as 'any person paying emoluments' and 'any person in receipt of emoluments'. *1 Sch 6(1)* provides that 'every employer, on making . . . payment of emoluments in respect of which earnings-related contributions are payable . . . may deduct earnings-related contributions in accordance with [the] Regulations'.

The second is where the bonus is paid to an employee of a UK company by a non-group overseas company with which the UK company does *not* carry on business in association (see 5.4 AGGREGATION OF EARNINGS) and the overseas company bears the full cost. In such circumstances, the amount is *not* to be regarded as earnings for contribution purposes, even if the payment is made via the UK company. (CWG2 (2000), Page 72, Item (118)). But, again, the only justification for such treatment would seem to be the special rules on tips and gratuities described at 28.33 below.

28.32 Examination awards and scholarships

DSS guidance was originally that examination awards were earnings for contribution purposes if paid by an employer who had an organised scheme for making such awards or if the employed earner could have expected to receive such an award on passing an examination. (NI 269 (April 1989 edition), Page 59, Item 22). Although this accords with the general principle laid down at 28.30 above, the guidance was wrong as examination awards are not normally made for 'acting as or being an employee' (*Ball v Johnson (1971) 47 TC 155*). In the case referred to, Midland Bank Ltd required certain of its employees to sit for (though not necessarily to pass) the Institute of Bankers examinations and, though it did not consider itself bound to do so, Midland Bank made awards to employees who succeeded in passing the examinations. The DSS subsequently corrected its guidance and said that examination awards are earnings only if the employee's contract of service or terms of employment require the examinations to be passed for the employment to continue. (See 1995 leaflet CA 28, Page 83, Item (74)).

Scholarships funded by employers and awarded on a discretionary basis to employees' children are not earnings of the employee because they are paid neither 'to' nor 'for the benefit of' the employee as would be required by *SSCBA 1992, s 6(1)* if a Class 1 liability were to arise. Save for Class 1A contributions, where various tax definitions form the basis of the charge, there are no 'connected person' rules in contribution law that enable the benefit received by another family member to be imputed in such circumstances to the earner.

Example

Billum & Bedunwithit (Solicitors) take on Billum's son as an employee and provide, as part of his contract of employment, for him to attend law school in Guildford to qualify as a solicitor. The firm contracts to pay the fees with the law school but as Billum's son will, at semesters and on graduation, work in Bedunwithit's litigation department the 'connected person' rules do not apply to him. As the contract is between the employer and the law school then Class 1A NICs will be relevant. See 16.18 CLASS 1A CONTRIBUTIONS. If Billum had contracted with the law school any scholarship and fees would be subject to Class 1 NICs and PAYE would be applied.

28.33 Gratuities, tips and service charges

A payment made to an employed earner in respect of gratuities or offerings is to be entirely excluded from earnings for contribution purposes provided that the payment is neither directly nor indirectly

(*a*) made by the secondary contributor (i.e. the employer) and does not comprise or represent sums previously paid to the secondary contributor; or

(*b*) allocated by the secondary contributor to the earner.

[*Contributions Regs, Reg 19(1)(c)(i)(ii)*].

Although tips have been held not to be earnings within the meaning of *Employment Protection (Consolidation) Act 1978, s 8* and may not, in some circumstances, be earnings for the purpose of the *National Minimum Wage Act 1998*, they have been held to be remuneration chargeable to income tax as emoluments under Schedule E. (*Confone v Spaghetti House* [*1980*] *ICR 155; Calvert v Wainwright* [*1947*] *1 AER 282; Figael Ltd v Fox* [*1990*] *STC 583*). In all likelihood, therefore, tips and gratuities would, but for *Reg 19(1)(c)*, be earnings for contribution purposes. The effect of *Reg 19(1)(c)* is, however, to exclude from an employed earner's earnings any tip or gratuity paid to him directly by a consumer or paid into a staff box or to someone acting independently of his employer, e.g. a troncmaster or tronc committee, *unless*

(i) the employer decides how the amount of tips collected in that way are to be divided among the employees; *and*

(ii) the employer is involved in the payment process.

(CWG2 (2000), Page 30 and Item (42) on Page 31).

It should be noted that this treatment differs from the tax treatment. Payments made through a tronc are subject to PAYE deductions at the hand of a troncmaster even if free from contribution liability.

A gratuity or tip is essentially a *voluntary* payment which the payer is under no obligation to make. Accordingly, any amount which a customer is required by the management of an hotel, restaurant, etc. to pay for services is *not* a tip, gratuity or offering but a *service charge* and, as such, if distributed to employees, is part of their earnings for contribution purposes. (CWG2 (2000), Page 30). Until 7 August 1980, the DSS treated service charges as a type of gratuity which might be excluded from earnings for contribution purposes. On that date, however, the DSS changed its views as a result of legal advice. (DSS Press Release, 7 August 1980).

See 5.12 AGGREGATION OF EARNINGS for the treatment of gratuities, tips, etc. which, though earnings for contribution purposes in accordance with the rules described above, are paid separately from other earnings.

It must be noted that the gratuities and offerings to which *Reg 19(1)(c)* relates are not subject to any limitation either as to amount or to the type of business or circumstances in which they are received. Thus the provisions may apply to any voluntary third party payment to an employed earner (see 28.31 above)—even, perhaps, from trustees (see 28.42 below).

28.34 Honoraria

An honorarium is usually taken to mean a voluntary fee paid for services; and the DSS followed this in referring to payments made for services which are not within an employee's contract of service or terms of employment and giving as an example voluntary payments made to an employee who serves in an unpaid capacity as the secretary of the firm's sports club. Guidance is that such payments are not earnings for contribution purposes. (See CWG2 (2000), Page 76). The rationale for this is that if a person's working arrangement in any particular capacity is such that he has no *entitlement* to reward, the arrangement cannot constitute a contract of service or an office with emoluments and the person cannot, therefore, be an employed earner within the terms of *SSCBA 1992, s 2* (see 14.2 CATEGORISATION). But if that is so, there is no employment from which he can derive remuneration or profit and it follows, therefore, that anything he does derive from his activity cannot be earnings within *SSCBA 1992, s 3*.

28.35 Incentive payments

In certain circumstances, an employer may make payments to an employee which are best described as 'sweeteners'. They do not relate to the service rendered by the employee but are intended to make changes in the terms and conditions of the employment more acceptable to the employee, e.g. a change from weekly to monthly pay, a change from cash payments to bank credits, a change in working hours or work times or even an inducement to the employee to accept lower pay. All such payments are earnings for Class 1 purposes because they are payments made to the person 'for

... being an employee' (see 28.2 above). (See 1995 leaflet CA 28, Page 78, Items (42) and (43) and CA Specialist Conference written responses, 20 February 1996.)

28.36 Offerings etc to clergy

Offerings, fees, etc. made to, and received directly by, a MINISTER OF RELIGION (43) (e.g. Easter, Christmas offerings, baptism, marriage, funeral fees), are to be excluded from his earnings for Class 1 purposes, provided they do not form part of his stipend or salary. [*Contributions Regs, Reg 19(1)(h)*].

28.37 Prizes and incentives

A cash prize awarded to an employee as a result of a competition which his employer runs in connection with his business (but which, presumably, is open only to employees) is earnings for Class 1 purposes on general principles (see 28.2 above). (CWG2 (2000), Page 23, Item (29)).

Likewise, any percentage of prize money which is paid to an employee of a horse racing stable is earnings for contribution purposes. In such cases, the trainer will be the as regards the share of prize money whether he is the employer or not.

Where an employer operates an incentive scheme for employees or third parties which does not provide cash rewards, the incentive or award is not earnings for contribution purposes because of the general payment in kind rules, see 28.24 PAYMENTS IN KIND. If the employer meets all or part of his employee's tax liability in respect of the award, this forms part of earnings for contribution purposes, whether or not the award was provided by the employer or by a third party. If, however, it is a third party, with whom the employee has no contract of employment, who meets the tax liability, that tax does not constitute earnings for contributions purposes. If the award itself is in cash, normal earnings rules apply so that if the award is from a third party it will not constitute earnings for contributions purposes. [*SSCBA 1992, s 6(1)*].

28.38 Staff suggestion scheme payments

Awards made under a staff suggestion scheme are not regarded as forming part of earnings for contribution purposes provided

(*a*) the making of suggestions is outside the scope of the employee's normal duties;

(*b*) there is no contractual entitlement to the awards;

(*c*) there is no expectation that an award will be made in any particular case; and

(*d*) awards are conditional upon discretion as to

    (i) the eligibility of the suggestion,

    (ii) the acceptance/rejection of the suggestion, and

    (iii) the award made.

(CWG2 (2000), Page 78).

28.39 Profit-related pay

Despite the fact that part of an employee's pay may be linked to, and vary with, the profits of his employer's business, the whole of that pay is earnings for contribution purposes on general principles (see 28.2 above).

The fact that the profit-related pay may be paid under a registered scheme and may thus, until 31 December 2000, be partly exempt from tax under *ICTA 1988, ss 169–184* is of no relevance for contribution purposes. (CWG2 (2000), Page 95). It should not, however, be overlooked that any emoluments on which no secondary Class 1 contributions have been paid will not be exempt from income tax as PRP, unless the reason for the Class 1 nil liability is simply that earnings do not reach the lower earnings limit or that, from 6 April 1999, they comprise the first £66 per week (or equivalent) of earnings. (*ICTA 1988, s 172(2)(3)*).

One matter that has arisen in the past is how should salary sacrifices made as part of a PRP scheme be treated for NIC purposes? It is clearly the case that, in a salary sacrifice scheme, the employee's contract terms have been varied so that the gross pay is a lower figure. There is no higher rate of pay from which PRP has been deducted. PRP must then, although tax-free (within limits), be subjected to NIC at the time of payment. The CA's written response states that the former rate of gross pay (prior to the introduction of PRP) is to be subject to NICs in full. Furthermore, the CA stated, the PRP is subject to NIC again when paid. This is fundamentally incorrect.

Under *FA 1997, 18 Sch Pt VI(3)* the repeal of *ss 169–184* will mean that the references to profit-related pay and NICs will become redundant after 31 December 2000.

28.40 Profit-sharing scheme payments

Any payment by way of, or derived from, shares appropriated under a profit-sharing scheme to which *ICTA 1988, s 186* applies is to be excluded from earnings for Class 1 purposes. [*Contributions Regs, Reg 19(1)(l)*].

28.41 Surrender of share option payments

From 6 April 1999, such payments are liable to national insurance contributions. [*SSCBA 1992, s 4(4) as introduced by Social Security Act 1998, s 50*].

Some payments arising on and after 6 April 1999 but which derive from rights acquired before that date, will be excluded from earnings by *Regs 19(1)(zl) or 19(1)(zm) as inserted by Social Security Contributions, Statutory Maternity Pay and Statutory Sick Pay (Miscellaneous Amendments) Regs 1999, Reg 3(2)*. See also 28.26 above re shares.

As regards such payments received before 6 April 1999, the DSS view was that, where an employee is paid by a third party (e.g. a company acquiring the company with which the employee is under a contract of service) for relinquishing personal rights in his employer's share option scheme, such a payment does *not* constitute earnings for contribution purposes as it cannot be said to be 'derived' from the employment (see 28.2 above). However, where such a payment is made by the employer of the employee concerned, the DSS view was that the payment *does* constitute earnings for contribution purposes as it is 'received in recognition of the loss of specified rights which were connected to the employment'. (DSS Letter, 7 January 1991).

The second view is surely wrong. On the basis of the decision in *Abbott v Philbin* (see 28.2 above), the payment of earnings to the employee takes place when the option is granted, not when it is exercised, assigned or released. The amount received in consideration of the surrender of a share option is a 'gain' which, for tax purposes, is chargeable to tax under Sch E only by virtue of *ICTA 1988, s 135*. This constitutes recognition, by the Inland Revenue at any rate, that it is not an emolument from an office or employment, and, by the same token, it is not earnings derived from an employment for contribution purposes. The right being surrendered is a property right in an asset, not an employment right.

The exception under *Reg 19(1)(zm)* from 6 April 1999, however, does not limit who the payer might be in order that the exception might apply.

28.42 Trust fund payments

Until 6 October 1987, payments *to* trustees (other than payments in connection with an occupational sick pay scheme—see 28.20 above) were to be excluded from earnings for contribution purposes, provided any share of the payments which an earner was entitled to have paid to him was, or may have been, dependent not on the secondary contributor concerned but on the exercise by the trustees of a discretion or the performance by them of a duty arising under the trust; and payments *by* trustees were, in those circumstances, also to be excluded from earnings. [*Contributions Regs, Reg 19(1)(e) as amended by Contributions Amendment No 4 Regs 1983, Reg 3(a) and as now revoked by Contributions Amendment No 3 Regs 1987, Reg 2*].

Between 6 October 1987 and 6 April 1990, such payments by trustees were, in certain circumstances, to continue to be excluded from earnings if the establishment of the trust (or a predecessor trust) pre-dated 6 April 1985. [*Contributions Regs, Reg 19A as amended by Contributions Amendment No 3 Regs 1987, Reg 3*].

The exclusion from earnings of payments to and by trustees was withdrawn by legislation because it had become a popular means of contribution avoidance for an employer to settle on trust for his employees amounts which the trustees would then distribute to the employees as beneficiaries. But it must be questioned whether that avoidance route has, in fact, been closed and whether, in the case of purely *discretionary* employee trusts, *Reg 19(1)(e)* was ever needed to open it! If the trustees of a trust make gratuitous, discretionary payments to the employees of the settlor, free from any interference by the settlor as to how much each or any employee shall receive, are not the payments gratuities which fall squarely within the excluding provisions of *Reg 19(1)(c)(ii)* (see 28.33 above)? If that is correct, DSS guidance to the effect that, from 6 April 1990, payments from all trust funds will be earnings subject to Class 1 was incorrect. (See 1995 leaflet CA 28, Page 83, Item (72)).

28.43 Damages payments

Where an employer makes payments to recompense an employee for injuries sustained in the course of his employment, the payments do not constitute earnings for contribution purposes unless the employer has a contractual liability to make such payments. (Leaflet CWG2 (2000), Page 76). The measures were widened by the Inland Revenue to cover situations in which a third party may discharge the damages which would fall outside the scope of the current tax exemption. (See Inland Revenue Press Release 29 February 1996).

28.44 LOANS AND DEBT PAYMENTS

Guidance on loans is that a loan made by an employer to an employee is not earnings unless and until it is written off, in whole or in part, at which point the amount which is written off becomes earnings. (CWG2 (2000), Page 77). This applies not only to loans which the employer funds himself but also to loans funded by a third party in accordance with arrangements made by an employer.

The guidance is of questionable validity, however. The mere making of a book entry pursuant to a decision by an employer not to seek repayment of a loan is not sufficient to extinguish the loan in law. The debt can be abandoned by the employer only by a release under seal or in return for some consideration by the employee—and whether the current services of the employee are sufficient consideration for that purpose without any agreement being made to that effect is open to question.

The DSS was silent as to the position where a loan by an employer to an employee becomes statute-barred under the *Limitation Act 1980* by a lapse of six years. Such debts are not extinguished, they merely become unenforceable, so, arguably, they can never give rise to earnings. However, see the former Chief Executive, Mrs Faith Boardman's comments in Payroll Manager's Review, April 1996 on this point and 14.13 CATEGORISATION.

Repayments of capital and/or interest made by an employer in respect of a loan obtained by an employee from a third party, e.g. a bank, building society or other financial institution, are earnings for contribution purposes as they constitute a discharge by the employer of the employee's personal debt (see 28.45 below).

Where an employer who has himself made a loan to an employee assigns to a bank, building society etc. the *chose in action* (i.e. the right to interest and repayment of principal) created by the loan and, in consequence, pays interest additional to the interest payable by the employee, that additional interest is *not* earnings of the employee for contribution purposes.

28.45 Discharge of personal debts

Where an employer discharges a debt which his employee owes to a third party, the amount paid by the employer is money's worth in the hands of the employee and is, accordingly, earnings for contribution purposes. (See *Hartland v Diggines (1926) 10 TC 247; Nicoll v Austin (1935) 19 TC 531*). But, as previous DSS guidance has rightly emphasised, it is important in this context to determine whether a debt being discharged by the employer *is* the employee's debt or is the *employer's* debt. The question to be asked is: Who has made the contract? (CWG2 (2000), Page 78). The same problem arises with credit cards (see 28.47 below). If the employer makes the contract and discharges the liability which arises under it, then, to any extent to which the employee enjoys or consumes or utilises the services or goods contracted for, the employee receives a payment in kind (see 28.24 above). If, however, the employee makes the contract and the employer discharges it, the employee receives earnings (but see 22.3 COMPANY DIRECTORS).

Examples of payments which are commonly made by an employer but which, because they discharge an employee's debts, are earnings of the employee, are the payment of home telephone bills (see 28.57 below), private credit card accounts, home electricity bills, premiums on annuity contracts entered into by the employee, employee's premiums under personal pension policies, premiums on private medical cover arranged by the employee, club membership fees, school fees for the employee's children (CWG2 (2000), Page 78 and Tolley's National Insurance Brief, February 1997). In some instances, typically for example, home telephone and school fees, it may be possible for the original contract for the supply of services to be made with the employer, or for the original contract with the employee to be replaced by one with the employer. Great care is required to ensure that what is intended in this regard is, as a matter of contract law, actually achieved. [Case Study 4]. At one point the former CA asserted that the *Education Acts* do not permit parents to delegate responsibilities regarding education to others so that an employer's contract with the school is impossible. This view is incorrect. *Education Act 1944, s 36*, merely imposes a duty on parents 'to cause' their children to receive education. Education other than by attendance at school is permitted and the Act appears to be silent as to the manner in which education at school is obtained. The Secretary of State subsequently accepted in a determination pre-1 April 1999 (see 9 APPEALS AND REVIEWS) that the *Education Act* could not be interpreted in that way and that the CA was wrong. See WORKING CASE STUDY (58).

From 6 April 2000, such items paid under an employer's contract will attract a Class 1A charge.

A problem which DSS guidance never addressed is that of joint liability. An employee may enter into a contract as an agent for his employer as an undisclosed principal and thereupon the employer becomes primarily liable to discharge the debt that is created. If, however, the employer will not or cannot pay, the employee himself is liable—though with a right of indemnity against the employer. If, in such circumstances, the employer *does* pay, can it be said that he has discharged the employee's debt and thus made a payment of earnings? Surely not, for the employee's debt was only contingent and was in any case balanced by the right of indemnity and *both* are extinguished when the employer pays. The employee gains no money's worth. The DSS *implicitly* took a contrary view, however, as evidenced by its view on petrol purchases in earlier years (see 28.64 below).

See 28.75 for details of the relief for payments in respect of employee liabilities and indemnity insurance.

28.46 Discharge of tax

Discharge of an employee's tax liabilities by an employer constitutes a payment of earnings in accordance with the principle described at 28.45 above (See *Hartland v Diggines (1926) 10 TC 247*). (CWG2 (2000), Page 21). The wording of Item (66) was misleading in the equivalent publication in 1993 (NI 269). It stated that NICs were due on gross pay not net pay where an employer paid the tax but then went on to say that 'this' applied even if the employer paid the tax on a payment which itself was exempt from NICs. The implication was that contributions were due on the gross amount of a taxable but non-NICable payment whereas, of course, contributions are due only on the *tax* paid by the employer in such a case. The word 'this' was dropped from the guidance in CA 28 (1995) but unfortunately the paragraph was still misleading!

Under the stated rule, contribution liability will also arise on the tax which providers of awards under a *taxed award scheme* pay on behalf of their own employees.

More problematical is the position where an employer makes a settlement with the Inland Revenue which is based on estimated, undeclared and unpaid liabilities of employees and which has the effect of extinguishing such liabilities. This was often referred to as a Class 6 settlement. Does such a settlement by the employer constitute a payment of earnings equal to the tax element of the settlement? The DSS believed that it does; but it is arguable that that is not so (see 37.4 INLAND REVENUE: CO-ORDINATION WITH THE DSS). The matter is left beyond doubt where payment is made in an organised way e.g. through a PAYE Settlement Agreement (see 17 CLASS 1B CONTRIBUTIONS: PAYE SETTLEMENT AGREEMENTS), but there may still be grounds for the non-liability view to be taken in some other circumstances e.g. where a settlement is made following a PAYE audit.

28.47 Credit card transactions

If an employer discharges the balance on an employee's personal credit card, that is clearly a payment of earnings on the general principle described at 28.45 above. Where, however, the employer has supplied his employee with a company credit card and the employer discharges the balance on that card, the situation is more complex.

Guidance is that, where a company credit card is used to pay for actual business expenses, payment to the card company by the employer in respect of that part of the balance on the card will not constitute earnings. (CWG2 (2000), Page 76). So far as the payment of *non*-business expenses by company credit card is concerned, however, the position is more complex.

Until 6 April 1994, the DSS view, as set out in a letter dated 8 August 1989, was that an employee could never be acting as agent for his employer as either a disclosed or undisclosed principal when he purchased goods or services which were wholly or partly for private or personal use—even if his employer had authorised him to do so. Accordingly, an employee who used a company card to obtain private goods or services was, until 6 April 1994, regarded by the DSS as incurring a personal debt to the supplier which was then discharged by the card company. (See *Re Charge Card Services Ltd [1988] 3 AER 702*). When the employer then reimbursed the card company he thus (in the DSS's view) became a creditor of the employee under the employee's agreement (express or implied) to reimburse the employer for any private purchases made on the card unless the employer waived that obligation.

The DSS changed its mind and subsequently considered that if an employee is given prior authority to make a non-business purchase and if the employee reaches agreement with the supplier in advance of the contract being made that the purchase is to be made on behalf of the employer, the value of the goods or services so purchased does not form part of earnings for NI purposes (See 1995 leaflet CA 28, Page 74, Item (14) and CA National Insurance News, Issue 3, p 4). The current position is, therefore, that if the contract for the supply of goods or services is clearly between the employer and the supplier, with the employee acting as agent for his employer, then the goods or services become the property of the employer from the outset and, if the employee is allowed to retain them without being called upon by his employer to pay for them, they become a payment in kind (see 28.24 above).

Unfortunately, the revised guidance does not include any indication of when the contract is regarded as being entered into. This will depend on the nature and circumstances of the transaction. In the case of the purchase of car fuel, the contract is entered at the point of fill-up on the station forecourt (*Richardson v Worrall [1985] STC 693; R v DSS ex p Overdrive Credit Card Ltd [1991] STC 129*). The procedure described in the previous paragraph is referred to as 'the litany' and derives from the *Overdrive* case (see below). However, some petrol station forecourts have the option to pay at the kiosk or swipe the credit card at the pump—this results in the purchase becoming the property of the employee in both cases unless 'the employee explained in advance of the contract being made *and* the supplier accepted that the purchase was made on your [the employer's] behalf.' (CWG2 (2000), Page 76). Likewise, it seems, that a contract for a meal in a restaurant will be entered at the point at which an order for food, wine, etc. is given. But in a self-service store (just as in any other kind of shop) the contract is entered at the till, i.e. when (and only when) the customer offers to buy the goods in question, the offer is accepted and consideration is exchanged (*Pharmaceutical Society of Great Britain v Boots Cash Chemists (Southern) Ltd [1952] 2 AER 456*).

From a date shortly after enactment of the Child Support, Pensions and Social Security Bill 1999 (expected Summer 2000), new Regulations will specifically provide that a Class 1 liability will arise in respect of the use of an employer's credit card, etc. in order to obtain personal goods and services (CWG5, January 2000, page 8).

28.48 INSURANCE PREMIUMS

The general rule concerning the discharge by an employer of an employee's debts applies in most instances where an employer pays the premiums under an insurance contract entered into by the employee including insured sick pay schemes (see 28.45 above). (CWG2 (2000), Pages 77 and 83). However, see paragraph 28.69 below for the exclusion of NICs liability of insurance for medical costs/expenses for a period when an employee carries out duties abroad.

One exception to that rule arises where contributions are paid by an employer under approved personal pension arrangements made by his employee. Under *ICTA 1988, s 643(1)*, such contributions are not to be regarded as emoluments of the employment chargeable to tax under Schedule E and, where that is the case, the payment is to be excluded from earnings for contribution purposes also. [*Contributions Regs, Reg 19(1)(k) as inserted by Contributions Amendment No 4 Regs 1988, Reg 2*]. (CWG2

(2000), Page 77). The fact that, under a personal pension contract, contributions can be made by either the employee or the employer or both of them often causes confusion. It is essential that where the employer wishes to pay a premium the insurance company's application form is correctly completed showing the relevant amount as an *employer's* contribution. Although the number of personal pension contracts where the employer makes a contribution is thought to be in the minority where that is so it is often found, on an audit visit, that the contributions have been stated to be *employee's* contributions and treated as such by the insurance company. Where that is so the employer is meeting the personal obligation of the employee and contributions are due (see 28.45 above). The matter can easily be rectified for the future by varying the employee's contribution downwards and the employer then contracting to make an *employer's* contribution. Where the employer merely bears the cost of an employee's contribution then, as well as attracting an unnecessary Class 1 charge, there could be other tax difficulties. An employee's contribution is made net of basic rate tax whereas an employer should make payments gross. Similarly, even though the net contribution will have been declared on the employee's Form P11D, the Inland Revenue could possibly argue that whilst the benefit is assessable, the balancing 'expense' of the employee is not allowable because the employee has not actually paid the premium.

Where an employer pays contributions to an approved occupational pension scheme, which may include provision for death-in-service benefit of up to four times salary to be paid to the deceased employee's dependants, no indebtedness of the employee is being discharged nor is the employee acquiring anything other than a future entitlement to pension. Accordingly, such contributions are still regarded as a payment in kind (see 28.24 above), although if the DSS and CA's new views regarding FURBS (see 28.17 above) are correct, that interpretation should equally have applied to other forms of pension contribution. However, contributions to Inland Revenue approved schemes are, from 6 April 1999, specifically excluded from earnings. [*Reg 19(1)(zn) as inserted by Social Security (Contributions and Credits) (Miscellaneous Amendments) Regs 1999, Reg 9(2)*].

Where an employer pays a premium on a life policy and then assigns the policy to an employee, a payment of earnings takes place (see 28.26 above).

See 28.49 below for details of the relief given in respect of employee liabilities and indemnity insurance.

28.49 Employee liabilities and indemnity insurance

Directors and officers of companies may incur a liability to a third party by carrying out their official duties. Costs and losses may be incurred by them in a personal capacity, e.g. where the third party brings an action for actual or alleged breach of trust, breach of duty, neglect, error, misstatement, misleading statement or omission. Further liabilities may arise from fraud, dishonesty or malicious conduct, although these are actions of a different kind. Since the introduction of new provisions in *Companies Act 1989*, it has been possible for an employer to insure against a liability to indemnify directors or officers for losses or costs resulting from their actions as such, although agreements to indemnify against certain liabilities may be void under *Companies Act 1985, s 310, as amended by Companies Act 1989, s 137*.

Where the employer reimburses the employee's personal liabilities, a Class 1 charge may arise unless it can be shown that the reimbursement is a specific and distinct payment of, or contribution towards, expenses actually incurred by the employee in carrying out the employment, excluded from earnings by *Reg 19(4)(b)*. This may not be impossible, but for income tax purposes such payments would not pass the strict test in *ICTA 1988, s 198* as representing expenses incurred wholly, exclusively and necessarily in the performance of the duties. After the Inland Revenue had conducted a consultation exercise in early 1994, *FA 1995, s 91* created *ICTA 1988, s 201AA* to give specific relief for such payments, whether made by employer or employee, where they relate to a 'qualifying liability' or a claim that the officer is subject to such a liability. [*s 201AA(1)(a), (b)*]. A 'qualifying liability' in relation to an office or employment is a liability to someone other than the employer, imposed either (a) in respect of acts or omissions of a person in his capacity as an office-holder or in any other capacity in which he acts in the performance of the duties of that employment or office; or (b) in connection with any proceedings relating to or arising out of a claim that a person is subject to a liability imposed in respect of any such acts or omissions. [*s 201AA(2)*]. Relief is denied where it would be illegal for the employer to insure against a liability to indemnify the employee. [*s 201AA(8)*].

It was announced in 1994 Budget Press Release IR 20 that the DSS would bring forward regulations to parallel the new tax exemption. Regulations based on the new *s 201AA* could not be laid before Royal Assent to *FA 1995*. However, the regulations did come into force on 18 July 1995 where *Reg 19(1)(t)* was inserted by *Social Security (Contributions) Amendment (No 5) Regulations 1995, Reg 2* and ensures that employee liability and indemnity insurance is similarly treated. [*ICTA 1988, ss 200A, 201AA; Contributions Regs, Reg 19(1)(t)*]. (See also CA National Insurance News, Issue 4, page 10 and IR Leaflet 480 (2000) paras 7.10–11).

Where employers insure against their liability to indemnify a director or officer, the proceeds of a claim paid to the employee's creditor would, assuming *Reg 19(4)(b)* could not apply, represent Class 1 earnings were it not for the new relief. The premium paid by the employer would be to cover its own liabilities and would be of no relevance to the employee's income tax or Class 1 contributions position. However, some policies cover not only the employer for liabilities to indemnify employees, but also the employees directly for costs the employer may not legally reimburse. Before *s 201AA* was introduced, the payment of a premium by the employer for such cover represented a taxable benefit to the employee, as it was not necessary for such insurance to be carried. In practice, the total premium was often apportioned for tax purposes on a negotiated basis between company cover (no benefit) and officer cover (to be reported on P11D). As the premium was a payment in kind, no Class 1 liability arose in respect of it. If a claim was made by the employee under the 'employee cover' part of the policy, the proceeds were non-taxable, as he was the insured person and the premiums had been taxed at the inception of the policy. Again, no Class 1 liability would arise as no 'earnings' were paid. Under *s 201AA*, even the premiums for employee cover, to the extent that they relate to qualifying liabilities, are now exempt from income tax, [*s 201AA(1)(c)*].

In addition, liability insurance reimbursed by the employer from 18 July 1995 will not be liable for NICs. Also, the CA did not seek NICs for payments made in the period 6 April to 17 July 1995 (CA 28 supplement April 1996).

28.50 RELOCATION PAYMENTS

If an employer requires an employee to relocate for the purposes of his employment, the employer will normally make various payments in connection with the move. To the extent that such payments are specific and distinct payments of, or contributions towards, expenses actually incurred by the employee in carrying out his employment they will not be earnings for contribution purposes. [*Contributions Regs, Reg 19(4)(b)*].

DSS guidance up to 6 April 1998 was that reimbursement of absolutely necessary expenses such as solicitor's fees, estate agent's commission and removal expenses will fall within the terms of that excluding regulation, as will a lump sum payment or periodic payments made to cover specific additional expenses incurred as a result of the move such as higher mortgage or higher rent, but only to the extent that the excesses relate to accommodation equivalent to that from which the move has taken place. Any payments made which relate to an improved accommodation element are to be treated as earnings for contribution purposes, as are lump sum payments or periodic payments to cover a general increase in the employee's cost of living, such as a London weighting allowance. However, during 1997 the DSS/CA changed their views and considered that in fact all relocation allowances have, since 1975, been liable to NICs. Although the existing guidance remained unchanged and previous liabilities will not, in practice, be enforced, this change of view led to the new rules which took effect on 6 April 1998 (see below).

Where an employee moves to an area in which the council tax is higher, the DSS always argued that this is a personal liability of the occupier, not a relocation expense which may be excluded when reimbursed. This was also the case with the Personal Community Charge (NI 269, April 1991, Page 55). However, in the case of the Standard Community Charge, which was a charge on property rather than on the individual, DSS guidance was that no liability would arise where, for example, the Standard Community Charge became payable because the employee was unable to sell his old property, or because he stayed in temporary accommodation while seeking a property in the new location, and the employer paid or contributed towards the change. Reimbursement of Standard Community Charge in respect of transit accommodation where the employee was relocated only temporarily was only free of liability for up to twelve months and then only if it was not expected from the outset that the absence on detached duty would last for more than twelve months. (NI 269 April 1991 edition, Page 55, Item (9)).

The April 1993 edition of NI 269 was printed before details of the council tax were known. Accordingly, it directed employers who paid employees' council tax to refer to their local Social Security office for instructions. (NI 269/CA 28, Page 56, Item 11). Until 29 November 1993, the Contributions Agency took the line that, as the occupier of property is liable for the council tax relating to that property, an employer who pays the tax on behalf of an employee is discharging the employee's pecuniary liability and is thus making a payment of earnings for contribution purposes. (See 28.45). However, from 30 November 1993, council tax paid by employers for employees living in accommodation provided by the employer, and which falls within the income tax exemption of *ICTA 1988, s 145(4)*, will not be classed as earnings for contribution purposes. [*Contributions Regs, Reg 19(1)(r)*]. (CWG2 (2000), Page 75).

It should be noted that neither Inland Revenue Extra-Statutory Concession A5(a) nor the £8,000 limit on removal expenses set by the *ICTA 1988, 11A Sch 24(9)* had, until 6 April 1998,any application so far as exemption from contribution liability was concerned (see 37.4 INLAND REVENUE: CO-ORDINATION WITH THE DSS and also IR Leaflet 480 (2000) paras 5.2–5.12, Appendix 7).

In order to align NICs closer with the tax rules on relocation expenses national insurance contributions will from 6 April 1998 be collected on those relocation allowances that are not eligible for tax relief. This will mean that allowances such as legal and estate agent's fees, stamp duty and removal expenses, etc. exceeding £8,000 for each relocation under *ICTA 1988, 11A Sch* will not incur a NICs charge even though a tax liability exists. Where relocations were already planned before 6 April 1998, these changes will not affect employees who started a job in a new location before 6 April 1998 nor their employers. This treatment is despite the Department's original belief that the payment of relocation expenses in the past have generally been subject to NICs. It is also pointed out that where these contributions have not been paid then the benefits position of some employees may have been affected. It is difficult to imagine many cases where this might be applicable but the DSS stated that any employee who considers this may have applied to them should contact their local CA office. See DSS Press Release 97/142, 30 July 1997; CA Press

Release CA10/98, 16 March 1998; CWG2 (2000), page 89. [*Contributions Amendment (No 2) Regs 1998*].

Some employers make relocation payments in accordance with a scheme devised for the purpose. Until 6 April 1998 the DSS was prepared to accept that scheme payments fell within the terms of *Reg 19(4)(b)* if

(*a*) the scheme has no overall element of profit;

(*b*) payments are based on an accurate survey of the costs involved;

(*c*) the scheme is designed to allow for movements in prices; and

(*d*) the payments are reasonable in relation to the employment involved.

(CWG2 (1999), Page 78).

28.51 SUBSISTENCE AND OTHER ALLOWANCES

If an employer requires an employee to work away from his main place of work or to work from home, the employer will usually make payments to cover accommodation, meals and incidental expenses. To the extent that such payments are specific and distinct payments of, or contributions towards, expenses actually incurred by the employee in carrying out his employment they will not be earnings for contribution purposes. [*Contributions Regs, Reg 19(4)(b)*].

Guidance is that reimbursement of the actual amount spent will fall within the terms of that excluding regulation, as will any part of a round sum allowance which corresponds to an actual, identifiable business expense. (CWG2 (2000), Page 88 and IR Booklet 490, Paras 9.6–9.7).

Where travel and subsistence payments are made under a working rule agreement agreed with the Inland Revenue, from 6 April 1993 the DSS accepted that they do not constitute earnings for contribution purposes. Before this date the DSS considered the position case by case. (See 1995 leaflet CA 28, Page 92, Item (106) and IR Booklet 490).

Regulations were introduced to reflect the *Finance Act 1995, s 93* provision of relief for employees who incur incidental expenses when they are away from home up to a maximum of £5 per night in the UK and £10 per night outside the UK. (IR Leaflet 480 (2000), para 8.1, Appendix 8). The relief for personal incidental expenses was introduced into *ICTA 1988, s 155* and *s 200A* because items such as newspapers and telephone calls home, when paid for by an employer (whether by non-cash voucher, credit tokens, cash payments, etc.), would not qualify for relief under *s 198* as they were not *necessarily* incurred in the performance of the duties. Although the new tax relief is now paralleled in contributions regulations, it is questionable whether the change is necessary, as the test in *Reg 19(4)(b)* is arguably less strict than the income tax equivalent in *s 198* and would arguably allow the exclusion from earnings of costs incurred because the employee was carrying out the employment away from home. However, the NIC exemption introduced by *Contributions Regs 1979, Reg 19(1)(s)* applies from 18 July 1995 and not 6 April 1995 as for tax purposes but the CA did not pursue a claim for NICs for the interim period 6 April to 17 July 1995 (See CA press release 17 July 1995 and CA 28 Supplement April 1996). [*Contributions Amendment Regs (No 5) 1995, Reg 2*].

In line with the changes to the legislation affecting the tax position on travel and subsistence the DSS decided to mirror the position for NICs. In view of this the DSS reviewed the subsistence payments made to employees who are unexpectedly recalled to work. This applies to such employees who work in the construction and computer industries amongst others and such payments are regarded as earnings for NICs purposes. From 6 April 1998, all reasonable reimbursed subsistence allowances will not be liable to NICs. It is not clear what constitutes 'reasonable' in this instance but the CA stated that 'reasonable' in connection with mileage rates means the FPCS rates and IR Booklet 480(2000) states it includes alcoholic refreshments as well as non-alcoholic. This would indicate that using a standard agreed model is sufficient and therefore the use of the dispensation (Form 490 (DIS)) will facilitate this by enabling rates paid for food, accommodation, etc, to be agreed in advance as being 'reasonable'. (See CA Specialist Conference notes, 29 October 1997; CA National Insurance News, Winter 1997-98 and IR Booklet 490 'Employee Travel—A Tax and NIC's Guide for Employers').

28.52 Board and lodging

Where an employer provides free board and lodging for an employee, the board and lodging are to be excluded from earnings for contribution purposes. [*Contributions Regs, Reg 19(1)(d)*]. Note that any *reimbursement* of board and lodging costs, as opposed to direct provision under a contract made by the employer, will only be excluded from earnings if it is a specific and distinct payment of, or contribution towards, expenses actually incurred by an employed earner in carrying out his employment. [*Contributions Regs, Reg 19(4)(b)*]. (See 38.7 LABOUR-ONLY CONTRACTORS in respect of agricultural workers.)

A payment of, or contribution towards, expenses incurred by an employee in staying in board and lodging near his place of work does not form part of earnings for contribution purposes if those expenses were incurred as the result of a disruption to public transport caused by a strike or other form of industrial action. [*Contributions Amendment No 4 Regs 1993, Reg 2*].

28.53 Bounties etc. to serving members of the forces

Certain allowances, bounties and gratuities paid to serving members of the forces are to be *excluded* from earnings for contribution purposes (see 11.3 ARMED FORCES).

28.54 Club membership fees

The DSS considered that the joining of a club or society by an employee, even if the membership has a business motivation, always confers some personal benefit on the member. Accordingly, DSS guidance was that, unless the employer contracts for the membership of his employee, any subscription paid by the employer will be earnings for contribution purposes in accordance with the principle described at 28.45 above. (CWG2 (2000), Page 78).

28.55 Concessionary fuel for miners

Under Inland Revenue Extra-Statutory Concession A6 free coal supplied to miners or cash allowances in lieu of such free coal are exempt from income tax. Free coal is excluded from earnings for contribution purposes also as a payment in kind (see 28.24 above) but, strictly, a cash allowance in lieu was not. DSS guidance was formerly to the effect that payments in lieu *were* to be excluded from earnings for contribution purposes. (NI 269 April 1989 edition, Page 59, Item (16)). It having been noted in the 1990–91 edition of this work that that was presumably an extra-statutory concession (37.5) by the DSS (which it was not allowed to make), there was no mention of fuel for miners in the subsequent editions of DSS Leaflet CA 28 until CA 28 Supplement, April 1996, when it was stated categorically that 'Do not include in gross pay any cash payments to miners in lieu of free coal to which they are entitled because of their employment'. This statement reflects the change of regulations announced in CA Press Release 96/1, 15 March 1996 [*Social Security (Contributions) Amendment (No 3) Regulations 1996, Reg 3*].

28.56 Earnings

28.56 Councillor's attendance allowance

Attendance allowances paid to local councillors are earnings. This was determined in an unemployment benefit case (*R(U) 2/94*) and confirmed similar earlier decisions based on different legislation. In a supplementary decision there was held to be a rebuttable presumption that expenses incurred by a councillor are referable to attendance at council meetings and therefore deductible from attendance allowance. However, basic and special responsibilities allowances are not earnings [*Social Security (Computation of Earnings) Regulations 1978*] but include a substantial element of re-imbursed expenses and need, therefore, to be taken into account before an expenses deduction is allocated against the payment of attendance allowance. Often, of course, such payments will fall below the lower earnings limit in any event.

28.57 Meal allowances

Meal allowances which are paid in connection with an employee's employment away from his main place of work are subsistence allowances (see 28.50 above) and their treatment has already been explained.

Other meal allowances are earnings for contribution purposes if the payment is made in cash or by a voucher which can be redeemed for cash or for cash or food. Only if a meal voucher is incapable of encashment would it not be earnings for contribution purposes and even then only until 5 April 1999, after which all non-cash vouchers became liable to NICs. The first 15p per day of a voucher exchangeable only for food and drink, and not for cash, is, however, still free of NIC! [*1C Sch as inserted by Social Security (Contributions) Amendment Regs 1999, Reg 5*]. (See 28.28 above).

28.58 Mortgage payments

A mortgage provided by an employer for his employee is a loan and its treatment for contribution purposes is as described at 28.44 above. (CWG2 (2000), Page 77).

Repayments by an employer of the interest on, or the principal of, a mortgage loan obtained by his employee are earnings of the employee for contribution purposes as they are a discharge or partial discharge by the employer of the employee's personal debt (see 28.45 above).

28.59 Police rent allowances

A police rent allowance is earnings for contribution purposes as is any grant paid to cover income tax on the allowance or on the value of the accommodation as a benefit in kind. (See 1995 leaflet CA 28, Page 78, Item (47)).

28.60 Telephone charges

DSS guidance on payments made in connection with an employee's home telephone has been as follows.

If the employer is the subscriber, i.e. the contract is between the employer and the telephone company, payments by the employer are not earnings for contribution purposes. (CWG2 (2000), Page 79). That is because such payments, to the extent that they benefit the employee, are payments in kind (see 28.24 and 28.45 above). From 6 April 2000, provision in this manner will attract a Class 1A charge.

If, however, the employee is the subscriber, i.e. the contract is between the employee and the telephone company, the whole of any payments by the employer in respect of the *rental* element of telephone bills will be earnings for contribution purposes, whether a record of private and business calls is maintained or not, *unless* a record is kept which shows that the telephone is used *exclusively* for business calls. Where payments are made by the employer in respect of *calls and other charges*, those payments, too, will be earnings for contribution purposes *unless and only to the extent that* they relate to business calls. In the past, the DSS required business calls to be identified as such by means of a log accurately maintained by the employee and recording the time spent on the individual calls concerned, or they can be identified from itemised bills. From 6 April 1993 the Contributions Agency accepted that if the employer had an Inland Revenue dispensation allowing all or part of reimbursed telephone bills to be disregarded for income tax purposes, then that agreement could be used for contributions purposes as well.

The basis of this guidance was, first, the general principle that, where an employer discharges an employee's personal debts, he is placing money's worth in the hands of the employee (see 28.45 above) and, secondly, that a payment in connection with a business expense may be excluded from earnings only if it is a specific and distinct payment of or contribution towards an expense actually incurred in carrying out the employment. [*Contributions Regs, Reg 19(4)(b)*]. The DSS was of the view that, whereas a business call made on a private telephone is an identifiable expense actually incurred in carrying out the employment, the expense of renting a telephone which is used in part for private purposes is incurred in the course of domestic living and not in carrying out the employment. Accordingly, in the DSS's view, no apportionment was possible.

The Contributions Agency adopted a policy in late 1991 of collecting arrears of contributions in respect of reimbursed private telephone bills for the current year and the last six years, collecting on the basis that 100% of the reimbursement related to private calls where no call logs or itemised bills were held as evidence of business use. It was pointed out to the Contributions Agency that the Employers' Guide, Leaflet NP 15, had made no reference to telephone bills before April 1987, but the Agency policy remained unchanged, as the underlying law itself had been unchanged for many years. In practice, a number of local office inspectors agreed to collect only with effect from 6 April 1987 and some agreed a reasonable apportionment between business and private calls even without logs or itemised bills.

The policy of treating the whole of a reimbursement as earnings where no evidence was held was felt by many to be unreasonable and harsh. It was announced in the April 1995 edition of CA 28 that the Contributions Agency had reviewed its past policy and concluded that its policy of insisting on detailed call logs or itemised bills had indeed been incorrect. It is now acknowledged that an Inland Revenue dispensation should have been accepted as evidence of business use before 6 April 1993 and employers who paid the claimed arrears despite the existence of such a dispensation before that date may now claim a refund on production of the evidence which would now be acceptable (See also Tolley's National Insurance Brief, February 1997).

See leaflet 480 (2000), Chapter 22 for mobile telephone benefit treatment for tax purposes and CWG2 (2000), Page 79 for NICs treatment.

28.61 MOTOR AND TRAVELLING

Many changes have taken place in the field of motor and travelling expenses and their NIC treatment in recent years. The following paragraphs summarise the position.

28.62 Home to work allowances

It is well established in income tax law that the costs incurred by an employee in travelling from his home to his normal place of work are expenses incurred in placing himself in a position to carry out his employment, not in carrying out the employment itself. Accordingly, any payment by an employer of, or as a contribution towards, any such expenses *incurred by the employee* is earnings for contribution purposes. See Booklets 480 (2000), Chapter 8 and 490, para 7.2.

There are four exceptions to the rule stated above.

The first arises where the employee is a *disabled person* for whom training or employment facilities (i.e. sheltered workshops) are being provided under the *Disabled Persons (Employment) Act 1944, s 15*. If an employer defrays or contributes towards the expenses which such an employee incurs in travelling from his home to his main place of work, the employer's payments are to be excluded from earnings for contribution purposes. [*Contributions Regs, Reg 19(1)(i)*]. See Booklet 480 (2000), para 5.1 and IR 490. This exception was introduced to bring disabled people in sheltered workshops into line with disabled people in open employment for whom state-provided help with travelling expenses does not count as earnings for contribution purposes. (DSS Press Release, 8 December 1987). Payments made by the Department of Employment or by an employer to assist with a disabled person's travel expenses are similarly excluded.

The second exception arises where the employee is temporarily working at some place of work other than his usual place of work, e.g. at the premises of one of his employer's clients or on detached duty at some branch of the business other than the branch at which he normally works. If the employer pays or contributes towards the expenses which such an employee incurs in travelling from his home to his temporary place of work and, at the outset, the temporary placement is not expected to last for more than 24 months, the employer's payments are, for up to twelve months, to be excluded from earnings for contribution purposes — this is the current position. Prior to 6 April 1998 this limit was twelve. There appeared to be some basis in law for this old rule. It would appear to lie in *Smith v Stages [1989] 1 AER 833* (a vicarious liability case) where it was held that an employee who, for a short time has to work for his employer at a different place of work some distance away from his usual place of work will be acting in the course of his employment when travelling from and returning to his ordinary residence if he travels in his employer's time. The DSS view was, in other words, that an employee temporarily working somewhere other than his normal place of work is being employed to travel there as well as work when he gets there, whereas an employee working at his normal place of work is being employed only to work when he gets there.

Under the old rules usually, when considering the term 'temporary place of work', the CA issued the following guidelines

'Occasionally the person with a normal place of work will have to travel to a temporary place of work. In such a case, as the expenses have been incurred necessarily in the performance of the duties; they should not be included in the gross pay for NICs. An employee cannot be regarded as temporarily absent from his normal place of work unless: (a) the absence is expected to be, and is in fact, less than twelve months; and (b) the employee returns to his normal place of work at the end of the period. If conditions (a) and (b) are not satisfied such payments should be included in gross payments for NICs.'

With effect from the tax year 1998–99 onwards those employees who travel between home and a temporary workplace are to be treated slightly differently, see examples below; whereas in the past it has been the practice to treat payments for up to twelve months as excluded from earnings for contributions purposes (see above) this is changed to 24 months. That is any period that is not expected to exceed 24 months will not require tax or NICs to be deducted from the payments. However, if the period at the temporary workplace is expected from the outset to exceed 24 months then the favourable treatment will not apply. In addition, it was previously a requirement under the old twelve month rule that, after the period of temporary work, the employee returned to the original permanent workplace. This is no longer a requirement under the new 24 month rule. The recurrence of temporary employment in manipulation of the 24-month period will not be allowed but travel between employments or offices in the same group of companies will be allowed (see Extra Statutory Concession A4 and CA National Insurance News, Winter 1997–98, Page 10 and IR Booklet 490(2000), Chapter 3). [*ICTA 1988, s 198(1),(1A) (1B), 198A and 12A Sch as inserted by FA 1997, s 63; FA 1998, s 61, 10 Sch*].

Example

Q works for 007 Support Ltd and normally works at and lives near the company's London site. He is asked to go to the Hereford site for a period of seventeen months from 1 August 1998. He commutes on a weekly basis and 007 Productions Ltd reimburses his travel costs. Under the old rules there would have been tax and Class 1 NIC liability on the travel expenses but since the 24 month limit came into effect on 6 April 1998 the Hereford site would count as a new permanent workplace and no such liabilities will arise.

Example

Ms R who is Q's assistant normally works at the London site but is required to travel to the Hereford site for one day, 18 May 2000. She normally travels into London using her season ticket. She drives directly to Hereford from her flat in Ashford which is a round trip of 436 miles. 007 Productions Ltd reimburses the full costs of her day's journey to Hereford. The theoretical round trip from London to Hereford is 296 miles which is significantly less than the actual costs incurred. Under the 'lesser of' rule on triangular travel she only gets a deduction for the 296 miles being the theoretical round trip from the office to Hereford. However, Ms R would be able to claim the deduction for the additional cost of the journey not originally allowed i.e. 140 miles because there has been no actual saving to her in view of the fact that she has a season ticket for the trip from Ashford to London. [*ICTA 1988, s 198A(1)(b) as inserted by FA 1997, s 62*].

Example

S is a salesman for the southern part of England for 007 Productions Ltd and will be working in the Hereford area for a week as back-up to Q. He is due to call on at least twenty companies including the one where Q will be working. S has what is known as a 'travelling appointment' and therefore the reimbursement of the costs of travelling have not been taxed and will continue to remain non-taxable under the new rules. No NICs are due in these circumstances.

Example

T, who is Q's boss, lives near Swindon and commutes daily to the London office but decides to visit Q at Hereford to chair a meeting with purchasers. The distance T has to travel is 150 miles round trip which is about the same distance to the Hereford client. 007 Productions Ltd pays T's commuting expenses to Hereford and no tax is paid. This is because under the 'lesser of' rule on triangular travel T can claim the full cost of the journey from home to Hereford as it is less than the cost of travelling there from London which is T's normal place of work. No tax or NICs have been payable on the cost previously. However, from 6 April 1998 T only gets a deduction for the additional cost of travel where the travel expenses are 'reasonable' otherwise an NI liability will arise.

Example

X who has been on leave at his home in Canterbury is suddenly called in to test a new flak jacket at the London office's testing ground. This recall to the office is unexpected due to the fact that he was covered for the week he was on leave. However, the person who was covering his leave period has been taken ill and hence X is recalled to the office. The cost of his travel from Canterbury to London is paid by the company but is tax and NIC-able from April 1998 onwards. Arrears of NICs in two similar circumstances will not be payable by 007 Productions Ltd where it relied on past guidance before 6 April 1998.

In a response to employers' representatives the Financial Secretary to the Treasury announced on 24 September 1997 that legislation will be introduced in the 1998 Finance Bill to amend the *FA 1997* rules covering employees' travelling and associated subsistence expenses that will make it simpler to apply the rules. This is now contained in *FA 1998, s 61*. The effect of these changes on NICs will be that no contributions will arise on payments to meet *reasonable* business travel costs of employees and that there will be no offset for commuting savings made. In practice, therefore, as long as the sums reimbursed, or paid on an employee's behalf by an employer, do no more than cover the costs necessarily incurred there will be no NICs liability. For employers it is clear that where the rules have not been operated correctly in the past there will be the opportunity for the Inland Revenue to apply for back tax and NICs will also be due in addition. As the new regulations did not come into force until 1 October 1998 (*Social Security (Contributions) Amendment (No 3) Regs 1998, Reg 6(4)*) the CA agreed that employers could apply the new rules from 6 April 1998 onwards so that they mirror the tax rules. [*ICTA 1988, s 61, 12A Sch as inserted by FA 1998, s 61, 10 Sch*]. See Inland Revenue Tax Bulletin, Issue 33, page 477–485; CA Press Release 10/98, 2 March 1998; CA National Insurance News, issue 9, page 10.

The third exception relates to car fuel acquired for use in a car made available to the employee in connection with his employment. *Contributions Regs, Reg 19(4)* was to be amended so that payments by an employer in respect of such fuel would, with effect from 6 April 1991, not be part of earnings for contribution purposes. Instead, in many instances, CLASS 1A CONTRIBUTIONS (16) are payable by the employer on a car fuel scale amount. However, despite the introduction of Class 1A regulations, the Class 1 amendments were not made until 1996 by inserting new *regulation 19(1)(y)* into the *1979 Regs* (CA Press Release 96/1, 15 March 1996) (*Social Security (Contributions) Amendment (No 3) Regulations 1996, Reg 3*). Whilst this change only has the force of law from 6 April 1996 it has been the policy not to collect Class 1 on fuel payments previously. The same logic should have extended to the admittedly rare circumstance that an employee was required to meet certain repair costs or arrange insurance for a company owned car. However, some employers had difficulty with the DSS on this issue. These other non-fuel costs are now covered by the new regulation from 6 April 1996.

The fourth exception applies, for 1993–94 onwards, when there is a disruption to public transport caused by a strike or some other form of industrial action, or when an employee has worked to 9 pm or later at the request of his employer and this has not happened more than 60 times already in that year and it does not then form part of the normal pattern of the employment. [*Contributions Amendment No 4 Regs, Reg 2*] and see also Booklet 490. This corresponds to the income tax exception set out in ESC A66. (See IR Leaflet 480 (2000) para 5.1). The exception also applies when travel (including foreign travel) expenses are paid under *ICTA 1988, ss 193, 194*. In other circumstances contributions liability could be avoided by having the employer make the contract with the taxi or car hire company, since this would be a payment in kind (see 28.24 above) although this might attract a Class 1A charge from 6 April 2000.

Where the employer (rather than the employee) incurs the expense of the employee's home to work travel—by, for example, arranging a taxi on the company account—the benefit enjoyed by the employee is also a payment in kind (see 28.24 above) and is *not* earnings for Class 1 purposes although a Class 1A charge could arise from 6 April 2000. The same comment was applicable to the purchase of, for example, a rail season ticket until 6 April 1999, but that is no longer so (see 28.64 below).

'Site based' employees such as those in the construction industry or computer industries are deemed to have no normal place of work as such. They work at various sites consecutively spending weeks or months at each site. The expenses of travel in getting from home to site is not incurred necessarily in the performance of the duties. These expenses should therefore have been included in gross pay for NICs until 6 April 1998. The employee was deemed to be travelling *to* the job as opposed to the travelling appointment situation, mentioned below, where he is travelling *on* the job. If the employee then has to travel between sites it will be treated as two (or more) places of work and is therefore in the course of employment. From 6 April 1998 the 'reasonable' reimbursed travelling expenses between sites will not be liable for NICs. See Inland Revenue Tax Bulletin, issue 33, page 477 *et seq*; CA Press Release 10/98; CA National Insurance News, issue 9, page 10.

A travelling appointment is basically where the employee has travel as part of his duties. He is travelling *on* the job rather than *to* the job, as in the case of a person with a normal place of employment. In such a case where a travelling appointment is applicable the employment generally will commence when the employee leaves home and therefore his travelling expenses are necessarily incurred in the performance of the duties. In these cases expenses paid should not be included in gross pay for NICs. Some travelling expenses will, from 6 April 1998, be liable to tax and NICs if the employee lives outside the area within which he is required to travel as part of his job (see Booklet 490).

In the case of offshore oil and gas rig workers the reimbursement of expenses incurred by those workers in the course of transferring to or from the mainland is to be disregarded for NIC purposes. This also includes the provision of overnight accommodation in the vicinity of the mainland departure point. See ESC A59 and Leaflet 480 (2000), para 5.1. [*Contributions Regs 1979, Reg 19(1)(v) as inserted by Social Security (Contributions) Amendment (No 3) Regulations 1996, Reg 3*].

28.63 Recall expenses

In the past if an employee was recalled from his home to work by his employer, his travelling expenses, if reimbursed by his employer, were not earnings for contribution purposes. (CWG2 (1997), Page 83, Item (147)). The basis for this rule lay in *Blee v LNER [1938] AC 126* where it was held that a man who is called out at night to deal with an emergency may be acting in the course of his employment when travelling from his home to his place of work to deal with the emergency. The exclusion did not apply where the employee was required by the terms of his contract of service to be on call. (CWG2 (1997), Page 84, Flowchart).

The CA's National Insurance News, Winter 1997–98, Page 10 stated that the new rules regarding employee's travel and subsistence payments in *Finance Act 1997* were to be mirrored by the DSS:

'However, the Department of Social Security has now concluded that all such payments should be subject to National Insurance contributions. This aligns the National Insurance contributions position with that for tax. The Contributions Agency will not be seeking any arrears from the employer who has relied on published past guidance and not paid National Insurance contributions on these payments, but new employer guidance from April 1998 will confirm National Insurance contributions are due in these circumstances.'

28.64 Season travel tickets

In accordance with the principles described at 28.45 above a reimbursement by an employer in respect of a season travel ticket purchased by an employee will be earnings for contribution purposes. Where, however, the employer himself purchases the ticket either by buying it from the supplier directly or by giving the employee a cheque made payable to the supplier, the payment is a payment in kind (see 28.24 above) and, until 6 April 1999, therefore attracted no NIC liability. However, even though the employer may arrange for an employer's contract, the handing over of the season ticket will, from 6 April 1999, constitute the provision of a 'voucher, token, stamp or similar document exchangeable for goods or services' and liability will arise. Similar remarks also now apply to the provision of holidays, etc. under an employer's contract. (CWG2 (2000), Pages 24 and 79).

Likewise, any voucher or warrant which is redeemable only for travel and not for cash is a payment in kind (see 28.28 above).

28.65 Use of company car

Where an employer provides an employee with a car for his use, the benefit enjoyed by the employee is a payment in kind (see 28.24 above). (CWG2 (2000), Page 75). From 6 April 1991, however, the employer of the person to whom the car is made available may be liable to pay CLASS 1A CONTRIBUTIONS (16) in respect of the car benefit and, if applicable, fuel scale charge.

28.66 Use-of-own-car allowances

Where an employee uses his own car for the purposes of his employment he may be recompensed in various ways and this may give rise to difficulties from a contribution point of view. For the Inland Revenue view see Booklet 480 (2000) paras 16.1–16.5 and IR125 'Using your own car for work'.

If the employee receives a round sum allowance and the actual expense he incurs in using his car for business purposes cannot be identified, then, subject to the concession described at 28.66 below, the whole sum will be earnings for contribution purposes. This is because the payments by the employer cannot be said to be specific payments of or contributions towards expenses which the employee has actually incurred in carrying out his employment. [*Contributions Regs, Reg 19(4)(b)*]. (CWG2 (2000), Page 87).

If an employer discharges specific debts which the employee incurs in connection with a car which he owns personally but uses for the purposes of his employment, e.g. road fund licence, insurance, servicing, AA/RAC membership, DSS guidance was that the whole of each payment is earnings for contribution purposes. The basis for that guidance is, first, the general principle that, where an employer discharges an employee's personal debts, he is placing money's worth in the hands of the employee (see 28.45 above) and, second, that a payment in connection with a business expense may be excluded from earnings only if it is a specific and distinct payment of or contribution towards an expense actually incurred in carrying out the employment. [*Contributions Regs, Reg 19(4)(b)*]. The DSS was of the view that a person's expenses incurred in running a car for private purposes are incurred in the course of domestic living and not in carrying out the employment so that, even though the car might be put to some business use, *Reg 19(4)(b)* is of no relevance.

Since April 1996 it has been the case that where employees are paid a mileage allowance for using their own cars on business trips and the FPCS rates (see 28.65) have been used then there will be no profit element applying and, leading on from this, no liability to NICs.

Lump sum mileage allowance payments are liable to NICs and Local Government (and some other) employers pay such amounts to 'essential car users'. In these circumstances the FPCS rate may be deducted from the essential car user allowance when computing the Class 1 liability. The CA stated at their Specialist Conference on 29 October 1997:

'If FPCS rates were used we would be quite happy. If people were using higher rates than FPCS then we would establish whether or not there was a profit to the individual and we would charge NICs, if there was. If there wasn't then we'd accept it.'

28.67 **Petrol**

The principal rule which the DSS imposed on 6 April 1989 and which it considered to be of effect from then until 8 February 1991, is that, unless an employee obtained his car fuel

(a) from his employer's own stocks of fuel,

(b) in exchange for non-encashable fuel vouchers supplied to him by his employer, or

(c) on an account maintained by his employer with the filling station from which he obtained his supplies,

the whole of the expenditure on fuel met by his employer was earnings for contribution purposes if there was *any* non-incidental private usage of any of the fuel obtained. (NI 269 April 1989 edition, Page 61, Item (68) and Supplement).

In circumstances (a) and (c), the DSS regarded the fuel as supplied to the employee by the employer and thus (to any extent to which it was used for non-business purposes) as constituting a payment in kind (see 28.24 above). Likewise, in circumstance (b), the fuel voucher itself (provided it was incapable of encashment by mere surrender) was also regarded as a payment in kind (see 28.28 above).

Where fuel was obtained by any other means, e.g.

(d) cash, with subsequent reimbursement by the employer,

(e) cheque, with subsequent reimbursement by the employer,

(f) personal credit card, with subsequent reimbursement by the employer,

(g) in exchange for an encashable voucher supplied by the employer,

(h) on a personal account maintained with a filling station, whether the employer settled the account, or the employee settled it and was subsequently reimbursed by the employer,

(i) a company credit card, or

(j) an agency card,

the DSS regarded the fuel as supplied initially under a personal contract which the employee entered with the filling station at the point of filling up his car's tank on the forecourt, and regarded any subsequent reimbursement, adoption or discharge of that personal liability by the employer as a payment of 'earnings' to the extent that the fuel was not used for either business purposes or incidental private purposes (see 28.45 and 28.47 above). (NI 269 April 1989 edition, Page 61, Item (68) and Supplement).

No great weight was allowed to the apparent concession for 'incidental private usage' of car fuel. The DSS said that it was using the term 'incidental' in this context to mean unanticipated and exceptional, so that where, for example, an employee filled his car's tank with petrol immediately before setting off on a long business trip but then received a telephone call which necessitated his returning home to deal with a domestic crisis, the private usage of the fuel was 'incidental' and could be regarded as business usage, but where an employee filled up with petrol for a long business trip *knowing* he would return home before setting off, the private usage of the fuel was 'non-incidental'. (Aide-Mémoire entitled 'Paying Employee's Petrol Expenses—NIC Liability' and supplied on request by the DSS).

Unless travel formed an integral part of an employee's duties and he had no normal place of work at which he had to report, the DSS generally regarded all journeys made by an employee between his home and his normal place of work as private journeys. Where an employee was required to work somewhere other than his normal place of work, however, the DSS regarded only the lesser of

(i) the distance travelled between the employee's home and the specified place of work, and

(ii) the distance between the employee's normal place of work and the specified place of work

as the length of the business journey. (Aide-Mémoire entitled 'Paying Employee's Petrol Expenses—NIC Liability').

The important point for every employer was that the DSS considered that the *whole cost* of any car fuel obtained by methods (*d*) to (*j*) above and used partly for non-incidental private purposes by an employee had to be treated as part of that employee's earnings for contribution purposes unless detailed mileage records covering both business and private usage were maintained and kept available for inspection by the DSS and the Inland Revenue (in which case only the cost of fuel attributable to non-incidental private usage needed to be treated as earnings).

Where the cost of car fuel was to be treated as earnings under those rules, the cost was net of VAT if, but only if, the employer was entitled to reclaim input VAT in respect of car fuel purchases. (Aide-Mémoire entitled 'Paying Employee's Petrol Expenses—NIC Liability').

While the DSS said it was prepared to consider and, if appropriate, approve other methods of calculating the 'earnings' element of fuel costs borne by an employer, it formally approved two alternative methods whereby the 'earnings' amount could be arrived at:

(A) The ratio of private mileage to total mileage revealed by the mileage records for the earnings period could be applied to the petrol costs paid by the employer in the earnings period, or

(B) the car manufacturer's quoted consumption rate for consumption at 56 mph could be applied to the private mileage figure revealed by the mileage records. (Aide-Mémoire entitled 'Paying Employee's Petrol Expenses—NIC Liability').

It is understood to have approved a third:

(C) an appropriate *petrol* mileage rate could be obtained from AA or other scales published by motoring organisations and applied to the business mileage figure revealed by the mileage records and the resulting amount could be deducted from the total petrol costs.

Where petrol was provided by means of a company credit card or an agency card, the DSS view was that the cost of the petrol was to be regarded as paid for by the employer in the earnings period in which he received the account from the credit card or agency card company, *not* (if the earnings period was a different one) when the account was actually paid. (Aide-Mémoire entitled 'Paying Employee's Petrol Expenses—NIC Liability').

In mid-1990, the DSS recognised that many employers had thereto failed to comply with those rules and, while insisting that the rules had to be followed precisely in 1990–91 and future tax years, it proposed (in an undated technical note entitled 'Special Arrangements for the 1989–90 Tax Year') a number of alternative methods for settling liabilities for 1989–90.

Where mileage records had been maintained for 1989–90 but no action had been taken to account for NIC on the private use element of car fuel costs borne by the employer, the DSS said that the employer should calculate the 'earnings' element of car fuel costs using the rules described.

Where mileage records had not been maintained for 1989–90, the DSS offered two extra-statutory bases for settlement. It said that the employer might either:

(1)   measure private car fuel costs per employee over a sample period of, say, one month and calculate an annual equivalent for 1989–90 on the basis of such a sample; or

(2)   assume that private car fuel costs per employee were equivalent to the Inland Revenue fuel scale charge for 1989–90 for the relevant car.

Whichever method was used, said the DSS, the total amount arrived at for the year had to be treated as an additional item of earnings for NIC purposes in the final earnings period for 1989–90 (normally either week 52 or month 12) and the additional Class 1 contributions had to be calculated and added to the figures declared on forms P14 and P35. If the end of year returns had already been forwarded to the Inland Revenue, the employer had to check whether supplementary returns might still be filed. If they could not, he had to contact his local DSS office and explain the position.

The DSS pointed out that, if a primary as well as a secondary Class 1 liability arose on the additional 'earnings' (because the employee's other earnings had not reached the upper earnings limit in the final earnings period), it was then too late to recover this from the employee and it had to be borne by the employer.

All this advice was, to some extent, modified in the wake of *R v DSS, ex p Overdrive Credit Card Ltd [1991] STC 129*. There, Overdrive sought an order that the aide-mémoire referred to in the foregoing paragraphs should be withdrawn and that declarations should be granted to the effect that

(I)   payment of an employee's petrol expenses by use of an employer's credit card or petrol agency card does not attract liability to primary or secondary Class 1 national insurance contributions; or, alternatively to (I),

(II)   no distinction was to be drawn in point of liability for contributions between payment of an employee's petrol expenses

(i)   by use of an employer's credit card, and

(ii)   by issuing to the employee vouchers which could not be exchanged for cash, and

(iii)   by charging such petrol to an employer's garage account;

or, alternatively to (I) or (II),

(III) the treatment for the purposes of NICs of payment of an employee's petrol expenses whether such payment is made by the use of an employer's credit card or petrol agency card or by the issue to the employee of vouchers which cannot be exchanged for cash or by charging such petrol to an employer's garage account depends upon whether or not the employee is liable as principal for the price of the petrol in the first instance and that such treatment is the same whichever method is used, namely that a liability for the NICs is attracted if the employee is so liable as principal and there is no liability for NICs if the employee is not so liable as principal.

The court granted the order for the withdrawal of the aide-mémoire and, because the DSS had conceded prior to the judicial review that there was no distinction to be drawn between the three methods of payment set out at (II), the court also granted the declaration at (II). The declaration at (I) was refused, however, but the declaration at (III) was granted on the grounds that, where an employee makes it clear to the forecourt attendant, before filling up with petrol, that he is acting as agent for his employer, the value of the petrol purchased does not form part of the employee's earnings for contribution purposes, but where there is no such declaration of agency the employee contracts as principal and a contribution liability may arise if, and to the extent that, the goods are used for non-business purposes.

In the light of that judicial review, the DSS modified its views so that, for the period from 8 February 1991 onwards (or, in the case of fuel relating only to company cars, to 5 April 1991), (*b*) and (*c*) above joined (*d*) to (*j*) as methods of obtaining fuel which attract contribution liabilities in the circumstances described; but no liability was to be pursued in the case of fuel purchased by use of a company credit card, a company agency card, a voucher or a garage account on the assumption that a pre-fill-up declaration of agency would have been made by an employee in every case where such payment methods were used.

The DSS was, initially at least, emphatic that, for the period from 6 April 1989 to 8 February 1991, contribution liability had to be assessed in accordance with the pre-*Overdrive* rules and that such liabilities would continue to be pursued where they had not already been settled. The position became clearer with the publication in April 1992 of a Supplement to NI 269, which contained the table below in relation to petrol expenses for periods before 6 April 1991. The table was then included as Table A on Page 65 of NI 269 in April 1993, but has been omitted since the April 1995 edition of the equivalent guides

Method of fuel supply	Liability
1 Employer's credit card/agency card.	Class 1 primary and secondary NICs on any private mileage element. But if business and private mileage elements cannot be identified from logs, treat the full value of fuel as earnings for Class 1 NICs.
2 Employer's garage account.	As in 1 above—but see footnote.
3 Petrol vouchers.	As in 1 above—but see footnote.
4 Reimbursement of fuel bills paid by employee.	As in 1 above.
5 Round sum allowances.	Class 1 primary and secondary NICs. The full allowance should be treated as earnings for NICs.
6 Mileage allowances—business mileage only.	Class 1 primary and secondary NICs on any allowance paid in excess of AA/RAC recommended rates.
7 Mileage allowances—business and private mileage included.	Class 1 primary and secondary NICs on any private mileage element. If business mileage element can be identified from logs, no NICs due if below AA/RAC recommended rates. If business/private elements cannot be identified from logs, treat whole allowance as earnings for Class 1 NICs.
8 Company fuel pump.	No liability.

Footnote: Methods 2 and 3 If you are able to demonstrate you have relied on past guidance to the effect that there was no NIC liability in these circumstances payment will not be pursued.

Employers who supplied fuel to employees under method 1 were informed on the same page of NI 269 that there was *no* liability if *before filling the tank* the garage attendant/cashier was told, and accepted, that the fuel was being bought on behalf of the employer. It was stressed, however, that each case was dealt with on its own merits and the quality of the evidence supporting the employer's claim would be critically examined.

Following legal advice, the DSS stated that in view of the terms in which the department gave guidance for tax years 1989–90 and 1990–91, it would not take enforcement action for either of those tax years for any NICs due in respect of payments of the cost of fuel provided for private use and paid for by employer's credit card or fuel agency card, garage account or non-cash vouchers. (Press Release 93/163, 24 September 1993). This practice recognises that questions of justice and fairness arise if collection is pursued in respect of periods when DSS guidance was, at best, misleading. The Department did, however, refuse to refund contributions already paid in similar circumstances so that employers who followed DSS guidance were effectively put at a financial disadvantage when compared with those who challenged the DSS view and therefore delayed, or ignored, demands for payment. It is not consistent with the Contributor's Charter (see 40.3 LEAFLETS) that one group of contributors should be treated more fairly than others! However, in a written response in February 1996 the CA stated 'Some employers who paid [NICs] have suggested that, because other employers will not now be required to pay, they should have a refund on the grounds of equitable treatment. As NICs were correctly paid refunds cannot be given and no question of equity arises.' (CA Specialist Conference written responses, 20 February 1996.)

In a further twist there is evidence that some contributors in this position have had their contributions refunded (see Taxation 25 April 1996, page 111). The Agency pointed to their new recognition of what is acceptable evidence of a business expense (see 1995 leaflet CA 28, Page 84, para 163) as an alternative means whereby *some* employers *may* be able to obtain a full or partial refund of such payments made. It should be noted that repayments for 1989–90 and 1990–91 will be debarred if no claim was made by 5 April 1996 or 5 April 1997 respectively (*Reg 32(5)*) unless the Secretary of State can be satisfied that all these circumstances constitute a 'good reason for delay' and allows a period of longer than six years for making the claim. (See also CA National Insurance News, Issue 3, Page 4.) In a written reply to a question put by a delegate at the CA Conference in February 1997 the CA stated

'Looking first at refunds, regulation 32 of the Social Security (Contributions) Regulations 1979 permits refunds only when contributions have been paid in error. There is no other provision, statutory or otherwise, which enables contributions which have been properly paid to be refunded. The case of *R v The Department of Social Security ex parte Overdrive Credit Cards Limited 1991 WLR 635* established that NICs were correctly due in respect of fuel purchased by means of:

- employers' credit or fuel agency card

- employers' garage account

- vouchers not exchangeable for cash

unless the employee indicated to the garage attendant before making the purchase that said purchase was being made on behalf of the employer. As liability was confirmed, with the result that contributions were properly paid, there is no basis on which such contributions can be refunded.

The decision not to enforce payment from those who did not pay in these circumstances—or, indeed, any others—is, as stated above, an entirely separate issue. Like any other creditor, the Department has to make a business decision as to whether or not to pursue a debt. That decision will be influenced by a number of factors, not least of which is the economics of enforcement. That said, the Department is in no different position to any other creditor and will no more return payment X to a payer just because it does not pursue debt Y. The fact that debt Y

is not pursued for sound business reasons does not amount to a justification or reason to return sums paid in the discharge of a liability.'

CA Specialist Conference written response, February 1997.

Where fuel is purchased on or after 6 April 1991 for use in a car made available to an employee by his employer or a third party in connection with his employment, DSS did not pursue the Class 1 liability that strictly has arisen in addition to the Class 1A charge. This policy has the force of law from 6 April 1996 (*Social Security (Contribution) Amendment (No 3) Regulations 1996*). The DSS had expressed its intention that this will be so whether or not liability for CLASS 1A CONTRIBUTIONS (16) arises in respect of the car and car fuel in question and that, from 6 April 1991, the revised post-*Overdrive* rules should be applied only to fuel costs borne by an employer in connection with an employee's *own* car.

The table below (from the 1995 edition of CA 28, Pages 93 and 94) sets out the DSS policy since 6 April 1991 for both employer-supplied cars and employee-supplied cars.

It should be noted that, where appropriate, the comments about what constitutes acceptable evidence of a business expense may be borne in mind.

Method of fuel supply	Employer supplied cars	Employee supplied cars or vehicles on which Class 1A NICs are not payable
Employer's credit card/ agency card/petrol vouchers/employer's garage account.	No Class 1 NICs will be collected.	No Class 1 NIC liability if it was explained in advance that fuel was being bought on behalf of the employer.
Supply from company fuel pump.	No Class 1 NIC liability.	No Class 1 NIC liability, fuel is benefit in kind.
Reimbursement of fuel bills paid by employee, including use of employee credit cards.	No Class 1 NICs will be collected.	There is no Class 1 NIC liability if only business mileage is involved. If both business and private mileage are involved, Class 1 NICs are due on the full amount paid. But if the actual business mileage can be identified, the amount on which NICs is due can be reduced by that business element. NICs will then be due on the private element only.
Round sum allowance.	A Class 1 NIC liability on whole amount. If any specific and distinct business expense can be identified, the amount on which NICs is due can be reduced by the business element.	Class 1 NIC liability on whole amount. If any specific and distinct business expense can be subsequently identified, the amount on which NICs is due can be reduced by the business element.

Mileage allowance—business mileage only.	A Class 1 NIC liability may arise. Ask the Contributions Agency at your local Social Security office how this is calculated.	Class 1 NIC liability arises on the balance of any business mileage allowance paid in excess of the rates recommended by either the AA for 10,000 miles or the Inland Revenue Fixed Profit Car Scheme rates. See paragraph 164(85).
Mileage allowance—business and private mileage included.	A Class 1 NIC liability may arise. Ask the Contributions Agency at your local Social Security office how this is calculated.	Class 1 NICs are due on the amount paid if both business *and* private mileage are involved. *But*, if the *actual* business mileage can be identified, the amount on which NICs is due can be reduced by the business element *if* the rates paid do not exceed those quoted by either the AA for 10,000 miles or the Inland Revenue Fixed Profit Car Scheme rates. See paragraph 164(85).

28.68 Mileage allowances for business travel

In an effort to simplify the mileage allowance arrangements for NICs purposes from 6 April 1996 onwards the FPCS rates for up to 4,000 miles will be the standard measure of allowable motoring costs including pedal cycles and motorcycles from 6 April 2000. In 1995–96 employers could use the FPCS rates or those of the AA for 10,000 miles or keep their own records. For 1996–97 onwards there is less choice and employers are obliged to use the FPCS rates or keep their own records without the option of using the AA rates. Administratively, the change will help the employer because the AA rates were not available until after the tax year had commenced and this inevitably created problems. Also, the FPCS rates apply equally to petrol and diesel cars whereas the AA rates made a distinction between the two with varying rates.

Where an employee who uses his own vehicle and his own fuel for the purposes of his employment is paid a mileage allowance by his employer based on recorded business mileage, the payments made will not be earnings for contribution purposes unless they exceed an amount arrived at by applying to recorded business mileage the Fixed Profit Car Scheme rates (also termed 'Inland Revenue Authorised Mileage rates') for up to 4,000 miles of business travel per year. (See CWG2 (2000), Pages 86 and 87). These particular rates apply for NIC purposes *regardless* of the number of business miles actually travelled by the employees. Alternatively, if the employer can identify the actual business expense this can be excluded from gross pay. If payment is

- over the Inland Revenue's Authorised Mileage rates, or if higher
- for more than the actual business expense incurred, or
- for private travel

then the excess should be included in the employee's gross pay. (See CA National Insurance News, Issue 4, Page 7, and IR Leaflet 480 (2000) paras 16.1–5). The relevant rates for 1997–98 to 2000–2001 are shown below (see CWG1 (2000), Cards 13, 14 and 15):

FPCS rates for NICs in 1997–98
Engine capacity (cc)

up to 1000	1001 to 1500	1501 to 2000	over 2000
28p	35p	45p	63p

Inland Revenue Authorised rates for NICs for 1998–99 to 2000–2001 inclusive
Engine capacity (cc)

up to 1000	1001 to 1500	1501 to 2000	over 2000
28p	35p	45p	63p

Note: These rates apply to leaded, unleaded petrol and diesel cars. Where the same mileage rate is paid to all employees regardless of their car's engine size the average of the two middle FPCS rates is used e.g. $\frac{35p + 45p}{2} = 40p$

In the case of pedal cycles the rate is 12p per mile from 6 April 1999 and for motorcyles it is 24p per mile from 6 April 2000. NICs do not arise if employees are paid at or below these rates for business use of their pedal cycles or motorcycles.

Also, the FPCS, etc. rates for over 4,000 miles are not relevant to NIC and are not reproduced. For AA rates for 1995–96 and previous years and details of the methods of application see earlier years' editions of this work.

Example
Frank works at different sites and has no permanent workplace. He travels in his own 1600cc car to and from the sites where he is working. Over the whole of the tax year he travels 8,000 miles on business to and from the different sites. He is entitled to tax relief for the cost of his travel.

Frank's employer pays him 50 pence a mile for his business travel. This is more than the Inland Revenue authorised mileage rate for a 1,501–2,000cc car. For the particular tax year (2000–01) the authorised rates are 45 pence for each of the first 4,000 business miles and 25 pence for each mile over 4,000. Frank gets a tax return. Frank's employer does not operate a FPCS. So his P11D shows the full mileage allowances of £4,000 he has been paid (50 pence x 8,000 miles) for the tax year.

Frank can choose to calculate the tax relief for his business travel by

- using the Inland Revenue's authorised mileage rates. The cost of 8,000 business miles using these rates is £2,800 (the first 4,000 miles at 45 pence = £1,800, plus the next 4,000 miles at 25 pence = £1,000); or

- using his actual costs of business motoring. Frank has kept full records of his costs and these show that his business travel in his own car has cost £2,935. The relief due for the 8,000 business miles by using his actual costs is £2,935.

For NICs purposes Frank's employer will have to include in earnings the sum of gross pay of £400 (i.e. 50 pence – 45 pence × 8,000 miles).

Mileage allowances which are not related to actual business mileage are merely round sum allowances (see 28.63 above). (CWG2 (2000), Pages 87 and 88).

The DSS did not regard payments made to employees to cover the additional expense of carrying passengers and/or equipment specifically relating to the employment in the employee's car as part of earnings for contribution purposes. (See 1995 leaflet CA 28, Page 88, Item 87).

As an alternative to FPCS, etc. rates, the employer may exclude the actual business expense from earnings, if it can be identified. (See Inland Revenue Press Release, 9 December 1996 and leaflet IR125 'Using your car for work').

28.69 Essential car user's allowances

Some employers (typically, until recently, local authorities) make two forms of payment to employees who use their own cars for the purposes of their employment. The first is a periodic round sum allowance representing a proportion of the vehicle standing charges (often known as an essential car user's allowance) and the second is a (usually low) mileage allowance. If (as will normally be the case) the mileage rate used is less than the relevant FPCS rate, the excess of the FPCS rate over the rate used may be applied to the relevant business mileage and the resulting amount may be deducted from the round-sum allowance. By concession, only the reduced round sum allowance will then be regarded as earnings. Special notes were available from the DSS to assist local authorities etc. in making the necessary calculations. The NJC 'Purple Book' rates of allowance were *not* accepted by the DSS as an alternative to FPCS rates.

However, at the CA Specialist Conference in Newcastle on 27 October 1997 this point was addressed with the following reply:

'We would look at what was paid and was it reasonable in the circumstances. If FPCS rates were used we would be quite happy. If people [Local Government] were using higher rates than FPCS then we would establish whether or not there was a profit to the individual and we would charge NICs if there was. If there wasn't then we'd accept it.'

28.70 Parking fees and fines

An employer's reimbursement of parking fees incurred by an employee in connection with business-related journeys does not form part of earnings for contribution purposes because they are expenses actually incurred by the employee in carrying out his employment. [*Contributions Regs, Reg 19(4)*]. (CWG2 (2000), Page 75). The DSS required evidence of the parking fees incurred, however, and, in the absence of such evidence, the reimbursements must be included in gross pay.

An employer's reimbursement or payment of parking fees incurred by an employee at his normal place of work constitutes earnings for contribution purposes on general principles. (CWG2 (2000), Page 75). This is so despite statutory exemption for PAYE income tax purposes.

Where an employer contracts with a car park or uses his own land to provide car parking facilities for his employees, no contribution liability arises as the facility is a payment in kind. (CWG2 (2000), Page 75).

A contract made by the employer may nonetheless attract Class 1 contributions from 6 April 1999 if a ticket (i.e. a non-cash voucher) is provided or, if not, a Class 1A charge from 6 April 2000.

Fines incurred for illegal parking are not generally regarded as expenses incurred in carrying out an employment and any payment or reimbursement by an employer in that regard will normally constitute earnings for contribution purposes if the employee is liable to pay the fine. If, instead, a 'notice to owner' is issued by virtue of which the employer becomes liable to pay the fine no liability to Class 1 contributions arises.

Exceptionally, in a Secretary of State's determination under the pre-1 April 1999 procedures (see 9 APPEALS AND REVIEWS), parking fines were held not to be earnings where the employee's duties were to empty gaming machines, etc. at customers' premises in central London and his written contract of employment specifically required that the vehicle be parked as near the customer's entrance as physically possible, regardless of any parking restrictions, for security reasons.

28.71 OVERSEAS EARNINGS

If an employee is, or is treated as being, an employed earner for contribution purposes, the fact that he receives payments from an overseas source does not prevent those payments being earnings for contribution purposes if they would otherwise be earnings in accordance with the rules described in this chapter. (See also OVERSEAS MATTERS (49)).

If the earnings are paid in a foreign currency the amount of the earnings is to be determined by converting them into their sterling equivalent using the exchange rate current at the time of payment. (See leaflet NI 132, April 1999, page 6).

According to NI 269 in April 1993, where an employee in the UK receives a payment from an overseas company the DSS did not expect contributions to be accounted for by a UK employer if the overseas company is not trading in association with the UK company or its parent company when the overseas company actually makes the payment to the employee or via the UK company *and* incurs the full cost of the payment. (The question of who bears the cost was not mentioned in CA 28, April 1995.) The rationale of this view is discussed at 28.31 above. Payments from overseas *must*, however, be included in gross pay if the UK employer carries on business in association with the overseas company and the overseas employer has a place of business in the UK, in which case AGGREGATION OF EARNINGS (5.5) is required.

28.72 Overseas expenses and allowances

An employer's specific and distinct payment of or contribution towards expenses which an employee actually incurs in carrying out his employment while overseas is to be excluded from earnings for contribution purposes in accordance with the normal rule. [*Contributions Regs, Reg 19(4)(b)*]. Because an employee may have difficulty in obtaining receipts for all such expenditure, however, the DSS accepted a declaration by the employee that the expenses claimed were actually incurred. (See 1995 leaflet CA 28, Page 91, Item (101) and CA 28 Supplement April 1996).

Round sum allowances paid by an employer to an employee who is or has been working overseas do not fall within the excluding provisions of *Reg 19(4)(b)* (except to the extent that actual expenses covered by the allowance are identified) and they are, therefore, earnings for Class 1 contribution purposes. The DSS gave as examples of such round sum allowances payments to compensate for the higher cost of living abroad; payments as an inducement to persuade the employee to work abroad; and bonuses for working abroad.

It should be noted, however, that increased cost of living payments made to employees working overseas in accordance with scales prepared by employers' organisations may constitute subsistence allowances (see 28.50 above) and the use of such scales may constitute a scheme which satisfies all the conditions under which scheme payments are not regarded as earnings. Despite this, the CA stated that 'Cost of living allowances (COLAs) . . . are generally based on a shopping basket of goods and services (more highly) priced in the country where the employee is working and compared with the UK equivalent. They are not therefore incurred as an expense . . .' and therefore must be taken into account for NIC purposes on earnings. (See CA National Insurance News, Issue 4, page 9 and CA Specialist Conference written responses, 20 February 1996 and this was reaffirmed by the CA Specialist Conference written responses, 4 February 1997.)

A tax equalisation payment to an employee by his employer will normally cover an actual liability incurred but the DSS did not regard such a liability as an expense incurred by the employee in carrying out his employment. Accordingly, it cannot be excluded from earnings by virtue of *Reg 19(4)(b)*. (See 1995 leaflet CA 28, Page 82, Item (68)).

CWG2 (1997) referred employers to their local Contributions Agency Office for advice on paying travel expenses for employees and/or their families returning to the UK on home leave. The advice for 1998 and subsequent years is contained in booklet 490 'Employee Travel — A Tax and NICs Guide for Employers'. Any payment of, or contribution towards, expenses which, under *ICTA 1988, s 193(3), (4) or (6)* or *s 194* (travel expenses and foreign travel expenses where the duties of an office or employment are performed wholly or partly outside the UK) are deductible from the emoluments of the employment chargeable to tax under Schedule E is excluded from earnings for Class 1 purposes. [*Contributions Regs, Reg 19(1)(q)*, introduced by *Contributions Amendment No 4 Regs 1993* with effect from 6 April 1993].

Note also that where employees or directors, although fit enough to carry out duties at their normal place of work in the UK, but because of their poor state of health cannot undertake travel abroad on business without being accompanied, then the cost of the spouse's travel will not be charged to NICs. The CA took the view that legislation to mirror ESC A4(d) was not required because they were advised that the terms of *Reg 19(4)(b)* are wide enough to cover this matter (CA Specialist Conference, 20 February 1996 and see also IR Leaflet 480 (2000) paras 10.1–6).

From 6 April 1998 onwards the payment of medical expenses by an employer to an employee in respect of expenses they incur when carrying out duties abroad is removed from NICs liability. This applies to actual medical costs and expenses or insurance against such costs. CA Press Release CA10/98, 16 March 1998 and *Contributions Regs, Reg 19 (1)(zb)* inserted by *Contributions Amendment (No 2) Regs 1998, Reg 2.*

28.73 Special payments to mariners

Certain special payments made to mariners while incapacitated overseas are to be *excluded* from earnings for contribution purposes (see 42.6 MARINERS).

28.74 TRAINING EXPENSES

Payments made by an employer to an employee to reimburse him for fees, books, travel, etc. in connection with courses which are work-related or are required or encouraged by the employer (e.g. first aid courses) are not earnings for contribution purposes. (CWG2 (2000), Page 79 and see also IR Leaflet 480 (2000) para 5.1).

Following the introduction of the *Health and Safety (Display Screen Equipment) Regs 1992*, the Contributions Agency stated that it would not regard as 'earnings' the reimbursement by an employer of an employee's expenditure on an eyesight test when the employee is required to use a VDU in the course of his employment. Nor will Class 1 contributions be sought in respect of the provision or reimbursement of the cost of spectacles needed solely for use with a VDU in the course of the duties of an employment. Where a general need for spectacles is identified and, in addition to the special prescription for VDU use, the employer discharges the whole of the employee's liability for the spectacles acquired, the cost in excess of the VDU-only prescription will be regarded as earnings. If, however, the spectacles are purchased under a contract between the employer and the optician, the provision of the spectacles to the employee will be a payment in kind which will attract no contribution liability (see 28.24 above) until 6 April 2000, when a Class 1A charge then arises.

28.75 **VAT**

Where goods or services on which VAT is chargeable are supplied by an employed earner in the course of his employment and earnings paid to him in respect of that employment include the remuneration for the supply of those goods or services, an amount equal to the VAT so chargeable is to be excluded from his earnings for contribution purposes. Any VAT which forms part of a payment of earnings, for example, VAT on an employee's telephone bill which has been paid by the employer, forms part of earnings for contribution purposes. [*Contributions Regs, Reg 19(2)*].

28.76 **Nominee directors' fees**

A payment by a company to or for the benefit of one of its directors, in respect of any employed earner's employment of the director with the company, is to be excluded from the computation of the director's earnings for contribution purposes provided that

(*a*) the director was appointed to his office either

(i) by a company which had the right to make the appointment by virtue of its shareholding in, or agreement with, the company making the payment, or

(ii) by a company which is not the company making the payment and which is not controlled by the director and/or any person connected with him, and

(*b*) the director, by virtue of an agreement with the company which appointed him, is required to account for the payment to that company, and

(*c*) the payment forms part of the profits brought into charge for corporation tax or income tax of the company that appointed him.

[*Contributions Regs, Reg 19B(1)(2)(3)(4) as inserted by Contributions Amendment No 4 Regs 1987, Reg 4*].

For these purposes, control has the meaning attached to it in *ICTA 1988, s 840*, and 'any person connected with the director' has the meaning of spouse, parent, child, son-in-law or daughter-in-law of the director. [*Contributions Regs, Reg 19B(5) as inserted by Contributions Amendment No 4 Regs 1987, Reg 4*].

This regulation, which was made on 6 January 1988, corresponds almost exactly to Inland Revenue ESC A37 Paras 2 and 3 and gives the force of law to the DSS concession which was available before that date. From 6 April 1996 contribution law and the ESCs are brought fully into line by adopting for the purpose of *Reg 19B* the definition of 'company' that is contained in *ICTA 1988, s 832(1)(2)*. [*Social Security (Contributions) Amendment (No 3) Regulations 1996, Reg 3*].

The position is summarised in Leaflet CA 44, Para 58 and explained in a flowchart.

The rules can give rise to difficulty where the company which makes the appointment has no UK presence whatsoever, since the fees for which the director must account to that company may be included in profits which are subject to neither corporation tax nor income tax.

28.77 **EARNINGS FOR CLASS 2 PURPOSES**

Although CLASS 2 CONTRIBUTIONS (18) are not earnings-related, it becomes necessary to ascertain earnings for Class 2 purposes where exception from liability is sought on the grounds that those earnings are less than a specified amount, or where it is sought to demonstrate by reference to earnings that the earner is not ordinarily self-employed at all (see 14.10 CATEGORISATION and 18.3 CLASS 2 CONTRIBUTIONS).

The earnings to be compared with the limit set for a tax year are the earnings *in respect of* that year. [*Contributions Regs, Reg 25(1)*]. In this connection, earnings means the applicant's *net earnings* from employment as a self-employed earner. [*Reg 25(2)(a)*] and, in calculating those earnings, where the contributor also has earnings from employed earner's employment in the same year which are shown in the accounts of his business, those earnings are disregarded. [*Reg 25(2)(b)*]. The exclusion of Class 1 earnings for this purpose was introduced with effect from 6 July 1994 by *Contributions Amendment No 2 Regs 1994*. Before that date, Class 1 earnings paid into a business taxed under Schedule D were, arguably incorrectly, treated as part of profits for the purposes of small earnings exception. This led to the problem outlined further below.

The term 'net earnings' was interpreted by the DSS as meaning the figure which would appear in a profit and loss account prepared in accordance with normal accounting principles. Accordingly, deductions may be made from gross earnings for expenses incurred in running the business and an allowance may be made for depreciation. No deduction may, however, be made for income tax payments or for Class 2 or Class 4 contributions payable; an enterprise allowance paid under *Employment and Training Act 1973, s 2(2)(d)* and income from any source other than self-employment must be disregarded; and adjustments must be made for drawings from the business (including any 'salary' drawn by the earner) and the value of any withdrawals from stock for the person's own use. (Leaflet CA 02). The application for exception is to be accompanied by an estimate of gross earnings and expenses prepared in this way and until 27 May 1996 it was also necessary to enclose evidence of earnings e.g. the last accounts or tax papers—these do not now need to be supplied unless requested subsequently (see form CF 10 in leaflet CA 02 and 5.16 AGGREGATION OF EARNINGS).

Where a figure of net earnings from self-employment has been required in connection with the application of the 'earnings rule' for benefit claim purposes, the National Insurance Commissioners have accepted that accounts which have clearly been drawn-up by someone versed in commercial accountancy are sufficient evidence that the net earnings are as shown by the net profit in those accounts (see reported decision *R(P) 1/76* in the pension series). They have also accepted, however, that where the accounts include income from capital assets (such as rents), the net profit should be reduced by such income (see reported decision *R(U) 3/77* in the unemployment benefit series). These decisions, though useful indicators of probable DSS thinking, were not binding on the Department in the contribution field (see 28.3 above).

It is important to note that although, as indicated above, one of the DSS's instructions to a person with earnings from self-employment was: 'Do not count as earnings any income . . . from sources other than self-employment', that instruction relates only to the way in which an account of earnings should be drawn-up. If a self-employed earner (or his accountants) ignores that advice and includes on revenue account receipts from a source other than self-employment, the DSS maintained that those moneys thereby become a receipt of the trade and thus part of the earner's income from self-employment. Treasury Counsel advised the DSS with particular reference to SUBPOSTMASTERS (55.3) that where a subpostmaster includes his PO remuneration (Class 1 earnings) in the accounts relating to his ancillary business,

> 'The payments he puts into his business are plainly receipts of the business. Indeed, the accounts show how the gross salary appears in the accounts as an undifferentiated receipt on revenue account. There would be no other way of dealing with them in accordance with proper commercial accounting practice. It would be different if the payments were appropriated to capital expenditure or by way of a loan (other than a short-term loan analogous to an overdraft) (see e.g. *Ryan v Crabtree Denims* [*1987*] *STC 402*)'.

The case referred to by Counsel concerned the correct treatment for tax purposes of an interest relief grant made to a company in difficulties by the DoT for the purpose of keeping the business alive. Hoffman J held that, because the grant was not specifically earmarked for either a revenue or a capital purpose (i.e. it was an undifferentiated receipt) and because there was nothing in the circumstances of the case to suggest that it was for a capital purpose, the grant fell to be treated as a revenue receipt.

The application of the principle in *Ryan* to the situation of subpostmasters etc. is surely open to challenge but a challenge now seems unnecessary following the amendment to the definition outlined above. See the CA National Insurance News, Issue 2, page 6 concerning the entitlement to relief for the small earnings exception by reference only to the actual earnings from the business itself and not to the total receipts of the business which would have included those other earnings. The change to *Reg 25(2)* noted above and detailed in SUBPOSTMASTERS (see 55.3) will affect subpostmasters and groups of mainly professional people such as accountants and doctors. The problem of whether exception should have been granted in the past may never now be settled. To avoid problems, a self-employed earner should, perhaps, have ensured that any of his earnings which were not from self-employment were paid into some bank account other than that used for the main business, and should then have made a capital introduction to the main business, taking care that the amount introduced did not appear in his trading and profit and loss account but in his capital account on the balance sheet as an introduction of capital. It is suggested that, in contradiction of Counsel's advice, this is an 'other way of dealing with' non-trading income 'in accordance with proper commercial accounting practice'. Where earnings of the kind in question have previously been included in the profits and, by concession, charged to tax under Schedule D, the tax computation will, of course, need to include an addition of those earnings to the profit shown by the accounts. It is assumed that, provided such an addition was made in the computation, the Inland Revenue would continue to permit the income concerned to be assessed under Schedule D, but, if that was not so, it should be noted that the increased tax liability would have generally outweighed the Class 2 savings and would have made the treatment suggested inappropriate. However, since 1995 Leaflet CA 02 has advised 'Where you also have earnings from employed earner's employment in the same year and those earnings are shown in the accounts of the business, as a business receipt, those earnings can be disregarded when calculating the profits from your self-employed business.'

The National Insurance Commissioners have accepted that, in connection with the application of the 'earnings rule', the net earnings relevant to a particular tax year are the 'actual net earnings for that year', even though those earnings may be taxed in a later tax year (see reported decision *R(P) 1/73* in the pension series). This is clearly the force of the phrase 'in relation to' in *Reg 25(1)*.

It will therefore be necessary, if a person's accounting period overlaps 5 April, to time-apportion the profits shown by his accounts in order to arrive at an earnings amount appropriate to a Class 2 exception application.

Example
Jerry is an unsuccessful builder. His accounting year ends on 30 June and his accounts for the last two years show results as follows

Year to		£
30.6.99	Profit	9,000
30.6.2000	Loss	(1,500)

For the purpose of an application for Class 2 exception, his profits for 1999–2000 are

	£
3/12 × £9,000	2,250
9/12 × £(1,500)	(1,125)
	£1,125

Where a person has more than one self-employment, the net earnings from each must be arrived at as illustrated, then aggregated (see 5.16 AGGREGATION OF EARNINGS). (Leaflet CA 02).

28.78 **EARNINGS FOR CLASS 4 PURPOSES**

A self-employed earner's earnings for Class 4 purposes are all annual profits or gains immediately derived from the carrying on or exercise of one or more trades, professions or vocations, being profits or gains *chargeable to income tax* under Case I or II of Schedule D for any year of assessment beginning on or after 6 April 1975. [*SSCBA 1992, s 15(1)*]. They are subject to various deductions, additions and reliefs as prescribed in *2 Sch 2, 3* and described at 28.79 to 28.86 below.

The effect of this provision is to exchange the actual basis on which earnings are otherwise assessed throughout the contribution scheme for whichever basis is adopted for Schedule D purposes. In the past this may have been an actual basis in the opening or closing years of a business (depending on the application of *ICTA 1988, ss 61, 63*), but more often a preceding year basis or, even, an average basis under *ICTA 1988, s 60(5)–(8) or s 96*. [*ICTA 1988, s 60(2)–(4)*]. For businesses that commenced on or after 6 April 1994, the current year basis (including the opening rules) under 'self-assessment' are applicable as they are to longer established businesses for 1997–98 onwards with a special, 'transitional' basis of assessment (broadly, the average of two years results) for 1996–97.

The departure from an actual basis may be of distinct advantage to a contributor (see 3.14 AGE EXCEPTION).

The reference in *SSCBA 1992, s 15(1)* to profits or gains chargeable to income tax under Case I or II of Schedule D is to be taken as including a reference to profits or gains consisting of a payment of enterprise allowance made

(*a*)   on or after 18 March 1986, or

(*b*)   before 18 March 1986 as part of a distinct series of payments of which one or more is made on or after that date

under *Employment and Training Act 1973, s 2(2)(d)* or *Enterprise and New Towns (Scotland) Act 1990, s 2(4)(c)* and chargeable to tax under Case VI of Schedule D by virtue of *ICTA 1988, s 127*. [*ICTA 1988, 29 Sch 14*].

A pre-18 March 1986 payment of enterprise allowance which did not fall within the above provisions was a trading receipt which formed part of profits chargeable to income tax under Case I or II of Schedule D and which, accordingly, was included in profits for Class 4 contribution purposes. (Inland Revenue Press Release reported in Tolley's Practical Tax, Vol 7, No 12, 11 June 1986, p 96). The effect was that prior to 1986 the Enterprise Allowance would have been subject to multiple assessment under the opening years provisions.

28.79 **Capital allowances**

First year, initial, writing-down and balancing allowances which, under the *Capital Allowances Act 1990, s 140(2)*, fall to be made as a deduction in charging profits or gains to tax, are a permitted deduction for Class 4 purposes also. [*SSCBA 1992, 2 Sch 2(a)(i)*]. The same applies to agricultural buildings allowances which, under *CAA 1990, s 141*, fall to be given by way of discharge or repayment of tax. [*2 Sch 2(a)(ii)*]. In either case, however, a deduction for Class 4 purposes is conditional upon the allowances having arisen from the activities of the relevant trade, profession or vocation.

Balancing charges which, under *CAA 1990, s 140(7)*, fall to be made for tax purposes are to be *added* to profits for Class 4 purposes also. [*2 Sch 2(b)*].

These provisions cease to be of practical application under 'self-assessment' as relief is obtained for capital allowances as if the amount computed were a deductible trading expense in arriving at profits/losses.

28.80 Stock relief

Where, in computing the amount of profits or gains of a trade, deductions in respect of stock relief (or additions in respect of stock relief recovery) fell to be made in charging those profits or gains to tax, such deductions (or additions) were to be made for Class 4 purposes also. [*FA 1976, 5 Sch 8; FA 1981, 9 Sch 11 now repealed*]. Stock relief was abolished by *FA 1984, s 48*.

Stock relief under earlier legislation was given by way of reduction in the closing stock of the business and was thus automatically taken into account for both tax and Class 4 purposes.

28.81 Loss relief

Loss relief available for tax purposes under *ICTA 1988, s 385* by carry-forward against subsequent profits is available for Class 4 purposes also, as is carry-back of terminal loss relief under *ICTA 1988, ss 388, 389*. [*SSCBA 1992, 2 Sch 3(1)(c)(d)*]. The fact that a loss may have originated before the introduction of Class 4 contributions (6 April 1975) does not affect its availability for use for Class 4 purposes under *2 Sch 3(1)(c)*.

Loss relief available for tax purposes under *ICTA 1988, s 380, 381* by set-off against general income is available for Class 4 purposes also, provided the loss arises from activities of which any profits or gains would have been earnings for Class 4 purposes. [*SSCBA 1992, 2 Sch 3(1)(a)*]. It may be augmented for Class 4 purposes, as it may for tax purposes under *ICTA 1988, s 383*, by capital allowances. [*SSCBA 1992, 2 Sch 3(1)(b)*]. This is of no application where capital allowances are already taken into account under 'self-assessment'.

In most instances where such relief is available, however, it will be claimed for tax purposes against income which is not profits or gains for Class 4 purposes (or against income which is not profits or gains of the person who incurred the loss). Accordingly, where, in any tax year beginning on or after 6 April 1975, a deduction in respect of a loss falls to be made in computing a person's total income (or, for 1989–90 or earlier years, that of his spouse) for tax purposes and all or part of the loss falls to be deducted from income other than his trading profit or gains, the loss is, to that extent, to be carried forward for Class 4 purposes and set off against the first available trading profit or gains for subsequent years. [*SSCBA 1992, 2 Sch 3(3)(4)*].

Example
Kit has a sportswear business. His trading results (adjusted for Schedule D Case I purposes) are

Year to		£
5 July 1998	Profit	12,000
5 July 1999	Loss	(17,200)
5 July 2000	Profit	4,000
5 July 2001	Profit	19,400

K is single and his assessable amounts of profit and other income are

	Sch D and Class 4	Investment Income
	£	£
1998–99	12,000	1,500
1999–2000	NIL	1,700
2000–01	4,000	1,800
2001–02	19,400	2,200

If K claims relief for his 1999–2000 loss of £17,200 under *Sec 380*, it will be apportioned against 1998–99 earned income i.e. £12,000 Schedule D, then against 1998–99 investment income i.e. £1,500 and then against 1999–2000 investment income i.e. £1,700. The balance of the loss (£2,000) is then carried forward against profits of the same trade only. This will result in revised assessable amounts of profit and income, thus

	Sch D	Investment Income
	£	£
1998–99	NIL	NIL
1999–2000	NIL	NIL
2000–01	2,000	1,800
2001–02	19,400	2,200

For Class 4 purposes, however, only £14,000 of the loss has been relieved (£12,000 in 1998–99 and £2,000 in 2000–01) and the remaining £3,200 must, therefore, also be carried forward to 2000–01 (and subsequent years, if necessary, as in the example), giving revised Class 4 profits as follows

	Class 4
	£
1998–99	NIL
1999–2000	NIL
2000–01	NIL
2001–02	18,200

No relief is available for Class 4 purposes for constructive losses available for tax purposes in respect of annual payments carried forward under *ICTA 1988, s 387* or interest carried forward or backward under *Sec 390*. [*SSCBA 1992, 2 Sch 3(2)(c)(d)*]. In the Inland Revenue Inspector's Manual it states that any loss which is allowed for income tax purposes against non-NIC income, e.g. PAYE income, will remain unrelieved for NIC purposes and will be carried forward to use against the first available subsequent year and so on until it is fully allowed. As a result trading tax losses carried forward may be different from NIC losses carried forward and NIC losses should be separately recorded. Also relief for a Schedule E loss may occasionally be given for income tax in an assessment on trading profits: it is not to be allowed for NIC. (See Inspector's Manual, para 6053, issue 12/97.)

28.82 Personal reliefs

No allowance for personal reliefs under *ICTA 1988, ss 256–278* may be made for Class 4 purposes. [*SSCBA 1992, 2 Sch 3(2)(a)*].

28.83 Retirement annuities and personal pension premiums

No relief for premiums or other considerations under annuity contracts and trust schemes under *ICTA 1988, ss 619, 620* may be given for Class 4 purposes [*SSCBA*

1992, 2 Sch 3(2)(f)] nor for personal pension contributions under *ICTA 1988, s 639.* *[SSCBA 1992, 2 Sch 3(2)(g)].* (*Maher v CIR* [1997] *STC SSCD 103*). Although the latter provision was not introduced until 1993, it is deemed to have had effect ever since personal pension plans were introduced by *F(No 2)A 1987* [*Social Security (Contributions) Act 1993, s 3(2)*].

28.84 **Interest and other annual payments**

Relief for payment of interest under *ICTA 1988, s 353* is not to be given *per se* for Class 4 purposes, but *is* to be given to the extent to which it falls within the relieving provision next described. [*SSCBA 1992, 2 Sch 3(2)(b)*].

Relief is to be allowed in respect of annuities and other annual payments under *ICTA 1988, ss 348, 349(1)* or payments of *interest* for which relief from income tax is or can be given under *ICTA 1988, s 353,* but only so far as incurred wholly or exclusively for the purpose of any relevant trade, profession or vocation. [*SSCBA 1992, 2 Sch 3(5)(a)(b)*].

There can be little doubt that the 'or' separating 'wholly' and 'exclusively' is a drafting error and that the intention was to reproduce the highly restrictive phrase of *ICTA 1988, s 74.* In the event, the intention failed and a much wider test of allowability lies in its place. 'Wholly' relates to the amount of the expenditure; 'exclusively' relates to the motive behind the expenditure. The 'and' of *ICTA 1988, s 74* ensures that both criteria must be met for tax allowability while the 'or' of *SSCBA 1992, 2 Sch 3(5)* clearly bears the meaning that satisfaction of either criterion will suffice.

Relief for payments which satisfy the prescribed conditions is to be given by deducting from profits or gains the gross amount of the payments made in the tax year concerned, and any such amounts which, because of an insufficiency of profits or gains, cannot be relieved in the year of payment are to be carried forward and relieved as soon as possible. [*SSCBA 1992, 2 Sch 3(5)*].

28.85 **Relief for absence on business abroad**

FA 1978, s 27 introduced a measure of relief from income tax for persons resident in the United Kingdom who, in the course of carrying on a trade, profession or vocation assessable under Sch D, Cases I or II, were absent from the United Kingdom for at least 30 qualifying days in the tax year. The relief was abolished for 1985–86 and later years, but during the period of its availability it was specifically provided that the relief was *not* to be available in computing profits or gains in respect of which Class 4 contributions were payable (see OVERSEAS MATTERS (49) for details of the contribution liability of those earners who derive income from activities outside the UK). [*SSA 1975, 2 Sch 3(2)(cc), as amended by FA 1978, 4 Sch 8 and as repealed by FA 1984, 23 Sch*].

28.86 **Professions: 'catching-up' charge under Finance Act 1998**

The 'catching-up' charge required as a result of the change to an accounting basis for non-corporate businesses of a true and fair view with effect from the period of account beginning after 6 April 1999 is taxable under Schedule D, Case VI and therefore not subject to Class 4 contributions. A negative adjustment is allowable as a deduction in computing profits and so will be deducted also in computing the amount on which Class 4 contributions are to be charged. [*FA 1998, ss 42, 44(1) and (2), Sch 6, paras 2(1), 2(2)(a), 2(2)(b)*].

Although the charge will not attract a Class 4 liability, it will nonetheless count as 'relevant earnings' for pension contribution purposes. [*FA 1998, Sch 6, 2(2)(c)*].

28.87 **Relief for Class 4 contributions payable**

ICTA 1988, s 617(5) provided for relief from income tax for 1985–86 and years up to and including 1995–96 on 50% of Class 4 contributions ultimately payable in respect of a year of assessment (see 20.8 CLASS 4 CONTRIBUTIONS). It was specifically provided, however, that such relief was not to be available in computing profits or gains for Class 4 purposes. [*SSCBA 1992, 2 Sch 3(2)(e)* as repealed by *FA 1996, 41 Sch 15*]. Whilst from 1996–97 (the introduction of self-assessment) the availability of tax relief on 50% of Class 4 contributions is withdrawn the rate of Class 4 contributions was reduced to 6% from 7.3% to apply from 6 April 1996 as a broad, compensatory measure. [*FA 1996, s 147; FA 1997, s 65(2)*]. The 6% rate was maintained until 6 April 2000.

29 Earnings Factors

Cross-references. See BENEFITS (13); CLASS 3 CONTRIBUTIONS (19); CREDITS (24); LATE-PAID CONTRIBUTIONS (39).

29.1 GENERAL CONSIDERATIONS

An earnings factor is the criterion for judging a person's

(*a*) satisfaction of contribution conditions for benefit entitlement (see 13.2 BENEFITS);

(*b*) eligibility for credits (see 24.1 CREDITS);

(*c*) need to pay Class 3 contributions (see 19.2 CLASS 3 CONTRIBUTIONS); and

(*d*) level of entitlement to the additional State pension (see 13.3 BENEFITS).

It is the notional amount of a person's earnings for a tax year calculated by reference to contributions paid and credited and (from 6 April 1987) to earnings payable or treated as paid. [*SSCBA 1992, s 22(1)(2)*].

The need for such a common unit of contribution measurement arises out of the fact that certain contributions are earnings-related (with contribution rates depending on the level of earnings) whereas others are not. Additionally, within certain classes of contribution, rates differ according to the status of the contributor without his entitlement to benefit being necessarily thereby reduced.

29.2 RELEVANT CONTRIBUTIONS AND EARNINGS

An earnings factor may be derived only from Class 2 contributions, Class 3 contributions and

(*a*) so far as 1986–87 and earlier tax years are concerned, primary Class 1 contributions paid at a rate other than the reduced rate (see REDUCED LIABILITY ELECTION (52)), and

(*b*) so far as 1987–88 and later tax years are concerned, earnings upon which primary Class 1 contributions are payable or treated as paid, (including, from 6 April 1999, the amount of earnings up to the lower earnings limit on which nothing is paid, and from 6 April 2000 the amount of earnings up to the employee's earnings threshold on which nothing is paid provided the lower earnings limit is equalled or exceeded) at a rate other than the reduced rate (see REDUCED LIABILITY ELECTION (52)).

[*SSCBA 1992, s 22(1)(2)(4) and s 6A, inserted by Welfare Reform and Pensions Act 1999, Sch 9, para 3*].

Secondary Class 1 contributions, Class 1A contributions, Class 1B and Class 4 contributions are ignored. The Secretary of State has authority to make regulations providing for reduced rate primary Class 1 contributions to yield an earnings factor but this has never yet been exercised. This power remains with the Secretary of State for Social Security notwithstanding the transfer of various powers and functions to the Inland Revenue and the Treasury under *SSC(T)A 1999*. [*SSCBA 1992, s 19(6)*].

29.3 COMPUTATIONAL PROCEDURE 1987–88 TO 2000–01

The calculation of an earnings factor must proceed in a prescribed manner. [*SSCBA 1992, ss 22(3), 23(1)(3); Earnings Factor Regs, Reg 2*]. For 1987–88 to 2000–01 it is necessary to

(1) calculate the earnings factor derived from earnings on which primary Class 1 contributions have been paid or treated as paid and from earnings credited (see 29.4 below);

(2) calculate separately the earnings factor derived from Class 2 and Class 3 contributions paid and from Class 3 contributions credited (see 29.5 below); and

(3) if there were earnings on which primary Class 1 contributions were paid or treated as paid, subject the aggregate earnings factor arrived at under (1) to various tests and increase that earnings factor as appropriate (see 29.6 below);

(4) combine earnings factors arrived at under (1) to (3) above.

29.4   Class 1 contributions

The earnings factor derived from

(a) earnings on which a person has paid, or is treated as having paid Class 1 contributions (see 15.6 CLASS 1 CONTRIBUTIONS; 21.3 COLLECTION and 39.3 and 39.4 LATE-PAID CONTRIBUTIONS), and

(b) earnings with which he has been credited (see 24.5, 24.8, 24.10 and 24.13–24.16 CREDITS)

is an amount equal to the amount of those actual and credited earnings rounded down to the nearest whole pound. [*Earnings Factor Regs, Reg 2, 1 Sch 2 as substituted by Earnings Factor Amendment Regs 1991, Reg 2*].

Where a person's earnings upon which Class 1 contributions have been paid or treated as paid fall to be recorded as separate sums (by reason, for example, of the person having two or more separate employments during the year), the earnings factor derived from those earnings is to be equal to the aggregate of the amounts arrived at by rounding down each sum separately to the nearest whole pound. [*Reg 2, 1 Sch 3 as substituted by Earnings Factor Amendment Regs 1991, Reg 3*].

Example
For the first four weeks of 2000–01, Amos is employed by Baruch and has earnings of £67.23, £30.31, £160.76 and £545.24. He is then made redundant and is unemployed for twelve weeks after which he is self-employed for 27 weeks before obtaining employment with Caleb for the remaining nine weeks at a weekly wage of £60.30. His earnings factor in respect of earnings credited and earnings on which Class 1 contributions are paid is calculated as follows.

	£
Earnings from B on which Class 1 contributions actually paid or treated as paid because the lower earnings limit was equalled or exceeded:	
£67.23 + £160.76 + £535.00 (N.B. £30.31 ignored as below LEL and £10.24 of £545.24 ignored as above UEL) = £762.99, rounded down to	762.00
Earnings credited during unemployment assuming that a successful claim to Jobseeker's Allowance was made:	
12 × £67.00	804.00
Earnings from C on which Class 1 contributions paid: None (£60.30 is below EEET)	—
	£1,566.00

29.5   Class 2 and Class 3 contributions

The earnings factor derived from Class 2 or Class 3 contributions paid or credited in respect of a year is the weekly lower earnings limit for the year for Class 1 purposes

29.6 Earnings Factors

(see EARNINGS LIMITS AND THRESHOLDS (30)) multiplied by the number of Class 2 or Class 3 contributions paid or credited for the year (see 24.6 and 24.17 CREDITS) and rounded to the nearest whole pound. [*Earnings Factor Regs, Reg 2, 1 Sch 8, 9*]. Since the DSS stated that in future the LEL will be a whole pound figure the provision for rounding to the nearest whole pound has been of no practical effect since 1985–86.

Example
Amos (see example at 29.4 above) pays Class 2 contribution of £2.00 for each of his 27 weeks of self-employment. His earnings factor derived from these contributions is 27 × £67 = £1,809. His aggregate earnings factor for the year then becomes, therefore, £1,809 + £1,566 = £3,375. *Note:* It is the employee's lower earnings limit rather than the primary earnings threshold that is relevant here.

29.6 Earnings factor shortfalls

Where a person has actual earnings upon which Class 1 contributions have been paid or treated as paid (as opposed to earnings merely credited) and

(a) his earnings factor derived from those earnings (see 29.4 above), or

(b) the aggregate of his earnings factors derived from those earnings and from any earnings credited and from Class 2 or Class 3 contributions paid or credited (see 29.4 and 29.5 above)

falls short of

(i) the qualifying earnings factor (see below) by an amount not exceeding £50, or

(ii) the standard level (see below) by an amount not exceeding £50, or

(iii) one-half of the standard level by an amount not exceeding £25,

the aggregate earnings factor is, *for the purpose of satisfying the contribution conditions of benefit entitlement only* (see 29.1 above), to be increased by the amount of the shortfall and rounded up to the next whole pound. [*Earnings Factor Regs, Reg 2, 1 Sch 4 as amended by Earnings Factor Amendment Regs 1991, Reg 3*].

The 'qualifying earnings factor' is an earnings factor equal to the weekly lower earnings limit for the year in question multiplied by 52 (see EARNINGS LIMITS AND THRESHOLDS (30)). [*SSCBA 1992, s 122(1)*].

The 'standard level' is a level equal to the weekly lower earnings limit for the year multiplied by 50 (see EARNINGS LIMITS AND THRESHOLDS (30)). [*Earnings Factor Regs 1 Sch 1(1)*].

For 1995–96 to 2000–01 the shortfall criteria are:

	1995–96	1996–97	1997–98	1998–99	1999–2000	2000–01
	£	£	£	£	£	£
Qualifying earnings factor (52 × £LEL)	3,016	3,172	3,224	3,328	3,432	3,484
Standard level (50 × £LEL)	2,900	3,050	3,100	3,200	3,300	3,350
1/2 standard level	1,450	1,525	1,550	1,600	1,650	1,675

Example
Amos (see previous example) has an earnings factor derived from actual earnings in respect of which Class 1 contributions have been paid of £762 and an aggregate earnings factor derived from such earnings and from credited earnings and from Class 2 contributions paid of £3,375. The aggregate earnings factor falls short of the qualifying earnings factor for 2000–01 by £109 and, since this is greater than £50, his aggregate earnings factor is (for benefit purposes only) unable to be

increased to £3,484. If Amos were to pay a single Class 3 contribution of £6.55 this will increase the aggregate earnings factor to £3,442 since it is equivalent to earnings of £67 on which Class 1 contributions have been paid (see 29.5 above). This still falls short of the 'qualifying earnings factor' by £42, but this shortfall now falls within the limits mentioned above such that for benefit claim purposes the earnings factor may be increased to the amount of £3,484 that may be required for a successful claim as regards certain benefits.

29.7 COMPUTATIONAL PROCEDURE 1985–86 and 1986–87

For details of how to calculate a person's earnings factor for 1985–86 or 1986–87 see Tolley's National Insurance Contributions 1995–96, page 295.

29.8 Class 1 contributions paid

The earnings factor derived from a person's Class 1 contributions actually paid in respect of any year before 1987–88 was to be equal or approximate to the minimum actual earnings sufficient to yield contributions of that amount. [*SSA 1975, s 13(5)(a)*]. For further details and calculations see Tolley's National Insurance Contributions 1995–96, page 296 *et seq*.

29.9 NOTIFICATION OF DEFICIENT EARNINGS FACTOR

It is NICO practice to notify a contributor of a deficient earnings factor for a year by means of a statement of contributions paid or credited (RD 170). If that factor falls short of the qualifying earnings factor, the NICO will inform him of the number of Class 3 contributions he will need to pay to rectify matters. Such a statement may be requested if, as may happen, one is not automatically received. The RD 170 is produced automatically by the computer in the next-but-one tax year to the one in which the deficiency arose, but *only if* at least one contribution was paid or credited for that year. The notice specifies the contributions paid as an employed person, the number of Class 2 and Class 3 contributions and the number of credited contributions on the contributions record for the year. If the record is deficient (i.e. the year will not count for pension purposes), the notice invites payment of Class 3 contributions of a specified amount and recommends payment by the following 5 April, warning that the contributions may still be paid after that date but may be at a higher rate. Where Class 3 contributions are paid in response to the notice, a confirmation letter (RD 1296) is sent to the contributor. In the case of Amos (see 29.4 above) it is likely that he would receive his RD 170 in the second half of 2002 or very early in 2003.

In view of the difficulties in implementing the new NIRS 2 computer, few RD170 notices will have been issued in 1999 and 2000.

30   Earnings Limits and Thresholds

Cross-references. See 5.3 AGGREGATION OF EARNINGS for anti-avoidance rule relating to lower earnings limit in multiple employments; 13.2 BENEFITS for use of lower earnings limit in setting contribution conditions; CLASS 1 CONTRIBUTIONS (15); CLASS 4 CONTRIBUTIONS (20); 23.3 CONTRACTED-OUT EMPLOYMENT for significance of lower earnings limit in relation to basic component of State pensions; 24.2 CREDITS for use of lower earnings limit in setting value of Class 1 credits; 29.6 EARNINGS FACTORS for use of lower earnings limit in setting qualifying earnings factor and standard level of contribution; EARNINGS PERIODS (31) for relation of earnings limits to earnings periods; 51.2 and 51.7 RATES AND LIMITS.

30.1   CLASS 1 LIMITS

For every tax year there is set both a lower and an upper earnings limit ('UEL') for Class 1 contributions purposes. The lower earnings limit ('LEL') is the level of weekly EARNINGS (28) at which, until 6 April 2000, a liability for primary and, until 6 April 1999, secondary Class 1 contributions arises in respect of earnings from an employed earner's employment. The upper earnings limit ('UEL') is the maximum amount of weekly earnings in respect of which *primary* Class 1 contributions are payable. Until 6 October 1985, the UEL governed secondary Class 1 contribution liabilities also, but that is no longer the case. [*SSCBA 1992, s 5(1)* now amended by the *Welfare Reform and Pensions Act 1999*].

The LEL marks the level of weekly earnings entitlement to basic contributory benefits is secured (see 13.2 BENEFITS).

From 6 April 1999, there is a secondary, i.e. employer's, earnings threshold (*ERET*), intended to be aligned with the tax allowance and therefore set at £83 per week/£4,335 per annum for 1999–2000 and £84 per week/£4,385 per annum for 2000–01(see 13.2 BENEFITS).

From 6 April 2000, there is also a primary earnings threshold (EEET), which for 2000–01 represents the point at which employees' liability begins. This is set at £76 for 2000–01. For 2001–02, it is expected that the primary and secondary earnings thresholds will be equalised. *Sections 73* and *74* of the *Welfare Reform and Pensions Act 1999* create the legal framework in Britain and Northern Ireland for the new primary earnings threshold. The provisions are brought into force by the *Welfare Reform and Pensions Act 1999, (Commencement No 2) Order 1999 SI 1999/3420* and *Social Security (Contributions) (Amendment) Regs 2000, SI 2000/175*. The lower earnings limit is retained due to the government policy of protecting the contributory benefit entitlement of those earning from the lower earnings limit up to the primary earnings threshold, even though no contributions are payable by the employee in such circumstances.

30.2   Prescribed amounts

Both the lower and upper earnings limits are to be set annually by regulations and the lower earnings limit is to be linked to the amount of the basic category A retirement pension at the start of the tax year for which the earnings limits are being set (or the immediately following 6 May if an increase in the basic component is to take effect by then). The upper earnings limit is linked to the secondary (i.e. employer's) earnings threshold. [*SSCBA 1992, s 5(1)(2)*].

In the case of the *lower earnings limit*, the weekly amount prescribed must be an amount equal to or not more than 99p less than the basic pension. [*SSCBA 1992, s 5(2)*]. As the basic pension payable from the week commencing 10 April 2000 is £67.50, the LEL for 2000–01 could have been £66.51 or £67.50 or any amount between. It has, in fact, been set at £67.50. [*Contributions Regs, Reg 7; Contributions Amendment Regs 2000, SI 2000/175; Reg 2*].

For the *upper earnings limit*, until 5 April 2000, the weekly amount prescribed must have been equal to seven times the basic pension or must exceed or fall short of that sum by not more than half the basic pension. [*SSCBA 1992, s 5(3)*]. From 6 April 2000, it must fall within the same parameters but measured against the primary earnings threshold rather than the lower earnings limit (*Welfare Reform and Pensions Act 1999, s 73*). The UEL for 2000–01 would, therefore, have been set at £494.00 or £570.00 or any amount between. It has, in fact, been set at £535.00. [*Contributions Regs, Reg 7; Contributions Amendment Regs 2000, SI 2000/175; Reg 2*].

For practical purposes the DSS stated that in future the LEL will be a whole pound figure and the UEL will be in multiples of £5.

For prescribed amounts for 1999–2000 and earlier years see 51.2 RATES AND LIMITS.

The earnings thresholds are specified quite separately and the employer's threshold is intended to match the weekly equivalent of the personal tax allowance (i.e. £4,385) and the employee's earnings threshold will also do so from 6 April 2001. For 2000–01 it has been set at a weekly amount of £84.00 and the employee's threshold has been set at a weekly amount of £76.00. [*Reg 7(c) and (d), as inserted by Social Security (Contributions) (Amendments) Regs 2000, SI 2000/175, Reg 2*].

30.3   Pro-rata earnings limits and threshold

Where an employed earner's EARNINGS PERIOD (31) is other than a week, the weekly LEL and UEL are to be replaced by a prescribed equivalent. [*SSCBA 1992, s 6(1)(b)*]. The equivalent limits are as follows.

(*a*)   Where the earnings period is a multiple of a week, the weekly limits multiplied by that multiple.

(*b*)   Where the earnings period is a month, the weekly limits multiplied by 41/3.

(*c*)   Where the earnings period is a multiple of a month, the monthly limits (before rounding, see below) multiplied by that multiple.

(*d*)   In any other case, one-seventh of the weekly limits multiplied by the number of days in the earnings period concerned.

[*Contributions Regs, Reg 8(1)(2)(a)–(d) as amended by Social Security (Contributions) (Amendment) Regs 2000, SI 2000/175 Reg 3*].

The amounts determined under (*b*) and (*c*) above are, if not whole pounds, to be rounded up to the next whole pound, whereas the calculation under (*d*) is to be made to the nearest penny and any amount of one-half penny or less is to be disregarded. [*Reg 8(2A)(3) as amended by Contributions Amendment No 2 Regs 1987, Reg 4*]. Thus, for 2000–01, the monthly and yearly LEL and UEL are

	LEL		UEL
Monthly:			
£67 × 4⅓ = £290.33 =	£291.00	£535 × 4⅓ = £2,318.33 =	£2,319.00
Yearly:			
£67 × 4⅓ × 12 =	£3,484.00	£535 × 4⅓ × 12	£27,820.00

The new earnings thresholds, from 6 April 1999, are not, however, computed for longer earnings periods in the same way. The equivalent thresholds are specified in regulations. Those for 2000–01 are contained in *Social Security (Contributions) (Amendment) Regs 2000, SI 2000/175 Reg 3* as follows:

Employer's threshold

●   £84 per week, where the earnings period is a week;

30.4   Earnings Limits and Thresholds

- £365 per month, where the earnings period is a month;
- £4,385 per year, where the earnings period is a year;

Employee's threshold

- £76 per week, where the earnings period is a week;
- £329 per month, where the earnings period is a month;
- £3,952 per year, where the earnings period is a year;

and, in either case

- where the earnings period is a whole number of weeks, divide the annual limit by 52, multiply by the number of weeks contained in the earnings period and round up to the next whole pound;
- where the earnings period is a whole number of months, divide the annual limit by 12, multiply by the number of months contained in the earning period and round up to the next whole pound;
- in any other case, divide the annual limit by 365, multiply by the number of days in the earnings period and round up to the nearest penny (1/2p being rounded down).

For the monthly and yearly employer's threshold for 1999–2000, see 51.3 RATES AND LIMITS.

[*Social security (Contributions) (Amendment) Regs 2000, SI 2000/175 Reg 3*].

30.4   CLASS 1 EARNINGS BRACKETS 6.10.85 TO 5.4.99

Until 6 October 1985, Class 1 contributions were levied at a single primary percentage rate and a single secondary percentage rate on earnings equal to the upper earnings limit or, if earnings were less than the upper earnings limit but not less than the lower earnings limit, on the actual amount of earnings paid (see, in either case, 30.1 above). From 6 October 1985 to 4 October 1989 the rate at which a liability for primary and secondary Class 1 contributions arose for any particular week was determined by reference to the primary earnings bracket and the secondary earnings bracket applicable for the week in which the earnings in question were paid.

Subsequently, until 5 April 1999, secondary Class 1 contributions continued to be calculated in the above manner but primary contributions comprised two parts—an initial primary percentage applied to earnings up to the LEL and a main primary percentage applied to earnings between the LEL and the UEL. [*SSCBA 1992, s 8(1)*].

30.5   Prescribed amounts

Unlike earnings limits, earnings brackets were *not* linked to the amount of the basic category A retirement pension (see 30.2 above) but, having been set by Parliament for 1985–86 may be (and have been) changed by order of the Secretary of State. [*SSCBA 1992, s 9(3)*]. These were last amended with effect from April 1996 and so were, for 1998–99 (as well as for 1996–97 and 1997–98)

Primary			*Secondary*		
	Weekly earnings	*%*	*EB*	*Weekly earnings*	*%*
Initial	Up to £64.00	2	1	Current LEL to £109.99	3
Main	£64.01 to £485.00	10	2	£110.00 to £154.99	5
			3	£155.00 to £209.99	7
			4	£210.00 or more	10

[*SSCBA 1992, s 9(3), as amended by Contributions Re-rating and National Insurance Fund Payments Order 1996, Art 2*].

For prescribed earnings brackets for 1995–96 and earlier years, see 51.3 RATES AND LIMITS.

30.6 **Pro-rata earnings brackets**

Where an employed earner's EARNINGS PERIOD (31) is other than a week, the weekly primary and secondary earnings brackets were to be replaced by prescribed equivalents. [*SSCBA 1992, s 9(2)*]. For the lower weekly amount specified in relation to each earnings bracket, the equivalent amount is as follows.

(*a*) Where the earnings period is a multiple of a week, the lower weekly amount multiplied by that multiple.

(*b*) Where the earnings period is a month, the lower weekly amount multiplied by 4⅓.

(*c*) Where the earnings period is a multiple of a month, the amount is calculated by multiplying each lower bracket by 4⅓ and multiplying each product by the corresponding multiple.

(*d*) In any other case, one-seventh of the weekly amount multiplied by the number of days in the earnings period.

[*Contributions Regs, Reg 8A(1)–(3), as amended by Contributions Transitional Regs 1985, Reg 5(3) and Contributions Amendment (No 4) Regs 1987, Reg 3(a)*].

The amounts determined under (*b*) and (*c*) above are, if not whole pounds, to be rounded up to the next whole pound, whereas the calculation under (*d*) is to be made to the nearest penny and any amount of one-half penny or less is to be disregarded. [*Reg 8A(3B) as amended by Contributions Amendment No 2 Regs 1987, Reg 5(a), and Reg 8A(4) as amended by Contributions Transitional Regs 1985, Reg 5(3) and Contributions Amendment No 2 Regs 1987, Reg 5(b)*]. Thus, for 1996–97, 1997–98 and 1998–99, the monthly and yearly lower amounts specified in relation to secondary earnings brackets 2 and 3 were

	EB2		EB3
Monthly:			
£110 × 4⅓ = £476.67 =	£477.00	£155 × 4⅓ = £671.67 =	£672.00
Yearly:			
£110.00 × 4⅓ × 12 =	£5,720.00	£155 × 4⅓ × 12 =	£8,060.00

and the monthly and yearly lower amounts specified in relation to secondary earnings bracket 4 are

	EB4
Monthly: £210 × 4⅓ =	£910.00
Yearly: £210 × 4⅓ × 12 =	£10,920.00

For the higher weekly amount specified in relation to secondary earnings brackets 1, 2 and 3, the equivalent amount is one penny less than the next succeeding bracket's lower amount. [*Reg 8A(5), as amended by Contributions Transitional Regs 1985, Reg 5(3)*].

30.7 **THE SIGNIFICANCE OF THE EARNINGS LIMITS, THRESHOLD AND BRACKETS**

The LEL did not (until 6 April 1999) create a contribution-free band of earnings; it merely provided a trip-wire whereby liability would be triggered on all earnings (including those below the LEL) insofar as, in the case of Class 1 *primary* contributions, those earnings do not exceed the UEL. The rate at which liability will arise was determined by reference to the earnings band in which the earnings fall.

As there was no form of tapering relief, there existed, inevitably, bands of earnings beginning with and lying immediately above

30.7 Earnings Limits and Thresholds

(a) the LEL, and

(b) in the case of secondary contributions only, the sum with which each of earnings brackets 2 and 3,

which attracted contribution liabilities sufficiently significant, in relative terms, to cause the primary and secondary contributors to consider carefully their effects. In the case of (a), the liabilities arising may not only eliminate part of the earnings above the LEL but also some part of the earnings lying immediately *below* that limit. In the case of (b), the secondary contributor may find that his contribution liabilities increase by more than the value of a pay rise which he grants to an employee.

From 6 April 1999, the position is more straightforward. For example, in 2000–01 as no liability arises on the first £76 per week (or other equivalent) of earnings so far as the employee is concerned (i.e. the Primary Earnings Threshold) or on the first £84 per week (or other equivalent) of earnings so far as the employer is concerned (i.e. the Secondary Earnings Threshold).

Example
Albright, Bellini, Chagall and Dali are all employed by El Greco Ltd (E). In the week ended 28 April 2000, A earns £76.00, B earns £76.06, C earns £84.00 and D earns £84.05. The Class 1 contribution liabilities arising are as follows:

		Primary £	Secondary £
A	£76.00 (EEET)	—	—
B	£76.06 – £76 = £0.06 × 10% (rounded)	0.01	
	£76.06 – less than ERET		—
C	£84 – £76 = £8 × 10%	0.80	
	£84 (*ERET*)		—
D	£84.05 – £76 = £8.05 × 10%	0.80	
	£84.05 – £84 = £0.05 × 12.2% (rounded)		0.01

In 1999–2000 only, earnings by B of £66.01, £66.02, £66.03, £66.04 or £66.05 weekly would each have attracted a primary contribution of one penny, due to a special rounding rule which has the no effect after 5 April 2000.

In the past the LEL and the earnings brackets other than the highest such bracket could have been turned to advantage by

(i) remunerating lower-paid earners at a level which would take their earnings either below the LEL or into an earnings bracket lower than the bracket into which their earnings would otherwise have fallen and making up any shortfall by providing benefits in kind which, not being EARNINGS (28), attracted no contribution liability; or

(ii) engaging, in place of one full-time earner, two or more part-time earners with earnings which fell below the LEL or in an earnings bracket lower than the bracket in which the full-time earner's earnings would have fallen; or,

(iii) where the employer had associates with whom he did *not* actually carry on business in association (see 5.4 AGGREGATION OF EARNINGS) or where, even if business *was* carried on in association by the employer and his associates, the payroll arrangements were such as to render it impracticable to aggregate the earnings of a person paid by the employer and one or more of his associates (see 5.7 AGGREGATION OF EARNINGS), fragmenting an earner's earnings between the employer and his associates so as to take the component parts of earnings below the LEL or into earnings brackets lower than the earnings bracket into which the combined earnings would have fallen.

Note, however, that where earnings fell below the LEL, entitlement to contributory BENEFITS (13) may have been jeopardised.

The earnings bracket 'trap' ceased to apply from 6 April 1999 from which date contributions are simply charged at a percentage rate on earnings above a specified lower limit, which is different for primary and secondary contributors. It may still be possible in a small number of cases to employ several people each earning less than the LEL so that neither employees' nor employers' contributions arise or, better still, at rates between the LEL and an earnings threshold so that either no employer's — nor possibly — employee's contributions arise and full benefit entitlement is thereby earned. See Tolley's National Insurance Brief, April 1998 and *Social Security Act 1998, s 51.*

30.8   CLASS 4 LIMITS

Class 4 contributions are calculated at a percentage rate on so much of the adjusted profits or gains as falls between a *lower annual limit* and an *upper annual limit* (see 28.78 to 28.86 EARNINGS). [*SSCBA 1992, s 15(3)*]. These limits may be altered by order of the Treasury (Secretary of State for Social Security prior to 1 April 1999) as a result of the review of contributions and general level of earnings which, in the absence of statutory direction to the contrary, must be carried out annually. [*SSAA 1992, s 141(3)(4)(d)*]. For 2000–01 those limits have been changed to £4,385 and £27,820 respectively. [*Contributions Re-rating Order 2000, Reg 4*].

For limits for 2000–01 and earlier years see 51.13 RATES AND LIMITS.

Whereas the LEL for Class 1 purposes served, until 6 April 1999, to subject *all* earnings below the UEL to contribution liability once earnings exceed the LEL (see 30.2 above), the lower annual limit for Class 4 purposes has always been a true threshold and no Class 4 contributions are, nor were, payable on earnings below that limit even where earnings exceed it. In effect, Class 2 contributions (though not related to earnings) are levied in place of Class 4 contributions on profits below the Class 4 annual limit. For a discussion of the complex actuarial links between Class 2, Class 4 and Class 1 contributions see DSS discussion document 'The Self Employed and National Insurance', 1980, Paras 27 to 31.

31 Earnings Periods

Cross-references. See 5.10 AGGREGATION OF EARNINGS for establishment of common earnings period; CLASS 1 CONTRIBUTIONS (15); COMPANY DIRECTORS (22); EARNINGS (28); EARNINGS LIMITS AND THRESHOLDS (30).

Other Sources. Simon's NIC, Part I, Section 2, Chapter 7; Tolley's National Insurance Brief, March 1997, pages 17–19; Leaflets CWG2 (2000), CA24, CA25, CA38, CA39, CA43, CWG1 (Card 2).

31.1 GENERAL CONSIDERATIONS

An earnings period is a period to which earnings paid to or for the benefit of an employed earner are deemed to relate, irrespective of the period over which those earnings are earned, and by reference to which assessment of contribution liability takes place. Where earnings are paid at *regular intervals*, the earnings period is determined by the periodicity of such payments but, where payment is *irregular*, the earnings period is determined by the application of certain rules provided by regulations made under *SSCBA 1992, 1 Sch 2*. Special rules apply to company directors whether their earnings are paid at regular intervals or not (see 31.11 below) and to mariners who are paid in respect of voyage periods (see 31.12 below).

An earnings period cannot be *less than seven days* in length and the first earnings period in any tax year is deemed to begin on the first day of that tax year. [*Contributions Regs, Reg 3(1)(a)(iii)(b) as amended by Contributions Amendment Regs 1984, Reg 2(b)*]. Where an earnings period is either a week or a month or a multiple of a week or a month, its end will, therefore, always correspond with the end of either a tax week or a tax month in the PAYE calendar. See CWG1 Card 2. Any period between the end of the last earnings period of normal length and the beginning of the next tax year is itself to be treated as an earnings period of normal length however short it might actually be. [*Reg 3(3)*]. Where the normal earnings period is a week, the final earnings period of a week in a tax year will always contain either one or two days, but no more.

In accordance with the rule stated in the foregoing paragraph, the earnings period of an employed earner who is paid at intervals of less than a week is a week and it will, therefore, be necessary to aggregate all payments made to him during each contribution week in order to calculate any Class 1 contribution liabilities on his earnings. (CWG2 (2000), Pages 8 and 9).

Not all employees are paid either weekly or monthly. An employee may, for example, be paid every ten days, and, in that event, he will have 37 earnings periods in the year: 36 of ten days each and the thirty-seventh of five or six days. Class 1 contribution liabilities on earnings paid in each of those 37 such earnings periods will be ascertained by reference to the upper earnings limit multiplied by 10/7 and earnings thresholds of £3,952 ÷ 365 × 10 = £108.27 and £4,385 ÷ 365 × 10 = £120.14 (see 30.3 and 30.6 EARNINGS LIMITS AND THRESHOLDS). In these circumstances, employers may only use the exact percentage method of calculation. (CWG2 (2000), Pages 10 and 11).

Some employees may work and be paid only every other week or every other fortnight during the year. In such cases, the employee should be treated as having a two- or four-weekly earnings period and his earnings should be divided by two (if he works every other week) or four (if he works every other fortnight) and Class 1 contribution liabilities should be calculated by looking up the weekly figure in the tables and then multiplying the answer by 2 or 4 as appropriate. (Leaflets CA 38, Page 3, CA39, Page 4 and CA 43, Page 4).

In the case of the earnings threshold, special rules apply for determining these equivalent amounts (see 30.3 EARNINGS LIMITS AND THRESHOLDS).

Regulations ensure that under normal circumstances (but for exceptions see 31.7, 31.8 and 31.11 below) an earner can, at any one time, have but one earnings period per employment and that he is never outside an earnings period.

31.2 PAY PATTERNS

Single regular pay pattern

'Regular intervals' are intervals of substantially equal length at which, in accordance with an express or implied arrangement between an employed earner and a secondary contributor, payments of earnings normally fall to be made. A 'regular pay pattern' is established where there is a succession of such intervals, each of which begins immediately after the end of the interval which precedes it. Where only one such pattern exists in relation to a particular earner, that earner's earnings period is identical to his normal pay interval. [*Contributions Regs, Regs 1(2), 3(1)(a)(i) as amended by Contributions Amendment Regs 1984, Reg 2(b)*]. See Leaflet CWG2 (2000), Page 34, item (60).

Example

Aubrey and Beardsley both work in an art studio. A is paid £77 per week and B is paid £292 per month; therefore A's earnings period is one week and B's earnings period is one month. A's first earnings period in the tax year will begin on 6 April and end on 12 April (see 31.1 above). His second will start on 13 April and end on 19 April. B's first earnings period will begin on 6 April and end on 5 May. His second will start on 6 May and end on 5 June. If A's weekly wage of £77 is paid to him on 14 April it will, therefore, fall in and be related to his second earnings period for the tax year, i.e. PAYE week 2 ended 19 April. If B's monthly salary of £292 is paid to him on 8 May it will fall in and be related to his second earnings period for the tax year also, i.e. PAYE month 2 ended 5 June.

31.3 Multiple regular pay pattern

Because an earner (other than an ex-company director-see 31.11 below) may not at one and the same time have two or more earnings periods as regards a single employment (see 31.1 above), difficulties arise where *two or more regular pay patterns run concurrently*. The difficulties are resolved, except where a direction is issued, by equating the earnings period with the length of the *shorter or shortest* interval at which any part of earnings is paid or treated as paid-except in certain circumstances where earnings fall to be aggregated (see 5.10 AGGREGATION OF EARNINGS). [*Contributions Regs, Reg 3(1)(a)(ii) as amended by Contributions Amendment Regs 1984, Reg 2(b)*].

Example

Clive is a salesman for Dubbleglays Ltd. He is paid a monthly salary, a quarterly commission and an annual bonus and has, therefore, three regular pay intervals: a month, a quarter and a year. As the shortest of these is a month, C's earnings period is a month and all the earnings paid to him in a year will be related to one or other of the twelve such periods it contains. If, therefore, he is paid £830 commission on 8 May for the quarter ended 31 March, £500 salary on 15 May for the month of May and £1,500 bonus on 29 May for the year ended 31 December of the preceding year, his earnings for the earnings period from 6 May to 5 June (PAYE month 2) will be £2,830, irrespective of the fact that only £500 of the total is earned within the month and the remainder relates to previous tax years and was earned over a period of between three and twelve months.

31.3 Earnings Periods

It will be observed that, because an earnings period of one month attracts an upper earnings limit appropriate to only one month (2000–01, £2,319, see 30.3 EARNINGS LIMITS AND THRESHOLDS), £511 of the earnings in PAYE month 2 in the above example escapes Class 1 *primary* contribution liability entirely (but *not* Class 1 *secondary* liability), and that, as a matter of general principle, the greater the amount of earnings paid at the longer pay intervals of a multiple regular pay interval earnings arrangement, the greater the Class 1 primary contribution avoidance which may be achieved. In order that such avoidance activity may be countered, however, the Inland Revenue is empowered, where satisfied that the greater part of earnings is normally paid at intervals of greater length than the shorter or shortest, to reverse the rule by merely notifying the earner and the secondary contributor that it is doing so. Thereafter (but not retrospectively), the length of the *longer or longest* interval will be the length of the earnings period. [*Reg 3(2) as amended by Contributions Amendment Regs 1984, Reg 2(c)*]. Where that longer or longest interval is a year, the first earnings period following a *Reg 3(2)* direction is to consist of the number of weeks remaining in the tax year, commencing with the week in which the direction takes effect. [*Reg 3(2A) as amended by Contributions Amendment Regs 1984, Reg 2(d)*].

Example
If, for the tax year, Everard (one of Clive's colleagues—see above example) had earnings of £15,200 consisting of

	£	Pay interval
Salary	7,200	month
Commission	4,000	quarter
Bonus	4,000	year

and a similar pattern had subsisted at least during the preceding tax year the Inland Revenue will, because the greater part of earnings were paid at quarterly and annual intervals, be able to direct that, from the date of the direction onwards, and for all future years, E is to have an annual earnings period. If such a direction were to be made on, say, 5 June, E's earnings periods for the tax year would be

1 month to	5 May
1 month to	5 June
44-week period to	5 April

and his earnings period for the next and all future tax years would be the tax year concerned. (For this purpose, the last day, or last two days in a leap year, is usually to be ignored—Leaflet CA 44, Page 10, para 24.)

Until 6 April 1984, a *Reg 3(2)* direction could only be made where the *greatest* (not greater) part of earnings was paid at intervals of greater length than the shortest interval. The rule was changed with effect from 6 April 1984 because three-part earnings arrangements (such as that illustrated) were becoming a popular means of reducing contribution liabilities while remaining beyond the reach of *Reg 3(2)*.

The use of the qualification 'normally' in the wording of *Reg 3(2)* would suggest that the Inland Revenue will be unable to use its powers under that regulation until an arrangement to which the regulation would otherwise apply has been repeated sufficiently to establish it as the rule rather than the exception.

Where the Inland Revenue is unable to issue a *Reg 3(2)* direction (e.g. because less than half the earnings are paid at the longer interval), it may instead issue a similar direction under *Reg 22*, which applies where the Inland Revenue is satisfied as to the existence of a practice in respect of the payment of earnings whereby the incidence of Class 1 contributions is avoided or reduced by means of irregular or unequal payments (see 8.8 ANTI-AVOIDANCE).

31.4   Irregular payments treated as paid at regular intervals

Where a payment of earnings which would normally fall to be made at a regular interval is made at some other interval it is to be treated as made on the date on which it would normally fall to be made. [*Contributions Regs, Reg 6(1)(a), (2)(a)*]. (CWG2 (2000), Page 34, item (61) and chart on pages 8 to 11).

> *Example*
> Fred works for Gimlet, a self-employed joiner, and is paid £80 per week. G falls ill and for three weeks F is unpaid. In the fourth week G is again able to attend to his business and F is paid £320. For Class 1 purposes, however, F is to be treated as receiving £80 on each normal pay day and his earnings period remains a week.

In the same way, earnings paid at irregular intervals are to be treated as paid at regular intervals if the pay arrangement in force ensures that *one and only one* payment is made in *each* of a succession of periods consisting of the same number of days, weeks or calendar months. The deemed date of payment in such a case will be the last day of the deemed regular interval. [*Reg 6(1)(b), (2)(b)*]. (Leaflet CWG2 (2000), Page 34, item (61) and chart on pages 8 to 11). The DSS said that payments are made at regular intervals if, for example, payments are normally made at 17-day intervals and some of the payments are made at 16-day or 18-day intervals.

> *Example*
> Henry is paid on the last Thursday of each calendar month. He is, therefore, to be treated as paid at regular monthly intervals corresponding with PAYE months and the deemed pay day will be the last day of each such month.

Where earnings are paid *in respect of regular intervals* but at *irregular intervals*, each payment is to be treated as made on the last day of the regular interval in respect of which it is due. [*Reg 6(1)(c),(2)(b)*].

Where earnings are paid irregularly, e.g. at intervals of 4–4–5 weeks, perhaps because of the need for quarterly accounting, the earnings periods will be 4–4–5 weeks. Where, however, employees are paid monthly but the calculation differs because sometimes they are paid for four weeks and sometimes five, the earnings period is a month. (Leaflet CWG2 (2000), Page 34, item (61) and chart on pages 8 to 11).

The only circumstance in which these rules are *not* to apply is where, in consequence of treating an irregular payment of earnings as paid at a regular interval, a payment of earnings made in one tax year would be treated as made in another. [*Reg 6(3)*].

> *Example*
> Ingrid starts work on 2 March 2000 but the payment of £1,000 due to be made to her on 31 March 2000 is made to her with her April salary of £1,000 on 28 April 2000. Under the rule stated earlier, £1,000 of this would have been treated as paid on 31 March 2000 but as it was actually paid in a different tax year this is not possible. Although the payments are kept separate for NIC purposes the rates and limits to be used are those in force at the time of payment and the £2,000 is treated as having been paid in the later tax year. Ingrid is in not contracted-out employment and not eligible to pay the reduced rate. The total contributions due are, from CA38, page 19, £144.79 (contributions due on £1,000) times two.

In such a case, however, the earnings have to be shown separately so that an earner may, if he wishes, apply to the Secretary of State for the contributions paid in the year to which the earnings do not truly belong to be allocated to the other year for benefit entitlement purposes. [*SSCBA 1975, 1 Sch 8(1)(e); Contributions Regs, Reg 37*]. See also CA National Insurance News, summer 1997 pages 8 and 9.

31.5   Other irregular payments

A special rule applies where earnings are paid at irregular intervals but earnings neither follow nor can be treated as following a regular pay pattern. In such cases, the earnings period is to be the length of that part of the employment for which the earnings are paid or a week, whichever is the longer. [*Contributions Regs, Reg 4(a) as amended by Contributions Amendment Regs 1984, Reg 3*]. (Leaflet CWG2 (2000), Page 34, item (62)).

Example (1)
On 15 July, Jack is employed by Kwest Films Ltd as a researcher. He is to be paid £5 per hour and to work in his own time and at his own convenience. He has, however, to meet the following deadlines

'Health Service' material	31 August
'Aids' material	28 October
'Disarmament' material	31 October

J works 106 hours on the first project, 151 hours on the second and 12 hours on the third. Earnings periods and earnings will be as follows

	£
48 days from 15 July to 31 August	530
58 days from 1 September to 28 October	755
Week ended 1 November (though only a four-day fixed period)	60

Example (2)
Logan is employed by Mulch Ltd as a gardener. He is paid on an irregular basis for occasional attendance at various locations at such times and for such periods as he considers necessary. His rate of pay is £5 per hour. Part of his work record is

23 October to 5 November	80 hours
18 November	6 hours
30 November to 10 December	63 hours

L's earnings periods and earnings are as follows

	£
14 days to 5 November	400
Week ended 22 November	30
11 days to 10 December	315

Where it is not reasonably practicable to determine the period of that part of the employment for which earnings are paid, the earnings period is to be the period from the date of the last preceding payment of earnings in respect of the employment to the date of payment. Where there has been no previous payment, the period is to be measured from the date the employment began. In any event, the minimum length of the earnings period must be one week. [*Reg 4(b)(i) as amended by Contributions Amendment Regs 1984, Reg 3*]. Where such a payment is made before the related employment begins or after it ends, the earnings period is to be a week. [*Reg 4(b)(ii) as amended by Contributions Amendment Regs 1984, Reg 3*]. (Leaflet CWG2 (2000), Page 15).

Each session of a person in a sessional fee-paid office is to be treated as a separate employment and, accordingly, under *Reg 3(1)(a)(iii)* a weekly earnings period is to apply unless, exceptionally, a session lasts for longer than a week. In that event, the earnings period is, instead, to be the length of the session. (Leaflet CWG2 (2000), Pages 10 and 11).

In practice, persons paid per session are normally paid on a regular basis. For example, a teacher at a night school may work on Tuesday, Thursday and Friday evenings but payment is made on a weekly or, more often, a monthly basis. The payments in such cases are aggregated and the earnings period will be a week or a month.

Each payment per session may sometimes have a separate earnings period of a week, for example, in the case of a relief barmaid who fills in at short notice for someone who has failed to turn up. At the end of the session she may receive £10 and at that time it is not known if she will work again. If she does in fact work again that day or week the payments are not aggregated.

31.6   PAYMENTS UNDER EMPLOYMENT PROTECTION LEGISLATION

Special earnings period rules are to be applied to payments made under employment protection legislation (see 28.11 EARNINGS).

In the case of *awards under orders for reinstatement or re-engagement or for the continuation of a contract of employment*, the earnings period is to be the period to which the award relates or a week, whichever is the longer. [*Reg 5(a)(ii) as amended by Contributions Amendment Regs 1984, Reg 4(a)*]. If certain amounts due under the order are payable by instalments those instalments are to be aggregated and the rule is to be applied as stated. Where the award is paid with the first regular payment of earnings following reinstatement or re-engagement, the award must be assessed separately according to the stated rule. (Leaflet CWG2 (2000), Pages 95 and 96).

In the case of a *protective award*, the earnings period is to be the protected period or that part of it for which the sum is paid or a week, whichever is the longer. [*Reg 5(a)(iii, as amended by Contributions Amendment Regs 1984, Reg 4(a)*]. Where, therefore, earnings have been paid to an earner for part of the protected period, the earnings period to be applied in relation to wages paid for the remaining part of the protected period is to be that remaining part of the protected period. Any earnings paid during the period covered by the award (e.g. overtime arrears) must be dealt with separately for contribution purposes. (Leaflet CWG2 (2000), Page 96).

Where, in consequence of these rules, an earnings period falls wholly or partly in a tax year or years other than that in which relevant contributions are paid, contributions may, on request and in order to protect the earner's contribution record for the purposes of benefit entitlement, be treated as paid proportionately in respect of the year or years in which the earnings period falls. [*Reg 5(b) as amended by Contributions Amendment Regs 1984, Reg 4(b)*].

Where a payment of statutory sick pay or statutory maternity pay is paid by the Inland Revenue on behalf of the Secretary of State for Social Security rather than by an employer (e.g. where the employer has become insolvent and a period of entitlement or a maternity pay period has not expired), the earnings period is, in the case of such a payment of statutory sick pay, a week or the period for which the payment is made, whichever is the longer, and, in the case of such a payment of statutory maternity pay for any week, the earnings period is a week. [*Reg 6B as amended by Contributions Amendment No 2 Regs 1987, Reg 3*].

31.7   CHANGE OF REGULAR PAY INTERVAL

Where, because of a change in the regular interval at which any part of an employed earner's earnings is paid or treated as paid, an earner's earnings period is changed and the new earnings period is longer than the old, a payment of earnings at the old interval may fall within the first new earnings period. In that event, contributions on all payments made during the new earnings period are not to exceed the contribution which would have been payable had all those payments been made at the new interval. [*Contributions Regs, Reg 14*]. Accordingly, employers are instructed to calculate the Class 1 contribution liabilities on the total of all payments of earnings made in the new earnings period and then to deduct from those amounts the contribution liabilities already calculated on payments of earnings made at the old interval within the new earnings period. (Leaflet CWG2 (2000), Page 12).

Example
Nuthatch and Osprey are both employed by Partridge Ltd. N is paid £390 per week and O is paid £90 per week. In May 2000, they become salaried employees and begin to be paid monthly at £1,800 and £540 per month, respectively. The last weekly wage is paid to each of them on 6 May and their first monthly salaries are paid on 3 June. The first new earnings period is the month from 6 May to 5 June and their last payments of weekly wage fall within this period. Contributions have already been calculated on that wage as follows.

		Primary		Secondary*	
		%	£	%	£
N	£390	Nil/10	31.40	Nil/12.2	37.33
O	£90	Nil/10	1.40	Nil/12.2	0.73

If contributions on the payment of salary on 5 June are calculated without regard to that wage payment, those contributions will be

		Primary		Secondary*	
		%	£	%	£
N	£1,800	Nil/10	147.10	Nil/12.2	175.07
O	£540	Nil/10	21.10	Nil/12.2	21.35

If, however, contributions are calculated on the total payments in the earnings period, contributions will be

		Primary		Secondary*	
		%	£	%	£
N	£2,190	Nil/10	186.10	Nil/12.2	222.65
O	£630	Nil/10	30.10	Nil/12.2	32.33

*First £365 (monthly) or £84 (weekly) at Nil%

Under *Reg 14*, the contributions due on the two separate parts of earnings are not to exceed the contributions due on the total and they do not. However, the CWG2 guidance requires the recalculation to be performed regardless of any comparison and thus, N's separate contributions (primary, £31.40 + £147.10 = £178.50 and secondary, £37.33 + £175.07 = £212.40) become primary, £186.10 and secondary £222.65, and O's separate contributions (primary £1.40 + £21.10 = £22.50 and secondary, £0.73 + £21.35 = £22.08) are, under *Reg 14*, to be uplifted to £30.10 primary and £32.33 secondary. Thus, according to CWG2, primary contributions of £154.70 (£186.10 – £31.40) and secondary contributions of £185.32 (£222.65 – £37.33) are to be paid on the first payment of monthly salary to N, while primary contributions of £28.70 (£30.10 – £1.40) and secondary contributions of £31.60 (£32.33 – £0.73) are to be paid on the first payment of monthly salary to O.
The legal validity of the instruction in CWG2 in these circumstances is highly questionable.
If, in the circumstances described above, the date of the change to a longer pay interval is also the date of a change from not contracted-out employment to CONTRACTED-OUT EMPLOYMENT (23), the Class 1 liabilities on the total payments in the new earnings period must be calculated at contracted-out rates. (Leaflet CWG2 (2000), Page 12).

It should be noted that, provided the regular interval in respect of which earnings are paid remains unchanged, a mere change of pay day or a change in 'week in hand' or 'lying-time' arrangements does *not* bring the *Reg 14* rule into operation. This is because the earnings period (which is determined by the regular pay interval) also remains unchanged. Instructions are, therefore, that, where in consequence of such a change, two regular payments fall within the same earnings period, contribution liabilities are to be calculated on each payment separately (Leaflet CWG2 (2000), Page 13).

Example

Quail is employed by Roadrunner Ltd and is paid, on a Friday, a weekly wage of £100 for the week ended seven days previous. In the earnings period ended 26 July 2000, the arrangement is changed and, having received £100 on 21 July (in respect of the working week ended 14 July), Q also receives £100 on Tuesday 25 July (in respect of the working week ended 21 July) in accordance with the new arrangement. It follows, therefore, that Q has received two payments in his one-week earnings period ended 26 July. Were these payments to be aggregated, Class 1 liabilities would be

Primary   £200 @ Nil%/10%   = £12.40
Secondary   £200 @ Nil%/12.2%   = £14.15

Instead, however, liabilities are to be

Primary   2 × (£100 @ Nil%/10%)   = £4.80
Secondary   2 × (£100 @ Nil%/12.2%)= £3.90

This same principle of separate assessment is applicable where an employed earner's regular pay interval is changed so that the new interval is shorter than the old interval and, in consequence, the first of the new earnings periods is contained within the last of the old earnings periods. (Leaflet CWG2 (2000), Page 12).

Example

Snipe is employed by Teal Ltd at a salary of £500 per month. He receives £500 on 18 August 2000 but then, from 1 September 2000, his pay arrangement is changed to one under which he receives a weekly wage of £125 per week. His first weekly wage under the new arrangement is paid on 2 September 2000. It follows that, in the contribution month ended 5 September, S has received two payments of earnings. Were these payments to be aggregated and treated as relating to the monthly earnings period ended 5 September 2000, Class 1 liabilities would be

Primary   £625 @ Nil%/10%   = £29.60
Secondary   £625 @ Nil%/12.2%   = £31.72

Instead, however, liabilities are to be

Primary   (on a monthly earnings period basis) £500 @ Nil%/10% =   17.10
                 (on a weekly earnings period basis) £125 @ Nil%/10% =   4.90
                                                                                                                    £22.00

Secondary (on a monthly earnings period basis) £500 @ Nil%/12.2% =   16.47
                 (on a weekly earnings period basis) £125 @ Nil%/12.2% =   5.00
                                                                                                                    £21.47

31.8 HOLIDAY PAY

Where a payment of earnings (other than a payment on termination of the employment) includes a payment in respect of one or more week's holiday (see 28.21 EARNINGS), the earnings period may be the length of the interval in respect of which the payment is made. Alternatively, the holiday pay may simply be treated for contribution purposes as pay in the weeks in which earnings would normally have

31.8   Earnings Periods

been paid. [*Contributions Regs, Regs 6(1)(a), 15 as amended by Contributions Amendment Regs 1984, Reg 7*].

The first method is referred to as 'method B' and the second as 'method A'. (Leaflet CWG2 (2000), Pages 25 and 26). Where method B is adopted and the length of the interval in respect of which the payment is made includes a fraction of a week, that fraction is to be treated as a whole week. [*Reg 15 as amended by Contributions Amendment Regs 1984, Reg 7*].

Where, having received holiday pay on which contributions have been calculated, an employed earner decides not to take his holiday but to work instead, the additional contribution liability on earnings for the holiday weeks is to be calculated as follows.

If method A was used, the earnings for each week are to be aggregated with the holiday pay apportioned to each week and contribution liabilities are to be calculated on the weekly aggregate amounts. The contribution liability for each week as already calculated on the holiday pay is then to be deducted from the contribution liability on the aggregated amount, and the result will be the contributions due on the earnings for the week. (Leaflet CWG2 (2000), Page 25, item (36)).

If method B was used, the contributions are to be calculated in the normal manner using the National Insurance Tables on the earnings for each week of holiday without taking any account of contributions paid on the holiday pay already paid for the holiday period. (Leaflet CWG2 (2000), Page 26, item (36)).

Where, although an employed earner takes the holiday for which he has been paid, payments fall due to him during his holiday period (e.g. overtime payable one week after the week in which it was earned), liability for contributions on those payments is to be calculated as follows.

If method A was used, the payment falling due for each week is to be aggregated with the holiday pay apportioned to each week and contribution liabilities are to be calculated on the weekly aggregated amounts. The contribution liability for each week as already calculated on the holiday pay is then to be deducted from the contribution liability on the aggregated amount, and the result will be the contributions due on the payment falling due in the week. (Leaflet CWG2 (2000), Pages 25 and 26). When the payment which fell due during the holiday period is actually paid, it must, of course, be excluded from earnings for contribution purposes.

If method B was used, payments falling due during the holiday period are not to be taken into account as earnings for contribution purposes until they are actually paid, whereupon they are to be aggregated with any other earnings paid in the same earnings period. (Leaflet CWG2 (2000), Page 26).

Example
Utrillo and Vermeer are both employed by Whistler Ltd. Both are paid a wage of £90 and holiday pay (for the following two weeks) of £220 on 8 July 2000. U works during his holiday period and earns £80 paid to him on 15 July and £120 paid to him on 22 July. His wage on 29 July is £110. V takes his holiday but £40 in overtime pay becomes due for payment to him on 15 July. This is paid (along with a wage of £90) on 29 July after his return to work.
If W adopts *method A*, final calculations will be as follows.

U	£	*Primary*	£	*Secondary*	£
8 July 2000	90	Nil%/10%	1.40	Nil%/12.2%	0.73
15 July 2000	190	Nil%/10%	11.40	Nil%/12.2%	12.93
22 July 2000	230	Nil%/10%	15.40	Nil%/12.2%	17.81
29 July 2000	110	Nil%/10%	3.40	Nil%/12.2%	3.17
	£620		£31.60		£34.64

V	£	Primary	£	Secondary	£
8 July 2000	90	Nil%/10%	1.40	Nil%/12.2%	0.73
15 July 2000	150	Nil%/10%	7.40	Nil%/12.2%	8.05
22 July 2000	110	Nil%/10%	3.40	Nil%/12.2%	3.17
29 July 2000	90	Nil%/10%	1.40	Nil%/12.2%	0.73
	£440		£13.60		£12.68

If W adopts *method B*, final calculations will be as follows.

U	£	Primary	£	Secondary	£
8 July 2000	310/3		2.73		2.36
	= 103.33	Nil%/10%	× 3 =	Nil%/12.2%	× 3 =
			8.19		7.08
15 July 2000	80	Nil%/10%	0.40	Nil%/12.2%	Nil
22 July 2000	120	Nil%/10%	4.40	Nil%/12.2%	4.39
29 July 2000	110	Nil%/10%	3.40	Nil%/12.2%	3.17
	£620		£16.39		£14.64

V	£	Primary	£	Secondary	£
8 July 2000	310/3		2.73		2.36
	= 103.33	Nil%/10%	× 3 =	Nil%/12.2%	× 3 =
			8.19		7.08
15 July 2000	—	—	—	—	—
22 July 2000	—	—	—	—	—
29 July 2000	130	Nil%/10%	5.40	Nil%/12.2%	5.61
	£440		£13.59		£12.69

31.9 AGGREGABLE EARNINGS

Where earnings paid in respect of two or more employed earner's employments fall to be aggregated, special rules apply for the purpose of establishing a common earnings period (see 5.10 AGGREGATION OF EARNINGS).

31.10 EARNINGS PAID ON OR AFTER CESSATION OF EMPLOYMENT

The rules which follow are in accordance with *Contributions Regs* and guidance, but they disregard the fact that, as explained at 28.5 EARNINGS, payments made after an employment has ended are, it seems, no longer within the ambit of the Class 1 contribution charge.

Where an employment in respect of which earnings have been paid or treated as paid according to a regular pay pattern comes to an end and, at the end of the employment, two or more payments of earnings are made in respect of regular pay intervals, the payments should *not* be aggregated and treated as falling into a single earnings period but each payment should be regarded as falling into a separate earnings period (determined according to general rules) and contributions should be calculated accordingly. (Leaflet CWG2 (2000), Page 15).

Example

Xerxes is employed by Yesteryear Ltd on a weekly wage of £105 payable each Friday in respect of the working week ended on the previous Friday. He leaves the employment on 26 May 2000 which falls within the earnings period Thursday 25 May to Wednesday 31 May (see 31.2 above). On the day he leaves, 26 May, he is paid his wage for the working week ended 19 May 2000 and also for the working week ended 26 May 2000. His earnings for the earnings period ended 31 May

2000 are £105, *not* £210, and his earnings for the earnings period ended 7 June 2000 are (although by then he has left his employment) £105 also.

If, in addition to regular earnings, holiday pay is paid to an employed earner when he leaves his employment, the way in which it should be treated for contribution purposes will depend on whether the employed earner's contract of service terminates on the date he leaves or only after a period of holiday following his last day of work. In the latter event, contribution liability on the holiday pay may be calculated using either of the normal methods (see 31.8 above). In the former event, however, it should be aggregated with regular earnings paid at the date of leaving.

Where an employment in respect of which earnings have been paid or treated as paid according to a regular pay pattern comes to an end and, after the end of the employment, a payment of earnings which is *not* in respect of a regular interval is made by way of an addition to a payment of earnings made before the employment ended (see 28.18 EARNINGS), the earnings period in respect of those additional earnings is to be the *week* in which the payment is made regardless of what the length of the regular pay interval has been. [*Contributions Regs, Reg 3(4), as amended by Contributions Amendment Regs 1984, Reg 2(e)*]. Examples of such payments are arrears of pay from a back-dated pay increase, holiday pay in respect of a holiday which an employee has not taken by the time he leaves his employment, and a one-off payment such as an unexpected bonus. (Leaflet CWG2 (2000), Page 15). The same principle applies where statutory maternity pay paid after a contract of service has ended is paid at a different interval from that at which regular earnings were paid or is paid in a lump sum. (Leaflet CWG2 (2000), Page 20, item (23)).

Where a payment of earnings made to an employed earner after he has left his employment *is* in respect of a regular pay interval, the earnings period into which the payment falls is an earnings period determined according to the general rules. If, for example, a monthly-paid employed earner leaves his employment part way through a month and his final monthly salary payment is made at the end of that month, his earnings period as regards that payment is the month in which he leaves, just as it would be had he continued in the employment. (Leaflet CWG2 (2000), Page 15). Likewise, the earnings period into which there falls a payment of statutory maternity pay paid after a contract of service has ended is to be of the same length as the earnings period in use before the employee left if the statutory maternity pay is paid at the same interval as that at which regular earnings were paid. (Leaflet CWG2 (2000), Page 20). Any payment of statutory maternity pay made when a contract of service ends is, if paid with the last regular payment of earnings, to be aggregated with that last regular payment of earnings.

31.11 PAYMENTS TO COMPANY DIRECTORS AND EX-COMPANY DIRECTORS

Until 6 April 1983, COMPANY DIRECTORS (22) were subject to the same earnings periods rules as all other employed earners. Where, however, on or after 6 April 1983, a person is, or is appointed, or ceases to be, a director of a company, the amount (if any) of Class 1 contributions payable in respect of earnings paid to or for his benefit in respect of any employed earner's employment with *that* company (whether the employment is as a director or not) are to be assessed on the amount of all such earnings paid (whether at regular intervals or not) in the earnings period specified under the following special rules. [*Contributions Regs, Reg 6A(1) as amended by Contributions Amendment Regs 1983, Reg 4*].

Where a person is a company director at the beginning of a tax year, the earnings period in respect of his earnings is to be *that tax year*, whether or not he remains a director throughout the year (see 22.4 COMPANY DIRECTORS). [*Contributions Regs, Reg 6A(3) as amended by Contributions Amendment Regs 1983, Reg 4*].

Example

Anchovy is a director of Barracuda Ltd. His drawings (treated as earnings) are £2,600 per month. On 30 June 2000 he resigns his office and begins to work as an ordinary employee of Carp Ltd (a completely unconnected company) who pay him a weekly wage. An earnings period of one year is to apply to his earnings for the months April, May and June 2000 of £7,800 from B. A weekly earnings period will then apply in respect of his earnings from C.

Reg 6A(3) is designed to ensure that any payments made to an ex-director in the year in which his directorship ceases will not escape the April 1983 rules (e.g. a bonus paid by B to A in August 2000, in the example above).

Any payments to an ex-director in any year *after* that in which his directorship ceased are, if they are in respect of any period during which he was a company director, also caught by the rules in that the earnings period in respect of those earnings is to be the *tax year* in which they are paid. [*Reg 6A(5)(b) as amended by Contributions Amendment Regs 1983, Reg 4*].

Example

Anchovy (see previous example) continues to work for C in the next tax year but in May of that year is paid a bonus of £5,000 by B in respect of the year ended 31 March. The bonus will attract an annual earnings period and, as the annual upper earnings limit for the later year will inevitably be in excess of £5,000, will be fully subject to contribution liability, on the excess over the earnings threshold or thresholds for 2001–02, irrespective of the level of earnings received from C during that year. Only if the total contributions paid for the later year exceed the annual maximum for that year will a repayment of excess primary contributions be made.

Where (on one or more than one occasion) a person is appointed a company director during the course of a tax year, the earnings period in respect of such earnings as are paid in so much of the year as remains in the period commencing with the week in which he is appointed (or, as the case may be, first appointed) is to be the number of weeks in that period. [*Reg 6A(2) as amended by Contributions Amendment Regs 1983, Reg 4*]. 'Week' means tax week. [*Reg 1(2)*].

Example

Dace is appointed a director of Eel Ltd on 5 June. He resigns on 31 August and becomes a salaried employee of E. He is re-appointed a director on 1 December of that same year. 5 June lies in the tax week commencing 1 June (Tax week 9) and the number of tax weeks to 5 April is, therefore, 44. (NB. There are 53 tax weeks in *every* tax year although the last 'week' will consist of only one or two days but the odd day or two days can, generally, be ignored (CA44, Para 24)). Despite his resignation and subsequent re-appointment, D will have a 44 week earnings period by reference to which all his earnings from E (whether in respect of his directorships or not) will be assessed.

It should be noted that it is the date of *appointment* that is relevant, not the date on which a company *begins to trade* or (following a period of suspension) recommences trading.

Example

Moby Ltd was formed on 26 April 2000 and Dick was appointed a director on that date. The company begins to trade on 1 March 2001 and on 31 March 2001 Dick is paid £20,000. Dick's earnings period is 50 weeks (UEL: 50 × £535 = £26,750), not 5 weeks (UEL: 5 × £535 = £2,675), and thus the whole of the £20,000 falls below the UEL and suffers Class 1 contributions on the excess above the earnings threshold.

It should be noted that in practice employers are instructed to assume a basis of a 52-week year in carrying out the pro-rata calculation. However, if the director is appointed in week 53, the pro-rata period is one week. (Leaflet CA 44, Paras 23–27).

Special earnings periods rules apply where earnings of a company director fall to be aggregated, and aggregation is actually prohibited in certain circumstances where a person has been, but is no longer, a company director (see 5.8, 5.10 AGGREGATION OF EARNINGS).

31.12 PAYMENTS TO MARINERS

Where MARINERS (42) are paid at regular intervals (e.g. a week or a month), the length of the earnings period by reference to which contributions are to be calculated will be ascertained in the normal way (see 31.2 etc. above). Where (as is more usual), however, a mariner receives a general settlement of his earnings at the end of a voyage, his earnings period is to be determined by reference to the voyage period and special rules have applied from 6 April 1982. [*Contributions Regs, Reg 90(1) as amended by Contributions (Mariners) Amendment Regs 1982, Reg 2*].

A 'voyage period' is a pay period comprising an entire voyage or series of voyages and it includes any period of paid leave which immediately follows the day on which the termination of the voyage or series of voyages occurs. It is measured in weeks which are periods of seven consecutive days. [*Reg 86*].

The length of a 'voyage-paid' mariner's earnings period will depend on whether the voyage period falls wholly in one tax year or partly in one and partly in one or more other tax years and whether or not, during the voyage period, one or more than one *relevant change* occurs. A 'relevant change' is a change (other than a change in the amount of the mariner's earnings or in contribution rates or earnings limits) affecting the calculation of Class 1 contributions, e.g. the mariner attaining pensionable age. [*Reg 90(2) as amended by Contributions (Mariners) Amendment Regs 1982, Reg 2; Contributions Transitional Regs 1989, Reg 3*].

Where a voyage period falls wholly in one year and, during the voyage period, no relevant change occurs, the earnings period is to be the voyage period. [*Reg 90(3)(a) as amended by Contributions (Mariners) Amendment Regs 1982, Reg 2*].

Where a voyage period falls wholly in one year but, during the voyage period, one or more than one relevant change occurs, earnings periods are to be

(*a*) the period beginning with the day on which the voyage began and ending with the day immediately before the first change occurs;

(*b*) each period beginning with the day on which the immediately preceding change occurs and ending on the day immediately before the next succeeding change occurs; and

(*c*) so much of the voyage period as remains.

[*Reg 90(3)(b) as amended by Contributions (Mariners) Amendment Regs 1982, Reg 2*].

Where a voyage period falls partly in one and partly in one or more other tax years but, during the voyage period, no relevant change occurs, the earnings periods are to correspond with the parts of the voyage period falling in each tax year. [*Reg 90(4) as amended by Contributions (Mariners) Amendment Regs 1982, Reg 2*].

Where a voyage period falls partly in one and partly in one or more other tax years but, during the voyage period, one or more than one relevant change occurs, the earnings periods are to be periods corresponding to the parts of the voyage period between its beginning and end arrived at by allowing each relevant change and each tax year-end to act as a division point. [*Reg 90(5) as amended by Contributions (Mariners) Amendment Regs 1982, Reg 2*].

Where a voyage period does not comprise an exact number of weeks, any remaining period of three days or less are ignored. Any remaining period four, five or six days is treated as a further whole week. [*Reg 90(6)*].

Example

Flounder was engaged by Gudgeon Ltd to serve on a voyage which began on 14 December 1999. The voyage ends on 15 April 2000 and F is then paid £3,500 which includes leave pay to 17 June 2000. F attained the age of 65 on 15 March 2000. His earnings are attributable to periods of work and leave as follows.

	£
14 December 1999 to 14 March 2000	1,800
15 March 2000 to 5 April 2000	400
6 April 2000 to 15 April 2000	200
16 April 2000 to 17 June 2000	1,100

In accordance with the rules described above, F's earnings periods and the bases of contribution calculation are as follows.

Earnings period 1.	14 December 1999 to 14 March 2000 (13 weeks): primary and secondary Class 1 contributions due at 1999–2000 rates on £1,800.
Earnings period 2.	15 March 2000 to 5 April 2000 (3 weeks): secondary Class 1 contributions due at 1999–2000 rates on £400.
Earnings period 3.	6 April 2000 to 17 June 2000 (10 weeks): secondary Class 1 contributions due at 2000–01 rates on £1,300.

32 Enforcement

Cross-references. See ADMINISTRATION (2); APPEALS AND REVIEWS (9); ARREARS OF CONTRIBUTIONS (12); COLLECTION (21).

Other Sources. Simon's NIC, Part I, Section 11, Chapter 58; IR Enforcement Manuals, vols I–IV.

32.1 OFFICERS OF THE INLAND REVENUE

The Inland Revenue may authorise any of its officers to exercise powers to monitor and enforce compliance with contribution law. [*SSAA 1992, s 110ZA*]. Additionally, the Secretary of State may make arrangements with the Inland Revenue or some other department for any of the powers or duties of his inspectors to be carried out by an inspector or officer employed by the Inland Revenue or that other department. [*SSAA 1992, s 110(5) as amended by Social Security Contributions (Transfer of Functions, etc.) Act 1999, 5 Sch 2, 3*].

32.2 Right of entry

An Inland Revenue officer has the right of entry at all reasonable times to any premises (except a private dwelling-house not used for the purposes of trade or business) where he has reasonable grounds for supposing that persons are employed or that an employment agency or similar business is being carried on. [*SSAA 1992, s 110ZA(2)(a)(3)*]. A private dwelling-house is not within the exception unless it is in use as such at the time and it is for the person challenging an inspector's right of entry to prove that is so. (*Stott v Hefferon [1974] 3 AER 673*).

Where an inspector or officer of, or under the control of, some other Government department has a similar right of entry to any premises the Inland Revenue may make arrangements with that department (e.g. DSS) for such a person to have the powers and carry out the duties of the Inland Revenue officer. [*Sec 110(5) as amended by SSC(T)A 1999, 5 Sch 2*]. This right of entry is wide ranging and can extend to farmhouses, private property, nursing homes, lodging houses, etc.

Every officer is furnished with a certificate of his appointment and must, on applying for admission to premises, produce it if asked to do so. [*Sec 110(4) and Sec 110ZA(4)*]. The fact that there might be no one on the premises to whom the certificate can be produced does not, however, negate right of entry to those premises. (*Grove v Eastern Gas Board [1951] 2 AER 1051*).

Obstruction of an officer properly seeking entry is an offence and carries a penalty (see 32.5 below), but entry cannot be forced if refused and social security legislation makes no provision for obtaining of search warrants. [*Sec 111(1)(a) as amended by SSC(T)A 1999, 5 Sch 4(2)(3)*].

However, where documents are promised but the information is not forthcoming the Inland Revenue can apply for 'a notice to produce' document.

32.3 Right of examination and inquiry

An officer has the right of examination and inquiry to whatever extent is necessary for the purpose of ascertaining whether or not the requirements of social security legislation have been, or are being, complied with. [*SSAA 1992, s 110ZA(2)(b)*]. This right extends to the examination (alone, if the inspector thinks fit) of anyone whom he finds on premises he has entered *or* anyone whom he has reason to believe is, or has been, liable to pay contributions. [*Sec 110ZA(2)(c)*]. Thus, a person who, being found in premises which an officer has entered, admits to being an employee commits an offence if he refuses to disclose the identity of his employer. (*Smith v Hawkins [1972] 1 AER 910*).

32.4 Right to require information and documents

There is a duty to give an inspector information when he reasonably requires it. Anyone

(*a*) who is the occupier of premises liable to inspection (see 32.2 above);

(*b*) who is, or has been, employing another;

(*c*) who is carrying on an employment agency or similar business;

(*d*) who is a servant or agent of any person falling within (*a*) to (*c*) above;

(*e*) who is, or has been, liable to pay contributions; or

(*f*) who is, or has been, a trustee or manager of a personal or occupational pension scheme,

must furnish an officer with all such information, and produce for his inspection all such documents, as he may reasonably require for the purpose of ascertaining whether any contributions due are payable, have been payable, or have been duly paid, by, or in respect of, any person. This includes all wages sheets, deduction working sheets and other documents and records relating to the calculation of earnings, earnings-related contributions and Class 1A contributions. [*SSAA 1992, s 110ZA(6)(7); Contributions Regs, 1 Sch 32(1); SSC(T)A 1999*]. Any documents reasonably required must be produced at the prescribed place. [*1 Sch 32(1)*]. This means such place in Great Britain as the employer and the officer may agree upon. If no agreement is reached, they must be produced at the place in Great Britain at which they are normally kept or, if there is no such place, at the employer's principal place of business in Great Britain. [*1 Sch 32(1A)*]. The officer is empowered to take copies of, or make extracts from, any documents produced to him and, if it appears to him to be necessary, at a reasonable time and for a reasonable period, take away any such document, providing a receipt to the employer. If any of the documents removed is reasonably required for the conduct of the business, the officer must provide a copy, free of charge, within seven days of its being taken away. [*1 Sch 32(1B)*].

Example
Joyce Jones, an appointed officer of the Inland Revenue visits Profit Bros Ltd after meeting Elsa Smith at her home (see 32.5 below). A review of the wage sheets reveals a deficiency of SMP and the Inspector extracts the following signed statement from the employee:

Statement of employee

I, Elsa Doreen Smith, state that I have not received Statutory Maternity Pay from Profit Bros Ltd for the period 19 October 1998 to 21 February 1999.

Signed: Elsa Smith

No one is, however, to be required to answer any question or to give any evidence tending to incriminate himself or herself or his or her spouse. [*Sec 110(7)*].

32.5 OFFENCES AND PENALTIES

A person commits an offence if he

(*a*) wilfully delays or obstructs an inspector in the exercise of any of his powers; or

(*b*) refuses or neglects to

(i) answer any question, or

(ii) furnish any information, or

(iii) produce any document

when contribution law requires him to do so, and he becomes liable on summary conviction to a fine of up to £1,000 (level 3 on the standard scale). [*SSAA 1992, s 111(1); Criminal Justice Act 1982, ss 37(2), 46(1); Criminal Justice Act 1991, s 17*]. If after conviction of an offence under (*b*) above, he continues in his refusal or neglect, he is guilty of a further offence and liable on summary conviction to a fine of up to £40 a day. [*Sec 111(2)*].

To obstruct is to do any act which makes it more difficult for an inspector to carry out his duty, but *wilfully* to obstruct is to obstruct intentionally and without lawful excuse. (*Rice v Connolly [1966] 2 AER 649*). Where the obstruction consists of a positive act, the law does not require that the act be unlawful independent of its operation as an obstruction. (*Ingleton v Dibble [1972] 1 AER 275*).

To knowingly furnish wrong information may incur a penalty of up to £5,000 (level 5 on the standard scale) and/or 3 months imprisonment.

32.6 False statements or documents

A person commits an offence if, for any purpose connected with contribution law, he

(*a*) knowingly makes any false statement or false representation; or

(*b*) produces or furnishes, or causes or knowingly allows to be produced or furnished, any document or information which he knows to be false in a material particular. (*Barras v Reeve [1980] 3 AER 705*).

A statement or representation will be false if, even though no specific part of it is untrue, the statement or representation, looked at as a whole, intentionally gives a false impression. (*Aaron's Reefs v Twiss [1896] AC 273*). It follows that an omission from an otherwise true statement or representation will, if that omission creates, clearly and intentionally, an impression and belief which is wrong, render the statement or representation false. (*R v Bishirgian [1936] 1 AER 586*). It will be false 'not because of what it states, but because of what it does not state, because of what it implies'. (*R v Kylsant [1932] 1 KB 442*).

A corporate body, even though it itself is incapable of having a wrongful intent, will be guilty of making false statements or representations if it makes such statements or representations through its human agents. (*DPP v Kent and Sussex Contractors Ltd [1944] 1 AER 119*).

32.7 Contravention of regulations

If a person contravenes or fails to comply with any requirement of contribution regulations and no *special* penalty is provided, he is liable, from 20 April 1999, to a penalty of £100 and such penalty is recoverable as if it were contributions payable to the Inland Revenue. [*Reg 132 as amended by Social Security (Contributions) Amendment (No 3) Regs 1999, Reg 3*]. Previously, he was liable on summary conviction to a penalty of up to £1,000 (level 3 on the standard scale) or, where the offence continues after conviction, up to £40 a day. [*SSAA 1992, s 113; Criminal Justice Act 1982, ss 46(1), 37(2); Criminal Justice Act 1991, s 17; Contributions Regs, Reg 132, as amended by Contributions Amendment No 5 Regs 1991, Reg 4*]. An employer may properly delegate his duties of compliance to another, but if he does so and that other person fails to carry out the duties, the employer is nonetheless guilty of the offence. (*Godman v Crofton (1913) 110 LTR 387*).

It was the *Social Security Act 1998* which enabled the previous *criminal* offence for a breach of regulations to be replaced by the new civil penalty.

Introduction of the following new penalties has been deferred:

- where there are multiple inaccuracies in returns e.g. missing national insurance numbers on Forms P14 (OCR), incorrect NI Table letter, etc. *even though no underpayment may have arisen. (SSA 1998, s 60)*;

- late payment of Class 2 quarterly bill [*SSA 1998, s 60*];

- failure to notify commencement of self-employment within three months, even though no underpayment may arise because, for example, the contributor is entitled to small earnings exception in the early period of the business. [*SSA 1998, s 60*].

See CA Press Release, CA 05/99, 30 March 1999.

SSA 1998, s 61 introduced, by way of new *SSAA 1992, s 114A* and with effect from 6 April 1999, a new criminal offence of fraudulent evasion of NICs. Although aimed at large scale and repeated evasion, and the non-compliance of directors of 'phoenix' companies the provision is far wider covering far more circumstances than merely that situation. In addition, it extends to 'any person' involved with fraudulent evasion, which could include professional advisers, on the one hand, or junior payroll clerks, on the other. There are other methods which provide, in certain circumstances, for contribution and associated penalty and interest debts to be transferred to directors personally (see 12.1 and 12.4 ARREARS OF CONTRIBUTIONS).

32.8 Non-payment of contributions

For the offence of failure to pay a contribution which is due see 12.4 ARREARS OF CONTRIBUTIONS, and for offences in connection with contribution cards or stamps see 21.9 and 21.10 COLLECTION as well as 20.10 COLLECTION of earlier editions of this work.

32.9 PROSECUTION

Proceedings for an offence under contribution law may be conducted before a magistrates' court by anyone authorised for that purpose by the Inland Revenue, or before the county courts even if the person authorised is not a barrister or solicitor. [*SSC(T)A 1999, s 4, 4 Sch*].

32.10 Laying an information

A duly authorised officer will commence proceedings by attending the court of the Office of the Clerk to the Justices and laying an information under *Magistrates' Courts Act 1980, s 127* alleging the offence. It is the duty of the clerk to ensure that authorisation is produced but, if it is not and if no objection is raised before the case for the prosecution is closed, the summons must be considered good. (*Price v Humphries [1958] 2 AER 725*).

32.11 Time limits

Proceedings must be brought before a magistrates' court not later than the first anniversary of the day on which the contribution became due, except in the case of Class 2 contributions (or interest or penalties in respect of Class 2 contributions) when the time limit is the end of the year following the tax year in which the contributions fell due.

Provided an information is received at the Office of the Clerk to the Justices for the relevant area within the time limit allowed, it is 'laid' within the time, even though it may not be personally considered by a magistrate or the clerk to the justices until after the time limit has expired. (*R v Dartford Justices, ex p Dhesi, [1982] 3 WLR 331*).

The certificate of an authorised officer as to unpaid contributions, interest or penalties shall be sufficient evidence in any proceedings before any court, until the contrary is proved. [*SSAA 1992, s 118 as amended by Social Security Act 1998, s 62*].

32.12 The summons

Following an information being laid, a summons will, without delay prejudicial to the defendant and within a reasonable time before the hearing, be issued and served on the person cited in the information. It will state the general matter of the information and the place and time the defendant is to appear. The summons must be issued by the justices before whom the information was laid. (*R v Fairford JJ, ex p Brewster [1975] 2 AER 757; R v Jenkins (1862) 26 JP 775; Dixon v Wells (1890) 54 JP 725*).

If the alleged offender is a limited company, the company itself must be summoned, and where, instead, a director or the company secretary is summoned the case must be dismissed. (*City of Oxford Tramway Co v Sankey (1890) 54 JP 564*). A summons will be properly served on a company only if it is left at, or posted to, its registered office. In the case of a company registered in Scotland carrying on business in England and Wales, a summons may be served at its principal place of business in England and Wales if process is served through an English or Welsh court, but the person issuing the summons must send a copy of it by post to the company's registered office. [*Companies Act 1985, s 725*].

An error in the defendant's name as it appears in the summons will not invalidate the proceedings provided it is *idem sonans* or the defendant appears to the summons.

Where a summons is defective because of a clerical error (e.g. the statement therein of the wrong section number of the relevant enactment under which the offence is alleged to have taken place) but the person summoned has not been misled by the error and pleads guilty when the charge is put to him without reference to either the section of the enactment or the enactment itself, the justices are entitled to amend the summons before the final disposal of the case. (*R v Eastbourne Justices, ex p Kisten, The Times, 22 December 1984*).

32.13 Representation

The case will be heard in open court. [*Magistrates' Courts Act 1980, s 4(2)*]. An Inland Revenue officer, although not a barrister or a solicitor, may prosecute or conduct the proceedings for the offence before the magistrates or county court. [*SSAA 1992, s 116(1) as amended by SSC(T)A 1999, 1 Sch 21 and 4 Sch 3(2)*]. The proceedings will not be invalidated if they are conducted by a different officer to the one who laid the information which gave rise to the summons. (*R v Northumberland Justices, ex p Thompson (1923) 87 JP 95*). Either party may be represented by a barrister or a solicitor and an absent party so represented is deemed to be present. The court may, however, proceed in the absence of the defendant even where he is unrepresented provided it is proved to the satisfaction of the court that the summons was served on the accused within a reasonable time before the trial. [*MCA 1980, s 11*].

32.14 Witnesses

Either party may call witnesses and is able to seek a witness summons if a required witness is unwilling to attend voluntarily. Such a summons may require the production of documents, etc.

33   Entertainers

Cross-references. See CATEGORISATION (14); 20.4 CLASS 4 CONTRIBUTIONS for relief for Class 1 contributions paid by a self-employed earner.

Other Sources. Simon's NIC, Part I, Section 2, Chapters 3, 4.95–4.97, 5.122, and Part V, 101, 102 and 121; Tolley's Tax Planning 2000–01 and Tolley's National Insurance Brief, August 1996, specialist sector.

33.1   GENERAL CONSIDERATIONS

The categorisation of entertainers (which includes actor, singer, musician, or any similar performing capacity) for contribution purposes has been a continual source of difficulty and several cases have come before the Secretary of State and the courts. Even where an entertainer is provided through an agency the categorisation question was not always resolved as the categorisation regulations which provide that certain agency workers are to be treated as employed earners specifically excluded

— entertainers

— fashion models

— photographic models

— artist's models

but the position was reversed for entertainers from 17 July 1998 (see 33.2 below).

[Categorisation Regs, Reg 2, 1 Sch Pt I Para 2(b) as amended by Social Security (Categorisation of Earners) Amendment Regs 1998, SI 1998 No 1728, Reg 3]. It follows that the employment status of all such persons must be decided in accordance with the common law.

33.2   ACTORS AND STAGE AND SCREEN PERFORMERS

Almost all the published decisions in this area have been arrived at by application of the control test (see 14.5 CATEGORISATION). As the degree of control exerted over an entertainer tends to be much greater in the case of extended or resident (rather than short or single) engagements, the duration of the contract is of great significance. Entertainers who appear regularly in a radio or TV series normally have a contract of service and are therefore treated as employed earners. This applies even though they may do other work which is classed as that of a self-employed earner.

In *Gould v Minister of National Insurance [1951] 1 AER 368*, the engagement of Gould and his partner was for one week and the only control of any significance was a reserved right on the part of the theatre management to prohibit the whole or part of Gould's act. The performing of the act itself was, however, quite outside the management's control and rested solely on Gould's skill, personality and artistry. Gould was, accordingly, held to be a *self-employed* earner.

In *Stagecraft Ltd v Minister of National Insurance [1952] SC 288*, however, the engagement was for almost six months and the two comedians involved were under the direction of a producer and were obliged to collaborate with other artists involved in the performances produced. The two comedians were, accordingly, held to be *employed* earners.

Similarly, in *Campbell v Minister of National Insurance (1952)* (unreported except as part of the Minister of State's formal decision *M28 (1952)* against which the case was brought on appeal), a film actress was held to be an *employed* earner as her contract with the film company by which she was engaged extended over two years during which time the company had complete control over her. The fact that the actress had to bring her personal talents to her performance was held to have no bearing on the situation.

Similarly, in *Fall v Hitchen [1973] 1 AER 368* (a tax case), a professional ballet dancer was held to be an *employed* earner because the company by which he was engaged had secured his virtually exclusive services for a minimum period of rehearsals plus 22 weeks during which the dancer was to work specified hours for a regular salary.

In *Davies v Braithwaite (1932) 18 TC 198* (also a tax case), the important point was made that if a person finds a method of earning a livelihood which does not involve acquiring a post and continuing to occupy it, but which involves rather 'a series of engagements' and moving from one to the other, each of those engagements cannot be considered an employment but is a mere *engagement in the course of exercising a profession* (per Rowlatt J at p 203). This principle is embodied in the economic reality test (see 14.6 CATEGORISATION) and also accords with the decision in *Hall v Lorimer* (see 38.10 LABOUR-ONLY CONTRACTORS). Although that test was applied only in the *Fall* case of those referred to above, it would, it is suggested, have produced results consistent with the decisions reached. For an example of its recent application in a national insurance case see 33.3 below.

The present position concerning stage performers is one of great difficulty. Publicity during the early part of 1990 highlighted a hardening of the Inland Revenue's attitude towards theatrical performers, in that any performer working under the standard Equity contract is now automatically treated as an employee for income tax purposes but is allowed, by virtue of *ICTA 1988, s 201A (introduced by FA 1990, s 77 and amended by FA 1991, s 69)*, a deduction for certain agents' fees. Attempts during the Finance Bill debates to grant automatic or voluntary Schedule D status to actors came to nothing. On a purely concessionary basis, however, the Inland Revenue agreed that any such performer who could prove that he or she had been dealt with before 6 April 1987 under Schedule D could continue on that basis indefinitely (known as 'reserved Schedule D status'), but any new entrant to the profession after that date will now automatically be dealt with under Schedule E.

The Inland Revenue bases its position on the *Fall v Hitchen* case (see above) which established that the Esher Standard Contract for Ballet (a standard Equity contract) was a contract of service rather than a contract for services. In the past, it was furthermore argued that any contract which extended over three months or more (whether or not an Equity contract and whatever the true nature of the Equity contract might be) could not be regarded as merely one of a series of successive contracts which were entered into in the course of exercising a profession such as that which was found to be exercised in the *Davies v Braithwaite* case (see above).

The DSS view continued to be that the Equity contract is clearly a contract of service, however long the engagement, principally because it gives a very detailed degree of control over the performer and it requires personal service to be provided. The Inland Revenue's past treatment of performers and its current treatment of those with reserved Schedule D status were seen by the DSS as purely concessionary, aimed at simplifying the collection of tax and no more. The DSS expected the producer in each case to deduct and account for Class 1 contributions, irrespective of the income tax treatment unless it is a clear cut case of Schedule D status. In September 1993 the Special Commissioners ruled that live theatre work by actors Sam West and Alec McCowan should be taxed under Schedule D and not Schedule E. The Inland Revenue stated that they would not appeal against the Commissioners' decision. The basis of the decision was understood to be that a series of roles played amounted to incidents in a professional self-employed career, which enabled the Special Commissioners to distinguish the case from *Fall v Hitchen*. This accords with the decision in *Hall v Lorimer* (see 38.10 LABOUR-ONLY CONTRACTORS).

It is submitted that, until the *McCowan* and *West* decisions (see 38.10 LABOUR-ONLY CONTRACTORS), neither the DSS nor the Inland Revenue gave due weight to the *Davies v Braithwaite* decision and that any performer who wishes to establish or retain self-employed status should, where possible, enter into only renewable short-term contracts and should consider not using the Equity standard contract but rather a contract drawn up with different terms and conditions which supports any claim to self-employed status.

In answer to a delegate's question on 'status' at the CA Specialist Conference on 27 October 1997 it was stated:

'The matter is being looked at as we speak. It has been under review for quite some time. It was under review with the previous Government as most people will know, it was not resolved before the election. It is being put to present Government and additional discussions have been taking place with interested parties in the industry. Particularly the likes of Equity and I can assure you that an announcement will be made very quickly after a decision is reached by Ministers. I couldn't give you a date.'

On 20 November 1997, Mr Denham, then Secretary of State for Social Security said in the House of Commons:

'We are considering the status of actors for National Insurance purposes and an announcement will be made in due course.'

This announcement was made on 15 July 1998.

After many years of prevarication, the DSS admitted in Press Release 98/202 (15 July 1998) that its view that actors and musicians are always employees could not, in fact, be sustained. However, many such persons are, with effect from 17 July 1998 to be categorised specially as if they were employees for NICs purposes. This will not affect the income tax position where status will continue to be determined according to basic case law principles. These regulations were to cease to have effect on 1 February 1999 but that cessation date was subsequently removed by further regulations. [*Categorisation Amendments Regs 1999*].

The advantage of Class 1 liability to performers is, of course, that they may qualify when they are 'resting' for contributions based jobseeker's allowance, which would not be the case for Class 2 contributors. It is possible that this may be the underlying reason for any enthusiasm shown by actors' representatives for treatment as employees. The disadvantage is that each engagement will be treated as a separate employment for Class 1 purposes with the result that contributions in excess of the ANNUAL MAXIMUM (see 7.2) may be paid. In certain circumstances, of course, Class 1 DEFERMENT OF PAYMENT (see 27.2) may be available or repayments obtained (see REPAYMENT AND REALLOCATION (53)).

33.3   MUSICIANS

A number of decisions have been made by the courts concerning the employment status of musicians who play in bands and orchestras.

In the early case of *Performing Right Society Ltd v Mitchell & Booker (Palais de Danse) Ltd [1924] 1 KB 762* it was held that the members of a dance band were *employed earners* because the band was subject to 'continuous dominant and detailed control on every point, including the nature of the music to be played'.

In the Minister of State's decision *M14 (1950)*, it was held that the leader of a dance band engaged by an hotel was a *self-employed* earner but that the members of his band were *employed earners* by reason of the fact that, while the leader was not himself subject to detailed control, he exercised detailed control over the members, handled the hotel's complaints concerning the band, and paid them wages from the weekly engagement fee which he received from the hotel.

That decision contrasts with that of the Employment Appeal Tribunal in *Winfield v London Philharmonic Orchestra Ltd [1979] ICR 726* (an employment law case) where it was held that the members of the orchestra were *self-employed earners*. That conclusion followed from the finding that the relationship between the company and the individual players was not that of 'a boss and his musician employees' but that an orchestra was 'a cooperative of distinguished musicians running themselves with self and mutual discipline'.

In *Addison v London Philharmonic Orchestra Ltd [1981] ICR 261* (an employment law case), it was held that an associate player and three additional players of the London Philharmonic Orchestra were *self-employed* earners. This was because, when playing with the orchestra, each remained essentially a freelance musician and pursued his or her own profession as an instrumentalist. Their skills and interpretative powers were contributed by them to the orchestra as independent contractors.

Similarly, in *Midland Sinfonia Concert Society Ltd v Secretary of State for Social Services [1981] ICR 454*, it was held that musicians engaged to perform in an orchestra in individual concerts and rehearsals by separate invitation and remunerated solely in respect of each engagement are *self-employed* earners. That decision reversed the determination by the Secretary of State on 21 July 1978 that the individuals concerned were employed earners.

The most recent 'musician' case concerning status is *Jowitt v London Symphony Orchestra Ltd, 5 November 1990, EAT 301/90*. Mr Jowitt was co-principal clarinettist with the London Symphony Orchestra. Although he was being treated as self-employed for tax and national insurance purposes and was registered for VAT, upon having his appointment terminated by the LSO because of a disagreement, he complained to an industrial tribunal that, as an *employee* of the orchestra, he had been unfairly dismissed within the terms of the *Employment Protection (Consolidation) Act 1978*.

The question of Mr Jowitt's true status fell to be determined by the Employment Appeals Tribunal and, on the basis of the following facts, the EAT decided that Mr Jowitt was indeed *self-employed*.

(*a*) He was subject to rules and regulations for performing members of the orchestra, including a rule which gave the orchestra director power, on giving a member six months' notice, to require that member to 'block off' specific periods during which he would have to give the orchestra his 'exclusive services'.

(*b*) He was, in practice, 'blocked off' only for some two or three months of each year and at other times was free to organise his musical life as he wished.

(*c*) During his free time, he played solo or for other orchestras and only ever accepted about two out of every three 'calls to play' offered by the LSO outside of 'blocked off' periods.

The EAT decided that

(i) the 'control' factor which, according to Mr Jowitt, meant that he was really an employee was not decisive in that it was only the minimum amount of control necessary to 'get an orchestra sufficiently made up' to play an engagement; and

(ii) the 'exclusivity' factor, which again, according to Mr Jowitt, made him an employee was not decisive of employee status either. Very importantly, the EAT decided that *there was no reason why a self-employed person should not say by agreement 'I will give my services to you (the employer or payer) for a given period of time'*.

The status of individual club musicians is more problematical because 'the forms of engagement of musicians working in clubs vary and the employment status of any individual musician will depend on the particular facts'. (Hansard 5 December 1983 Vol 150 Col 26). Where, however, the facts reveal (as they often will) that the engagement is an ongoing one and that the musician is closely controlled by the management of the club in which he performs and that such control extends beyond the mere dictation of the dates, times and duration of his appearances, to the dictation of the very content and style of his performances (see 14.5 CATEGORISATION), it will be difficult to resist the contention that the musician is an employed earner under a (possibly unwritten) contract of service to the club. In 1984 the Chancellor of the Exchequer revealed that over 300 club musicians had recently had their self-employed status withdrawn by the Inland Revenue and had been reclassified as employed earners. (Hansard 16 January 1984 Vol 52 Col 14).

In *Warner Holidays Ltd v Secretary of State for Social Services [1983] ICR 440*, two musicians (and a comedian) were held to be *employed earners*. The case was distinguished from the various 'orchestra' cases referred to above in that it did not concern concert or session musicians but musicians who were holiday camp entertainers. Warners had full and exclusive control over them and paid them fixed salaries. The economic reality test was applied and it was found that none of the persons were performing their services as persons in business on their own account. Following the July 1998 announcement by the DSS, the position for musicians will be as set out in 33.2 above.

33.4 CIRCUS PERFORMERS

In *Whittaker v Minister of Pensions and National Insurance [1966] 3 AER 531*, it was held that a trapeze artist engaged by Bertram Mills Circus and paid by the performance was an *employed* earner. Although on the basis of the *Gould* case (see 33.2 above) it had been decided by the Minister of State that Miss Whittaker was self-employed, there were additional factors which made that decision incorrect. Miss Whittaker had a dual role with the circus, being under contract to act as an usherette when not performing and to assist in moving the circus when it transferred to a new location. These factors clearly pointed to control by the company in a sufficient degree to make the contract one of service.

In the Minister of State's decision *M66 (1958)*, it was similarly held that a circus clown engaged not only to clown but also to drive one of the circus vehicles and to assist in erecting and dismantling tents was an *employed* earner.

Perhaps significantly, the entertainers in the *Warner* case (see 33.3 above) had also accepted a dual role: each had general duties in addition to his obligations as a performer.

34 Examiners

Cross-reference. See CATEGORISATION (14).

Other Sources. Leaflet CA 26; Tolley's National Insurance Brief, June 1995.

34.1 Anyone who is gainfully employed as an examiner (other than through an agency—see 4.1 AGENCY WORKERS) will, irrespective of whether or not his employment is under a contract of service or in an office with emoluments chargeable to tax under Schedule E, be treated as falling into the category of *self-employed earner* provided

    (*a*) the person employing him is responsible for the conduct or administration of an examination leading to a certificate, diploma, degree or professional qualification, *and*

    (*b*) his duties are to examine, moderate, invigilate or act in a similar capacity, or to set questions or tests for examinations of the kind referred to in (*a*), *and*

    (*c*) his contract is one under which the whole of the work to be performed is to be performed in less than twelve months.

[SSCBA 1992, s 2(2)(b), Categorisation Regs, Reg 2(3); 1 Sch Pt II Para 6].

This regulation is of particular application to those persons who are given short-term (even if renewable) contracts relating to particular examinations, e.g. GCSE and college and university examinations. Its effect is to give most examiners dual status: employed earner status for tax purposes and self-employed earner status for national insurance purposes. In the years leading up to 1984, many examiners were treated as self-employed for tax purposes also but, over those years, more than 100,000 were re-categorised as employed by the Inland Revenue. (Hansard 16 January 1984 Vol 52 Col 14).

Examiners to whom this chapter applies are, if their earnings are sufficiently high, liable for special Class 4 contributions (see 20.5 CLASS 4 CONTRIBUTIONS) based on those earnings.

35 Homeworkers and Outworkers

Cross-reference. See CATEGORISATION (14).

Other Sources. Simon's NIC, Part I, Section 2, Chapter 4.94; Leaflet CA 25.

35.1 CATEGORISATION

A person who performs services in his own home or on other premises not under the control or management of the person for whom he performs them may be either an employed earner or a self-employed earner depending on the nature of the relationship between the parties and whether that relationship indicates the presence of a contract of service or of a contract for services (see CATEGORISATION (14)).

The Secretary of State for Social Security has formally decided, for example, that a person making rugs in her own home for a company engaging disabled persons is not under a contract of service and is, therefore, a *self-employed earner. (M17 (1951))*. He has also decided that a person making-up coats for a tailor, unsupervised, in his own home is *self-employed, (M25 (1952))*, and that an outworker engaged in scissor grinding and finishing who employed his own assistants, supplied his own tools, equipment and materials, was free to process goods for whom he wished, chose his own production methods, was paid by the piece processed, and was unsupervised, was a *self-employed earner*, despite the fact that he rented and occupied premises in the factory of his main customer and undertook the whole of that customer's grinding and finishing work. *(M35 (1953))*.

In *Westall Richardson Ltd v Roulson [1954] 2 AER 448*, the court held that another outworker in the Sheffield cutlery trade—a mirror finisher of cutlery whose working arrangements were virtually identical with those described in *M35* above—was also a *self-employed earner* for, although there was 'some element of service or servitude in his position' there was 'a far greater element of independence and freedom'.

Conversely, an industrial tribunal found in *D'Ambrogio v Hyman Jacobs [1978] IRLR 236* that a machinist working at home and using equipment and materials supplied to her by the person for whom she worked was an *employed earner* because the person for whom she worked called at her home daily and exercised a high degree of control over her—something the Secretary of State had found lacking in the two cases referred to earlier.

Although control is of great importance, however, lack of it will not be decisive. In *Airfix Footwear Ltd v Cope [1978] ICR 1210*, the Employment Appeal Tribunal upheld a finding that a person who assembled shoe parts in her own home was an *employed earner* and in *Nethermere (St Neots) Ltd v Gardiner [1984] ICR 615* the Court of Appeal upheld an Employment Appeal Tribunal decision that a person who made-up boys' trousers in her own home was an *employed earner*. In both these cases, the courts emphasised the failure of the economic reality test of self-employment (see 14.6 CATEGORISATION) and stressed the ongoing and dependent nature of the working relationship between the persons concerned and the persons for whom they worked. It will be noted that, had the economic reality test been applied in *Westall Richardson Ltd v Roulson* (see above), it would have fully supported the outcome.

35.2 AGENCY WORKERS

The only circumstance in which the categorisation of a homeworker or outworker is in no doubt is where the person falls within the AGENCY WORKERS (see 4.1) category and is, by *reason of the nature of the services he renders*, required to render that service in his own home or on other premises not under the control or management of the person to whom he is supplied. Such a person is to be categorised as an *employed earner*. [*SSCBA 1992, s 2(2)(b); Categorisation Regs, Reg 2(2), 1 Sch Pt I Para 2(2)(a)*].

One example of such a situation will arise where an audit clerk supplied by an agency to an accountant is, according to normal practice, sent to work on an audit at the premises of one of the accountant's clients. (Leaflet CA 25).

Anyone who, though an agency worker and though working at home or on other premises not under the control or management of the person to whom he is supplied, does not do so by reason of the nature of the services is, however, to be categorised according to whether he is under a contract of service or not, and *not* under the special rules relating to AGENCY WORKERS (see 4.5). [*Categorisation Regs, Reg 2(2), 1 Sch Pt I Para 2(2)(a)*].

36   Husband and Wife

Cross-references. See CATEGORISATION (14); CLASS 1 CONTRIBUTIONS (15); CLASS 2 CONTRIBUTIONS (18); CLASS 4 CONTRIBUTIONS (20); PARTNERS (50).

Other Sources. Tolley's Partnership Taxation; Tolley's Income Tax 2000–01; Tolley's Tax Planning 2000–01.

36.1   EMPLOYMENT BY SPOUSE

A person who is employed by his or her spouse for the purpose of the spouse's employment is to be treated as falling within the category of employed earner despite the probable absence of a contract of service. [*SSCBA 1992, s 2(2)(a); Categorisation Regs, Reg 2(2), 1 Sch Pt I Para 3*]. Employment of a person by his or her spouse otherwise than for the purpose of the spouse's employment is to be entirely disregarded whether under a contract of service or not. [*SSCBA 1992, s 2(2)(b); Categorisation Regs, Reg 2(4), 1 Sch Pt III Para 8*].

Where a person is to be treated as an employed earner under these regulations, that person's spouse will fall to be treated as the *secondary contributor*. [*SSCBA 1992, s 7(2); Categorisation Regs, Reg 5, 3 Sch 3*]. He will be responsible for paying and accounting for contributions in the normal way (see CLASS 1 CONTRIBUTIONS (15), COLLECTION (21)).

Where a husband and wife in fact run a business jointly (e.g. a public house), it may be that the wife is in partnership with her husband (rather than being employed by him) and is entitled to a half share in the profits whether she has ever claimed a share or not. (*Nixon v Nixon [1969] 1 WLR 1676, Re Cummins [1972] Ch 62, R(P)1/76*). In that event both the husband and the wife should be self-employed earners and a Class 2 and Class 4 liability may accordingly arise for each of them unless the NICO argues that one spouse spends so little time working in the business (e.g. less than an hour or two per week) that he or she is to be treated as being other than ordinarily self-employed and accordingly has no Class 2 liability, however much is received as a share of the profits. It should be noted that such a decision would apparently contradict the advice given previously to Adjudication Officers, which is that 'the owner of a business, representing to the Inland Revenue that the profits from the business are income, should be regarded as gainfully employed continuously in the business *even if taking little or no direct part in the running of it*.' (Author's italics) (AOG Vol 6, 50065).

The expression 'spouse's employment' in the *Categorisation Regs* is not confined to spouse's self-employment (though that is the usual case where this regulation applies) but extends to spouse's employed earner's employment also.

Example
On 25 October 2000 Alf, a sales representative, is disqualified from driving and, in order not to lose his job, employs Bet, his wife, as his chauffeuse. He pays B £97 a week. B will suffer a primary Class 1 contribution of £2.10 (i.e. £76 @ Nil% + £21 @ 10%) and A will have to pay a secondary Class 1 contribution of £1.59 (i.e. £84 @ Nil% + £13 @ 12.2%).

NB. It *may* be that both A and B will escape contribution liability entirely if B is unremunerated and A's employer, discovering that B is acting as his unpaid chauffeuse, pays B, on his own volition and merely in token recognition of the help she is giving A, £97 a week. A wife who helped her public school housemaster husband in his work was thus sent monthly cheques by the school bursar in monetary recognition of her contribution to the school and the Secretary of State formally decided that she was neither gainfully employed by her husband nor under a contract of service with the school nor ordinarily self-employed for the purposes of gain (*M47 (1956)*).

It is generally accepted by both the Inland Revenue and, in the past, the DSS that a self-employed earner's spouse has an almost inevitable involvement in the business (e.g. telephone answering, book-keeping, making appointments). This being so, remuneration at a modest level will usually be justifiable and should be physically paid. (*Copeman v William Flood & Sons Ltd (1940) 24 TC 53; Abbot v IRC (1996) STC SSCD 41 Sp C 58*). It will avoid complications with tax and national insurance if such remuneration is below the level at which either would be levied. For 2000–01 this is the amount of the employee's earnings threshold i.e. £76 per week for contribution purposes. It should not, however, be overlooked that payment below the LEL i.e. £67 for 2000-01, which does not attract a contribution liability, prevents the accumulation of a contribution record which in turn affects future benefit entitlement of the spouse (see EARNINGS FACTORS (29)). With the introduction of the *National Minimum Wage Act 1998* currently at £3.60 per hour (£3.70 per hour from October 2000) the employer husband/wife should ensure that not only does their calculation come below the earnings threshold but also it should not come below the minimum national wage for the hours actually worked. There are certain exclusions from the Act but these are not within the scope of this book.

36.2   JOINT EMPLOYMENT

Where a husband and wife are jointly employed in employed earner's employment (e.g. as wardens of a hostel or managers of a hotel) and earnings in respect of that employment are paid to them jointly, the amount of the earnings of each is, for Class 1 contribution purposes, to be calculated on the same basis as that on which it is calculated for tax purposes. (See Leaflet CWG2 (2000), Page 16). In the absence of such a calculation, it will be calculated upon such basis as the Inland Revenue may approve. [*Contributions Regs, Reg 16*]. In ascertaining the amount of earnings for benefit claim purposes, the Social Security Commissioners divided such sums according to the proportion of the work performed by each spouse. (AOG Vol 6, 50341).

A wife who worked with her husband (and children) as a cherry picker on a farm was held to be an employed earner in joint employment with her husband, even though the husband alone was paid for their combined pickings. (*M8 (1950)*).

Both spouses will be treated as gainfully employed where they are appointed jointly to an employment or, where only one has been appointed, there is an express or implied term of the contract of service that the other should assist in the duties. In the absence of any such term, the spouse's services are deemed voluntary and gratuitous. He or she is then deemed not to be gainfully employed. (AOG Vol 6, 50113-4).

36.3   SELF-EMPLOYED WIFE

For Class 4 contribution purposes, a wife's profits or gains for years of assessment up to 5 April 1990 were to be computed as if *ICTA 1988, s 279* did *not* apply. [*SSA 1975, 2 Sch 4(3) repealed for 1990–91 onwards by FA 1988, s 148, 14 Sch, Pt VIII*]. (*ICTA 1988, s 279* provided that, in the absence of an approved application under *ICTA 1988, s 283* for separate assessment of husband and wife for tax purposes or an election under *ICTA 1988, s 287* for separate taxation of a wife's earnings, a wife's profits or gains from self-employment were to be treated as part of her husband's income for tax purposes.) The need for such a deeming provision was obviated by the introduction on 6 April 1990 of the system of independent taxation of husband and wife. It remains the case, therefore, that a self-employed wife is, irrespective of her tax position, to be regarded as a *femme sole* for the purpose of *calculating* her Class 4 contribution liability and that, for example, any losses which her husband has incurred in self-employment, cannot be set off against her profits. Once calculation of the Class 4 liability has taken place, that liability is now to be *assessed on and recovered from* her whereas, under the former rules, her husband would have been liable in the absence of an election for separate assessment or separate taxation of her earnings. [*SSA 1975, 2 Sch 4(1)(3) repealed for 1990–91 onwards by FA 1988, s 148, 14 Sch, Pt VIII*] (see also Inspector's Manual, para 6030, issue 12/94).

Where a husband was liable to pay Class 4 contributions in respect of his wife's profits or gains under the rules formerly in force, the *Contribution Regs* concerning Class 4 contributions (except those relating to assessment, appeals or claims under the Income Tax Acts or certification by the Inland Revenue) were nonetheless to apply as if the wife were separately assessed. [*Contribution Regs, Reg 79 now revoked by Contributions Amendment No 5 Regs 1991, Reg 3*].

An application or election for separate assessment or taxation of a wife's earnings was not possible for Class 4 purposes only. [*2 Sch 4(2) repealed for 1990–91 onwards by FA 1988, s 148, 14 Sch, Pt VIII*].

36.4   PARTNERSHIP

The principles stated at 36.3 above apply equally where a husband and wife carry on business together in partnership. Each is liable to pay Class 2 contributions unless specifically excepted from such liability (see CLASS 2 CONTRIBUTIONS (18)) or unless, in the case of the wife, a reduced rate election is in force (see REDUCED LIABILITY ELECTIONS (52)). The husband will now no longer be liable to pay any Class 4 contributions arising on his wife's share of the profits or gains which, prior to 6 April 1990, would have been the case even in the absence of an application or election for separate assessment or taxation of his wife's earnings. This was so despite the fact that each spouse's share of profits or gains was to be separately computed and to be separately subjected to Class 4 EARNINGS LIMITS (see 30.6) in the same way as in any partnership (see PARTNERS (50)).

37   Inland Revenue: Co-ordination with the DSS

Cross-references. See ARREARS OF CONTRIBUTIONS (12) for Inland Revenue enforcement powers and role of collector of taxes regarding Class 1 contributions; 14.11 CATEGORISATION for relevance of treatment of contributors; COLLECTION (21).

37.1   COLLECTION

From 1 April 1999, national insurance administration is dealt with by the Inland Revenue following *SSC(T)A 1999*. Information obtained for tax purposes may therefore be readily passed to colleagues in other sections of the Inland Revenue, including those dealing with national insurance contributions, and *vice versa*. The DSS and the Inland Revenue are entirely separate departments of Government but, because until 1 April 1999 they had an area of common concern, i.e. the collection of taxes and contributions levied by Parliament on a common portion of the subject's income, the function of the DSS was, in that area, performed (though not completely) by the Inland Revenue. Thus, the Inland Revenue collected almost all primary and secondary Class 1 contributions and Class 4 contributions due to the DSS and, from time to time, paid these over to the National Insurance Fund (see COLLECTION (21)).

Following the transfer, there remain areas of common interest, including:

- the possibility that Inland Revenue officers may, under arrangements made with the Secretary of State for Social Security, carry out duties under *SSAA 1992, s110* in connection with benefit matters (see 37.3);

- the operation of NIRS 2, the contribution recording system, which lies with the Inland Revenue following the transfer, although the Benefits Agency and other parts of DSS are major users;

- the need for liaison if the Benefits Agency are to allow a claim for contributory benefit if the required contributions were not paid on time due to misinformation or other error on the part of Inland Revenue NICO.

37.2   DISCLOSURE OF INFORMATION

The obligation of secrecy imposed on persons employed in relation to Inland Revenue and Customs & Excise (or by a person providing services to both of these) was not to prevent information obtained or held in connection with the assessment and collection of income tax from being disclosed (by or under Inland Revenue authority) to the DSS in connection with the calculation or collection of national insurance contributions. [*SSAA 1992, s 122(1) as amended by Social Security Contributions (Transfer of Functions, etc.) Act 1999, 6 Sch 2*]. Information held by the Inland Revenue in connection with contributions, SSP or SMP may be supplied, and must be supplied if requested, to the DSS in connection with social security, child support or war pensions matters. Similarly, information held by DSS in those connections may be disclosed to the Inland Revenue for contributions, SSP and SMP purposes. [*SSAA 1992, ss 121E, 121F as inserted by SSC(T)A 1999*]. Once information is disclosed to the DSS the Department is as bound as the Inland Revenue not to disclose that information further, unless such further disclosure is for the purpose of civil or criminal proceedings in relation to contribution law or the determination of a question by the Secretary of State. [*Sec 122(3)*]. The Field Operations Manual of the former CA, paragraphs 9000-9002 stated at:

9000 All civil servants are bound by a duty of confidentiality. All information received in the course of duty must be used for official purposes for which it was obtained.

9001 Information given by customers, insured persons and others is obtained and held by the Department in strictest confidence.

9002 Members of the public must be able to rely absolutely on that confidence being maintained or the work and reputation of the Department will inevitably suffer.

and under paragraph 9400 the following:

9400 The *Social Security Administration Act 1992 (section 122)* permits the Inland Revenue to disclose information to the Secretary of State, the Northern Ireland Department, or to an officer of either Department who is authorised to receive that information in connection with any matters either under the *Social Security Contributions and Benefits Act 1992* or the *Social Security Administration Act 1992* or their Northern Ireland equivalents. It does not provide for a mutual exchange of information.

As the Inland Revenue and the Customs and Excise are authorised to disclose to each other information relevant to their respective duties, it may be that, in some circumstances, information passed to the DSS will have originated in Customs and Excise files. [*FA 1972, s 127*].

The *Social Security Contributions (Transfer of Functions, etc.) Act 1999, 6 Sch 3* inserts a new *SSAA 1992, s 122AA* which lifts the secrecy imposition on the Inland Revenue relating to contributions (also SMP and SSP). Disclosure may be made to the Health and Safety Executive, Government Actuary's Department, Office for National Statistics and Occupational Pensions Regulatory Authority.

Example
The DSS have, following the receipt of information on their newly set up fraud hotline, received information that individual X has been claiming benefit and that he is married and for the past four years he has been receiving unemployment benefit/income support (now Jobseeker's Allowance) relevant to a married person. However, on investigation by the DSS Inspector the marriage certificate is proved to be a forgery and a prosecution is instigated by the DSS. Although the DSS may inform the Inland Revenue who may wish to investigate previous claims for the married couple's allowance on tax returns, neither the DSS or IR can at this stage advise the Registrar General of Births, Deaths and Marriages who would be obliged to undertake proceedings under the *Perjury Act 1911, s 3(1)*.

37.3   INSPECTION

Where premises are liable to be inspected by the Inland Revenue under *SSAA 1992, s 110ZA* (see 32 ENFORCEMENT) the Secretary of State for Social Security may make arrangements for powers or duties of inspectors for social security, child support or war pensions functions to be carried out by the Inland Revenue officer(s). [*SSAA 1992, s 110(5) as inserted by SSC(T)A 1999*].

During 1983–84 a pilot scheme was implemented under which DSS inspectors, when examining wages records for contribution purposes, conducted a PAYE examination also and reported to the Inland Revenue any irregularities which were brought to light. The object was to assess whether such a scheme would reduce the number of official visits to employers' premises and whether many follow-up visits by the Inland Revenue's own PAYE audit inspection teams would be required. (Hansard Vol 44 No 4 Col 56). The scheme was so successful that, on 13 December 1985, a decision was taken to implement it on a nationwide basis. (Inland Revenue Press Release). The scheme remained fully operational and has resulted in 'closer coordination between PAYE auditors and National Insurance inspectors in planning visits to employers' premises' which should 'relieve employers from unnecessarily separate visits from the two Departments'. ('Building businesses ... not barriers' Cmnd 9794 Para 6.12). It also meant, however, that more employers would be visited with greater frequency than would otherwise be the case, and that there was a far greater chance of non-compliance with the requirements of contribution law being discovered. One problem which was, however, reported is that an auditor or investigator from one department is not trained in the legislation governing the other department's operations. Therefore, although an Inland Revenue inspection may include an examination of the contribution records, employers were entitled to ensure that a settlement in respect of underpayments was not reached on false premises, e.g. income tax law applied where contribution law is required. Indeed, it is open to an employer to insist that any matter of dispute relating to contribution liability be referred to the DSS rather than be dealt with by the Inland Revenue team.

It remains the case, from 1 April 1999, notwithstanding that it is the Inland Revenue who now administer the national insurance system, that national insurance liability can only be determined under social security legislation. The legislation, if producing a different effect for tax purposes, is of no relevance.

It became routine that any determination made by the Inland Revenue under *Income Tax (Employments) Regs 1993, Reg 49* in respect of under-declarations of PAYE was copied to the DSS so that appropriate action is taken to recover any associated Class 1 arrears, see *R v CIR ex parte McVeigh [1996] STC 91*. This process is no doubt be even more automatic following the transfer on 1 April 1999. In *Pawlowski v Dunnington [1999] STC 550* the taxpayer waited until the Collector was seeking payment through the County Court before arguing that the Collector had not put forward any evidence to support the determinations. The Collector's claim was dismissed and it was held that the taxpayer was able to put forward a public law defence.

Following the tripartite announcement on 19 September 1995 (Tax and National Insurance Red Tape Cut for Business) there was a single audit visit carried out with each employer concerning both PAYE and NIC. In an interview with Payroll Manager's Review in early 1996, Mrs Faith Boardman, the former Chief Executive of the CA, said

'. . . we have actually started joint visits. It's quite early days yet and we have not done very many. The initial feedback suggests that they have been well-received, particularly by larger employers . . . . The first step is very much concentrated on trying to ensure that our Inspectors have sufficient working knowledge of PAYE to identify problems but equally to identify areas which aren't problems. Our wish is to keep the follow-up visits and queries which we pass on to our Inland Revenue colleagues to the minimum.'

Later, in 1997 it was stated:

'The single audit joint working project has ensured that a visit by both the Contributions Agency and the Inland Revenue within 12 months does not occur. Procedures are in place for each Department to forward copies of prospective visits to their respective Departments ahead of notification to the employer. As a consequence, each can then ensure that employers earmarked for visit are not visited if the other Department has them on their itinerary. Discussion takes place between the two Departments to ensure that the visit is undertaken by the most appropriate Department. The single audit should ensure that when CA decide to refer a case to IR they will do so within 10 days of notifying the employer that it is to be referred. The IR will acknowledge the receipt of that referral within 10 days and make contact with the employer within 1 month in 75% of all referrals and 2 months in 95% of all cases.'

Feedback from statistical returns shows that these targets are being met.

A project was set up to examine the working practises of each Department in terms of their approach to Audit.

Reports from CA and IR Regions revealed that instances of duplicate visits were minimal and that employers, where they commented, were pleased with the approach that both Departments took with regard to Joint Working.

The IR's National Audit Group deals with roughly the 3,000 largest employers in the UK. The former CA's Large Employers Unit (LEU but now the Large Employers Compliance Office) will have included the same employers in its own database. The LECO and NAG agreed a programme of joint visits. Latterly employers with more than 1,000 employees or groups of companies were being visited jointly. The LEU were committed to an increasing schedule of joint visits. To achieve this the working practises of both Departments were examined by a joint steering group with the intention that operational methods were aligned wherever possible. A joint opening letter to employers was used and identical best practice guidance notes were issued to all the staff within LEU and NAG.

Three regions have been selected for trials of a wider payroll cleanse; these are Scotland (for all employers), Anglia (employers with over 25 employees) and North East Thames (employers with over 200 employees).

CA Specialist Conference written responses, item 8d, 4 February 1997 and CA Specialist Conference, 29 October 1997.

Following the transfer on 1 April 1999, the former CA Large Employers Unit has been subsumed into Schedule E Compliance Office, operating out of West Midlands and Newcastle.

37.4 Class 6 Settlements

If, as a result of a PAYE inspection during which income tax underpayments are discovered, an employer is invited to make a voluntary offer in consideration of the Board of Inland Revenue agreeing not to take formal proceedings to recover tax, interest and penalties (referred to by the Inland Revenue as a Class 6 settlement), it is Inland Revenue practice to augment the figure for lost income tax by (currently) 12.2% to represent a hypothetical secondary Class 1 liability on the tax borne by the employer on the grounds that he is meeting what should have been the employee's liability if PAYE had been operated correctly. Under the rule in *Hartland v Diggines [1926] 10 TC 247* the discharge of employees' tax liabilities is equivalent to cash payments to those employees. From 6 April 1999, the figure of 12.2% will be used even for years where the employer's rate was 10.4% and subsequently 10.2% and then 10%, since the calculation must be performed at the time of the payment of the alleged liability, not when that liability is claimed to have arisen.

The statutory authority for this practice is weak because a Class 1 liability can only arise where in any tax week earnings are paid to or for the benefit of an earner in respect of any one employment of his which is employed earner's employment (*SSCBA 1992, s 6(1)*). In the case of such a settlement the payment is made in order that the Revenue will waive its right to recover the tax lost by assessment; the payment is not earnings paid to or for the benefit of an earner and so there are no grounds for levying Class 1 contributions. The DSS always rejected this view on the grounds that the voluntary nature of the offer means that the contract, of which it forms part, is merely an administrative easement which cannot be allowed to remove a legal liability for contributions. (Letter from DSS dated 2 September 1993). It is, however, unclear how a valid contract can be entered into other than voluntarily. A second objection is that the settlement figure is rarely calculated precisely enough to establish the exact amount attributable to each employee so that the requirements of *s 6(1)* are satisfied.

Where a Class 1 liability arises on cash payments to employees which should have been payrolled, that liability is not subject to the same objections and may be due at 10.4% where the payments were made before 6 April 1993, 10.2% between 6 April

1993 and 5 April 1997, 10% between 6 April 1997 and 5 April 1999 and 12.2% thereafter. A primary contribution may also be collected.

The introduction of legislation concerning Annual Voluntary Settlements, now called PAYE settlement agreements (PSAs), which enables the Inland Revenue to exact the tax liability from the employer without recourse to the employee, impacts on NICs treatment in such a more regulated environment. [*ICTA 1988, s 206A as inserted by FA 1996, s 110*]. See 17 CLASS 1B CONTRIBUTIONS. In settlement cases, however, the Inland Revenue practice of charging NIC on the tax settlement remains questionable.

37.5   EXTRA-STATUTORY CONCESSIONS

In order to facilitate the working of the tax system and to avoid undue harshness in the application of certain provisions of tax law, the Inland Revenue has published a large number of extra-statutory concessions (IR 1, January 2000) and statements of practice (IR 131, January 2000). It must not be assumed, however, that, where there is an area of common concern to both tax and national insurance contributions, such concession will apply to contribution (either before or after the transfer on 1 April 1999). (See 22.3 COMPANY DIRECTORS.) The Inland Revenue's authority for making concessions for tax is weak, but the DSS's authority was non-existent. Concessions made by the DSS in the past have, therefore, tended to be given statutory force by secondary legislation, although the series of concessions underlying a number of statements in CA 28 Supplement April 1996 states that to mirror the tax treatment the DSS introduced regulations which remove NIC liability on certain Inland Revenue ESCs. [*Contributions Regs 1979, Reg 19(1)(u)(v)(w)(x)*]. Further, at the CA Specialist Conference on 20 February 1996 the CA stated that ESC A4(d) is in any case covered by *Contributions Regs 1979, Reg 19(4)(b)*. The *Social Security (Contributions) Amendment (No 3) Regs 1996, Reg 3* gives the force of law to ESC A6, A65 and A90 from 6 April 1996. Mrs Faith Boardman, the former Chief Executive, when interviewed in February 1996 by Payroll Manager's Review on this subject said

> 'There are a number of specific areas, like AVSs and ESCs, where we both have and will be taking further steps in the public domain. Many of the other areas are technically quite difficult and they would also involve a number of winners and losers, inevitably because the base for the income tax and NICs is so different at present.'

There remain, however, a number of ESCs which have not been mirrored in contribution law and, at the time of the merger, the DSS had no plans for further such harmonisation. (See also CA Press Release 96/1, 15 March 1996.)

37.6   TAX/NICs HARMONISATION

In September 1993, the DSS published a report prepared by a 'Tax/NICs Working Group', set up by the Secretary of State earlier that year under the Deregulation Initiative, to consider how, while respecting both the contributory principle and the need to broaden the tax base, the tax and contributions systems could be more closely aligned so as to remove a perceived burden on business, i.e. the need to operate two sets of rules on one set of earnings. The group comprised Inland Revenue and DSS staff, together with representatives of the DTI Deregulation Unit and a range of employers' representatives, including professional bodies.

The fundamental conclusion of the group was that the Class 1 definition of earnings should be brought as closely as possible into line with the Schedule E definition of emoluments. As a corollary of this, tax dispensations and extra-statutory concessions would be extended to Class 1.

The report offered four options for a change:

Option 1

- PAYE and primary Class 1 contributions would use the same thresholds and the PAYE code for the single personal allowance would be used for Class 1. The LEL would become a contributions-free band like the personal allowance. A second PAYE code would be used to cover tax allowances not relevant to Class 1 (e.g. married couple's allowance, blind person's allowance).

- Year-end adjustments for errors in PAYE codes would apply for Class 1.

- Secondary Class 1 would be calculated as a percentage of gross payroll, with a further charge on taxable benefits and expenses.

Option 2

- Similar to Option 1, but the PAYE code would not apply for Class 1, which would continue as at present with a lower earnings limit, except that the measure of 'earnings' would be the taxable emoluments.

- Both primary and secondary Class 1, collected annually, would apply to benefits and taxable expenses.

Option 3

- PAYE and Class 1 would both continue as at present, except for harmonisation of the definitions of earnings and emoluments, but primary and secondary Class 1 would apply annually to benefits and taxable expenses.

Option 4

- As Option 3, but only secondary contributions would apply to benefits and taxable expenses, effectively applying Class 1A contributions to P11D benefits.

Comments on the report were invited, although no formal consultation process followed publication. However, an informal series of meetings with interested parties took place in late 1994 and early 1995 to discuss how the issues were to be progressed. Nothing was ever published about those discussions and the matter has been superseded by subsequent developments.

There are difficulties with all the options outlined in the report, not least with achieving the alleged aim of deregulation. Many changes seem possible, but it is questionable whether anything other than complete harmonisation would be deregulatory. The restructuring of the LEL into a NIC-free band would entail some restructuring of the contributory benefits system, and this did not find favour with ministers until after the 1997 General Election. Similarly, if full harmonisation were to be achieved, the deduction of pension contributions from 'earnings' would have a significant impact on the SERPS system. There are also numerous difficulties in the international context, since the two charges would then have to be separately identified and calculated where a tax treaty exempted income from tax but a social security treaty or EC regulations led to a Class 1 charge or *vice versa*.

There are also numerous difficulties associated with charging Class 1 contributions on benefits while respecting the contributory principle. An annual Class 1 charge would be a radical departure from the earnings period basis, leaving problems over allocating earnings factors and applying the upper earnings limit.

It is understood that the question of proceeding with complete harmonisation under any of the four options listed above is not considered to be viable by Ministers.

However, several positive results of the more general harmonisation process were seen in the intervening period: acceptance of Inland Revenue dispensations for Class 1, the promise to incorporate extra-statutory concessions for tax into Class 1 regulations and better co-ordination of visits to employers by the Contributions Agency and PAYE Audit (see 37.2 above). The *FA 1995* changes relieving from

Schedule E liability personal incidental expenses and payments to directors and officers under indemnity and insurance arrangements have now been reflected in Class 1 regulations as have other matters mentioned at 37.5 above. Further progress has been reported from time to time e.g. IR Tax Bulletin, Issue 21, page 289 and CA National Insurance News, Issue 5, page 3.

A report 'Work Incentives; A Report by Martin Taylor', having been commissioned by the incoming Government of 1997, was published on 17 March 1998. As regards national insurance contributions, it recommended

1.   The lower earnings limit to become an allowance rather than a limit;

2.   The employer's lower earnings limit to be equalised with the single person's tax allowance (then £81 per week);

3.   The employee's lower earnings limit to be equalised with the single person's allowance (then £81 per week);

4.   National Insurance to be charged on all benefits in kind;

5.   Class 2 to be abolished and replaced with a more appropriate Class 4 regime for the self-employed;

6.   The functions of the Contributions Agency to be carried out by the Inland Revenue.

Items 1, 3 and 4 above were, in fact, amongst the various options set out in the report of September 1993. The Chancellor of the Exchequer, Mr Gordon Brown, announced on 17 March 1998 that items 1,2 and 6 would be adopted with effect from 6 April 1999 (see *SSA 1998, s 51; SSC(T)A, 8 Sch 4*) and item 3 at a later date once the means have been identified to protect the benefit entitlement of those earning between the lower earnings limit and the new earnings threshold. The Chancellor would also consider further items 4 and 5. Then, in the economic and fiscal strategy report 'Budget 99' it was stated that

'From April 2000, the threshold of earnings above which people will pay NICs will increase to £76 per week. A zero rate of NICs will apply on earnings between the previous lower limit and the new threshold, to protect benefit entitlement. The threshold of earnings above which employees will pay no NICs (the upper earnings limit, UEL) will increase to £535 per week. (12)'

and in respect of item 4 the report stated

'From April 2000, employer NICs will be extended to those benefits-in-kind which are already subject to income tax.'

Further, although Class 2 is not abolished it is considerably reduced from 6 April 2000, although by far outweighed by increases in Class 4 contributions for those with higher profits.

As regards item 4, such a change does no more than raise extra revenue for the Government. Harmonisation and co-ordination as regards the tax and national insurance system entails ensuring that those items which are subject to PAYE are also subject to national insurance and those that are *not* subject to PAYE are also *not* subject to national insurance contributions. To impose a national insurance charge where PAYE is not applicable (probably because it has been recognised that either it is not possible to make a deduction from the item in question because of its nature or else it is not possible to quantify the amount at the time that deduction is required) simply because, ultimately, the item is a taxable item does nothing to harmonise the systems from the employer's perspective. It is anticipated that the charge on all benefits in kind will be achieved by extending the current Class 1A charge. That being so, the difficulties mentioned above will be alleviated, but there remain many areas where the operation is inconsistent, not least of which is the newly introduced charge on non-cash vouchers with effect from 6 April 1999 (see EARNINGS (28)).

38   Labour-Only Contractors

Cross-references. See AGENCY WORKERS (4); CATEGORISATION (14); 20.4 CLASS 4 CONTRIBUTIONS for relief for Class 1 contributions paid by a self-employed earner; 21.14 COLLECTION for treatment of deductions made by contractors from amounts paid to subcontractors in the construction industry; ENTERTAINERS (33); EXAMINERS (34); HOMEWORKERS AND OUTWORKERS (35); LECTURERS, TEACHERS AND INSTRUCTORS (41); WORKING CASE STUDY (58).

Other Sources. Simon's NIC, Part I; IR Tax Bulletin, April 1997, pages 405–413; Leaflets IR 148/CA 69, IR 56/NI 39 and IR 157.

38.1   GENERAL CONSIDERATIONS

By 'labour-only contractor' is meant anyone who purports to supply services consisting entirely of his own labour to another, not as an employee but as an independent contractor. It does, therefore, include persons working in the building and construction industry, but is by no means confined to such persons.

Persons within the scope of this definition tend to be viewed with some suspicion by the Inland Revenue since the contracts or agreements on which their status rests may be found to be matters of mere form disguising their true status as employed earners and devised with the objective of reducing contribution liability (see 8.1 ANTI-AVOIDANCE). This suspicion on the part of the Inland Revenue was further underlined by the Budget Day press release (IR35) on 9 March 1999; the now notorious 'IR35' regarding the restriction placed on personal service companies from 6 April 2000. The Inland Revenue have issued draft tax legislation and final NIC regulations so that those undertaking such services will have additional or, in some cases, new PAYE and NICs deductions to account for. This is a continuing attack on the self-employed. See 14.17 CATEGORISATION and *www.inlandrevenue. gov.uk.IR35*. [See draft Finance Act 2000, clause 59 and Sch 12; *Social Security Contributions (Intermediaries) Regs 2000, SI 2000/727; Welfare Reform and Pensions Act 1999, ss 75 and 76* and *Welfare Reform and Pensions Act 1999 (Commencement No 2) Order 1999, SI 1999/3420*].

Of particular importance in the wider group of labour-only contractors are casual workers. The case of *O'Kelly v Trusthouse Forte plc* (discussed at 38.7 below) underlined the fact that the employment status of a casual worker who works regularly for one employer will depend on whether or not there exists an ongoing obligation on the part of the person who employs him to supply him with work and an ongoing obligation on the part of the worker to take work which is offered (see 14.4 CATEGORISATION). In the absence of such mutual obligations there can be no 'umbrella' contract of service and each engagement (however regular) will generally constitute a contract for services rather than a contract of service. In those circumstances, the casual worker will (unless he obtains his engagements through an agency under the conditions described at 4.1 AGENCY WORKERS) fall to be categorised as a *self-employed earner*.

38.2   CATEGORIES OF LABOUR-ONLY CONTRACTORS

Sales representatives

Commercial agents who are remunerated on a commission-only basis are a source of categorisation difficulty in that the terms under which they perform their services are seldom conclusive evidence of employment or self-employment.

In *Egginton v Reader [1936] 3 AER 7* it was held that a sales representative who was remunerated by commission only, sought sales where he thought fit, was free to act as a representative of other companies, and was not subject to any orders or directions from the company which he represented, was a *self-employed earner*. A sales representative operating on similar terms was also held to be a *self-employed earner* in *Chadwick v Pioneer Private Telephone Co Ltd [1941] 1 AER 522*.

In *Willy Scheidegger Swiss Typewriting School (London) Ltd v Minister of Social Security (1968) 5 KIR 65* it was decided, following *Rolls Razor v Cox [1967] 1 QB 552*, that sales representatives who were paid only by results, were liable to dismissal if sales targets were not reached, worked to no fixed hours or days, had to meet their own expenses, and were at liberty to undertake non-competitive work, were, despite an obligation to pursue the sales policies of the company and to obey all its lawful orders, *self-employed* earners.

In the formal determination against which the *Scheidegger* case was an appeal, the Minister had, on those facts, decided that the sales representatives were employed earners, emphasising the control implicit in the terms relating to the carrying out of sales policies and obedience to lawful orders.

Control (or lack of it) was the deciding factor in two earlier determinations by the Secretary of State relating to the status of sales representatives. In *M9 (1950)* a commercial agent who was remunerated on a commission-only basis, visited only such persons and firms as he thought fit, and held another non-competing agency, was held to be a *self-employed* earner. In *M22 (1952)*, however, a commercial agent who, though remunerated on a commission-only basis, was bound by contract to serve the company faithfully and at all times to obey instructions, was held to be an *employed* earner.

Those decisions were reinforced by the Employment Appeal Tribunal decision in *Tyne & Clyde Warehouses Ltd v Hamerton [1978] ICR 661*. There it was held that a sales representative who, each week, was instructed when and where to work and was required to follow detailed selling techniques laid down for him in a staff manual, was held to be subject to a sufficient degree of control for him to be regarded as an *employed earner*, despite the fact that he was remunerated solely by commission.

38.3 Drivers and driving instructors

In *Ready Mixed Concrete (South East) Ltd v Minister of Pensions [1968] 1 AER 433*, a person contracted to carry concrete in a vehicle provided by himself for the purpose was held to be *self-employed*, even though he was obliged to wear the uniform and colours of the concrete manufacturer and work to his orders. The contract was held to be inconsistent with a contract of service (and to be, in fact, a contract of carriage) in that control did not extend far enough for the person to cease to be an independent contractor.

In contrast, in *Global Plant Ltd v Secretary of State for Health and Social Security [1971] 3 AER 385*, a driver of a hired-out industrial plant vehicle, who regarded himself as a self-employed earner and purported to be engaged on a contract which gave him freedom to work when he chose and to send a suitably qualified substitute to work in his stead, was held to be an *employed earner* since, in practice, he worked the normal hours of a full-time employee, attended sites as directed by the company, submitted to the instructions of site foremen, was remunerated on an hourly basis and generally behaved in all respects as would an employee.

Many heavy goods vehicle drivers, having entered into arrangements for the lease of the vehicles they operate from the haulage firm for which they principally work, have operated as self-employed earners, but the status of such drivers was the subject of a concerted attack by the DSS with the result that many such drivers have been recategorised as *employed earners*.

38.4 Labour-Only Contractors

The employment status of a taxicab driver will depend on the arrangements under which he works. At one extreme there are drivers who merely operate cabs owned by some other person in accordance with contracts of service under which they receive a wage; such drivers are *employed earners*. At the other extreme, there are owner-drivers who are independent of any other person; such drivers are *self-employed earners*. Between these two extremes, however, there are two other kinds of taxicab drivers— 'settle' drivers and 'off-the-clock' drivers—the status of whom is problematical. Under a settle agreement a driver pays for his own fuel and hires his cab from the owner for a fixed weekly amount which entitles him to its use for twelve hours of every day in the week and to all his takings. Under an off-the-clock agreement the owner of the cab pays for all fuel and at the end of each week receives from the driver a percentage of the fares registered on the clock. The driver is left with the remainder of the registered fares and any tips he has received. The consensus of judicial thought seems to be that in neither case will the driver be the employee of the cab owner since neither type of contract is a contract of service. The relationship in both cases is probably that of bailor and bailee (*Smith v General Motor Cab Co Ltd [1911] AC 188*; *London General Cab Co v CIR [1950] 2 AER 566; Challinor v Taylor [1972] ICR 129*), so that, in the absence of a categorisation regulation which imposes employed earner status (such as that, long since repealed, which existed under *National Insurance (Classification) Regulations 1948*), drivers under either type of agreement will now, under normal circumstances, be regarded as *self-employed earners* for contribution purposes.

The employment status of motorcycle despatch riders will also depend on the arrangements under which they operate. Where (as is usually the case) the rider owns his own motorcycle, provides his own protective clothing, personally bears the costs of road tax, insurance, fuel, repairs etc., and is remunerated only by reference to actual mileage and/or the contract price, it is arguable on the basis of the economic reality test (see 14.7 CATEGORISATION) that he is truly in business on his own account and is a self-employed earner fulfilling contracts for carriage. Against this, however, must be set the fact that the rider will generally obtain work only from a single firm which will, itself, obtain the contracts for the delivery of mail or goods which the rider will then execute. Furthermore, the rider's radio will usually be hired to him by the firm for which he works, and the firm will usually insure itself in respect of general liability for the goods etc. carried.

Prior to 1978 the DSS had decided categorisation questions concerning driving instructors largely on the basis that if the instructor provided his own vehicle he was a self-employed earner whereas if he merely gave instruction in a car provided by a motoring school he was an employed earner. This test had, however, to be abandoned following *BSM (1257) Ltd v Secretary of State for Social Services [1978] 2 AER 576* where it was held that a written contract between a driving instructor and a car-owning operating company expressly intended to establish the instructor as a self-employed earner succeeded in doing so since the terms of the contract itself were consistent with the relationship of employer and independent contractor and the relationship was in fact as stated by the contract, i.e. the instructor would be available at stated times but could notify the office that he would not be available and could send a substitute if necessary; payment would be by the lesson and the operating company would make no provision for sickness, holidays or pension.

38.4 Construction workers

Although the construction industry tax deduction scheme introduced in 1975 is of no direct application for contribution purposes, the DSS had, historically, stated that it would normally accept a certificate issued under the scheme as evidence of self-employment unless investigation reveals that a contract of service is in existence. (Hansard 13 November 1981 Vol 12 No 8 Pt II Col 188). Whether a contract of service does exist or not will be determined by application of the usual tests (see 14.3 to 14.6 CATEGORISATION).

Thus, in *Ferguson v John Dawson & Partners (Contractors) Ltd [1976] 3 AER 817*, a 'lump labourer' who regarded himself as a self-employed earner was held to be under a contract of service (and, accordingly, an *employed earner*) as his employers controlled not only the work he did but also the method and manner in which he did it, even supplying him with the necessary tools.

DSS practice then moved towards disregarding a 714 certificate issued by the Inland Revenue. It was presumed that the Inland Revenue had not made detailed enquiries into a subcontractor's employment status before issuing a 714 certificate, unless there was evidence to the contrary.

The Government announced in February 1994 plans for changes in the construction industry tax deduction scheme and enabling powers were included in *FA 1995, s 139, 27 Sch; FA 1996, s 178*. The changes were originally due to take effect from 1 August 1998 and were intended to restrict gross payment for labour to 'businesses of substance' rather than allowing small, often one-man, businesses to obtain a 714 certificate. The implementation of proposed changes to the tax certification of subcontractors was delayed until 1 August 1999. Draft regulations setting out the changes to the construction industry deduction scheme were published on 1 March 1995, further draft regulations were issued on 5 February 1998 and full regulations issued on 23 October 1998. See Inland Revenue Press Releases 5 February 1998 and regulations in *Income Tax (Sub-contractors in the Construction Industry)(Amendment) Regs 1998, SI 1998 No 2622; Income Tax (Sub-contractors in the Construction Industry)(Amendment No 2) Regs 1999, SI 1999/2159*. These changes restrict the number of exemption certificates issued to subcontractors above a turnover limit and with a satisfactory tax and NICs record. The turnover limit has been set at £30,000 per annum (net of materials) and legislation was included in the *Finance Act 1999* to allow all construction income to form the basis of turnover tests. [*ICTA 1988, ss 562–565 as amended by FA 1999, s 53*]. Exemption from the scheme applies in respect of small payments made by deemed contractors, which do not exceed £1,000. Partnerships, including husband and wife partnerships and most companies, will have to multiply the turnover limit by the number of partners, etc to obtain the overall figure with the alternative turnover threshold being set at £200,000. Those not qualifying will have to register. Exemption certificates issued in the final years of the pre-August 1999 regime were still shown as being valid for three years, even though this will take expiry dates beyond the 1 August 1999 implementation date. However, regardless of the actual, later expiry date shown on such certificates they nonetheless ceased to be valid with effect from 1 August 1999. [*ICTA 1988, ss 564, 565; FA 1998, s 57, 8 Sch 3,4*]. (See IR Press Releases, 28 July 1997, 5 February 1998, 9 June 1998, 6 October 1998 and 23 October 1998; Inland Revenue Tax Bulletin, April 1999 Pages 635–636). From August 1999, subcontractors in the construction industry who are unable to qualify for exemption certificates will present a registration card to contractors who will inspect and record details from the card (CIS 4) or certificates (CIS 5 or CIS 6). Failure to comply with the requirements will attract penalties of up to £3,000 for failure to record accurately or completely the information. [*ICTA 1988, s 566(2A–F); FA 1996, s 178*]. The Paymaster General announced on 25 February 2000 that the rate of deduction is to fall from 23% to 18% from 6 April 2000. This deduction only applies in those cases where subcontractors have been granted a certificate. The rate of 18% is a flat rate which is applied to the net payments after the deduction of materials but needed to take into account personal allowances and lower rate band. See IR Press Release, 25 February 2000.

All these changes may well be a result of the Inland Revenue's much-publicised interest in the case concerning a construction worker: *Lee Ting Sang v Chung Chi-Keung [1990] ICR 409*. Mr Lee was a mason who was injured while working for

Chung Chi-Keung, a subcontractor, on a construction site in Hong Kong. His application for compensation under the Hong Kong Employees' Compensation Ordinance was refused on the grounds that he was a self-employed worker, not an employee. On appeal from the judgment of the Court of Appeal of Hong Kong, the Privy Council held that Mr Lee was, in fact, an *employed earner*. Referring with approval to the tests laid down by Cooke J in *Market Investigations Ltd v Minister of Social Security* (see 14.7 CATEGORISATION), Lord Griffiths said: 'The applicant did not provide his own equipment, the equipment was provided by his employer. He did not hire his own helpers; this emerged with clarity in his evidence when he explained that he gave priority to [Chung Chi-Keung's] work and if asked by [Chung Chi-Keung] to do an urgent job he would tell those he was working for that they would have to employ someone else: if he was an independent contractor in business on his own account, one would expect that he would attempt to keep both contracts by hiring others to fill the contract he had to leave. He had no responsibility for investment in, or management of, the work on the construction site, he simply turned up for work and chipped off concrete to the required depth upon the beams indicated to him on a plan by [Chung Chi-Keung]. There is no suggestion in the evidence that he priced the job which is normally a feature of the business approach of a subcontractor; he was paid either a piece-work rate or a daily rate according to the nature of the work he was doing. It is true that he was not supervised in his work, but this is not surprising, he was a skilled man and he had been told the beams upon which he was to work and the depth to which they were to be cut and his work was measured to see that he had achieved that result. There was no question of his being called upon to exercise any skill or judgment as to which beams required chipping or as to the depths that they were to be cut. He was simply told what to do and left to get on with it . . . Taking all the foregoing considerations into account the picture emerges of a skilled artisan earning his living by working for more than one employer as an employee and not as a small businessman venturing into business on his own account as an independent contractor with all its attendant risks. The applicant ran no risk whatsoever save that of being unable to find employment . . .'

Lord Griffiths specifically advised that the application of the 'integration' test (see 14.6 CATEGORISATION) (which had been relied on in the Hong Kong courts) is likely to be misleading in the context of the employment status of construction workers.

Probably as a result of the uncertainty in this area the leaflet IR 148/CA 69 'Are your workers employed or self-employed?' was issued in the latter part of 1995 and to some extent reveals the Inland Revenue and former Contribution Agency's joint view of the position. Whilst the leaflet reiterates the standard tests of control (see 14.5 CATEGORISATION), mutual obligations (see 14.4 CATEGORISATION) and integration (see 14.6 CATEGORISATION) it does go into the practicalities of the industry in determining whether someone is an employee or self-employed. In this connection, the leaflet summarises the common industry indicators as follows:

Employment

- supply of own **small** tools
- no monetary risk or financial loss
- no business organisation (or, presumably premises) such as yard, stock, workers, etc.
- paid by the hour, day, week or month

Self-employment

- supply of materials, plant or **heavy** equipment
- bidding for the job and incurring the additional loss if the bid is too low
- right to hire other people who are answerable to and paid by him/her

- an agreed amount is paid for the job regardless of how long it takes
- the right to decide how and when the work is done within an overall deadline.

Needless to say the above lists are not conclusive and in certain cases the fact that an exemption certificate is already held by the subcontractor has no bearing on the current decision as to whether they are self-employed or not; the determining factor will be the actual terms and conditions that apply to that particular job. The transition from apprenticeship to normal working will not normally result in the individual being self-employed unless there is a material change in the terms and conditions applying.

The obvious criteria that employers might be advised to concentrate on are:

- hourly/daily paid subcontractors;
- continuous employment periods e.g. exceeding two years;
- transport provided to and from home;
- holiday and sick pay provided.

Other matters should also be taken into account and the IR 148/CA 69 is quite specific on this. The recategorisation should be reviewed by the employer in light of IR 148/CA 69 especially where there is no CA written status ruling. See also Taxation magazine, 25 July 1996, pages 450–452.

Example
Subbies Ltd has taken on John, Paul and George to service a new contract to build a motel on the outskirts of Guildford. Following a recent joint IR/CA visit the current work force are being correctly treated as employees and Class 1 contributions are being deducted. However, the new workers all declare that they are subcontractors with existing exemption certificates. John runs his own small business and will be providing the work in building the slipway off the dual carriageway leading to the motel. Paul is to provide electrical and plumbing expertise for the duration of the contract and is expected to be on site for three months. George is a self-employed site supervisor and estimator who provides his services on an irregular basis for Subbies Ltd from his office at home and has previously had an Industrial Tribunal decision declare him to be self-employed.
Clearly a lot more information is required from Subbies Ltd on the terms of the engagements but initially the likely view by reference to IR 148/CA 69 might be that John could be self-employed; if the circumstances indicate that he provides his own heavy equipment and workforce to do the slip road this would be a factor, and, if there was a penalty clause for delays in the completion of the road which might delay the building of the motel, this would further reinforce a determination of self-employment.

Paul's situation seems to indicate that he will supply his own small tools with no financial risk amongst other things. He will be an employee for the duration of the contract even though it is relatively short.

George is providing hard hat and white collar services and is already classed as self-employed. However, these facts do not mean that Subbies Ltd should treat him as self-employed even though he may provide white collar services from his home base. Also, the Industrial Tribunal determination has no binding force on the decision by the Contributions Agency in these particular circumstances.

Subbies Ltd should have Forms P46 completed by Paul and George and deduct tax and Class 1 NICs from the first and subsequent payments. John's situation should be reviewed with the IR/CA status officer with the full facts and supporting documents as quickly as possible. See IR Tax Bulletin, April 1997, page 413.

38.4 Labour-Only Contractors

During May and June 1996 a number of contractors received visits from IR/CA compliance teams who were checking the employment status of their workers in the construction industry. The compliance teams were charged with the review of the employment status of the workers of the company they visited. These compliance teams, it appeared, had no definitive guidance other than IR 148/CA 69 mentioned above which had been issued to those in the construction industry to correct cases of miscategorisation and get future employment status correct. There was some confusion for a period as the CA/IR field operatives were not issued with the final instructions until 15 August 1996. The Inland Revenue instructions to their operatives state 'consider reviewing the status of workers in cases of clear miscategorisation' and to concentrate on the longer term workers with particular reference to holders of 714 certificates. If such a review results in certain workers being recategorised as employees the employer must apply PAYE/NIC to all future payments. The position with regard to earlier years payments is set out in IR 148/CA 69 which is not to reassess liabilities for past years unless there has been evidence of fraud, or tax for earlier years had been evaded and this is confirmed in the Annex to the IR Press Release dated 19 November 1996 and IR Tax Bulletin, April 1997, page 405. This leaves the collection of the PAYE/NIC by the employer from all future payments.

At the CA Specialist Conference 15 October 1996 the CA stated the following:
'We have advocated an even-handed approach and have emphasised the need to maximise the use of our respective finite resources.

- We will carry out a programme of educational visits/seminars and review visits. It is not planned to increase the volume of visits—in the region of 9,000 in the construction industry last year—but the IR will return to their former levels. We will focus on employment status issues assisting engagers to get it right *from now*.

- We are to encourage contractors to seek advice without fear of reprisal in the shape of arrears *before* the current year, 1996–97.

- We will expect to see evidence that contractors have reviewed their working practices. The question of arrears will only arise where there has been deliberate evasion.

- The reality is that most people know there is some kind of change going on and the longer time elapses the more difficult it will be for a contractor to plead ignorance of the change.
Some employers may need time to make the change and it may be reasonable in some circumstances but this depends upon the circumstances.'

See also CA National Insurance News, Issue 6, page 2. From 2 December 1996 a helpline (0345 335588) is available for contractors and workers who need general assistance with employment status queries.

The CA expected all engagers of workers in the construction industry to have reviewed status before 6 April 1997. Although they accept that circumstances may necessitate a change of status (where that is found to be so) to take place after 6 April 1996 and may not always, therefore, seek arrears from that date, arrears will be sought back to at least 6 April 1997 in all cases where a subsequent visit reveals 'self-employed' workers to be, genuinely, employees. However, the CA stated that despite efforts to help contractors, ongoing consultation with the industry has indicated that a significant number of construction firms are failing to meet their legal liabilities. In view of this where the Inland Revenue Inspectors now find that PAYE and Class 1 NICs are due because contractors have not reviewed the employment status of their workforce and made necessary changes, they will seek to recover arrears of PAYE and Class 1 NICs back to *at least* 6 April 1997. In appropriate cases interest and penalties will also be sought. CA National Insurance News, Issue 9, Page 7.

The position of agencies in the construction industry was unusual as although workers would usually be subject to Class 1 NIC there was no equivalent provision for income tax and they were still treated as self-employed for tax purposes, liable to Schedule D, Case I and Class 4 NICs (see 4.11 Construction industry workers and also IR Tax Bulletin No. 28, April 1997, page 405). However, this inconsistency is removed from 6 April 1998. Class 1 liability will continue as before but the exception of the building trade from the usual agency rules for PAYE is removed from that date. Such workers now therefore suffer both PAYE and Class 1 deductions and will no longer find themselves in a more favourable position simply because they are employed by an agency rather than engaged directly. (*Finance Act 1998, ss 55, 56*; IR Press Releases 25 September 1997, 9 February 1998 and 17 March 1998).

A joint Inland Revenue/Contribution Agency Press Release issued on 25 September 1997 announced various extra measures to police the construction industry including a greater number of survey/audit visits than the authorities had previously anticipated would be appropriate. This has also been supported by the introduction of a fraud telephone line ('Business Anti Fraud Hotline') 0800 788887. A number of employers are being investigated some of whom are in the construction industry. See DSS Press Releases 98/009, 20 January 1998 and 98/036, 23 February 1998.

38.5 Market researchers

The Secretary of State formerly determined that a woman conducting surveys on the listening and viewing habits of the public was not an employed earner because she was given only general guidance in her duties and was not subject to detailed control. (*M48 (1956)*). However, it was held in *Market Investigations Ltd v Minister of Social Security [1969] 3 AER 732* that, because of the degree of control exercised by Market Investigations Ltd over their interviewers and because, approaching matters from a different angle, the interviewers could not truly be said to be performing their services as persons in business on their own account, the interviewers were *employed earners* (see 14.7 CATEGORISATION). At page 737 of the *Market Investigations Ltd* case, Cooke, J describes the 'economic reality test'.

> 'The fundamental test to be applied is this: "Is the person who has engaged himself to perform these services performing them as a person in business on his own account?" If the answer to that question is "yes", then the contract is a contract for services. If the answer is "no", then the contract is a contract of service. No exhaustive list has been compiled and perhaps no exhaustive list can be compiled of considerations which are relevant in determining that question, nor can strict rules be laid down as to the relative weight which the various considerations should carry in particular cases. The most that can be said is that control will no doubt always have to be considered, although it can no longer be regarded as the sole determining factor; and that factors, which may be of importance, are such matters as whether the man performing the services provides his own equipment, whether he hires his own helpers, what degree of financial risk he takes, what degree of responsibility for investment and management he has, and whether and how far he has an opportunity of profiting from sound management in the performance of his task.'

It is clear from the decision in *Hall v Lorimer* (see 38.10 below) that Cooke, J's list is *not* a checklist but merely an indication of the factors to be weighed in any case and this is clear from the IR/CA Leaflet wording which uses words such as 'probably', 'usually' and 'guidelines'. (See IR 156/NI 39 pages 2 and 3).

38.6   **Office workers**

In *Rennison v Minister of Social Security (1970) 10 KIR 65* it was held that employees of a firm of solicitors remained *employed earners* despite their entering into a contract with the firm which stipulated that they were to be treated as self-employed earners in partnership with each other. The arrangement involved the weekly payment of a lump sum to the cashier (who was one of the parties to the arrangement) and his division of it between himself and the others on the basis of hours worked at an hourly rate. The arrangement would now be caught by the rules relating to AGENCY WORKERS (4) but the case is of importance in showing that arrangements which are clearly artificial and which do not change the reality of a relationship will almost always be overturned by the court.

38.7   **Catering staff**

In *O'Kelly v Trusthouse Forte plc [1983] 3 AER 456* the Court of Appeal restored the decision of an industrial tribunal that so-called 'regular casuals' (i.e. casual staff engaged on a regular basis to such an extent that some of their number had no other work) who formed the main part of the banqueting staff of the banqueting business carried on by Trusthouse Forte at the Grosvenor House Hotel were in business on their own account as independent contractors supplying services to the company. Although the regular casuals were remunerated for work actually performed; performed their work under the direction and control of Trusthouse Forte; were (when they attended functions) part of Trusthouse Forte's organisation and were represented in the staff consultation process; wore clothing and used equipment provided by Trusthouse Forte; were paid weekly in arrears under deduction of income tax and national insurance contributions; were organised on the basis of a weekly rota and required permission to take time off from rostered duties; were subject to a disciplinary and grievance procedure and received holiday pay or an incentive bonus calculated by reference to past service, *there was no obligation on Trusthouse Forte to offer them work and there was no obligation on them to take the work offered.* In the absence of such mutual obligations, there could be no 'umbrella' contract of service and each engagement constituted a separate contract for services.

In such circumstances, no liability for Class 1 contributions can arise unless the persons concerned are categorised as employed earners by regulation (see 14.14 CATEGORISATION).

It should be noted, however, that mutual obligations may arise out of custom and almost certainly will so arise where a worker is offered and accepts work on a day-in, day-out basis over a significant period of time. (*Airfix Footwear Ltd v Cope [1978] ICR 1210; Nethermere (St Neots) Ltd v Gardiner [1984] ICR 615*). Even work offered and accepted on a week-in, week-out basis where the number of days varies will, in some instances, suffice. In *Four Seasons (Inn on the Park) Ltd v Hamarat 17.4.85 EAT 369/84*, for example, mutual obligations were held to have come into existence between a wine waiter and a hotel for which, since 1976, he had worked exclusively for between one or two and six days a week. The industrial tribunal (distinguishing the case from the *O'Kelly* case) found that 'if the applicant had not undertaken work offered to him by the respondent, further work would have been withheld. Equally, if the respondent had not offered further work to the applicant, he would have removed his services to some other form of employment'. The tribunal's decision that Mr Hamarat was, therefore, an employed earner was upheld by the Employment Appeal Tribunal.

Even where mutual obligations are found to be absent in situations where there is a regular succession of short-term contracts, each contract may (exceptionally) be found to be a contract of service rather than a contract for services. Thus, in *Letheby and Christopher Ltd v Bangurah 19 May 1987 EAT 639/86*, a Mrs Bangurah who worked on a regular but casual basis as a waitress and barmaid for a race-course catering company was found to have worked under a series of individual contracts which the EAT, though not having to decide the point, seems to have regarded as contracts of employment.

38.8   Agricultural workers

The employment status of most agricultural workers is determinable, without difficulty, by application of the normal tests (see CATEGORISATION (14)). Regular full-time farm workers will be under contracts of service and will be *employed earners*, while contractors such as threshers, ploughers and hauliers who supply their own equipment and perform their tasks unsupervised and in their own way will generally be *self-employed earners*. A statement involving 16 questions slanted towards employment status was obtained in some cases by the former CA from the farmer as to the working arrangements of the farm worker and it is often this statement that forms the basis of contentious issues. In the case of contract milkers a specific contract (Agreement LL 12) is entered into if they are to be self-employed and this was the result of discussions between the former CA, National Farmer's Union and Milk Marketing Board (at the time). The CA contended that the self-employed milker must adhere strictly to the contract and if they do not they become relief milkers and are counted as employees. Former Inland Revenue Leaflet, P5, Para 15, (now withdrawn) advised that gangmasters who supply and pay squads for potato, onion and beet-lifting, pea, fruit and hop-picking, etc. were to be regarded as *self-employed earners* provided they were not in the regular employment of the grower to whom they supplied the services in question, as were milkers who contracted to milk cows at a price per gallon or per cow and rat catchers, rabbit catchers, thatchers etc. who went from farm to farm performing their services.

Although most of that advice is probably still sound, the question of the status of a gangmaster must now always be considered in the light of *Andrews v King [1991] STC 481*. There it was held that Mr Andrews, a master of a potato picking and/or grading gang was *not* a self-employed earner. For a period of just over two years, Mr Andrews was engaged on various days by J W Stanberry Ltd, potato merchants, in connection with potato picking and/or grading. He would telephone the company on an evening and if he found there was work available for the following day, he would contact the men necessary, supply transport and arrange for them and himself to be on site the next morning. Payment was made to Mr Andrews who, after deducting petrol contributions, divided the pay between himself and the gang members. Referring with approval to the tests laid down by Cooke J in *Market Investigations Ltd v Minister of Social Security* (see 14.7 CATEGORISATION), Sir Nicolas Browne-Wilkinson V-C said: 'Beyond the selection of the members of the gang the taxpayer had no rights of control. Where and when the work was to be done were matters for Stanberrys. The work of the whole gang including the taxpayer was supervised by Stanberrys. There is no indication that [Mr Andrews] had any powers of control over the members of the gang. The evidence was that he was subject to the control of Stanberrys. Turning to the question whether the taxpayer provided equipment for carrying out the work, it is clear that he did not. The only equipment he provided was a van which was not used to do the work but to get to the place of work. Even in relation to the van, the direct cost of getting there in the form of petrol was not paid by him alone but was shared by the other members of the gang. As to the question whether or not he hired his own helpers, he certainly selected them but he did not himself pay them any wages. He did not engage men, pay them and then provide a gang *en bloc* to Stanberrys in return for a fixed charge. Having selected his gang, they all went together to the place of work selected by Stanberrys and the total sum paid for the work by Stanberrys was a sum which all the members of the gang had agreed, not [Mr Andrews] by himself. The net proceeds, after deduction of petrol money, were divided equally between them. In my judgment it is impossible to call that "hiring helpers". As to the question whether or not [Mr Andrews] was running any financial risk, I can see none beyond the risk run by many casual labourers in agriculture that if there is no work because of weather conditions there is no payment. There was no question of investment or management so far as [Mr Andrews] was concerned. There was no question of his profiting from sound management since he took the same reward as all other members of the gang. He had no extra remuneration reflecting in any way the quality of his management in the selection and production of the gang at the workplace. Looking at those elements and standing back and considering the case as a whole, one asks the basic question: Was [Mr Andrews] in business on his own account? I cannot see that he was carrying on any business . . .'.

Where a gangmaster *is* self-employed, he has a responsibility to deduct and account for PAYE and Class 1 national insurance contributions on the amounts he pays to the individual squad members. (See Leaflet CWG2 (2000), Page 71, item 115). Because many gangmasters fail to discharge that responsibility, the Inland Revenue established an Agricultural Compliance Unit (currently located in Leeds) which is charged with the task of enforcing compliance. (See 37.3 INLAND REVENUE for the Inland Revenue's role in enforcing compliance in the area of national insurance contributions). The Inland Revenue says:

'Agricultural gangmasters are middle men who supply casual labour for farmers, canning factories and other agricultural concerns at peak times. Gangmasters should normally operate PAYE and account for national insurance contributions on the wages they pay to work forces they supply. They should also account for tax on their own business profits. There is fierce competition for work among gangmasters. Many gangmasters do fulfil all their tax obligations, but others do not. They may also disregard social security, employment, and health and safety laws. Their overheads are thus substantially lower than the 'legitimate' gangmasters, who may find their prices are undercut, and their businesses threatened.' (IR Press Release, 2 September 1988).

Workers engaged for a fixed sum payable at the end of a six-month or annual 'hiring', e.g. at Whitsun or Martinmas, are *employed earners*.

Where a farmer provides his workers with free board and lodging, this is a benefit in kind and is disregarded for Class 1 contribution purposes (see 28.52 EARNINGS). However, where a board and lodging allowance is paid, whether to the employee or, after deduction from wages, to the accommodation provider, contributions are due on the gross wage (See Leaflet CWG2 (2000), Page 69).

Particular difficulties arise in relation to *irregular casual workers* engaged for no fixed period in the field or orchard in work such as fruit picking and remunerated on a piece-work basis. In such circumstances, the grower generally has no way of identifying individual workers, controlling their hours of work or recording their earnings, and, accordingly, in 1975, the National Farmers' Union negotiated a working arrangement with the then DHSS under which the DHSS agreed not to seek contributions in respect of such workers. In 1978, further discussions between the NFU and the DSS resulted in a DSS agreement not to disturb the earlier working arrangement. (NFU Cyclo 918/74/78 Econ Y57 of 17 May 1978). This position was confirmed in Parliament in 1983. (Hansard 28 July 1983 Col 591). In 1984, the issue was again reviewed by the NFU and the DSS with the result that, so far as the irregular casual category of workers was concerned:

'The previously agreed arrangements for national insurance contributions, as set out in the May 1978 statement, remain unchanged except that since the original agreement was reached the DSS have made clear that the simple notation of names and addresses will not necessarily make irregular casuals ineligible for this category.'

(NFU Cyclo 456/29/84 Econ O29 of 29 February 1984).

The DSS was at pains to point out, however, that

'it is not a case of irregular casuals having no liability for NICs. Rather, the department has taken a realistic approach to the particular characteristics and difficulties of this industry, and has decided not to attempt to enforce liability'. (Letter from DSS, 5 June 1987).

In other words, the forms of engagement of most casual crop pickers are such that they will generally be *employed earners*. (Hansard 5 December 1983 Vol 50 Col 26). They are merely treated as non-employed as a matter of convenience.

Regular casual workers also are regarded as *employed earners* but in their case no concessionary treatment is available. A regular casual is regarded as a person who is known to the grower, is usually paid weekly and will normally move from one casual job to another as the season proceeds. The DSS required that Class 1 contribution liabilities are accounted for in the normal way as regards earnings paid to such persons (Hansard 28 July 1983 Col 591) and this continues to be reflected in current guidance. See Leaflet CWG2 (2000), Pages 69 and 70, item 114.

The Agricultural Compliance Unit, it is understood, has been taking an interest in large fruit farms with large numbers of casual pickers. Where, for example, foreign students are recruited overseas by an agency offering work for a particular season, the ACU argues that they are not casual harvest employees and that full PAYE and NIC procedures should be operated.

The true status of both regular and irregular casuals is, in any event, questionable following the decision in *O'Kelly v Trusthouse Forte plc.* (See 38.7 above).

The forms of engagement of dairy herdsmen vary in practice and the employment status of any individual herdsman will depend on the particular facts. (Hansard 5 December 1983 Vol 50 Col 26).

In Minister of State's decision *M34 (1953)* it was decided that a father and son who cleared areas of standing timber as dictated by the forest manager were *self-employed earners* since they determined their own methods of performance of their task and supplied most of their own equipment. By contrast, it was held in *M40 (1953)* that two timber fellers who were more closely controlled, in that the company foreman would dictate the trees to be felled and the method of felling, were *employed earners*.

38.9 **Journalists**

In *Beloff v Pressdram Ltd [1973] 1 AER 243*, it was held that a political and lobby correspondent of the Observer newspaper was an *employed earner* even though the Observer exercised little control over her work and even though she engaged in other forms of journalism and authorship while working for the Observer newspaper. The court applied both the 'integration test' (see 14.6 CATEGORISATION) and the 'economic reality test' (see 14.7 CATEGORISATION) and found that the woman in question was 'an integral part of the business' carried on by the Observer and was not in business on her own account.

Earlier, the Secretary of State had determined that a newspaper correspondent who worked in Great Britain for an Italian newspaper was an *employed earner*. (*M33 (1953)*). Although he worked here without supervision, his activities were subjected to a high degree of control in that he was required not only to devote substantially the whole of his time to the regular transmission of news but was required also to submit one or two special articles each month and to write articles on given subjects when instructed to do so.

Although a number of journalists enjoyed self-employed status previously, Inland Revenue activity in the years leading up to 1984 resulted in more than 700 being re-categorised as employed earners. (Hansard 16 January 1984 Vol 52 Col 14). However, the General Commissioners found that the shifts that journalist Margaret Leslie worked on a national newspaper were not contracts of service but that she was self-employed. Factors that led to the Commissioner's decision included the facts that (a) she had no guarantee of work beyond her eight hour shift, and (b) that she was not subject to established disciplinary and grievance procedures. (Tolley's Practical NIC, Vol 3, Number 11, p 87).

38.10 Film and TV industry workers

On 30 March 1983, the Inland Revenue announced that, having carried out a review of the employment status of workers engaged on 'freelance' terms within the film and allied industries and having had an extensive series of discussions with representative bodies within the industry, it had come to the conclusion that 'a number of workers engaged on "freelance" terms within the industry are engaged as employees under contracts of service, either written or oral' and that, where those workers had been treated as self-employed, re-categorisation would take place from 6 April 1983. (Press Release). By the end of 1983, over 7,000 such workers had been recategorised as employed earners. (Hansard 16 January 1984 Vol 52 Col 14). The Inland Revenue identified in June 1996 the following casual and freelance staff in the film, television and production industry as genuinely *self-employed*:

advance riggers[2]; animal handlers[1]; animation directors[1]; animation production co-ordinators[1]; animators[2 and 3]; animatronic model designers[1]; art directors[1]; assistant art directors[3]; associate producers[1] (except where they are engaged solely for general research); auditioners[1];

background artists[3];

camera operators/cameramen/model cameras[2]; casting directors[1]; chaperones[1]; choreographers[1]; composers[1]; continuity workers (where script breakdown is an integral part of the engagement); contributors (who are paid on a per-contribution basis); costume designers/assistant costume designers[2 or 3]; cricket scorers[1];

directors[1]; dressmakers[3]; drivers[2];

editors[1]; executive producers[1];

fight arrangers[1]; film stylists[1]; first assistant director[1];

gaffers[2]; graphic artists and graphic designers[3]; grips[2];

hairdressers[2 or 3]; heads of art departments[1]; HOD riggers[2];

language assessors (when used occasionally to check the style and delivery of foreign language broadcasts); lettering artists/designers[3]; lighting directors/ lighting cameramen[1] (where they are responsible for designing the lighting or photography); line producers[1]; location managers[3];

make-up artists[2 or 3]; matrons[1]; model designers and model makers[2 or 3]; modellers[1]; musical arrangers/copyists[3]; musical associates[1]; musical directors[1]; musical score readers[1];

nurses[1];

painters[3]; photographic stylists[1]; post-production supervisors[1]; producers and co-producers[1]; production accountants[3]; production assistants (where script breakdown is an integral part of the engagement); production buyers[1]; production designers[1]; production managers[1]; production supervisors[1]; property masters/prop hands[2]; providers of occasional information (e.g. tip-offs, racing tips, news and sport); publicists[1];

scenic artists/designers[3]; script readers[3]; script supervisors (where script break-down is an integral part of the engagement); scriptwriters[1] (other than those merely engaged in reporting); sculptors[1]; senior floor manager[1]; senior special effects technician[1]; set decorators/set dressers[3]; sound maintenance engineers[2]; sound recordists/sound mixers[2]; special effects wiremen[2]; specialist researchers (who have an existing profession outside broadcasting and films, e.g. a University professor or legal expert, or who have specialist knowledge of the subject to be researched, are engaged for specific projects and are only occasional contributors); stage managers[2]; statisticians[1] (in sport); stills photographers[2]; story board artists[1]; story writers[1] (other than those merely engaged in reporting);

tracers[3]; transcript typists[3]; translators[3]; transport managers[2]; translators[1];

video technicians[2];

wardrobe workers[2 or 3]; warm-ups[1]; wigmakers[3]; wiremen[2]; writers[1] (other than those merely engaged in reporting).

Notes
The numbers in the list indicate the specific requirements a grade must satisfy, in order to qualify for self-employed status. These are as follows.

1   To be non-permanent, casual and freelance.

2   To provide 'substantial or major' equipment.

3   Not to use the payer's facilities.

See Tolley's National Insurance Brief, Specialist Sector, July 1996.

Workers in the film industry who do not fall within any of the categories listed are regarded by the Inland Revenue as employees, and the Inland Revenue's view has been adopted by the Customs and Excise since April 1988. Under the 'Common Approach', the DSS should accept the status agreed by the Inland Revenue.

It should also be noted that the Inland Revenue has instructed film companies to continue to treat as employees individuals who fall outside the categories listed above and operate through a partnership or a limited company. Such persons may also, from 6 April 2000, be affected by the 'intermediaries' provisions, see 14.17 CATEGORISATION.

The DSS attitude to voice-over artists was that they are employed earners because of the right of close supervision and control over method and manner of performance which is available to producers. No account is taken of the brevity of any particular voice-over contract, since each engagement is regarded in itself as an employed earner's employment, although this policy is thought to be under review following the decisions in *Hall v Lorimer* (see below) and the Special Commissioners' hearing on the status of actors Alec McCowan and Sam West (see 33.2 ENTERTAINERS).

From 6 April 1993 to 5 April 1995, the following casual and freelance staff in the television industry were to be regarded as self-employed for contribution purposes. The list does not include assistants, or staff who were engaged on a regular succession of contracts.

animal handlers, animators, auditioners who are brought in from outside, camera operators and cameramen who supply all major and basic pieces of equipment, casting directors and choreographers engaged for specific projects, chaperones, contributors to concerts and associated publicity material, cricket scorers and sports statisticians, directors and producers who are engaged either for a specific project or series lasting less than six months, but excluding those contracted to work in a general programme department, editors engaged for specific projects because of particular talents, fight arrangers, make-up artists brought in for one-off jobs or because of particular skills, gaffers who provide all major and basic pieces of equipment, news and sports reporters and commentators including those paid on a per contribution basis, but not those who present their finished work on the air, lighting directors engaged for a specific project, matrons, musical associates and production designers for specific projects, providers of occasional information, script writers and short story writers (but not reporters), sound recordists who usually provide all major and basic pieces of equipment, stage managers engaged for specific projects because of special talents, stills photographers who provide cameras, stand-ins for performers, warm-ups.

The following freelance personnel were also included if they worked from their home or a studio outside the television company's premises:

costume and scenic designers, dressmakers, graphic artists and graphic designers, musical arrangers and copyists, photographers, production buyers, specialist researchers engaged for specific and occasional projects and who are outside the control and management of the television company, translators and language assessors, wigmakers.

In November 1993, the Court of Appeal confirmed the 1992 High Court decision that, on the particular facts of the case, a freelance vision mixer was self-employed (*Hall v Lorimer [1993] BTC 473*). He worked over a four year period on 580 separate engagements for a maximum number at any one time of 22 clients. He was free to accept or reject offers of work and when engagements clashed he sometimes provided a substitute with the consent of the TV company. The Inland Revenue believed the decision of the single Special Commissioner who had heard the case had been incorrect in law. Lorimer did not provide any equipment, and except for a few occasions he provided no staff. He worked where and when he was required and was subject to the control of the programme's director. There was allegedly no economic risk other than that of having no work and he could not profit from sound management of his business. It was contended that these facts clearly showed him to have undertaken a series of contracts of employment. Mummery J accepted that the Inland Revenue's argument that Lorimer was not a small businessman was formidable and that the distinction between Schedule E and Schedule D was very fine, especially where only personal services were provided, but the Special Commissioner had applied the correct tests to the established facts and had been entitled to reach the conclusion that Lorimer was self-employed.

There were a number of factors weighing against self-employed status:

- the production company controlled the time, place and duration of the work;

- Lorimer provided no equipment and only rarely provided staff;

- he ran no financial risk, other than the possibility of an occasional bad debt and of not being able to find work; and

- he had no part in the investment and management of the production and no opportunity for profit.

Importantly, the judgment acknowledged these alleged weaknesses but pointed out that these things were the production company's business but *not part of Lorimer's business*. His business was different:

- he had his own office;

- he exploited his abilities in the market place;

- he bore his own financial risk, which was higher than that of an employee;

- his opportunity to profit from being a good vision mixer was through using his skill and efficiency to increase demand for his services; and

- he incurred substantial costs which an employee would not incur: bad debts, car running costs, office costs, all different in nature and scale from those likely to be incurred by an employee.

The Inland Revenue asserted that the case did not change the law, but many commentators disagree. The Inland Revenue issued a note on 17 August 1994 on the application of the case to the film and TV industry, implicitly trying to restrict the scope of the decision, but it is arguably of application wherever labour-only subcontractors work.

In December 1992 the Contributions Agency published a note stating that it was now instructing its staff to use the Inland Revenue's lists of behind the camera/microphone workers in the television, radio, film and video industries as a basis for identifying those who are most likely to be self-employed. It said that the lists may also be used by employers in the industries as a guide to employment status for NI purposes, but should not be used to override special terms agreed between the worker and the company. In cases of dispute the Agency would investigate and provide a formal ruling on status but the right of either party to seek a formal determination by the Secretary of State was not affected (now replaced by the appeals procedure, see 9 APPEALS AND REVIEWS).

Where a retrospective change to self-employed status is appropriate, and is consented to by the worker concerned, NICO accepts that a refund of Class 1 NICs may be due, subject to the employee's paying Class 2 and Class 4 contributions. Provision has been made in the *Pensions Act 1995* for self-employed persons wrongly categorised as employed earners to forego a refund of primary contributions in order to preserve entitlement to additional benefits. This does not preclude the 'employer' reclaiming the associated secondary contributions. (DSS Press Release, 23 June 1995). Claims should be made to NICO, Refunds Group, Longbenton, Newcastle upon Tyne, NE98 1ZZ (tel 08459 154260). See also DSS Press Release, 14 May 1996.

The Inland Revenue announced revised arrangements in early 1995 under which production companies from 6 April 1995 may pay without deduction of tax where any engagement of a person in the listed categories is for less than seven days. However, the guidance notes issued instruct the companies to apply Class 1 to payments even if no tax is deducted. The list of freelance grades for the TV and film industries were also revised (see above).

38.11 Domestic workers

A domestic worker, or a cleaner who is employed in a private household or elsewhere, will generally be categorised as an *employed earner* simply by reason of the contract of service which will normally exist between that person and the person for whom he works (see CATEGORISATION (14)). Thus a handyman working seven hours a week has been held by the Secretary of State to be an *employed earner*, as has a jobbing gardener working two days a week and as has a resident housekeeper. (*M21 (1952), M64 (1958)* and *M58 (1958)*). Where, however, circumstances are such that a contract of service does not exist or its existence is difficult to establish, categorisation rules operate to resolve the categorisation questions which arise.

38.12 Employment by a close relative

Where a person is employed in a private dwelling-house in which both he and his employer reside and the employer is the person's parent, step-parent, grandparent, child, step-child, grandchild, brother, sister, half-brother or half-sister, the employment is to be entirely *disregarded* for contribution purposes, provided it is not employment for the purposes of any trade or business carried on in the house by the employer. [*SSCBA 1992, s 2(2)(a); Categorisation Regs, Reg 2(4), 1 Sch Pt III Para 7*].

38.13 Labour-Only Contractors

The kind of employments to which this regulation may relate include employment outdoors as a gardener, chauffeur or handyman or employment indoors as a cook, cleaner, secretary, housekeeper or companion. (DSS Leaflet NI 11, now withdrawn).

Employment by one's *spouse* is also to be disregarded in similar circumstances (but see 36.1 HUSBAND AND WIFE). [*1 Sch Pt III Para 8*].

The regulation makes no reference to the employment of a person by a *close relative of his spouse* and, in such circumstances, the question as to whether or not the person is an employed earner will have to be determined by reference to the legal relationship, if any, which has been created between the parties. If the relationship is, and was intended to be, merely domestic (see *Simpkins v Pays [1955] 3 AER 110*), no contract of service will exist and the person will not be an employed earner.

38.13 Cleaners of commercial or industrial premises

Employment as an office cleaner or in any similar capacity in any premises other than those used as a private dwelling-house is an employment in respect of which a person is to be treated as an *employed earner* irrespective of whether or not a contract of service exists between the person employed and the person for whom the services are performed. [*SSCBA 1992, s 2(2)(b); Categorisation Regs, Reg 2(2), 1 Sch Pt I Para 1*].

This special categorisation rule does not apply to proprietors of office cleaning businesses even if they perform some cleaning activities themselves. Nor does it apply to window cleaners. (See 38.14 below). The rule *does* apply to telephone kiosk cleaners, however. (See 38.15 below).

Where the person employed is supplied by, or through, an agency and is remunerated from or through the agency, the agency is to be treated as the secondary contributor (see 14.15 CATEGORISATION). In any other case, the person with whom the person employed contracted to do the work is to be treated as the secondary contributor, unless that person is a company in voluntary liquidation, when the liquidator will be the secondary contributor. [*Categorisation Regs, 3 Sch 1, 4*].

38.14 Window cleaners

The DSS did not regard the special categorisation rule described at 38.13 above as applying to window cleaners. Accordingly, their employment status falls to be determined by application of the normal CATEGORISATION (14) rules.

38.15 Kiosk cleaners

Following an inquiry (see 9.11 APPEALS AND REVIEWS) held in London on 31 January 1989, the Secretary of State decided that British Telecom telephone kiosk cleaners subcontracted to do their work by a contract cleaning firm *do* fall within the special categorisation rule described at 38.13 above. The Secretary of State conceded that, but for the special rule, such cleaners would have been self-employed earners as they used their own materials and invoiced the principal contractor for the work done on a monthly basis; but he held that the special rule applied because telephone kiosks—even the open hood-covered types—are 'premises' within the meaning of *Categorisation Regs, 1 Sch Pt I Para I* and because—even though the kiosk cleaners did more than merely clean the kiosks—they were employed 'in a similar capacity' to office cleaners, again within the meaning of that paragraph. Despite that decision, however, the *Categorisation Regs* have been amended with effect from 16 October 1990 to ensure the employed earner status of anyone employed as 'a cleaner of any telephone apparatus and associated fixtures' other than of apparatus or fixtures in a private house. [*Categorisation Regs, 1 Sch Pt I Para 1(b) as amended by Categorisation Amendment Regs 1990, Reg 2*]. The secondary contributor is identified under the rules described at 38.13 above.

38.16 **Au pairs**

If the arrangement under which an 'au pair' works in a private household is one which satisfies the conditions of stay laid down by the Home Office in rule 33 of its Immigration Rules, and the 'au pair' is female, she is regarded as not being gainfully employed and thus no contribution liabilities will arise. The relevant conditions are that the 'au pair'

(a) is aged 17 or more but not older than 27;

(b) is a national of a West European state (including Malta, Cyprus and Turkey);

(c) has come to the UK to learn English and to live in an English-speaking household for up to two years;

(d) does housework (including looking after the children of the household) for no more than 5 hours a day with at least two full days off per week;

(e) receives free board and lodging and pocket money; and

(f) is without dependants and does not have close relatives in the UK.

If these conditions are *not* met, the normal CATEGORISATION (14) rules will apply. (See *M67(1958)*). See also *Asylum and Immigration Act 1996, s 8*.

Until 3 July 1993 the Immigration Rules excluded male 'au pairs'. Despite the relaxation of the rules, it is understood that the DSS did not alter its departmental practice to reflect this, although this arguably contravenes European Community law on equal treatment, at least for EEA nationals.

38.17 **Locum doctors, dentists, opticians etc.**

The DSS did not generally regard a locum as being an employed earner unless he or she enters a contract of service with the person for whom he or she is 'standing in'. Although it might be expected that attacks by the Inland Revenue on locum opticians might have changed DSS attitudes, this did not appear to have been the case.

In April 1989, charges for sight-tests were introduced and test fees began to be paid by Specialeyes (Optical Services) Ltd (a major high-street chain of dispensing opticians) to the opticians who it engaged to carry out sight-testing on a self-employed basis at its various branches. In a case taken before the Special Commissioners the Inland Revenue contended that the 'self-employed' opticians were, in fact, employees of Specialeyes Ltd.

On the basis of the following facts, the Special Commissioners decided that the locum opticians were *self-employed*:

(a) The opticians negotiated a fixed fee for each test performed and were paid on the basis of a monthly claim supported by their own invoices.

(b) Specialeyes provided all major items of non-portable equipment but the opticians provided their own retinoscopes and ophthalmoscopes.

(c) The opticians attended the branches to perform sight tests only and (unlike employee opticians at some of the branches) undertook no other duties.

(d) Specialeyes was not obliged to offer any of the opticians work and the opticians were free to refuse engagements offered without penalty and to stipulate their own hours of availability; though, in practice, many worked up to six days a week.

(e) The locum opticians received none of the benefits enjoyed by employee opticians: fixed salary, sick pay, holiday pay, medical insurance, company car.

(f) The opticians insured themselves against malpractice claims.

(g) Some of the opticians had their own practices elsewhere.

The Special Commissioners accepted Specialeyes' contention that there was no global contract between it and any particular optician but that there was rather a series of individual contracts each of which covered but a single engagement; and they further agreed with Specialeyes that each such individual contract was a contract for services rather than a contract of service—mainly on the grounds that Specialeyes had very little control over the activities of the opticians.

The Special Commissioners were dismissive of the suggestion that, as the opticians were clearly part of Specialeyes' 'team', the application of the 'integration test' (see 14.6 CATEGORISATION) showed that the opticians were employees of Specialeyes. The Commissioners held that the fact that the company could not function without the opticians did *not* mean that the opticians were 'part and parcel' of Specialeyes' organisation.

It is understood to be current Inland Revenue policy to categorise locum pharmacists according to the status of the pharmacists they replace, so that the local chemist shop may treat a locum as self-employed when he or she replaces the self-employed proprietor, while the pharmacy chains would be expected to treat the locums as casual employees. This policy, while a convenient rule of thumb, has no basis in law. The status of the locum will depend solely on the tests discussed above and on the terms of the contract under which the work is carried out.

39 Late-Paid Contributions

Cross-references. See ARREARS OF CONTRIBUTIONS (12); BENEFITS (13); COLLECTION (21); 26.4 DEATH OF CONTRIBUTOR; ENFORCEMENT (32); WORKING CASE STUDY (58).

Other Sources. Leaflet CA 07.

39.1 GENERAL CONSIDERATIONS

There is a 'due date' of payment for every Class 1, Class 1A, Class 1B, Class 2 or Class 4 contribution for which liability arises (see 21.3, 21.8 and 21.13 COLLECTION). If payment is not made on or before that date, collection may be enforced and the person from whom the payment is due may (subject to *Limitation Act 1980, s 9(1)*) be proceeded against for recovery of the ARREARS OF CONTRIBUTIONS (12). There is also a 'required date' by which Class 3 contributions are to be made by anyone entitled to pay them (see 21.12 COLLECTION).

Where the due or required date for payment has passed, however, a contribution then paid may nevertheless, in certain circumstances, be admitted for the purpose of satisfying the contribution conditions for benefit entitlement. In effect, the provisions relating to such late-paid contributions impose a secondary 'due date'.

39.2 RULES WHERE GOOD REASONS FOR DELAY

Delay due to ignorance or error

Where a person who is entitled to pay a Class 3 contribution or is entitled, but not liable, to pay a Class 2 contribution, fails to pay that contribution by its due or required date and the Inland Revenue is satisfied that the failure is attributable to *ignorance or error* and not to failure to exercise due care and diligence, the contribution may be paid within such further period as the Inland Revenue may allow. [*Contribution Regs, Regs 29, 40 as amended by SSC(T)A 1999, 2 Sch*].

The CA Field Operations Manual, paragraph 5150 states:

5150 You can only extend the time limits for paying NICs and for them counting for benefit if ... the contributor:

   1.   did not know when to pay the NICs;

   2.   made a mistake with the payments; and

   3.   took reasonable steps to find out what, and when, payments should have been due.

In assessing whether a contributor had failed to exercise due care and diligence, the Inland Revenue might be expected to take into account the person's circumstances. For example, youth and inexperience or age and infirmity may explain why a person failed to pay a contribution on time. Similarly, the contributor's level of intelligence and standard of education might be taken into account.

The CA Field Operations Manual, paragraphs 5158–5160 indicate a rather stricter approach *viz*;

5158 The Department expects anyone working in this country to know that they must pay NICs to receive benefit, *without reminder from the Department*.

5159 The Department expects anyone who is not working but wants to pay voluntary NICs to know that they must contact the Department.

5160 Cases where self-employed or non-employed contributor comes from abroad need special consideration. In these cases, consider:

39.3 Late-Paid Contributions

1. how much publicity, leaflets and advice are available; and

2. whether the contributor came from a country which had a similar insurance scheme.

Furthermore, where the time has passed within which a late-paid contribution is, for benefit entitlement purposes, to be recognised as paid (see 39.5 to 39.6 below), the Secretary of State for Social Security may, if similarly satisfied, direct that the late-paid contribution is to be treated as paid on such earlier day as he considers appropriate. [*Reg 41*].

39.3 Delay or failure attributable to secondary contributor

Where a primary Class 1 contribution which is payable on a contributor's behalf by a secondary contributor (see 21.3 COLLECTION) is paid after the due date or is not paid and the Secretary of State for Social Security is satisfied that the failure or delay was neither consented to, nor connived at by, nor attributable to any negligence on the part of, the primary contributor then the primary contribution is to be treated as paid on the due date. [*SSCBA 1992, 1 Sch 8(1)(c); Contributions Regs, Reg 39*]. To connive at something is to 'wink at' it or to take no exception to it. It has been described as intentional concurrence. (*Godfrey v Godfrey [1964] 3 AER 154*).

Because of the nature of a *director's* responsibilities in relation to the business of his company, however, Class 1 contributions unpaid by a company will generally *not* be treated as having been paid so far as the company's directors are concerned. (Hansard 12 April 1984 Vol 58 No 141 Cols 376–377).

Where, in these circumstances, payment is not made relative to, and before a day in respect of which, contributions based jobseeker's allowance, short-term incapacity benefit or maternity allowance is claimed, the primary contribution is, for the purpose of the first contribution condition of entitlement (see 13.2 BENEFITS), to be treated as paid on the date on which the earnings to which it relates are paid and for any other contribution condition treated as paid on the due date. [*Reg 39 as amended by Contributions Amendment No 2 Regs 1987, Reg 10, Contributions Amendment No 4 Regs 1987, Reg 7 and Incapacity Benefit (Consequential and Transitional Amendments and Savings) Regs 1995, Reg 13(5)*].

39.4 Delay by reason of a deferral arrangement

Class 1 or Class 2 contributions which, under an approved deferral or other arrangement, are paid after the date on which they would otherwise have fallen due for payment are, for the purpose of the contribution conditions for entitlement to benefits, to be treated as paid on that due date. [*SSCBA 1992, 1 Sch 8(1)(d); Contributions Regs, Reg 42*].

39.5 OTHER RULES

General rule in other circumstances

Subject to the provisions described in 39.1 to 39.4 above, any Class 2 or Class 3 contribution which is paid before the end of the second tax year following the tax year in which its due or required date lies is, for the purpose of satisfying contribution conditions for entitlement to benefit in respect of periods after payment of the contribution, to be treated as paid on the date on which it is *actually* paid. If it is paid after the end of that second year, it is (subject to an extension) to be treated for benefit purposes as *not* paid. From 6 April 1985, the period for payment is extended from two to six years in the case of Class 2 contributions, the due date for which fell after 5 April 1983, and in the case of Class 3 contributions, the required date for which fell after 5 April 1982. [*SSCBA 1992, 1 Sch 8(1)(d); Contributions*

Regs, Regs 27(3)(b)(i), 38(1A)(2)(5), as amended by Contributions Amendment Regs 1984, Regs 9(a), 13]. See Tolley's National Insurance Contributions 1995–96, pages 358–9 as to relaxations as to the required timing of payments of Class 3 for 1981–82 and earlier years.

39.6 Special rules relating to short-term benefits

A late-paid Class 1 or Class 2 contribution may count towards satisfaction of the *second* contribution condition for the purpose of entitlement to

(*a*) contributions based jobseeker's allowance or short-term incapacity benefit only if it is paid

    (i) before the start of the relevant benefit year, or

    (ii) if it is paid *after* the start of the relevant benefit year, only after 42 days have elapsed. In practice this means that benefit could be disallowed for up to six weeks;

and

(*b*) maternity allowance only if it is paid *before* the beginning of the period for which maternity allowance is payable.

[*Contributions Regs, Reg 38(6)(7) as amended by Contributions Amendment No 2 Regs 1987, Reg 9 and Incapacity Benefit Consequential and Transitional Amendments and Savings Regs 1995, Reg 13(4)*].

39.7 RATE AT WHICH OVERDUE CONTRIBUTIONS PAYABLE

As there are no provisions to the contrary, late-paid *Class 1* contributions will be payable at the rate current at the time when their payment was due.

Where a Class 2 contribution (including a contribution at other than the standard rate paid by share fishermen and volunteer development workers) is paid late but is paid within the tax year in which the contribution week to which it relates falls, the rate at which the contribution is payable is (there being no statutory provision to the contrary) the rate at which the contribution would have been payable had it been paid on its due date.

The rate at which late-paid *Class 2* contributions are payable is determined according to the following rules:

(*a*) Where a Class 2 contribution is paid in respect of a contribution week falling in the tax year 1982–83 or in any earlier tax year, the rate at which that contribution is payable (regardless of how late it is paid) is the rate at which it would have been payable had it been paid on its due date. [*Contributions Regs, Reg 43A as amended by Contributions Amendment No 2 Regs 1985, Reg 4*].

(*b*) Where (*a*) does not apply and the Inland Revenue (previously, the Secretary of State for Social Security) has agreed to accept payment of arrears by instalments in accordance with an undertaking made by the contributor, the rate at which a Class 2 contribution payable in accordance with that undertaking is to be paid in respect of any particular contribution week is

    (i) if the undertaking was entered into in the tax year in which the contribution week fell or in the immediately following tax year, the rate at which it would have been payable had it been paid on its due date; or

    (ii) if the undertaking was entered into in any tax year other than those stated in (i) and payment is before 22 September 1991, the rate applicable at the date of the undertaking; or

    (iii) if the undertaking was entered into in any tax year other than those stated in (i) and payment is on or after 22 September 1991, the highest rate in the period from the due date to the date of the undertaking.

[Reg 43B as amended by Contributions Amendment No 2 Regs 1985, Reg 4 and Contributions Amendment No 5 Regs 1991, Reg 2 and SSC(T)A 1999, 2 Sch].

(c) Where (a) does not apply and the Inland Revenue (previously, the Secretary of State for Social Security) has agreed to accept payment of arrears by instalments in accordance with an undertaking made by the contributor, the rate at which a Class 2 contribution payable *otherwise than* in accordance with that undertaking is to be paid in respect of any particular contribution week is

    (i) if the contribution is paid in accordance with a further undertaking entered into in a later year and payment is before 22 September 1991, the rate applicable at the date of the further undertaking; or

    (ii) if the contribution is paid in accordance with a further undertaking entered into in a later year and payment is on or after 22 September 1991, the highest rate in the period from the due date to the date of the further undertaking; or

    (iii) if there has been a further undertaking but the contribution is paid *otherwise than* in accordance with that further undertaking and payment is before 22 September 1991, the rate applicable at the date of payment; or

    (iv) if there has been a further undertaking but the contribution is paid *otherwise than* in accordance with that further undertaking and payment is on or after 22 September 1991, the highest rate in the period from the due date to the date of payment.

[Reg 43B as amended by Contributions Amendment No 2 Regs 1985, Reg 4 and Contributions Amendment No 5 Regs 1991, Reg 2 and SSC(T)A 1999, 2 Sch].

(d) Where, following notification by the Inland Revenue in the last month of a tax year of the amount, a Class 2 contribution is paid within one calendar month from the date of notification but in the tax year immediately following notification, the rate at which that contribution is payable is the rate at which it would have been payable had it been paid on the last day of the tax year of notification. *[Contributions Regs Reg 43C, as amended by Contributions Amendment No 2 Regs 1985, Reg 4, Contributions Transitional Regs 1985, Reg 5(8) and SSC(T)A 1999, 2 Sch].*

(e) Where a Class 2 contribution is paid late but it is shown to the satisfaction of the Inland Revenue that the late payment was attributable to ignorance or error on the part of the contributor (other than ignorance or error due to his failure to exercise due care and diligence), the rate at which that contribution is payable is the rate at which it would have been payable had it been paid on the date on which the period to which it relates commenced. *[Contributions Regs, Reg 43D as amended by Contributions Amendment No 2 Regs 1985, Reg 4, Contributions Transitional Regs 1985, Reg 5(9) and SSC(T)A 1999, 2 Sch].*

(f) Where a Class 2 contribution is paid late but (a) to (e) do not apply, the rate at which that contribution is payable is

    (i) if it is paid in the tax year in which it is due or in the immediately following tax year, the rate at which it would have been payable had it been paid on its due date; or

    (ii) if it is paid at a date later than that stated in (i), the highest rate in the period from the due date to the date of payment. This is not necessarily the same as the rate in force on the date of payment.

[SSCBA 1992, s 12(3)].

Example

Alec became self-employed on 6 April 1992 and, knowing he was liable to pay Class 2 contributions, failed to do so. On 30 June 2000, the Inland Revenue discovers the failure and requires Alec to pay the arrears. The Class 2 weekly rate was £5.55 from 6 April 1993 to 5 April 1994, £5.65 from 6 April 1994 to 5 April 1995, £5.75 from 6 April 1995 to 5 April 1996, £6.05 from 6 April 1996 to 5 April 1997, £6.15 from 6 April 1997 to 5 April 1998, £6.35 from 6 April 1998 to 5 April 1999, £6.55 from 6 April 1999 to 5 April 2000 and £2.00 from 6 April 2000 to the date of payment. The payment of the contributions for the contribution year 1993–94 is taking place after the end of the tax year following the contribution year and the rate at which those contributions must be paid is, therefore, the highest (as in (*f*) (ii) above) of all the rates stated, i.e. £6.55 for each of the 52 weeks. The payment of the contributions for the contribution years 1994–95, 1995–96, 1996–97, 1997–98 and 1998–99 is also taking place after the end of the tax year following the contribution year and the rate at which those contributions must be paid is, therefore, the highest of the seven rates, £5.65, £5.75, £6.05, £6.15, £6.35, £6.55 and £2.00, i.e. £6.55. The payment of the contributions for the contribution year 1999–2000 and for the period from 6 April 2000 to 30 June 2000 is, however, taking place before the end of the tax year following the contribution year and the rates at which those contributions must be paid are, therefore, the rates at which they would have been paid had they been paid on their due dates, i.e. £6.55 per week and £2.00 per week, respectively. By reason of special rule (*b*) above, this position will remain unchanged even if Alec enters into an arrangement with the Inland Revenue and, under that arrangement, pays some or all of the arrears in an even later tax year when contribution rates may have increased once again, unless he fails to honour the undertaking.

Where a Class 3 contribution is paid late but is paid within the two tax years immediately following that to which it relates, the rate at which the contribution is payable is the rate at which the contribution would have been payable had it been paid in the tax year to which it relates. [*SSCBA 1992, s 13(4)(6)*]. Where, however, a Class 3 contribution is paid late and the payment is made after the end of the second tax year after that to which it relates, the rate at which the contribution is payable is, unless the contribution is of a kind referred to in the special rules set out below, the highest of the Class 3 contribution rate which would have applied had the contribution been paid in the tax year to which it relates, the Class 3 contribution rate applying at the date of payment or any other Class 3 contribution rate applying in the intervening period. [*SSCBA 1992, s 13(6)*].

The special rules referred to above are as follows:

(i) Where a Class 3 contribution is paid in respect of the tax year 1982–83 or in respect of any earlier tax year, the rate at which that contribution is payable (regardless of how late it is paid) is the rate at which it would have been payable had it been paid on its required date. [*Contributions Regs, Reg 43A as amended by Contributions Amendment No 2 Regs 1985, Reg 4*].

(ii) Where, following notification by the Inland Revenue (previously, the Secretary of State for Social Security) in the last month of a tax year of the amount, a Class 3 contribution is paid within one calendar month from the date of notification but in the tax year immediately following notification, the rate at which that contribution is payable is the rate at which it would have been payable had it been paid on the last day of the tax year of notification. [*Contributions Regs, Reg 43C as amended by Contributions Amendment No 2 Regs 1985, Reg 4, Contributions Transitional Regs 1985, Reg 5(8) and SSC(T)A 1999, 2 Sch*].

(iii) Where a Class 3 contribution is paid late but it is shown to the satisfaction of the Inland Revenue (previously the Secretary of State for Social Security) that the late payment was attributable to ignorance or error on the part of the contributor (other than ignorance or error due to his failure to exercise due care and diligence), the rate at which that contribution is payable is the rate applicable to the period for which the contribution is paid. [*Contributions Regs, Reg 43D(3)(a) as amended by Contributions Amendment No 2 Regs 1985, Reg 4, Contributions Transitional Regs 1985, Reg 5(9) and SSC(T)A 1999, 2 Sch*].

(iv) Where a Class 3 contribution is paid late and it is shown to the satisfaction of the Inland Revenue (previously, the Secretary of State for Social Security) that there was a period commencing at some date subsequent to the end of the second tax year after the tax year within which the contribution was due, where the contribution was not paid during those two subsequent tax years because of ignorance or error on the part of the contributor (other than ignorance or error due to his failure to exercise due care and diligence), the rate at which that contribution is payable is the rate at which it would have been payable had it been paid on the date at which the period of non-payment through ignorance or error began. [*Contributions Regs, Reg 43D(3)(b) as amended by Contribution Amendment No 2 Regs 1985, Reg 4, Contributions Transitional Regs 1985, Reg 5(9) and SSC(T)A 1999, 2 Sch*].

39.8   TREATMENT OF CONTRIBUTION ARREARS RECOVERED THROUGH THE COURT

Although unpaid contributions are recoverable through the court as a penalty (see 12.8 ARREARS OF CONTRIBUTIONS), the amount recovered is to be treated as being the contributions which it represents. [*SSAA 1992, s 121(4)(5)*]. Insofar as the amount represents primary Class 1 or Class 2 contributions, it is to be treated as contributions paid in respect of the persons with regard to whom they were originally payable. [*Sec 121(6)*]. Accordingly, the provisions described in this chapter will apply to such recoveries in the same way and to the same extent as they apply to other late-paid contributions.

39.9   INTEREST ON OVERDUE CONTRIBUTIONS

A person who fails to pay contributions by their due date may be proceeded against summarily (see ARREARS OF CONTRIBUTIONS (12)). He may also, from 19 April 1993, be liable for interest on overdue amounts of Class 1 and Class 1A contributions and on Class 4 contributions which attract an interest charge under *TMA 1970, s 86* (see Inspector's Manual, para 6035, issue 12/97 and Enforcement Manual, para 2514, issue 10/97). [*SSCBA 1992, 1 Sch 6(2)*]. Interest is charged on late-paid primary and secondary Class 1 contributions in respect of 1992–93 and subsequent years, and on Class 1A contributions for 1991–92 and subsequent years from the reckonable date until payment. It is also charged on late payments of Class 1B contributions for 1999–2000 onwards. (*Contributions Regs 1979 Sch 1, Regs 28A, 28B as inserted by Contributions Amendment No 5 Regs 1993 and as amended by The Social Security Contributions, Statutory Maternity Pay and Statutory Sick Pay (Miscellaneous Amendment) Regs 1999, Reg 4*).

In the case of Class 1 primary or secondary contributions the reckonable date is the fourteenth day after the end of the year in respect of which the contributions were due, and in the case of a Class 1A contribution it is the fourteenth day after the end of the year in which it was due to be paid. Interest will therefore run from 19 April 2000 in respect of late-paid 1998–99 Class 1A contributions if paid via the PAYE documentation. The position is now different if the 'Alternative Payment Method' is used — see 16.21 CLASS 1A: CONTRIBUTIONS: BENEFITS IN KIND. Interest is charged at the same rate as for late-paid income tax. [*SSCBA 1992, 1 Sch 6(3)* which refers to *FA 1989, s 178* as amended by the *Taxes (Interest Rate) (Amendment No 4) Regs 1996, No 3187*]. (See IR Press Release, 28 January 1997 and CA Press Release, 25

February 1999). Where an assessment has been made for the purpose of making good to the Crown a loss of tax wholly or partly attributable to a failure or an error on the part of the taxpayer, and a related Class 4 assessment is made also, the contributions charged by the Class 4 assessment already carry interest, just as the tax carries interest, under *TMA 1970, s 88(1)*, and the tax provisions in that section relating to the discretionary mitigation of interest, the staying or compounding of proceedings for its recovery, and the determination of the date from which it is to run, apply as regards the interest on Class 4 contributions also. (See also IR Press Release 1 April 1996). [*SSCBA 1992, 2 Sch 6 as amended by SS(CP)A 1992, 4 Sch 8*].

It should be noted that there may be a separate penalty under *TMA 1970, s 7* (failure to notify liability) in relation to Class 4 contributions. It has been known for the Inland Revenue, on occasions, to attempt to impose a double penalty: e.g., before 6 April 1988, £100 in respect of failure to notify a liability to tax, £100 in respect of failure to notify a liability to Class 4 contributions; it is questionable whether the imposition of the latter penalty is invalid, but the penalty provisions of *TMA 1970, Pt X* are specifically stated to apply to Class 4 contributions '*as if those contributions were*' Schedule D, Case I or II income tax. [*SSCBA 1992, s 16(1)*]. This is interpreted by some Inspectors of Taxes as meaning that they are added to the income tax liability and by others as meaning that the liability is separate and distinct and, therefore, open to additional penalties. The position since 6 April 1988 has been that the maximum penalty for failure to notify is the tax liability in respect of income from each undeclared source for a year under assessments made more than twelve months after the end of the year. The penalty in respect of Class 4 liability assessed in this way may therefore equal the contributions due in respect of the undeclared income.

The *Social Security Act 1998* amends *SSCBA 1992, 2 Sch 6(1)* so that references to *TMA 1970, s 88* in that section are repealed, this interest charging provision now being effectively redundant under the 'self-assessment' income tax regime. [*SSCBA 1992, 2 Sch 6 as repealed by Social Security Act 1998, s 59*].

Before 1 April 1999, interest was not charged on disputed amounts of NICs pending a determination by the Secretary of State under *SSAA 1992, s 17*. Under the new NICs appeals procedure which came into effect on 1 April 1999 (see APPEALS AND REVIEWS (9)) the amount of the disputed NICs liability and the interest on it need not be paid while an appeal to the tax appeal Commissioners is pending. If the liability is confirmed the whole amount becomes payable, together with the interest on the debt calculated under normal rules e.g. in the case of Class 1 contributions, from 14 days after the end of the tax year in which it becomes due.

For details of repayment supplement payable where refunds of contributions are received late, see 53.2 and 53.7 REPAYMENT AND RE-ALLOCATION.

40 Leaflets

40.1 ESTOPPEL

Each leaflet carries the warning that it gives general guidance only and should not be treated as a complete and authoritative statement of the law. There is no estoppel against the Crown and as the Inland Revenue and DSS cannot, therefore, be prevented from denying statements contained in their leaflets, no legal reliance may be placed in their contents. (*Southend-on-Sea Corporation v Hodgson (Wickford) Ltd [1961] 2 AER 46*). If, however, the Inland Revenue and DSS were to ignore considerations which, according to one of its leaflets, were relevant and were to reach a decision based on other considerations, it would have misdirected itself according to its own criteria and its decision could be quashed by an order of *certiorari*. (*R v Secretary of State for the Home Department ex p Khan [1985] 1 AER 45*).

40.2 LEAFLETS

The Inland Revenue, DSS and Benefits Agency produce various leaflets, many of which are specifically aimed at employers (i.e. manuals, tables and fact cards) and these are listed below.

Leaflets regarding National Insurance Contributions are issued by the Inland Revenue (except for SA series leaflets, which are issued by the Benefits Agency) and can be obtained from

*local Inland Revenue (NIC) offices

+ coastal Inland Revenue offices

++ International Services, NICO, Longbenton, NEWCASTLE UPON TYNE NE98 1ZZ or Department of Social Security, Pensions and Overseas Benefits Directorate, Customer Service Unit, Room TC 109, NEWCASTLE UPON TYNE NE98 1BA.

** Contracted-out Employments Group, NICO, Longbenton, NEWCASTLE UPON TYNE NE98 1ZZ.

Employers Orderline (08457 646 646)

Contributions Agency Leaflets

Number	Data	Name
*CA 01	Apr 00	National Insurance contributions for employees
*CA 02	Apr 00	National Insurance contributions for self-employed people with small earnings 2000–2001
*CA 04	Apr 00	Class 2 and Class 3 National Insurance contributions Direct Debit the easier way to pay
*CA 07	Apr 99	NIC unpaid and late paid contributions
*CA 08	Apr 00	NIC Voluntary contributions
*CA 09	Jun 99	National Insurance contributions for widows
*CA 10	Jun 99	National Insurance contributions for divorced women
+CA 11	Apr 99	National Insurance contributions for share fishermen
*CA 12	Sep 99	Training for further employment and your National Insurance record
*CA 13	Jun 99	NIC for married women
**CA 14	Apr 99	Termination of Contracted-out Employment Manual for Salary Related Pension Schemes and Salary Related Parts of Mixed Benefits Schemes
**CA 14A	Apr 99	Termination of Contracted-out Employment Manual for Money Purchase Pension Schemes and Money Purchase Parts of Mixed Benefits Schemes

Number	Data	Name
**CA 14B	Apr 97	Contracted-out Guidance on re-elections for Salary Related Pension Schemes and Salary Related Overseas Schemes
**CA 14C	Apr 99	Contracted-out Guidance for Salary Related Pension Schemes and Salary Related Overseas Schemes
**CA 14D	Apr 99	Contracted-out Guidance for Money Purchase Pension Schemes and Money Purchase Overseas Schemes
**CA 14E	Apr 99	Contracted-out Guidance for Mixed Benefit Pension Schemes and Mixed Benefit Overseas Schemes
**CA 14F	Jul 99	Technical Guidance on Contracted-Out Decision Making and Appeals
**CA 15	Apr 99	Cessation of Contracted-out Pension Schemes Manual
**CA 16	Apr 99	Appropriate Personal Pension Scheme Manual—Procedural Guidance
**CA 16A	Apr 99	Appropriate Personal Pension Scheme Manual—Guidance for Scheme Managers
**CA 17	Apr 00	Employee's guide to minimum contributions
**CA 19	Apr 99	Using the Accrued GMP Liability Service
**CA 20	Apr 99	Using the Contracted-out Contributions/Earnings Information Service
**CA 21	Jun 99	Using the National Insurance Number/Date of Birth Checking Service
**CA 22	Jun 99	Contracted-out Data Transactions Using Magnetic Media
+CA 23	Apr 00	National Insurance contributions for mariners
+CA 24	Apr 00	National Insurance contributions for masters and employers of mariners
*CA 25	Jun 99	National Insurance contributions for agencies and people working through agencies
*CA 26	Jun 99	National Insurance contributions for examiners, lecturers, teachers and instructors
*/#CA 29	Apr 00	Statutory Maternity Pay Manual for employers
*/#CA 30	Apr 00	Statutory Sick Pay Manual for employers
*/#CA 33	Apr 00	Cars and Fuel Manual
*/#CA 34	Apr 00	Provision of National Insurance related information and services (Class 1A APM application form)
*/#CA 35/36	Apr 00	Statutory Sick Pay and Statutory Maternity Pay Tables
*CA 37	Apr 00	Simplified Deductions Scheme for employers
*/#CA 38	Apr 00	Not contracted-out contributions for employers
**CA 39	Apr 00	Contracted-out contributions for employers with Contracted-out Salary Related Schemes
*CA 40	Apr 99	Employee only contributions tables for employers
+CA 42	Apr 99	Foreign-going Mariner's deep-sea fishermen's contributions tables for employers
**CA 43	Apr 00	Contracted-out contributions and minimum payments for employers with contracted-out Money Purchase Schemes
*/#CA 44	Apr 00	National Insurance for Company Directors (Employer's Manual)
*CA 47	Apr 99	Charter for National Insurance contributors
*CA 49	Apr 99	Make your end of year easier End of year returns by Magnetic Media
*CA 50	Apr 99	Making Year End Returns on Tape or Disc—General Guide
*CA 51/52	Apr 00	Making Year End Returns on Tape or Disc
*/++CA 65	Sep 99	National Insurance contributions for people working for embassies, consulates and overseas employers
*CA 66	May 97	Surveys of National Insurance Records — A Code of Practice
*CA 67	1998	Contributions Agency Business Plan 1998-1999
*CA 68	1998	Contributions Agency Annual Report 1997-1998
*CA 69	Oct 95	Are your workers employed or self-employed? (construction industry)
*CA 72	Apr 00	National Insurance contributions deferring payment

40.2 Leaflets

Number	Data	Name
*CA 76	Sep 99	National Insurance abroad—A guide for employers of employees from abroad
*CA 83	Apr 00	National Insurance Contributions Office — Quality Service through people
*CA 86	Apr 00	Employee's Guide to Statutory Sick Pay
*CA 87	Apr 00	National Insurance contributions and the Welsh Language
*CA 88	Apr 00	Payroll Cleaning. What is it and what can it do for you?
*COP 1	Apr 99	Mistakes by the Inland Revenue
*COP 3	Apr 99	Inland Revenue: Reviews of employers' and contractors' records
*COP 10	Apr 99	Inland Revenue: Information and advice
*/#CWG 1	Apr 00	Employer's quick guide to PAYE and NICs
*/#CWG 2	Jan 00	Employer's Further Guide to PAYE and NICs
*/#CWG 3	Jan 00	The Employer's Annual Pack
*/#CWG 5	Jan 00	Class 1A National Insurance contributions on Benefits in Kind—A preliminary guide for employers to proposed changes for 2000–01
*CWL 1	Mar 99	Starting your own business?
*CWL 2	Mar 99	National Insurance contributions for self-employed people. Class 2 and Class 4
*CWL 3	Oct 97	Thinking of taking someone on?
*IR 37	Apr 99	Appeals against tax, National Insurance contributions, Statutory Sick Pay and Statutory Maternity Pay
*IR 56	Apr 99	Employed or self-employed?
*NE 1	Mar 99	First steps as a new employer
*/++NI 38	Apr 99	Social Security abroad
*/++NI 132	Apr 99	National Insurance for employers of people working abroad
*NIC 2	Jun 99	National Insurance contributions Holiday Scheme Getting back to work and saving you money?
++SA 4	Apr 99	Social security agreement between United Kingdom and Jersey and Guernsey
++SA 5	Aug 96	Social security agreement between United Kingdom and Australia
++SA 6	May 99	Social security agreement between United Kingdom and Switzerland
++SA 8	Oct 96	Social security agreement between United Kingdom and New Zealand
++SA 9	Dec 94	Social security agreement between United Kingdom and Sweden
++SA 11	Apr 99	Social security agreement between United Kingdom and Malta
++SA 12	Apr 99	Social security agreement between United Kingdom and Cyprus
++SA 14	Aug 96	Social security agreement between United Kingdom and Israel
++SA 17	Apr 97	Social security agreement between United Kingdom and the Republics of the former Yugoslavia
++SA 19	Jan 95	Social security agreement between United Kingdom and Finland
++SA 20	Apr 98	Social security agreement between United Kingdom and Canada
++SA 22	Jan 95	Social security agreement between United Kingdom and Turkey
++SA 23	Dec 96	Social security agreement between United Kingdom and Bermuda
++SA 24	Dec 94	Social security agreement between United Kingdom and Iceland
++SA 25	Jan 95	Social security agreement between United Kingdom and Austria
++SA 27	Apr 97	Social security agreement between United Kingdom and Jamaica
++SA 29	Aug 98	Your social security insurance, benefits and healthcare rights in the European Community, and in Iceland, Liechtenstein and Norway
++SA 33	Sep 97	Social security agreement between United Kingdom and United States of America

Number	Data	Name
++SA 38	Apr 99	Social security agreement between United Kingdom and Mauritius
++SA 42	Apr 97	Social security agreement between United Kingdom and Philippines
++SA 43	Feb 97	Social security agreement between United Kingdom and Barbados

Other social security leaflets are available from local social security offices, except where indicated

* only available from Child Support Literature Line, Room 164E, DSS Longbenton, NEWCASTLE UPON TYNE NE98 1YX (phone 08457 133133)

+ only available from Department of Health, PO Box 777, LONDON SE1 6XH

++ DSS Pensions, FREEPOST BS5555/1, BRISTOL BS99 1BL (phone 08457 31 32 33, textphone 08456 040210)

** Phone 0800 555 777

only available from War Pensions Agency Distrbution Unit, Room 403A, Norcross, BLACKPOOL FY5 3WP

Number	Date	Name
AC 2	Apr 97	How would you like your child benefit to arrive?
BC 1	Apr 00	Babies and children
BC 2	Oct 99	Expecting a baby?
BC 3	Apr 00	Bringing up children?
BTWB 20	Mar 98	Back to Work Bonus
CF 411	Oct 99	Home Responsibilities Protection
CH 1	Oct 99	Child Benefit
CH 4	Sep 97	Child Benefit for children away from home
CH 4A	Apr 97	Social security and children being looked after by a local authority
CH 5	Sep 97	Child Benefit for people entering Britain
CH 6	Apr 97	Child Benefit for people leaving Britain
CH 7	Dec 98	Child Benefit for children aged 16 and over
CH 11	Jul 98	Child Benefit for lone parents
CMB 20	Oct 98	Child Maintenance Bonus
*CSA 2001	Nov 99	Child Support for parents who live apart
*CSA 2002	Nov 99	Changes in child maintenance Advice to Employers
*CSA 2084	Oct 98	A catalogue of CSA leaflets, audio tapes, posters and information
CUST 1	Nov 99	Benefits Agency—Customer Charter
D 49	Feb 99	What to do after a death in England and Wales
DAP 01	Jan 97	Benefits Agency national fax and textphone directory
DS 702	Oct 97	Attendance Allowance
DS 704	Oct 97	Disability Living Allowance – You could benefit
DS 706	Apr 97	Disability Living Allowance for children
++EQP 1a	Feb 96	Equality in State Pension Age
GL 12	Oct 99	Going into hospital?
GL 13	Oct 99	Separated or divorced?
GL 14	Oct 99	Widowed?
GL 16	Apr 00	Help with your rent
GL 17	Oct 99	Help with your council tax
GL 18	Oct 99	Help from the Social Fund
GL 19	Oct 99	School-leavers and students
GL 21	Jul 99	A helping hand for benefits?
GL 22	Jul 99	Tell us your comments and complaints
GL 23	Apr 00	Social security benefit rates
GL 24	Jul 99	If you think our decision is wrong
GL 25	Oct 99	How to prove your identity for social security
GL 26	Oct 99	Service families
GL 27	Oct 99	Compensation and social security benefits
GL 28	Oct 99	Coming from abroad and social security benefits

40.2 Leaflets

Number	Data	Name
GL 29	Oct 99	Going abroad and social security benefits
HB 3	Oct 99	Vaccine damage payments
HB 5	Oct 99	Non-Contributory Benefits for Disabled People
+HB 6	Nov 98	A Practical Guide for Disabled People
+HC 11	Apr 98	Are you entitled to help with health costs?
+HC 12	Apr 99	NHS charges and optical voucher values
+HC 13	Jan 98	Help with health costs
IB 202	Sep 99	Incapacity Benefit—Information for new customers
IB 203	Sep 99	Incapacity benefit—Getting back to work
IB 214	Apr 97	Incapacity benefit—The all work test
IS 1	Apr 98	Income support
IS 9	Jan 98	Direct payment
IS 20	Oct 98	Income Support
JSA 8	Jan 99	Jobseeker's Allowance and Income Support if you are 16 or 17 years old
JSA 9	Oct 99	Jobseeker's Hardship provision
JSAL 5	Feb 99	Jobseeker's Allowance—Helping You Back To Work
JSAL 6	Oct 99	Jobseeker's Allowance Over 60? Nearing age 60?
JSAL 7	Mar 97	Jobseeker's Allowance – Voluntary work when you're unemployed
JSAL 22	Jan 97	Jobseeker's Allowance People going abroad or coming from abroad
JSAL 74	Jan 97	Jobseeker's Allowance Short term working or temporarily laid off from work
LP 15	Sep 99	New deal for lone parents
NI 14	Oct 99	Guardian's Allowance
NI 17A	Oct 99	A guide to Maternity Benefits
NI 92	Feb 97	Giving up your right to Retirement Pension to earn extra
NI 105	Aug 97	Your Retirement Pension or widow's benefits paid straight into an account
NI 260 DMA	Oct 99	A guide to Dispute, Supersession and Appeal
NP 45	Sep 99	A guide to Widow's Benefits
NP 46	Nov 99	A guide to Retirement Pensions
++PEC 1	Aug 98	Information about pensions
++PEC 5	Aug 96	Occupational pension schemes and the Pensions Act 1995 – How to appoint member-nominated trustees A guide for trustees and employers
++PEC 6	Apr 96	Occupational pension schemes and the Pensions Act 1995 – A guide for trustees, employers and scheme administrators
++PM 1	Jan 00	Don't leave your pension to chance
++PM 2	Jan 00	You and state pensions
++PM 3	Jan 00	You and occupational pensions
++PM 4	Jan 00	You and personal pensions
++PM 5	Jan 00	Pensions for the self-employed
++PM 6	Jan 00	Pensions for women
++PM 7	Jan 00	Understanding contracted-out pensions
++PM 8	Jan 00	Making the most of your personal pension
++PP 4	Oct 94	A guide to the Financial Services Act for employers
PRIS 1	Dec 98	Prisoners and their families A guide to benefits
RM 1	Oct 99	Retirement
RM 2	Oct 99	Approaching retirement?
RM 3	Oct 99	Retired?
RR 2	Oct 98	Housing Benefit and Council Tax Benefit
SB 16	Nov 99	A guide to The Social Fund
SD 1	Apr 00	Sick or disabled
SD 2	Oct 99	Sick and unable to work?
SD 3	Oct 99	Long-term ill or disabled?
SD 4	Oct 99	Caring for someone?
SD 6	Oct 99	Ill or disabled because of a disease or deafness caused by work?

Number	Data	Name
SD 7	Oct 99	Disabled because of an accident at work?
*T 6	Mar 99	Health advice for Travellers
TD 1	Feb 94	Income Support Trade disputes Notes for employers
WFP 5	Sep 99	Winter Fuel Payments 1999
WK 1	Apr 00	Financial help if you work or are looking for work
WK 2	Oct 99	Financial help if you are looking for work
WK 3	Oct 99	Need help starting work or getting back to work?
WK 4	Oct 99	Financial help if you are working or doing voluntary work
+WMV: G1	Mar 96	Welfare milk and vitamins
#WPA 1	Oct 99	Notes about the War Disablement Pension and War Widow's Pension
#WPA 2	Oct 99	Notes for people getting a war pension living in the United Kingdom
#WPA 3	Oct 99	Notes for people getting a war pension living overseas
#WPA 4	Oct 99	Notes for people not getting a war pension living in the United Kingdom
#WPA 5	Oct 99	Notes for people not getting a war pension living overseas
#WPA 6	Nov 99	Notes for War Pensioners and War Widows going abroad
#WPA 7	May 99	Notes for Ex-Far East and Korean Prisoners of War
#WPA 9	Apr 99	Rates of War Pensions and allowances 1999–2000
#WPA 10	Jun 98	Notes about War Pension claims for deafness
#WPA 11	Apr 98	How we decide who receives a War Disablement Pension
Z 1	Nov 99	Recovery of benefits – Procedures for liaison with the Compensation Recovery Unit
Z 2	Jan 98	Recovery of benefits Appeal Guide

40.3   Inland Revenue Tax Bulletin

The IR Tax Bulletin is published every other month and, from April 1999, contains relevant national insurance material. This is in place of the CA 'National Insurance News', the final issue of which was No 12, Winter 1998–99. Extracts from CA National Insurance News are reproduced at the back of this book. To subscribe to the Tax Bulletin send a crossed cheque for £22, payable to 'Inland Revenue', to Inland Revenue, Finance Division, Barrington Road, WORTHING, West Sussex BN12 4XH.

40.4   Contributors' Charter

In the Inland Revenue booklet CA47 'Charter for National Insurance contributors' the Charter, reproduced below, has been produced after consultation with staff and customers.

Our service commitment to you

The Inland Revenue and Customs & Excise are committed to serving your needs well by

Acting fairly and impartially

We

- Treat your affairs in strict confidence, within the law

- Want you to pay or receive the right amount due.

Communicating effectively with you

We aim to provide

- Clear and simple forms and guidance

- Accurate and complete information in a helpful and appropriate way.

Providing good quality service

We aim to

- Handle your affairs promptly and accurately
- Be accessible in ways that are convenient to you
- Keep your costs to the minimum necessary
- Take reasonable steps to meet special needs
- Be courteous and professional

Taking responsibility for our service

- We publish annually our customer service aims and achievements.
- If you wish to comment, or make a complaint, we want to hear from you so we can improve our service. We advise you how to do this.

We can provide better service if you help us by

- Keeping accurate and up-to-date records
- Letting us know if your personal/business circumstances change
- Giving us correct and complete information when we ask for it
- Paying on time what you should pay.

Further information on customer service is available at Inland Revenue and Customs & Excise local offices, set out in our Charters, complaints leaflets (IR120 and Notice 1000) and Codes of Practice.

Our overall approach to customer service

This Charter covers customer affairs relating to individual contributors' National Insurance, for which we aim to provide an efficient effective and fair service. The service is provided through the Inland Revenue's National Insurance Contributions Office and a network of Inland Revenue (National Insurance Contributions) offices and Inland Revenue Enquiry Centres based in the ten Inland Revenue regions. The Benefits Agency* also provides information and basic advice.

The Charter has been developed after consultation with our customers and staff and sets out:

- How we will provide you with the help and assistance
- The standards of service you can expect
- How you can help us deliver an effective service and make suggestions for further improvement
- Where you can obtain information about your legal rights relating to National Insurance and other entitlements, and
- How to complain if you are unhappy with the service we provide.

Providing you with help and assistance

We provide help:

- Through a wide range of clearly written leaflets and booklets. Each explains a particular aspect of National Insurance, or what to do in specific circumstances (for example, if you wish to make voluntary contributions). These leaflets and booklets are available from all Inland Revenue (National Insurance Contributions) offices and a selection is available from Inland Revenue Enquiry Centres and most Benefit Agency offices. Information is also available on the National Insurance page of the Inland Revenue Internet website at **www.inlandrevenue.gov.uk**

- Over the telephone, in person at the Inland Revenue Enquiry Centres, Benefits Agency offices and in writing. The Inland Revenue leaflet 'How to contact the Inland Revenue', available from all Inland Revenue offices, sets out the main sources of Inland Revenue help and advice available to you.

Contacting us

Opening hours

Inland Revenue Enquiry Centres are open for at least 40 hours a week. Most are open from 8.30 am to 4.30 pm, Monday to Friday, and some are also open outside these hours.

Many Inland Revenue (National Insurance Contributions) offices are shared with the Benefits Agency. These shared offices are open for at least 36 hours a week, including the period between 9.00 am to 3.30 pm, Monday to Friday, although offices will open earlier or close later to meet customer needs.

Telephone service

Switchboards in Inland Revenue (National Insurance Contributions) offices are also open for at least 36 hours a week, including the period between 9.00 am to 3.30 pm, Monday to Friday, although offices will open earlier or close later to meet customer needs.

Addresses

The address of the National Insurance Contributions Office, where all National Insurance records are kept is:

> National Insurance Contributions Office
> Longbenton
> Newcastle upon Tyne
> NE98 1ZZ
> (Telephone 0191 213 5000, E-mail **www.dss.gov.uk**)

The address and telephone number of locally based Inland Revenue (National Insurance Contributions) offices will be at the top of any correspondence they have sent to you; alternatively, details can be found in your telephone directory under 'Contributions Agency' or, in some cases, 'Inland Revenue'. In Northern Ireland, these will be listed in the phone book as 'Social Security Agency, Contributions Unit', under 'Government of Northern Ireland—Department of Health and Social Services'.

Our standards of service

If you **telephone** us, we aim to:

- Answer within 30 seconds (ten rings) at the switchboard
- Connect you to the right extension first time (unless your call has gone direct).

If you **visit** any of our Inland Revenue Enquiry Centres, we aim to see you within 15 minutes of arrival if you have not previously made an appointment. The Benefits Agency will also aim to see you within 10 minutes or, at particularly busy times, within 30 minutes.

Many Inland Revenue (National Insurance Contributions) offices are shared with the Benefits Agency and the receptionist you see works for them. Benefits Agency staff can answer basic National Insurance enquiries, but if your question is complex they will make an appointment for an Inland Revenue member of staff specialising in National Insurance Contributions to see you or to contact you by telephone.

If you **write** to us, we aim to provide a full reply within 28 calendar days. Where this is not possible, we will tell you why and when you can expect a full reply.

However you contact us, we will:

- Provide a clear, accurate and helpful response
- Make clear what action you need to take next, and by what date
- Give you our names and telephone numbers, and
- Be courteous and professional.

In addition, we aim to:

- get every aspect of your affairs right the first time by making full and correct use of the information available to us
- tell you what we are doing to put things right, if there are any problems.

Specific targets and previous year's results

The National Insurance Contributions Office works with the ten Regional Executive Offices (whose contact details are given in the back of this leaflet) to deliver a national service on National Insurance Contributions.

In this first year as part of the Inland Revenue, the National Insurance Contributions Office will produce a leaflet showing its customers service targets for the year. In future, it will continue to publish these standards, as well as performance against the previous year's targets.

Customer service leaflets are available from the National Insurance Contributions Office and all Inland Revenue (National Insurance Contributions) offices. The information is also published in the Department's annual report available from The Stationery Office and on the Internet.

Privacy and confidentiality

In handling your affairs, we will:

- deal with them on a strictly confidential basis, within the law
- respect your privacy
- if you visit us, find a private room or space for you to discuss your affairs, should you prefer it.

Any special needs

If you have special needs (for example, related to a disability) we will provide whatever help we reasonably can. Most Inland Revenue Enquiry Centres and Inland Revenue (National Insurance Contributions) offices have already been equipped with ramps, hearing loops and other aids, and we are installing Minicom systems (for people with hearing difficulties). Some leaflets are being converted, on a rolling programme, to Braille, audio and large print. Details of specific services can be found in the Regional Executive Office Customer Service leaflets (available from the Inland Revenue Enquiry Centres).

If you need to see us, but you have a disability which prevents you from coming to our office, please phone or write explaining the problem and what you need from us. We will make the necessary arrangements to visit you.

Please discuss any other requirements with the Customer Service Manager of the office with which you are dealing (you can get their name from any member of staff in the office). They will explain what they can offer to help you.

Your legal rights and our Codes of Practice

The Inland Revenue produces Codes of Practice explaining our approach and procedures in certain areas of work (some of which apply to National Insurance). The Codes set out, as appropriate, your legal rights and the rights of the Inland Revenue, and explain what you can expect to happen. Copies of the Codes are available from local Inland Revenue offices, and those which refer specifically to National Insurance from the National Insurance Contributions Office.

How you can help us

We need to maintain your National Insurance records accurately and securely. Please make sure that your National Insurance number does not get into the wrong hands. If you have any doubts about giving it to someone, please contact your nearest Inland Revenue (National Insurance Contributions) office for advice.

If you contact us, please quote your National Insurance number (which is unique to you). You can find this on your payslip. You should also give your full name and, if possible, a phone or fax number which we can use if we need more information. If you have forgotten your National Insurance number, contact the nearest Inland Revenue or Benefits Agency office.

It is also important that you tell the National Insurance Contributions office when your circumstances change – for example, if you change your name or address. This will allow us to continue to record your contributions accurately.

Make sure you give your employer your National Insurance number as soon as you start work for them: without this, the contributions deducted from your pay may be recorded on the wrong account and so cause you delay, should you want to claim benefit.

If you are self-employed, please tell us as soon as possible if you:

- expect your self-employed earnings in your first year of trading to be low

- work for an employer as well as being self-employed

- stop being self-employed.

What to do if you disagree with us

You may disagree with our interpretation of the law or the way we have applied it to your particular circumstances. If so, you should let us know why you disagree. Alternatively, if we have already made a formal decision on your contributions liability, you are entitled to appeal against what we have done. The letter we send advising you of the formal decision will explain how to do this. If we can not resolve your appeal, you can refer the matter to the General or Special Commissioners – independent appeals tribunals whose decision is binding on both parties. Appeals on the Commissioners' interpretation of the law can be made through the civil courts.

If you wish to complain

If you are unhappy about the way we have dealt with your affairs (because, for example, of delays, mistakes or failure to act on information you have given us), you should complain first of all to the Officer in Charge of the office or unit you are dealing with (their name is displayed at the head of all correspondence) **or** to the Officer in Charge of the Business Unit (if you are dealing with the National Insurance Contributions Office).

If you are still not satisfied, you can refer the complaint to the Director with overall responsibility for that office or unit (the name and address of the Director is shown in the leaflet IR120 and can also be obtained from any Revenue office) **or** to the Director of the National Insurance Contributions Office if you are dealing with the National Insurance Contributions Office.

If you are dissatisfied with the Director's response, you can ask the Adjudicator to look at your complaint. Finally, you can ask your MP to refer your case to the independent Parliamentary Commissioner for Administration (the Ombudsman). The Ombudsman will accept referral from any MP, but you should approach your own MP first. The Inland Revenue leaflet IR 120 'You and the Inland Revenue' explains these options.

The Adjudicator's Office also produces leaflet, AO3 (AO4 for Northern Ireland) explaining its role and procedures. Copies of the Adjudicator's leaflet are available from the Adjudicator's Office (Haymarket House, 28 Haymarket, London SW1Y 4SP) and all Inland Revenue offices.

Listening to your suggestions

We welcome your suggestions and use them to improve our service and supporting processes. We supplement this with:

- an annual national postal survey, covering all major customer groups
- local surveys, as appropriate
- feedback from complaints.

Please make any suggestions for improvement (including this Charter) direct to the Customer Service Manager at your Inland Revenue (National Insurance Contributions) office, Inland Revenue Enquiry Centre or the National Insurance Contributions Office.

Revision date

This Charter came into force at 1 April 1999; it will be reviewed annually and (if not amended before then) will be reissued at 1 April 2002.

Useful addresses and phone numbers

National Insurance Contributions Office

George Bertram, National Insurance Contributions Office, Longbenton, Newcastle upon Tyne NE98 1YX tel 0191 213 5000.

Regional Offices

East — Stephen Banyard, Inland Revenue East, Churchgate, New Road, Peterborough PE1 1TD tel 01733 754321.

North West — Geoff Lunn, Inland Revenue North West, The Triad, Stanley Road, Bootle, Merseyside L75 2DD tel 0151 300 3000.

London — John Carling, Inland Revenue London, New Court, 48 Carey Street, London WC2A 2JE tel 0171 324 1222.

South East — Tony Sleeman, Inland Revenue South East, Duke's Court, Duke Street, Woking GU21 1BT tel 01483 258600.

North — Richard Cooke, Inland Revenue North, Dunedin House, Columbia Drive, Stockton-on-Tees TS17 6QZ tel 01642 637700.

South West — Roger Hurcombe, Inland Revenue South West, Longbrook House, New North Road, Exeter EX4 4QU tel 01392 663210.

South Yorkshire — Mary Hay, Inland Revenue South Yorkshire, Concept House, 5 Young Street, Sheffield, S1 4LF tel 0114 296 9696.

Wales and Midlands — Malcolm Kirk, Inland Revenue Wales and Midlands, 1st Floor, Ty Glas, Llanishen, Cardiff CF4 5TS tel 02920 325000.

Northern Ireland — David Hinstridge, Inland Revenue Northern Ireland, Dorchester House, 52–58 Great Victoria Street, Belfast BT2 7QE tel 01232 245123.

Scotland — Ian Gerrie, Inland Revenue Scotland, Clarendon House, 114–116 George Street, Edinburgh EH2 4LH tel 0131 473 4000.

We produce a wide range of leaflets, booklets and helpsheets designed to explain different aspects of the tax system in plain English and to assist in the completion of tax returns. Most of them are free.

Our leaflet IR120 'You and the Inland Revenue' tells you more about the standard of service you can expect and the steps to take if you want to comment on the service you receive, or complain about the way we have handled your tax affairs.

Our IR List 'Catalogue of leaflets and booklets' gives further information about our publications, most of which you can get from any Inland Revenue Enquiry Centre or Tax Office. Addresses are in your local phone book under 'Inland Revenue'. Most offices are open to the public from 8.30 am to 4.30 pm, Monday to Friday, and some are also open outside these hours.

Our leaflet 'How to contact the Inland Revenue', available from all Inland Revenue offices, sets out the main sources of help and information available to you.

Your local library or Citizens' Advice Bureau may also have copies of our leaflets.

You can also get our Self Assessment leaflets by calling our Orderline on **0645 000404** between 8.00 am and 10.00 pm, seven days a week (except Christmas Day)

fax on **0645 000604**

e-mail on **saorderline.ir@gtnet.gov.uk** or

writing to **PO Box 37, St Austell, Cornwall PL25 5YN**

Many leaflets are also available on the Internet at **www.inlandrevenue.gov.uk**

Helpline and Orderline calls are charged at local rates.

---

* Please note that all references to the Benefits Agency should be read as Social Security Agency in Northern Ireland.

41 Lecturers, Teachers and Instructors

Cross-references. See ANNUAL MAXIMUM (7); CATEGORISATION (14); CLASS 1 CONTRIBUTIONS (15); CLASS 2 CONTRIBUTIONS (18); DEFERMENT (27); 38.3 LABOUR-ONLY CONTRACTORS for the position of driving instructors.

Other Sources. Simon's NIC, Part I, Section 2, Chapter 4.131–136; Leaflet CA 26.

41.1 GENERAL CONSIDERATIONS

Most lecturers, teachers and instructors will indisputably fall to be categorised as employed earners by reason of their being employed under contracts of service or holding offices with emoluments chargeable to income tax under Schedule E (see 14.2 to 14.9 CATEGORISATION). The main exceptions will be teachers in private schools which are being run by those teachers in partnership and head teachers who are the proprietors of the private schools in which they teach. Such teachers will fall to be categorised as self-employed earners.

Student teachers will, if they are gainfully employed in Great Britain, generally be categorised as employed earners on normal principles (see 41.3 below). So, too, will most part-time teachers because of the degree of control to which they will be subject. Even if a particular part-time teacher would fall to be categorised as self-employed on general principles, however, he or she may fall to be *treated* as an employed earner by virtue of regulations (see 41.2 below).

The fact that a member of a religious order who is employed as a teacher may arrange for the whole of his or her remuneration to be paid to the order will not prevent that person falling to be categorised as an employed earner if he or she has a contractual entitlement to the remuneration in question.

41.2 CATEGORISATION

Employed earners by regulation

Anyone who, on or after 6 April 1978, is employed as a lecturer, teacher, instructor or in any similar capacity in an educational establishment (see below for definition) by any person providing education is to be treated as falling within the category of employed earner *provided*

(*a*) he is not an agency worker (see AGENCY WORKERS (4)); and

(*b*) the instruction is not given as public lectures; and

(*c*) the number of days on which the instruction is given has not been limited, by prior agreement, to three days or less in three consecutive months; and

(*d*) he gives the instruction in the presence of the person to whom the instruction is given, except where the employment is in the Open University; and

(*e*) his earnings are paid by, or on behalf of, the person providing the education.

[*SSCBA 1992, s 2(2)(b); Categorisation Regs, Reg 2(2), 1 Sch Pt I Para 4 as amended by Categorisation Amendment Regs 1984, Reg 2*].

Where the person *is* an agency worker (see AGENCY WORKERS (4)) he will still fall to be categorised as an employed earner but under those special categorisation rules and not under these rules.

A lecture is regarded as 'public' if members of the public may attend whether they do or not and whether or not they are charged for admission. A lecture that is part of a course or that is only open to a particular group of persons or to the members of a particular society is not regarded as 'public'.

An 'educational establishment' includes any place where instruction is provided in any course or part of a course designed to lead to a certificate, diploma, degree or professional qualification, or any like place where courses are substantially similar but do not lead to a certificate, etc. [*Categorisation Regs, Reg 1(2)*]. The term accordingly covers universities, colleges and schools of all kinds including schools of arts and crafts and languages. (Leaflet CA 26). The DSS did not regard a teacher's own home as an educational establishment.

The phrase 'in three consecutive months' is presumably intended to mean in an *overall* period of three months but could also be interpreted as meaning in each of three consecutive months. The DSS rejected this latter interpretation.

The clause 'in the presence of the person to whom instruction is given' precludes instruction by correspondence and videotape (except where the educational establishment is the Open University); and the qualification concerning pay precludes the payment of fees directly to the instructor by individual students. (Leaflet CA 26).

The former Contributions Agency used the regulations in relation to self-employed peripatetic music teachers giving instruction in non-local authority schools. If the teacher is paid by or on behalf of the school, Class 1 contributions are due from both the individual and the school. However, if the teacher contracts directly with the parents of the children in question and receives payment directly from the parents, the arrangement is outside the scope of the regulations.

The position is similar in relation to university lecturers, etc. whose employers were also been to special interest by the Agency.

The person falling to be treated as the secondary contributor in a case falling within these provisions is the person providing the education. [*Categorisation Regs, Reg 5, 3 Sch 6 as amended by Categorisation Amendment Regs 1984, Reg 4*].

41.3 Other lecturers, teachers and instructors

Where a person does not fall to be categorised as an employed earner under the regulation described at 41.2 above and is not in an office with emoluments chargeable to income tax under Schedule E, the normal tests must be applied to determine whether he is, in fact, under a contract of service (see 14.4 to 14.7 CATEGORISATION).

In 1954, the Secretary of State determined that a golf professional who was paid a weekly salary by a golf club and provided with a shop and workshop rent-free, with free heating and lighting, was a *self-employed earner* since the club exercised no control over the way in which he performed his duties, imposed no fixed hours of attendance, imposed no constraints on his outside activities, and left it to him to agree tuition times and fees with club members. (*M44 (1954)*).

Similarly, in 1955, the Secretary of State determined that a professional lawn tennis coach appointed by the Lawn Tennis Association to give instruction to school-teachers and youth leaders on the teaching of lawn tennis was a *self-employed earner* since the coach was not controlled in his methods of teaching, was not obliged to accept engagements for any particular course, and was remunerated by a fee for each tuition session. (*M51 (1956)*).

The leading case concerning part-time lecturers etc. is *Argent v Minister of Social Security [1968] 3 AER 208*. Argent gave acting instruction at the Guildhall School of Music and Drama and was remunerated at an hourly rate. He was free to undertake other engagements, was given no guidance as to his teaching methods and had no administrative duties. On the facts it was held that, applying all three tests described at 14.4 to 14.7 CATEGORISATION, Argent was a *self-employed earner*.

The *Argent* case contrasts with an earlier case in which the Secretary of State held that a self-employed architect and surveyor who was also a part-time lecturer in the

Department of Building in a College of Technology was an *employed earner* as regards his lecturing post by reason of the degree of control which the college exercised over him. Unlike Argent, he was obliged to carry out various specific administrative duties, to adhere to the syllabus laid down in the college prospectus, and to be subject to the head of the department in which he taught (*M20 (1952)*).

In *Davis v New England College of Arundel [1977] ICR 6* it was found that Davis, who had previously been a freelance self-employed lecturer, had, upon his engagement by the college, come under its control, been integrated into its organisation and become an *employed earner*, despite the fact that, at his own request, he had been treated as self-employed by the college.

In *Narich Pty Ltd v Commissioner of Pay-roll Tax [1984] ICR 286*, the Judicial Committee of the Privy Council held that lecturers who conducted weight watchers classes in New South Wales pursuant to contracts with a company which was the franchisee throughout Australia of Weight Watchers International Inc. were employees of that company despite a clause in their contracts that they were independent contractors and not employees. The lecturer was 'tied hand and foot' by the contract with regard to the manner of performing the work under it and in those circumstances the only possible conclusion was that the lecturer was an employee.

In *Sidey v Phillips [1987] STC 87*, it was held that a barrister who lectured part-time for both Thames Polytechnic and the Inner London Education Authority was an *employed earner* in relation to both engagements. The contracts which regulated the relationship between Mr Sidey and those who paid him, though not closely adhered to, pointed 'inescapably to the establishment of master and servant relationships'. There was lawful authority to command so far as there was scope for it.

42 Mariners

Cross-references. See CLASS 1 CONTRIBUTIONS (15); COLLECTION (21); EARNINGS (28); EARNINGS PERIODS (31); OVERSEAS MATTERS (49); 51.3 RATES AND LIMITS; SHARE FISHERMEN (54).

Other Sources. Simon's NIC, Part I, Section 2, Chapter 11; Tolley's Payroll Handbook 2000; Leaflets CA 23, CA 24.

42.1 GENERAL CONSIDERATIONS

The social security system is, like the tax system, subject to territorial limitations (see 49.2 OVERSEAS MATTERS). Where an insured person works outside the UK, he ceases to be 'gainfully employed in Great Britain', with the result that he can be neither an 'employed earner' nor a 'self-employed earner' for contributions purposes (see 14.2 and 14.10 CATEGORISATION). This implies that there is no liability to pay Class 1, Class 2 or Class 4 contributions. In the absence of special rules to change the position, UK residents employed in the shipping and fishing industries would often cease to be compulsorily insured when they left UK territorial waters and might have to rely on voluntary contributions under Class 3 to maintain their entitlement to the basic state pension.

The system copes with many temporary overseas absences for those normally within Class 1 liability by deeming the individuals concerned to continue to be 'employed earners' for 52 weeks after departure from the UK. There is a corresponding 52-week period of non-liability for those sent to work only temporarily in the UK by non-UK employers (see 49.8 OVERSEAS MATTERS). [*Contributions Regs, Regs 119(2), 120(2)(a)*].

Workers in the shipping and fishing industries, however, do not fit neatly into that framework. Because of the brevity of their stays in many different jurisdictions and the length of time they spend outside national jurisdictions, they may not qualify for the protection of any state's social security system. To provide such protection for essentially UK-based workers in fishing and international sea transport, the *Contributions Regs, Regs 86–89* include provisions governing the UK national insurance liabilities of 'mariners', broadly limiting liability to those domiciled in the UK or resident in the UK, subject to the provisions of reciprocal agreements and EC regulations as they apply to nationals, etc. of EEA members.

42.2 DEFINITION

A mariner is a person who is or has been in employment under a contract of service

(*a*) as a master or member of the crew of any ship or vessel; or

(*b*) on board any ship or vessel in some other capacity (i.e. as a supernumerary, e.g. a cattleman, shop assistant, hairdresser—see Leaflet CA 23) for the purposes of the ship, vessel, her crew or any passengers, cargo or mails she carries, provided the contract was entered into in the UK with a view to its whole or part performance while the ship or vessel is on her voyage.

[*Contributions Regs, Reg 86*].

The term includes a radio officer, but not any member of the ARMED FORCES (11). A 'radio officer' is a mariner employed in connection with the radio apparatus of any ship or vessel and holding a certificate of competence in radio telephony granted by the Inland Revenue, or by an authority empowered in that behalf by the legislature in some part of the Commonwealth or of the Republic of Ireland and recognised by the

Inland Revenue as equivalent to a certificate granted by it. [*Reg 86 as amended by SSC(T)A 1999, 2 Sch*].

The terms 'ship' and 'vessel' are not further defined for national insurance purposes, except to include hovercraft for the purposes of certain of the mariners' rules. [*Reg 86*]. However, in merchant shipping law, a 'vessel' is any ship, boat or other vessel used in navigation, and a 'ship' is any vessel used in navigation not propelled by oars. [*Merchant Shipping Act 1995, s 313*]. In a recent Special Commissioners case it was determined that an oil drilling rig which was being towed by two tugs to its drilling site could be classed as a 'ship' for the purposes of *ICTA 1988, s 192A(3)*. The fact that the drilling unit 'does not appear at first glance to be what the layman would describe as a ship' and it had no rudder, the oil rig 'was operating as a ship' and its 'movements were under the control of a master mariner' on the bridge of the unit — it was therefore, for these purposes, a ship. (See *Lavery v MacLeod [2000] STC SSCD 118 Sp C 230*).

Crew members will include deck and engine room hands, navigating and engineering officers, cooks and stewards.

42.3   **CATEGORISATION**

Not all members of the crew of a ship etc. are under contracts of service and, if they are not, they are neither employed earners nor mariners within the terms of *Reg 86*, and the rules described in this chapter do not apply to them. It was held, for instance, in *McLeod v Hellyer Brothers Ltd [1987] IRLR 232* that trawlermen who worked under crew agreements regulated by the *Merchant Shipping Act 1970* are *self-employed* earners if their agreements terminated at the end of each voyage and thereupon the shipping company had no obligation to offer further work and the trawlermen had no obligation to take any further work which was offered. This is because the agreements which trawlermen sign on engagement aboard a fishing vessel are contracts for services. Where, however, a series of such agreements is entered into between the same parties and covers a substantial period of time *and* the minimum of mutual obligations necessary to support a contract of service exist during the interval between the individual crew agreements, it is open to a court to infer the existence of an overriding arrangement which governs the whole relationship and which constitutes a global or umbrella contract of service. (*Boyd Line Ltd v Pitts [1986] ICR 244*).

Although, by definition (see 42.2 above), a mariner is a person under a contract of service, that alone is not sufficient to result in his categorisation as an employed earner: it is also necessary that he be gainfully employed *in Great Britain* (see 42.1 above). [*SSCBA 1992, s 2(1)(a)*]. Because any mariner (other than one employed exclusively in British territorial waters) would necessarily fail to comply with this requirement, however, regulations have been made under *SSCBA 1992, s 117* which provide that a mariner is to be *treated as* an employed earner (although not necessarily liable to Class 1 contributions – see 42.4 below for exception) if he is employed as a mariner on board either

(*a*)   a *British ship*; or

(*b*)   a non-British ship where

    (i)   the employment on board is under a contract entered into in the UK with a view to its whole or part performance while the ship is on her voyage, *and*

    (ii)   the person paying his earnings (or, if the mariner is the ship's master or a crew member (but not a supernumerary), the ship's 'owner' or managing 'owner') has a place of business in Great Britain.

[*Contributions Regs, Reg 88(a)(i)–(iii)*].

A mariner who does not fall to be treated as an employed earner under these provisions is nonetheless to be so treated if he is employed on any ship etc. as either

(A) a radio officer and

(i) his contract is entered into in the UK, and

(ii) his employer or the person paying his earnings has a place of business in Great Britain;

or

(B) a master, crew member or radio officer (but not as a supernumerary), and

(i) his contract is not entered into in the UK, but

(ii) the person paying his earnings has his principal place of business in Great Britain.

[*Reg 88(b)(i)(ii)*].

A 'British ship' is any ship or vessel in the service of the Crown, any ship or vessel registered at a port in Great Britain, or any hovercraft registered in Great Britain. [*Reg 86*]. Accordingly, ships of the Royal Navy, cable ships, weather ships, Customs and Excise launches are all included, as are ships held by Her Majesty by Demise Charter or requisition.

For the meaning of 'place of business' see 49.7 OVERSEAS MATTERS.

The term 'owner' has an extended meaning for the purposes of the mariners' rules. In relation to a ship or vessel it means both

(*a*) the person to whom the ship belongs and who, subject to the right of control of the captain or master of the ship, is entitled to full control of that ship; and

(*b*) where the ship has been demised, the person who for the time being is entitled as charterer to possession and, subject to the right of control of the captain or master, to control of the ship by virtue of the demise or any sub-demise.

The 'managing owner' is the owner of the ship who, where there is more than one owner, is responsible for its control and management.

[*Reg 86*].

42.4 EXCEPTION FROM LIABILITY UNDER BRITISH SCHEME

The conditions of residence or presence in Great Britain which must normally be fulfilled for contribution liabilities to arise, set by *Regs 119–123*, do not apply in the case of mariners. [*SSCBA 1992, s 117; Contributions Regs, Reg 87(1)(a)*]. Subject to EC regulations and reciprocal agreements providing to the contrary, a mariner's liability is to be conditional on him being domiciled or resident in Great Britain. [*Reg 87(1)(c)*].

It was formerly the case that mariners who signed crew agreements in Great Britain under National Maritime Board conditions were treated as having a place of residence in Great Britain whether or not they had such a place. A mariner who does not live in Great Britain but stays in the country between voyages is not treated as UK-resident, even if paid while ashore, provided that he works for a shipping company as a mariner and does not take up work ashore. (Leaflet CA 23).

In addition, by virtue of the joint arrangements made for the purpose of co-ordinating the social security schemes of Great Britain and Northern Ireland and the agreement between Great Britain and the Isle of Man, a mariner employed on a Northern Irish ship is treated as working on a British ship and *vice versa* and a similar arrangement operates with Isle of Man ships. (Leaflet CA 24, pages 8 and 9). [*SSAA 1992, ss 177–179; Reciprocal Agreements—Isle of Man, Art 2*].

Because the normal rules on residence and presence in *Reg 119* are disapplied for mariners and their employers, the 'host employer' rule in *Categorisation Regs 1978, 3 Sch 9* (see 49.9 OVERSEAS MATTERS) cannot apply to deem the UK user of the personal services of a mariner employed by a non-UK employer to be the secondary contributor in relation to the mariner's earnings.

42.5 EC regulations and reciprocal agreement provisions

In practice, the identity of the insuring state in relation to most mariners will be determined under the provisions of the EC regulations or the reciprocal agreements between Great Britain and foreign states, and only where such regulations or agreements are of no application will the rules stated at 42.4 above apply.

The EC regulations direct that a mariner employed on board a vessel flying the flag of the EC/EEA member states is to be subject to the contribution legislation of that state [*EC Reg 1408/71, Art 13(2)(c)*] *unless*

(*a*) he has been posted on board that vessel by his employer to perform work there for his employer but is normally employed in another state or on board a vessel flying another state's flag, in which case he is to remain subject to the contribution legislation of that other state [*EC Reg 1408/71, Art 14b(1)*]; or

(*b*) that vessel is in a port of, or within the territorial waters of, another member state and the mariner concerned is not normally employed at sea, in which case he is to be subject to the contribution legislation of that other state [*EC Reg 1408/71, Art 14b(3)*];

(*c*) he is resident in another member state and paid by an employer or other person whose registered office or place of business is also in that other member state, in which case he is to be subject to the contribution legislation of that other state [*EC Reg 1408/71, Art 14b(4)*].

EEA member states may, by mutual agreement, provide for exception to these provisions in the interests of certain mariners or groups of mariners, but, to date, no states have made any such provision. [*EC Reg 1408/71, Art 17*].

The reciprocal agreements currently in force between the United Kingdom and Barbados, Bermuda, Cyprus, Israel, Jamaica, Jersey and Guernsey, Malta, Mauritius, Switzerland, Turkey, the USA, and the former Yugoslavia and its successor states all make special provisions concerning mariners. Reciprocal agreements with several of the EEA member states make such special provision also, but those agreements are in many cases superseded by the EC regulations referred to above in the case of EEA nationals.

42.6 Certificate of mariner's non-liability

A mariner who, after application of all these rules, finds himself not liable to pay contributions under the British scheme should (if he is to be employed on a British ship etc.) apply for a certificate of mariner's non-liability on form CA 3644 available from Inland Revenue, National Insurance Contributions Office, International Services, Longbenton, Newcastle upon Tyne NE98 1ZZ.

42.7 EARNINGS

A mariner's earnings are to be calculated according to the normal rules (see EARNINGS (28)) and, in particular, any interim payment by way of an advance or any payment of part of his earnings to some other person at his behest, are to be disregarded until the earnings they represent actually fall due. [*Contributions Regs, Reg 94(1)(a)(b)(2) as amended by Contributions (Mariners) Amendment Regs 1982, Reg 3*].

A special payment (as defined by the National Maritime Board) made to a mariner who has to be left abroad because of sickness or the risk of infection is, however, to be excluded from earnings entirely. [*Reg 94(1)(c) as amended by Contributions (Mariners) Amendment Regs, Reg 3*].

42.8   CALCULATION OF CONTRIBUTIONS

Calculation of primary and secondary Class 1 contribution liabilities in respect of the earnings of a mariner proceeds largely in the same manner as does the calculation of the contribution liabilities in respect of the earnings of any other employed earner *except that*

(*a*)   where a mariner is paid his earnings in the form of a general settlement at the end of a voyage or series of voyages, special rules are to be applied for the ascertainment of his earnings periods and the apportionment of earnings to those periods (see 31.12 EARNINGS PERIODS); and

(*b*)   where the mariner is the master or crew member of a 'foreign-going' ship, secondary Class 1 contribution liability will arise at reduced rates (see 42.10 below).

Special tables (see 15.5 CLASS 1 CONTRIBUTIONS) are prepared by the Inland Revenue to facilitate the complex calculations to which (*a*) and (*b*) above may, on occasions give rise, though contributions may be calculated using the exact percentage method if this is preferred (see 15.5 CLASS 1 CONTRIBUTIONS). [*Contributions Regs, Reg 91(1)(2)*].

Collection procedures (see COLLECTION (21)) are modified only insofar as the employer is required to submit a special post-voyage period return to the Inland Revenue within 14 days of the end of a voyage or series of voyages. [*Contributions Regs, 1 Sch 30A, as amended by Contributions (Mariners) Amendment Regs 1982, Reg 4 as amended by SSC(T)A 1999, 2 Sch*].

42.9   The prescribed secondary contributor

The shipowner will, as a mariner's employer, usually fall to be treated as the secondary contributor in relation to earnings paid to a mariner, but only if he is resident or has a place of business (see 49.4 and 49.9 OVERSEAS MATTERS) in Great Britain. [*Contributions Regs, Reg 87(1)(c)*]. If the employer of a mariner does not satisfy either of these conditions but the person who actually pays the mariner does, that person (even if he is acting merely as agent for the employer) is to be treated as the secondary contributor in the employer's stead. [*Contributions Regs, Reg 93*].

A radio officer is usually employed by a marine radio company rather than by a shipowner. Where that is the case, the marine radio company will fall to be treated as the secondary contributor. (Leaflet CA 24, Page 13).

42.10   Contribution rates

Primary and secondary Class 1 contributions in respect of a mariner's earnings are normally payable at the same rates as would be applicable were the mariner an ordinary employed earner (see 51.3 RATES AND LIMITS). Where, however, a mariner is a master or crew member on a 'foreign-going' ship (see 42.12 below), secondary Class 1 contributions (at either contracted-out or not contracted-out rate) are reduced and for these purposes see the special Mariners' contribution tables CA 42.

42.11 Redundancy rebated contributions

For contribution years up to and including 1987–88, the primary and secondary Class 1 contribution rates were reduced in respect of certain mariners who had no redundancy rights under the *Employment Rights Act 1996, Part XI and sections 199(2) or 209.*

The appropriate percentage rate of the primary and the secondary Class 1 contributions payable on the earnings of any mariner who was affected was reduced, from 6 April 1984 to 5 April 1988, by 0.25 in the case of the primary contribution rate and by 0.15 in the case of the secondary contribution rate. [*Contributions Regs, Reg 89(1)(a) as amended by SS(C)A 1982, s 4(3), 1 Sch 3(2)(b) and Contributions Transitional Regs 1985, Reg 6(c)(ii)*]. The reductions from 6 April 1982 to 5 April 1984 were 0.35 and 0.15 respectively. From 6 April 1980 to 5 April 1982 they were nil and 0.15 and prior to 6 April 1980 they were nil and 0.2 (see 45.13 NATIONAL INSURANCE FUND). The reduction was abolished from 6 April 1988. [*Contributions Amendment No 2 Regs 1988, Reg 2*].

42.12 Foreign-going rebated contributions

Where a mariner is a master or crew member of a foreign-going ship, the appropriate percentage rate of the secondary Class 1 contributions payable in respect of his earnings is reduced in tables R, T, W, N and O, from 6 April 1984 onwards, and also in tables H, K and V from 6 April 1997 onwards, by 0.5. [*Reg 89(1) as substituted by Contributions Amendment No 2 Regs 1988, Reg 2*]. Prior to 6 April 1984 the rebate was 0.6.

A 'foreign-going ship' is (in contradistinction to a home-trade ship) a ship or vessel which is employed in trading or going beyond the UK (including, for this purpose, the Irish Republic), the Channel Islands, the Isle of Man and the continent of Europe between the river Elbe and Brest inclusive; and any fishing vessel proceeding beyond the limits of, on the south, latitude 48°30' N, on the west, longitude 12°W, on the north, latitude 61°N. [*Reg 86*]. If the employment is partly on a foreign-going ship but also partly on a home-trade ship, the appropriate rate of secondary contribution payable (standard or rebated) will be determined by the nature of the voyage at the time the payment of earnings is made. [*Reg 89(2) as substituted by Contributions Amendment No 2 Regs 1988, Reg 2*]. See also CA Specialist Conference, written response item 18, 4 February 1997.

'Employment' in this context includes any period of leave, other than study leave, accruing from the employment. [*Reg 89(3) as substituted by Contributions Amendment No 2 Regs 1988, Reg 2*].

Where home-trade agreements are opened between successive foreign-going voyages rebated secondary contributions may be made in respect of all the earnings arising provided the home-trade agreements are merely incidental to the distribution and collection of foreign cargo at ports within the home-trade limits and the ship is not actually engaged in trade between those ports. (Leaflet CA 24, page 12).

42.13 MODIFICATION OF COMPLIANCE RULES

Where a mariner is unable, because of his absence from Great Britain by reason of his employment as a mariner, to comply with any time limits on acts which he is liable to perform under contribution law, he is to be treated as complying if he performs the acts as soon as is reasonably practicable. [*Contributions Regs, Reg 96(1)*].

43 Ministers of Religion

Cross-reference. See CATEGORISATION (14).

Other Sources. Simon's NIC, Part I, Section 2, Chapter 4; Tolley's National Insurance Brief, December 1995, page 89.

43.1 CATEGORISATION

As a matter of general law, Church of England clergy and stipendiary readers in the Church of England are office holders and ministers of the Methodist Church, ministers of the Congregational Church, ministers of the Presbyterian Church, officers of the Salvation Army, Sikh *granthis* or priests and Islamic *khateebs* are neither office holders nor employees under contracts of service. *(Re Employment of Church of England Curates [1912] 2 Ch 563; Barthorpe v Exeter Diocesan Board of Finance [1979] ICR 900; Re Employment of Methodist Ministers (1912) 107 LTR 143; Methodist Conference (President) v Parfitt [1983] 3 AER 747; Parker v Orr (1966) 1 ITR 488; Lewis v Scunthorpe Congregational Church (1978) unreported; Davies v Presbyterian Church of Wales [1986] 1 AER 705; Rogers v Booth [1937] 2 AER 751; Santokh Singh v Guru Nanak Gurdwara [1990] ICR 309; Birmingham Mosque Trust Ltd v Alavi [1992] ICR 435).*

For contribution purposes, however, *any* 'minister of religion' is to be treated as falling within the category of employed earners unless his remuneration in respect of his employment (disregarding any payment in kind) does not consist wholly or mainly of stipend or salary. [*Categorisation Regs, 1 Sch Pt I Para 5*].

The term 'minister of religion' is defined neither in *SSCBA 1992* nor in the *Categorisation Regs* but it has been held by the courts that to be a minister of religion a person must be 'set apart in sacred matters as superior to the rest of the religious community, the laity'. It must be 'for them and them alone to perform the important sacred rites . . . to preach and interpret the gospel and the doctrines of the church with authority'. The 'dominant feature' must be 'the differentiation between clergy on the one hand and laity on the other'. (*Walsh v Lord Advocate [1956] 3 AER 129, per Lord Patrick and Lord Mackintosh*). It follows from this that remunerated 'apostles', 'elders' and the like in the unstructured, charismatic, non-denominational churches are not 'ministers of religion' since a feature of such churches is the absence of a distinction between clergy and laity: any member may teach, preach and administer the sacraments. Similarly, a member of the Jehovah's Witnesses — though termed 'a minister of God' — is not a 'minister of religion' since *all* members are termed 'ministers of God'. Likewise, a Sikh priest (i.e. a *granthi*) should probably not (contrary to practice) be regarded as a 'minister of religion' in this context because there is no system of ordination or formal training for the priesthood in the Sikh religion. The employment status of all such persons falls, therefore, to be decided according to normal criteria. Persons who will be regarded as ministers of religion by application of the stated test are ordained ministers and deaconesses of any denomination, trained deaconesses of the Methodist Church and the Baptist Church, evangelists under the Home Missions Committee of the Methodist Church, commissioned officers of the Salvation Army, Jewish ministers and rabbis and Muslim imams.

A stipend or salary or any regular payment of a similar kind, however described, must be payable *as of right* for it to be recognised as such for the purpose of the categorisation rule and must form the *major* part (i.e. over half) of the minister's remuneration. In deciding whether or not the stipend or salary represents over half of a minister's total remuneration, such benefits as free housing, the provision of a motor vehicle etc. are to be disregarded.

Because the remuneration payable to ministers of the Elim Pentecostal Church is, under the constitution of that church, the last call on church funds and is not payable if no funds remain after all other expenses have been met, that remuneration does not constitute 'stipend or salary' for the purposes of the regulations and, accordingly, an Elim Pentecostal minister — though a 'minister of religion' — is excluded from the categorisation rules and is, according to normal criteria, regarded as a self-employed earner. A Roman Catholic priest has likewise for many years been regarded as self-employed because of the absence of a right to remuneration, although some small stipends may be payable and the matter is known to have been under review.

For the purposes of EC social security legislation, a missionary priest who is supported by contributions from his parishioners is to be regarded as *self-employed*. (*Van Roosmalen v Bestuur van de Bedrijfsvereniging voor de Gezondheid, Geestelijke en Maatschappelijke Belangen, Case 300/84, 29 October 1986, The Times*).

In *R(P)7/54* (a reported decision of the National Insurance Commissioner in the retirement pension series) it was accepted that members of an enclosed devotional order are neither employed under contracts of service nor under contracts for services. The recent view of the DSS has been, however, that such persons are employed earners and that Class 1 contribution liabilities arise on the whole of their earnings even if those earnings are covenanted in whole or in part to the order. (Letter from DSS 5 June 1987 and the 1996 edition of DSS Leaflet CA 28, Page 79, Item (53)).

A minister of religion may, of course, also be employed in some other capacity and may thus be an employed earner on general principles. Thus, the Secretary of State has formally determined that a member of the Church of England clergy appointed director of education for a diocese of the Church of England is engaged under a contract of service and is an *employed earner*. (*M60 (1958)*). Similarly, it has been held that an ordained priest appointed Church of England chaplain at a general hospital by a Hospital Management Committee is engaged under a contract of service and is an *employed earner*. (*M61 (1958)*).

43.2   SECONDARY CONTRIBUTORS

In the case of employment as a minister of the Church of England, the *Church Commissioners* for England fall to be treated as the secondary contributor. [*Categorisation Regs, 3 Sch 7*].

The secondary contributor in relation to any other employment as a minister of religion is, however, to be identified by examining the source of his remuneration and, in this connection, 'remuneration' includes any payment in respect of stipend or salary which would be earnings for contribution purposes under the normal rules *excluding* any specific or distinct payment made towards the maintenance or education of a dependant of the person receiving the payment (see EARNINGS (28)). [*Categorisation Regs, Reg 1(2)*].

Where the whole of such remuneration is paid from one fund, the person responsible for the administration of that fund is to be treated as the secondary contributor. [*3 Sch 8(a)*]. This will be so even if the fund is assisted by another fund in order to be enabled to make the payment.

Where, however, a minister is remunerated directly from one fund but receives *regular additional payments* from one or more other funds, the person responsible for the administration of the fund out of which such payments are made to the greater, or greatest, number of ministers is to be treated as the secondary contributor. [*3 Sch 8(b)(i)(ii)*]. This generally means, in practice, that where some payments are made from a local fund and others from a central fund, the person responsible for administering the central fund falls to be treated as the secondary contributor, irrespective of the comparative values of the local and central payments.

Where a minister is remunerated from more than one fund but each fund makes payments to an equal number of ministers, the person responsible for administering the fund from which a minister first receives a payment of remuneration in the tax year is to be treated as the secondary contributor. [*3 Sch 8(b)(iii)*].

There will be a secondary contributor as regards each separate employment in which a minister of religion is engaged and for which he is separately remunerated (e.g. the Church Commissioners with regard to stipend and a local authority with regard to teaching work undertaken). Where, however, a minister has but one employment there will be but one secondary contributor identified according to the rules stated and that secondary contributor will be responsible for paying and accounting for *all* contributions due in respect of payments made to the minister, however many funds are involved.

43.3 Compensatory payments

In order to clarify the NIC treatment of compensatory payments made to individuals who resign from the Church of England, the Contributions Agency Technical Services issued a circular in November 1995 setting out the position [CA Field Operations Manual Circular 89/95].

The Church of England's decision to allow the ordination of women priests has meant that a number of the clergy consider that they have no option but to resign on the grounds that their conscience does not allow their continuance in the Church. The scheme to draw up a system of benefits to compensate those that felt they had to resign was introduced in early 1994 under the Ordination of Women (Financial Provisions) Measure but it only covers the Church of England. To benefit from the measure, introduced those clergy resigning as a matter of conscience must do so between 25 August 1993 and 24 February 2004. On resignation the individual must have been in paid ecclesiastical service of not less than five years within the Province of Canterbury or the Province of York (this covers the whole of England, Europe, the Channel Islands and the Isle of Man but nowhere else within Great Britain and Northern Ireland). The individual resigning must

- cease to hold employment or ecclesiastical office, and
- cease to receive remuneration in the form of stipend or salary.

Three categories of payment arise from the Measure and these are periodical payments, resettlement grants and discretionary retraining grants. The payments made under the provision of the Measure are compensatory payments, not rewards for past services or inducements to continue to perform services, and therefore are not earnings. As a result there is no NIC liability on these payments.

44 Multiple Employments

Cross-references. See AGGREGATION OF EARNINGS (5); ANNUAL MAXIMUM (7); CLASS 1 CONTRIBUTIONS (15); CLASS 2 CONTRIBUTIONS (18); DEFERMENT OF PAYMENT (27); REPAYMENT AND RE-ALLOCATION (53).

Other Sources. Simon's NIC, Part I, Section 8, Chapter 52.58–52.60; Tolley's Payroll Handbook 2000; Leaflets CA 01 and CA 72.

44.1 GENERAL CONSIDERATIONS

It is a general principle of contribution law that a separate potential liability is to arise in respect of each employed earner's employment in which a person is engaged and in respect of any self-employment. [*SSCBA 1992, ss 2(5), 6(4)*]. (NB. All self-employments in which a person may engage are treated as one since a person has only one 'self' by whom he may be employed.)

In some circumstances, earnings from one or more of a person's employed earner's employments may, or must, be *aggregated* (see AGGREGATION OF EARNINGS (5)) in which case those multiple employments become effectively a single employment.

In other circumstances, where it is clear that contributions paid in one or more employed earner's employments will comfortably exceed the annual maximum contribution liability of the contributor concerned, liability on earnings from any remaining employments and self-employments may be deferred and those earnings ultimately excepted from liability (see ANNUAL MAXIMUM (7) and DEFERMENT OF PAYMENT (27)).

Where there are employments with earnings which may neither be aggregated with other earnings nor temporarily disregarded under a liability-deferment arrangement, however, contributions in excess of the annual maximum contribution liability may well be paid and, in that event, a repayment of contributions will need to be obtained (see 53.5 REPAYMENT AND RE-ALLOCATION).

44.2 AVOIDANCE OF EXCESSIVE SECONDARY CONTRIBUTIONS

Although the effect of the various provisions referred to at 44.1 above is to limit an earner's combined primary Class 1 contribution liabilities to an annual maximum, secondary Class 1 contribution liabilities arising on the earner's earnings remain completely unaffected.

Until 6 October 1985 (when the upper earnings limit as regards secondary contributions was removed), it was possible for connected potential secondary contributors to mitigate their combined secondary contribution liability as regards the earnings of an earner employed by each of them by arranging for the earner to be remunerated by only one of them at an amount equivalent to the total of the amounts which would otherwise have been paid by them individually, and for the distribution of the remuneration burden to be achieved by service charges to the non-remunerating employers. A full description and illustration of arrangements of this kind is given in Tolley's National Insurance Contributions 1984–85 and 1985–86.

From 6 October 1985, such arrangements will actually *increase* secondary (and primary) contribution liabilities by — at first — lifting the level of earnings to one at which there is attracted a higher contribution rate than the earnings would have attracted had they been paid by the individual employers and then in more recent times by allowing only one slice of earnings up to the earnings thresholds to be charged at 0%, and previously only one slice of earnings liable to the initial 2% primary rate.

Example

Angelica is a director of Basil Ltd, Camomile Ltd and Dill Ltd. For the year 2000–01, director's fees on which Class 1 liability arises are £2,000 from B, £4,000 from C, and £6,000 from D. Class 1 contribution liabilities were as follows.

		Primary		*Secondary*	
	£	%	£	%	£
B	2,000 (below ERET)	—	—	—	—
C	4,000 (below ERET, but not EEET)	Nil/10	4.80	Nil/12.2	—
D	6,000	Nil/10	204.80	Nil/12.2	197.03
	12,000		209.60		197.03

If, however, B, C and D had made (or perpetuated) an arrangement whereunder all A's fees were paid through, say, B (with B making service charges to C and D to recover their share of such fees), Class 1 contribution liabilities would have been

B	12,000	Nil/10	804.80	Nil/12.2	929.03

As such an arrangement will nearly triple the primary Class 1 liability and more than quadruple the secondary Class 1 liability, it should, of course, be avoided. If it *is* avoided, however, the Inland Revenue may attempt to enforce the higher liability by contending that B, C and D are carrying on business in association and by insisting that, in those circumstances, AGGREGATION OF EARNINGS (5) must take place. In that event, the impracticability exemption should be pleaded where appropriate (see 5.7 AGGREGATION OF EARNINGS).

It follows that, where companies are economically unassociated (i.e. are *not* carrying on business in association for contribution purposes) but are constitutionally associated to a sufficient degree to permit the making of advantageous arrangements between themselves, the fragmentation of a single employment into multiple employments may prove extremely beneficial, subject to convincing the National Insurance Contributions Office that any recharges do not mean that the companies are sharing personnel and therefore 'carrying on business in association'. If, for instance, using the facts in the above example, A was a director only of B with director's fees of £12,000, the contribution bill could have been substantially reduced by reducing her fees from B to £2,000 p.a. and appointing her a director of C and D with fees of £4,000 p.a. and £6,000 p.a. respectively.

At the CA Specialist Conference in Newcastle on 29 October 1997 it was stated:

'There are many aspects that we would need to look at to arrive at a decision on trading in association, such as: whether or not they are sharing resources; whether or not they are sharing staff; if they are involved in contracts where they would both share - it is not enough to merely identify premises and directors.'

44.3 APPORTIONMENT OF SECONDARY CONTRIBUTIONS

Where a single payment of earnings is made in respect of two or more employed earners' employments under different secondary contributors, and those secondary contributors are *not* carrying on business in association with each other, the payment of earnings is to be *apportioned* to the secondary contributors in proportion to the earnings due from each and contribution liability is to be calculated accordingly. [*SSCBA 1992, 1 Sch 1(7); Contributions Regs, Reg 13(b)*].

Where the secondary contributors *are* carrying on business in association *as regards the two or more employments in question*, contribution liability may be determined by treating the entire payment as due from the secondary contributor by whom it is made. [*Reg 13(a)*]. As has been noted, the NICO applies an economic, not a

44.3 Multiple Employments

constitutional test, in determining whether or not businesses are being carried on in association (see 5.4 AGGREGATION OF EARNINGS).

45   National Insurance Fund

Cross-references. See ADMINISTRATION (2); 13.1 BENEFITS for description of benefits payable out of the National Insurance Fund; 47.1 NATIONAL INSURANCE SURCHARGE for destination of surcharge.

Other Sources. Simon's NIC, Part I, Sections 1 and 2, Chapters 1 and 8.1; Tolley's Practical NIC Service, January 1999, page 6 and May 2000, page 40.

45.1   INTRODUCTION

On 1 April 1975, the National Insurance (Reserve) Fund (established under *National Insurance Act 1946*) and the Industrial Injuries Fund (established under *National Insurance (Industrial Injuries) Act 1946*) were wound up and their assets and liabilities were transferred to the National Insurance Fund. This fund was previously under the control and management of the Secretary of State for Social Security and, periodically, accounts of the fund were prepared at Treasury direction and, after being examined, certified and reported on by the Comptroller and Auditor-General, and laid before Parliament. Upon the transfer on 1 April 1999, the National Insurance Fund now comes under the control and management of the Inland Revenue. [*SSAA 1992, s 161 as amended by SSC(T)A, 3 Sch 5*].

45.2   QUINQUENNIAL REVIEW

Every five years the fund and the social security scheme in general are to be subjected to a review by the Government Actuary who, having regard to current contribution rates, expected future contribution yields and other relevant factors, is to determine the extent to which the fund may be expected to bear a proper relationship to the demands made upon it in respect of benefits, and is to report to the Treasury (Secretary of State prior to 1 April 1999) who then lays the report before Parliament. [*SSAA 1992, s 166 as amended by SSC(T)A 1999, 3 Sch 55*]. Quinquennial reviews covered the periods from 6 April 1975 to 5 April 1980, 6 April 1980 to 5 April 1985, 6 April 1985 to 5 April 1990 and 6 April 1990 to 5 April 1995. One of the major items settled by the quinquennial review is the appropriate level of the contracting-out rebate for the next five years. The five-yearly pattern of review of the contracting-out rebate has been broken, with a further change to this rebate from 6 April 1997 simultaneous with the other major pension reforms, including the introduction of contracted-out money purchase schemes.

45.3   ANNUAL REVIEW

In practice, the National Insurance Fund is reported upon each year (though less fully than under the quinquennial review), because a report by the Government Actuary is required whenever a draft order for changes in contribution rates etc. is to be made by the Treasury (previously the Secretary of State for Social Security). In each tax year there is required to be carried out a review of the general level of earnings, taking into account changes in that level which have taken place since the last review, with a view to determining whether an order should be made varying for the ensuing tax year the weekly rate of Class 2 contributions (see 18.5 CLASS 2 CONTRIBUTIONS), the Class 2 exception level (see 18.3 CLASS 2 CONTRIBUTIONS), the rate of Class 3 contributions (see 19.4 CLASS 3 CONTRIBUTIONS), and/or the annual lower and upper profits limits for Class 4 contribution purposes (see 20.6 CLASS 4 CONTRIBUTIONS). [*SSAA 1992, s 141*]. Following such a review, there may, if it is thought expedient to do so, be made an order changing (within defined limits) the various rates and levels mentioned and also the maximum percentage rates for primary and secondary Class

45.4 National Insurance Fund

1 contributions (see 15.4 CLASS 1 CONTRIBUTIONS) and the percentage rate for Class 4 contributions (see 20.6 CLASS 4 CONTRIBUTIONS). [*SSAA 1992, s 143*]. Whenever there is laid a draft of any such order before Parliament, there must, however, be laid with it a copy of a report by the Government Actuary on the likely effects of the order on the National Insurance Fund. [*SSAA 1992, ss 142(1), 144(1) as amended by SSC(T)A 1999, 3 Sch 45 and 3 Sch 48 respectively*].

45.4 THE 2000–01 ESTIMATES

On the basis of figures set out in the Government Actuary's report (Cm 4587) on the *Social Security Benefits Up-rating Order 2000* and the *Social Security (Contributions) (Re-rating and National Insurance Funds Payments) Order 1999*, the income and outgoings of the National Insurance Fund for 2000–01 are likely to be as set out below.

	£ million	£ million	£ million		£ million
Balance b/f (see 45.5)			13,786		
Contributions (see 45.6)				Retirement pensions	38,554
Class 1 primary	26,044			Widows' benefit	962
Less c-o rebates	(2,155)			Incapacity benefit	6,779
		23,889		Maternity allowance	47
				Contribution based	
Class 1 secondary	37,112			Jobseeker's allowance	525
less c-o rebates	(3,926)			Guardian's allowance and	
		33,186		child's special allowance	2
Class 1A		896		Pensioners' Christmas	
Class 1B		12		bonus	121
Class 2		332			46,990
Class 3		64			
Class 4		1,048		Personal pension rebates	
			59,427	and incentives (see 45.16)	2,686
				Redundancy payments	
Treasury grant (see 45.7)			NIL	(see 45.13)	148
					49,824
Consolidated fund				SSP and SMP (see 45.11)	620
(see 45.7 and 45.11)			616	National Health Service	
				(see 45.12)	6,600
State scheme premiums				Northern Ireland transfers	
(see 45.8)			98	(see 45.14)	200
				Administration (see 45.15)	1,112
Investment income			853		
Other net receipts			235	Balance c/f (see 45.5)	16,659
			75,015		75,015

45.5 Balance

The National Insurance Fund is not a true fund in that it has no significant balance available for investment. The balance in hand at the end of 2000–01 will be sufficient to support only about *eighteen* weeks of benefit expenditure and the remainder of fund expenditure must be met from current contributions and other fund income. For this reason the scheme is described as a 'pay-as-you-go' scheme.

Nonetheless, the balance on the Fund has tended to grow over recent years, the balance previously sometimes only being sufficient to cover six to eight weeks benefit expenditure.

45.6 Contributions

It will be noted that, together, primary and secondary Class 1 contributions account for over 96% of total contributions. It is not surprising, therefore, that because the fund's largest outlay relates to retirement benefits, the contribution scheme is sometimes described as an unfunded pension scheme supported by a payroll tax. Contributions in respect of employees in contracted-out occupational pension schemes or contracted-out money purchase schemes are received net of the contracted-out rebate.

45.7 Consolidated Fund and Treasury Grant

Until 6 April 1989, the National Insurance Fund was subsidised from general taxation by means of a treasury supplement. That supplement was abolished by *SSA 1989, s 3* but, to compensate for the resulting loss of fund income, industrial injuries benefits, statutory sick pay and statutory maternity pay became payable out of general taxation rather than (as formerly) the National Insurance Fund. This change came into force with effect from 1 April 1990. [*SSCBA 1992, ss 1(5); SSAA 1992, s 165(1)*]. Recovery of SSP was abolished for most employers from 6 April 1994 (see 45.11) but the relief given by the Percentage Threshold Scheme for 1995–96 and subsequent years is funded from taxation, although employers will initially recover it through their contributions remittances. The *Social Security Act 1993, s 2*, reintroduced the Treasury grant for 1993–94 onwards. However, no Treasury Grant is expected to be required in 2000–01 (as in 1998–99 and 1999–2000). In 1997–98 it was estimated at an amount equivalent to 2.2% of benefit expenditure (4.6% in 1996–97 and 8.8% in 1995–96). (Government Actuary's report on the drafts of the *Social Security Benefits Up-rating Order 2000* and the *Social Security (Contributions) (Re-rating and National Insurance Funds Payments) Order 2000*, Cm 4587).

45.8 State scheme premiums

State scheme premiums are compensation payments which an employer must make to the State if, having taken responsibility for an employee's pension through a contracted-out pension scheme (see CONTRACTED-OUT EMPLOYMENT (23)), he subsequently transfers the responsibility for that employee's pension back to the State.

45.9 Investment income

At Treasury direction, monies in the National Insurance Fund may, from time to time, be paid over to the National Debt Commissioners for investment within a permitted range of securities. [*SSAA 1992, s 165(3)*]. Because there is never a significant amount of fund income available for investment, however, the income generated by investment never represents more than 3% of total fund income (see 45.5 above) and is less than 1½% for 2000–01.

45.10 Benefits

Not all State benefits are paid from the National Insurance Fund. In particular, the non-contributory benefits listed at 13.1 BENEFITS are not so paid. See also 45.7 above as regards industrial injuries benefits.

45.11 Statutory sick pay and statutory maternity pay

Under the *SSCBA 1992, Pt XI*, an employee's entitlement to sickness (now incapacity) benefit for the first 28 weeks of a period of incapacity for work (8 weeks for 1985–86 and earlier years) is removed but a corresponding responsibility is imposed on his employer to pay him statutory sick pay during that period at specified levels. Until 5 April 1994 the employer recovered 80% of the statutory sick pay so paid (100% before 6 April 1991). From 6 April 1995 only employers qualifying under the Percentage Threshold Scheme are entitled to recover statutory sick pay paid to employees. The reduction in the rate of Class 1 secondary contributions from 10.4% to 10.2% from 6 April 1994 was stated to compensate for the additional payroll cost arising from the abolition of the 80% recovery. In cases where it applies, the recovery is effected by the employer deducting an equivalent amount from Class 1 contributions due to be remitted to the Collector of Taxes. Thus in some cases the National Insurance Fund actually receives an amount of secondary class 1 contributions *net* of statutory sick pay. The same principle (but with 104% recovery for all employers up to 3 September 1994, reducing to 92% from 4 September 1994 for all except those eligible for small employers' relief) operates in relation to statutory maternity pay which, from 6 April 1987, replaced maternity allowance (except for those women who do not qualify for statutory maternity pay) and is payable by an employer, usually for 18 weeks, to any female employee who is expecting a child. This provision came into force for employees expecting a child on or after 21 June 1987.

The fund estimates at 45.4 above show the gross contributions as outgo while the payments of SSP and SMP are shown as income from the Consolidated Fund as they are now made from general taxation as explained at 45.7 above.

45.12 National health service

A part of contributions received by the National Insurance Fund is allocated as a contribution to health service funds. In the case of primary and secondary Class 1 contributions, the part so allocated is a specified percentage applied to an amount of *earnings*; in the case of Class 2 and Class 3 contributions, a specified percentage of the *total contributions* of those classes and, in the case of Class 4 contributions, a specified percentage applied to the amount of earnings in respect of which the contributions have been paid [*SSAA 1992, s 162(5)(6)*]. Until 5 April 2000, the percentages applied to the amount of earnings above the LEL on which contributions had been paid. From 6 April 2000, the allocation in respect of secondary contributions is the specified percentage applied to all earnings in respect of employees with earnings above the employee's earnings threshold. In respect of primary contributions the allocation is based on earnings between the employee's earnings threshold and the upper earnings limit. The relevant percentages may be varied by order of the Treasury, provided the increase or decrease is, in the case of primary or secondary Class 1 contributions and Class 4 contributions, not more than 0.1% and 0.2% respectively of the relevant earnings; in the case of Class 1A contributions, not more than 0.1% of the amount estimated to be the aggregate of the cash equivalents of the benefits of the cars and car fuel used in calculating those contributions; and, in the case of Class 2 and Class 3 contributions, not more than 4% of the relevant contributions. [*SSAA 1992, s 162(7)(8)*]. Prior to 1 April 1999, such variations were to be made by the Secretary of State for Social Security, with the consent of the Treasury. [*SSAA 1992, s 162 (7) as amended by SSC(TF)A 1999, s 2 and Sch 3, para 52(7)*]. Variations which go beyond these limits require full legislation. In the case of Class 1B contributions the *Social Security Act 1998* states that not more than 0.9% will be the relevant percentage of the amount estimated to be the aggregate of the emoluments and the amounts of income tax in respect of which those contributions were paid. [*SSAA 1992, s 163(4) as inserted by Social Security Act 1998, s 65*]. Where secondary Class 1 contributions are reduced in the case of MARINERS (42), the health service allocation is reduced to 0.6%. [*SSAA 1992, s 162(12); Contributions Regs, Reg 134(a); Contributions (Re-rating) Order 1989, Art 6*]. The various percentage rates are set out below.

| | Class 1 | | Class 1A | Class 1B | Class 2 | Class 3 | Class 4 |
| | Primary | Secondary | | | | | |
	%	%	%	%	%	%	%
2000–01	1.05	0.90	0.90	0.90	15.50	15.50	1.15
1999–2000	1.05	0.90	0.90	0.90	15.50	15.50	1.15
1998–99	1.05	0.90	0.90	0.90	15.50	15.50	1.15
1997–98	1.05	0.90	0.90	—	15.50	15.50	1.15
1996–97	1.05	0.90	0.90	—	15.50	15.50	1.15
1995–96	1.05	0.90	0.90	—	15.50	15.50	1.00
1994–95	1.05	0.90	0.90	—	15.50	15.50	1.15
1993–94	1.05	0.90	0.90	—	15.50	15.50	1.15
1992–93	1.05	0.90	0.90	—	15.50	15.50	1.15
1991–92	1.05	0.90	0.90	—	15.50	15.50	1.15
1990–91	1.05	0.90	—	—	15.50	15.50	1.15
1989–90	1.05	0.90	—	—	15.50	15.50	1.15
1988–89	0.95	0.80	—	—	15.50	15.50	1.15
1987–88	0.85	0.70	—	—	15.50	15.50	1.15
1986–87	0.75	0.60	—	—	11.50	11.50	0.95
1985–86	0.75	0.60	—	—	11.50	11.50	0.95
1984–85	0.75	0.60	—	—	11.50	11.50	0.95
1983–84	0.75	0.60	—	—	11.50	11.50	0.95
1982–83	0.75	0.60	—	—	11.50	11.50	0.95
1981–82	0.65	0.60	—	—	11.50	11.50	0.85
1980–81	0.40	0.60	—	—	8.00	8.00	0.60
1979–80	0.40	0.60	—	—	8.00	8.00	0.60
1978–79	0.40	0.60	—	—	8.00	8.00	0.60
1977–78	0.40	0.60	—	—	8.00	8.00	0.60
1976–77	0.40	0.60	—	—	8.00	8.00	0.60
1975–76	0.40	0.60	—	—	8.00	8.00	0.60

[*SSAA 1992, s 162(1)(5)*].

45.13 Redundancy Fund

On 31 January 1991 the Redundancy Fund was merged with the National Insurance Fund. Redundancy payments made by the state from that date now form part of benefit expenditure as shown.

45.14 Northern Ireland transfers

The Joint Authority which co-ordinates the operation of social security in Great Britain and Northern Ireland is empowered to make financial adjustments between the National Insurance Fund and the Northern Ireland National Insurance Fund. [*SSAA 1992, s 177(3)*]. See 49.18 OVERSEAS MATTERS.

45.15 Pension scheme rebates and incentives

Contributions in respect of employees who contract out of SERPS by means of an appropriate personal pension are paid at the not contracted-out rate. The DSS then responsible for paying all the contracted-out rebate, any related incentives and (where relevant) age related rebates (see 23.2 CONTRACTED-OUT EMPLOYMENT) to the personal pension provider. Similar arrangements also apply in the case of contracted-out money purchase arrangements.

46 National Insurance Number

Cross-reference. See ADMINISTRATION (2); WORKING CASE STUDY (58).

Other Sources. Simon's NIC, Part I, chapter 54; Tolley's Payroll Handbook 2000; Leaflet CWG2 (2000), CWG1 (2000) Card 3 and Home Office Leaflet 'Prevention of illegal working—guidance for employers'.

46.1 GENERAL CONSIDERATIONS

Under arrangements authorised by the Secretary of State, a national insurance number is generally notified to a person within the year preceding his sixteenth birthday. [*Contributions Regs, Reg 44(3)*]. It is notified to him on an NI number card which is given to him shortly before his school-leaving date is reached. Cards issued after January 1984 are plastic and resemble a credit or cheque guarantee card. Exceptionally, due to problems with the new NIRS 2 computer, some young people who were due to receive such notification between June 1998 and January 1999 did not do so. This situation was remedied by Summer 1999 (see Tolley's Practical NIC, July 1999, p 52). The notification of a national insurance number marks a person's registration with the State social security scheme. Employees who have never been given an NI number can apply in person to their local Social Security Office and at that time produce documentary evidence e.g. passport, EC identity card, Home Office standard acknowledgement letter, or Home Office forms EL3, EL3(D), or EL3(P). Once the application has been made the employee will be sent form CA 5404 (CF 197) which can be shown to the employer as verification that the employee has applied for a number. It should be noted that under the *Asylum and Immigration Act 1996, s 8* such forms would not be sufficient as specified documents and thereby fail as a defence. (See also Leaflet CWG2 (2000), Page 6, item 4).

A national insurance number consists of two prefix letters (see later), six figures and a suffix letter (e.g. AB123456C) and it is by this number as it appears on returns, claims, elections and contribution collection documentation that a person's contribution record (against which claims to benefit are checked) is maintained and updated in the NIRS 2 computer at Records Division (see 2.3 ADMINISTRATION).

National insurance numbers are, furthermore, used as reference numbers in the separate computerised PAYE system, and the Inland Revenue had transferred names, addresses, dates of birth and titles of contributors from the DSS' predecessor computer to the NIRS 2. Contrary to popular belief, the numbers issued do not represent a code that reflects the holder's age, employer, address, etc.

Where the income tax office issues forms showing NI numbers, in some cases the NI number shown differs from that already in use by an employer. This has arisen as a result of the cross-checking of Inland Revenue and former DSS files and the new number should be correct. However, advice in such cases is as follows.

(*a*) If the NI number issued by the tax/PAYE office is similar to the one already held (e.g. LM has become ML or '64' has become '04'), employers should use the 'new' number.

(*b*) If the NI number issued by the tax/PAYE office is completely different, use the 'new' number if the person concerned is over State pension age, since no further contributions will be added to the NIRS 2 record.

(*c*) In any other case, the matter should be referred to the local Inland Revenue National Insurance Contributions Office for clarification.

Where the DSS cannot issue an NI number, but a PAYE record is required (e.g. a young child in receipt of a dependant's pension from an occupational pension scheme), the Inland Revenue will issue and use a temporary number until such time as the DSS is able to issue a true NI number. The temporary number will be made up of the letters TN (i.e. temporary number) followed by the person's date of birth and a suffix of M (male) or F (female). An employer who uses a computerised payroll system and needs a number to enter the new employee on the payroll can also use this procedure.

Example
Kite Design Systems Ltd has a computerised payroll system and two new joiners in July 2000 who have no NI numbers. Jane is a university graduate born on 27 September 1978 and Bill a previously long-term expatriate born on 1 January 1944. For the purposes of the payroll the following temporary numbers will be allocated

Jane: TN 27 09 78 F.
Bill: TN 01 01 44 M.

However, by the time the year-end return is made the temporary numbers must be replaced by actual NI numbers. If Jane and/or Bill do not produce an NI number shortly after starting work the payroll manager can ask the local National Insurance Contributions Office to find the number by completing the 'Number trace' form CA 6855. Supplies of this form can be obtained from local offices and from the Employers Orderline. If Jane has claimed Social Security benefits since leaving school, she should already know her NI number.

46.2 RULES RELATING TO NI NUMBERS

Application for NI number

Anyone who is resident or present in Great Britain (see 49.3 and 49.4 OVERSEAS MATTERS) and over the age of 16 must, if he has not received notification as described at 46.1 above and is an employed earner or a self-employed earner or wishes to pay a Class 3 contribution, apply to the Secretary of State for a number. [*SSCBA 1992, 1 Sch 8(1)(p); Contributions Regs, Reg 44(1)(2)*]. In practical terms, such an application will be made to a person's local DSS office on form CF 8. Where a person is neither an employed earner nor a self-employed earner, there is no obligation to apply for an NI number unless and until that person wishes to pay a Class 3 contribution.

46.3 Disclosure

Anyone who has a national insurance number must supply it to anyone who is liable to pay earnings-related contributions in his respect. [*Contributions Regs, Regs 45, 72(1)*]. The Contributions Agency National Insurance News, Issue 2, page 4 explains the workings of national insurance numbers and how they should be used by employers. It also mentions that some employers believe that a new employee must have an NI number before they can be taken on but this view is incorrect.

A secondary contributor who is unable to obtain a national insurance number from an employee of his should, if the number cannot be obtained from the tax office, instruct the employee to contact the local DSS office, and, if no number has been supplied within eight weeks of the employee starting work, contact the local National Insurance Contributions Office. CWG 1 (2000), Card 3 explains how to obtain a missing NI number for an employee.

Currently a person needs to produce one of a number of singularly acceptable documents in support of their application to be registered for national insurance purposes by the employer. These documents are listed in detail in Appendix A of the Home Office's leaflet 'Prevention of illegal working—guidance for employers' and this includes:

- current valid passport
- standard acknowledgement letter issued by the Home Office
- EL3
- an identity card issued by an EU/EEA member state.

If the person is unable to provide these documents an interview will normally take place and the individual will be asked to provide as much documentary evidence as possible including birth certificate, marriage certificate (if applicable), full driving licence (if applicable) and paid fuel/telephone bills in the person's name.

The *Asylum and Immigration Act 1996, s 8* creates a criminal offence for an employer of employing someone without the necessary immigration entitlement to work in the UK. This impacts on the employer who may be committing an offence unwittingly but those employers who have made the NI number checks would not be liable to prosecution and a possible maximum fine of £5,000 per illegal employee if, despite having taken those steps, it turned out that they were employing an illegal worker (CA Specialist Conference, 4 February 1997).

Whilst the employer is making checks on a potential new employee the checks must be consistent with the *Race Relations Act 1979*. There is guidance issued by the Home Office on the *Asylum and Immigration Act 1996, s 8* (see above) and this guidance includes advice on how to ensure that checks are not carried out in a racially discriminatory way by employers.

Example

Death's Door Ltd have decided to take on extra staff as from 25 September 2000 and have interviewed a number of candidates. Having decided to make two of the applicants an offer of employment the *Asylum and Immigration Act 1996* obligations apply from 27 January 1997 and are dealt with by Death's Door Ltd's personnel department by an insertion in the letter of offer as follows:

Dear ....

Following your interview with .... I am pleased to offer you the position of........... in the .... with this Company commencing on Monday, 25 September 2000. The salary offered for the position is £ ...... per annum.

Under the Asylum and Immigration Act 1996, we require evidence that you are permitted to work in the United Kingdom. A documented National Insurance number (e.g. P45, P60 or payslip), British Passport or British birth certificate would also fulfil this requirement. A copy of the original form will be made for our records or alternatively the form may be retained by us if you do not need it. If you do not have any of the above documents please contact the Personnel Department as there are other documents which will also suffice for this purpose. The document should be sent with your other acceptance documents or brought with you on your date of start.

Please confirm your acceptance by signing and returning to me the attached copy of this letter and the Schedule of Principal Terms, together with other starter forms enclosed.

Etc.

46.4 DEPARTMENTAL RECORDS

Local National Insurance Contributions offices are all eventually to have direct access to contribution records at Records Division by Dataline terminal, though presently details have, in many offices, to be obtained by telephone. More functions of the new NIRS 2 computer are being made available to local offices at regular intervals and should have been completed by April 2000. Not all functions may be fully used, however, until April 2001. Any individual or his personal advisers may obtain details of his contribution record through a local office, but such information is not available to other third parties.

The CA Specialist Conference in Newcastle on 29 October 1997 stated:

'We try and identify discrepancies and look into any differences, in terms of the National Insurance number we check - does it relate to that person? Is it correct? We want to make sure the names fully match those recorded against the National Insurance number. We check the address and also run against other Departmental records, for example Jobseeker's Allowance, Income Support records, to see if there is any overlap, such as someone working and claiming benefit. This is part of the Department's anti-fraud efforts.'

Inaccuracies may sometimes occur in NICO records, though such inaccuracies are, in many cases, attributable to errors or omissions in the end-of-year returns made by employers (see 21.5 COLLECTION). At the 1996 Contributions Agency Specialist Conference, for instance, it was mentioned that about ten million of the returns received each year are *partially deficient* so that contributions could not immediately be credited to any particular contributor. Of these, about one million are such that it is necessary to contact the employer to resolve matters. Many of those one million have the employee's national insurance number missing and this is the only defect. It has been the case, since 6 April 1981, that the DSS does not try to trace the identity of individual contributors where computer techniques alone have failed and the contributions in question do not exceed the contributions which would be payable on earnings up to twice the lower earnings limits. (Hansard 6th Series Vol 1 Col 123).

The DSS record may be difficult to challenge and any such challenge will constitute a for a decision of an officer of the Board of Inland Revenue and subject to appeal (see APPEALS AND REVIEWS (9)).

Direct independent access to the records is, however, available to the Parliamentary Commissioner for Administration and, on one occasion, certain errors and omissions were found. (House of Commons Paper 395, Session 1980–81, p 55, Case C 135/80). The Parliamentary Commissioner may only investigate a matter when a complaint made to a member of the House of Commons by a member of the public who claims to have sustained injustice in consequence of maladministration is referred to him. [*Parliamentary Commissioner Act 1967, ss 5(1), 8*].

In the effort to trace individuals' national insurance records the revamped form P46 signed by new employees who do not have a form P45 includes a second page which duplicates relevant information. The Inland Revenue tax office will then send this on to the NICO for their attention and this is expected to assist in the tracing and anti-fraud measures which are carried out (*Income Tax (Employments) Regs 1993*, and Inland Revenue Press Release, 9 October 1996). If the National Insurance number stated on the form is incorrect, or where no number is stated, the employer will be informed, within 7–10 days, of the correct number.

46.5 VALID NATIONAL INSURANCE PREFIXES

Where an employee provides a National Insurance number the employer may wish to check the number against the valid NI number prefixes. These prefixes are shown in the Table below:

46.5 National Insurance Number

Valid National Insurance Number Prefixes
AA AB AE AH AK AL AM AP AR AT AW AX AY AZ
BA BB BE BH BK BL BM BT
CA CB CE CH CK CL CR
EA EB EE EH EK EL EM EP ER ES ET EW EX EY EZ
GY
HA HB HE HH HK HL HM HP HR HS HT HW HX HY HZ
JA JB JC JE JG JH JJ JK JL JM JN JP JR JS JT JW JX JY JZ
KA KB KE KH KK KL KM KP KR KS KT KW KX KY KZ
LA LB LE LH LK LL LM LP LR LS LT LW LX LY LZ
MA MX
NA NB NE NH NL NM NP NR NS NW NX NY NZ
OA OB OE OH OK OL OM OP OR OS OX
PA PB PC PE PW PX
RA RB RE RH RK RM RP RR RS RT RW RX RY RZ
SA SB SM SW
TA TB TE TH TK TL TM TP TR TS TT TW TY TZ
WA WB WE WK WL WM WP
YA YB YE YH YK YL YM YP YR YS YT YW YX YY YZ
ZA ZB ZE ZH ZK ZL ZM ZP ZR ZS ZT ZW ZX ZY

TN (Temporary Number) is also feasible but should only be used as a temporary measure until a correct National Insurance number is obtained.

(NI Guidance for Software Developers for 2000–01).

47 National Insurance Surcharge

Cross-references. See CLASS 1 CONTRIBUTIONS (15); 51.7 RATES AND LIMITS.

47.1 GENERAL CONSIDERATIONS

Until 1 October 1984 (6 April 1985 in the case of local authorities etc.), any person who paid, or was liable to pay, a secondary Class 1 contribution on earnings was liable to pay with that secondary contribution a surcharge, with the exception of charities within the meaning of *ICTA 1970, s 360*. [*National Insurance Surcharge Act 1976, s 1(1); FA 1977, s 57(1)*].

Although the surcharge was, in law, distinguishable from the secondary contributions to which it was attached (and had, in fact, a different destination in State funds, being paid to the Exchequer), the surcharge was effectively an increase in the secondary Class 1 contribution and was treated as such. Accordingly, the secondary Class 1 contribution rate for the first half of 1984–85 was generally stated as being 11.45% rather than 10.45% plus 1% surcharge.

The surcharge was abolished with effect from 6 April 1985 as regards local authorities etc. and with effect from 1 October 1984 as regards all other secondary contributors. [*FA 1984, s 117*].

47.2 RATES

As regards earnings paid *after 31 July 1983*, the surcharge was 1% of the amount of earnings in respect of which a secondary Class 1 contribution was paid or payable [*NISA 1976, s 1(1), as amended by NISA 1982, s 1(1) and FA 1983, s 42(1)*] unless the secondary contributor was a local authority, police authority, probation or after-care committee, magistrates' court committee or, in Scotland, regional, island or district council or fire authority, when the surcharge was 2.5%. [*FA 1982, s 143(4) and NISA 1982, s 1(2)*].

For rates prior to 31 July 1983 see 51.7 RATES AND LIMITS.

48 Oil-Rig Workers, Divers, Etc.

Cross-references. See MARINERS (42); OVERSEAS MATTERS (49); SHARE FISHERMEN (54).

48.1 GENERAL CONSIDERATIONS

As the continental shelf is outside the territorial waters of the UK, employment there is not employment in Great Britain and would, therefore, apart from regulations made under *SSCBA 1992, s 120*, be beyond the scope of contribution legislation, since anyone working outside the UK falls outside the definition of 'employed earner' unless he is deemed by regulation to be present in the UK (see 14.2 CATEGORISATION and 49.2 OVERSEAS MATTERS). Anyone who is employed (whether under a contract of service or not) in connection with the exploitation of resources or the exploration of the sea bed and subsoil in any area designated under *Continental Shelf Act 1964, s 1(7)* (i.e. by *Continental Shelf (Designation of Areas) Orders*) is, however, to be treated for contribution purposes as if those areas *are* in Great Britain, where the employment is in connection with any activity mentioned in *Oil and Gas (Enterprise) Act 1982, s 23(2)*. Compliance with the general requirements of residence or presence is to be judged accordingly (see 49.3 and 49.4 OVERSEAS MATTERS). [*Contributions Regs, Reg 85(1)(2)*]. Thus, anyone who would be an employed earner/self-employed earner were he engaged in relevant activities in Great Britain will be an employed earner/self-employed earner for contribution purposes if he is engaged in those activities in a designated area of the continental shelf. Oil-rig workers, divers and diving supervisors will be the main types of worker to whom these provisions apply. It should be noted that the deeming regulation applies only to persons in 'prescribed employment'. A person's own liability is to be determined as if the designated area were in Great Britain, but this is not extended to his employer, who may operate in the North Sea without having a place of business in the UK.

The Orders made under the *Continental Shelf Act 1964* are

SI 1964 No 697	North Sea
SI 1965 No 1531	North Sea, English Channel, Irish Sea, Orkneys and Shetlands
SI 1968 No 891	Irish Sea, St George's Channel and Bristol Channel
SI 1971 No 594	English Channel, West Coast of Scotland, Shetlands
SI 1974 No 1489	West Coast of Scotland
SI 1976 No 1153	South of Cornwall and English Channel
SI 1977 No 1871	English Channel and South Western Approaches
SI 1978 No 178	North West of Shetland Isles
SI 1978 No 1029	South Western Approaches to the English Channel
SI 1979 No 1447	North Sea
SI 1982 No 1072	English Channel, Southern North Sea and West and North West of the Shetland Isles
SI 1989 No 2398	English Channel, Irish Sea, West Coast of Scotland
SI 1993 No 599	North Sea
SI 1993 No 1782	North Sea
SI 1997 No 268	Orkneys and Shetlands

48.2 DIVERS AND DIVING SUPERVISORS

For 1978–79 and subsequent years a diver or diving supervisor working as an employee in the designated areas referred to at 48.1 above is to be treated as carrying on a trade for tax purposes. [*ICTA 1988, s 314*]. Although, in consequence, his earnings are assessed under Case I of Schedule D and should, therefore, attract a Class 4 contribution liability, he is, if he is under a contract of service, to retain his status as an employed earner for contribution purposes and is to be excepted from such contributions on so much of his profits or gains as are derived from that employment and his earnings will attract a Class 1 contribution liability under the normal rules (see CLASS 4 CONTRIBUTIONS (20)). [*Contributions Regs, Reg 59*]. Divers and diving supervisors submit their accounts to Aberdeen District, which issues guidance notes on their tax treatment. The current notes state that the rules do not extend to 'diving superintendents', although that term is not further defined and some confusion may arise where an employer uses the term to describe a 'diving supervisor' (also not defined).

48.3   **RIG-WORKERS**

It is generally the case that rig-workers spend a number of weeks on a rig followed by a short period of leave and then repeat the cycle. Payment is made for hours worked and includes an element of leave pay. For the NIC treatment of reimbursed expenses of cost of travel and subsistence see 28.51 EARNINGS.

Because of this work-pattern, primary Class 1 contribution liabilities may be minimised if a *weekly* pay interval is established wherever possible (see below). This may be achieved, however, only by actually *paying* earnings at weekly intervals (either by delivery to the rig or by transfer of pay to the credit of a rig-worker's bank account): mere weekly *calculation* followed by, say, a monthly payment is not sufficient. A weekly pay interval will establish an EARNINGS PERIOD (31) of a week and, as a rig-worker will frequently earn an amount in excess of the weekly upper earnings limit (see EARNINGS LIMITS AND THRESHOLDS (30)) in the weeks he is actually working, this will result in earnings escaping a primary contribution liability which (because of the period of leave a monthly or longer earnings period would include) they would otherwise wholly or partly attract.

Example
Angus works as a mud technician on a rig in Morecambe Bay. His earnings in the four weeks to 27 November 2000 are as follows:

	£
6 November 2000	650
13 November 2000	665
20 November 2000	685
27 November 2000	Nil
	£2,000

If A is paid weekly, Class 1 liabilities will arise as follows:

W/ended	Earnings	Main Primary (ET to UEL) Nil/10%	Secondary Nil/12.2%
	£		£
6.11.00	650	On £459 = 45.90	on £566 = 69.05
13.11.00	665	On £459 = 45.90	on £581 = 70.88
20.11.00	685	On £459 = 45.90	on £601 = 73.32
27.11.00	Nil	—	—
	£2,000	£137.70	£213.25

If A is paid monthly, however, the contribution liabilities would become

27.11.00	£2,000	on £1,671 = £167.10	on £1,635 = £199.47

A would lose £29.40 (£167.10 – £137.70), although his employer would gain £13.78 (£213.25 – £199.47).

48.4 MODIFICATION OF COMPLIANCE RULES

Where a person in prescribed employment on the continental shelf is, because of his employment in that capacity and by reason of his being outside Great Britain (see 49.2 OVERSEAS MATTERS), unable to comply with any time limit imposed on acts which, under contribution law, he is required to perform, he is to be deemed to have complied if he performs the acts as soon as is reasonably practicable. [*Contributions Regs, Reg 85(3)*].

48.5 NORWEGIAN CONTINENTAL SHELF

Until 31 December 1993, the contribution liability of individuals sent to work on the Norwegian Continental Shelf who were previously insured in either the UK or Norway was governed by the reciprocal agreement on social security with Norway. Under that agreement it is a basic rule that a worker is insured where he is 'gainfully occupied', in an employed or self-employed capacity. If a self-employed person works in both the UK and Norway, his liability falls to be determined under the legislation of the state where he is ordinarily resident. [*Social Security (Norway) Order 1991, Art 5*].

Where any person insured in the UK or Norway and employed by an employer with a place of business in either state was, before 1 January 1994, sent by his employer to work in the other state (i.e. onshore or within the 12-mile limit) for a period not expected to last for more than three years, home state liability continued for the period of the detached duty. No host state liability arose. It was a condition that the home state employer had to continue to pay the worker and that application for a certificate of continuing liability was requested from the home authorities within four months and was presented to the host state authorities within two months of its issue. In practice, the treaty time limits are closely monitored by the Norwegian authorities.

Workers ordinarily resident in the UK whose employment offshore on the Norwegian Continental Shelf began before 1 January 1994 and whose employer had a UK place of business may have benefited from the above rule without the three-year time limit. [*Art 6*]. Similar provisions applied to Norwegian residents working in the British sector for an employer with a Norwegian place of business. [*Art 6(5)*]. Self-employed persons ordinarily resident in the UK could continue to pay UK contributions without time limit when going to work in the Norwegian offshore sector, before 1 January 1994, despite not fulfilling the necessary conditions of residence or presence in the UK. [*Art 6(6)*].

With the ratification of the treaty establishing the European Economic Area on 1 January 1994 (see 49.17 below), the EC regulations now govern the contribution liabilities of cross-border workers, insofar as nationals of EEA member countries are concerned. Transitional provisions ensured that workers already working within Norway on 1 January 1994 would not be subject to the EC regulations until the expiry of the existing three-year period within their home scheme. [*Art 2A*].

The EC regulations are more restrictive than the reciprocal agreement between the UK and Norway in that the latter provides for automatic cover by the 'home' scheme for three years, whereas the EC regulations only provide for a period of twelve months with a twelve months extension. [*EC Reg 1408/71, Art 14*]. However, *EC Reg 1408/71, Art 17*, permits this period to be extended by agreement between the appropriate national authorities. It is not yet known how the British and Norwegian social security agencies will implement this provision.

However, it is now known that the British and Norwegian social security authorities have agreed that the designated areas of the continental shelf outside the 12-mile limit will *not* be classed as within the EEA. Offshore workers in international waters are therefore still subject to the provisions of the UK–Norway reciprocal agreement.

48.6   NETHERLANDS AND DENMARK

The UK and the Netherlands have agreed that their respective sectors in the designated areas should not be treated as part of the EC/EEA. *EC Reg 1408/71* therefore does not apply to offshore staff transferred between the UK and the Dutch sector. However, in contrast the UK and Denmark have agreed to regard the UK and Danish sectors as covered by the EC regulations.

48.7   EXPENSES

The Inland Revenue concession ESC A65 has the force of law for contribution purposes with effect from 6 April 1996. [*Regulation 19(1)(v) inserted by The Social Security (Contributions) Amendment (No 3) Regulations 1996*]. Where the employee incurs expenses of travel from the mainland to offshore oil and gas rigs or platforms (or vice versa) or in respect of overnight accommodation in the vicinity of the mainland departure point and the employer re-imburses such expenses no contribution liability is to arise (see IR Leaflet 480 (2000), para 5.1). Clearly, if the employer contracted for the provision of these items they would be payments in kind (see 28.24 EARNINGS and Booklet 490, Chapter 8).

49 Overseas Matters

Cross-references. See AIRMEN (6); ARMED FORCES (11); CROWN SERVANTS AND STATUTORY EMPLOYEES (25); LEAFLETS (40); MARINERS (42); OIL-RIG WORKERS, DIVERS, ETC. (48); SHARE FISHERMEN (54).

Other Sources. Simon's NIC, Part I, Section 2, Chapters 5, 46, 47.21, 48.3–5, 51.88 and 61; Tolley's Tax Planning 2000–01; Tolley's National Insurance Brief, January 1996; Leaflets CA 65, CA 76, NI 38, NI 132, SA 29.

49.1 GENERAL CONSIDERATIONS

Whenever an individual or his employer has any overseas involvement the national insurance contribution position can become very complicated. Responsibility for regulating this 'overseas connection' in relation to contribution liabilities lies with the NICO International Services Section (see 2.3 ADMINISTRATION), now part of the Inland Revenue. It has 260 staff, dealing solely with the contributions of those UK nationals who are abroad temporarily or permanently, and those foreign nationals who are visiting these shores. Whatever the circumstances surrounding the individual's crossing of international borders, certain basic principles must be understood.

First, as far as the UK social security regulations are concerned (see 49.2 below for the territorial boundaries of the United Kingdom) the rest of the world can be divided into three distinct groups:

(*a*) the member states of the European Economic Area ('EEA'), comprising the fifteen member states of the European Union together with Iceland, Norway and Liechtenstein;

(*b*) non-EEA countries with which the UK has reciprocal agreements or social security treaties, as listed at 49.21 below, and;

(*c*) other non-EEA countries with which there are no reciprocal agreements (see below).

Although the term 'European Union' is now widely used following the ratification of the Treaty on European Union (Maastricht) as from 1 November 1993, the 'union' is based on the European Communities and has no direct effect on social security matters. *Art G(1)* of the Maastricht Treaty provided that the term 'European Community' would replace 'European Economic Community' in the Treaty of Rome under which the original EEC was established. All directives and regulations affecting social security in the EU are made by the Council of the European Communities. For this reason, references below are to the 'EC' rather than the 'EU'.

The purpose of the EC regulations, which extend to EEA member states, and the reciprocal agreements is to coordinate the provision of social security cover for migrant workers. The Treaty of Rome, *Art 48* provides for freedom of movement for workers within the Community and the abolition of any discrimination based on nationality between workers of the member states as regards employment, remuneration and other conditions of work and employment. The aim of the social security regulations is to remove a barrier to that free movement by providing for non-discrimination, protecting benefit entitlements and preventing dual contribution liability (see *Terhoeve v Inspecteur van de Belastingdienst Particulieren/ Ondernemingen Buitenland, ECJ C-18/95*).

Secondly, the EC regulations and reciprocal agreements use certain terms repeatedly and it is important that their meaning is understood. The terms 'presence' (see 49.3 below), 'residence and ordinary residence' (see 49.4 below) and 'domicile' (see 49.5

below) are all vital to the understanding of how the overseas agreements will affect a particular individual. For the employer (the secondary contributor—see 49.9 below) one of the key phrases is 'place of business' (see 49.7 below).

Finally, subject to certain conditions, an individual who moves abroad may, even if not *liable* to contribute to the UK scheme, continue to do so on a *voluntary* basis and thus maintain his entitlement to some UK state benefits, e.g. the basic retirement pension. Such voluntary contributions will be either of Class 2 or Class 3 and are discussed at 49.10 and 49.11 below.

49.2   TERRITORIAL CONNECTING FACTORS

SSCBA 1992, SSAA 1992 and *SS(CP)A 1992* relate to England, Wales and Scotland and, for a small number of provisions, to Northern Ireland (see 49.18 below). [*SSAA 1992, s 192; SSCBA 1992, s 177*]. England, Wales and Scotland are to be described collectively as Great Britain. [*Royal and Parliamentary Titles Act 1927*]. The United Kingdom consists of Great Britain and Northern Ireland. [*Interpretation Act 1978, 1 Sch*]. The CA Field Operations Manual defines 'Great Britain' as follows:

1101   Unless otherwise stated, the following table shows what is and is not included in Great Britain for the purposes of this Guide:

Included
ENGLAND **SCOTLAND** **WALES** **the ISLANDS ROUND THE COAST, e.g. SHETLANDS** **NORTHERN IRELAND** **the ISLE OF MAN**
Excluded
the CHANNEL ISLANDS **IRELAND (formerly IRISH REPUBLIC)** **SHIPS AT SEA** **BRITISH EMBASSIES, CONSULATES OR LEGATIONS**

Northern Ireland has its own social security system (see 49.18). The regulations dealing with the international aspects of social security contain mixed references to Great Britain and the UK and, because of joint arrangements between the Secretary of State for Social Security and the Northern Ireland Office, the two terms are effectively interchangeable in nearly all cases. References in the legislation to Great Britain are to be treated as including a reference to the territorial waters of the United Kingdom adjacent to Great Britain. [*SSCBA 1992, s 172(a)*]. References to the United Kingdom include a reference to the territorial waters of the United Kingdom. [*SSCBA 1992, s 172(b)*].

The Scilly Isles, Orkney, Shetland and the Western Isles are all part of Great Britain but the Isle of Man and the Channel Islands are not (see 49.19 and 49.20 below).

The territorial waters of the United Kingdom include inland waters, the area of sea which lies upon the landward side of the low water line along the coast, and any part of the open sea which lies within twelve nautical miles on the seaward side of the low water line. [*Territorial Waters Order in Council 1964, Arts 2–5; Territorial Sea Act 1987, s 1*]. Note that the twelve nautical mile territorial limit does not equate with the Continental Shelf which has implications for oil-rig workers working on the Norwegian Continental Shelf. See 48.5 OIL-RIG WORKERS, DIVERS, ETC.

Whether or not a person is prima facie subject to British contribution legislation is to depend on whether or not he is present, resident or ordinarily resident in Great Britain. [*SSCBA 1992, s 1(6)*]. In the case of an airman or mariner it may also depend on whether or not he is domiciled in either England and Wales or Scotland (see 6.3 AIRMEN and 42.4 MARINERS). In the case of employers, a key term is 'place of business'.

49.3 Presence

Whether or not an individual is present in Great Britain at any particular time is a matter of *fact*. (*Colt Industries v Sarlie [1966] 1 AER 673*). Presence on a British ship on the high seas or in the territorial waters of a foreign state or presence in a British embassy overseas is, therefore, not presence in Great Britain. (National Insurance Commissioners' decisions *R(S) 23/52, R(U) 18/60* and *R(I) 44/61; Haughton v Olau Lines (UK) Ltd, The Times, 8 March 1986*). As there are no express provisions to the contrary, however, a company registered in England and Wales or Scotland will be present in Great Britain even if all its business activities take place overseas. [*Companies Act 1985, s 725*].

In determining whether or not a non-resident and non-ordinarily-resident director of a British company is present here for *contribution* purposes, the Inland Revenue has regard to contribution law, not tax law, and considers where the director lives and/or works, and the number, length and purpose of his visits in the particular tax year concerned. If the director lives and/or works in one or more EEA member states (see 49.13 to 49.16 below), including the UK, or in a state with which the UK has a reciprocal agreement on social security (see 49.17 to 49.22 below), the provisions of the appropriate regulations or agreement govern the contribution liability of both director and company. The position of a director from a state other than an EEA state or a reciprocal agreement state is, however, governed by an extra-statutory practice. If a director who usually lives overseas (i.e. is neither resident nor ordinarily resident in the UK) visits merely to attend board meetings and his visits are only fleeting visits (extending over no more than two days each) which number ten or less in the tax year, the visits will be ignored and the director will be regarded as not being present here. Alternatively, if there is only one board meeting in a tax year and that visit does not last more than two weeks, the visit will also be ignored. However, if neither condition is met, the director will be regarded as present here and contribution liabilities on fees etc. paid to him in the tax year will ensue. (Leaflet CA 44, Page 36, Para 70). Three points of interest are worthy of note. First, the wording of the guidance appears to preclude from the concessionary treatment a non-resident director who visits for only one board meeting of between three and fourteen days' duration where the company in fact holds more than one board meeting in a tax year. This would seem a strange result, since the concession is aimed at allowing temporary presence to be ignored, so it is to be hoped that clarification will be provided on this point in due course. Secondly, the policy is stated in CA 44 to be that it 'does not seek payment of Class 1 NICs' (CA 44, Para 70), highlighting the concessionary nature of the policy. Thirdly, Leaflet CA 44 makes a distinction between those directors ordinarily resident in an EEA member state or a reciprocal agreement country and those ordinarily resident elsewhere; international agreements and the EC Regulations on Social Security are looked at by NICO prior to the test at paragraph 69 of leaflet CA 44.

49.4 Residence and ordinary residence

Neither residence nor ordinary residence is defined in the legislation and the terms must, therefore, carry their ordinary meanings. As the ordinary meaning of these terms has been much debated in the context of income tax law, however, and as regard may be had to decisions on the ordinary meaning of words in one statute when considering the meaning of those words in another statute, it is suggested that the accepted meanings of the terms for tax purposes must carry great weight in the present context. (*Goodman v J Eban Ltd [1954] 1 AER 763*). It is worth observing, however, that a person may be found to be not ordinarily resident for contribution purposes when he is ordinarily resident for tax purposes. (*R(P) 1/78*). This position will not change simply by virtue of the transfer of the former Contributions Agency on 1 April 1999 to the Inland Revenue and leaflet IR20 re-iterates the point at page 61, para 11.2 of the December 1999 edition.

Residence is something more than mere presence (see 49.3 above). However, there cannot be residence without physical presence occurring at some time during the period of residence. (*Lloyd v Sulley (1884) 2 TC 37; Reed v Clark [1985] STC 323*). If a person maintains a fixed place of abode in Great Britain, he will be resident for any tax year in which he makes any visit, however brief, and non-ownership of the property will not prevent this being so, though the maintenance of a fixed place of abode is by no means an essential of residence. (*Cooper v Cadwalader (1904) 5 TC 101; Loewenstein v De Salis (1926) 10 TC 424; Lysaght v CIR (1928) 13 TC 511*). A person's intentions and wishes have no bearing on whether he is resident or not, for residence is a matter of *degree* and *fact*. Family ties, though on their own not conclusive, may indicate where a person is resident, though a person may be resident in more than one place at one time. (*Inchiquin (Lord) v CIR (1948) 31 TC 125; Turnbull v Foster (1904) 6 TC 206*).

In *Levene v CIR (1928) 13 TC 486* it was stated that 'to dwell permanently or for a considerable time; to have one's settled or usual abode; to live in or at a particular place' is an accurate meaning of the word reside.

Days of arrival and departure are days of residence for contribution purposes. (*R(S)1/66*).

The change to the tax definition of residence from 6 April 1993 (i.e. regarding the existence of 'available accommodation') is of no direct application in considering residence for contribution purposes. [*FA 1993, s 208*].

Ordinary residence is something other than mere residence and, indeed, it is clear from *Contribution Regs, Reg 119(1)* (where ordinary residence is prescribed as an alternative condition to residence for contribution liability to arise) that a person may be ordinarily resident in Great Britain when he is neither resident nor present here.

The consensus of judicial thought is that 'ordinary' contrasts with casual or occasional or extraordinary and that 'ordinarily resident' refers to 'a man's abode in a particular place or country which he has adopted voluntarily and for settled purposes as part of the regular order of his life for the time being, whether of short or long duration'. (*Shah v Barnet London BC [1983] 1 AER 226, per Lord Scarman at p 235*). It follows that a person may be outside Great Britain for extensive periods of time and yet still be ordinarily resident here.

The DSS generally used to regard a person as continuing to be ordinarily resident in Great Britain where he is absent for up to five years, provided the intention to return is not abandoned. If the intention to return is abandoned during the five years, ordinary residence ceases. (*R(G)1/54*). Where the absence extends, or is likely to extend, beyond five years, however, the DSS considered each case individually taking into account the intended length of absence, whether a home or accommodation is being maintained in Great Britain and whether personal effects and furniture are being stored or disposed of. This guidance was formerly given in DSS Leaflet NI 38, but more recent editions of the leaflet make no reference to a period of five years since that old rule is no longer used by NICO.

The ordinary residence indicators at page 11 of the current edition of Leaflet NI38 give the type of factors which are used currently to decide on ordinary residence. Legal advice was received by the former CA to the effect that the five year rule would no longer be sustained. Ordinary residence is a matter of fact, and each case must be decided on its own merits. The CA transfer to the Inland Revenue may mean that the question of ordinary residence will be re-visited in due course (because of the different rules which applied between the CA and the Inland Revenue) but this has not happened yet (see IR 20, page 61, para 11.2).

For the meaning of 'habitual residence' see 49.15 below.

49.5 Domicile

Unlike presence, residence and ordinary residence, domicile is a matter of law not of fact. Furthermore, it is a matter of general law and neither tax law nor social security law. A person is domiciled in the country in which he is considered, under English law, to have his *permanent home*. Every person has a domicile but no person may have more than one. (*IRC v Bullock [1976] 3 AER 353*). At birth each person acquires a *domicile of origin* which, regardless of the country of birth, is that of the father if the father is alive and married to the mother at the time of birth, or that of the mother if the father is dead, the parents are divorced, or the child is illegitimate. (*Forbes v Forbes (1854) Kay 341; Udny v Udny (1869) LR 1 Sc & Div 441*).

After birth, a child's domicile normally follows that of the person on whom he is legally dependent. (*D'Etchegoyen v D'Etchegoyen (1888) 13 PD 132*). Where, however, his father and mother are alive but living apart, his domicile is that of his mother if he has his home with her and has no home with his father. [*Domicile and Matrimonial Proceedings Act 1973, s 4*].

Once a child attains the age of 16 or marries under that age (i.e. under foreign law), he may set aside his domicile of origin (or dependency if different to his domicile of origin) by acquiring a *domicile of choice*, but only by positive, unambiguous action and intent. [*DMPA 1973, s 3(1)*]. However, if that domicile of choice is then abandoned in *actuality*, whether by intent or not, the domicile of origin and not the domicile of dependency, if different, will revive. (*Udny v Udny (1869) LR 1 Sc & Div 441*).

Until 31 December 1973, a woman automatically acquired the domicile of her husband on marriage but, from 1 January 1974, the domicile of a married woman is to be ascertained by reference to the same factors as in the case of any other individual capable of having an independent domicile, except that a woman already married at that date will retain her husband's domicile until it is changed by acquisition or revival of another domicile. [*DMPA 1973, ss 1, 17(5)*].

A woman married on or before 31 December 1973 who is widowed retains her late husband's domicile unless and until she later acquires a domicile of choice. (*CIR v Duchess of Portland [1982] STC 149*).

FA 1996, s 200(2) introduced, for certain Inheritance Tax purposes, a relief whereby a person living overseas and registering to vote in the UK would not have that factor taken into account. Since, however, domicile is a matter of general law (see above), this Inheritance Tax change would seem to have no bearing on contribution matters whatsoever and the domicile concept for all purposes other than Inheritance Tax, including contributions purposes, will continue to follow general law principles.

Domicile is generally relevant only to AIRMEN (6) and MARINERS (42) for social security purposes.

49.6 Nationality

Nationality is not prescribed as a connecting factor under the British contribution scheme but may be such a factor under certain of the EC regulations and under reciprocal agreement rules. For the purposes of the EC regulations, each member state defines the scope of its own nationality laws and, in the case of the UK, the definition includes

(*a*) British citizens;

(*b*) persons who are British subjects by virtue of *British Nationality Act 1981, Pt IV* and who have the right of abode in the UK and are therefore exempt from UK immigration control;

(*c*) British Dependent Territories citizens who acquire their citizenship from a connection with Gibraltar.

Other British Subjects and British Dependent Territories citizens are excluded, as are Commonwealth Citizens who do not fall within the headings above and British Overseas Citizens and British protected persons.

Channel Islanders and Manxmen are generally excluded under the above rules but an exception is made in the case of any Channel Islander or Manxman if

(i) he, a parent or grandparent was born, adopted, naturalised or registered in the UK, or

(ii) he has at any time been ordinarily resident in the UK for 5 years.

[*Act of Accession, Protocol No 3, Art 2*].

Under the provisions of *BNA 1981*, those persons who, immediately before the commencement of the Act, were Citizens of the UK and Colonies *and* had the right of abode in the UK under the provisions of *Immigration Act 1971*, were reclassified as 'British citizens'. See also the *Asylum and Immigration Act 1996*.

Children born in the UK on or after 1 January 1983 are 'British citizens' if one or both parents is a British citizen or settled in the UK at the time of the birth. A child born in the UK may be registered as a British citizen before he or she reaches the age of eighteen if either parent becomes a British citizen or becomes settled, or if the child has spent the first ten years of his or her life in the UK, with no more than 90 days' absence in any one year.

A child born outside the UK on or after 1 January 1983 is a British citizen if, at the time of the birth, one parent is a British citizen otherwise than by descent (i.e. birth, adoption, registration or naturalisation). The child will also be a British citizen if, at the time of the birth, one parent was a British citizen in Crown Service under the UK Government or in service designated as closely associated with HM Government's activities outside the UK, provided the parent was recruited for that service in the UK. A similar rule applies where, at the time of birth, one parent was a British citizen serving outside the UK under a European Community institution, provided the parent was recruited in a EC member state.

A person holding British citizenship continues to hold that status without time limit unless it is formally renounced or, in exceptional circumstances, the Home Secretary exercises a discretionary power to deprive that person of British citizenship (e.g. in cases of treason).

Under reciprocal agreements between the UK and other states, a definition of British nationality may apply which differs from that in the context of EC regulations. All of the bilateral agreements with EC states, for example, define a 'UK national' as 'a citizen of the United Kingdom and Colonies'. This category of nationality was abolished by *British Nationality Act 1981* with effect from 1 January 1983 and was replaced by three categories: 'British Citizen', 'British Dependent Territories Citizen' and 'British Overseas Citizen'. Under *BNA 1981, s 51(2)*, however, the term 'citizen of the United Kingdom and Colonies' is, in any enactment passed before 1983, to be deemed to include the three new categories. This means, therefore, that each agreement covers not only the average UK-resident British citizen but also includes, e.g. approximately 3,000,000 Hong Kong citizens who are now BDT citizens and approximately 1,300,000 Malaysians who are also British Overseas citizens, together with citizens of numerous island relics of Britain's imperial past.

Other reciprocal agreements refer to 'British subjects' and 'British protected persons' (e.g. the UK/Austrian agreement), which brings what are now Commonwealth citizens within the scope of their provisions.

The UK is also a signatory to the two 'European Interim Agreements on Social Security Schemes' brought into force for UK purposes in 1959. The agreements were drawn up under the auspices of the Council of Europe to cover, in one case, old age, invalidity and survivors' benefits and, in the other, short-term benefits for sickness, maternity, employment injury, unemployment and family allowances. Their effect is limited to persons not already covered by the EC regulations or a reciprocal agreement. Nationals of the participating states are granted favoured status, so that they are not to be prejudiced by reason of nationality and they are to receive the benefits of agreements entered into by other participating states. In effect, until the advent of the European Economic Area this meant that Norwegians, Swedes and Icelanders were allowed to benefit from the provisions of the UK's reciprocal agreements, where they were not otherwise covered by a treaty of their own, by means of granting them deemed UK nationality. The agreements imposed an ordinary residence qualification, however, so they were intended to apply in practice only to those who had moved on a permanent basis between states.

49.7 Place of business

A 'place of business' is regarded for contributions purposes as being any place from which a person can, as of right, conduct his business, or from which his agent has power to conduct business on his behalf. A business incorporated in Great Britain under the *Companies Acts* is normally regarded as a place of business. (Leaflet NI 132, Page 3). Under the *Companies Act 1985, s 691(1)*, any overseas company which establishes a place of business within Great Britain must, within one month of so doing, deliver to the registrar of companies a list of the names and addresses of some one or more persons resident in Great Britain authorised to accept service of process on behalf of the company. The DSS previously confirmed (see below) that the delivery to the registrar of such a list will be 'a strong indication' though 'not in itself conclusive proof' of the existence of a place of business in Great Britain, but failure to deliver such a list will not be evidence that a place of business does not exist.

The premises occupied by a UK subsidiary of an overseas parent company or by the UK parent company of an overseas subsidiary are *not* regarded (see below) as constituting a place of business of the overseas company unless there is tangible evidence that the overseas company has the legal right to occupy part of the UK company's premises for business purposes. This view has been upheld in Canadian law. (*Imperial Oil v Oil Workers International Union 69 WWR 702*).

The courts have held that, in deciding whether a company has established a place of business in Great Britain for the purposes of the Companies Acts, one must see whether the company has here 'a local habitation of its own'. (*Lord Advocate v Huron and Erie Loan and Savings Co 1911 SC 612*). The concept is of 'some more or less permanent location, not necessarily owned or even leased by the company, but at least associated with the company and from which habitually and with some degree of regularity business is conducted'. Thus, the meeting of clients or potential customers in an hotel room may constitute the carrying on of business but the company will not have, in the hotel room, a place of business. (*Re Morris (1884) 4 TLR 452; Re Oriel Ltd [1985] 3 AER 216, per Oliver LJ*). This accords with the judgment in *South India Shipping Corporation Ltd v Export-Import Bank of Korea [1985] 2 AER 219* that a place of business is some specific location readily identifiable with the company by members of the public from which it can be deduced that some substantial business activity is being carried on. In line with these later definitions, a fixed address from which activity such as the sending out of advertisements or the soliciting of finance is conducted has been held to be a place of business, while mere ownership of property in Great Britain or the retention of books and records here has been held not to be evidence of the establishment of a place of business here. (*A/S Dampskib 'Hercules' v Grand Trunk Pacific Railway Co [1912] 1 KB 222; Badcock v Cumberland Gap Park Co [1893]1 Ch 362*).

A 'visible sign or physical indication' that the company has a connection with particular premises will be indicative of the establishment of a place of business, but the absence of such signs or indications will not be conclusive evidence that a place of business has not been established. (*Deverall v Grant Advertising Inc [1954] 3 AER 389*).

The DSS had in the past asserted that the use of a desk and chair may result in that furniture constituting a place of business, but from 6 April 1995 it said that whether an employer has a place of business is a question of fact and may depend on how the business operates: 'Generally an employer can be said to have a place of business in the UK if they have a fixed address or occupy premises where they are, or are present with the consent of, the lawful owner or tenant, *and* an activity takes place which need not necessarily be remunerative in itself, but is in furtherance of the purposes of the business. The business does not need to be of a trading or commercial nature.' (Leaflet CWG2 (2000), Page 71). The pointers that will be looked for in deciding whether there is a fixed address of the kind described are a name plate on the door or premises; headed letter paper; an entry in the telephone directory; a lease or rent agreement or some sort of financial transaction for the use of the premises; a registered office; registration as a company incorporated outside the UK, but with a place of business in the UK for the purposes of the *Companies Act 1985*; and the existence of any other premises in Great Britain. In a note supplied to the ICAEW by the DSS, the DSS said that so far as the 'carrying out of a business activity' is concerned 'it is not necessary for the staff in this country to be carrying out the main activity of the company, e.g. a foreign bank may have a branch in this country which is not actually banking; a foreign building firm may have an office here which is not actually building etc. [but] as long as the office in Great Britain is carrying out some sort of activity for the company, e.g. collecting orders and posting them on to the foreign company, this is sufficient for it to be said that the company is carrying out its business here.' The DSS note stresses that an overseas organisation may have a place of business in Great Britain even if it has no employees under contract of service here, e.g. where partners or office-holding directors of the overseas entity work from a UK base. [ICAEW Faculty of Taxation Technical Release Tax 21/92, Annex F, December 1992].

Leaflet NI 132, April 1999 edition says, with regard to the occupation of premises, that the person must be the 'lawful tenant or occupier' if those premises are to constitute a place of business.

The DSS maintained that an embassy in Great Britain is a place of business of the relevant overseas government and this is probably correct.

49.8   Employed earners

Unless the EC regulations or a reciprocal agreement is of application and provides to the contrary, anyone who falls to be categorised as an employed earner by reason of being gainfully employed in Great Britain (see 14.2 CATEGORISATION) is, subject to the exceptions stated below, to be liable for primary Class 1 contributions in respect of the earnings from his employment if, at the time of his employment, he is

(*a*)   resident in Great Britain (see 49.4 above); or

(*b*)   present or but for any temporary absence would be present in Great Britain (see 49.3 above); or

(*c*)   ordinarily resident in Great Britain (see 49.4 above).

[*Contributions Regs, Reg 119(1)(a)*].

It should be noted that the fact that a person's contract of employment may be made under foreign law or that his employer may be located overseas is irrelevant. It is the location in which a person works that determines where he is gainfully employed.

Where an employed earner would be liable to pay contributions under this rule by reason of falling within (*a*) or (*b*) above, but does not fall within (*c*), no primary or secondary Class 1 liability is to arise in respect of earnings from the employment until a continuous period of 52 weeks of residence have elapsed beginning with the contribution week following the date of his last entry into Great Britain, provided

(i)   he is *not ordinarily employed* in Great Britain, and

(ii)   the employment concerned is *mainly* employment *outside the UK* by an employer whose *place of business* (see 49.7 above) is *outside the UK* (whether or not he also has a place of business in the UK).

[*Reg 119(2)*].

In the context of employment law, it has been said that in deciding where a person ordinarily works one should look at the terms of his contract, express or implied, in order to ascertain where, looking at the whole period contemplated by the contract, his *base* is to be; and that, where the contract is of no assistance the matter should be resolved by looking at the conduct of the parties and the way they have operated the contract. (*Maulik v Air India [1974] ICR 528; Wilson v Maynard Shipbuilding Consultants AB [1978] ICR 376; Todd v British Midland Airways Ltd [1978] ICR 959; Janata Bank v Ahmed [1981] ICR 719; Sonali Bank v Rahman [1989] ICR 314*). It is suggested that this approach is equally valid in deciding whether or not a person is ordinarily employed in Great Britain.

The meaning of 'place of business' is discussed at 49.7 above, but the phrasing of *Reg 119(2)* suggests that the expression, where first used, denotes the *principal* place of business, i.e. the *siege sociale* or central seat of government and control of a corporation.

A 'contribution week' is a period of seven days beginning with midnight between Saturday and Sunday. [*Reg 1(2)*].

The DSS considered that the reference in the Regulation to 'the date of the earner's last entry' should not be looked at in isolation—but should be considered in the context of the Regulation as a whole. The 'continuous period of 52 weeks' is, in NICO's view, a test of continuous residence and not a test of continuous presence in the UK. The test of 52 weeks continuous residence has been applied to seconded workers from abroad since 1948 when the National Insurance scheme began, and the policy intention has not changed since then. Once the worker has been resident in the UK for a continuous period of 52 weeks after having been sent here 'for a time', Class 1 NICs become due. The date of the worker's last entry in the UK for this purpose will be the date of the worker's last entry in order to take up the employment 'for a time'. (Letter from the Contributions Agency, 11 February 1994). Accordingly, the DSS rejected any suggestion that a short period of absence from the territory of Great Britain in, say, the fifty-first week of residence will trigger off a fresh 52-week period of non-liability. It is understood that this view was supported in a determination of a question by the Secretary of State in 1994 on the contribution liabilities of a Japanese employer with a number of Japanese employees in the UK for varying periods. The essence of the decision was that the words 'last entry' should be taken to mean 'last entry at or before the commencement of such employment', i.e. *first* entry to take up the employment in the UK. (See Tolley's National Insurance

Brief, Vol 4, No 1, pages 1–3). However, the matter is far from resolved, as the determination by the Secretary of State is open to challenge through the courts as being unreasonable. It may be argued that 'last' cannot possibly have meant 'first' and that the plain English of the regulation should only take a different meaning if the result of the natural meaning of the words is absurd.

See 10.7 APPRENTICES, TRAINEES AND STUDENTS for a similar 52-week exception in the case of certain students and apprentices not ordinarily resident in Great Britain.

Example
Pak-lok, a Malay engineer who is ordinarily employed in Kuala Lumpur for a Malay company, is sent to Birmingham for a nine-month period of service with an associated British company. His sister accompanies him and finds employment in a restaurant.

P's sister is 'present' during the nine months and falls to be categorised as an employed earner by reason of her contract of service with the proprietor of the restaurant for whom she works. Her earnings will, therefore, attract primary and secondary Class 1 contribution liabilities from the outset. P's earnings will, however, attract no contribution liabilities under the British contribution scheme for, although he, like his sister, is 'present' and falls to be categorised as an employed earner during the period of presence, he is neither 'ordinarily resident' in Great Britain, nor 'ordinarily employed' in Great Britain, nor employed in Great Britain for a *continuous* period of 52 or more weeks, *and* his employment is 'mainly outside the UK' by an employer whose place of business is outside the UK.

Where a person is gainfully employed outside Great Britain in an employment which, were it in Great Britain, would be an employed earner's employment, that employment is to be *treated as* an employed earner's employment and primary and secondary Class 1 liabilities are to arise in respect of the person's earnings for the employment if

(A) the employer has a place of business in Great Britain (see 49.7 above); and

(B) the earner is ordinarily resident in Great Britain (see 49.4 above); and

(C) immediately before the commencement of the employment the earner was resident in Great Britain (see 49.4 above).

Such liability will continue, however, only during the period of 52 contribution weeks from the beginning of the contribution week in which the overseas employment commenced. [*Reg 120(1)(2)*].

The 52 weeks of continuing liability are, according to NICO, to include weeks of sickness or leave or temporary duty for which the employee is remunerated. This is surely correct. The DSS previously asserted that weeks of *unpaid* leave in GB were not to be included—an assertion which seemed wrong in law. The August 1995 and subsequent editions of Leaflet NI 132, the latest being April 1999, now agree that the 52–week period of liability is *not* extended if periods of unpaid leave fall within it (page 8). Again, the DSS formerly asserted that where an employee was to return abroad after a remunerated period of sickness or leave in GB and the 52 weeks of continuing liability came to an end before or during that leave, etc. Class 1 liability would be treated as arising again after the leave, etc. had lasted for 26 weeks and that a further 52–week period of liability would begin—even if no actual duties had been performed in GB. Again there appeared to be no grounds in law for imposing such liabilities since paid leave in the UK does not bring the employment outside the UK to an end. Leaflet NI 132 (August 1995 edition onwards) is no longer so presumptive and seems to suggest that a fresh period of 52 week liability will only occur when:

(I) a quite separate and distinct secondment abroad takes place, or

(II) the return to the UK is other than on temporary duty, incidental to the overseas employment (e.g. a briefing or further training), or

(III) the return to the UK is other than on temporary duty, *not* incidental to the overseas employment but the stay in the UK is for six weeks or less.

The period of six weeks mentioned above does not have the force of law but it is admitted in the leaflet to be a concession to ease administration.

The earnings upon which Class 1 liabilities continue to arise for 52 weeks are the gross earnings from the employment concerned (converted into their sterling equivalent, if necessary, at the rate of exchange applicable at the date of payment) irrespective of where, or by whom, those earnings are paid.

Example
Mary, who is employed by Quite Ltd in the UK, is seconded to Contrary, Q's Taiwan subsidiary, for eighteen months. She is paid £800 a month by Q and 2,000 NT$ by C. On the date of her first payment by Q and C, the exchange rate is 43.55 NT$ to the £. Her earnings for Class 1 contribution purposes are £845.92. The actual exchange rate needs to be similarly dealt with on the occasion of future payments where Class 1 liability exists. There is no such liability, however, in respect of payments made *after* the first 52 weeks have elapsed.

The question whether (and which) overseas allowances form part of earnings for contribution purposes is discussed at 49.24 below.

It is important to note that 'employer' in the context of *Reg 120(1)(2)* means the employer to whom the earner is under a contract of service while overseas. (DSS Leaflet CF(N) 1030, Para 1 (now withdrawn)). Accordingly, whenever an employee is seconded overseas to work for an associated or subsidiary company, it will be important to decide whether or not the employee remains under contract to the UK company or whether that contract has been replaced by a contract with the overseas company. If it has, and if the overseas company has no place of business in Great Britain (see 49.7 above), Class 1 liability will *not* continue after the date on which the contract with the UK company was terminated. In cases where the position is in doubt, International Services will look at the precise terms of employment overseas and consider whether the employer/employee relationship implicit in a contract of service still exists between the original employer and employee or whether in fact that relationship now exists between the employee and the associate or subsidiary company overseas. In coming to a decision, International Services will ask four principal questions.

(1) Which company has the right to dictate what work the employee will perform during his time overseas and the manner in which he will perform it?

(2) Which company has the right to suspend or dismiss the employee?

(3) Is the UK company able to recall the employee at any time?

(4) By which company are the employee's earnings funded?

The DSS acknowledged that an employee's continued membership of a UK company's pension scheme while he is overseas is a factor in deciding with which company his contract lies, but said that 'it should not be taken as decisive'. (DSS Leaflet CF(N) 1030, Para 3 (now withdrawn)). See also Leaflet CWG2 (2000), Page 72.

Where an employee sent overseas by a UK employer changes jobs with the same employer, the 52-week period of continuing liability is brought to an end, because condition (C) above is not met in relation to the new job.

Example
Ralph, who works for Albert Ltd in London, is posted to become general manager of the personnel office of Albert's Sydney office. Liability to Class 1 contributions should continue for the first 52 weeks, but Ralph is moved after six months onto a dam-building project in Malaysia as foreman. Class 1 liability ceases at this point, even though Ralph is still employed by Albert.

In instances where there is a fresh employment with an overseas employer, anomalous results can arise from the breadth of the 'place of business' definition at (A) above. Employees and overseas employers may be unaware of the existence of a deemed place of business in Great Britain (see 49.7 above) so that direct collection of primary and secondary Class 1 contributions is due, but overlooked.

Example
Bill is unable to find work in the UK but goes to Saudi Arabia and is immediately taken on by X Ltd, who recruit him locally, on a three-year contract. Unbeknown to Bill, X Ltd has a place of business in Manchester at Y Ltd and, when Bill applies to pay voluntary Class 3 contributions, this fact is picked up by the NICO. Accordingly, because all the conditions for 52 weeks of the UK Class 1 liability as laid down in *Reg 120(1)* are met, the NICO approaches the UK place of business of X Ltd at Y Ltd (who has never heard of Bill) and asks for Class 1 contributions in respect of Bill's earnings from X Ltd.

Whilst collection of both primary and secondary contributions can be enforced against the entity having a UK place of business, the diplomatic immunity enjoyed by embassy officials prevents this being effective where an embassy is a UK place of business. In such a case, collection of secondary contributions cannot be enforced against the employee, and whilst he is outside the UK, it is not possible to enforce collection of his primary contributions, either. Collection can, however, be enforced when he is within the UK, e.g. upon his return at the end of the contract. [*Contributions Regs, 1 Sch Reg 50*]. It should be possible to avoid the unexpected liabilities described in these paragraphs if condition (C) above is not met. This can be achieved by a period of time elapsing between the employee ceasing to be resident in the UK and the employment overseas commencing. As mentioned above, EC regulations and reciprocal agreements may override the provisions of *Reg 120*.

Where a person takes up overseas employed earner's employment with an employer who has no place of business in the UK, neither employee nor employer is liable to contribute to the UK national insurance scheme in respect of that employment. This means that, on his return to the UK, the employee may not (depending on the length of time spent overseas) be eligible for short-term social security benefits (e.g. contributions based jobseeker's allowance, incapacity benefit) and his state pension entitlement may also be prejudiced by the lack of a contribution record. The long-term benefit position may be safeguarded by the payment of Class 3 voluntary contributions (see 49.11 below). The individual's entitlement to short-term incapacity benefit, maternity allowance and widow's payment may be protected, subject to certain requirements as to past residence or past payment of contributions, by the payment of voluntary *Class 2* contributions in respect of each year relevant to benefit entitlement for which his or her contribution record or EARNINGS FACTOR (29) is deficient. [*Contributions Regs 1979, Reg 121(1)(a)*]. Such contributions must be paid within six years of the end of the fiscal year for which they are paid. [*Contributions Regs, Reg 122*]. In practice, contributions should be paid promptly as late payment may result in otherwise valid claims to short-term benefit becoming inadmissible.

Example
George and Mildred have both worked in the UK for many years. George obtains a new job in Saudi Arabia where he is recruited locally for three years. He leaves his old job, as does Mildred, and they both move to accommodation in Saudi for

the three years. Mildred does not obtain any employment during the three years, but pays Class 3 (voluntary) contributions (see 49.11 below) to protect her benefit entitlement. This only covers retirement pension, however. George's income from employment is not subject to UK Class 1 contributions but he is entitled to pay Class 3 contributions. Because he is working, however, he is also entitled to pay Class 2 contributions (but not both). He pays Class 2 contributions. Two months before the end of George's contract, both he and his wife fall seriously ill and George is unable to complete his contract. After a further month George and Mildred return to the UK i.e. one month early. Whilst ill in Saudi, neither George nor Mildred can receive UK short-term incapacity benefit as it is a benefit requirement that they are present in the UK. On return George can claim benefit but Mildred cannot as she did not pay, nor was entitled to pay, contributions which give rise to eligibility for incapacity benefit. Had the three–year job been in Germany rather than Saudi, George could have claimed benefit for the whole of the two months as under EC law presence in another EEA member state is required to be treated as presence in the UK.

Class 2 contributions cost only 10 pence per week more than Class 3 contributions until 6 April 2000 and are considerably cheaper thereafter, and should be considered for the last two complete tax years ended before the start of the calendar year of return to the UK, upon which the conditions for short-term benefit entitlement are based (see 13.2).

Where a person continues to pay UK contributions under the 52–week rule described above, the entitlement to contributions based jobseeker's allowance and short-term incapacity benefit is already protected, subject to certain conditions, by virtue of *Social Security (Unemployment, Sickness and Invalidity Benefit) Regs 1983, Reg 20.*

Where an employee works overseas for several years, it is likely that a gap will be created in his or her contribution record. However, in the year of departure (and, if the 52-week rule applies, the following year), it is possible that enough Class 1 contributions will be paid from 6 April to the point of departure to make the year a qualifying year for all basic benefit purposes (although SERPS entitlements may be reduced), since the year qualifies if Class 1 contributions are paid on earnings equal to the LEL for the year. Similarly, in the year of return, unless the return to UK employment is shortly before 5 April, it is possible that enough Class 1 contributions will be paid in that year to make the year qualify. For instance, an employee paid £535 per week or more (or monthly or other equivalent) in 2000–01 needs to be paid such an amount for only seven weeks ($7 \times £535 = £3,745$) since he will then have paid contributions on the LEL for the equivalent of a whole year ($52 \times £67 = £3,484$). In either case, if the year does not qualify, the NICO will automatically issue a deficiency notice (RD 170) to the contributor after the end of the year inviting payment of voluntary contributions. Such a notice will not be issued automatically for any of the years where *no* contributions are paid.

Example
Lionel is seconded to his firm's South African subsidiary company for four years from 12 July 2000. His wife Jean gives up her current employment and finds new employment in South Africa beginning on 1 September 2000. Lionel's income is subject to primary and secondary contributions for the first fifty two weeks only. When he returns to the UK on 12 July 2004 he is immediately covered for short-term benefits so he does not need to pay Class 2 contributions whilst abroad. As regards state pension entitlement, his earnings at the start of 2000–01 are sufficient for that year to become a 'qualifying year'. A similar position applies at the end of 2004–05. Lionel needs to consider payment of Class 3 contributions for 2001–02, 2002–03 and 2003–04 to enhance basic state pension and widow's benefit entitlement. As Class 2 contributions cost only £2.00 per week from 6 April 2000, but Class 3 contributions cost £6.55 per week, the former will be preferred.

On becoming employed in September 2000, Jean is entitled to pay Class 2 contributions and does so throughout the remainder of their time in South Africa. Jean is expecting a baby in August 2004. She cannot make a valid claim for Maternity Allowance whilst in South Africa as she has to be present in the UK, so she defers her claim until arrival back in the UK. Had Lionel's secondment been to Luxembourg and Jean had worked there and paid Class 2 contributions she could have claimed UK Maternity Allowance from 11 weeks before the birth as presence in a fellow EEA member state satisfies, under EC law, the conditions as to presence for UK benefit entitlement. Had Jean paid only Class 3 contributions while in either South Africa or Luxembourg no Maternity Allowance would be due as Class 3 buys only entitlement to state pension (and, in the case of a man, widow's benefits).

Because the payment of Class 1 contributions under the 52-week rule provides short-term benefit protection, Class 2 contributions may not be paid voluntarily in such circumstances.

49.9   Secondary contributors

A person who would be the secondary contributor in respect of earnings paid to an employed earner (taking no account of questions of residence and presence) *is* to be the secondary contributor and is to be liable to pay secondary Class 1 contributions and collect primary Class 1 contributions in the normal way *if*, at the time the contributions become due, he is either resident (see 49.4 above), or present (see 49.3 above), or has a place of business (see 49.7 above), in Great Britain. [*Contributions Regs, Reg 119(1)(b)*]. (See CLASS 1 CONTRIBUTIONS (15) and 21.3 COLLECTION.)

Where a liability for *primary* Class 1 contributions arises but not (by virtue of *Reg 119(1)(b)*) a liability for secondary Class 1 contributions, the person who would otherwise have been liable for secondary contributions may pay them *voluntarily* if he wishes to do so and will then also collect the primary contributions due. [*Reg 119(1)(b)*]. If he declines to do so, however, direct collection from the earner of the primary Class 1 contributions will be arranged (see 21.7 COLLECTION).

New rules applied from 6 April 1994 under which a UK employer may be treated as the secondary contributor in relation to workers seconded to him by a foreign employer who has no place of business in the UK. The rules provide that where a person is employed by a foreign employer and, in pursuance of that employment, his personal service is first made available to a host employer on or after 6 April 1994 and is rendered for the purposes of the host employer's business, the host employer to whom the personal service is made available is to be treated as the secondary Class 1 contributor. [*Categorisation Regs, 3 Sch 9 as inserted by Categorisation Amendment Regs 1994, Reg 4*]. For this purpose, a 'foreign employer' is a person who does not fulfil the conditions as to residence or presence in Great Britain described earlier and who, if he did fulfil those conditions, would be the secondary contributor in relation to any payment of earnings to or for the benefit of the person employed; and a 'host employer' is a person who has a place of business in Great Britain. [*Categorisation Regs, Reg 1(2) as amended by Categorisation Amendment Regs 1994, Reg 2*].

It should be noted that the new rules are of no application where the seconded worker was already working for the UK employer on 6 April 1994 and that, even where they are of application by reason of a seconded worker beginning to work for a UK employer on or after that date, no primary or secondary Class 1 liability will generally be imposed on the host employer until 52 weeks of the secondment has elapsed. (See *Contributions Regs, Reg 119(2)* as described at 49.8 above).

However, it should not be overlooked that the rules do not only apply to seconded workers. Employees hired locally in the UK on or after 6 April 1994 by a 'foreign employer' for work in the UK with a UK 'host employer' will have an immediate primary Class 1 liability. As the 'host' is deemed to be the secondary contributor in relation to the earnings paid, there will also be an immediate secondary liability. (Leaflet CWG2 (1997), Page 62, item 120).

49.10 Self-employed earners

Unless the EC regulations or a reciprocal agreement is of application and provides to the contrary, anyone who falls to be categorised as a self-employed earner by reason of being gainfully self-employed in Great Britain (see 14.2 CATEGORISATION) is to be liable to pay a Class 2 contribution for a contribution week if

(a) he is ordinarily resident in Great Britain (see 49.4 above); or

(b) he has been resident in Great Britain (see 49.4 above) for at least 26 of the 52 immediately preceding contribution weeks.

He is, however, *entitled* to pay such a contribution for any contribution week in which he is merely present in Great Britain (see 49.3 above). [*Contributions Regs, Reg 119(1)(c)(d)*].

Example
Miguel arrives in Great Britain from Mexico on 1 September 1999. He takes a short lease on some premises in Leeds (intending to return to Mexico in a year or two) and starts a hairdressing business. As he is not 'ordinarily resident' in Great Britain, the first week for which he will be *liable* to pay a Class 2 contribution is that ending 4 March 2000, for not until then will he have been 'resident' for 26 of the immediately preceding 52 weeks. He will, however, be *entitled* to pay Class 2 contributions, if he so wishes, from the date he begins to trade.

A person who is self-employed outside Great Britain is also entitled to pay Class 2 contributions (but only to the extent to which he would be entitled to make such contributions were he present in Great Britain) if immediately before he last left Great Britain he was ordinarily an employed earner or a self-employed earner *and*

(a) he has been resident in Great Britain (see 49.4 above) for a continuous period of three or more years at some time prior to the period for which the Class 2 contributions are to be paid; *or*

(b) he has in each of any three earlier tax years paid

   (i) contributions of any Class from which an earnings factor of at least 52 times the then-current lower earnings limit for Class 1 purposes has been derived (see EARNINGS FACTORS (29)); or

   (ii) where one or more of those years falls before 6 April 1975, an average of 52 contributions of any class under the former principal Act.

[*Reg 121(1)(a)(2)(3)*].

Time spent in another EEA country and/or Turkey may help to meet condition (a) above.

This entitlement is subject to the contributions being paid within the time limits relating to Class 3 contributions set down at 39.5 LATE-PAID CONTRIBUTIONS. [*Reg 122(a)*].

49.11 Class 3 contributors

Unless the EC regulations or a reciprocal agreement is of application and provides to the contrary, anyone who wishes to pay Class 3 contributions may, subject to normal constraints, do so if he is resident in Great Britain during the course of the tax year for which they are to be paid (see 19.2 CLASS 3 CONTRIBUTIONS). [*Contributions Regs, Reg 119(1)(e)*]. *Note*: the meaning of 'during the course of' is ambiguous.

Where a person is gainfully employed in an employed earner's employment *outside Great Britain* which is to be treated as an employed earner's employment attracting Class 1 contribution liabilities for the first 52 weeks (see 49.8 above), that person is entitled to pay Class 3 contributions for any tax year during the whole or part of which the overseas employment subsists, provided he would be entitled to make such contributions were he present in Great Britain. [*Regs 120(2)(b), 122(b)*].

The payment of Class 3 contributions provides cover for UK basic pension rights. Class 3 NICs can be paid by direct debit, annual remittance or by an agent in the UK (see below) acting on behalf of the contributor. There is an application form CF83 at the back of the leaflet NI 38. If the contributor is also paying into a foreign Social Security scheme it could still be advantageous to pay Class 3 contributions into the UK scheme, where this is permitted, as this will continue to protect the UK pension rights.

An employer may agree to act as the employee's agent for the payment of Class 3 contributions and arrangements may be made for payment to be made annually to the NICO International Services Section. (Leaflet NI 38).

Apart from the entitlement described, any person who fulfils the past-contribution or past-residence conditions under which a self-employed earner outside Great Britain may voluntarily pay Class 2 contributions (see 49.10 above) may pay Class 3 contributions, provided he would be entitled to make such contributions were he present in Great Britain. [*Regs 121(1)(b)(2)(3), 122(b)*].

These entitlements are subject to the contributions being paid within the time limits set down at 39.5 LATE-PAID CONTRIBUTIONS. [*Reg 122(a)*].

49.12 Class 4 contributors

Any earner who, for tax purposes, is not resident in the UK in a year of assessment is to be excepted from liability for Class 4 contributions. [*Contributions Regs, Reg 58(b)*].

49.13 EC REGULATIONS

For social security purposes (but not necessarily for other purposes) the European Community presently consists of Austria (from 1 January 1995); Belgium; Denmark (excluding the Faroe Islands and including Greenland from 1.4.73 to 31.1.85 but not thereafter); Finland (from 1 January 1995); France (including Corsica, Guadeloupe, Martinique, Réunion, French Guiana and Saint-Pierre et Miquelon, but excluding Monaco); Germany (consisting of, until 3.10.90, the Federal Republic, i.e. West Germany and West Berlin but, thereafter, both the former Federal Republic and the former German Democratic Republic); Greece (including Crete and the Greek Islands i.e. Macedonia, Thrace, Epirus, Thessaly, the Peloponese, the Dodecanese, the Cyclades, the Ionian Islands and the Aegean Islands); Irish Republic; Italy (including Sicily, Sardinia, Trieste and Elba, but excluding Vatican City and San Marino); Luxembourg; the Netherlands (excluding the Netherlands Antilles); Portugal (including Madeira and the Azores); Spain (including the Balearic Islands of Majorca, Minorca, Ibiza and Formantara, the Canary Islands and the Spanish enclaves of Ceuta and Melilla in North Africa); Sweden (from 1 January 1995); and the United Kingdom of Great Britain and Northern Ireland (including Gibraltar but excluding the Isle of Man and the Channel Islands).

A European Economic Area Agreement was reached in Oporto on 2 May 1992 between the seven EFTA states (Austria, Finland, Iceland, Liechtenstein, Norway, Sweden and Switzerland) which was intended to promote co-operation between the

EC and EFTA, including in the area of social security co-ordination, with effect from 1 January 1993. However, following a referendum in December 1992, Switzerland failed to ratify the agreement and implementation by the remaining participants was therefore delayed until 1 January 1994. Liechtenstein ratified the agreement but, because its economy was so closely bound up with the Swiss economy, could not participate from that later date but eventually became an EEA member on 1 May 1995.

From 1 January 1994, the EC social security regulations 1408/71 and 574/72 (see below) applied to the other five EFTA states as if they were EC members. Austria, Finland and Sweden became full members of the EU on 1 January 1995, leaving only Norway, Iceland and Liechtenstein as EFTA members covered by the EC regulations under the EEA Agreement.

All articles of EC Treaties and Regulations which are of relevance to British contribution law take direct effect in Great Britain under *European Communities Act 1972, s 2* and decisions of the European Court of Justice on contribution matters also take direct effect here under *ECA 1972, s 3*.

The principal regulations are *EC Reg 1408/71* (dealing with the application of social security schemes of member states to employed persons and their families moving within the Community) and *EC Reg 574/72* (fixing the procedure for implementing *EC Reg 1408/71*) as amended, inter alia, by *EC Reg 1390/81* (extending *EC Reg 1408/71* to self-employed persons), *EC Reg 3795/81* (extending the implementing regulation), *EC Reg 2332/89* (extending *EC Reg 1408/71* in respect of minimum periods of insurance) and *EC Reg 2195/91*. All these regulations were made under *EC Treaty 1957, Art 51*.

The regulations (as amended) prevail over inconsistent internal law of a member state and over prior bilateral and multilateral agreements unless these are expressly excepted. It should be noted that EC Regulations apply only to EC nationals or stateless persons and refugees residing within the Community, whereas the coverage of other reciprocal agreements depends on their specific terms. A list of all bilateral agreements between the UK and other states is given at 49.21 below and those relating to EC member states are **in bold**. Apart from the agreements with the Federal Republic of Germany (in which case certain articles have been retained in accordance with *EC Reg 1408/71 Annex III, Point 39*) *none* of the agreements has been excepted and *all* are superseded by EC regulations.

The regulations distinguish between employed persons and self-employed persons and provide specifically that all persons who are employed earners or self-employed earners within the meaning of the legislation of Great Britain are to be regarded as employed persons and self-employed persons respectively under EC regulations. [*EC Reg 1408/71, Annex I, Point L*]. Accordingly, the European Court will not interfere with the determination of status or an appeal under the new procedures effective from 1 April 1999 (see APPEALS AND REVIEWS (9)).

The fundamental principle underlying the regulations is that a person should at no time be subject to the contribution legislation of more than one member state unless *Article 14c(b)* applies. [*EC Reg 1408/71, Art 13(1)*]. (*Nonnenmacher v Bestuur der Sociale Verzekeringsbank Case 92/63 [1964] ECR 281*). He should normally be subject to the contribution law of the state in whose territory he is employed or self-employed even though he may reside in another state or even though (if he is an employed person) the registered office or place of business of his employer may be situated in another state. [*Art 13(2)*]. In *Bestuur der Sociale Verzekeringsbank v van der Vecht Case 19/67 [1967] ECR 345* the court held that this principle must be upheld even where a worker who is employed in the territory of a member state other than that in which he resides and in which his employer's undertaking is situated travels at his employer's cost between his place of residence and his place of work.

In accordance with this principle, the state in which a person resides cannot enforce payment of contributions on earnings on which the earner has already paid contributions in the state of his employment (being another state). (*Perenboom v Inspecteur der Directe Belastingen, Nijmegen Case 102/76 [1977] ECR 815*).

In a case that was put to the Contributions Agency International Services with regard to the UK insurability position of a group of workers in the UK who are all now employed by a company operating from the Netherlands: the question arose as to the treatment for NICs purposes of the workers who were from the Netherlands (EEA nationals) and those from non-EEA countries. The CA replied that workers coming to the UK from other EEA countries, such as the Netherlands, are liable to pay UK Class 1 contributions from the outset under *EC Reg 1408/71, Art 13(2)(a)* provided they are EEA nationals. The EEA workers are not exempt from their first 52 weeks contribution liability under the terms of *Contributions Regs, Reg 119(2)* due to the application of *Art 13(2)(a)* mentioned above. The EC Regulations take precedence over domestic legislation and aim to protect the Social Security position of those workers covered. Similarly, the UK employer is due to pay secondary contributions from the outset. Workers coming to the UK from other EEA countries, like the Netherlands, and who are non-EEA nationals may be covered under the terms of any reciprocal agreement. However, as at present the reciprocal agreement between the Netherlands and the UK covers mainly nationals of either country, any non-EEA nationals come under the UK domestic legislation. An exemption from the payment of UK contributions may be allowed for the first 52 weeks although a revised agreement is expected to come into force in the near future and this may affect the position.

Throughout the EC, liability as a secondary contributor in respect of earnings paid to an employed person *follows* the primary liability of *the earner*, and is unaffected by the fact that the secondary contributor may reside in a state other than that under the contribution law of which the earner's liabilities arise. Thus, it was held that a French football club employing German musicians not subject to French contribution law was under no liability to pay contributions to the Caisse under French contribution law in respect of earnings paid to the musicians but was liable to pay contributions under the legislation to which the musicians were subject. (*Caisse Primaire d'Assurance Maladie, Sélestet v Association du Football Club D'Andlau Case 8/75 [1975] ECR 739*).

Clearly, this raises enforcement problems which *EC Reg 1408/71, Art 92* partially resolves by providing for the collection and enforcement of contribution payments due to one member state in the territory of any other member state under inter-state agreements scheduled in *EC Reg 574/72, Annex 5*. No such agreements have yet been made with the UK and, indeed, because of the way in which the British scheme effectively resigns itself to the foregoing of secondary contributions where the secondary contributor is outside the jurisdiction (see 49.9 above), are unnecessary.

In the absence of such agreements, however, it would seem that contributions due to another state cannot be recovered through an English or Scottish court and, conversely, that contributions due to the Inland Revenue cannot be recovered through a foreign court. Prior to the UK's accession to the Treaty of Rome, the Court of Session in Scotland disallowed a claim by a foreign government to recover arrears of contributions to the foreign country's scheme of health insurance, relying on the rule that no action lies in a Scottish (or English) court to recover foreign taxes. (*Metal Industries (Salvage) Ltd v Owners of the S T Harle (1962) SLT 114*).

The general principle (enunciated earlier in this section) that the contribution legislation to which a person is to be subject is to be identified by the location of his employment, is modified in relation to certain types of earner by *EC Reg 1408/71, Art 14*, as explained in ensuing sections.

49.14 **Temporary trans-frontier employments**

Where an earner who is employed in the territory of one member state by an undertaking to which he is normally attached is sent by his employer to work in another member state, he is to remain subject to the contribution laws of the first state provided that

(a) the period of employment in the second state is not expected to last for a period in excess of twelve months; and

(b) he is not being sent to replace another person whose period of employment in the second state is at an end.

[*EC Reg 1408/71, Art 14(1)(a)*].

See also below regarding EC Administrative Decision 162 which extends *Art 14(1)* and *Art 14b(1)* to ensure that there must be a direct relationship between the worker and employer.

An employed earner's continuing liability to pay contributions under the contribution legislation of the member state in which he was employed before being posted to another member state is certified by the first member state on a form E101. UK employers must apply to International Services in Newcastle for the certificate, using new versions of forms CA3821 and CA3822 obtained from them. It is often International Services practice, where an employer applies for an E101 certificate for the first time, to ask the local Inland Revenue (NIC) office to visit the employer to verify the information given in the application. The CA gave the example (CA Specialist conference, 4 February 1997) that where a work force is substantially in another country and all that constitutes the UK employer is, say, a typist and fax machine, no E101s will be issued.

It is a popular misconception that the certificate E101 is issued *only* in temporary secondment situations. This is not so. The document certifies continuing Social Security coverage in the 'home' state and is of equal application where work is carried out in more than one EEA state (see 49.15 below). In all, over 50,000 E101s are issued each year.

In the event of the period of employment unexpectedly exceeding twelve months, the contribution laws of the first state may continue to apply for a further period of up to twelve months provided a request that that might be so is made to the appropriate authority in the second state before the first period of twelve months has elapsed and provided that the authority consents to the extension, certified on form E102. Consent cannot, however, be given for an extension in excess of twelve months unless the two states have entered into a special agreement permitting longer extensions and have notified the Commission of the Communities of that agreement. [*Arts 14(1)(b), 17*].

Extensions under *Art 17* are available in appropriate circumstances wherever an EEA national moves within the EEA. On 12 December 1984, the Administrative Commission on Social Security for Migrant Workers recommended to all member states that they should 'conclude . . . agreements pursuant to Article 17 . . . applicable to employed persons who, by virtue of their special knowledge and skills or because of special objectives set by the undertaking . . . with which they are employed are posted abroad to a member state other than the one in which they are normally employed . . . for a period exceeding 12 months. These agreements should lay down that these employed persons remain subject to the legislation of the sending state for the full duration of their assignment provided that the workers concerned agree to this condition'. [*ACR 16*]. International Services follows the recommendation in granting E101 coverage for up to five years where it is satisfied that the various conditions laid down in *ACR 16* are met. It is understood that, in exceptional circumstances, an even longer extension may be granted. This does, however, also require the consent of the authorities in the other state concerned. In the case of some states considerable delays can occur.

In the recent European Court case (*C-202/97*) of *Fitzwilliam Executive Search Ltd (t/a Fitzwilliam Technical Services) v Bestuur van het Landelijk Instituut Sociale Verzekeringen [2000] All ER (EC) 144* an Irish company's workers in the Netherlands who were in possession of E101s issued by the Irish state were also subjected to the Netherland's system and the company were required by the Netherland authorities to pay the employer's contributions. The Advocate General in the case stated:

> 'In my view, the host state may not impose its own social security system unless and until the E101 certificate issued by the other state has been withdrawn by the issuing authority. The fact that the certificate is based on a standard form drawn up by the Administrative Commission whose decisions cannot bind national authorities is irrelevant since it is the completion of that form by the competent institution which constitutes the certificate and the certificate draws its authority from art 11 of Regulation 574/72 (compare, however, the reasoning of the court in *Knoch*'s case (paras 50–54)).'

It is clear therefore that one state may not usurp a competent institution of a member state to its workers in the host member state. A member state to which workers are posted must take account of the fact that those workers are already subject to the social security legislation of the state in which the undertaking employing them is established. See also *Knoch v Bundesanstalt fur Arbeit C-102/91 [1992] ECR I-4341*.

An earner is employed in the territory of one member state if the relationship between him and the person paying him is that of employer and employee and the employment commenced in that state. It is irrelevant that the employee may have been engaged for the sole purpose of working in the second state (*Bestuur der Sociale Verzekeringsbank v Van der Vecht Case 19/67 [1967] ECR 345*) and that the employer may have had an existing commitment to supply labour in that second state. (*Manpower v Caisse Primaire d'Assurance Maladie, Strasbourg Case 35/70 [1970] ECR 1251*). It is sufficient that a direct relationship continues to exist between the employer and the employee. (Administrative Commission Decision 128 OJ 1986 C 141, but see below as this decision has been superseded by AC Admin Decision 162).

In accordance with *Art 14(1) and Art 14b (1)* and the judgments of the European Court cited above, therefore, NICO takes the view that
> 'consideration can only be given to the provision of a form E101 (by this Department) where either,

(*a*) a person has been sent to another EEA country in continuation of his United Kingdom employment, i.e. has been sent abroad by the employer he normally works for in the United Kingdom, *or*

(*b*) a person has been recruited in the United Kingdom with a view to immediate employment elsewhere within the EEA by a United Kingdom employer who normally carries out activities in this country comparable to those upon which the person sent abroad is to be employed and there is a direct relationship between the United Kingdom employer and the person concerned during his employment in the other EEA country. If the services of the person are hired to an undertaking in another EEA country and that undertaking makes the person's services available to another undertaking, then the direct relationship will be deemed to have broken and United Kingdom social security legislation will not be applicable.'

These quotations are taken from the standard response to a request for the issue of a form E101 in circumstances where the direct relationship between employer and employee appears to International Services to have been broken. This view reflects the contents of Decision 128 referred to above. They are of particular relevance to the not-infrequently encountered arrangement under which the services of a UK national are made available, on a labour-only sub-contract basis, to an EEA undertaking through an EEA intermediary, but where the whole arrangement is channelled, for tax purposes, through a 'one-man' company formed in the UK to 'employ' and 'post overseas' the UK national concerned. From 6 April 2000, such arrangements may also be inhibited by the intermediaries legislation — see 14.17 CATEGORISATION.

Following EC Administrative Decision 162 (dated 31 May 1996) it means that for workers posted to other EEA countries the competent State (i.e. the State where contributions are paid) can exercise more control over those companies and employment agencies employing people for immediate posting abroad. This applies to employment agencies which must usually carry out similar work in the UK to that undertaken abroad and seeks to prevent 'fly by night' agencies being set up with no presence in the UK. For other companies (e.g. contract work) they must undertake *substantial* business in the UK. This seeks to prevent the situation where a foreign employer sets up business in the UK and recruits workers for immediate posting abroad. In this case the employer gets form E101 from the NICO International Services but then the employer returns abroad having paid no NICs. Following on from this, the new form E101 is currently available taking account of Decision 162 together with information regarding EEA countries. In the meantime, Forms CA3821 and CA3822, mentioned above, will be issued to employers as appropriate.

Where an employment situation meets the criteria of International Services set out above, a form E101 will be issued provided the employer of the employed earner concerned supplies International Services with the full details of the posting.

This is now usually done by completing the application forms CA3821 and CA3822 obtainable from International Services.

In addition to the certificate E101 confirming continuing liability to contributions under the British scheme the NICO will issue a certificate E128 confirming entitlement to full health care cover for the worker and any accompanying family. It is not a registration form but is presented at the time health care treatment is required. An application for any extension of the period of continuing liability should be made in quadruplicate on form E102, available from International Services. (See 'National Insurance Contributions and the European Connection', Tolley's Practical Tax Vol 4, No 22, 26 October 1983).

A person who, though normally *self-employed* in one member state, performs work in another member state for an anticipated period not exceeding twelve months is to remain subject to the contribution law of the state in which he is normally self-employed. See *Banks and Others v Théâtre Royal de la Monnaie C-178/97 [2000] TLR 5 April 2000.* Also, as in the case of an employed earner, if owing to unforeseeable circumstances, the duration of the work to be done extends beyond the duration originally anticipated and exceeds twelve months, continuing liability may be extended for a further period of not more than twelve months, provided a request for the extension is made to the appropriate authority before the end of the initial twelve-month period. [*Art 14a(1)*].

From 6 April 1994, the rules for issuing E101 certificates to British construction workers were applied more rigorously. The DSS formerly received over 1,000 E101 applications a week from supposedly self-employed British construction workers going to work overseas in response to press advertisements by recruitment agencies. From 6 April 1994, E101s were issued only to those who were *normally* self-employed in the UK. (DSS Press Release, 24 March 1994). The rules were further tightened on 2 January 1998. The number of E101 applications from self-employed British construction workers has reduced substantially as certificates are issued only to those who have been self-employed in the UK for the majority of the last 24 months and provided they were not working in employed earners employment immediately prior to going abroad. (CA Press Release, 2 February

1998). See also 'UK Construction Workers in Germany' Tolley's National Insurance Brief, January 1996. It should be noted that the potential for a worker to be *normally* self-employed in the building trade in the UK is now further limited in view of the 'new approach' of the Inland Revenue (see AGENCY WORKERS (4) and LABOUR-ONLY CONTRACTORS (38)). From 1998, E101's will only be issued where the construction worker has been self-employed for the majority of the previous 24 months. (CA Press Release, 9 February 1998).

A major review of *EC Reg 1408/71* is being conducted which is set to streamline administration. Insurability matters will be looked at as well as benefits but because there are eighteen EEA countries involved the results will not be known for several years and implementation may take much longer still.

49.15 Multi-state employments

A person who normally pursues his employment in the territory of two or more EEA member states is to be subject to the contribution law of the state in which he resides if

(*a*) he partly pursues his employment there, or

(*b*) he is attached to several businesses or employers and those businesses or employers have their registered offices or places of business in a number of member states.

[*EC Reg 1408/71, Art 14(2)(b)(i)*].

In any other case, he is to be subject to the contribution law of the state in which his employer has his place of business or its registered office. [*Art 14(2)(b)(ii)*]. For the meaning of 'place of business' see 49.7 above.

Example
Gerald has his home in Manchester but has for many years worked as a sales representative in France for Rheinwein GmbH, a German wine producer which has its registered office in Hamburg and a branch in Manchester. In accordance with the requirements of the *Companies Act 1985, s 691(1)*, R had, upon setting up the Manchester branch, filed with the Registrar of Companies the name and address of a British resident whom it authorised to accept service of process on its behalf. On 1 July 1992, G's territory had been extended to cover Belgium and, on 1 August 1996, it was again extended; this time to cover Great Britain.

Until 30 June 1992, G's earnings would have been subject to French contribution law under *EC Reg 1408/71, Art 13(2)(a)* (see 49.13 above). From 1 July 1992, however, they will have been subject to German contribution law under *Art 14(2)(b)(ii)*, and, from 1 August 1996, they became subject to British contribution law under *Art 14(2)(b)(i)*. From 1 August 1996, R was the secondary contributor under the British scheme in accordance with both *Contributions Regs, Reg 119(1)(b)* (see 49.9 above) and the general EEA principle that liability as a secondary contributor follows the primary liability of the earner (see 49.13 above). Collection of contributions will, if necessary, be enforced against R through the person authorised to accept service of process for its Manchester branch.

Article 14(2) has been held to apply in the case of a person who is employed in several member states by *different* employers. It thus covers a German national resident in Germany and employed in Germany by a German company but also employed in France by a French company. (*Bentzinger v Steinbruchs Berufsgenossenschaft Case 73/72 [1973] ECR 283*).

The meaning of 'resides' in this context has been considered by the Court of Justice. According to *Art 1(h)* 'residence means habitual residence' and, in the light of that definition, the European Court held in *Angenieux v Hakenberg Case 13/73 [1973]*

ECR 935, that Hakenberg, a French national who worked in Germany as a business representative for several French undertakings, was resident in France despite the fact that for nine months of each year he lived in a caravan in Germany. The court decided that the state in which a person must be held to reside is the state with which a person has the strongest personal connections. Such connections need not be numerous but must have a degree of permanency greater than any connections with other states. The question to be asked is with which country is the person most closely and permanently connected? Where are his roots? The length of stay in a particular state is not the only factor to be considered. Other considerations of fact which establish a recognisable connection between the person himself and a territory must also be taken into account. Thus, in *di Paolo v Office National de l'Emploi Case 76/76 [1977] ECR 315*, it was held that the state in which a worker resides is the state in which, although occupied in another state, he continues *habitually* to reside *and where the habitual centre of his interests is also situated*. In *Rigsadvokaten v Ryborg Case 297/89*, it was held that the fact that a person spent nights and weekends for more than a year with a girlfriend in one state while maintaining accommodation and working in another state was not, in itself, sufficient reason to conclude that the person had moved the permanent centre of his interests to the first-mentioned state. In a judgment in February 1999 the Court of Justice held that British law could not prevent a British national, who had spent a considerable time working abroad, claiming Income Support immediately upon return to Britain with the intention of residing here for the foreseeable future. *Article 10a* prevented the operation of the restriction in income support law as regards persons from abroad since its operation would discriminate against those that exercised their right to freedom of movement. (*Swaddling v Adjudication Officer, ECJ Case C-90/97*).

The former CA historically took such habitual residence as being broadly equivalent to the concept of 'ordinary residence' in English law (see 49.4 above) but it must be questioned whether it was correct to do so. For example, a German national will, it seems, be regarded by the NICO as ordinarily resident in the UK if he is employed here for substantial tours of duty in each of six successive years, yet he may well not be 'habitually resident' here in the sense in which the European Court construes those words. If Germany remains the permanent centre of his interests and the place to which he returns when the demands of his work permit it, he is habitually resident in Germany, and, that being so, he will, if he has employment in Germany as well as in the UK, be subject to German contribution legislation only, not UK contribution legislation. See CA Specialist Conference reply 8, 4 February 1997 concerning the continued non-alignment of the two terms 'ordinarily resident' and 'habitually resident'. However, despite this, the August 1998 edition of Leaflet SA29 (Para 4) now refers to 'normally live' in the UK rather than being 'ordinarily resident'.

In 1985, the National Insurance Commissioners held (in a benefit case) that the view of the Inland Revenue on ordinary residence for tax purposes 'has no relevance whatsoever to the determination of habitual residence' (*R(U)7/85*) and, in another case, they gave detailed consideration to, and then applied, the judgment in the *di Paolo case* referred to above. (*R(U)7/85*).

In the more recent House of Lord's decision of *Nessa v Chief Adjudication Officer HL, [1999] TLR 27 October 1999* (another benefit case) it was held that it was not sufficient to merely arrive with the intention of settling in the UK to achieve 'habitual residence'. Habitual residence in the context of social security legislation has to be construed as a matter of ordinary language so that the claimant had to take up residence and live in the UK for a period which showed that the residence was in fact 'habitual'. Voluntariness of presence and an intention to reside do not establish habitual residence.

The provisions of *Art 14(2)(b)* are not to apply to anyone who is employed in two or more EEA member states as a member of the travelling personnel of an undertaking engaged in the international transport of passengers or goods by road, rail, inland waterway or air whose registered office or place of business is in one of those member states. Such a person is to be subject to the contribution legislation of *that member state*, unless

(i)   the undertaking has a branch or permanent representation in a state other than that in which it has its registered office or place of business and the employee is employed by that branch or permanent representation, in which case the employee is to be subject to the law of that state; or

(ii) the employee is employed principally in the member state in which he resides, in which case he is to be subject to the law of that state, whether or not the employer has a branch or permanent representation in that state.

[*Art 14(2)(a)*].

A person who is simultaneously employed in one member state and self-employed in another is generally subject to the legislation of the state in which he is in paid employment. [*Art 14c*]. A dual contribution liability arises in certain cases set out in *Annex VII* to *EC Reg 1408/71*. This rule may have a somewhat unexpected consequence due to the differing treatment of company directors in some EEA states. In German law, for example, a company director who is also a shareholder in the company may be treated as self-employed. If the German company has a UK subsidiary of which he is a paid director, *Art 14c* makes the director liable only to UK contribution law, despite the fact that he habitually resides in Germany but International Services would consider the application of *Article 17* of *Reg 1408/71* to retain him under German Social Security legislation.

A person who is normally self-employed in two or more member states is to be subject to the contribution law of the state in which he resides if he pursues any part of his activity there. Otherwise he is to be subject to the contribution law of the state in which he pursues his main activity. [*Art 14a(2)*]. The *exception* is that if, in its application, this rule would prevent the person joining a pension scheme, even on a voluntary basis, he may choose to be subject to the contribution law of the other state or, if there are two or more other states, the law of whichever state those states themselves decide upon. [*Art 14a(4)*]. In deciding where a self-employed earner pursues his main activity, account is taken, first and foremost, of the locality in which the fixed and permanent premises from which the person pursues his activities is situated. If this approach is inconclusive, however, account is then taken of criteria such as the usual nature or duration of the activities pursued, the number of services rendered, and the income arising from those activities. [*EC Reg 574/72, Art 12a(5)(d)*].

49.16 Frontier employments

A person who is employed in an undertaking which straddles a frontier common to two member states is to be subject to the contribution law of the state in which the employer has his registered office or place of business or, if the person is self-employed, the state in which he himself has his place of business. [*EC Reg 1408/71, Arts 14(3), 14a(3)*].

49.17 BILATERAL AGREEMENTS

Agreements providing for reciprocity in matters of social security between Great Britain and other nations are from time to time entered into by the Crown and given effect to by Order in Council under *SSAA 1992, s 179*. All such agreements entered into with other EEA member states have been superseded by the EC regulations in respect of EEA nationals. [*EC Reg 1408/71, Art 6*]. In *R(U)7/85* and *R(U)4/86*, the National Insurance Commissioners held that bilateral agreements were irrelevant where the states concerned were EC member states. There is nothing to prevent agreements with such states being made in the future, however, and, provided they are based on the principles and in the spirit of the EC regulations and are notified to the President of the EC Council, they will be of full effect. [*Arts 5, 97*].

The amended European Economic Agreement treaty between the EC and European Free Trade Association member states, excluding Switzerland, was ratified with effect from 1 January 1994. From that date the relevant reciprocal agreements ceased to apply to persons to whom the EC regulations on social security [*EC Reg 1408/71 and EC Reg 574/72*] are applicable.

In the case of the reciprocal agreement with Norway, the provisions covering Continental Shelf workers are still necessary, as Norway does not accept that its designated areas are within the scope of EC rules.

Because Switzerland did not ratify the treaty establishing the EEA, *SI 1969 No 384* will remain in force.

It should be noted that the reciprocal agreements may be of wider application than the EC rules, and if there is no conflict with the EC rules the reciprocal agreement will still apply. Similarly, the reciprocal agreements will continue to apply to EEA (but non-EC) nationals whose detached duty overseas had already begun on 1 January 1994, and will continue as long as necessary to give effect to existing treaty commitments.

A description of the usual form of a reciprocal agreement and the topics normally covered is given at 49.21 below together with a list of the current agreements.

The bi-lateral Social Security Agreement (Reciprocal Agreement) with the Netherlands has been revised to cover non-EC/EEA nationals particularly the Channel Islanders and is expected to come into effect in the near future.

49.18 **Northern Ireland**

Although quite separate from the British contribution scheme, the Northern Ireland scheme is virtually identical to it and currently operates under *Social Security (Northern Ireland) Act 1975* and its accompanying regulations. Rates of contributions are, and must be, maintained at the same level as the British rates. [*SS(NI)A 1975, s 120*].

There is no reciprocal agreement between Great Britain and Northern Ireland but reciprocity and co-ordination of the two schemes is secured by joint arrangements made by the Secretary of State with the Northern Ireland Department, the object of which is to ensure that the legislation provides a single system of social security for the UK. Such joint arrangements are given effect to by a Joint Authority consisting of the Secretary of State and the Head of the Northern Ireland Department. [*SSAA 1992, s 177*].

49.19 **Isle of Man**

As in the case of Northern Ireland, the Isle of Man has a contribution scheme separate from but very similar to that of Great Britain. The link is not, however, as strong as that binding Great Britain and Northern Ireland but consists of merely an Exchange of Letters which have been introduced into the British scheme by *Social Security (Isle of Man) Orders 1946, 1948, 1977 and 1989* and by *Social Security (Isle of Man) No 2 Order 1989* and under which rights acquired in one country are to be fully honoured in the other country on a reciprocal basis.

49.20 Channel Islands

Two separate and dissimilar social security schemes subsist in the Channel Islands: that of Jersey and that applying to the Bailiwick of Guernsey including Alderney, Herm and Jethou, but excluding Sark. Reciprocity with the British scheme is effected by *Social Security (Jersey and Guernsey) Orders 1994.* (See Leaflet SA 4.)

49.21 Reciprocal Agreements

Reciprocal agreements currently exist between the United Kingdom and the following countries.

Australia	(see Leaflet SA 5)	*SI 1992 No 1312*
		SI 1995 No 2699
Austria		*SI 1981 No 605*
		SI 1987 No 1830
		SI 1992 No 3209
Barbados	(see Leaflet SA 43)	*SI 1992 No 812*
Belgium		*SI 1951 No 1801*
		SI 1958 No 771
Bermuda	(see Leaflet SA 23)	*SI 1969 No 1686*
Bosnia-Herzegovinia	(see Leaflet SA 17)	*SI 1958 No 1263*
Canada	(see Leaflet SA 20)	*SI 1995 No 2699*
		SI 1998 No 263
Croatia	(see above entry for Bosnia)	
Cyprus	(see Leaflet SA 12)	*SI 1983 No 1698*
		SI 1994 No 1646
Denmark		*SI 1960 No 211*
Finland		*SI 1984 No 125*
		SI 1992 No 3210
France		*SI 1951 No 972*
		SI 1958 No 597
Germany		*SI 1961 No 1202*
		SI 1961 No 1513
Gibraltar		*SI 1974 No 555*
Iceland (*now EEA*)		*SI 1985 No 1202*
		SI 1992 No 3211
Ireland (formerly Irish Republic)		*SI 1960 No 707*
		SI 1966 No 270
		SI 1968 No 1655
		SI 1971 No 1742
Israel	(see Leaflet SA 14)	*SI 1957 No 1879*
		SI 1984 No 354
Italy		*SI 1953 No 884*
Jamaica	(see Leaflet SA 27)	*SI 1997 No 871*
Jersey/Guernsey	(see Leaflet SA 4)	*SI 1994 No 2802*

Luxembourg		*SI 1955 No 420*
Macedonia (former Yugoslavia)	(see above entry for Bosnia)	
Malta	(see Leaflet SA 11)	*SI 1996 No 1927*
Mauritius	(see Leaflet SA 38)	*SI 1981 No 1542*
Netherlands		*SI 1951 No 972*
		SI 1955 No 874
New Zealand	(see Leaflet SA 8)	*SI 1983 No 1894*
Norway (*now EEA*)		*SI 1991 No 767*
		SI 1992 No 3212
Philippines	(see Leaflet SA 42)	*SI 1989 No 2002*
Portugal		*SI 1979 No 921*
		SI 1982 No 1528
		SI 1987 No 1831
Slovenia	(see above entry for Bosnia)	
Spain		*SI 1975 No 415*
		SI 1976 No 1916
Sweden		*SI 1988 No 590*
		SI 1992 No 3213
Switzerland	(see Leaflet SA 6)	*SI 1969 No 384*
Turkey	(see Leaflet SA 22)	*SI 1961 No 584*
United States of America	(see Leaflet SA 33)	*SI 1984 No 1817*
		SI 1997 No 1778
Yugoslavia (Federal Republic of) (including Serbia and Montenegro)	(see above entry for Bosnia)	

A number of these agreements have been amended by *SI 1976 No 225*; *SI 1979 No 290*; *SI 1982 No 1528*; *SI 1988 No 591*; *SI 1995 No 767* and/or *SI 1996 No 1928*; all those **in bold** involve EC member states and have been superseded for most purposes by the *EC Regs*; and all those bearing an underlined SI number contain articles relating to contribution (as distinct from benefit) matters.

The leaflets mentioned above can be obtained from:

> Inland Revenue
> National Insurance Contributions Office
> International Services
> Longbenton
> Newcastle-upon-Tyne
> NE98 1ZZ
> Telephone 084591 54811
> Fax 084591 57800

The latest issue date of each leaflet is listed in 40.2 LEAFLETS.

Information regarding the above and some leaflets can be found on the internet at **http://www.inlandrevenue.gov.uk.**

Double contributions conventions (DCC) with Korea and Japan have been concluded and it is expected that these will come into force later in 2000–2001 once the administrative arrangements have been signed. Also, a DCC came into force with Canada on 1 April 1998 but it does not apply to Quebec. Chile, Greece, Poland and Slovak Republic are all expressing an interest in DCCs with the UK and talks between officials have already taken place. A number of other existing agreements are currently being re-negotiated.

A reciprocal agreement begins by defining its territorial scope, the persons to whom it relates (e.g. nationals of the contracting states or 'insured persons') and the branches of social security law involved. It then sets out the rules for determining under which state's contribution law a person connected with both states is to fall. The principle usually (but not invariably) adopted is that

(*a*) an employed person who is employed in the territory of one party is to be subject to the legislation of that party even if he is *resident* (see 49.4 above) in the territory of the other party or even if the person or undertaking by which he is employed has its principal place of business or is resident in the territory of the other party; and

(*b*) a self-employed person who follows his occupation in the territory of one party is to be subject to the legislation of that party even if he resides in the territory of the other party.

Example
Alex, Bill and Sandy are employed by Shipfitters Ltd who provide internal servicing for maritime vessels. A large contract is undertaken by their representative office in Valletta, Malta. The three are required to work in Malta on the contract for eight months and then return to the UK. As the three workers are not going to be working in Malta for more than three years they will continue to be within the UK contributions scheme. Shipfitters Ltd must apply to International Services for a certificate which is then retained at the Valletta office for inspection, if required, by the Maltese authorities and UK contributions liability continues. During the first three months Bill is injured and Sandy is released from his contract. Under the Malta/UK reciprocal agreement as both have paid sufficient contributions into the UK scheme they can claim short-term incapacity benefit and jobseeker's allowance respectively. Under the agreement the short-term incapacity benefit can be claimed by Bill for up to 28 weeks and contributions based jobseeker's allowance will be paid to Sandy in Malta. See SA 11 and *The National Insurance and Industrial Injuries (Malta) Order 1956, SI 1956 No 1897, Arts 12, 13 and SI 1996 No 1927.*

These general rules are then followed by various derogations from them dealing with

(i) temporary postings from the territory of one party to the other (the provisions usually being similar to those described at 49.14 above);

(ii) workers in international transport (the provisions usually being similar to those described at 49.15 above);

(iii) MARINERS (42.5);

(iv) CROWN SERVANTS AND STATUTORY EMPLOYEES (25);

(v) ARMED FORCES (11.2).

The remainder of the agreement then deals with entitlement to benefits.

49.22 **THE UK/USA RECIPROCAL AGREEMENT**

On 13 February 1984, agreement was reached between the UK government and the government of the United States of America as to reciprocity between the two nations in matters of social security. The agreement became part of English law on 22 November 1984 and, for the most part, took effect on 1 January 1985. A number of amendments to the agreement were announced from 1 September 1997 onwards. As far as contribution matters are concerned, the agreement prevents dual liability arising by providing that:

'*Where a person who is covered under the laws of coverage of one Party and is normally employed by an employer in the territory of that Party is sent by that employer to work in the territory of the other Party, the person shall be subject only to the laws on coverage of the former Party . . . provided that the period of work . . . is not expected to exceed 5 years. . . .*'.

The UK authorities interpret the above to mean that the employer has to be in the UK but the employee(s) to whom Article 4(2) is to apply can already be abroad on another assignment. See CA Specialist Conference, 20 February 1996. The US authority's interpretation is that six months FICA contributions are usually required before they will consider that the provisions cover the employee. Also, in the above quotation from Article 4(2) the insertion of the word *normally* from 1 September 1997 is a shift of emphasis so that the UK employer may no longer take on an employee and send him/her straight to the US and expect the provisions of the agreement to apply. There will be at least a few months of employment required by the UK employer, not weeks, before the employee is sent to the US. Ideally, six months is considered a starting point although International Services have confirmed to the author that there is no actual period but each case will be looked at on its own merits. The period of work referred to in *Art 4(2)* is to be measured from 1 January 1985. [*Art 24(4)*]. This will mean that where, for example, a person subject to UK contribution law was, in, say, 1980, sent by his UK employer to work in the USA for seven years, that person was subject only to UK contribution law from 1 January 1985 since, measured from that date, the expected period of work in the USA does not exceed five years. The first five-year certificates of continuing liability expired on 31 December 1989.

Where an employee has two contracts, one with a UK company for work in the UK and the other with a US affiliate for work in the US, the UK earnings will generally be subject to UK NICs while the US earnings will be insurable in the USA under FICA. There is considered to be no dual contribution liability under such circumstances and the treaty accordingly provides no relief.

The provisions described do not apply to MARINERS (42) or AIRMEN (6). [*Art 4(2)*]. Such persons are, if they would otherwise be subject to the contribution law of both parties, to be subject only to the contribution law of the party in whose territory they ordinarily reside (see 49.4 above). [*Art 4(5)*].

A person who is *self-employed* and would otherwise be subject to contribution law of both parties to the agreement is to be subject to the contribution law of the party in whose territory he ordinarily resides, *viz*:

'*A person who is covered under the laws on coverage of either Party with respect to self-employment shall be subject only to the laws on the coverage of the Party in whose territory he ordinarily resides*'.

This above amendment to the old Article 4(3) will mean that a UK national falling within the provisions will only pay the flat rate Class 2 contributions in the UK rather than the high US contributions as was likely to happen under the old Article 4(3) before the amendment was made. The change does not affect those US individuals coming to the UK who will continue to pay their contributions in the US. See also Tolley's Practical NIC, Vol 6, No 9. [*Art 4(3)*]. The criterion of ordinary residence is similarly to be applied where a person who, in relation to a single activity, is regarded as self-employed under the contribution law of one of the parties and regarded as employed under the contribution law of the other party. [*Art 4(4)*].

A person who ordinarily resides in the UK and who is neither employed nor self-employed is to be subject only to UK contribution law. [*Art 4(6)*].

If none of these provisions applies, a person employed within the territory of one of the parties is, as regards that employment, to be subject to the contribution laws of only that party, and, if that means he is subject only to UK contribution law, he is to be treated as ordinarily resident in the UK for the purpose of UK contribution law (see 49.4 above). [*Art 4(1)*].

Government employees of one party to the agreement are, if they are employed in the territory of the other party and do not fall within the special rules relating to CROWN SERVANTS AND STATUTORY EMPLOYEES (25), to be subject only to the contribution law of the first party. [*Art 5(1)(2)*].

Where, because of the provisions described above, the contribution laws of one of the parties to the agreement are applicable, the appropriate agency of that party (e.g. the Inland Revenue, now, in the UK) is, upon the request of an employer, employee or self-employed person, to issue a certificate stating that to be the case. That certificate must then be accepted by the other party as proof of exemption from its contribution law of the person concerned. [*2 Sch, Art 3(1)(2)*].

49.23 MULTILATERAL AGREEMENTS

Apart from the EC Treaty itself, the most important multilateral treaties affecting contribution law are the EC Co-operation Agreements entered into between the EC and Algeria, Morocco and Tunisia, i.e. Maghreb. When these treaties are fully implemented EC regulations on contribution law will extend to those states.

49.24 THE EXPATRIATE PROBLEM AFTER 6 OCTOBER 1985

It is frequently the case that where a UK company posts one of its employees overseas, liability for contributions on that employee's earnings is to continue by reason of the rules laid down in *Contributions Regs, Reg 120(1)(2)* (see 49.8 above), *EC Reg 1408/71, Art 14(1)(a)* (see 49.14 above), or in the reciprocal agreement (if any) between the UK and the country to which the employee is posted (see, for example, 49.22 above). Until 6 October 1985, this presented an employer with few difficulties as the secondary Class 1 contribution liability was limited to contributions on earnings at the upper earnings limit, however great the employee's earnings might be. Following the removal of the upper earnings limit for secondary Class 1 contribution purposes on 6 October 1985, however, the position changed completely. Expatriate remuneration arrangements are usually such as to compensate the employee for cost of living, accommodation, child education, and taxation increases, and such compensation will usually result in the employee's gross pay entitlement being significantly larger than that of his UK counterpart.

Example

Henry worked for International Widgets Ltd at a salary of £27,000 p.a. On 6 April 2000 he was posted to America for a period of four years. IW agreed with H that, to maintain his earnings level at the equivalent of £27,000, he should, while working in America, be paid £69,000. IW's increased contribution costs are £5,114, being 12.2% × (£69,000 − £27,000). Had the upper earnings limit remained applicable for secondary Class 1 contribution purposes, there would have been an increased cost of only £100.04 (i.e. 12.2% × (£27,820 − £27,000)) as H's earnings, whether at the UK level or at the American equivalent, would have been limited to £27,820 for contribution purposes.

Faced with increases of this order, UK companies operating on an international level may now need to consider breaking the direct relationship between themselves and the employees whom they wish to post overseas, and to arrange for such employees to terminate their employment and to enter employment overseas with, for example, an expatriate employment bureau or an overseas associated or subsidiary company which has no place of business in Great Britain (see 49.7 above). In the above example if the UK company paid £27,000 and the balance was paid from the US company the balance may not be liable to PAYE (see *Wilson v Bye [1996] SSCD 58*).

If the direct relationship is not broken, then the UK employer will no doubt wish to exclude as much of the increased cost from earnings for NIC purposes as possible. Overseas payments and allowances may, however, be excluded from earnings only if they are specific and distinct payments of or contributions towards such items as hotel accommodation, meals, clothing or if they are payments made in accordance with a scheme that complies with the requirements laid down in connection with a subsistence allowance scheme. NICs should be charged on payments described as compensation for working abroad (i.e. not business expenses), inducements, or bonuses for working abroad as well as COLAs (see 28.72 EARNINGS and DSS 1996 Leaflet CA 28, April 1995, Page 91, Items (100) and (101), CA 28 Supplement (1996) April 1996, page 8). See also CA Specialist Conference, written response 24, 4 February 1997.

The practice followed by some companies of calculating contribution liabilities only on the notional UK equivalent of earnings paid to an employee who has been posted overseas is incorrect and has no foundation in law or International Services practice. The authorities are aware of the practice of accounting for contributions on such 'phantom salaries' and assess arrears due in appropriate cases.

50   Partners

Cross-references. See CATEGORISATION (14); COLLECTION (21); EARNINGS (28); HUSBAND AND WIFE (36).

Other Sources. Simon's NIC, Part I, Section 2, Chapters 4.291, 13.37, 13.193 and 17.96; Tolley's Partnership Taxation, Third edition, chapter 25; Tolley's Practical NIC, Vol 3 No 8, page 61; IR Inspector's Manual, para 6025.

50.1   CATEGORISATION

Partnership is the relationship which subsists between persons carrying on a business in common with a view of profit. [*Partnership Act 1890, s 1*]. It is a question of *fact* whether a particular person is truly a party to such a relationship or is merely a senior employee who is being held out as a partner (see 50.2 below). The usual tests must, therefore, be applied in order to establish the truth of the relationship (see 14.4 to 14.7 CATEGORISATION).

If the truth of the relationship is that the person *is* a partner but that he merely invests capital in the firm and takes no part in its management, he is neither an employed earner nor a self-employed earner for contribution purposes since he is not *gainfully employed* either under a contract of service or otherwise. [*SSCBA 1992, s 2(1)*]. This will apply to limited partners (unless there is some actual involvement in the running of the business) and to sleeping partners.

If the truth of the relationship is that a contract of service exists (whether disguised by a partnership deed or not) the person will be an employed earner liable to pay primary Class 1 contributions on the earnings paid to him (whether described as profits or not). In that event, the true partners will be liable as secondary contributors in respect of his employment (see 14.15 CATEGORISATION and 50.3 below) (see also 'Profit sharing arrangements with employees' Tolley's Practical NIC, Vol 3, No 8, p 61).

If the truth of the relationship is that the person is a partner in the full sense of the word he will be a self-employed earner liable to pay Class 2 contributions unless his share of the actual profits is sufficiently low for him to be excepted from liability (see 18.3 CLASS 2 CONTRIBUTIONS). He will also be liable for Class 4 contributions on his share of profits or gains chargeable to income tax under Case I or II of Schedule D (see CLASS 4 CONTRIBUTIONS (20) and 50.4 below).

50.2   Salaried partners

The term 'salaried partner' is used to denote a person who is held out to the world as being a partner with his name appearing on a firm's notepaper etc. but who, instead of receiving a share of profits, receives a salary as remuneration and, possibly, some profit-related bonus. Whether or not such a person is truly a partner will depend on the facts, and the substance of the relationship between the person and the other parties must be examined. If there is clearly a contract of service only qualified by the fact that the servant is being held out as a partner, he is no true partner. If, however, though paid a fixed salary not dependent on profits, the person is party to a full partnership deed and is entitled to share in the profits on a winding-up, he may well be a true partner. (*Stekel v Ellice [1973] 1 AER 465*).

If such a person is a true partner, his share of profits or gains for Class 4 purposes will be his salary.

50.3   PARTNERS AS SECONDARY CONTRIBUTORS

Although a partnership is not, in English law, a separate legal entity, it (rather than the individual partners) will be treated as the secondary contributor in relation to earnings paid to its employees. If the partnership defaults in the payment of contributions, therefore, it is submitted that there is but one offence but that the Inland Revenue may proceed against one or more of the partners who may be separately fined and ordered to pay an amount equal to the unpaid contributions (see 12.4 ARREARS OF CONTRIBUTIONS), or against all the partners who may then be jointly convicted and ordered to pay the sum in question.

Partners may also become liable as secondary contributors where one of their number is supplied by the partnership to work for someone else within the terms of *Categorisation Regs, Reg 5 and 3 Sch 2(a)* (see 4.3 AGENCY WORKERS).

50.4   CLASS 4 CONTRIBUTIONS

Where a trade or profession is carried on in partnership, the liability of any partner in respect of Class 4 contributions is to arise in respect of his share of the profits or gains of that trade or profession; and, for this purpose, his share is to be *aggregated* with his share of the profits or gains of any other trade, profession or vocation (see 5.17 AGGREGATION OF EARNINGS). [*SSCBA 1992, 2 Sch 4(1)*].

Under tax law, the profits of a partnership set up and commenced before 6 April 1994 must be allocated to each partner in accordance with the profit-sharing ratio prevailing in the year of assessment and not that applying to the accounts forming the basis of assessment [*ICTA 1988, s 277*] (see *Lewis v CIR (1933) 18 TC 174*). For such partnerships, this remains the case for 1996–97, the transitional year under self-assessment. As Class 4 contributions are payable in respect of profits chargeable to tax, a partner's share of profits must be arrived at on this basis for Class 4 purposes also. From 1997–98 onwards the share of profits is determined on the basis of the profit sharing arrangements *in the basis period*.

Example
Alder, Birch and Cypress are in partnership as arboriculturists. Their profit for the year ended 30 June 2000 is £34,000 and during that year C is a salaried partner while A and B share the remaining profit in equal shares. The Sch D Case I assessment for 2000–01 is £34,000. Although A and B continue to share profits on the same basis, however, C's salary for the year ended 30 June 2000 is £12,000 and for the year ended 30 June 2001 is £14,000. For Class 4 purposes the 2000–01 assessment is to be

		£
C	=	12,000
A ½ × (£34,000 – £12,000)	=	11,000
B ½ × (£34,000 – £12,000)	=	11,000
		£34,000

Under self-assessment Class 4 contributions are, like income tax, self-assessed individually with each partner having been notified by the partnership of his/her share of assessable profit. Further, for long-established partnerships there is no joint or several liability in respect of tax and national insurance liabilities for 1997–98 onwards. The same is true, *from commencement*, for partnerships which started after 5 April 1994. See Inland Revenue Tax Bulletin, issue 22, page 293.

The Class 4 contributions for which a partner was liable prior to self-assessment and in accordance with the rules described could either be charged on him separately or, to the extent only that the liability arose in respect of the profits or gains of that partnership, be the subject of a joint assessment to contributions made in the partnership name. [*SSCBA 1992, 2 Sch 4(2)*]. The Inland Revenue Inspector's Manual states that in these circumstances the Inspector is advised for convenience to assess the partners jointly in one sum on the same assessment set as the income tax assessment. However, if exceptionally, the Inspector wishes to adopt the alternative method of assessing the partners individually he should contact Business Profits Division 4 if the Inspector is in doubt how to proceed. (See Inspector's Manual, para 6025, issue 12/94.)

Example

Diamond and Emerald are in partnership as jewellers sharing profits in the ratio of 1:1 until 30 September 1998 and in the ratio of 1:2 after that date. Diamond also runs a nightclub. The partnership profits for the years to 30 September 1998, 30 September 1999 and 30 September 2000 are £15,000, £21,000 and £27,000. D's profits from his nightclub are £19,000 for 1998–99, £23,000 for 1999–2000 and £15,000 for 2000–01.

D and E will each separately self-assess their tax and Class 4 national insurance liabilities. In the case of D, this will be based on the total income from both sources of self-employment income.

D's Class 4 liability for 1998–99 is

	£
£15,000 × $\frac{1}{2}$	7,500
Nightclub	19,000
	26,500
Less: Excess over upper annual limit (£25,220)	1,280
	25,220
Less: Lower annual limit	7,310
	£17,910

£17,910 @ 6.0% = £1,074.60

E's Class 4 liability for 1998–99 is

	£
£15,000 × $\frac{1}{2}$	7,500
Less: Lower annual limit	7,310
	£190

£190 @ 6.0% = £11.40

D's Class 4 liability for 1999–2000 is

	£
£21,000 × $\frac{1}{3}$	7,000
Nightclub	23,000
	30,000
Less: Excess over upper annual limit (£26,000)	4,000
	26,000
Less: Lower annual limit	7,530
	£18,470

£18,470 @ 6.0% = £1,108.20

E's Class 4 liability for 1999–2000 is

	£
£21,000 × $\frac{2}{3}$	14,000
Less: Lower annual limit	7,530
	£6,470

£6,470 @ 6.0% = £388.20

D's Class 4 liability for 2000–01 is

	£
£27,000 × $\frac{1}{3}$	9,000
Nightclub	15,000
	24,000
Less: Lower annual limit	4,385
	£19,615

£19,615 @ 7.0% = £1,373.05

E's Class 4 liability for 2000–01 is

	£
£27,000 × $\frac{2}{3}$	18,000
Less: Lower annual limit	4,385
	£13,615

£13,615 @ 7.0% = £953.05

D and E's Class 4 liabilities for 1998–99 was payable in two equal interim instalments on 31 January and 31 July 1999 based on the 1997–98 assessments, with the balance payable on 31 January 2000. Similarly, their Class 4 liability for 1999–2000 is payable in two equal instalments on 31 January and 31 July 2000 based on the 1998–99 assessment, with the balance payable on 31 January 2001 and so on.

The self-assessment payments will, therefore, include the following amounts in relation to Class 4 contributions

	D	E
	£	£
31 January 2000 (1999–2000 POA)	537.30	5.70
31 July 2000 (1999–2000 POA)	537.30	5.70
31 January 2001 (1999–2000 balance)	33.60	376.80
31 January 2001 (2000–01 POA)	554.10	194.10
31 July 2001 (2000–01 POA)	554.10	194.10
31 January 2002 (2000–01 balance)	264.85	564.85
31 January 2002 (2001–02 POA)	686.52	476.52
31 July 2002 (2001–02 POA)	686.53	476.53

51   Rates and Limits

Cross-references. See ADMINISTRATION (2); ANNUAL MAXIMUM (7); CLASS 1 CONTRIBUTIONS (15); CLASS 1A CONTRIBUTIONS (16); CLASS 2 CONTRIBUTIONS (18); CLASS 3 CONTRIBUTIONS (19); CLASS 4 CONTRIBUTIONS (20); CONTRACTED-OUT EMPLOYMENT (23); EARNINGS LIMITS AND THRESHOLDS (30); MARINERS (42); NATIONAL INSURANCE SURCHARGE (47); REDUCED LIABILITY ELECTIONS (52); SHARE FISHERMEN (54); VOLUNTEER DEVELOPMENT WORKERS (57).

Other Sources. Tolley's Social Security and State Benefits Handbook 2000–01; Leaflet GL 23.

51.1   CHANGES IN RATES, LIMITS, THRESHOLDS AND BRACKETS

As explained in the various chapters to which cross-references are given above, the power to change the rates, limits and brackets which govern contribution liability is, provided the changes lie within defined parameters, in the hands of the Treasury (the Secretary of State for Social Security until 1 April 1999). Normally, the majority of such changes are announced in November and take effect from the beginning of the following tax year, but mid-year changes are possible. Where changes lie outside the powers of the Secretary of State they are achieved by an Act of Parliament.

Alterations in the rate of national insurance surcharge (now abolished) were effected through the annual Finance Act and were normally announced as part of the Chancellor of the Exchequer's budget statement.

51.2   CLASS 1 CONTRIBUTIONS

Earnings limits

See 30.2 EARNINGS LIMITS AND THRESHOLDS for the factors affecting the level at which these limits may be set and 30.3 EARNINGS LIMITS AND THRESHOLDS for the formulae whereby earnings limits for periods of other than one week are to be calculated.

Lower earnings limits (see below for Earnings Thresholds)

Tax year	Weekly £	Monthly £	Annual £
2000–01	67.00	291.00	3,484.00
1999–2000	66.00	286.00	3,432.00
1998–99	64.00	278.00	3,328.00
1997–98	62.00	269.00	3,224.00
1996–97	61.00	265.00	3,172.00
1995–96	58.00	252.00	3,016.00
1994–95	57.00	247.00	2,964.00
1993–94	56.00	243.00	2,912.00
1992–93	54.00	234.00	2,808.00
1991–92	52.00	226.00	2,704.00
1990–91	46.00	200.00	2,392.00
1989–90	43.00	187.00	2,236.00
1988–89	41.00	178.00	2,132.00
1987–88	39.00	169.00	2,028.00
1986–87	38.00	164.67	1,976.04
1985–86	35.50	153.83	1,845.96
1984–83	34.00	147.33	1,767.96
1983–84	32.50	140.83	1,689.96
1982–83	29.50	127.83	1,533.96
1981–82	27.00	117.00	1,404.00

51.3 Rates and Limits

Upper earnings limits

Tax year	Weekly £	Monthly £	Annual £
2000–01	535.00	2,319.00	27,820.00
1999–2000	500.00	2,167.00	26,000.00
1998–99	485.00	2,102.00	25,220.00
1997–98	465.00	2,015.00	24,180.00
1996–97	455.00	1,972.00	23,660.00
1995–96	440.00	1,907.00	22,880.00
1994–95	430.00	1,864.00	22,360.00
1993–94	420.00	1,820.00	21,840.00
1992–93	405.00	1,755.00	21,060.00
1991–92	390.00	1,690.00	20,280.00
1990–91	350.00	1,517.00	18,200.00
1989–90	325.00	1,409.00	16,900.00
1988–89	305.00	1,322.00	15,860.00
1987–88	295.00	1,279.00	15,340.00
1986–87	285.00	1,235.00	14,820.00
1985–86	265.00	1,148.33	13,779.96
1984–85	250.00	1,083.33	12.999.96
1983–84	235.00	1,018.33	12,219.96
1982–83	220.00	953.33	11,439.96
1981–82	200.00	866.67	10,400.04

51.3 Earnings thresholds

Employee's Earnings Threshold

Tax year	Weekly £	Monthly £	Annual £
2000–01	76.00	329.00	3,952.00

Employer's Earnings Threshold

Tax Year	Weekly £	Monthly £	Annual £
2000–01	84.00	365.00	4,385.00
1999–2000	83.00	361.00	4,335.00

51.4 Earnings brackets

See 30.6 EARNINGS LIMITS AND THRESHOLDS for the formulae whereby earnings brackets for periods of other than one week are to be calculated.

Primary	EB1	EB2	EB3

From 5 October 1989 primary earnings brackets were abolished and replaced by an initial primary percentage (2%) on earnings up to the LEL and a main primary percentage (9%) on earnings between the LEL and the UEL. From 6 April 1994 the main primary percentage was increased to 10%, but the initial primary percentage remains at 2%.

1989–90 (to 4 October 1989)

	EB1	EB2	EB3
Week	LEL to £74.99	£75.00 to £114.99	£115.00 to £325.00
Month	LEL to £324.99	£325.00 to £498.99	£499.00 to £1,409.00
Year	LEL to £3,899.99	£3,900.00 to £5,979.99	£5,980.00 to £16,900.00

Primary	EB1	EB2	EB3
1988–89			
Week	LEL to £69.99	£70.00 to £104.99	£105.00 to £305.00
Month	LEL to £303.99	£304.00 to £454.99	£455.00 to £1,322.00
Year	LEL to £3,639.99	£3,640.00 to £5,459.99	£5,460.00 to £15,860.00
1987–88			
Week	LEL to £64.99	£65.00 to £99.99	£100.00 to £295.00
Month	LEL to £281.99	£282.00 to £433.99	£434.00 to £1,279.00
Year	LEL to £3,379.99	£3,380.00 to £5,199.99	£5,200.00 to £15,340.00
1986–87			
Week	LEL to £59.99	£60.00 to £94.99	£95.00 to £285.00
Month	LEL to £259.99	£260.00 to £411.66	£411.67 to £1,235.00
Year	LEL to £3,119.99	£3,120.00 to £4,940.03	£4,940.04 to £14,820.00
1985–86 (from 6.10.85)			
Week	LEL to £54.99	£55.00 to £89.99	£90.00 to £265.00
Month	LEL to £238.32	£238.33 to £389.99	£390.00 to £1,148.33
Year	LEL to £2,859.95	£2,859.96 to £4,679.99	£4,680.00 to £13,779.96

Secondary	EB1	EB2	EB3	EB4
1997–98 and 1998–99				
Week	LEL to £109.99	£110.00 to £154.99	£155.00 to £209.99	£210.00 or more
Month	LEL to £476.99	£477.00 to £671.99	£672.00 to £909.99	£910.00 or more
Year	LEL to £5,719.99	£5,720.00 to £8,059.99	£8,060.00 to £10,919.99	£10,920.00 or more
1996–97				
Week	LEL to £109.99	£110.00 to £154.99	£155.00 to £209.99	£210.00 or more
Month	LEL to £476.99	£477.00 to £671.99	£672.00 to £909.99	£910.00 or more
Year	LEL to £5,719.99	£5,720.00 to £8,059.99	£8,060.00 to £10,919.99	£10,920.00 or more
1995–96				
Week	LEL to £104.99	£105.00 to £149.99	£150.00 to £204.99	£205.00 or more
Month	LEL to £454.99	£455.00 to £649.99	£650.00 to £888.99	£889.00 or more
Year	LEL to £5,459.99	£5,460.00 to £7,799.99	£7,800.00 to £10,659.99	£10,660.00 or more
1994–95				
Week	LEL to £99.99	£100.00 to £144.99	£145.00 to £199.99	£200.00 or more
Month	LEL to £433.99	£434.00 to £628.99	£629.00 to £866.99	£867.00 or more
Year	LEL to £5,199.99	£5,200.00 to £7,539.99	£7,540.00 to £10,399.99	£10,400.00 or more
1993–94				
Week	LEL to £94.99	£95.00 to £139.99	£140.00 to £194.99	£195.00 or more
Month	LEL to £411.99	£412.00 to £606.99	£607.00 to £844.99	£845.00 or more
Year	LEL to £4,939.99	£4,940.00 to £7,279.99	£7,280.00 to £10,139.99	£10,140.00 or more
1992–93				
Week	LEL to £89.99	£90.00 to £134.99	£135.00 to £189.99	£190.00 or more
Month	LEL to £389.99	£390.00 to £584.99	£585.00 to £823.99	£824.00 or more
Year	LEL to £4,679.99	£4,680.00 to £7,019.99	£7,020.00 to £9,879.99	£9,880.00 or more
1991–92				
Week	LEL to £84.99	£85.00 to £129.99	£130.00 to £184.99	£185.00 or more
Month	LEL to £368.99	£369.00 to £563.99	£564.00 to £801.99	£802.00 or more
Year	LEL to £4,419.99	£4,420.00 to £6,759.99	£6,760.00 to £9,619.99	£9,620.00 or more
1990–91				
Week	LEL to £79.99	£80.00 to £124.99	£125.00 to £174.99	£175.00 or more
Month	LEL to £346.99	£347.00 to £541.99	£542.00 to £758.99	£759.00 or more
Year	LEL to £4,159.99	£4,160.00 to £6,499.99	£6,500.00 to £9,099.99	£9,100.00 or more
1989–90				
Week	LEL to £74.99	£75.00 to £114.99	£115.00 to £164.99	£165.00 or more
Month	LEL to £324.99	£325.00 to £498.99	£499.00 to £714.99	£715.00 or more
Year	LEL to £3,899.99	£3,900.00 to £5,979.99	£5,980.00 to £8,579.99	£8,580.00 or more

51.5 Rates and Limits

Secondary	EB1	EB2	EB3	EB4
1988–89				
Week	LEL to £69.99	£70.00 to £104.99	£105.00 to £154.99	£155.00 or more
Month	LEL to £303.99	£304.00 to £454.99	£455.00 to £671.99	£672.00 or more
Year	LEL to £3,639.99	£3,640.00 to £5,459.99	£5,460.00 to £8,059.99	£8,060.00 or more
1987–88				
Week	LEL to £64.99	£65.00 to £99.99	£100.00 to £149.99	£150.00 or more
Month	LEL to £281.99	£282.00 to £433.99	£434.00 to £649.99	£650.00 or more
Year	LEL to £3,379.99	£3,380.00 to £5,199.99	£5,200.00 to £7,799.99	£7,800.00 or more
1986–87				
Week	LEL to £59.99	£60.00 to £94.99	£95.00 to £139.99	£140.00 or more
Month	LEL to £259.99	£260.00 to £411.66	£411.67 to £606.66	£606.67 or more
Year	LEL to £3,119.99	£3,120.00 to £4,940.03	£4,940.04 to £7,280.03	£7,280.04 or more
1985–86 (from 6.10.85)				
Week	LEL to £54.99	£55.00 to £89.99	£90.00 to £129.99	£130.00 or more
Month	LEL to £238.32	£238.33 to £389.99	£390.00 to £563.32	£563.33 or more
Year	LEL to £2,859.95	£2,859.96 to £4,679.99	£4,680.00 to £6,759.96	£6,759.97 or more

51.5 Class 1 contribution rates from 6.4.99

The table below sets out the contribution rates for normal employed earners and their secondary contributors which apply to earnings from the appropriate earnings threshold (lower earnings limit in the case of primary contributions for 1999–2000 only) up to the upper earnings limit in the case of primary contributions and on all earnings above the employer's earnings threshold in the case of secondary contributions. [*Social Security (Contributions) Amendment Regs 2000, SI 2000/175*].

Where an employee is in contracted-out employment, primary contributions are payable at the contracted-out rate. Secondary contributions are payable at the contracted-out rate on earnings between the employer's earnings threshold and the upper earnings limit and at the next contracted-out rate on any balance of earnings above the upper earnings limit. In addition a rebate of employer's contributions applies in respect of the slice of earnings from the lower earnings limit to the employer's earnings threshold, at the appropriate rate. From 6 April 2000, a primary contracted-out rebate is also applicable in respect of earnings between the lower earnings limit and the employee's earnings threshold. The rebate is treated as set out in 23.3 CONTRACTED-OUT EMPLOYMENT.

Where a married woman or widow has a valid reduced rate election in force, her primary contributions are payable at the *reduced rate* on earnings between the lower and upper earnings limits but the secondary contributions are calculated as set out above, either not contracted-out or contracted-out.

Secondary contributions only are payable in respect of earnings paid to an earner over pensionable age and neither primary nor secondary contributions are payable in respect of earnings paid to an earner who is under the age of 16 (see 3.1 and 3.7 AGE EXCEPTION).

| | *Primary* | | | | *Secondary* | | |
	RR	SR	COR		SR	COSR	COMP
	%	%	%		%	%	%
2000–2001	3.85	10.00	8.40		12.2	9.2	11.6
1999–2000	3.85	10.00	8.40		12.2	9.2	11.6

	Primary rebate on LEL to EEET (COSR and COMP)	Secondary rebate on LEL to ERET	
		COSR	COMP
2000–01	(1.60)	(3.00)	(0.60)
1999–2000		(3.00)	(0.60)

51.6 Class 1 contribution rates from 6.10.85 to 5.4.99

The table below sets out, by reference to the earnings brackets (see 51.4 above) in which their earnings for their earnings periods fall, the contribution rates for normal employed earners and their secondary contributors. The rates as stated are reduced in the case of certain MARINERS (see 42.9 to 42.11) and, until 5 April 1996, in the case of members of the ARMED FORCES (see 11.5).

From 6 April 1982 until 5 April 1988, the appropriate percentage rate of primary and secondary class 1 contributions in respect of earnings paid to a registered dockworker who had no general entitlement to redundancy pay under *Employment Rights Act 1996, Part XI* and *sections 199(2)* or *209*, was reduced by 0.35 and 0.15 respectively. [*Contributions Regs, Reg 133(1) as amended by Social Security (Contributions) Act 1982, 1 Sch 3(4)(a)(b)*].

Where an employee is in contracted-out employment, contributions are payable at the appropriate *standard rate* on earnings at the lower earnings limit and then at *contracted-out rates* on the balance of earnings to the upper earnings limit. On earnings above the upper earnings limit secondary contributions only are payable, at the highest standard rate. An employee who contracts out through an appropriate personal pension pays contributions, as does his employer, at the not contracted-out rate (see 23.3 CONTRACTED-OUT EMPLOYMENT).

Where a married woman or widow has a valid reduced rate election in force, her primary contributions are payable at a single *reduced rate* but the secondary contribution is (if she is in not contracted-out employment) at the appropriate *standard rate* or (if she is in contracted-out employment) at the appropriate *standard rate* on earnings at the lower earnings limit and *contracted-out rate* on the balance of earnings (see REDUCED LIABILITY ELECTIONS (52)).

Secondary contributions only are payable in respect of earnings paid to an earner over pensionable age and neither primary nor secondary contributions are payable in respect of earnings paid to an earner who is under the age of 16 (see 3.1, 3.7 AGE EXCEPTION).

		Primary				*Secondary*	
EB	RR	SR	COR	EB	SR	COSR	COMP
	%	%	%		%	%	%
1997–98 and 1998–99							
Up to LEL	3.85	2.00	2.00	1	3.00	—	1.50
LEL to UEL	3.85	10.00	8.40	2	5.00	2.00	3.50
				3	7.00	4.00	5.50
				4	10.00	7.00/10.00	8.50/10.00

EB	RR	SR	COR	EB	SR	COR
	%	%	%		%	%
1996–97						
Up to LEL	3.85	2.00	2.00	1	3.00	—
LEL to UEL	3.85	10.00	8.20	2	5.00	2.00
				3	7.00	4.00
				4	10.20	7.20/10.20
1995–96						
Up to LEL	3.85	2.00	2.00	1	3.00	—
LEL to UEL	3.85	10.00	8.20	2	5.00	2.00
				3	7.00	4.00
				4	10.20	7.20/10.20
1994–95						
Up to LEL	3.85	2.00	2.00	1	3.60	0.60
LEL to UEL	3.85	10.00	8.20	2	5.60	2.60
				3	7.60	4.60
				4	10.20	7.20/10.20

51.7 Rates and Limits

EB	RR %	SR %	COR %	EB	SR %	COR %
1993–94						
Up to LEL	3.85	2.00	2.00	1	4.60	1.60
LEL to UEL	3.85	9.00	7.20	2	6.60	3.60
				3	8.60	5.60
				4	10.40	7.40/10.40
1991–92 and 1992–93						
Up to LEL	3.85	2.00	2.00	1	4.60	0.80
LEL to UEL	3.85	9.00	7.00	2	6.60	2.80
				3	8.60	4.80
				4	10.40	6.60/10.40
1989–90 (from 5 October 1989) and 1990–91						
Up to LEL	3.85	2.00	2.00	1	5.00	1.20
LEL to UEL	3.85	9.00	7.00	2	7.00	3.20
				3	9.00	5.20
				4	10.45	6.65/10.45
1988–89 and 1989–90 (to 4 October 1989)						
1	3.85	5.00	3.00	1	5.00	1.20
2	3.85	7.00	5.00	2	7.00	3.20
3	3.85	9.00	7.00	3	9.00	5.20
				4	10.45	6.65/10.45
1987–88, 1986–87 and 1985–86 (from 6 October 1985)						
1	3.85	5.00	2.85	1	5.00	0.90
2	3.85	7.00	4.85	2	7.00	2.90
3	3.85	9.00	6.85	3	9.00	4.90
				4	10.45	6.35/10.45

51.7 Class 1 contribution rates to 6.10.85

The table below sets out the contribution rates for normal employed earners and their secondary contributors under the national insurance scheme as it operated before 6 October 1985. The notes at 51.6 above concerning contracted-out contributions, reduced rate contributions, and the contributions of certain mariners, members of the armed forces and dock workers, apply in their entirety except that, before 6 October 1985, no primary or secondary contributions were payable on earnings above the upper earnings limit and, before 6 April 1982, a dockworker's primary percentage rate was subject to no reduction but his secondary contributor's percentage rate was reduced by 0.2%.

	Primary			*Secondary*	
	RR %	SR %	COR %	SR %	COR %
1985–86 (to 6.10.85)	3.85	9.00	6.85	10.45	6.35
1984–85	3.85	9.00	6.85	10.45	6.35
1983–84	3.85	9.00	6.85	10.45	6.35
1982–83	3.20	8.75	6.25	10.20	5.70
1981–82	2.75	7.75	5.25	10.20	5.70

51.8 Class 1A contribution rates

The Class 1A contribution rate is the standard secondary Class 1 rate (the Class 1 rate appropriate for the highest secondary earnings bracket until 5 April 1999) for the tax year in which the car (and fuel) was provided, with *no* reduction where the employment is contracted-out. [*SSCBA 1992, s 10(5)*].

	%
2000–01	12.20
1999–2000	12.20
1998–99	10.00
1997–98	10.00
1996–97	10.20
1995–96	10.20
1994–95	10.20
1993–94	10.40
1992–93	10.40
1991–92	10.40

51.9   Class 1B contribution rates

The Class 1B contribution rate is set as follows:

	%
2000–01	12.20
1999–2000	12.20

[*SSCBA 1992, s 10A as inserted by SSA 1998, s 53 and amended by Welfare Reform and Pensions Act 1999, s 77–78*].

51.10   National insurance surcharge

The surcharge was completely abolished with effect from 6 April 1985 (local authorities etc.) and 1 October 1984 (others).

See NATIONAL INSURANCE SURCHARGE (47) for the exemption of charities and for details of the organisations which were subject to the local authorities etc. rates.

Period	Local authorities etc.	Others
	%	%
1.10.84 to 5.4.85	2.5	—
1.8.83 to 30.9.84	2.5	1.0
6.4.83 to 31.7.83	2.5	1.5
2.8.82 to 5.4.83	3.5	2.0*
2.10.78 to 1.8.82	3.5	3.5*

*Although the surcharge to be applied to earnings from 2 August 1982 to 5 April 1983 was 2% as stated, this was an expedient and approximate means whereby a true surcharge of 2.5% was charged on earnings throughout 1982–83. [*FA 1972, s 143(1)(2)*]. That 2.5% was itself then effectively reduced to approximately 2% by a rebating arrangement in accordance with which remittances to the Collector of Taxes in the last three months of 1982–83 were reduced by an amount equal to 3% of an employer's total primary and secondary contribution and surcharge liability for the whole year. [*National Insurance Surcharge Act 1982, s 1(4)–(6)*]. This 3% rebate is not reflected in the above table.

51.11   CLASS 2 RATE AND SMALL EARNINGS EXCEPTION LIMIT

See 54.3 SHARE FISHERMEN for reason for increased contribution rate, 57.3 VOLUNTEER DEVELOPMENT WORKERS for reason for reduced contribution rate, and 18.3 CLASS 2 CONTRIBUTIONS for circumstances in which exception on the grounds of small earnings may be claimed.

51.12   Rates and Limits

Tax year	Normal weekly rate	Share fisherman's special rate	Volunteer development worker's special rate	Small earnings exception limit
	£	£	£	£
2000–01	2.00	2.65	3.35	3,825
1999–2000	6.55	7.20	3.30	3,770
1998–99	6.35	7.00	3.20	3,590
1997–98	6.15	6.80	3.10	3,480
1996–97	6.05	7.20	3.05	3,430
1995–96	5.75	7.30	2.90	3,260
1994–95	5.65	7.75	3.76	3,200
1993–94	5.55	7.75	3.70	3,140
1992–93	5.35	7.00	3.56	3,030
1991–92	5.15	6.20	3.43	2,900
1990–91	4.55	6.15	3.22	2,600
1989–90	4.25	5.80	4.30	2,350
1988–89	4.05	6.55	6.55	2,250
1987–88	3.85	6.55	6.55	2,125
1986–87	3.75	6.55	—	2,075
1985–86 (from 6.10.85)	3.50	7.55	—	1,925
1985–86 (to 6.10.85)	4.75	7.55	—	1,925
1984–85	4.60	7.20	—	1,850
1983–84	4.40	7.00	—	1,775
1982–83	3.75	5.85	—	1,600
1981–82	3.40	5.15	—	1,475

51.12 CLASS 3 CONTRIBUTIONS

Class 3 contribution rates are as follows.

Tax year	Weekly rate
	£
2000–01	6.55
1999–2000	6.45
1998–99	6.25
1997–98	6.05
1996–97	5.95
1995–96	5.65
1994–95	5.55
1993–94	5.45
1992–93	5.25
1991–92	5.05
1990–91	4.45
1989–90	4.15
1988–89	3.95
1987–88	3.75
1986–87	3.65
1985–86 (from 6.10.85)	3.40
1985–86 (to 6.10.85)	4.65
1984–85	4.50
1983–84	4.30
1982–83	3.65
1981–82	3.30

51.13 CLASS 4 RATES AND ANNUAL PROFIT LIMITS

Class 4 rates and profits limits are as follows.

Tax year	Rate %	Lower limit £	Upper limit £
2000–01	7.00	4,385	27,820
1999–2000	6.00	7,530	26,000
1998–99	6.00	7,310	25,220
1997–98	6.00	7,010	24,180
1996–97	6.00	6,860	23,660
1995–96	7.30	6,640	22,880
1994–95	7.30	6,490	22,360
1993–94	6.30	6,340	21,840
1992–93	6.30	6,120	21,060
1991–92	6.30	5,900	20,280
1990–91	6.30	5,450	18,200
1989–90	6.30	5,050	16,900
1988–89	6.30	4,750	15,860
1987–88	6.30	4,590	15,340
1986–87	6.30	4,450	14,820
1985–86	6.30	4,150	13,780
1984–85	6.30	3,950	13,000
1983–84	6.30	3,800	12,000
1982–83	6.00	3,450	11,000
1981–82	5.75	3,150	10,000

51.14 ANNUAL MAXIMA

Overall annual maximum

Subject to what is said at 7.1 ANNUAL MAXIMUM, no individual earner is required to pay total contributions in excess of the figure stated (see 7.2 ANNUAL MAXIMUM).

Tax year	Maximum £	Tax year	Maximum £
2000–01	2,432.70	1990–91	1,498.84
1999–2000	2,300.20	1989–90	1,468.98
1998–99	2,299.14	1988-89	1,454.85
1997–98	2,201.62	1987–88	1,407.15
1996–97	2,152.86	1986–87	1,359.45
1995–96	2,086.08	1985–86	1,264.05
1994–95	2,037.32	1984–85	1,192.50
1993–94	1,795.64	1983–84	1,120.95
1992–93	1,731.51	1982–83	1,020.25
1991–92	1,667.38	1981–82	821.50

51.15 Class 4 limiting maximum

If an individual's Class 1 and Class 2 contributions in a tax year total to less than the figure stated below, any Class 4 liability which would arise is to be limited to the difference between the Class 1 and Class 2 contributions paid and the figure stated below (see 7.3 ANNUAL MAXIMUM).

51.15 Rates and Limits

Tax year	Maximum £	Tax year	Maximum £
2000–01	1,746.45	1990–91	1,044.40
1999–2000	1,455.35	1989–90	971.80
1998–99	1,411.15	1988-89	914.58
1997–98	1,356.15	1987–88	881.30
1996–97	1,328.65	1986–87	852.06
1995–96	1,490.27	1985–86	824.69
1994–95	1,457.96	1984–85	813.95
1993–94	1,270.65	1983–84	750.80
1992–93	1,224.77	1982–83	651.75
1991–92	1,178.89	1981–82	574.07

52 Reduced Liability Elections

Cross-references. See CLASS 1 CONTRIBUTIONS (15); CLASS 2 CONTRIBUTIONS (18); CREDITS (24); HUSBAND AND WIFE (36); 51.6 RATES AND LIMITS.

Other Sources. Tolley's Payroll Handbook 2000; Leaflets CA 09, CA 10, CA 13 and CWG2 (2000).

52.1 GENERAL CONSIDERATIONS

The position of a married woman or widow under contribution law is now, in general, no different from that of any other person but, until 11 May 1977 (and for a transitional period thereafter in the case of certain widows and married women within a year of retirement age), a married woman or widow had the right to elect not to participate in the contribution scheme and many such elections continue in force at the present day.

The women to whom the making of such an election was open were those who, on 10 April 1977, were married or were widowed and entitled to either widow's benefits under the State scheme or industrial or war widow's pensions at a rate equivalent to or greater than the standard rate of basic widow's pension (£67.50 per week from 10 April 2000). [*Contributions Regs, Reg 100(1)(8)*].

Earlier elections made under *Contributions Regs 1975, Regs 91, 94* and in force at 6 April 1977, or under *Married Women Regs 1973, Regs 2(1)(a), 3(1)(a)* or *Contributions Regs 1969, Reg 9(3)(4A)* and in force at 6 April 1975, were continued under current regulations. [*Contributions Regs, Regs 102, 108*].

In 1995–96, the most recent year for which detailed figures are currently available, 339,000 women paid Class 1 contributions at the reduced rate. Of this number 159,000 will reach the age 60 by 5 April 2001. (Contributions and Qualifying Years for Retirement Pension 1995–96, Government Statistical Service, May 1998). In addition to these women, there are others who are self-employed only and who do not therefore pay a Class 2 contribution (see 52.3 below).

52.2 CERTIFICATES OF ELECTION

Whilst an election of the kind described at 52.1 above had to be made in writing to the Secretary of State on a form CF9 supported by a marriage certificate and other relevant documentation, in the case of a woman who, before 6 April 1975 was married and self-employed but who had *not* elected to pay Class 2 contributions, a reduced rate election is deemed to have been made on 6 April 1975. This deemed election will continue in force until a terminating event occurs, see 52.5 below. Where a married woman was employed before 6 April 1975 and had elected *not* to pay the flat rate Class 1 contributions, she was also deemed to have made a reduced rate election at a later date. [*National Insurance Act 1965, s 10(1), National Insurance (Married Women) Regs 1973, Reg 3(1)(a), Contributions Regs 1975, Regs 91, 100, Contributions Regs 1979, Regs 100(5)(7), 108*]. If a married woman was employed by her husband before 1975, that employment was disregarded *unless* the employment was in a trade or business in which she was ordinarily engaged for 24 hours or more in a contribution week. Where she was so engaged, she was, under *National Insurance Act 1965, s 1(3)* and *National Insurance (Classification) Regs 1972, 1 Sch Pt II, para 17* treated as *self-employed* provided her weekly earnings from the activity were ordinarily £4 or more [*para 22*] (increased to £8 from August 1974). A woman deemed to be self-employed in this way would have been deemed to have made a reduced rate election on 6 April 1975 if she had not elected to pay Class 2 contributions.

52.2   Reduced Liability Elections

There are still many women who were either employed by their husband or self-employed before 6 April 1975 and, because their circumstances have not changed or changed little since then, do not actually possess a certificate of reduced liability. *Reg 108*, a regulation giving transitional relief, provides that they are entitled to one (unless they have subsequently ceased to qualify to continue to pay the reduced rate (see 52.5 below)). This transitional provision is not widely known by NICO staff, and individuals may be able to readily fend off an approach for arrears if their circumstances enable them to send the following letter:

National Insurance Contributions Office

....

....

Dear Sirs,

Either I have remained in continuous self-employment since before 6 April 1975.

Or I was employed by my husband until 5 April 1975 (and therefore not allowed to pay contributions) and have been continuously self-employed since 6 April 1975.

I am therefore covered by the transitional regulation 108 of the Social Security (Contributions) Regulations 1979 and request that you now issue me with a 'Certificate of Election' (CA4139).

Yours faithfully,

....

Note to the letter

Limited gaps after 6 April 1978 and/or a cessation of self-employment replaced by employment at or above the LEL may also result in an individual retaining entitlement (see below). In suitable cases, the first sentence in the above letter should be adapted accordingly.

An election, latterly, has resulted in the issue of a certificate of election, CF 383 or CA 4139. If its holder is an employed earner, it has to be handed to the secondary contributor in relation to her employment as authority for primary Class 1 contributions to be paid in respect of her earnings at a reduced rate (see 52.3 below). (The rate of secondary contributions is unaffected.) Where a woman has more than one employed earner's employment, certificates are required for each. [*Reg 106(1)(3)(6)*].

Where a reduced rate election is renewed after 5 April 1987 a new form of certificate is issued but an unexpired old-type certificate, CF 383, remains valid until replaced. The validity of a new or old type of certificate CF 383 may be checked by reference to the contents of boxes A and B thereon. Earlier evidence of a reduced rate election consisted of either a certificate CF 380, a tear-off form CF 2AR(TO) from a 1974–75 special national insurance card or a CF 380A (printed in green). The first two of these should have been exchanged for current certificates by 5 April 1980 and are *no longer valid*. They must not, therefore, be accepted as proof that an election is currently in force. The last remains valid only if the holder has continued in the employment of the employer by whom she was employed on 5 April 1980 at a level of earnings equal to or exceeding the lower earnings limit (see EARNINGS LIMITS AND THRESHOLDS (30)). (Leaflet CWG2 (2000), Page 61, item 82).

The person who is the secondary contributor in relation to earnings paid to a woman is responsible for any underpayment of contributions which arises as a result of giving effect to an invalid reduced rate election certificate. (Leaflet CWG2 (2000), Page 62, item 84). In practice, the Inland Revenue will hold a secondary contributor responsible if a properly organised payroll system *would* have alerted the secondary contributor to the fact that a woman's election must have been brought to an end, e.g. where a woman has reverted to using her maiden name or has told a member of the personnel department that she has become divorced. (Leaflet CWG2 (2000), Page 62, item 84). This is clearly of concern to an employer when a married woman gets divorced and omits to tell him; the consequence of this is that a considerable amount of contributions can go unpaid and it is the current practice to demand the underpaid contributions from the employer. If the employer refuses to pay because he or she was not aware that the employee was divorcing then the NICO will usually come to some mediated agreement with both the parties to resolve the situation. (CA Specialist Conference 11 October 1994). As the idea of the divorce courts being required to notify the authorities direct has been discounted in the past, the onus is probably on the employer to educate his or her employees as to the importance of an early disclosure of a change of their personal circumstances. Some employers require an annual declaration to be signed by any woman who claims to hold a reduced rate election to the effect that it is still valid and that she has not divorced during the year.

Each certificate remains the property of the Inland Revenue and, if it ceases to be of effect (see 52.4 below), the woman is to notify the secondary contributor, retrieve the certificate from him and return it to the Inland Revenue, which in practice means the NICO Class 1 Caseworker. [*Reg 106(1)(c), (4) as amended by SSC(T)A 1999, 2 Sch*].

The secondary contributor should return a woman's certificate to her if

(*a*) the woman leaves his employment, or

(*b*) the woman tells him that her marriage has ended in divorce or annulment, or

(*c*) the woman reaches the age of 60, or

(*d*) the expiry date shown on the certificate has passed, or

(*e*) the woman has paid no contributions for two consecutive tax years because her earnings have not, during that time, reached or exceeded the lower earnings limit, or

(*f*) the woman has changed her name, or

(*g*) she remarries, or

(*h*) she asks for it back (in which case, standard rate contributions must be deducted from any subsequent payment of earnings).

If the certificate cannot be returned to a person who has left, it should be sent with a note of explanation to the Inland Revenue National Insurance Contributions Office, Refunds Group, Longbenton, Newcastle upon Tyne NE98 1ZZ.

(Leaflet CWG2 (2000), Page 62, item 85).

Example
Sickly Ltd has a number of married women and widows on their payroll and holds apparently valid forms CF383 and CA4139. Sickly Ltd notes that such employees must have their reduced rate certificate returned under the circumstances above. However, Sickly Ltd was not aware that it will be liable for any NICs underpaid where an employee is paying reduced rate contributions unless the employee was at fault or that the underpayment was not due to negligence on Sickly's behalf and

52.3   Reduced Liability Elections

this includes having inadequate arrangements in place for the employee to say that they are no longer entitled to pay NICs at the reduced rate. Sickly Ltd therefore immediately issues the following letter to the relevant female employees:

To:...........................

From: Sickly Ltd, Payroll Department

Dated:

Dear ....

Married women's and widow's reduced rate elections

Your reduced rate election certificate to pay lower national insurance contributions was lodged with this department on .... [Date] ....

As you may be aware you are required by law to tell us if you are no longer entitled to pay national insurance contributions at the reduced rate and return the certificate, which we currently hold, to the National Insurance Contributions Office. There are a number of reasons why a reduced rate certificate may no longer be valid and these include

(a)   divorce or annulment of your marriage

(b)   you becoming widowed but not being entitled to Widow's Benefit after an initial period

(c)   you losing your right to Widow's Benefit for a reason other than marriage

If any of the above apply in your case will you sign Part A of the slip below stating the reason and return it to the Payroll Department immediately. If none of the above apply please sign Part B stating that this is the case and then return Part B immediately to the Payroll Department. All the information you supply on this form is confidential and protected under the Data Protection Act 1998.

Failure to observe these requirements is, unlike other compliance failures in relation to contribution regulations, *not* an offence for which proceedings may be taken. [*Reg 132*].

52.3 **EFFECT OF AN ELECTION**

Where a woman has made such an election as is described at 52.1 above and that election is currently in force,

(*a*)   any primary Class 1 contributions payable in respect of earnings paid to her or for her benefit are to be at a reduced rate which is the same (3.85%) whether or not the employment is contracted-out;

(*b*)   she is to be under *no* liability to pay any Class 2 contribution;

(*c*)   she is to be precluded from paying Class 3 contributions for any year in respect of the whole of which the election has effect;

(*d*)   she is not to be entitled to credited contributions (see CREDITS (24));

(*e*)   she is not to be entitled to home responsibility protection in relation to retirement pension for any year in respect of which the election has effect (see Tolley's Social Security and State Benefits Handbook 2000–01);

(*f*)   she is to derive no earnings factor (see EARNINGS FACTORS (29)) from any contributions paid at a reduced rate.

[*Contributions Regs, Regs 100(3), 104, 105; Home Responsibilities Regs 1978, Reg 2(4)(a); SSCBA 1992, s 22(4); SSPA 1975, s 27(5)*].

Such women are, however, capable of receiving Statutory Sick Pay and Statutory Maternity Pay if all the other qualifying conditions are met. Liability for Class 4 contributions is entirely unaffected by such an election.

In respect of (c) above the CA Field Operations Manual states at paragraphs 3010 and 3011:

3010 Do not accept Class 3 NICs if the contributor is married or a widow with a reduced rate election in force. If you do not know the election position, obtain a RD18(CA714). If it does not show an election, send form MF15 to obtain details of the elections shown on the record sheet RF1 (see FOM Vol 2 Part 6).

3011 Do not accept Class 3 NICs if the contributor is a widow who is aged 55 or over, or will still receive Widowed Mother's Allowance (WMA) when they reach age 55, and is receiving Widow's Pension (WP), other than an age related WP, unless BA have told them to pay.

52.4   REVOCATION OF ELECTION

An election may, by notice in writing on Form CF9 contained in Leaflet CA 13, be *revoked* by the woman who made it and any such revocation may be cancelled by notice in writing to the Inland Revenue before the date on which the notice of revocation is to have effect. Revocation will take effect from the Sunday following the date of the notice or such later Sunday as may be specified in that notice. [*Contributions Regs, Reg 100(5)(6) as amended by Contribution Amendment No 3 Regs 1983, Reg 2 and SSC(T)A 1999, 2 Sch*].

52.5   CESSATION OF ELECTIONS

An election will continue in force until one or other of the following terminating events occurs.

(a)   The woman ceases to be married other than by reason of her husband dying, e.g. by divorce or annulment. In the case of divorce, the relevant date will be that of the decree absolute.

(b)   The ending of the tax year in which a woman ceases to be a widow who fulfils the conditions as regards entitlement to widow's benefits etc. (see 52.1 above), unless she remarries or again becomes a qualifying widow before the end of the tax year concerned.

(c)   The ending of two consecutive tax years which begin on or after 6 April 1978 and in which the woman has no earnings in respect of which any primary Class 1 contributions are payable (or would be payable but for the fact that, from 6 April 2000, they fall between the lower earnings limit and the employee's earnings threshold) and in which she is at no time a self-employed earner. This is known as the two-year test. Earnings from an employed earner's employment during the two years will not prevent the election being terminated if those earnings at no time reach the lower earnings limit. Whilst the certificate may be withdrawn by the Inland Revenue when its computer checks show that there are two consecutive blank years, it is almost certain that such action will take place well into the third year. Employers should therefore keep a check on this matter because they will be liable to pay any arrears.

(d)   The ending of the week in which the woman gives notice to the Inland Revenue of revocation of her election or, if the woman wishes and so specifies in her notice, the ending of any subsequent week in the same tax year, unless the woman cancels her revocation before such a week ends (see 52.4 above).

(e)   The ending of a tax year in which an erroneous payment on account of primary Class 1 contributions at the contracted-out rate is made by or on behalf of the woman, provided that the woman wishes to pay contributions at the standard rate from the beginning of the next tax year.

(f) The date (not being earlier than 6 April 1982) on which an erroneous payment (or, if there is more than one such payment, the date on which the first erroneous payment) on account of primary Class 1 contributions at the not contracted-out rate is made by or on behalf of the woman, provided

   (i) she wishes to pay contributions at the standard rate from that date; and

   (ii) after 5 April 1983 and on or before 31 December in the next complete calendar year following the end of the tax year in which the erroneous payment was made she notifies the Inland Revenue of that wish; and

   (iii) from the time of the erroneous payment to the time she notifies the Inland Revenue of that wish, no contributions have been paid by her or on her behalf at the reduced rate and no contributions have been payable by her or on her behalf in respect of any contracted-out employment; and

   (iv) she has not procured a refund in respect of any erroneous payment (see 53.2 REPAYMENT AND RE-ALLOCATION).

[*Contributions Regs, Reg 101(1)(a)–(f), (2) as amended by Contributions Amendment No 3 Regs 1983, Reg 3(a) and SSC(T)A 1999, 2 Sch*].

53   Repayment and Re-Allocation

Cross-references. See ANNUAL MAXIMUM (7); MULTIPLE EMPLOYMENTS (44); RATES AND LIMITS (51).

Other Sources. Simon's NIC, Part I, Sections 2, 3, 4 and 10, Chapters 9, 12, 14, 56 and 57; Tolley's Practical Tax, Vol 8 No 12.

53.1   RE-ALLOCATION OF CONTRIBUTIONS

The fact that a person has paid contributions which he was not liable to pay does not, of itself, entitle that person to a repayment of the contributions in question.

Where contributions are paid which are of the wrong class, or at the wrong rate, or of the wrong amount, the Inland Revenue is entitled (and may be expected) to treat them as paid on account of contributions properly payable under contribution law. [*SSCBA 1992, 1 Sch 8(1)(g); Contributions Regs, Regs 31, 68 and 77 as amended by SSC(T)A 1999, 2 Sch*]. Where Class 1A or Class 1B contributions fall to be repaid, they may be reallocated as a payment on account only of secondary Class 1 or Class 2 contributions properly payable. [*Reg 31(2) as amended by The Social Security Contributions, Statutory Maternity Pay and Statutory Sick Pay (Miscellaneous Amendments) Regs 1999, Reg 4*]. Such adjustments will be made before, and are to be reflected in, any calculation relating to a repayment. [*Regs 35(1)(a), 69(1)*].

53.2   REPAYMENTS

Repayment of contributions paid in error

Subject to the rule stated at 53.1 above, Class 1 or Class 2 contributions paid in error are to be returned by the Inland Revenue to the person or secondary contributor who paid them, provided

(*a*)   the error was made at the time of payment and related to some then-present or then-past matter; *and*

(*b*)   the amount of the contributions (other than Class 1A or Class 1B contributions) to be returned exceeds one-fifteenth of a standard rate contribution payable on earnings at the upper earnings limit in respect of primary Class 1 contributions prescribed for the last or only tax year in respect of which the contributions were paid, e.g. £2.56, 1994–95; £2.62, 1995–96; £2.70, 1996–97; £2.77, 1997–98; £2.89, 1998–99; £2.89, 1999–2000; £3.06, 2000–01; *and*

(*c*)   in the case of Class 1A or Class 1B contributions, the net amount to be returned is more than 50p.

[*SSCBA 1992, 1 Sch 8(1)(m); Contribution Regs, Reg 32(1)(6) as amended by Contributions Amendment Regs 1984, Reg 11(a), Contributions Transitional Regs 1985, Reg 5(6)(a), Contributions Amendment Regs 1992, Reg 3 Contributions Amendment No 6 Regs 1992, Reg 2 and the Social Security Contributions Statutory Maternity Pay and Statutory Sick Pay (Miscellaneous Amendments) Regs 1999, Reg 5*].

A mistaken belief that income would be treated as arising from self-employment when, in fact, the Inland Revenue treated it as arising for tax purposes from employment, in consequence of which Class 2 contributions were paid and no claim for small earnings exception from Class 2 liability was made, was an error within the terms of *Reg 32* and the Class 2 contributions paid were repayable. Payment of Class 2 contributions in circumstances where losses (not quantified until later) from a self-employed activity would, if they had been quantified at the time when Class 2 liability arose, have enabled a claim for small earnings exception to succeed was, however, not an error within the terms of *Reg 32*. (*Morecombe v Secretary of State for Social Services, The Times, 12 December 1987*). The effects of this judgment have now been remedied by regulation as described at 53.6 below.

Contributions paid by a secondary contributor in respect of an earner whom the Inland Revenue had already categorised as self-employed would be covered by this regulation, but contributions paid in respect of an earner who was later categorised as self-employed would not.

Recovery of overpaid Class 1A contributions is governed by *Contributions Regs, Reg 33A* (see 16.19 CLASS 1A CONTRIBUTIONS: BENEFITS IN KIND).

Primary contributions paid by a secondary contributor in error or (subject to what is said at 7.1 ANNUAL MAXIMUM) in excess of the ANNUAL MAXIMUM (7) will normally be returned to the secondary contributor provided he has not already recovered them from the primary contributor (e.g. by deduction from earnings paid). Where such contributions have already been recovered from the primary contributor they will be returned to the primary contributor unless he consents in writing to their return to the secondary contributor. [*Reg 32(4) as amended by Contributions Amendment No 4 Regs 1987, Reg 6*].

An application for repayment of contributions made in error must be made (in such form and manner as the Inland Revenue directs) within six years from the end of the year in which the contributions were paid, or, if the Inland Revenue is satisfied that there has been good reason for delay, within such longer period as he may allow. [*Reg 32(5) as amended by SSC(T)A 1999, 2 Sch*].

The *Social Security Act 1998* provides for contributions by way of Class 1, 1A or 1B which are paid by or for an earner in error because the earner is not an employed earner so that they may be treated as if the earner was nonetheless actually employed in employed earners employment throughout the period. This applies to contributions paid in error in a period in 1998–99 or any subsequent tax year. In certain prescribed circumstances such contributions shall not be treated as those of an employed earner in cases of contributions paid in error. [*SSCBA 1992, s19A inserted by Social Security Act 1998, s 54*]. This will effectively stop the NICO from having to make significant contribution refunds on re-categorisation such as in the case of the 'behind-the-camera' workers a few years ago. (See 38.10 LABOUR-ONLY CONTRACTORS). This onerous provision is, however, overridden from 6 April 2000 where, by the end of the second year, either

- an application had been made for a determination by the Secretary of State for Social Security (i.e. under the pre–1 April 1999 quasi–appeals procedure);

- a question of law arising in connection with the above has been referred to a Court under *SSAA 1992, s 18*;

- a written request has been made to an officer of the Board of Inland Revenue for a decision under *SSC(TF)A 1999, s 8(1)(a)* or for such a decision to be varied;

- a tax appeal is under way in respect of any associated Class 1B liability;

and the question, reference, request or appeal has not been finally settled by the end of the second year. [*SI 1979/591, Reg 37A, inserted by The Social Security (Contributions) (Amendment No 3) Regs 2000, SI 2000/736*].

In calculating the amount to be returned, any amount of contributory benefit paid because of, and attributable to, the contributions paid in error is to be deducted after being abated by any income support, etc. which would have been paid had the contributory benefit in question not been received. [*Reg 35(1)(b) as amended by Contributions Amendment Regs 1984, Reg 12*]. Any minimum contributions or incentive payments paid by the Secretary of State to a personal pension scheme under *Pension Schemes Act 1993, ss 42A(3) and 44(1)*, are also to be deducted. [*Reg 35(1)(e)(f)(g) as inserted by Contributions Amendment No 4 Regs 1988, Reg 4 and Contributions Amendment No 5 Regs 1996, Reg 5*].

Class 4 contributions paid in error are also returnable to the person who paid them but, if the error is one which affects both tax and contributions (e.g. an error in the financial accounts on which the assessment to both tax and Class 4 contributions was made), recovery must be sought from the Inland Revenue tax office under *Taxes Management Act 1970, s 33* instead of from the NICO. [*Regs 68(b), 69(1), 78(1)*].

The time limit within which application for repayment of erroneously paid ordinary Class 4 contributions must be made was previously six years from the end of the year of assessment in respect of which the payment was made or two years from the end of the tax year in which the payment was made. In the case of special Class 4 contributions the limit was six years from the end of the tax year in which the payment was made. [*Regs 69(2), 78(3) as amended by SSC(T)A 1999, 2 Sch*]. However, due to the changes arising out of self-assessment the time limit of 'six years from the end of the tax year in which the payment was made' is, from 6 April 1996, changed. It changed to 'five years after the 31 January next following the year of assessment' for any year of assessment commencing after 5 April 1996 but for any year of assessment ending on or before that date the existing limit of six years continues to apply. The two year limit mentioned above also continues as it relates to contributions that are paid late. [*Social Security Contributions Amendment (No 5) Regs 1996*].

Until 6 April 1995, no repayment supplement was available in respect of any repaid Class 4 contributions. [*Contributions Regs, Reg 70*]. However from 6 April 1995 onwards, the provisions of *ICTA 1988, s 824* apply to Class 4 contributions repayments by virtue of *2 Sch 6 and Contributions Amendment No 3 Regs 1995, Reg 2*. See also Inland Revenue Press Releases 25 January 1996, 1 April 1996 and the *Taxes (Interest Rate) (Amendment No 4) Regs 1996*. The current rate is 4% per annum applicable from 21 February 2000. See 53.7 below as regards interest on repayments of Class 1 and Class 1A contributions. Also, see 39.9 for interest supplement paid on disputed NICs liability subsequently repaid. CA Press Release CAO2/99.

In the absence of statutory provisions governing the payment of interest on refunded contributions, the DSS was authorised to make extra-statutory payments known as *compensation for delay in payment*, in the following circumstances:

- where the delay is attributable to a clear and unambiguous error on the part of the DSS and has not been contributed to, even in part, by unreasonable inactivity on the part of the contributor or his representative; and

- where the delay in making the refund has exceeded twelve months; and

- a claim is made by the contributor.

The rate of interest was not published, but it was known to fluctuate, and was calculated on the amount of the refund for the period of delay in excess of twelve months.

Example
Roger Wilco overpays NICs and applies for a refund but does not receive the refund for eight months despite a number of reminders. He eventually receives the refund and applies for compensation and receives the following reply from the NICO:

53.3 Repayment and Re-Allocation

> Dear Mr Wilco
>
> *Compensation for late contribution refund*
>
> You asked for compensation because of the delay in paying your refund of National Insurance contributions. I am afraid we cannot pay you any compensation.
>
> Social Security law does not provide for us to pay compensation but we can pay if these three things apply:
>
> 1 Your refund was delayed for more than 12 months.
> 2 We owe you £50 or more.
> 3 The amount of the compensation would be more than £5.
>
> In your case:
> *(a) your refund was not delayed for 12 months.*
> (b) we owed you less than £5.
> (c) the amount of compensation would be less than £5.
>
> If you wish to discuss this further, please get in touch with us, quoting our reference number. Our phone number and address are at the top of this letter.
>
> **Further information**
>
> Please get in touch with the person or the manager of the section shown above if you need further information or are dissatisfied with the service you have received.
>
> Full details of our complaints system are given in Leaflet CA62 — 'Unhappy with our service?' available from this or any Inland Revenue office.
>
> Yours sincerely,
>
> Over Anout

53.3 Repayment of not contracted-out element in contributions

Where a secondary contributor has paid an amount on account of Class 1 contributions at the not contracted-out rate but the employment concerned is, or has become, a contracted-out employment, the Inland Revenue will, on the secondary contributor's application, return the amount so paid after deducting the amount of Class 1 contributions payable at the contracted-out rate. [*Contributions Regs, Reg 33(1) as amended by SSC(T)A 1999, 2 Sch*].

The primary element of the repayment will be repaid to the primary contributor unless he consents in writing to its return to the secondary contributor. [*Reg 33(2)*].

Application for a repayment in these circumstances must be made in an approved form and manner within six years from the end of the year in which the contracting-out certificate in respect of the employment was issued or, if the Inland Revenue is satisfied that there has been good reason for the delay, within such longer period as he may allow. [*Reg 33(3) as amended by SSC(T)A 1999, 2 Sch*].

53.4 Repayment of precluded Class 3 contributions

Where a Class 3 contributor has paid a Class 3 contribution which he was not entitled to pay, the Inland Revenue will, on written application being made to him in an approved manner, return that contribution to the contributor. [*Contributions Regs, Reg 34 as amended by SSC(T)A 1999, 2 Sch*]. Alternatively, the contribution may, with the consent of the contributor, be appropriated to the earnings factor of another year if there is an entitlement to pay Class 3 contributions in that other year (see 19.3 CLASS 3 CONTRIBUTIONS).

53.5   Repayment of excess contributions

Where contributions are paid in excess of the ANNUAL MAXIMUM (7) they are to be repaid by the Inland Revenue provided written application is made to it within the time limits stated at 53.2 above or extended as described there. No amount will be returned unless it exceeds, in the case of Class 1 or 2 contributions, one-fifteenth of a standard rate contribution payable on earnings at the upper earnings limit in respect of primary Class 1 contributions prescribed for the last or only tax year in respect of which the contributions were paid (see 53.2(b) above for yearly figures), and, in the case of Class 1A, Class 1B or Class 4 contributions, fifty pence. [*SSCBA 1992, s 19(2)(b); Contributions Regs, Regs 32(1), 69(1) and 78(1), as amended by Contributions Amendment Regs 1984, Reg 11(a) Contributions Transitional Regs 1985, Reg 5(6)(a) and Social Security Contributions, Statutory Maternity Pay and Statutory Sick Pay (Miscellaneous Amendments) Reg 1999, Reg 6*].

Contributions are returned to the earner in a strictly prescribed order of priority. This is to ensure that where contracted-out employments are involved, the annual maximum amount of contributions which is retained contains the maximum amount of contributions at normal rate (i.e. 53 weeks contributions on earnings equal to the lower earnings limit) with only the balance at the contracted-out rate. Unless notice has been given to the Inland Revenue under *Pension Schemes Act 1993, s 44(1)* that the contributor concerned is or intends to become a member of a personal pension scheme, the order of priority is

(*a*)   ordinary and special Class 4 contributions [*Regs 67(1), 78(1)*];

(*b*)   primary Class 1 contributions at the reduced rate [*Reg 32(2)(a)*];

(*c*)   Class 2 contributions [*Reg 32(2)(b)*];

(*d*)   primary Class 1 contributions at the standard rate in respect of not contracted-out employments [*Reg 32(2)(c)*];

(*e*)   primary Class 1 contributions in respect of contracted-out salary related scheme (COSRS) and contracted-out money purchase scheme (COMPS) employments [*Reg 32(2)(d) and (e) as amended by Contributions Amendment No 5 Regs 1996, Reg 4*].

Where notice of membership of, or intention to join, a personal pension scheme has been given under *Pension Schemes Act 1993, s 44(1)*, paragraph (*d*) comes after (*e*) in the above priority listing. [*Reg 32(2A) as inserted by Contributions Amendment No 4 Regs 1988, Reg 3(b) and amended by Contributions Amendment No 5 Regs 1996, Reg 4*].

It should be noted as regards contracted-out contributions from 6 April 1997, that COSR contributions are repaid before COMP contributions. However, at present only the secondary contributors rate differs under the two contracted-out regimes. Since the rate of primary contributions is currently identical this elaboration can, in practice, be disregarded since secondary contributions are payable without any maximum limit.

The amount returnable in respect of contributions falling within (*e*) above is dependent on the amount of contributions paid at contracted-out rates. If the amount paid at contracted-out rates is

(i)   not less than 53 times the amount payable at the contracted-out rate on maximum upper band earnings for the year (i.e. earnings between the lower and upper earnings limits), there is to be returned (to the extent that a repayment remains due)

(A)   any amount paid at contracted-out rates, and

    (B) the excess of the amount paid at standard rates over 53 times the amount payable at the initial primary percentage rate (from 6 October 1989 to 5 April 1999) or at the highest standard rate (to 5 October 1989) on earnings at the weekly lower earnings limit;

  (ii) nil or less than 53 times the amount payable at the contracted-out rate on maximum upper band earnings, there is to be returned (to the extent that a repayment remains due) the amount paid at standard rates.

[*Reg 32(2)(d) as amended by Contributions Transitional Regs 1985, Reg 5(6) and by Contributions Transitional Regs 1989, Reg 3(5)*].

In the case of primary Class 1 contributions within (*b*), (*d*) or (*e*) above, the order of priority is

(A) contributions at the special ARMED FORCES (11.5) rate;

(B) contributions at the special MARINERS (42.10) rate;

(C) other primary Class 1 contributions as specified.

Until 6 April 1988, contributions might have been paid at the 'registered dock workers' rate. [*Reg 133, reduced by Contributions Amendment Regs 1988, Reg 3*]. If these became repayable, they were to be repaid after (A) and (B) but before (C) above. With the expiry of the six-year time limit on refund applications for 1987–88, this regulation is of no current relevance.

[*Reg 32(3), as amended by Contributions Amendment Regs 1984, Reg 11(b)*].

Example
Throughout 2000–01 Auk is employed by Bunting Ltd, Curlew Ltd and Dipper Ltd. Until 5 October 2000 he was also self-employed. His employments with C and D were contracted-out. His assessable profits for 2000–01 are £13,000 and earnings from B, C and D are £7,000, £15,000 and £23,500 respectively. Each employer pays weekly. He paid contributions as follows

	Class 2	Class 4	Class 1	
			Not contracted-out employment (n-c-o)	Contracted-out employment (c-o)
	£	£	£	£
S/employment	52.00	603.05		
B (n-c-o)			304.80	
C (c-o)				928.03
D (c-o)				1,642.03
	£52.00	£603.05	£304.80	£2,570.06

The overall annual maximum for 2000–01 is £2,432.70 (see 51.14 RATES AND LIMITS) and it is clear that this has been exceeded. In order to ascertain by how much it has been exceeded it is, however, necessary to convert to standard rate any Class 1 contributions paid at other rates (see 7.2 ANNUAL MAXIMUM).

	£
Class 1 (Not contracted-out rate)	304.80
Class 1 (Contracted-out rate £2,570.06 × 10/8.4)	3,059.60
Class 2	52.00
Class 4	603.05
	4,019.45
Annual maximum	2,432.70
Excessive *notional* contributions	£1,586.75

It is on this *notional* figure of £1,586.75 that the repayment calculation is based.

	£	*Repayment due* £
Excessive notional contributions	1,586.75	
Repay: Class 4	603.05	603.05
	983.70	
Repay: Class 2	52.00	52.00
	931.70	
Repay: Class 1 (not contracted-out)	304.80	304.80
	626.90	
	626.90 × 8.4/10	526.60
Total repayment due		£1,486.45

For an illustration of the effect on a repayment of the 2% bands of Class 1 contribution on earnings up to the LEL see the 1998–99 edition of this work.

A contributor who over-contributes as regards Class 1 or Class 2 contributions (e.g. by being concurrently employed in employment and self-employment or in two or more employed earner's employments and failing, or not being permitted, to defer a sufficient amount of his liability to prevent contributions in excess of the annual maximum being paid) will be informed of the fact by the NICO and invited to apply for repayment provided the excess payment is at least equal to half the current LEL. Smaller amounts are left to individual contributors to claim. Any delay may be avoided by applying directly, without awaiting notification of overpayment, to the Refunds Group, Longbenton, Newcastle upon Tyne, NE98 1ZZ. Repayment will be expedited if the application is supported by evidence of contribution payments (i.e. forms P60 or detailed statements from the secondary contributors concerned).

Where over-contribution extends to Class 4 contributions positive action on the part of the contributor is not only desirable but essential. This is because no records are kept by the NICO of Class 4 contributions as they do not count for benefit purposes and are mainly collected by the Inland Revenue offices dealing with tax functions. Any over-contribution will, therefore, remain undetected and unrepaid unless and until it is claimed. It should be noted that the NICO has no statutory duty to check for over-payments and that the onus of obtaining repayment is placed on the contributor. Repayment claims should be made to the Class 4 Group (see 2.3 ADMINISTRATION).

The DSS confirmed that

'Details of Class 1 and Class 2 contributions paid are held by this Department. Any excess is automatically identified and refund is invited. However the Social Security Regulations state that it is the responsibility of the contributor to apply for a refund of Class 4 contributions'.

(Tolley's Practical Tax, Vol 8, No 12, 17 June 1987).

A pro-forma which incorporates all the rules of repayment calculation (other than those involving volunteer development workers, mariners, members of the armed forces and dockworkers) is given at the end of this chapter. The pro-forma assumes that no notice of membership of a personal pension scheme has been given (see above).

53.6 Class 2 repayment for low earners

With effect from 27 September 1990, any self-employed earner who discovers that he has paid Class 2 contributions in respect of a period which is, or falls within, a tax year when exception from Class 2 liability could have been obtained had it been applied for in time (see 18.3 CLASS 2 CONTRIBUTIONS), may, under certain conditions, obtain repayment of the Class 2 contributions paid.

The conditions are that the application

(*a*) must be in writing to the Inland Revenue;

(*b*) must be supported by evidence of the earnings (i.e. profits) of the tax year in respect of which a repayment of Class 2 contributions is sought;

(*c*) must not be made before the beginning of the following tax year;

(*d*) must be made by 31 December in that following tax year.

[*Contributions Regs 1979, Reg 26A(1)(2) as inserted by Contributions Amendment No 3 Regs 1990, Reg 2 and amended by SSC(T)A 1999, 2 Sch*].

In a note from the DSS to the ICAEW, the DSS justified the relatively short time limit for refund applications on the grounds that difficulties could otherwise arise in connection with a subsequent claim to a contributions-related benefit. Appreciating the practical problems involved in producing formal accounts within such a short time scale the DSS said that it will accept evidence other than formal accounts as long as it covers the period for which a refund has been sought, but that it had no plans to extend the time limit. (ICAEW Technical Release 12/92, Annex G).

Condition (*d*) above was modified so far as applications relating to the years 1988–89 and 1989–90 are concerned. Such applications were to be made not later than 30 June 1991. [*Contributions Regs 1979, Reg 26A(3) as inserted by Contributions Amendment No 3 Regs 1990, Reg 2*].

Where, upon submission of an application within the time limits laid down, the Inland Revenue finds that exception from Class 2 liability on the grounds of small earnings would have been available to the contributor had he applied for it, he will be granted exception retrospectively and the Class 2 contributions will be repaid, less any amount paid by way of contributory benefits which would not have been paid but for the Class 2 contributions which are now being repaid. [*Contributions Regs 1979, Reg 26A(4)–(6) as inserted by Contributions Amendment No 3 Regs 1990, Reg 2 and amended by SSC(T)A 1999, 2 Sch*].

Example
Ernest is a self-employed joiner. His accounts for the years ended 31 May 2000 and 31 May 2001 are prepared on 31 October 2001 and show net profits of £2,000 and £2,400 respectively. The actual profit for the tax year 2000–01 will, on the time apportionment basis which must be used, be £2,333 (i.e. $\frac{1}{6} \times £2,000 + \frac{5}{6} \times$ £2,400) and, because those profits are below the small earnings exception limit for that year (£3,825), Ernest may, at any time before 31 December 2001, apply for retrospective exception and repayment of Class 2 contributions paid during that year.

Exception and repayment prevent the year from being a qualifying year for benefit purposes on the basis of Class 2 contributions (see 13.2 BENEFITS: CONTRIBUTION REQUIREMENTS and 29.5 EARNINGS FACTORS).

53.7 Interest on Class 1, Class 1A and Class 1B repayments

Repayments of Class 1 contributions for 1992–93 onwards, Class 1A for 1991–92 onwards and Class 1B for 1999–2000 carry interest at the same rate as income tax refunds (see 39.9 LATE-PAID CONTRIBUTIONS) from the relevant date until the repayment order is issued. The relevant date is the last day of the year after the year in respect of which the contribution was paid, unless the contribution was paid more than twelve months after the end of the year in respect of which it was made, in which case interest runs from the last day of the tax year in which it was paid. [*Contributions Regs, 1 Sch 28B*].

Example

Mogen Ltd pays its 1997–98 Class 1A contribution due on 19 June 1998, on 27 April 2000. It subsequently turns out that this includes an overpayment of £195 and a repayment order is issued on 7 December 2000.

There will be no interest included with the repayment because the payment itself was made more than twelve months after 5 April 1999 and interest does not begin to run in this case until 6 April 2001. If the overpayment had been made on 27 March 2000, however, interest would have run from 6 April 2000 until 7 December 2000.

It should be noted that the above position would be different under the new rules effective from 20 April 1999 in respect of Class 1A payments made under the 'Alternative Payment Method' see 16 CLASS 1A CONTRIBUTIONS.

Interest will be refunded if charged incorrectly [*Reg 28C*] and will be remitted if the contribution in respect of which it is charged was paid late as a result of an error by an Inland Revenue official. In this context an error is a mistake or omission which neither the employer nor any person acting on his behalf has caused or materially contributed towards. [*Reg 28D*]. The remission is for the period from the normal reckonable date (see 39.9 LATE-PAID CONTRIBUTIONS) or the date of the error if that is later, until fourteen days after the employer is advised in writing that the error has been rectified.

Interest was also be remitted from the date when a question was submitted to the Secretary of State under the pre-1 April 1999 procedure (see 9 APPEALS AND REVIEWS) until fourteen days after the question is determined, and when a question of law arising in connection with such a question is referred to the High Court or the Court of Session (see 9.13 APPEALS AND REVIEWS) in which case the remission is for the period from the date of referral to the court until fourteen days after the reference is finally disposed of (*Reg 28D*).

Whilst no *de minimis* limit is specified below which interest payable or receivable will be ignored, there are lower limits on the amount of contributions which will be repaid (see 53.2).

TAX YEAR 2000 — 2001

CONTRIBUTIONS PAID:

	£	£
Class 1 primary at:		
reduced rate	× sr/rr	...... (*a*)
standard/main rates		
(n-c-o e)		...... (*b*)
initial rates* (n-c-o e)		...... (*c*)
initial rates* (c-o e)		...... (*d*)
standard rates (c-o e)		...... (*e*)
contracted-out/main		
rates	(*f*) × sr/cor	...... (*g*)
Class 2		...... (*h*)
		...... (*i*)
Class 4		...... (*j*)
		...... (*k*)

ANNUAL MAXIMUM (w, if i exceeds w; x, if any Class 4 contributions payable and x exceeds i but does not exceed k; k, if any Class 4 contributions payable and x exceeds both i and k; otherwise i)   ...... (l)

EXCESS NOTIONAL CONTRIBUTIONS
   (k–l)   ...... (m)   **ACTUAL REPAYMENT**

NOTIONAL REPAYMENT

£

Class 4 (lesser of j and m)   ......
   ...... (n)   ......

Class 1 at rr (lesser of a and n)   ...... $\times$ rr/sr = ...
   ...... (o)

Class 2 (lesser of h and o)   ....
   ...... (p)

Class 1 at sr/main rates in n-c-o e
   (lesser of b and p)   ....
   ...... (q)

Class 1 at initial rates* in n-c-o e
   (lesser of c and q)   ....
   ...... (r)

Class 1 at sr in c-o e (if f greater than y, lesser of (e–z) and r; if f is equal to or less than y, lesser of f and r)   ....
   ...... (s)

Class 1 at initial rates* in c-o e
   (lesser of d and s)   ....
   ...... (t)

Class 1 at cor/main rates (lesser of g and t)   ...... $\times \dfrac{\text{cor/main rate}}{\text{sr}}$ = ...

REPAYMENT DUE   ======

Notes
* initial rates are applicable only up to 5 April 1999
w = overall annual maximum (see 50.14 RATES AND LIMITS)
x = Class 4 limiting maximum (see 50.15 RATES AND LIMITS)
y = 53 $\times$ (cor $\times$ (weekly upper earnings limit — weekly lower earnings limit))
z = 53 $\times$ (weekly lower earnings limit @ sr)

It should also be noted that the different COMPS/COSRS contracted-out rates from 6 April 1997 have their own priority. However, since the primary contributors' rates are currently the same (i.e. only the secondary contributors' rates differ) the procedure in the above chart is not currently affected.

54   Share Fishermen

Cross-references. See CATEGORISATION (14); CLASS 2 CONTRIBUTIONS (18); MARINERS (42).

Other Sources. Simon's NIC, Part I, Section 2, Chapter 11; Tolley's National Insurance Brief, November 1996, page 84; Leaflets CA 11, CA72, CWL1.

54.1   DEFINITION OF 'SHARE FISHERMAN'

A share fisherman is

(a) any person who is ordinarily employed in the fishing industry otherwise than under a contract of service (see 14.3 CATEGORISATION) as a master or member of the crew of any British fishing boat manned by more than one person, and remunerated in respect of that employment in whole or in part by a share of the profits or gross earnings of the fishing boat (i.e. a sea-going share fisherman for benefit regulation purposes); or

(b) any person who has been ordinarily so employed but who by reason of age or infirmity permanently ceases to be so employed and becomes ordinarily engaged in employment ashore in Great Britain otherwise than under a contract of service making or mending any gear appurtenant to a British fishing boat or performing other services ancillary to or in connection with that boat and is remunerated in respect of that employment in whole or in part by a share of the profit or gross earnings of that boat (i.e. an on-shore share fisherman).

[*Contributions Regs, Reg 86*].

A 'British fishing boat' is a vessel whose port of registry is in Great Britain. [*Merchant Shipping Act 1894, s 373*].

For the meaning of 'ordinarily employed' see 14.10 CATEGORISATION.

The National Insurance Commissioners have held that ordinary employment as a share fisherman ceases when a person otherwise within the above definition is stood-down from the crew of a boat of which he is not an owner or when the boat of which he is an owner and for which he works is offered for sale. (Decisions *R(U) 29/58, R(U) 6/63* in the unemployment benefit series).

54.2   CATEGORISATION

Under the normal rules of categorisation, a person must be gainfully employed in Great Britain if he is to be categorised as an employed earner or as a self-employed earner. [*SSCBA 1992, s 2(1)*]. He must also fulfil certain conditions of residence or presence here if he is then to be liable to pay contributions (see 49.3 and 49.4 OVERSEAS MATTERS). A share fisherman, however, though he might not meet these conditions because of the intrinsic nature of his employment, is nonetheless to be categorised as a self-employed earner and is to be subject to the same conditions of domicile and residence as are MARINERS (see 42.4) so far as actual liability to contributions is concerned. [*SSCBA 1992, s 117; Contributions Regs, Reg 98*].

54.3   RATE OF CONTRIBUTION

Share fishermen are (unlike other self-employed earners) liable to pay an increased rate of Class 2 contribution in order that they may acquire a contribution record which will entitle them to contributions based jobseeker's allowance (unemployment benefit prior to October 1996). [*Contributions Regs, Reg 98(c)*].

54.4 Share Fishermen

From 6 April 2000 the rate of a share fisherman's Class 2 contribution is £2.65. [*Contributions Re-rating Consequential Amendment Regs 2000, SI 2000/760 Reg 2*].

Rates for earlier years are stated at 51.11 RATES AND LIMITS.

A share fisherman unable to go fishing but who takes on alternative self-employment is only liable to pay the *ordinary* Class 2 contribution for the weeks in question.

54.4 ANNUAL MAXIMUM

The special Class 2 rate referred to at 54.3 above is to be substituted for the normal rate in any calculations connected with the ANNUAL MAXIMUM (7) contributions of a share fisherman. [*Contributions Regs, Reg 98(d)*].

54.5 CLASS 2 EXCEPTION

The circumstances under which a self-employed earner might be excepted from liability to pay a Class 2 contribution are to be extended, in the case of a share fisherman, so as to include any week in which he is entitled to contribution based jobseeker's allowance (previously unemployment benefit) or would be so entitled were his contribution record adequate (see 18.4 CLASS 2 CONTRIBUTIONS). [*Contributions Regs, Reg 98(e)*].

54.6 COLLECTION

Although due at different rates, collection is by the same method as for other Class 2 payments (see 18.6 CLASS 2 CONTRIBUTIONS: SELF-EMPLOYED EARNERS) although payment by direct debit is not yet available. Until April 1993, special contributions cards, available only from those offices dealing with share fishermen, were used. Those offices are listed in Leaflet CA 11.

54.7 CLASS 4 CONTRIBUTIONS

Insofar as Class 4 contributions in respect of a share fisherman's profits or gains are not collected by the Inland Revenue, the special direct collection procedure described at 21.16 COLLECTION is to apply. [*Contributions Regs, Reg 98(g)*].

A new scheme has been launched at the request of the Fishing Industry whereby share fishermen can have money deducted from their earnings and paid directly into an interest bearing account with Barclays. Twice a year the money will be allocated in payment of tax and NICs. See Inland Revenue Press Release, 31 May 2000.

55   Subpostmasters

Cross-references. See ANNUAL MAXIMUM (7); CATEGORISATION (14); 20.4 CLASS 4 CONTRIBUTIONS for exception of Class 1 contributors in respect of earnings chargeable to tax under Schedule D; DEFERMENT OF PAYMENT (27); REPAYMENT AND RE-ALLOCATION (53).

Other Sources. Simon's NIC, Part I, chapters 4.232, 11.291–296, 12.202, 13.31, 13.205; Tolley's National Insurance Brief, February 1995, page 14; Tolley's Practical NIC, June 1999, page 44; IR Inspector's Manual, IM3150; Leaflets CA72, CWL2.

55.1   CATEGORISATION

A subpostmaster almost invariably enjoys a dual employment status for contribution purposes. He is an *employed earner* by reason of the relationship he enjoys with the Post Office (see below) and he is a *self-employer earner* by reason of the fact that he is gainfully employed other than as an employed earner in running an ancillary business (e.g. a newsagency) from the premises in which he performs his duties as a subpostmaster (see 14.10 CATEGORISATION). Only if the business is carried on through the medium of a limited company will this not be the case (see 55.4 below).

Until the *Post Office Act 1969* transformed the Post Office into a statutory corporation, a subpostmaster was a CROWN SERVANT (25) who held an appointment which was terminable at the Crown's pleasure. Since 1969, however, that has no longer been the case. (*Malins v The Post Office [1975] ICR 60*). Now a subpostmaster is under a contract for services (*Hitchcock v Post Office [1980] ICR 100*) but that does not mean that he is a self-employed earner. A subpostmaster continues to occupy an office by Post Office appointment and, as that office is an office with emoluments chargeable to tax under Schedule E, it takes precedence over his contract for services and takes him into the category of *employed earner*. [*SSCBA 1992, s 2(1)(a)*]. (See 14.2 and 14.9 CATEGORISATION.)

As an employed earner, a subpostmaster is liable to pay CLASS 1 CONTRIBUTIONS (15) (and such contributions are, in fact, deducted from his earnings by the Post Office), while, as a self-employed earner, a subpostmaster is liable to pay CLASS 2 CONTRIBUTIONS (18) and profits-related CLASS 4 CONTRIBUTIONS (20).

The anomalies to which dual status can give rise have twice led to investigations by the Parliamentary Commissioner, but the position of a subpostmaster remains unchanged. (See *C43/J, HC Paper 49, Session 1974–75, p 81; 3A/624/77, HC Paper 246, Session 1977–78, p 156*). A determination in 1984 by the Secretary of State did, however, bring about one revision of DSS practice which will partly relieve a subpostmaster's contribution burdens in certain instances (see 55.5 below).

55.2   SUBPOSTMASTERS AS SOLE TRADERS OR IN PARTNERSHIP

It is common practice for a subpostmaster who is in business on his own account or in partnership, to include in his accounts as trading income not only the receipts he obtains from retail sales but also the gross amount of the remuneration he receives from the Post Office. (This practice is encouraged and facilitated by Inland Revenue tax offices which will issue a 'no-tax' code to the Post Office so as to ensure that earnings are paid gross.) Against that total income he will set the cost of goods sold and the establishment and running expenses of the business. The resulting net profit (after any adjustments required under the Taxes Acts) would then provide the basis for the calculation of Class 4 contributions. The orthodox view for many years was that a subpostmaster who follows the procedure described above may claim exception from Class 4 contributions for a year of assessment on profits equal to an amount of earnings calculated by reference to the Class 1 primary contributions which he has (or, but for deferment, would have) paid in that year of assessment. The effect of this would frequently have been to reduce the Class 4 assessment to nil.

Although this practical and fair approach was applied for many years, the CA took a different view more recently. This is because as explained at 20.2–20.4 (CLASS 4 CONTRIBUTIONS), the rules applied above are strictly applicable only where profits *chargeable* to income tax under Schedule D include earnings which attract a liability for Class 1 contributions. [*SSCBA 1992, s 15(1); Contributions Regs, Reg 61(1)*]. 'Chargeable' means 'chargeable in law' yet a subpostmaster's remuneration from the Post Office is not, in law, chargeable to tax under Schedule D. It is, as the CA rightly pointed out when levying Class 1 contributions on that remuneration, *chargeable* (though not actually *charged*) to tax under Schedule E. The charge to tax under Schedule D is a mere expediency.

In other words, because the precise terms of *SSCBA 1992, s 15(1)* are not sufficiently wide to bring the Post Office remuneration into charge, the Class 4 profits should, in law, be determined by merely eliminating from the profits on which the Schedule D assessment is based the remuneration from the Post Office which has been included in those profits, and *Contributions Regs, Reg 61* should be ignored as irrelevant in this particular context. There will be a multiplicity of circumstance in which such an approach will greatly benefit a subpostmaster yet it seems that the Secretary of State was never challenged as to the validity of the seemingly incorrect approach to these matters which was taken by his Department.

However, in a letter viewed by the author sent by a Manager of the CA's Parliamentary, Adjudicator & Chief Executive (PACE) Unit the following statement was issued in respect of Class 4 liability:

> 'In the case of sub-postmasters the key issue is the fact that they chose to pay the Post Office salary into the separate business of the store. Once the salary is paid into the business it effectively loses its identity as Class 1 earnings and becomes part of the assessable profits of the business regardless of the fact that the salary has already been subjected to deductions of Class 1 contributions. Regulation 61 is necessary to prevent a Class 1 and Class 4 contribution becoming payable on the same *earnings*. For example, a worker supplied through an agency who is subject to the right of supervision should not be liable in respect of the same earnings to a Class 4 contribution without taking account of his Class 1 liability. This is because there is no question in such a case of the use of earnings from one source to supplement the receipts of a separate business. Regulation 61 therefore provides for a genuine case of double liability as given in this example. In the case of sub-postmasters however, earnings are paid into a business and therefore become part of the assets of that business. As such, those earnings are correctly liable to Class 4 contributions when the assessments made on the earnings of the business.

> It should be noted however, that where a contributor is liable to both employed and self-employed contributions, the overall National Insurance liability is restricted to an annual maximum, and because of this there is the facility for deferment of payment to be granted.'

Of course, if the authorities are correct that relief is not due because the earnings are not *chargeable* to Schedule D, then logic dictates that you simply subtract *all* the Class 1 earnings (not just those subject to primary contributions) in arriving at the profit liable to Class 4. As the extract from the PACE letter suggests, the authorities do not subscribe to this view as the income, they say, loses its identity. Yet if that argument holds water, how are Enterprise Allowance payments to be excluded for Class 2 purposes or, to give the specific statutory relief (see 55.3 below), Post Office salary — since if its identity is lost through the mere act of including it in the business, then surely it can no longer be identified for the purpose of excluding it! And if it is identifiable for Class 2 purposes then the same information can be used also for Class 4! Even the guidance booklet CA72 (Deferring payment) is hopelessly muddled. On page 14 of the latest edition (and earlier editions from the Contributions Agency were similar), under the heading 'Class 1 contributions on Schedule D earnings' it says that you can apply for deferment or a refund of Class 4 if there is income on which Class 1 has been paid but which is *assessed* (our emphasis added) under Schedule D. In contrast, the claim form for deferment (CA72B) then goes back at question 12c to use of the phrase 'chargeable to income tax under Schedule D'.

The intransigent approach in the PACE letter does not take into account the full implications of the employee's right to be taxed under Schedule E; this is clearly laid out in both the Inland Revenue Inspector's Manual at paragraph IM 3150 (12/95) and the Schedule E Manual at paragraph SE 7781 (8/96) which state, 'Where a sub-postmaster also carrying on a trade requests the statutory basis of assessment for both sources of income, the trade profits should be assessed under Schedule D and the remuneration assessed under Schedule E.' Whilst this would have no effect on the actual NICs deducted in respect of the Class 1 contributions from the Post Office remuneration, the statutory basis would then enable the Schedule D profit to be reduced. In addition, the increase in the workload of the Inland Revenue in applying the statutory basis in the case of most subpostmasters wishing to switch would put resources at the few Inland Revenue Districts dealing with Post Office employees under intolerable strain. It seems, therefore, that the former CA's approach in this matter may need to be reassessed in the not too distant future. Indeed, it is understood that some cases are scheduled for hearing before the General Commissioners.

Example
Pat is a subpostmaster in business on his own account. His accounting year ends on 5 April and his trading accounts for the years ended 5 April 1998, 1999, 2000 and 2001 are, in summary, as follows

	1998	*1999*	*2000*	*2001*
Post Office fees	29,000	33,000	32,000	34,000
Sales etc.	13,000	15,000	20,000	20,000
	42,000	48,000	52,000	54,000
Expenses	13,000	11,000	18,000	19,000
Net profit	£29,000	£37,000	£34,000	£35,000

Class 1 primary contributions deducted from the Post Office fees in each year were

£2,160.08   £2,255.76   £2,256.80   £2,388.00

The amounts of earnings which these contributions represent are, accordingly

£24,180   £25,220   £26,000   £27,820

The discrepancy between these amounts and the gross amount of fees actually received according to the accounts is attributable to the fact that the fees actually received exceeded the upper earnings limit.

Class 4 profits and the amounts of those profits which might be excepted from Class 4 liability on the previous orthodox view, now rejected by the CA and NICO, would have been as follows:

Tax year	*Profits*	*Excepted*	*Balance*
	£	£	£
1997–98	29,000	24,180	4,820
1998–99	37,000	25,220	11,780
1999–2000	34,000	26,000	8,000
2000–01	35,000	27,820	7,180

As the balance for 1997–98 is below the lower annual Class 4 limit for that year, no Class 4 liability will arise. It should be noted that even if the balance exceeds the lower annual Class 4 limit for the year — as it does for 1998–99, 1999–2000 and 2000–01 — no Class 4 liability would arise as the Class 4 limitation rule—see 7.3 ANNUAL MAXIMUM—would come into effect.)

Class 2 liability could have been deferred for 1998–99, 1999–2000 and 2000–01 (since the fees liable to Class 1 contributions in those years exceeded the upper earnings limit). See 27.8 DEFERMENT OF PAYMENT. If the fees for any year had not exceeded the upper earnings limit for that year, however, Class 2 contributions for that year would have had to be paid — though a repayment in respect of these may have later become due (see 53.5 REPAYMENT AND RE-ALLOCATION).

If, for example, fees for 2000–01 had been £24,000, liability would have arisen as follows:

Class 1 primary paid		2,005.20
Class 2 paid	52 × £2.00 =	104.00
		2,109.20
Less: Annual maximum		2,432.70
		£323.50

If the authorities current view is correct their Class 4 of £323.50 is chargeable with no relief, other than the application of the ANNUAL MAXIMUM (7) rules referred to in the example.

This cannot, however, surely be correct for if it is accepted that the Post Office salary is correctly chargeable to Schedule E then it should merely be omitted from the profits computed for Class 4 purposes. The amounts by reference to which any Class 4 liability is to be determined would then be:

1997–98	NIL	(i.e. £29,000 – £29,000)
1998–99	£4,000	(i.e. £37,000 – £33,000)
1999–2000	£2,000	(i.e. £34,000 – £32,000)
2000–01	£1,000	(i.e. £35,000 – £34,000)

No one had ever formerly challenged the authorities approach by requesting a decision from the Secretary of State nor has any formal challenge been made under the new appeals procedure effective from 1 April 1999. It is understood that a number of cases are in the appeals pipeline.

However, a 1999 case that came before the Employment Tribunal may eventually clarify the matter. A subpostmistress in the Highlands of Scotland claimed that she was entitled to have her pay from Post Office Counters raised from £2.22 per hour to £3.60 per hour (the national adult minimum wage, until 1 October 2000 when it becomes £3.70) as an employee. Post Office Counters stated that the subpostmistress was self-employed and as a consequence they were not liable to pay the amount of (then) £3.60 per hour. The argument put forward by Post Office Counters was that the she was not contracted to provide personal services. The Post Office Counters agency development manager also stressed that subpostmasters were agents and not employees. However, the industrial tribunal in Inverness ruled that the purpose of the *National Minimum Wage Act 1998* was to ensure that adult workers were paid at least the minimum amount unless they were genuinely 'self-employed' and they conclude that the subpostmistress was an employee for this purpose. Post Office Counters are appealing to the Employment Appeals Tribunal. The case, whilst not directly related to NICs, does highlight the problems faced when trying to determine the actual status of subpostmasters — this seems to be determined by the Post Office, NICO and Inland Revenue according to the result that produces the least financial burden to, or greatest tax/NICs gain for the respective bodies. The divergence of treatment in this latest case only serves to underline the confusion in the area of subpostmasters. It is pleasing to note that a number of formal decisions under *SSC(TF)A 1999, s 8* have been made in respect of subpostmasters and once the implications have been fully rehearsed by the Inland Revenue in terms of tax and NICs the position may be a bit clearer.

These same principles apply equally when computing the liabilities of a subpostmaster who carries on business in partnership (see PARTNERS (50)).

In the interesting income tax case of *Dhendsa v Richardson [1997] SSCD 265 (Sp C 134)* the taxpayer signed form P931 'Acknowledgement of Appointment as Sub Postmaster' which stated:

I hereby accept appointment as Subpostmaster at [. . .].

I understand that the appointment is made under a contract for services. Consequently a Subpostmaster is not an employee of Post Office Counters Ltd and does not entitle me to compensation for loss of office or to a pension; that it does not entitle me to sick or annual leave at the expense of Post Office Counters Ltd, although I may be eligible to claim assistance towards the cost of providing a substitute during my annual holiday.

I understand that, if it be deemed necessary at any time to alter the duties, to withdraw any part of the business conducted at the Office, or to introduce an alternative method of payment I have no claim to compensation for any disappointment which may result from the change.

I understand that I must not look for reimbursement for any expenditure incurred on improvements of the premises or on fittings.

I understand that the initial payment advertised will be adjustable up or down, with effect from the date of my appointment, in accordance with the emoluments found to be warranted on the basis of (a) the first six and twelve months' figures of business; (b) the current vacancy revision.

There follow details of certain administrative procedures and then the form continues:

I agree that should I desire to resign my Office, I must give three calendar months' notice in writing, failing which I shall be liable to bear any expenses incurred by Post Office Counters Ltd in consequence, and the agreement may be determined by the Post Office at any time in case of Breach of Condition by me or non-performance of my obligations or non-performance of Sub-Post Office services, but otherwise may be determined by Post Office Counters on not less than three months' notice.

I understand that if, on resignation of my appointment as Subpostmaster, I dispose of my private business and/or premises in which the Post Office business is conducted, the successor to the private business and/or premises will have no claim to the post of Subpostmaster, the filling of which is a matter entirely for the Post Office Counters Ltd.

Form continues

Commenting on the circumstances the Special Commissioner states that 'For the Crown, Mr Ali [Inland Revenue Solicitor] concedes that the assessments under appeal cannot bring into charge the taxpayer's remuneration from his post of sub-postmaster since that income, being properly chargeable to tax under Sch E, cannot be charged (concession aside) under Sch D which charges other types of profits'. The loss of identity of Class 1 earnings as alleged above by the Manager of the CA's Parliamentary, Adjudicator & Chief Executive Unit would not seem to fit in with the Special Commissioner's statement that remuneration 'cannot be charged (concession aside) under Sch D' and which therefore confirms that the identity is not lost. The case also confirmed that the subpostmasters' introductory payment received from Post Office Counters Ltd is *not* to be treated as an expense in calculating Schedule D Case 1 profits. This, therefore, has the added effect that the payment cannot reduce the profit for the purposes of Class 4 contributions.

55.3   SMALL EARNINGS EXCEPTION

The practice of including Post Office fees in the general accounts of the business as described at 55.2 above also used to give rise to problems in connection with a claim for Class 2 exception on the grounds of small earnings. (See 28.77 EARNINGS.) However, with effect from 6 July 1994 *Reg 25* was amended to ensure that where a person with a business also has earnings from employed earner's employment, and those earnings are shown in the accounts of the business as a receipt, that amount must be disregarded in assessing earnings for the purposes of the small earnings exception. The new provisions affect

(*a*)   application for small earnings exception for 1994–95 and later tax years, and

(*b*)   application for refunds of contributions on the grounds of small earnings for 1993–94 and later tax years made on or after 6 July 1994.

(CA National Insurance News, Issue 2, page 6). *Contributions Regs, Reg 25 as amended by Contributions Amendment No 2 Regs 1994, Reg 2*].

In the CA Field Operations Manual at paragraphs 8507–8509 it states:

8507   If a sub-postmaster pays Class 2 contributions and then claims a refund on account of low earnings, the application must be made after 6/7/94 and on or before 31 December after the tax year in which the contributions were paid.

8508   The earliest tax year for which an application for a refund of Class 2 contributions can be accepted from a sub-postmaster is the 1993–94 tax year, provided they apply after 6/7/94 and on or before 31/12/94.

8509   Provided the application for a refund is timeous, Class 2 Group will exclude **all** earnings from employed earner's employment paid into the business from the relevant results, including pro-rata calculations.

In any event, the March 1995, March 1996, April 1997, April 1998, April 1999 and April 2000 editions of Leaflet CA 02 now give the following advice— 'Where you also have earnings from employed earners employment in the same year and those earnings are shown in the accounts of the business, as a business receipt, those earnings can be disregarded when calculating the profits from the business'. Given the previous views of the DSS, it is difficult to see the reason for this view being expounded currently, except in the case of subpostmasters where the change of law referred to above makes the position clear. This statement is also at variance with the comments made in 55.2 above regarding the Class 4/Class 1 interaction.

55.4   SUBPOSTMASTER TRADING IN PARTNERSHIP WITH SPOUSE

One situation which can give rise to difficulties if the historical view of the incidence of Class 4 contribution liability in the case of subpostmasters is taken (see 55.2 above), is that in which a subpostmaster and his wife (or a subpostmistress and her husband) trade in partnership (see PARTNERS (50)). An appointment to the office of subpostmaster is an *individual* appointment and the remuneration paid by the Post Office is the remuneration of the person holding the appointment only. Accordingly, if Class 4 liability is ascertained by reference to profits *charged* to tax under Schedule D and relief is claimed under *Contributions Regs, Reg 61*, relief will be available only to the member of the partnership who holds the Post Office appointment.

Example

George is subpostmaster of Hopefuleigh and runs the business in partnership with his wife Iris. They share profits equally. For the year 2000–01 their profits were £22,720. Those profits required no adjustment for tax purposes and reflect G's remuneration from the Post Office of £16,000 in the year to 5 April 2001. On the historical basis, the Class 4 profit for 2000–01 is £22,720 divided between G and I in accordance with their profit-sharing arrangement for 2000–01, i.e. G £11,360, I £11,360. The lower annual profit limit for Class 4 contributions in 2000–01 is £4,385 so that G and I each have a liability of 7.0% on £6,975. Relief amounting to £16,000 may, however, be claimed under *Reg 61* (but see 55.2 above) by G only, thus eliminating his Class 4 liability entirely. But I's liability remains, and G's unused relief of £9,025 (£16,000 – (£11,360 – £4,385)) is lost.

G could request that the statutory basis (see 55.2 above) apply to his earnings and they be taken out of the profits leaving a Schedule D profit of £6,720 shared between G and I of £3,360 each. This income for 2000–01 would be covered by the Class 4 lower annual profit limit and the Class 2 exception limit would also be applicable. The tax, accounting and pension contributions implications of such action are beyond the scope of this book but should also be considered.

Alternatively, it will be seen that, adopting the historical approach to these matters, George and Iris would be well-advised to have an agreement that George receives a partner's salary equivalent to his Post Office remuneration for the ensuing year and that only the remaining profits are then shared equally. Given such an agreement for 2000–01, George's profit share for Class 4 purposes will be £16,000 + (½ × £6,720) = £19,360 while Iris's share will be ½ × £6,720 = £3,360. After deducting the lower annual limit, Iris would have had no Class 4 liability and George's liability would have been 7.0% on £14,975. George would then have claimed *Reg 61* relief of £16,000 and his liability would also have been extinguished.

The DSS have subsequently stated that their historical view is incorrect (see 55.2 above) but never acknowledged that Class 4 is therefore to be calculated by simply deducting the Class 1 earnings included in accounting profits. Were they to make that acknowledgement, then the problem disappears without the need for any variation to the equal-share agreement. George's and Iris's Class 4 profits become ½ × (£22,720 – £16,000) = £3,360 each and any Class 4 liability is eliminated by the lower annual profit limit of £4,385.

55.5 SUBPOSTMASTER TRADING THROUGH A LIMITED COMPANY

Where a sub-post office is operated through the medium of a limited company, great difficulties may be encountered. A limited company cannot itself be appointed by the Post Office as subpostmaster, so the normal procedure is for the company to nominate one of its directors or senior employees for the office. That individual is then appointed subpostmaster but holds the office as a nominee for the limited company.

At one time, the Inland Revenue, faced with such an arrangement, would insist that the subpostmaster's remuneration was charged to tax under Schedule E since there could be no *personal* Schedule D assessment on profits within which it could be included. The Inland Revenue did, however, review its treatment of subpostmasters in limited company situations and recognised the problems caused, particularly in the case of some large companies where a single director holds a number of appointments as subpostmaster. It was then decided that, provided a subpostmaster is required by the company of which he is a director to hand over his Post Office remuneration to the company, and does in fact do so, the concessionary treatment accorded to subpostmasters who carry on trades will be extended to such nominee subpostmasters also. Publication of this extended concession (which, it will be noted, does for nominee subpostmasters what Extra-Statutory Concession A37 does for nominee directors who are required to hand over their fees to a company — see 28.76 EARNINGS) was under consideration by the Inland Revenue as long ago as February 1986 but has not yet taken place. However, with the publication of the Inland Revenue Manuals it is possible to review the written instructions issued to IR Inspectors. Inland Revenue Inspector's Manual, Para IM 3150 (12/95) states, 'Where a retail trade or business is carried on by a company from the same premises as a sub-post office, the Post Office salary is the income of the sub-postmaster and not of the company. In practice, however, no objection should be raised to a request to treat the Post Office salary as income of the company provided that the sub-postmaster is required to, and does, hand over his remuneration to the company.' See also IR Schedule E Manual, Para SE 7781 (8/96).

The present position, then, is that a subpostmaster who is a director of a company to which he hands over his Post Office remuneration receives that remuneration without deduction of tax, and the remuneration forms part of the profits of the company for corporation tax purposes. That is unobjectionable from a taxation point of view but is a disastrous arrangement from a contribution point of view. The problem arises out of the requirement in law that primary and secondary Class 1 contributions must be accounted for on the Post Office remuneration paid to a subpostmaster, whether he is a nominee subpostmaster or not. (The legislation referred to at 28.76 (EARNINGS) which extinguishes Class 1 liabilities on fees handed over to a company by a nominee director, thus giving legal effect in the contribution field to Inland Revenue Extra-statutory Concession A37 (see also CA 28 Supplement April 1996) does not extend to nominee subpostmasters who hand over their Post Office remuneration to a company.) In consequence, Post Office remuneration taken into a company's trading account will already have suffered a charge to Class 1 contributions yet that remuneration will then, effectively, in whole or in part, be paid out by the company in the form of wages, salaries or directors' remuneration, all of which again attract primary and secondary Class 1 liabilities. Thus, the charge for both primary and secondary Class 1 contributions will frequently be wholly or partly duplicated.

Example
Jane is subpostmistress of Kwietspot but runs her business through Letterbox Ltd, a company in which J owns all the shares except for one which is owned by her mother. L's accounts for the year ended 31 March 2001 reveal profits of £25,500 which include J's Post Office remuneration of £16,500 but take no director's remuneration into account. Remuneration of £16,500 is then voted to J for the year, and the profit is reduced to £9,000. In other words, J and L are, on the face of it, restored to the same positions they would each have occupied had J never brought her Post Office remuneration into the company. Yet that is far from the result. The £16,500 director's remuneration voted to J attracts a primary Class 1 contribution of £1,254.80 which J must suffer and a secondary Class 1 contribution of £1,478.03 which L must suffer. J has, however, already suffered a primary Class 1 deduction of £1,254.80 at the hands of the Post Office when her Post Office remuneration was paid to her, and the Post Office has already suffered a secondary Class 1 contribution charge of £1,478.03 on that same remuneration. It is, of course, true that J will be able to recover primary Class 1 contributions which she has paid in excess of £2,432.70—the ANNUAL MAXIMUM (7) for 2000–01—but, even after that recovery, the Inland Revenue will have obtained primary Class 1 contributions of £2,432.70 on earnings of £16,500 (a 14.74% levy) and secondary Class 1 contributions of £2,576.03 on the same earnings (a 17.92% levy)! In other words, J will have paid £1,177.90 of unnecessary contributions and her company will have paid £1,478.03 of unnecessary contributions.

One apparent solution to the problem illustrated is to treat the Post Office remuneration introduced into the company as what, in law, it is: a loan to the company by the subpostmaster. Then, the 'director's remuneration' which would otherwise have been voted should be reduced by the amount of that loan with only the remainder (if any) being voted, the balance being treated as what, in law, it truly is: a repayment of the loan. But if that were to be done, the Post Office remuneration would escape the tax net. Accordingly, in a case such as Jane's, the correct solution to the problem is simply for the subpostmaster to advise the Inland Revenue that he should be assessed to tax on his Post Office remuneration under Schedule E and to keep his Post Office remuneration out of the company.

In the case of a large company with a number of sub-post offices and but a single nominee subpostmaster there *is* no solution, simple or otherwise. The only remedy in such a case — which, whilst technically correct, may be quite impracticable — is to re-arrange matters so that a different director is appointed subpostmaster of each sub-post office run by the company and for each such director to be selected on a basis which ensures that he becomes subpostmaster of a sub-post office which yields remuneration of a lesser amount than the director's remuneration he might be expected to receive. Post Office remuneration would then be left out of the company's account; each director/ subpostmaster would, by arrangement with the Inland Revenue, be assessed to tax on his Post Office remuneration under Schedule E; and director's remuneration would be voted by the company only on a 'top-up' basis.

It is understood that, following a determination by the Secretary of State (reported in *National Federation of Self Employed and Small Businesses Press Release, 10 December 1984*), the DSS permitted 'remuneration' paid to a subpostmaster by his company to be regarded (to the extent that it does not exceed Post Office fees introduced to the company by the subpostmaster) as a loan repayment and not as earnings liable to either primary or secondary Class 1 contributions, but only where the 'remuneration' has not been voted by the company in general meeting. Once voting has taken place, the amount voted will acquire the quality of true remuneration (see 15.3 CLASS 1 CONTRIBUTIONS) and will become earnings for contribution purposes, irrespective of the fact that its source may have been earnings already subjected to Class 1 contributions.

Example
Michael, Nigel, Oliver and Peter are directors of Quickstamp Ltd. M is also a nominee subpostmaster for Q of sub-post offices in Riverlea, Streamton, Treesthwaite and Underedge. In the year ended 31 March 2001, M receives PO remuneration in respect of R, S, T and U of £12,000, £10,000, £14,000 and £15,000 respectively, which he hands over (net of £2,432.70 maximum Class 1 primary contributions) to Q. Each director (including M) receives director's fees of £15,000 for the year. Q pays Class 1 secondary contributions on those fees at 12.2% on the excess over the earnings threshold, i.e. £5,180.12, and its accounts show:

PO Remuneration		£47,567
Non-PO Income		100,000
		147,567
Expenses	£50,000	
Directors' Remuneration	60,000	
NIC on Directors' Remuneration	5,180	
		115,180
		£32,387

If N, O and P had been appointed subpostmasters of S, T and U respectively (leaving M as subpostmaster of R only) and the arrangement for handing over PO remuneration to Q had been brought to an end, a further £8,538 (i.e. £40,925 – £32,387) of profit could have been retained for the year at no detriment to any of the directors. M, N, O and P would each have retained their PO remuneration and would have been paid director's fees of only £3,000 (M), £5,000 (N), £1,000 (O) and nil (P), to bring their total remuneration up to £15,000 each, and Q would have paid secondary Class 1 contributions of only £5,000 – £4,385 × 12.2% = £75.03. (M and O fell below the LEL). The accounts would have shown:

Non-PO Income		£100,000
Expenses	£50,000	
Directors' Remuneration	9,000	
NIC on Directors' Remuneration	75	
		59,075
		£40,925

55.6 Relief subpostmasters

A relief subpostmaster will normally be regarded as an employee of the subpostmaster unless, by reference to the tests of employment status (see CATEGORISATION (14)), he is found to be a person who is in business on his own account as a relief subpostmaster. Those tests will generally be regarded as satisfied if the relief subpostmaster charges fees for providing relief cover for a number of sub-post offices and their associated businesses and for looking after the related property and contents.

56 Underwriters at Lloyd's

Cross-references. See ANNUAL MAXIMUM(7); CLASS 2 CONTRIBUTIONS(18); CLASS 4 CONTRIBUTIONS(20).

Other sources. Tolley's Taxation of Lloyd's Underwriters, eighth edition.

56.1 Exclusions

At the start of 1997 the DSS confirmed their view that external members of Lloyd's Underwriters, i.e. non-working Names, are subject to Class 4 and Class 2 contributions on their Lloyd's profits where they exceed the appropriate thresholds. The DSS stated that it was not seeking to collect arrears for earlier years but those who wish to pay arrears of Class 2 to enhance their benefits e.g. retirement pension, may do so and the DSS will consider extending the normal time limits for payment for this purpose (see Lloyd's Market Bulletin, 20 January 1997). From then, the NICs position for external Names is that Class 4 contributions will be due from the year 1997–98 (when self-assessment commenced) and will be collected through the Inland Revenue as normal. Class 2 contributions are due from 1 January 1997 unless that Name:

- is abroad, or
- is over pension age, or
- has been granted the small earnings exception, or
- is a married woman/widow with a reduced rate liability, or
- is getting a deferment on account of other earnings.

Names and their advisers should check the Class 2 contribution position of the Name and advise the NICO of the self-employed status and arrange to pay NICs or seek deferral where applicable. The NICO provide a starter pack for those Names who have not previously registered with regard to Class 2 contributions.

56.2 Non-working Names

This new view adopted by the CA is questionable and may yet be challenged. Most non-working Names will not consider that they are 'gainfully' employed as *Social Security Contributions and Benefits Act 1992, s 2(1)(b)* requires but, rather, making a passive investment.

Were the Agency's view to be correct, their statement that Class 2 need not be paid if the Name is abroad is equally highly questionable. If there is any 'gainful employment' as regards Lloyd's of London then it no less continues to take place in Great Britain just because the Name is abroad on an extended holiday or working for some employer completely unconnected with underwriting activities.

At a joint Lloyd's and Inland Revenue seminar for Lloyd's Names in May 1997 the imposition of Class 4 NICs on Names was explained by the Inland Revenue even though this was then within the ambit of the CA. It was stated that the CA had looked at the role of the managing agent in the *Gooda Walker* case and much store had been placed in Gibson LJ's comment that 'On general principles a principal who employs an agent to carry on a trade nevertheless owns and carries on that trade, even though the income received by the principal from it is not immediately derived from the carrying on by him of the trade'. See *Deeny and others v Gooda Walker Ltd (in voluntary liquidation) and others (IRC third party) [1996] STC 39.* The *obiter dictum* of Gibson LJ in this case was viewed by the CA as a peg on which to hang their Class 4 hat.

56.3   Tax return

The 2000–01 Notes to the tax return (pages LUN 9 and 10) give information on Class 4 NICs stating that for external Names (or non-working Names), the Department of Social Security view is that Lloyd's profits are and always have been chargeable to Class 4. They also state that sometimes where both Class 1 and Class 4 contributions are payable the latter may not be due because a deferment operates until such time as the overall contributions may be determined. Only the Inland Revenue National Insurance Contributions Office can agree to the deferment and for this Leaflet CA 72 may be used.

57   Volunteer Development Workers

Cross-references. See ANNUAL MAXIMUM (7); CLASS 2 CONTRIBUTIONS (18); LATE-PAID CONTRIBUTIONS (39); OVERSEAS MATTERS (49).

Other Sources. Leaflet NI 38.

57.1   GENERAL CONSIDERATIONS

At a meeting held on 25 and 26 June 1984, the EC Council called on EC Member States to take steps to encourage young people to participate in development projects organised by the EC beyond its frontiers, to bring together young Europeans who wish to work in developing countries, to support the creation of national committees of European volunteers for such development work, and to provide social protection for such volunteer development workers. (Council Recommendation 85/308 13 July 1985). One response of the UK parliament has been to bring into force the legislation described in this chapter.

57.2   CATEGORISATION

Any person who

(*a*)   is certified by the Inland Revenue as being a volunteer development worker, and

(*b*)   is ordinarily resident in Great Britain (see 49.4 OVERSEAS MATTERS), and

(*c*)   is employed outside Great Britain in circumstances under which no liability for Class 1 contributions arises in respect of his earnings,

is to be included in the category of self-employed earner for contribution purposes. [*Contribution Regs, Regs 123A and 123B as amended by Contributions Amendment Regs 1986, Reg 2 and SSC(T)A 1999, 2 Sch*].

The effect of (*c*) above and *Contributions Regs, Reg 120(1)(2)* is to exclude from this categorisation provision, for the first 52 weeks of his employment abroad, anyone who, though ordinarily resident in Great Britain and certified as an overseas development worker, is gainfully employed overseas by an employer who has a place of business in Great Britain (see 49.8 OVERSEAS MATTERS).

The DSS formerly recognised some 50 organisations as sending volunteer workers to 100 or so developing countries; though the one supplying most such workers is Voluntary Services Overseas.

57.3   CONTRIBUTION LIABILITIES AND OPTIONS

Once a person is categorised as a self-employed earner, a liability to pay Class 2 contributions will arise, subject to the person fulfilling conditions of residence and presence in Great Britain (see 18.2 CLASS 2 CONTRIBUTIONS and 49.10 OVERSEAS MATTERS). A volunteer development worker who is so categorised is, however, excepted from normal Class 2 liability but is entitled to pay a Class 2 contribution, free from the normal constraints of residence and presence requirements, at a special rate for any contribution week during which he is ordinarily employed as a volunteer development worker (see 49.8 OVERSEAS MATTERS). [*Contribution Regs, Regs 123C and 123D(a) as amended by Contributions Amendment Regs 1986, Reg 2*].

The special weekly rate of the optional Class 2 contribution is calculated for 2000–01 by applying a rate of 5% to the lower earnings limit for the week concerned, i.e. 5% × £67 = £3.35. [*Reg 123D(1)(b)*]. Class 2 contributions paid at this special rate will, as in the case of SHARE FISHERMEN (54), enable the contributor to acquire or maintain a contribution record on the basis of which he will be entitled to contributions based jobseeker's allowance (previously unemployment benefit). [*Benefit Persons Abroad Regs 1975, Reg 13B as inserted by Benefit Persons Abroad Amendment Regs 1986, Reg 2*].

The normal rules concerning method of, and time for, payment of Class 2 contributions and Class 3 contributions (see 21.8 to 21.10 COLLECTION) do not apply to volunteer development workers who wish to pay special Class 2 contributions. [*Reg 123D(d) as amended by Contributions Amendment Regs 1993, Reg 6*]. Instead, a volunteer development worker should complete a form CF 83 (contained in Leaflet NI 38) indicating that he wishes to pay special Class 2 contributions and he should give the completed form to the organisation through whom he has been recruited for work overseas. That organisation will then submit the form to the Inland Revenue and will act as agent in paying special Class 2 contributions.

It should be noted that these special provisions are of no application to a volunteer development worker who is under a contract of service to an employer who has a place of business in Great Britain. Such a VDW will be an employed earner in accordance with the normal rules and, when he is sent overseas, his contribution liability (if any) will be determined in accordance with the rules set out at 49.8 OVERSEAS MATTERS.

57.4   LATE-PAID CONTRIBUTIONS

The normal rules relating to the late payment of Class 2 contributions do not apply in the case of volunteer development workers [*Contribution Regs, Reg 123E(2) as amended by Contributions Amendment Regs 1986, Reg 2*]. Instead, a special Class 2 contribution paid by a volunteer development worker after the end of the tax year immediately following the tax year in which there falls the week to which the contribution relates, is to be paid at the highest of all special Class 2 rates which have applied in the period from the week to which the contribution relates to the date of payment, unless the rate at the beginning and end of that period is the same. [*Reg 123E(4) as amended by Contributions Amendment Regs 1986, Reg 2*]. A late paid contribution paid in the tax year in which there falls the week to which the contribution relates, or paid in the tax year immediately following, is payable at the special rate which applied for the week in question. [*Reg 123E(1)(3) as amended by Contributions Amendment Regs 1986, Reg 2*].

57.5   ANNUAL MAXIMUM

In the case of a volunteer development worker, the ANNUAL MAXIMUM (7) which serves to limit the total amount of contributions payable for a year is reduced by the amount of any special Class 2 contributions which are paid in respect of that year. [*Contributions Regs, Reg 123D(c) as amended by Contributions Amendment Regs 1986, Reg 2*]. The effect of this is to ensure that, where contributions are paid in excess of the maximum, any return of contributions to him will consist entirely of contributions *other than* special Class 2 contributions, thus preserving any entitlement to contributions based jobseeker's allowance (previously unemployment benefit) which those special Class 2 contributions have created.

58 Working Case Study

Cross-references. See ADMINISTRATION (2); AGE EXCEPTION (3); ANNUAL MAXIMUM (7); APPEALS AND REVIEWS (9); APPRENTICES, TRAINEES AND STUDENTS (10); ARREARS OF CONTRIBUTION (12); CATEGORISATION (14); CLASS 1 CONTRIBUTIONS (15); CLASS 1A CONTRIBUTIONS (16); CLASS 2 CONTRIBUTIONS (18); COMPANY DIRECTORS (22); EARNINGS (28); EARNINGS LIMITS AND THRESHOLDS (30); ENFORCEMENT (32); HUSBAND AND WIFE (36); INLAND REVENUE: CO-ORDINATION WITH THE DSS (37); LABOUR-ONLY CONTRACTORS (38); OVERSEAS MATTERS (49); RATES AND LIMITS (51); REDUCED LIABILITY CONTRIBUTIONS (52); REPAYMENT AND RE-ALLOCATION (53).

Other Sources. Tolley's Payroll Managers Review; Simon's Weekly Tax Intelligence; Employer's Bulletin, Issue 4; Leaflets CWG1 (2000) Cards 1–23; CWG2 (2000); CWG5 (2000), Issue 1; CA33; CA35/36; CA38; CA39; CA40; CA44; WFTC/EG.

58.1 INTRODUCTION

Benevolent Ltd (B Ltd) is a company that manufactures a range of gift items for retail supply to United Kingdom and overseas purchasers of corporate and personal luxury gifts. The company is quoted on the Alternative Investment Market (AIM) and has 500 employees some of whom work abroad in a sales capacity, others in administration but the main bulk of employees are on the production, sales and distribution side of the business. During the year 2000–01 a number of employees come and go for different reasons which have an impact on the payroll of the company generally and in particular the National Insurance contributions burdens of both the business and the employees.

For instance, in May 2000 Alex Slipman **[Case Study 1]**, previously self-employed, is appointed a senior marketing manager with the promise of a bonus on performance if he achieves results before the company's year-end of 31 December 2000. Alex achieves this bonus, payable in February 2001, but is made a director from 1 January 2001 and receives share options in an existing unapproved scheme. In August 2000 a University graduate, Roger Coxon, joins the company as a trainee **[Case Study 2]**. He arrives with no P45 or National Insurance number but indicates to payroll that he has had a Student Loan whilst at university. In July, Janet Johns **[Case Study 3]**, a long-term unemployed divorced mother of two, is taken on as a canteen assistant. She states that she signed an NIC exemption certificate many years ago and provides a photocopy. The change in the charity laws result in three members, Mark, Luke and John, of the sales team being made redundant in September **[Case Study 4]**. In November 2000 Alan Bransdon-Smith **[Case Study 5]**, the managing director, decides that his usual director's bonus should be paid by way of dividend this year. He has a son at Select independent school and the company decides that it will contract with the school this year for the fees to be paid by the company. On 5 August 2000 the United Kingdom sales force **[Case Study 6]** upgrade their company cars under a new lease company for their petrol-driven 1,600 cc cars costing £16,000 to be replaced by four wheel-drive diesel cars of 2,000 cc costing £20,000 each. The lease takes immediate effect and therefore the sales force will have two cars available from August 2000 to 31 December 2000 when the existing lease expires. The four-wheel drive vehicles have discreet advertising on the back windows and the company will benefit in the accounts under the new lease scheme. Also the company provides fuel from its own pumps which includes private use.

In September 2000 Benevolent Ltd takes over a small French executive gifts manufacturer in Paris called 'Le Gift, Paris' and undertakes a marketing personnel exchange from 1 January 2000 for a period of 12 months. Tony Hudson goes to the Paris office on that date and Francois Dubois comes to the UK for the same period **[Case Study 7]**.

58.2 Working Case Study

In October 2000 the Managing Director's wife, Angela Bransdon-Smith [**Case Study 8**], who is a self-employed entertainment hostess, supplies the company with corporate entertaining consultancy services. On 15 April 2001 a PAYE/NIC audit [**Case Study 9**] is instigated and various matters come to light.

58.2 CASE STUDIES

The following case studies look at the National Insurance contributions position of the employees and Benevolent Ltd. Where the tax position and Budget 2000 has an impact then this too will be mentioned. Each case study is cross-referenced to chapters in the earlier part of the book and some examples pertinent to the case study are to be located in the relevant chapters. In addition, where applicable, useful internet websites of the Inland Revenue/DSS and other sites will be shown for additional access to source information. Each case study is then summarised with any tax and National Insurance planning suggestions which although comprehensive should be read in conjunction with the relevant chapters referred to in the earlier part of this work.

58.3 CASE STUDY 1 — ALEX SLIPMAN

Alex's self-employed earnings from 1 September 1999 until he joined Benevolent Ltd on 5 May 2000 amounted to £28,000. He joined without a form P45 and therefore completes a form P46 ticking the box 'This is my only job' on the basis that self-employment has ceased. His salary and other details are as follows:

- Salary of £2,500 payable monthly.
- Commission of £7,000 payable on 31 December 2000.
- Bonus of £16,000 for the period ended 31 December 2000, payable on 31 March 2001.
- Fees of £5,000 payable from 1 January 2000.

Alex is appointed a director on 1 January 2001 and he joins the existing unapproved share option scheme securing 50,000 ordinary 25 pence shares valued at £1.50 per share. The unapproved option scheme was set up in 1997 and is a greater than ten year scheme. A copy of the Directors' resolution is detailed below:

Directors' Resolution			
IT WAS RESOLVED THAT options be hereby granted under the Benevolent Ltd (Unapproved) Scheme 1997 to the following Executive:			
Name and address of Optionholder Alex Slipman	*Number of shares allocated* 50,000 ord 25 pence	*Exercise price* £4.50 pence per share	*Terms or Performance Targets* ABI earnings per share growth target ...

Note: Alex is only able to join the existing scheme because the rules (ABI 1995) and the Memorandum and Articles of Association allow an allocation of existing options to him, following a previous director's dismissal due to fraud, and his shares were allocated to Alex.

58.4 Compliance undertakings

The wages department must ensure that the P46 is completed and submitted to the tax office without delay on Alex's joining the company. A form P11 deduction working sheet must be completed to record his salary payment and the tax code of 438 L Week 1 basis (emergency code) will be operational until the tax office advises otherwise on form P6. The commission is paid after he becomes a director and is assessable to PAYE and NIC in the month it is paid i.e. December 2000. The unapproved share option offered to him in the existing scheme is slightly anomalous as he is joining it whilst it is an already existing scheme. However, notwithstanding this it may constitute a 'readily convertible asset'. See 28.26 EARNINGS. Normally, no income tax would be due under PAYE if the grant of an option was for an unapproved scheme with less than ten years but Alex has been given options in the old scheme that stipulates a twelve-year period. The other Directors benefit from the fact that this unapproved scheme commenced before 27 November 1996 but Alex does not so benefit.

PAYE should be deducted by the company using the code number issued to Alex by the Inland Revenue [**www.inlandrevenue.gov.uk/rates/rates2000.htm**]. Therefore with the shares standing at £2.78 and the option at £1.50 there is likely, subject to the NICs planning and mitigation below, to be subject to PAYE of £25,600 (i.e. 50,000 shares multiplied by £1.28 = £64,000 x 40%).

In addition, employer's Class 1 NICs are also due of £3,123 (i.e. £25,600 x 12.2%) which the company must pay with the PAYE to the Collector of Taxes within 14 days of the end of the relevant tax month, *viz* £28,723 before 20 January 2001. The amount of the unapproved option must be reported and Alex will need to make an entry on his tax return for 2000–01 on the share scheme supplementary pages.

58.5 NIC planning and mitigation

The bonus of £16,000 received by Alex after he becomes a director is treated under the annual earnings rule and 'spreading' is applied unless he agrees to pay on account using regular monthly earnings period as per *SSA 1998, s 49* [**www.inlandrevenue.gov.uk/nic/class1/nidirec.htm**], whereas if the bonus had been paid before he becomes a director it would have had employee contributions limited to the monthly upper earnings limit. The NICs treatment of the director's fees can be seen at 22.3 COMPANY DIRECTORS.

The share option has proved expensive for the company in terms of PAYE and NICs which have to be deducted and accounted for almost immediately to the Collector of Taxes. The problem has been the fact that Alex joined an existing scheme that exceeds the ten-year period and therefore falls foul of the *Finance Act 1998* rules. It would have been better if Alex had been given a new approved option scheme or an unapproved scheme that is exercisable in less than seven years. The company, having paid the tax and any employee NICs, will now have to try to recoup those payments from Alex by way of joint election. Any shortfall not recovered from Alex proves to be a further benefit on which tax and NICs must be payable! See IR Press Release 19 May 2000.

Alex was previously self-employed so during the year 2000–01 he has made Class 1, Class 2 and Class 4 NIC contributions [**www.inlandrevenue.gov.uk/rates/nic1.htm**]. He is over the maximum threshold for NICs and therefore a refund is relevant.

Example
Alex was a self-employed marketing consultant whose 2000–01 assessable Class 4 profits were £28,000 up until 5 May 2000. He is, however, now employed by Benevolent Ltd at an amount of £2,500 per month and expects the commission payment of £7,000 to be paid on 31 December 2000. His anticipated contribution liability for 2000–01 prior to his becoming a director is, therefore,

	£
Class 1: say £27,500 : Nil% on £76 × 48 weeks	0.00
+ 10% on £22,032 (balance)	2,203.20
Class 2: 4 × £2.00	8.00
	2,211.20
Class 4: £27,820 – £4,385 (lower limit) × 7%	1,640.45
	£3,851.65

58.5 Working Case Study

As the estimated Class 1 and Class 2 total (£2,211.20) exceeds the 2000–01 Class 4 limiting amount (£1,746.45) (see 7.3 ANNUAL MAXIMUM), Class 4 contributions will be reduced to nil. Because the amount may not be determined with accuracy until 6 April 2000 or later, however, he may apply for deferment of all Class 4 liability. In practice, the Inland Revenue does not make refunds of 50p or less and therefore works on a limiting amount of £1,746.95.

A contributor who over-contributes as regards Class 1 or Class 2 contributions (e.g. by being concurrently employed in employment and self-employment or in two or more employed earner's employments and failing, or not being permitted, to defer a sufficient amount of his liability to prevent contributions in excess of the annual maximum being paid) will be informed of the fact by the NICO and invited to apply for repayment provided the excess payment is at least equal to half the current weekly LEL . Smaller amounts are left to individual contributors to claim. Any delay may be avoided by applying directly, without awaiting notification of overpayment, to the Refunds Group, Longbenton, Newcastle upon Tyne, NE98 1ZZ. Repayment will be expedited if the application is supported by evidence of contribution payments (i.e. forms P60 or detailed statements from the secondary contributors concerned).

Where over-contribution extends to Class 4 contributions positive action on the part of the contributor is not only desirable but essential. This is because no records are kept by the NICO of Class 4 contributions as they do not count for benefit purposes and are mainly collected by the Inland Revenue offices dealing with tax functions. Any over-contribution will, therefore, remain undetected and unrepaid unless and until it is claimed. It should be noted that the NICO has no statutory duty to check for over-payments and that the onus of obtaining repayment is placed on the contributor. Repayment claims should be made to the Class 4 Group (see 2.3 ADMINISTRATION).

Contributions Agency Deferment Group's decision on form CA 2717 and deferment certificates (CA 2700) are sent to the secondary contributors in the employments to which the deferment is to relate. (See CWG2 (2000), Page 58). The certificate informs the secondary contributor of the period to which it relates and instructs the secondary contributor that, during that period, he is no longer to deduct primary Class 1 contributions from the earnings paid to the earner in question, unless he is given written notification that the arrangement has been cancelled (CA 2702), though it offers him no explanation as to why that should be so and gives him no indication that the earner has one or more other employments. [*Contributions Regs, Reg 48*]. Nonetheless, although the Form CA2700 itself may remain silent on the matter, the astute employer who is conversant with the instructions on Page 58 of CWG2 will be only too well aware that his employee probably has at least one other job.

The secondary contributor himself is unaffected by the arrangement and must continue to pay and account for *secondary* Class 1 contributions on the earner's earnings as normal, using Table C, S, or V for the purpose of his calculations (see 15.5 CLASS 1 CONTRIBUTIONS and CWG2 (2000), Page 58).

A secondary contributor to whom a deferment certificate has been issued in respect of one of his employees is asked to maintain a record of both the primary Class 1 contribution liabilities which would have arisen had the deferment certificate not been issued and the relevant earnings. Such a record should be retained for three years after the end of the tax year concerned and may be required by the Deferment Group at Newcastle upon Tyne on form CA 2701 (CWG2 (2000), Page 58).

Where an application is approved *after 6 April*, one or more pay days may have passed before a deferment certificate can be sent to the secondary contributor (or contributors) concerned. In that event, the secondary contributor will be instructed to repay to the earner concerned all primary contributions thus far deducted from earnings paid to that earner since the previous 6 April. The secondary contributor will then be permitted to recoup from the next remittance relating to the earnings period in which the deduction is made to the Collector of Taxes amounts already paid to the collector in respect of those refunded primary Class 1 contributions. Any unrecouped amount outstanding at the end of the tax year will be repaid by the Collector direct to the employee.

58.6 CASE STUDY 2 — ROGER COXON

Roger Coxon joins Benevolent Ltd on 5 August 2000 as a graduate from Southampton University. He has no P45 but does say he has had a university student loan for the two years he was at university amounting to £6,250. He will receive a graduate salary with Benevolent Ltd amounting to £17,000 per year payable monthly in arrears. In addition, he will go on a company sponsored training course in November 2000 costing the company £2,500.

58.7 Compliance undertakings

As Roger does not have a form P45 then a form P46 should be completed and sent to the Tax Office. It is important that the National Insurance number (NINO) be inserted on the form. If the payroll office does not know it then a temporary one should be placed on the P46. See 46 NATIONAL INSURANCE NUMBER [**www.inlandrevenue.gov.uk/nic/nitrace.htm**]. Any investigation uncovering missing or incorrect NINOs may incur a penalty in the future, but may also prompt a visit currently, notwithstanding that the imposition of such penalties continues to be deferred (see Tax Bulletin, April 2000). See [**Case Study 9**]. As Roger had been on a three year course commencing before August 1998 he would normally pay the loan back to the Student Loan Office independently with no involvement of Benevolent Ltd. However, Roger did not take out a loan in his first year at university so in fact he does come within the post-August 1998 rules for new borrowers from that date. Benevolent Ltd do not, however, have to apply the new rules until they are notified by the Inland Revenue PAYE Office to do so. [**www.inlandrevenue.gov.uk/rates/ tables.htm**]. Roger's starting salary is £17,000 per annum which is over the £10,000 annual threshold so deductions will be made from his salary when a 'Start Notice' SL1 is received. As Roger has not handed in a P45 there is no way of checking the loan position because the P45 would normally have had a 'Y' in the student loan box in cases such as Roger's. On receipt of the advice SL1, a repayment at the rate of 9% of the pay above £10,000 p.a. liable to NICs should be deducted. The amount deducted, which should be triggered from the Inland Revenue on receipt of form P46, must be shown on Roger's payslip and form P11. The deduction must be paid over to the Inland Revenue together with the tax and NICs deductions on the normal remittance date. A record of student loan deductions must be kept for a period of three years. In Roger's case his monthly deductions will be £52 (i.e. £17,000 − £10,000 x 9% ÷ 12 months) Using the student loan deduction tables SL3 that come with the annual employer's PAYE pack, Roger's monthly pay of £1,417 (£17,000 per annum ÷ 12 months) falls in the band in the Table on page 3 of £1,412 − £1,422. The loan deduction is confirmed at £52 per month from the Table.

The company sponsored training course is tax and NICs free but will be an allowable deduction in the company's accounts. See CWG5 (2000) and Table at 16 CLASS 1A CONTRIBUTIONS.

58.8 NIC planning and mitigation

The payment of £2,500 for the training course in November 2000 is not treated as earnings for PAYE/NICs purposes. However, the immediate large salary that Roger has secured brings its own problems i.e. higher taxes and NICs and student loan repayment deductions. The £52 per month student loan repayment might be settled by making Roger a loan from the company interest free of up to £5,000 (tax and NIC free) to repay the loan and then Roger repay the loan back to the company over a greater length of time. The payroll department should contact the National Insurance Contributions Office P46 section at Longbenton for a form CA6855 in order to trace the NI number. See CWG1 (2000), card 3.

Finally, it will be beneficial to give Roger benefits, other than those subject to Class 1 NICs, instead of salary as this would not affect the student loan position because the value of those benefits are not included in the £10,000 threshold figure for collection purposes. However, Class 1 or Class 1A NICs are also due on most benefits from 6 April 2000. See 16.18 CLASS 1A CONTRIBUTIONS; 28.26 EARNINGS.

The actual cost in terms of NICs under Class 1A on £7,000 worth of benefits will be £71 per month. Clearly the student loan repayments may not be deferred indefinitely but deductions in the future from incremental pay rises may be more measured.

58.9 CASE STUDY 3 — JANET JOHNS

Janet joins Benevolent Ltd on 17 July 2000 after a long period of unemployment and she hands over a photocopy of a married woman's reduced rate certificate but not the actual form itself. Her salary is £150 (net) per week for 26 hours work in the canteen at Benevolent Ltd. Her youngest two children aged 10 and 17 years both live at home. She has a child minder for some of the five days she works at Benevolent Ltd costing £50.

58.10 Compliance undertakings

The fact that Janet does not have an original exception certificate and she is now divorced should ensure that the circumstances are reviewed by the payroll department. See 52.2 REDUCED LIABILITY ELECTIONS. As Benevolent Ltd would be responsible for any shortfall in Class 1 NICs they would best deduct normal Class 1 NICs pending the receipt of forms CF383 or CA4139 and instruct the employee that they will only recognise a current, valid, original certificate. It is quite possible that such a certificate would not be forthcoming in the circumstances mentioned. [**www.inlandrevenue.gov.uk/wftc/index.htm**].

The calculation of Janet John's WFTC per week is shown in the example below.

Example

Weekly Income (net of tax and NICs)		£150.00
Add:	£	
Basic Tax credit	53.15	
Child Care Credit (child under 11 years)	21.25	
Child Care Credit (Child between 16–18 years)	26.35	
Child Care Tax Credit (70% × £50)	35.00	
Total	135.75	
Less 55% of income in excess of £90	(33.00)	102.75
(i.e. £150 – 90 × 55%)		
Janet's net weekly income from Benevolent Ltd		252.75

Benevolent Ltd will receive form 'TCO1', the employer's green start notification. WFTC is deducted from PAYE and student loans before it is accounted for to the Collector of Taxes as per form P32 employer's payment record. Form TC11 may be completed if there is not enough PAYE/NIC available and the employer wishes to obtain advance funding. Under the new tax credits (leaflet WFTC/EG) legislation penalties have been introduced to deter irregularities arising from fraud or negligence (up to £3,000 per employee). See [**Case Study 9**]. [**www.fsb.org.uk**].

58.11 NICs planning

Benevolent Ltd could perhaps offer free canteen meals, crèche facilities, work's bus transport which would be tax and NICs free or childcare vouchers which would be NICs free. Following the Budget 2000 proposals payments to childcare providers or registered childminders contracted by Benevolent Ltd will also be free of Class 1A liabilities freeing up companies such as Benevolent Ltd from liability in these cases. As Janet is earning more than £8,500 gross per annum other benefits could not be made available to her tax and NICs free such as private medical, etc. as Class 1A is payable in respect of benefits to employees earning over that limit.

There are still many women who were either employed by their husband or self-employed before 6 April 1975 and, because their circumstances have not changed or changed little since then, do not actually possess a certificate of reduced liability. *Reg 108*, a regulation giving transitional relief, provides that they are entitled to one (unless they have subsequently ceased to qualify to continue to pay the reduced rate). This transitional provision is not widely known by NICO staff, and individuals may be able to readily fend off an approach for arrears if their circumstances enable them to send the following letter:

> National Insurance Contributions Office
>
> ....
>
> ....
>
> Dear Sirs,
>
> *Either* I have remained in continuous self-employment since before 6 April 1975.
>
> *Or* I was employed by my husband until 5 April 1975 (and therefore not allowed to pay contributions) and have been continuously self-employed since 6 April 1975.
>
> I am therefore covered by the transitional regulation 108 of the Social Security (Contributions) Regulations 1979 and request that you now issue me with a 'Certificate of Election' (CA4139).
>
> Yours faithfully,
>
> ....

Limited gaps after 6 April 1978 and/or a cessation of self-employment replaced by employment at or above the LEL may also result in an individual retaining entitlement (see below). In suitable cases, the first sentence in the above letter should be adapted accordingly.

An election, latterly, has resulted in the issue of a certificate of election, CF 383 or CA 4139. If its holder is an employed earner, it has to be handed to the secondary contributor in relation to her employment as authority for primary Class 1 contributions to be paid in respect of her earnings between the primary threshold and the upper earnings limit at a reduced rate. (The rate of secondary contributions is unaffected.) Where a woman has more than one employed earner's employment, certificates are to be issued for each. [*Reg 106(1)(3)(6)*].

58.12 CASE STUDY 4 — MARK, LUKE and JOHN

The direct sales department offering charity-inscribed merchandise are immediately made redundant following the Chancellor's changes to tax relief for charitable giving. It is decided that they should leave the company immediately rather than serve their full three months' notice and they will receive a Payment In Lieu of Notice (PILON) as well as their month's salary and a redundancy payment of one month's pay for each year served with the company as follows:

	PILON	**Redundancy**	**TOTAL**
Mark	£4,500	£15,000	£19,500
Luke	3,700	11,250	14,950
John	5,400	27,000	32,400

Their staff handbook states that '*You will be expected to work your full period of notice before leaving the company. The company reserves the right to make payment of the equivalent salary in lieu of notice and to terminate employment without notice or payment in lieu for gross misconduct*'.

The redundancy letter sent by Benevolent Ltd to the employees is along the following lines:

Dear Mark/Luke/John

I refer to my letter of [. . .] and our meeting today.

I confirm that the position remains as set out in my letter. The company, with regret, does not see any practical alternative to the reorganisation and thus the reduction in staff which, unfortunately, means that your employment will end because of redundancy.

While careful thought has been given to the points raised by you, these do not change our view that your redundancy is unavoidable in the circumstances.

Since there is currently no work for you to perform and there is no likelihood of the overall situation changing, the company will not ask you to work your notice but will pay you in lieu of it. Your employment will therefore end today. You will receive the following payments:

£[. . .] week's pay in lieu of notice

£[. . .] redundancy payment based on [. . .] years' service, your age and a weekly wage of £[. . .].

Letter continues

58.13 Compliance undertakings

Forms P45 should be issued to the men on their departure. See CWG1 (2000) Card 21. However, the PILON should be included as pay and subjected to PAYE /NICs following the *EMI v Coldicot* case. This arises from the fact that the staff hand book states that they are entitled to PILON, *viz* ' . . .*the company reserves*. . .' etc. The redundancy payments are tax free within the £30,000 limit and NICs free but should be notified to the Inland Revenue at the end of the tax year.

Where no tax is due because the redundancy payment is below the £30,000 limit as in the case of all three men above then the amounts should not be included in gross pay either on form P11 or form P45. If tax is due because the payment is over the £30,000 limit or it is a PILON then the payroll department of Benevolent Ltd should make the payment to the employees when or before they leave the company. The taxable amount should be included in gross pay on form P11 and PAYE operated in the normal way by including the taxable amount on form P45. A letter might also be sent to the PAYE Tax Office with Part 1 of form P45 advising them of the amount and date of the lump sum payment. The PAYE Tax

Office will then contact the employee if there is a refund due. If the payment is made after the employee leaves then Benevolent's payroll department should include the taxable amount in gross pay on form P11 for the tax week or month the payment is made i.e. September 2000. The tax code that should be operated is BR (basic rate) WK 1 basis. A P45 should not be issued but instead the payroll department should write to the PAYE Tax Office and advise them of the date of the lump sum payment and the amount of tax deducted (the former employees receiving a copy of the letter). Mark, Luke and John, in these circumstances should be provided with a copy of the letter sent to the Tax Office.

NICs should be worked out on the regular earnings period for the employment when the employee leaves. In the case of Mark, Luke and John who have left already the NICs should be worked out using the minimum contributions period of 7 days, the contribution rates and limits current at the time of payment and the usual contribution Table letter. If the employees were in contracted-out employment (not the case here) and the payment is made more than six weeks after they leave the NICs should be worked out using the equivalent not contracted-out rate. Where the payment comprises two or more items, after the employee leaves the earnings periods are dependent on what those payments are. If all the payments are salary and wages the payroll department should work out the NICs on the total using the usual earnings period for the payment of salary. If all payments are irregular sums, add them together and work out NICs using the weekly earnings period.

58.14 NICs planning

Mark, Luke and John's PILONs are assessable to tax and Class 1 NICs as they currently stand but the redundancy payment is covered by the £30,000 exemption to tax which is not fully utilised leaving scope for further planning. See CWG (2000), Page 92, Item 6. The company should reappraise its staff handbook and instructions regarding its right to make PILONs. CWG (2000) states that 'a single payment is often made up of more than one element. For example, one payment might cover redundancy pay, accrued holiday pay and a payment in lieu of notice. Each element must be considered separately.' In this connection the payroll department must also contact the PAYE Tax Office for guidance on calculating the taxable amount if it is intended that anything other than cash e.g. car is given or any payment or part payment is made by another company.

Another alternative is to ensure that the payment is made NICs free is as damages for breach of contract. For example, if Benevolent Ltd did not give the employee proper notice and there was no entitlement to a PILON (not the case here) then a payment is not NICable. Alternatively, If the Courts/Employment Tribunal rule that the employee was unfairly or wrongly dismissed then that amount will be PAYE and NICs free. If, though, it is ordered or Benevolent Ltd agrees to make a payment that is part of a settlement of damages to pay wages then these must still be included in gross pay for PAYE and NICs purposes. So, if Mark, Luke and John take Benevolent Ltd to the Employment Tribunal on the basis that the company made them redundant and there was no basis for such an action and it was unlawful a correctly worded decision would ensure that the payments were damages and PAYE and NICs free. Unfortunately, the particular circumstances of their situation can be likened to that in the House of Lords decision in *Murray and another v Foyle Meats Ltd [1999] IRLR 562* so an application to the Industrial Tribunal (Form IT1) would probably be inappropriate. However, in some cases the company may be in a unsafe position with regard to unfair dismissal and could agree with the employee as follows:

Company Headed Paper

[EMPLOYEE'S NAME]

[EMPLOYEE'S ADDRESS]

Dear [Employee],

Without Prejudice

We write following the termination of your employment with Benevolent Ltd ('the Company') on [Date]. The Company is prepared to offer to you the sum of £[...] in full and final settlement of all and any claims arising out of your employment with the Company on the termination of your employment. The sum would be paid on or shortly after [. . .insert date approximately three and a half months after the effective date of termination of employment. . .], so long as, at that date, you have not commenced or threatened to commence legal proceedings against the company in any court or tribunal or elsewhere, arising out of your employment or its termination.

Letter continues

If you wish to accept this offer, please sign the enclosed duplicate copy of this letter and return it in the envelope provided. Although headed 'Without Prejudice', this will, upon signature by you and return to us, be an open agreement binding on both parties.

In CWG2 (2000), Page 93, Item 7 such a payment, as damages because the employee was unfairly or wrongly dismissed, would not be NICable and providing the payment is under £30,000 no PAYE would attach.

58.15 CASE STUDY 4 — ALAN BRANSDON-SMITH

Alan's decision to have a dividend instead of a £50,000 discretionary bonus payment (see Introduction) and the contract between the Company and his son's school for fees has both tax and NICs implications on both the company and the Director. The school fees contract has been drawn up over the year between the school and the company as follows:

This agreement is made between the Governors of [**Select Independent School**] by their duly authorised officer [**A. Bursar**] (hereinafter called 'the school') of the first part; and [**Benevolent Ltd**] Company/plc of the second part.

Whereas it is proposed that the [**Benevolent Ltd**] Company/plc do make periodical payments of school fees to the school until [**Alan Bransdon-Smith's**] son [**Robert Bransdon-Smith**] completes full time education (or as the case may be). Such said fees shall be paid to the school by the Company/plc in advance of each term and the receipt by the school shall be sufficient discharge.

1. In consideration of the payment by the Company/plc of the said school fees the school agrees to keep a place open for the child [**Robert Bransdon-Smith**] until they have completed full time education or cease such education at the agreement of the contracting parties.

2. Any case of default of payment of the said fees shall be submitted to the Headmaster/Bursar for arbitration and if the said fees remain unpaid the child shall no longer occupy a place at the said school. If sufficient discharge be provided after arbitration then such amount of discharge shall include interest at [**3%**] above LIBOR for the period the said fees have been outstanding.

Etc.

The dividend payment instead of the usual bonus will attract no contribution liability and, because the corporation tax rate for small companies is presently 20% and no additional rate of income tax is charged on an individual's investment income, no adverse tax consequences will follow, provided the company profits out of which it is paid do not exceed £300,000 (for the year to 31 March 2001) i.e. the level of profits beyond which the fully-reduced small companies rate of corporation tax ceases to apply. [*ICTA 1988, s 13*]. For 2000–01 the tax credit for individuals is 10% and since dividend income is taxed at either this rate of 10% or the rate of 32 ½%—for higher rate taxpayers (but not at basic rate), only higher rate taxpayers will suffer an additional tax charge.

Example
Alan Bransdon-Smith and Geoff Legit are directors of Benevolent Ltd and each holds 500 £1 shares in that company. On 17 July 2000 it is clear that the corporation tax profits of W for the accounting period to 31 July 2000 will be approximately £170,000 and it is decided to pay T and V £50,000 each immediately. This might be achieved by the payment of either £100,000 in bonuses or £80,000 in dividends that will carry £8,888 (10% of the gross equivalent) in related tax credits. (Since the 10% tax credit for dividends attracts no further liability to a basic rate taxpayer this is as good as the 20% tax credit on most other forms of savings income).

From 6 April 1999, there is no longer any ACT payable by the company when it pays a dividend. The dividend figure of £80,000 rather than £90,000 (i.e. equivalent to £100,000 gross) is appropriate because of the reduced tax credit and tax liability on dividends for 40% taxpayers which leaves the same total liability in the hands of such a taxpayer now as was the case when the tax credit was actually 20%. This gives an additional income tax advantage to those still wholly or partially below the 40% income tax bracket.

A comparison of the two routes is as follows:

	Bonus route £	Bonus route £	Dividend route £	Dividend route £
B				
Pre-bonus profit		170,000		170,000
Gross bonuses	(100,000)			
Class 1 secondary @ Nil/12.2%	(11,130)			—
		(111,130)		
Post-bonus profit		58,870		170,000
Corporation tax @ 20%		(11,774)		(34,000)*
Post-tax profit		47,098		136,000
Dividend		—		(80,000)
Retained Profit		£47,098		£56,000
Bransdon-Smith and Legit				
Gross bonuses		100,000		—
Class 1 primary @ Nil%/10% on UEL £27,820 × 2		(4,774)		—
Post-NIC bonuses		95,226		—
Dividends		—		80,000
Post-NIC dividends and bonuses		95,226		80,000
Income tax*		(25,904)	(13,258)	
Tax credits		—	8,888	
				(4,370)
Post-tax and NI income		£69,322		£75,630

58.16 Working Case Study

Assuming reliefs of £4,385 each, income tax would be charged for each individual as follows:

	Bonus route £		*Dividend route* £
Taxable income	50,000		44,444
Personal allowances	(4,385)		(4,385)
	45,615		40,059

1,520 @ 10% = £152		28,400 @ 10% = £2,840		
26,880 @ 22% = £5,914		— @ 22%		
17,215 @ 40% = £6,886		11,659 @ 32½% = £3,789		
Liability before credits	12,952			6,629
Tax credits	—	£40,000 @ ⅑%		4,444
Tax not collected at source	—			2,185

The individual's tax liability in the above example is affected (in both cases) by the availability of personal allowances and (under the dividend route) by the lack of income other than dividend income. If other income covered the allowances and the lower and basic rate bands, the tax liability under both routes would be identical. The only difference in net income would then be the primary contribution liability (if any) on the bonuses.

58.16 Compliance undertakings

The cost incurred by the company in respect of school fees should be entered at section N (other items) on the Form P11D. Whilst the contract is between the employer and the school there is no Class 1 liability. [**www.inlandrevenue.gov.uk/nic/class1/nidirec.htm**]. The National Insurance News, February 1997, Issue 7 stated:

'As a general rule, NIC liability on the provision of education and the payment of school fees depends on who has contracted with the school to provide the education, and who is liable to pay the fees ... this does not detract from the fact that there is a benefit here to the employee and, depending upon the nature of the transaction in providing that benefit, there may be liability for NICs.'

Therefore the settlement of fees between the employer and the employee would be characterised as the employee's debt being discharged by the employer and becomes earnings for NICs purposes (see *Hartland v Diggines [1926] 10 TC 247* and *Nicol v Austin [1935] 19 TC 531*). The fact that some employers and their advisers held the view that payments to an employee are never earnings because the employee has never actually profited himself is incorrect in the NICO's view. Their view is that there is a benefit to the employee and, depending on the nature of the transaction in providing that benefit there may be a liability for NICs. In the school fees case of *Glynn v IRC [1990] STC 227* held on appeal from Hong Kong that:

'an identifiable sum of money required to be extended by an employer pursuant to a contract of service for the benefit of the employee, is money paid at the request of the employee and is either part of the employee's salary or is a monetary perquisite taxable as such ...'

In order to attract liability for National Insurance contributions, it is necessary for the employee to be ultimately liable to the school in the event of the employer defaulting and there being an ultimate personal pecuniary liability on which to charge NICs. If the employer cannot or will not pay the school fees then the employee must pay and this creates a joint liability but in these circumstances the default would normally occur where the employer is unable to pay because of, say, the company going into liquidation. The school may be willing to accept an arrangement such as that detailed below on the basis that any default by the employer would result in the employee's child being excluded from the school for the next term with the loss to the school of only one term's fees. Such a circumstance e.g. liquidation of the company and subsequent dismissal of the employees would in any case lead to a possible claim by the parent for a Bursary award or other assistance.

58.17 NICs planning

For the company, the benefit of the dividend route is the post-tax saving of secondary NIC liability, reduced by the excess of the corporation tax relief lost by not paying the bonus.

Where a company's profits are such that it pays corporation tax at the full rate of 30% or marginal rate of 32½% (2000–01), the payment of a bonus rather than a dividend will result in an absolute saving of corporation tax, as the bonus is deductible from profits for Schedule D purposes. In contrast, dividends are paid out of post-tax earnings.

It should be noted that, where directors require income at regular intervals throughout the year, e.g. monthly, interim dividends might be paid at the required intervals. In the above example, for instance, Bransdon-Smith and Legit could have received an interim monthly dividend of £3,704 (including related tax credit) each.

Where it is undesirable that all shareholders should participate *pro rata* in any profits which are to be distributed, waivers (or part waivers) may be obtained from non- (or only part-) participating shareholders as necessary. Possible drawbacks to arrangements of the kind described should not be overlooked. These include the

(*a*) possibility that a dividend declared *before* the end of the accounting period to which it relates will (because the profits are not finally ascertainable at the time of payment) exceed the profits ultimately found to have been available for distribution and will thus be wholly or partly illegal. [*Companies Act 1985, ss 263–268*];

(*b*) possibility that the value of any minority shareholdings will be enhanced if a high dividend record is established by the company;

(*c*) fact that dividends are neither remuneration for occupational pension scheme purposes nor relevant earnings for retirement annuity or personal pension purposes. This must be a major point for consideration in the case of any director who is approaching retirement age or a younger director who wishes to take maximum advantage of a good trading year to direct earnings into a tax-free savings scheme;

(*d*) fact that entitlement to State benefits will be impaired unless remuneration by way of salary is maintained at a level equal to or above the lower earnings limit (see 13.2 BENEFITS AND 30.1 EARNINGS LIMITS AND THRESHOLDS).

In February 1994, the Contributions Agency issued a note to the ICAEW and other professional bodies in which they admitted that, until August 1992, their view had been that *disproportionate* dividends were not genuine dividends but earnings. The note confirms, however, that, from that date, their view has been that a lawful dividend (i.e. one paid in accordance with the rights laid down in a company's Memorandum and Articles of Association and out of profits available for distribution) should not (even if disproportionate by reason of waivers) be regarded as earnings for contribution purposes. The note also goes on to state that an unlawful dividend *will* be regarded as earnings, but there seems to be no justification for such a stance. A dividend, whether lawful or unlawful, is derived from shares, not from an employment, and is not therefore within the terms of *SSCBA 1992, s 3(1)*.

The CA took the view that in cases above where there is a contract between the employer and the school for the education of an employee's child the *Education Acts* state the parents cannot delegate their responsibilities for that child; therefore, following on from this point, the parents are responsible for the payment of the fees ultimately. This is a fine point but nowhere in the *Education Act 1944* or the *Education Act 1996* does it mention that the parents are responsible for and must pay the school fees of their child. In the *Education Act 1944, section 36* it states that;

'... it shall be the duty of the parent of every child of compulsory school age to **cause** him to receive efficient ...'

In this respect it cannot be said that the word 'cause' either means or implies that the parent should pay for education or be liable for payment. Therefore, the CA's arguments appear to be unfounded and the matter may need to go to the Tax Commissioners for their determination.

58.18 CASE STUDY 6 — SALES FORCE CARS

The new car lease being undertaken by Benevolent Ltd prior to the expiry of the old lease provides financial savings for the company but has adverse impact on the employees tax and NICs position. It is likely that both cars will be 'available' for the employee although it is likely that the new cars will be the required car because of the advertising on them. There is the private fuel aspect that needs to be covered bearing in mind the sales force do over 18,000 business miles per year. Also, the strict emissions tests proposed in the Budget 2000 will from, 6 April 2002, result in penalising the sales force by way of higher deduction in the long term.

For *tax* purposes, the cash equivalent of the car, but not car fuel, is to be *reduced* if it is shown to the Inspector of Taxes' satisfaction that the employee was required by the nature of his employment to make (and did in fact make) use of the car for business travel amounting to at least 2,500 miles (proportionally reduced for periods of unavailability) in the relevant tax year. Where business travel is shown to be at least 2,500, but less than 18,000, miles benefit is 25% of the car's price. Business mileage in excess of 17,999 a year attracts a charge of 15% of the car's price. [*ICTA 1988, Sch 6, para 2 as amended by FA 1999, s 47*].

For the year 2000–01, the car benefit is 15% of the car's list price.

The same rule applies for Class 1A purposes, but the person liable to pay the Class 1A contribution must treat the employee's business mileage as giving rise to a charge at 35% unless he, the Class 1A contributor, has information to the contrary. [*SSCBA 1992, s 10(6)(b)(i)* and also CWG1 (2000), Card 14].

From 6 April 1993, for income tax purposes the fuel scale charge was not to be adjusted to reflect business travel of more than 18,000 miles. [**www.inlandrevenue.gov.uk/rates/fuel.htm**]. The same change was applied to Class 1A contributions, but because of the way the legislative amendments were made, opinion was divided as to whether the abolition of the reduction for Class 1A purposes took effect from 6 April 1993 or only from 30 November 1993 when the amending regulations were laid. The DSS took the former view, so that the fuel scale charge for 1993–94 *et seq.* is not adjusted for Class 1A purposes in respect of business travel of 18,000 miles or more.

If, for *tax* purposes, a charge arises in respect of two or more cars which are made available concurrently, the car benefit in respect of each of the cars, other than the one used to the greatest extent for the employee's business travel, is not to be reduced when business travel is at least 2,500 but less than 18,000 miles, and is only to be reduced to 25% of the list price when business travel is 18,000 miles or more. [*ICTA 1988, Sch 6, para 4 as amended by FA 1999, s 47*]. The same rule applies for Class 1A purposes, except that *no* car is to be treated as the one used to the greatest extent for the employee's business travel unless the person liable to pay the Class 1A contribution has information to show the contrary. [*SSCBA 1992, s 10(6)(c)*]. As it stands, this rule gives rise to one or more increased Class 1A liabilities even where two or more cars are concurrently made available for private use by reason of different employed earner's employments under different employers who are *not* 'associated'.

If, for any part of the relevant tax year, the car in question was 'unavailable', the car benefits are, for *tax* purposes, to be *reduced* by multiplying them by the fraction

$$\frac{365 - \textit{number of days of unavailability}}{365}$$

A car is to be treated as 'unavailable' for a particular day if

(i)   it was not made available to the employee until after that day; or

(ii) it had ceased to be available to him before that day; or

(iii) it was incapable of being used at all throughout a period of not less than 30 consecutive days of which that day was one.

[*ICTA 1988, s 158(5) and 6 Sch 9* and see also CWG1 (2000), Card 14; CA33 (2000), Pages 12, 44 and 45]

58.19 Compliance undertakings

As an employer Benevolent Ltd is liable to pay Class 1A contributions for cars provided to directors employees paid at a rate of £8,500 or more a year including taxable benefits and taxable expenses. Also, where members of the individual's family or household including spouses, children and their spouses, parents, dependants, servants and guests receive a taxable benefit a report on Form P11D should be made. As two cars will be available for five months of the year to each of the sales force the double car benefit charge should be included at section 2 of the P11D WS2 (2000) as well as the car fuel at section 3. The calculation will be as follows:

Example

Metro is employed by Benevolent Ltd throughout 2000–01. B Ltd makes available for Metro's use two cars: one (car 1) of 1,600 cc costing £16,000 until 31 December 2000 and another (car 2) of 2,000 cc costing £20,000 from 5 August 2000, and B Ltd also provides petrol for business and private motoring in both cars.

			£
Car 1	£16,000 × 15% × 122/365	=	802
Car 1	£16,000 × 35% × 148/365	=	2,271
Car 2	£20,000 × 15% × 243/365	=	1,997
Fuel 1	£2,170 × 270/365	=	1,605
Fuel 2	£2,170 × 243/365	=	1,445
			£8,120

58.20 NICs planning

B Ltd should try to plan that the sales force are not left with a double charge for fuel and car benefit for the year. The intention is for the second new car with advertising to be used by the sales force and therefore the first car is superfluous unless it is to be used by the salesman's family. Either way there is going to be a double tax car benefit and fuel charge. Therefore, the car should be formally withdrawn from the employees and pounded. This will reduce the Class 1A NICs charge and benefits. The company should perhaps have considered using the Fixed Profit Car Scheme rates instead of company cars or alternatively made loans to the sales force for them to buy their own cars on which allowances would be due. [**www.inlandrevenue.gov.uk/ rates/fpcs.htm**]. In the long term the emissions test will need to be addressed and either the new cars reassessed as being 'tax efficient' or replaced with an alternative scheme as mentioned. [**www.roads.detr.gov.uk**]

The Contributions Agency confirmed that the car would not be regarded as unavailable for use when the employee/director is disqualified from driving, nor when he is on an overseas business trip lasting more than 30 days, unless the car is in fact no longer available to the employee/director or his family. (*Letter from CA to local General Practitioners Group*).

The same rules apply for Class 1A purposes except that a car is *not* to be regarded as unavailable for a day under (iii) above unless the person liable to pay the Class 1A contribution has information to show that the condition specified at (iii) is satisfied as regards the day in question. [*SSCBA 1992, s 10(6)(a)*].

A specimen letter is shown below:

Benevolent Ltd

Kadette

....

....

Dear K,

Provision of company car and fuel

The company has decided that, with immediate effect, it shall no longer pro- vide you with company vehicle [. . .Reg . . .] for either business and/or private use.

You are required to return the vehicle .... [make, model] .... [Reg no.] .... to .... [Name] .... at .... [Location] .... by .... [Time] .... on .... [Date] .... along with all sets of ignition and related keys. You will wish to remove all personal possessions before doing so.

If, however, B Ltd obtains the letters above to show that car 1 was withdrawn at the same time that car 2 was provided and that business mileage in cars 1 and 2 had been proportionately over 18,000 business miles (thus bringing potential entitlement to a reduction to 15% of list price) the cash equivalent for Class 1A purposes will be as follows:

			£
Car 1	£16,000 × 15% × 122/365	=	802
Car 2	£20,000 × 15% × 243/365	=	1,997
Fuel 1	£2,170 × 122/365	=	725
Fuel 2	£2,170 × 243/365	=	1,445
			£4,969

58.21 CASE STUDY 7 — TONY HUDSON AND FRANCOIS DUBOIS

The take-over of the French company gives Benevolent Ltd a foot in Europe and the consequences of complying with European working practices. The work exchange between Mr Hudson and Monsieur Dubois is for a period of twelve months.

The DSS generally used to regard a person as continuing to be ordinarily resident in Great Britain where he is absent for up to five years, provided the intention to return is not abandoned. If the intention to return is abandoned during the five years, ordinary residence ceases. This is somewhat outdated now following the issue of NI138 and NI132 booklets. Where the absence extends, or is likely to extend, beyond five years, however, the DSS considered each case individually taking into account the intended length of absence, whether a home or accommodation is being maintained in Great Britain and whether personal effects and furniture are being stored or disposed of. This guidance was formerly given in Inland Revenue Leaflet NI 38, but current editions of the leaflet make no reference to a period of five years since that old rule is no longer used by NICO. In the case of Tony Hudson he is not going to be going abroad in excess of a twelve-month stay.

Unless the EC regulations or a reciprocal agreement is of application and provides to the contrary, anyone who falls to be categorised as an employed earner by reason of being gainfully employed in Great Britain (see 14.2 CATEGORISATION) is, subject to the exceptions stated below, to be liable for primary Class 1 contributions in respect of the earnings from his employment if, at the time of his employment, he is

(a) resident in Great Britain; or

(b) present or but for any temporary absence would be present in Great Britain; or

(c) ordinarily resident in Great Britain.

[*Contributions Regs, Reg 119(1)(a)*].

It should be noted that the fact that a person's contract of employment may be made under foreign law or that his employer may be located overseas is irrelevant. It is the location in which a person works that determines where he is gainfully employed.

Where an employed earner would be liable to pay contributions under this rule by reason of falling within (a) or (b) above, but does not fall within (c), no primary or secondary Class 1 liability is to arise in respect of earnings from the employment until a continuous period of 52 weeks of residence have elapsed beginning with the contribution week following the date of his last entry into Great Britain, provided

(i) he is *not ordinarily employed* in Great Britain, and

(ii) the employment concerned is *mainly* employment *outside the UK* by an employer whose *place of business* is *outside the UK* (whether or not he also has a place of business in the UK).

[*Reg 119(2)*].

In the context of employment law, it has been said that in deciding where a person ordinarily works one should look at the terms of his contract, express or implied, in order to ascertain where, looking at the whole period contemplated by the contract, his *base* is to be; and that, where the contract is of no assistance the matter should be resolved by looking at the conduct of the parties and the way they have operated the contract. It is suggested that this approach is equally valid in deciding whether or not a person is ordinarily employed in Great Britain.

Where a person is gainfully employed outside Great Britain in an employment which, were it in Great Britain, would be an employed earner's employment, that employment is to be *treated as* an employed earner's employment and primary and secondary Class 1 liabilities are to arise in respect of the person's earnings for the employment if

(A) the employer has a place of business in Great Britain; and

(B) the earner is ordinarily resident in Great Britain; and

(C) immediately before the commencement of the employment the earner was resident in Great Britain.

Such liability will continue, however, only during the period of 52 contribution weeks from the beginning of the contribution week in which the overseas employment commenced. [*Reg 120(1)(2)*].

The 52 weeks of continuing liability are, according to NICO, to include weeks of sickness or leave or temporary duty for which the employee is remunerated. This is surely correct. The DSS previously asserted that weeks of *unpaid* leave in GB were not to be included—an assertion which seemed wrong in law. The August 1995 and subsequent editions of Leaflet NI 132, the latest being April 1999, now agree that the 52 week period of liability is *not* extended if periods of unpaid leave fall within it (page 8). Again, the DSS formerly asserted that where an employee was to return abroad after a remunerated period of sickness or leave in GB and the 52 weeks of continuing liability came to an end before or during that leave, etc. Class 1 liability would be treated as arising again after the leave, etc. had lasted for 26 weeks and that a further 52 week period of liability would begin—even if no actual duties had been performed in GB. Again there appeared to be no grounds in law for imposing such liabilities since paid leave in the UK does not bring the employment outside the UK to an end. Leaflet NI 132 (August 1995 edition onwards) is no longer so presumptive and seems to suggest that a fresh period of 52 week liability will only occur when:

(I) a quite separate and distinct secondment abroad takes place, or

(II) the return to the UK is other than on temporary duty, incidental to the overseas employment (e.g. a briefing or further training), or

(III) the return to the UK is other than on temporary duty, *not* incidental to the overseas employment but the stay in the UK is for six weeks or less.

The period of six weeks mentioned above does not have the force of law but it is admitted in the leaflet to be a concession to ease administration.

Where an earner such as Francois Dubois who is employed in the territory of one member state by an undertaking to which he is normally attached is sent by his employer to work in another member state, he is to remain subject to the contribution laws of the first state provided that

(*a*) the period of employment in the second state is not expected to last for a period in excess of twelve months; and

(*b*) he is not being sent to replace another person whose period of employment in the second state is at an end.

[*EC Reg 1408/71, Art 14(1)(a)*].

An earner is employed in the territory of one member state if the relationship between him and the person paying him is that of employer and employee and the employment commenced in that state. It is irrelevant that the employee may have been engaged for the sole purpose of working in the second state and that the employer may have had an existing commitment to supply labour in that second state. It is sufficient that a direct relationship continues to exist between the employer and the employee. (Administrative Commission Decision 128 OJ 1986 C 141 but see below as this decision has been superseded by AC Admin Decision 162).

58.22 NICs compliance undertakings

Both the departing and arriving employees will be covered by the EC Regulations and E101s will be needed. That for Tony Hudson will need to be obtained from International Services, National Insurance Contributions Office, Newcastle and that for Monsieur Dubois from the equivalent French authorities.

The earnings upon which Class 1 liabilities continue to arise are the gross earnings from the employment concerned (converted into their sterling equivalent, if necessary, at the rate of exchange applicable at the date of payment) irrespective of where, or by whom, those earnings are paid. [**www.inlandrevenue.gov.uk/nic/intserv/osc.htm**].

Example

Tony Hudson, who is employed by B Ltd in the UK, is seconded to Le Gift, B's Paris subsidiary, for twelve months. He is paid £1,800 a month by B Ltd and 5,000 FF by Le Gift. On the date of his first payment by B Ltd and Le Gift, the exchange rate is 9.5 FF to the £. His earnings for Class 1 contribution purposes are £526.31 + £1,800. The actual exchange rate needs to be similarly dealt with on the occasion of future payments where Class 1 liability exists.

Tony Hudson's continuing liability to pay contributions under the contribution legislation of the member state in which he was employed, i.e. the UK, before being posted to another member state is certified by the first member state on a form E101. UK employers must therefore apply to International Services in Newcastle for the certificate, using new versions of forms CA3821 and CA3822 obtained from them. It is often International Services practice, where an employer applies for an E101 certificate for the first time, to ask the local Inland Revenue (NIC) office to visit the employer to verify the information given in the application.

In the event of the period of employment unexpectedly exceeding twelve months, the contribution laws of the first state may continue to apply for a further period of up to twelve months provided a request that that might be so is made to the appropriate authority in the second state before the first period of twelve months has elapsed and provided that the authority consents to the extension, certified on form E102. Consent cannot, however, be given for an extension in excess of twelve months unless the two states have entered into a special agreement permitting longer extensions and have notified the Commission of the Communities of that agreement. [*Arts 14(1)(b), 17*].

In accordance with *Art 14(1)* and *Art 14b (1)* and the judgments of the European Court cited above, therefore, NICO takes the view that

'consideration can only be given to the provision of a form E101 (by this Department) where either,

(*a*)   a person has been sent to another EEA country in continuation of his United Kingdom employment, i.e. has been sent abroad by the employer he normally works for in the United Kingdom, *or*

(*b*)   a person has been recruited in the United Kingdom with a view to immediate employment elsewhere within the EEA by a United Kingdom employer who normally carries out activities in this country comparable to those upon which the person sent abroad is to be employed and there is a direct relationship between the United Kingdom employer and the person concerned during his employment in the other EEA country. If the services of the person are hired to an undertaking in another EEA country and that undertaking makes the person's services available to another undertaking, then the direct relationship will be deemed to have broken and United Kingdom social security legislation will not be applicable.'

These quotations are taken from the standard response to a request for the issue of a form E101 in circumstances where the direct relationship between employer and employee appears to International Services to have been broken. This view reflects the contents of Decision 128 referred to above. They are of particular relevance to the not-infrequently encountered arrangement under which the services of a UK national are made available, on a labour-only subcontract basis, to an EEA undertaking through an EEA intermediary, but where the whole arrangement is channelled, for tax purposes, through a 'one-man' company formed in the UK to 'employ' and 'post overseas' the UK national concerned.

Where an employment situation meets the criteria of International Services set out above, a form E101 will be issued provided the employer of the employed earner concerned supplies International Services with the full details of the posting.

This is now usually done by completing the application forms CA3821 and CA3822 obtainable from International Services.

In addition to the certificate E101 confirming continuing liability to contributions under the British scheme the NICO will issue a certificate E128 confirming entitlement to full health care cover for the worker and any accompanying family. It is not a registration form but is presented at the time health care treatment is required. An application for any extension of the period of continuing liability should be made in quadruplicate on form E102, available from International Services. (See 'National Insurance Contributions and the European Connection').

International Services follows the recommendation in granting E101 coverage for up to five years where it is satisfied that the various conditions laid down in *ACR 16* are met. It is understood that, in exceptional circumstances, an even longer extension may be granted. This does, however, also require the consent of the authorities in the other state concerned. In the case of some states considerable delays can occur.

Extensions under *Art 17* are available in appropriate circumstances wherever an EEA national moves within the EEA. On 12 December 1984, the Administrative Commission on Social Security for Migrant Workers recommended to all member states that they should 'conclude . . . agreements pursuant to Article 17 . . . applicable to employed persons who, by virtue of their special knowledge and skills or because of special objectives set by the undertaking . . . with which they are employed are posted abroad to a member state other than the one in which they are normally employed . . . for a period exceeding 12 months. These agreements should lay down that these employed persons remain subject to the legislation of the sending state for the full duration of their assignment provided that the workers concerned agree to this condition'. [*ACR 16*]. Where an earner such as Francois Dubois is employed in the territory of one member state (France) by an undertaking to which he is normally attached is sent by his employer to work in another member state (UK), he is to remain subject to the contribution laws of the first state provided that

(*a*) the period of employment in the second state is not expected to last for a period in excess of twelve months; and

(*b*) he is not being sent to replace another person whose period of employment in the second state is at an end.

[*EC Reg 1408/71, Art 14(1)(a)*].

58.23 **NICs Planning**

It is frequently the case that where a UK company such as Benevolent Ltd posts one of its employees overseas, liability for Class 1 contributions on that employee's earnings is to continue by reason of the rules laid down in *Contributions Regs, Reg 120(1)(2), EC Reg 1408/71, Art 14(1)(a)*, or in the reciprocal agreement (if any) between the UK and the country to which the employee is posted. Until 6 October 1985, this presented an employer with few difficulties as the secondary Class 1 contribution liability was limited to contributions on earnings at the upper earnings limit, however great the employee's earnings might be. Following the removal of the upper earnings limit for secondary Class 1 contribution purposes on 6 October 1985, however, the position changed completely. Expatriate remuneration arrangements are usually such as to compensate the employee for cost of living, accommodation, child education, and taxation increases, and such compensation will usually result in the employee's gross pay entitlement being significantly larger than that of his UK counterpart.

Example

If Hudson worked for Benevolent Ltd at a salary of £21,600 p.a. when he is posted to France for a period of twelve months then to maintain his earnings/standard of living level at the equivalent of £21,600, he should, while working in France, be paid £39,000 p.a. B's increased contribution costs are £2,123, being 12.2% × (£39,000 – £21,600). Had the upper earnings limit remained applicable for secondary Class 1 contribution purposes, there would have been a smaller increased cost as H's earnings, whether at the UK level or at the French equivalent, would have been limited to £27,820 for all contribution purposes, as they so remain for employees contributions.

Faced with increases of this order, UK companies operating on an international level may now need to consider breaking the direct relationship between themselves and the employees whom they wish to post overseas, and to arrange for such employees to terminate their employment and to enter employment overseas with, for example, an expatriate employment bureau or an overseas associated or subsidiary company which has no place of business in Great Britain. In the above example if the UK company paid £27,820 and the balance was paid from the French company the balance may not be liable to PAYE.

If the direct relationship is not broken, then the UK employer will no doubt wish to exclude as much of the increased cost from earnings for NIC purposes as possible. Overseas payments and allowances may, however, be excluded from earnings only if they are specific and distinct payments of or contributions towards such items as hotel accommodation, meals, clothing or if they are payments made in accordance with a scheme that complies with the requirements laid down in connection with a subsistence allowance scheme. NICs should be charged on payments described as compensation for working abroad (i.e. not business expenses), inducements, or bonuses for working abroad as well as COLAs (see 28.50 EARNINGS and DSS 1996 Leaflet CA 28, Page 91, Items (100) and (101), CA 28 Supplement (1996) April 1996, page 8). The practice followed by some companies of calculating contribution liabilities only on the notional UK equivalent of earnings paid to an employee who has been posted overseas is incorrect and has no foundation in law or International Services practice. The authorities are aware of the practice of accounting for contributions on such 'phantom salaries' and are assessing arrears due in appropriate cases.

58.24 CASE STUDY 8 — ANGELA BRANSDON-SMITH

Mrs Bransdon-Smith has provided corporate hospitality services for Benevolent Ltd since 27 October 2000 where the entertaining involved organising both in-house and outside hospitality events for customers and staff. Mrs Bransdon-Smith has a HND in 'Corporate and Personal Hospitality Studies' as well as having worked as an airhostess in previous years before setting up her self–employed business. The wages clerk at Benevolent Ltd has been told by Mr Bransdon-Smith that all payments for work undertaken by his wife should be paid 'gross' to his wife.

58.25 NICs compliance undertakings

The wages clerk at Benevolent Ltd has written to the NICO asking for their determination on the employment status of the Managing Director's wife who is to provide consultancy [**www.inlandrevenue.gov.uk/ir35/index.htm**] services to the company for the period 27 October 2000 to 15 April 2001. The NICO replies to the wages officer as follows:

Dear Sir,

Under the provisions of Section 2(1)(a) of the Social Security Contributions and Benefits Act 1992 ('the 1992 Act') the distinction between employed earner's employment and self-employment depends mainly on the existence of a contract of service.

Where there is a contract of service then, in general, the person is regarded as an employee.

A contract of service need not be in writing. Section 122 of the 1992 Act provides that it can also be an oral agreement and can be an expressed one or one implied from the working arrangements.

There is however no precise legal definition of what constitutes a contract of service, i.e. what makes the relationship in law between the two parties that of employer and employee.

The National Insurance Contributions Office relies on principles established from the case law of the Courts over many years and applies these to the facts of the individual case concerned.

Some of the facts which the Courts consider important are:

1.   is the person in business on their own account;

2.   must the person give personal service for which they are paid;

3.   can the 'employer' control what the person does, when they do it and how they do it, even if the control is not exercised;

4.   is the person part and parcel of the 'employer's' business or organisation;

5.   does the person supply tools, equipment and materials and, if so, to what extent;

6.   who makes a profit or loss from work;

7.   is the person paid for the job or for the hours or days they work;

8.   can the 'employer' select, suspend or dismiss the person; and

9.   is the self-employment the intention of both parties.

The National Insurance Contributions Office weighs all the factors in a working relationship, including those mentioned above, before deciding if a contract of service exists.

A person may say that they are self-employed or work on a casual basis but this does not alter the fact that if the work is carried out under conditions which amount to a contract of service the person is an employed earner under the 1992 Act.

Our ruling

In this case Jennifer Bransdon-Smith

I consider the weight of evidence of these factors in the working relationship between 27 October 2000 and 15 April 2001 shows that there is a contract of service.

National Insurance contributions and income tax may be payable on a different basis.

Keep this letter safe in a case you have to show it to the Inland Revenue tax office.

Further information

If you think this decision or ruling is incorrect, please let us know, in writing within 28 days. Please include:

- reasons why you think it is wrong and

- any further information and/or documentation which you think is relevant.

Letter continues

CA National Insurance News, summer 1997 page 4 states that if new information is put forward the CA, as it then was, will consider whether the ruling can be changed. If not, there is a right to have the matter formally considered by the Tax Commissioners on appeal (see 9 APPEALS AND REVIEWS).

58.26 NICs planning

Assuming that Angela Bransdon-Smith fails the 'badges of trade' test then she is likely to be classed as an employee. See IR Schedule E Manual, paras SE 635–701. Tax case law may provide sustainable argument that indeed Mrs Bransdon-Smith is self-employed. In the case of *Express and Echo Publications v Tanton* (see 14.5 CATEGORISATION) the issue of substitution is important and the requirement for Mrs Bransdon-Smith to provide a substitute in case of sickness or holiday would be an important factor. The consequences of Angela Bransdon-Smith being classified as having always been an employee will result in current and retrospective PAYE and NICs being payable. There may also be penalties and interest involved as well. The fact that Mrs Bransdon-Smith is the wife of the director should not be a bar to putting a (arguable) case for self-employment status. The case may not be clear cut and the Inland Revenue may be prepared to concede earlier years' (only one in this case!) self-employed status for current and future Schedule E and Class 1 NICs treatment. Such a recategorisation under Schedule E will be inevitably more costly from a PAYE and NICs aspect. However, the use of NICs-free benefits, pension payments, share schemes in the future may compensate for the potential switch from self–employment to employment recategorisation.

58.27 CASE STUDY 9 — PAYE/NICs AUDIT

On 7 April 2001 the Large Employer's Compliance Unit, 'Full Audit' Department, notifies Benevolent Ltd that it will be making a visit for PAYE/NIC audit purposes as follows:

PAYE, NATIONAL INSURANCE AND DEDUCTIONS FROM SUBCONTRACTORS INSPECTION OF EMPLOYERS/CONTRACTORS RECORDS

It is proposed to inspect the records of Benevolent Ltd and the subsidiary companies which form the group [if applicable].

As an inspection may present certain practical problems, I would welcome the opportunity to discuss the matter at a preliminary meeting. It would be helpful if the following information could be made available at the meeting.

Locations of subsidiaries holding records such as payrolls, petty cash vouchers, expenses claims and so on.

The name and telephone number of a contact at each location together with the status of that person.

The approximate number of employees at each location.

The PAYE reference numbers for each location operating a payroll (as shown in the Inland Revenue payslip booklet).

Whether any of the locations have been the subject of a previous inspection.

The Tax District which deals with Group's Corporation tax and the reference number.

Would you please advise me of the date and time, if possible between [date] and [date], when it would be convenient for a preliminary meeting to take place with you or an appropriate officer of the company.

When this information is available, would you please contact me to arrange a convenient date and time for a preliminary meeting with you or an appropriate officer of the company.

I enclose a copy of the Inland Revenue's Code of Practice regarding the inspection of Employers' and Contractors' records.

OFFICER IN CHARGE

On 15 April two members of staff from the Audit section arrive and commence to inspect the records with the payroll manager, accountant and a personnel officer of Benevolent Ltd. It turns out that the visit has been precipitated by four factors: (a) the lack of NINOs on P46s (b) the decision relating to Mrs Bransdon-Smith (see **[Case Study 8]**) (c) persistent late filing of end of year forms and (d) the possible back tax and NICs for the school fees paid by the company for the Bransdon-Smith child. See **[Case Study 4]**.

The factors that arise during the investigation of the records and procedures at Benevolent Ltd are:

(a) CWG1 (2000), Card 3 states that where an employer is unable to find the employee's number 'keep a record of their full name *surname and forenames,* address, date of birth, sex **and** ... send a form P46 to the Tax office. Investigation shows that no records have been kept prior to the sending of the P46s to the Tax Office;

(b) The self-employment categorisation of Mrs Bransdon-Smith is incorrect and she should be classed as an employee of Benevolent Ltd with the consequence that there is a shortfall of Class 1 contributions for the relevant periods concerned;

(c) The persistent late filing of the end of year returns may have been due to very good reasons but the penalty for late filing has resulted in the audit;

(d) The possible back tax and NICs exigible regarding the school fees contract may be subject of appeal but the issue of the decision **[Case Study 4]** means that subject to an appeal being successful the £11,220 (i.e. £55,490 – £44,270) is payable.

The payment of the Director's child's school fees has naturally led to an enquiry and led to a decision to charge the company in respect of the Class 1 NICs. See below for Form DAA1(A).

58.28 NICs compliance undertakings

Decisions are issued on Form DAA1(A) (see 9 APPEALS AND REVIEWS) [www.inlandrevenue.gov.uk/nic/class1/appeals.htm] and it tells the recipient to let their professional adviser or agent, if they have one, see it. Copies will be issued direct to agents, if acting. Where copies have to be sent to more than one person, the notes on the face of the notice will be varied on each copy to reflect the differing effects of the decision on different categories of people affected, e.g. where copies are sent to employers and one or more employees. The Notice of Decision also includes a payslip for making payment of the National Insurance contributions in question and will be sent with a letter of explanation which will, in practice, usually be a summary of what has been established in previous correspondence. A guide, DAA2 'A Guide to Your Notice of Decision' will also be sent to every recipient.

INLAND REVENUE
B Ltd
10 Any Road
Any Town
Any County
AN10 2YZ

Date of Issue 1 April 2001

NOTICE OF DECISION
Inland Revenue (NI) Contributions Office
Class 1 Caseworker
Instructions and Planning Team
Room H2002
Longbenton
Newcastle Upon Tyne NE98 1YZ

Tel 0191 225 8159 Fax. 0191 225 8344
Reference
AB123456C

Please use this reference if you write or call it will help avoid delay

National Insurance contributions, Statutory Sick Pay or Statutory Maternity Pay

My decision is as follows:

1. That B Ltd is liable to pay primary and secondary Class 1 contributions for the period 6 April 1998 to 5 April 2000 in respect of the earnings of Mr Bransdon-Smith.

2. The amount that B Ltd is liable to pay in respect of those earnings is £55,490.

3. The amount that B Ltd has paid in respect of those earnings is £44,270.

4. The difference is due to Class 1 contributions on school fees.

A N Other
Officer of the Board

Notes
General
This Notice of Decision is addressed to you personally as required by law. If you have a professional adviser or agent Please let them see this notice at once.

This notice contains my formal decision. You will find details of how the decision has been reached and additional information in the accompanying letter and/or *DAA2 Guide*, 'A Guide to your Notice of Decision'.

Payment
If you accept this decision please pay any outstanding amount of National Insurance contributions due from you using the enclosed payslip. Pay any Statutory Sick Pay or Statutory Maternity Pay to the employee.
DAA1(A)

Appeals
If you do not accept this decision please appeal telling us why you think the decision is wrong. The appeal must be made in writing to me within 30 days of the date of issue shown above.

If agreement cannot be reached we will arrange for your appeal and any other appeal to be heard by the Appeal Commissioners who are an independent tribunal. See page 4 of the *DAA2 Guide*.

Variation of Decision
A decision is varied when agreement has been reached or the decision is incorrect. See page 6 of the *DAA2 Guide*.

Interest Charges on late payment
Interest may be charged on National Insurance Contributions paid late. See page 6 of the *DAA2 Guide*.

58.29 **NICs planning**

With regard to the ruling in both (b) and (d) above in 58.28 there is the opportunity for an appeal to be lodged against the decisions. The CA National Insurance News, Summer 1997, page 4 states that if new information is put forward CA, as it then was, will consider whether the ruling can be changed. If not, there is a right to have the matter formally considered by the Tax Commissioners on appeal (see 9 APPEALS AND REVIEWS).

Benevolent Ltd should take advantage of the Payroll Cleansing department of the Inland Revenue. This is a service for large payrolls and this contact should be done before the next end of year return is submitted.

Each employee on the payroll will have their name, national insurance number, date of birth, etc. provided to the Payroll Cleansing department at King's Lynn (tel. 01553 666866) or at Newcastle (tel. 0191 225 6110). The information supplied by Benevolent Ltd will then be compared with each individual's National Insurance identity information held on the Departmental Central Index. Any discrepancies or omissions are investigated and corrected. The advantage to Benevolent Ltd is that after such a check the end of year return submitted is accurate with regard to existing employees.

For the employees the advantage is that their National Insurance account will be fully up to date (address, contributions for benefits/pension is correct) after the cleanse.

59   National Insurance News Extracts

Note.—The Contributions Agency NI News extracts were published by kind permission of the Contributions Agency. NI News is no longer published following the merger between the Inland Revenue and Contributions Agency. National Insurance matters are included in editions of the Tax Bulletin from time to time. Interpretations of the law contained within it will normally be applied in relevant cases, but this is subject to a number of qualifications. Individual cases may turn on their own facts, or context, and because not every possible situation can be covered, there may be circumstances in which the interpretation given here will not apply. The Inland Revenue's view of the law might change in the future. In the event of any change, readers will be notified in future editions.

Autumn/Winter 1994 – Issue 2 NI News extracts

Cash alternatives to company cars – Liability for Class 1A NICs

Where employees are provided with company cars which are available for private use, they are usually taxed on the benefit of the car under the special income tax rules contained in TA 1988 s 157 under s 10 SSCBA 1992, the employer is required to pay Class 1A contributions on the benefit of a car which is taxable under TA 1988 s 157.

In some instances, where the benefit of the car is freely convertible into cash, the benefit of providing a car is taxable under the general income tax rules rather than the special provisions for company cars. This leaves no amount chargeable under the special company cars rules so that liability for Class 1A NICs does not arise.

By adopting these cash alternative schemes, some employers have avoided their Class 1A NIC liability.

To prevent further loss to the National Insurance Fund new legislation is to be introduced. This will ensure that—

- where a car would otherwise be within the special income tax rules for company cars; and

- a cash alternative to the benefit is offered,

the fact that the alternative is offered will not make the benefit of the car chargeable under the normal income tax rules. The employer will pay NICs on what the employee actually gets, Class 1A NICs if they have the benefit of a car or Class 1 NICs if they take the cash.

The new legislation is intended to apply from 6 April 1995.

When the new legislation receives Royal Assent, liability will exist from 6 April 1995 in respect of all employees, including those who leave between the start of the 1995–96 tax year and the date on which the proposed legislation becomes law. This means that employers will be liable for Class 1A National Insurance Contributions (NICs) in respect of those employees who leave the employment after 6 April 1995 but prior to Royal Assent being given.

Current rules will apply to companies which operate cash alternatives schemes and who cease to trade before the new legislation becomes law.

The Agency intends to publicise this change in a supplement to leaflet CA 33 'Car and fuel manual for employers' which will be included with the annual NIC pack in February/March 1995.

National Insurance Numbers

The National Insurance (NI) number is the unique reference number we use to identify a customer's NI contribution record. It is used to make sure that NI contributions paid by and credited to a customer are put on the right record so that they get the correct benefit when they make a claim.

Employers are responsible for putting employees' NI numbers on the deduction working documents. To help us ensure contributions are put on the correct record we also ask them to put the number on their end of year summaries (forms P14 etc) before they send them off to the Inland Revenue or Contributions Agency. It is therefore important that they ask employees to tell them their number as soon as possible after they start work.

Where an employee does not produce a NI number shortly after starting work, employers can ask the local Contributions Agency office to find the number for them. The leaflet NI 269 *'National Insurance contributions—Manual for employers'*, tells employers what information to give the local Contributions Agency when they need to use the tracing service.

Employers who use computerised payroll systems and need a number to put a new employee onto their system can create a temporary number. They do this by using the letters TN followed by the employee's date of birth and then the letter M or F according to sex. Thus the temporary number for a woman born on 16 November 1977 would be TN161177F, and that for a man born on 6 May 1978 would be TN060578M. Whilst this temporary number is useful for payroll purposes we still need a proper NI number when returns are made at the end of the year. Employees are under an obligation imposed by Regulations to give NI number to their employers and all employers should therefore ensure that their employees comply with this obligation. We have recently received a number of letters which suggest that some employers believe that new employees must have a NI number before they can be taken on. Whilst this might be considered useful, there is no legal requirement for a number to be provided or even for the employee to apply for one before employment begins. Some of these letters also reveal that there are misunderstandings about the significance of a NI number. The NI number card which we issue should not be accepted by anyone as evidence of a person's identity. Nor does the possession of such a number confirm anyone's right to work, or even to be in this country. Earners are required to apply to us for a number and when we issue one, we do so purely on the basis of it being needed for our business. It is not a 'passport' to employment.

Spring/Summer 1995 – Issue 3 NI News Extracts

The treatment of expenses payments for NICs purposes

In response to feedback from employers and their advisers, the Agency has carried out a review to clarify the position and improve its guidance in respect of evidence to substantiate expenses for NICs purposes.

Legal advice has indicated that particular practises adopted by the Agency in the past may have been incorrect, particularly with regard to petrol and telephone expenses.

The law

Class 1 NICs are calculated on the amounts of earnings. In order to be earnings a payment must constitute salary or other personal benefit or gain to an employee, and be derived from employment.

The reimbursement of an expense which an employee incurs in carrying out his employment does not represent any profit or gain, so does not constitute earnings. Regulation 19(4)(*b*) of the Social Security (Contributions) Regulations 1979 confirms this, providing:

'For the avoidance of doubt, in the calculation of earnings paid to or for the benefit of an earner in respect of any employed earner's employment, there shall be disregarded—

(b) any specific and distinct payment of, or contribution towards, expenses actually incurred by an employed earner in carrying out his employment.'

This ensures that payments made to cover business expenses incurred by an employee can be excluded from gross pay for NICs purposes. Payments from employment which are made to cover other personal expenses are gains or benefits to the employee, and therefore earnings which do have to be included in gross pay.

Evidence identifying business expenses

Class 1 NICs are payable to the Secretary of State, who is entitled to receive what is due to be paid. Although the onus is on employers to ensure that NICs are calculated on the right amount of earnings, the Secretary of State is equally entitled to verify that the calculation has been based on the correct amount of earnings.

To provide this verification employers need to ensure they have evidence to identify the business expenses actually incurred, and so demonstrate:

- the amount of the expenses involved;
- that the expenses were incurred as part of the employee's work; and therefore
- that the amount disregarded was correctly excluded from gross pay.

The type of evidence clearly depends upon the individual item(s) of business expenditure. It may be, for example:

- a log of business telephone calls or visits;
- credit card bills.

Other acceptable evidence includes:

- receipts;
- work diaries showing engagements etc;
- representative surveys of the costs involved;
- Inland Revenue dispensations.

This list is not exhaustive and other forms of evidence will be considered.

Inland Revenue dispensations

The inclusion of Revenue dispensations in the above list of examples follows an announcement made by the Secretary of State for Social Security on 30 November 1994. As part of a package aimed at aligning more closely the NICs and income tax systems, it was announced that employers would be allowed to take account of Inland Revenue dispensations. Provided the circumstances under which the dispensation was issued have not changed, it may be used as evidence to prove that the payments it covers are expenses incurred in carrying out the employer's business and not earnings for NICs purposes.

Previous practices

In the past the Agency generally held that maintenance of a log was the only acceptable way for an employee to identify the amount of business calls made or business miles travelled. This view was reflected in the guidance issued to both Agency staff and employers. But it is now accepted that the Agency was wrong to be so prescriptive about the type of evidence required to identify and quantify business expenses. As legal advice has indicated, if a log has not been kept the Agency could and should have considered other evidence identifying the amount of business calls or miles. The Agency will in future take account of such evidence. Moreover, any employer who thinks it can be shown that NICs have been overpaid because a log was not maintained and that the Agency did not take account of other acceptable evidence held, should now contact the Contributions Agency through their local Social Security office. Acceptance of Inland Revenue dispensations also reflects a change in the Agency's approach to the type of evidence needed to identify business expenses. Any employer who thinks it can be shown that NICs were previously paid on payments covered by a dispensation which, in the light of the revised approach, should not have been paid should also contact the Agency.

Autumn/Winter 1995 – Issue 4 NI News extracts

Class 1A NICs: List price of cars

If you provide a director or employee, or member of their family or household, with a car which they can use privately you may have to pay Class 1A NICs.

Class 1A NICs due from 6 April 1994 are based on a car's price. The starting point for this is usually the manufacturer's, importer's or distributor's list price of the car on the day before it was first registered. Delivery charges and taxes such as VAT and car tax (up to 12 November 1992), but not vehicle excise duty (road tax), are included in the price. So is the list price of qualifying accessories and the cost of fitting them.

As an employer, it is up to you to ensure that Class 1A NICs are based on the correct "list price". Contribution Agency Inspectors are entitled to verify that you have done so. We do not believe in dictating what records you should keep, but you can help our Inspectors (and yourself!) if you have some evidence to support your calculations. The purchase invoice for the vehicle will usually be taken as the best evidence of all. But other helpful pointers include:

- specialist lists of prices in book form or computer disk (eg, as published by Glass's Guide Services Limited);

- organisations offering specialist services providing prices for list of cars (eg GAP Nationwide Motor Research Limited);

- price lists from manufacturer's or importer's special telephone contact points, (eg Ford and Vauxhall);

- leasing companies, some of whom are providing advice on prices for client companies.

Cars are treated as "classic" cars if they are 15 years old or more with an open market value of at least £15,000 and this exceeds their original list price. Values may be arrived at from recent valuations (eg for insurance purposes) or prices in the market, or published prices.

For second hand cars, Class 1A NICs are calculated in the same way as for new cars. Because is usually harder to find records of list prices and accessories for second hand cars, we will wherever possible accept the reported price used for tax purposes.

Personal incidental expenses and employee liabilities and indemnity insurance

New regulations made in June bring the treatment of tax and NI closer together on payments made by employers in respect of employees' *personal incidental expenses and liabilities* and *indemnity insurance*.

Personal incidental expenses

Employees staying away from home overnight whilst on business often incur personal incidental expenses which are met either wholly or in part by their employer. Common examples are newspapers, laundry and telephone calls home.

Up until now these *should* normally have been treated as earnings on which NI contributions are due. Such payments will no longer attract liability. This change is intended to ease the burden on employers and will cover *any* personal incidental expenses (including alcoholic drinks) paid by employers *within prescribed limits*.

These limits are:

- £5 for overnight stays within the United Kingdom, and

- £10 for overnight stays outside the United Kingdom.

The exemptions cover all possible ways in which employers pay for employees' personal incidental expenses O payments by non cash vouchers, credit tokens (eg credit cards), benefits in kind (eg where the employer arranges with a hotel to pay the hotel bill) and cash payments (eg allowances, reimbursed expenses or where the employer meets the employees' bills).

The prescribed limits must be strictly observed. Any payment made in excess of them renders the *whole* amount subject to NI contributions. The only variation to this is where an employee spends more than one night away from home in an unbroken run of consecutive nights. In that case, it is the aggregate of personal incidental expenses paid that matters.

For example, say an employee spends 4 nights away from home and claims £5, £5, £6, and £4 respectively. Although the claim for only one of those nights exceeds £5, the total NIC free amount claimable for the 4 night period is £20, ie 4 x £5. But, if the aggregate of £21 for all 4 nights is claimed, then the whole amount would be subject of NICs.

The aggregation rule can apply only to an unbroken run of consecutive nights. Employers may not choose to break-up a period of (say) 5 nights into one consecutive period of 4 nights plus one "stand alone" night. All consecutive nights away must be taken together in determining whether the exemption applies.

Employee Liabilities Insurance/Uninsured Liabilities

Some employees and company directors take out liability insurance, or they meet the cost of uninsured liabilities in connection with the work they do for their employer. Examples of this are Director's and Officer's liability insurance, and professional indemnity insurance. The objective is to cover themselves against possible claims being made against them personally by third parties.

Employers who reimburse an employee's liabilities insurance premiums, or meet the cost of uninsured liabilities, *should* in many cases have been treating those payments as earnings for NIC purposes. The new regulations mean that such payments become NIC free. This change mirrors an Inland Revenue easement exempting such payments from liability to tax.

Legislation

The regulations — Social Security (Contributions) Amendment (No 5) Regulations 1995 (SI 1995 1570) came in to force on 18 July 1995. Regulation 2 inserts regulations 19(1)*(s)* and 19(1)*(t)* into the principal Contributions Regulations, the Social Security (Contributions) Regulations 1979.

Regulation 19(1)*(s)* provides that there shall be excluded from the computation of a person's earnings for NI contributions purposes:

- a payment which by virtue of TA 1988 s 200A (incidental overnight expenses) is not regarded as an emolument of the employment chargeable to income tax under Schedule E.

Regulations 19(1)*(t)* provides that there shall be excluded from the computation of a person's earnings for NI contributions purposes:

- a payment which by virtue of TA 1988 s 201AA (employee liabilities and indemnity insurance) is deductible from the emoluments of the employments chargeable to income tax under Schedule E.

Autumn 1996 – Issue 6 NI News extracts

Construction industry encouraged to get their house in order

The Contributions Agency is urging those in the building trade to get their house in order by taking a second look at the employment status of their workers.

To encourage more people in the industry to address their concern about this issue, the Contribution Agency and the Inland Revenue produced a joint IR148/CA69 leaflet "Are Your Workers Employed or Self Employed?" in October 1995.

Targeted at the construction industry this leaflet offers general guidance on how to determine if a worker should be treated as employed or self-employed.

Contribution Agency and Revenue officers have also recently been given guidance specifically covering this technical area.

Neither of these moves mean that the construction industry is about to become the subject of a purge by Inspectors. It does however mean that the construction industry is to be treated in the same way as any other industry, and that employment status be considered during the course of normal compliance visits.

While it recognised that there is still substantial scope for self-employment within the construction industry, not every worker falls into this category. Where doubts about status arise, compliance officers will investigate and rule accordingly. Where a ruling is made that a worker is an employee, PAYE tax and Class 1 contributions should be made.

If any arrears are identified they will be pursued from a date where it can be determined that the engager could have been expected to have put his house in order concerning status.

Unless there is evidence that payment has been deliberately evaded the Contributions Agency will not normally pursue payment for arrears in past years.

It should be stressed that it is the actual terms and conditions of engagement which determine employment status and that under this new approach it does *not* mean that all workers are considered to be employees.

Any ruling however is subject to challenge. Anyone not satisfied with a ruling on employment status does have the right to ask for a formal determination by the Secretary of State under section 17(1) of the Social Security Administration Act 1992. Further details are given in leaflet CA64 "Dissatisfied with our Ruling."

Reduced rate contributions for married women

Prior to 11 May 1977, married women and certain widows could elect to pay a reduced rate NIC. While no new elections could be made after this date, existing elections can continue until one of the following terminating events occur:

- Termination of a marriage other than by widowhood, ie divorce, or annulment.
- Widow ceases to be a qualifying widow, ie no longer in receipt of Widows Benefit.
- No contributions are paid for two or more consecutive tax years.
- The woman voluntarily revokes her election.

An employer must be in possession of a valid Certificate of Election (CF383), before Reduced Rate Contributions are deducted. When an election ends, the Contributions Agency (CA) will request the return of the CF383 from the current employer, and advise them that full rate contributions are due.

One of the major problems for the Contributions Agency is caused by the payment of reduced rate contributions by women who have been divorced, and are therefore no longer entitled to pay reduced rate. This situation usually occurs because either this Agency or the employer are unaware of a change in marital status, and reduced rate contributions continue to be deducted, often for many years.

When reduced rate contributions have been paid in error, we have to undertake lengthy enquiries with both the contributor and the employer to establish which party is responsible for the debt. This is a costly, time consuming procedure for both the

Contributions Agency and the employer. As well as the extra work involved, there is also the possibility that the employer will be found to be responsible for any arrears, and this could ultimately result in legal proceedings to recover the debt.

What employers can do to help

As the secondary contributor, an employer will be held liable should reduced rate contributions be deducted without a valid certificate. Some of the most common reasons for certificates being invalid are as follows:

- A CF380 or C3F380A certificate, which was issued prior to 5 April 1980, is no longer valid except for women whose current employment began before 5 April 1980.

- The name shown on a certificate must exactly match that of the employee. If an employee is notified of a change in name for any reason, the certificate should be returned to the contributor, who should in turn contact the Contributions Agency.

- The certificate must not be used if either of the dates shown have passed. If an employer is presented with an expired certificate, you should return it to the contributor.

Many employers find it worthwhile to write, on an annual basis, to all employees who are paying reduced rate contributions. They:

- Remind them that reduced rate is no longer applicable after divorce.

- Remind them of the procedures they have in place for notifying any change in circumstances; and

- Request that they sign a statement to the effect that their election is still valid and there has been no change in their marital status.

If there is no response within a specified period, the employer automatically starts to deduct full rate.

If at a later date, it transpires that a woman has indeed ceased to be liable for reduced rate contributions, and the employer, having a set procedure in place, can prove that this information was withheld, then responsibility for any debt would lie with the employee and not the employer.

It therefore follows that it is beneficial for employers to set procedures in place for the notification of any change in the marital status of their personnel.

If you have any doubt about the validity of a reduced rate certificate, deduct full rate contributions and contact this Agency for further advice.

What CA can do to help

If you would like us to validate the election of any employee paying reduced rate contributions, please contact us with name, address and NI number of the employee concerned. Once we have confirmed that an employee is still eligible to pay reduced rate NICs, we will inform you in writing.

February 1997 – Issue 7 NI News extracts

NICs on shares

Shares and options were brought into NICs in 1991 but, until recently, certain own company shares and options remained excluded from NICs. Following the Chancellor's Budget announcement restricting the exclusion from PAYE for certain own company shares, the DSS has introduced matching NICs regulations.

NEW REGULATIONS—WITH EFFECT FROM 5 DECEMBER 1996

Narrowing of the exclusion for certain own company shares and options

The exclusion for certain shares and options has been further restricted. New regulations (SI 1996/3031) introduced with effect from 5 December 1996 limit the exclusion from NICs for payments by way of own company shares and the grant of share options. Payments which will continue to be excluded from NICs are those where the shares form part of the ordinary share capital of the secondary contributor or a company owning or controlling that secondary contributor; and they are,

- under schemes approved by the Inland Revenue under TA 1988, Sch 9;
- by way of unlisted shares, had options for unlisted shares, where no trading arrangements exist.

Shares

NICs must therefore be operated on any payment of earnings in the form of own company shares, provided they are outside an approved scheme, where the shares are tradeable assets. Shares will be tradeable assets if:

- the shares can be sold or otherwise realised on a recognised investment exchange, such as the Stock Exchange; or
- trading arrangements are in place in respect of the shares at the time the assessable income is provided.

Options

NICs must be operated on any payment of earnings in the form of the grant of an option over own company shares, provided outside an approved scheme, where the option or the underlying shares are tradeable assets. Shares and options will be tradeable assets if:

- they can be sold or otherwise realised on a recognised investment exchange, such as the Stock Exchange; or
- trading arrangements are in place at the time the assessable income is provided.

Shares obtained by exercising an option

Where an employee is paid by way of the grant of an option and later exercises that option to obtain shares, NICs are charged on the grant of the option (valued by reference to the shares) rather than on the shares eventually obtained by exercising the option.

Trading arrangements

Trading arrangements are any arrangements for the purpose of enabling the persons to whom the asset is provided to obtain an amount greater than, equal to or not substantially less than the expense incurred in the provision of the asset. They include arrangements put in place by employers, employee share option trusts or other bodies to create a market in the shares of an unlisted company.

How much is subject to NICs?

Where a payment of earnings is made in the form of shares the amount on which NICs must operated is as follows:

- The open market price. (If the asset is not quoted on a recognised exchange, the price which a reasonably prudent purchaser might pay if purchased at arm's length.)
- If listed on the Stock Exchange Daily Official list — the "quarter up value" or the "mid bargain point".
- If the Stock Exchange provides a more active market elsewhere — what it might reasonably be expected to fetch on that market where the asset is one which can

be sold on a recognised investment exchange and would not otherwise be NICable–the amount for which it is capable of being sold or realised on that exchange.

- Where the asset is one for which trading arrangements are in place — the amount obtained by the employee under those arrangements, or the valuation provisions above, which ever is the greater.

Where a payment of earnings is made in the form of an option for shares the amount on which NICs must operated is calculated by reference to the value of the shares on the day the option is conferred. A deduction may be made for the consideration for which the option is acquired.

Vouchers

The regulations also apply to NICs vouchers for those shares and options which have been brought into NICs.

Operation of NICs

Where should payments be recorded?

Payments of earnings in the form of shares or options should be included in gross earnings and entered on the deductions working sheet, or equivalent payroll record, for the pay period in which the payment occurs. NICs should be calculated in the normal way.

What can the NICs be deducted from?

NICs must be deducted from any actual payments (ie cash) made at the same time as the payment, and from any other actual payments paid later in the same pay period (such as monthly salary).

What if it is not possible to deduct all the NICs on the payment?

All the NICs due on the payment has to be accounted for to the Collector (along with ordinary PAYE deductions for that period) 14 days after the end of the pay period in which the payment was paid. Liability for primary and secondary NICs is in the first instance the liability of the employer. The employer may deduct the primary NICs from the employee. If the employer is unable to deduct sufficient primary NICs from the employee in the pay period the employer is responsible for the balance.

What should be included in end of year pay and tax details?

There are no special recording requirement for shares or options. The total of gross earnings from the P11 should be transferred to the P14, P35 and P60 and where appropriate P45s, to include the payment in the same way as other pay.

PAYE tax

The NICs regulations parallel changes to PAYE regulations introduced with effect from 27 November 1996 (SI 2969/1996). The tax changes are explained in the January issue of Tax Bulletin.

Reimbursement of the costs of school fees incurred by employees

Periodically, the Department is asked whether the reimbursement by employers of the cost of school fees incurred by their employees is *earnings* for NIC purposes, and whether this attracts liability for NICs.

There are many scenarios where such reimbursement might take place; one example might be the situation where an employee is seconded abroad. They may take their family with them, but their children are at a critical point in their education. The employee prefers the children to be educated in the UK, and decides to send them to boarding school. This example is mentioned only because it is the most common, but CA have received enquires where the circumstances have been very different.

As a general rule, NIC liability on the provision of the education and the payment of school fees depends on who has contracted with the school to provide the education, and who is liable to pay the fees.

Some employers and their advisers hold the view that payments such as these are never earnings. It is argued that the employee has not profited; all the employer has done is to assist with a personal cost to the employee to enable that employee to continue in their employment. In the case of the employee sent abroad who wants his children to continue their education in the UK, it might be argued that it is only reasonable that the employer should meet the cost, particularly if it is they who require the employee to work abroad.

The Department does not disagree with this; it is reasonable, and many employees do it. However, this does not detract from the fact that there is a benefit here to the employee and, depending upon the nature of the transaction in providing that benefit, there may be liability for NICs.

In effect, "remuneration or profit" includes anything an employee receives for giving their services. The payment is from the employment:

- the employment is the cause of the payment;
- the payment is made by the employer with an interest in the performance of the contract; and
- it is made in return for the employee's services.

It is a personal payment, an inducement to enter or continue in the employment, and therefore it is earnings.

There are other examples of payments made to employees to reimburse them of costs incurred to enable them to perform their duties; for example, home to work commuting costs, cost of living allowances, London weighting and so on. None of these are free of liability for NICs. Such payments are made to enable employees to perform their duties, but they are not costs incurred in carrying them out. Only those costs which are "..... *specific and distinct payment of, or contribution toward, expenses actually incurred in carrying out his employment.....*" may be excluded from the computation of earnings for NICs purposes — regulations 19(4)(*b*) of the Social Security (Contributions) Regulations 1979. Payments which cannot be *excluded* necessarily fall to be *included*.

Similar questions have been raised about the payment of school fees by an employer to an employee who has been seconded to the UK from abroad. Provided the employee is in employed earners employment in which there is liability for UK NICs, then the general rules are the same.

Current guidance appears in the "What is and is not included in gross pay" section of the Employers Manual on NICs, leaflet CA 28, paragraph 162(40) headed "Payment of bills".

Interest rates paid on late and overpaid NICs

Inland Revenue is to introduce regulations with effect from 31 January 1997 to alter the method of calculating interest rates for the purposes of late paid and overpaid tax. The present alignment of the rates of interest used for the purposes of tax and NICs is to continue and the revised rates resulting from the new method of calculation will apply also to NICs.

The method of calculating interest rates for income tax is set out in the Taxes (Interest Rate) Regulations 1989. The rates so calculated apply also to Class 1 and Class 1A NICs in view of Social Security Contributions and Benefits Act 1992 Sch 1 para 6(3), which provides for the rate of interest for NICs to be the rate prescribed for that purpose under FA 1989 s 178 (ie the rate calculated under regulation 3 of the Interest Rate Regulations). They also apply to Class 4 NICs in accordance with

Social Security Contributions and Benefits Act 1992 s 16, which provides for all the provisions of the Income Tax Acts to apply to such contributions.

At present, the method of calculating interest rates results in interest being charged on overdue tax and NICs and paid on overpaid tax and NICs which fall to be refunded at the same rate — currently 6.25%.

The change will mean that from 31 January 1997 the rate of interest applying to overdue tax and NICs will be different to that applying to tax and NICs which are overpaid. The rate charged on late paid tax and NICs will be nearer to the average rate for borrowing and the rate of interest paid on overpaid tax and NICs will be nearer to the average rate of return on deposits.

With effect from 31 January 1997, the rate chargeable on overdue sums will, on current bank rates, rise to 8.5% while the rate payable in connection with overpaid tax and NICs will fall to 4%.

Summer 1997 – Issue 8 NI News extracts

Construction industry – an update

Issue 6 of National Insurance News explained that in response to requests from construction industry representatives, the Contributions Agency and Inland Revenue had given information and advice to help contractors with the question of whether their workers were employed or self-employed. In November 1996, following further discussions with the industry representatives, Ministers announced additional measures to help the construction industry review the employment status of their workers–These included that:

- contractors would, where necessary, be given a reasonable time to review the employment status of workers and set up PAYE arrangements;

- all contractors were expected *to have completed* these reviews by 5 April 1997 at the latest, and where appropriate, be accounting for PAYE and NICs by that date;

- after 5 April 1997, where contractors are found not to be accounting for PAYE and NICs in respect of payments to employees, the Contributions Agency and Inland Revenue would normally seek payment of arrears back to 5 April 1997. Payment would be sought for earlier years only where there is a clear evidence of evasion;

- the present level of compliance visits by both the Contributions Agency and the Inland Revenue will be maintained.

- a telephone help line–(0345) 335588–would be available to provide general assistance for contractors and workers.

What happens next

By now contractors should have completed reviews of their workers' status and be accounting for PAYE/NICs where appropriate. Compliance staff from both the CA and Inland Revenue will be looking closely at employment status when visiting contractors to conduct compliance checks. They will expect reviews to have been carried out. Ongoing consultation and feedback from the industry has suggested workers may benefit from a better understanding of general NI issues. A further leaflet is to be issued to address workers' most common NI concerns.

Help in deciding

Substantial advice about employment status in the construction industry was given in issue 28 of the Inland Revenue's Tax Bulletin. This article also reflects the views of the Contributions Agency.

Agencies — a special case

There are specific provisions within the *Social Security (Categorisation of Earners) Regulations 1978*, which govern the NI liabilities of certain workers who provide their services through a labour agency. Provided the relevant conditions are satisfied, where a person gets work through an agency or other third party and is not an employee of the client, they are treated as an employee of the agency. This means that the agency is required to account for Class 1 NI Contributions in respect of payments to these workers.

In brief the relevant conditions are:

● there is a continuing financial relationship between the agency and worker and

● the worker has to give personal service and

● there is a right to supervise, direct or control the worker as to how the work is carried out (even if the client firm does not exercise this right).

Further information is contained in the leaflet CA25 'NI Contributions for Agencies and People Finding Work Through Agencies'.

The services of some workers are provided to contractors through labour agencies. The normal rule is that agencies must account for PAYE and NICs in relation to payments made to the workers whose services they provide. But where an agency provides the services of a worker in construction, and there is no contract of employment between the agency and worker or between the contractor and worker, there is no obligation to account for PAYE. Instead the agency may make payments with no tax deducted if the worker holds a valid 714 certificate and must deduct and account for SC60 tax from payments made to uncertified sub-contractors. *But agencies are obliged to account for Class 1 NICs, both primary and secondary, in respect of payments they make to construction workers.*

In this situation workers may find themselves being charged Class 4 contributions on earnings which are subject to Class 1. Social Security legislation allows such earnings to be excluded from the calculation of Class 4 and to avoid any potential problems in the future, workers should apply for a certificate of exemption. Special application forms for agency supplied workers to the construction industry are available from Contributions Agency, Deferment Group, Construction Industry Section, Room A1301, Newcastle upon Tyne NE98 1YX. Anyone who wants to know more about deferment can contact the Helpline 0645 157141.

In the past there has been some confusion over the requirement for agencies to account for NICs but the legal position is clear. Agencies which supply labour—only workers to the construction industry should examine their procedures to ensure that they are accounting for NICs. The CA and the Inland Revenue will be looking closely at this aspect of agencies when they carry out compliance checks. Any agency which wants to know more about its obligations in relation to NICs, particularly the accounting arrangements for Class 1 contributions, should contact its local CA office.

Employed or Self-employed?

Whether or not someone is employed or self-employed depends on the terms and conditions of the engagement and the way they carry out their work. Engagers and workers are free to agree contractual arrangements which suit them, but a worker cannot just call him or herself employed or self-employed without the facts to support this.

There is no definition in Social Security law of employment or self-employment, but the Courts have looked at the matter on many occasions and have identified the sort of factors which must be taken into account.

Broadly, it is a question of whether someone is in business on their own account. These general tests, which are explained in the leaflet (IR56/NI39) *'Employed or Self-employed'* are the same for National Insurance and tax purposes.

What the legislation says

Section 2 (1) of the Social Security Contributions and Benefits Act 1992 defines an *employed earner* as 'a person who is gainfully employed in Great Britain either under a contract of service, or in an office (including elective office) with emoluments chargeable to income tax under Schedule E'. A *self-employed earner* is defined in section 2(1) as 'a person who is gainfully employed in Great Britain otherwise than in employed earner's employment' whether or not he is also employed in such employment.

How the CA makes a decision

In most cases it will be quite clear whether someone is employed or self-employed. For example, someone who runs their own shop is clearly self–employed. On the other hand, someone working for the shop owner would be an employee. But there are cases on the borderline between employment and self-employment where the decision is more difficult.

When looking at employment status the CA relies on tests which have emerged from case law over many years, and applies these to the facts of the individual case concerned. After weighing up all the factors, a ruling is given as to whether a worker is employed or self-employed.

When giving this ruling the CA will explain the reasoning behind it and also explain what someone can do if they are dissatisfied. If the new information is put forward the CA will consider whether the ruling can be changed. If not, there is a right to have the matter formally determined by the Secretary of State under Section 17(1) of the Social Security Administration Act 1992.

Winter 1997–98 – Issue 9 NI News extracts

The Construction industry — ensuring there is a level playing field

In response to numerous requests to 'level playing field', Contributions Agency and Inland Revenue have decided to increase the number of visits to be made to construction firms during 1997–98 to check that contractors are deducting and accounting for Pay As You Earn and National Insurance contributions in line with revised guidelines.

Before ...

Issues No. 6 and No. 8 of National Insurance News explained the changes to the employment status of construction industry workers and the measures available to help contractors address the question of whether their workers were employed or self-employed. Contractors have subsequently been given a reasonable amount of time to review the employment status of their workers. They were expected to have completed their reviews and, where appropriate, be accounting for Pay As You Earn and National Insurance contributions by 5 April 1997 at the latest.

In order to help contractors to carry out these reviews with the minimum disruption both Contributions Agency and Inland Revenue agreed initially that they would not specifically target the construction industry over and above the normal level of compliance visits.

Despite efforts to help contractors, ongoing consultation with the industry has indicated that a significant number of construction firms are failing to meet their legal liabilities and may thereby be obtaining a commercial advantage.

Now ...

Where Contributions Agency and/or Inland Revenue inspectors find that Pay As You Earn and Class 1 National Insurance are due because contractors have not reviewed the employment status of their workforce and made the necessary changes, they will seek to recover arrears of PAYE and Class 1 NICs back to at least 6 April 1997. In appropriate cases interest and penalties will also be sought. Situations where arrears are recovered for periods earlier than 6 April 1997 are set out in issue No.8 of National Insurance News.

Whether someone is employed or self-employed depends on the terms and conditions of their engagement. The same general rule applies to the construction industry as to other industries and are set out in leaflet IR56/NI39 'Employed or self-employed'. Leaflet IR148/CA69 'Are your workers employed or self-employed?' explains how the general rules on employment status apply to the particular circumstances of the construction industry. These leaflets continue to be available from local offices of the Contributions Agency and Inland Revenue.

New leaflet

A new information leaflet CA80 'Workers in building and construction' has recently been introduced to assist employees and subcontractors with their National Insurance. Copies of this leaflet are available from Social Security offices, telephone numbers and addresses are listed in the Phone Book under Contributions Agency.

Medical expenses of employees abroad

Subject to Parliamentary Approval, the Department of Social Security intends to bring forward an amendment to regulations which will exclude from the computation of an employee's earnings payments which cover medical expenses abroad, or insurance against such expenses. This change will take effect from 6 April 1998 and ensures that there is no liability for National Insurance contributions on these payments.

Employee travel and subsistence payments

In the 1997 Finance Act, Inland Revenue brought forward changes to the legislation dealing with employee's travelling and subsistence payments. The new rules which come into force from 6 April 1998 are to be further amended in the next Finance Bill.

The Department of Social Security has decided to mirror these changes and subject to Parliamentary Approval intends to introduce new regulations to mirror the new Tax legislation. Those employees most affected by the changes are listed below.

In addition, but not as part of the proposed legislative changes, the Department of Social Security has reviewed its rules on the treatment of travel and subsistence payments made to employees who are unexpectedly recalled to work.

Site-based employees

Site-based employees have no permanent place of work. They work for a period at one location, then move on to another location when the job is finished. Typically, employees work in the construction and computer industries.

At present, any expenses paid for travel and subsistence in these circumstances are regarded as earnings and attract liability for National Insurance contributions.

Triangular travel

When an employee with a normal, permanent place of work travels directly between their permanent place of work, the term Triangular Travel is used. Under current practice, the employee can claim Tax and National Insurance–free allowances of:

- costs of travelling between the normal work place and the temporary work place; or

- actual costs incurred,

whichever is less.

From 6 April 1998, any amounts paid by the employer which do no more than cover the employee's reasonable travel and subsistence costs will not attract liability for National Insurance contributions.

Temporary absence from a normal, permanent place of work

At present, the term 'temporarily absent from a normal, permanent place of work' is defined as less than 12 months.

From 6 April 1998, the term will mean 24 months or less.

Home to work expenses when employee unexpectedly recalled to work

As part of the review of its policy in the field of travel and subsistence, the Department of Social Security has also looked at reimbursement of home to work expenses when an employee is unexpectedly recalled to work.

The Department of Social Security had previously taken the view that reimbursement of expenses in these circumstances could be disregarded, unless an employee's conditions of service or contract of employment required them occasionally to return to work in the same working day.

However, the Department of Social Security has now concluded that all such payments should be subject to National Insurance contributions. This aligns the National Insurance contributions position with that for Tax.

The Contributions Agency will not be seeking any arrears from any employer who has relied on published past guidance and not paid National Insurance contributions on these payments, but new employer guidance from April 1998 will confirm National Insurance contributions are due in these circumstances.

Relocation allowances

Background

In the past, the department held the view that in general, the payment of relocation allowances did not attract a liability for Class 1 National Insurance contributions. However, following receipt of legal advice, it is now clear that this interpretation was flawed and a liability for National Insurance contributions does arise under existing legislation.

In light of this, on 30 July 1997, the Government announced that implementation of the current liability will be delayed until 6 April 1998 and in addition, announced proposals for new legislation which would limit the scope of liability to only some relocation allowances.

The existing legislative position

The Department's revised view is that relocation allowances are generally earnings under section 3(1) of the Social Security Contributions and Benefits Act 1992. NICs are therefore payable under section 6(1) of that Act. Currently no specific legislation exists to exclude these payments from earnings. However, the Contributions Agency will not be seeking to recover any arrears from any employer who has relied on published guidance and not paid National Insurance contributions in respect of these allowances.

The proposals

New regulations will be introduced to limit the scope of the current power to charge National Insurance contributions by specifically excluding some relocation allowances from earnings. So what is not excluded will fall to be considered for National Insurance contributions.

It is proposed that all allowances and expenses listed in Schedule 11A to the Income and Corporation Taxes Act 1988 will be excluded from earnings. These allowances are listed in Appendix 7 of the 1997 edition of the Inland Revenue publication, *Expenses and benefits — A Tax Guide, 480.* The regulations are to refer to the tax legislation for consistency and simplicity, but will differ in two important respects.

The most important difference is in relation to the £8,000 cap. While Inland Revenue only exclude from tax the first £8,000 worth of qualifying expenses and benefits, the full amount of these allowances will be excluded for National Insurance contributions purposes. This is in recognition of the difficulty employers would face in operating such a cap on a pay period basis.

Secondly, tax legislation requires payments to be made on or before the 'relevant day' to be considered towards the £8,000 exclusion. This is normally the 5 April in the tax year following the one in which the employee starts work at their new location. For National Insurance contributions purposes, the relevant day provisions will not apply, thus allowing employees who have problems relocating to continue to receive appropriate allowances National Insurance contributions free. For employees who have already started work in their new location before 6 April 1998, it is proposed that the new legislation will specifically exclude the payment of further reasonable relocation allowances, in line with existing guidance. However, if the conditions of the relocation package are varied after 5 April 1998, so that the allowances are increased in number or amount or both, then the additional sums would attract a liability for National Insurance contributions unless the allowances concerned would otherwise be excluded because they are listed in Schedule 11A.

The current position

The proposals and draft regulations were put to the Social Security Advisory Committee (SSAC) on 7 January 1998. SSAC is the major UK advisory body responsible for advising the Secretary of State on most social security issues. SSAC have asked for the draft regulations to be the subject of full consultation prior to the report to the Secretary of State. The consultative period started on 12 January 1998 and the report is expected to be completed by mid March, at which time Ministers will consider and respond to the report before proceeding.

National Insurance Tracing and Verification Service

About a year ago, the 'P46 section' was established because employers wanted a more efficient and rapid means of obtaining their employees National Insurance numbers. The section deals with form P46 sent to the Contributions Agency by the Inland Revenue and form CA6855 which is a tracing form sent to the Contributions Agency by employers. *The CA6855 is for use when completion of form P46 is not appropriate* e.g. to trace/verify an existing employees National Insurance number.

How it works

When the P46 or form CA6855 is received and the National Insurance number is not known or is incorrect and a National Insurance number is subsequently traced, a National Insurance number notification form CA6856 is sent automatically to the employer. This form asks the employer to amend their records and advise the employee of their National Insurance number.

Schedules

National Insurance number trace requests can now be sent to the Contributions Agency in schedule form. We have devised the CA6855 schedule for use in cases where employers wish to trace National Insurance numbers for more than one employee. However, employers may still submit form CA6855 in respect of each employee if they prefer. To help P46 section to input the schedules to the National Insurance Recording System it is important that the employee's details are in the *correct format.* Employers wishing to use the schedule service should contact their local Contributions Agency or Inland Revenue office that will provide details of the required format.

Response Times

The Contributions Agency aims to respond to *straight forward* tracing requests in 10 working days. Requests for National Insurance numbers may only be made in writing, and regretfully we cannot process tracing requests made by telephone.

Spring 1998 — Issue 10 NI News Extracts

Transfer of Contributions Agency from DSS to Inland Revenue

In the Budget on 17 March 1998, The Chancellor of the Exchequer announced a decision to transfer the Contributions Agency from the Department of Social Security to the Inland Revenue in April 1999.

The Government has expressed a long-term objective for greater alignment between Tax and National Insurance contributions and this move takes a step forward in that direction by bringing Tax and National Insurance under one organisation.

Both departments believe this approach will:

- enable us to progressively reduce the burden on business and people so they can sort out taxes and contributions through a single organisation
- enable us to combine our efforts on customer service
- help us share experience, knowledge and skills in combating Tax and National Insurance contributions avoidance
- build on the successful Joint Working Programme that already exists between the two organisations.

A Joint Programme Team has been set up to ensure a seamless and successful transfer, laying strong foundations for our combined organisation.

Both departments welcome this opportunity to further improve the service they provide to business and to the public through greater alignment of the Tax and National Insurance systems. It is our aim to ensure successful implementation and therefore we welcome any thoughts you may have or issues you would like us to focus on as we plan to merge the two organisations.

Help for new employers to reduce costs and create jobs

The Chancellor announced that a new service from Inland Revenue and the Contributions Agency would be introduced to provide one stop, one-to-one help for new employers to become familiar with tax, National Insurance contributions and benefits. This will include elements of pay such as Statutory Sick Pay/Statutory Maternity Pay, expenses, payments in kind etc. In particular, it will provide rapid response tailor-made help with an employer's first payday.

The intention is that the service will reduce one of the major barriers to setting up and running a business, making it cheaper and easier for small businesses to take on their first employee(s).

There is a pilot scheme currently operating in Leicester. The intention is that the service will become more widely available in other parts of the country during the next year, becoming nationwide from April 1999. Inland Revenue has issued a Press Release about the service – reference Inland Revenue 43.

Funded Unapproved Retirement Benefit Schemes

On 17 November 1997 a Press Release was issued to clarify the Contributions Agency's approach towards payments made into Funded Unapproved Retirement Benefit Schemes. From 6 April 1998, most payments by an employer into a Funded

Unapproved Retirement Benefit Schemes will be subject to National Insurance contributions.

Background

Funded Unapproved Retirement Benefit Schemes, unapproved in so far as they fall outside the scope of Inland Revenue taxed approved retirement benefit schemes are usually designed to enable an employer:

to secure future benefit rights through an insurance policy – these are common in the case of death benefit schemes, under which the insurance policy is written into trust for an employee. In practice, employers make contributions which the trustees apply towards the acquisition of an insurance policy providing a lump sum death benefit on the death of a specified person

to set up a separate trust fund specifically for participating members, i.e. employees. This type of Funded Unapproved Retirement Benefit Scheme is much more common.

These schemes were effectively created by the introduction of an "earnings cap" in 1989, setting a limit on the amount of earnings in respect of which contributions may be paid into a tax-approved pension scheme. The earnings cap is increased each year in line with the Retail Prices Index (£87,500 for 1998/99).

Payments described as Funded Unapproved Benefit Schemes which are not Funded Unapproved Retirement Benefit Schemes

The label "Retirement Benefit" can be misleading. Not every trust described by an employer as a Funded Unapproved Retirement Benefit Schemes will provide a genuine occupational pension. They are also increasingly being used by employers as a National Insurance contribution avoidance measure. Some alleged Funded Unapproved Retirement Benefit Schemes are set up with the sole purpose of deferring a payment of earnings to a future date in a disguised format in the belief that it escapes National Insurance contribution liability.

An example of such a scheme is where the employer sets up a trust for an individual employee (often the company director) into which a lump sum is paid (equivalent to the annual bonus). Rather than using the money paid in to provide a pension, the trustees pay the money out to the employee a few days or a few weeks later. Some commentators have described this as "washing an annual bonus through a trust".

Past National Insurance contributions position

In correspondence with employers, accountants and other professional organisations, the Contributions Agency has always reserved its right to charge National Insurance contributions where a Funded Unapproved Retirement Benefit Schemes is not used to provide pensions, but rather to pay bonuses to employees, including ex-employees, whilst avoiding contributions.

Although the Press Release in November 1997 was accompanied by further guidance for employers about Funded Unapproved Retirement Benefit Schemes in general, the Contributions Agency's current and previously published guidance does not contain any specific mention of Funded Unapproved Retirement Benefit Schemes.

Revised National Insurance contributions position

In that Press Release, the Contributions Agency announced its view that payments into Funded Unapproved Retirement Benefit Schemes are in most cases, **"earnings"** under section 3(1) of the Social Security Contributions and Benefits Act 1992.

"Earnings" are defined as "... **including any remuneration or profit derived from an employment** ...", attracting liability for National Insurance contributions under section 6(1) of the same Act " ... **earnings paid to or for the benefit of an earner in respect of any one employment of his which is employed earner's employment** ..."

The Press Release was accompanied by additional guidance to explain the current legal position. However, because the Contributions Agency's previously published guidance makes no specific mention of Funded Unapproved Retirement Benefit Schemes, it has been decided that we will not act retrospectively to enforce arrears for previous tax years except in limited circumstances. We will enforce arrears of National Insurance contributions only on payments made into Funded Unapproved Retirement Benefit Schemes before 6 April 1998 in cases where the scheme does not in fact provide a pension, i.e. money goes into and out of the trust and is paid to employees, including ex-employees.

The Contributions Agency will enforce in respect of payments to Funded Unapproved Retirement Benefit Schemes which are liable to National Insurance contributions and where payment is made on or after 6 April 1998. The Agency's view is that earnings for National Insurance contributions purposes encompasses payments made directly to an employee and also payments made by others to or for their benefit. As well as the most obvious avoidance schemes of alleged Funded Unapproved Retirement Benefit Schemes described earlier, existing legislation also catches the following:

Separate trusts for each employee

Payment by an employer into the separate trust for each employee's Funded Unapproved Retirement Benefit Schemes is earnings for National Insurance contributions purposes. It is " ... **remuneration or profit derived from an employment**..." for the purposes of section 3(1) of the Social Security and Benefits Act 1992, and " ... **paid to or for the benefit of** ..." an employed earner for the purposes of section 6(1) of the act. The same view is taken where a third party makes a payment into a Funded Unapproved Retirement Benefit Schemes in respect of an individual.

Where a payment out of a funded Unapproved Retirement Benefit Schemes is earnings derived from employment (i.e. the individual receives the payment by virtue of being an employee and not simply as a beneficiary), and is not otherwise exempt in regulations, liability for National Insurance contributions arises by virtue of section 6(1). For instance, payments out in the form of a pension are exempt from the computation of earnings for Class 1 National Insurance contributions purposes by virtue of regulation 19(1)(g) of the Social Security (Contributions) Regulations 1979. The Agency considers that payment by way of pension for the purposes of regulation 19(1)(g) can include pensions commuted to a lump sum, which is the usual form of payment from a Funded Unapproved Retirement Benefit Schemes.

Single trust fund – employees having a distinct and separate share

The same points apply to payments in and out of the scheme as above under "Separate trusts for each employee".

Single trust fund – Discretionary Benefit Funded Unapproved Retirement Benefit Schemes

A discretionary trust is a flexible device which allows the trustees to choose how, when, what and to whom they make payment, in accordance with the terms of any trust deed. The Contributions Agency will closely scrutinise Funded Unapproved Retirement Benefit Schemes constructed under discretionary trust arrangements. If the Agency can establish a payment of earnings to or for the benefit of an employee, it will challenge the scheme and seek National Insurance contributions.

Further changes from 6 April 1999

Under Clause 48 of the Social Security Bill, the Government intends to introduce new regulations to provide for apportionment of payments into Funded Unapproved Retirement Benefit Schemes made for the benefit of two or more employed earners.

Subject to Parliamentary approval, these new regulations will come into effect by 6 April 1999.

Regulations to ensure alignment of National Insurance contributions with the tax treatment of unapproved schemes

The clarification of liability in respect of Funded Unapproved Retirement Benefit Schemes will not apply to certain retirement benefit schemes which, although they are outside the regime for tax approval receive special tax treatment. Employees are not charged tax on the employer's contributions to these schemes in accordance with legislative provision, concession or Inland Revenue practice. Therefore, in line with the policy aim of aligning the tax and National Insurance contributions systems, a package of new regulations will be introduced shortly after April 1998 to exclude payments to certain types of non-approved scheme for National Insurance contributions liability. A further announcement will be made at that time.

Contributions to tax-approved schemes will also remain excluded from liability.

Between 6 April 1998 and these new regulations coming into force, the Contributions Agency will not enforce National Insurance contributions in the circumstances to be covered by the regulations. The schemes to which payments will not attract liability for National Insurance contributions are as follows:

- Tax approved retirement benefit schemes
- Schemes granted provisional tax approval
- Relevant Statutory Schemes
- Schemes set up by a non-UK government for its employees
- Schemes granted "corresponding approval"
- Pilots' Schemes
- Approved schemes which are wound up (i.e. the Inland Revenue allow them to be abandoned and regard them as having been unapproved, and the contents of the trust are refunded).

Relocation allowances

Issue No 9 explained that the Social Security Advisory Committee had asked for the draft regulations governing the proposed changes in the treatment of certain relocation allowances to be the subject of a full consultation exercise, prior to a report to the Secretary of State.

Details of the final proposals were publicised in CA Press Release 10/98 issued on 16 March 1998. The regulatory amendments are contained in the Social Security (Contributions) Amendment (No. 2) Regulations 1998, Statutory Instrument 1998/680.

Following consultation a further concession was offered. Relocation allowances that are taxed through Inland Revenue PAYE Settlement Agreements will be excluded from National Insurance contributions liability for a further year, i.e. the 1998/99 tax year. With effect from 6 April 1999, subject to the current Social Security Bill receiving Royal Assent, in line with all other items taxed through PAYE Settlement Agreements, relevant relocation allowances will be subject to the new Class 1B National Insurance contribution.

In addition, legislation has been clarified to ensure that relevant qualifying relocation allowances (those listed in the tax legislation) paid to employees relocating abroad will not attract National Insurance contributions liability.

Effects on benefits entitlement

The DSS believes that payment of relocation allowances should generally have been subject to National Insurance contributions in the past, and recognises that where these contributions have not been paid, the benefits position of some employees may have been affected.

Those employees who think that their benefits entitlement may have been affected should contact their nearest Social Security office for advice. In Northern Ireland, they should contact the Contributions Unit Headquarters.

The only employees affected will be those who have received relocation allowances on which National Insurance contributions were not paid. Their normal earnings would also need to have been less than the Upper Earnings Limit in the earnings period in which the relocation allowances were paid.

Liability for National Insurance contributions on payments after employment terminated

In recent years the Contributions Agency has occasionally been challenged over its practice of assessing National Insurance contributions on payments which are made to employees after their contract of employment with an employer has come to an end.

This article aims to clarify the issue by explaining in detail the legislation that provides for the charging of National Insurance contributions in the above circumstances. Although this article refers specifically to payments made after the end of the employment, it also applies to the less common situation of payments made to an individual before the commencement of their employment.

The Legislation

The duty to pay contributions in respect of earnings derived from employment is imposed by section 6(1) of the Social Security Contributions and Benefits Act 1992. Section 6(1) provides that a primary and secondary Class 1 contribution is payable **"where in any tax week earnings are paid to or for the benefit of an earner in respect of any one employment which is employed earner's employment"**.

The use of the present tense in section 6(1) has led some commentators to the view that the phrase **"which is employed earner's employment"** can be construed as applying only to the present, and so only relates to employment in which the person was engaged at the time the payment was made. The Department's view is that this interpretation is incorrect for the following reasons:

Section 2(1)(a) of the Social Security Contributions and Benefits Act 1992 defines **"employed earner"** as **"a person who is gainfully employed in Great Britain ..."**, and section 3(1) defines **"earnings"** as including **"any remuneration or profit derived from an employment"** . The use of the present tense in Section 6(1) "which *is* employed earner's employment" concerns the nature of the employment when the payment is made, not whether the individual is in employment at the time when that payment is made. The use of the phrase **"which is"** relates to whether, when the payment is made, the employment is employed earner's employment as opposed to some other type of employment (e.g. self-employment).

This interpretation is supported by the previous statutory provisions. Whereas section 6(1) of the 1992 Act uses the phrase **"which is employed earner's employment"**, section 2(2) of the Social Security Act 1973 and section 4(2) of the Social Security Act 1975 referred to employment **"being employed earner's employment"**. This alteration was not intended to have substantive significance, rather it was simply a more modern way of expressing the same meaning, and as the 1992 Act was primarily a consolidation measure it was not intended to alter the previous law in this respect.

In the Department's view, section 6(1) is to be construed so as to advance the purpose indicated by section 3(1), namely, to bring within the scope of the statutory regime **"any remuneration or profit derived from an employment"**. Therefore, despite the use of the present tense in section 6(1), this provision imposes a duty to pay

National Insurance contributions in respect of earnings derived from employment even if those earnings are paid after the employment terminates.

Summer 1998 — Issue 11 NI News Extracts.

Welfare to Work

Background

In March this year, the Chancellor of the Exchequer announced benefit changes to encourage disabled people to return to work, in his Budget statement and the Welfare Reform Green Paper "New Ambitions for our Country: A New Contract for Welfare."

The changes are part of the Government's New Deal for disabled people. the regulations seek to encourage those who might want to return to work by:

- the introduction of a new rule linking periods of incapacity for 52 weeks for those who move into work. This protects their benefit position if they have to reclaim during that period, and will reduce the risk and uncertainty faced by those who are considering a move into work

- the removal of the 16 hour a week limit on voluntary work for those on incapacity benefits. This will allow people to make a greater contribution and perhaps to act as a first step towards a return to paid work.

Effect on Statutory Sick Pay

The Statutory Sick Pay Regulations will be amended by the Social Security (Welfare to Work) Regulations 1998, so that employers are not liable for Statutory Sick Pay, for employees who:

- are treated as Welfare to Work beneficiaries, **and**

- who become incapable of work again within 52 weeks.

The Social Security (Welfare to Work) Regulations are expected to come into force from 5 October 1998.

Employers will not need to take any additional action because of these regulations. A person who qualifies as a Welfare to Work beneficiary will be given a form from the Benefits Agency, known as a 'linking letter', in the same way as any other employee who has recently claimed Social Security benefit, which they should then give to their employer.

The only difference between the normal linking letter and this one used for the Welfare to Work beneficiaries, is that it will bear a date **52 weeks** after the benefit claim ended, instead of the **normal 8 weeks.**

If the employee falls sick before this date they will not be entitled to Statutory Sick Pay and the employer should complete form SSP1 to enable the employee to claim Incapacity Benefit.

Employer's Manual on Statutory Sick Pay, CA 30

The Employer's Manual on Statutory Sick Pay, CA30, will not be amended until April 1999. In the meantime employers should note the contents of this article against paragraph 35, page 26 of the April 1997 edition.

Business Anti-Fraud Hotline

Since the Business Anti-Fraud Hotline was launched in January 1998, it has taken over 40,000 calls leading to more than 3,000 referrals to Contributions Agency inspectors.

With the launch of the hotline, lawful employers now have the means to report those competitors they believe are defaulting on National Insurance contributions and gaining an unfair business advantage.

All calls to the hotline on **0800 788 887** are free and confidential. Lines are open from 8.30am to 6.30pm Monday to Friday.

Performers – Press Release 98/202

Social Security Minister, John Denham, recently announced changes to the National Insurance rules for actor, musicians and other entertainers.

Following legal advice that existing National Insurance contribution treatment was no longer sustainable, regulations to treat the majority of performers as employees came into force from 17 July 1998.

Performers and engagers who consider they incorrectly paid National Insurance contributions over the past six years, in the belief that those previously treated as employees should have been treated as self-employed, are able to apply for a refund.

Enquiries can be made to:

Refunds Group, Contributions Agency, Room 107B, Longbenton, Newcastle-upon-Tyne NE98 1YX.

Alternatively telephone 06451 53443, calls charged at local rate. Guidance notes are available from CA local offices.

Winter 1998/99 – Issue 12 NI News Extracts

Class 1A National Insurance Contributions and Unremunerated Employees and Directors

Liability for Class 1A National Insurance contributions may arise when an employee or director receives the benefit of a company as a result of their employment, which they can also use privately.

When an employee or director receives no payment of earnings, even though they receive the benefit of a company car, there may be no liable secondary contributor who can be held responsible for the payment of Class 1A National Insurance contributions.

Section 52 of the Social Security Act 1998 states:
> Class 1A National Insurance contributions shall be payable in respect of company cars provided to employees and directors who are taxed under section 157 of the Income and Corporation Taxes Act 1988, even if the benefit of the car is the only payment earnings made.

The person liable to pay Class 1A National Insurance contributions in these circumstances, will be the person who would normally have been liable to pay secondary Class 1 National Insurance contributions had the benefit of the car been earnings. This change came into force on **8 September 1998**.

Although the contributions will not become due until **19 July 1999**, to ensure compliance, employers will need to keep records now about unremunerated employees and directors.

Discretionary Payments in Lieu of Notice (PILONS)

There is an error in the current CWG2 guidance. This guidance incorrectly states that National Insurance contributions are not payable on discretionary Payments in Lieu of Notice (PILONS). In fact a **National Insurance contributions liability on such payments does exist**.

This is an alignment with the tax position and the CWG2 will be amended in 1999. Meanwhile any enquiries should be directed to your nearest Social Security office.

Class 1A National Insurance contributions – Calculating Business Mileage Where Two or More cars are provided Consecutively

Class 1A National Insurance contributions are payable by employers who provide their employees with company cars and/or fuel, which they can also use privately.

From 6 April 1994, Class 1A National Insurance contributions have been calculated by referring to the cash equivalent of providing these cars.

The cash equivalent, sometimes referred to as the taxable or car benefit, is adjusted with reference to the amount of business mileage travelled in the tax year, and into which, of the three available mileage bands a car falls.

Generally, the higher the business mileage travelled, the greater the adjustment available. When more than one car is consecutively provided to an employee in a tax year, each car must be treated individually. The business mileage recorded in each car was available to the employee. The business mileage of each car must **not** be aggregated when determining which mileage band adjustment to use.

For Example:

From April 1997 to December 1997 the employee travels 16,000 business miles in car A. In January the employee is promoted and is given a new car in which he travels a further 4,000 miles.

When assessing the amount of Class 1A National Insurance contributions due, each car must be treated separately, the high/low pro–rata business mileage thresholds calculated for each car.

Payment of travel and subsistence expenses

The regulations in respect of the treatment of travel and subsistence for National Insurance contributions came into force on 1 October 1998.

The national Insurance regulations are based in income tax legislation contained in Finance Act 1998, which means that the changes maintain general alignment between the National Insurance and tax positions on these payments.

Employers have been able to apply the new rules for National Insurance as well as tax from 6 April 1998.

Assessment of National Insurance contributions for company directors

The liability for National Insurance contributions for directors is based on annual pay rather than weekly or monthly pay as for most other employees. With effect from 6 April 1999, employers may spread payments over the whole of the year by paying contributions on account using a weekly or monthly pay interval.

Payments in non-cash form

Some employers set up schemes whereby they 'pay' employees by providing assets which can be readily converted into cash. The purpose of such schemes is to place cash in the hands of the employees but take the remuneration outside the scope for National Insurance contributions and Pay As You Earn tax. Since 1994, increasingly complex schemes have been set up based on the narrow interpretation of the law. The Contributions Agency does not accept that payments made via these schemes successfully avoid National Insurance.

However, to place the matter beyond doubt and dissuade the possible introduction of new schemes, the contributions regulations have been changed – changes which mirror in effect income tax law introduced in the Finance Act 1998.

Readily convertible assets

The regulations that provide that readily convertible assets are subject to National Insurance came into force with effect from 1 October 1998. The definition of readily convertible assets for tax purposes as per section 203F(2) of ICTA 1988 as amended by Finance Act 1998.

It includes:

- an asset capable of being sold or otherwise realised on (I) a recognised investment exchange or on the London Bullion Market (ii) a market for the time being specified in Pay As You Earn Regulations (this includes the New York Stock Exchange)
- money debts
- an asset subject to a fiscal warehousing regime i.e. assets held in 'bond'
- assets that give rise to cash without any action being taken by the employee
- an asset for which trading arrangements are in existence, **or**
- assets for which trading arrangements are likely to come into existence in accordance with other arrangements, or an understanding in place when the asset was provided to the employee.

The new provisions also ensure payments to employees which enhance the value of a readily convertible asset, a National Insurance contribution liability will arise in respect of that asset. The amount on which to assess National Insurance contributions will be the best estimate that the employer can reasonably make of income likely to be chargeable to tax under Schedule E and to be accounted for via Pay As You Earn.

Payments by way of shares subject to forfeiture or conversion

Shares subject to forfeiture

Many companies offer their employees shares in the company they work for as part of their earnings. These shares often form part of a Long Term Investment Plan where the employee's ownership of the shares can be conditional on the employee meeting relevant conditions i.e. meeting performance targets.

With effect from 9 April 1998, if the shares are readily convertible assets and are not issued via the Inland Revenue approved scheme:

- there will normally be no National Insurance liability when shares subject to forfeiture are first awarded, **but**
- there will be a liability based on the market value of the shares at the time when the risk of forfeiture is lifted, or if sooner, when the shares are sold, less any consideration previously paid. It is at this point that the value of the shares can most easily be determined and that the employee is often able to realise the value of the shares.

There will also be a National Insurance liability if the shares can be subject to risk of forfeiture more than five years after they were first awarded. This is intended to stop National Insurance liability from being postponed indefinitely but as most Long Term Investment Plans run for five years or less, few employees will actually pay National Insurance contributions when conditional shares are first awarded.

Convertible shares

Convertible shares of a certain class, which can subsequently convert into another class. For example, some have different voting or dividend rights. An employer may grant one class of share which can then be converted to a more valuable class.

With effect from 9 April 1998, if such shares are not issued via an Inland Revenue approved scheme and are readily convertible assets, a National Insurance contribution liability will arise on the gain from the conversion. Generally, the gain is the best estimate of the difference between the market value of the converted share and any consideration previously paid including any amount on which any National Insurance contributions paid when the shares were first awarded.

These changes generally mirror tax changes introduced in the Finance Act 1998 and have the effect that the amount on which National Insurance contributions are due is the same as the amount on which Pay As You Earn must be operated.

Age Related Rebates for Contracted–out Money Purchase schemes including the Money Purchase Part of a Contracted–out Mixed Benefit Scheme

Since 6 April 1997, members who contracted–out of the States Earnings Related Pension Scheme via Contracted–out Mixed Benefit Scheme, have been eligible for a rebate on their National Insurance contributions based on their age.

With the introduction of these age related rebates, new contributions categories for members of Contracted–out Money Purchase Schemes came into force on 6 April 1997. these categories included:

F — Contracted–out standard rate

G — Contracted–out reduced rate

H — Contracted–out standard rate — mariner

K — Contracted–out reduced rate — mariner

S — Contracted–out notional rate

V — Contracted–out notional rate — mariner

If you operate a Contracted–out Money Purchase Scheme, including the Contracted–out Money Purchase part of a Contracted–out Mixed Benefit, and have deducted the wrong rate of National Insurance for the 1997/98 tax year, contact Contracted–out Employments Group, on telephone number (0191) 22 50172.

Table of Statutes

Table of Statutes

Table of Statutes

Table of Statutes

61　Table of Statutory Instruments

Categorisation Amendment Regs 1980: Social Security (Categorisation of Earners) Amendment Regulations 1980, SI 1980 No 1713

Categorisation Amendment Regs 1984: Social Security (Categorisation of Earners) Amendment Regulations 1984, SI 1984 No 350

Categorisation Amendment Regs 1990: Social Security (Categorisation of Earners) Amendment Regulations 1990, SI 1990 No 1894

Categorisation Amendment Regs 1994: Social Security (Categorisation of Earners) Amendment Regulations 1994, SI 1994 No 726

Categorisation Amendment Regs 1998: Social Security (Categorisation of Earners) Amendment Regulations 1998, SI 1998 No 1728   14.15, 33.1

Categorisation Amendment Regs 1999: Social Security (Categorisation of Earners) Amendment Regulations 1999, SI 1999 No 3   33.2

Consequential Provisions Act 1992 Appointed Day Order: Social Security (Consequential Provisions) Act 1992, Appointed Day Order 1993, SI 1993 No 1025 12.3; 21.20

Continental Shelf (Designation of Areas) Orders: Continental Shelf (Designation of Areas) Order 1964, SI 1964 No 687; Continental Shelf (Designation of Additional Areas) Orders 1965, SI 1965 No 1531; 1968, SI 1968 No 891; 1971, SI 1971 No 594; 1974, SI 1974 No 1489; 1976, SI 1976 No 1153; 1977, SI 1977 No 1871; 1978, SI 1978 Nos 178; 1029; 1979, SI 1979 No 1447; 1982, SI 1982 No 1072   48.1

Contracted-out Percentages Orders: Social Security (Class 1 — Contracted-out Percentages) Order 1987, SI 1987 No 656 Art 2; Social Security (Class 1 Contributions — Contracted-out Percentages) Order 1992, SI 1992 No 795, Arts 1, 2   23.3

Contracting-Out (Recovery of Class 1 Contributions) Regs 1982: Contracting-out (Recovery of Class 1 Contributions) Regulations 1982, SI 1982 No 1033

Contributions Regs 1969: National Insurance (Contributions) Regulations 1969, SI 1969 No 1696

Contributions Regs 1975: Social Security (Contributions) Regulations 1975, SI 1975 No 492

Table of Statutory Instruments

Table of Statutory Instruments

Table of Statutory Instruments

Table of Statutory Instruments

Table of Statutory Instruments

Table of Statutory Instruments

Table of Statutory Instruments

Table of Cases

Table of Cases

Table of Cases

63 Published Decisions

References are to *Selected Decisions of the Minister on Questions of Classification and Insurability.*

The index is referenced to the chapter and paragraph number. The entries printed in bold capitals are chapter headings in the text.

Index

Index

Index

Index

Index

Index

decree absolute, 24.14

Dock workers, reduced Class 1 rate for, 51.6

Documents, inspectors' right to require, 32.4

Dodecanese, 49.13

Domestic law, effect of EC regulations, 49.1, 49.13

Domestic workers, 38.11–38.16
agency, employed through, 38.13
au pair girls, 38.12
categorisation, 38.11
close relatives, employed by, 38.12
handyman, 38.11
housekeeper, 38.11
industrial premises, employed in, 38.13
jobbing gardener, 38.11

Domicile,
airmen, 6.3
jurisdictional link, 49.5
mariners, 42.4
share fishermen, 54.2

Double liability, avoidance of, 28.5, 49.13, 55.3

Drivers,
concrete vehicle, 38.3
despatch, 38.3
heavy goods vehicle, 38.3
industrial plant, 38.3
taxicab, 38.3

Driving instructors, 38.3

Due date,
Class 1, 21.2
Class 2, 21.9
Class 3, 21.13
Class 4, 21.14

E

E101, 49.14

E102, 49.14

E111, 49.14

Earner (*see also* Employed earner, Self-employed earner), 14.1

EARNINGS, 28
abroad, absence on business, 28.85
absence, pay during, 28.18–28.23
accommodation, provision of, 28.52
accommodation, relocation of, 28.50
accrued holiday pay, 28.8
advances on account of, 15.3, 28.5
advances re damages, 28.23
alcoholic liquor, 28.26
anniversary gifts, 28.30
annual payments, 28.84
armed forces, members of, 11.3, 28.53

arrears of pay, 28.18, 28.11
assignment of, 28.6
awards, 28.2, 28.29–28.42
balancing charges, 28.78
beneficial payment of, 15.3
benefits in kind, 8.4, 28.24–28.28
birthday presents, 28.30
board and lodging, provision of, 28.52
bonuses, 28.31
bounties, 11.3, 28.53
capital allowances, 28.79
car parking fees, 28.70
car user allowances, 28.66–28.69
cash vouchers, provision of, 28.28
certificates of deposit, provision of, 28.26
charge card, company, 15.3, 28.47
charitable payments, 28.4, 28.6
Class 1, 28.2–28.76
Class 2, for exception purposes, 5.14, 18.3, 28.77
Class 4, 28.77–28.86
club membership, provision of, 28.54
commodities, 28.27
Community Charge paid by employer, 28.50
company directors, 22.3
compensation for breach of contract, 28.9
compensation for loss of amateur status, 28.7
compensation for loss of office, 28.9, 28.12
concessionary fuel for miners, 28.55
conditional payments, 15.3
contract continuation order, payments under, 28.11
contract of service, consideration relating to, 28.2
contract of service, after termination of, 28.8
cost of living overseas allowances, 28.72
council tax, paid by employer, 28.50
councillors, 28.26
covenant, restrictive, payments under, 28.16
covenanted to charity, 28.6
credit card, company, 15.3, 28.47
damages advances, 28.23
damages for breach of contract, 28.9, 28.10, 28.14
damages, personal injuries, 28.43
debt instruments as, 28.26
debts settled by employer, as, 15.3, 28.45, 28.66

Index

Index

Index

Index

Index

Index

Index

Index

Index

Twelve-year Summary of Rates and Limits (continued)

The paragraph numbers below correspond to paragraphs in the text. See those paragraphs for further details.

	1989–90	1990–91	1991–1992	1992–93
CLASS 2 CONTRIBUTION RATES AND LIMITS				
Normal weekly rate (see 18.5)	£4.25	£4.55	£5.15	£5.35
Share fisherman's special rate (see 54.3)	£5.80	6.15	£6.20	£7.00
Volunteer development worker's special rate (see 56.3)	£4.30	£3.22	£3.43	£3.56
Small earnings exception limit (see 18.3)	£2,350.00	£2,600.00	£2,9000.00	£3,030.00
De-categorisation limit (see 14.10)	£800.00	£800.00	£800.00	£800.00
CLASS 3 CONTRIBUTION RATES				
Normal rate (see 19.4)	£4.15	£4.45	£5.05	£5.25
CLASS 4 CONTRIBUTION RATES AND LIMITS				
Lower annual limit (see 30.6)	£5,050.00	£5,450.00	£5,900.00	£6,120.00
Upper annual limit (see 30.6)	£16,900.00	£18,200.00	£20,280.00	£21,060.00
Rate (see 20.6)	6.3%	6.3%	6.3%	6.3%
Limiting amount (see 7.3)	£971.80	£1,044.00	£1,178.89	£1,224.77
Share fisherman's limiting amount (see 7.3)	£1,053.95	£1,129.20	£1,234.54	£1,312.22
CLASS 1, 2, 3 and 4 LIMITING AMOUNT				
Annual maximum (see 7.2)	£1,468.98	£1,498.84	£1,667.38	£1,731.51
SSP AND SMP RECOVERY				
Statutory sick pay (see 15.7)	107.5%	107%	80%	80%
Higher rate			100%*	100%*
Statutory maternity pay (see 15.7)	107.5%	107%	104.5%	104.5%
Higher rate				

*Higher rate **only** if small employer's relief applies (see 15.7)
‡From 4.9.94 104% **only** if small employer's relief applies (see 15.7), otherwise 92%
†Recovery determined by the Percentage Threshold Scheme (15.7)